THE OXFORD

FRENCH

DICTIONARY

THE OXFORD

FRENCH
DICTIONARY

French–English   français–anglais
English–French   anglais–français

Michael Janes
Dora Carpenter
Edwin Carpenter

BERKLEY BOOKS, NEW YORK

THE OXFORD FRENCH DICTIONARY

A Berkley Book / published in mass-market paperback by arrangement with Oxford University Press, Inc.

PRINTING HISTORY
Oxford University Press edition published 1994
Berkley edition / August 1997

Copyright © 1986, 1993, 1997 by Oxford University Press.
Second edition first published in 1993 as *The Oxford French Minidictionary.*
First published in 1989 as *The Oxford Paperback French Dictionary.*
Second edition 1994.
Oxford is a registered trademark of Oxford University Press.
All rights reserved. No part of this publication may be reproduced, stored in a retrieval system, or transmitted, in any form or by any means, electronic, mechanical, photocopying, recording, or otherwise, without the prior permission of Oxford University Press.
For information contact: Oxford University Press, 198 Madison Avenue, New York, New York 10016.

The Penguin Putnam Inc. World Wide Web site address is http://www.penguinputnam.com

ISBN: 0-425-16010-6

BERKLEY®
Berkley Books are published by
The Berkley Publishing Group, a division of Penguin Putnam Inc., 375 Hudson Street, New York, New York 10014.
BERKLEY and the "B" design are trademarks belonging to Penguin Putnam Inc.

PRINTED IN THE UNITED STATES OF AMERICA

15   14   13   12

Preface

This is the second edition of *The Oxford Paperback French Dictionary*. It remains largely the work of Michael Janes, the compiler of the first edition, but some entries have been substantially revised and we have been able to incorporate a large proportion of new material. We hope to have kept to the aim of the original: to provide users requiring a compact dictionary with the maximum amount of useful material.

Dora Latiri-Carpenter
Edwin Carpenter

Introduction

When you look up a word, you will find a pronunciation, a grammatical part of speech, and the translation. Sometimes more than one translation is given, and material in brackets in *italics* is included to help you choose the right one. For example, under **cabin** you will see (*hut*) and (*in ship, aircraft*). When a word has more than one part of speech, this can affect the translation. For example **praise** is translated one way when it is a verb (*v.t.*) and another way when it is a noun (*n.*).

A swung dash (~) represents the entry word, or the part of it that comes before a vertical bar (as in **libert|y**). You will see it in examples using the entry word and words based on it. For example, under **good** you will find **as ~ as** and **~-looking**.

Translations are given in their basic form. You will find tables at the end showing verb forms. Irregular verbs are marked on the French to English side with †. This side also shows the plurals of nouns and the feminine forms of adjectives when they do not follow the normal rules.

Abbreviations · Abréviations

abbreviation	*abbr., abrév.*	abréviation
adjective(s)	*a. (adjs.)*	adjectif(s)
adverb(s)	*adv(s).*	adverbe(s)
American	*Amer.*	américain
anatomy	*anat.*	anatomie
approximately	*approx.*	approximativement
archaeology	*archaeol., archéol.*	archéologie
architecture	*archit.*	architecture
automobile	*auto.*	automobile
auxiliary	*aux.*	auxiliaire
aviation	*aviat.*	aviation
botany	*bot.*	botanique
computing	*comput.*	informatique
commerce	*comm.*	commerce
conjunction(s)	*conj(s)*	conjonction(s)
cooking	*culin.*	culinaire
electricity	*electr., électr.*	électricité
feminine	*f.*	féminin
familiar	*fam.*	familier
figurative	*fig.*	figuré
geography	*geog., géog.*	géographie
geology	*geol., géol.*	géologie
grammar	*gram.*	grammaire
humorous	*hum.*	humoristique
interjection(s)	*int(s).*	interjection(s)
invariable	*invar.*	invariable
legal, law	*jurid.*	juridique
language	*lang.*	langue
masculine	*m.*	masculin
medicine	*med., méd.*	médecine
military	*mil.*	militaire
music	*mus.*	musique
noun(s)	*n(s).*	nom(s)
nautical	*naut.*	nautique
oneself	*o.s.*	se, soi-même
proprietary term	*P.*	marque déposée
pejorative	*pej., péj.*	péjoratif
philosophy	*phil.*	philosophie
photography	*photo.*	photographie
plural	*pl.*	pluriel
politics	*pol.*	politique
possessive	*poss.*	possessif
past participle	*p.p.*	participe passé
prefix	*pref., préf.*	préfixe
preposition(s)	*prep(s)., prép(s).*	préposition(s)
present participle	*pres. p.*	participe présent
pronoun	*pron.*	pronom
psychology	*psych.*	psychologie
past tense	*p.t.*	passé
something	*qch.*	quelque chose
someone	*qn.*	quelqu'un
railroad	*rail.*	chemin de fer
religion	*relig.*	religion
relative pronoun	*rel. pron., pron. rel.*	pronom relatif

school, scholastic	*schol., scol.*	scolaire
singular	*sing.*	singulier
slang	*sl.*	argot
someone	*s.o.*	quelqu'un
something	*sth.*	quelque chose
technical	*techn.*	technique
television	*TV*	télévision
university	*univ.*	université
auxiliary verb	*v. aux.*	verbe auxiliaire
intransitive verb	*v.i.*	verbe intransitif
pronominal verb	*v. pr.*	verbe pronominal
transitive verb	*v.t.*	verbe transitif

Note on proprietary status

This dictionary includes some words which have, or are asserted to have, proprietary status as trademarks or otherwise. Their inclusion dose not imply that they have acquired for legal purposes a non-proprietary or general significance, nor any other judgment concerning their legal status In cases where the editorial staff have some evidence that a word has proprietary status this is indicated in the entry for that word by the symbol Ⓡ, but no judgment concerning the legal status of such words is made or implied thereby.

Pronunciation of French

Phonetic symbols

Vowels

i	vie	y	vêtu
e	pré	ø	peu
ɛ	lait	œ	peur
a	plat	ə	de
ɑ	bas	ɛ̃	matin
ɔ	mort	ɑ̃	sans
o	mot	ɔ̃	bon
u	genou	œ̃	lundi

Consonants and semi-consonants

p	payer	ʒ	je
b	bon	m	main
t	terre	n	nous
d	dans	l	long
k	cou	r	rue
g	gant	ɲ	agneau
f	feu	ŋ	camping
v	vous	j	yeux
s	sale	w	oui
z	zéro	ɥ	huile
ʃ	chat		

Note: ' before the pronunciation of a word beginning with *h* indicates no liaison or elision.
An asterisk immediately following an apostrophe in some words like **qu'*** shows that this form of the word is used before a vowel or mute 'h'.

Français · Anglais
French · English

A

a /a/ *voir* avoir.

à /a/ *prép.* (*à* + *le* = *au*, *à* + *les* = *aux*) in, at; (*direction*) to; (*temps*) at; (*jusqu'à*) to, till; (*date*) on; (*époque*) in; (*moyen*) by, on; (*prix*) for; (*appartenance*) of; (*mesure*) by. **donner**/*etc.* **à qn.**, give/*etc.* to s.o. **apprendre**/*etc.* **à faire**, learn/*etc.* to do. **l'homme à la barbe,** the man with the beard. **à la radio,** on the radio. **c'est à moi**/*etc.*, it is mine/*etc.* **c'est à vous**/*etc.* **de,** it is up to you/*etc.* to; (*en jouant*) it is your/*etc.* turn to. **à six km d'ici,** six km. away. **dix km à l'heure,** ten km. an *ou* per hour. **il a un crayon à la main,** he's got a pencil in his hand.

abaissement /abɛsmã/ *n.m.* (*baisse*) drop, fall.

abaisser /abese/ *v.t.* lower; (*levier*) pull *ou* push down; (*fig.*) humiliate. **s'~** *v. pr.* go down, drop; (*fig.*) humiliate o.s. **s'~ à,** stoop to.

abandon /abãdɔ̃/ *n.m.* abandonment; desertion; (*sport*) withdrawal; (*naturel*) abandon. **à l'~,** in a state of neglect. **~ner** /-ɔne/ *v.t.* abandon, desert; (*renoncer à*) give up, abandon; (*céder*) give (**à,** to). **s'~ner à,** give o.s. up to.

abasourdir /abazurdir/ *v.t.* stun.

abat-jour /abaʒur/ *n.m. invar.* lampshade.

abats /aba/ *n.m. pl.* offal.

abattement /abatmã/ *n.m.* dejection; (*faiblesse*) exhaustion; (*comm.*) allowance.

abattis /abati/ *n.m. pl.* giblets.

abattoir /abatwar/ *n.m.* slaughter-house, abattoir.

abattre† /abatr/ *v.t.* knock down; (*arbre*) cut down; (*animal*) slaughter; (*avion*) shoot down; (*affaiblir*) weaken; (*démoraliser*) dishearten. **s'~** *v. pr.* come down, fall (down). **se laisser ~,** let things get one down.

abbaye /abei/ *n.f.* abbey.

abbé /abe/ *n.m.* priest; (*supérieur d'une abbaye*) abbot.

abcès /apsɛ/ *n.m.* abscess.

abdi|quer /abdike/ *v.t./i.* abdicate. **~cation** *n.f.* abdication.

abdom|en /abdɔmɛn/ *n.m.* abdomen. **~inal** (*m. pl.* **~inaux**) *a.* abdominal.

abeille /abɛj/ *n.f.* bee.

aberrant, ~e /abɛrã, -t/ *a.* absurd.

aberration /abɛrasjɔ̃/ *n.f.* aberration; (*idée*) absurd idea.

abêtir /abetir/ *v.t.* make stupid.

abhorrer /abɔre/ *v.t.* loathe, abhor.

abîme /abim/ *n.m.* abyss.

abîmer /abime/ *v.t.* damage, spoil. **s'~** *v. pr.* get damaged *ou* spoilt.

abject /abʒɛkt/ *a.* abject.

abjurer /abʒyre/ *v.t.* abjure.

ablation /ablasjɔ̃/ *n.f.* removal.

ablutions /ablysjɔ̃/ *n.f. pl.* ablutions.

aboiement /abwamã/ *n.m.* bark (ing). **~s,** barking.

abois (aux) /(oz)abwa/ *adv.* at bay.

abol|ir /abɔlir/ *v.t.* abolish. **~ition** *n.f.* abolition.

abominable /abɔminabl/ *a.* abominable.

abond|ant, ~ante /abɔ̃dã, -t/ *a.* abundant, plentiful. **~amment** *adv.* abundantly. **~ance** *n.f.* abundance; (*prospérité*) affluence.

abonder /abɔ̃de/ *v.i.* abound (**en,** in). **~ dans le sens de qn.,** completely agree with s.o.

abonn|er (s') /(s)abɔne/ *v. pr.* subscribe (**à,** to). **~é, ~ée** *n.m., f.* subscriber; season-ticket holder. **~ement** *n.m.* (*à un journal*) subscription; (*de bus, théâtre, etc.*) season-ticket.

abord /abɔr/ *n.m.* access. **~s,** surroundings. **d'~,** first.

abordable /abɔrdabl/ *a.* (*prix*) reasonable; (*personne*) approachable.

abordage /abɔrdaʒ/ *n.m.* (*accident: naut.*) collision. **prendre à l'~,** (*navire*) board, attack.

aborder /abɔrde/ v.t. approach; (*lieu*) reach; (*problème etc.*) tackle. ● v.i. reach land.

aborigène /abɔriʒɛn/ n.m. aborigine, aboriginal.

aboutir /abutir/ v.i. succeed, achieve a result. **~ à,** end (up) in, lead to. **n'~ à rien,** come to nothing.

aboutissement /abutismɑ̃/ n.m. outcome.

aboyer /abwaje/ v.i. bark.

abrasi|f, ~ve /abrazif, -v/ a. & n.m. abrasive.

abrégé /abreʒe/ n.m. summary.

abréger /abreʒe/ v.t. (*texte*) shorten, abridge; (*mot*) abbreviate, shorten; (*visite*) cut short.

abreuv|er /abrœve/ v.t. water; (*fig.*) overwhelm (**de,** with). **s'~er** v. pr. drink. **~oir** n.m. watering-place.

abréviation /abrevjasjɔ̃/ n.f. abbreviation.

abri /abri/ n.m. shelter. **à l'~,** under cover. **à l'~ de** sheltered from.

abricot /abriko/ n.m. apricot.

abriter /abrite/ v.t. shelter; (*recevoir*) house. **s'~** v. pr. (take) shelter.

abroger /abrɔʒe/ v.t. repeal.

abrupt /abrypt/ a. steep, sheer; (*fig.*) abrupt.

abruti, ~e /abryti/ n.m., f. (*fam.*) idiot.

abrutir /abrytir/ v.t. make ou drive stupid, dull the mind of.

absence /apsɑ̃s/ n.f. absence.

absent, ~e /apsɑ̃, -t/ a. absent, away; (*chose*) missing. ● n.m., f. absentee. **il est toujours ~,** he's still away. **d'un air ~,** absently. **~éisme** /-teism/ n.m. absenteeism. **~éiste** /-teist/ n.m./f. absentee.

absenter (s') /(s)apsɑ̃te/ v. pr. go ou be away; (*sortir*) go out, leave.

absolu /apsɔly/ a. absolute. **~ment** adv. absolutely.

absolution /apsɔlysjɔ̃/ n.f. absolution.

absor|ber /apsɔrbe/ v.t. absorb; (*temps etc.*) take up. **~bant, ~bante** a. (*travail etc.*) absorbing; (*matière*) absorbent. **~ption** n.f. absorption.

absoudre /apsudr/ v.t. absolve.

absten|ir (s') /(s)apstənir/ v. pr. abstain. **s'~ir de,** refrain from. **~tion** /-ɑ̃sjɔ̃/ n.f. abstention.

abstinence /apstinɑ̃s/ n.f. abstinence.

abstr|aire /apstrɛr/ v.t. abstract. **~action** n.f. abstraction. **faire ~action de,** disregard. **~ait, ~aite** a. & n.m. abstract.

absurd|e /apsyrd/ a. absurd. **~ité** n.f. absurdity.

abus /aby/ n.m. abuse, misuse; (*injustice*) abuse. **~ de confiance,** breach of trust. **~ sexuel,** sexual abuse.

abuser /abyze/ v.t. deceive. ● v.i. go too far. **s'~** v. pr. be mistaken. **~ de,** abuse, misuse; (*profiter de*) take advantage of; (*alcool etc.*) over-indulge in.

abusi|f, ~ve /abyzif, -v/ a. excessive; (*usage*) mistaken.

acabit /akabi/ n.m. **du même ~,** of that sort.

académicien, ~ne /akademisjɛ̃, -jɛn/ n.m., f. academician.

académ|ie /akademi/ n.f. academy; (*circonscription*) educational district. **A~ie,** Academy. **~ique** a. academic.

acajou /akaʒu/ n.m. mahogany.

acariâtre /akarjɑtr/ a. cantankerous.

accablement /akɑbləmɑ̃/ n.m. despondency.

accabl|er /akɑble/ v.t. overwhelm. **~er d'impôts,** burden with taxes. **~er d'injures,** heap insults upon. **~ant, ~ante** a. (*chaleur*) oppressive.

accalmie /akalmi/ n.f. lull.

accaparer /akapare/ v.t. monopolize; (*fig.*) take up all the time of.

accéder /aksede/ v.i. **~ à,** reach; (*pouvoir, requête, trône, etc.*) accede to.

accélér|er /akselere/ v.i. (*auto.*) accelerate. ● v.t., **s'~er** v. pr. speed up. **~ateur** n.m. accelerator. **~ation** n.f. acceleration; speeding up.

accent /aksɑ̃/ n.m. accent; (*sur une syllabe*) stress, accent; (*ton*) tone. **mettre l'~ sur,** stress.

accent|uer /aksɑ̃tɥe/ v.t. (*lettre, syllabe*) accent; (*fig.*) emphasize, accentuate. **s'~uer** v. pr. become more pronounced, increase. **~uation** n.f. accentuation.

accept|er /aksɛpte/ v.t. accept. **~er de,** agree to. **~able** a. acceptable. **~ation** n.f. acceptance.

acception /aksɛpsjɔ̃/ n.f. meaning.

accès /aksɛ/ n.m. access; (*porte*) entrance; (*de fièvre*) attack; (*de colère*) fit; (*de joie*) (out)burst. **les ~ de,** (*voies*) the approaches to. **facile d'~,** easy to get to.

accessible /aksesibl/ *a.* accessible; (*personne*) approachable.

accession /aksɛsjɔ̃/ *n.f.* **~ à,** accession to.

accessit /aksesit/ *n.m.* honourable mention.

accessoire /akseswar/ *a.* secondary. ● *n.m.* accessory; (*théâtre*) prop.

accident /aksidã/ *n.m.* accident. **~ de train/d'avion,** train/plane crash. **par ~,** by accident. **~é** /-te/ *a.* damaged *ou* hurt (in an accident); (*terrain*) uneven, hilly.

accidentel, ~le /aksidãtɛl/ *a.* accidental.

acclam|er /aklame/ *v.t.* cheer, acclaim. **~ations** *n.f. pl.* cheers.

acclimat|er /aklimate/ *v.t.,* **s'~er** *v. pr.* acclimatize; (*Amer.*) acclimate. **~ation** *n.f.* acclimatization; (*Amer.*) acclimation.

accolade /akɔlad/ *n.f.* embrace; (*signe*) brace, bracket.

accommodant, ~e /akɔmɔdã, -t/ *a.* accommodating.

accommodement /akɔmɔdmã/ *n.m.* compromise.

accommoder /akɔmɔde/ *v.t.* adapt (**à,** to); (*cuisiner*) prepare; (*assaisonner*) flavour. **s'~ de,** put up with.

accompagn|er /akɔ̃paɲe/ *v.t.* accompany. **s'~er de,** be accompanied by. **~ateur, ~atrice** *n.m., f.* (*mus.*) accompanist; (*guide*) guide. **~ement** *n.m.* (*mus.*) accompaniment.

accompli /akɔ̃pli/ *a.* accomplished.

accompl|ir /akɔ̃plir/ *v.t.* carry out, fulfil. **s'~ir** *v. pr.* be carried out, happen. **~issement** *n.m.* fulfilment.

accord /akɔr/ *n.m.* agreement; (*harmonie*) harmony; (*mus.*) chord. **être d'~,** agree (**pour,** to). **se mettre d'~,** come to an agreement, agree. **d'~!,** all right!, OK!

accordéon /akɔrdeɔ̃/ *n.m.* accordion.

accord|er /akɔrde/ *v.t.* grant; (*couleurs etc.*) match; (*mus.*) tune. **s'~er** *v. pr.* agree. **s'~er avec,** (*s'entendre avec*) get on with. **~eur** *n.m.* tuner.

accoster /akɔste/ *v.t.* accost; (*navire*) come alongside.

accotement /akɔtmã/ *n.m.* roadside, verge; (*Amer.*) shoulder.

accoter (s') /(s)akɔte/ *v. pr.* lean (**à,** against).

accouch|er /akuʃe/ *v.i.* give birth (**de,** to); (*être en travail*) be in labour. ● *v.t.* deliver. **~ement** *n.m.* childbirth; (*travail*) labour. **(médecin) ~eur** *n.m.* obstetrician. **~euse** *n.f.* midwife.

accoud|er (s') /(s)akude/ *v. pr.* lean (one's elbows) on. **~oir** *n.m.* armrest.

accoupl|er /akuple/ *v.t.* couple; (*faire copuler*) mate. **s'~er** *v. pr.* mate. **~ement** *n.m.* mating; coupling.

accourir /akurir/ *v.i.* run up.

accoutrement /akutrəmã/ *n.m.* (strange) garb.

accoutumance /akutymãs/ *n.f.* habituation; (*méd.*) addiction.

accoutum|er /akutyme/ *v.t.* accustom. **s'~er** *v. pr.* get accustomed. **~é** *a.* customary.

accréditer /akredite/ *v.t.* give credence to; (*personne*) accredit.

accro /akro/ *n.m./f.* (*drogué*) addict; (*amateur*) fan.

accroc /akro/ *n.m.* tear, rip; (*fig.*) hitch.

accroch|er /akrɔʃe/ *v.t.* (*suspendre*) hang up; (*attacher*) hook, hitch; (*déchirer*) catch; (*heurter*) hit; (*attirer*) attract. **s'~er** *v. pr.* cling, hang on; (*se disputer*) clash. **~age** *n.m.* hanging; hooking; (*auto.*) collision; (*dispute*) clash; (*mil.*) encounter.

accroissement /akrwasmã/ *n.m.* increase (**de,** in).

accroître /akrwatr/ *v.t.,* **s'~** *v. pr.* increase.

accroup|ir (s') /(s)akrupir/ *v. pr.* squat. **~i** *a.* squatting.

accru /akry/ *a.* increased, greater.

accueil /akœj/ *n.m.* reception, welcome.

accueill|ir† /akœjir/ *v.t.* receive, welcome; (*aller chercher*) meet. **~ant, ~ante** *a.* friendly.

acculer /akyle/ *v.t.* corner. **~ à,** force *ou* drive into *ou* against *ou* close to.

accumul|er /akymyle/ *v.t.,* **s'~er** *v. pr.* accumulate, pile up. **~ateur** *n.m.* accumulator. **~ation** *n.f.* accumulation.

accus /aky/ *n.m. pl.* (*fam.*) battery.

accusation /akyzasjɔ̃/ *n.f.* accusation; (*jurid.*) charge. **l'~,** (*magistrat*) the prosecution.

accus|er /akyze/ *v.t.* accuse (**de,** of); (*blâmer*) blame (**de,** for); (*jurid.*) charge (**de,** with); (*fig.*) show, emphasize. **~er reception de,**

acknowledge receipt of. **~ateur,** **~atrice** *a.* incriminating; *n.m.,* *f.* accuser. **~é, ~ée** *a.* marked; *n.m.,* *f.* accused.

acerbe /asɛrb/ *a.* bitter.

acéré /asere/ *a.* sharp.

achalandé /aʃalɑ̃de/ *a.* **bien ~,** well-stocked.

acharn|é /aʃarne/ *a.* relentless, ferocious. **~ement** *n.m.* relentlessness.

acharner (s') /(s)aʃarne/ *v. pr.* **s'~ sur,** set upon; (*poursuivre*) hound. **s'~ à faire,** keep on doing.

achat /aʃa/ *n.m.* purchase. **~s,** shopping. **faire l'~ de,** buy.

acheminer /aʃmine/ *v.t.* dispatch, convey. **s'~ vers,** head for.

achet|er /aʃte/ *v.t.* buy. **~er à,** buy from; (*pour*) buy for. **~eur, ~euse** *n.m., f.* buyer; (*client de magasin*) shopper.

achèvement /aʃɛvmɑ̃/ *n.m.* completion.

achever /aʃve/ *v.t.* finish (off). **s'~** *v. pr.* end.

acid|e /asid/ *a.* acid, sharp. ● *n.m.* acid. **~ité** *n.f.* acidity. **~ulé** *a.* slightly acid.

acier /asje/ *n.m.* steel. **aciérie** *n.f.* steelworks.

acné /akne/ *n.f.* acne.

acolyte /akɔlit/ *n.m.* (*péj.*) associate.

acompte /akɔ̃t/ *n.m.* deposit, part-payment.

à-côté /akote/ *n.m.* side-issue. **~s,** (*argent*) extras.

à-coup /aku/ *n.m.* jolt, jerk. **par ~s,** by fits and starts.

acoustique /akustik/ *n.f.* acoustics. ● *a.* acoustic.

acqu|érir† /akerir/ *v.t.* acquire, gain; (*biens*) purchase, acquire. **~éreur** *n.m.* purchaser. **~isition** *n.f.* acquisition; purchase.

acquiescer /akjese/ *v.i.* acquiesce, agree.

acquis, ~e /aki, -z/ *n.m.* experience. ● *a.* acquired; (*fait*) established; (*faveurs*) secured. **~ à,** (*projet*) in favour of.

acquit /aki/ *n.m.* receipt. **par ~ de conscience,** for peace of mind.

acquitt|er /akite/ *v.t.* acquit; (*dette*) settle. **s'~er de,** (*promesse, devoir*) carry out. **s'~er envers,** repay. **~ement** *n.m.* acquittal; settlement.

âcre /ɑkr/ *a.* acrid.

acrobate /akrɔbat/ *n.m./f.* acrobat.

acrobatie /akrɔbasi/ *n.f.* acrobatics. **~ aérienne,** aerobatics. **acrobatique** /-tik/ *a.* acrobatic.

acte /akt/ *n.m.* act, action, deed; (*théâtre*) act; (*de naissance, mariage*) certificate. **~s,** (*compte rendu*) proceedings. **prendre ~ de,** note.

acteur /aktœr/ *n.m.* actor.

acti|f, ~ve /aktif, -v/ *a.* active. ● *n.m.* (*comm.*) assets. **avoir à son ~f,** have to one's credit *ou* name. **~vement** *adv.* actively.

action /aksjɔ̃/ *n.f.* action; (*comm.*) share; (*jurid.*) action. **~naire** /-jɔnɛr/ *n.m./f.* shareholder.

actionner /aksjone/ *v.t.* work, activate.

activer /aktive/ *v.t.* speed up; (*feu*) boost. **s'~** *v. pr.* hurry, rush.

activiste /aktivist/ *n.m./f.* activist.

activité /aktivite/ *n.f.* activity. **en ~,** active.

actrice /aktris/ *n.f.* actress.

actualiser /aktɥalize/ *v.t.* update.

actualité /aktɥalite/ *n.f.* topicality. **l'~,** current events. **les ~s,** news. **d'~,** topical.

actuel, ~le /aktɥel/ *a.* present; (*d'actualité*) topical. **~lement** *adv.* at the present time.

acuité /akɥite/ *n.f.* acuteness.

acupunct|ure /akypɔ̃ktyr/ *n.f.* acupuncture. **~eur** *n.m.* acupuncturist.

adage /adaʒ/ *n.m.* adage.

adapt|er /adapte/ *v.t.* adapt; (*fixer*) fit. **s'~er** *v. pr.* adapt (o.s.); (*techn.*) fit, **~ateur, ~atrice** *n.m., f.* adapter; *n.m.* (*électr.*) adapter. **~ation** *n.f.* adaptation.

additif /aditif/ *n.m.* (*note*) rider; (*substance*) additive.

addition /adisjɔ̃/ *n.f.* addition; (*au café etc.*) bill; (*Amer.*) check. **~nel, ~nelle** /-jɔnɛl/ *a.* additional. **~ner** /-jɔne/ *v.t.* add; (*totaliser*) add (up).

adepte /adɛpt/ *n.m./f.* follower.

adéquat, ~e /adekwa, -t/ *a.* suitable.

adhérent, ~e /aderɑ̃, -t/ *n.m., f.* member.

adhé|rer /adere/ *v.i.* adhere, stick (à, to). **~rer à,** (*club etc.*) be a member of; (*s'inscrire à*) join. **~rence** *n.f.* adhesion. **~sif, ~sive** *a. & n.m.* adhesive. **~sion** *n.f.* membership; (*accord*) adherence.

adieu (*pl.* **~x**) /adjø/ *int. & n.m.* goodbye, farewell.

adipeu|x, ~**se** /adipø, -z/ *a.* fat; (*tissu*) fatty.

adjacent, ~**e** /adʒasɑ̃, -t/ *a.* adjacent.

adjectif /adʒɛktif/ *n.m.* adjective.

adjoindre /adʒwɛ̃dr/ *v.t.* add, attach; (*personne*) appoint. **s'**~ *v. pr.* appoint.

adjoint, ~**e** /adʒwɛ̃, -t/ *n.m.*, *f.* & *a.* assistant. ~ **au maire,** deputy mayor.

adjudant /adʒydɑ̃/ *n.m.* warrant-officer.

adjuger /adʒyʒe/ *v.t.* award; (*aux enchères*) auction. **s'**~ *v. pr.* take.

adjurer /adʒyre/ *v.t.* beseech.

admettre† /admɛtr/ *v.t.* let in, admit; (*tolérer*) allow; (*reconnaître*) admit; (*candidat*) pass.

administrati|f, ~**ve** /administratif, -v/ *a.* administrative.

administr|er /administre/ *v.t.* run, manage; (*justice, biens, antidote, etc.*) administer. ~**ateur,** ~**atrice** *n.m.*, *f.* administrator, director. ~**ation** *n.f.* administration. **A**~**ation,** Civil Service.

admirable /admirabl/ *a.* admirable.

admirati|f, ~**ve** /admiratif, -v/ *a.* admiring.

admir|er /admire/ *v.t.* admire. ~**ateur,** ~**atrice** *n.m.*, *f.* admirer. ~**ation** *n.f.* admiration.

admissible /admisibl/ *a.* admissible; (*candidat*) eligible.

admission /admisjɔ̃/ *n.f.* admission.

adolescen|t, ~**te** /adɔlesɑ̃, -t/ *n.m.*, *f.* adolescent. ~**ce** *n.f.* adolescence.

adonner (s') /(s)adɔne/ *v. pr.* **s'**~ **à,** devote o.s. to; (*vice*) take to.

adopt|er /adɔpte/ *v.t.* adopt. ~**ion** /-psjɔ̃/ *n.f.* adoption.

adopti|f, ~**ve** /adɔptif, -v/ *a.* (*enfant*) adopted; (*parents*) adoptive.

adorable /adɔrabl/ *a.* delightful, adorable.

ador|er /adɔre/ *v.t.* adore; (*relig.*) worship, adore. ~**ation** *n.f.* adoration; worship.

adosser /adɔse/ *v.t.* **s'**~ *v. pr.* lean back (**à, contre,** against).

adouci|r /adusir/ *v.t.* soften; (*boisson*) sweeten; (*personne*) mellow; (*chagrin*) ease. **s'**~**r** *v. pr.* soften; mellow; ease; (*temps*) become milder. ~**ssant** *n.m.* (fabric) softener.

adresse /adrɛs/ *n.f.* address; (*habileté*) skill.

adresser /adrese/ *v.t.* send; (*écrire l'adresse sur*) address; (*remarque etc.*) address. ~ **la parole à,** speak to. **s'**~ **à,** address; (*aller voir*) go and ask *ou* see; (*bureau*) enquire at; (*viser, intéresser*) be directed at.

adroit, ~**e** /adrwa, -t/ *a.* skilful, clever. ~**ement** /-tmɑ̃/ *adv.* skilfully, cleverly.

aduler /adyle/ *v.t.* adulate.

adulte /adylt/ *n.m./f.* adult. ● *a.* adult; (*plante, animal*) fully- grown.

adultère /adyltɛr/ *a.* adulterous. ● *n.m.* adultery.

advenir /advənir/ *v.i.* occur.

adverbe /advɛrb/ *n.m.* adverb.

adversaire /advɛrsɛr/ *n.m.* opponent, adversary.

adverse /advɛrs/ *a.* opposing.

adversité /advɛrsite/ *n.f.* adversity.

aérateur /aeratœr/ *n.m.* ventilator.

aér|er /aere/ *v.t.* air; (*texte*) lighten. **s'**~**er** *v. pr.* get some air. ~**ation** *n.f.* ventilation. ~**é** *a.* airy.

aérien, ~**ne** /aerjɛ̃, -jɛn/ *a.* air; (*photo*) aerial; (*câble*) overhead; (*fig.*) airy.

aérobic /aerɔbik/ *m.* aerobics.

aérodrome /aerɔdrom/ *n.m.* aerodrome.

aérodynamique /aerɔdinamik/ *a.* streamlined, aerodynamic.

aérogare /aerɔgar/ *n.f.* air terminal.

aéroglisseur /aerɔglisœr/ *n.m.* hovercraft.

aérogramme /aerɔgram/ *n.m.* air-mail letter; (*Amer.*) aerogram.

aéronautique /aerɔnotik/ *a.* aeronautical. ● *n.f.* aeronautics.

aéronavale /aerɔnaval/ *n.f.* Fleet Air Arm; (*Amer.*) Naval Air Force.

aéroport /aerɔpɔr/ *n.m.* airport.

aéroporté /aerɔpɔrte/ *a.* airborne.

aérosol /aerɔsɔl/ *n.m.* aerosol.

aérospat|ial (*m. pl.* ~**iaux**) /aerɔspasjal, -jo/ *a.* aerospace.

affable /afabl/ *a.* affable.

affaibl|ir /afeblir/ *v.t.*, **s'**~**ir** *v. pr.* weaken. ~**issement** *n.m.* weakening.

affaire /afɛr/ *n.f.* matter, affair; (*histoire*) affair; (*transaction*) deal; (*occasion*) bargain; (*firme*) business; (*jurid.*) case. ~**s,** affairs; (*comm.*) business; (*effets*) belongings. **avoir** ~ **à,** (have to) deal with. **c'est mon** ~**, ce sont mes** ~**s,** that is my business. **faire l'**~**,** do the job. **tirer**

qn. d'~, help s.o. out. **se tirer d'~**, manage.

affair|er (s') /(s)afere/ v. pr. bustle about. ~é a. busy.

affaiss|er (s') /(s)afese/ v. pr. (sol) sink, subside; (poutre) sag; (personne) collapse. ~ement /-ɛsmɑ̃/ n.m. subsidence.

affaler (s') /(s)afale/ v. pr. slump (down), collapse.

affam|er /afame/ v.t. starve. ~é a. starving.

affect|é /afɛkte/ a. affected. ~ation[1] n.f. affectation.

affect|er /afɛkte/ v.t. (feindre, émouvoir) affect; (destiner) assign; (nommer) appoint, post. ~ation[2] n.f. assignment; appointment, posting.

affecti|f, ~ve /afɛktif, -v/ a. emotional.

affection /afɛksjɔ̃/ n.f. affection; (maladie) ailment. ~ner /-jɔne/ v.t. be fond of.

affectueu|x, ~se /afɛktɥø, -z/ a. affectionate.

affermir /afɛrmir/ v.t. strengthen.

affiche /afiʃ/ n.f. (public) notice; (publicité) poster; (théâtre) bill.

affich|er /afiʃe/ v.t. (annonce) put up; (événement) announce; (sentiment etc, comput.) display. ~age n.m. billposting; (électronique) display.

affilée (d') /(d)afile/ adv. in a row, at a stretch.

affiler /afile/ v.t. sharpen.

affil|ier (s') /(s)afilje/ v. pr. become affiliated. ~iation n.f. affiliation.

affiner /afine/ v.t. refine.

affinité /afinite/ n.f. affinity.

affirmati|f, ~ve /afirmatif, -v/ a. affirmative. ● n.f. affirmative.

affirm|er /afirme/ v.t. assert. ~ation n.f. assertion.

affleurer /aflœre/ v.i. appear on the surface.

affliction /afliksjɔ̃/ n.f. affliction.

afflig|er /afliʒe/ v.t. grieve. ~é a. distressed. ~é de, afflicted with.

affluence /aflyɑ̃s/ n.f. crowd(s).

affluent /aflyɑ̃/ n.m. tributary.

affluer /aflye/ v.i. flood in; (sang) rush.

afflux /afly/ n.m. influx, flood; (du sang) rush.

affol|er /afɔle/ v.t. throw into a panic. **s'~er** v. pr. panic. ~ant, ~ante a. alarming. ~ement n.m. panic.

affranch|ir /afrɑ̃ʃir/ v.t. stamp; (à la machine) frank; (esclave) emancipate; (fig.) free. ~issement n.m. (tarif) postage.

affréter /afrete/ v.t. charter.

affreu|x, ~se /afrø, -z/ a. (laid) hideous; (mauvais) awful. ~sement adv. awfully, hideously.

affriolant, ~e /afrijɔlɑ̃, -t/ a. enticing.

affront /afrɔ̃/ n.m. affront.

affront|er /afrɔ̃te/ v.t. confront. **s'~er** v. pr. confront each other. ~ement n.m. confrontation.

affubler /afyble/ v.t. rig out (de, in).

affût /afy/ n.m. **à l'~**, on the watch (de, for).

affûter /afyte/ v.t. sharpen.

afin /afɛ̃/ prép. & conj. ~ **de/que**, in order to/that.

african|, ~e /afrikɛ̃, -ɛn/ a. & n.m., f. African.

Afrique /afrik/ n.f. Africa. ~ **du Sud**, South Africa.

agacer /agase/ v.t. irritate, annoy.

âge /aʒ/ n.m. age. **quel ~ avez-vous?**, how old are you? ~ **adulte**, adulthood. ~ **mûr**, middle age. **d'un certain ~**, past one's prime.

âgé /aʒe/ a. elderly. ~ **de cinq ans**/etc., five years/etc. old.

agence /aʒɑ̃s/ n.f. agency, bureau, office; (succursale) branch. ~ **d'interim**, employment agency. ~ **de voyages**, travel agency.

agenc|er /aʒɑ̃se/ v.t. organize, arrange. ~ement n.m. organization.

agenda /aʒɛ̃da/ n.m. diary; (Amer.) datebook.

agenouiller (s') /(s)aʒnuje/ v. pr. kneel (down).

agent /aʒɑ̃/ n.m. agent; (fonctionnaire) official. ~ **(de police)**, policeman. ~ **de change**, stockbroker.

agglomération /aglɔmerasjɔ̃/ n.f. built-up area, town.

aggloméré /aglɔmere/ n.m. (bois) chipboard.

agglomérer /aglɔmere/ v.t., **s'~** v. pr. pile up.

agglutiner /aglytine/ v.t., **s'~** v. pr. stick together.

aggraver /agrave/ v.t., **s'~** v. pr. worsen.

agil|e /aʒil/ a. agile, nimble. ~ité n.f. agility.

agir /aʒir/ v.i. act. **il s'agit de faire**, it is a matter of doing; (il faut) it is necessary to do. **dans ce livre il s'agit de,** this book is about. **dont il s'agit,** in question.

agissements /aʒismɑ̃/ *n.m. pl.* (*péj.*) dealings.

agité /aʒite/ *a.* restless, fidgety; (*troublé*) agitated; (*mer*) rough.

agit|er /aʒite/ *v.t.* (*bras etc.*) wave; (*liquide*) shake; (*troubler*) agitate; (*discuter*) debate. **s'~er** *v. pr.* bustle about; (*enfant*) fidget; (*foule, pensées*) stir. **~ateur, ~atrice** *n.m.,* f. agitator. **~ation** *n.f.* bustle; (*trouble*) agitation.

agneau (*pl.* **~x**) /aɲo/ *n.m.* lamb.

agonie /agɔni/ *n.f.* death throes.

agoniser /agɔnize/ *v.i.* be dying.

agraf|e /agraf/ *n.f.* hook; (*pour papiers*) staple. **~er** *v.t.* hook (up); staple. **~euse** *n.f.* stapler.

agrand|ir /agrɑ̃dir/ *v.t.* enlarge. **s'~ir** *v. pr.* expand, grow. **~issement** *n.m.* extension; (*de photo*) enlargement.

agréable /agreabl/ *a.* pleasant. **~ment** /-əmɑ̃/ *adv.* pleasantly.

agré|er /agree/ *v.t.* accept. **~er à,** please. **~é** *a.* authorized.

agrég|ation /agregɑsjɔ̃/ *n.f.* agrégation (*highest examination for recruitment of teachers*). **~é, ~ée** /-ʒe/ *n.m.,* f. agrégé (*teacher who has passed the agrégation*).

agrément /agremɑ̃/ *n.m.* charm; (*plaisir*) pleasure; (*accord*) assent.

agrémenter /agremɑ̃te/ *v.t.* embellish (**de,** with).

agrès /agrɛ/ *n.m. pl.* (gymnastics) apparatus.

agress|er /agrese/ *v.t.* attack. **~eur** /-ɛsœr/ *n.m.* attacker; (*mil.*) aggressor. **~ion** /-ɛsjɔ̃/ *n.f.* attack; (*mil.*) aggression.

agressi|f, ~ve /agresif, -v/ *a.* aggressive. **~vité** *n.f.* aggressiveness.

agricole /agrikɔl/ *a.* agricultural; (*ouvrier etc.*) farm.

agriculteur /agrikyltœr/ *n.m.* farmer.

agriculture /agrikyltyr/ *n.f.* agriculture, farming.

agripper /agripe/ *v.t.,* **s'~ à,** grab, clutch.

agroalimentaire /agrɔalimɑ̃tɛr/ *n.m.* food industry.

agrumes /agrym/ *n.m. pl.* citrus fruit(s).

aguerrir /agerir/ *v.t.* harden.

aguets (aux) /(oz)agɛ/ *adv.* on the look-out.

aguicher /agiʃe/ *v.t.* entice.

ah /a/ *int.* ah, oh.

ahur|ir /ayrir/ *v.t.* dumbfound. **~issement** *n.m.* stupefaction.

ai /e/ *voir* avoir.

aide /ɛd/ *n.f.* help, assistance, aid. ● *n.m./f.* assistant. **à l'~ de,** with the help of. **~ familiale,** home help. **~-mémoire** *n.m. invar.* handbook of facts. **~ sociale,** social security; (*Amer.*) welfare. **~-soignant, ~-soignante** *n.m.,* f. auxiliary nurse. **venir en ~ à,** help.

aider /ede/ *v.t./i.* help, assist. **~ à faire,** help to do. **s'~ de,** use.

aïe /aj/ *int.* ouch, ow.

aïeul, ~e /ajœl/ *n.m.,* f. grandparent.

aïeux /ajø/ *n.m. pl.* forefathers.

aigle /ɛgl/ *n.m.* eagle.

aigr|e /ɛgr/ *a.* sour, sharp; (*fig.*) sharp. **~e-doux, ~e-douce** *a.* bitter-sweet. **~eur** *n.f.* sourness; (*fig.*) sharpness. **~eurs d'estomac,** heartburn.

aigrir /egrir/ *v.t.* embitter; (*caractère*) sour. **s'~** *v. pr.* turn sour; (*personne*) become embittered.

aigu, ~ë /egy/ *a.* acute; (*objet*) sharp; (*voix*) shrill. (*mus.*) **les ~s,** the high notes.

aiguillage /eguijaʒ/ *n.m.* (*rail.*) points; (*rail., Amer.*) switches.

aiguille /eguij/ *n.f.* needle; (*de montre*) hand; (*de balance*) pointer.

aiguill|er /eguije/ *v.t.* shunt; (*fig.*) steer. **~eur** *n.m.* pointsman; (*Amer.*) switchman. **~eur du ciel,** air traffic controller.

aiguillon /eguijɔ̃/ *n.m.* (*dard*) sting; (*fig.*) spur. **~ner** /-jɔne/ *v.t.* spur on.

aiguiser /eg(ɥ)ize/ *v.t.* sharpen; (*fig.*) stimulate.

ail (*pl.* **~s**) /aj/ *n.m.* garlic.

aile /ɛl/ *n.f.* wing.

ailé /ele/ *a.* winged.

aileron /ɛlrɔ̃/ *n.m.* (*de requin*) fin.

ailier /elje/ *n.m.* winger; (*Amer.*) end.

aille /aj/ *voir* aller[1].

ailleurs /ajœr/ *adv.* elsewhere. **d'~,** besides, moreover. **par ~,** moreover, furthermore. **partout ~,** everywhere else.

ailloli /ajɔli/ *n.m.* garlic mayonnaise.

aimable /ɛmabl/ *a.* kind. **~ment** /-əmɑ̃/ *adv.* kindly.

aimant [1] /ɛmɑ̃/ *n.m.* magnet. **~er** /-te/ *v.t.* magnetize.

aimant [2], **~e** /ɛmɑ̃, -t/ *a.* loving. **j'aimerais faire,** I'd like to do. **~ bien,** quite like. **~ mieux** *ou* **autant,** prefer.

aine /ɛn/ *n.f.* groin.

aîné, ~e /ene/ *a.* eldest; (*entre deux*) elder. ● *n.m., f.* eldest (child); elder (child). **~s** *n.m. pl.* elders. **il est mon ~,** he is older than me *ou* my senior.

ainsi /ɛ̃si/ *adv.* thus; (*donc*) so. **~ que,** as well as; (*comme*) as. **et ~ de suite,** and so on. **pour ~ dire,** so to speak, as it were.

air /ɛr/ *n.m.* air; (*mine*) look, air; (*mélodie*) tune. **~ conditionné,** air-conditioning. **avoir l'~ de,** look like. **avoir l'~ de faire,** appear to be doing. **en l'~,** (up) in the air; (*promesses etc.*) empty.

aire /ɛr/ *n.f.* area. **~ d'atterrissage,** landing-strip.

aisance /ɛzɑ̃s/ *n.f.* ease; (*richesse*) affluence.

aise /ɛz/ *n.f.* joy. ● *a.* **bien ~ de/ que,** delighted about/that. **à l'~,** (*sur un siège*) comfortable; (*pas gêné*) at ease; (*fortuné*) comfortably off. **mal à l'~,** uncomfortable; ill at ease. **aimer ses ~s,** like one's comforts. **se mettre à l'~,** make o.s. comfortable.

aisé /eze/ *a.* easy; (*fortuné*) well-off. **~ment** *adv.* easily.

aisselle /ɛsɛl/ *n.f.* armpit.

ait /ɛ/ *voir* avoir.

ajonc /aʒɔ̃/ *n.m.* gorse.

ajourn|er /aʒurne/ *v.t.* postpone; (*assemblée*) adjourn. **~ement** *n.m.* postponement; adjournment.

ajout /aʒu/ *n.m.* addition.

ajouter /aʒute/ *v.t.* **s'~** *v. pr.* add (**à,** to). **~ foi à,** lend credence to.

ajust|er /aʒyste/ *v.t.* adjust; (*coup*) aim; (*cible*) aim at; (*adapter*) fit. **s'~er** *v. pr.* fit. **~age** *n.m.* fitting. **~é** *a.* close-fitting. **~ement** *n.m.* adjustment. **~eur** *n.m.* fitter.

alambic /alɑ̃bik/ *n.m.* still.

alanguir (s') /(s)alɑ̃gir/ *v. pr.* grow languid.

alarme /alarm/ *n.f.* alarm. **donner l'~,** sound the alarm.

alarmer /alarme/ *v.t.* alarm. **s'~** *v. pr.* become alarmed (**de,** at).

alarmiste /alarmist/ *a. & n.m.* alarmist.

albâtre /albɑtr/ *n.m.* alabaster.

albatros /albatros/ *n.m.* albatross.

album /albɔm/ *n.m.* album.

albumine /albymin/ *n.f.* albumin.

alcali /alkali/ *n.m.* alkali.

alcool /alkɔl/ *n.m.* alcohol; (*eau de vie*) brandy. **~ à brûler,** methylated spirit. **~ique** *a. & n.m./f.* alcoholic. **~isé** *a.* (*boisson*) alcoholic. **~isme** *n.m.* alcoholism.

alcootest /alkɔtɛst/ *n.m.* (P.) breath test; (*appareil*) breathalyser.

alcôve /alkov/ *n.f.* alcove.

aléa /alea/ *n.m.* hazard.

aléatoire /aleatwar/ *a.* uncertain; (*comput.*) random.

alentour /alɑ̃tur/ *adv.* around. **~s** *n.m. pl.* surroundings. **aux ~s de,** round about.

alerte /alɛrt/ *a.* agile. ● *n.f.* alert. **~ à la bombe,** bomb scare.

alerter /alɛrte/ *v.t.* alert.

algarade /algarad/ *n.f.* altercation.

alg|èbre /alʒɛbr/ *n.f.* algebra. **~ébrique** *a.* algebraic.

Alger /alʒe/ *n.m./f.* Algiers.

Algérie /alʒeri/ *n.f.* Algeria.

algérien, ~ne /alʒerjɛ̃, -jɛn/ *a. & n.m., f.* Algerian.

algue /alg/ *n.f.* seaweed. **les ~s,** (*bot.*) algae.

alias /aljas/ *adv.* alias.

alibi /alibi/ *n.m.* alibi.

aliéné, ~e /aljene/ *n.m., f.* insane person.

alién|er /aljene/ *v.t.* alienate; (*céder*) give up. **s'~er** *v. pr.* alienate. **~ation** *n.f.* alienation.

aligner /aline/ *v.t.* (*objets*) line up, make lines of; (*chiffres*) string together. **~ sur,** bring into line with. **s'~** *v. pr.* line up. **s'~ sur,** align o.s. on. **alignement** /-əmɑ̃/ *n.m.* alignment.

aliment /alimɑ̃/ *n.m.* food. **~aire** /-tɛr/ *a.* food; (*fig.*) bread-and-butter.

aliment|er /alimɑ̃te/ *v.t.* feed; (*fournir*) supply; (*fig.*) sustain. **~ation** *n.f.* feeding; supply(ing); (*régime*) diet; (*aliments*) groceries.

alinéa /alinea/ *n.m.* paragraph.

aliter (s') /(s)alite/ *v. pr.* take to one's bed.

allaiter /alete/ *v.t.* feed. **~ au biberon,** bottle-feed. **~ au sein,** breast-feed; (*Amer.*) nurse.

allant /alɑ̃/ *n.m.* verve, drive.

allécher /aleʃe/ *v.t.* tempt.

allée /ale/ *n.f.* path, lane; (*menant à une maison*) drive(way). **~s et venues,** comings and goings.

allégation /alegɑsjɔ̃/ *n.f.* allegation.

allég|er /aleʒe/ *v.t.* make lighter; (*poids*) lighten; (*fig.*) alleviate. **~é** *a.* (*diététique*) light.

allègre /alɛgr/ *a.* gay; (*vif*) lively, jaunty.

allégresse /alegrɛs/ *n.f.* gaiety.

alléguer /alege/ *v.t.* put forward.

Allemagne /almaɲ/ *n.f.* Germany. **~ de l'Ouest,** West Germany.

allemand, ~e /almɑ̃, -d/ *a. & n.m., f.* German. ● *n.m.* (*lang.*) German.

aller†[1] /ale/ (*aux. être*) go. **s'en ~** *v. pr.* go away. **~ à,** (*convenir à*) suit; (*s'adapter à*) fit. **~ faire,** be going to do. **comment allez-vous?, (comment) ça va?,** how are you? **ça va!,** all right! **il va bien,** he is well. **il va mieux,** he's better. **allez-y!,** go on! **allez!,** come on! **allons-y!,** let's go!

aller[2] /ale/ *n.m.* outward journey; **~ (simple),** single (ticket); (*Amer.*) one-way (ticket). **~ (et) retour,** return journey; (*Amer.*) round trip; (*billet*) return (ticket); (*Amer.*) round trip (ticket).

allerg|ie /alɛrʒi/ *n.f.* allergy. **~ique** *a.* allergic.

alliage /aljaʒ/ *n.m.* alloy.

alliance /aljɑ̃s/ *n.f.* alliance; (*bague*) wedding-ring; (*mariage*) marriage.

allié, ~e /alje/ *n.m., f.* ally; (*parent*) relative (by marriage).

allier /alje/ *v.t.* combine; (*pol.*) ally. **s'~** *v. pr.* combine; (*pol.*) become allied; (*famille*) become related (**à**, to).

alligator /aligatɔr/ *n.m.* alligator.

allô /alo/ *int.* hallo, hello.

allocation /alɔkɑsjɔ̃/ *n.f.* allowance. **~ (de) chômage,** unemployment benefit. **~s familiales,** family allowance.

allocution /alɔkysjɔ̃/ *n.f.* speech.

allongé /alɔ̃ʒe/ *a.* elongated.

allongement /alɔ̃ʒmɑ̃/ *n.m.* lengthening.

allonger /alɔ̃ʒe/ *v.t.* lengthen; (*bras, jambe*) stretch (out). **s'~** *v. pr.* get longer; (*s'étendre*) stretch (o.s.) out.

allouer /alwe/ *v.t.* allocate.

allum|er /alyme/ *v.t.* light; (*radio, lampe, etc.*) turn on; (*pièce*) switch the light(s) on in; (*fig.*) arouse. **s'~er** *v. pr.* (*lumière*) come on. **~age** *n.m.*

lighting; (*auto.*) ignition. **~e-gaz** *n.m. invar.* gas lighter.

allumette /alymɛt/ *n.f.* match.

allure /alyr/ *n.f.* speed, pace; (*démarche*) walk; (*prestance*) bearing; (*air*) look. **à toute ~,** at full speed. **avoir de l'~,** have style.

allusion /alyzjɔ̃/ *n.f.* allusion (**à**, to); (*implicite*) hint (**à**, at). **faire ~ à,** allude to; hint at.

almanach /almana/ *n.m.* almanac.

aloi /alwa/ *n.m.* **de bon ~,** sterling; (*gaieté*) wholesome.

alors /alɔr/ *adv.* then. ● *conj.* so, then. **~ que,** when, while; (*tandis que*) whereas. **ça ~!,** well! **et ~?,** so what?

alouette /alwɛt/ *n.f.* lark.

alourdir /alurdir/ *v.t.* weigh down.

aloyau (*pl. ~x*) /alwajo/ *n.m.* sirloin.

alpage /alpaʒ/ *n.m.* mountain pasture.

Alpes /alp/ *n.f. pl.* **les ~,** the Alps.

alpestre /alpɛstr/ *a.* alpine.

alphab|et /alfabɛ/ *n.m.* alphabet. **~étique** *a.* alphabetical.

alphabétiser /alfabetize/ *v.t.* teach to read and write.

alphanumérique /alfanymerik/ *a.* alphanumeric.

alpin, ~e /alpɛ̃, -in/ *a.* alpine.

alpinis|te /alpinist/ *n.m./f.* mountaineer. **~me** *n.m.* mountaineering.

altér|er /altere/ *v.t.* falsify; (*abîmer*) spoil; (*donner soif à*) make thirsty. **s'~er** *v. pr.* deteriorate. **~ation** *n.f.* deterioration.

alternati|f, ~ve /altɛrnatif, -v/ *a.* alternating. ● *n.f.* alternative. **~vement** *adv.* alternately.

altern|er /altɛrne/ *v.t./i.* alternate. **~ance** *n.f.* alternation. **en ~ance,** alternately. **~é** *a.* alternate.

Altesse /altɛs/ *n.f.* Highness.

alt|ier, ~ière /altje, -jɛr/ *a.* haughty.

altitude /altityd/ *n.f.* altitude, height.

alto /alto/ *n.m.* viola.

aluminium /alyminjɔm/ *n.m.* aluminium; (*Amer.*) aluminum.

alvéole /alveɔl/ *n.f.* (*de ruche*) cell.

amabilité /amabilite/ *n.f.* kindness.

amadouer /amadwe/ *v.t.* win over.

amaigr|ir /amegrir/ *v.t.* make thin(ner). **~issant, ~issante** *a.* (*régime*) slimming.

amalgam|e /amalgam/ *n.m.* combination. **~er** *v.t.* combine, amalgamate.

amande /amɑ̃d/ *n.f.* almond; (*d'un fruit à noyau*) kernel.

amant /amɑ̃/ *n.m.* lover.

amarr|e /amar/ *n.f.* (mooring) rope. **~es,** moorings. **~er** *v.t.* moor.

amas /amɑ/ *n.m.* heap, pile.

amasser /amase/ *v.t.* amass, gather; (*empiler*) pile up. **s'~** *v. pr.* pile up; (*gens*) gather.

amateur /amatœr/ *n.m.* amateur. **~ de,** lover of. **d'~,** amateur; (*péj.*) amateurish. **~isme** *n.m.* amateurism.

amazone (en) /(ɑ̃)amazon/ *adv.* side-saddle.

Amazonie /amazɔni/ *n.f.* Amazonia.

ambages (sans) /(sɑ̃z)ɑ̃baʒ/ *adv.* in plain language.

ambassade /ɑ̃basad/ *n.f.* embassy.

ambassa|deur, ~drice /ɑ̃basadœr, -dris/ *n.m.*, *f.* ambassador.

ambiance /ɑ̃bjɑ̃s/ *n.f.* atmosphere.

ambiant, ~e /ɑ̃bjɑ̃, -t/ *a.* surrounding.

ambigu, ~ë /ɑ̃bigy/ *a.* ambiguous. **~ïté** /-ɥite/ *n.f.* ambiguity.

ambitieu|x, ~se /ɑ̃bisjø, -z/ *a.* ambitious.

ambition /ɑ̃bisjɔ̃/ *n.f.* ambition. **~ner** /-jɔne/ *v.t.* have as one's ambition (**de,** to).

ambivalent, ~e /ɑ̃bivalɑ̃, -t/ *a.* ambivalent.

ambre /ɑ̃br/ *n.m.* amber.

ambulanc|e /ɑ̃bylɑ̃s/ *n.f.* ambulance. **~ier, ~ière** *n.m.*, *f.* ambulance driver.

ambulant, ~e /ɑ̃bylɑ̃, -t/ *a.* itinerant.

âme /ɑm/ *n.f.* soul. **~ sœur,** soul mate.

amélior|er /ameljɔre/ *v.t.*, **s'~er** *v. pr.* improve. **~ation** *n.f.* improvement.

aménag|er /amenaʒe/ *v.t.* (*arranger*) fit out; (*transformer*) convert; (*installer*) fit up; (*territoire*) develop. **~ement** *n.m.* fitting out; conversion; fitting up; development; (*modification*) adjustment.

amende /amɑ̃d/ *n.f.* fine. **faire ~ honorable,** make an apology.

amend|er /amɑ̃de/ *v.t.* improve; (*jurid.*) amend. **s'~er** *v. pr.* mend one's ways. **~ement** *n.m.* (*de texte*) amendment.

amener /amne/ *v.t.* bring; (*causer*) bring about. **~ qn. à faire,** cause sb. to do. **s'~** *v. pr.* (*fam.*) come along.

amenuiser (s') /(s)amənɥize/ *v. pr.* dwindle.

amer, amère /amɛr/ *a.* bitter.

américain, ~e /amerikɛ̃, -ɛn/ *a.* & *n.m.*, *f.* American.

Amérique /amerik/ *n.f.* America. **~ centrale/latine,** Central/ Latin America. **~ du Nord/Sud,** North/South America.

amertume /amɛrtym/ *n.f.* bitterness.

ameublement /amœbləmɑ̃/ *n.m.* furniture.

ameuter /amøte/ *v.t.* draw a crowd of; (*fig.*) stir up.

ami, ~e /ami/ *n.m.*, *f.* friend; (*de la nature, des livres, etc.*) lover. ● *a.* friendly.

amiable /amjabl/ *a.* amicable. **à l'~** *adv.* amicably; *a.* amicable.

amiante /amjɑ̃t/ *n.m.* asbestos.

amic|al (*m. pl.* **~aux**) /amikal, -o/ *a.* friendly. **~alement** *adv.* in a friendly manner.

amicale /amikal/ *n.f.* association.

amidon /amidɔ̃/ *n.m.* starch. **~ner** /-ɔne/ *v.t.* starch.

amincir /amɛ̃sir/ *v.t.* make thinner. **s'~** *v. pr.* get thinner.

amir|al (*pl.* **~aux**) /amiral, -o/ *n.m.* admiral.

amitié /amitje/ *n.f.* friendship. **~s,** kind regards. **prendre en ~,** take a liking to.

ammoniac /amɔnjak/ *n.m.* (*gaz*) ammonia.

ammoniaque /amɔnjak/ *n.f.* (*eau*) ammonia.

amnésie /amnezi/ *n.f.* amnesia.

amnistie /amnisti/ *n.f.* amnesty.

amniocentèse /amniɔsɛ̃tɛz/ *n.f.* amniocentesis.

amocher /amɔʃe/ *v.t.* (*fam.*) mess up.

amoindrir /amwɛ̃drir/ *v.t.* diminish.

amollir /amɔlir/ *v.t.* soften.

amonceler /amɔ̃sle/ *v.t.*, **s'~** *v.pr.* pile up.

amont (en) /(ɑ̃)amɔ̃/ *adv.* upstream.

amorc|e /amɔrs/ *n.f.* bait; (*début*) start; (*explosif*) fuse, cap; (*de pistolet d'enfant*) cap. **~er** *v.t.* start; (*hameçon*) bait; (*pompe*) prime.

amorphe /amɔrf/ *a.* (*mou*) listless.

amortir /amɔrtir/ *v.t.* (*choc*) cushion; (*bruit*) deaden; (*dette*) pay off; (*objet acheté*) make pay for itself.

amortisseur /amɔrtisœr/ *n.m.* shock absorber.

amour /amur/ *n.m.* love. **pour l'~de,** for the sake of. **~-propre** *n.m.* self-respect.

amouracher (s') /(s)amuraʃe/ *v. pr.* become infatuated (**de,** with).

amoureu|x, ~se /amurø, -z/ *a.* (*ardent*) amorous; (*vie*) love. ● *n.m., f.* lover. **~x de qn.,** in love with s.o.

amovible /amɔvibl/ *a.* removable.

ampère /ɑ̃pɛr/ *n.m.* amp(ere).

amphibie /ɑ̃fibi/ *a.* amphibious.

amphithéâtre /ɑ̃fiteatr/ *n.m.* amphitheatre; (*d'université*) lecture hall.

ample /ɑ̃pl/ *a.* ample; (*mouvement*) broad. **~ment** /-əmɑ̃/ *adv.* amply.

ampleur /ɑ̃plœr/ *n.f.* extent, size; (*de vêtement*) fullness.

ampli /ɑ̃pli/ *n.m.* amplifier.

amplif|ier /ɑ̃plifje/ *v.t.* amplify; (*fig.*) expand, develop. **s'~ier** *v.pr.* expand, develop. **~icateur** *n.m.* amplifier.

ampoule /ɑ̃pul/ *n.f.* (*électrique*) bulb; (*sur la peau*) blister; (*de médicament*) phial.

ampoulé /ɑ̃pule/ *a.* turgid.

amput|er /ɑ̃pyte/ *v.t.* amputate; (*fig.*) reduce. **~ation** *n.f.* amputation; (*fig.*) reduction.

amuse-gueule /amyzgœl/ *n.m. invar.* appetizer.

amus|er /amyze/ *v.t.* amuse; (*détourner l'attention de*) distract. **s'~er** *v. pr.* enjoy o.s.; (*jouer*) play. **~ant, ~ante** *a.* (*blague*) funny; (*soirée*) enjoyable, entertaining. **~ement** *n.m.* amusement; (*passe-temps*) diversion. **~eur** *n.m.* (*péj.*) entertainer.

amygdale /amidal/ *n.f.* tonsil.

an /ɑ̃/ *n.m.* year. **avoir dix/etc. ans,** be ten/*etc.* years old.

anachronisme /anakrɔnism/ *n.m.* anachronism.

analgésique /analʒezik/ *a. & n.m.* analgesic.

analog|ie /analɔʒi/ *n.f.* analogy. **~ique** *a.* analogical, (*comput.*) analogue.

analogue /analɔg/ *a.* similar.

analphabète /analfabɛt/ *a. & n.m./f.* illiterate.

analy|se /analiz/ *n.f.* analysis; (*de sang*) test. **~ser** *v.t.* analyse. **~ste** *n.m./f.* analyst. **~tique** *a.* analytical.

ananas /anana(s)/ *n.m.* pineapple.

anarch|ie /anarʃi/ *n.f.* anarchy. **~ique** *a.* anarchic. **~iste** *n.m./f.* anarchist.

anatom|ie /anatɔmi/ *n.f.* anatomy. **~ique** *a.* anatomical.

ancestr|al (*m. pl.* **~aux**) /ɑ̃sɛstral, -o/ *a.* ancestral.

ancêtre /ɑ̃sɛtr/ *n.m.* ancestor.

anche /ɑ̃ʃ/ *n.f.* (*mus.*) reed.

anchois /ɑ̃ʃwa/ *n.m.* anchovy.

ancien, ~ne /ɑ̃sjɛ̃, -jɛn/ *a.* old; (*de jadis*) ancient; (*meuble*) antique; (*précédent*) former, ex-, old; (*dans une fonction*) senior. ● *n.m., f.* senior; (*par l'âge*) elder. **~ combattant,** ex-serviceman. **~nement** /-jɛnmɑ̃/ *adv.* formerly. **~neté** /-jɛnte/ *n.f.* age; seniority.

ancr|e /ɑ̃kr/ *n.f.* anchor. **jeter/lever l'~e,** cast/weigh anchor. **~er** *v.t.* anchor; (*fig.*) fix. **s'~er** *v.pr.* anchor.

andouille /ɑ̃duj/ *n.f.* sausage filled with chitterlings; (*idiot: fam.*) nitwit.

âne /ɑn/ *n.m.* donkey, ass; (*imbécile*) ass.

anéantir /aneɑ̃tir/ *v.t.* destroy; (*exterminer*) annihilate; (*accabler*) overwhelm.

anecdot|e /anɛkdɔt/ *n.f.* anecdote. **~ique** *a.* anecdotal.

aném|ie /anemi/ *n.f.* anaemia. **~ié, ~ique** *adjs.* anaemic.

ânerie /ɑnri/ *n.f.* stupidity; (*parole*) stupid remark.

ânesse /ɑnɛs/ *n.f.* she-ass.

anesthés|ie /anɛstezi/ *n.f.* (*opération*) anaesthetic. **~ique** *a. & n.m.* (*substance*) anaesthetic.

ang|e /ɑ̃ʒ/ *n.m.* angel. **aux ~es,** seventh heaven. **~élique** *a.* angelic.

angélus /ɑ̃ʒelys/ *n.m.* angelus.

angine /ɑ̃ʒin/ *n.f.* throat infection.

anglais, ~e /ɑ̃glɛ, -z/ *a.* English. ● *n.m., f.* Englishman, Englishwoman. ● *n.m.* (*lang.*) English.

angle /ɑ̃gl/ *n.m.* angle; (*coin*) corner.

Angleterre /ɑ̃glətɛr/ *n.f.* England.

anglicisme /ɑ̃glisism/ *n.m.* anglicism.

angliciste /ɑ̃glisist/ *n.m./f.* English specialist.

anglo- /ɑ̃glɔ/ *préf.* Anglo-.

anglophone /ɑ̃glɔfɔn/ *a.* English-speaking. ● *n.m./f.* English speaker.

anglo-saxon, ~ne /ɑ̃glɔsaksɔ̃, -ɔn/ *a. & n.m., f.* Anglo-Saxon.

angoiss|e /ãgwas/ *n.f.* anxiety. **~ant,
~ante** *a.* harrowing. **~é** *a.* anxious.
~er *v.t.* make anxious.

anguille /ãgij/ *n.f.* eel.

anguleux, ~se /ãgylø, -z/ *a.* (*traits*)
angular.

anicroche /anikrɔʃ/ *n.f.* snag.

anim|al (*pl.* **~aux**) /animal, -o/ *n.m.*
animal. ● *a.* (*m. pl.* **~aux**) animal.

anima|teur, ~trice /animatœr,
-tris/ *n.m., f.* organizer, leader; (*TV*)
host, hostess.

anim|é /anime/ *a.* lively; (*affairé*)
busy, (*être*) animate. **~ation** *n.f.*
liveliness; (*affairement*) activity; (*cinéma*) animation.

animer /anime/ *v.t.* liven up; (*mener*)
lead; (*mouvoir, pousser*) drive; (*encourager*) spur on. **s'~** *v. pr.* liven
up.

animosité /animozite/ *n.f.* animosity.

anis /anis/ *n.m.* (*parfum, boisson*)
aniseed.

ankylos|er (s') /(s)ãkiloze/ *v. pr.* go
stiff. **~é** *a.* stiff.

anneau (*pl.* **~x**) /ano/ *n.m.* ring; (*de
chaîne*) link.

année /ane/ *n.f.* year.

annexe /anɛks/ *a.* attached; (*question*) related. (*bâtiment*) adjoining.
● *n.f.* annexe; (*Amer.*) annex.

annex|er /anɛkse/ *v.t.* annex; (*docu-
ment*) attach. **~ion** *n.f.* annexation.

annihiler /aniile/ *v.t.* annihilate.

anniversaire /aniverser/ *n.m.* birthday; (*d'un événement*) anniversary.
● *a.* anniversary.

annonc|e /anɔ̃s/ *n.f.* announcement;
(*publicitaire*) advertisement; (*indice*) sign. **~er** *v.t.* announce; (*dénoter*) indicate. **s'~er bien/mal,** look
good/bad. **~eur** *n.m.* advertiser;
(*speaker*) announcer.

Annonciation /anɔ̃sjasjɔ̃/ *n.f.* **l'~,**
the Annunciation.

annuaire /anɥɛr/ *n.m.* year-book. **~
(téléphonique),** (telephone) directory.

annuel, ~le /anɥɛl/ *a.* annual,
yearly. **~lement** *adv.* annually,
yearly.

annuité /anɥite/ *n.f.* annual payment.

annulaire /anɥlɛr/ *n.m.* ringfinger.

annul|er /anyle/ *v.t.* cancel; (*contrat*)
nullify; (*jugement*) quash. **s'~er** *v.
pr.* cancel each other out. **~ation**
n.f. cancellation.

anodin, ~e /anɔdɛ̃, -in/ *a.* insignificant; (*blessure*) harmless.

anomalie /anɔmali/ *n.f.* anomaly.

ânonner /anone/ *v.t./i.* mumble,
drone.

anonymat /anɔnima/ *n.m.* anonym-
ity.

anonyme /anɔnim/ *a.* anonymous.

anorak /anɔrak/ *n.m.* anorak.

anorexie /anɔreksi/ *n.f.* anorexia.

anorm|al (*m. pl.* **~aux**) /anɔrmal, -o/
a. abnormal.

anse /ãs/ *n.f.* handle; (*baie*) cove.

antagonis|me /ãtagɔnism/ *n.m.*
antagonism. **~te** *n.m./f.* antagonist;
a. antagonistic.

antan (d') /(d)ãtã/ *a.* of long ago.

antarctique /ãtarktik/ *a. & n.m.*
Antarctic.

antenne /ãtɛn/ *n.f.* aerial; (*Amer.*)
antenna; (*d'insecte*) antenna; (*succursale*) agency; (*mil.*) outpost;
(*auto., méd.*) emergency unit. **à
l'~,** on the air. **sur l'~ de,** on the
wavelength of.

antérieur /ãterjœr/ *a.* previous, earlier; (*placé devant*) front. **~ à,** prior
to. **~ement** *adv.* earlier. **~ement à,**
prior to. **antériorité** /-jɔrite/ *n.f.*
precedence.

anthologie /ãtɔlɔʒi/ *n.f.* anthology.

anthropolo|gie /ãtrɔpɔlɔʒi/ *n.f.*
anthropology. **~gue** *n.m./f.* anthro-
pologist.

anthropophage /ãtrɔpɔfaʒ/ *a.*
cannibalistic. ● *n.m./f.* cannibal.

anti- /ãti/ *préf.* anti-.

antiadhési|f, ~ve /ãtiadezif, -v/ *a.*
non-stick.

antiaérien, ~ne /ãtiaerjɛ̃, -jɛn/ *a.*
anti-aircraft. **abri ~,** air-raid shelter.

antiatomique /ãtiatɔmik/ *a.* **abri ~,**
fall-out shelter.

antibiotique /ãtibjɔtik/ *n.m.* antibiotic.

anticancéreu|x, ~se /ãtikãserø, -z/
a. (anti-)cancer.

antichambre /ãtiʃãbr/ *n.f.* waiting-
room, antechamber.

anticipation /ãtisipasjɔ̃/ *n.f.* **d'~,**
(*livre, film*) science fiction. **par ~,**
in advance.

anticipé /ãtisipe/ *a.* early.

anticiper /ãtisipe/ *v.t./i.* **~ (sur),**
anticipate.

anticonceptionnel, ~le /ãtikɔ̃-
sɛpsjɔnɛl/ *a.* contraceptive.

anticorps /ãtikɔr/ *n.m.* antibody.

anticyclone /ãtisiklon/ n.m. anticyclone.

antidater /ãtidate/ v.t. backdate, antedate.

antidote /ãtidɔt/ n.m. antidote.

antigel /ãtiʒɛl/ n.m. antifreeze.

antihistaminique /ãtiistaminik/ a. & n.m. antihistamine.

antillais, ~e /ãtijɛ, -z/ a. & n.m., f. West Indian.

Antilles /ãtij/ n.f. pl. **les ~,** the West Indies.

antilope /ãtilɔp/ n.f. antelope.

antimite /ãtimit/ n.m. moth repellent.

antipath|ie /ãtipati/ n.f. antipathy. **~ique** a. unpleasant.

antipodes /ãtipɔd/ n.m. pl. antipodes. **aux ~ de,** (fig.) poles apart from.

antiquaire /ãtikɛr/ n.m./f. antique dealer.

antiqu|e /ãtik/ a. ancient. **~ité** n.f. antiquity; (objet) antique.

antirouille /ãtiruj/ a. & n.m. rustproofing.

antisémit|e /ãtisemit/ a. anti-Semitic. **~isme** n.m. anti-Semitism.

antiseptique /ãtisɛptik/ a. & n.m. antiseptic.

antithèse /ãtitɛz/ n.f. antithesis.

antivol /ãtivɔl/ n.m. anti-theft lock ou device.

antre /ãtr/ n.m. den.

anus /anys/ n.m. anus.

anxiété /ãksjete/ n.f. anxiety.

anxieu|x, ~se /ãksjø, -z/ a. anxious. ● n.m., f. worrier.

août /u(t)/ n.m. August.

apais|er /apeze/ v.t. calm down, (douleur, colère) soothe (faim) appease. **s'~er** v. pr. (tempête) die down. **~ement** n.m. appeasement; soothing. **~ements** n.m. pl. reassurances.

apanage /apanaʒ/ n.m. **l'~ de,** the privilege of.

aparté /aparte/ n.m. private exchange; (théâtre) aside. **en ~,** in private.

apath|ie /apati/ n.f. apathy. **~ique** a. apathetic.

apatride /apatrid/ n.m./f. stateless person.

apercevoir† /apɛrsəvwar/ v.t. see. **s'~ de,** notice. **s'~ que,** notice ou realize that.

aperçu /apɛrsy/ n.m. general view ou idea; (intuition) insight.

apéritif /aperitif/ n.m. aperitif.

à-peu-près /apøprɛ/ n.m. invar. approximation.

apeuré /apœre/ a. scared.

aphone /afɔn/ a. voiceless.

aphte /aft/ n.m. mouth ulcer.

apit|oyer /apitwaje/ v.t. move (to pity). **s'~oyer sur,** feel pity for. **~oiement** n.m. pity.

aplanir /aplanir/ v.t. level; (fig.) smooth out.

aplatir /aplatir/ v.t. flatten (out). **s'~** v. pr. (s'allonger) lie flat; (s'humilier) grovel; (tomber: fam.) fall flat on one's face.

aplomb /aplɔ̃/ n.m. balance; (fig.) self-possession. **d'~,** (en équilibre) steady, balanced.

apogée /apɔʒe/ n.m. peak.

apologie /apɔlɔʒi/ n.f. vindication.

a posteriori /apɔsterjɔri/ adv. after the event.

apostolique /apɔstɔlik/ a. apostolic.

apostroph|e /apɔstrɔf/ n.f. apostrophe; (appel) sharp address. **~er** v.t. address sharply.

apothéose /apɔteoz/ n.f. final triumph.

apôtre /apotr/ n.m. apostle.

apparaître† /aparɛtr/ v.i. appear. **il apparaît que,** it appears that.

apparat /apara/ n.m. pomp. **d'~,** ceremonial.

appareil /aparɛj/ n.m. apparatus; (électrique) appliance; (anat.) system; (téléphonique) phone; (dentaire) brace; (auditif) hearing-aid; (avion) plane; (culin.) mixture. **l'~ du parti,** the party machinery. **c'est Gabriel à l'~,** it's Gabriel on the phone. **~(-photo),** camera. **~ électroménager,** household electrical appliance.

appareiller[1] /apareje/ v.i. (navire) cast off, put to sea.

appareiller[2] /apareje/ v.t. (assortir) match.

apparemment /aparamã/ adv. apparently.

apparence /aparãs/ n.f. appearance. **en ~,** outwardly; (apparemment) apparently.

apparent, ~e /aparã, -t/ a. apparent; (visible) conspicuous.

apparenté /aparãte/ a. related; (semblable) similar.

appariteur /aparitœr/ n.m. (univ.) attendant, porter.

apparition /aparisjɔ̃/ *n.f.* appearance; (*spectre*) apparition.

appartement /apartəmɑ̃/ *n.m.* flat; (*Amer.*) apartment.

appartenance /apartənɑ̃s/ *n.f.* membership (**à**, of), belonging (**à**, to).

appartenir† /apartənir/ *v.i.* belong (**à**, to) **il lui/vous/***etc.* **appartient de**, it is up to him/you/*etc.* to.

appât /apɑ/ *n.m.* bait; (*fig.*) lure. **~er** /-te/ *v.t.* lure.

appauvrir /apovrir/ *v.t.* impoverish. **s'~** *v. pr.* grow impoverished.

appel /apel/ *n.m.* call; (*jurid.*) appeal; (*mil.*) call-up. **faire ~,** appeal. **faire ~ à**, (*recourir à*) call on; (*invoquer*) appeal to; (*évoquer*) call up; (*exiger*) call for. **faire l'~,** (*scol.*) call the register; (*mil.*) take a roll-call. **~ d'offres,** (*comm.*) invitation to tender. **faire un ~ de phares,** flash one's headlights.

appelé /aple/ *n.m.* conscript.

appel|er /aple/ *v.t.* call; (*nécessiter*) call for. **s'~er** *v. pr.* be called. **~é à,** (*désigné à*) marked out for. **en ~er à,** appeal to. **il s'appelle,** his name is. **~lation** /apelasjɔ̃/ *n.f.* designation.

appendic|e /apɛ̃dis/ *n.m.* appendix. **~ite** *n.f.* appendicitis.

appentis /apɑ̃ti/ *n.m.* lean-to.

appesantir /apəzɑ̃tir/ *v.t.* weigh down. **s'~** *v. pr.* grow heavier. **s'~ sur,** dwell upon.

appétissant, ~e /apetisɑ̃, -t/ *a.* appetizing.

appétit /apeti/ *n.m.* appetite.

applaud|ir /aplodir/ *v.t./i.* applaud. **~ir à,** applaud. **~issements** *n.m. pl.* applause.

applique /aplik/ *n.f.* wall lamp.

appliqué /aplike/ *a.* painstaking.

appliquer /aplike/ *v.t.* apply; (*loi*) enforce. **s'~** *v. pr.* apply o.s. (**à**, to). **s'~ à,** (*concerner*) apply to. **applicable** /-abl/ *a.* applicable. **application** /-asjɔ̃/ *n.f.* application.

appoint /apwɛ̃/ *n.m.* contribution. **d'~,** extra. **faire l'~,** give the correct money.

appointements /apwɛ̃tmɑ̃/ *n.m. pl.* salary.

apport /apɔr/ *n.m.* contribution.

apporter /apɔrte/ *v.t.* bring.

apposer /apoze/ *v.t.* affix.

appréciable /apresjabl/ *a.* appreciable.

appréc|ier /apresje/ *v.t.* appreciate; (*évaluer*) appraise. **~iation** *n.f.* appreciation; appraisal.

appréhen|der /apreɑ̃de/ *v.t.* dread, fear; (*arrêter*) apprehend. **~sion** *n.f.* apprehension.

apprendre† /aprɑ̃dr/ *v.t./i.* learn; (*être informé de*) hear of. **~ qch. à qn.,** teach s.o. sth.; (*informer*) tell s.o. sth. **~ à faire,** learn to do. **~ à qn. à faire,** teach s.o. to do. **~ que,** learn that; (*être informé*) hear that.

apprenti, ~e /aprɑ̃ti/ *n.m.*, *f.* apprentice.

apprentissage /aprɑ̃tisaʒ/ *n.m.* apprenticeship; (*d'un sujet*) learning.

apprêté /aprete/ *a.* affected.

apprêter /aprete/ *v.t.*, **s'~** *v. pr.* prepare.

apprivoiser /aprivwaze/ *v.t.* tame.

approba|teur, ~trice /aprɔbatœr, -tris/ *a.* approving.

approbation /aprɔbasjɔ̃/ *n.f.* approval.

approchant, ~e /aprɔʃɑ̃, -t/ *a.* close, similar.

approche /aprɔʃ/ *n.f.* approach.

approché /aprɔʃe/ *a.* approximate.

approcher /aprɔʃe/ *v.t.* (*objet*) move near(er) (**de**, to); (*personne*) approach. ● *v.i.* **~ (de),** approach. **s'~ de,** approach, move near(er) to.

approfond|ir /aprɔfɔ̃dir/ *v.t.* deepen; (*fig.*) go into thoroughly. **~i** *a.* thorough.

approprié /aprɔprije/ *a.* appropriate.

approprier (s') /(s)aprɔprije/ *v. pr.* appropriate.

approuver /apruve/ *v.t.* approve; (*trouver louable*) approve of; (*soutenir*) agree with.

approvisionn|er /aprɔvizjɔne/ *v.t.* supply. **s'~er** *v. pr.* stock up. **~ement** *n.m.* supply.

approximati|f, ~ve /aprɔksimatif, -v/ *a.* approximate. **~vement** *adv.* approximately.

approximation /aprɔksimasjɔ̃/ *n.f.* approximation.

appui /apɥi/ *n.m.* support; (*de fenêtre*) sill; (*pour objet*) rest. **à l'~ de,** in support of. **prendre ~,** support o.s. on.

appuie-tête /apɥitɛt/ *n.m.* headrest.

appuyer /apɥije/ *v.t.* lean, rest; (*presser*) press; (*soutenir*) support, back. ● *v.i.* **~ sur,** press (on); (*fig.*) stress. **s'~ sur,** lean on; (*compter sur*) rely on.

âpre /ɑpr/ a. harsh, bitter. **~ au gain,** grasping.

après /aprɛ/ prép. after; (au-delà de) beyond. ● adv. after(wards); (plus tard) later. **~ avoir fait,** after doing. **~ qu'il est parti,** after he left. **~ coup,** after the event. ● **tout,** after all. **d'~,** (selon) according to. **~-demain** adv. the day after tomorrow. **~-guerre** n.m. postwar period. **~-midi** n.m./f. invar. afternoon. **~-rasage** n.m. aftershave. **~-ski** n.m. moonboot. **~-vente** a. aftersales.

a priori /aprijɔri/ adv. in principle, without going into the matter. ● n.m. preconception.

à-propos /aprɔpo/ n.m. timeliness; (fig.) presence of mind.

apte /apt/ a. capable (**à,** of).

aptitude /aptityd/ n.f. aptitude, ability.

aquarelle /akwarɛl/ n.f. water-colour, aquarelle.

aquarium /akwarjɔm/ n.m. aquarium.

aquatique /akwatik/ a. aquatic.

aqueduc /akdyk/ n.m. aqueduct.

arabe /arab/ a. Arab; (lang.) Arabic; (désert) Arabian. ● n.m./f. Arab. ● n.m. (lang.) Arabic.

Arabie /arabi/ n.f. **~ Séoudite,** Saudi Arabia.

arable /arabl/ a. arable.

arachide /araʃid/ n.f. peanut.

araignée /areɲe/ n.f. spider.

arbitraire /arbitrɛr/ a. arbitrary.

arbitr|e /arbitr/ n.m. referee; (cricket, tennis) umpire; (maître) arbiter; (jurid.) arbitrator. **~age** n.m. arbitration; (sport) refereeing. **~er** v.t. (match) referee; (jurid.) arbitrate.

arborer /arbɔre/ v.t. display; (vêtement) sport.

arbre /arbr/ n.m. tree; (techn.) shaft.

arbrisseau (pl. **~x**) /arbriso/ n.m. shrub.

arbuste /arbyst/ n.m. bush.

arc /ark/ n.m. (arme) bow; (voûte) arch. **~ de cercle,** arc of a circle.

arcade /arkad/ n.f. arch. **~s,** arcade, arches.

arc-boutant (pl. **arcs-boutants**) /arkbutɑ̃/ n.m. flying buttress.

arc-bouter (s') /(s)arkbute/ v. pr. lean (for support), brace o.s.

arceau (pl. **~x**) /arso/ n.m. hoop; (de voûte) arch.

arc-en-ciel (pl. **arcs-en-ciel**) /arkɑ̃sjɛl/ n.m. rainbow.

archaïque /arkaik/ a. archaic.

arche /arʃ/ n.f. arch. **~ de Noé,** Noah's ark.

archéolo|gie /arkeɔlɔʒi/ n.f. archaeology. **~gique** a. archaeological. **~gue** n.m./f. archaeologist.

archer /arʃe/ n.m. archer.

archet /arʃɛ/ n.m. (mus.) bow.

archétype /arketip/ n.m. archetype.

archevêque /arʃəvɛk/ n.m. archbishop.

archi- /arʃi/ préf. (fam.) tremendously.

archipel /arʃipɛl/ n.m. archipelago.

architecte /arʃitɛkt/ n.m. architect.

architecture /arʃitɛktyr/ n.f. architecture.

archiv|es /arʃiv/ n.f. pl. archives. **~iste** n.m./f. archivist.

arctique /arktik/ a. & n.m. Arctic.

ardemment /ardamɑ̃/ adv. ardently.

ard|ent, ~ente /ardɑ̃, -t/ a. burning; (passionné) ardent; (foi) fervent. **~eur** n.f. ardour; (chaleur) heat.

ardoise /ardwaz/ n.f. slate.

ardu /ardy/ a. arduous.

are /ar/ n.m. are (= 100 square metres).

arène /arɛn/ n.f. arena. **~(s),** (pour courses de taureaux) bullring.

arête /arɛt/ n.f. (de poisson) bone; (bord) ridge.

argent /arʒɑ̃/ n.m. money; (métal) silver. **~ comptant,** cash. **prendre pour ~ comptant,** take at face value. **~ de poche,** pocket money.

argenté /arʒɑ̃te/ a. silver(y); (métal) (silver-)plated.

argenterie /arʒɑ̃tri/ n.f. silverware.

argentin, ~e /arʒɑ̃tɛ̃, -in/ a. & n.m., f. Argentinian, Argentine.

Argentine /arʒɑ̃tin/ n.f. Argentina.

argil|e /arʒil/ n.f. clay. **~eux, ~euse** a. clayey.

argot /argo/ n.m. slang. **~ique** /-ɔtik/ a. (terme) slang; (style) slangy.

arguer /argɥe/ v.i. **~ de,** put forward as a reason.

argument /argymɑ̃/ n.m. argument. **~er** /-te/ v.i. argue.

aride /arid/ a. arid, barren.

aristocrate /aristɔkrat/ n.m./f. aristocrat.

aristocrat|ie /aristɔkrasi/ n.f. aristocracy. **~ique** /-atik/ a. aristocratic.

arithmétique /aritmetik/ *n.f.*
arithmetic. ● *a.* arithmetical.

armateur /armatœr/ *n.m.* ship-
owner.

armature /armatyr/ *n.f.* framework;
(*de tente*) frame.

arme /arm/ *n.f.* arm, weapon. **~s,**
(*blason*) arms. **~ à feu,** firearm.

armée /arme/ *n.f.* army. **~ de l'air,**
Air Force. **~ de terre,** Army.

armement /arməmã/ *n.m.* arms.

armer /arme/ *v.t.* arm; (*fusil*) cock;
(*navire*) equip; (*renforcer*) reinforce; (*photo.*) wind on. **~ de,** (*garnir de*) fit with. **s'~ de,** arm o.s.
with.

armistice /armistis/ *n.m.* armistice.

armoire /armwar/ *n.f.* cupboard;
(*penderie*) wardrobe; (*Amer.*) closet.

armoiries /armwari/ *n.f. pl.* (coat of)
arms.

armure /armyr/ *n.f.* armour.

arnaque /arnak/ *n.f.* (*fam.*)
swindling. **c'est de l'~,** it's a swindle *ou* con (*fam.*). **~r** *v.t.* swindle,
con (*fam.*).

arnica /arnika/ *n.f.* (*méd.*) arnica.

aromate /arɔmat/ *n.m.* herb, spice.

aromatique /arɔmatik/ *a.* aromatic.

aromatisé /arɔmatize/ *a.* flavoured.

arôme /arom/ *n.m.* aroma.

arpent|er /arpãte/ *v.t.* pace up and
down; (*terrain*) survey. **~eur** *n.m.*
surveyor.

arqué /arke/ *a.* arched; (*jambes*)
bandy.

arraché (à l') /(al)araʃe/ *adv.* with a
struggle, after a hard struggle.

arrache-pied (d') /(d)araʃpje/ *adv.*
relentlessly.

arrach|er /araʃe/ *v.t.* pull out *ou* off;
(*plante*) pull *ou* dig up; (*cheveux,
page*) tear *ou* pull out; (*par une
explosion*) blow off. **~er à,** (*enlever
à*) snatch from; (*fig.*) force *ou* wrest
from. **s'~er qch.,** fight over sth.
~age /-aʒ/ *n.m.* pulling *ou* digging
up.

arraisonner /arɛzɔne/ *v.t.* inspect.

arrangeant, ~e /arãʒã, -t/ *a.* obli-
ging.

arrangement /arãʒmã/ *n.m.* arrangement.

arranger /arãʒe/ *v.t.* arrange, fix up;
(*réparer*) put right; (*régler*) sort out;
(*convenir à*) suit. **s'~** *v. pr.* (*se
mettre d'accord*) come to an arrangement; (*se débrouiller*) manage (**pour,**
to).

arrestation /arɛstasjɔ̃/ *n.f.* arrest.

arrêt /arɛ/ *n.m.* stopping (**de,** of);
(*lieu*) stop; (*pause*) pause; (*jurid.*)
decree. **~s,** (*mil.*) arrest. **à l'~,**
stationary. **faire un ~,** (make a)
stop. **sans ~,** without stopping. **~
maladie,** sick leave. **~ de travail,**
(*grève*) stoppage; (*méd.*) sick leave.
rester *ou* **tomber en ~,** stop short.

arrêté /arete/ *n.m.* order.

arrêter /arete/ *v.t./i.* stop; (*date, regard*) fix; (*appareil*) turn off; (*ap-
préhender*) arrest. **s'~** *v. pr.* stop.
(s')~ de faire, stop doing.

arrhes /ar/ *n.f. pl.* deposit.

arrière /arjɛr/ *n.m.* back, rear; (*football*) back. ● *a. invar.* back, rear.
à l'~, in *ou* at the back. **en ~,**
behind; (*marcher*) backwards. **en
~ de,** behind. **~-boutique** *n.f.*
back room (of the shop). **~-garde**
n.f. rearguard. **~-goût** *n.m.* after-
taste. **~-grand-mère** *n.f.* great-
grandmother. **~-grand-père** (*pl.
~-grands-pères*) *n.m.* great-grand-
father. **~-pays** *n.m.* backcountry.
~-pensée *n.f.* ulterior motive. **~-
plan** *n.m.* background.

arriéré /arjere/ *a.* backward. ● *n.m.*
arrears.

arrimer /arime/ *v.t.* rope down; (*cargaison*) stow.

arrivage /arivaʒ/ *n.m.* consignment.

arrivant, ~e /arivã, -t/ *n.m., f.* new
arrival.

arrivée /arive/ *n.f.* arrival; (*sport*)
finish.

arriver /arive/ *v.i.* (*aux. être*) arrive,
come; (*réussir*) succeed; (*se produire*) happen. **~ à,** (*atteindre*)
reach. **~ à faire,** manage to do. **en
~ à faire,** get to the stage of doing. **il
arrive que,** it happens that. **il lui
arrive de faire,** he (sometimes) does.

arriviste /arivist/ *n.m./f.* self-seeker.

arrogan|t, ~te /arɔgã, -t/ *a.* ar-
rogant. **~ce** *n.f.* arrogance.

arroger (s') /(s)arɔʒe/ *v. pr.* assume
(without justification).

arrondir /arɔ̃dir/ *v.t.* (make) round;
(*somme*) round off. **s'~** *v. pr.* become round(ed).

arrondissement /arɔ̃dismã/ *n.m.*
district.

arros|er /aroze/ *v.t.* water; (*repas*)
wash down; (*rôti*) baste; (*victoire*)
celebrate with a drink. **~age** *n.m.*
watering. **~oir** *n.m.* watering-can.

arsen|al (*pl.* **~aux**) /arsənal, -o/ *n.m.* arsenal; (*naut.*) dockyard.

arsenic /arsənik/ *n.m.* arsenic.

art /ar/ *n.m.* art. **~s et métiers,** arts and crafts. **~s ménagers,** domestic science.

artère /artɛr/ *n.f.* artery. **(grande) ~,** main road.

artériel, ~le /arterjɛl/ *a.* arterial.

arthrite /artrit/ *n.f.* arthritis.

arthrose /artroz/ *n.f.* osteoarthritis.

artichaut /artiʃo/ *n.m.* artichoke.

article /artikl/ *n.m.* article; (*comm.*) item, article. **à l'~ de la mort,** at death's door. **~ de fond,** feature (article). **~s d'ameublement,** furnishings. **~s de voyage,** travel requisites *ou* goods.

articul|er /artikyle/ *v.t.*, **s'~er** *v. pr.* articulate. **~ation** *n.f.* articulation; (*anat.*) joint.

artifice /artifis/ *n.m.* contrivance.

artificiel, ~le /artifisjɛl/ *a.* artificial. **~lement** *adv.* artificially.

artill|erie /artijri/ *n.f.* artillery. **~eur** *n.m.* gunner.

artisan /artizã/ *n.m.* artisan, craftsman. **l'~ de,** (*fig.*) the architect of. **~al** (*m. pl.* **~aux**) /-anal, -o/ *a.* of *ou* by craftsmen, craft; (*amateur*) home-made. **~at** /-ana/ *n.m.* craft; (*classe*) artisans.

artist|e /artist/ *n.m./f.* artist. **~ique** *a.* artistic.

as¹ /a/ *voir* avoir.

as² /ɑs/ *n.m.* ace.

ascendant¹, ~e /asãdã, -t/ *a.* ascending, upward.

ascendant² /asãdã/ *n.m.* influence. **~s,** ancestors.

ascenseur /asãsœr/ *n.m.* lift; (*Amer.*) elevator.

ascension /asãsjõ/ *n.f.* ascent. **l' A~,** Ascension.

ascète /asɛt/ *n.m./f.* ascetic.

ascétique /asetik/ *a.* ascetic.

aseptique /asɛptik/ *a.* aseptic.

aseptis|er /asɛptize/ *v.t.* disinfect; (*stériliser*) sterilize. **~é** (*péj.*) sanitized.

asiatique /azjatik/ *a.* & *n.m./f.*, **Asiate** /azjat/ *n.m./f.* Asian.

Asie /azi/ *n.f.* Asia.

asile /azil/ *n.m.* refuge; (*pol.*) asylum; (*pour malades, vieillards*) home.

aspect /aspɛ/ *n.m.* appearance; (*fig.*) aspect. **à l'~ de,** at the sight of.

asperge /aspɛrʒ/ *n.f.* asparagus.

asper|ger /aspɛrʒe/ *v.t.* spray. **~sion** *n.f.* spray(ing).

aspérité /asperite/ *n.f.* bump, rough edge.

asphalt|e /asfalt/ *n.m.* asphalt. **~er** *v.t.* asphalt.

asphyxie /asfiksi/ *n.f.* suffocation.

asphyxier /asfiksje/ *v.t.*, **s'~** *v. pr.* suffocate, asphyxiate; (*fig.*) stifle.

aspic /aspik/ *n.m.* (*serpent*) asp.

aspirateur /aspiratœr/ *n.m.* vacuum cleaner.

aspir|er /aspire/ *v.t.* inhale; (*liquide*) suck up. ● *v.i.* **~er à,** aspire to. **~ation** *n.f.* inhaling; suction; (*ambition*) aspiration.

aspirine /aspirin/ *n.f.* aspirin.

assagir /asaʒir/ *v.t.*, **s'~** *v. pr.* sober down.

assaill|ir /asajir/ *v.t.* assail. **~ant** *n.m.* assailant.

assainir /asenir/ *v.t.* clean up.

assaisonn|er /asɛzɔne/ *v.t.* season. **~ement** *n.m.* seasoning.

assassin /asasɛ̃/ *n.m.* murderer; (*pol.*) assassin.

assassin|er /asasine/ *v.t.* murder; (*pol.*) assassinate. **~at** *n.m.* murder; (*pol.*) assassination.

assaut /aso/ *n.m.* assault, onslaught. **donner l'~ à, prendre d'~,** storm.

assécher /aseʃe/ *v.t.* drain.

assemblée /asãble/ *n.f.* meeting; (*gens réunis*) gathering; (*pol.*) assembly.

assembl|er /asãble/ *v.t.* assemble, put together; (*réunir*) gather. **s'~er** *v. pr.* gather, assemble. **~age** *n.m.* assembly; (*combinaison*) collection; (*techn.*) joint. **~eur** *n.m.* (*comput.*) assembler.

assener /asene/ *v.t.* (*coup*) deal.

assentiment /asãtimã/ *n.m.* assent.

asseoir† /aswar/ *v.t.* sit (down), seat; (*affermir*) establish; (*baser*) base. **s'~** *v. pr.* sit (down).

assermenté /asɛrmãte/ *a.* sworn.

assertion /asɛrsjõ/ *n.f.* assertion.

asservir /asɛrvir/ *v.t.* enslave.

assez /ase/ *adv.* enough; (*plutôt*) quite, fairly. **~ grand/rapide** *etc.*, big/fast/*etc.* enough (**pour,** to). **~ de,** enough. **j'en ai ~ (de),** I've had enough (of).

assid|u /asidy/ *a.* (*zèle*) assiduous; (*régulier*) regular. **~u auprès de,** attentive to. **~uité** /-ɥite/ *n.f.* assiduousness; regularity. **~ûment** *adv.* assiduously.

assiéger /asjeʒe/ v.t. besiege.

assiette /asjɛt/ n.f. plate; (*équilibre*) seat. **~ anglaise**, assorted cold meats. **~ creuse/plate**, soup-/dinner-plate. **ne pas être dans son ~**, feel out of sorts.

assiettée /asjete/ n.f. plateful.

assigner /asiɲe/ v.t. assign; (*limite*) fix.

assimil|er /asimile/ v.t., **s'~er** v. pr. assimilate. **~er à**, liken to; (*classer*) class as. **~ation** n.f. assimilation; likening; classification.

assis, ~e /asi, -z/ *voir* asseoir. ● a. sitting (down), seated.

assise /asiz/ n.f. (*base*) foundation. **~s**, (*tribunal*) assizes; (*congrès*) conference, congress.

assistance /asistɑ̃s/ n.f. audience; (*aide*) assistance. **l'A~ (publique)**, government child care service.

assistant, ~e /asistɑ̃, -t/ n.m., f. assistant; (*univ.*) assistant lecturer. **~s**, (*spectateurs*) members of the audience. **~ social, ~e sociale**, social worker.

assist|er /asiste/ v.t. assist. ● v.i. **~er à**, attend, be (present) at; (*scène*) witness. **~é par ordinateur**, computer-assisted.

association /asɔsjasjɔ̃/ n.f. association.

associé, ~e /asɔsje/ n.m., f. partner, associate. ● a. associate.

associer /asɔsje/ v.t. associate; (*mêler*) combine (**à**, with). **~ qn. à**, (*projet*) involve s.o. in; (*bénéfices*) give s.o. a share of. **s'~** v. pr. (*sociétés, personnes*) become associated, join forces (**à**, with); (*s'harmoniser*) combine (**à**, with). **s'~ à**, (*joie de qn.*) share in; (*opinion de qn.*) share; (*projet*) take part in.

assoiffé /aswafe/ a. thirsty.

assombrir /asɔ̃brir/ v.t. darken; (*fig.*) make gloomy. **s'~** v. pr. darken; become gloomy.

assommer /asɔme/ v.t. knock out; (*tuer*) kill; (*animal*) stun; (*fig.*) overwhelm; (*ennuyer: fam.*) bore.

Assomption /asɔ̃psjɔ̃/ n.f. Assumption.

assorti /asɔrti/ a. matching; (*objets variés*) assorted.

assort|ir /asɔrtir/ v.t. match (**à**, with, to). **~ir de**, accompany with. **s'~ir (à)**, match. **~iment** n.m. assortment.

assoup|ir (s') /(s)asupir/ v. pr. doze off; (*s'apaiser*) subside. **~i** a. dozing.

assouplir /asuplir/ v.t. make supple; (*fig.*) make flexible.

assourdir /asurdir/ v.t. (*personne*) deafen; (*bruit*) deaden.

assouvir /asuvir/ v.t. satisfy.

assujettir /asyʒetir/ v.t. subject, subdue. **~ à**, subject to.

assumer /asyme/ v.t. assume.

assurance /asyrɑ̃s/ n.f. (self-) assurance; (*garantie*) assurance; (*contrat*) insurance. **~-maladie** n.f. health insurance. **~s sociales**, National Insurance. **~-vie** n.f. life assurance *ou* insurance.

assuré, ~e /asyre/ a. certain, assured; (*sûr de soi*) (self-)confident, assured. ● n.m., f. insured. **~ment** adv. certainly.

assurer /asyre/ v.t. ensure; (*fournir*) provide; (*exécuter*) carry out; (*comm.*) insure; (*stabiliser*) steady; (*frontières*) make secure. **~ à qn. que**, assure s.o. that. **~ qn. de**, assure s.o. of. **~ la gestion de**, manage. **s'~ de**, make sure of/ that. **s'~ qch.**, (*se procurer*) secure *ou* ensure sth. **assureur** /-œr/ n.m. insurer.

astérisque /asterisk/ n.m. asterisk.

asthm|e /asm/ n.m. asthma. **~atique** a. & n.m./f. asthmatic.

asticot /astiko/ n.m. maggot.

astiquer /astike/ v.t. polish.

astre /astr/ n.m. star.

astreignant, ~e /astreɲɑ̃, -t/ a. exacting.

astreindre /astrɛ̃dr/ v.t. **~ qn. à qch.**, force sth. on s.o. **~ à faire**, force to do.

astringent, ~e /astrɛ̃ʒɑ̃, -t/ a. astringent.

astrolo|gie /astrɔlɔʒi/ n.f. astrology. **~gue** n.m./f. astrologer.

astronaute /astrɔnot/ n.m./f. astronaut.

astronom|ie /astrɔnɔmi/ n.f. astronomy. **~e** n.m./f. astronomer. **~ique** a. astronomical.

astuce /astys/ n.f. smartness; (*truc*) trick; (*plaisanterie*) wisecrack.

astucieu|x, ~se /astysjø, -z/ a. smart, clever.

atelier /atəlje/ n.m. workshop; (*de peintre*) studio.

athé|e /ate/ n.m./f. atheist. ● a. atheistic. **~isme** n.m. atheism .

athl|ète /atlɛt/ *n.m./f.* athlete. **~étique** *a.* athletic. **~étisme** *n.m.* athletics.

atlantique /atlɑ̃tik/ *a.* Atlantic. ● *n.m.* **A~,** Atlantic (Ocean).

atlas /atlɑs/ *n.m.* atlas.

atmosph|ère /atmɔsfɛr/ *n.f.* atmosphere. **~érique** *a.* atmospheric.

atome /atom/ *n.m.* atom.

atomique /atɔmik/ *a.* atomic.

atomiseur /atɔmizœr/ *n.m.* spray.

atout /atu/ *n.m.* trump (card); (*avantage*) great asset.

âtre /ɑtr/ *n.m.* hearth.

atroc|e /atrɔs/ *a.* atrocious. **~ité** *n.f.* atrocity.

atroph|ie /atrɔfi/ *n.f.* atrophy. **~ié** *a.* atrophied.

attabler (s') /(s)atable/ *v. pr.* sit down at table.

attachant, ~e /ataʃɑ̃, -t/ *a.* likeable.

attache /ataʃ/ *n.f.* (*agrafe*) fastener; (*lien*) tie.

attach|é /ataʃe/ *a.* **être ~é à,** (*aimer*) be attached to. ● *n.m., f.* (*pol.*) attaché. **~é-case** *n.m.* attaché case. **~ement** *n.m.* attachment.

attacher /ataʃe/ *v.t.* tie (up); (*ceinture, robe, etc.*) fasten; (*étiquette*) attach. **~ à,** (*attribuer à*) attach to. ● *v.i.* (*culin.*) stick. **s'~ à,** (*se lier à*) become attached to; (*se consacrer à*) apply o.s. to.

attaque /atak/ *n.f.* attack. **~ (cérébrale),** stroke. **il va en faire une ~,** he'll have a fit. **~ à main armée,** armed attack.

attaqu|er /atake/ *v.t./i.*, **s'~er à,** attack; (*problème, sujet*) tackle. **~ant, ~ante** *n.m., f.* attacker; (*football*) striker; (*football, Amer.*) forward.

attardé /atarde/ *a.* backward; (*idées*) outdated; (*en retard*) late.

attarder (s') /(s)atarde/ *v. pr.* linger.

atteindre† /atɛ̃dr/ *v.t.* reach; (*blesser*) hit; (*affecter*) affect.

atteint, ~e /atɛ̃, -t/ *a.* **~ de,** suffering from.

atteinte /atɛ̃t/ *n.f.* attack (à, on). **porter ~ à,** make an attack on.

attel|er /atle/ *v.t.* (*cheval*) harness; (*remorque*) couple. **s'~er à,** get down to. **~age** *n.m.* harnessing; coupling; (*bêtes*) team.

attelle /atɛl/ *n.f.* splint.

attenant, ~e /atnɑ̃, -t/ *a.* **~ (à),** adjoining.

attendant (en) /(ɑ̃n)atɑ̃dɑ̃/ *adv.* meanwhile.

attendre /atɑ̃dr/ *v.t.* wait for; (*bébé*) expect; (*être le sort de*) await; (*escompter*) expect. ● *v.i.* wait. **~ que qn. fasse,** wait for s.o. to do. **s'~ à,** expect.

attendr|ir /atɑ̃drir/ *v.t.* move (to pity). **s'~ir** *v. pr.* be moved to pity. **~issant, ~issante** *a.* moving.

attendu /atɑ̃dy/ *a.* (*escompté*) expected; (*espéré*) long-awaited. **~ que,** considering that.

attentat /atɑ̃ta/ *n.m.* murder attempt. **~ (à la bombe),** (bomb) attack.

attente /atɑ̃t/ *n.f.* wait(ing); (*espoir*) expectation.

attenter /atɑ̃te/ *v.i.* **~ à,** make an attempt on; (*fig.*) violate.

attenti|f, ~ve /atɑ̃tif, -v/ *a.* attentive; (*scrupuleux*) careful. **~f à,** mindful of; (*soucieux*) careful of. **~vement** *adv.* attentively.

attention /atɑ̃sjɔ̃/ *n.f.* attention; (*soin*) care. **~ (à)!,** watch out (for)! **faire ~ à,** (*professeur*) pay attention to; (*marche*) mind. **faire ~ à faire,** be careful to do. **~né** /-jɔne/ *a.* considerate.

attentisme /atɑ̃tism/ *n.m.* wait-and-see policy.

atténuer /atenɥe/ *v.t.* (*violence*) tone down; (*douleur*) ease; (*faute*) mitigate. **s'~** *v. pr.* subside.

atterrer /atere/ *v.t.* dismay.

atterr|ir /aterir/ *v.i.* land. **~issage** *n.m.* landing.

attestation /atɛstasjɔ̃/ *n.f.* certificate.

attester /atɛste/ *v.t.* testify to. **~ que,** testify that.

attifé /atife/ *a.* (*fam.*) dressed up.

attirail /atiraj/ *n.m.* (*fam.*) gear.

attirance /atirɑ̃s/ *n.f.* attraction.

attirant, ~e /atirɑ̃, -t/ *a.* attractive.

attirer /atire/ *v.t.* draw, attract; (*causer*) bring. **s'~** *v. pr.* bring upon o.s.; (*amis*) win.

attiser /atize/ *v.t.* (*feu*) poke; (*sentiment*) stir up.

attitré /atitre/ *a.* accredited; (*habituel*) usual.

attitude /atityd/ *n.f.* attitude; (*maintien*) bearing.

attraction /atraksjɔ̃/ *n.f.* attraction.

attrait /atrɛ/ *n.m.* attraction.

attrape-nigaud /atrapnigo/ *n.m.* (*fam.*) con.

attraper /atrape/ *v.t.* catch; (*habitude, style*) pick up; (*duper*) take in; (*gronder*: *fam.*) tell off.

attrayant, **~e** /atrɛjɑ̃, -t/ *a.* attractive.

attrib|uer /atribɥe/ *v.t.* award; (*donner*) assign; (*imputer*) attribute. **s'~uer** *v. pr.* claim. **~ution** *n.f.* awarding; assignment. **~utions** *n.f. pl.* attributions.

attrister /atriste/ *v.t.* sadden.

attroup|er (s') /(s)atrupe/ *v. pr.* gather. **~ement** *n.m.* crowd.

au /o/ *voir* à.

aubaine /obɛn/ *n.f.* (stroke of) good fortune.

aube /ob/ *n.f.* dawn, daybreak.

aubépine /obepin/ *n.f.* hawthorn.

auberg|e /obɛrʒ/ *n.f.* inn. **~e de jeunesse,** youth hostel. **~iste** *n.m./ f.* innkeeper.

aubergine /obɛrʒin/ *n.f.* aubergine; (*Amer.*) egg-plant.

aucun, **~e** /okœ̃, okyn/ *a.* no, not any; (*positif*) any. ● *pron.* none, not any; (*positif*) any. **~ des deux,** neither of the two. **d'~s,** some. **~ement** /okynmɑ̃/ *adv.* not at all.

audace /odas/ *n.f.* daring; (*impudence*) audacity.

audacieu|x, **~se** /odasjø, -z/ *a.* daring.

au-delà /odla/ *adv.,* **~ de** *prép.* beyond.

au-dessous /odsu/ *adv.,* **~ de** *prép.* below; (*couvert par*) under.

au-dessus /odsy/ *adv.,* **~ de** *prép.* above.

au-devant (de) /odvɑ̃(də)/ *prép.* **aller ~ de qn.,** go to meet s.o.

audience /odjɑ̃s/ *n.f.* audience; (*d'un tribunal*) hearing; (*intérêt*) attention.

Audimat /odimat/ *n.m.* (P.) **l'~,** the TV ratings.

audiotypiste /odjotipist/ *n.m./f.* audio typist.

audio-visuel, **~le** /odjovizɥɛl/ *a.* audio-visual.

audi|teur, **~trice** /oditœr, -tris/ *n.m., f.* listener.

audition /odisjɔ̃/ *n.f.* hearing; (*théâtre, mus.*) audition. **~ner** /-jɔne/ *v.t./i.* audition.

auditoire /oditwar/ *n.m.* audience.

auditorium /oditɔrjɔm/ *n.m.* (*mus., radio*) recording studio.

auge /oʒ/ *n.f.* trough.

augment|er /ogmɑ̃te/ *v.t./i.* increase; (*employé*) increase the pay of. **~ation** *n.f.* increase. **~ation (de salaire),** (pay) rise; (*Amer.*) raise.

augure /ogyr/ *n.m.* (*devin*) oracle. **être de bon/mauvais ~,** be a good/ bad sign.

auguste /ogyst/ *a.* august.

aujourd'hui /oʒurdɥi/ *adv.* today.

aumône /omon/ *n.f.* alms.

aumônier /omonje/ *n.m.* chaplain.

auparavant /oparavɑ̃/ *adv.* before (-hand).

auprès (de) /oprɛ(də)/ *prép.* by, next to; (*comparé à*) compared with; (*s'adressant à*) to.

auquel, **~le** /okɛl/ *voir* lequel.

aura, aurait /ora, orɛ/ *voir* avoir.

auréole /oreɔl/ *n.f.* halo.

auriculaire /orikylɛr/ *n.m.* little finger.

aurore /orɔr/ *n.f.* dawn.

ausculter /ɔskylte/ *v.t.* examine with a stethoscope.

auspices /ɔspis/ *n.m. pl.* auspices.

aussi /osi/ *adv.* too, also; (*comparaison*) as; (*tellement*) so. ● *conj.* (*donc*) therefore. **~ bien que,** as well as.

aussitôt /osito/ *adv.* immediately. **~ que,** as soon as. **~ arrivé/levé**/*etc.*, as soon as one has arrived/got up/ *etc.*

aust|ère /ostɛr/ *a.* austere. **~érité** *n.f.* austerity.

austral (*m. pl.* **~s**) /ostral/ *a.* southern.

Australie /ɔstrali/ *n.f.* Australia.

australien, **~ne** /ostraljɛ̃, -jɛn/ *a. & n.m., f.* Australian.

autant /otɑ̃/ *adv.* (*travailler, manger, etc.*) as much (**que,** as). **~ (de),** (*quantité*) as much (**que,** as); (*nombre*) as many (**que,** as); (*tant*) so much; so many. **~ faire,** one had better do. **d'~ plus que,** all the more since. **en faire ~,** do the same. **pour ~,** for all that.

autel /otɛl/ *n.m.* altar.

auteur /otœr/ *n.m.* author. **l'~ du crime,** the person who committed the crime.

authentifier /otɑ̃tifje/ *v.t.* authenticate.

authenti|que /otɑ̃tik/ *a.* authentic. **~cité** *n.f.* authenticity.

auto /oto/ *n.f.* car. **~s tamponneuses,** dodgems, bumper cars.

auto- /oto/ *préf.* self-, auto-.

autobiographie /otɔbjɔgrafi/ *n.f.* autobiography.

autobus /otɔbys/ *n.m.* bus.

autocar /otɔkar/ *n.m.* coach.

autochtone /otɔktɔn/ *n.m./f.* native.

autocollant, ~e /otɔkɔlã, -t/ *a.* self-adhesive. ● *n.m.* sticker.

autocratique /otɔkratik/ *a.* autocratic.

autocuiseur /otɔkɥizœr/ *n.* pressure cooker.

autodéfense /otɔdefãs/ *n.f.* self-defence.

autodidacte /otɔdidakt/ *a.* & *n.m./f.* self-taught (person).

auto-école /otɔekɔl/ *n.f.* driving school.

autographe /otɔgraf/ *n.m.* autograph.

automate /otɔmat/ *n.m.* automaton, robot.

automatique /otɔmatik/ *a.* automatic. ~**ment** *adv.* automatically.

automat|iser /otɔmatize/ *v.t.* automate. ~**ion** /-mɑsjõ/ *n.f.* ~**isation** *n.f.* automation.

automne /otɔn/ *n.m.* autumn; (*Amer.*) fall.

automobil|e /otɔmɔbil/ *a.* motor, car. ● *n.f.* (motor) car. l'~**e**, (*sport*) motoring. ~**iste** *n.m./f.* motorist.

autonom|e /otɔnɔm/ *a.* autonomous. ~**ie** *n.f.* autonomy.

autopsie /otɔpsi/ *n.f.* post-mortem, autopsy.

autoradio /otɔradjo/ *n.m.* car radio.

autorail /otɔrɑj/ *n.m.* railcar.

autorisation /otɔrizasjõ/ *n.f.* permission, authorization; (*permis*) permit.

autoris|er /otɔrize/ *v.t.* authorize, permit; (*rendre possible*) allow (of). ~**é** *a.* (*opinions*) authoritative.

autoritaire /otɔritɛr/ *a.* authoritarian.

autorité /otɔrite/ *n.f.* authority. **faire** ~, be authoritative.

autoroute /otɔrut/ *n.f.* motorway; (*Amer.*) highway.

auto-stop /otɔstɔp/ *n.m.* hitch-hiking. **faire de l'**~, hitch-hike. **prendre en** ~, give a lift to. ~**peur**, ~**peuse** *n.m.,* f. hitch-hiker.

autour /otur/ *adv.,* ~ **de** *prép.* around. **tout** ~, all around.

autre /otr/ *a.* other. **un** ~ **jour/***etc.*, another day/*etc.* ● *pron.* **un** ~, **une** ~, another (one). l'~, the other

(one). **les** ~**s**, the others; (*autrui*) others. **d'**~**s**, (some) others. **l'un l'**~, each other. **l'un et l'**~, both of them. ~ **chose/part**, sth./somewhere else. **qn./rien d'**~, s.o./nothing else. **quoi d'**~?, what else? **d'**~ **part**, on the other hand. **vous** ~**s Anglais**, you English. **d'un jour/***etc.* **à l'**~, (*bientôt*) any day/*etc.* now. **entre** ~**s**, among other things.

autrefois /otrəfwa/ *adv.* in the past.

autrement /otrəmã/ *adv.* differently; (*sinon*) otherwise; (*plus*) far more. ~ **dit**, in other words.

Autriche /otriʃ/ *n.f.* Austria.

autrichien, ~**ne** /otriʃjɛ̃, -jɛn/ *a.* & *n.m.,* f. Austrian.

autruche /otryʃ/ *n.f.* ostrich.

autrui /otrɥi/ *pron.* others.

auvent /ovã/ *n.m.* canopy.

aux /o/ *voir* à.

auxiliaire /oksiljɛr/ *a.* auxiliary. ● *n.m./f.* (*assistant*) auxiliary. ● *n.m.* (*gram.*) auxiliary.

auxquel|s, ~**les** /okɛl/ *voir* lequel.

aval (en) /(ɑ̃)naval/ *adv.* downstream.

avalanche /avalɑ̃ʃ/ *n.f.* avalanche.

avaler /avale/ *v.t.* swallow.

avance /avãs/ *n.f.* advance; (*sur un concurrent*) lead. ~ **(de fonds)**, advance. **à l'**~, **d'**~, in advance. **en** ~, early; (*montre*) fast. **en** ~ **(sur)**, (*menant*) ahead (of).

avancement /avãsmã/ *n.m.* promotion.

avanc|er /avãse/ *v.i.* move forward, advance; (*travail*) make progress; (*montre*) be fast; (*faire saillie*) jut out. ● *v.t.* (*argent*) advance; (*montre*) put forward. **s'**~**er** *v. pr.* move forward, advance; (*se hasarder*) commit o.s. ~**é**, ~**ée** *a.* advanced; *n.f.* projection.

avanie /avani/ *n.f.* affront.

avant /avã/ *prép* & *adv.* before. ● *a. invar.* front. ● *n.m.* front; (*football*) forward. ~ **de faire**, before doing. ~ **qu'il (ne) fasse**, before he does. **en** ~, (*mouvement*) forward. **en** ~ **(de)**, (*position, temps*) in front (of). ~ **peu**, before long. ~ **tout**, above all. **bien** ~ **dans**, very deep(ly) *ou* far into. ~**-bras** *n.m. invar.* forearm. ~**-centre** *n.m.* centre-forward. ~**-coureur** *a. invar.* precursory, foreshadowing. ~**-dernier**, ~**-dernière** *a.* & *n.m.,* f. last but one. ~**-garde** *n.f.* (*mil.*) vanguard; (*fig.*)

avant-garde. **~-goût** *n.m.* foretaste. **~-guerre** *n.m.* pre-war period. **~-hier** /-tjɛr/ *adv.* the day before yesterday. **~-poste** *n.m.* outpost. **~-première** *n.f.* preview. **~-propos** *n.m.* foreword. **~-veille** *n.f.* two days before.

avantag|e /avɑ̃taʒ/ *n.m.* advantage; (*comm.*) benefit. **~er** *v.t.* favour; (*embellir*) show off to advantage.

avantageu|x, ~se /avɑ̃taʒø, -z/ *a.* attractive.

avar|e /avar/ *a.* miserly. ● *n.m./f.* miser. **~e de,** sparing of. **~ice** *n.f.* avarice.

avarié /avarje/ *a.* (*aliment*) spoiled.

avaries /avari/ *n.f. pl.* damage.

avatar /avatar/ *n.m.* (*fam.*) misfortune.

avec /avɛk/ *prép.* with; (*envers*) towards. ● *adv.* (*fam.*) with it *ou* them.

avenant, ~e /avnɑ̃, -t/ *a.* pleasing.

avenant (à l') /(al)avnɑ̃/ *adv.* in a similar style.

avènement /avɛnmɑ̃/ *n.m.* advent; (*d'un roi*) accession.

avenir /avnir/ *n.m.* future. **à l'~,** in future. **d'~,** with (future) prospects.

aventur|e /avɑ̃tyr/ *n.f.* adventure; (*sentimentale*) affair. **~eux, ~euse** *a.* adventurous; (*hasardeux*) risky. **~ier, ~ière** *n.m.*, *f.* adventurer.

aventurer (s') /(s)avɑ̃tyre/ *v. pr.* venture.

avenue /avny/ *n.f.* avenue.

avérer (s') /(s)avere/ *v. pr.* prove (to be).

averse /avɛrs/ *n.f.* shower.

aversion /avɛrsjɔ̃/ *n.f.* aversion.

avert|ir /avɛrtir/ *v.t.* inform; (*mettre en garde, menacer*) warn. **~i** *a.* informed. **~issement** *n.m.* warning.

avertisseur /avɛrtisœr/ *n.m.* (*auto.*) horn. **~ d'incendie,** fire-alarm.

aveu (*pl.* **~x**) /avø/ *n.m.* confession. **de l'~ de,** by the admission of.

aveugl|e /avœgl/ *a.* blind. ● *n.m./f.* blind man, blind woman. **~ement** *n.m.* blindness. **~ément** *adv.* blindly. **~er** *v.t.* blind.

aveuglette (à l') /(al)avœglɛt/ *adv.* (*à tâtons*) blindly.

avia|teur, ~trice /avjatœr, -tris/ *n.m.*, *f.* aviator.

aviation /avjasjɔ̃/ *n.f.* flying; (*industrie*) aviation; (*mil.*) air force. **d'~,** air.

avid|e /avid/ *a.* greedy (**de,** for); (*anxieux*) eager (**de,** for). **~e de faire,** eager to do. **~ité** *n.f.* greed; eagerness.

avilir /avilir/ *v.t.* degrade.

avion /avjɔ̃/ *n.m.* plane, aeroplane, aircraft; (*Amer.*) airplane. **~ à réaction,** jet.

aviron /avirɔ̃/ *n.m.* oar. **l'~,** (*sport*) rowing.

avis /avi/ *n.m.* opinion; (*renseignement*) notification; (*comm.*) advice. **à mon ~,** in my opinion. **changer d'~,** change one's mind. **être d'~ que,** be of the opinion that.

avisé /avize/ *a.* sensible. **bien/mal ~ de,** well-/ill-advised to.

aviser /avize/ *v.t.* notice; (*informer*) advise. ● *v.i.* decide what to do (**à,** about). **s'~ de,** suddenly realize. **s'~ de faire,** take it into one's head to do.

aviver /avive/ *v.t.* revive.

avocat[1]**, ~e** /avɔka, -t/ *n.m.*, *f.* barrister; (*Amer.*) attorney; (*fig.*) advocate. **~ de la défense,** counsel for the defence.

avocat[2] /avɔka/ *n.m.* (*fruit*) avocado (pear).

avoine /avwan/ *n.f.* oats.

avoir† /avwar/ *v. aux.* have. ● *v.t.* have; (*obtenir*) get; (*duper*: *fam.*) take in. ● *n.m.* assets. **je n'ai pas de café,** I haven't (got) any coffee; (*Amer.*) I don't have any coffee. **est-ce que tu as du café?,** have you (got) any coffee?; (*Amer.*) do you have any coffee? **~ à faire,** have to do. **tu n'as qu'à l'appeler,** all you have to do is call her. **~ chaud/faim**/*etc.*, be hot/hungry/*etc.* **~ dix/**etc. **ans,** be ten/*etc.* years old. **~ lieu,** take place. **~ lieu de,** have good reason to. **en ~ contre qn.,** have a grudge against s.o. **en ~ assez,** have had enough. **en ~ pour une minute**/*etc.*, be busy for a minute/*etc.* **il en a pour cent francs,** it will cost him one hundred francs. **qu'est-ce que vous avez?,** what is the matter with you? **on m'a eu!,** I've been had.

avoisin|er /avwazine/ *v.t.* border on. **~ant, ~ante** *a.* neighbouring.

avort|er /avɔrte/ *v.i.* (*projet etc.*) miscarry. **(se faire) ~er,** have an abortion. **~é** *a.* abortive. **~ement** *n.m.* (*méd.*) abortion.

avou|er /avwe/ v.t. confess (to). ● v.i.
confess. **~é** a. avowed; n.m. solicitor; (Amer.) attorney.

avril /avril/ n.m. April.

axe /aks/ n.m. axis; (essieu) axle;
(d'une politique) main line(s), basis.
~ (routier), main road.

axer /akse/ v.t. centre.

axiome /aksjom/ n.m. axiom.

ayant /ɛjɑ̃/ voir avoir.

azimuts /azimyt/ n.m. pl. **dans tous
les ~,** (fam.) all over the place.

azote /azɔt/ n.m. nitrogen.

azur /azyr/ n.m. sky-blue.

B

ba-ba /beaba/ n.m. **le ~ (de)**, the
basics (of).

baba /baba/ n.m. **~ (au rhum)**, rum
baba. **en rester ~,** (fam.) be flabbergasted.

babil /babi(l)/ n.m. babble. **~ler** /-ije/
v.i. babble.

babines /babin/ n.f. pl. **se lécher les
~,** lick one's chops.

babiole /babjol/ n.f. knick-knack.

bâbord /babɔr/ n.m. port (side).

babouin /babwɛ̃/ n.m. baboon.

baby-foot /babifut/ n.m. invar. table
football.

baby-sitt|er /bebisitœr/ n.m./f. baby-
sitter. **~ing** n.m. **faire du ~ing,**
babysit.

bac [1] /bak/ n.m. = **baccalauréat.**

bac [2] /bak/ n.m. (bateau) ferry; (récipient) tub; (plus petit) tray.

baccalauréat /bakalɔrea/ n.m.
school leaving certificate.

bâch|e /baʃ/ n.f. tarpaulin. **~er** v.t.
cover (with a tarpaulin).

bachel|ier, ~ière /baʃəlje, -jɛr/ n.m.,
f. holder of the baccalauréat.

bachot /baʃo/ n.m. (fam.) =
baccalauréat. **~er** /-ɔte/ v.i. cram
(for an exam).

bâcler /bakle/ v.t. botch (up).

bactérie /bakteri/ n.f. bacterium.

badaud, ~e /bado, -d/ n.m., f. (péj.)
onlooker.

badigeon /badiʒɔ̃/ n.m. whitewash.
~ner /-ɔne/ v.t. whitewash; (barbouiller) daub.

badin, ~e /badɛ̃, -in/ a. light-
hearted.

badiner /badine/ v.i. joke (**sur, avec,**
about).

badminton /badmintɔn/ n.m. badminton.

baffe /baf/ n.f. (fam.) slap.

baffle /bafl/ n.m. speaker.

bafouer /bafwe/ v.t. scoff at.

bafouiller /bafuje/ v.t./i. stammer.

bâfrer /bafre/ v.i. (fam.) gobble. **se ~**
v.pr. stuff o.s.

bagage /bagaʒ/ n.m. bag; (fig.) (store
of) knowledge. **~s,** luggage, baggage.
~s à main, hand luggage.

bagarr|e /bagar/ n.f. fight. **~er** v.i.,
se ~er v. pr. fight.

bagatelle /bagatɛl/ n.f. trifle;
(somme) trifling amount.

bagnard /baɲar/ n.m. convict.

bagnole /baɲɔl/ n.f. (fam.) car.

bagou(t) /bagu/ n.m. **avoir du ~,**
have the gift of the gab.

bagu|e /bag/ n.f. (anneau) ring. **~er**
v.t. ring.

baguette /bagɛt/ n.f. stick; (de chef
d'orchestre) baton; (chinoise) chopstick; (magique) wand; (pain) stick of
bread. **~ de tambour,** drumstick.

baie /bɛ/ n.f. (géog.) bay; (fruit)
berry. **~ (vitrée),** picture window.

baign|er /beɲe/ v.t. bathe; (enfant)
bath. ● v.i. **~er dans,** soak in; (être
enveloppé dans) be steeped in. **se
~er** v. pr. go swimming (ou)
bathing. **~é de,** bathed in; (sang)
soaked in. **~ade** /bɛɲad/ n.f. bathing, swimming. **~eur, ~euse**
/bɛɲœr, -øz/ n.m., f. bather.

baignoire /beɲwar/ n.f. bath(-tub).

bail (pl. **baux** /baj, bo/ n.m. lease.

bâill|er /baje/ v.i. yawn; (être ouvert)
gape. **~ement** n.m. yawn.

bailleur /bajœr/ n.m. **~ de fonds,**
(comm.) backer.

bâillon /bajɔ̃/ n.m. gag. **~ner**
/bajone/ v.t. gag.

bain /bɛ̃/ n.m. bath; (de mer) bathe.
~(s) de soleil, sunbathing. **~-
marie** (pl. **~s-marie**) n.m. double
boiler. **~ de bouche,** mouthwash.
mettre qn. dans le ~, (compromettre) drop s.o. in it; (au courant)
put s.o. in the picture. **se remettre
dans le ~,** get back into the swim
of things. **prendre un ~ de
foule,** mingle with the crowd.

baiser /beze/ n.m. kiss. ● v.t. (main)
kiss; (fam.) screw.

baisse /bɛs/ n.f. fall, drop. **en ~,**
falling.

baisser /bese/ v.t. lower; (radio, lampe, etc.) turn down. ● v.i. go down, fall; (santé, forces) fail. **se ~** v. pr. bend down.

bajoues /baʒu/ n.f. pl. chops.

bakchich /bakʃiʃ/ n.m. (fam.) bribe.

bal (pl. **~s**) /bal/ n.m. dance; (habillé) ball; (lieu) dance-hall. **~ costumé,** fancy-dress ball.

balad|e /balad/ n.f. stroll; (en auto) drive. **~er** v.t. take for a stroll. **se ~er** v. pr. (go for a) stroll; (excursionner) wander around. **se ~er (en auto),** go for a drive.

baladeur /baladœr/ n.m. personal stereo.

balafr|e /balafr/ n.f. gash; (cicatrice) scar. **~er** v.t. gash.

balai /balɛ/ n.m. broom. **~-brosse** n.m. garden broom.

balance /balãs/ n.f. scales. **la B~,** Libra.

balancer /balãse/ v.t. swing; (doucement) sway; (lancer: fam.) chuck; (se débarrasser de: fam.) chuck out. ● v.i., **se ~** v. pr. swing; sway. **se ~ de,** (fam.) not care about.

balancier /balãsje/ n.m. (d'horloge) pendulum; (d'équilibriste) pole.

balançoire /balãswar/ n.f. swing; (bascule) see-saw.

balay|er /baleje/ v.t. sweep (up); (chasser) sweep away; (se débarrasser de) sweep aside. **~age** n.m. sweeping; (cheveux) highlights. **~eur, ~euse** n.m., f. road sweeper.

balbut|ier /balbysje/ v.t./i. stammer. **~iement** n.m. stammering.

balcon /balkɔ̃/ n.m. balcony; (théâtre) dress circle.

baleine /balɛn/ n.f. whale.

balis|e /baliz/ n.f. beacon; (bouée) buoy; (auto.) (road) sign. **~er** v.t. mark out (with beacons); (route) signpost.

balistique /balistik/ a. ballistic.

balivernes /balivɛrn/ n.f. pl. balderdash.

ballade /balad/ n.f. ballad.

ballant, ~e /balã, -t/ a. dangling.

ballast /balast/ n.m. ballast.

balle /bal/ n.f. (projectile) bullet; (sport) ball; (paquet) bale.

ballerine /balrin/ n.f. ballerina.

ballet /balɛ/ n.m. ballet.

ballon /balɔ̃/ n.m. balloon; (sport) ball. **~ de football,** football.

ballonné /balɔne/ a. bloated.

ballot /balo/ n.m. bundle; (nigaud: fam.) idiot.

ballottage /balɔtaʒ/ n.m. second ballot (due to indecisive result).

ballotter /balɔte/ v.t./i. shake about, toss.

balnéaire /balneɛr/ a. seaside.

balourd, ~e /balur, -d/ n.m., f. oaf. ● a. oafish.

balustrade /balystrad/ n.f. railing(s).

bambin /bãbɛ̃/ n.m. tot.

bambou /bãbu/ n.m. bamboo.

ban /bã/ n.m. round of applause. **~s,** (de mariage) banns. **mettre au ~ de,** cast out from. **publier les ~s,** have the banns called.

banal (m. pl. **~s**) /banal/ a. commonplace, banal. **~ité** n.f. banality.

banane /banan/ n.f. banana.

banc /bã/ n.m. bench; (de poissons) shoal. **~ des accusés,** dock. **~ d'essai,** test bed; (fig.) testing-ground.

bancaire /bãkɛr/ a. banking; (chèque) bank.

bancal (m. pl. **~s**) /bãkal/ a. wobbly; (raisonnement) shaky.

bandage /bãdaʒ/ n.m. bandage. **~ herniaire,** truss.

bande[1] /bãd/ n.f. (de papier etc.) strip; (rayure) stripe; (de film) reel; (radio) band; (pansement) bandage. **~ (magnétique),** tape. **~ dessinée,** comic strip. **~ sonore,** sound-track. **par la ~,** indirectly.

bande[2] /bãd/ n.f. (groupe) bunch, band, gang.

bandeau (pl. **~x**) /bãdo/ n.m. headband; (sur les yeux) blindfold.

bander /bãde/ v.t. bandage; (arc) bend; (muscle) tense. **~ les yeux à,** blindfold.

banderole /bãdrɔl/ n.f. banner.

bandit /bãdi/ n.m. bandit. **~isme** /-tism/ n.m. crime.

bandoulière (en) /(ã)bãduljɛr/ adv. across one's shoulder.

banjo /bã(d)ʒo/ n.m. banjo.

banlieu|e /bãljø/ n.f. suburbs. **de ~e,** suburban. **~sard, ~sarde** /-zar, -zard/ n.m., f. (suburban) commuter.

bannière /banjɛr/ n.f. banner.

bannir /banir/ v.t. banish.

banque /bãk/ n.f. bank; (activité) banking. **~ d'affaires,** merchant bank.

banqueroute /bãkrut/ n.f. (fraudulent) bankruptcy.

banquet /bãkɛ/ n.m. dinner; (fastueux) banquet.

banquette /bãkɛt/ n.f. seat.

banquier /bãkje/ n.m. banker.

bapt|ême /batɛm/ n.m. baptism; christening. **~iser** v.t. baptize, christen; (appeler) christen.

baquet /bakɛ/ n.m. tub.

bar /bar/ n.m. (lieu) bar.

baragouin /baragwɛ̃/ n.m. gibberish, gabble. **~er** /-wine/ v.t./i. gabble; (langue) speak a few words of.

baraque /barak/ n.f. hut, shed; (boutique) stall; (maison: fam.) house. **~ments** n.m. pl. huts.

baratin /baratɛ̃/ n.m. (fam.) sweet ou smooth talk. **~er** /-ine/ v.t. (fam.) chat up; (Amer.) sweet-talk.

barbar|e /barbar/ a. barbaric. ● n.m./f. barbarian. **~ie** n.f. (cruauté) barbarity.

barbe /barb/ n.f. beard. **~ à papa,** candy-floss; (Amer.) cotton candy. **la ~!,** (fam.) blast (it)! **quelle ~!,** (fam.) what a bore!

barbecue /barbəkju/ n.m. barbecue.

barbelé /barbəle/ a. **fil ~,** barbed wire.

barber /barbe/ v.t. (fam.) bore.

barbiche /barbiʃ/ n.f. goatee.

barbiturique /barbityrik/ n.m. barbiturate.

barboter [1] /barbɔte/ v.i. paddle, splash.

barboter [2] /barbɔte/ v.t. (voler: fam.) pinch.

barbouill|er /barbuje/ v.t. (peindre) daub; (souiller) smear; (griffonner) scribble. **avoir l'estomac ~é ou se sentir ~é** feel liverish.

barbu /barby/ a. bearded.

barda /barda/ n.m. (fam.) gear.

barder /barde/ v.i. **ça va ~,** (fam.) sparks will fly.

barème /barɛm/ n.m. list, table; (échelle) scale.

baril /baril/ n.m. barrel; (de poudre) keg.

bariolé /barjɔle/ a. motley.

barman /barman/ n.m. barman; (Amer.) bartender.

baromètre /barɔmɛtr/ n.m. barometer.

baron, ~ne /barɔ̃, -ɔn/ n.m., f. baron, baroness.

baroque /barɔk/ a. (fig.) weird; (archit., art) baroque.

baroud /barud/ n.m. **~ d'honneur,** gallant last fight.

barque /bark/ n.f. (small) boat.

barrage /baraʒ/ n.m. dam; (sur route) road-block.

barre /bar/ n.f. bar; (trait) line, stroke; (naut.) helm.

barreau (pl. **~x**) /baro/ n.m. bar; (d'échelle) rung. **le ~,** (jurid.) the bar.

barrer /bare/ v.t. block; (porte) bar; (rayer) cross out; (naut.) steer. **se ~** v. pr. (fam.) hop it.

barrette /barɛt/ n.f. (hair-)slide.

barricad|e /barikad/ n.f. barricade. **~er** v.t. barricade. **se ~er** v. pr. barricade o.s.

barrière /barjɛr/ n.f. (porte) gate; (clôture) fence; (obstacle) barrier.

barrique /barik/ n.f. barrel.

baryton /baritɔ̃/ n.m. baritone.

bas, basse /ba, bas/ a. low; (action) base. ● n.m. bottom; (chaussette) stocking. ● n.f. (mus.) bass. ● adv. low. **à ~,** down with. **au ~ mot,** at the lowest estimate. **en ~,** down below; (dans une maison) downstairs. **en ~ âge,** young. **en ~ de,** at the bottom of. **plus ~,** further ou lower down. **~-côté** n.m. (de route) verge; (Amer.) shoulder. **~ de casse** n.m. invar. lower case. **~ de laine,** nest-egg. **~-fonds** n.m. pl. (eau) shallows; (fig.) dregs. **~-morceaux,** (viande) cheap cuts. **~-relief** n.m. low relief. **~-ventre** n.m. lower abdomen. **mettre ~,** give birth (to).

basané /bazane/ a. tanned.

bascule /baskyl/ n.f. (balance) scales. **cheval/fauteuil à ~,** rocking-horse/-chair.

basculer /baskyle/ v.t./i. topple over; (benne) tip up.

base /baz/ n.f. base; (fondement) basis; (pol.) rank and file. **de ~,** basic.

baser /baze/ v.t. base. **se ~ sur,** base o.s. on.

basilic /bazilik/ n.m. basil.

basilique /bazilik/ n.f. basilica.

basket(-ball) /baskɛt(bol)/ n.m. basketball.

basque /bask/ a. & n.m./f. Basque.

basse /bas/ voir bas.

basse-cour (pl. **basses-cours**) /baskur/ n.f. farmyard.

bassement /basmã/ adv. basely.

bassesse /basɛs/ n.f. baseness; (action) base act.

bassin /basɛ̃/ *n.m.* bowl; (*pièce d'eau*) pond; (*rade*) dock; (*géog.*) basin; (*anat.*) pelvis. **~ houiller,** coalfield.

basson /basɔ̃/ *n.m.* bassoon.

bastion /bastjɔ̃/ *n.m.* bastion.

bat /ba/ *voir* battre.

bât /bɑ/ *n.m.* **là où le ~ blesse,** where the shoe pinches.

bataill|e /batɑj/ *n.f.* battle; (*fig.*) fight. **~er** *v.i.* fight.

bataillon /batajɔ̃/ *n.m.* battalion.

bâtard, **~e** /bɑtar, -d/ *n.m.*, *f.* bastard. ● *a.* (*solution*) hybrid.

bateau (*pl.* **~x**) /bato/ *n.m.* boat. **~-mouche** (*pl.* **~x-mouches**) *n.m.* sightseeing boat.

bâti /bɑti/ *a.* **bien ~,** well-built.

batifoler /batifɔle/ *v.i.* fool about.

bâtiment /bɑtimɑ̃/ *n.m.* building; (*navire*) vessel; (*industrie*) building trade.

bâtir /bɑtir/ *v.t.* build; (*coudre*) baste.

bâtisse /batis/ *n.f.* (*péj.*) building.

bâton /bɑtɔ̃/ *n.m.* stick. **à ~s rompus,** jumping from subject to subject. **~ de rouge,** lipstick.

battage /bataʒ/ *n.m.* (*publicité*: *fam.*) (hard) plugging.

battant /batɑ̃/ *n.m.* (*vantail*) flap. **porte à deux ~s,** double door.

battement /batmɑ̃/ *n.m.* (*de cœur*) beat(ing); (*temps*) interval.

batterie /batri/ *n.f.* (*mil.*, *électr.*) battery; (*mus.*) drums. **~ de cuisine,** pots and pans.

batteur /batœr/ *n.m.* (*mus.*) drummer; (*culin.*) whisk.

battre† /batr/ *v.t./i.* beat; (*blé*) thresh; (*cartes*) shuffle; (*parcourir*) scour; (*faire du bruit*) bang. **se ~** *v. pr.* fight. **~ des ailes,** flap its wings. **~ des mains,** clap. **~ en retraite,** beat a retreat. **~ la semelle,** stamp one's feet. **~ pavillon britannique/***etc.*, fly the British/*etc.* flag. **~ son plein,** be in full swing.

battue /baty/ *n.f.* (*chasse*) beat; (*de police*) search.

baume /bom/ *n.m.* balm.

bavard, **~e** /bavar, -d/ *a.* talkative. ● *n.m.*, *f.* chatterbox.

bavard|er /bavarde/ *v.i.* chat; (*jacasser*) chatter, gossip. **~age** *n.m.* chatter, gossip.

bav|e /bav/ *n.f.* dribble, slobber; (*de limace*) slime. **~er** *v.i.* dribble, slobber. **~eux, ~euse** *a.* dribbling; (*omelette*) runny.

bav|ette /bavɛt/ *n.f.*, **~oir** *n.m.* bib. **tailler une ~ette,** (*fam.*) have a chat.

bavure /bavyr/ *n.f.* smudge; (*erreur*) mistake. **~ policière,** (*fam.*)police cock-up. **sans ~,** flawless(ly).

bazar /bazar/ *n.m.* bazaar; (*objets*: *fam.*) clutter.

bazarder /bazarde/ *v.t.* (*vendre*: *fam.*) get rid of, flog.

BCBG *abrév.* (*bon chic bon genre*) posh.

BD *abrév.* (*bande dessinée*) comic strip.

béant, **~e** /beɑ̃, -t/ *a.* gaping.

béat, **~e** /bea, -t/ *a.* (*hum.*) blissful; (*péj.*) smug. **~itude** /-tityd/ *n.f.* (*hum.*) bliss.

beau *ou* **bel*, belle** (*m. pl.* **~x**) /bo, bɛl/ *a.* fine, beautiful; (*femme*) beautiful; (*homme*) handsome; (*grand*) big. ● *n.f.* beauty; (*sport*) deciding game. **au ~ milieu,** right in the middle. **bel et bien,** well and truly. **de plus belle,** more than ever. **faire le ~,** sit up and beg. **on a ~ essayer/insister/***etc.*, however much one tries/insists/*etc.*, it is no use trying/insisting/*etc.* **~x-arts** *n.m. pl.* fine arts. **~-fils** (*pl.* **~x-fils**) *n.m.* son-in-law; (*remariage*) stepson. **~-frère** (*pl.* **~x-frères**) *n.m.* brother-in-law. **~père** (*pl.* **~x-pères**) *n.m.* father-in-law; stepfather. **~x-parents** *n.m. pl.* parents-in-law.

beaucoup /boku/ *adv.* a lot, very much. ● *pron.* many (people). **~ de,** (*nombre*) many; (*quantité*) a lot of. **pas ~ (de),** not many; (*quantité*) not much. **~ plus/***etc.*, much more/*etc.* **~ trop,** much too much. **de ~,** by far.

beauté /bote/ *n.f.* beauty. **en ~,** magnificently. **tu es en ~,** you are looking good.

bébé /bebe/ *n.m.* baby. **~-éprouvette,** test-tube baby.

bec /bɛk/ *n.m.* beak; (*de plume*) nib; (*de bouilloire*) spout; (*de casserole*) lip; (*bouche*: *fam.*) mouth. **~-de-cane** (*pl.* **~s-de-cane**) door-handle. **~ de gaz,** gas lamp (*in street*).

bécane /bekan/ *n.f.* (*fam.*) bike.

bécasse /bekas/ *n.f.* woodcock.

bêche /bɛʃ/ *n.f.* spade.

bêcher /beʃe/ *v.t.* dig.

bécoter /bekɔte/ *v.t.*, **se ~** *v. pr.* (*fam.*) kiss.

becquée /beke/ *n.f.* **donner la ~ à,** (*oiseau*) feed; (*fig.*) spoonfeed.

bedaine /bədɛn/ *n.f.* paunch.

bedeau (*pl. ~x*) /bədo/ *n.m.* beadle.

bedonnant, ~e /bədɔnɑ̃, -t/ *a.* paunchy.

beffroi /befrwa/ *n.m.* belfry.

bégayer /begeje/ *v.t./i.* stammer.

bègue /bɛg/ *n.m./f.* stammerer. **être ~,** stammer.

bégueule /begœl/ *a.* prudish.

béguin /begɛ̃/ *n.m.* **avoir le ~ pour,** (*fam.*) have a crush on.

beige /bɛʒ/ *a. & n.m.* beige.

beignet /bɛɲɛ/ *n.m.* fritter.

bel /bɛl/ *voir* beau.

bêler /bele/ *v.i.* bleat.

belette /bəlɛt/ *n.f.* weasel.

belge /bɛlʒ/ *a. & n.m./f.* Belgian.

Belgique /bɛlʒik/ *n.f.* Belgium.

bélier /belje/ *n.m.* ram. **le B~,** Aries.

belle /bɛl/ *voir* beau.

belle|-fille (*pl. ~s-filles*) /bɛlfij/ *n.f.* daughter-in-law; (*remariage*) stepdaughter. **~-mère** (*pl. ~s-mères*) *n.f.* mother-in-law; stepmother. **~-sœur** (*pl. ~s-sœurs*) *n.f.* sister-in-law.

belligérant, ~e /beliʒerɑ̃, -t/ *a. & n.m.* belligerent.

belliqueu|x, ~se /belikø, -z/ *a.* warlike.

belote /bəlɔt/ *n.f.* belote (*card game*).

belvédère /bɛlvedɛr/ *n.m.* (*lieu*) viewing spot, viewpoint.

bémol /bemɔl/ *n.m.* (*mus.*) flat.

bénédiction /benediksjɔ̃/ *n.f.* blessing.

bénéfice /benefis/ *n.m.* (*gain*) profit; (*avantage*) benefit.

bénéficiaire /benefisjɛr/ *n.m./f.* beneficiary.

bénéficier /benefisje/ *v.i.* **~ de,** benefit from; (*jouir de*) enjoy, have.

bénéfique /benefik/ *a.* beneficial.

Bénélux /benelyks/ *n.m.* Benelux.

benêt /bənɛ/ *n.m.* simpleton.

bénévole /benevɔl/ *a.* voluntary.

bén|in, ~igne /benɛ̃, -iɲ/ *a.* mild, slight; (*tumeur*) benign.

bén|ir /benir/ *v.t.* bless. **~it, ~ite** *a.* (*eau*) holy; (*pain*) consecrated.

bénitier /benitje/ *n.m.* stoup.

benjamin, ~e /bɛ̃ʒamɛ̃, -in/ *n.m., f.* youngest child.

benne /bɛn/ *n.f.* (*de grue*) scoop; (*amovible*) skip. **~ (basculante),** dump truck.

benzine /bɛ̃zin/ *n.f.* benzine.

béotien, ~ne /beɔsjɛ̃, -jɛn/ *n.m., f.* philistine.

béquille /bekij/ *n.f.* crutch; (*de moto*) stand.

bercail /bɛrkaj/ *n.m.* fold.

berceau (*pl. ~x*) /bɛrso/ *n.m.* cradle.

bercer /bɛrse/ *v.t.* (*balancer*) rock; (*apaiser*) lull; (*leurrer*) delude.

berceuse /bɛrsøz/ *n.f.* lullaby.

béret /berɛ/ *n.m.* beret.

berge /bɛrʒ/ *n.f.* (*bord*) bank.

berg|er, ~ère /bɛrʒe, -ɛr/ *n.m., f.* shepherd, shepherdess. **~erie** *n.f.* sheep-fold.

berlingot /bɛrlɛ̃go/ *n.m.* boiled sweet; (*emballage*) carton.

berne (en) /(ɑ̃)bɛrn/ *adv.* at half-mast.

berner /bɛrne/ *v.t.* hoodwink.

besogne /bəzɔɲ/ *n.f.* task, job, chore.

besoin /bəzwɛ̃/ *n.m.* need. **avoir ~ de,** need. **au ~,** if need be.

best|ial (*m. pl. ~iaux*) /bɛstjal, -jo/ *a.* bestial.

bestiaux /bɛstjo/ *n.m. pl.* livestock.

bestiole /bɛstjɔl/ *n.f.* creepy-crawly.

bétail /betaj/ *n.m.* farm animals.

bête¹ /bɛt/ *n.f.* animal. **~ noire,** pet hate, pet peeve. **~ sauvage,** wild beast. **chercher la petite ~,** be overfussy.

bête² /bɛt/ *a.* stupid. **~ment** *adv.* stupidly.

bêtise /betiz/ *n.f.* stupidity; (*action*) stupid thing.

béton /betɔ̃/ *n.m.* concrete. **~ armé,** reinforced concrete. **~nière** /-ɔnjɛr/ *n.f.* cement-mixer, concrete-mixer.

betterave /bɛtrav/ *n.f.* beetroot. **~ sucrière,** sugar-beet.

beugler /bøgle/ *v.i.* bellow, low; (*radio*) blare.

beur /bœr/ *n.m./f. & a.* (*fam.*) young French North African.

beurr|e /bœr/ *n.m.* butter. **~er** *v.t.* butter. **~ier** *n.m.* butter-dish. **~é, a** buttered; (*fam.*) drunk.

bévue /bevy/ *n.f.* blunder.

biais /bjɛ/ *n.m.* (*fig.*) expedient; (*côté*) angle. **de ~, en ~,** at an angle. **de ~,** (*fig.*) indirectly.

biaiser /bjeze/ *v.i.* hedge.

bibelot /biblo/ *n.m.* curio.

biberon /bibrɔ̃/ *n.m.* (feeding-) bottle. **nourrir au ~,** bottle-feed.

bible /bibl/ *n.f.* bible. **la B~,** the Bible.

bibliographie /biblijɔgrafi/ *n.f.* bibliography.

bibliophile /biblijɔfil/ n.m./f. book-lover.

biblioth|èque /biblijɔtɛk/ n.f. library; (meuble) bookcase; ~écaire n.m./f. librarian.

biblique /biblik/ a. biblical.

bic /bik/ n.m. (P.) biro (P.).

bicarbonate /bikarbɔnat/ n.m. ~ (de soude), bicarbonate (of soda).

biceps /bisɛps/ n.m. biceps.

biche /biʃ/ n.f. doe.

bichonner /biʃɔne/ v.t. doll up.

bicoque /bikɔk/ n.f. shack.

bicyclette /bisiklɛt/ n.f. bicycle.

bide /bid/ n.m. (ventre: fam.) belly; (théâtre: fam.) flop.

bidet /bidɛ/ n.m. bidet.

bidon /bidɔ̃/ n.m. can. ● a. invar. (fam.) phoney. **c'est pas du ~,** (fam.) it's the truth, it's for real.

bidonville /bidɔ̃vil/ n.f. shanty town.

bidule /bidyl/ n.m. (fam.) thing.

bielle /bjɛl/ n.f. connecting rod.

bien /bjɛ̃/ adv. well; (très) quite, very. ● n.m. good; (patrimoine) possession. ● a. invar. good; (passable) all right; (en forme) well; (à l'aise) comfortable; (beau) attractive; (respectable) nice, respectable. ● conj. ~ que, (al)though. ~ que ce soit/que ça ait, although it is/it has. ~ du, (quantité) a lot of, much. ~ des, (nombre) many. **il l'a ~ fait,** (intensif) he did do it. **ce n'est pas ~ de,** it is not right to. ~ **sûr,** of course. ~**s de consommation,** consumer goods. ~**-aimé, ~aimée** a. & n.m., f. beloved. ~**-être** n.m. well-being. ~**-fondé** n.m. soundness. ~**-pensant, ~-pensante** a. & n.m., f. (péj.) right-thinking.

bienfaisan|t, -te /bjɛ̃fəzɑ̃, -t/ a. beneficial. ~**ce** n.f. charity. **fête de ~ce,** fête.

bienfait /bjɛ̃fɛ/ n.m. (kind) favour; (avantage) benefit.

bienfai|teur, ~trice /bjɛ̃fɛtœr, -tris/ n.m., f. benefactor.

bienheureu|x, ~se /bjɛ̃nœrø, -z/ a. happy, blessed.

bienséan|t, ~te /bjɛ̃seɑ̃, -t/ a. proper. ~**ce** n.f. propriety.

bientôt /bjɛ̃to/ adv. soon. **à ~,** see you soon.

bienveillan|t, ~te /bjɛ̃vɛjɑ̃, -t/ a. kind(ly). ~**ce** n.f. kind(li)ness.

bienvenu, ~e /bjɛ̃vny/ a. welcome. ● n.f. welcome. ● n.m., f. **être le ~,** être la ~**e,** be welcome. **souhaiter la ~e à,** welcome.

bière /bjɛr/ n.f. beer; (cercueil) coffin. ~ **blonde,** lager. ~ **brune,** stout, brown ale. ~ **pression,** draught beer.

biffer /bife/ v.t. cross out.

bifteck /biftɛk/ n.m. steak.

bifur|quer /bifyrke/ v.i. branch off, fork. ~**cation** n.f. fork, junction.

bigam|e /bigam/ a. bigamous. ● n.m./f. bigamist. ~**ie** n.f. bigamy.

bigarré /bigare/ a. motley.

big-bang /bigbɑ̃g/ n.m. big bang.

bigot, ~e /bigo, -ɔt/ n.m., f. religious fanatic. ● a. over-pious.

bigoudi /bigudi/ n.m. curler.

bijou (pl. ~**x**) /biʒu/ n.m. jewel. ~**terie** n.f. (boutique) jeweller's shop; (comm.) jewellery. ~**tier,** ~**tière** n.m., f. jeweller.

bikini /bikini/ n.m. bikini.

bilan /bilɑ̃/ n.m. outcome; (d'une catastrophe) (casualty) toll; (comm.) balance sheet. **faire le ~ de,** assess. ~ **de santé,** check-up.

bile /bil/ n.f. bile. **se faire de la ~,** (fam.) worry.

bilieu|x, ~se /biljø, -z/ a. bilious; (fig.) irascible.

bilingue /bilɛ̃g/ a. bilingual.

billard /bijar/ n.m. billiards; (table) billiard-table.

bille /bij/ n.f. (d'enfant) marble; (de billard) billiard-ball.

billet /bijɛ/ n.m. ticket; (lettre) note; (article) column. ~ (**de banque**), (bank)note. ~ **d'aller et retour,** return ticket; (Amer.) round trip ticket. ~ **de faveur,** complimentary ticket. ~ **aller simple,** single ticket; (Amer.) one-way ticket.

billetterie /bijɛtri/ n.f. cash dispenser.

billion /biljɔ̃/ n.m. billion (= 10^{12}); (Amer.) trillion.

billot /bijo/ n.m. block.

bimensuel, ~le /bimɑ̃sɥɛl/ a. fortnightly, bimonthly.

bin|er /bine/ v.t. hoe. ~**ette** n.f. hoe; (fam.) face.

biochimie /bjoʃimi/ n.f. biochemistry.

biodégradable /bjodegradabl/ a. biodegradable.

biograph|ie /bjɔgrafi/ n.f. biography. ~**e** n.m./f. biographer.

biolog|ie /bjɔlɔʒi/ n.f. biology. ~**ique** a. biological. ~**iste** n.m./f. biologist.

bipède /bipɛd/ *n.m.* biped.

bis [1], **bise** /bi, biz/ *a.* greyish brown.

bis [2] /bis/ *a.invar.* (*numéro*) A, a. ● *n.m.* & *int.* encore.

bisbille (en) /(ã)bisbij/ *adv.* (*fam.*) at loggerheads (**avec,** with).

biscornu /biskɔrny/ *a.* crooked; (*bizarre*) weird.

biscotte /biskɔt/ *n.f.* rusk.

biscuit /biskɥi/ *n.m.* (*salé*) biscuit; (*Amer.*) cracker; (*sucré*) biscuit; (*Amer.*) cookie. ~ **de Savoie,** sponge-cake.

bise [1] /biz/ *n.f.* (*fam.*) kiss.

bise [2] /biz/ *n.f.* (*vent*) north wind.

bison /bizɔ̃/ *n.m.* (American) buffalo, bison.

bisou /bizu/ *n.m.* (*fam.*) kiss.

bisser /bise/ *v.t.* encore.

bistouri /bisturi/ *n.m.* lancet.

bistre /bistr/ *a.* & *n.m.* dark brown.

bistro(t) /bistro/ *n.m.* café, bar.

bit /bit/ *n.m.* (*comput.*) bit.

bitume /bitym/ *n.m.* asphalt.

bizarre /bizar/ *a.* odd, peculiar. ~**ment** *adv.* oddly. ~**rie** *n.f.* peculiarity.

blafard, ~e /blafar, -d/ *a.* pale.

blagu|e /blag/ *n.f.* joke. ~**e à tabac,** tobacco-pouch. ~**er** *v.i.* joke; *v.t.* tease. ~**eur, ~euse** *n.m.*, *f.* joker; *a.* jokey.

blaireau (*pl.* ~**x**) /blɛro/ *n.m.* shaving-brush; (*animal*) badger.

blâm|e /blɑm/ *n.m.* rebuke, blame. ~**able** *a.* blameworthy. ~**er** *v.t.* rebuke, blame.

blanc, blanche /blã, blãʃ/ *a.* white; (*papier, page*) blank. ● *n.m.* white; (*espace*) blank. ● *n.m.*, *f.* white man, white woman. ● *n.f.* (*mus.*) minim. ~ (**de poulet**), breast, white meat (of the chicken). **le ~,** (*linge*) whites. **laisser en ~,** leave blank.

blancheur /blãʃœr/ *n.f.* whiteness.

blanch|ir /blãʃir/ *v.t.* whiten; (*linge*) launder; (*personne: fig.*) clear; (*culin.*) blanch. ~**ir (à la chaux),** whitewash. ● *v.i.* turn white. ~**issage** *n.m.* laundering. ~**isserie** *n.f.* laundry. ~**isseur, ~isseuse** *n.m.*, *f.* laundryman, laundress.

blasé /blaze/ *a.* blasé.

blason /blazɔ̃/ *n.m.* coat of arms.

blasph|ème /blasfɛm/ *n.m.* blasphemy. ~**émer** *v.t./i.* blaspheme.

blatte /blat/ *n.f.* cockroach.

blazer /blɛzœr/ *n.m.* blazer.

blé /ble/ *n.m.* wheat.

bled /blɛd/ *n.m.* (*fam.*) dump, hole.

blême /blɛm/ *a.* (sickly) pale.

bless|er /blese/ *v.t.* injure, hurt; (*par balle*) wound; (*offenser*) hurt, wound. **se ~er** *v. pr.* injure *ou* hurt o.s. ~**ant, ~ante** /blesã, -t/ *a.* hurtful. ~**é, ~ée** *n.m.*, *f.* casualty, injured person.

blessure /blesyr/ *n.f.* wound.

blet, ~te /blɛ, blɛt/ *a.* over-ripe.

bleu /blø/ *a.* blue; (*culin.*) very rare. ~ **marine,** navy blue. ● *n.m.* blue; (*contusion*) bruise. ~**(s),** (*vêtement*) overalls. ~**ir** *v.t./i.* turn blue.

bleuet /bløɛ/ *n.m.* cornflower.

bleuté /bløte/ *a.* slightly blue.

blind|er /blɛ̃de/ *v.t.* armour (-plate); (*fig.*) harden. ~**é** *a.* armoured; (*fig.*) immune (**contre,** to); *n.m.* armoured car, tank.

blizzard /blizar/ *n.m.* blizzard.

bloc /blɔk/ *n.m.* block; (*de papier*) pad; (*système*) unit; (*pol.*) bloc. à ~, hard, tight. **en ~,** all together. ~**-notes** (*pl.* ~**s-notes**) *n.m.* notepad.

blocage /blɔkaʒ/ *n.m.* (*des prix*) freeze, freezing; (*des roues*) locking; (*psych.*) block.

blocus /blɔkys/ *n.m.* blockade.

blond, ~e /blɔ̃, -d/ *a.* fair, blond. ● *n.m.*, *f.* fair-haired *ou* blond man *ou* woman. ~**eur** /-dœr/ *n.f.* fairness.

bloquer /blɔke/ *v.t.* block; (*porte, machine*) jam; (*freins*) slam on; (*roues*) lock; (*prix, crédits*) freeze; (*grouper*) put together. **se ~** *v. pr.* jam; (*roues*) lock.

blottir (se) /(sə)blɔtir/ *v. pr.* snuggle, huddle.

blouse /bluz/ *n.f.* smock.

blouson /bluzɔ̃/ *n.m.* lumber-jacket; (*Amer.*) windbreaker.

blue-jean /bludʒin/ *n.m.* jeans.

bluff /blœf/ *n.m.* bluff. ~**er** *v.t./i.* bluff.

blush /blœʃ/ *n.m.* blusher.

boa /bɔa/ *n.m.* boa.

bobard /bɔbar/ *n.m.* (*fam.*) fib.

bobine /bɔbin/ *n.f.* reel; (*sur machine*) spool; (*électr.*) coil.

bobo /bɔbo/ *n.m.* (*fam.*) sore, cut. **avoir ~,** have a pain.

bocage /bɔkaʒ/ *n.m.* grove.

boc|al (*pl.* ~**aux**) /bɔkal, -o/ *n.m.* jar.

bock /bɔk/ *n.m.* beer glass; (*contenu*) glass of beer.

body /bɔdi/ *n.m.* leotard.

bœuf /pl. ~s/ /bœf, bø/ n.m. ox; (viande) beef. **~s,** oxen.

bogue /bɔg/ n.m. (comput.) bug.

bohème /bɔɛm/ a. & n.m./f. unconventional.

boire† /bwar/ v.t./i. drink; (absorber) soak up. **~ un coup,** have a drink.

bois [1] /bwa/ voir boire.

bois [2] /bwa/ n.m. (matériau, forêt) wood. **de ~, en ~,** wooden.

boisé /bwaze/ a. wooded.

bois|er /bwaze/ v.t. (chambre) panel. **~eries** n.f. pl. panelling.

boisson /bwasɔ̃/ n.f. drink.

boit /bwa/ voir boire.

boîte /bwat/ n.f. box; (de conserves) tin, can; (firme: fam.) firm. **~ à gants,** glove compartment. **~ aux lettres,** letter-box. **~ de nuit,** nightclub. **~ postale,** post-office box. **~ de vitesses,** gear box.

boiter /bwate/ v.i. limp; (meuble) wobble.

boiteu|x, ~se /bwato, -z/ a. lame; (meuble) wobbly; (raisonnement) shaky.

boîtier /bwatje/ n.m. case.

bol /bɔl/ n.m. bowl. **un ~ d'air,** a breath of fresh air. **avoir du ~,** (fam.) be lucky.

bolide /bɔlid/ n.m. racing car.

Bolivie /bɔlivi/ n.f. Bolivia.

bolivien, ~ne /bɔlivjɛ̃, -jɛn/ a. & n.m., f. Bolivian.

bombance /bɔ̃bɑ̃s/ n.f. **faire ~,** (fam.) revel.

bombard|er /bɔ̃barde/ v.t. bomb; (par obus) shell; (nommer: fam.) appoint unexpectedly (as). **~er qn. de,** (fig.) bombard s.o. with. **~ement** n.m. bombing; shelling. **~ier** n.m. (aviat.) bomber.

bombe /bɔ̃b/ n.f. bomb; (atomiseur) spray, aerosol.

bombé /bɔ̃be/ a. rounded; (route) cambered.

bomber /bɔ̃be/ v.t. **~ la poitrine,** throw out one's chest.

bon, bonne /bɔ̃, bɔn/ a. good; (qui convient) right; (prudent) wise. **~ à/ pour,** (approprié) fit to/for. **tenir ~,** stand firm. ● n.m. (billet) voucher, coupon; (comm.) bond. **du ~,** some good. **pour de ~,** for good. **à quoi ~?,** what's the good ou point? **bonne année,** happy New Year. **~ anniversaire,** happy birthday. **~ appétit/voyage,** enjoy your meal/trip.

bonne chance/nuit, good luck/ night. **bonne femme,** (péj.) woman. **bonne-maman** (pl. bonnes-mamans) n.f. (fam.) granny. **~-papa** (pl. ~s-papas) n.m. (fam.) grand-dad. **~ sens,** common sense. **~ vivant,** bon viveur. **de bonne heure,** early.

bonbon /bɔ̃bɔ̃/ n.m. sweet; (Amer.) candy. **~nière** /-ɔnjɛr/ n.f. sweet box; (Amer.) candy box.

bonbonne /bɔ̃bɔn/ n.f. demijohn; (de gaz) canister.

bond /bɔ̃/ n.m. leap. **faire un ~,** leap in the air; (de surprise) jump.

bonde /bɔ̃d/ n.f. plug; (trou) plughole.

bondé /bɔ̃de/ a. packed.

bondir /bɔ̃dir/ v.i. leap; (de surprise) jump.

bonheur /bɔnœr/ n.m. happiness; (chance) (good) luck. **au petit ~,** haphazardly. **par ~,** luckily.

bonhomme [1] (pl. bonshommes) /bɔnɔm, bɔzɔm/ n.m. fellow. **~ de neige,** snowman.

bonhom|me [2] /bɔnɔm/ a. invar. good-hearted. **~ie** n.f. good-heartedness.

bonifier (se) /(sə)bɔnifje/ v. pr. improve.

boniment /bɔnimɑ̃/ n.m. smooth talk.

bonjour /bɔ̃ʒur/ n.m. & int. hallo, hello, good morning ou afternoon.

bon marché /bɔ̃marʃe/ a. invar. cheap. ● adv. cheap(ly).

bonne [1] /bɔn/ a.f. voir bon.

bonne [2] /bɔn/ n.f. (domestique) maid. **~ d'enfants,** nanny.

bonnement /bɔnmɑ̃/ adv. **tout ~,** quite simply.

bonnet /bɔnɛ/ n.m. hat; (de soutiengorge) cup. **~ de bain,** swimming cap.

bonneterie /bɔnɛtri/ n.f. hosiery.

bonsoir /bɔ̃swar/ n.m. & int. good evening; (en se couchant) good night.

bonté /bɔ̃te/ n.f. kindness.

bonus /bɔnys/ n.m. (auto.) no claims bonus.

boom /bum/ n.m. (comm.) boom.

boots /buts/ n.m. pl. ankle boots.

bord /bɔr/ n.m. edge; (rive) bank. **à ~ (de),** on board. **au ~ de la mer,** at the seaside. **au ~ des larmes,** on the verge of tears. **~ de la route,** roadside. **~ du trottoir,** kerb; (Amer.) curb.

bordeaux /bɔrdo/ *n.m. invar.* Bordeaux (wine), claret. ● *a. invar.* maroon.

bordée /bɔrde/ *n.f.* ~ **d'injures,** torrent of abuse.

bordel /bɔrdɛl/ *n.m.* brothel; (*désordre: fam.*) shambles.

border /bɔrde/ *v.t.* line, border; (*tissu*) edge; (*personne, lit*) tuck in.

bordereau (*pl.* ~x) /bɔrdəro/ *n.m.* (*liste*) note, slip; (*facture*) invoice.

bordure /bɔrdyr/ *n.f.* border. **en ~ de,** on the edge of.

borgne /bɔrɲ/ *a.* one-eyed; (*fig.*) shady.

borne /bɔrn/ *n.f.* boundary marker. ~ **(kilométrique),** (*approx.*) milestone. ~**s,** limits.

borné /bɔrne/ *a.* narrow; (*personne*) narrow-minded.

borner /bɔrne/ *v.t.* confine. **se ~** *v. pr.* confine o.s. (**à,** to).

bosquet /bɔskɛ/ *n.m.* grove.

bosse /bɔs/ *n.f.* bump; (*de chameau*) hump. **avoir la ~ de,** (*fam.*) have a gift for. **avoir roulé sa ~,** have been around.

bosseler /bɔsle/ *v.t.* emboss; (*endommager*) dent.

bosser /bɔse/ *v.i.* (*fam.*) work (hard). ● *v.t.* (*fam.*) work (hard) at.

bossu, ~e /bɔsy/ *n.m., f.* hunchback.

botani|que /bɔtanik/ *n.f.* botany. ● *a.* botanical. ~**ste** *n.m./f.* botanist.

bott|e /bɔt/ *n.f.* boot; (*de fleurs, légumes*) bunch; (*de paille*) bundle, bale. ~**s de caoutchouc,** wellingtons. ~**ier** *n.m.* boot-maker.

botter /bɔte/ *v.t.* (*fam.*) **ça me botte,** I like the idea.

Bottin /bɔtɛ̃/ *n.m.* (P.) phone book.

bouc /buk/ *n.m.* (billy-)goat; (*barbe*) goatee. ~ **émissaire,** scapegoat.

boucan /bukɑ̃/ *n.m.* (*fam.*) din.

bouche /buʃ/ *n.f.* mouth. ~ **bée,** open-mouthed. ~ **d'égout,** manhole. ~ **d'incendie,** (fire) hydrant. ~ **de métro,** entrance to the underground *ou* subway (*Amer.*). ~**-à-bouche** *n.m.* mouth-to-mouth resuscitation.

bouché /buʃe/ *a.* **c'est ~,** (*profession, avenir*) it's a dead end.

bouchée /buʃe/ *n.f.* mouthful.

boucher[1] /buʃe/ *v.t.* block; (*bouteille*) cork. **se ~** *v. pr.* get blocked. **se ~ le nez,** hold one's nose.

bouch|er[2], ~**ère** /buʃe, -ɛr/ *n.m., f.* butcher. ~**erie** *n.f.* butcher's (shop); (*carnage*) butchery.

bouche-trou /buʃtru/ *n.m.* stopgap.

bouchon /buʃɔ̃/ *n.m.* stopper; (*en liège*) cork; (*de bidon, tube*) cap; (*de pêcheur*) float; (*de circulation: fig.*) hold-up.

boucle /bukl/ *n.f.* (*de ceinture*) buckle; (*forme*) loop; (*de cheveux*) curl. ~ **d'oreille,** ear-ring.

boucl|er /bukle/ *v.t.* fasten; (*terminer*) finish off; (*enfermer: fam.*) shut up; (*encercler*) seal off; (*budget*) balance. ● *v.i.* curl. ~**é** *a.* (*cheveux*) curly.

bouclier /buklije/ *n.m.* shield.

bouddhiste /budist/ *a. & n.m./f.* Buddhist.

boud|er /bude/ *v.i.* sulk. ● *v.t.* steer clear of. ~**erie** *n.f.* sulkiness. ~**eur, ~euse** *a. & n.m.,* f. sulky (person).

boudin /budɛ̃/ *n.m.* black pudding.

boudoir /budwar/ *n.m.* boudoir.

boue /bu/ *n.f.* mud.

bouée /bwe/ *n.f.* buoy. ~ **de sauvetage,** lifebuoy.

boueu|x, ~se /bwø, -z/ *a.* muddy. ● *n.m.* dustman; (*Amer.*) garbage collector.

bouff|e /buf/ *n.f.* (*fam.*) food, grub. ~**er** *v.t./i.* (*fam.*) eat; (*bâfrer*) gobble.

bouffée /bufe/ *n.f.* puff, whiff; (*méd.*) flush; (*d'orgueil*) fit.

bouf† /bufi/ *a.* bloated.

bouffon, ~ne /bufɔ̃, -ɔn/ *a.* farcical. ● *n.m.* buffoon.

bouge /buʒ/ *n.m.* hovel; (*bar*) dive.

bougeoir /buʒwar/ *n.m.* candlestick.

bougeotte /buʒɔt/ *n.f.* **la ~,** (*fam.*) the fidgets.

bouger /buʒe/ *v.t./i.* move; (*agir*) stir. **se ~** *v. pr.* (*fam.*) move.

bougie /buʒi/ *n.f.* candle; (*auto.*) spark(ing)-plug.

bougon, ~ne /bugɔ̃, -ɔn/ *a.* grumpy. ~**ner** /-ɔne/ *v.i.* grumble.

bouillabaisse /bujabɛs/ *n.f.* bouillabaisse.

bouillie /buji/ *n.f.* porridge; (*pour bébé*) baby food; (*péj.*) mush. **en ~,** crushed, mushy.

bouill|ir† /bujir/ *v.i.* boil. ● *v.t.* **(faire) ~ir,** boil. ~**ant, ~ante** *a.* boiling; (*très chaud*) boiling hot.

bouilloire /bujwar/ *n.f.* kettle.

bouillon /bujɔ̃/ n.m. (*aliment*) stock.
~ cube, stock cube. **~ner** /-jɔne/ v.i.
bubble.

bouillote /bujɔt/ n.f. hot-water bottle.

boulang|er, ~ère /bulɑ̃ʒe, -ɛr/ n.m.,
f. baker. **~erie** n.f. bakery. **~erie-
pâtisserie** n.f. baker's and confectioner's shop.

boule /bul/ n.f. ball; (*de machine à
écrire*) golf ball. **~s,** (*jeu*) bowls.
jouer aux ~s, play bowls. **une ~
dans la gorge,** lump in one's throat.
~ de neige, snowball. **faire ~ de
neige,** snowball.

bouleau (*pl. ~x*) /bulo/ n.m. (silver)
birch.

bouledogue /buldɔg/ n.m. bulldog.

boulet /bulɛ/ n.m. (*de canon*) cannon-ball; (*de forçat:* fig.) ball and
chain.

boulette /bulɛt/ n.f. (*de papier*) pellet; (*aliment*) meat ball.

boulevard /bulvar/ n.m. boulevard.

boulevers|er /bulvɛrse/ v.t. turn up-
side down; (*pays, plans*) disrupt;
(*émouvoir*) distress, upset. **~ant,
ante** a. deeply moving. **~ement**
n.m. upheaval.

boulier /bulje/ n.m. abacus.

boulimie /bulimi/ n.f. compulsive
eating; (*méd.*) bulimia.

boulon /bulɔ̃/ n.m. bolt.

boulot[1] /bulo/ n.m. (*travail:* fam.)
work.

boulot[2], **~te** /bulo, -ɔt/ a. (*rond:*
fam.) dumpy.

boum /bum/ n.m. & int. bang. ● n.f.
(*réunion:* fam.) party.

bouquet /bukɛ/ n.m. (*de fleurs*)
bunch, bouquet; (*d'arbres*) clump.
c'est le ~!, (fam.) that's the last
straw!

bouquin /bukɛ̃/ n.m. (fam.) book.
~er /-ine/ v.t./i. (fam.) read. **~iste**
/-inist/ n.m./f. second-hand bookseller.

bourbeu|x, ~se /burbø, -z/ a.
muddy.

bourbier /burbje/ n.m. mire.

bourde /burd/ n.f. blunder.

bourdon /burdɔ̃/ n.m. bumble-bee.

bourdonn|er /burdɔne/ v.i. buzz.
~ement n.m. buzzing.

bourg /bur/ n.m. (market) town.

bourgade /burgad/ n.f. village.

bourgeois, ~e /burʒwa, -z/ a. &
n.m., f. middle-class (person); (péj.)

bourgeois. **~ie** /-zi/ n.f. middle
class(es).

bourgeon /burʒɔ̃/ n.m. bud. **~ner**
/-ɔne/ v.i. bud.

bourgogne /burgɔɲ/ n.m. burgundy.
● n.f. **la B~,** Burgundy.

bourlinguer /burlɛ̃ge/ v.i. (fam.) travel about.

bourrade /burad/ n.f. prod.

bourrage /buraʒ/ n.m. **~ de crâne,**
brainwashing.

bourrasque /burask/ n.f. squall.

bourrati|f, ~ve /buratif, -v/ a. filling, stodgy.

bourreau (*pl. ~x*) /buro/ n.m.
executioner. **~ de travail,** workaholic.

bourrelet /burlɛ/ n.m. weather-strip,
draught excluder; (*de chair*) roll of
fat.

bourrer /bure/ v.t. cram (**de,** with);
(*pipe*) fill. **~ de,** (*nourriture*) stuff
with. **~ de coups,** thrash. **~ le
crâne à qn.,** fill s.o.'s head with
nonsense.

bourrique /burik/ n.f. ass.

bourru /bury/ a. surly.

bours|e /burs/ n.f. purse; (*subvention*) grant. **la B~e,** the Stock
Exchange. **~ier, ~ière** a. Stock
Exchange; **—** n.m., f. holder of a grant.

boursoufler /bursufle/ v.t., **se ~** v.
pr. puff up, swell.

boyscul|er /buskyle/ v.t. (*pousser*)
jostle; (*presser*) rush; (*renverser*)
knock over. **~ade** n.f. rush; (*cohue*)
crush.

bouse /buz/ n.f. (cow) dung.

bousiller /buzije/ v.t. (fam.) mess up.

boussole /busɔl/ n.f. compass.

bout /bu/ n.m. end; (*de langue, bâton*) tip; (*morceau*) bit. **à ~,**
exhausted. **à ~ de souffle,** out of
breath. **à ~ portant,** point-blank. **au
~ de,** (*après*) after. **~ filtre,** filter-
tip. **venir à ~ de,** (*finir*) manage to
finish.

boutade /butad/ n.f. jest; (*caprice*)
whim.

boute-en-train /butɑ̃trɛ̃/ n.m. invar.
joker, live wire.

bouteille /butɛj/ n.f. bottle.

boutique /butik/ n.f. shop; (*de mode*)
boutique.

bouton /butɔ̃/ n.m. button; (*pustule*)
pimple; (*pousse*) bud; (*de porte,
radio, etc.*) knob. **~ de manchette,**
cuff-link. **~-d'or** n.m. (*pl. ~s-d'or*)
buttercup. **~ner** /-ɔne/ v.t. button

(up). ~**nière** /-ɔnjɛr/ n.f. buttonhole.
~**-pression** (pl. ~**s-pression**) n.m.
press-stud; (Amer.) snap.
boutonneu|x, ~se /butɔnø, -z/ a.
pimply.
bouture /butyr/ n.f. (plante) cutting.
bovin, ~e /bɔvɛ̃, -in/ a. bovine. ~**s**
n.m. pl. cattle.
bowling /boliŋ/ n.m. bowling; (salle)
bowling-alley.
box (pl. ~ ou **boxes**) /bɔks/ n.m. lock-
up garage; (de dortoir) cubicle;
(d'écurie) (loose) box; (jurid.) dock.
box|e /bɔks/ n.f. boxing. ~**er** v.t./i.
box. ~**eur** n.m. boxer.
boyau (pl. ~**x**) /bwajo/ n.m. gut;
(corde) catgut; (galerie) gallery; (de
bicyclette) tyre; (Amer.) tire.
boycott|er /bɔjkɔte/ v.t. boycott.
~**age** n.m. boycott.
BP abrév. (boîte postale) PO Box.
bracelet /braslɛ/ n.m. bracelet; (de
montre) strap.
braconn|er /brakɔne/ v.i. poach.
~**ier** n.m. poacher.
brad|er /brade/ v.t. sell off. ~**erie** n.f.
open-air sale.
braguette /bragɛt/ n.f. fly.
braille /braj/ n.m. & a. Braille.
brailler /braje/ v.t./i. bawl.
braire /brɛr/ v.i. bray.
braise /brɛz/ n.f. embers.
braiser /breze/ v.t. braise.
brancard /brãkar/ n.m. stretcher;
(bras) shaft. ~**ier** /-dje/ n.m.
stretcher-bearer.
branch|e /brãʃ/ n.f. branch. ~**ages**
n.m. pl. (cut) branches.
branché /brãʃe/ a. (fam.) trendy.
branch|er /brãʃe/ v.t. connect;
(électr.) plug in. ~**ement** n.m. connection.
branchies /brãʃi/ n.f. pl. gills.
brandir /brãdir/ v.t. brandish.
branle /brãl/ n.m. **mettre en ~,** set
in motion. **se mettre en ~,** get
started. ~**-bas (de combat)** n.m.
invar. bustle.
branler /brãle/ v.i. be shaky. ● v.t.
shake.
braquer /brake/ v.t. aim; (regard)
fix; (roue) turn; (banque: fam.) hold
up. ~ **qn. contre,** turn s.o. against.
● v.i. (auto.) turn (the wheel). ● v.
pr. **se ~,** dig one's heels in.
bras /bra/ n.m. arm. ● n.m. pl. (fig.)
labour, hands. **à ~-le-corps** adv.
round the waist. ~ **dessus bras
dessous,** arm in arm. ~ **droit,**

(fig.) right-hand man. **en ~ de
chemise,** in one's shirtsleeves.
brasier /brazje/ n.m. blaze.
brassard /brasar/ n.m. arm-band.
brasse /bras/ n.f. (breast-)stroke; (mesure) fathom.
brassée /brase/ n.f. armful.
brass|er /brase/ v.t. mix; (bière)
brew; (affaires) handle a lot of.
~**age** n.m. mixing; brewing. ~**erie**
n.f. brewery; (café) brasserie. ~**eur**
n.m. brewer. ~**eur d'affaires,** big
businessman.
brassière /brasjɛr/ n.f. (baby's) vest.
bravache /bravaʃ/ n.m. braggart.
bravade /bravad/ n.f. **par ~,** out of
bravado.
brave /brav/ a. brave; (bon) good.
~**ment** adv. bravely.
braver /brave/ v.t. defy.
bravo /bravo/ int. bravo. ● n.m.
cheer.
bravoure /bravur/ n.f. bravery.
break /brɛk/ n.m. estate car; (Amer.)
station-wagon.
brebis /brəbi/ n.f. ewe. ~ **galeuse,**
black sheep.
brèche /brɛʃ/ n.f. gap, breach. **être
sur la ~,** to be on the go.
bredouille /brəduj/ a. empty-
handed.
bredouiller /brəduje/ v.t./i. mumble.
bref, brève /brɛf, -v/ a. short, brief.
● adv. in short. **en ~,** in short.
Brésil /brezil/ n.m. Brazil.
brésilien, ~ne /breziljɛ̃, -jɛn/ a. &
n.m., f. Brazilian.
Bretagne /brətaɲ/ n.f. Brittany.
bretelle /brətɛl/ n.f. (shoulder-) strap;
(d'autoroute) access road. ~**s,** (pour
pantalon) braces; (Amer.) suspen-
ders.
breton, ~ne /brətɔ̃, -ɔn/ a. & n.m., f.
Breton.
breuvage /brœvaʒ/ n.m. beverage.
brève /brɛv/ voir bref.
brevet /brəvɛ/ n.m. diploma. ~ **(d'invention),** patent.
brevet|er /brəvte/ v.t. patent. ~**é** a.
patented.
bribes /brib/ n.f. pl. scraps.
bric-à-brac /brikabrak/ n.m. invar.
bric-à-brac.
bricole /brikɔl/ n.f. trifle.
bricol|er /brikɔle/ v.i. do odd (do-it-
yourself) jobs. ● v.t. fix (up). ~**age**
n.m. do-it-yourself (jobs). ~**eur,**
~**euse** n.m., f. handyman, handy-
woman.

brid|e /brid/ n.f. bridle. **tenir en ~e,**
keep in check. **~er** v.t. (cheval)
bridle; (fig.) keep in check, bridle;
(culin.) truss.

bridé /bride/ a. **yeux ~s,** slit eyes.

bridge /bridʒ/ n.m. (cartes) bridge.

briève|ment /brijɛvmɑ̃/ adv. briefly.
~té n.f. brevity.

brigad|e /brigad/ n.f. (de police)
squad; (mil.) brigade; (fig.) team.
~ier n.m. (de police) sergeant.

brigand /brigɑ̃/ n.m. robber. **~age**
/-daʒ/ n.m. robbery.

briguer /brige/ v.t. seek (after).

brill|ant, ~ante /brijɑ̃, -t/ a. (cou-
leur) bright; (luisant) shiny; (remarquable) brilliant. ● n.m. (éclat)
shine; (diamant) diamond. **~am-
ment** adv. brilliantly.

briller /brije/ v.i. shine.

brim|er /brime/ v.t. bully, harass. **se
sentir brimé,** feel put down. **~ade**
n.f. vexation.

brin /brɛ̃/ n.m. (de corde) strand; (de
muguet) sprig. **~ d'herbe,** blade of
grass. **un ~ de,** a bit of.

brindille /brɛ̃dij/ n.f. twig.

bringuebaler /brɛ̃gbale/ v.i. (fam.)
wobble about.

brio /brijo/ n.m. brilliance. **avec ~,**
brilliantly.

brioche /brijɔʃ/ n.f. brioche (small
round sweet cake); (ventre: fam.)
paunch.

brique /brik/ n.f. brick.

briquer /brike/ v.t. polish.

briquet /brikɛ/ n.m. (cigarette-)
lighter.

brisant /brizɑ̃/ n.m. reef.

brise /briz/ n.f. breeze.

bris|er /brize/ v.t. break. **se ~er** v. pr.
break. **~e-lames** n.m. invar.
breakwater. **~eur de grève** n.m.
strikebreaker.

britannique /britanik/ a. British.
● n.m./f. Briton. **les B~s,** the British.

broc /bro/ n.m. pitcher.

brocant|e /brɔkɑ̃t/ n.f. second-hand
goods. **~eur, ~euse** n.m., f. second-
hand goods dealer.

broche /brɔʃ/ n.f. brooch; (culin.)
spit. **à la ~,** spit-roasted.

broché /brɔʃe/ a. paperback(ed).

brochet /brɔʃɛ/ n.m. (poisson) pike.

brochette /brɔʃɛt/ n.f. skewer.

brochure /brɔʃyr/ n.f. brochure,
booklet.

brod|er /brɔde/ v.t. embroider. ● v.i.
(fig.) embroider the truth. **~erie** n.f.
embroidery.

broncher /brɔ̃ʃe/ v.i. **sans ~,** without turning a hair.

bronch|es /brɔ̃ʃ/ n.f. pl. bronchial
tubes. **~ite** n.f. bronchitis.

bronze /brɔ̃z/ n.m. bronze.

bronz|er /brɔ̃ze/ v.i., **se ~er** v. pr. get
a (sun-)tan. **~age** n.m. (sun-)tan. **~é**
a. (sun-)tanned.

brosse /brɔs/ n.f. brush. **~ à dents,**
toothbrush. **~ à habits,** clothes-
brush. **en ~,** (coiffure) in a crew cut.

brosser /brɔse/ v.t. brush; (fig.)
paint. **se ~ les dents/les cheveux,**
brush one's teeth/hair.

brouette /bruɛt/ n.f. wheelbarrow.

brouhaha /bruaa/ n.m. hubbub.

brouillard /brujar/ n.m. fog.

brouille /bruj/ n.f. quarrel.

brouill|er /bruje/ v.t. mix up; (vue)
blur; (œufs) scramble; (radio) jam;
(amis) set at odds. **se ~er** v. pr.
become confused; (ciel) cloud over;
(amis) fall out. **~on[1], ~onne** a.
untidy.

brouillon[2] /brujɔ̃/ n.m. (rough)
draft.

broussailles /brusaj/ n.f. pl. undergrowth.

brousse /brus/ n.f. **la ~,** the bush.

brouter /brute/ v.t./i. graze.

broutille /brutij/ n.f. trifle.

broyer /brwaje/ v.t. crush; (moudre)
grind.

bru /bry/ n.f. daughter-in-law.

bruin|e /brɥin/ n.f. drizzle. **~er** v.i.
drizzle.

bruire /brɥir/ v.i. rustle.

bruissement /brɥismɑ̃/ n.m. rus-
tling.

bruit /brɥi/ n.m. noise; (fig.) rumour.

bruitage /brɥitaʒ/ n.m. sound effects.

brûlant, ~e /brylɑ̃, -t/ a. burning
(hot); (sujet) red-hot; (ardent) fiery.

brûlé /bryle/ a. (démasqué: fam.)
blown. ● n.m. burning. **ça sent le
~,** I can smell sth. burning.

brûle-pourpoint (à) /(a)bryl-
purpwɛ̃/ adv. point-blank.

brûl|er /bryle/ v.t./i. burn; (essence)
use (up); (signal) go through ou past
(without stopping); (dévorer: fig.)
consume. **se ~er** v. pr. burn o.s.
~eur n.m. burner.

brûlure /brylyr/ n.f. burn. **~s d'estomac,** heartburn.

brum|e /brym/ *n.f.* mist. **~eux,** **~euse** *a.* misty; (*idées*) hazy.

brun, ~e *pl.* /brœ̃, bryn/ *a.* brown, dark. ● *n.m.* brown. ● *n.m., f.* dark-haired person. **~ir** /brynir/ *v.i.* turn brown; (*se bronzer*) get a tan.

brunch /brœnʃ/ *n.m.* brunch.

brushing /brœʃiŋ/ *n.m.* blow-dry.

brusque /brysk/ *a.* (*soudain*) sudden, abrupt; (*rude*) abrupt. **~ment** /-əmɑ̃/ *adv.* suddenly, abruptly.

brusquer /bryske/ *v.t.* rush.

brut /bryt/ *a.* (*diamant*) rough; (*soie*) raw; (*pétrole*) crude; (*comm.*) gross.

brut|al (*m. pl.* **~aux**) /brytal, -o/ *a.* brutal. **~aliser** *v.t.* treat roughly *ou* violently, manhandle. **~alité** *n.f.* brutality.

brute /bryt/ *n.f.* brute.

Bruxelles /brysɛl/ *n.m./f.* Brussels.

bruy|ant, ~ante /brɥijɑ̃, -t/ *a.* noisy. **~amment** *adv.* noisily.

bruyère /bryjɛr/ *n.f.* heather.

bu /by/ *voir* boire.

bûche /byʃ/ *n.f.* log. **~ de Noël,** Christmas log. **(se) ramasser une ~,** (*fam.*) come a cropper.

bûcher[1] /byʃe/ *n.m.* (*supplice*) stake.

bûch|er[2] /byʃe/ *v.t./i.* (*fam.*) slog away (at). **~eur, ~euse** *n.m., f.* (*fam.*) slogger.

bûcheron /byʃrɔ̃/ *n.m.* woodcutter.

budg|et /bydʒɛ/ *n.m.* budget. **~étaire** *a.* budgetary.

buée /bɥe/ *n.f.* mist, condensation.

buffet /byfɛ/ *n.m.* sideboard; (*réception, restaurant*) buffet.

buffle /byfl/ *n.m.* buffalo.

buis /bɥi/ *n.m.* (*arbre, bois*) box.

buisson /bɥisɔ̃/ *n.m.* bush.

buissonnière /bɥisɔnjɛr/ *a.f.* **faire l'école ~,** play truant.

bulbe /bylb/ *n.m.* bulb.

bulgare /bylgar/ *a. & n.m./f.* Bulgarian.

Bulgarie /bylgari/ *n.f.* Bulgaria.

bulldozer /byldozɛr/ *n.m.* bulldozer.

bulle /byl/ *n.f.* bubble.

bulletin /byltɛ̃/ *n.m.* bulletin, report; (*scol.*) report; (*billet*) ticket. **~ d'information,** news bulletin. **~ météorologique,** weather report. **~ (de vote),** ballot paper. **~ de salaire,** pay-slip. **~-réponse** *n.m.* (*pl.* **~s-réponses**) reply slip.

buraliste /byralist/ *n.m./f.* tobacconist; (*à la poste*) clerk.

bureau (*pl.* **~x**) /byro/ *n.m.* office; (*meuble*) desk; (*comité*) board. **~ de location,** booking-office; (*théâtre*) box-office. **~ de poste,** post office. **~ de tabac,** tobacconist's (shop). **~ de vote,** polling station.

bureaucrate /byrokrat/ *n.m./f.* bureaucrat.

bureaucrat|ie /byrokrasi/ *n.f.* bureaucracy. **~ique** /-tik/ *a.* bureaucratic.

bureautique /byrotik/ *n.f.* office automation.

burette /byrɛt/ *n.f.* (*de graissage*) oilcan.

burin /byrɛ̃/ *n.m.* (cold) chisel.

burlesque /byrlɛsk/ *a.* ludicrous; (*théâtre*) burlesque.

bus /bys/ *n.m.* bus.

busqué /byske/ *a.* hooked.

buste /byst/ *n.m.* bust.

but /by(t)/ *n.m.* target; (*dessein*) aim, goal; (*football*) goal. **avoir pour ~ de,** aim to. **de ~ en blanc,** point-blank. **dans le ~ de,** with the intention of.

butane /bytan/ *n.m.* butane, Calor gas (P.).

buté /byte/ *a.* obstinate.

buter /byte/ *v.i.* **~ contre,** knock against; (*problème*) come up against. ● *v.t.* antagonize. **se ~** *v. pr.* (*s'entêter*) become obstinate.

buteur /bytœr/ *n.m.* striker.

butin /bytɛ̃/ *n.m.* booty, loot.

butiner /bytine/ *v.i.* gather nectar.

butoir /bytwar/ *n.m.* **~ (de porte),** doorstop.

butor /bytɔr/ *n.m.* (*péj.*) lout.

butte /byt/ *n.f.* mound. **en ~ à,** exposed to.

buvard /byvar/ *n.m.* blotting-paper.

buvette /byvɛt/ *n.f.* (refreshment) bar.

buveu|r, ~se /byvœr, -øz/ *n.m., f.* drinker.

C

c' /s/ *voir* ce[1].

ça /sa/ *pron.* it, that; (*pour désigner*) that; (*plus près*) this. **ça va?,** (*fam.*) how's it going? **ça va!,** (*fam.*) all right! **où ça?,** (*fam.*) where? **quand ça?,** (*fam.*) when? **c'est ça,** that's right.

çà /sa/ *adv.* **çà et là,** here and there.

caban|e /kaban/ *n.f.* hut; (*à outils*) shed. **~on** *n.m.* hut; (*en Provence*) cottage.

cabaret /kabarɛ/ *n.m.* night-club.

cabas /kabɑ/ *n.m.* shopping bag.

cabillaud /kabijo/ *n.m.* cod.

cabine /kabin/ *n.f.* (*à la piscine*) cubicle; (*à la plage*) (beach) hut; (*de bateau*) cabin; (*de pilotage*) cockpit; (*de camion*) cab; (*d'ascenseur*) cage. **~ (téléphonique),** phone-booth, phone-box.

cabinet /kabinɛ/ *n.m.* (*de médecin*) surgery; (*Amer.*) office; (*d'avocat*) office; (*clientèle*) practice; (*pol.*) Cabinet; (*pièce*) room. **~s,** (*toilettes*) toilet. **~ de toilette,** bathroom.

câble /kɑbl/ *n.m.* cable; (*corde*) rope.

câbler /kɑble/ *v.t.* cable.

cabosser /kabɔse/ *v.t.* dent.

cabot|age /kabɔtaʒ/ *n.m.* coastal navigation. **~eur** *n.m.* coaster.

cabotin, ~e /kabɔtɛ̃, -in/ *n.m., f.* (*théâtre*) ham; (*fig.*) play-actor. **~age** /-inaʒ/ *n.m.* ham acting; (*fig.*) play-acting.

cabrer /kabre/ *v.t.,* **se ~** *v. pr.* (*cheval*) rear up. **se ~ contre,** rebel against.

cabri /kabri/ *n.m.* kid.

cabriole /kabrijɔl/ *n.f.* (*culbute*) somersault. **faire des ~s,** caper about.

cacahuète /kakaɥɛt/ *n.f.* peanut.

cacao /kakao/ *n.m.* cocoa.

cachalot /kaʃalo/ *n.m.* sperm whale.

cache /kaʃ/ *n.m.* mask; (*photo.*) lens cover.

cachemire /kaʃmir/ *n.m.* cashmere.

cach|er /kaʃe/ *v.t.* hide, conceal (**à,** from). **se ~er** *v. pr.* hide; (*se trouver caché*) be hidden. **~e-cache** *n.m. invar.* hide-and-seek. **~e-nez** *n.m. invar.* scarf. **~e-pot** *n.m.* cache-pot.

cachet /kaʃɛ/ *n.m.* seal; (*de la poste*) postmark; (*comprimé*) tablet; (*d'artiste*) fee; (*fig.*) style.

cacheter /kaʃte/ *v.t.* seal.

cachette /kaʃɛt/ *n.f.* hiding-place. **en ~,** in secret.

cachot /kaʃo/ *n.m.* dungeon.

cachott|eries /kaʃɔtri/ *n.f. pl.* secrecy. **faire des ~eries,** be secretive. **~ier, ~ière** *a.* secretive.

cacophonie /kakɔfɔni/ *n.f.* cacophony.

cactus /kaktys/ *n.m.* cactus.

cadavérique /kadaverik/ *a.* (*teint*) deathly pale.

cadavre /kadavr/ *n.m.* corpse.

caddie /kadi/ *n.m.* trolley.

cadeau (*pl.* **~x**) /kado/ *n.m.* present, gift. **faire un ~ à qn.,** give s.o. a present.

cadenas /kadnɑ/ *n.m.* padlock. **~ser** /-ase/ *v.t.* padlock.

cadenc|e /kadɑ̃s/ *n.f.* rhythm, cadence; (*de travail*) rate. **en ~e,** in time. **~é** *a.* rhythmic(al).

cadet, ~te /kadɛ, -t/ *a.* youngest; (*entre deux*) younger. ● *n.m., f.* youngest (child); younger (child).

cadran /kadrɑ̃/ *n.m.* dial. **~ solaire,** sundial.

cadre /kadr/ *n.m.* frame; (*milieu*) surroundings; (*limites*) scope; (*contexte*) framework. ● *n.m./f.* (*personne: comm.*) executive. **les ~s,** (*comm.*) the managerial staff.

cadrer /kadre/ *v.i.* **avec,** tally with. ● *v.t.* (*photo*) centre.

cadu|c, ~que /kadyk/ *a.* obsolete.

cafard /kafar/ *n.m.* (*insecte*) cockroach. **avoir le ~,** (*fam.*) be feeling low. **~er** /-de/ *v.i.* (*fam.*) tell tales.

caf|é /kafe/ *n.m.* coffee; (*bar*) café. **~é au lait,** white coffee. **~etière** *n.f.* coffee-pot.

caféine /kafein/ *n.f.* caffeine.

cafouiller /kafuje/ *v.i.* (*fam.*) bumble, flounder.

cage /kaʒ/ *n.f.* cage; (*d'escalier*) well; (*d'ascenseur*) shaft.

cageot /kaʒo/ *n.m.* crate.

cagibi /kaʒibi/ *n.m.* storage room.

cagneu|x, ~se /kaɲø, -z/ *a.* knock-kneed.

cagnotte /kaɲɔt/ *n.f.* kitty.

cagoule /kagul/ *n.f.* hood.

cahier /kaje/ *n.m.* notebook; (*scol.*) exercise-book.

cahin-caha /kaɛ̃kaa/ *adv.* **aller ~,** (*fam.*) jog along.

cahot /kao/ *n.m.* bump, jolt. **~er** /kaɔte/ *v.t./i.* bump, jolt. **~eux, ~euse** /kaɔtø, -z/ *a.* bumpy.

caïd /kaid/ *n.m.* (*fam.*) big shot.

caille /kɑj/ *n.f.* quail.

cailler /kɑje/ *v.t./i.,* **se ~** *v. pr.* (*sang*) clot; (*lait*) curdle.

caillot /kɑjo/ *n.m.* (blood) clot.

caillou (*pl.* **~x**) /kaju/ *n.m.* stone; (*galet*) pebble. **~teux, ~teuse** *a.* stony. **~tis** *n.m.* gravel.

caisse /kɛs/ n.f. crate, case; (*tiroir*, *machine*) till; (*guichet*) pay-desk; (*bureau*) office; (*mus.*) drum. ~ **enregistreuse**, cash register. ~ **d'épargne**, savings bank. ~ **de retraite**, pension fund.

caiss|ier, ~ière /kesje, -jɛr/ n.m., f. cashier.

cajol|er /kaʒɔle/ v.t. coax. **~eries** n.f. pl. coaxing.

cake /kɛk/ n.m. fruit-cake.

calamité /kalamite/ n.f. calamity.

calandre /kalɑ̃dr/ n.f. radiator grill.

calanque /kalɑ̃k/ n.f. creek.

calcaire /kalkɛr/ a. (*sol*) chalky; (*eau*) hard.

calciné /kalsine/ a. charred.

calcium /kalsjɔm/ n.m. calcium.

calcul /kalkyl/ n.m. calculation; (*scol.*) arithmetic; (*différentiel*) calculus. ~ **biliaire**, gallstone.

calcul|er /kalkyle/ v.t. calculate. **~ateur** n.m. (*ordinateur*) computer, calculator. **~atrice** n.f. (*ordinateur*) calculator. **~ette** n.f. (pocket) calculator.

cale /kal/ n.f. wedge; (*de navire*) hold. ~ **sèche**, dry dock.

calé /kale/ a. (*fam.*) clever.

caleçon /kalsɔ̃/ n.m. underpants; (*de femme*) leggings. ~ **de bain**, (bathing) trunks.

calembour /kalɑ̃bur/ n.m. pun.

calendrier /kalɑ̃drije/ n.m. calendar; (*fig.*) timetable.

calepin /kalpɛ̃/ n.m. notebook.

caler /kale/ v.t. wedge; (*moteur*) stall. ● v.i. stall.

calfeutrer /kalføtre/ v.t. stop up the cracks of.

calibr|e /kalibr/ n.m. calibre; (*d'un œuf, fruit*) grade. **~er** v.t. grade.

calice /kalis/ n.m. (*relig.*) chalice; (*bot.*) calyx.

califourchon (à) /(a)kalifurʃɔ̃/ adv. astride. ● *prép.* **à ~ sur**, astride.

câlin /kɑlɛ̃/ a. (*fam.*) endearing, cuddly. **~er** /-ine/ v.t. cuddle.

calmant /kalmɑ̃/ n.m. sedative.

calm|e /kalm/ a. calm ● n.m. calm(ness). **du ~e!**, calm down! **~er** v.t., **se ~er** v. pr. (*personne*) calm (down); (*diminuer*) ease.

calomn|ie /kalɔmni/ n.f. slander; (*écrite*) libel. **~ier** v.t. slander; libel. **~ieux, ~ieuse** a. slanderous; libellous.

calorie /kalɔri/ n.f. calorie.

calorifuge /kalɔrifyʒ/ a. (heat-) insulating. ● n.m. lagging.

calot /kalo/ n.m. (*mil.*) forage-cap.

calotte /kalɔt/ n.f. (*relig.*) skullcap; (*tape: fam.*) slap.

calqu|e /kalk/ n.m. tracing; (*fig.*) exact copy. **~er** v.t. trace; (*fig.*) copy. **~er sur**, model on.

calvaire /kalvɛr/ n.m. (*croix*) calvary; (*fig.*) suffering.

calvitie /kalvisi/ n.f. baldness.

camarade /kamarad/ n.m./f. friend; (*pol.*) comrade. ~ **de jeu**, playmate. **~rie** n.f. good companionship.

cambiste /kɑ̃bist/ n.m./f. foreign exchange dealer.

cambouis /kɑ̃bwi/ n.m. (engine) oil.

cambrer /kɑ̃bre/ v.t. arch. **se ~** v. pr. arch one's back.

cambriol|er /kɑ̃brijɔle/ v.t. burgle. **~age** n.m. burglary. **~eur, ~euse** n.m., f. burglar.

cambrure /kɑ̃bryr/ n.f. curve.

came /kam/ n.f. **arbe à ~s**, camshaft.

camée /kame/ n.m. cameo.

camelot /kamlo/ n.m. street vendor.

camelote /kamlɔt/ n.f. junk.

camembert /kamɑ̃bɛr/ n.m. Camembert (cheese).

caméra /kamera/ n.f. (*cinéma, télévision*) camera.

caméra|man (*pl.* **~men**) /kameraman, -mɛn/ n.m. cameraman.

camion /kamjɔ̃/ n.m. lorry, truck. **~-citerne** n.m. tanker. **~nage** /-jɔnaʒ/ n.m. haulage. **~nette** /-jɔnɛt/ n.f. van. **~neur** /-jɔnœr/ n.m. lorry ou truck driver; (*entrepreneur*) haulage contractor.

camisole /kamizɔl/ n.f. ~ **(de force)**, strait-jacket.

camoufl|er /kamufle/ v.t. camouflage. **~age** n.m. camouflage.

camp /kɑ̃/ n.m. camp; (*sport*) side.

campagn|e /kɑ̃paɲ/ n.f. country (side); (*mil., pol.*) campaign. **~ard, ~arde** a. country; n.m., f. countryman, countrywoman.

campanile /kɑ̃panil/ n.m. belltower.

camp|er /kɑ̃pe/ v.i. camp. ● v.t. plant boldly; (*esquisser*) sketch. **se ~er** v. pr. plant o.s. **~ement** n.m. encampment. **~eur, ~euse** n.m., f. camper

camphre /kɑ̃fr/ n.m. camphor.

camping /kɑ̃piŋ/ n.m. camping. **faire du ~**, go camping. **~-car** n.m. camper-van; (*Amer.*) motorhome.

~-gaz *n.m. invar.* (P.) camping-gaz.
(terrain de) ~, campsite.
campus /kãpys/ *n.m.* campus.
Canada /kanada/ *n.m.* Canada.
canadien, ~ne /kanadjɛ̃, -jɛn/ *a. & n.m.,* f. Canadian. ● *n.f.* fur-lined jacket.
canaille /kanɑj/ *n.f.* rogue.
can|al (*pl.* **~aux**) /kanal, -o/ *n.m.* (*artificiel*) canal; (*bras de mer*) channel; (*techn., TV*) channel. **par le ~al de,** through.
canalisation /kanalizasjɔ̃/ *n.f.* (*tuyaux*) main(s).
canaliser /kanalize/ *v.t.* (*eau*) canalize; (*fig.*) channel.
canapé /kanape/ *n.m.* sofa.
canard /kanar/ *n.m.* duck; (*journal*: *fam.*) rag.
canari /kanari/ *n.m.* canary.
cancans /kãkã/ *n.m. pl.* malicious gossip.
canc|er /kãsɛr/ *n.m.* cancer. **le C~er,** Cancer. **~éreux, ~éreuse** *a.* cancerous. **~érigène** *a.* carcinogenic.
cancre /kãkr/ *n.m.* dunce.
cancrelat /kãkrəla/ *n.m.* cockroach.
candélabre /kãdelabr/ *n.m.* candelabrum.
candeur /kãdœr/ *n.f.* naïvety.
candidat, ~e /kãdida, -t/ *n.m., f.* candidate; (*à un poste*) applicant, candidate (**à,** for). **~ure** /-tyr/ *n.f.* application; (*pol.*) candidacy. **poser sa ~ure pour,** apply for.
candide /kãdid/ *a.* naïve.
cane /kan/ *n.f.* (female) duck. **~ton** *n.m.* duckling.
canette /kanɛt/ *n.f.* (*de bière*) bottle.
canevas /kanva/ *n.m.* canvas; (*plan*) framework, outline.
caniche /kaniʃ/ *n.m.* poodle.
canicule /kanikyl/ *n.f.* hot summer days.
canif /kanif/ *n.m.* penknife.
canin, ~e /kanɛ̃, -in/ *a.* canine. ● *n.f.* canine (tooth).
caniveau (*pl.* **~x**) /kanivo/ *n.m.* gutter.
cannabis /kanabis/ *n.m.* cannabis.
canne /kan/ *n.f.* (walking-)stick. **~ à pêche,** fishing-rod. **~ à sucre,** sugar-cane.
cannelle /kanɛl/ *n.f.* cinnamon.
cannibale /kanibal/ *a. & n.m./f.* cannibal.
canoë /kanɔe/ *n.m.* canoe; (*sport*) canoeing.

canon /kanɔ̃/ *n.m.* (big) gun; (*d'une arme*) barrel; (*principe, règle*) canon. **~nade** /-ɔnad/ *n.f.* gunfire. **~nier** /-ɔnje/ *n.m.* gunner.
canot /kano/ *n.m.* boat. **~ de sauvetage,** lifeboat. **~ pneumatique,** rubber dinghy.
canot|er /kanɔte/ *v.i.* boat. **~age** *n.m.* boating. **~ier** *n.m.* boater.
cantate /kãtat/ *n.f.* cantata.
cantatrice /kãtatris/ *n.f.* opera singer.
cantine /kãtin/ *n.f.* canteen.
cantique /kãtik/ *n.m.* hymn.
canton /kãtɔ̃/ *n.m.* (*en France*) district; (*en Suisse*) canton.
cantonade (à la) /(ala)kãtɔnad/ *adv.* for all to hear.
cantonner /kãtɔne/ *v.t.* (*mil.*) billet. **se ~ dans,** confine o.s. to.
cantonnier /kãtɔnje/ *n.m.* roadman, road mender.
canular /kanylar/ *n.m.* hoax.
caoutchou|c /kautʃu/ *n.m.* rubber; (*élastique*) rubber band. **~c mousse,** foam rubber. **~té** *a.* rubberized. **~teux, ~teuse** *a.* rubbery.
cap /kap/ *n.m.* cape, headland; (*direction*) course. **doubler *ou* franchir le ~ de,** go beyond (the point of). **mettre le ~ sur,** steer a course for.
capable /kapabl/ *a.* able, capable. **~ de qch.,** capable of sth. **~ de faire,** able to do, capable of doing.
capacité /kapasite/ *n.f.* ability; (*contenance*) capacity.
cape /kap/ *n.f.* cape. **rire sous ~,** laugh up one's sleeve.
capillaire /kapilɛr/ *a.* (*lotion, soins*) hair. **(vaisseau) ~,** capillary.
capilotade (en) /(ã)kapilɔtad/ *adv.* (*fam.*) reduced to a pulp.
capitaine /kapitɛn/ *n.m.* captain.
capit|al, ~ale (*m. pl.* **~aux**) /kapital, -o/ *a.* major, fundamental; (*peine, lettre*) capital. ● *n.m.* (*pl.* **~aux**) (*comm.*) capital; (*fig.*) stock. **~aux,** (*comm.*) capital. ● *n.f.* (*ville, lettre*) capital.
capitalis|te /kapitalist/ *a. & n.m./f.* capitalist. **~me** *n.m.* capitalism.
capiteu|x, ~se /kapitø, -z/ *a.* heady.
capitonné /kapitɔne/ *a.* padded.
capitul|er /kapityle/ *v.i.* capitulate. **~ation** *n.f.* capitulation.
capor|al (*pl.* **~aux**) /kapɔral, -o/ *n.m.* corporal.

capot /kapo/ n.m. (auto.) bonnet; (auto., Amer.) hood.

capote /kapɔt/ n.f. (auto.) hood; (auto., Amer.) (convertible) top; (fam.) condom.

capoter /kapɔte/ v.i. overturn.

câpre /kɑpr/ n.f. (culin.) caper.

capric|e /kapris/ n.m. whim, caprice. ~ieux, ~ieuse a. capricious; (appareil) temperamental.

Capricorne /kaprikɔrn/ n.m. le ~, Capricorn.

capsule /kapsyl/ n.f. capsule; (de bouteille) cap.

capter /kapte/ v.t. (eau) tap; (émission) pick up; (fig.) win, capture.

capti|f, ~ve /kaptif, -v/ a. & n.m., f. captive.

captiver /kaptive/ v.t. captivate.

captivité /kaptivite/ n.f. captivity.

captur|e /kaptyr/ n.f. capture. ~er v.t. capture.

capuch|e /kapyʃ/ n.f. hood. ~on n.m. hood; (de stylo) cap.

caquet /kakɛ/ n.m. rabattre le ~ à qn., take s.o. down a peg or two.

caquet|er /kakte/ v.i. cackle. ~age n.m. cackle.

car¹ /kar/ conj. because, for.

car² /kar/ n.m. coach; (Amer.) bus.

carabine /karabin/ n.f. rifle.

caracoler /karakɔle/ v.i. prance.

caract|ère /karaktɛr/ n.m. (nature, lettre) character. ~ères d'imprimerie, block letters. ~ériel, ~érielle a. character; n.m., f. disturbed child.

caractérisé /karakterize/ a. well-defined.

caractériser /karakterize/ v.t. characterize. se ~ par, be characterized by.

caractéristique /karakteristik/ a. & n.f. characteristic.

carafe /karaf/ n.f. carafe; (pour le vin) decanter.

caraïbe /karaib/ a. Caribbean. les C~s, the Caribbean.

carambol|er (se) /(sə)karɑ̃bɔle/ v. pr. (voitures) smash into each other. ~age n.m. multiple smash-up.

caramel /karamɛl/ n.m. caramel. ~iser v.t./i. caramelize.

carapace /karapas/ n.f. shell.

carat /kara/ n.m. carat.

caravane /karavan/ n.f. (auto.) caravan; (auto., Amer.) trailer; (convoi) caravan.

carbone /karbɔn/ n.m. carbon; (double) carbon (copy). (papier) ~, carbon (paper).

carboniser /karbɔnize/ v.t. burn (to ashes).

carburant /karbyrɑ̃/ n.m. (motor) fuel.

carburateur /karbyratœr/ n.m. carburettor; (Amer.) carburetor.

carcan /karkɑ̃/ n.m. (contrainte) yoke.

carcasse /karkas/ n.f. carcass; (d'immeuble, de voiture) frame.

cardiaque /kardjak/ a. heart. ● n.m./f. heart patient.

cardigan /kardigɑ̃/ n.m. cardigan.

cardin|al (m. pl. ~aux) /kardinal, -o/ a. cardinal. ● n.m. (pl. ~aux) cardinal.

Carême /karɛm/ n.m. Lent.

carence /karɑ̃s/ n.f. inadequacy; (manque) deficiency.

caressant, ~e /karɛsɑ̃, -t/ a. endearing.

caress|e /karɛs/ n.f. caress. ~er /-ese/ v.t. caress, stroke; (espoir) cherish.

cargaison /kargɛzɔ̃/ n.f. cargo.

cargo /kargo/ n.m. cargo boat.

caricatur|e /karikatyr/ n.f. caricature. ~al (m. pl. ~aux) a. caricature-like.

car|ie /kari/ n.f. cavity. la ~ie (dentaire), tooth decay. ~ié a. (dent) decayed.

carillon /karijɔ̃/ n.m. chimes; (horloge) chiming clock. ~ner /-jɔne/ v.i. chime, peal.

caritati|f, ~ve /karitatif, -v/ a. association ~ve, charity.

carlingue /karlɛ̃g/ n.f. (d'avion) cabin.

carnage /karnaʒ/ n.m. carnage.

carnass|ier, ~ière /karnasje, -jɛr/ a. flesh-eating.

carnaval (pl. ~s) /karnaval/ n.m. carnival.

carnet /karnɛ/ n.m. notebook; (de tickets etc.) book. ~ de chèques, cheque-book. ~ de notes, school report.

carotte /karɔt/ n.f. carrot.

carotter /karɔte/ v.t. (argot) swindle. ~ qch. à qn., (argot) wangle sth. from s.o.

carpe /karp/ n.f. carp.

carpette /karpɛt/ n.f. rug.

carré /kare/ a. (forme, mesure) square; (fig.) straightforward. ● n.m. square; (de terrain) patch.

carreau (pl. ~x) /karo/ n.m. (window) pane; (par terre, au mur) tile; (dessin) check; (cartes) diamonds. à ~x, check(ed).

carrefour /karfur/ n.m. crossroads.

carrel|er /karle/ v.t. tile. ~age n.m. tiling; (sol) tiles.

carrelet /karlɛ/ n.m. (poisson) plaice.

carrément /karemɑ̃/ adv. straight; (dire) straight out.

carrer (se) /(sə)kare/ v. pr. settle firmly (dans, in).

carrière /karjɛr/ n.f. career; (terrain) quarry.

carrossable /karɔsabl/ a. suitable for vehicles.

carrosse /karɔs/ n.m. (horse-drawn) coach.

carross|erie /karɔsri/ n.f. (auto.) body(work). ~ier n.m. (auto.) bodybuilder.

carrure /karyr/ n.f. build; (fig.) calibre.

cartable /kartabl/ n.m. satchel.

carte /kart/ n.f. card; (géog.) map; (naut.) chart; (au restaurant) menu. ~s, (jeu) cards. à la ~, (manger) à la carte. ~ **blanche**, a free hand. ~ **de crédit**, credit card. ~ **des vins**, wine list. ~ **de visite**, (business) card. ~ **grise**, (car) registration card. ~ **postale**, postcard.

cartel /kartɛl/ n.m. cartel.

cartilage /kartilaʒ/ n.m. cartilage.

carton /kartɔ̃/ n.m. cardboard; (boîte) (cardboard) box. ~ **à dessin**, portfolio. **faire un** ~, (fam.) take a pot-shot. ~nage /-ɔnaʒ/ n.m. cardboard packing. ~-**pâte** n.m. pasteboard. **en** ~-**pâte**, cardboard.

cartonné /kartɔne/ a. (livre) hardback.

cartouch|e /kartuʃ/ n.f. cartridge; (de cigarettes) carton. ~ière n.f. cartridge-belt.

cas /kɑ/ n.m. case. **au** ~ **où**, in case. ~ **urgent**, emergency. **en aucun** ~, on no account. **en** ~ **de**, in the event of, in case of. **en tout** ~, in any case. **faire** ~ **de**, set great store by. ~ **de conscience** matter of conscience.

casan|ier, ~ière /kazanje, -jɛr/ a. home-loving.

casaque /kazak/ n.f. (de jockey) shirt.

cascade /kaskad/ n.f. waterfall; (fig.) spate.

cascad|eur, ~euse /kaskadœr, -øz/ n.m., f. stuntman, stuntgirl.

case /kɑz/ n.f. hut; (compartiment) pigeon-hole; (sur papier) square.

caser /kaze/ v.t. (mettre) put; (loger) put up; (dans un travail) find a job for; (marier: péj.) marry off.

caserne /kazɛrn/ n.f. barracks.

cash /kaʃ/ adv. **payer** ~, pay (in) cash.

casier /kazje/ n.m. pigeon-hole, compartment; (meuble) cabinet; (à bouteilles) rack. ~ **judiciaire**, criminal record.

casino /kazino/ n.m. casino.

casqu|e /kask/ n.m. helmet; (chez le coiffeur) (hair-)drier. ~e **à écouteurs)**, headphones. ~é a. wearing a helmet.

casquette /kaskɛt/ n.f. cap.

cassant, ~e /kasɑ̃, -t/ a. brittle; (brusque) curt.

cassation /kasasjɔ̃/ n.f. **cour de** ~, appeal court.

casse /kɑs/ n.f. (objets) breakages. **mettre à la** ~, scrap.

cass|er /kɑse/ v.t./i. break; (annuler) annul. **se** ~er v. pr. break. ~er la **tête à**, (fam.) give a headache to. ~e-**cou** n.m. invar. daredevil. ~e-**croûte** n.m. invar. snack. ~e-**noisettes** ou ~e-**noix** n.m. invar. nutcrackers. ~e-**pieds** n.m./f. invar. (fam.) pain (in the neck). ~e-**tête** n.m. invar. (problème) headache; (jeu) brain teaser.

casserole /kasrɔl/ n.f. saucepan.

cassette /kasɛt/ n.f. casket; (de magnétophone) cassette; (de video) video tape.

cassis[1] /kasi(s)/ n.m. black currant.

cassis[2] /kasi(s)/ n.m. (auto.) dip.

cassoulet /kasulɛ/ n.m. stew (of beans and meat).

cassure /kasyr/ n.f. break.

caste /kast/ n.f. caste.

castor /kastɔr/ n.m. beaver.

castr|er /kastre/ v.t. castrate. ~ation n.f. castration.

cataclysme /kataklism/ n.m. cataclysm.

catalogu|e /katalɔg/ n.m. catalogue. ~er v.t. catalogue; (personne: péj.) label.

catalyseur /katalizœr/ n.m. catalyst.

cataphote /katafɔt/ n.m. reflector.

cataplasme /kataplasm/ n.m. poultice.

catapult|e /katapylt/ *n.f.* catapult.
~er *v.t.* catapult.

cataracte /katarakt/ *n.f.* cataract.

catastroph|e /katastrɔf/ *n.f.* disaster, catastrophe. **~ique** *a.* catastrophic.

catch /katʃ/ *n.m.* (all-in) wrestling. **~eur, ~euse** *n.m.,* *f.* (all-in) wrestler.

catéchisme /kateʃism/ *n.m.* catechism.

catégorie /kategɔri/ *n.f.* category.

catégorique /kategɔrik/ *a.* categorical.

cathédrale /katedral/ *n.f.* cathedral.

catholi|que /katɔlik/ *a.* Catholic. **~cisme** *n.m.* Catholicism. **pas très ~que,** a bit fishy.

catimini (en) /(ɑ̃)katimini/ *adv.* on the sly.

cauchemar /koʃmar/ *n.m.* nightmare.

cause /koz/ *n.f.* cause; (*jurid.*) case. **à ~ de,** because of. **en ~,** (*en jeu, concerné*) involved. **pour ~ de,** on account of.

caus|er /koze/ *v.t.* cause. ● *v.i.* chat. **~erie** *n.f.* talk. **~ette** *n.f.* **faire la ~ette,** have a chat.

caustique /kostik/ *a.* caustic.

caution /kosjɔ̃/ *n.f.* surety; (*jurid.*) bail; (*appui*) backing; (*garantie*) deposit. **sous ~,** on bail.

cautionn|er /kosjɔne/ *v.t.* guarantee; (*soutenir*) back.

cavalcade /kavalkad/ *n.f.* (*fam.*) stampede, rush.

cavalerie /kavalri/ *n.f.* (*mil.*) cavalry; (*au cirque*) horses.

caval|ier, ~ière /kavalje, -jɛr/ *a.* offhand. ● *n.m., f.* rider; (*pour danser*) partner. ● *n.m.* (*échecs*) knight.

cave [1] /kav/ *n.f.* cellar.

cave [2] /kav/ *a.* sunken.

caveau (*pl.* **~x**) /kavo/ *n.m.* vault.

caverne /kavɛrn/ *n.f.* cave.

caviar /kavjar/ *n.m.* caviare.

cavité /kavite/ *n.f.* cavity.

CD (*abrév.*) (*compact disc*) CD.

ce [1], **c'*** /sə, s/ *pron.* it, that. **c'est, it** *ou* that is. **ce sont,** they are. **c'est moi,** it's me. **c'est un chanteur/une chanteuse/***etc.*, he/she is a singer/ *etc.* **ce qui, ce que,** what. **ce que c'est bon/***etc.***!,** how good/*etc.* it is! **tout ce qui, tout ce que,** everything that.

ce [2] *ou* **cet*, cette** (*pl.* **ces**) /sə, sɛt, se/ *a.* that; (*proximité*) this. **ces,** those; (*proximité*) these.

CE *abrév.* (Communauté européenne) EC.

ceci /səsi/ *pron.* this.

cécité /sesite/ *n.f.* blindness.

céder /sede/ *v.t.* give up. ● *v.i.* (*se rompre*) give way; (*se soumettre*) give in.

cédille /sedij/ *n.f.* cedilla.

cèdre /sɛdr/ *n.m.* cedar.

CEE *abrév.* (*Communauté économique européenne*) EEC.

ceinture /sɛtyr/ *n.f.* belt; (*taille*) waist; (*de bus, métro*) circle (line). **~ de sauvetage,** lifebelt. **~ de sécurité,** seat-belt.

ceinturer /sɛtyre/ *v.t.* seize round the waist; (*entourer*) surround.

cela /səla/ *pron.* it, that; (*pour désigner*) that. **~ va de soi,** it is obvious.

célèbre /selɛbr/ *a.* famous.

célébr|er /selebre/ *v.t.* celebrate. **~ation** *n.f.* celebration (**de,** of).

célébrité /selebrite/ *n.f.* fame; (*personne*) celebrity.

céleri /sɛlri/ *n.m.* (*en branches*) celery. **~(-rave),** celeriac.

céleste /selɛst/ *a.* celestial.

célibat /seliba/ *n.m.* celibacy.

célibataire /selibatɛr/ *a.* unmarried. ● *n.m.* bachelor. ● *n.f.* unmarried woman.

celle, celles /sɛl/ *voir* celui.

cellier /selje/ *n.m.* store-room (*for wine*).

cellophane /selɔfan/ *n.f.* (P.) Cellophane (P.).

cellul|e /selyl/ *n.f.* cell. **~aire** *a.* cell. **fourgon** *ou* **voiture ~aire,** prison van.

celui, celle (*pl.* **ceux, celles**) /səlɥi, sɛl, sø/ *pron.* the one. **~ de mon ami,** my friend's. **~-ci,** this (one). **~-là,** that (one). **ceux-ci,** these (ones). **ceux-là,** those (ones).

cendr|e /sɑ̃dr/ *n.f.* ash. **~é** *a.* (*couleur*) ashen. **blond ~é,** ash blond.

cendrier /sɑ̃drije/ *n.m.* ashtray.

censé /sɑ̃se/ *a.* **être ~ faire,** be supposed to do.

censeur /sɑ̃sœr/ *n.m.* censor; (*scol.*) assistant headmaster.

censur|e /sɑ̃syr/ *n.f.* censorship. **~er** *v.t.* censor; (*critiquer*) censure.

cent (*pl.* **~s**) /sɑ̃/ (*generally* /sɑ̃t/ *pl.* /sɑ̃z/ *before vowel*) *a. & n.m.* (a) hundred. **~ un** /sɑ̃œ̃/ a hundred and one.

centaine /sātɛn/ *n.f.* hundred. **une ~ (de),** (about) a hundred.

centenaire /sātnɛr/ *n.m.* (*anniversaire*) centenary.

centième /sātjɛm/ *a. & n.m./f.* hundredth.

centigrade /sātigrad/ *a.* centigrade.

centilitre /sātilitr/ *n.m.* centilitre.

centime /sātim/ *n.m.* centime.

centimètre /sātimɛtr/ *n.m.* centimetre; (*ruban*) tape-measure.

centr|al, ~ale (*m. pl.* **~aux**) /sātral, -o/ *a.* central. ● *n.m.* (*pl.* **~aux**). **~al (téléphonique),** (telephone) exchange. ● *n.f.* power-station. **~aliser** *v.t.* centralize.

centr|e /sātr/ *n.m.* centre. **~e-ville** *n.m.* town centre. **~er** *v.t.* centre.

centuple /sātypl/ *n.m.* **le ~ (de),** a hundredfold. **au ~,** a hundredfold.

cep /sɛp/ *n.m.* vine stock.

cépage /sepaʒ/ *n.m.* (variety of) vine.

cèpe /sɛp/ *n.m.* (edible) boletus.

cependant /səpādā/ *adv.* however.

céramique /seramik/ *n.f.* ceramic; (*art*) ceramics.

cerceau (*pl.* **~x**) /sɛrso/ *n.m.* hoop.

cercle /sɛrkl/ *n.m.* circle; (*cerceau*) hoop. **~ vicieux,** vicious circle.

cercueil /sɛrkœj/ *n.m.* coffin.

céréale /sereal/ *n.f.* cereal.

cérébr|al (*m. pl.* **~aux**) /serebral, -o/ *a.* cerebral.

cérémonial (*pl.* **~s**) /seremɔnjal/ *n.m.* ceremonial.

cérémon|ie /seremɔni/ *n.f.* ceremony. **~ie(s),** (*façons*) fuss. **~ieux, ~ieuse** *a.* ceremonious.

cerf /sɛr/ *n.m.* stag.

cerfeuil /sɛrfœj/ *n.m.* chervil.

cerf-volant (*pl.* **cerfs-volants**) /sɛrvɔlā/ *n.m.* kite.

ceris|e /sriz/ *n.f.* cherry. **~ier** *n.m.* cherry tree.

cerne /sɛrn/ *n.f.* ring.

cern|er /sɛrne/ *v.t.* surround; (*question*) define. **les yeux ~és,** with rings under one's eyes.

certain, ~e /sɛrtɛ̃, -ɛn/ *a.* certain; (*sûr*) certain, sure (**de,** of; **que,** that). ● *pron.* **~s,** certain people. **d'un ~ âge,** past one's prime. **un ~ temps,** some time.

certainement /sɛrtɛnmā/ *adv.* certainly.

certes /sɛrt/ *adv.* indeed.

certificat /sɛrtifika/ *n.m.* certificate.

certif|ier /sɛrtifje/ *v.t.* certify. **~ier qch. à qn.,** assure s.o. of sth. **~ié** *a.* (*professeur*) qualified.

certitude /sɛrtityd/ *n.f.* certainty.

cerveau (*pl.* **~x**) /sɛrvo/ *n.m.* brain.

cervelas /sɛrvəla/ *n.m.* saveloy.

cervelle /sɛrvɛl/ *n.f.* (*anat.*) brain; (*culin.*) brains.

ces /se/ *voir* ce².

césarienne /sezarjɛn/ *n.f.* Caesarean (section).

cessation /sɛsasjɔ̃/ *n.f.* suspension.

cesse /sɛs/ *n.f.* **n'avoir de ~ que,** have no rest until. **sans ~,** incessantly.

cesser /sese/ *v.t./i.* stop. **~ de faire,** stop doing.

cessez-le-feu /seselfø/ *n.m. invar.* cease-fire.

cession /sɛsjɔ̃/ *n.f.* transfer.

c'est-à-dire /setadir/ *conj.* that is (to say).

cet, cette /sɛt/ *voir* ce².

ceux /sø/ *voir* celui.

chacal (*pl.* **~s**) /ʃakal/ *n.m.* jackal.

chacun, ~e /ʃakœ̃, -yn/ *pron.* each (one), every one; (*tout le monde*) everyone.

chagrin /ʃagrɛ̃/ *n.m.* sorrow. **avoir du ~,** be distressed. **~er** /-ine/ *v.t.* distress.

chahut /ʃay/ *n.m.* row, din. **~er** /-te/ *v.i.* make a row; *v.t.* be rowdy with. **~eur, ~euse** /- tœr, -tøz/ *n.m., f.* rowdy.

chaîn|e /ʃɛn/ *n.f.* chain; (*de télévision*) channel. **~e de montagnes,** mountain range. **~e de montage/ fabrication,** assembly/production line. **~e hi-fi,** hi-fi system. **en ~e,** (*accidents*) multiple. **~ette** *n.f.* (small) chain. **~on** *n.m.* link.

chair /ʃɛr/ *n.f.* flesh. **bien en ~,** plump. **en ~ et en os,** in the flesh. **~ à saucisses,** sausage meat. **la ~ de poule,** goose-flesh. ● *a. invar.* (**couleur**) **~,** flesh-coloured.

chaire /ʃɛr/ *n.f.* (*d'église*) pulpit; (*univ.*) chair.

chaise /ʃɛz/ *n.f.* chair. **~ longue,** deck-chair.

chaland /ʃalā/ *n.m.* barge.

châle /ʃal/ *n.m.* shawl.

chalet /ʃalɛ/ *n.m.* chalet.

chaleur /ʃalœr/ *n.f.* heat; (*moins intense*) warmth; (*d'un accueil, d'une couleur*) warmth. **~eux, ~euse** *a.* warm.

challenge /ʃalāʒ/ *n.m.* contest.

chaloupe /ʃalup/ *n.f.* launch, boat.

chalumeau (*pl.* ~x) /ʃalymo/ *n.m.* blowlamp; (*Amer.*) blowtorch.

chalut /ʃaly/ *n.m.* trawl-net. ~**ier** /-tje/ *n.m.* trawler.

chamailler (se) /(sə)ʃamaje/ *v. pr.* squabble.

chambarder /ʃɑ̃barde/ *v.t.* (*fam.*) turn upside down.

chambre /ʃɑ̃br/ *n.f.* (bed)room; (*pol., jurid.*) chamber. **faire ~ à part,** sleep in different rooms. ~ **à air,** inner tube. ~ **d'amis,** spare *ou* guest room. ~ **à coucher,** bedroom. ~ **à un lit/deux lits,** single/double room. ~ **forte,** strong-room.

chambrer /ʃɑ̃bre/ *v.t.* (*vin*) bring to room temperature.

chameau (*pl.* ~x) /ʃamo/ *n.m.* camel.

chamois /ʃamwa/ *n.m.* chamois. **peau de ~,** chamois leather.

champ /ʃɑ̃/ *n.m.* field. ~ **de bataille,** battlefield. ~ **de courses,** racecourse.

champagne /ʃɑ̃paɲ/ *n.m.* champagne.

champêtre /ʃɑ̃pɛtr/ *a.* rural.

champignon /ʃɑ̃piɲɔ̃/ *n.m.* mushroom; (*moisissure*) fungus. ~ **de Paris,** button mushroom.

champion, ~ne /ʃɑ̃pjɔ̃, -jɔn/ *n.m., f.* champion. ~**nat** /-jɔna/ *n.m.* championship.

chance /ʃɑ̃s/ *n.f.* (good) luck; (*possibilité*) chance. **avoir de la ~,** be lucky. **quelle ~!,** what luck!

chanceler /ʃɑ̃sle/ *v.i.* stagger; (*fig.*) falter.

chancelier /ʃɑ̃səlje/ *n.m.* chancellor.

chanceu|x, ~se /ʃɑ̃sø, -z/ *a.* lucky.

chancre /ʃɑ̃kr/ *n.m.* canker.

chandail /ʃɑ̃daj/ *n.m.* sweater.

chandelier /ʃɑ̃dəlje/ *n.m.* candlestick.

chandelle /ʃɑ̃dɛl/ *n.f.* candle. **dîner aux ~s,** candlelight dinner.

change /ʃɑ̃ʒ/ *n.m.* (foreign) exchange.

changeant, ~e /ʃɑ̃ʒɑ̃, -t/ *a.* changeable.

changement /ʃɑ̃ʒmɑ̃/ *n.m.* change. ~ **de vitesses,** gears.

changer /ʃɑ̃ʒe/ *v.t./i.* change. **se ~** *v. pr.* change (one's clothes). ~ **de nom/voiture,** change one's name/car. ~ **de place/train,** change places/trains. ~ **de direction,** change direction. ~ **d'avis** *ou*

d'idée, change one's mind. ~ **de vitesses,** change gear.

changeur /ʃɑ̃ʒœr/ *n.m.* ~ **automatique,** (money) change machine.

chanoine /ʃanwan/ *n.m.* canon.

chanson /ʃɑ̃sɔ̃/ *n.f.* song.

chant /ʃɑ̃/ *n.m.* singing; (*chanson*) song; (*religieux*) hymn.

chantage /ʃɑ̃taʒ/ *n.m.* blackmail. ~ **psychologique,** emotional blackmail.

chant|er /ʃɑ̃te/ *v.t./i.* sing. **si cela vous ~e,** (*fam.*) if you feel like it. **faire ~,** (*délit*) blackmail. ~**eur,** ~**euse** *n.m., f.* singer.

chantier /ʃɑ̃tje/ *n.m.* building site. ~ **naval,** shipyard. **mettre en ~,** get under way, start.

chantonner /ʃɑ̃tɔne/ *v.t./i.* hum.

chanvre /ʃɑ̃vr/ *n.m.* hemp.

chao|s /kao/ *n.m.* chaos. ~**tique** /kaɔtik/ *a.* chaotic.

chaparder /ʃaparde/ *v.t.* (*fam.*) filch.

chapeau (*pl.* ~x) /ʃapo/ *n.m.* hat. ~!, well done!

chapelet /ʃaplɛ/ *n.m.* rosary; (*fig.*) string.

chapelle /ʃapɛl/ *n.f.* chapel. ~ **ardente,** chapel of rest.

chapelure /ʃaplyr/ *n.f.* breadcrumbs.

chaperon /ʃaprɔ̃/ *n.m.* chaperon. ~**ner** /-ɔne/ *v.t.* chaperon.

chapiteau (*pl.* ~x) /ʃapito/ *n.m.* (*cirque*) big top; (*de colonne*) capital.

chap|itre /ʃapitr/ *n.m.* chapter; (*fig.*) subject.

chapitrer /ʃapitre/ *v.t.* reprimand.

chaque /ʃak/ *a.* every, each.

char /ʃar/ *n.m.* (*mil.*) tank; (*de carnaval*) float; (*charrette*) cart; (*dans l'antiquité*) chariot.

charabia /ʃarabja/ *n.m.* (*fam.*) gibberish.

charade /ʃarad/ *n.f.* riddle.

charbon /ʃarbɔ̃/ *n.m.* coal. ~ **de bois,** charcoal. ~**nages** /-ɔnaʒ/ *n.m. pl.* coal-mines.

charcut|erie /ʃarkytri/ *n.f.* pork-butcher's shop; (*aliments*) (cooked) pork meats. ~**ier,** ~**ière** *n.m., f.* pork-butcher.

chardon /ʃardɔ̃/ *n.m.* thistle.

charge /ʃarʒ/ *n.f.* load, burden; (*mil., électr., jurid.*) charge; (*mission*) responsibility. ~**s,** expenses; (*de locataire*) service charges. **être à la ~ de,** be the responsibility of. ~**s sociales,** social security contributions. **prendre en ~,** take charge of; (*transporter*) give a ride to.

chargé /ʃarʒe/ *a.* (*journée*) busy; (*langue*) coated. ● *n.m.*, *f.* **~ de mission.** head of mission. **~ d'affaires,** chargé d'affaires, **~ de cours,** lecturer.

charger /ʃarʒe/ *v.t.* load; (*attaquer*) charge; (*batterie*) charge. ● *v.i.* (*attaquer*) charge. **se ~ de,** take charge *ou* care of. **~ qn. de,** weigh. s.o. down with; (*tâche*) entrust s.o. with. **~ qn. de faire,** instruct s.o. to do. **chargement** /-əmɑ̃/ *n.m.* loading; (*objets*) load.

chariot /ʃarjo/ *n.m.* (*à roulettes*) trolley; (*charrette*) cart.

charitable /ʃaritabl/ *a.* charitable.

charité /ʃarite/ *n.f.* charity. **faire la ~,** give to charity. **faire la ~ à,** give to.

charlatan /ʃarlatɑ̃/ *n.m.* charlatan.

charmant, ~e /ʃarmɑ̃, -t/ *a.* charming.

charm|e /ʃarm/ *n.m.* charm. **~er** *v.t.* charm. **~eur, ~euse** *n.m.*, *f.* charmer.

charnel, ~le /ʃarnɛl/ *a.* carnal.

charnier /ʃarnje/ *n.m.* mass grave.

charnière /ʃarnjɛr/ *n.f.* hinge. **à la ~ de,** at the meeting point between.

charnu /ʃarny/ *a.* fleshy.

charpent|e /ʃarpɑ̃t/ *n.f.* framework; (*carrure*) build. **~é a.** built.

charpentier /ʃarpɑ̃tje/ *n.m.* carpenter.

charpie (en) /(ɑ̃)ʃarpi/ *adv.* in(to) shreds.

charretier /ʃartje/ *n.m.* carter.

charrette /ʃarɛt/ *n.f.* cart.

charrier /ʃarje/ *v.t.* carry.

charrue /ʃary/ *n.f.* plough.

charte /ʃart/ *n.f.* charter.

charter /ʃartɛr/ *n.m.* charter flight.

chasse /ʃas/ *n.f.* hunting; (*au fusil*) shooting; (*poursuite*) chase; (*recherche*) hunt. **~ (d'eau),** (toilet) flush. **~ sous-marine,** underwater fishing.

châsse /ʃas/ *n.f.* shrine, reliquary.

chass|er /ʃase/ *v.t./i.* hunt; (*faire partir*) chase away; (*odeur, employé*) get rid of. **~e-neige** *n.m. invar.* snow-plough. **~eur, ~euse** *n.m.*, *f.* hunter; *n.m.* page-boy; (*avion*) fighter.

châssis /ʃasi/ *n.m.* frame; (*auto.*) chassis.

chaste /ʃast/ *a.* chaste. **~té** /-əte/ *n.f.* chastity.

chat, ~te /ʃa, ʃat/ *n.m.*, *f.* cat.

châtaigne /ʃatɛɲ/ *n.f.* chestnut.

châtaignier /ʃatɛɲe/ *n.m.* chestnut tree.

châtain /ʃatɛ̃/ *a. invar.* chestnut (brown).

château (*pl.* **~x**) /ʃato/ *n.m.* castle; (*manoir*) manor. **~ d'eau,** water-tower. **~ fort,** fortified castle.

châtelain, ~e /ʃatlɛ̃, -ɛn/ *n.m.*, *f.* lord of the manor, lady of the manor.

châtier /ʃatje/ *v.t.* chastise; (*style*) refine.

châtiment /ʃatimɑ̃/ *n.m.* punishment.

chaton /ʃatɔ̃/ *n.m.* (*chat*) kitten.

chatouill|er /ʃatuje/ *v.t.* tickle. **~ement** *n.m.* tickling.

chatouilleu|x, ~se /ʃatujø, -z/ *a.* ticklish; (*susceptible*) touchy.

chatoyer /ʃatwaje/ *v.i.* glitter.

châtrer /ʃatre/ *v.t.* castrate.

chatte /ʃat/ *voir* chat.

chaud, ~e /ʃo, ʃod/ *a.* warm; (*brûlant*) hot; (*vif: fig.*) warm. ● *n.m.* heat. **au ~,** in the warm(th). **avoir ~,** be warm; be hot. **il fait ~,** it is warm; it is hot. **pour te tenir ~,** to keep you warm. **~ement** /-dmɑ̃/ *adv.* warmly; (*disputé*) hotly.

chaudière /ʃodjɛr/ *n.f.* boiler.

chaudron /ʃodrɔ̃/ *n.m.* cauldron.

chauffage /ʃofaʒ/ *n.m.* heating. **~ central,** central heating.

chauffard /ʃofar/ *n.m.* (*péj.*) reckless driver.

chauff|er /ʃofe/ *v.t./i.* heat (up). **se ~er** *v. pr.* warm o.s. (up). **~e-eau** *n.m. invar.* water-heater.

chauffeur /ʃofœr/ *n.m.* driver; (*aux gages de qn.*) chauffeur.

chaum|e /ʃom/ *n.m.* (*de toit*) thatch.

chaussée /ʃose/ *n.f.* road(way).

chauss|er /ʃose/ *v.t.* (*chaussures*) put on; (*enfant*) put shoes on (to). **se ~er** *v. pr.* put one's shoes on. **~er bien,** (*aller*) fit well. **~er du 35/etc.,** take a size 35/etc. shoe. **~e-pied** *n.m.* shoehorn. **~eur** *n.m.* shoemaker.

chaussette /ʃosɛt/ *n.f.* sock.

chausson /ʃosɔ̃/ *n.m.* slipper; (*de bébé*) bootee. **~ (aux pommes),** (apple) turnover.

chaussure /ʃosyr/ *n.f.* shoe. **~s de ski,** ski boots. **~s de marche,** hiking boots.

chauve /ʃov/ *a.* bald.

chauve-souris (*pl.* **chauves-souris**) /ʃovsuri/ *n.f.* bat.

chauvin, ~**e** /ʃovɛ̃, -in/ *a.* chauvinistic. ● *n.m., f.* chauvinist. ~**isme** /-inism/ *n.m.* chauvinism.

chaux /ʃo/ *n.f.* lime.

chavirer /ʃavire/ *v.t./i.* (*bateau*) capsize.

chef /ʃɛf/ *n.m.* leader, head; (*culin.*) chef; (*de tribu*) chief. ~ **d'accusation,** (*jurid.*) charge. ~ **d'équipe,** foreman; (*sport*) captain. ~ **d'État,** head of State. ~ **de famille,** head of the family. ~ **de file,** (*pol.*) leader. ~ **de gare,** station-master. ~ **d'orchestre,** conductor. ~ **de service,** department head. ~**-lieu** (*pl.* ~**s-lieux**) *n.m.* county town.

chef-d'œuvre (*pl.* **chefs-d'œuvre**) /ʃɛdœvr/ *n.m.* masterpiece.

cheik /ʃɛk/ *n.m.* sheikh.

chemin /ʃmɛ̃/ *n.m.* path, road; (*direction, trajet*) way. **beaucoup de** ~ **à faire,** a long way to go. ~ **de fer,** railway. **en** *ou* **par** ~ **de fer,** by rail. ~ **de halage,** towpath. ~ **vicinal,** by-road. **se mettre en** ~, start out.

cheminée /ʃmine/ *n.f.* chimney; (*intérieure*) fireplace; (*encadrement*) mantelpiece; (*de bateau*) funnel.

chemin|er /ʃmine/ *v.i.* plod; (*fig.*) progress. ~**ement** *n.m.* progress.

cheminot /ʃmino/ *n.m.* railwayman; (*Amer.*) railroad man.

chemis|e /ʃmiz/ *n.f.* shirt; (*dossier*) folder; (*de livre*) jacket. ~**e de nuit,** night-dress. ~**ette** *n.f.* short-sleeved shirt.

chemisier /ʃmizje/ *n.m.* blouse.

chen|al (*pl.* ~**aux**) /ʃənal, -o/ *n.m.* channel.

chêne /ʃɛn/ *n.m.* oak.

chenil /ʃni(l)/ *n.m.* kennels.

chenille /ʃnij/ *n.f.* caterpillar.

chenillette /ʃnijɛt/ *n.f.* tracked vehicle.

cheptel /ʃɛptɛl/ *n.m.* livestock.

chèque /ʃɛk/ *n.m.* cheque. ~ **de voyage,** traveller's cheque.

chéquier /ʃekje/ *n.m.* cheque-book.

cher, chère /ʃɛr/ *a.* (*coûteux*) dear, expensive; (*aimé*) dear. ● *adv.* (*coûter, payer*) a lot (of money). ● *n.m., f.* **mon** ~, **ma chère,** my dear.

chercher /ʃɛrʃe/ *v.t.* look for; (*aide, paix, gloire*) seek. **aller** ~, go and get

ou fetch, go for. ~ **à faire,** attempt to do. ~ **la petite bête,** be finicky.

chercheu|r, ~**se** /ʃɛrʃœr, -øz/ *n.m., f.* research worker.

chèrement /ʃɛrmɑ̃/ *adv.* dearly.

chéri, ~**e** /ʃeri/ *a.* beloved. ● *n.m., f.* darling.

chérir /ʃerir/ *v.t.* cherish.

cherté /ʃɛrte/ *n.f.* high cost.

chéti|f, ~**ve** /ʃetif, -v/ *a.* puny.

chev|al (*pl.* ~**aux**) /ʃval, -o/ *n.m.* horse. ~**al (vapeur),** horsepower. **à** ~**al,** on horseback. **à** ~**al sur,** straddling. **faire du** ~**al,** ride (a horse). ~**al-d'arçons** *n.m. invar.* (*gymnastique*) horse.

chevaleresque /ʃvalrɛsk/ *a.* chivalrous.

chevalerie /ʃvalri/ *n.f.* chivalry.

chevalet /ʃvalɛ/ *n.m.* easel.

chevalier /ʃvalje/ *n.m.* knight.

chevalière /ʃvaljɛr/ *n.f.* signet ring.

chevalin, ~**e** /ʃvalɛ̃, -in/ *a.* (*boucherie*) horse; (*espèce*) equine.

chevauchée /ʃvoʃe/ *n.f.* (horse) ride.

chevaucher /ʃvoʃe/ *v.t.* straddle. ● *v.i.,* **se** ~ *v. pr.* overlap.

chevelu /ʃəvly/ *a.* hairy.

chevelure /ʃəvlyr/ *n.f.* hair.

chevet /ʃvɛ/ *n.m.* **au** ~ **de,** at the bedside of.

cheveu (*pl.* ~**x**) /ʃvø/ *n.m.* (*poil*) hair. ~**x,** (*chevelure*) hair. **avoir les** ~**x longs,** have long hair.

cheville /ʃvij/ *n.f.* ankle; (*fiche*) peg, pin; (*pour mur*) (wall) plug.

chèvre /ʃɛvr/ *n.f.* goat.

chevreau (*pl.* ~**x**) /ʃəvro/ *n.m.* kid.

chevreuil /ʃəvrœj/ *n.m.* roe(-deer); (*culin.*) venison.

chevron /ʃəvrɔ̃/ *n.m.* (*poutre*) rafter. **à** ~**s,** herring-bone.

chevronné /ʃəvrone/ *a.* experienced, seasoned.

chevrotant, ~**e** /ʃəvrotɑ̃, -t/ *a.* quavering.

chewing-gum /ʃwiŋgom/ *n.m.* chewing-gum.

chez /ʃe/ *prép.* at *ou* to the house of; (*parmi*) among; (*dans le caractère ou l'œuvre de*) in. ~ **le boucher/*etc.*,** at the butcher's/ *etc.* ~ **soi,** at home; (*avec direction*) home. ~**-soi** *invar.* home.

chic /ʃik/ *a. invar.* smart; (*gentil*) kind. **sois** ~, do me a favour. ● *n.m.* style. **avoir le** ~ **pour,** have the knack of. ~ **(alors)!,** great!

chicane /ʃikan/ *n.f.* zigzag. **chercher** ~ **à qn,** needle s.o.

chiche /ʃiʃ/ *a.* mean (**de,** with). ~ **(que je le fais)!,** (*fam.*) I bet you I will, can, *etc.*

chichis /ʃiʃi/ *n.m. pl.* (*fam.*) fuss.

chicorée /ʃikɔre/ *n.f.* (*frisée*) endive; (*à café*) chicory.

chien, ~ne /ʃjɛ̃, ʃjɛn/ *n.m.* dog. ● *n.f.* dog, bitch. ~ **de garde,** watchdog. **~-loup** *n.m.* (*pl.* **~s-loups**) wolfhound.

chiffon /ʃifɔ̃/ *n.m.* rag.

chiffonner /ʃifɔne/ *v.t.* crumple; (*préoccuper*: *fam.*) bother.

chiffonnier /ʃifɔnje/ *n.m.* rag-and-bone man.

chiffre /ʃifr/ *n.m.* figure; (*code*) code. **~s arabes/romains,** Arabic/roman numerals. ~ **d'affaires,** turnover.

chiffrer /ʃifre/ *v.t.* set a figure to, assess; (*texte*) encode. **se** ~ **à,** amount to.

chignon /ʃiɲɔ̃/ *n.m.* bun, chignon.

Chili /ʃili/ *n.m.* Chile.

chilien, ~ne /ʃiljɛ̃, -jɛn/ *a. & n.m., f.* Chilean.

chim|ère /ʃimɛr/ *n.f.* fantasy. **~érique** *a.* fanciful.

chim|ie /ʃimi/ *n.f.* chemistry. **~ique** *a.* chemical. **~iste** *n.m./f.* chemist.

chimpanzé /ʃɛ̃pɑ̃ze/ *n.m.* chimpanzee.

Chine /ʃin/ *n.f.* China.

chinois, ~e /ʃinwa, -z/ *a. & n.m., f.* Chinese. ● *n.m.* (*lang.*) Chinese.

chiot /ʃjo/ *n.m.* pup(py).

chiper /ʃipe/ *v.t.* (*fam.*) swipe.

chipoter /ʃipɔte/ *v.i.* (*manger*) nibble; (*discuter*) quibble.

chips /ʃips/ *n.m. pl.* crisps; (*Amer.*) chips.

chiquenaude /ʃiknod/ *n.f.* flick.

chiromanc|ie /kirɔmɑ̃si/ *n.f.* palmistry. **~ien, ~ienne** *n.m., f.* palmist.

chirurgic|al (*m. pl.* **~aux**) /ʃiryrʒikal, -o/ *a.* surgical.

chirurg|ie /ʃiryrʒi/ *n.f.* surgery. **~ie esthétique,** plastic surgery. **~ien** *n.m.* surgeon.

chlore /klɔr/ *n.m.* chlorine.

choc /ʃɔk/ *n.m.* (*heurt*) impact, shock; (*émotion*) shock; (*collision*) crash; (*affrontement*) clash; (*méd.*) shock.

chocolat /ʃɔkɔla/ *n.m.* chocolate; (*à boire*) drinking chocolate. ~ **au lait,** milk chocolate. ~ **chaud,** hot chocolate.

chœur /kœr/ *n.m.* (*antique*) chorus; (*chanteurs, nef*) choir. **en** ~, in chorus.

chois|ir /ʃwazir/ *v.t.* choose, select. **~i** *a.* carefully chosen; (*passage*) selected.

choix /ʃwa/ *n.m.* choice, selection. **au** ~, according to preference. **de** ~, choice. **de premier** ~, top quality.

choléra /kɔlera/ *n.m.* cholera.

chômage /ʃomaʒ/ *n.m.* unemployment. **en** ~, unemployed. **mettre en** ~ **technique,** lay off.

chôm|er /ʃome/ *v.i.* be unemployed; (*usine*) lie idle. **~eur, ~euse** *n.m., f.* unemployed person. **les ~eurs,** the unemployed.

chope /ʃɔp/ *n.f.* tankard.

choper /ʃɔpe/ *v.t.* (*fam.*) catch.

choquer /ʃɔke/ *v.t.* shock; (*commotionner*) shake.

choral, ~e (*m. pl.* **~s**) /kɔral/ *a.* choral. ● *n.f.* choir, choral society.

chorégraph|ie /kɔregrafi/ *n.f.* choreography. **~e** *n.m./f.* choreographer.

choriste /kɔrist/ *n.m./f.* (*à l'église*) chorister; (*opéra, etc.*) member of the chorus *ou* choir.

chose /ʃoz/ *n.f.* thing. **(très) peu de** ~, nothing much.

chou (*pl.* **~x**) /ʃu/ *n.m.* cabbage. ~ **(à la crème),** cream puff. **~x de Bruxelles,** Brussels sprouts. **mon petit** ~, (*fam.*) my little dear.

choucas /ʃuka/ *n.m.* jackdaw.

chouchou, ~te /ʃuʃu, -t/ *n.m., f.* pet, darling. **le** ~ **du prof.,** the teacher's pet.

choucroute /ʃukrut/ *n.f.* sauerkraut.

chouette[1] /ʃwɛt/ *n.f.* owl.

chouette[2] /ʃwɛt/ *a.* (*fam.*) super.

chou-fleur (*pl.* **choux-fleurs**) /ʃuflœr/ *n.m.* cauliflower.

choyer /ʃwaje/ *v.t.* pamper.

chrétien, ~ne /kretjɛ̃, -jɛn/ *a. & n.m., f.* Christian.

Christ /krist/ *n.m.* **le** ~, Christ.

christianisme /kristjanism/ *n.m.* Christianity.

chrom|e /krom/ *n.m.* chromium, chrome. **~é** *a.* chromium-plated.

chromosome /krɔmozom/ *n.m.* chromosome.

chroniqu|e /krɔnik/ *a.* chronic. ● *n.f.* (*rubrique*) column; (*nouvelles*) news; (*annales*) chronicle.

~eur *n.m.* columnist; (*historien*) chronicler.

chronolog|ie /krɔnɔlɔʒi/ *n.f.* chronology. **~ique** *a.* chronological.

chronom|ètre /krɔnɔmɛtr/ *n.m.* stopwatch. **~étrer** *v.t.* time.

chrysanthème /krizɑ̃tɛm/ *n.m.* chrysanthemum.

chuchot|er /ʃyʃɔte/ *v.t./i.* whisper. **~ement** *n.m.* whisper(ing).

chuinter /ʃɥɛ̃te/ *v.i.* hiss.

chut /ʃyt/ *int.* shush.

chute /ʃyt/ *n.f.* fall; (*déchet*) scrap. **~ (d'eau)**, waterfall. **~ du jour,** nightfall. **~ de pluie,** rainfall. **la ~ des cheveux,** hair loss.

chuter /ʃyte/ *v.i.* fall.

Chypre /ʃipr/ *n.f.* Cyprus.

-ci /si/ *adv.* (*après un nom précédé de ce, cette, etc.*) **cet homme-ci,** this man. **ces maisons-ci,** these houses.

ci- /si/ *adv.* here. **ci-après,** hereafter. **ci-contre,** opposite. **ci-dessous,** below. **ci-dessus,** above. **ci-gît,** here lies. **ci-inclus, ci-incluse, ci-joint, ci-jointe,** enclosed.

cible /sibl/ *n.f.* target.

ciboul|e /sibul/ *n.f.,* **~ette** *n.f.* chive(s).

cicatrice /sikatris/ *n.f.* scar.

cicatriser /sikatrize/ *v.t.,* **se ~** *v. pr.* heal (up).

cidre /sidr/ *n.m.* cider.

ciel (*pl.* **cieux, ciels**) /sjɛl, sjø/ *n.m.* sky; (*relig.*) heaven. **cieux,** (*relig.*) heaven.

cierge /sjɛrʒ/ *n.m.* candle.

cigale /sigal/ *n.f.* cicada.

cigare /sigar/ *n.m.* cigar.

cigarette /sigarɛt/ *n.f.* cigarette.

cigogne /sigɔɲ/ *n.f.* stork.

cil /sil/ *n.m.* (eye)lash.

ciller /sije/ *v.i.* blink.

cime /sim/ *n.f.* peak, tip.

ciment /simɑ̃/ *n.m.* cement. **~er** /-te/ *v.t.* cement.

cimetière /simtjɛr/ *n.m.* cemetery. **~ de voitures,** breaker's yard.

cinéaste /sineast/ *n.m./f.* film-maker.

ciné-club /sineklœb/ *n.m.* film society.

cinéma /sinema/ *n.m.* cinema. **~tographique** *a.* cinema.

cinémathèque /sinematɛk/ *n.f.* film library; (*salle*) film theatre.

cinéphile /sinefil/ *n.m./f.* film lover.

cinétique /sinetik/ *a.* kinetic.

cinglant, ~e /sɛ̃glɑ̃, -t/ *a.* biting.

cinglé /sɛ̃gle/ *a.* (*fam.*) crazy.

cingler /sɛ̃gle/ *v.t.* lash.

cinq /sɛ̃k/ *a.* & *n.m.* five. **~ième** *a.* & *n.m./f.* fifth.

cinquantaine /sɛ̃kɑ̃tɛn/ *n.f.* **une ~ (de),** about fifty.

cinquant|e /sɛ̃kɑ̃t/ *a.* & *n.m.* fifty. **~ième** *a.* & *n.m./f.* fiftieth.

cintre /sɛ̃tr/ *n.m.* coat-hanger; (*archit.*) curve.

cintré /sɛ̃tre/ *a.* (*chemise*) fitted.

cirage /siraʒ/ *n.m.* (wax) polish.

circoncision /sirkɔ̃sizjɔ̃/ *n.f.* circumcision.

circonférence /sirkɔ̃ferɑ̃s/ *n.f.* circumference.

circonflexe /sirkɔ̃flɛks/ *a.* circumflex.

circonscription /sirkɔ̃skripsjɔ̃/ *n.f.* district. **~ (électorale),** constituency.

circonscrire /sirkɔ̃skrir/ *v.t.* confine; (*sujet*) define.

circonspect /sirkɔ̃spɛkt/ *a.* circumspect.

circonstance /sirkɔ̃stɑ̃s/ *n.f.* circumstance; (*occasion*) occasion. **~s atténuantes,** mitigating circumstances.

circonstancié /sirkɔ̃stɑ̃sje/ *a.* detailed.

circonvenir /sirkɔ̃vnir/ *v.t.* circumvent.

circuit /sirkɥi/ *n.m.* circuit; (*trajet*) tour, trip.

circulaire /sirkylɛr/ *a.* & *n.f.* circular.

circul|er /sirkyle/ *v.i.* circulate; (*train, automobile, etc.*) travel; (*piéton*) walk. **faire ~er,** (*badauds*) move on. **~ation** *n.f.* circulation; (*de véhicules*) traffic.

cire /sir/ *n.f.* wax.

ciré /sire/ *n.m.* oilskin; waterproof.

cir|er /sire/ *v.t.* polish, wax. **~euse** *n.f.* (*appareil*) floor-polisher.

cirque /sirk/ *n.m.* circus; (*arène*) amphitheatre; (*désordre: fig.*) chaos.

cirrhose /siroz/ *n.f.* cirrhosis.

cisaille(s) /sizaj/ *n.f.* (*pl.*) shears.

ciseau (*pl.* **~x**) /sizo/ *n.m.* chisel. **~x,** scissors.

ciseler /sizle/ *v.t.* chisel.

citadelle /sitadɛl/ *n.f.* citadel.

citadin, ~e /sitadɛ̃, -in/ *n.m., f.* city dweller. ● *a.* city.

cité /site/ *n.f.* city. **~ ouvrière,** (workers') housing estate. **~ universitaire,** (university) halls of residence. **~-dortoir** *n.f.* (*pl.* **~s-dortoirs**) dormitory town.

cit|er /site/ v.t. quote, cite; (*jurid.*) summon. **~ation** n.f. quotation; (*jurid.*) summons.

citerne /sitɛrn/ n.f. tank.

cithare /sitar/ n.f. zither.

citoyen, ~ne /sitwajɛ̃, -jɛn/ n.m., f. citizen. **~neté** /-jɛnte/ n.f. citizenship.

citron /sitrɔ̃/ n.m. lemon. **~ vert,** lime. **~nade** /-ɔnad/ n.f. lemon squash *ou* drink, (still) lemonade.

citrouille /sitruj/ n.f. pumpkin.

civet /sivɛ/ n.m. stew. **~ de lièvre/ lapin,** jugged hare/rabbit.

civette /sivɛt/ n.f. (*culin.*) chive(s).

civière /sivjɛr/ n.f. stretcher.

civil /sivil/ a. civil; (*non militaire*) civilian; (*poli*) civil. ● n.m. civilian. **dans le ~,** in civilian life. **en ~,** in plain clothes.

civilisation /sivilizasjɔ̃/ n.f. civilization.

civiliser /sivilize/ v.t. civilize. **se ~** v. pr. become civilized.

civi|que /sivik/ a. civic. **~sme** n.m. civic sense.

clair /klɛr/ a. clear; (*éclairé*) light, bright; (*couleur*) light; (*liquide*) thin. ● adv. clearly. ● n.m. **~ de lune,** moonlight. **le plus ~ de,** most of. **~ement** adv. clearly.

claire-voie (à) /(a)klɛrvwa/ adv. with slits to let the light through.

clairière /klɛrjɛr/ n.f. clearing.

clairon /klɛrɔ̃/ n.m. bugle. **~ner** /-ɔne/ v.t. trumpet (forth).

clairsemé /klɛrsəme/ a. sparse.

clairvoyant, ~e /klɛrvwajɑ̃, -t/ a. clear-sighted.

clamer /klame/ v.t. utter aloud.

clameur /klamœr/ n.f. clamour.

clan /klɑ̃/ n.m. clan.

clandestin, ~e /klɑ̃dɛstɛ̃, -in/ a. secret; (*journal*) underground. **passager ~,** stowaway.

clapet /klapɛ/ n.m. valve.

clapier /klapje/ n.m. (rabbit) hutch.

clapot|er /klapɔte/ v.i. lap. **~is** n.m. lapping.

claquage /klakaʒ/ n.m. strained muscle.

claque /klak/ n.f. slap. **en avoir sa ~ (de),** (*fam.*) be fed up (with).

claqu|er /klake/ v.i. bang; (*porte*) slam, bang; (*fouet*) snap, crack; (*se casser: fam.*) conk out; (*mourir: fam.*) snuff it. ● v.t. (*porte*) slam, bang; (*dépenser: fam.*) blow; (*fatiguer: fam.*) tire out. **~er des doigts,**

snap one's fingers. **~er des mains,** clap one's hands. **il claque des dents,** his teeth are chattering. **~ement** n.m. bang(ing); slam(ming); snap(ping).

claquettes /klakɛt/ n.f. pl. tap-dancing.

clarifier /klarifje/ v.t. clarify.

clarinette /klarinɛt/ n.f. clarinet.

clarté /klarte/ n.f. light, brightness; (*netteté*) clarity.

classe /klɑs/ n.f. class; (*salle: scol.*) class(-room). **aller en ~,** go to school. **~ ouvrière/moyenne,** working/middle class. **faire la ~,** teach.

class|er /klɑse/ v.t. classify; (*par mérite*) grade; (*papiers*) file; (*affaire*) close. **se ~er premier/dernier,** come first/last. **~ement** n.m. classification; grading; filing; (*rang*) place, grade; (*de coureur*) placing.

classeur /klɑsœr/ n.m. filing cabinet; (*chemise*) file.

classif|ier /klasifje/ v.t. classify. **~ication** n.f. classification.

classique /klasik/ a. classical; (*de qualité*) classic(al); (*habituel*) classic. ● n.m. classic; (*auteur*) classical author.

clause /kloz/ n.f. clause.

claustration /klostrasjɔ̃/ n.f. confinement.

claustrophobie /klostrɔfɔbi/ n.f. claustrophobia.

clavecin /klavsɛ̃/ n.m. harpsichord.

clavicule /klavikyl/ n.f. collar-bone.

clavier /klavje/ n.m. keyboard.

claviste /klavist/ n.m./f. keyboarder.

clé, clef /kle/ n.f. key; (*outil*) spanner; (*mus.*) clef. ● a. invar. key. **~ anglaise,** (monkey-)wrench. **~ de contact,** ignition key. **~ de voûte,** keystone. **prix ~s en main,** (*voiture*) on-the-road price.

clémen|t, ~te /klemɑ̃, -t/ a. (*doux*) mild; (*indulgent*) lenient. **~ce** n.f. mildness; leniency.

clémentine /klemɑ̃tin/ n.f. clementine.

clerc /klɛr/ n.m. (*de notaire etc.*) clerk; (*relig.*) cleric.

clergé /klɛrʒe/ n.m. clergy.

cléric|al (*m. pl.* **~aux**) /klerikal, -o/ a. clerical.

cliché /kliʃe/ n.m. cliché; (*photo.*) negative.

client, ~e /klijɑ̃, -t/ n.m., f. customer; (*d'un avocat*) client; (*d'un*

médecin) patient; (*d'hôtel*) guest.
~èle /-tɛl/ *n.f.* customers, clientele;
(*d'un avocat*) clientele, clients, practice; (*d'un médecin*) practice, patients; (*soutien*) custom.

cligner /kliɲe/ *v.i.* **~ des yeux,** blink.
~ de l'œil, wink.

clignot|er /kliɲɔte/ *v.i.* blink; (*lumière*) flicker; (*comme signal*) flash.
~ant *n.m.* (*auto.*) indicator; (*auto.*, *Amer.*) directional signal.

climat /klima/ *n.m.* climate. **~ique**
/-tik/ *a.* climatic.

climatis|ation /klimatizɑsjɔ̃/ *n.f.* air-conditioning. **~é** *a.* air-conditioned.

clin d'œil /klɛ̃dœj/ *n.m.* wink. **en un
~,** in a flash.

clinique /klinik/ *a.* clinical. ● *n.f.*
(private) clinic.

clinquant, **~e** /klɛ̃kɑ̃, -t/ *a.* showy.

clip /klip/ *n.m.* video.

clique /klik/ *n.f.* clique; (*mus.*, *mil.*)
band.

cliquet|er /klikte/ *v.i.* clink. **~is** *n.m.*
clink(ing).

clitoris /klitɔris/ *n.m.* clitoris.

clivage /klivaʒ/ *n.m.* cleavage.

clochard, **~e** /klɔʃar, -d/ *n.m.*, *f.*
tramp.

cloch|e[1] /klɔʃ/ *n.f.* bell. **~ à fromage,** cheese-cover. **~ette** *n.f.* bell.

cloche[2] /klɔʃ/ *n.f.* (*fam.*) idiot.

cloche-pied (à) /(a)klɔʃpje/ *adv.* hopping on one foot.

clocher[1] /klɔʃe/ *n.m.* bell-tower;
(*pointu*) steeple. **de ~,** parochial.

clocher[2] /klɔʃe/ *v.i.* (*fam.*) be wrong.

cloison /klwazɔ̃/ *n.f.* partition; (*fig.*)
barrier. **~ner** /-ɔne/ *v.t.* partition;
(*personne*) cut off.

cloître /klwatr/ *n.m.* cloister.

cloîtrer (se) /(sə)klwatre/ *v. pr.* shut
o.s. away.

clopin-clopant /klɔpɛ̃klɔpɑ̃/ *adv.*
hobbling.

cloque /klɔk/ *n.f.* blister.

clore /klɔr/ *v.t.* close.

clos, **~e** /klo, -z/ *a.* closed.

clôtur|e /klotyr/ *n.f.* fence; (*fermeture*) closure. **~er** *v.t.* enclose;
(*festival, séance, etc.*) close.

clou /klu/ *n.m.* nail; (*furoncle*) boil;
(*de spectacle*) star attraction. **~ de
girofle,** clove. **les ~s,** (*passage*)
zebra *ou* pedestrian crossing. **~er**
v.t. nail down; (*fig.*) pin down.
être ~é au lit, be confined to
one's bed. **~er le bec à qn.,** shut
s.o. up.

clouté /klute/ *a.* studded.

clown /klun/ *n.m.* clown.

club /klœb/ *n.m.* club.

coaguler /kɔagyle/ *v.t./i.*, **se ~** *v. pr.*
coagulate.

coaliser (se) /(sə)kɔalize/ *v. pr.* join
forces.

coalition /kɔalisjɔ̃/ *n.f.* coalition.

coasser /kɔase/ *v.i.* croak.

cobaye /kɔbaj/ *n.m.* guinea-pig.

coca /kɔka/ *n.m.* (P.) Coke.

cocagne /kɔkaɲ/ *n.f.* **pays de ~,** land
of plenty.

cocaïne /kɔkain/ *n.f.* cocaine.

cocarde /kɔkard/ *n.f.* rosette.

cocard|ier, **~ière** /kɔkardje, -jɛr/ *a.*
chauvinistic.

cocasse /kɔkas/ *a.* comical.

coccinelle /kɔksinɛl/ *n.f.* ladybird;
(*Amer.*) ladybug; (*voiture*) beetle.

cocher[1] /kɔʃe/ *v.t.* tick (off), check.

cocher[2] /kɔʃe/ *n.m.* coachman.

cochon, **~ne** /kɔʃɔ̃, -ɔn/ *n.m.* pig.
● *n.m.*, *f.* (*personne: fam.*) pig. ● *a.*
(*fam.*) filthy. **~nerie** /-ɔnri/ *n.f.*
(*saleté: fam.*) filth; (*marchandise:
fam.*) rubbish.

cocktail /kɔktɛl/ *n.m.* cocktail; (*réunion*) cocktail party.

cocon /kɔkɔ̃/ *n.m.* cocoon.

cocorico /kɔkɔriko/ *n.m.* cock-a-doodle-doo.

cocotier /kɔkɔtje/ *n.m.* coconut palm.

cocotte /kɔkɔt/ *n.f.* (*marmite*)
casserole. **~ minute,** (P.) pressure-cooker. **ma ~,** (*fam.*) my sweet, my
dear.

cocu /kɔky/ *n.m.* (*fam.*) cuckold.

code /kɔd/ *n.m.* code. **~s, phares ~,**
dipped headlights. **~ de la route,**
Highway Code. **se mettre en ~,** dip
one's headlights.

coder /kɔde/ *v.t.* code.

codifier /kɔdifje/ *v.t.* codify.

coéquip|ier, **~ière** /kɔekipje, -jɛr/
n.m., *f.* team-mate.

cœur /kœr/ *n.m.* heart; (*cartes*)
hearts. **~ d'artichaut,** artichoke
heart. **~ de palmier,** heart of palm.
à ~ ouvert, (*opération*) open-heart;
(*parler*) freely. **avoir bon ~,** be
kind-hearted. **de bon ~,** with a good
heart. **par ~,** by heart. **avoir mal au
~,** feel sick. **je veux en avoir le ~
net,** I want to be clear in my own
mind (about it).

coexist|er /kɔɛgziste/ *v.i.* coexist.
~ence *n.f.* coexistence.

coffre /kɔfr/ n.m. chest; (*pour argent*) safe; (*auto.*) boot; (*auto.*, *Amer.*) trunk. **~-fort** (*pl.* **~-forts**) n.m. safe.

coffrer /kɔfre/ v.t. (*fam.*) lock up.

coffret /kɔfrɛ/ n.m. casket, box.

cognac /kɔɲak/ n.m. cognac.

cogner /kɔɲe/ v.t./i. knock. **se ~** v. pr. knock o.s.

cohabit|er /kɔabite/ v.i. live together. **~ation** n.f. living together.

cohérent, ~e /kɔerɑ̃, -t/ a. coherent.

cohésion /kɔezjɔ̃/ n.f. cohesion.

cohorte /kɔɔrt/ n.f. troop.

cohue /kɔy/ n.f. crowd.

coi, coite /kwa, -t/ a. silent.

coiffe /kwaf/ n.f. head-dress.

coiff|er /kwafe/ v.t. do the hair of; (*chapeau*) put on; (*surmonter*) cap. **~er qn. d'un chapeau,** put a hat on s.o. **se ~er** v. pr. do one's hair. **~é de,** wearing. **bien/mal ~é,** with tidy/untidy hair. **~eur, ~euse** n.m., f. hairdresser; n.f. dressing-table.

coiffure /kwafyr/ n.f. hairstyle; (*chapeau*) hat; (*métier*) hairdressing.

coin /kwɛ̃/ n.m. corner; (*endroit*) spot; (*cale*) wedge; (*pour graver*) die. **au ~ du feu,** by the fireside. **dans le ~,** locally. **du ~,** local. **le boulanger du ~,** the local baker.

coincer /kwɛ̃se/ v.t. jam; (*caler*) wedge; (*attraper: fam.*) catch. **se ~** v. pr. get jammed.

coïncid|er /kɔɛ̃side/ v.i. coincide. **~ence** n.f. coincidence.

coing /kwɛ̃/ n.m. quince.

coït /kɔit/ n.m. intercourse.

coite /kwat/ voir coi.

coke /kɔk/ n.m. coke.

col /kɔl/ n.m. collar; (*de bouteille*) neck; (*de montagne*) pass. **~ roulé,** polo-neck; (*Amer.*) turtle-neck. **~ de l'utérus,** cervix.

coléoptère /kɔleɔptɛr/ n.m. beetle.

colère /kɔlɛr/ n.f. anger; (*accès*) fit of anger. **en ~,** angry. **se mettre en ~,** lose one's temper.

colér|eux, ~euse /kɔlerø, -z/, **~ique** adjs. quick-tempered.

colibri /kɔlibri/ n.m. humming-bird.

colifichet /kɔlifiʃɛ/ n.m. trinket.

colimaçon (en) /(ɑ̃)kɔlimasɔ̃/ adv. spiral.

colin /kɔlɛ̃/ n.m. (*poisson*) hake.

colin-maillard /kɔlɛ̃majar/ n.m. **jouer à ~,** play blind man's buff.

colique /kɔlik/ n.f. diarrhoea; (*méd.*) colic.

colis /kɔli/ n.m. parcel.

collabor|er /kɔlabɔre/ v.i. collaborate (**à,** on). **~er à,** (*journal*) contribute to. **~ateur, ~atrice** n.m., f. collaborator; contributor. **~ation** n.f. collaboration (**à,** on); contribution (**à,** to).

collant, ~e /kɔlɑ̃, -t/ a. skin-tight; (*poisseux*) sticky. ● n.m. (*bas*) tights; (*de danseur*) leotard.

collation /kɔlasjɔ̃/ n.f. light meal.

colle /kɔl/ n.f. glue; (*en pâte*) paste; (*problème: fam.*) poser; (*scol., argot*) detention.

collect|e /kɔlɛkt/ n.f. collection. **~er** v.t. collect.

collecteur /kɔlɛktœr/ n.m. (*égout*) main sewer.

collecti|f, ~ve /kɔlɛktif, -v/ a. collective; (*billet, voyage*) group. **~vement** adv. collectively.

collection /kɔlɛksjɔ̃/ n.f. collection.

collectionn|er /kɔlɛksjɔne/ v.t. collect. **~eur, ~euse** n.m., f. collector.

collectivité /kɔlɛktivite/ n.f. community.

coll|ège /kɔlɛʒ/ n.m. (secondary) school; (*assemblée*) college. **~égien, ~égienne** n.m., f. schoolboy, schoolgirl.

collègue /kɔlɛg/ n.m./f. colleague.

coll|er /kɔle/ v.t. stick; (*avec colle liquide*) glue; (*affiche*) stick up; (*mettre: fam.*) stick; (*scol., argot*) keep in; (*par une question: fam.*) stump. ● v.i. stick (**à,** to); (*être collant*) be sticky. **~er à,** (*convenir à*) fit, correspond to. **être ~é à,** (*examen: fam.*) fail.

collet /kɔlɛ/ n.m. (*piège*) snare. **~ monté,** prim and proper. **prendre qn. au ~,** collar s.o.

collier /kɔlje/ n.m. necklace; (*de chien*) collar.

colline /kɔlin/ n.f. hill.

collision /kɔlizjɔ̃/ n.f. (*choc*) collision; (*lutte*) clash. **entrer en ~ (avec),** collide (with).

colloque /kɔlɔk/ n.m. symposium.

collyre /kɔlir/ n.m. eye drops.

colmater /kɔlmate/ v.t. seal; (*trou*) fill in.

colombe /kɔlɔ̃b/ n.f. dove.

Colombie /kɔlɔ̃bi/ n.f. Colombia.

colon /kɔlɔ̃/ n.m. settler.

colonel /kɔlɔnɛl/ n.m. colonel.

colon|ial, **~iale** (*m. pl.* **~iaux**) /kɔlɔnjal, -jo/ *a.* & *n.m.*, *f.* colonial.

colonie /kɔlɔni/ *n.f.* colony. **~ de vacances,** children's holiday camp.

coloniser /kɔlɔnize/ *v.t.* colonize.

colonne /kɔlɔn/ *n.f.* column. **~ vertébrale,** spine. **en ~ par deux,** in double file.

color|er /kɔlɔre/ *v.t.* colour; (*bois*) stain. **~ant** *n.m.* colouring. **~ation** *n.f.* (*couleur*) colour(ing).

colorier /kɔlɔrje/ *v.t.* colour (in).

coloris /kɔlɔri/ *n.m.* colour.

coloss|al (*m. pl.* **~aux**) /kɔlɔsal, -o/ *a.* colossal.

colosse /kɔlɔs/ *n.m.* giant.

colport|er /kɔlpɔrte/ *v.t.* hawk. **~eur, ~euse** *n.m.*, *f.* hawker.

colza /kɔlza/ *n.m.* rape(-seed).

coma /kɔma/ *n.m.* coma. **dans le ~,** in a coma.

combat /kɔ̃ba/ *n.m.* fight; (*sport*) match. **~s,** fighting.

combati|f, **~ve** /kɔ̃batif, -v/ *a.* eager to fight; (*esprit*) fighting.

combatt|re† /kɔ̃batr/ *v.t./i.* fight. **~ant, ~ante** *n.m.*, *f.* fighter; (*mil.*) combatant.

combien /kɔ̃bjɛ̃/ *adv.* **~ (de),** (*quantité*) how much; (*nombre*) how many; (*temps*) how long. **~ il a changé!,** (*comme*) how he has changed! **~y a-t-il d'ici à ...?,** how far is it to ...?

combinaison /kɔ̃binɛzɔ̃/ *n.f.* combination; (*manigance*) scheme; (*de femme*) slip; (*bleu de travail*) boiler suit; (*Amer.*) overalls; (*de plongée*) wetsuit. **~ d'aviateur,** flying-suit.

combine /kɔ̃bin/ *n.f.* trick; (*fraude*) fiddle.

combiné /kɔ̃bine/ *n.m.* (*de téléphone*) receiver.

combiner /kɔ̃bine/ *v.t.* (*réunir*) combine; (*calculer*) devise.

comble [1] /kɔ̃bl/ *a.* packed.

comble [2] /kɔ̃bl/ *n.m.* height. **~s,** (*mansarde*) attic, loft. **c'est le ~!,** that's the (absolute) limit!

combler /kɔ̃ble/ *v.t.* fill; (*perte, déficit*) make good; (*désir*) fulfil; (*personne*) gratify. **~ qn. de cadeaux/etc.,** lavish gifts/*etc.* on s.o.

combustible /kɔ̃bystibl/ *n.m.* fuel.

combustion /kɔ̃bystjɔ̃/ *n.f.* combustion.

comédie /kɔmedi/ *n.f.* comedy. **~ musicale,** musical. **jouer la ~,** put on an act.

comédien, **~ne** /kɔmedjɛ̃, -jɛn/ *n.m.*, *f.* actor, actress.

comestible /kɔmɛstibl/ *a.* edible. **~s** *n.m. pl.* foodstuffs.

comète /kɔmɛt/ *n.f.* comet.

comique /kɔmik/ *a.* comical; (*genre*) comic. **~** *n.m.* (*acteur*) comic; (*comédie*) comedy; (*côté drôle*) comical aspect.

comité /kɔmite/ *n.m.* committee.

commandant /kɔmɑ̃dɑ̃/ *n.m.* commander; (*armée de terre*) major. **~ (de bord),** captain. **~ en chef,** Commander-in-Chief.

commande /kɔmɑ̃d/ *n.f.* (*comm.*) order. **~s,** (*d'avion etc.*) controls.

command|er /kɔmɑ̃de/ *v.t.* command; (*acheter*) order. **•** *v.i.* be in command. **~er à,** (*maîtriser*) control. **~er à qn. de,** command s.o. to. **~ement** *n.m.* command; (*relig.*) commandment.

commando /kɔmɑ̃do/ *n.m.* commando.

comme /kɔm/ *conj.* as. **•** *prép.* like. **•** *adv.* (*exclamation*) how. **~ ci comme ça,** so-so. **~ d'habitude, ~ à l'ordinaire,** as usual. **~ il faut,** proper(ly). **~ pour faire,** as if to do. **~ quoi,** to the effect that. **qu'avez-vous ~ amis/etc.?,** what have you in the way of friends/*etc.*? **~ c'est bon!,** it's so good! **~ il est mignon!** isn't he sweet!

commémor|er /kɔmemɔre/ *v.t.* commemorate. **~ation** *n.f.* commemoration.

commenc|er /kɔmɑ̃se/ *v.t.* begin, start. **~er à faire,** begin *ou* start to do. **~ement** *n.m.* beginning, start.

comment /kɔmɑ̃/ *adv.* how. **~?,** (*répétition*) pardon?; (*surprise*) what? **~ est-il?,** what is he like? **le ~ et le pourquoi,** the whys and wherefores.

commentaire /kɔmɑ̃tɛr/ *n.m.* comment; (*d'un texte*) commentary.

comment|er /kɔmɑ̃te/ *v.t.* comment on. **~ateur, ~atrice** *n.m.*, *f.* commentator.

commérages /kɔmeraʒ/ *n.m. pl.* gossip.

commerçant, **~e** /kɔmɛrsɑ̃, -t/ *a.* (*rue*) shopping; (*personne*) business-minded. **•** *n.m.*, *f.* shopkeeper.

commerce /kɔmɛrs/ *n.m.* trade, commerce; (*magasin*) business. **faire du ~,** trade.

commerc|ial (m. pl. ~iaux) /kɔ-mɛrsjal, -jo/ a. commercial. ~iali-ser v.t. market. ~ialisable a. mar-ketable.

commère /kɔmɛr/ n.f. gossip.

commettre /kɔmɛtr/ v.t. commit.

commis /kɔmi/ n.m. (de magasin) assistant; (de bureau) clerk.

commissaire /kɔmisɛr/ n.m. (sport) steward. ~ (de police), (police) superintendent. ~-priseur (pl. ~s-priseurs) n.m. auctioneer.

commissariat /kɔmisarja/ n.m. ~ (de police), police station.

commission /kɔmisjɔ̃/ n.f. commis-sion; (course) errand; (message) message. ~s, shopping. ~naire /-jɔnɛr/ n.m. errand-boy.

commod|e /kɔmɔd/ a. handy; (facile) easy. pas ~e, (personne) a difficult customer. ● n.f. chest (of drawers). ~ité n.f. convenience.

commotion /kɔmosjɔ̃/ n.f. ~ (céré-brale), concussion. ~né /-jɔne/ a. shaken.

commuer /kɔmɥe/ v.t. commute.

commun, ~e /kɔmœ̃, -yn/ a. com-mon; (effort, action) joint; (frais, pièce) shared. ● n.f. (circonscrip-tion) commune. ~s n.m. pl. out-houses, outbuildings. **avoir** ou **mettre en ~**, share. **le ~ des mortels**, ordinary mortals. ~al (m. pl. ~aux) /-ynal, -o/ a. of the com-mune, local. ~ément /-ynemɑ̃/ adv. commonly.

communauté /kɔmynote/ n.f. community. ~ **des biens** (entre époux) shared estate.

commune /kɔmyn/ voir commun.

communiant, ~e /kɔmynjɑ̃, -t/ n.m., f. (relig.) communicant.

communicati|f, ~ve /kɔmynikatif, -v/ a. communicative.

communication /kɔmynikɑsjɔ̃/ n.f. communication; (téléphonique) call. ~ **interurbaine**, long-distance call.

commun|ier /kɔmynje/ v.i. (relig.) receive communion; (fig.) com-mune. ~ion n.f. communion.

communiqué /kɔmynike/ n.m. com-muniqué.

communiquer /kɔmynike/ v.t. pass on, communicate; (mouvement) impart. ● v.i. communicate. se ~ à, spread to.

communis|te /kɔmynist/ a. & n.m./f. communist. ~me n.m. communism.

commutateur /kɔmytatœr/ n.m. (électr.) switch.

compact /kɔpakt/ a. dense; (voiture) compact.

compact disc /kɔ̃paktdisk/ n.m. (P.) compact disc.

compagne /kɔ̃paɲ/ n.f. companion.

compagnie /kɔ̃paɲi/ n.f. company. **tenir ~ à**, keep company.

compagnon /kɔ̃paɲɔ̃/ n.m. compa-nion; (ouvrier) workman. ~ **de jeu**, playmate.

comparaître /kɔ̃parɛtr/ v.i. (jurid.) appear (**devant**, before).

compar|er /kɔ̃pare/ v.t. compare. ~er qch./qn. à ou et compare sth./ s.o. with ou and; se ~er v. pr. be compared. ~able a. comparable. ~aison n.f. comparison; (littéraire) simile. ~atif, ~ative a. & n.m. comparative. ~é a. comparative.

comparse /kɔ̃pars/ n.m./f. (péj.) stooge.

compartiment /kɔ̃partimɑ̃/ n.m. compartment. ~er /-te/ v.t. divide up.

comparution /kɔ̃parysjɔ̃/ n.f. (jurid.) appearance.

compas /kɔ̃pa/ n.m. (pair of) com-passes; (boussole) compass.

compassé /kɔ̃pase/ a. stilted.

compassion /kɔ̃pasjɔ̃/ n.f. compas-sion.

compatible /kɔ̃patibl/ a. compatible.

compatir /kɔ̃patir/ v.i. sympathize. ~ **à**, share in.

compatriote /kɔ̃patrijɔt/ n.m./f. compatriot.

compens|er /kɔ̃pɑse/ v.t. compensate for, make up for. ~ation n.f. com-pensation.

compère /kɔ̃pɛr/ n.m. accomplice.

compéten|t, ~te /kɔpetɑ̃, -t/ a. competent. ~ce n.f. competence.

compétiti|f, ~ve /kɔ̃petitif, -v/ a. competitive.

compétition /kɔ̃petisjɔ̃/ n.f. competi-tion; (sportive) event. **de ~**, compe-titive.

complainte /kɔ̃plɛ̃t/ n.f. lament.

complaire (se) /(sə)kɔ̃plɛr/ v. pr. se ~ **dans**, delight in.

complaisan|t, ~te /kɔ̃plɛzɑ̃, -t/ a. kind; (indulgent) indulgent. ~ce n.f. kindness; indulgence.

complément /kɔ̃plemɑ̃/ n.m. com-plement; (reste) rest. ~ (**d'objet**), (gram.) object. ~ **d'information**, further information. ~aire /-tɛr/ a.

complementary; (*renseignements*) supplementary.

compl|et [1], **~ète** /kɔ̃plɛ, -t/ *a.* complete; (*train, hôtel, etc.*) full. **~ètement** *adv.* completely.

complet [2] /kɔ̃plɛ/ *n.m.* suit.

compléter /kɔ̃plete/ *v.t.* complete; (*agrémenter*) complement. **se ~** *v. pr.* complement each other.

complex|e [1] /kɔ̃plɛks/ *a.* complex. **~ité** *n.f.* complexity.

complex|e [2] /kɔ̃plɛks/ *n.m.* (*sentiment, bâtiments*) complex. **~é** *a.* hung up.

complication /kɔ̃plikɑsjɔ̃/ *n.f.* complication; (*complexité*) complexity.

complic|e /kɔ̃plis/ *n.m.* accomplice. **~ité** *n.f.* complicity.

compliment /kɔ̃plimɑ̃/ *n.m.* compliment. **~s,** (*félicitations*) congratulations. **~er** /-te/ *v.t.* compliment.

compliqu|er /kɔ̃plike/ *v.t.* complicate. **se ~er** *v. pr.* become complicated. **~é** *a.* complicated.

complot /kɔ̃plo/ *n.m.* plot. **~er** /-ɔte/ *v.t./i.* plot.

comporter [1] /kɔ̃pɔrte/ *v.t.* contain; (*impliquer*) involve.

comport|er [2] (se) /(sə)kɔ̃pɔrte/ *v. pr.* behave; (*joueur*) perform. **~ement** *n.m.* behaviour; (*de joueur*) performance.

composé /kɔ̃poze/ *a.* compound; (*guindé*) affected. ● *n.m.* compound.

compos|er /kɔ̃poze/ *v.t.* make up, compose; (*chanson, visage*) compose; (*numéro*) dial. ● *v.i.* (*scol.*) take an exam; (*transiger*) compromise. **se ~er de,** be made up *ou* composed of. **~ant** *n.m.,* **~ante** *n.f.* component.

composi|teur, **~trice** /kɔ̃pozitœr, -tris/ *n.m., f.* (*mus.*) composer.

composition /kɔ̃pozisjɔ̃/ *n.f.* composition; (*examen*) test, exam.

composter /kɔ̃pɔste/ *v.t.* (*billet*) punch.

compot|e /kɔ̃pɔt/ *n.f.* stewed fruit. **~e de pommes,** stewed apples. **~ier** *n.m.* fruit dish.

compréhensible /kɔ̃preɑsibl/ *a.* understandable.

compréhensi|f, **~ve** /kɔ̃preɑsif, -v/ *a.* understanding.

compréhension /kɔ̃preɑsjɔ̃/ *n.f.* understanding, comprehension.

comprendre† /kɔ̃prɑ̃dr/ *v.t.* understand; (*comporter*) comprise. **ça se comprend,** that is understandable.

compresse /kɔ̃prɛs/ *n.f.* compress.

compression /kɔ̃prɛsjɔ̃/ *n.f.* (*physique*) compression, (*réduction*) reduction. **~ de personnel,** staff cuts.

comprimé /kɔ̃prime/ *n.m.* tablet.

comprimer /kɔ̃prime/ *v.t.* compress; (*réduire*) reduce.

compris, **~e** /kɔ̃pri, -z/ *a.* included; (*d'accord*) agreed. **~ entre,** (contained) between. **service (non) ~,** service (not) included, (not) including service. **tout ~,** (all) inclusive. **y ~,** including.

compromettre /kɔ̃prɔmɛtr/ *v.t.* compromise.

compromis /kɔ̃prɔmi/ *n.m.* compromise.

comptab|le /kɔ̃tabl/ *a.* accounting. ● *n.m.* accountant. **~ilité** *n.f.* accountancy; (*comptes*) accounts; (*service*) accounts department.

comptant /kɔ̃tɑ̃/ *adv.* (*payer*) (in) cash; (*acheter*) for cash.

compte /kɔ̃t/ *n.m.* count; (*facture, à la banque, comptabilité*) account; (*nombre exact*) right number. **demander/rendre des ~s,** ask for/give an explanation. **à bon ~,** cheaply. **s'en tirer à bon ~,** get off lightly. **à son ~,** (*travailler*) for o.s., on one's own. **faire le ~ de,** count. **pour le ~ de,** on behalf of. **sur le ~ de,** about. **~ à rebours,** countdown. **~-gouttes** *n.m. invar.* (*méd.*) dropper. **au ~-gouttes,** (*fig.*) in dribs and drabs. **~ rendu,** report; (*de film, livre*) review. **~-tours** *n.m. invar.* rev counter.

compter /kɔ̃te/ *v.t.* count; (*prévoir*) reckon; (*facturer*) charge for; (*avoir*) have; (*classer*) consider. ● *v.i.* (*calculer, importer*) count. **~ avec,** reckon with. **~ faire,** expect to do. **~ parmi,** (*figurer*) be considered among. **~ sur,** rely on.

compteur /kɔ̃tœr/ *n.m.* meter. **~ de vitesse,** speedometer.

comptine /kɔ̃tin/ *n.f.* nursery rhyme.

comptoir /kɔ̃twar/ *n.m.* counter; (*de café*) bar.

compulser /kɔ̃pylse/ *v.t.* examine.

comt|e, **~esse** /kɔ̃t, -ɛs/ *n.m., f.* count, countess.

comté /kɔ̃te/ *n.m.* county.

con, conne /kɔ̃, kɔn/ *a.* (*argot*) bloody foolish. ● *n.m., f.* (*argot*) bloody fool.

concave /kɔ̃kav/ *a.* concave.

concéder /kɔ̃sede/ *v.t.* grant, concede.

concentr|er /kɔ̃sɑ̃tre/ *v.t.*, **se ~er** *v. pr.* concentrate. **~ation** *n.f.* concentration. **~é** *a.* concentrated; (*lait*) condensed; (*personne*) absorbed; *n.m.* concentrate.

concept /kɔ̃sɛpt/ *n.m.* concept.

conception /kɔ̃sɛpsjɔ̃/ *n.f.* conception.

concerner /kɔ̃sɛrne/ *v.t.* concern. **en ce qui me concerne,** as far as I am concerned.

concert /kɔ̃sɛr/ *n.m.* concert. **de ~,** in unison.

concert|er /kɔ̃sɛrte/ *v.t.* organize, prepare. **se ~er** *v. pr.* confer. **~é** *a.* (*plan etc.*) concerted.

concerto /kɔ̃sɛrto/ *n.m.* concerto.

concession /kɔ̃sesjɔ̃/ *n.f.* concession; (*terrain*) plot.

concessionnaire /kɔ̃sesjɔnɛr/ *n.m./ f.* (authorized) dealer.

concevoir† /kɔ̃svwar/ *v.t.* (*imaginer, engendrer*) conceive; (*comprendre*) understand.

concierge /kɔ̃sjɛrʒ/ *n.m./f.* caretaker.

concile /kɔ̃sil/ *n.m.* council.

concil|ier /kɔ̃silje/ *v.t.* reconcile. **se ~ier** *v. pr.* (*s'attirer*) win (over). **~iation** *n.f.* conciliation.

concis, ~e /kɔ̃si, -z/ *a.* concise. **~ion** /-zjɔ̃/ *n.f.* concision.

concitoyen, ~ne /kɔ̃sitwajɛ̃, -jɛn/ *n.m., f.* fellow citizen.

concl|ure† /kɔ̃klyr/ *v.t./i.* conclude. **~ure à,** conclude in favour of. **~uant, ~uante** *a.* conclusive. **~usion** *n.f.* conclusion.

concocter /kɔ̃kɔkte/ *v.t.* (*fam.*) cook up.

concombre /kɔ̃kɔ̃br/ *n.m.* cucumber.

concorde /kɔ̃kɔrd/ *n.f.* concord.

concord|er /kɔ̃kɔrde/ *v.i.* agree. **~ance** *n.f.* agreement; (*analogie*) similarity. **~ant, ~ante** *a.* in agreement.

concourir /kɔ̃kurir/ *v.i.* compete. **~ à,** contribute towards.

concours /kɔ̃kur/ *n.m.* competition; (*examen*) competitive examination; aid; (*de circonstances*) combi-

concr|et, ~ète /kɔ̃krɛ, -t/ *a.* concrete. **~ètement** *adv.* in concrete terms.

concrétiser /kɔ̃kretize/ *v.t.* give concrete form to. **se ~** *v. pr.* materialize.

conçu /kɔ̃sy/ *a.* **bien/mal ~,** (*appartement etc.*) well/badly planned.

concubinage /kɔ̃kybinaʒ/ *n.m.* cohabitation.

concurrenc|e /kɔ̃kyrɑ̃s/ *n.f.* competition. **faire ~e à,** compete with. **jusqu'à ~e de,** up to. **~er** *v.t.* compete with.

concurrent, ~e /kɔ̃kyrɑ̃, -t/ *n.m., f.* competitor; (*scol.*) candidate. ● *a.* competing.

condamn|er /kɔ̃dane/ *v.t.* (*censurer, obliger*) condemn; (*jurid.*) sentence; (*porte*) block up. **~ation** *n.f.* condemnation; (*peine*) sentence. **~é** *a.* (*fichu*) without hope, doomed.

condens|er /kɔ̃dɑ̃se/ *v.t.*, **se ~er** *v. pr.* condense. **~ation** *n.f.* condensation.

condescendre /kɔ̃desɑ̃dr/ *v.i.* condescend (**à,** to).

condiment /kɔ̃dimɑ̃/ *n.m.* condiment.

condisciple /kɔ̃disipl/ *n.m.* classmate, schoolfellow.

condition /kɔ̃disjɔ̃/ *n.f.* condition. **~s,** (*prix*) terms. **à ~ de** *ou* **que,** provided (that). **sans ~,** unconditional(ly). **sous ~,** conditionally. **~nel, ~nelle** /-jɔnɛl/ *a.* conditional. **~nel** *n.m.* conditional (tense).

conditionnement /kɔ̃disjɔnmɑ̃/ *n.m.* conditioning; (*emballage*) packaging.

conditionner /kɔ̃disjɔne/ *v.t.* condition; (*emballer*) package.

condoléances /kɔ̃dɔleɑ̃s/ *n.f. pl.* condolences.

conduc|teur, ~trice /kɔ̃dyktœr, -tris/ *n.m., f.* driver.

conduire† /kɔ̃dɥir/ *v.t.* lead; (*auto.*) drive; (*affaire*) conduct. ● *v.i.* drive. **se ~** *v. pr.* behave. **~ à,** (*accompagner à*) take to.

conduit /kɔ̃dɥi/ *n.m.* (*anat.*) duct.

conduite /kɔ̃dɥit/ *n.f.* conduct; (*auto.*) driving; (*tuyau*) main. **~ à droite,** (*place*) right-hand drive.

cône /kon/ *n.m.* cone.

confection /kɔ̃fɛksjɔ̃/ *n.f.* making. **de ~,** ready-made. **la ~,** the clothing industry. **~ner** /-jɔne/ *v.t.* make.

confédération /kɔ̃federasjɔ̃/ *n.f.* confederation.

conférenc|e /kɔ̃ferɑ̃s/ *n.f.* conference; (*exposé*) lecture. ~e au sommet, summit conference. ~ier, ~ière *n.m.*, *f.* lecturer.

conférer /kɔ̃fere/ *v.t.* give; (*décerner*) confer.

confess|er /kɔ̃fese/ *v.t.*, se ~er *v. pr.* confess. ~eur *n.m.* confessor. ~ion *n.f.* confession; (*religion*) denomination. ~ionnal (*pl.* ~ionnaux) *n.m.* confessional. ~ionnel, ~ionnelle *a.* denominational.

confettis /kɔ̃feti/ *n.m. pl.* confetti.

confiance /kɔ̃fjɑ̃s/ *n.f.* trust. avoir ~ en, trust.

confiant, ~e /kɔ̃fjɑ̃, -t/ *a.* (*assure*) confident; (*sans défiance*) trusting. ~ en *ou* dans, confident in.

confiden|t, ~te /kɔ̃fidɑ̃, -t/ *n.m.*, *f.* confidant, confidante. ~ce *n.f.* confidence.

confidentiel, ~le /kɔ̃fidɑ̃sjɛl/ *a.* confidential.

confier /kɔ̃fje/ *v.t.* ~ à qn., entrust s.o. with; (*secret*) confide to s.o. se ~ à, confide in.

configuration /kɔ̃figyrasjɔ̃/ *n.f.* configuration.

confiner /kɔ̃fine/ *v.t.* confine. ● *v.i.* ~ à, border on. se ~ *v. pr.* confine o.s. (à, dans, to).

confins /kɔ̃fɛ̃/ *n.m. pl.* confines.

confirm|er /kɔ̃firme/ *v.t.* confirm. ~ation *n.f.* confirmation.

confis|erie /kɔ̃fizri/ *n.f.* sweet shop. ~eries, confectionery. ~eur, ~euse *n.m.*, *f.* confectioner.

confis|quer /kɔ̃fiske/ *v.t.* confiscate. ~cation *n.f.* confiscation.

confit, ~e /kɔ̃fi, -t/ *a.* (*culin.*) candied. fruits ~s, crystallized fruits. ● *n.m.* ~ d'oie, goose liver conserve.

confiture /kɔ̃fityr/ *n.f.* jam.

conflit /kɔ̃fli/ *n.m.* conflict.

confondre /kɔ̃fɔ̃dr/ *v.t.* confuse, mix up; (*consterner, étonner*) confound. se ~ *v. pr.* merge. se ~ en excuses, apologize profusely.

confondu /kɔ̃fɔ̃dy/ *a.* (*déconcerté*) overwhelmed, confounded.

conforme /kɔ̃fɔrm/ *a.* ~ à, in accordance with.

conformément /kɔ̃fɔrmemɑ̃/ *adv.* ~ à, in accordance with.

conform|er /kɔ̃fɔrme/ *v.t.* adapt. se ~er à, conform to. ~ité *n.f.* conformity.

conformis|te /kɔ̃fɔrmist/ *a.* & *n.m.*/*f.* conformist. ~me *n.m.* conformism.

confort /kɔ̃fɔr/ *n.m.* comfort. tout ~, with all mod cons. ~able /-tabl/ *a.* comfortable.

confrère /kɔ̃frɛr/ *n.m.* colleague.

confrérie /kɔ̃freri/ *n.f.* brotherhood.

confront|er /kɔ̃frɔ̃te/ *v.t.* confront; (*textes*) compare. se ~er à *v. pr.* confront. ~ation *n.f.* confrontation.

confus, ~e /kɔ̃fy, -z/ *a.* confused; (*gêné*) embarrassed.

confusion /kɔ̃fyzjɔ̃/ *n.f.* confusion; (*gêné*) embarrassment.

congé /kɔ̃ʒe/ *n.m.* holiday; (*arrêt momentané*) time off; (*mil.*) leave; (*avis de départ*) notice. ~ de maladie, sick-leave. ~ de maternité, maternity leave. jour de ~, day off. prendre ~ de, take one's leave of.

congédier /kɔ̃ʒedje/ *v.t.* dismiss.

congel|er /kɔ̃ʒle/ *v.t.* freeze. les ~elés, frozen food. ~élateur *n.m.* freezer.

congénère /kɔ̃ʒenɛr/ *n.m.*/*f.* fellow creature.

congénit|al (*m. pl.* ~aux) /kɔ̃ʒenital, -o/ *a.* congenital.

congère /kɔ̃ʒɛr/ *n.f.* snow-drift.

congestion /kɔ̃ʒɛstjɔ̃/ *n.f.* congestion. ~ cérébrale, stroke, cerebral haemorrhage. ~ner /-jɔne/ *v.t.* congest; (*visage*) flush.

congrégation /kɔ̃gregasjɔ̃/ *n.f.* congregation.

congrès /kɔ̃grɛ/ *n.m.* congress.

conifère /kɔnifɛr/ *n.m.* conifer.

conique /kɔnik/ *a.* conic(al).

conjectur|e /kɔ̃ʒɛktyr/ *n.f.* conjecture. ~er *v.t.*/*i.* conjecture.

conjoint, ~e[1] /kɔ̃ʒwɛ̃, -t/ *n.m.*, *f.* spouse.

conjoint, ~e[2] /kɔ̃ʒwɛ̃, -t/ *a.* joint. ~ement /-tmɑ̃/ *adv.* jointly.

conjonction /kɔ̃ʒɔ̃ksjɔ̃/ *n.f.* conjunction.

conjonctivite /kɔ̃ʒɔ̃ktivit/ *n.f.* conjunctivitis.

conjoncture /kɔ̃ʒɔ̃ktyr/ *n.f.* circumstances; (*économique*) economic climate.

conjugaison /kɔ̃ʒygɛzɔ̃/ *n.f.* conjugation.

conjug|al (*m. pl.* ~aux) /kɔ̃ʒygal, -o/ *a.* conjugal.

conjuguer /kɔ̃ʒyge/ *v.t.* (*gram.*) conjugate; (*efforts*) combine. **se ~** *v. pr.* (*gram.*) be conjugated.

conjur|er /kɔ̃ʒyre/ *v.t.* (*éviter*) avert; (*implorer*) entreat. **~ation** *n.f.* conspiracy. **~é, ~ée** *n.m., f.* conspirator.

connaissance /kɔnɛsɑ̃s/ *n.f.* knowledge; (*personne*) acquaintance. **~s,** (*science*) knowledge. **faire la ~ de,** meet; (*personne connue*) get to know. **perdre ~,** lose consciousness. **sans ~,** unconscious.

connaisseur /kɔnɛsœr/ *n.m.* connoisseur.

connaître† /kɔnɛtr/ *v.t.* know; (*avoir*) have. **se ~** *v. pr.* (*se rencontrer*) meet. **faire ~,** make known. **s'y ~ à** *ou* **en,** know (all) about.

conne|cter /kɔnɛkte/ *v.t.* connect. **~xion** *n.f.* connection.

connerie /kɔnri/ *n.f.* (*argot*) (*remarque*) rubbish. **faire une ~,** do sth. stupid. **dire une ~,** talk rubbish. **quelle ~!,** how stupid!

connivence /kɔnivɑ̃s/ *n.f.* connivance.

connotation /kɔnɔtasjɔ̃/ *n.f.* connotation.

connu /kɔny/ *a.* well-known.

conquér|ir /kɔ̃kerir/ *v.t.* conquer. **~ant, ~ante** *n.m., f.* conqueror.

conquête /kɔ̃kɛt/ *n.f.* conquest.

consacrer /kɔ̃sakre/ *v.t.* devote; (*relig.*) consecrate; (*sanctionner*) establish. **se ~** *v. pr.* devote o.s. (**à,** to).

consciemment /kɔ̃sjamɑ̃/ *adv.* consciously.

conscience /kɔ̃sjɑ̃s/ *n.f.* conscience; (*perception*) consciousness. **avoir/ prendre ~ de,** be/become aware of. **perdre ~,** lose consciousness. **avoir bonne/mauvaise ~,** have a clear/guilty conscience.

consciencieu|x, ~se /kɔ̃sjɑ̃sjø, -z/ *a.* conscientious.

conscient, ~e /kɔ̃sjɑ̃, -t/ *a.* conscious. **~ de,** aware *ou* conscious of.

conscrit /kɔ̃skri/ *n.m.* conscript.

consécration /kɔ̃sekrasjɔ̃/ *n.f.* consecration.

consécuti|f, ~ve /kɔ̃sekytif, -v/ *a.* consecutive. **~f à,** following upon. **~vement** *adv.* consecutively.

conseil /kɔ̃sɛj/ *n.m.* (piece of) advice; (*assemblée*) council, committee; (*séance*) meeting; (*personne*) consultant. **~ d'administration,** board of directors. **~ des ministres,** Cabinet. **~ municipal,** town council.

conseiller[1] /kɔ̃seje/ *v.t.* advise. **~ à qn. de,** advise s.o. to. **~ qch. à qn.,** recommend sth. to s.o.

conseill|er[2], **~ère** /kɔ̃seje, -ɛjɛr/ *n.m., f.* adviser, counsellor. **~er municipal,** town councillor.

consent|ir /kɔ̃sɑ̃tir/ *v.i.* agree (**à,** to). ● *v.t.* grant. **~ement** *n.m.* consent.

conséquence /kɔ̃sekɑ̃s/ *n.f.* consequence. **en ~,** consequently; (*comme il convient*) accordingly.

conséquent, ~e /kɔ̃sekɑ̃, -t/ *a.* logical; (*important: fam.*) sizeable. **par ~,** consequently.

conserva|teur, ~trice kɔ̃sɛrvatœr, -tris/ *a.* conservative. ● *n.m., f.* (*pol.*) conservative. ● *n.m.* (*de musée*) curator. **~tisme** *n.m.* conservatism.

conservatoire /kɔ̃sɛrvatwar/ *n.m.* academy.

conserve /kɔ̃sɛrv/ *n.f.* tinned *ou* canned food. **en ~,** tinned, canned.

conserv|er /kɔ̃sɛrve/ *v.t.* keep; (*en bon état*) preserve; (*culin.*) preserve. **se ~er** *v. pr.* (*culin.*) keep. **~ation** *n.f.* preservation.

considérable /kɔ̃siderabl/ *a.* considerable.

considération /kɔ̃siderasjɔ̃/ *n.f.* consideration; (*respect*) regard. **prendre en ~,** take into consideration.

considérer /kɔ̃sidere/ *v.t.* consider; (*respecter*) esteem. **~ comme,** consider to be.

consigne /kɔ̃siɲ/ *n.f.* (*de gare*) left luggage (office); (*Amer.*) (baggage) checkroom; (*scol.*) detention; (*somme*) deposit; (*ordres*) orders. **~ automatique,** (left-luggage) lockers; (*Amer.*) (baggage) lockers.

consigner /kɔ̃siɲe/ *v.t.* (*comm.*) charge a deposit on; (*écrire*) record; (*élève*) keep in; (*soldat*) confine.

consistan|t, ~te /kɔ̃sistɑ̃, -t/ *a.* solid; (*épais*) thick. **~ce** *n.f.* consistency; (*fig.*) solidity.

consister /kɔ̃siste/ *v.i.* **~ en/dans,** consist of/in. **~ à faire,** consist in doing.

consœur /kɔ̃sœr/ *n.f.* colleague; fellow member.

consol|er /kɔ̃sɔle/ *v.t.* console. **se ~er** *v. pr.* be consoled (**de,** for). **~ation** *n.f.* consolation.

consolider /kɔ̃sɔlide/ v.t. strengthen; (fig.) consolidate.

consomma|teur, ~trice /kɔ̃sɔmatœr, -tris/ n.m., f. (comm.) consumer; (dans un café) customer.

consommé [1] /kɔ̃sɔme/ a. consummate.

consommé [2] /kɔ̃sɔme/ n.m. (bouillon) consommé.

consomm|er /kɔ̃sɔme/ v.t. consume; (user) use, consume; (mariage) consummate. ● v.i. drink. ~ation n.f. consumption; consummation; (boisson) drink. **de ~ation,** (comm.) consumer.

consonne /kɔ̃sɔn/ n.f. consonant.

consortium /kɔ̃sɔrsjɔm/ n.m. consortium.

conspir|er /kɔ̃spire/ v.i. conspire. ~ateur, ~atrice n.m., f. conspirator. ~ation n.f. conspiracy.

conspuer /kɔ̃spɥe/ v.t. boo.

const|ant, ~ante /kɔ̃stɑ̃, -t/ a. constant. ● n.f. constant. ~amment /-amɑ̃/ adv. constantly. ~ance n.f. constancy.

constat /kɔ̃sta/ n.m. (official) report.

constat|er /kɔ̃state/ v.t. note; (certifier) certify. ~ation n.f. observation, statement of fact.

constellation /kɔ̃stelasjɔ̃/ n.f. constellation.

constellé /kɔ̃stele/ a. ~ de, studded with.

constern|er /kɔ̃stɛrne/ v.t. dismay. ~ation n.f. dismay.

constip|é /kɔ̃stipe/ a. constipated; (fig.) stilted. ~ation n.f. constipation.

constitu|er /kɔ̃stitɥe/ v.t. make up, constitute; (organiser) form; (être) constitute. **se ~er prisonnier,** give o.s. up. **~é de,** made up of.

constituti|f, ~ve /kɔ̃stitytif, -v/ a. constituent.

constitution /kɔ̃stitysjɔ̃/ n.f. formation; (d'une équipe) composition; (pol., méd.) constitution. ~nel, ~nelle /-jɔnɛl/ a. constitutional.

constructeur /kɔ̃stryktœr/ n.m. manufacturer.

constructi|f, ~ve /kɔ̃stryktif, -v/ a. constructive.

constr|uire† /kɔ̃strɥir/ v.t. build; (système, phrase, etc.) construct. ~uction n.f. building; (structure) construction.

consul /kɔ̃syl/ n.m. consul. ~aire a. consular. ~at n.m. consulate.

consult|er /kɔ̃sylte/ v.t. consult. ● v.i. (médecin) hold surgery; (Amer.) hold office hours. **se ~er** v. pr. confer. ~ation n.f. consultation; (réception: méd.) surgery; (Amer.) office.

consumer /kɔ̃syme/ v.t. consume. **se ~** v. pr. be consumed.

contact /kɔ̃takt/ n.m. contact; (toucher) touch. **au ~ de,** on contact with; (personne) by contact with, by seeing. **mettre/couper le ~,** (auto.) switch on/off the ignition. **prendre ~ avec,** get in touch with. ~er v.t. contact.

contag|ieux, ~ieuse /kɔ̃taʒjø, -z/ a. contagious. ~ion n.f. contagion.

container /kɔ̃tɛnɛr/ n.m. container.

contamin|er /kɔ̃tamine/ v.t. contaminate. ~ation n.f. contamination.

conte /kɔ̃t/ n.m. tale. **~ de fées,** fairy tale.

contempl|er /kɔ̃tɑ̃ple/ v.t. contemplate. ~ation n.f. contemplation.

contemporain, ~e /kɔ̃tɑ̃pɔrɛ̃, -ɛn/ a. & n.m., f. contemporary.

contenance /kɔ̃tnɑ̃s/ n.f. (contenu) capacity; (allure) bearing; (sang-froid) composure.

conteneur /kɔ̃tnœr/ n.m. container.

contenir† /kɔ̃tnir/ v.t. contain; (avoir une capacité de) hold. **se ~** v. pr. contain o.s.

content, ~e /kɔ̃tɑ̃, -t/ a. pleased (de, with). **~ de faire,** pleased to do.

content|er /kɔ̃tɑ̃te/ v.t. satisfy. **se ~er de,** content o.s. with. ~ement n.m. contentment.

contentieux /kɔ̃tɑ̃sjø/ n.m. matters in dispute; (service) legal department.

contenu /kɔ̃tny/ n.m. (de contenant) contents; (de texte) content.

conter /kɔ̃te/ v.t. tell, relate.

contestataire /kɔ̃tɛstatɛr/ n.m./f. protester.

conteste (sans) /(sɑ̃)kɔ̃tɛst/ adv. indisputably.

contest|er /kɔ̃tɛste/ v.t. dispute; (s'opposer) protest against. ● v.i. protest. ~able a. debatable. ~ation n.f. dispute; (opposition) protest.

conteu|r, ~se /kɔ̃tœr, -øz/ n.m., f. story-teller.

contexte /kɔ̃tɛkst/ n.m. context.

contigu, ~ë /kɔ̃tigy/ *a.* adjacent (à, to).

continent /kɔ̃tinɑ̃/ *n.m.* continent. ~al (*m. pl.* ~aux) /-tal, -to/ *a.* continental.

contingences /kɔ̃tɛ̃ʒɑ̃s/ *n.f. pl.* contingencies.

contingent /kɔ̃tɛ̃ʒɑ̃/ *n.m.* (*mil.*) contingent; (*comm.*) quota.

continu /kɔ̃tiny/ *a.* continuous.

continuel, ~le /kɔ̃tinɥɛl/ *a.* continual. ~lement *adv.* continually.

contin|uer /kɔ̃tinɥe/ *v.t.* continue. ● *v.i.* continue, go on. ~uer à *ou de* faire, carry on *ou* go on *ou* continue doing. ~uation *n.f.* continuation.

continuité /kɔ̃tinɥite/ *n.f.* continuity.

contorsion /kɔ̃tɔrsjɔ̃/ *n.f.* contortion. se ~ner *v. pr.* wriggle.

contour /kɔ̃tur/ *n.m.* outline, contour. ~s, (*d'une route etc.*) twists and turns, bends.

contourner /kɔ̃turne/ *v.t.* go round; (*difficulté*) get round.

contracepti|f, ~ve /kɔ̃trasɛptif, -v/ *a. & n.m.* contraceptive.

contraception /kɔ̃trasɛpsjɔ̃/ *n.f.* contraception.

contract|er /kɔ̃trakte/ *v.t.* (*maladie, dette*) contract; (*muscle*) tense, contract; (*assurance*) take out. se ~er *v. pr.* contract. ~é *a.* tense. ~ion /-ksjɔ̃/ *n.f.* contraction.

contractuel, ~le /kɔ̃traktɥɛl/ *n.m., f.* (*agent*) traffic warden.

contradiction /kɔ̃tradiksjɔ̃/ *n.f.* contradiction.

contradictoire /kɔ̃tradiktwar/ *a.* contradictory; (*débat*) open.

contraignant, ~e /kɔ̃trɛɲɑ̃, -t/ *a.* restricting.

contraindre† /kɔ̃trɛ̃dr/ *v.t.* compel.

contraint, ~e /kɔ̃trɛ̃, -t/ *a.* constrained. ● *n.f.* constraint.

contraire /kɔ̃trɛr/ *a. & n.m.* opposite. ~ à, contrary to. au ~, on the contrary. ~ment *adv.* ~ment à, contrary to.

contralto /kɔ̃tralto/ *n.m.* contralto.

contrar|ier /kɔ̃trarje/ *v.t.* annoy; (*action*) frustrate. ~iété *n.f.* annoyance.

contrast|e /kɔ̃trast/ *n.m.* contrast. ~er *v.i.* contrast.

contrat /kɔ̃tra/ *n.m.* contract.

contravention /kɔ̃travɑ̃sjɔ̃/ *n.f.* (parking-)ticket. en ~, in contravention (à, of).

contre /kɔ̃tr(ə)/ *prép.* against; (*en échange de*) for. par ~, on the other hand. tout ~, close by. ~-attaque *n.f.,* ~-attaquer *v.t.* counter-attack. ~-balancer *v.t.* counterbalance. ~-courant *n.m.* aller à ~-courant de, swim against the current of. ~indiqué *a.* (*méd.*) contra-indicated; (*déconseillé*) not recommended. à ~-jour *adv.* against the (sun)light. ~-offensive *n.f.* counter-offensive. prendre le ~-pied, do the opposite; (*opinion*) take the opposite view. à ~-pied *adv.* (*sport*) on the wrong foot. ~plaqué *n.m.* plywood. ~-révolution *n.f.* counter-revolution. ~-torpilleur *n.m.* destroyer.

contreband|e /kɔ̃trəbɑ̃d/ *n.f.* contraband. faire la ~e de, passer en ~e, smuggle. ~ier *n.m.* smuggler.

contrebas (en) /(ɑ̃)kɔ̃trəba/ *adv. & prép.* en ~ (de), below.

contrebasse /kɔ̃trəbas/ *n.f.* double-bass.

contrecarrer /kɔ̃trəkare/ *v.t.* thwart.

contrecœur (à) /(a)kɔ̃trəkœr/ *adv.* reluctantly.

contrecoup /kɔ̃trəku/ *n.m.* consequence.

contredire† /kɔ̃trədir/ *v.t.* contradict. se ~ *v. pr.* contradict o.s.

contrée /kɔ̃tre/ *n.f.* region, land.

contrefaçon /kɔ̃trəfasɔ̃/ *n.f.* (*objet imité, action*) forgery.

contrefaire /kɔ̃trəfɛr/ *v.t.* (*falsifier*) forge; (*parodier*) mimic; (*déguiser*) disguise.

contrefait, ~e /kɔ̃trəfɛ, -t/ *a.* deformed.

contreforts /kɔ̃trəfɔr/ *n.m. pl.* foothills.

contremaître /kɔ̃trəmɛtr/ *n.m.* foreman.

contrepartie /kɔ̃trəparti/ *n.f.* compensation. en ~, in exchange, in return.

contrepoids /kɔ̃trəpwa/ *n.m.* counterbalance.

contrer /kɔ̃tre/ *v.t.* counter.

contresens /kɔ̃trəsɑ̃s/ *n.m.* misinterpretation; (*absurdité*) nonsense. à ~, the wrong way.

contresigner /kɔ̃trəsiɲe/ *v.t.* countersign.

contretemps /kɔ̃trətɑ̃/ *n.m.* hitch. **à ~,** at the wrong time.

contrevenir /kɔ̃trəvnir/ *v.i.* **~ à,** contravene.

contribuable /kɔ̃tribɥabl/ *n.m./f.* taxpayer.

contribuer /kɔ̃tribɥe/ *v.t.* contribute (**à,** towards).

contribution /kɔ̃tribysjɔ̃/ *n.f.* contribution. **~s,** (*impôts*) taxes; (*administration*) tax office.

contrit, ~e /kɔ̃tri, -t/ *a.* contrite.

contrôl|e /kɔ̃trol/ *n.m.* check; (*des prix, d'un véhicule*) control; (*poinçon*) hallmark; (*scol.*) test. **~e continu,** continuous assessment. **~e de soi-même,** self-control. **~e des changes,** exchange control. **~e des naissances** birth-control. **~er** *v.t.* check; (*surveiller, maîtriser*) control. **se ~er** *v. pr.* control o.s.

contrôleu|r, ~se /kɔ̃trolœr, -øz/ *n.m., f.* (bus) conductor *ou* conductress; (*de train*) (ticket) inspector.

contrordre /kɔ̃trɔrdr/ *n.m.* change of orders.

controvers|e /kɔ̃trɔvɛrs/ *n.f.* controversy. **~é** *a.* controversial.

contumace (par) /(par)kɔ̃tymas/ *adv.* in one's absence.

contusion /kɔ̃tyzjɔ̃/ *n.f.* bruise. **~né** /-jɔne/ *a.* bruised.

convaincre† /kɔ̃vɛ̃kr/ *v.t.* convince. **~ qn. de faire,** persuade s.o. to do.

convalescen|t, ~te /kɔ̃valesɑ̃, -t/ *a. & n.m., f.* convalescent. **~ce** *n.f.* convalescence. **être en ~ce,** convalesce.

convenable /kɔ̃vnabl/ *a.* (*correct*) decent, proper; (*approprié*) suitable.

convenance /kɔ̃vnɑ̃s/ *n.f.* **à sa ~,** to one's satisfaction. **les ~s,** the proprieties.

convenir† /kɔ̃vnir/ *v.i.* be suitable. **~ à** suit. **~ de/que,** (*avouer*) admit (to)/that. **~ de qch.,** (*s'accorder sur*) agree on sth. **~ de faire,** agree to do. **il convient de,** it is advisable to; (*selon les bienséances*) it would be right to.

convention /kɔ̃vɑ̃sjɔ̃/ *n.f.* convention. **~s,** (*convenances*) convention. **de ~,** conventional. **~ collective,** industrial agreement. **~né** *a.* (*prix*) official; (*médecin*) health service (*not private*). **~nel, ~nelle** /-jɔnɛl/ *a.* conventional.

convenu /kɔ̃vny/ *a.* agreed.

converger /kɔ̃vɛrʒe/ *v.i.* converge.

convers|er /kɔ̃vɛrse/ *v.i.* converse. **~ation** *n.f.* conversation.

conver|tir /kɔ̃vɛrtir/ *v.t.* convert (**à,** to; **en,** into). **se ~tir** *v. pr.* be converted, convert. **~sion** *n.f.* conversion. **~tible** *a.* convertible.

convexe /kɔ̃vɛks/ *a.* convex.

conviction /kɔ̃viksjɔ̃/ *n.f.* conviction.

convier /kɔ̃vje/ *v.t.* invite.

convive /kɔ̃viv/ *n.m./f.* guest.

conviv|ial (*m. pl.* **~iaux**) /kɔ̃vivjal, -jo/ *a.* convivial; (*comput.*) userfriendly.

convocation /kɔ̃vɔkasjɔ̃/ *n.f.* summons to attend; (*d'une assemblée*) convening; (*document*) notification to attend.

convoi /kɔ̃vwa/ *n.m.* convoy; (*train*) train. **~ (funèbre),** funeral procession.

convoit|er /kɔ̃vwate/ *v.t.* desire, covet, envy. **~ise** *n.f.* desire, envy.

convoquer /kɔ̃vɔke/ *v.t.* (*assemblée*) convene; (*personne*) summon.

convoy|er /kɔ̃vwaje/ *v.t.* escort. **~eur** *n.m.* escort ship. **~eur de fonds,** security guard.

convulsion /kɔ̃vylsjɔ̃/ *n.f.* convulsion.

cool /kul/ *a. invar.* cool, laidback.

coopérati|f, ~ve /kɔɔperatif, -v/ *a.* co-operative. ● *n.f.* co-operative (society).

coopér|er /kɔɔpere/ *v.i.* co-operate (**à, in**). **~ation** *n.f.* co-operation. **la C~ation,** civilian national service.

coopter /kɔɔpte/ *v.t.* co-opt.

coordination /kɔɔrdinasjɔ̃/ *n.f.* co-ordination.

coordonn|er /kɔɔrdɔne/ *v.t.* co-ordinate. **~ées** *n.f. pl.* co-ordinates; (*adresse*: *fam.*) particulars.

copain /kɔpɛ̃/ *n.m.* (*fam.*) pal; (*petit ami*) boyfriend.

copeau (*pl.* **~x**) /kɔpo/ *n.m.* (*lamelle de bois*) shaving.

cop|ie /kɔpi/ *n.f.* copy; (*scol.*) paper. **~ier** *v.t./i.* copy. **~ier sur,** (*scol.*) copy *ou* crib from.

copieu|x, ~se /kɔpjø, -z/ *a.* copious.

copine /kɔpin/ *n.f.* (*fam.*) pal; (*petite amie*) girlfriend.

copiste /kɔpist/ *n.m./f.* copyist.

coproduction /kɔprɔdyksjɔ̃/ *n.f.* co-production.

copropriété /kɔprɔprijete/ *n.f.* co-ownership.

copulation /kɔpylasjɔ̃/ *n.f.* copulation.

coq /kɔk/ *n.m.* cock. **~-à-l'âne** *n.m. invar.* abrupt change of subject.

coque /kɔk/ *n.f.* shell; (*de bateau*) hull.

coquelicot /kɔkliko/ *n.m.* poppy.

coqueluche /kɔklyʃ/ *n.f.* whooping cough.

coquet, **~te** /kɔkɛ, -t/ *a.* flirtatious; (*élégant*) pretty; (*somme. fam.*) tidy. **~terie** /-tri/ *n.f.* flirtatiousness.

coquetier /kɔktje/ *n.m.* egg-cup.

coquillage /kɔkijaʒ/ *n.m.* shellfish; (*coquille*) shell.

coquille /kɔkij/ *n.f.* shell; (*faute*) misprint. **~ Saint-Jacques,** scallop.

coquin, **~e** /kɔkɛ̃, -in/ *a.* naughty. ● *n.m., f.* rascal.

cor /kɔr/ *n.m.* (*mus.*) horn; (*au pied*) corn.

cor|ail (*pl.* **~aux**) /kɔraj, -o/ *n.m.* coral.

Coran /kɔrɑ̃/ *n.m.* Koran.

corbeau (*pl.* **~x**) /kɔrbo/ *n.m.* (*oiseau*) crow.

corbeille /kɔrbɛj/ *n.f.* basket. **~ à papier,** waste-paper basket.

corbillard /kɔrbijar/ *n.m.* hearse.

cordage /kɔrdaʒ/ *n.m.* rope. **~s,** (*naut.*) rigging.

corde /kɔrd/ *n.f.* rope; (*d'arc, de violon, etc.*) string. **~ à linge,** washing line. **~ à sauter,** skipping-rope. **~ raide,** tightrope. **~s vocales,** vocal cords.

cordée /kɔrde/ *n.f.* roped party.

cord|ial (*m. pl.* **~iaux**) /kɔrdjal, -jo/ *a.* warm, cordial. **~ialité** *n.f.* warmth.

cordon /kɔrdɔ̃/ *n.m.* string, cord. **~-bleu** (*pl.* **~s-bleus**) *n.m.* first-rate cook. **~ de police,** police cordon.

cordonnier /kɔrdɔnje/ *n.m.* shoe mender.

Corée /kɔre/ *n.f.* Korea.

coreligionnaire /kɔrəliʒjɔnɛr/ *n.m./ f.* person of the same religion.

coriace /kɔrjas/ *a.* (*aliment*) tough. ● *a. & n.m.* tenacious and tough (person).

corne /kɔrn/ *n.f.* horn.

cornée /kɔrne/ *n.f.* cornea.

corneille /kɔrnɛj/ *n.f.* crow.

cornemuse /kɔrnəmyz/ *n.f.* bagpipes.

corner[1] /kɔrne/ *v.t.* (*page*) make dog-eared. ● *v.i.* (*auto.*) hoot; (*auto., Amer.*) honk.

corner[2] /kɔrnɛr/ *n.m.* (*football*) corner.

cornet /kɔrnɛ/ *n.m.* (paper) cone; (*crème glacée*) cornet, cone.

corniaud /kɔrnjo/ *n.m.* (*fam.*) nitwit.

corniche /kɔrniʃ/ *n.f.* cornice; (*route*) cliff road.

cornichon /kɔrniʃɔ̃/ *n.m.* gherkin.

corollaire /kɔrɔlɛr/ *n.m.* corollary.

corporation /kɔrpɔrasjɔ̃/ *n.f.* professional body.

corporel, **~le** /kɔrpɔrɛl/ *a.* bodily; (*châtiment*) corporal.

corps /kɔr/ *n.m.* body; (*mil., pol.*) corps. **~ à corps,** hand to hand. **~ électoral,** electorate. **~ enseignant,** teaching profession. **faire ~ avec,** form part of.

corpulen|t, **~te** /kɔrpylɑ̃, -t/ *a.* stout. **~ce** *n.f.* stoutness.

correct /kɔrɛkt/ *a.* proper, correct; (*exact*) correct; (*tenue*) decent. **~ement** *adv.* properly; correctly; decently.

correc|teur, **~trice** /kɔrɛktœr, -tris/ *n.m., f.* (*d'épreuves*) proof-reader; (*scol.*) examiner. **~teur d'orthographe,** spelling checker.

correction /kɔrɛksjɔ̃/ *n.f.* correction; (*punition*) beating.

corrélation /kɔrelasjɔ̃/ *n.f.* correlation.

correspondan|t, **~te** /kɔrɛspɔ̃dɑ̃, -t/ *a.* corresponding. ● *n.m., f.* correspondent; (*au téléphone*) caller. **~ce** *n.f.* correspondence; (*de train, d'autobus*) connection. **vente par ~ce,** mail order.

correspondre /kɔrɛspɔ̃dr/ *v.i.* (*s'accorder, écrire*) correspond; (*chambres*) communicate.

corrida /kɔrida/ *n.f.* bullfight.

corridor /kɔridɔr/ *n.m.* corridor.

corrig|er /kɔriʒe/ *v.t.* correct; (*devoir*) mark, correct; (*punir*) beat; (*guérir*) cure. **se ~er de,** cure o.s. of. **~é** *n.m.* (*scol.*) correct version, model answer.

corroborer /kɔrɔbɔre/ *v.t.* corroborate.

corro|der /kɔrɔde/ *v.t.* corrode. **~sion** /-ozjɔ̃/ *n.f.* corrosion.

corromp|re† /kɔrɔ̃pr/ *v.t.* corrupt; (*soudoyer*) bribe. **~u** *a.* corrupt.

corrosi|f, **~ve** /kɔrozif, -v/ *a.* corrosive.

corruption /kɔrypsjɔ̃/ *n.f.* corruption.

corsage /kɔrsaʒ/ *n.m.* bodice; (*chemisier*) blouse.

corsaire /kɔrsɛr/ *n.m.* pirate.

Corse /kɔrs/ *n.f.* Corsica.

corse /kɔrs/ *a. & n.m./f.* Corsican.

corsé /kɔrse/ *a.* (*vin*) full-bodied; (*scabreux*) spicy.

corset /kɔrsɛ/ *n.m.* corset.

cortège /kɔrtɛʒ/ *n.m.* procession.

cortisone /kɔrtizɔn/ *n.f.* cortisone.

corvée /kɔrve/ *n.f.* chore.

cosaque /kɔzak/ *n.m.* Cossack.

cosmétique /kɔsmetik/ *n.m.* cosmetic.

cosmique /kɔsmik/ *a.* cosmic.

cosmonaute /kɔsmɔnot/ *n.m./f.* cosmonaut.

cosmopolite /kɔsmɔpɔlit/ *a.* cosmopolitan.

cosmos /kɔsmos/ *n.m.* (*espace*) (outer) space; (*univers*) cosmos.

cosse /kɔs/ *n.f.* (*de pois*) pod.

cossu /kɔsy/ *a.* (*gens*) well-to-do; (*demeure*) opulent.

costaud, **~e** /kɔsto, -d/ *a.* (*fam.*) strong. ● *n.m.* (*fam.*) strong man.

costum|e /kɔstym/ *n.m.* suit; (*théâtre*) costume. **~é** *a.* dressed up.

cote /kɔt/ *n.f.* (classification) mark; (*en Bourse*) quotation; (*de cheval*) odds (**de**, on); (*de candidat, acteur*) rating. **~ d'alerte,** danger level.

côte /kot/ *n.f.* (*littoral*) coast; (*pente*) hill; (*anat.*) rib; (*de porc*) chop. **~ à côte,** side by side. **la C~ d'Azur,** the (French) Riviera.

côté /kote/ *n.m.* side; (*direction*) way. **à ~,** nearby; (*voisin*) next-door. **à ~ de,** next to; (*comparé à*) compared to; (*cible*) wide of. **aux ~s de,** by the side of. **de ~,** aside; (*regarder*) sideways. **mettre de ~,** put aside. **de ce ~,** this way. **de chaque ~,** on each side. **de tous les ~s,** on every side; (*partout*) everywhere. **du ~ de,** towards; (*proximité*) near; (*provenance*) from.

coteau (*pl.* **~x**) /kɔto/ *n.m.* hill.

côtelette /kotlɛt/ *n.f.* chop.

coter /kɔte/ *v.t.* (*comm.*) quote; (*apprécier, noter*) rate.

coterie /kɔtri/ *n.f.* clique.

côt|ier, **~ière** /kotje, -jɛr/ *a.* coastal.

cotis|er /kɔtize/ *v.i.* pay one's contributions (**à**, to); (*à un club*) pay one's subscription. **se ~er** *v. pr.* club together. **~ation** *n.f.* contribution(s); subscription.

coton /kɔtɔ̃/ *n.m.* cotton. **~ hydrophile,** cotton wool.

côtoyer /kotwaje/ *v.t.* skirt, run along; (*fréquenter*) rub shoulders with; (*fig.*) verge on.

cotte /kɔt/ *n.f.* (*d'ouvrier*) overalls.

cou /ku/ *n.m.* neck.

couchage /kuʃaʒ/ *n.m.* sleeping arrangements.

couchant /kuʃɑ̃/ *n.m.* sunset.

couche /kuʃ/ *n.f.* layer; (*de peinture*) coat; (*de bébé*) nappy. **~s,** (*méd.*) childbirth. **~s sociales,** social strata.

coucher /kuʃe/ *n.m.* **~ (du soleil),** sunset. ● *v.t.* put to bed; (*loger*) put up; (*étendre*) lay down. **~ (par écrit),** set down. ● *v.i.* sleep. **se ~** *v. pr.* go to bed; (*s'étendre*) lie down; (*soleil*) set. **couché** *a.* in bed; (*étendu*) lying down.

couchette /kuʃɛt/ *n.f.* (*rail.*) couchette; (*naut.*) bunk.

coucou /kuku/ *n.m.* cuckoo.

coude /kud/ *n.m.* elbow; (*de rivière etc.*) bend. **~ à coude,** side by side.

cou-de-pied (*pl.* **cous-de-pied**) /kudpje/ *n.m.* instep.

coudoyer /kudwaje/ *v.t.* rub shoulders with.

coudre† /kudr/ *v.t./i.* sew.

couenne /kwan/ *n.f.* (*de porc*) rind.

couette /kwɛt/ *n.f.* duvet, continental quilt.

couffin /kufɛ̃/ *n.m.* Moses basket.

couiner /kwine/ *v.i.* squeak.

coulant, **~e** /kulɑ̃, -t/ *a.* (*indulgent*) easy-going; (*fromage*) runny.

coulée /kule/ *n.f.* **~ de lave,** lava flow.

couler [1] /kule/ *v.i.* flow, run; (*fromage, nez*) run; (*fuir*) leak. ● *v.t.* (*sculpture, métal*) cast; (*vie*) pass, lead. **se ~** *v. pr.* (*se glisser*) slip.

couler [2] /kule/ *v.t./i.* (*bateau*) sink.

couleur /kulœr/ *n.f.* colour; (*peinture*) paint; (*cartes*) suit. **~s,** (*teint*) colour. **de ~,** (*homme, femme*) coloured. **en ~s,** (*télévision, film*) colour.

couleuvre /kulœvr/ *n.f.* (grass *ou* smooth) snake.

coulis /kuli/ *n.m.* (*culin.*) coulis.

couliss|e /kulis/ *n.f.* (*de tiroir etc.*) runner. **~es,** (*théâtre*) wings. **à ~e,** (*porte, fenêtre*) sliding. **~er** *v.i.* slide.

couloir /kulwar/ *n.m.* corridor; (*de bus*) gangway; (*sport*) lane.

coup /ku/ *n.m.* blow; (*choc*) knock; (*sport*) stroke; (*de crayon, chance, cloche*) stroke; (*de fusil, pistolet*) shot; (*fois*) time; (*aux échecs*) move. **à ~ sûr,** definitely. **après ~,** after the event. **boire un ~,** have a drink. **~ de chiffon,** wipe (with a rag). **~ de coude,** nudge. **~ de couteau,** stab. **~ d'envoi,** kick-off. **~ d'état** (*pol.*) coup. **~ de feu,** shot. **~ de fil,** phone call. **~ de filet,** haul. **~ de frein,** sudden braking. **~ de grâce,** coup de grâce. **~ de main,** helping hand. **avoir le ~ de main,** have the knack. **~ d'œil,** glance. **~ de pied,** kick. **~ de poing,** punch. **~ de sang,** (*méd.*) stroke. **~ de soleil,** sunburn. **~ de sonnette,** ring (on a bell). **~ de téléphone,** (tele)phone call. **~ de tête,** wild impulse. **~ de théâtre,** dramatic event. **~ de tonnerre,** thunderclap. **~ de vent,** gust of wind. **~ franc,** free kick. **~ sur coup,** in rapid succession. **d'un seul ~,** in one go. **du premier ~,** first go. **sale ~,** dirty trick. **sous le ~ de,** under the influence of. **sur le ~,** immediately. **tenir le coup,** take it.

coupable /kupabl/ *a.* guilty. ● *n.m./f.* culprit.

coupe [1] /kup/ *n.f.* cup; (*de champagne*) goblet; (*à fruits*) dish.

coupe [2] /kup/ *n.f.* (*de vêtement etc.*) cut; (*dessin*) section. **~ de cheveux,** haircut.

coupé /kupe/ *n.m.* (*voiture*) coupé.

coup|er /kupe/ *v.t./i.* cut; (*arbre*) cut down; (*arrêter*) cut off; (*voyage*) break; (*appétit*) take away; (*vin*) water down. **~er par,** take a short cut via. **se ~er** *v. pr.* cut o.s.; (*routes*) intersect. **~er la parole à,** cut short. **~e-papier** *n.m. invar.* paper-knife.

couperosé /kuproze/ *a.* blotchy.

couple /kupl/ *n.m.* couple.

coupler /kuple/ *v.t.* couple.

couplet /kuplɛ/ *n.m.* verse.

coupole /kupɔl/ *n.f.* dome.

coupon /kupɔ̃/ *n.m.* (*étoffe*) remnant; (*billet, titre*) coupon.

coupure /kupyr/ *n.f.* cut; (*billet de banque*) note; (*de presse*) cutting. **~ (de courant),** power cut.

cour /kur/ *n.f.* (court)yard; (*de roi*) court; (*tribunal*) court. **~ (de ré-**

création), playground. **~ martiale,** court martial. **faire la ~ à,** court.

courag|e /kuraʒ/ *n.m.* courage. **~eux, ~euse** *a.* courageous.

couramment /kuramã/ *adv.* frequently; (*parler*) fluently.

courant [1], **~e** /kurã, -t/ *a.* standard, ordinary; (*en cours*) current.

courant [2] /kurã/ *n.m.* current; (*de mode, d'idées*) trend. **~ d'air,** draught. **dans le ~ de,** in the course of. **être/mettre au ~ de,** know/tell about; (*à jour*) be/bring up to date on.

courbatur|e /kurbatyr/ *n.f.* ache. **~é** *a.* aching.

courbe /kurb/ *n.f.* curve. ● *a.* curved.

courber /kurbe/ *v.t./i.,* **se ~** *v. pr.* bend.

coureu|r, ~se /kurœr, -øz/ *n.m., f.* (*sport*) runner. **~r automobile,** racing driver. ● *n.m.* womanizer.

courge /kurʒ/ *n.f.* marrow; (*Amer.*) squash.

courgette /kurʒɛt/ *n.f.* courgette; (*Amer.*) zucchini.

courir† /kurir/ *v.i.* run; (*se hâter*) rush; (*nouvelles etc.*) go round. ● *v.t.* (*risque*) run; (*danger*) face; (*épreuve sportive*) run *ou* compete in; (*fréquenter*) do the rounds of; (*filles*) chase.

couronne /kurɔn/ *n.f.* crown; (*de fleurs*) wreath.

couronn|er /kurɔne/ *v.t.* crown. **~ement** *n.m.* coronation, crowning; (*fig.*) crowning achievement.

courrier /kurje/ *n.m.* post, mail; (*à écrire*) letters; (*de journal*) column.

courroie /kurwa/ *n.f.* strap; (*techn.*) belt.

courroux /kuru/ *n.m.* wrath.

cours /kur/ *n.m.* (*leçon*) class; (*série de leçons*) course; (*prix*) price; (*cote*) rate; (*déroulement, d'une rivière*) course; (*allée*) avenue. **au ~ de,** in the course of. **avoir ~,** (*monnaie*) be legal tender; (*fig.*) be current; (*scol.*) have a lesson. **~ d'eau,** river, stream. **~ du soir,** evening class. **~ magistral,** (*univ.*) lecture. **en ~,** current; (*travail*) in progress. **en ~ de route,** on the way.

course /kurs/ *n.f.* run(ning); (*épreuve de vitesse*) race; (*entre rivaux: fig.*) race; (*de projectile*) flight; (*voyage*) journey; (*commission*) errand. **~s,**

(*achats*) shopping; (*de chevaux*) races.

cours|ier, ~ère /kursje, -jɛr/ *n.m.*, *f.* messenger.

court [1], **~e** /kur, -t/ *a.* short. ● *adv.* short. **à ~ de**, short of. **pris de ~**, caught unawares. **~-circuit** (*pl.* **~s-circuits**) *n.m.* short circuit.

court [2] /kur/ *n.m.* **~ (de tennis)**, (tennis) court.

court|ier, ~ière /kurtje, -jɛr/ *n.m.*, *f.* broker.

courtisan /kurtizɑ̃/ *n.m.* courtier.

courtisane /kurtizan/ *n.f.* courtesan.

courtiser /kurtize/ *v.t.* court.

courtois, ~e /kurtwa, -z/ *a.* courteous. **~ie** /-zi/ *n.f.* courtesy.

couscous /kuskus/ *n.m.* couscous.

cousin, ~e /kuzɛ̃, -in/ *n.m.*, *f.* cousin. **~ germain**, first cousin.

coussin /kusɛ̃/ *n.m.* cushion.

coût /ku/ *n.m.* cost.

couteau (*pl.* **~x**) /kuto/ *n.m.* knife. **~ à cran d'arrêt**, flick-knife.

coutellerie /kutɛlri/ *n.f.* (*magasin*) cutlery shop.

coût|er /kute/ *v.t./i.* cost. **~e que coûte**, at all costs. **au prix ~ant**, at cost (price). **~eux, ~euse** *a.* costly.

coutum|e /kutym/ *n.f.* custom. **~ier, ~ière** *a.* customary.

coutur|e /kutyr/ *n.f.* sewing; (*métier*) dressmaking; (*points*) seam. **~ier** *n.m.* fashion designer. **~ière** *n.f.* dressmaker.

couvée /kuve/ *n.f.* brood.

couvent /kuvɑ̃/ *n.m.* convent; (*de moines*) monastery.

couver /kuve/ *v.t.* (*œufs*) hatch; (*personne*) pamper; (*maladie*) be coming down with, be sickening for. ● *v.i.* (*feu*) smoulder; (*mal*) be brewing.

couvercle /kuvɛrkl/ *n.m.* (*de marmite, boîte*) lid; (*d'objet allongé*) top.

couvert [1], **~e** /kuvɛr, -t/ *a.* covered (**de**, with); (*habillé*) covered up; (*ciel*) overcast. ● *n.m.* (*abri*) cover. **à ~ de**, (*mil.*) under cover. **à ~ de**, (*fig.*) safe from.

couvert [2] /kuvɛr/ *n.m.* (*à table*) place-setting; (*prix*) cover charge. **~s**, (*couteaux etc.*) cutlery. **mettre le ~**, lay the table.

couverture /kuvɛrtyr/ *n.f.* cover; (*de lit*) blanket; (*toit*) roofing. **~ chauffante**, electric blanket.

couveuse /kuvøz/ *n.f.* **~ (artificielle)**, incubator.

couvreur /kuvrœr/ *n.m.* roofer.

couvr|ir† /kuvrir/ *v.t.* cover. **se ~ir** *v. pr.* (*s'habiller*) cover up; (*se coiffer*) put one's hat on; (*ciel*) become overcast. **~e-chef** *n.m.* hat. **~e-feu** (*pl.* **~e-feux**) *n.m.* curfew. **~e-lit** *n.m.* bedspread.

cow-boy /kɔbɔj/ *n.m.* cowboy.

crabe /krab/ *n.m.* crab.

crachat /kraʃa/ *n.m.* spit(tle).

cracher /kraʃe/ *v.i.* spit; (*radio*) crackle. ● *v.t.* spit (out).

crachin /kraʃɛ̃/ *n.m.* drizzle.

crack /krak/ *n.m.* (*fam.*) wizard, ace, prodigy.

craie /krɛ/ *n.f.* chalk.

craindre† /krɛ̃dr/ *v.t.* be afraid of, fear; (*être sensible à*) be easily damaged by.

crainte /krɛ̃t/ *n.f.* fear. **de ~ de/que**, for fear of/that.

crainti|f, ~ve /krɛ̃tif, v/ *a.* timid.

cramoisi /kramwazi/ *a.* crimson.

crampe /krɑ̃p/ *n.f.* cramp.

crampon /krɑ̃pɔ̃/ *n.m.* (*de chaussure*) stud.

cramponner (se) /(sə)krɑ̃pɔne/ *v. pr.* **se ~ à**, cling to.

cran /krɑ̃/ *n.m.* (*entaille*) notch; (*trou*) hole; (*courage: fam.*) pluck.

crâne /krɑn/ *n.m.* skull.

crâner /krɑne/ *v.i.* (*fam.*) swank.

crapaud /krapo/ *n.m.* toad.

crapul|e /krapyl/ *n.f.* villain. **~eux, ~euse** *a.* sordid, foul.

craqu|er /krake/ *v.i.* crack, snap; (*plancher*) creak; (*couture*) split; (*fig.*) break down; (*céder*) give in. ● *v.t.* **~er une allumette**, strike a match. **~ement** *n.m.* crack(ing), snap(ping); creak(ing); striking.

crass|e /kras/ *n.f.* grime. **~eux, ~euse** *a.* grimy.

cratère /kratɛr/ *n.m.* crater.

cravache /kravaʃ/ *n.f.* horsewhip.

cravate /kravat/ *n.f.* tie.

crawl /krol/ *n.m.* (*nage*) crawl.

crayeu|x, ~se /krɛjø, -z/ *a.* chalky.

crayon /krɛjɔ̃/ *n.m.* pencil. **~ (de couleur)**, crayon. **~ à bille**, ball-point pen. **~ optique**, light pen.

créanc|ier, ~ière /kreɑ̃sje, -jɛr/ *n.m.*, *f.* creditor.

créa|teur, ~trice /kreatœr, -tris/ *a.* creative. ● *n.m.*, *f.* creator.

création /kreasjɔ̃/ *n.f.* creation; (*comm.*) product.

créature /kreatyr/ *n.f.* creature.

crèche /kʀɛʃ/ n.f. day nursery; (*re-lig.*) crib.

crédibilité /kʀedibilite/ n.f. credibility.

crédit /kʀedi/ n.m. credit; (*banque*) bank. **~s**, funds. **à ~**, on credit. **faire ~**, give credit (**à**, to). **~er** /-te/ v.t. credit. **~eur, ~euse** /-tœʀ, -tøz/ a. in credit.

credo /kʀedo/ n.m. creed.

crédule /kʀedyl/ a. credulous.

créer /kʀee/ v.t. create.

crémation /kʀemɑsjɔ̃/ n.f. cremation.

crème /kʀɛm/ n.f. cream; (*dessert*) cream dessert. ● a. invar. cream. ● n.m. (*café*) **~**, white coffee. **~ anglaise**, fresh custard. **~ à raser**, shaving-cream.

crémeu|x, ~se /kʀemø, -z/ a. creamy.

crém|ier, ~ière /kʀemje, -jɛʀ/ n.m., f. dairyman, dairywoman. **~erie** /kʀɛmʀi/ n.f. dairy.

créneau (*pl.* **~x**) /kʀeno/ n.m. (*trou, moment*) slot; (*dans le marché*) gap; **faire un ~**, park between two cars.

créole /kʀeɔl/ n.m./f. Creole.

crêpe[1] /kʀɛp/ n.f. (*galette*) pancake. **~rie** n.f. pancake shop.

crêpe[2] /kʀɛp/ n.m. (*tissu*) crêpe; (*matière*) crêpe (rubber).

crépit|er /kʀepite/ v.i. crackle. **~ement** n.m. crackling.

crépu /kʀepy/ a. frizzy.

crépuscule /kʀepyskyl/ n.m. twilight, dusk.

crescendo /kʀeʃɛndo/ adv. & n.m. invar. crescendo.

cresson /kʀesɔ̃/ n.m. (water)cress.

crête /kʀɛt/ n.f. crest; (*de coq*) comb.

crétin, ~e /kʀetɛ̃, -in/ n.m., f. cretin.

creuser /kʀøze/ v.t. dig; (*évider*) hollow out; (*fig.*) go deeply into. **se ~ (la cervelle)**, (*fam.*) rack one's brains.

creuset /kʀøzɛ/ n.m. (*lieu*) melting-pot.

creu|x, ~se /kʀø, -z/ a. hollow; (*heures*) off-peak. ● n.m. hollow; (*de l'estomac*) pit.

crevaison /kʀəvɛzɔ̃/ n.f. puncture.

crevasse /kʀəvas/ n.f. crack; (*de glacier*) crevasse; (*de la peau*) chap.

crevé /kʀəve/ a. (*fam.*) worn out.

crève-cœur /kʀɛvkœʀ/ n.m. invar. heart-break.

crever /kʀəve/ v.t./i. burst; (*pneu*) puncture burst; (*exténuer: fam.*)

exhaust; (*mourir: fam.*) die; (*œil*) put out.

crevette /kʀəvɛt/ n.f. **~ (grise)**, shrimp. **~ (rose)**, prawn.

cri /kʀi/ n.m. cry; (*de douleur*) scream, cry.

criant, ~e /kʀijɑ̃, -t/ a. glaring.

criard, ~e /kʀijaʀ, -d/ a. (*couleur*) garish; (*voix*) bawling.

crible /kʀibl/ n.m. sieve, riddle.

criblé /kʀible/ a. **~ de**, riddled with.

cric /kʀik/ n.m. (*auto.*) jack.

crier /kʀije/ v.i. (*fort*) shout, cry (out); (*de douleur*) scream; (*grincer*) creak. ● v.t. (*ordre*) shout (out).

crim|e /kʀim/ n.m. crime; (*meurtre*) murder. **~inalité** n.f. crime. **~inel, ~inelle** a. criminal; n.m., f. criminal; (*assassin*) murderer.

crin /kʀɛ̃/ n.m. horsehair.

crinière /kʀinjɛʀ/ n.f. mane.

crique /kʀik/ n.f. creek.

criquet /kʀikɛ/ n.m. locust.

crise /kʀiz/ n.f. crisis; (*méd.*) attack; (*de colère*) fit. **~ cardiaque**, heart attack. **~ de foie**, bilious attack.

crisp|er /kʀispe/ v.t., **se ~er** v. pr. tense; (*poings*) clench. **~ation** n.f. tenseness; (*spasme*) twitch. **~é** a. tense.

crisser /kʀise/ v.i. crunch; (*pneu*) screech.

crist|al (*pl.* **~aux**) /kʀistal, -o/ n.m. crystal.

cristallin, ~e /kʀistalɛ̃, -in/ a. (*limpide*) crystal-clear.

cristalliser /kʀistalize/ v.t./i., **se ~** v. pr. crystallize.

critère /kʀitɛʀ/ n.m. criterion.

critique /kʀitik/ a. critical. ● n.f. criticism; (*article*) review. ● n.m. critic. **la ~**, (*personnes*) the critics.

critiquer /kʀitike/ v.t. criticize.

croasser /kʀɔase/ v.i. caw.

croc /kʀo/ n.m. (*dent*) fang; (*crochet*) hook.

croc-en-jambe (*pl.* **crocs-en-jambe**) /kʀɔkɑ̃ʒɑ̃b/ n.m. = **croche-pied**.

croche /kʀɔʃ/ n.f. quaver. **double ~**, semiquaver.

croche-pied /kʀɔʃpje/ n.m. **faire un ~ à**, trip up.

crochet /kʀɔʃɛ/ n.m. hook; (*détour*) detour; (*signe*) (square) bracket; (*tricot*) crochet. **faire au ~**, crochet.

crochu /kʀɔʃy/ a. hooked.

crocodile /kʀɔkɔdil/ n.m. crocodile.

crocus /kʀɔkys/ n.m. crocus.

croire† /krwar/ *v.t./i.* believe (**à, en,**
in); (*estimer*) think, believe (**que,**
that).

croisade /krwazad/ *n.f.* crusade.

croisé /krwaze/ *a.* (*veston*) double-
breasted. ● *n.m.* crusader.

croisée /krwaze/ *n.f.* window. **~ des
chemins,** crossroads.

crois|er¹ /krwaze/ *v.t.*, **se ~er** *v. pr.*
cross; (*passant, véhicule*) pass (each
other). **(se) ~er les bras,** fold one's
arms. **(se) ~er les jambes,** cross
one's legs. **~ement** *n.m.* crossing;
passing; (*carrefour*) crossroads.

crois|er² /krwaze/ *v.i.* (*bateau*)
cruise. **~eur** *n.m.* cruiser. **~ière**
n.f. cruise.

croissan|t¹, **~te** /krwasã, -t/ *a.*
growing. **~ce** *n.f.* growth.

croissant² /krwasã/ *n.m.* crescent;
(*pâtisserie*) croissant.

croître† /krwatr/ *v.i.* grow; (*lune*)
wax.

croix /krwa/ *n.f.* cross. **~ gammée,**
swastika. **C~-Rouge,** Red Cross.

croque-monsieur /krɔkməsjø/ *n.m.*
invar. toasted ham and cheese sandwich.

croque-mort /krɔkmɔr/ *n.m.* (*fam.*)
undertaker's assistant.

croqu|er /krɔke/ *v.t./i.* crunch; (*des-
siner*) sketch. **chocolat à ~er,** plain
chocolate. **~ant, ~ante** *a.* crunchy.

croquet /krɔkɛ/ *n.m.* croquet.

croquette /krɔkɛt/ *n.f.* croquette.

croquis /krɔki/ *n.m.* sketch.

crosse /krɔs/ *n.f.* (*de fusil*) butt;
(*d'évêque*) crook.

crotte /krɔt/ *n.f.* droppings.

crotté /krɔte/ *a.* muddy.

crottin /krɔtɛ̃/ *n.m.* (horse) dung.

crouler /krule/ *v.i.* collapse; (*être en
ruines*) crumble.

croupe /krup/ *n.f.* rump; (*de colline*)
brow. **en ~,** pillion.

croupier /krupje/ *n.m.* croupier.

croupir /krupir/ *v.i.* stagnate.

croustill|er /krustije/ *v.i.* be crusty.
~ant, ~ante *a.* crusty; (*fig.*) spicy.

croûte /krut/ *n.f.* crust; (*de fromage*)
rind; (*de plaie*) scab. **en ~,** (*culin.*)
en croûte.

croûton /krutɔ̃/ *n.m.* (*bout de pain*)
crust; (*avec potage*) croûton.

croyable /krwajabl/ *a.* credible.

croyan|t, ~te /krwajã, -t/ *n.m.*, *f.*
believer. **~ce** *n.f.* belief.

CRS *abrév.* (*Compagnies républicaines
de sécurité*) French state security
police.

cru¹ /kry/ *voir* croire.

cru² /kry/ *a.* raw; (*lumière*) harsh;
(*propos*) crude. ● *n.m.* vineyard;
(*vin*) wine.

crû /kry/ *voir* croître.

cruauté /kryote/ *n.f.* cruelty.

cruche /kryʃ/ *n.f.* pitcher.

cruc|ial (*m. pl.* **~iaux**) /krysjal, -jo/ *a.*
crucial.

crucif|ier /krysifje/ *v.t.* crucify.
~ixion *n.f.* crucifixion.

crucifix /krysifi/ *n.m.* crucifix.

crudité /krydite/ *n.f.* (*de langage*)
crudeness. **~s,** (*culin.*) raw vegetables.

crue /kry/ *n.f.* rise in water level. **en
~,** in spate.

cruel, ~le /kryɛl/ *a.* cruel.

crûment /krymã/ *adv.* crudely.

crustacés /krystase/ *n.m. pl.* shellfish.

crypte /kript/ *n.f.* crypt.

Cuba /kyba/ *n.m.* Cuba.

cubain, ~e /kybɛ̃, -ɛn/ *a. & n.m., f.*
Cuban.

cub|e /kyb/ *n.m.* cube. ● *a.* (*mètre
etc.*) cubic. **~ique** *a.* cubic.

cueill|ir† /kœjir/ *v.t.* pick, gather;
(*personne*: *fam.*) pick up. **~ette**
n.f. picking, gathering.

cuill|er, ~ère /kɥijɛr/ *n.f.* spoon.
~er à soupe, soup-spoon; (*mesure*)
tablespoonful. **~erée** *n.f.* spoonful.

cuir /kɥir/ *n.m.* leather. **~ chevelu,**
scalp.

cuirassé /kɥirase/ *n.m.* battleship.

cuire /kɥir/ *v.t./i.* cook; (*picoter*)
smart. **~ (au four),** bake. **faire ~,**
cook.

cuisine /kɥizin/ *n.f.* kitchen; (*art*)
cookery, cooking; (*aliments*) cooking. **faire la ~,** cook.

cuisin|er /kɥizine/ *v.t./i.* cook;
(*interroger*: *fam.*) grill. **~ier,
~ière** *n.m., f.* cook; *n.f.* (*appareil*)
cooker, stove.

cuisse /kɥis/ *n.f.* thigh; (*de poulet,
mouton*) leg.

cuisson /kɥisɔ̃/ *n.m.* cooking.

cuit, ~e /kɥi, -t/ *a.* cooked. **bien ~,**
well done *ou* cooked. **trop ~,** over-
done.

cuivr|e /kɥivr/ *n.m.* copper. **~e
(jaune),** brass. **~es,** (*mus.*) brass.
~é *a.* coppery.

cul /ky/ *n.m.* (*derrière*: *fam.*) backside, bum.

culasse /kylas/ *n.f.* (*auto.*) cylinder head; (*arme*) breech.

culbut|e /kylbyt/ *n.f.* somersault; (*chute*) tumble. **~er** *v.i.* tumble; *v.t.* knock over.

cul-de-sac (*pl.* **culs-de-sac**) /kydsak/ *n.m.* cul-de-sac.

culinaire /kylinɛr/ *a.* culinary; (*recette*) cooking.

culminer /kylmine/ *v.i.* reach the highest point.

culot [1] /kylo/ *n.m.* (*audace*: *fam.*) nerve, cheek.

culot [2] /kylo/ *n.m.* (*fond*: *techn.*) base.

culotte /kylɔt/ *n.f.* (*de femme*) knickers; (*Amer.*) panties. **~ (de cheval)**, (riding) breeches. **~ courte,** short trousers.

culpabilité /kylpabilite/ *n.f.* guilt.

culte /kylt/ *n.m.* cult, worship; (*religion*) religion; (*protestant*) service.

cultivé /kyltive/ *a.* cultured.

cultiv|er /kyltive/ *v.t.* cultivate; (*plantes*) grow. **~ateur, ~atrice** *n.m., f.* farmer.

culture /kyltyr/ *n.f.* cultivation; (*de plantes*) growing; (*agriculture*) farming; (*éducation*) culture. **~s,** (*terrains*) lands under cultivation. **~ physique,** physical training.

culturel, ~le /kyltyrɛl/ *a.* cultural.

cumuler /kymyle/ *v.t.* (*fonctions*) hold simultaneously.

cupide /kypid/ *a.* grasping.

cure /kyr/ *n.f.* (course of) treatment, cure.

curé /kyre/ *n.m.* (parish) priest.

cur|er /kyre/ *v.t.* clean. **se ~er les dents/ongles,** clean one's teeth/nails. **~e-dent** *n.m.* toothpick. **~e-pipe** *n.m.* pipe-cleaner.

curieu|x, ~se /kyrjø, -z/ *a.* curious. ● *n.m.,* f. (*badaud*) onlooker. **~sement** *adv.* curiously.

curiosité /kyrjozite/ *n.f.* curiosity; (*objet*) curio; (*spectacle*) unusual sight.

curriculum vitae /kyrikylɔm vite/ *n.m. invar.* curriculum vitae.

curseur /kyrsœr/ *n.m.* cursor.

cutané /kytane/ *a.* skin.

cuve /kyv/ *n.f.* tank.

cuvée /kyve/ *n.f.* (*de vin*) vintage.

cuvette /kyvɛt/ *n.f.* bowl; (*de lavabo*) (wash-)basin; (*des cabinets*) pan, bowl.

CV /seve/ *n.m.* CV.

cyanure /sjanyr/ *n.m.* cyanide.

cybernétique /sibɛrnetik/ *n.f.* cybernetics.

cycl|e /sikl/ *n.m.* cycle. **~ique** *a.* cyclic(al).

cyclis|te /siklist/ *n.m./f.* cyclist. ● *a.* cycle. **~me** *n.m.* cycling.

cyclomoteur /syklɔmɔtœr/ *n.m.* moped.

cyclone /siklon/ *n.m.* cyclone.

cygne /siɲ/ *n.m.* swan.

cylindr|e /silɛ̃dr/ *n.m.* cylinder. **~ique** *a.* cylindrical.

cylindrée /silɛ̃dre/ *n.f.* (*de moteur*) capacity.

cymbale /sɛ̃bal/ *n.f.* cymbal.

cystite /sistit/ *n.f.* cystitis.

cyni|que /sinik/ *a.* cynical. ● *n.m.* cynic. **~sme** *n.m.* cynicism.

cyprès /siprɛ/ *n.m.* cypress.

cypriote /siprijɔt/ *a. & n.m./f.* Cypriot.

D

d' /d/ *voir* de.

d'abord /dabɔr/ *adv.* first; (*au début*) at first.

dactylo /daktilo/ *n.f.* typist. **~(graphie)** *n.f.* typing. **~graphe** *n.f.* typist. **~graphier** *v.t.* type.

dada /dada/ *n.m.* hobby-horse.

dahlia /dalja/ *n.m.* dahlia.

daigner /deɲe/ *v.t.* deign.

daim /dɛ̃/ *n.m.* (fallow) deer; (*cuir*) suede.

dall|e /dal/ *n.f.* paving stone, slab. **~age** *n.m.* paving.

daltonien, ~ne /daltɔnjɛ̃, -jɛn/ *a.* colour-blind.

dame /dam/ *n.f.* lady; (*cartes, échecs*) queen. **~s,** (*jeu*) draughts; (*jeu: Amer.*) checkers.

damier /damje/ *n.m.* draught-board; (*Amer.*) checker-board. **à ~,** chequered.

damn|er /dɑne/ *v.t.* damn. **~ation** *n.f.* damnation.

dancing /dɑ̃siŋ/ *n.m.* dance-hall.

dandiner (se) /(sə)dɑ̃dine/ *v. pr.* waddle.

Danemark /danmark/ *n.m.* Denmark.

danger /dɑ̃ʒe/ *n.m.* danger. **en ~,** in danger. **mettre en ~,** endanger.

dangereu|x, ~se /dɑ̃ʒʁø, -z/ *a.* dangerous.

danois, ~e /danwa, -z/ *a.* Danish. ● *n.m., f.* Dane. ● *n.m.* (*lang.*) Danish.

dans /dɑ̃/ *prép.* in; (*mouvement*) into; (*à l'intérieur de*) inside, in; (*approximation*) about. **~ dix jours,** in ten days' time. **prendre/boire/etc. ~,** take/drink/*etc.* out of *ou* from.

dans|e /dɑ̃s/ *n.f.* dance; (*art*) dancing. **~er** *v.t./i.* dance. **~eur, ~euse** *n.m., f.* dancer.

dard /dar/ *n.m.* (*d'animal*) sting.

darne /darn/ *n.f.* steak (*of fish*).

dat|e /dat/ *n.f.* date. **~e limite,** deadline; **~e limite de vente,** sell-by date; **~e de péremption,** expiry date. **~er** *v.t./i.* date. **à ~er de,** as from.

datt|e /dat/ *n.f.* (*fruit*) date. **~ier** *n.m.* date-palm.

daube /dob/ *n.f.* casserole.

dauphin /dofɛ̃/ *n.m.* (*animal*) dolphin.

davantage /davɑ̃taʒ/ *adv.* more; (*plus longtemps*) longer. **~ de,** more. **~ que,** more than; longer than.

de, d'* /də, d/ *prép.* (*de + le = du, de + les = des*) of; (*provenance*) from; (*moyen, manière*) with; (*agent*) by. ● *article* some; (*interrogation*) any, some. **le livre de mon ami,** my friend's book. **un pont de fer,** an iron bridge. **dix mètres de haut,** ten metres high. **du pain,** (some) bread; **une tranche de pain,** a slice of bread. **des fleurs,** (some) flowers.

dé /de/ *n.m.* (*à jouer*) dice; (*à coudre*) thimble. **dés,** (*jeu*) dice.

dealer /dilər/ *n.m.* (*drug*) dealer.

débâcle /debɑkl/ *n.f.* (*mil.*) rout.

déball|er /debale/ *v.t.* unpack; (*montrer, péj.*) spill out. **~age** *n.m.* unpacking.

débarbouiller /debarbuje/ *v.t.* wash the face of. **se ~** *v. pr.* wash one's face.

débarcadère /debarkadɛr/ *n.m.* landing-stage.

débardeur /debardœr/ *n.m.* docker; (*vêtement*) tank top.

débarqu|er /debarke/ *v.t./i.* disembark, land; (*arriver: fam.*) turn up. **~ement** *n.m.* disembarkation.

débarras /debara/ *n.m.* junk room. **bon ~!,** good riddance!

débarrasser /debarase/ *v.t.* clear (**de, of**). **~ qn. de,** take from s.o.; (*défaut, ennemi*) rid s.o. of. **se ~ de,** get rid of, rid o.s. of.

débat /deba/ *n.m.* debate.

débattre† [1] /debatr/ *v.t.* debate. ● *v.i.* **~ de,** discuss.

débattre† [2] **(se)** /(sə)debatr/ *v. pr.* struggle (**to get free**).

débauch|e /deboʃ/ *n.f.* debauchery; (*fig.*) profusion. **~er** [1] *v.t.* debauch.

débaucher [2] /deboʃe/ *v.t.* (*licencier*) lay off.

débile /debil/ *a.* weak; (*fam.*) stupid. ● *n.m./f.* moron.

débit /debi/ *n.m.* (rate of) flow; (*de magasin*) turnover; (*élocution*) delivery; (*de compte*) debit. **~ de tabac,** tobacconist's shop; **~ de boissons,** licensed premises.

débi|ter /debite/ *v.t.* cut up; (*fournir*) produce; (*vendre*) sell; (*dire: péj.*) spout; (*compte*) debit. **~teur, ~trice** *n.m., f.* debtor; *a.* (*compte*) in debit.

débl|ayer /debleje/ *v.t.* clear. **~aiement, ~ayage** *n.m.* clearing.

déblo|quer /debloke/ *v.t.* (*prix, salaires*) free. **~cage** *n.m.* freeing.

déboires /debwar/ *n.m. pl.* disappointments.

déboiser /debwaze/ *v.t.* clear (of trees).

déboîter /debwate/ *v.i.* (*véhicule*) pull out. ● *v.t.* (*membre*) dislocate.

débord|er /deborde/ *v.i.* overflow. ● *v.t.* (*dépasser*) extend beyond. **~er de,** (*joie etc.*) be overflowing with. **~é** *a.* snowed under (**de,** with). **~ement** *n.m.* overflowing.

débouché /debuʃe/ *n.m.* opening; (*carrière*) prospect; (*comm.*) outlet; (*sortie*) end, exit.

déboucher /debuʃe/ *v.t.* (*bouteille*) uncork; (*évier*) unblock. ● *v.i.* emerge (**de,** from). **~ sur,** (*rue*) lead into.

débourser /deburse/ *v.t.* pay out.

déboussolé /debusole/ *a.* (*fam.*) disorientated, disoriented.

debout /dəbu/ *adv.* standing; (*levé, éveillé*) up. **être ~, se tenir ~,** be standing, stand. **se mettre ~,** stand up.

déboutonner /debutone/ *v.t.* unbutton. **se ~** *v. pr.* unbutton o.s.; (*vêtement*) come undone.

débraillé /debraje/ *a.* slovenly.

débrancher /debrɑ̃ʃe/ *v.t.* unplug, disconnect.

débray|er /debreje/ v.i. (auto.) de-
clutch; (faire grève) stop work.
~age /debrɛjaʒ/ n.m. (pédale)
clutch; (grève) stoppage.

débris /debri/ n.m. pl. fragments;
(détritus) rubbish, debris.

débrouill|er /debruje/ v.t. disentan-
gle; (problème) sort out. **se ~er** v.
pr. manage. **~ard, ~arde** a. (fam.)
resourceful.

débroussailler /debrusaje/ v.t. clear
(of brushwood).

début /deby/ n.m. beginning. **faire
ses ~s,** (en public) make one's
début.

début|er /debyte/ v.i. begin; (dans un
métier etc.) start out. **~ant, ~ante**
n.m., f. beginner.

déca /deka/ n.m. decaffeinated coffee.

décafeiné /dekafeine/ a. decaffeinated. ● n.m. **du ~,** decaffeinated coffee.

deçà (en) /(ɑ̃)dəsa/ adv. this side.
● prép. **en ~ de,** this side of.

décacheter /dekaʃte/ v.t. open.

décade /dekad/ n.f. ten days; (décennie) decade.

décaden|t, ~te /dekadɑ̃, -t/ a.
decadent. **~ce** n.f. decadence.

décalcomanie /dekalkɔmani/ n.f.
transfer; (Amer.) decal.

décal|er /dekale/ v.t. shift. **~age** n.m.
(écart) gap. **~age horaire,** time
difference.

décalquer /dekalke/ v.t. trace.

décamper /dekɑ̃pe/ v.i. clear off.

décanter /dekɑ̃te/ v.t. allow to settle.
se ~ v. pr. settle.

décap|er /dekape/ v.t. scrape down;
(surface peinte) strip. **~ant** n.m.
chemical agent; (pour peinture)
paint stripper.

décapotable /dekapɔtabl/ a. convertible.

décapsul|er /dekapsyle/ v.t. take the
cap off. **~eur** n.m. bottle- opener.

décarcasser (se) /(sə)dekarkase/ v.
pr. (fam.) work o.s. to death.

décathlon /dekatlɔ̃/ n.m. decathlon.

décéd|er /desede/ v.i. die. **~é** a.
deceased.

décel|er /desle/ v.t. detect; (dé-
montrer) reveal. **~able** a. detect-
able.

décembre /desɑ̃br/ n.m. December.

décennie /deseni/ n.f. decade.

déc|ent, ~ente /desɑ̃, -t/ a. decent.
~emment /-amɑ̃/ adv. decently.
~ence n.f. decency.

décentralis|er /desɑ̃tralize/ v.t.
decentralize. **~ation** n.f. decentrali-
zation.

déception /desɛpsjɔ̃/ n.f. disappointment.

décerner /deserne/ v.t. award.

décès /desɛ/ n.m. death.

décev|oir† /desvwar/ v.t. disappoint.
~ant, ~ante a. disappointing.

déchaîn|er /deʃene/ v.t. (violence
etc.) unleash; (enthousiasme) arouse
a good deal of. **se ~er** v. pr. erupt.
~ement /-ɛnmɑ̃/ n.m. (de passions)
outburst.

décharge /deʃarʒ/ n.f. (salve) volley
of shots. **~ (électrique),** electrical
discharge. **~ (publique),** rubbish
tip.

décharg|er /deʃarʒe/ v.t. unload;
(arme, accusé) discharge. **~er de,**
release from. **se ~er** v. pr. (batterie,
pile) go flat. **~ement** n.m. unload-
ing.

décharné /deʃarne/ a. bony.

déchausser (se) /(sə)deʃose/ v. pr.
take off one's shoes; (dent) work
loose.

dèche /dɛʃ/ n.f. (fam.) **dans la ~,**
broke.

déchéance /deʃeɑ̃s/ n.f. decay.

déchet /deʃɛ/ n.m. (reste) scrap;
(perte) waste. **~s,** (ordures) refuse.

déchiffrer /deʃifre/ v.t. decipher.

déchiqueter /deʃikte/ v.t. tear to
shreds.

déchir|ant, ~ante /deʃirɑ̃, -t/ a.
heart-breaking. **~ement** n.m.
heart-break; (conflit) split.

déchir|er /deʃire/ v.t. tear; (lacérer)
tear up; (arracher) tear off ou out;
(diviser) tear apart; (oreilles: fig.)
split. **se ~er** v. pr. tear. **~ure** n.f.
tear.

déch|oir /deʃwar/ v.i. demean o.s.
~oir de, (rang) lose, fall from. **~u**
a. fallen.

décibel /desibɛl/ n.m. decibel.

décid|er /deside/ v.t. decide on; (per-
suader) persuade. **~er que/de,** decide that/to. ● v.i. decide. **~er de**
qch., decide on sth. **se ~er** v. pr.
make up one's mind (à, to). **~é** a.
(résolu) determined; (fixé, marqué)
decided. **~ément** adv. really.

décim|al, ~ale (m. pl. **~aux**) /de-
simal, -o/ a. & n.f. decimal.

décimètre /desimɛtr/ n.m. decimetre.

décisi|f, ~ve /desizif, -v/ a. decisive.

décision /desizjɔ̃/ n.f. decision.

déclar|er /deklare/ v.t. declare; (*naissance*) register. **se ~er** v. pr. (*feu*) break out. **~er forfait,** (*sport*) withdraw. **~ation** n.f. declaration; (*commentaire politique*) statement. **~ation d'impôts,** tax return.

déclasser /deklɑse/ v.t. (*coureur*) relegate; (*hôtel*) downgrade.

déclench|er /deklɑ̃ʃe/ v.t. (*techn.*) release, set off; (*lancer*) launch; (*provoquer*) trigger off. **se ~er** v. pr. (*techn.*) go off. **~eur** n.m. (*photo.*) trigger.

déclic /deklik/ n.m. click; (*techn.*) trigger mechanism.

déclin /deklɛ̃/ n.m. decline.

déclin|er¹ /dekline/ v.i. decline. **~aison** n.f. (*lang.*) declension.

décliner² /dekline/ v.t. (*refuser*) decline; (*dire*) state.

déclivité /deklivite/ n.f. slope.

décocher /dekɔʃe/ v.t. (*coup*) fling; (*regard*) shoot.

décoder /dekɔde/ v.t. decode.

décoiffer /dekwafe/ v.t. (*ébouriffer*) disarrange the hair of.

décoincer /dekwɛ̃se/ v.t. free.

décoll|er¹ /dekɔle/ v.i. (*avion*) take off. **~age** n.m. take-off.

décoller² /dekɔle/ v.t. unstick.

décolleté /dekɔlte/ a. low-cut. ● n.m. low neckline.

décolor|er /dekɔlɔre/ v.t. fade; (*cheveux*) bleach. **se ~er** v. pr. fade. **~ation** n.f. bleaching.

décombres /dekɔ̃br/ n.m. pl. rubble.

décommander /dekɔmɑ̃de/ v.t. cancel.

décompos|er /dekɔ̃poze/ v.t. break up; (*substance*) decompose; (*visage*) contort. **se ~er** v. pr. (*pourrir*) decompose. **~ition** n.f. decomposition.

decompt|e /dekɔ̃t/ n.m. deduction; (*détail*) breakdown. **~er** v.t. deduct.

déconcerter /dekɔ̃sɛrte/ v.t. disconcert.

décongel|er /dekɔ̃ʒle/ v.t. thaw. **~ation** n.f. thawing.

décongestionner /dekɔ̃ʒɛstjɔne/ v.t. relieve congestion in.

déconseill|er /dekɔ̃seje/ v.t. **~er qch. à qn.,** advise s.o. against sth. **~é** a. not advisable, inadvisable.

décontenancer /dekɔ̃tnɑ̃se/ v.t. disconcert.

décontract|er /dekɔ̃trakte/ v.t., **se ~** v. pr. relax. **~é** a. relaxed.

déconvenue /dekɔ̃vny/ n.f. disappointment.

décor /dekɔr/ n.m. (*paysage, théâtre*) scenery; (*cinéma*) set; (*cadre*) setting; (*de maison*) décor.

décorati|f, **~ve** /dekɔratif, -v/ a. decorative.

décor|er /dekɔre/ v.t. decorate. **~ateur,** **~atrice** n.m., f. (interior) decorator. **~ation** n.f. decoration.

décortiquer /dekɔrtike/ v.t. shell; (*fig.*) dissect.

découdre (se) /(sə)dekudr/ v. pr. come unstitched.

découler /dekule/ v.i. **~ de,** follow from.

découp|er /dekupe/ v.t. cut up; (*viande*) carve; (*détacher*) cut out. **se ~er sur,** stand out against. **~age** n.m. (*image*) cut-out.

décourag|er /dekuraʒe/ v.t. discourage. **se ~er** v. pr. become discouraged. **~ement** n.m. discouragement. **~é** a. discouraged.

décousu /dekuzy/ a. (*vêtement*) falling apart; (*idées etc.*) disjointed.

découvert, **~e** /dekuver, -t/ a. (*tête etc.*) bare; (*terrain*) open. ● n.m. (*de compte*) overdraft. ● n.f. discovery. **à ~,** exposed; (*fig.*) openly. **à la ~e de,** in search of.

découvrir† /dekuvrir/ v.t. discover; (*enlever ce qui couvre*) uncover; (*voir*) see; (*montrer*) reveal. **se ~** v. pr. uncover o.s.; (*se décoiffer*) take one's hat off; (*ciel*) clear.

décrasser /dekrase/ v.t. clean.

décrépit, **~e** /dekrepi, -t/ a. decrepit. **~ude** n.f. decay.

décret /dekrɛ/ n.m. decree. **~er** /-ete/ v.t. decree.

décrié /dekrije/ v.t. decried.

décrire† /dekrir/ v.t. describe.

décrisp|er (se) /(sə)dekrispe/ v. pr. become less tense. **~ation** n.f. lessening of tension.

décroch|er /dekrɔʃe/ v.t. unhook; (*obtenir*: fam.) get. ● v.i. (*abandonner*: fam.) give up. **~er (le téléphone),** pick up the phone. **~é** a. (*téléphone*) off the hook.

décroître /dekrwatr/ v.i. decrease.

décrue /dekry/ n.f. going down (of river water).

déçu /desy/ a. disappointed.

décupl|e /dekypl/ n.m. **au ~e,** tenfold. **le ~e de,** ten times. **~er** v.t./i. increase tenfold.

dédaign|er /dedeɲe/ v.t. scorn. ~**er de faire,** consider it beneath one to do. ~**eux,** ~**euse** /dedeɲø, -z/ a. scornful.

dédain /dedɛ̃/ n.m. scorn.

dédale /dedal/ n.m. maze.

dedans /dədɑ̃/ adv. & n.m. inside. **au ~ (de),** inside. **en ~,** on the inside.

dédicac|e /dedikas/ n.f. dedication, inscription. ~**er** v.t. dedicate, inscribe.

dédier /dedje/ v.t. dedicate.

dédommag|er /dedɔmaʒe/ v.t. compensate (**de,** for). ~**ement** n.m. compensation.

dédouaner /dedwane/ v.t. clear through customs.

dédoubler /deduble/ v.t. split into two. ~ **un train,** put on a relief train.

déd|uire† /deduir/ v.t. deduct; (conclure) deduce. ~**uction** n.f. deduction; ~**uction d'impôts** tax deduction.

déesse /deɛs/ n.f. goddess.

défaillance /defajɑ̃s/ n.f. weakness; (évanouissement) black-out; (panne) failure.

défaill|ir /defajir/ v.i. faint; (forces etc.) fail. ~**ant,** ~**ante** a. (personne) faint; (candidat) defaulting.

défaire† /defɛr/ v.t. undo; (valise) unpack; (démonter) take down; (débarrasser) rid. **se ~ de,** rid o.s. of. **se ~** v. pr. come undone.

défait, ~**e**[1] /defɛ, -t/ a. (cheveux) ruffled; (visage) haggard.

défaite[2] /defɛt/ n.f. defeat.

défaitisme /defetizm/ n.m. defeatism.

défaitiste /defetist/ a. & n.m./f. defeatist.

défalquer /defalke/ v.t. (somme) deduct.

défaut /defo/ n.m. fault, defect; (d'un verre, diamant, etc.) flaw; (carence) lack; (pénurie) shortage. **à ~ de,** for lack of. **en ~,** at fault. **faire ~,** (argent etc.) be lacking. **par ~,** (jurid.) in one's absence.

défav|eur /defavœr/ n.f. disfavour. ~**orable** a. unfavourable.

défavoriser /defavɔrize/ v.t. put at a disadvantage.

défection /defɛksjɔ̃/ n.f. desertion. **faire ~,** desert.

défect|ueux, ~**ueuse** /defɛktɥø, -z/ a. faulty, defective. ~**uosité** n.f. faultiness; (défaut) fault.

défendre /defɑ̃dr/ v.t. defend; (interdire) forbid. ~ **à qn. de,** forbid s.o. to. **se ~** v. pr. defend o.s.; (se débrouiller) manage; (se protéger) protect o.s. **se ~ de,** (refuser) refrain from.

défense /defɑ̃s/ n.f. defence; (d'éléphant) tusk. ~ **de fumer**/etc., no smoking/etc.

défenseur /defɑ̃sœr/ n.m. defender.

défensi|f, ~**ve** /defɑ̃sif, -v/ a. & n.f. defensive.

déféren|t, ~**te** /deferɑ̃, -t/ a. deferential. ~**ce** n.f. deference.

déférer /defere/ v.t. (jurid.) refer. ● v.i. ~ **à,** (avis etc.) defer to.

déferler /defɛrle/ v.i. (vagues) break; (violence etc.) erupt.

défi /defi/ n.m. challenge; (refus) defiance. **mettre au ~,** challenge.

déficeler /defisle/ v.t. untie.

déficience /defisjɑ̃s/ n.f. deficiency.

déficient /defisjɑ̃/ a. deficient.

déficit /defisit/ n.m. deficit. ~**aire** a. in deficit.

défier /defje/ v.t. challenge; (braver) defy. **se ~ de,** mistrust.

défilé[1] /defile/ n.m. procession; (mil.) parade; (fig.) (continual) stream. ~ **de mode,** fashion parade.

défilé[2] /defile/ n.m. (géog.) gorge.

défiler /defile/ v.i. march (past); (visiteurs) stream; (images) flash by. **se ~** v. pr. (fam.) sneak off.

défini /defini/ a. definite.

définir /definir/ v.t. define.

définissable /definisabl/ a. definable.

définiti|f, ~**ve** /definitif, -v/ a. final; (permanent) definitive. **en ~ve,** in the final analysis. ~**vement** adv. definitively, permanently.

définition /definisjɔ̃/ n.f. definition; (de mots croisés) clue.

déflagration /deflagrasjɔ̃/ n.f. explosion.

déflation /deflasjɔ̃/ n.f. deflation. ~**niste** /-jɔnist/ a. deflationary.

défoncer /defɔ̃se/ v.t. (porte etc.) break down; (route, terrain) dig up; (lit) break the springs of. **se ~** v. pr. (fam.) work like mad; (drogué) get high.

déform|er /defɔrme/ v.t. put out of shape; (membre) deform; (faits, pensée) distort. ~**ation** n.f. loss of shape; deformation; distortion.

défouler (se) /(sə)defule/ v. pr. let off steam.

défraîchir (se) /(sə)defreʃir/ v. pr. become faded.

défrayer /defreje/ v.t. (payer) pay the expenses of.

défricher /defriʃe/ v.t. clear (for cultivation).

défroisser /defrwase/ v.t. smooth out.

défunt, ∼e /defœ̃, -t/ a. (mort) late. ● n.m., f. deceased.

dégagé /degaʒe/ a. clear; (ton) free and easy.

dégag|er /degaʒe/ v.t. (exhaler) give off; (désencombrer) clear; (délivrer) free; (faire ressortir) bring out. ● v.i. (football) kick the ball (down the pitch ou field). **se ∼er** v. pr. free o.s.; (ciel, rue) clear; (odeur etc.) emanate. **∼ement** n.m. giving off; clearing; freeing; (espace) clearing; (football) clearance.

dégainer /degene/ v.t./i. draw.

dégarnir /degarnir/ v.t. clear, empty. **se ∼** v. pr. clear, empty; (crâne) go bald.

dégâts /degɑ/ n.m. pl. damage.

dégel /deʒɛl/ n.m. thaw. **∼er** /deʒle/ v.t./i. thaw (out). **(faire) ∼er,** (culin.) thaw.

dégénér|er /deʒenere/ v.i. degenerate. **∼é, ∼ée** a. & n.m., f. degenerate.

dégingandé /deʒɛ̃gɑ̃de/ a. gangling.

dégivrer /deʒivre/ v.t. (auto.) de-ice; (réfrigérateur) defrost.

déglacer /deglase/ v.t. (culin.) deglaze.

déglingu|er /deglɛ̃ge/ (fam.) v.t. knock about. **se ∼er** v. pr. fall to bits. **∼é** adj. falling to bits.

dégonfl|er /degɔ̃fle/ v.t. let down, deflate. **se ∼er** v. pr. (fam.) get cold feet. **∼é** a. (pneu) flat; (lâche: fam.) yellow.

dégorger /degɔrʒe/ v.i. **faire ∼,** (culin.) soak.

dégouliner /deguline/ v.i. trickle.

dégourdi /degurdi/ a. smart.

dégourdir /degurdir/ v.t. (membre, liquide) warm up. **se ∼ les jambes,** stretch one's legs.

dégoût /degu/ n.m. disgust.

dégoût|er /degute/ v.t. disgust. **∼er qn. de qch.,** put s.o. off sth. **∼ant, ∼ante** a. disgusting. **∼é** a. disgusted. **∼é de,** sick of. **faire le ∼é,** look disgusted.

dégradant /degradɑ̃/ a. degrading.

dégrader /degrade/ v.t. degrade; (abîmer) damage. **se ∼** v. pr. (se détériorer) deteriorate.

dégrafer /degrafe/ v.t. unhook.

degré /dəgre/ n.m. degree; (d'escalier) step.

dégressi|f, ∼ve /degresif, -v/ a. gradually lower.

dégrèvement /degrɛvmɑ̃/ n.m. **∼ fiscal** ou **d'impôts,** tax reduction.

dégrever /degrəve/ v.t. reduce the tax on.

dégringol|er /degrɛ̃gɔle/ v.i. tumble (down). ● v.t. rush down. **∼ade** n.f. tumble.

dégrossir /degrosir/ v.t. (bois) trim; (projet) rough out.

déguerpir /degɛrpir/ v.i. clear off.

dégueulasse /degœlas/ a. (argot) disgusting, lousy.

dégueuler /degœle/ v.t. (argot) throw up.

déguis|er /degize/ v.t. disguise. **se ∼er** v. pr. disguise o.s.; (au carnaval etc.) dress up. **∼ement** n.m. disguise; (de carnaval etc.) fancy dress.

dégust|er /degyste/ v.t. taste, sample; (savourer) enjoy. **∼ation** n.f. tasting, sampling.

déhancher (se) /(sə)deɑ̃ʃe/ v. pr. sway one's hips.

dehors /dəɔr/ adv. & n.m. outside. ● n.m. pl. (aspect de qn.) exterior. **au ∼ (de),** outside. **en ∼ de,** outside; (hormis) apart from. **jeter/ mettre/etc. ∼,** throw/put/etc. out.

déjà /deʒa/ adv. already; (avant) before, already.

déjà-vu /deʒavy/ n.m. inv. déjà vu.

déjeuner /deʒœne/ v.i. (have) lunch; (le matin) (have) breakfast. ● n.m. lunch. **(petit) ∼,** breakfast.

déjouer /deʒwe/ v.t. thwart.

delà /dəla/ adv. & prép. **au ∼ (de), en ∼ (de), par ∼,** beyond.

délabrer (se) /(sə)delabre/ v. pr. become dilapidated.

délacer /delase/ v.t. undo.

délai /dele/ n.m. time-limit; (attente) wait; (sursis) extension (of time). **sans ∼,** without delay. **dans les plus brefs ∼s,** as soon as possible.

délaisser /delese/ v.t. desert.

délass|er /delase/ v.t., **se ∼er** v. pr. relax. **∼ement** n.m. relaxation.

délation /delasjɔ̃/ n.f. informing.

délavé /delave/ a. faded.

délayer /deleje/ v.t. mix (with liquid); (idée) drag out.

delco /dɛlko/ n.m. (P., auto.) distributor.

délecter (se) /(sə)delɛkte/ v. pr. se ~ de, delight in.

délégation /delegɑsjɔ̃/ n.f. delegation.

délégu|er /delege/ v.t. delegate. ~é, ~ée n.m., f. delegate.

délibéré /delibere/ a. deliberate; (résolu) determined. ~ment adv. deliberately.

délibér|er /delibere/ v.i. deliberate. ~ation n.f. deliberation.

délicat, ~e /delika, -t/ a. delicate; (plein de tact) tactful; (exigeant) particular. ~ement /-tmɑ̃/ adv. delicately; tactfully. ~esse /-tɛs/ n.f. delicacy; tact. ~esses /-tɛs/ n.f. pl. (kind) attentions.

délice /delis/ n.m. delight. ~s n.f. pl. delights.

délicieu|x, ~se /delisjø, -z/ a. (au goût) delicious; (charmant) delightful.

délié /delje/ a. fine, slender; (agile) nimble.

délier /delje/ v.t. untie; (délivrer) free. se ~ v. pr. come untied.

délimit|er /delimite/ v.t. determine, demarcate. ~ation n.f. demarcation.

délinquan|t, ~te /delɛ̃kɑ̃, -t/ a. & n.m., f. delinquent. ~ce n.f. delinquency.

délire /delir/ n.m. delirium; (fig.) frenzy.

délir|er /delire/ v.i. be delirious (de, with); (déraisonner) rave. ~ant, ~ante a. delirious; (frénétique) frenzied; (fam.) wild.

délit /deli/ n.m. offence, crime.

délivr|er /delivre/ v.t. free, release; (pays) deliver; (remettre) issue. ~ance n.f. release; deliverance; issue.

déloger /delɔʒe/ v.t. force out.

déloy|al (m. pl. ~aux) /delwajal, -jo/ a. disloyal; (procédé) unfair.

delta /dɛlta/ n.m. delta.

deltaplane /dɛltaplan/ n.m. hang-glider.

déluge /delyʒ/ n.m. flood; (pluie) downpour.

démagogie /demagɔʒi/ n.m. demagogy.

démagogue /demagɔg/ n.m./f. demagogue.

demain /dmɛ̃/ adv. tomorrow.

demande /dmɑ̃d/ n.f. request; (d'emploi) application; (exigence) demand. ~ en mariage, proposal (of marriage).

demandé /dmɑ̃de/ a. in demand.

demander /dmɑ̃de/ v.t. ask for; (chemin, heure) ask; (emploi) apply for; (nécessiter) require. ~ que/si, ask that/if. ~ qch. à qn., ask s.o. for sth. ~ à qn. de, ask s.o. to. ~ en mariage, propose to. se ~ si/où/etc., wonder if/where/etc.

demandeu|r, ~se /dmɑ̃dœr, -øz/ n.m., f. les ~rs d'emploi job seekers.

démang|er /demɑ̃ʒe/ v.t./i. itch. ~eaison n.f. itch(ing).

démanteler /demɑ̃tle/ v.t. break up.

démaquill|er (se) /(sə)demakije/ v. pr. remove one's make-up. ~ant n.m. make-up remover.

démarcation /demarkɑsjɔ̃/ n.f. demarcation.

démarchage /demarʃaʒ/ n.m. door-to-door selling.

démarche /demarʃ/ n.f. walk, gait; (procédé) step. faire des ~s auprès de, make approaches to.

démarcheu|r, ~se /demarʃœr, -øz/ n.m., f. (door-to-door) canvasser.

démarr|er /demare/ v.i. (moteur) start (up); (partir) move off; (fig.) get moving. ● v.t. (fam.) get moving. ~age n.m. start. ~eur n.m. starter.

démasquer /demaske/ v.t. unmask.

démêlant /demelɑ̃/ n.m. conditioner.

démêler /demele/ v.t. disentangle.

démêlés /demele/ n.m. pl. trouble.

déménag|er /demenaʒe/ v.i. move (house). ● v.t. (meubles) remove. ~ement n.m. move; (de meubles) removal. ~eur n.m. removal man; (Amer.) furniture mover.

démener (se) /(sə)demne/ v. pr. move about wildly; (fig.) exert o.s.

démen|t, ~te /demɑ̃, -t/ a. insane. ● n.m., f. lunatic. ~ce n.f. insanity.

démenti /demɑ̃ti/ n.m. denial.

démentir /demɑ̃tir/ v.t. refute; (ne pas être conforme à) belie. ~ que, deny that.

démerder (se) /(sə)demɛrde/ (fam.) manage.

démesuré /deməzyre/ a. inordinate.

démettre /demɛtr/ v.t. (poignet etc.) dislocate. ~ qn. de, dismiss s.o. from. se ~ v. pr. resign (de, from).

demeure /dəmœr/ *n.f.* residence. **mettre en ~ de,** order to.

demeurer /dəmœre/ *v.i.* live; (*rester*) remain.

demi, ~e /dmi/ *a.* half(-). ● *n.m., f.* half. ● *n.m.* (*bière*) (half-pint) glass of beer; (*football*) half-back. ● *n.f.* (*à l'horloge*) half-hour. ● *adv.* **à ~,** half; (*ouvrir, fermer*) half-way. **à la ~e,** at half-past. **une heure et ~e,** an hour and a half; (*à l'horloge*) half past one. **une ~-journée/-livre/***etc.*, half a day/pound/*etc.*, a half-day/-pound/*etc.* **~-cercle** *n.m.* semicircle. **~-finale** *n.f.* semifinal. **~-frère** *n.m.* stepbrother. **~-heure** *n.f.* half-hour, half an hour. **~-jour** *n.m.* half-light. **~-mesure** *n.f.* half-measure. **à ~-mot** *adv.* without having to express every word. **~-pension** *n.f.* half-board. **~-pensionnaire** *n.m./f.* day-boarder. **~-sel** *a. invar.* slightly salted. **~-sœur** *n.f.* stepsister. **~-tarif** *n.m.* half-fare. **~-tour** *n.m.* about turn; (*auto.*) U-turn. **faire ~-tour,** turn back.

démis, ~e /demi, -z/ *a.* dislocated. **~ de ses fonctions,** removed from his post.

démission /demisjɔ̃/ *n.f.* resignation. **~ner** /-jɔne/ *v.i.* resign.

démobiliser /demɔbilize/ *v.t.* demobilize.

démocrate /demɔkrat/ *n.m./f.* democrat. ● *a.* democratic.

démocrat|ie /demɔkrasi/ *n.f.* democracy. **~ique** /-atik/ *a.* democratic.

démodé /demɔde/ *a.* old-fashioned.

démographi|e /demɔgrafi/ *n.f.* demography. **~que** *a.* demographic.

demoiselle /dəmwazɛl/ *n.f.* young lady; (*célibataire*) spinster. **~ d'honneur,** bridesmaid.

démol|ir /demɔlir/ *v.t.* demolish. **~ition** *n.f.* demolition.

démon /demɔ̃/ *n.m.* demon. **le D~,** the Devil.

démoniaque /demɔnjak/ *a.* fiendish.

démonstra|teur, ~trice /demɔ̃stratœr, -tris/ *n.m., f.* demonstrator. **~tion** /-asjɔ̃/ *n.f.* demonstration; (*de force*) show.

démonstrati|f, ~ve /demɔ̃stratif, -v/ *a.* demonstrative.

démonter /demɔ̃te/ *v.t.* take apart, dismantle; (*installation*) take down; (*fig.*) disconcert. **se ~** *v. pr.* come apart.

démontrer /demɔ̃tre/ *v.t.* show, demonstrate.

démoraliser /demɔralize/ *v.t.* demoralize.

démuni /demyni/ *a.* impoverished. **~ de,** without.

démunir /demynir/ *v.t.* **~ de,** deprive of. **se ~ de,** part with.

démystifier /demistifje/ *v.t.* enlighten.

dénaturer /denatyre/ *v.t.* (*faits etc.*) distort.

dénégation /denegasjɔ̃/ *n.f.* denial.

dénicher /denife/ *v.t.* (*trouver*) dig up; (*faire sortir*) flush out.

dénigr|er /denigre/ *v.t.* denigrate. **~ement** *n.m.* denigration.

dénivellation /denivɛlasjɔ̃/ *n.f.* (*pente*) slope.

dénombrer /denɔ̃bre/ *v.t.* count; (*énumérer*) enumerate.

dénomination /denɔminasjɔ̃/ *n.f.* designation.

dénommé, ~e /denɔme/ *n. m., f.* **le ~ X,** the said X.

dénonc|er /denɔ̃se/ *v.t.* denounce; (*scol.*) tell on. **se ~er** *v. pr.* give o.s. up. **~iateur, ~iatrice** *n.m., f.* informer; (*scol.*) tell-tale. **~iation** *n.f.* denunciation.

dénoter /denɔte/ *v.t.* denote.

dénouement /denumɑ̃/ *n.m.* outcome; (*théâtre*) dénouement.

dénouer /denwe/ *v.t.* unknot, undo. **se ~** *v. pr.* (*nœud*) come undone.

dénoyauter /denwajote/ *v.t.* stone; (*Amer.*) pit.

denrée /dɑ̃re/ *n.f.* foodstuff.

dens|e /dɑ̃s/ *a.* dense. **~ité** *n.f.* density.

dent /dɑ̃/ *n.f.* tooth; (*de roue*) cog. **faire ses ~s,** teethe. **~aire** /-tɛr/ *a.* dental.

dentelé /dɑ̃tle/ *a.* jagged.

dentelle /dɑ̃tɛl/ *n.f.* lace.

dentier /dɑ̃tje/ *n.m.* denture.

dentifrice /dɑ̃tifris/ *n.m.* toothpaste.

dentiste /dɑ̃tist/ *n.m./f.* dentist.

dentition /dɑ̃tisjɔ̃/ *n.f.* teeth.

dénud|er /denyde/ *v.t.* bare. **~é** *a.* bare.

dénué /denye/ *a.* **~ de,** devoid of.

dénuement /denymɑ̃/ *n.m.* destitution.

déodorant /deɔdɔrɑ̃/ *a.m. & n.m.* **(produit) ~,** deodorant.

déontologi|e /deɔ̃tɔlɔʒi/ *n.f.* code of practice. **~que** *a.* ethical.

dépann|er /depane/ v.t. repair; (fig.) help out. **~age** n.m. repair. **de ~age**, (service etc.) breakdown. **~euse** n.f. breakdown lorry; (Amer.) wrecker.

dépareillé /depareje/ a. odd, not matching.

départ /depar/ n.m. departure; (sport) start. **au ~**, at the outset.

départager /departaʒe/ v.t. settle the matter between.

département /departəmɑ̃/ n.m. department.

dépassé /depase/ a. outdated.

dépass|er /depase/ v.t. go past, pass; (véhicule) overtake; (excéder) exceed; (rival) surpass; (dérouter: fam.) be beyond. ● v.i. stick out; (véhicule) overtake. **~ement** n.m. overtaking.

dépays|er /depeize/ v.t. disorientate, disorient. **~ant, ~e** a. disorientating. **~ement** n.m. disorientation; (changement) change of scenery.

dépêch|e /depɛʃ/ n.f. dispatch. **~er¹** /-eʃe/ v.t. dispatch.

dépêcher² (se) /(sə)depeʃe/ v. pr. hurry (up).

dépeindre /depɛ̃dr/ v.t. depict.

dépendance /depɑ̃dɑ̃s/ n.f. dependence; (bâtiment) outbuilding.

dépendre /depɑ̃dr/ v.t. take down. ● v.i. depend (de, on). **~ de**, (appartenir à) belong to.

dépens (aux) /(o)depɑ̃/ prép. **aux ~ de**, at the expense of.

dépens|e /depɑ̃s/ n.f. expense; expenditure. **~er** v.t./i. spend; (énergie etc.) expend. **se ~er** v. pr. exert o.s.

dépens|ier, ~ière /depɑ̃sje, -jɛr/ a. **être ~ier**, be a spendthrift.

dépérir /deperir/ v.i. wither.

dépêtrer (se) /(sə)depetre/ v. pr. get o.s. out (de, of).

dépeupler /depœple/ v.t. depopulate. **se ~** v. pr. become depopulated.

déphasé /defaze/ a. (fam.) out of touch.

dépilatoire /depilatwar/ a. & n.m. depilatory.

dépist|er /depiste/ v.t. detect; (criminel) track down; (poursuivant) throw off the scent. **~age** n.m. detection.

dépit /depi/ n.m. resentment. **en ~ de**, despite. **en ~ du bon sens**,

against all common sense. **~é** /-te/ a. vexed.

déplacé /deplase/ a. out of place.

déplac|er /deplase/ v.t. move. **se ~er** v. pr. move; (voyager) travel. **~ement** n.m. moving; travel(-ling).

déplaire /deplɛr/ v.i. **~ à**, (irriter) displease. **ça me déplaît**, I dislike that.

déplaisant, ~e /deplezɑ̃, -t/ a. unpleasant, disagreeable.

déplaisir /deplezir/ n.m. displeasure.

dépliant /deplijɑ̃/ n.m. leaflet.

déplier /deplije/ v.t. unfold.

déplor|er /deplore/ v.t. (trouver regrettable) deplore; (mort) lament. **~able** a. deplorable.

dépl|oyer /deplwaje/ v.t. (ailes, carte) spread; (courage) display; (armée) deploy. **~oiement** n.m. display; deployment.

déport|er /deporte/ v.t. (exiler) deport; (dévier) carry off course. **~ation** n.f. deportation.

déposer /depoze/ v.t. put down; (laisser) leave; (passager) drop; (argent) deposit; (installation) dismantle; (plainte) lodge; (armes) lay down; (roi) depose. ● v.i. (jurid.) testify. **se ~** v. pr. settle.

dépositaire /depozitɛr/ n.m./f. (comm.) agent.

déposition /depozisjɔ̃/ n.f. (jurid.) statement.

dépôt /depo/ n.m. (garantie, lie) deposit; (entrepôt) warehouse; (d'autobus) depot; (d'ordures) dump. **laisser en ~**, give for safe keeping.

dépotoir /depotwar/ n.m. rubbish dump.

dépouille /depuj/ n.f. skin, hide. **~ (mortelle)**, mortal remains. **~s**, (butin) spoils.

dépouiller /depuje/ v.t. go through; (votes) count; (écorcher) skin. **~ de**, strip of.

dépourvu /depurvy/ a. **~ de**, devoid of. **prendre au ~**, catch unawares.

dépréc|ier /depresje/ v.t., **se ~ier** v. pr. depreciate. **~iation** n.f. depreciation.

déprédations /depredasjɔ̃/ n.f. pl. damage.

dépr|imer /deprime/ v.t. depress. **~ession** n.f. depression. **~ession nerveuse**, nervous breakdown.

depuis /dəpɥi/ prép. since; (durée) for; (à partir de) from. ● adv. (ever) since. ~ **que**, since. ~ **quand attendez-vous?**, how long have you been waiting?

députation /depytasjɔ̃/ *n.f.* deputation.

député, ~**e** /depyte/ *n.m.*, *f.* Member of Parliament.

déraciné, ~**e** /derasine/ *a. & n.m.*, *f.* rootless (person).

déraciner /derasine/ *v.t.* uproot.

déraill|er /deraje/ *v.i.* be derailed; (*fig.*, *fam.*) be talking nonsense. **faire ~er**, derail. ~**ement** *n.m.* derailment. ~**eur** *n.m.* (*de vélo*) gear mechanism, *dérailleur*.

déraisonnable /derɛzɔnabl/ *a.* unreasonable.

dérang|er /derɑ̃ʒe/ *v.t.* (*gêner*) bother, disturb; (*dérégler*) upset, disrupt. **se ~er** *v. pr.* put o.s. out. **ça vous ~e si . . .?**, do you mind if . . .? ~**ement** *n.m.* bother; (*désordre*) disorder, upset. **en ~ement**, out of order.

dérap|er /derape/ *v.i.* skid; (*fig.*) get out of control. ~**age** *n.m.* skid.

déréglé /deregle/ *a.* (*vie*) dissolute; (*estomac*) upset; (*pendule*) (that is) not running properly.

dérégler /deregle/ *v.t.* put out of order. **se ~** *v. pr.* go wrong.

dérision /derizjɔ̃/ *n.f.* mockery. **par ~**, derisively. **tourner en ~**, mock.

dérisoire /derizwar/ *a.* derisory.

dérivatif /derivatif/ *n.m.* distraction.

dériv|e /deriv/ *n.f.* **aller à la ~e**, drift. ~**er**[1] *v.i.* (*bateau*) drift; *v.t.* (*détourner*) divert.

dériv|er[2] /derive/ *v.i.* ~**er de**, derive from. ~**é** *a.* derived; *n.m.* derivative; (*techn.*) by-product.

dermatolo|gie /dɛrmatɔlɔʒi/ *n.f.* dermatology. ~**gue** /-g/ *n.m./f.* dermatologist.

dern|ier, ~**ière** /dɛrnje, -jɛr/ *a.* last; (*nouvelles, mode*) latest; (*étage*) top. ● *n.m.*, *f.* last (one). **ce ~ier**, the latter. **en ~ier**, last. **le ~ier cri**, the latest fashion.

dernièrement /dɛrnjɛrmɑ̃/ *adv.* recently.

dérobé /derɔbe/ *a.* hidden. **à la ~e**, stealthily.

dérober /derɔbe/ *v.t.* steal; (*cacher*) hide (**à**, from). **se ~** *v. pr.* slip away. **se ~ à**, (*obligation*) shy away from; (*se cacher à*) hide from.

dérogation /derɔgasjɔ̃/ *n.f.* exemption.

déroger /derɔʒe/ *v.i.* ~ **à**, go against.

dérouiller (se) /(sə)deruje/ *v. pr.* **se ~ les jambes** to stretch one's legs.

déroul|er /derule/ *v.t.* (*fil etc.*) unwind. **se ~er** *v. pr.* unwind; (*avoir lieu*) take place; (*récit, paysage*) unfold. ~**ement** *n.m.* (*d'une action*) development.

déroute /derut/ *n.f.* (*mil.*) rout.

dérouter /derute/ *v.t.* disconcert.

derrlère /dɛrjɛr/ *prép. & adv.* behind. ● *n.m.* back, rear; (*postérieur*) behind. **de ~**, back, rear; (*pattes*) hind. **par ~**, (from) behind, at the back *ou* rear.

des /de/ *voir* de.

dès /dɛ/ *prép.* (right) from, from the time of. ~ **lors**, from then on. ~ **que**, as soon as.

désabusé /dezabyze/ *a.* disillusioned.

désaccord /dezakɔr/ *n.m.* disagreement. ~**é** /-de/ *a.* out of tune.

désaffecté /dezafɛkte/ *a.* disused.

désaffection /dezafɛksjɔ̃/ *n.f.* alienation (**pour**, from).

désagréable /dezagreabl/ *a.* unpleasant.

désagréger (se) /(sə)dezagreʒe/ *v. pr.* disintegrate.

désagrément /dezagremɑ̃/ *n.m.* annoyance.

désaltérant /dezalterɑ̃/ *a.* thirst-quenching, refreshing.

désaltérer /dezaltere/ *v.i.*, **se ~** *v. pr.* quench one's thirst.

désamorcer /dezamɔrse/ *v.t.* (*situation, obus*) defuse.

désapprlouver /dezapruve/ *v.t.* disapprove of. ~**obation** *n.f.* disapproval.

désarçonner /dezarsɔne/ *v.t.* disconcert, throw; (*jockey*) unseat, throw.

désarmant /dezarmɑ̃/ *a.* disarming.

désarm|er /dezarme/ *v.t./i.* disarm. ~**ement** *n.m.* (*pol.*) disarmament.

désarroi /dezarwa/ *n.m.* confusion.

désarticulé /dezartikyle/ *a.* dislocated.

désastr|e /dezastr/ *n.m.* disaster. ~**eux**, ~**euse** *a.* disastrous.

désavantag|e /dezavɑ̃taʒ/ *n.m.* disadvantage. ~**er** *v.t.* put at a disadvantage. ~**eux**, ~**euse** *a.* disadvantageous.

désaveu (*pl.* ~**x**) /dezavø/ *n.m.* repudiation.

désavouer /dezavwe/ *v.t.* repudiate.

désaxé, ~e /dezakse/ *a. & n.m., f.* unbalanced (person).

descendan|t, ~te /desɑ̃dɑ̃, -t/ *n.m., f.* descendant. **~ce** *n.f.* descent; (*enfants*) descendants.

descendre /desɑ̃dr/ *v.i.* (*aux. être*) go down; (*venir*) come down; (*passager*) get off *ou* out; (*nuit*) fall. **~ de**, (*être issu de*) be descended from. **~ à l'hôtel,** go to a hotel. ● *v.t.* (*aux. avoir*) (*escalier etc.*) go *ou* come down; (*objet*) take down; (*abattre, fam.*) shoot down.

descente /desɑ̃t/ *n.f.* descent; (*pente*) (downward) slope; (*raid*) raid. **~ de lit,** bedside rug.

descripti|f, ~ve /dɛskriptif, -v/ *a.* descriptive.

description /dɛskripsjɔ̃/ *n.f.* description.

désemparé /dezɑ̃pare/ *a.* distraught.

désemplir /dezɑ̃plir/ *v.i.* **ne pas ~,** be always crowded.

désendettement /dezɑ̃dɛtmɑ̃/ *n.m.* getting out of debt.

désenfler /dezɑ̃fle/ *v.i.* go down.

déséquilibre /dezekilibr/ *n.m.* imbalance. **en ~,** unsteady.

déséquilibr|er /dezekilibre/ *v.t.* throw off balance. **~é, ~ée** *a. & n.m., f.* unbalanced (person).

désert¹ ~e /dezɛr, -t/ *a.* deserted.

désert² /dezɛr/ *n.m.* desert. **~ique** /-tik/ *a.* desert.

déserter /dezɛrte/ *v.t./i.* desert. **~eur** *n.m.* deserter. **~ion** /-ɛrsjɔ̃/ *n.f.* desertion.

désespér|er /dezɛspere/ *v.i.*, **se ~er** *v. pr.* despair. **~er de**, despair of. **~ant, ~ante** *a.* utterly disheartening. **~é** *a.* in despair; (*état, cas*) hopeless; (*effort*) desperate. **~ément** *adv.* desperately.

désespoir /dezɛspwar/ *n.m.* despair. **au ~,** in despair. **en ~ de cause,** as a last resort.

déshabill|er /dezabije/ *v.t.* **se ~er** *v. pr.* undress, get undressed. **~é** *a.* undressed; *n.m.* négligée.

déshabituer (se) /(sə)dezabitɥe/ *v. pr.* **se ~ de**, get out of the habit of.

désherb|er /dezɛrbe/ *v.t.* weed. **~ant** *n.m.* weed-killer.

déshérit|er /dezerite/ *v.t.* disinherit. **~é** *a.* (*région*) deprived. **les ~és** *n.m. pl.* the underprivileged.

déshonneur /dezɔnœr/ *n.m.* dishonour.

déshonor|er /dezɔnɔre/ *v.t.* dishonour. **~ant, ~ante** *a.* dishonourable.

déshydrater /dezidrate/ *v.t.*, **se ~** *v. pr.* dehydrate.

désigner /deziɲe/ *v.t.* (*montrer*) point to *ou* out; (*élire*) appoint; (*signifier*) indicate.

désillusion /dezilyzjɔ̃/ *n.f.* disillusionment.

désincrust|er /dezɛ̃kryste/ *v. pr.* (*chaudière*) descale; (*peau*) exfoliate. **~ant** *a.* **produit ~ant**, (skin) scrub.

désinence /dezinɑ̃s/ *n.f.* (*gram.*) ending.

désinfect|er /dezɛ̃fɛkte/ *v.t.* disinfect. **~ant** *n.m.* disinfectant.

désinfection /dezɛ̃fɛksjɔ̃/ *n.f.* disinfection.

désintégrer /dezɛ̃tegre/ *v.t.*, **se ~** *v. pr.* disintegrate.

désintéressé /dezɛ̃terese/ *a.* disinterested.

désintéresser (se) /(sə)dezɛ̃terese/ *v. pr.* **se ~ de**, lose interest in.

désintoxication /dezɛ̃tɔksikasjɔ̃/ *n.f.* detoxification. **cure de ~,** detoxification course.

désintoxiquer /dezɛ̃tɔksike/ *v.t.* cure of an addiction; (*régime*) purify.

désinvolt|e /dezɛ̃vɔlt/ *a.* casual. **~ure** *n.f.* casualness.

désir /dezir/ *n.m.* wish, desire; (*convoitise*) desire.

désirer /dezire/ *v.t.* want; (*convoiter*) desire. **~ faire**, want *ou* wish to do.

désireu|x, ~se /dezirø, -z/ *a.* **~x de**, anxious to.

désist|er (se) /(sə)deziste/ *v. pr.* withdraw. **~ement** *n.m.* withdrawal.

désobéir /dezɔbeir/ *v.i.* **~ (à)**, disobey.

désobéissan|t, ~te /dezɔbeisɑ̃, -t/ *a.* disobedient. **~ce** *n.f.* disobedience.

désobligeant, ~e /dezɔbliʒɑ̃, -t/ *a.* disagreeable, unkind.

désodé /desɔde/ *a.* sodium-free.

désodorisant /dezɔdɔrizɑ̃/ *n.m.* air freshener.

désœuvr|é /dezœvre/ *a.* idle. **~ement** *n.m.* idleness.

désolé /dezɔle/ *a.* (*région*) desolate.

désol|er /dezɔle/ *v.t.* distress. **être ~é**, (*regretter*) be sorry. **~ation** *n.f.* distress.

désopilant, ~e /dezɔpilɑ̃, -t/ a. hilarious.

désordonné /dezɔrdɔne/ a. untidy; (mouvements) uncoordinated.

désordre /dezɔrdr/ n.m. disorder; (de vêtements, cheveux) untidiness. **mettre en ~,** make untidy.

désorganiser /dezɔrganize/ v.t. disorganize.

désorienté /dezɔrjɑ̃te/ a. disorientated.

désorienter /dezɔrjɑ̃te/ v.t. disorientate, disorient.

désormais /dezɔrmɛ/ adv. from now on.

désosser /dezɔse/ v.t. bone.

despote /dɛspɔt/ n.m. despot.

desquels, desquelles /dekɛl/ voir lequel.

dessécher /deseʃe/ v.t., **se ~** v. pr. dry out ou up.

dessein /desɛ̃/ n.m. intention. **à ~,** intentionally.

desserrer /desere/ v.t. loosen. **sans ~ les dents,** without opening his/her mouth. **se ~** v. pr. come loose.

dessert /desɛr/ n.m. dessert.

desserte /desɛrt/ n.f. (transports) service, servicing.

desservir /desɛrvir/ v.t./i. clear away; (autobus) provide a service to, serve.

dessin /desɛ̃/ n.m. drawing; (motif) design; (contour) outline. **~ animé,** (cinéma) cartoon. **~ humoristique,** cartoon.

dessin|er /desine/ v.t./i. draw; (fig.) outline. **se ~er** v. pr. appear, take shape. **~ateur, ~atrice** n.m., f. artist; (industriel) draughtsman.

dessoûler /desule/ v.t./i. sober up.

dessous /dsu/ adv. underneath.
● n.m. under-side, underneath.
● n.m. pl. underclothes. **du ~,** bottom; (voisins) downstairs. **en ~, par ~,** underneath. **~-de-plat** n.m. invar. (heat-resistant) table-mat. **~-de-table** n.m. invar. backhander.

dessus /dsy/ adv. on top (of it), on it.
● n.m. top. **du ~,** top; (voisins) upstairs. **en ~,** above. **par ~,** over (it). **avoir le ~,** get the upper hand. **~-de-lit** n.m. invar. bedspread.

destabilis|er /destabilize/ v.t. destabilize. **~ation** n.f. destabilization.

destin /dɛstɛ̃/ n.m. (sort) fate; (avenir) destiny.

destinataire /dɛstinatɛr/ n.m./f. addressee.

destination /dɛstinasjɔ̃/ n.f. destination; (emploi) purpose. **à ~ de,** (going) to.

destinée /dɛstine/ n.f. (sort) fate; (avenir) destiny.

destin|er /dɛstine/ v.t. **~er à,** intend for; (vouer) destine for; (affecter) earmark for. **être ~é à faire,** be intended to do; (condamné, obligé) be destined to do. **se ~er à,** (carrière) intend to take up.

destit|uer /dɛstitɥe/ v.t. dismiss (from office). **~ution** n.f. dismissal.

destruc|teur, ~trice /dɛstryktœr, -tris/ a. destructive.

destruction /dɛstryksjɔ̃/ n.f. destruction.

dés|uet, ~uète /dezɥɛ, -t/ a. outdated.

désunir /dezynir/ v.t. divide.

détachant /detaʃɑ̃/ n.m. stain-remover.

détach|é /detaʃe/ a. detached. **~ement** n.m. detachment.

détacher /detaʃe/ v.t. untie; (ôter) remove, detach; (déléguer) send (on assignment ou secondment). **se ~** v. pr. come off, break away; (nœud etc.) come undone; (ressortir) stand out.

détail /detaj/ n.m. detail; (de compte) breakdown; (comm.) retail. **au ~,** (vendre etc.) retail. **de ~,** (prix etc.) retail. **en ~,** in detail.

détaillé /detaje/ a. detailed.

détaill|er /detaje/ v.t. (articles) sell in small quantities, split up. **~ant, ~ante** n.m., f. retailer.

détaler /detale/ v.i. (fam.) make tracks, run off.

détartrant /detartrɑ̃/ n.m. descaler.

détaxer /detakse/ v.t. reduce the tax on.

détect|er /detɛkte/ v.t. detect. **~eur** n.m. detector. **~ion** /-ksjɔ̃/ n.f. detection.

détective /detɛktiv/ n.m. detective.

déteindre /detɛ̃dr/ v.i. (couleur) run (sur, on to). **~ sur,** (fig.) rub off on.

détend|re /detɑ̃dr/ v.t. slacken; (ressort) release; (personne) relax. **se ~re** v. pr. become slack, slacken; be released; relax. **~u** a. (calme) relaxed.

détenir† /detnir/ v.t. hold; (secret, fortune) possess.

détente /detɑ̃t/ *n.f.* relaxation; (*pol.*) détente; (*saut*) spring; (*gâchette*) trigger; (*relâchement*) release.

déten|teur, **~trice** /detɑ̃tœr, -tris/ *n.m.,* *f.* holder.

détention /detɑ̃sjɔ̃/ *n.f.* **~ préventive,** custody.

détenu, **~e** /detny/ *n.m.,* *f.* prisoner.

détergent /detɛrʒɑ̃/ *n.m.* detergent.

détérior|er /deterjɔre/ *v.t.* damage. **se ~er** *v. pr.* deteriorate. **~ation** *n.f.* damaging; deterioration.

détermin|er /detɛrmine/ *v.t.* determine. **se ~er** *v. pr.* make up one's mind **(à,** to). **~ation** *n.f.* determination. **~é** *a.* (*résolu*) determined; (*précis*) definite.

déterrer /detere/ *v.t.* dig up.

détersif /detɛrsif/ *n.m.* detergent.

détestable /detɛstabl/ *a.* foul.

détester /detɛste/ *v.t.* hate. **se ~** *v. pr.* hate each other.

déton|er /detɔne/ *v.i.* explode, detonate. **~ateur** *n.m.* detonator. **~ation** *n.f.* explosion, detonation.

détonner /detɔne/ *v.i.* clash.

détour /detur/ *n.m.* bend; (*crochet*) detour; (*fig.*) roundabout means.

détourné /deturne/ *a.* roundabout.

détourn|er /deturne/ *v.t.* divert; (*tête, yeux*) turn away; (*avion*) hijack; (*argent*) embezzle. **se ~er de,** stray from. **~ement** *n.m.* hijack(ing); embezzlement.

détrac|teur, **~trice** /detraktœr, -tris/ *n.m.,* *f.* critic.

détraquer /detrake/ *v.t.* break, put out of order; (*estomac*) upset. **se ~** *v. pr.* (*machine*) go wrong.

détresse /detrɛs/ *n.f.* distress.

détriment /detrimɑ̃/ *n.m.* detriment.

détritus /detrity(s)/ *n.m. pl.* rubbish.

détroit /detrwa/ *n.m.* strait.

détromper /detrɔpe/ *v.t.* undeceive, enlighten.

détruire† /detrɥir/ *v.t.* destroy.

dette /dɛt/ *n.f.* debt.

deuil /dœj/ *n.m.* mourning; (*perte*) bereavement. **porter le ~,** be in mourning.

deux /dø/ *a. & n.m.* two. **~ fois,** twice. **tous (les) ~,** both. **~- pièces** *n.m. invar.* (*vêtement*) two-piece; (*logement*) two-room flat *or* apartment. **~-points** *n.m. invar.* (*gram.*) colon. **~-roues** *n.m. invar.* two-wheeled vehicle.

deuxième /døzjɛm/ *a. & n.m./f.* second. **~ment** *adv.* secondly.

dévaler /devale/ *v.t./i.* hurtle down.

dévaliser /devalize/ *v.t.* rob, clean out.

dévaloriser /devalɔrize/ *v.t.,* **se ~** *v. pr.* reduce in value.

dévalorisant, **~e** /devalɔrizɑ̃, -t/ *a.* demeaning.

déval|uer /devalɥe/ *v.t.,* **se ~uer** *v. pr.* devalue. **~uation** *n.f.* devaluation.

devancer /dəvɑ̃se/ *v.t.* be *ou* go ahead of; (*arriver*) arrive ahead of; (*prévenir*) anticipate.

devant /dvɑ̃/ *prép.* in front of; (*distance*) ahead of; (*avec mouvement*) past; (*en présence de*) before; (*face à*) in the face of. **●** *adv.* in front; (*à distance*) ahead. **●** *n.m.* front. **prendre les ~s,** take the initiative. **de ~,** front. **par ~,** at *ou* from the front, in front. **aller au ~ de qn.,** go to meet sb. **aller au ~ des désirs de qn.,** anticipate sb.'s wishes.

devanture /dvɑ̃tyr/ *n.f.* shop front; (*étalage*) shop-window.

dévaster /devaste/ *v.t.* devastate.

déveine /devɛn/ *n.f.* bad luck.

développ|er /devlɔpe/ *v.t.,* **se ~er** *v. pr.* develop. **~ement** *n.m.* development; (*de photos*) developing.

devenir† /dəvnir/ *v.i.* (*aux. être*) become. **qu'est-il devenu?,** what has become of him?

dévergondé /devɛrgɔ̃de/ *a.* shameless.

déverser /devɛrse/ *v.t.,* **se ~** *v. pr.* empty out, pour out.

dévêtir /devetir/ *v.t.,* **se ~** *v. pr.* undress.

déviation /devjɑsjɔ̃/ *n.f.* diversion.

dévier /devje/ *v.t.* divert; (*coup*) deflect. **●** *v.i.* (*ballon, balle*) veer; (*personne*) deviate.

devin /dəvɛ̃/ *n.m.* fortune-teller.

deviner /dvine/ *v.t.* guess; (*apercevoir*) distinguish.

devinette /dvinɛt/ *n.f.* riddle.

devis /dvi/ *n.m.* estimate.

dévisager /devizaʒe/ *v.t.* stare at.

devise /dviz/ *n.f.* motto. **~s,** (*monnaie*) (foreign) currency.

dévisser /devise/ *v.t.* unscrew.

dévitaliser /devitalize/ *v.t.* (*dent*) kill the nerve in.

dévoiler /devwale/ *v.t.* reveal.

devoir [1] /dvwar/ *n.m.* duty; (*scol.*) homework; (*fait en classe*) exercise.

devoir†² /dvwar/ *v.t.* owe. ● *v. aux.*
~ faire, (*nécessité*) must do, have
(got) to do; (*intention*) be due to do.
~ être, (*probabilité*) must be. **vous
devriez,** you should. **il aurait dû,** he
should have.

dévolu /devɔly/ *n.m.* **jeter son ~ sur,**
set one's heart on. ● *a.* **~ à,** allotted
to.

dévorer /devɔre/ *v.t.* devour.

dévot, ~e /devo, -ɔt/ *a.* devout.

dévotion /devosjɔ̃/ *n.f.* (*relig.*) devotion.

dévou|er (se) /(sə)devwe/ *v. pr.* de-
vote o.s. (**à,** to); (*se sacrifier*) sacrifice o.s. **~é** *a.* devoted. **~ement** /-
vumɑ̃/ *n.m.* devotion.

dextérité /dɛksterite/ *n.f.* skill.

diab|ète /djabɛt/ *n.m.* diabetes.
~étique *a.* & *n.m./f.* diabetic.

diab|le /djɑbl/ *n.m.* devil. **~olique** *a.*
diabolical.

diagnosti|c /djagnɔstik/ *n.m.* dia-
gnosis. **~quer** *v.t.* diagnose.

diagon|al, ~ale (*m. pl.* **~aux**) /dja-
gɔnal, -o/ *a.* & *n.f.* diagonal. **en ~ale,**
diagonally.

diagramme /djagram/ *n.m.* diagram;
(*graphique*) graph.

dialecte /djalɛkt/ *n.m.* dialect.

dialogu|e /djalɔg/ *n.m.* dialogue. **~er**
v.i. (*pol.*) have a dialogue.

diamant /djamɑ̃/ *n.m.* diamond.

diamètre /djamɛtr/ *n.m.* diameter.

diapason /djapazɔ̃/ *n.m.* tuning-fork.

diaphragme /djafragm/ *n.m.* diaphragm.

diapo /djapo/ *n.f.* (colour) slide.

diapositive /djapozitiv/ *n.f.* (colour)
slide.

diarrhée /djare/ *n.f.* diarrhoea.

dictat|eur /diktatœr/ *n.m.* dictator.
~ure *n.f.* dictatorship.

dict|er /dikte/ *v.t.* dictate. **~ée** *n.f.*
dictation.

diction /diksjɔ̃/ *n.f.* diction.

dictionnaire /diksjɔnɛr/ *n.m.* dictionary.

dicton /diktɔ̃/ *n.m.* saying.

dièse /djɛz/ *n.m.* (*mus.*) sharp.

diesel /djezɛl/ *n.m.* & *a. invar.* diesel.

diète /djɛt/ *n.f.* (*régime*) diet.

diététicien, ~ne /djetetisjɛ̃, -jɛn/
n.m., f. dietician.

diététique /djetetik/ *n.f.* dietetics.
● *a.* **produit** *ou* **aliment ~,** dietary
product.

dieu (*pl.* **~x**) /djø/ *n.m.* god. **D~,**
God.

diffamatoire /difamatwar/ *a.* defa-
matory.

diffam|er /difame/ *v.t.* slander; (*par
écrit*) libel. **~ation** *n.f.* slander;
libel.

différé (en) /(ɑ̃)difere/ *adv.* (*émission*) recorded.

différemment /diferamɑ̃/ *adv.* differently.

différence /diferɑ̃s/ *n.f.* difference. **à
la ~ de,** unlike.

différencier /diferɑ̃sje/ *v.t.* differentiate. **se ~ de,** (*différer de*)
differ from.

différend /diferɑ̃/ *n.m.* difference (of
opinion).

différent, ~e /diferɑ̃, -t/ *a.* different
(**de,** from).

différentiel, ~le /diferɑ̃sjɛl/ *a.* &
n.m. differential.

différer¹ /difere/ *v.t.* postpone.

différer² /difere/ *v.i.* differ (**de,**
from).

difficile /difisil/ *a.* difficult. **~ment**
adv. with difficulty.

difficulté /difikylte/ *n.f.* difficulty.

difform|e /difɔrm/ *a.* deformed. **~ité**
n.f. deformity.

diffus, ~e /dify, -z/ *a.* diffuse.

diffus|er /difyze/ *v.t.* broadcast;
(*lumière, chaleur*) diffuse. **~ion** *n.f.*
broadcasting; diffusion.

dig|érer /diʒere/ *v.t.* digest;
(*endurer: fam.*) stomach. **~este,
~estible** *adjs.* digestible. **~estion**
n.f. digestion.

digesti|f, ~ve /diʒɛstif, -v/ *a.*
digestive. ● *n.m.* after-dinner liqueur.

digit|al (*m. pl.* **~aux**) /diʒital, -o/ *a.*
digital.

digne /diɲ/ *a.* (*noble*) dignified; (*honnête*) worthy. **~ de,** worthy of. **~ de
foi,** trustworthy.

dignité /diɲite/ *n.f.* dignity.

digression /digresjɔ̃/ *n.f.* digression.

digue /dig/ *n.f.* dike.

diktat /diktat/ *n.m.* diktat.

dilapider /dilapide/ *v.t.* squander.

dilat|er /dilate/ *v.t.*, **se ~er** *v. pr.*
dilate. **~ation** /-asjɔ̃/ *n.f.* dilation.

dilemme /dilɛm/ *n.m.* dilemma.

dilettante /diletɑ̃t/ *n.m., f.* amateur.

diluant /dilɥɑ/ *n.m.* thinner.

diluer /dilɥe/ *v.t.* dilute.

diluvien, ~ne /dilyvjɛ̃, -ɛn/ *a.*
(*pluie*) torrential.

dimanche /dimɑ̃ʃ/ *n.m.* Sunday.

dimension /dimãsjõ/ *n.f.* (*taille*) size; (*mesure*) dimension.

dimin|uer /diminɥe/ *v.t.* reduce, decrease; (*plaisir, courage, etc.*) lessen; (*dénigrer*) lessen. ● *v.i.* decrease. ~**ution** *n.f.* decrease (**de**, in).

diminutif /diminytif/ *n.m.* diminutive; (*surnom*) pet name *ou* form.

dinde /dɛ̃d/ *n.f.* turkey.

dindon /dɛ̃dɔ̃/ *n.m.* turkey.

dîn|er /dine/ *n.m.* dinner. ● *v.i.* have dinner. ~**eur**, ~**euse** *n.m.*, *f.* diner.

dingue /dɛ̃g/ *a.* (*fam.*) crazy.

dinosaure /dinozɔr/ *n.m.* dinosaur.

diocèse /djɔsɛz/ *n.m.* diocese.

diphtérie /difteri/ *n.f.* diphtheria.

diphtongue /diftɔ̃g/ *n.f.* diphthong.

diplomate /diplɔmat/ *n.m.* diplomat. ● *a.* diplomatic.

diplomat|ie /diplɔmasi/ *n.f.* diplomacy. ~**ique** /-atik/ *a.* diplomatic.

diplôm|e /diplom/ *n.m.* certificate, diploma; (*univ.*) degree. ~**é** *a.* qualified.

dire† /dir/ *v.t.* say; (*secret, vérité, heure*) tell; (*penser*) think. ~ **que**, say that. ~ **à qn. que/de**, tell s.o. that/to. **se** ~ *v. pr.* (*mot*) be said; (*fatigué etc.*) say that one is. **ça me/vous/***etc.* **dit de faire**, I/you/*etc.* feel like doing. **on dirait que**, it would seem that, it seems that. **dis/dites donc!**, hey! ● *n.m.* **au** ~ **de**, **selon les** ~**s de**, according to.

direct /dirɛkt/ *a.* direct. **en** ~, (*émission*) live. ~**ement** *adv.* directly.

direc|teur, ~**trice** /dirɛktœr, -tris/ *n.m.*, *f.* director; (*chef de service*) manager, manageress; (*d'école*) headmaster, headmistress.

direction /dirɛksjɔ̃/ *n.f.* (*sens*) direction; (*de société etc.*) management; (*auto.*) steering. **en** ~ **de**, (going) to.

directive /dirɛktiv/ *n.f.* instruction.

dirigeant, ~**e** /diriʒɑ̃, -t/ *n.m.*, *f.* (*pol.*) leader; (*comm.*) manager. ● *a.* (*classe*) ruling.

diriger /diriʒe/ *v.t.* run, manage, direct; (*véhicule*) steer; (*orchestre*) conduct; (*braquer*) aim; (*tourner*) turn. **se** ~ *v. pr.* guide o.s. **se** ~ **vers**, make one's way to.

dirigis|me /diriʒism/ *n.m.* interventionism. ~**te** /-ist/ *a.* & *n.m./f.* interventionist.

dis /di/ *voir* **dire**.

discern|er /disɛrne/ *v.t.* discern. ~**ement** *n.m.* discernment.

disciple /disipl/ *n.m.* disciple.

disciplin|e /disiplin/ *n.f.* discipline. ~**aire** *a.* disciplinary. ~**er** *v.t.* discipline.

discontinu /diskɔ̃tiny/ *a.* intermittent.

discontinuer /diskɔ̃tinɥe/ *v.i.* **sans** ~, without stopping.

discordant, ~**e** /diskɔrdɑ̃, -t/ *a.* discordant.

discorde /diskɔrd/ *n.f.* discord.

discothèque /diskɔtɛk/ *n.f.* record library; (*club*) disco(thèque).

discount /diskunt/ *n.m.* discount.

discourir /diskurir/ *v.i.* (*péj.*) hold forth, ramble on.

discours /diskur/ *n.m.* speech.

discréditer /diskredite/ *v.t.* discredit.

discr|et, ~**ète** /diskrɛ, -t/ *a.* discreet. ~**ètement** *adv.* discreetly.

discrétion /diskresjɔ̃/ *n.f.* discretion. **à** ~, as much as one desires.

discrimination /diskriminasjɔ̃/ *n.f.* discrimination.

discriminatoire /diskriminatwar/ *a.* discriminatory.

disculper /diskylpe/ *v.t.* exonerate. **se** ~ *v. pr.* prove o.s. innocent.

discussion /diskysjɔ̃/ *n.f.* discussion; (*querelle*) argument.

discuté /diskyte/ *a.* controversial.

discut|er /diskyte/ *v.t.* discuss; (*contester*) question. ● *v.i.* (*parler*) talk; (*répliquer*) argue. ~**er de**, discuss. ~**able** *a.* debatable.

disette /dizɛt/ *n.f.* (food) shortage.

diseuse /dizøz/ *n.f.* ~ **de bonne aventure**, fortune-teller.

disgrâce /disgrɑs/ *n.f.* disgrace.

disgracieu|x, ~**se** /disgrasjø, -z/ *a.* ungainly.

disjoindre /disʒwɛ̃dr/ *v.t.* take apart. **se** ~ *v. pr.* come apart.

dislo|quer /dislɔke/ *v.t.* (*membre*) dislocate; (*machine etc.*) break (apart). **se** ~**quer** *v. pr.* (*parti, cortège*) break up; (*meuble*) come apart. ~**cation** *n.f.* (*anat.*) dislocation.

dispar|aître† /disparɛtr/ *v.i.* disappear; (*mourir*) die. **faire** ~**aître**, get rid of. ~**ition** *n.f.* disappearance; (*mort*) death. ~**u**, ~**ue** *a.* (*soldat etc.*) missing; *n.m.*, *f.* missing person; (*mort*) dead person.

disparate /disparat/ *a.* ill-assorted.

disparité /disparite/ *n.f.* disparity.

dispensaire /dispɑ̃sɛr/ *n.m.* clinic.

dispense /dispɑ̃s/ *n.f.* exemption.

dispenser /dispɑ̃se/ *v.t.* exempt (**de,** from). **se ~ de (faire),** avoid (doing).

disperser /dispɛrse/ *v.t.* (*éparpiller*) scatter; (*répartir*) disperse. **se ~** *v. pr.* disperse.

disponib|le /dispɔnibl/ *a.* available. **~ilité** *n.f.* availability.

dispos, **~e** /dispo, -z/ *a.* **frais et ~,** fresh and alert.

disposé /dispoze/ *a.* **bien/mal ~,** in a good/bad mood. **~ à,** prepared to. **~ envers,** disposed towards.

disposer /dispoze/ *v.t.* arrange. **~ à,** (*engager à*) incline to. ● *v.i.* **~ de,** have at one's disposal. **se ~ à,** prepare to.

dispositif /dispozitif/ *n.m.* device; (*plan*) plan of action. **~ anti-parasite,** suppressor.

disposition /dispozisjɔ̃/ *n.f.* arrangement; (*humeur*) mood; (*tendance*) tendency. **~s,** (*préparatifs*) arrangements; (*aptitude*) aptitude. **à la ~ de,** at the disposal of.

disproportionné /disprɔpɔrsjone/ *a.* disproportionate.

dispute /dispyt/ *n.f.* quarrel.

disputer /dispyte/ *v.t.* (*match*) play; (*course*) run in; (*prix*) fight for; (*gronder: fam.*) tell off. **se ~** *v. pr.* quarrel; (*se battre pour*) fight over; (*match*) be played.

disquaire /diskɛr/ *n.m./f.* record dealer.

disqualif|ier /diskalifje/ *v.t.* disqualify. **~ication** *n.f.* disqualification.

disque /disk/ *n.m.* (*mus.*) record; (*sport*) discus; (*cercle*) disc, disk. **~ dur,** hard disk.

disquette /diskɛt/ *n.f.* (floppy) disk.

dissection /disɛksjɔ̃/ *n.f.* dissection.

dissemblable /disɑ̃blabl/ *a.* dissimilar.

disséminer /disemine/ *v.t.* scatter.

disséquer /diseke/ *v.t.* dissect.

dissertation /disɛrtasjɔ̃/ *n.f.* (*scol.*) essay.

disserter /disɛrte/ *v.i.* **~ sur,** comment upon.

dissiden|t, **~te** /disidɑ̃, -t/ *a. & n.m., f.* dissident. **~ce** *n.f.* dissidence.

dissimul|er /disimyle/ *v.t.* conceal (**à,** from). **se ~er** *v. pr.* conceal o.s. **~ation** *n.f.* concealment; (*fig.*) deceit.

dissipé /disipe/ *a.* (*élève*) unruly.

dissip|er /disipe/ *v.t.* (*fumée, crainte*) dispel; (*fortune*) squander; (*personne*) lead into bad ways. **se ~er** *v. pr.* disappear. **~ation** *n.f.* squandering; (*indiscipline*) misbehaviour.

dissolution /disɔlysjɔ̃/ *n.f.* dissolution.

dissolvant /disɔlvɑ̃/ *n.m.* solvent; (*pour ongles*) nail polish remover.

dissonant, **~e** /disɔnɑ̃, -t/ *a.* discordant.

dissoudre† /disudr/ *v.t.*, **se ~** *v. pr.* dissolve.

dissua|der /disɥade/ *v.t.* dissuade (**de,** from). **~sion** /-ɥɑzjɔ̃/ *n.f.* dissuasion. **force de ~sion,** deterrent force.

dissuasi|f, **~ve** /disɥazif, -v/ *a.* dissuasive.

distance /distɑ̃s/ *n.f.* distance; (*écart*) gap. **à ~,** at *ou* from a distance.

distancer /distɑ̃se/ *v.t.* leave behind.

distant, **~e** /distɑ̃, -t/ *a.* distant.

distendre /distɑ̃dr/ *v.t.*, **se ~** *v. pr.* distend.

distill|er /distile/ *v.t.* distil. **~ation** *n.f.* distillation.

distillerie /distilri/ *n.f.* distillery.

distinct, **~e** /distɛ̃(kt), -ɛ̃kt/ *a.* distinct. **~ement** /-ɛ̃ktəmɑ̃/ *adv.* distinctly.

distincti|f, **~ve** /distɛ̃ktif, -v/ *a.* distinctive.

distinction /distɛ̃ksjɔ̃/ *n.f.* distinction.

distingué /distɛ̃ge/ *a.* distinguished.

distinguer /distɛ̃ge/ *v.t.* distinguish.

distraction /distraksjɔ̃/ *n.f.* absent-mindedness; (*oubli*) lapse; (*passe-temps*) distraction.

distraire† /distrɛr/ *v.t.* amuse; (*rendre inattentif*) distract. **se ~** *v. pr.* amuse o.s.

distrait, **~e** /distrɛ, -t/ *a.* absent-minded. **~ement** *a.* absent-mindedly.

distrayant, **~e** /distrɛjɑ̃, -t/ *a.* entertaining.

distrib|uer /distribɥe/ *v.t.* hand out, distribute; (*répartir, amener*) distribute; (*courrier*) deliver. **~uteur** *n.m.* (*auto., comm.*) distributor. **~uteur (automatique),** vending-machine; (*de billets*) (cash) dispenser. **~ution** *n.f.* distribution; (*du courrier*) delivery; (*acteurs*) cast.

district /distrikt/ *n.m.* district.

dit [1], **dites** /di, dit/ *voir* dire.

dit [2], **~e** /di, dit/ *a.* (*décidé*) agreed; (*surnommé*) called.

diurétique /djyretik/ *a. & n.m.* diurétic.

diurne /djyrn/ *a.* diurnal.

divagu|er /divage/ *v.i.* rave. **~ations** *n.f. pl.* ravings.

divan /divã/ *n.m.* divan.

divergen|t, ~te /divɛrʒã, -t/ *a.* divergent. **~ce** *n.f.* divergence.

diverger /divɛrʒe/ *v.i.* diverge.

divers, ~e /divɛr, -s/ *a.* (*varié*) diverse; (*différent*) various. **~ement** /-səmã/ *adv.* variously.

diversifier /divɛrsifje/ *v.t.* diversify.

diversion /divɛrsjõ/ *n.f.* diversion.

diversité /divɛrsite/ *n.f.* diversity.

divert|ir /divɛrtir/ *v.t.* amuse. **se ~ir** *v. pr.* amuse o.s. **~issement** *n.m.* amusement.

dividende /dividãd/ *n.m.* dividend.

divin, ~e /divɛ̃, -in/ *a.* divine.

divinité /divinite/ *n.f.* divinity.

divis|er /divize/ *v.t.*, **se ~er** *v. pr.* divide. **~ion** *n.f.* division.

divorc|e /divɔrs/ *n.m.* divorce. **~é ~ée** *a.* divorced; *n.m., f.* divorcee. **~er** *v.i.* **~er (d'avec)**, divorce.

divulguer /divylge/ *v.t.* divulge.

dix /dis/ (/di/ *before consonant,* /diz/ *before vowel*) *a. & n.m.* ten. **~ième** /dizjɛm/ *a. & n.m./f.* tenth.

dix-huit /dizɥit/ *a. & n.m.* eighteen. **~ième** *a. & n.m./f.* eighteenth.

dix-neu|f /diznœf/ *a. & n.m.* nineteen. **~vième** *a. & n.m./f.* nineteenth.

dix-sept /disɛt/ *a. & n.m.* seventeen. **~ième** *a. & n.m./f.* seventeenth.

dizaine /dizɛn/ *n.f.* (about) ten.

docile /dɔsil/ *a.* docile.

docilité /dɔsilite/ *n.f.* docility.

dock /dɔk/ *n.m.* dock.

docker /dɔkɛr/ *n.m.* docker.

doct|eur /dɔktœr/ *n.m.* doctor. **~oresse** *n.f.* (*fam.*) lady doctor.

doctorat /dɔktɔra/ *n.m.* doctorate.

doctrin|e /dɔktrin/ *n.f.* doctrine. **~aire** *a.* doctrinaire.

document /dɔkymã/ *n.m.* document. **~aire** /-tɛr/ *a. & n.m.* documentary.

documentaliste /dɔkymãtalist/ *n.m./f.* information officer.

document|er /dɔkymãte/ *v.t.* document. **se ~er** *v. pr.* collect information. **~ation** *n.f.* information, literature. **~é** *a.* well-documented.

dodo /dodo/ *n.m.* **faire ~**, (*langage enfantin*) go to byebyes.

dodu /dɔdy/ *a.* plump.

dogm|e /dɔgm/ *n.m.* dogma. **~atique** *a.* dogmatic.

doigt /dwa/ *n.m.* finger. **un ~ de**, a drop of. **à deux ~s de**, a hair's breadth away from. **~ de pied,** toe.

doigté /dwate/ *n.m.* (*mus.*) fingering, touch; (*adresse*) tact.

dois, doit /dwa/ *voir* devoir [2].

Dolby /dɔlbi/ *n.m. & a.* (P.) Dolby (P.).

doléances /dɔleãs/ *n.f. pl.* grievances.

dollar /dɔlar/ *n.m.* dollar.

domaine /dɔmɛn/ *n.m.* estate, domain; (*fig.*) domain.

dôme /dom/ *n.m.* dome.

domestique /dɔmɛstik/ *a.* domestic. ● *n.m./f.* servant.

domestiquer /dɔmɛstike/ *v.t.* domesticate.

domicile /dɔmisil/ *n.m.* home. **à ~,** at home; (*livrer*) to the home.

domicilié /dɔmisilje/ *a.* resident.

domin|er /dɔmine/ *v.t./i.* dominate; (*surplomber*) tower over, dominate; (*équipe*) dictate the game (to). **~ant, ~ante** *a.* dominant; *n.f.* dominant feature. **~ation** *n.f.* domination.

domino /dɔmino/ *n.m.* domino.

dommage /dɔmaʒ/ *n.m.* (*tort*) harm. **~(s),** (*dégâts*) damage. **c'est ~,** it's a pity. **quel ~,** what a shame. **~s-intérêts** *n.m. pl.* (*jurid.*) damages.

dompt|er /dõte/ *v.t.* tame. **~eur, ~euse** *n.m., f.* tamer.

don /dõ/ *n.m.* (*cadeau, aptitude*) gift.

dona|teur, ~trice /dɔnatœr, -tris/ *n.m., f.* donor.

donation /dɔnasjõ/ *n.f.* donation.

donc /dõk/ *conj.* so, then; (*par conséquent*) so, therefore.

donjon /dõʒõ/ *n.m.* (*tour*) keep.

donné /dɔne/ *a.* (*fixé*) given; (*pas cher: fam.*) dirt cheap. **étant ~ que,** given that.

données /dɔne/ *n.f. pl.* (*de science*) data; (*de problème*) facts.

donner /dɔne/ *v.t.* give; (*vieilles affaires*) give away; (*distribuer*) give out; (*récolte etc.*) produce; (*film*) show; (*pièce*) put on. ● *v.i.* **~ sur,** look out on to. **~ dans,** (*piège*) fall into. **ça donne soif/faim,** it makes one thirsty/ hungry. **~ à réparer** *etc.,* take to be repaired/*etc.* **~ lieu à,** give rise to. **se ~ à,** devote o.s. to. **se**

~ **du mal,** go to a lot of trouble
(**pour faire,** to do).

donneu|r, ~**se** /dɔnœr, -øz/ *n.m.,* f.
(*de sang*) donor.

dont /dɔ̃/ *pron. rel.* (*chose*) whose, of
which; (*personne*) whose; (*partie
d'un tout*) of whom; (*chose*) of
which; (*provenance*) from which;
(*manière*) in which. **le père ~ la
fille,** the father whose daughter. **ce
~,** what. **~ il a besoin,** which he
needs. **l'enfant ~ il est fier,** the
child he is proud of. **trois enfants ~
deux sont jumeaux,** three children,
two of whom are twins.

dopage /dɔpaʒ/ *n.m.* doping.

doper /dɔpe/ *v.t.* dope. **se ~** *v. pr.*
take dope.

doré /dɔre/ *a.* (*couleur d'or*) golden;
(*avec dorure*) gold. **la bourgeoisie
~e** the affluent middle class.

dorénavant /dɔrenavɑ̃/ *adv.* hence-
forth.

dorer /dɔre/ *v.t.* gild; (*culin.*) brown.

dorloter /dɔrlɔte/ *v.t.* pamper.

dorm|ir† /dɔrmir/ *v.i.* sleep; (*être
endormi*) be asleep. ~**eur,** ~**euse**
n.m., f. sleeper. **il dort debout,** he
can't keep awake. **une histoire à
~ir debout,** a cock-and-bull story.

dortoir /dɔrtwar/ *n.m.* dormitory.

dorure /dɔryr/ *n.f.* gilding.

dos /do/ *n.m.* back; (*de livre*) spine. **à
~ de,** riding on. **de ~,** from behind.
~ crawlé, backstroke.

dos|e /doz/ *n.f.* dose. ~**age** *n.m.*
(*mélange*) mixture. **faire le ~age
de,** measure out; balance. ~**er** *v.t.*
measure out; (*équilibrer*) balance.

dossard /dɔsar/ *n.m.* (*sport*) number.

dossier /dɔsje/ *n.m.* (*documents*) file;
(*de chaise*) back.

dot /dɔt/ *n.f.* dowry.

doter /dɔte/ *v.t.* ~ **de,** equip with.

douan|e /dwan/ *n.f.* customs. ~**ier,**
~**ière** *a.* customs; *n.m.,* f. customs
officer.

doubl|e /dubl/ *a. & adv.* double.
● *n.m.* (*copie*) duplicate; (*sosie*)
double. **le ~e (de),** twice as much
ou as many (as). **le ~e messieurs,**
the men's doubles. **~e décimètre,**
ruler. ~**ement**[1] *adv.* doubly.

doubl|er /duble/ *v.t./i.* double; (*dé-
passer*) overtake; (*vêtement*) line;
(*film*) dub; (*classe*) repeat; (*cap*)
round. ~**ement**[2] *n.m.* doubling.
~**ure** *n.f.* (*étoffe*) lining; (*acteur*)
understudy.

douce /dus/ *voir* doux.

douceâtre /dusɑtr/ *a.* sickly sweet.

doucement /dusmɑ̃/ *adv.* gently.

douceur /dusœr/ *n.f.* (*mollesse*) softness; (*de climat*) mildness; (*de personne*) gentleness; (*joie, plaisir*)
sweetness. ~**s,** (*friandises*) sweet
things. **en ~,** smoothly.

douch|e /duʃ/ *n.f.* shower. ~**er** *v.t.*
give a shower to. **se ~er** *v. pr.* have
ou take a shower.

doudoune /dudun/ *n.f.* (*fam.*) anorak.

doué /dwe/ *a.* gifted. **~ de,** endowed
with.

douille /duj/ *n.f.* (*électr.*) socket.

douillet, ~**te** /dujɛ, -t/ *a.* cosy,
comfortable; (*personne: péj.*) soft.

doul|eur /dulœr/ *n.f.* pain; (*chagrin*)
grief. ~**oureux,** ~**oureuse** *a.*
painful. **la ~oureuse** *n.f.* the bill.

doute /dut/ *n.m.* doubt. **sans ~,** no
doubt. **sans aucun ~,** without
doubt.

douter /dute/ *v.i.* ~ **de,** doubt. **se ~
de,** suspect.

douteu|x, ~**se** /dutø, -z/ *a.* doubtful.

Douvres /duvr/ *n.m./f.* Dover.

doux, douce /du, dus/ *a.* (*moelleux*)
soft; (*sucré*) sweet; (*clément, pas
fort*) mild; (*pas brusque, bienveillant*) gentle.

douzaine /duzɛn/ *n.f.* about twelve;
(*douze*) dozen. **une ~ d'œufs/etc.,** a
dozen eggs/etc.

douz|e /duz/ *a. & n.m.* twelve. ~**ième**
a. & n.m./f. twelfth.

doyen, ~**ne** /dwajɛ̃, -jɛn/ *n.m.,* f.
dean; (*en âge*) most senior person.

dragée /draʒe/ *n.f.* sugared almond.

dragon /dragɔ̃/ *n.m.* dragon.

dragu|e /drag/ *n.f.* (*bateau*) dredger.
~**er** *v.t.* (*rivière*) dredge; (*filles:
fam.*) chat up, try to pick up.

drain /drɛ̃/ *n.m.* drain.

drainer /drene/ *v.t.* drain.

dramatique /dramatik/ *a.* dramatic;
(*tragique*) tragic. ● *n.f.* (television)
drama.

dramatiser /dramatize/ *v.t.* drama-
tize.

dramaturge /dramatyrʒ/ *n.m./f.* dra-
matist.

drame /dram/ *n.m.* drama.

drap /dra/ *n.m.* sheet; (*tissu*) (wool-
len) cloth. **~-housse** /draus/ *n.m.*
fitted sheet.

drapeau (*pl.* ~**x**) /drapo/ *n.m.* flag.

draper /drape/ *v.t.* drape.

dress|er /drese/ v.t. put up, erect; (*tête*) raise; (*animal*) train; (*liste*) draw up. **se ~er** v. pr. (*bâtiment etc.*) stand; (*personne*) draw o.s. up. **~er l'oreille**, prick up one's ears. **~age** /drɛsaʒ/ n.m. training. **~eur, ~euse** /drɛsœr, -øz/ n.m., f. trainer.

dribbler /drible/ v.t./i. (*sport*) dribble.

drille /drij/ n.m. **un joyeux ~,** a cheery character.

drive /drajv/ n.m. (*comput.*) drive.

drogue /drɔg/ n.f. drug. **la ~,** drugs.

drogu|er /drɔge/ v.t. (*malade*) drug heavily, dose up; (*victime*) drug. **se ~er** v. pr. take drugs. **~é, ~ée** n.m., f. drug addict.

drogu|erie /drɔgri/ n.f. hardware and chemist's shop; (*Amer.*) drugstore. **~iste** n.m./f. owner of a *droguerie*.

droit [1] **~e** /drwa, -t/ a. (*non courbe*) straight; (*loyal*) upright; (*angle*) right. ● adv. straight. ● n.f. straight line.

droit [2] **~e** /drwa, -t/ a. (*contraire de gauche*) right. **à ~e,** on the right; (*direction*) (to the) right. **la ~e,** the right (side); (*pol.*) the right (wing). **~ier, ~ière** /-tje, -tjɛr/ a. & n.m., f. right-handed (person).

droit [3] /drwa/ n.m. right. **~(s),** (*taxe*) duty; (*d'inscription*) fee(s). **le ~,** (*jurid.*) law. **avoir ~ à,** be entitled to. **avoir le ~ de,** be allowed to. **être dans son ~,** be in the right. **~ d'auteur,** copyright. **~s d'auteur,** royalties.

drôle /drol/ a. funny. **~ d'air,** funny look. **~ment** adv. funnily; (*extrêmement: fam.*) dreadfully.

dromadaire /drɔmadɛr/ n.m. dromedary.

dru /dry/ a. thick. **tomber ~,** fall thick and fast.

drugstore /drœgstɔr/ n.m. drugstore.

du /dy/ voir de.

dû, due /dy/ voir devoir [2]. ● a. due. ● n.m. due; (*argent*) dues. **~ à,** due to.

duc, duchesse /dyk, dyʃɛs/ n.m., f. duke, duchess.

duel /dɥɛl/ n.m. duel.

dune /dyn/ n.f. dune.

duo /dɥo/ n.m. (*mus.*) duet; (*fig.*) duo.

dup|e /dyp/ n.f. dupe. **~er** v.t. dupe.

duplex /dyplɛks/ n.m. split-level apartment; (*Amer.*) duplex; (*émission*) link-up.

duplicata /dyplikata/ n.m. invar. duplicate.

duplicité /dyplisite/ n.f. duplicity.

duquel /dykɛl/ voir lequel.

dur /dyr/ a. hard; (*sévère*) harsh, hard; (*viande*) tough, hard; (*col, brosse*) stiff. ● adv. hard. ● n.m. tough guy. **~ d'oreille,** hard of hearing.

durable /dyrabl/ a. lasting.

durant /dyrɑ̃/ prép. during; (*mesure de temps*) for.

durc|ir /dyrsir/ v.t./i., **se ~ir** v. pr. harden. **~issement** n.m. hardening.

dure /dyr/ n.f. **à la ~,** the hard way.

durée /dyre/ n.f. length; (*période*) duration.

durement /dyrmɑ̃/ adv. harshly.

durer /dyre/ v.i. last.

dureté /dyrte/ n.f. hardness; (*sévérité*) harshness.

duvet /dyvɛ/ n.m. down; (*sac*) (down-filled) sleeping-bag.

dynami|que /dinamik/ a. dynamic. **~sme** n.m. dynamism.

dynamit|e /dinamit/ n.f. dynamite. **~er** v.t. dynamite.

dynamo /dinamo/ n.f. dynamo.

dynastie /dinasti/ n.f. dynasty.

dysenterie /disɑ̃tri/ n.f. dysentery.

E

eau (pl. **~x**) /o/ n.f. water. **~ courante/dormante,** running/still water. **~ de Cologne,** eau-de-Cologne. **~ dentifrice,** mouthwash. **~ de toilette,** eau de toilette. **~-de-vie** (pl. **~x-de-vie**) n.f. brandy. **~ douce/salée,** fresh/salt water. **~-forte** (pl. **~x-fortes**) n.f. etching. **~ potable,** drinking water. **~ de Javel,** bleach. **~ minérale,** mineral water. **~ gazeuse,** fizzy water. **~ plate,** still water. **~x usées,** dirty water. **tomber à l'~** (*fig.*) fall through. **prendre l'~,** take in water.

ébahi /ebai/ a. dumbfounded.

ébattre (s') /(s)ebatr/ v. pr. frolic.

ébauch|e /eboʃ/ n.f. outline. **~er** v.t. outline. **s'~er** v. pr. form.

ébène /ebɛn/ n.f. ebony.

ébéniste /ebenist/ n.m. cabinet-maker.

éberlué /ebɛrlɥe/ a. flabbergasted.

B.W.

éblou|ir /ebluir/ v.t. dazzle. **~issement** n.m. dazzle, dazzling; (*malaise*) dizzy turn.

éboueur /ebwœr/ n.m. dustman; (*Amer.*) garbage collector.

ébouillanter /ebujɑ̃te/ v.t. scald.

éboul|er (s') /(s)ebule/ v. pr. crumble, collapse. **~ement** n.m. landslide. **~is** n.m. pl. fallen rocks and earth.

ébouriffé /eburife/ a. dishevelled.

ébranler /ebrɑ̃le/ v.t. shake. **s'~** v. pr. move off.

ébrécher /ebreʃe/ v.t. chip.

ébriété /ebrijete/ n.f. intoxication.

ébrouer (s') /(s)ebrue/ v. pr. shake o.s.

ébruiter /ebrɥite/ v.t. spread about.

ébullition /ebylisjɔ̃/ n.f. boiling. **en ~,** boiling.

écaille /ekaj/ n.f. (*de poisson*) scale; (*de peinture, roc*) flake; (*matière*) tortoiseshell.

écailler /ekaje/ v.t. (*poisson*) scale. **s'~** v. pr. flake (off).

écarlate /ekarlat/ a. & n.f. scarlet.

écarquiller /ekarkije/ v.t. **~ les yeux,** open one's eyes wide.

écart /ekar/ n.m. gap; (*de prix etc.*) difference; (*embardée*) swerve; (*de conduite*) lapse (de, in). **à l'~,** out of the way. **tenir à l'~,** (*participant*) keep out of things. **à l'~ de,** away from.

écarté /ekarte/ a. (*lieu*) remote. **les jambes ~es,** (with) legs apart. **les bras ~s,** with one's arms out.

écartement /ekartəmɑ̃/ n.m. gap.

écarter /ekarte/ v.t. (*objets*) move apart; (*ouvrir*) open; (*éliminer*) dismiss. **~ qch. de,** move sth. away from. **~ qn. de,** keep s.o. away from. **s'~** v. pr. (*s'éloigner*) move away; (*quitter son chemin*) move aside. **s'~ de,** stray from.

ecchymose /ekimoz/ n.f. bruise.

ecclésiastique /eklezjastik/ a. ecclesiastical. ● n.m. clergyman.

écervelé, ~e /esɛrvəle/ a. scatterbrained. ● n.m., f. scatter-brain.

échafaud|age /eʃafodaʒ/ n.m. scaffolding; (*amas*) heap. **~er** v.t. (*projets*) construct.

échalote /eʃalɔt/ n.f. shallot.

échang|e /eʃɑ̃ʒ/ n.m. exchange. **en ~e (de),** in exchange (for). **~er** v.t. exchange (**contre,** for).

échangeur /eʃɑ̃ʒœr/ n.m. (*auto.*) interchange.

échantillon /eʃɑ̃tijɔ̃/ n.m. sample. **~nage** /-jɔnaʒ/ n.m. range of samples.

échappatoire /eʃapatwar/ n.f. (clever) way out.

échappée /eʃape/ n.f. (*sport*) breakaway.

échappement /eʃapmɑ̃/ n.m. exhaust.

échapper /eʃape/ v.i. **~ à,** escape; (*en fuyant*) escape (from). **s'~** v. pr. escape. **~ des mains de** ou **à,** slip out of the hands of. **l'~ belle,** have a narrow ou lucky escape.

écharde /eʃard/ n.f. splinter.

écharpe /eʃarp/ n.f. scarf; (*de maire*) sash. **en ~,** (*bras*) in a sling.

échasse /eʃas/ n.f. stilt.

échassier /eʃasje/ n.m. wader.

échaud|er /eʃode/ v.t. **se faire ~er, être ~é,** get one's fingers burnt.

échauffer /eʃofe/ v.t. heat; (*fig.*) excite. **s'~** v. pr. warm up.

échauffourée /eʃofure/ n.f. (*mil.*) skirmish; (*bagarre*) scuffle.

échéance /eʃeɑ̃s/ n.f. due date (for payment); (*délai*) deadline; (*obligation*) (financial) commitment.

échéant (le cas) /(ləkaz)eʃeɑ̃/ adv. if the occasion arises, possibly.

échec /eʃɛk/ n.m. failure. **~s,** (*jeu*) chess. **~ et mat,** checkmate. **en ~,** in check.

échelle /eʃɛl/ n.f. ladder; (*dimension*) scale.

échelon /eʃlɔ̃/ n.m. rung; (*de fonctionnaire*) grade; (*niveau*) level.

échelonner /eʃlɔne/ v.t. spread out, space out.

échevelé /eʃəvle/ a. dishevelled.

échine /eʃin/ n.f. backbone.

échiquier /eʃikje/ n.m. chessboard.

écho /eko/ n.m. echo. **~s,** (*dans la presse*) gossip.

échographie /ekɔgrafi/ n.f. ultrasound (scan).

échoir /eʃwar/ v.i. (*dette*) fall due; (*délai*) expire.

échoppe /eʃɔp/ n.f. stall.

échouer[1] /eʃwe/ v.i. fail.

échouer[2] /eʃwe/ v.t. (*bateau*) ground. ● v.i., **s'~** v. pr. run aground.

échu /eʃy/ a. (*délai*) expired.

éclabouss|er /eklabuse/ v.t. splash. **~ure** n.f. splash.

éclair /eklɛr/ n.m. (flash of) lightning; (*fig.*) flash; (*gâteau*) éclair. ● a. invar. lightning.

éclairag|e /eklɛraʒ/ n.m. lighting; (point de vue) light. **~iste** /-aʒist/ n.m. lighting technician.

éclaircie /eklɛrsi/ n.f. sunny interval.

éclairc|ir /eklɛrsir/ v.t. make lighter; (mystère) clear up. s'**~ir** v. pr. (ciel) clear; (mystère) become clearer. **~issement** n.m. clarification.

éclairer /eklere/ v.t. light (up); (personne) give some light to; (fig.) enlighten; (situation) throw light on. ● v.i. give light. s'**~** v. pr. become clearer. s'**~ à la bougie**, use candle-light.

éclaireu|r, **~se** /eklɛrœr, -øz/ n.m., f. (boy) scout, (girl) guide. ● n.m. (mil.) scout.

éclat /ekla/ n.m. fragment; (de lumière) brightness; (de rire) (out)-burst; (splendeur) brilliance.

éclatant, **~e** /eklatɑ̃, -t/ a. brilliant.

éclat|er /eklate/ v.i. burst; (exploser) go off; (verre) shatter; (guerre) break out; (groupe) split up. **~er de rire**, burst out laughing. **~ement** n.m. bursting; (de bombe) explosion; (scission) split.

éclipse /eklips/ n.f. eclipse.

éclipser /eklipse/ v.t. eclipse. s'**~** v. pr. slip away.

écl|ore /eklɔr/ v.i. (œuf) hatch; (fleur) open. **~osion** n.f. hatching; opening.

écluse /eklyz/ n.f. (de canal) lock.

écœurant, **~e** /ekœrɑ̃, -t/ a. (gâteau) sickly; (fig.) disgusting.

écœurer /ekœre/ v.t. sicken.

école /ekɔl/ n.f. school. **~ maternelle/primaire/secondaire**, nursery/primary/secondary school. **~ normale**, teachers' training college.

écol|ier, **~ière** /ekɔlje, -jɛr/ n.m., f. schoolboy, schoolgirl.

écolo /ekɔlo/ a. & n.m./f. (fam.) green.

écolog|ie /ekɔlɔʒi/ n.f. ecology. **~ique** a. ecological, green.

écologiste /ekɔlɔʒist/ n.m./f. ecologist.

éconduire /ekɔ̃dɥir/ v.t. dismiss.

économat /ekɔnɔma/ n.m. bursary.

économe /ekɔnɔm/ a. thrifty. ● n.m./f. bursar.

économ|ie /ekɔnɔmi/ n.f. economy. **~ies**, (argent) savings. **une ~ie de**, (gain) a saving of. **~ie politique**, economics. **~ique** a. (pol.) economic; (bon marché) economical.

~iser v.t./i. save. **~iste** n.m./f. economist.

écoper /ekɔpe/ v.t. bail out. **~ (de)**, (fam.) get.

écorce /ekɔrs/ n.f. bark; (de fruit) peel.

écorch|er /ekɔrʃe/ v.t. graze; (animal) skin. s'**~er** v. pr. graze o.s. **~ure** n.f. graze.

écossais, **~e** /ekɔsɛ, -z/ a. Scottish. ● n.m., f. Scot.

Écosse /ekɔs/ n.f. Scotland.

écosser /ekɔse/ v.t. shell.

écosystème /ekɔsistɛm/ n.m. ecosystem.

écouler[1] /ekule/ v.t. dispose of, sell.

écoul|er[2] (s') /(s)ekule/ v. pr. flow (out), run (off); (temps) pass. **~ement** n.m. flow.

écourter /ekurte/ v.t. shorten.

écoute /ekut/ n.f. listening. **à l'~ (de)**, listening in (to). **aux ~s**, attentive. **heures de grande ~**, peak time. **~s téléphoniques**, phone tapping.

écout|er /ekute/ v.t. listen to; (radio) listen (in) to. ● v.i. listen. **~eur** n.m. earphones; (de téléphone) receiver.

écran /ekrɑ̃/ n.m. screen. **~ total**, sun-block.

écrasant, **~e** /ekrazɑ̃, -t/ a. overwhelming.

écraser /ekraze/ v.t. crush; (piéton) run over. s'**~** v. pr. crash (contre, into).

écrémé /ekreme/ a. **lait ~**, skimmed milk. **lait demi-~**, semi-skimmed milk.

écrevisse /ekrevis/ n.f. crayfish.

écrier (s') /(s)ekrije/ v. pr. exclaim.

écrin /ekrɛ̃/ n.m. case.

écrire† /ekrir/ v.t./i. write; (orthographier) spell. s'**~** v. pr. (mot) be spelt.

écrit /ekri/ n.m. document; (examen) written paper. **par ~**, in writing.

écriteau (pl. **~x**) /ekrito/ n.m. notice.

écriture /ekrityr/ n.f. writing. **~s**, (comm.) accounts. **l'É~ (sainte)**, the Scriptures.

écrivain /ekrivɛ̃/ n.m. writer.

écrou /ekru/ n.m. nut.

écrouer /ekrue/ v.t. imprison.

écrouler (s') /(s)ekrule/ v. pr. collapse.

écru /ekry/ a. (couleur) natural; (tissu) raw.

Écu /eky/ n.m. invar. ecu.

écueil /ekœj/ *n.m.* reef; (*fig.*) danger.

éculé /ekyle/ *a.* (*soulier*) worn at the heel; (*fig.*) well-worn.

écume /ekym/ *n.f.* foam; (*culin.*) scum.

écum|er /ekyme/ *v.t.* skim; (*piller*) plunder. ● *v.i.* foam. ~**oire** *n.f.* skimmer.

écureuil /ekyrœj/ *n.m.* squirrel.

écurie /ekyri/ *n.f.* stable.

écuy|er, ~ère /ekɥije, -jɛr/ *n.m., f.* (horse) rider.

eczéma /ɛgzema/ *n.m.* eczema.

édenté /edɑ̃te/ *a.* toothless.

édifice /edifis/ *n.m.* building.

édif|ier /edifje/ *v.t.* construct; (*porter à la vertu, éclairer*) edify. ~**ication** *n.f.* construction; edification.

édit /edi/ *n.m.* edict.

édi|ter /edite/ *v.t.* publish; (*annoter*) edit. ~**teur, ~trice** *n.m., f.* publisher; editor.

édition /edisjɔ̃/ *n.f.* edition; (*industrie*) publishing.

éditor|ial (*pl.* ~**iaux**) /editɔrjal, -jo/ *n.m.* editorial.

édredon /edrədɔ̃/ *n.m.* eiderdown.

éducateur, ~trice /edykatœr, -tris/ *n.m., f.* teacher.

éducati|f, ~ve /edykatif, -v/ *a.* educational.

éducation /edykɑsjɔ̃/ *n.f.* education; (*dans la famille*) upbringing; (*manières*) manners. ~ **physique,** physical education.

édulcorant /edylkɔrɑ̃/ *n.m.* & *a.* (**produit**) ~, sweetener.

éduquer /edyke/ *v.t.* educate; (*à la maison*) bring up.

effac|é /efase/ *a.* (*modeste*) unassuming. ~**ement** *n.m.* unassuming manner; (*suppression*) erasure.

effacer /efase/ *v.t.* (*gommer*) rub out; (*par lavage*) wash out; (*souvenir etc.*) erase. **s'~** *v. pr.* fade; (*s'écarter*) step aside.

effar|er /efare/ *v.t.* alarm. ~**ement** *n.m.* alarm.

effaroucher /efaruʃe/ *v.t.* scare away.

effecti|f [1], ~ve /efɛktif, -v/ *a.* effective. ~**vement** *adv.* effectively; (*en effet*) indeed.

effectif [2] /efɛktif/ *n.m.* size, strength. ~**s,** numbers.

effectuer /efɛktɥe/ *v.t.* carry out, make.

efféminé /efemine/ *a.* effeminate.

effervescen|t, ~te /efɛrvesɑ̃, -t/ *a.* **comprimé ~t,** effervescent tablet. ~**ce** *n.f.* excitement.

effet /efɛ/ *n.m.* effect; (*impression*) impression. ~**s,** (*habits*) clothes, things. **en ~,** indeed. **faire de l'~,** have an effect, be effective. **faire bon/mauvais ~,** make a good/bad impression.

efficac|e /efikas/ *a.* effective; (*personne*) efficient. ~**ité** *n.f.* effectiveness; efficiency.

effigie /efiʒi/ *n.f.* effigy.

effilocher (s') /(s)efilɔʃe/ *v. pr.* fray.

efflanqué /eflɑ̃ke/ *a.* emaciated.

effleurer /eflœre/ *v.t.* touch lightly; (*sujet*) touch on; (*se présenter à*) occur to.

effluves /eflyv/ *n.m. pl.* exhalations.

effondr|er (s') /(s)efɔ̃dre/ *v. pr.* collapse. ~**ement** *n.m.* collapse.

efforcer (s') /(s)efɔrse/ *v. pr.* try (hard) (**de,** to).

effort /efɔr/ *n.m.* effort.

effraction /efraksjɔ̃/ *n.f.* **entrer par ~,** break in.

effray|er /efreje/ *v.t.* frighten; (*décourager*) put off. **s'~er** *v. pr.* be frightened. ~**ant, ~ante** *a.* frightening; (*fig.*) frightful.

effréné /efrene/ *a.* wild.

effriter (s') /(s)efrite/ *v. pr.* crumble.

effroi /efrwa/ *n.m.* dread.

effronté /efrɔ̃te/ *a.* impudent.

effroyable /efrwajabl/ *a.* dreadful.

effusion /efyzjɔ̃/ *n.f.* ~ **de sang,** bloodshed.

ég|al, ~ale (*m. pl.* ~**aux**) /egal, -o/ *a.* equal; (*surface, vitesse*) even. ● *n. m., f.* equal. **ça m'est/lui est ~al,** it is all the same to me/him. **sans égal,** matchless. **d'~ à égal,** between equals.

également /egalmɑ̃/ *adv.* equally; (*aussi*) as well.

égaler /egale/ *v.t.* equal.

égaliser /egalize/ *v.t./i.* (*sport*) equalize; (*niveler*) level out; (*cheveux*) trim.

égalit|é /egalite/ *n.f.* equality; (*de surface, d'humeur*) evenness. **à ~é (de points),** equal. ~**aire** *a.* egalitarian.

égard /egar/ *n.m.* regard. ~**s,** consideration. **à cet ~,** in this respect. **à l'~ de,** with regard to; (*envers*) towards. **eu ~ à,** in view of.

égar|er /egare/ *v.t.* mislay; (*tromper*) lead astray. **s'~er** *v. pr.* get lost; (*se* _tromper_) go astray. **~ement** n.m. loss; (_affolement_) confusion.

égayer /egeje/ v.t. (_personne_) cheer up; (_pièce_) brighten up.

égide /eʒid/ n.f. aegis.

églantier /eglɑ̃tje/ n.m. wild rose (-bush).

églefin /egləfɛ̃/ n.m. haddock.

église /egliz/ n.f. church.

égoïs|te /egoist/ a. selfish. ● n.m./f. egoist. **~me** n.m. selfishness, egoism.

égorger /egɔrʒe/ v.t. slit the throat of.

égosiller (s') /(s)egozije/ v. pr. shout one's head off.

égout /egu/ n.m. sewer.

égoutt|er /egute/ v.t./i., **s'~er** v. pr. (_vaisselle_) drain. **~oir** n.m. draining-board; (_panier_) dish drainer.

égratign|er /egratiɲe/ v.t. scratch. **~ure** n.f. scratch.

égrener /egrəne/ v.t. (_raisins_) pick off; (_notes_) sound one by one.

Égypte /eʒipt/ n.f. Egypt.

égyptien, ~ne /eʒipsjɛ̃, -jɛn/ a. & n.m., f. Egyptian.

eh /e/ int. hey. **eh bien,** well.

éjacul|er /eʒakyle/ v.i. ejaculate. **~ation** n.f. ejaculation.

éjectable a. **siège ~,** ejector seat.

éjecter /eʒɛkte/ v.t. eject.

élabor|er /elabɔre/ v.t. elaborate. **~ation** n.f. elaboration.

élaguer /elage/ v.t. prune.

élan[1] /elɑ̃/ n.m. (_sport_) run-up; (_vitesse_) momentum; (_fig._) surge.

élan[2] /elɑ̃/ n.m. (_animal_) moose.

élancé /elɑ̃se/ a. slender.

élancement /elɑ̃smɑ̃/ n.m. twinge.

élancer (s') /(s)elɑ̃se/ v. pr. leap forward, dash; (_se dresser_) soar.

élarg|ir /elarʒir/ v.t., **s'~ir** v. pr. widen. **~issement** n.m. widening.

élasti|que /elastik/ a. elastic. ● n.m. elastic band; (_tissu_) elastic. **~cité** n.f. elasticity.

élec|teur, ~trice /elɛktœr, -tris/ n.m., f. voter, elector.

élection /elɛksjɔ̃/ n.f. election.

élector|al (_m. pl._ **~aux**) /elɛktɔral, -o/ a. (_réunion etc._) election; (_collège_) electoral.

électorat /elɛktɔra/ n.m. electorate, voters.

électricien /elɛktrisjɛ̃/ n.m. electrician.

électricité /elɛktrisite/ n.f. electricity.

électrifier /elɛktrifje/ v.t. electrify.

électrique /elɛktrik/ a. electric (al).

électrocuter /elɛktrɔkyte/ v.t. electrocute.

électroménager /elɛktrɔmenaʒe/ n.m. l'**~,** household appliances.

électron /elɛktrɔ̃/ n.m. electron.

électronique /elɛktrɔnik/ a. electronic. ● n.f. electronics.

électrophone /elɛktrɔfɔn/ n.m. record-player.

élég|ant, ~ante /elegɑ̃, -t/ a. elegant. **~amment** adv. elegantly. **~ance** n.f. elegance.

élément /elemɑ̃/ n.m. element; (_meuble_) unit. **~aire** /-tɛr/ a. elementary.

éléphant /elefɑ̃/ n.m. elephant.

élevage /ɛlvaʒ/ n.m. (stock-)breeding.

élévation /elevasjɔ̃/ n.f. raising; (_hausse_) rise; (_plan_) elevation.

élève /elɛv/ n.m./f. pupil.

élevé /ɛlve/ a. high; (_noble_) elevated. **bien ~,** well-mannered.

élever /ɛlve/ v.t. raise; (_enfants_) bring up, raise; (_animal_) breed. **s'~** v. pr. rise; (_dans le ciel_) soar up. **s'~ à,** amount to.

éleveu|r, ~se /ɛlvœr, -øz/ n.m., f. (stock-)breeder.

éligible /eliʒibl/ a. eligible.

élimé /elime/ a. worn thin.

élimin|er /elimine/ v.t. eliminate. **~ation** n.f. elimination. **~atoire** a. eliminating; n.f. (_sport_) heat.

élire† /elir/ v.t. elect.

élite /elit/ n.f. élite.

elle /ɛl/ pron. she; (_complément_) her; (_chose_) it. **~-même** pron. herself; itself.

elles /ɛl/ pron. they; (_complément_) them. **~-mêmes** pron. themselves.

ellip|se /elips/ n.f. ellipse. **~tique** a. elliptical.

élocution /elɔkysjɔ̃/ n.f. diction.

élog|e /elɔʒ/ n.m. praise. **faire l'~e de,** praise. **~ieux, ~ieuse** a. laudatory.

éloigné /elwaɲe/ a. distant. **~ de,** far away from. **parent ~,** distant relative.

éloign|er /elwaɲe/ v.t. take away ou remove (**de,** from); (_personne aimée_) estrange (**de,** from); (_danger_) ward off; (_visite_) put off. **s'~er** v. pr. go ou move away (**de,** from); (_affectivement_) become estranged (**de,** from). **~ement** n.m. removal; (_distance_) distance; (_oubli_) estrangement.

élongation /elɔ̃gasjɔ̃/ *n.f.* strained muscle.

éloquen|t, ~te /elɔkɑ̃, -t/ *a.* eloquent. **~ce** *n.f.* eloquence.

élu, ~e /ely/ *a.* elected. ● *n.m., f.* (*pol.*) elected representative.

élucider /elyside/ *v.t.* elucidate.

éluder /elyde/ *v.t.* elude.

émacié /emasje/ *a.* emaciated.

ém|ail (*pl.* **~aux**) /emaj, -o/ *n.m.* enamel.

émaillé /emaje/ *a.* enamelled. **~ de,** studded with.

émancip|er /emɑ̃sipe/ *v.t.* emancipate. **s'~er** *v. pr.* become emancipated. **~ation** *n.f.* emancipation.

éman|er /emane/ *v.i.* emanate. **~ation** *n.f.* emanation.

émarger /emarʒe/ *v.t.* initial.

emball|er /ɑ̃bale/ *v.t.* pack, wrap; (*personne: fam.*) enthuse. **s'~er** *v. pr.* (*moteur*) race; (*cheval*) bolt; (*personne*) get carried away. **~age** *n.m.* package, wrapping.

embarcadère /ɑ̃barkadɛr/ *n.m.* landing-stage.

embarcation /ɑ̃barkasjɔ̃/ *n.f.* boat.

embardée /ɑ̃barde/ *n.f.* swerve.

embargo /ɑ̃bargo/ *n.m.* embargo.

embarqu|er /ɑ̃barke/ *v.t.* embark; (*charger*) load; (*emporter: fam.*) cart off. ● *v.i.,* **s'~er** *v. pr.* board, embark. **s'~er dans,** embark upon. **~ement** *n.m.* embarkation; loading.

embarras /ɑ̃bara/ *n.m.* obstacle; (*gêne*) embarrassment; (*difficulté*) difficulty.

embarrasser /ɑ̃barase/ *v.t.* clutter (up); (*gêner dans les mouvements*) hinder; (*fig.*) embarrass. **s'~ de,** burden o.s. with.

embauch|e /ɑ̃boʃ/ *n.f.* hiring; (*emploi*) employment. **~er** *v.t.* hire, take on.

embauchoir /ɑ̃boʃwar/ *n.m.* shoe tree.

embaumer /ɑ̃bome/ *v.t./i.* (make) smell fragrant; (*cadavre*) embalm.

embellir /ɑ̃belir/ *v.t.* brighten up; (*récit*) embellish.

embêt|er /ɑ̃bete/ *v.t.* (*fam.*) annoy. **s'~er** *v. pr.* (*fam.*) get bored. **~ant, ~ante** *a.* (*fam.*) annoying. **~ement** /ɑ̃bɛtmɑ̃/ *n.m.* (*fam.*) annoyance.

emblée (d') /(d)ɑ̃ble/ *adv.* right away.

emblème /ɑ̃blɛm/ *n.m.* emblem.

embobiner /ɑ̃bɔbine/ *v.t.* (*fam.*) get round.

emboîter /ɑ̃bwate/ *v.t.,* **s'~** *v. pr.* fit together. **(s')~ dans,** fit into. **~ le pas à qn.,** (*imiter*) follow suit.

embonpoint /ɑ̃bɔ̃pwɛ̃/ *n.m.* stoutness.

embouchure /ɑ̃buʃyr/ *n.f.* (*de fleuve*) mouth; (*mus.*) mouthpiece.

embourber (s') /(s)ɑ̃burbe/ *v. pr.* get bogged down.

embourgeoiser (s') /(s)ɑ̃burʒwaze/ *v. pr.* become middle-class.

embout /ɑ̃bu/ *n.m.* tip.

embouteillage /ɑ̃butejaʒ/ *n.m.* traffic jam.

emboutir /ɑ̃butir/ *v.t.* (*heurter*) crash into.

embranchement /ɑ̃brɑ̃ʃmɑ̃/ *n.m.* (*de routes*) junction.

embraser /ɑ̃braze/ *v.t.* set on fire, fire. **s'~** *v. pr.* flare up.

embrass|er /ɑ̃brase/ *v.t.* kiss; (*adopter, contenir*) embrace. **s'~er** *v. pr.* kiss. **~ades** *n.f. pl.* kissing.

embrasure /ɑ̃brazyr/ *n.f.* opening.

embray|er /ɑ̃breje/ *v.i.* let in the clutch. **~age** /ɑ̃brɛjaʒ/ *n.m.* clutch.

embrigader /ɑ̃brigade/ *v.t.* enrol.

embrocher /ɑ̃brɔʃe/ *v.t.* (*viande*) spit.

embrouiller /ɑ̃bruje/ *v.t.* mix up; (*fils*) tangle. **s'~** *v. pr.* get mixed up.

embroussaillé /ɑ̃brusaje/ *a.* (*poils, chemin*) bushy.

embryon /ɑ̃brijɔ̃/ *n.m.* embryo. **~naire** /-jɔnɛr/ *a.* embryonic.

embûches /ɑ̃byʃ/ *n.f. pl.* traps.

embuer /ɑ̃bɥe/ *v.t.* mist up.

embuscade /ɑ̃byskad/ *n.f.* ambush.

embusquer (s') /(s)ɑ̃byske/ *v. pr.* lie in ambush.

éméché /emeʃe/ *a.* tipsy.

émeraude /ɛmrod/ *n.f.* emerald.

émerger /emɛrʒe/ *v.i.* emerge; (*fig.*) stand out.

émeri /ɛmri/ *n.m.* emery.

émerveill|er /emɛrveje/ *v.t.* amaze. **s'~er de,** marvel at, be amazed at. **~ement** /-vɛjmɑ̃/ *n.m.* amazement, wonder.

émett|re† /emɛtr/ *v.t.* give out; (*message*) transmit; (*timbre, billet*) issue; (*opinion*) express. **~eur** *n.m.* transmitter.

émeut|e /emøt/ *n.f.* riot. **~ier, ~ière** *n.m., f.* rioter.

émietter /emjete/ *v.t.,* **s'~** *v. pr.* crumble.

émigrant, ~e /emigrã, -t/ *n.m., f.* emigrant.

émigr|er /emigre/ *v.i.* emigrate. **~ation** *n.f.* emigration.

émincer /emɛ̃se/ *v.t.* cut into thin slices.

émin|ent, ~ente /eminã, -t/ *a.* eminent. **~emment** /-amã/ *adv.* eminently. **~ence** *n.f.* eminence; (*colline*) hill. **~ence grise,** éminence grise.

émissaire /emisɛr/ *n.m.* emissary.

émission /emisjõ/ *n.f.* emission; (*de message*) transmission; (*de timbre*) issue; (*programme*) bro adcast.

emmagasiner /ãmagazine/ *v.t.* store.

emmanchure /ãmãʃyr/ *n.f.* armhole.

emmêler /ãmele/ *v.t.* tangle. **s'~** *v. pr.* get mixed up.

emménager /ãmenaʒe/ *v.i.* move in. **~ dans,** move into.

emmener /ãmne/ *v.t.* take; (*comme prisonnier*) take away.

emmerder /ãmɛrde/ *v.t.* (*argot*) bother. **s'~** *v. pr.* (*argot*) get bored.

emmitoufler /ãmitufle/ *v.t.,* **s'~** *v. pr.* wrap up (warmly).

émoi /emwa/ *n.m.* excitement.

émoluments /emɔlymã/ *n.m. pl.* remuneration.

émonder /emõde/ *v.t.* prune.

émoti|f, ~ve /emɔtif, -v/ *a.* emotional.

émotion /emosjõ/ *n.f.* emotion; (*peur*) fright. **~nel,** ~nelle /-jɔnɛl/ *a.* emotional.

émousser /emuse/ *v.t.* blunt.

émouv|oir /emuvwar/ *v.t.* move. **s'~oir** *v. pr.* be moved. **~ant,** ~ante *a.* moving.

empailler /ãpaje/ *v.t.* stuff.

empaqueter /ãpakte/ *v.t.* package.

emparer (s') /(s)ãpare/ *v. pr.* **s'~ de,** seize.

empâter (s') /(s)ãpate/ *v. pr.* fill out, grow fatter.

empêchement /ãpɛʃmã/ *n.m.* hitch, difficulty.

empêcher /ãpeʃe/ *v.t.* prevent. **~ de faire,** prevent *ou* stop (from) doing. **il ne peut pas s'~ de penser,** he cannot help thinking. **(il) n'empêche que,** still.

empêch|eur, ~euse /ãpeʃœr, -øz/ *n.m., f.* **~eur de tourner en rond,** spoilsport.

empeigne /ãpɛɲ/ *n.f.* upper.

empereur /ãprœr/ *n.m.* emperor.

empeser /ãpəze/ *v.t.* starch.

empester /ãpɛste/ *v.t.* make stink, stink out; (*essence etc.*) stink of. ● *v.i.* stink.

empêtrer (s') /(s)ãpetre/ *v. pr.* become entangled.

emphase /ãfaz/ *n.f.* pomposity.

empiéter /ãpjete/ *v.i.* **~ sur,** encroach upon.

empiffrer (s') /(s)ãpifre/ *v. pr.* (*fam.*) gorge o.s.

empiler /ãpile/ *v.t.,* **s'~** *v. pr.* pile (up).

empire /ãpir/ *n.m.* empire; (*fig.*) control.

empirer /ãpire/ *v.i.* worsen.

empirique /ãpirik/ *a.* empirical.

emplacement /ãplasmã/ *n.m.* site.

emplâtre /ãplatr/ *n.m.* (*méd.*) plaster.

emplettes /ãplɛt/ *n.f. pl.* purchase. **faire des ~,** do one's shopping.

emplir /ãplir/ *v.t.,* **s'~** *v. pr.* fill.

emploi /ãplwa/ *n.m.* use; (*travail*) job. **~ du temps,** timetable. **l'~,** (*pol.*) employment.

employ|er /ãplwaje/ *v.t.* use; (*personne*) employ. **s'~er** *v. pr.* be used. **s'~er à,** devote o.s. to. **~é,** ~ée *n.m., f.* employee. **~eur,** ~euse *n.m., f.* employer.

empocher /ãpɔʃe/ *v.t.* pocket.

empoigner /ãpwaɲe/ *v.t.* grab. **s'~** *v. pr.* come to blows.

empoisonn|er /ãpwazɔne/ *v.t.* poison; (*empuantir*) stink out; (*embêter: fam.*) annoy. **~ement** *n.m.* poisoning.

emport|é /ãpɔrte/ *a.* quicktempered. **~ement** *n.m.* anger.

emporter /ãpɔrte/ *v.t.* take (away); (*entraîner*) carry away; (*prix*) carry off; (*arracher*) tear off. **~ un chapeau/***etc.,* (*vent*) blow off a hat/*etc.* **s'~** *v. pr.* lose one's temper. **l'~,** get the upper hand (**sur,** of). **plat à ~,** take-away.

empoté /ãpɔte/ *a.* silly.

empourpré /ãpurpre/ *a.* crimson.

empreint, ~e /ãprɛ̃, -t/ *a.* **~e de,** marked with. ● *n.f.* mark. **~e (digitale),** fingerprint. **~e de pas,** footprint.

empress|er (s') /(s)ãprese/ *v. pr.* **s'~er auprès de,** be attentive to. **s'~er de,** hasten to. **~é** *a.* eager, attentive. **~ement** /ãprɛsmã/ *n.m.* eagerness.

emprise /ãpriz/ *n.f.* influence.

emprisonn|er /ɑ̃prizɔne/ v.t. imprison. **~ement** n.m. imprisonment.

emprunt /ɑ̃prœ̃/ n.m. loan. **faire un ~**, take out a loan.

emprunté /ɑ̃prœ̃te/ a. awkward.

emprunt|er /ɑ̃prœ̃te/ v.t. borrow (**à**, from); (*route*) take; (*fig.*) assume. **~eur, ~euse** n.m., f. borrower.

ému /emy/ a. moved; (*apeuré*) nervous; (*joyeux*) excited.

émulation /emylasjɔ̃/ n.f. emulation.

émule /emyl/ n.m./f. imitator.

émulsion /emylsjɔ̃/ n.f. emulsion.

en[1] /ɑ̃/ *prép.* in; (*avec direction*) to; (*manière, état*) in, on; (*moyen de transport*) by; (*composition*) made of. **en cadeau/médecin**/etc., as a present/doctor/etc. **en guerre**, at war. **en faisant**, by ou on ou while doing.

en[2] /ɑ̃/ *pron.* of it, of them; (*moyen*) with it; (*cause*) from it; (*lieu*) from there. **en avoir/vouloir**/etc., have/ want/etc. **ne pas en avoir/ vouloir**/etc., not have/want/etc. any. **où en êtes-vous?**, where are you up to?, how far have you got? **j'en ai assez**, I've had enough. **en êtes-vous sûr?**, are you sure?

encadr|er /ɑ̃kadre/ v.t. frame; (*entourer d'un trait*) circle; (*entourer*) surround. **~ement** n.m. framing; (*de porte*) frame.

encaiss|er /ɑ̃kese/ v.t. (*argent*) collect; (*chèque*) cash; (*coups: fam.*) take. **~eur** /ɑ̃kɛsœr/ n.m. debt-collector.

encart /ɑ̃kar/ n.m. **~ publicitaire**, (advertising) insert.

en-cas /ɑ̃ka/ n.m. (stand-by) snack.

encastré /ɑ̃kastre/ a. built-in.

encaustiqu|e /ɑ̃kɔstik/ n.f. wax polish. **~er** v.t. wax.

enceinte[1] /ɑ̃sɛ̃t/ a.f. pregnant. **~ de 3 mois**, 3 months pregnant.

enceinte[2] /ɑ̃sɛ̃t/ n.f. enclosure. **~ (acoustique)**, loudspeaker.

encens /ɑ̃sɑ̃/ n.m. incense.

encercler /ɑ̃sɛrkle/ v.t. surround.

enchaîn|er /ɑ̃ʃene/ v.t. chain (up); (*coordonner*) link (up). ● v.i. continue. **s'~er** v. pr. be linked (up). **~ement** /ɑ̃ʃɛnmɑ̃/ n.m. (*suite*) chain; (*liaison*) link(ing).

enchant|er /ɑ̃ʃɑ̃te/ v.t. delight; (*ensorceler*) enchant. **~é** a. (*ravi*) delighted. **~ement** n.m. delight; (*magie*) enchantment.

enchâsser /ɑ̃ʃase/ v.t. set.

enchère /ɑ̃ʃɛr/ n.f. bid. **mettre ou vendre aux ~s**, sell by auction.

enchevêtrer /ɑ̃ʃvetre/ v.t. tangle. **s'~** v. pr. become tangled.

enclave /ɑ̃klav/ n.f. enclave.

enclencher /ɑ̃klɑ̃ʃe/ v.t. engage.

enclin, ~e /ɑ̃klɛ̃, -in/ a. **~ à**, inclined to.

enclore /ɑ̃klɔr/ v.t. enclose.

enclos /ɑ̃klo/ n.m. enclosure.

enclume /ɑ̃klym/ n.f. anvil.

encoche /ɑ̃kɔʃ/ n.f. notch.

encoignure /ɑ̃kɔɲyr/ n.f. corner.

encoller /ɑ̃kɔle/ v.t. paste.

encolure /ɑ̃kɔlyr/ n.f. neck.

encombre /ɑ̃kɔ̃br/ n.m. **sans ~**, without any problems.

encombr|er /ɑ̃kɔ̃bre/ v.t. clutter (up); (*gêner*) hamper. **s'~er de**, burden o.s. with. **~ant, ~ante** a. cumbersome. **~ement** n.m. congestion; (*auto.*) traffic jam; (*volume*) bulk.

encontre de (à l') /(al)ɑ̃kɔ̃trədə/ *prép.* against.

encore /ɑ̃kɔr/ adv. (*toujours*) still; (*de nouveau*) again; (*de plus*) more; (*aussi*) also. **~ mieux/plus grand**/ etc., even better/larger/etc. **~ une heure/un café**/etc., another hour/ coffee/ etc. **pas ~**, not yet. **si ~**, if only.

encourag|er /ɑ̃kuraʒe/ v.t. encourage. **~ement** n.m. encouragement.

encourir /ɑ̃kurir/ v.t. incur.

encrasser /ɑ̃krase/ v.t. clog up (with dirt).

encr|e /ɑ̃kr/ n.f. ink. **~er** v.t. ink.

encrier /ɑ̃krije/ n.m. ink-well.

encroûter (s') /(s)ɑ̃krute/ v. pr. become doggedly set in one's ways. **s'~ dans**, sink into.

encyclopéd|ie /ɑ̃siklɔpedi/ n.f. encyclopaedia. **~ique** a. encyclopaedic.

endetter /ɑ̃dete/ v.t., **s'~** v. pr. get into debt.

endeuiller /ɑ̃dœje/ v.t. plunge into mourning.

endiablé /ɑ̃djɑble/ a. wild.

endiguer /ɑ̃dige/ v.t. dam; (*fig.*) check.

endimanché /ɑ̃dimɑ̃ʃe/ a. in one's Sunday best.

endive /ɑ̃div/ n.f. chicory.

endocrinolo|gie /ãdɔkrinɔlɔʒi/ *n.f.*
endocrinology. **~gue** *n.m./f.* endocrinologist.

endoctrin|er /ãdɔktrine/ *v.t.* indoctrinate. **~ement** *n.m.* indoctrination.

endommager /ãdɔmaʒe/ *v.t.* damage.

endorm|ir /ãdɔrmir/ *v.t.* send to sleep; (*atténuer*) allay. **s'~ir** *v. pr.* fall asleep. **~i** *a.* asleep; (*apathique*) sleepy.

endosser /ãdɔse/ *v.t.* (*vêtement*) put on; (*assumer*) assume; (*comm.*) endorse.

endroit /ãdrwa/ *n.m.* place; (*de tissu*) right side. **à l'~,** the right way round, right side out.

end|uire /ãdɥir/ *v.t.* coat. **~uit** *n.m.* coating.

endurance /ãdyrãs/ *n.f.* endurance.

endurant, ~e /ãdyrã, -t/ *a.* tough.

endurci /ãdyrsi/ *a.* **célibataire ~,** confirmed bachelor.

endurcir /ãdyrsir/ *v.t.* harden. **s'~** *v. pr.* become hard(ened).

endurer /ãdyre/ *v.t.* endure.

énerg|ie /enɛrʒi/ *n.f.* energy; (*techn.*) power. **~étique** *a.* energy. **~ique** *a.* energetic.

énervant, ~e /enɛrvã, -t/ *a.* irritating, annoying.

énerver /enɛrve/ *v.t.* irritate. **s'~** *v. pr.* get worked up.

enfance /ãfãs/ *n.f.* childhood. **la petite ~,** infancy.

enfant /ãfã/ *n.m./f.* child. **~ en bas âge,** infant. **~illage** /-tijaʒ/ *n.m.* childishness. **~in, ~ine** /-tɛ̃, -tin/ *a.* childlike; (*puéril*) childish; (*jeu, langage*) children's.

enfanter /ãfãte/ *v.t./i.* give birth (to).

enfer /ãfɛr/ *n.m.* hell.

enfermer /ãfɛrme/ *v.t.* shut up. **s'~** *v. pr.* shut o.s. up.

enferrer (s') /(s)ãfere/ *v. pr.* become entangled.

enfiévré /ãfjevre/ *a.* feverish.

enfilade /ãfilad/ *n.f.* string, row.

enfiler /ãfile/ *v.t.* (*aiguille*) thread; (*anneaux*) string; (*vêtement*) slip on; (*rue*) take; (*insérer*) insert.

enfin /ãfɛ̃/ *adv.* at last, finally; (*en dernier lieu*) finally; (*somme toute*) after all; (*résignation, conclusion*) well.

enflammer /ãflame/ *v.t.* set fire to; (*méd.*) inflame. **s'~** *v. pr.* catch fire.

enfl|er /ãfle/ *v.t./i.*, **s'~er** *v. pr.* swell. **~é** *a.* swollen. **~ure** *n.f.* swelling.

enfoncer /ãfɔ̃se/ *v.t.* (*épingle etc.*) push *ou* drive in; (*chapeau*) push down; (*porte*) break down; (*mettre*) thrust, put. ● *v.i.,* **s'~** *v. pr.* sink (**dans,** into).

enfouir /ãfwir/ *v.t.* bury.

enfourcher /ãfurʃe/ *v.t.* mount.

enfourner /ãfurne/ *v.t.* put in the oven.

enfreindre /ãfrɛ̃dr/ *v.t.* infringe.

enfuir† (s') /(s)ãfɥir/ *v. pr.* run off.

enfumer /ãfyme/ *v.t.* fill with smoke.

engagé /ãgaʒe/ *a.* committed.

engageant, ~e /ãgaʒã, -t/ *a.* attractive.

engag|er /ãgaʒe/ *v.t.* (*lier*) bind, commit; (*embaucher*) take on; (*commencer*) start; (*introduire*) insert; (*entraîner*) involve; (*encourager*) urge; (*investir*) invest. **s'~er** *v. pr.* (*promettre*) commit o.s.; (*commencer*) start; (*soldat*) enlist; (*concurrent*) enter. **s'~er à faire,** undertake to do. **s'~er dans,** (*voie*) enter. **~ement** *n.m.* (*promesse*) promise; (*pol., comm.*) commitment; (*début*) start; (*inscription: sport*) entry.

engelure /ãʒlyr/ *n.f.* chilblain.

engendrer /ãʒãdre/ *v.t.* beget; (*causer*) generate.

engin /ãʒɛ̃/ *n.m.* machine; (*outil*) instrument; (*projectile*) missile. **~ explosif,** explosive device.

englober /ãglɔbe/ *v.t.* include.

engloutir /ãglutir/ *v.t.* swallow (up). **s'~** *v. pr.* (*navire*) be engulfed.

engorger /ãgɔrʒe/ *v.t.* block.

engou|er (s') /(s)ãgwe/ *v. pr.* **s'~er de,** become infatuated with. **~ement** /-umã/ *n.m.* infatuation.

engouffrer /ãgufre/ *v.t.* devour. **s'~ dans,** rush into (with force).

engourd|ir /ãgurdir/ *v.t.* numb. **s'~ir** *v. pr.* go numb. **~i** *a.* numb.

engrais /ãgrɛ/ *n.m.* manure; (*chimique*) fertilizer.

engraisser /ãgrese/ *v.t.* fatten. **s'~** *v. pr.* get fat.

engrenage /ãgrənaʒ/ *n.m.* gears; (*fig.*) chain (of events).

engueuler /ãgœle/ *v.t.* (*argot*) curse, swear at, hurl abuse at.

enhardir (s') /(s)ãardir/ *v. pr.* become bolder.

énième /enjɛm/ *a.* (*fam.*) umpteenth.

énigm|e /enigm/ *n.f.* riddle, enigma. **~atique** *a.* enigmatic.

enivrer /ãnivre/ *v.t.* intoxicate. **s'~** *v. pr.* get drunk.

enjamb|er /ãʒãbe/ *v.t.* step over; (*pont*) span. **~ée** *n.f.* stride.

enjeu (*pl.* **~x**) /ãʒø/ *n.m.* stake(s).

enjôler /ãʒole/ *v.t.* wheedle.

enjoliver /ãʒolive/ *v.t.* embellish.

enjoliveur /ãʒolivœr/ *n.m.* hub-cap.

enjoué /ãʒwe/ *a.* cheerful.

enlacer /ãlase/ *v.t.* entwine.

enlaidir /ãledir/ *v.t.* make ugly. ● *v.i.* grow ugly.

enlèvement /ãlɛvmã/ *n.m.* removal; (*rapt*) kidnapping.

enlever /ãlve/ *v.t.* (*emporter*) take (away), remove (**à**, from); (*vêtement*) take off, remove; (*tache, organe*) take out, remove; (*kidnapper*) kidnap; (*gagner*) win.

enliser (s') /(s)ãlize/ *v. pr.* get bogged down.

enluminure /ãlyminyr/ *n.f.* illumination.

enneig|é /ãneʒe/ *a.* snow-covered. **~ement** /ãnɛʒmã/ *n.m.* snow conditions.

ennemi /ɛnmi/ *n.m. & a.* enemy. **~ de,** (*fig.*) hostile to. **l'~ public numéro un,** public enemy number one.

ennui /ãnɥi/ *n.m.* boredom; (*tracas*) trouble, worry. **il a des ~s,** he's got problems.

ennuyer /ãnɥije/ *v.t.* bore; (*irriter*) annoy; (*préoccuper*) worry. **s'~** *v. pr.* get bored.

ennuyeu|x, ~se /ãnɥijø, -z/ *a.* boring; (*fâcheux*) annoying.

énoncé /enõse/ *n.m.* wording, text; (*gram.*) utterance.

énoncer /enõse/ *v.t.* express, state.

enorgueillir (s') /(s)ãnɔrgœjir/ *v. pr.* **s'~ de,** pride o.s. on.

énorm|e /enɔrm/ *a.* enormous. **~ément** *adv.* enormously. **~ément de,** an enormous amount of. **~ité** *n.f.* enormous size; (*atrocité*) enormity; (*bévue*) enormous blunder.

enquérir (s') /(s)ãkerir/ *v. pr.* **s'~ de,** enquire about.

enquêt|e /ãkɛt/ *n.f.* investigation; (*jurid.*) inquiry; (*sondage*) survey. **mener l'~e,** lead the inquiry. **~er** /-ete/ *v.i.* **~er (sur),** investigate. **~eur, ~euse** *n.m., f.* investigator.

enquiquin|er /ãkikine/ *v.t.* (*fam.*) bother. **~ant, ~ante** *a.* irritating. **c'est ~ant,** it's a nuisance.

enraciné /ãrasine/ *a.* deep-rooted.

enrag|er /ãraʒe/ *v.i.* be furious. **faire ~er,** annoy. **~é** *a.* furious; (*chien*) mad; (*fig.*) fanatical. **~eant, ~eante** *a.* infuriating.

enrayer /ãreje/ *v.t.* check.

enregistr|er /ãrʒistre/ *v.t.* note, record; (*mus.*) record. **(faire) ~er,** (*bagages*) register, check in. **~ement** *n.m.* recording; (*des bagages*) registration.

enrhumer (s') /(s)ãryme/ *v. pr.* catch a cold.

enrich|ir /ãriʃir/ *v.t.* enrich. **s'~ir** *v. pr.* grow rich(er). **~issement** *n.m.* enrichment.

enrober /ãrɔbe/ *v.t.* coat (**de,** with).

enrôl|er /ãrole/ *v.t.*, **s'~** *v. pr.* enlist, enrol.

enrou|er (s') /(s)ãrwe/ *v. pr.* become hoarse. **~é** *a.* hoarse.

enrouler /ãrule/ *v.t.*, **s'~** *v. pr.* wind. **s'~ dans une couverture,** roll o.s. up in a blanket.

ensabler /ãsable/ *v.t.*, **s'~** *v. pr.* (*port*) silt up.

ensanglanté /ãsãglãte/ *a.* bloodstained.

enseignant, ~e /ãsɛɲã, -t/ *n.m., f.* teacher. ● *a.* teaching.

enseigne /ãsɛɲ/ *n.f.* sign.

enseignement /ãsɛɲmã/ *n.m.* teaching; (*instruction*) education.

enseigner /ãsɛɲe/ *v.t./i.* teach. **~ qch. à qn.,** teach s.o. sth.

ensemble /ãsãbl/ *adv.* together. ● *n.m.* unity; (*d'objets*) set; (*mus.*) ensemble; (*vêtements*) outfit. **dans l'~,** on the whole. **d'~,** (*idée etc.*) general. **l'~ de,** (*totalité*) all of, the whole of.

ensemencer /ãsmãse/ *v.t.* sow.

enserrer /ãsere/ *v.t.* grip (tightly).

ensevelir /ãsəvlir/ *v.t.* bury.

ensoleill|é /ãsoleje/ *a.* sunny. **~ement** /ãsɔlɛjmã/ *n.m.* (period of) sunshine.

ensommeillé /ãsɔmeje/ *a.* sleepy.

ensorceler /ãsɔrsəle/ *v.t.* bewitch.

ensuite /ãsɥit/ *adv.* next, then; (*plus tard*) later.

ensuivre (s') /(s)ãsɥivr/ *v. pr.* follow. **et tout ce qui s'ensuit,** and so on.

entaill|e /ãtaj/ *n.f.* notch; (*blessure*) gash. **~er** *v.t.* notch; gash.

entamer /ãtame/ *v.t.* start; (*inciser*) cut into; (*ébranler*) shake.

entass|er /ãtase/ *v.t.*, **s'~er** *v. pr.* pile up. **(s')~er dans,** cram (together) into. **~ement** *n.m.* (*tas*) pile.

entendement /ātādmā/ *n.m.* understanding. **ça dépasse l'~,** it defies one's understanding.

entendre /ātādr/ *v.t.* hear; (*comprendre*) understand; (*vouloir*) intend, mean; (*vouloir dire*) mean. **s'~** *v. pr.* (*être d'accord*) agree. **~ dire que,** hear that. **~ parler de,** hear of. **s'~ (bien),** get on (**avec,** with). **(cela) s'entend,** of course.

entendu /ātādy/ *a.* (*convenu*) agreed; (*sourire, air*) knowing. **bien ~,** of course. **(c'est) ~!,** all right!

entente /ātāt/ *n.f.* understanding. **à double ~,** with a double meaning.

entériner /āterine/ *v.t.* ratify.

enterr|er /ātere/ *v.t.* bury. **~ement** /ātɛrmā/ *n.m.* burial, funeral.

entêtant, ~e /ātɛtā, -t/ *a.* heady.

en-tête /ātɛt/ *n.m.* heading. **à ~,** headed.

entêt|é /ātete/ *a.* stubborn. **~ement** /ātɛtmā/ *n.m.* stubbornness.

entêter (s') /(s)ātete/ *v. pr.* persist (**à, dans,** in).

enthousias|me /ātuzjasm/ *n.m.* enthusiasm. **~mer** *v.t.* enthuse. **s'~mer pour,** enthuse over. **~te** *a.* enthusiastic.

enticher (s') /(s)ātiʃe/ *v. pr.* **s'~ de,** become infatuated with.

ent|ier, ~ière /ātje, -jɛr/ *a.* whole; (*absolu*) absolute; (*entêté*) unyielding. ● *n.m.* whole. **en ~ier,** entirely. **~ièrement** *adv.* entirely.

entité /ātite/ *n.f.* entity.

entonner /ātɔne/ *v.t.* start singing.

entonnoir /ātɔnwar/ *n.m.* funnel; (*trou*) crater.

entorse /ātɔrs/ *n.f.* sprain. **~ à,** (*loi*) infringement of.

entortiller /ātɔrtije/ *v.t.* wrap (up); (*enrouler*) wind, wrap; (*duper*) deceive.

entourage /āturaʒ/ *n.m.* circle of family and friends; (*bordure*) surround.

entourer /āture/ *v.t.* surround (**de,** with); (*réconforter*) rally round. **~ de,** (*écharpe etc.*) wrap round.

entracte /ātrakt/ *n.m.* interval.

entraide /ātrɛd/ *n.f.* mutual aid.

entraider (s') /(s)ātrede/ *v. pr.* help each other.

entrailles /ātraj/ *n.f. pl.* entrails.

entrain /ātrɛ̃/ *n.m.* zest, spirit.

entraînant, ~e /ātrɛnā, -t/ *a.* rousing.

entraînement /ātrɛnmā/ *n.m.* (*sport*) training.

entraîn|er /ātrene/ *v.t.* carry away *ou* along; (*emmener, influencer*) lead; (*impliquer*) entail; (*sport*) train; (*roue*) drive. **~eur** /ātrɛnœr/ *n.m.* trainer.

entrav|e /ātrav/ *n.f.* hindrance. **~er** *v.t.* hinder.

entre /ātr(ə)/ *prép.* between; (*parmi*) among(st). **~ autres,** among other things. **l'un d'~ nous/vous/eux,** one of us/you/them.

entrebâillé /ātrəbaje/ *a.* ajar.

entrechoquer (s') /(s)ātrəʃɔke/ *v. pr.* knock against each other.

entrecôte /ātrəkot/ *n.f.* rib steak.

entrecouper /ātrəkupe/ *v.t.* **~ de,** intersperse with.

entrecroiser (s') /(s)ātrəkrwaze/ *v. pr.* (*routes*) intersect.

entrée /ātre/ *n.f.* entrance; (*accès*) admission, entry; (*billet*) ticket; (*culin.*) first course; (*de données: techn.*) input. **~ interdite,** no entry.

entrefaites (sur ces) /(syrsez)-ātrəfɛt/ *adv.* at that moment.

entrefilet /ātrəfilɛ/ *n.m.* paragraph.

entrejambe /ātrəʒāb/ *n.m.* crotch.

entrelacer /ātrəlase/ *v.t.,* **s'~** *v. pr.* intertwine.

entremêler /ātrəmele/ *v.t.,* **s'~** *v. pr.* (inter)mingle.

entremets /ātrəmɛ/ *n.m.* dessert.

entremetteu|r, ~se /ātrəmɛtœr, -øz/ *n.m., f.* (*péj.*) go-between.

entre|mettre (s') /(s)ātrəmɛtr/ *v. pr.* intervene. **~mise** *n.f.* intervention. **par l'~mise de,** through.

entreposer /ātrəpoze/ *v.t.* store.

entrepôt /ātrəpo/ *n.m.* warehouse.

entreprenant, ~e /ātrəprənā, -t/ *a.* (*actif*) enterprising; (*séducteur*) forward.

entreprendre† /ātrəprādr/ *v.t.* start on; (*personne*) buttonhole. **~ de faire,** undertake to do.

entrepreneur /ātrəprənœr/ *n.m.* **~ (de bâtiments),** (building) contractor.

entreprise /ātrəpriz/ *n.f.* undertaking; (*société*) firm.

entrer /ātre/ *v.i.* (*aux. être*) go in, enter; (*venir*) come in, enter. **~ dans,** go *ou* come into, enter; (*club*) join. **~ en collision,** collide (**avec,** with). **faire ~,** (*personne*) show in. **laisser ~,** let in.

entresol /ātrəsɔl/ *n.m.* mezzanine.

entre-temps /ãtrətã/ *adv.* meanwhile.

entretenir† /ãtrətnir/ *v.t.* maintain; (*faire durer*) keep alive. **~ qn. de,** converse with s.o. about. **s'~** *v. pr.* speak (**de,** about; **avec,** to).

entretien /ãtrətjẽ/ *n.m.* maintenance; (*discussion*) talk; (*audience pour un emploi*) interview.

entrevoir /ãtrəvwar/ *v.t.* make out; (*brièvement*) glimpse.

entrevue /ãtrəvy/ *n.f.* interview.

entrouvrir /ãtruvrir/ *v.t.* half-open.

énumér|er /enymere/ *v.t.* enumerate. **~ation** *n.f.* enumeration.

envah|ir /ãvair/ *v.t.* invade, overrun; (*douleur, peur*) overcome. **~isseur** *n.m.* invader.

enveloppe /ãvlɔp/ *n.f.* envelope; (*emballage*) covering; (*techn.*) casing.

envelopper /ãvlɔpe/ *v.t.* wrap (up); (*fig.*) envelop.

envenimer /ãvnime/ *v.t.* embitter. **s'~** *v. pr.* become embittered.

envergure /ãvɛrgyr/ *n.f.* wing-span; (*importance*) scope; (*qualité*) calibre.

envers /ãvɛr/ *prép.* toward(s), to. ● *n.m.* (*de tissu*) wrong side. **à l'~,** upside down; (*pantalon*) back to front; (*chaussette*) inside out.

enviable /ãvjabl/ *a.* enviable. **peu ~,** unenviable.

envie /ãvi/ *n.f.* desire, wish; (*jalousie*) envy. **avoir ~ de,** want, feel like. **avoir ~ de faire,** want to do, feel like doing.

envier /ãvje/ *v.t.* envy.

envieu|x, ~se /ãvjø, -z/ *a. & n.m., f.* envious (person).

environ /ãvirõ/ *adv.* (round) about. **~s** *n.m. pl.* surroundings. **aux ~s de,** round about.

environnement /ãvirɔnmã/ *n.m.* environment.

environn|er /ãvirɔne/ *v.t.* surround. **~ant, ~ante** *a.* surrounding.

envisager /ãvizaʒe/ *v.t.* consider. **~ de faire,** consider doing.

envoi /ãvwa/ *n.m.* dispatch; (*paquet*) consignment.

envol /ãvɔl/ *n.m.* flight; (*d'avion*) take-off.

envoler (s') /(s)ãvɔle/ *v. pr.* fly away; (*avion*) take off; (*papiers*) blow away.

envoûter /ãvute/ *v.t.* bewitch.

envoyé, ~e /ãvwaje/ *n.m., f.* envoy; (*de journal*) correspondent.

envoyer† /ãvwaje/ *v.t.* send; (*lancer*) throw. **~ promener qn.,** give s.o. the brush-off.

enzyme /ãzim/ *n.m.* enzyme.

épagneul, ~e /epaɲœl/ *n.m., f.* spaniel.

épais, ~se /epɛ, -s/ *a.* thick. **~seur** /-sœr/ *n.f.* thickness.

épaissir /epesir/ *v.t./i.* **s'~** *v. pr.* thicken.

épanch|er (s') /(s)epãʃe/ *v. pr.* pour out one's feelings; (*liquide*) pour out. **~ement** *n.m.* outpouring.

épanoui /epanwi/ *a.* (*joyeux*) beaming, radiant.

épan|ouir (s') /(s)epanwir/ *v. pr.* (*fleur*) open out; (*visage*) beam; (*personne*) blossom. **~ouissement** *n.m.* (*éclat*) blossoming, full bloom.

épargne /eparɲ/ *n.f.* saving; (*somme*) savings. **caisse d'~,** savings bank.

épargn|er /eparɲe/ *v.t./i.* save; (*ne pas tuer*) spare. **~er qch. à qn.,** spare s.o. sth. **~ant, ~ante** *n.m., f.* saver.

éparpiller /eparpije/ *v.t.* scatter. **s'~** *v. pr.* scatter; (*fig.*) dissipate one's efforts.

épars, ~e /epar, -s/ *a.* scattered.

épat|er /epate/ *v.t.* (*fam.*) amaze. **~ant, ~ante** *a.* (*fam.*) amazing.

épaule /epol/ *n.f.* shoulder.

épauler /epole/ *v.t.* (*arme*) raise; (*aider*) support.

épave /epav/ *n.f.* wreck.

épée /epe/ *n.f.* sword.

épeler /ɛple/ *v.t.* spell.

éperdu /epɛrdy/ *a.* wild, frantic. **~ment** *adv.* wildly, frantically.

éperon /eprõ/ *n.m.* spur. **~ner** /-ɔne/ *v.t.* spur (on).

épervier /epɛrvje/ *n.m.* sparrow-hawk.

éphémère /efemɛr/ *a.* ephemeral.

éphéméride /efemerid/ *n.f.* tear-off calendar.

épi /epi/ *n.m.* (*de blé*) ear. **~ de cheveux,** tuft of hair.

épic|e /epis/ *n.f.* spice. **~é** *a.* spicy. **~er** *v.t.* spice.

épic|ier, ~ière /episje, -jɛr/ *n.m., f.* grocer. **~erie** *n.f.* grocery shop; (*produits*) groceries.

épidémie /epidemi/ *n.f.* epidemic.

épiderme /epidɛrm/ *n.m.* skin.

épier /epje/ *v.t.* spy on.

épilep|sie /epilɛpsi/ n.f. epilepsy.
~tique a. & n.m./f. epileptic.
épiler /epile/ v.t. remove unwanted
hair from; (sourcils) pluck.
épilogue /epilɔg/ n.m. epilogue; (fig.)
outcome.
épinard /epinar/ n.m. (plante)
spinach. **~s**, (nourriture) spinach.
épin|e /epin/ n.f. thorn, prickle;
(d'animal) prickle, spine. **~e dor-
sale**, backbone. **~eux**, **~euse** a.
thorny.
épingl|e /epɛ̃gl/ n.f. pin. **~e de
nourrice**, **~e de sûreté**, safety-pin.
~er v.t. pin; (arrêter: fam.) nab.
épique /epik/ a. epic.
épisod|e /epizɔd/ n.m. episode. **à
~es**, serialized. **~ique** a. occasional.
épitaphe /epitaf/ n.f. epitaph.
épithète /epitɛt/ n.f. epithet.
épître /epitr/ n.f. epistle.
éploré /eplɔre/ a. tearful.
épluche-légumes /eplyʃlegym/ n.m.
invar. (potato) peeler.
épluch|er /eplyʃe/ v.t. peel; (exa-
miner: fig.) scrutinize. **~age** n.m.
peeling; (fig.) scrutiny. **~ure** n.f.
piece of peel ou peeling. **~ures** n.f.
pl. peelings.
épong|e /epɔ̃ʒ/ n.f. sponge. **~er** v.t.
(liquide) sponge up; (surface)
sponge (down); (front) mop; (dettes)
wipe out.
épopée /epɔpe/ n.f. epic.
époque /epɔk/ n.f. time, period. **à
l'~**, at the time. **d'~**, period.
épouse /epuz/ n.f. wife.
épouser[1] /epuze/ v.t. marry.
épouser[2] /epuze/ v.t. (forme, idée)
assume, embrace, adopt.
épousseter /epuste/ v.t. dust.
époustouflant, **~e** /epustuflɑ̃, -t/ a.
(fam.) staggering.
épouvantable /epuvɑ̃tabl/ a. appal-
ling.
épouvantail /epuvɑ̃taj/ n.m. scarecrow.
épouvant|e /epuvɑ̃t/ n.f. terror. **~er**
v.t. terrify.
époux /epu/ n.m. husband. **les ~**, the
married couple.
éprendre (s') /(s)eprɑ̃dr/ v. pr. **s'~
de**, fall in love with.
épreuve /eprœv/ n.f. test; (sport)
event; (malheur) ordeal; (photo.)
print; (d'imprimerie) proof. **mettre
à l'~**, put to the test.
éprouvé /epruve/ a. (well-)proven.

éprouv|er /epruve/ v.t. test; (ressen-
tir) experience; (affliger) distress.
~ant, **~ante** a. testing.
éprouvette /epruvɛt/ n.f. test-tube.
bébé-~, test-tube baby.
épuis|er /epɥize/ v.t. (fatiguer, user)
exhaust. **s'~er** v. pr. become
exhausted. **~é** a. exhausted; (livre)
out of print. **~ement** n.m. exhaustion.
épuisette /epɥizɛt/ n.f. fishing-net.
épur|er /epyre/ v.t. purify; (pol.)
purge. **~ation** n.f. purification;
(pol.) purge.
équat|eur /ekwatœr/ n.m. equator.
~orial (m. pl. **~oriaux**) a. equator-
ial.
équation /ekwasjɔ̃/ n.f. equation.
équerre /ekɛr/ n.f. (set) square. **d'~**,
square.
équilibr|e /ekilibr/ n.m. balance.
être ou **se tenir en ~e**, (personne)
balance; (objet) be balanced. **~é** a.
well-balanced. **~er** v.t. balance.
s'~er v. pr. (forces etc.) counterbalance each other.
équilibriste /ekilibrist/ n.m./f. tightrope walker.
équinoxe /ekinɔks/ n.m. equinox.
équipage /ekipaʒ/ n.m. crew.
équipe /ekip/ n.f. team. **~ de nuit/
jour**, night/day shift.
équipé /ekipe/ a. **bien/mal ~**, well/
poorly equipped.
équipée /ekipe/ n.f. escapade.
équipement /ekipmɑ̃/ n.m.
equipment. **~s**, (installations) amenities, facilities.
équiper /ekipe/ v.t. equip (de, with).
s'~ v. pr. equip o.s.
équip|ier, **~ière** /ekipje, -jɛr/ n.m.,
f. team member.
équitable /ekitabl/ a. fair. **~ment**
/-əmɑ̃/ adv. fairly.
équitation /ekitasjɔ̃/ n.f. (horse-)
riding.
équité /ekite/ n.f. equity.
équivalen|t, **~te** /ekivalɑ̃, -t/ a.
equivalent. **~ce** n.f. equivalence.
équivaloir /ekivalwar/ v.i. **~ à**, be
equivalent to.
équivoque /ekivɔk/ a. equivocal;
(louche) questionable. ● n.f. ambiguity.
érable /erabl/ n.m. maple.
érafl|er /erafle/ v.t. scratch. **~ure** n.f.
scratch.
éraillé /eraje/ a. (voix) raucous.
ère /ɛr/ n.f. era.

érection /erɛksjɔ̃/ *n.f.* erection.

éreinter /erɛ̃te/ *v.t.* exhaust; (*fig.*) criticize severely.

ergoter /ɛrgɔte/ *v.i.* quibble.

ériger /eriʒe/ *v.t.* erect. **(s')~ en**, set (o.s.) up as.

ermite /ɛrmit/ *n.m.* hermit.

éroder /erɔde/ *v.t.* erode.

érosion /erozjɔ̃/ *n.f.* erosion.

éroti|que /erɔtik/ *a.* erotic. **~sme** *n.m.* eroticism.

errer /ɛre/ *v.i.* wander.

erreur /ɛrœr/ *n.f.* mistake, error. **dans l'~**, mistaken. **par ~**, by mistake. **~ judiciaire**, miscarriage of justice.

erroné /ɛrɔne/ *a.* erroneous.

ersatz /ɛrzats/ *n.m.* ersatz.

érudit, ~e /erydi, -t/ *a.* scholarly. ● *n.m., f.* scholar. **~ion** /-sjɔ̃/ *n.f.* scholarship.

éruption /erypsjɔ̃/ *n.f.* eruption; (*méd.*) rash.

es /ɛ/ *voir* être.

escabeau (*pl.* **~x**) /ɛskabo/ *n.m.* step-ladder; (*tabouret*) stool.

escadre /ɛskadr/ *n.f.* (*naut.*) squadron.

escadrille /ɛskadrij/ *n.f.* (*aviat.*) flight, squadron.

escadron /ɛskadrɔ̃/ *n.m.* (*mil.*) squadron.

escalad|e /ɛskalad/ *n.f.* climbing; (*pol., comm.*) escalation. **~er** *v.t.* climb.

escalator /ɛskalatɔr/ *n.m.* (P.) escalator.

escale /ɛskal/ *n.f.* (*d'avion*) stopover; (*port*) port of call. **faire ~ à**, (*avion, passager*) stop over at; (*navire, passager*) put in at.

escalier /ɛskalje/ *n.m.* stairs. **~ mécanique** *ou* **roulant**, escalator.

escalope /ɛskalɔp/ *n.f.* escalope.

escamotable /ɛskamɔtabl/ *a.* (*techn.*) retractable.

escamoter /ɛskamɔte/ *v.t.* make vanish; (*éviter*) dodge.

escargot /ɛskargo/ *n.m.* snail.

escarmouche /ɛskarmuʃ/ *n.f.* skirmish.

escarpé /ɛskarpe/ *a.* steep.

escarpin /ɛskarpɛ̃/ *n.m.* pump.

escient /esjɑ̃/ *n.m.* **à bon ~**, with good reason.

esclaffer (s') /(s)ɛsklafe/ *v. pr.* guffaw, burst out laughing.

esclandre /ɛsklɑ̃dr/ *n.m.* scene.

esclav|e /ɛsklav/ *n.m./f.* slave. **~age** *n.m.* slavery.

escompte /ɛskɔ̃t/ *n.m.* discount.

escompter /ɛskɔ̃te/ *v.t.* expect; (*comm.*) discount.

escort|e /ɛskɔrt/ *n.f.* escort. **~er** *v.t.* escort. **~eur** *n.m.* escort (ship).

escouade /ɛskwad/ *n.f.* squad.

escrim|e /ɛskrim/ *n.f.* fencing. **~eur, ~euse** *n.m., f.* fencer.

escrimer (s') /(s)ɛskrime/ *v. pr.* struggle.

escroc /ɛskro/ *n.m.* swindler.

escroqu|er /ɛskrɔke/ *v.t.* swindle. **~er qch. à qn.**, swindle s.o. out of sth. **~erie** *n.f.* swindle.

espace /ɛspas/ *n.m.* space. **~s verts**, gardens, parks.

espacer /ɛspase/ *v.t.* space out. **s'~** *v. pr.* become less frequent.

espadrille /ɛspadrij/ *n.f.* rope sandals.

Espagne /ɛspaɲ/ *n.f.* Spain.

espagnol, ~e /ɛspaɲɔl/ *a.* Spanish. ● *n.m., f.* Spaniard. ● *n.m.* (*lang.*) Spanish.

espagnolette /ɛspaɲɔlɛt/ *n.f.* (window) catch.

espèce /ɛspɛs/ *n.f.* kind, sort; (*race*) species. **~s**, (*argent*) cash. **~ d'idiot/de brute/etc.!**, you idiot/brute/*etc.*!

espérance /esperɑ̃s/ *n.f.* hope.

espérer /ɛspere/ *v.t.* hope for. **~ faire/que**, hope to do/that. ● *v.i.* hope. **~ en**, have faith in.

espiègle /ɛspjɛgl/ *a.* mischievous.

espion, ~ne /ɛspjɔ̃, -jɔn/ *n.m., f.* spy.

espionn|er /ɛspjɔne/ *v.t./i.* spy (on). **~age** *n.m.* espionage, spying.

esplanade /ɛsplanad/ *n.f.* esplanade.

espoir /ɛspwar/ *n.m.* hope.

esprit /ɛspri/ *n.m.* spirit; (*intellect*) mind; (*humour*) wit. **perdre l'~**, lose one's mind. **reprendre ses ~s**, come to. **vouloir faire de l'~**, try to be witty.

Esquimau, ~de (*m. pl.* **~x**) /ɛskimo, -d/ *n.m., f.* Eskimo.

esquinter /ɛskɛ̃te/ *v.t.* (*fam.*) ruin.

esquiss|e /ɛskis/ *n.f.* sketch; (*fig.*) suggestion. **~er** *v.t.* sketch; (*geste etc.*) make an attempt at.

esquiv|e /ɛskiv/ *n.f.* (*sport*) dodge. **~er** *v.t.* dodge. **s'~er** *v. pr.* slip away.

essai /esɛ/ *n.m.* testing; (*épreuve*) test, trial; (*tentative*) try; (*article*) essay. **à l'~**, on trial.

essaim /esɛ̃/ n.m. swarm. **~er** /eseme/ v.i. swarm; (fig.) spread.

essayage /esɛjaʒ/ n.m. (de vêtement) fitting. **salon d'~,** fitting room.

essayer /eseje/ v.t./i. try; (vêtement) try (on); (voiture etc.) try (out). **~ de faire,** try to do.

essence [1] /esɑ̃s/ n.f. (carburant) petrol; (Amer.) gas.

essence [2] /esɑ̃s/ n.f. (nature, extrait) essence.

essentiel, ~le /esɑ̃sjɛl/ a. essential. ● n.m. **l'~,** the main thing; (quantité) the main part. **~lement** adv. essentially.

essieu (pl. **~x**) /esjø/ n.m. axle.

essor /esɔr/ n.m. expansion. **prendre son ~,** expand.

essor|er /esɔre/ v.t. (linge) spin-dry; (en tordant) wring. **~euse** n.f. spin-drier.

essouffler v.t. make breathless. **s'~** v. pr. get out of breath.

ess|uyer [1] /esɥije/ v.t. wipe. **s'~uyer** v. pr. dry ou wipe o.s. **~uie-glace** n.m. invar. windscreen wiper; (Amer.) windshield wiper. **~uie-mains** n.m. invar. hand-towel.

essuyer [2] /esɥije/ v.t. (subir) suffer.

est [1] /ɛ/ voir être.

est [2] /ɛst/ n.m. east. ● a. invar. east; (partie) eastern; (direction) easterly.

estampe /ɛstɑ̃p/ n.f. print.

estampille /ɛstɑ̃pij/ n.f. stamp.

esthète /ɛstɛt/ n.m./f. aesthete.

esthéticienne /ɛstetisjɛn/ n.f. beautician.

esthétique /ɛstetik/ a. aesthetic.

estimable /ɛstimabl/ a. worthy.

estimation /ɛstimasjɔ̃/ n.f. valuation.

estime /ɛstim/ n.f. esteem.

estim|er /ɛstime/ v.t. (objet) value; (calculer) estimate; (respecter) esteem; (considérer) consider. **~ation** n.f. valuation; (calcul) estimation.

estiv|al (m. pl. **~aux**) /ɛstival, -o/ a. summer. **~ant, ~ante** n.m., f. summer visitor, holiday-maker.

estomac /ɛstɔma/ n.m. stomach.

estomaqué /ɛstɔmake/ a. (fam.) stunned.

estomper (s') /(s)ɛstɔ̃pe/ v. pr. become blurred.

estrade /ɛstrad/ n.f. platform.

estragon /ɛstragɔ̃/ n.m. tarragon.

estrop|ier /ɛstrɔpje/ v.t. cripple; (fig.) mangle. **~ié, ~iée** n.m., f. cripple.

estuaire /ɛstɥɛr/ n.m. estuary.

estudiantin, ~e /ɛstydjɑ̃tɛ̃, -in/ a. student.

esturgeon /ɛstyrʒɔ̃/ n.m. sturgeon.

et /e/ conj. and. **et moi/lui/etc.?,** what about me/him/etc.?

étable /etabl/ n.f. cow-shed.

établi [1] /etabli/ a. established. **un fait bien ~,** a well-established fact.

établi [2] /etabli/ n.m. work-bench.

établir /etablir/ v.t. establish; (liste, facture) draw up; (personne, camp, record) set up. **s'~** v. pr. (personne) establish o.s. **s'~ épicier/etc.,** set (o.s.) up as a grocer/etc. **s'~ à son compte,** set up on one's own.

établissement /etablismɑ̃/ n.m. (bâtiment, institution) establishment.

étage /etaʒ/ n.m. floor, storey; (de fusée) stage. **à l'~,** upstairs. **au premier ~,** on the first floor.

étager (s') /(s)etaʒe/ v. pr. rise at different levels.

étagère /etaʒɛr/ n.f. shelf; (meuble) shelving unit.

étai /etɛ/ n.m. prop, buttress.

étain /etɛ̃/ n.m. pewter.

étais, était /etɛ/ voir être.

étal (pl. **~s**) /etal/ n.m. stall.

étalag|e /etalaʒ/ n.m. display; (vitrine) shop-window. **faire ~e de,** show off **~iste** n.m./f. window-dresser.

étaler /etale/ v.t. spread; (journal) spread (out); (vacances) stagger; (exposer) display. **s'~** v. pr. (s'étendre) stretch out; (tomber: fam.) fall flat. **s'~ sur,** (paiement) be spread over.

étalon /etalɔ̃/ n.m. (cheval) stallion; (modèle) standard.

étanche /etɑ̃ʃ/ a. watertight; (montre) waterproof.

étancher /etɑ̃ʃe/ v.t. (soif) quench; (sang) stem.

étang /etɑ̃/ n.m. pond.

étant /etɑ̃/ voir être.

étape /etap/ n.f. stage; (lieu d'arrêt) stopover.

état /eta/ n.m. state; (liste) statement; (métier) profession; (nation) State. **en bon/mauvais ~,** in good/bad condition. **en ~ de,** in a position to. **hors d'~ de,** not in a position to. **en ~ de marche,** in working order. **~ civil,** civil status. **~-major** (pl. **~s-majors**) n.m. (officiers) staff.

faire ~ de, (*citer*) mention. **être dans tous ses ~s,** be in a state. **~ des lieux,** inventory.

étatisé /etatize/ *a.* State-controlled.

États-Unis /etazyni/ *n.m. pl.* **~ (d'Amérique),** United States (of America).

étau (*pl.* **~x**) /eto/ *n.m.* vice.

étayer /eteje/ *v.t.* prop up.

été[1] /ete/ *voir* être.

été[2] /ete/ *n.m.* summer.

étein|dre† /etɛ̃dr/ *v.t.* put out, extinguish; (*lumière, radio*) turn off. **s'~dre** *v. pr.* (*feu*) go out; (*mourir*) die. **~t, ~te** /etɛ̃, -t/ *a.* (*feu*) out; (*volcan*) extinct.

étendard /etɑ̃dar/ *n.m.* standard.

étendre /etɑ̃dr/ *v.t.* spread; (*journal, nappe*) spread out; (*bras, jambes*) stretch (out); (*linge*) hang out; (*agrandir*) extend. **s'~** *v. pr.* (*s'allonger*) stretch out; (*se propager*) spread; (*plaine etc.*) stretch. **s'~ sur,** (*sujet*) dwell on.

étendu, ~e /etɑ̃dy/ *a.* extensive. ● *n.f.* area; (*d'eau*) stretch; (*importance*) extent.

éternel, ~le /etɛrnɛl/ *a.* eternal. **~lement** *adv.* eternally.

éterniser (s') /(s)etɛrnize/ *v. pr.* (*durer*) drag on.

éternité /etɛrnite/ *n.f.* eternity.

étern|uer /etɛrnɥe/ *v.i.* sneeze. **~uement** /-ymɑ̃/ *n.m.* sneeze.

êtes /ɛt/ *voir* être.

éthique /etik/ *a.* ethical. ● *n.f.* ethics.

ethn|ie /ɛtni/ *n.f.* ethnic group. **~ique** *a.* ethnic.

éthylisme /etilism/ *n.m.* alcoholism.

étinceler /etɛ̃sle/ *v.i.* sparkle.

étincelle /etɛ̃sɛl/ *n.f.* spark.

étioler (s') /(s)etjole/ *v. pr.* wilt.

étiqueter /etikte/ *v.t.* label.

étiquette /etikɛt/ *n.f.* label; (*protocole*) etiquette.

étirer /etire/ *v.t.*, **s'~** *v. pr.* stretch.

étoffe /etɔf/ *n.f.* fabric.

étoffer /etɔfe/ *v.t.*, **s'~** *v. pr.* fill out.

étoil|e /etwal/ *n.f.* star. **à la belle ~e,** in the open. **~e de mer,** starfish. **~é** *a.* starry.

étonn|er /etone/ *v.t.* amaze. **s'~er** *v. pr.* be amazed (**de,** at). **~ant, ~ante** *a.* amazing. **~ement** *n.m.* amazement.

étouffée /etufe/ *n.f.* **cuire à l'~,** braise.

étouff|er /etufe/ *v.t./i.* suffocate; (*sentiment, révolte*) stifle; (*feu*) smother; (*bruit*) muffle. **on ~e,** it is stifling. **s'~er** *v. pr.* suffocate; (*en mangeant*) choke. **~ant, ~ante** *a.* stifling.

étourd|i, ~ie /eturdi/ *a.* unthinking, scatter-brained. ● *n.m., f.* scatter-brain. **~erie** *n.f.* thoughtlessness; (*acte*) thoughtless act.

étourd|ir /eturdir/ *v.t.* stun; (*griser*) make dizzy. **~issant, ~issante** *a.* stunning. **~issement** *n.m.* (*syncope*) dizzy spell.

étourneau (*pl.* **~x**) /eturno/ *n.m.* starling.

étrange /etrɑ̃ʒ/ *a.* strange. **~ment** *adv.* strangely. **~té** *n.f.* strangeness.

étrang|er, ~ère /etrɑ̃ʒe, -ɛr/ *a.* strange, unfamiliar; (*d'un autre pays*) foreign. ● *n.m., f.* foreigner; (*inconnu*) stranger. **à l'~er,** abroad. **de l'~er,** from abroad.

étrangler /etrɑ̃gle/ *v.t.* strangle; (*col*) stifle. **s'~** *v. pr.* choke.

être† /ɛtr/ *v.i.* be. ● *v. aux.* (*avec aller, sortir, etc.*) have. **~ donné/fait par,** (*passif*) be given/done by. ● *n.m.* (*personne, créature*) being. **~ humain,** human being **~ médecin/ tailleur**/*etc.*, be a doctor/a tailor/*etc.* **~ à qn.,** be s.o.'s. **c'est à faire,** it needs to be *ou* should be done. **est-ce qu'il travaille?,** is he working?, does he work? **vous travaillez, n'est-ce pas?,** you are working, aren't you?, you work, don't you? **il est deux heures**/*etc.*, it is two o'clock/*etc.* **nous sommes le six mai,** it is the sixth of May.

étrein|dre /etrɛ̃dr/ *v.t.* grasp; (*ami*) embrace. **~te** /-ɛ̃t/ *n.f.* grasp; embrace.

étrenner /etrene/ *v.t.* use for the first time.

étrennes /etrɛn/ *n.f. pl.* (*cadeau*) New Year's gift.

étrier /etrije/ *n.m.* stirrup.

étriqué /etrike/ *a.* tight; (*fig.*) small-minded.

étroit, ~e /etrwa, -t/ *a.* narrow; (*vêtement*) tight; (*liens, surveillance*) close. **à l'~,** cramped. **~ement** /-tmɑ̃/ *adv.* closely. **~esse** /-tɛs/ *n.f.* narrowness.

étude /etyd/ *n.f.* study; (*bureau*) office. **(salle d')~,** (*scol.*) prep room; (*scol., Amer.*) study hall. **à l'~,**

under consideration. **faire des ~s (de)**, study.

étudiant, ~e /etydjã, -t/ *n.m.*, *f.* student.

étudier /etydje/ *v.t./i.* study.

étui /etɥi/ *n.m.* case.

étuve /etyv/ *n.f.* steamroom. **quelle ~!**, it's like a hothouse in here.

étuvée /etyve/ *n.f.* **cuire à l'~**, braise.

etymologie /etimɔlɔʒi/ *n.f.* etymology.

eu, eue /y/ *voir* avoir.

eucalyptus /økaliptys/ *n.m.* eucalyptus.

euphémisme /øfemism/ *n.m.* euphemism.

euphorie /øfɔri/ *n.f.* euphoria.

Europe /ørɔp/ *n.f.* Europe.

européen, ~ne /ørɔpeẽ, -ɛɛn/ *a.* & *n.m.*, *f.* European.

euthanasie /øtanazi/ *n.f.* euthanasia.

eux /ø/ *pron.* they; (*complément*) them. **~-mêmes** *pron.* themselves.

évac|uer /evakɥe/ *v.t.* evacuate. **~uation** *n.f.* evacuation.

évad|er (s') /(s)evade/ *v. pr.* escape. **~é, ~ée** *a.* escaped; *n.m.*, *f.* escaped prisoner.

éval|uer /evalɥe/ *v.t.* assess. **~uation** *n.f.* assessment.

évang|ile /evãʒil/ *n.m.* gospel. **l'Évangile**, the Gospel. **~élique** *a.* evangelical.

évan|ouir (s') /(s)evanwir/ *v. pr.* faint; (*disparaître*) vanish. **~ouissement** *n.m.* (*syncope*) fainting fit.

évapor|er /evapɔre/ *v.t.*, **s'~er** *v. pr.* evaporate. **~ation** *n.f.* evaporation.

évasi|f, ~ve /evazif, -v/ *a.* evasive.

évasion /evazjõ/ *n.f.* escape; (*par le rêve etc.*) escapism.

éveil /evɛj/ *n.m.* awakening. **donner l'~ à**, arouse the suspicions of. **en ~**, alert.

éveill|er /eveje/ *v.t.* awake(n); (*susciter*) arouse. **s'~er** *v. pr.* awake(n); be aroused. **~é** *a.* awake; (*intelligent*) alert.

événement /evɛnmã/ *n.m.* event.

éventail /evãtaj/ *n.m.* fan; (*gamme*) range.

éventaire /evãtɛr/ *n.m.* stall, stand.

éventé /evãte/ *a.* (*gâté*) stale.

éventrer /evãtre/ *v.t.* (*sac etc.*) rip open.

éventualité /evãtɥalite/ *n.f.* possibility. **dans cette ~**, in that event.

éventuel, ~le /evãtɥɛl/ *a.* possible. **~lement** *adv.* possibly.

évêque /evɛk/ *n.m.* bishop.

évertuer (s') /(s)evɛrtɥe/ *v. pr.* **s'~ à**, struggle hard to.

éviction /eviksjõ/ *n.f.* eviction.

évidemment /evidamã/ *adv.* obviously; (*bien sûr*) of course.

évidence /evidãs/ *n.f.* obviousness; (*fait*) obvious fact. **être en ~**, be conspicuous. **mettre en ~**, (*fait*) highlight.

évident, ~e /evidã, -t/ *a.* obvious, evident.

évider /evide/ *v.t.* hollow out.

évier /evje/ *n.m.* sink.

évincer /evɛ̃se/ *v.t.* oust.

éviter /evite/ *v.t.* avoid (**de faire**, doing). **~ à qn.**, (*dérangement etc.*) spare s.o.

évoca|teur ~trice /evɔkatœr, -tris/ *a.* evocative.

évocation /evɔkasjõ/ *n.f.* evocation.

évolué /evɔlɥe/ *a.* highly developed.

évol|uer /evɔlɥe/ *v.i.* develop; (*se déplacer*) move, manœuvre; (*Amer.*) maneuver. **~ution** *n.f.* development; (*d'une espèce*) evolution; (*déplacement*) movement.

évoquer /evɔke/ *v.t.* call to mind, evoke.

ex- /ɛks/ *préf.* ex-.

exacerber /ɛgzasɛrbe/ *v.t.* exacerbate.

exact, ~e /ɛgza(kt), -akt/ *a.* exact, accurate; (*correct*) correct; (*personne*) punctual. **~ement** /-ktəmã/ *adv.* exactly. **~itude** /-ktityd/ *n.f.* exactness; punctuality.

ex aequo /ɛgzeko/ *adv.* (*classer*) equal. **être ~**, be equally placed.

exagéré /ɛgzaʒere/ *a.* excessive.

exagér|er /ɛgzaʒere/ *v.t./i.* exaggerate; (*abuser*) go too far. **~ation** *n.f.* exaggeration.

exaltation /ɛgzaltasjõ/ *n.f.* elation.

exalté, ~e /ɛgzalte/ *n.m.*, *f.* fanatic.

exalter /ɛgzalte/ *v.t.* excite; (*glorifier*) exalt.

examen /ɛgzamɛ̃/ *n.m.* examination; (*scol.*) exam(ination).

examin|er /ɛgzamine/ *v.t.* examine. **~ateur, ~atrice** *n.m.*, *f.* examiner.

exaspér|er /ɛgzaspere/ *v.t.* exasperate. **~ation** *n.f.* exasperation.

exaucer /ɛgzose/ *v.t.* grant; (*personne*) grant the wish(es) of.

excavateur /ɛkskavatœr/ *n.m.* digger.

excavation /ɛkskavɑsjɔ̃/ *n.f.* excavation.

excédent /ɛksedã/ *n.m.* surplus. ~ **de bagages,** excess luggage. ~ **de la balance commerciale,** trade surplus. ~**aire** /-tɛr/ *a.* excess, surplus.

excéder[1] /ɛksede/ *v.t.* (*dépasser*) exceed.

excéder[2] /ɛksede/ *v.t.* (*agacer*) irritate.

excellen|t, ~**te** /ɛksɛlã, -t/ *a.* excellent. ~**ce** *n.f.* excellence.

exceller /ɛksele/ *v.i.* excel (**dans,** in).

excentri|que /ɛksãtrik/ *a. & n.m./f.* eccentric. ~**cité** *n.f.* eccentricity.

excepté /ɛksɛpte/ *a. & prép.* except.

excepter /ɛksɛpte/ *v.t.* except.

exception /ɛksɛpsjɔ̃/ *n.f.* exception. **à l'~ de,** except for. **d'~,** exceptional. **faire ~,** be an exception. ~**nel, ~nelle** /-jɔnɛl/ *a.* exceptional. ~**nellement** /-jɔnɛlmã/ *adv.* exceptionally.

excès /ɛksɛ/ *n.m.* excess. ~ **de vitesse,** speeding.

excessi|f, ~**ve** /ɛksesif, -v/ *a.* excessive. ~**vement** *adv.* excessively.

excitant /ɛksitã/ *n.m.* stimulant.

excit|er /ɛksite/ *v.t.* excite; (*encourager*) exhort (**à,** to); (*irriter: fam.*) annoy. ~**ation** *n.f.* excitement.

exclam|er (s') /(s)ɛksklame/ *v. pr.* exclaim. ~**ation** *n.f.* exclamation.

exclu|re† /ɛksklyr/ *v.t.* exclude; (*expulser*) expel; (*empêcher*) preclude. ~**sion** *n.f.* exclusion.

exclusi|f, ~**ve** /ɛksklyzif, -v/ *a.* exclusive. ~**vement** *adv.* exclusively. ~**vité** *n.f.* (*comm.*) exclusive rights. **en** ~**vité à,** (*film*) (showing) exclusively at.

excrément(s) /ɛkskremã/ *n.m.* (*pl.*). excrement.

excroissance /ɛkskrwasãs/ *n.f.* (out)growth, excrescence.

excursion /ɛkskyrsjɔ̃/ *n.f.* excursion; (*à pied*) hike.

excuse /ɛkskyz/ *n.f.* excuse. ~**s,** apology. **faire des** ~**s,** apologize.

excuser /ɛkskyze/ *v.t.* excuse. **s'~** *v. pr.* apologize (**de,** for). **je m'excuse,** (*fam.*) excuse me.

exécrable /ɛgzekrabl/ *a.* abominable.

exécrer /ɛgzekre/ *v.t.* loathe.

exécut|er /ɛgzekyte/ *v.t.* carry out, execute; (*mus.*) perform; (*tuer*) execute. ~**ion** /-sjɔ̃/ *n.f.* execution; (*mus.*) performance.

exécuti|f, ~**ve** /ɛgzekytif, -v/ *a. & n.m.* (*pol.*) executive.

exemplaire /ɛgzãplɛr/ *a.* exemplary. ● *n.m.* copy.

exemple /ɛgzãpl/ *n.m.* example. **par** ~, for example. **donner l'~,** set an example.

exempt, ~e /ɛgzã, -t/ *a.* ~ **de,** exempt from.

exempt|er /ɛgzãte/ *v.t.* exempt (**de,** from). ~**ion** /-psjɔ̃/ *n.f.* exemption.

exercer /ɛgzɛrse/ *v.t.* exercise; (*influence, contrôle*) exert; (*métier*) work at; (*former*) train, exercise. **s'~ (à),** practise.

exercice /ɛgzɛrsis/ *n.m.* exercise; (*mil.*) drill; (*de métier*) practice. **en** ~, in office; (*médecin*) in practice.

exhaler /ɛgzale/ *v.t.* emit.

exhausti|f, ~**ve** /ɛgzostif, -v/ *a.* exhaustive.

exhiber /ɛgzibe/ *v.t.* exhibit.

exhibitionniste /ɛgzibisjɔnist/ *n.m./f.* exhibitionist.

exhorter /ɛgzɔrte/ *v.t.* exhort (**à,** to).

exigence /ɛgziʒãs/ *n.f.* demand.

exig|er /ɛgziʒe/ *v.t.* demand. ~**eant, ~eante** *a.* demanding.

exigu, ~ë /ɛgzigy/ *a.* tiny.

exil /ɛgzil/ *n.m.* exile. ~**é, ~ée** *n.m., f.* exile. ~**er** *v.t.* exile. **s'~er** *v. pr.* go into exile.

existence /ɛgzistãs/ *n.f.* existence.

exist|er /ɛgziste/ *v.i.* exist. ~**ant, ~ante** *a.* existing.

exode /ɛgzɔd/ *n.m.* exodus.

exonér|er /ɛgzɔnere/ *v.t.* exempt (**de,** from). ~**ation** *n.f.* exemption.

exorbitant, ~e /ɛgzɔrbitã, -t/ *a.* exorbitant.

exorciser /ɛgzɔrsize/ *v.t.* exorcize.

exotique /ɛgzɔtik/ *a.* exotic.

expansi|f, ~**ve** /ɛkspãsif, -v/ *a.* expansive.

expansion /ɛkspãsjɔ̃/ *n.f.* expansion.

expatr|ier (s') /(s)ɛkspatrije/ *v. pr.* leave one's country. ~**ié, ~iée** *n.m., f.* expatriate.

expectative /ɛkspɛktativ/ *n.f.* **dans l'~,** still waiting.

expédient, ~e /ɛkspedjã, -t/ *a. & n.m.* expedient. **vivre d'~s,** live by one's wits. **user d'~s,** resort to expedients.

expéd|ier /ɛkspedje/ v.t. send, dispatch; (*tâche: péj.*) dispatch. **~iteur, ~itrice** n.m., f. sender. **~ition** n.f. dispatch; (*voyage*) expedition.

expéditi|f, ~ve /ɛkspeditif, -v/ a. quick.

expérience /ɛksperjɑ̃s/ n.f. experience; (*scientifique*) experiment.

expérimenté /ɛksperimɑ̃te/ a. experienced.

expériment|er /ɛksperimɑ̃te/ v.t. test, experiment with. **~al** (*m. pl.* **~aux**) a. experimental. **~ation** n.f. experimentation.

expert, ~e /ɛkspɛr, -t/ a. expert. ● n.m. expert; (*d'assurances*) valuer; (*Amer.*) appraiser. **~-comptable** (*pl.* **~s-comptables**) n.m. accountant.

expertis|e /ɛkspɛrtiz/ n.f. expert appraisal. **~er** v.t. appraise.

expier /ɛkspje/ v.t. atone for.

expir|er /ɛkspire/ v.i. breathe out; (*finir, mourir*) expire. **~ation** n.f. expiry.

explicati|f, ~ve /ɛksplikatif, -v/ a. explanatory.

explication /ɛksplikasjɔ̃/ n.f. explanation; (*fig.*) discussion; (*scol.*) commentary. **~ de texte,** (*scol.*) literary commentary.

explicite /ɛksplisit/ a. explicit.

expliquer /ɛksplike/ v.t. explain. **s'~** v. pr. explain o.s.; (*discuter*) discuss things; (*être compréhensible*) be understandable.

exploit /ɛksplwa/ n.m. exploit.

exploitant /ɛksplwatɑ̃/ n.m. **~ (agricole),** farmer.

exploit|er /ɛksplwate/ v.t. (*personne*) exploit; (*ferme*) run; (*champs*) work. **~ation** n.f. exploitation; running; working; (*affaire*) concern. **~eur, ~euse** n.m., f. exploiter.

explor|er /ɛksplɔre/ v.t. explore. **~ateur, ~atrice** n.m., f. explorer. **~ation** n.f. exploration.

explos|er /ɛksploze/ v.i. explode. **faire ~er,** explode; (*bâtiment*) blow up. **~ion** n.f. explosion.

explosi|f, ~ve /ɛksplozif, -v/ a. & n.m. explosive.

export|er /ɛkspɔrte/ v.t. export. **~ateur, ~atrice** n.m., f. exporter; a. exporting. **~ation** n.f. export.

exposant, ~e /ɛkspozɑ̃, -t/ n.m., f. exhibitor.

exposé /ɛkspoze/ n.m. talk (**sur,** on); (*d'une action*) account. **faire l'~ de**

la situation, give an account of the situation.

expos|er /ɛkspoze/ v.t. display, show; (*expliquer*) explain; (*soumettre, mettre en danger*) expose (**à,** to); (*vie*) endanger. **~é au nord**/ *etc.,* facing north/ *etc.* **s'~er à,** expose o.s. to.

exposition /ɛkspozisjɔ̃/ n.f. display; (*salon*) exhibition. **~ à,** exposure to.

exprès¹ /ɛksprɛ/ adv. specially; (*délibérément*) on purpose.

expr|ès², ~esse /ɛksprɛs/ a. express. **~essément** adv. expressly.

exprès³ /ɛkspres/ a. invar. & n.m. **lettre ~,** express letter. **(par) ~,** sent special delivery.

express /ɛkspres/ a. & n.m. invar. **(café) ~,** espresso. **(train) ~,** fast train.

expressi|f, ~ve /ɛkspresif, -v/ a. expressive.

expression /ɛkspresjɔ̃/ n.f. expression. **~ corporelle,** physical expression.

exprimer /ɛksprime/ v.t. express. **s'~** v. pr. express o.s.

expuls|er /ɛkspylse/ v.t. expel; (*locataire*) evict; (*joueur*) send off. **~ion** n.f. expulsion; eviction.

expurger /ɛkspyrʒe/ v.t. expurgate.

exquis, ~e /ɛkski, -z/ a. exquisite.

extase /ɛkstaz/ n.f. ecstasy.

extasier (s') /(s)ɛkstazje/ v. pr. **s'~ sur,** be ecstatic about.

extensible /ɛkstɑ̃sibl/ a. expandable, extendible. **tissu ~,** stretch fabric.

extensi|f, ~ve /ɛkstɑ̃sif, -v/ a. extensive.

extension /ɛkstɑ̃sjɔ̃/ n.f. extension; (*expansion*) expansion.

exténuer /ɛkstenɥe/ v.t. exhaust.

extérieur /ɛksterjœr/ a. outside; (*signe, gaieté*) outward; (*politique*) foreign. ● n.m. outside, exterior; (*de personne*) exterior. **à l'~ (de),** outside. **~ement** adv. outwardly.

extérioriser /ɛksterjorize/ v.t. show, externalize.

extermin|er /ɛkstɛrmine/ v.t. exterminate. **~ation** n.f. extermination.

externe /ɛkstɛrn/ a. external. ● n.m./f. (*scol.*) day pupil.

extincteur /ɛkstɛ̃ktœr/ n.m. fire extinguisher.

extinction /ɛkstɛ̃ksjɔ̃/ n.f. extinction. **~ de voix,** loss of voice.

extirper /ɛkstirpe/ v.t. eradicate.

extor|quer /ɛkstɔrke/ *v.t.* extort.
~sion *n.f.* extortion.

extra /ɛkstra/ *a. invar.* first-rate.
● *n.m. invar.* (*repas*) (special) treat.

extra- /ɛkstra/ *préf.* extra-.

extrad|er /ɛkstrade/ *v.t.* extradite.
~ition *n.f.* extradition.

extr|aire† /ɛkstrɛr/ *v.t.* extract.
~action *n.f.* extraction.

extrait /ɛkstrɛ/ *n.m.* extract.

extraordinaire /ɛkstraɔrdinɛr/ *a.* extraordinary.

extravagan|t, ~te /ɛkstravagɑ̃, -t/
a. extravagant. **~ce** *n.f.* extravagance.

extraverti, ~e /ɛkstravɛrti/ *n.m.*, *f.*
extrovert.

extrême /ɛkstrɛm/ *a. & n.m.*
extreme. **E~-Orient** *n.m.* Far East.
~ment *adv.* extremely.

extrémiste /ɛkstremist/ *n.m.*, *f.* extremist.

extrémité /ɛkstremite/ *n.f.* extremity, end; (*misère*) dire straits. **~s,**
(*excès*) extremes.

exubéran|t, ~te /ɛgzyberɑ̃, -t/ *a.*
exuberant. **~ce** *n.f.* exuberance.

exulter /ɛgzylte/ *v.i.* exult.

exutoire /ɛgzytwar/ *n.m.* outlet.

F

F *abrév.* (*franc, francs*) franc, francs.

fable /fabl/ *n.f.* fable.

fabrique /fabrik/ *n.f.* factory.

fabri|quer /fabrike/ *v.t.* make; (*industriellement*) manufacture; (*fig.*)
make up. **~cant, ~cante** *n.m.*, *f.*
manufacturer. **~cation** *n.f.* making;
manufacture.

fabul|er /fabyle/ *v.i.* fantasize.
~ation *n.f.* fantasizing.

fabuleu|x, ~se /fabylø, -z/ *a.* fabulous.

fac /fak/ *n.f.* (*fam.*) university.

façade /fasad/ *n.f.* front; (*fig.*) façade.

face /fas/ *n.f.* face; (*d'un objet*) side.
en ~ (de), d'en ~, opposite. **en ~
de,** (*fig.*) faced with. **~ à,** facing;
(*fig.*) faced with. **faire ~ à,** face.

facétie /fasesi/ *n.f.* joke.

facette /fasɛt/ *n.f.* facet.

fâch|er /faʃe/ *v.t.* anger. **se ~er** *v. pr.*
get angry; (*se brouiller*) fall out. **~é**
a. angry; (*désolé*) sorry.

fâcheu|x, ~se /faʃø, -z/ *a.* unfortunate.

facil|e /fasil/ *a.* easy; (*caractère*)
easygoing. **~ement** *adv.* easily.
~ité *n.f.* easiness; (*aisance*) ease;
(*aptitude*) ability; (*possibilité*) facility. **~ités de paiement,** easy
terms.

faciliter /fasilite/ *v.t.* facilitate.

façon /fasɔ̃/ *n.f.* way; (*de vêtement*)
cut. **~s,** (*chichis*) fuss. **de cette ~,**
in this way. **de ~ à,** so as to. **de
toute ~,** anyway.

façonner /fasɔne/ *v.t.* shape; (*faire*)
make.

facteur[1] /faktœr/ *n.m.* postman.

facteur[2] /faktœr/ *n.m.* (*élément*) factor.

factice /faktis/ *a.* artificial.

faction /faksjɔ̃/ *n.f.* faction. **de ~,**
(*mil.*) on guard.

factur|e /faktyr/ *n.f.* bill; (*comm.*)
invoice. **~er** *v.t.* invoice.

facultati|f, ~ve /fakyltatif, -v/ *a.*
optional.

faculté /fakylte/ *n.f.* faculty; (*possibilité*) power; (*univ.*) faculty.

fade /fad/ *a.* insipid.

fagot /fago/ *n.m.* bundle of firewood.

fagoter /fagɔte/ *v.t.* (*fam.*) rig out.

faibl|e /fɛbl/ *a.* weak; (*espoir,
quantité, écart*) slight; (*revenu, intensité*) low. ● *n.m.* weakling;
(*penchant, défaut*) weakness. **~e
d'esprit,** feeble-minded. **~esse** *n.f.*
weakness. **~ir** *v.i.* weaken.

faïence /fajɑ̃s/ *n.f.* earthenware.

faille /faj/ *n.f.* (*géog.*) fault; (*fig.*)
flaw.

faillir /fajir/ *v.i.* **j'ai failli acheter**/
etc., I almost bought/*etc.*

faillite /fajit/ *n.f.* bankruptcy; (*fig.*)
collapse.

faim /fɛ̃/ *n.f.* hunger. **avoir ~,** be
hungry.

fainéant, ~e /feneɑ̃, -t/ *a.* idle.
● *n.m.*, *f.* idler.

faire† /fɛr/ *v.t.* make; (*activité*) do;
(*rêve, chute, etc.*) have; (*dire*) say. **ça
fait 20 F,** that's 20 F. **ça fait 3 ans,**
it's been 3 years. ● *v.i.* do; (*paraître*) look. **se ~,** *v. pr.* (*petit etc.*)
make o.s.; (*amis, argent*) make;
(*illusions*) have; (*devenir*) become.
~ du rugby/du violon/*etc.,* play
rugby/the violin/*etc.* **~ construire**/
punir/*etc.,* have *ou* get built/punished/*etc.,* **~ pleurer/tomber/** *etc.,*
make cry/fall/*etc.* **se ~ tuer**/*etc.,* get

killed/*etc.* **se ~ couper les cheveux,** have one's hair cut. **il fait beau/ chaud**/*etc.*, it is fine/hot/*etc.* **~ l'idiot,** play the fool. **ne ~ que pleurer**/*etc.*, (*faire continuellement*) do nothing but cry/*etc.* **ça ne fait rien,** it doesn't matter. **se ~ à,** get used to. **s'en ~,** worry. **ça se fait,** that is done. **~-part** *n.m. invar.* announcement.

fais, fait [1] /fɛ/ *voir* faire.

faisable /fəzabl/ *a.* feasible.

faisan /fəzɑ̃/ *n.m.* pheasant.

faisandé /fəzɑ̃de/ *a.* high.

faisceau (*pl.* ~x) /fɛso/ *n.m.* (*rayon*) beam; (*fagot*) bundle.

fait [2], ~e /fɛ, fɛt/ *a.* done; (*fromage*) ripe. **~ pour,** made for. **tout ~,** ready made. **c'est bien ~ pour toi,** it serves you right.

fait [3] /fɛ/ *n.m.* fact; (*événement*) event. **au ~ (de),** informed (of). **de ce ~,** therefore. **du ~ de,** on account of. **~ divers,** (*trivial*) news item. **~ nouveau,** new development. **sur le ~,** in the act.

faîte /fɛt/ *n.m.* top; (*fig.*) peak.

faites /fɛt/ *voir* faire.

faitout /fɛtu/ *n.m.* stew-pot.

falaise /falɛz/ *n.f.* cliff.

falloir† /falwar/ *v.i.* **il faut qch.**/**qn.**, we, you, *etc.* need sth./so. **il lui faut du pain,** he needs bread. **il faut rester,** we, you, *etc.* have to *ou* must stay. **il faut que j'y aille,** I have to *ou* must go. **il faudrait que tu partes,** you should leave. **il aurait fallu le faire,** we, you, *etc.* should have done it. **il s'en faut de beaucoup que je sois,** I am far from being. **comme il faut,** properly; *a.* proper.

falot, ~e /falo, -ɔt/ *a.* grey.

falsifier /falsifje/ *v.t.* falsify.

famélique /famelik/ *a.* starving.

fameu|x, ~se /famø, -z/ *a.* famous; (*excellent:* *fam.*) first-rate. **~se- ment** *adv.* (*fam.*) extremely.

famil|ial (*m. pl.* ~iaux) /familjal, -jo/ *a.* family.

familiar|iser /familjarize/ *v.t.* familiarize (**avec,** with). **se ~iser** *v. pr.* familiarize o.s. **~isé** *a.* familiar. **~ité** *n.f.* familiarity.

famil|ier, ~ière /familje, -jɛr/ *a.* familiar; (*amical*) informal. ● *n.m.* regular visitor. **~ièrement** *adv.* informally.

famille /famij/ *n.f.* family. **en ~,** with one's family.

famine /famin/ *n.f.* famine.

fanati|que /fanatik/ *a.* fanatical. ● *n.m./f.* fanatic. **~sme** *n.m.* fanaticism.

faner (se) /(sə)fane/ *v. pr.* fade.

fanfare /fɑ̃far/ *n.f.* brass band; (*musique*) fanfare.

fanfaron, **~ne** /fɑ̃farɔ̃, -ɔn/ *a.* boastful. ● *n.m.,* *f.* boaster.

fanion /fanjɔ̃/ *n.m.* pennant.

fantaisie /fɑ̃tezi/ *n.f.* imagination, fantasy; (*caprice*) whim. **(de) ~,** (*boutons etc.*) fancy.

fantaisiste /fɑ̃tezist/ *a.* unorthodox.

fantasme /fɑ̃tasm/ *n.m.* fantasy.

fantasque /fɑ̃task/ *a.* whimsical.

fantastique /fɑ̃tastik/ *a.* fantastic.

fantoche /fɑ̃tɔʃ/ *a.* puppet.

fantôme /fɑ̃tom/ *n.m.* ghost. ● *a.* (*péj.*) bogus.

faon /fɑ̃/ *n.m.* fawn.

faramineu|x, **~se** /faraminø, -z/ *a.* astronomical.

farc|e [1] /fars/ *n.f.* (practical) joke; (*théâtre*) farce. **~eur,** **~euse** *n.m.,* *f.* joker.

farc|e [2] /fars/ *n.f.* (*hachis*) stuffing. **~ir** *v.t.* stuff.

fard /far/ *n.m.* make-up. **piquer un ~,** blush. **~er** /-de/ *v.t.,* **se ~er** *v. pr.* make up.

fardeau (*pl.* ~x) /fardo/ *n.m.* burden.

farfelu, **~e** /farfəly/ *a. & n.m.,* *f.* eccentric.

farin|e /farin/ *n.f.* flour. **~eux,** **~euse** *a.* floury. **les ~eux** *n.m. pl.* starchy food.

farouche /faruʃ/ *a.* shy; (*peu sociable*) unsociable; (*violent*) fierce. **~ment** *adv.* fiercely.

fascicule /fasikyl/ *n.m.* volume.

fascin|er /fasine/ *v.t.* fascinate. **~ation** *n.f.* fascination.

fascis|te /faʃist/ *a. & n.m./f.* fascist. **~me** *n.m.* fascism.

fasse /fas/ *voir* faire.

faste /fast/ *n.m.* splendour.

fast-food /fastfud/ *n.m.* fast-food place.

fastidieu|x, **~se** /fastidjø, -z/ *a.* tedious.

fat|al (*m. pl.* ~als) /fatal/ *a.* inevitable; (*mortel*) fatal. **~alement** *adv.* inevitably. **~alité** *n.f.* (*destin*) fate.

fataliste /fatalist/ *n.m./f.* fatalist.

fatidique /fatidik/ *a.* fateful.

fatigant, ~e /fatigã, -t/ *a.* tiring; (*ennuyeux*) tiresome.

fatigue /fatig/ *n.f.* fatigue, tiredness.

fatigu|er /fatige/ *v.t.* tire; (*yeux, moteur*) strain. ● *v.i.* (*moteur*) labour. **se ~er** *v. pr.* get tired, tire (**de,** of). **~é** *a.* tired.

fatras /fatra/ *n.m.* jumble.

faubourg /fobur/ *n.m.* suburb.

fauché /foʃe/ *a.* (*fam.*) broke.

faucher /foʃe/ *v.t.* (*herbe*) mow; (*voler*: *fam.*) pinch. **~ qn.,** (*véhicule, tir*) mow s.o. down.

faucille /fosij/ *n.f.* sickle.

faucon /fokɔ̃/ *n.m.* falcon, hawk.

faudra, faudrait /fodra, fodrɛ/ *voir* falloir.

faufiler (se) /(sə)fofile/ *v. pr.* edge one's way.

faune /fon/ *n.f.* wildlife, fauna.

faussaire /fosɛr/ *n.m.* forger.

fausse /fos/ *voir* faux².

faussement /fosmã/ *adv.* falsely, wrongly.

fausser /fose/ *v.t.* buckle; (*fig.*) distort. **~ compagnie à,** sneak away from.

fausseté /foste/ *n.f.* falseness.

faut /fo/ *voir* falloir.

faute /fot/ *n.f.* mistake; (*responsabilité*) fault; (*délit*) offence; (*péché*) sin. **en ~,** at fault. **~ de,** for want of. **~ de quoi,** failing which. **sans faute,** without fail. **~ de frappe,** typing error. **~ de goût,** bad taste. **~ professionelle,** professional misconduct.

fauteuil /fotœj/ *n.m.* armchair; (*de président*) chair; (*théâtre*) seat. **~ roulant,** wheelchair.

fauti|f, ~ve /fotif, -v/ *a.* guilty; (*faux*) faulty. ● *n.m., f.* guilty party.

fauve /fov/ *a.* (*couleur*) fawn. ● *n.m.* wild cat.

faux¹ /fo/ *n.f.* scythe.

faux², fausse /fo, fos/ *a.* false; (*falsifié*) fake, forged; (*numéro, calcul*) wrong; (*voix*) out of tune. **c'est ~!,** that is wrong! **~ témoignage,** perjury. **faire ~ bond à qn.,** stand s.o. up. ● *adv.* (*chanter*) out of tune. ● *n.m.* forgery. **fausse alerte,** false alarm. **fausse couche,** miscarriage. **~-filet** *n.m.* sirloin. **~ frais,** *n.m. pl.* incidental expenses. **~-monnayeur** *n.m.* forger.

faveur /favœr/ *n.f.* favour. **de ~,** (*régime*) preferential. **en ~ de,** in favour of.

favorable /favɔrabl/ *a.* favourable.

favori, ~te /favɔri, -t/ *a.* & *n.m., f.* favourite. **~tisme** *n.m.* favouritism.

favoriser /favɔrize/ *v.t.* favour.

fax /faks/ *n.m.* fax. **~er** *v.t.* fax.

fébrile /febril/ *a.* feverish.

fécond, ~e /fekɔ̃, -d/ *a.* fertile. **~er** /-de/ *v.t.* fertilize. **~ité** /-dite/ *n.f.* fertility.

féMér|al (*m. pl.* **~aux**) /federal, -o/ *a.* federal.

fédération /federasjɔ̃/ *n.f.* federation.

fée /fe/ *n.f.* fairy.

féer|ie /fe(e)ri/ *n.f.* magical spectacle. **~ique** *a.* magical.

feindre† /fɛ̃dr/ *v.t.* feign. **~ de,** pretend to.

feinte /fɛ̃t/ *n.f.* feint.

fêler /fele/ *v.t.,* **se ~** *v. pr.* crack.

félicit|er /felisite/ *v.t.* congratulate (**de,** on). **~ations** *n.f. pl.* congratulations (**pour,** on).

félin, ~e /felɛ̃, -in/ *a.* & *n.m.* feline.

fêlure /felyr/ *n.f.* crack.

femelle /fəmɛl/ *a.* & *n.f.* female.

fémin|in, ~ine /feminɛ̃, -in/ *a.* feminine; (*sexe*) female; (*mode, équipe*) women's. ● *n.m.* feminine. **~ité** *n.f.* femininity.

féministe /feminist/ *n.m./f.* feminist.

femme /fam/ *n.f.* woman; (*épouse*) wife. **~ au foyer,** housewife. **~ de chambre,** chambermaid. **~ de ménage,** cleaning lady.

fémur /femyr/ *n.m.* thigh-bone.

fendiller /fãdije/ *v.t.,* **se ~** *v. pr.* crack.

fendre /fãdr/ *v.t.* (*couper*) split; (*fissurer*) crack; (*foule*) push through. **se ~** *v. pr.* crack.

fenêtre /fənɛtr/ *n.f.* window.

fenouil /fənuj/ *n.m.* fennel.

fente /fãt/ *n.f.* (*ouverture*) slit, slot; (*fissure*) crack.

féod|al (*m. pl.* **~aux**) /feɔdal, -o/ *a.* feudal.

fer /fɛr/ *n.m.* iron. **~ (à repasser),** iron. **~ à cheval,** horseshoe. **~-blanc** (*pl.* **~s-blancs**) *n.m.* tinplate. **~ de lance,** spearhead. **~ forgé,** wrought iron.

fera, ferait /fəra, fərɛ/ *voir* faire.

férié /ferje/ *a.* **jour ~,** public holiday.

ferme¹ /fɛrm/ *a.* firm. ● *adv.* (*travailler*) hard. **~ment** /-əmã/ *adv.* firmly.

ferme² /fɛrm/ *n.f.* farm; (*maison*) farm(house).

fermé /fɛrme/ a. closed; (*gaz, radio, etc.*) off.

ferment /fɛrmɑ̃/ n.m. ferment.

ferment|er /fɛrmɑ̃te/ v.i. ferment. **~ation** n.f. fermentation.

fermer /fɛrme/ v.t./i. close, shut; (*cesser d'exploiter*) close ou shut down; (*gaz, robinet*) turn off. **se ~** v. pr. close, shut.

fermeté /fɛrməte/ n.f. firmness.

fermeture /fɛrmətyr/ n.f. closing; (*dispositif*) catch. **~ annuelle,** annual closure. **~ éclair,** (P.) zip (-fastener); (*Amer.*) zipper.

ferm|ier, ~ière /fɛrmje, -jɛr/ n.m. farmer. ● n.f. farmer's wife. ● a. farm.

fermoir /fɛrmwar/ n.m. clasp.

féroc|e /ferɔs/ a. ferocious. **~ité** n.f. ferocity.

ferraille /fɛrɑj/ n.f. scrap-iron.

ferré /fɛre/ a. (*canne*) steel-tipped.

ferrer /fɛre/ v.t. (*cheval*) shoe.

ferronnerie /fɛrɔnri/ n.f. ironwork.

ferroviaire /fɛrɔvjɛr/ a. rail(way).

ferry(-boat) /fɛri(bot)/ n.m. ferry.

fertil|e /fɛrtil/ a. fertile. **~e en,** (*fig.*) rich in. **~iser** v.t. fertilize. **~ité** n.f. fertility.

féru, ~e /fery/ a. **~ de,** passionate about.

ferv|ent, ~ente /fɛrvɑ̃, -t/ a. fervent. ● n.m., f. enthusiast (**de,** of). **~eur** n.f. fervour.

fesse /fɛs/ n.f. buttock.

fessée /fese/ n.f. spanking.

festin /fɛstɛ̃/ n.m. feast.

festival (*pl.* **~s**) /fɛstival/ n.m. festival.

festivités /fɛstivite/ n.f. pl. festivities.

festoyer /fɛstwaje/ v.i. feast.

fêtard /fɛtar/ n.m. merry-maker.

fête /fɛt/ n.f. holiday; (*religieuse*) feast; (*du nom*) name-day; (*réception*) party; (*en famille*) celebration; (*foire*) fair; (*folklorique*) festival. **~ des Mères,** Mother's Day. **~ foraine,** fun-fair. **faire la ~,** make merry. **les ~s (de fin d'année),** the Christmas season.

fêter /fɛte/ v.t. celebrate; (*personne*) give a celebration for.

fétiche /fetiʃ/ n.m. fetish; (*fig.*) mascot.

fétide /fetid/ a. fetid.

feu¹ (*pl.* **~x**) /fø/ n.m. fire; (*lumière*) light; (*de réchaud*) burner. **~x (rouges),** (traffic) lights. **à ~ doux/**

vif, on a low/high heat. **du ~,** (*pour cigarette*) a light. **au ~!,** fire! **~ d'artifice,** firework display. **~ de joie,** bonfire. **~ rouge/vert/orange,** red/green/amber ou yellow (*Amer.*). **~ de position,** sidelight. **mettre le ~ à,** set fire to. **prendre ~,** catch fire. **jouer avec le ~,** play with fire. **ne pas faire long ~,** not last.

feu² /fø/ a. invar. (*mort*) late.

feuillage /fœjaʒ/ n.m. foliage.

feuille /fœj/ n.f. leaf; (*de papier, bois, etc.*) sheet; (*formulaire*) form.

feuillet /fœjɛ/ n.m. leaf.

feuilleter /fœjte/ v.t. leaf through.

feuilleton /fœjtɔ̃/ n.m. (*à suivre*) serial; (*histoire complète*) series.

feuillu /fœjy/ a. leafy.

feutre /føtr/ n.m. felt; (*chapeau*) felt hat; (*crayon*) felt-tip (pen).

feutré /føtre/ a. (*bruit*) muffled.

fève /fɛv/ n.f. broad bean.

février /fevrije/ n.m. February.

fiable /fjabl/ a. reliable.

fiançailles /fjɑ̃saj/ n.f. pl. engagement.

fianc|er (se) /(sə)fjɑ̃se/ v. pr. become engaged (**avec,** to). **~é, ~ée** a. engaged; n.m. fiancé; n.f. fiancée.

fiasco /fjasko/ n.m. fiasco.

fibre /fibr/ n.f. fibre. **~ de verre,** fibreglass.

ficeler /fisle/ v.t. tie up.

ficelle /fisɛl/ n.f. string.

fiche /fiʃ/ n.f. (index) card; (*formulaire*) form, slip; (*électr.*) plug.

ficher¹ /fiʃe/ v.t. (*enfoncer*) drive (**dans,** into).

ficher² /fiʃe/ v.t. (*faire: fam.*) do; (*donner: fam.*) give; (*mettre: fam.*) put. **se ~ de,** (*fam.*) make fun of. **~ le camp,** (*fam.*) clear off. **il s'en fiche,** (*fam.*) he couldn't care less.

fichier /fiʃje/ n.m. file.

fichu /fiʃy/ a. (*mauvais: fam.*) rotten; (*raté: fam.*) done for. **mal ~,** (*fam.*) terrible.

ficti|f, ~ve /fiktif, -v/ a. fictitious.

fiction /fiksjɔ̃/ n.f. fiction.

fidèle /fidɛl/ a. faithful. ● n.m./f. (*client*) regular; (*relig.*) believer. **~s,** (*à l'église*) congregation. **~ment** adv. faithfully.

fidélité /fidelite/ n.f. fidelity.

fier¹, fière /fjɛr/ a. proud (**de,** of). **fièrement** adv. proudly. **~té** n.f. pride.

fier² (se) /(sə)fje/ v. pr. **se ~ à,** trust.

fièvre /fjɛvr/ n.f. fever.

fiévreu|x, ~se /fjevrø, -z/ a. fever-
ish.
figé /fiʒe/ a. fixed; set; (*manières*)
stiff.
figer /fiʒe/ v.t./i., **se ~** v. pr. congeal.
~ sur place, petrify.
fignoler /fiɲɔle/ v.t. refine (upon),
finish off meticulously.
figu|e /fig/ n.f. fig. **~ier** n.m. fig-tree.
figurant, ~e /figyrɑ̃, -t/ n.m., f.
(*cinéma*) extra.
figure /figyr/ n.f. face; (*forme, personnage*) figure; (*illustration*) picture.
figuré /figyre/ a. (*sens*) figurative.
au ~, figuratively.
figurer /figyre/ v.i. appear. ● v.t.
represent. **se ~** v. pr. imagine.
fil /fil/ n.m. thread; (*métallique, électrique*) wire; (*de couteau*) edge; (*à
coudre*) cotton. **au ~ de,** with the
passing of. **au ~ de l'eau,** with the
current. **~ de fer,** wire. **au bout du
~,** on the phone.
filament /filamɑ̃/ n.m. filament.
filature /filatyr/ n.f. (textile) mill;
(*surveillance*) shadowing.
file /fil/ n.f. line; (*voie: auto.*) lane. **~
(d'attente),** queue; (*Amer.*) line. **en
~ indienne,** in single file. **se mettre
en ~,** line up.
filer /file/ v.t. spin; (*suivre*) shadow.
~ qch. à qn., (*fam.*) slip s.o. sth.
● v.i. (*bas*) ladder, run; (*liquide*)
run; (*aller vite: fam.*) speed along,
fly by; (*partir: fam.*) dash off. **~
doux,** do as one's told. **~ à l'anglaise,** take French leave.
filet /filɛ/ n.m. net; (*d'eau*) trickle;
(*de viande*) fillet. **~ (à bagages),**
(luggage) rack. **~ à provisions,**
string bag (*for shopping*).
fil|ial, ~iale (*m. pl.* **~iaux**) /filjal,
-jo/ a. filial. ● n.f. subsidiary
(company).
filière /filjɛr/ n.f. (official) channels;
(*de trafiquants*) network. **passer
par ou suivre la ~,** (*employé*) work
one's way up.
filigrane /filigran/ n.m. watermark.
en ~, between the lines.
filin /filɛ̃/ n.m. rope.
fille /fij/ n.f. girl; (*opposé à fils*)
daughter. **~-mère** (*pl.* **~s-mères**)
n.f. (*péj.*) unmarried mother.
fillette /fijɛt/ n.f. little girl.
filleul /fijœl/ n.m. godson. **~e** n.f.
god-daughter.
film /film/ n.m. film. **~ d'épou-
vante/muet/parlant,** horror/si-

lent/talking film. **~ dramatique,**
drama. **~er** v.t. film.
filon /filɔ̃/ n.m. (*géol.*) seam; (*situation*) source of wealth.
filou /filu/ n.m. crook.
fils /fis/ n.m. son.
filtr|e /filtr/ n.m. filter. **~er** v.t./i.
filter; (*personne*) screen.
fin [1] /fɛ̃/ n.f. end. **à la ~,** finally. **en ~
de compte,** all things considered. **~
de semaine,** weekend. **mettre ~ à,**
put an end to. **prendre ~,** come to
an end.
fin [2], **fine** /fɛ̃, fin/ a. fine; (*tranche,
couche*) thin; (*taille*) slim; (*plat*)
exquisite; (*esprit, vue*) sharp.
● adv. (*couper*) finely. **~es herbes,**
herbs.
fin|al, ~ale (*m. pl.* **~aux** *ou* **~als**)
/final, -o/ a. final. ● n.f. (*sport*) final; (*gram.*) final syllable. ● n.m.
(*pl.* **~aux** *ou* **~als**) (*mus.*) finale.
~alement adv. finally; (*somme
toute*) after all.
finaliste /finalist/ n.m./f. finalist.
financ|e /finɑ̃s/ n.f. finance. **~er** v.t.
finance. **~ier, ~ière** a. financial;
n.m. financier.
finesse /finɛs/ n.f. fineness; (*de
taille*) slimness; (*acuité*) sharpness.
~s, (*de langue*) niceties.
fini /fini/ a. finished; (*espace*) finite.
● n.m. finish.
finir /finir/ v.t./i. finish, end; (*arrêter*) stop; (*manger*) finish (up). **en
~ avec,** have done with. **~ par
faire,** end up doing. **ça va mal ~,**
it will turn out badly.
finition /finisjɔ̃/ n.f. finish.
finlandais, ~e /fɛ̃lɑ̃dɛ, -z/ a.
Finnish. ● n.m., f. Finn.
finlande /fɛ̃lɑ̃d/ n.f. Finland.
finnois, ~e /finwa, -z/ a. Finnish.
● n.m. (*lang.*) Finnish.
fiole /fjɔl/ n.f. phial.
firme /firm/ n.f. firm.
fisc /fisk/ n.m. tax authorities. **~al**
(*m. pl.* **~aux**) a. tax, fiscal. **~alité**
n.f. tax system.
fission /fisjɔ̃/ n.f. fission.
fissur|e /fisyr/ n.f. crack. **~er** v.t., **se
~er** v. pr. crack.
fiston /fistɔ̃/ n.m. (*fam.*) son.
fixation /fiksasjɔ̃/ n.f. fixing; (*complexe*) fixation.
fixe /fiks/ a. fixed; (*stable*) steady. **à
heure ~,** at a set time. **menu à prix
~,** set menu.

fix|er /fikse/ v.t. fix. **~er (du regard)**, stare at. **se ~er** v. pr. (s'installer) settle down. **être ~é**, (personne) have made up one's mind.

flacon /flakɔ̃/ n.m. bottle.

flageolet /flaʒɔlɛ/ n.m. (haricot) (dwarf) kidney bean.

flagrant, ~e /flagrɑ̃, -t/ a. flagrant. **en ~ délit**, in the act.

flair /flɛr/ n.m. (sense of) smell; (fig.) intuition. **~er** /flere/ v.t. sniff at; (fig.) sense.

flamand, ~e /flamɑ̃, -d/ a. Flemish. ● n.m. (lang.) Flemish. ● n.m., f. Fleming.

flamant /flamɑ̃/ n.m. flamingo.

flambant /flɑ̃bɑ̃/ adv. **~ neuf**, brand-new.

flambé, ~e /flɑ̃be/ a. (culin.) flambé.

flambeau (pl. **~x**) /flɑ̃bo/ n.m. torch.

flambée /flɑ̃be/ n.f. blaze; (fig.) explosion.

flamber /flɑ̃be/ v.i. blaze; (prix) shoot up. ● v.t. (aiguille) sterilize; (volaille) singe.

flamboyer /flɑ̃bwaje/ v.i. blaze.

flamme /flam/ n.f. flame; (fig.) ardour. **en ~s**, ablaze.

flan /flɑ̃/ n.m. custard-pie.

flanc /flɑ̃/ n.m. side; (d'animal, d'armée) flank.

flancher /flɑ̃ʃe/ v.i. (fam.) give in.

Flandre(s) /flɑ̃dr/ n.f. (pl.) Flanders.

flanelle /flanɛl/ n.f. flannel.

flân|er /flɑne/ v.i. stroll. **~erie** n.f. stroll.

flanquer /flɑ̃ke/ v.t. flank; (jeter: fam.) chuck; (donner: fam.) give. **~ à la porte**, kick out.

flaque /flak/ n.f. (d'eau) puddle; (de sang) pool.

flash (pl. **~es**) /flaʃ/ n.m. (photo.) flash; (information) news flash.

flasque /flask/ a. flabby.

flatt|er /flate/ v.t. flatter. **se ~er de**, pride o.s. on. **~erie** n.f. flattery. **~eur, ~euse** a. flattering; n.m., f. flatterer.

fléau (pl. **~x**) /fleo/ n.m. (désastre) scourge; (personne) bane.

flèche /flɛʃ/ n.f. arrow; (de clocher) spire. **monter en ~**, spiral. **partir en ~**, shoot off.

flécher /fleʃe/ v.t. mark ou signpost (with arrows).

fléchette /fleʃɛt/ n.f. dart.

fléchir /fleʃir/ v.t. bend; (personne) move. ● v.i. (faiblir) weaken; (poutre) sag, bend.

flegmatique /flɛgmatik/ a. phlegmatic.

flemm|e /flɛm/ n.f. (fam.) laziness. **j'ai la ~e de faire**, I can't be bothered doing. **~ard, ~arde** a. (fam.) lazy; n.m., f. (fam.) lazybones.

flétrir /fletrir/ v.t., **se ~** v. pr. wither.

fleur /flœr/ n.f. flower. **à ~ de terre/d'eau**, just above the ground/water. **à ~s**, flowery. **~ de l'âge**, prime of life. **en ~s**, in flower.

fleur|ir /flœrir/ v.i. flower; (arbre) blossom; (fig.) flourish. ● v.t. adorn with flowers. **~i** a. flowery.

fleuriste /flœrist/ n.m./f. florist.

fleuve /flœv/ n.m. river.

flexible /flɛksibl/ a. flexible.

flexion /flɛksjɔ̃/ n.f. (anat.) flexing.

flic /flik/ n.m. (fam.) cop.

flipper /flipœr/ n.m. pinball (machine).

flirter /flœrte/ v.i. flirt.

flocon /flɔkɔ̃/ n.m. flake.

flopée /flɔpe/ n.f. (fam.) **une ~ de**, masses of.

floraison /flɔrɛzɔ̃/ n.f. flowering.

flore /flɔr/ n.f. flora.

florissant, ~e /flɔrisɑ̃, -t/ a. flourishing.

flot /flo/ n.m. flood, stream. **être à ~**, be afloat. **les ~s**, the waves.

flottant, ~e /flɔtɑ̃, -t/ a. (vêtement) loose; (indécis) indecisive.

flotte /flɔt/ n.f. fleet; (pluie: fam.) rain; (eau: fam.) water.

flottement /flɔtmɑ̃/ n.m. (incertitude) indecision.

flott|er /flɔte/ v.i. float; (drapeau) flutter; (nuage, parfum, pensées) drift; (pleuvoir: fam.) rain. **~eur** n.m. float.

flou /flu/ a. out of focus; (fig.) vague.

fluc|tuer /flyktɥe/ v.i. fluctuate. **~uation** n.f. fluctuation.

fluet, ~te /flyɛ, -t/ a. thin.

fluid|e /flɥid/ a. & n.m. fluid. **~ité** n.f. fluidity.

fluor /flyɔr/ n.m. (pour les dents) fluoride.

fluorescent, ~e /flyɔresɑ̃, -t/ a. fluorescent.

flût|e /flyt/ n.f. flute; (verre) champagne glass. **~iste** n.m./f. flautist; (Amer.) flutist.

fluv|ial (*m. pl.* **~iaux**) /flyvjal, -jo/ *a.* river.

flux /fly/ *n.m.* flow. **~ et reflux,** ebb and flow.

FM /ɛfɛm/ *abrév. f.* FM.

foc /fɔk/ *n.m.* jib.

fœtus /fetys/ *n.m.* foetus.

foi /fwa/ *n.f.* faith. **être de bonne/ mauvaise ~,** be acting in good/bad faith. **ma ~!,** well (indeed)! **digne de ~,** reliable.

foie /fwa/ *n.m.* liver. **~ gras,** foie gras.

foin /fwɛ̃/ *n.m.* hay. **faire tout un ~,** (*fam.*) make a fuss.

foire /fwar/ *n.f.* fair. **faire la ~,** (*fam.*) make merry.

fois /fwa/ *n.f.* time. **une ~,** once. **deux ~,** twice. **à la ~,** at the same time. **des ~,** (*parfois*) sometimes. **une ~ pour toutes,** once and for all.

foison /fwazɔ̃/ *n.f.* abundance. **à ~,** in abundance. **~ner** /-ɔne/ *v.i.* abound (**de,** in).

fol /fɔl/ *voir* fou.

folâtrer /fɔlatre/ *v.i.* frolic.

folichon, ~ne /fɔliʃɔ̃, -ɔn/ *a.* **pas ~,** (*fam.*) not much fun.

folie /fɔli/ *n.f.* madness; (*bêtise*) foolish thing, folly.

folklor|e /fɔlklɔr/ *n.m.* folklore. **~ique** *a.* folk; (*fam.*) picturesque.

folle /fɔl/ *voir* fou.

follement /fɔlmɑ̃/ *adv.* madly.

fomenter /fɔmɑ̃te/ *v.t.* foment.

fonc|er[1] /fɔ̃se/ *v.t./i.* darken. **~é** *a.* dark.

foncer[2] /fɔ̃se/ *v.i.* (*fam.*) dash along. **~ sur,** (*fam.*) charge at.

fonc|ier, ~ière /fɔ̃sje, -jɛr/ *a.* fundamental; (*comm.*) real estate. **~ièrement** *adv.* fundamentally.

fonction /fɔ̃ksjɔ̃/ *n.f.* function; (*emploi*) position; (*obligations*) duties. **en ~ de,** according to. **~ publique,** civil service. **voiture de ~,** company car.

fonctionnaire /fɔ̃ksjɔnɛr/ *n.m./f.* civil servant.

fonctionnel, ~le /fɔ̃ksjɔnɛl/ *a.* functional.

fonctionn|er /fɔ̃ksjɔne/ *v.i.* work. **faire ~er,** work. **~ement** *n.m.* working.

fond /fɔ̃/ *n.m.* bottom; (*de salle, magasin, etc.*) back; (*essentiel*) basis; (*contenu*) content; (*plan*) background. **à ~,** thoroughly. **au ~,** basically. **de ~,** (*bruit*) background;

(*sport*) long-distance. **de ~ en comble,** from top to bottom. **au *ou* dans le ~,** really.

fondament|al (*m. pl.* **~aux**) /fɔ̃damɑ̃tal, -o/ *a.* fundamental.

fondation /fɔ̃dasjɔ̃/ *n.f.* foundation.

fond|er /fɔ̃de/ *v.t.* found; (*baser*) base (**sur,** on). **(bien) ~é,** well-founded. **~é à,** justified in. **se ~er sur,** be guided by, place one's reliance on. **~ateur, ~atrice** *n.m., f.* founder.

fonderie /fɔ̃dri/ *n.f.* foundry.

fondre /fɔ̃dr/ *v.t./i.* melt; (*dans l'eau*) dissolve; (*mélanger*) merge. **se ~** *v. pr.* merge. **faire ~,** melt; dissolve. **~ en larmes,** burst into tears. **~ sur,** swoop on.

fondrière /fɔ̃drijɛr/ *n.f.* pot-hole.

fonds /fɔ̃/ *n.m.* fund. ● *n.m. pl.* (*capitaux*) funds. **~ de commerce,** business.

fondu /fɔ̃dy/ *a.* melted; (*métal*) molten.

font /fɔ̃/ *voir* faire.

fontaine /fɔ̃tɛn/ *n.f.* fountain; (*source*) spring.

fonte /fɔ̃t/ *n.f.* melting; (*fer*) cast iron. **~ des neiges,** thaw.

foot /fut/ *n.m.* (*fam.*) football.

football /futbol/ *n.m.* football. **~eur** *n.m.* footballer.

footing /futiŋ/ *n.m.* fast walking.

forage /fɔraʒ/ *n.m.* drilling.

forain /fɔrɛ̃/ *n.m.* fairground entertainer. **(marchand) ~,** stall-holder (*at a fair or market*).

forçat /fɔrsa/ *n.m.* convict.

force /fɔrs/ *n.f.* force; (*physique*) strength; (*hydraulique etc.*) power. **~s,** (*physiques*) strength. **à ~ de,** by sheer force of. **de ~, par la ~,** by force. **~ de dissuasion,** deterrent. **~ de frappe,** strike force, deterrent. **~ de l'âge,** prime of life. **~s de l'ordre,** police (force).

forcé /fɔrse/ *a.* forced; (*inévitable*) inevitable.

forcément /fɔrsemɑ̃/ *adv.* necessarily; (*évidemment*) obviously.

forcené, ~e /fɔrsəne/ *a.* frenzied. ● *n.m., f.* maniac.

forceps /fɔrsɛps/ *n.m.* forceps.

forcer /fɔrse/ *v.t.* force (**à faire,** to do); (*voix*) strain. ● *v.i.* (*exagérer*) overdo it. **se ~** *v. pr.* force o.s.

forcir /fɔrsir/ *v.i.* fill out.

forer /fɔre/ *v.t.* drill.

forest|ier, ~ière /fɔrɛstje, -jɛr/ *a.* forest.

foret /fɔrɛ/ *n.m.* drill.

forêt /fɔrɛ/ *n.f.* forest.

forfait /fɔrfɛ/ *n.m.* (*comm.*) inclusive price. **~aire** /-tɛr/ *a.* (*prix*) inclusive.

forge /fɔrʒ/ *n.f.* forge.

forger /fɔrʒe/ *v.t.* forge; (*inventer*) make up.

forgeron /fɔrʒərɔ̃/ *n.m.* blacksmith.

formaliser (se) /(sə)fɔrmalize/ *v. pr.* take offence (**de**, at).

formalité /fɔrmalite/ *n.f.* formality.

format /fɔrma/ *n.m.* format.

formater /fɔrmate/ *v.t.* (*comput.*) format.

formation /fɔrmasjɔ̃/ *n.f.* formation; (*de médecin etc.*) training; (*culture*) education. **~ permanente** *ou* **continue,** continuing education. **~ professionnelle,** professional training.

forme /fɔrm/ *n.f.* form; (*contour*) shape, form. **~s,** (*de femme*) figure. **en ~,** (*sport*) in good shape, on form. **en ~ de,** in the shape of. **en bonne et due ~,** in due form.

formel, ~le /fɔrmɛl/ *a.* formal; (*catégorique*) positive. **~lement** *adv.* positively.

former /fɔrme/ *v.t.* form; (*instruire*) train. **se ~** *v. pr.* form.

formidable /fɔrmidabl/ *a.* fantastic.

formulaire /fɔrmylɛr/ *n.m.* form.

formul|e /fɔrmyl/ *n.f.* formula; (*expression*) expression; (*feuille*) form. **~e de politesse,** polite phrase, letter ending. **~er** *v.t.* formulate.

fort¹, ~e /fɔr, -t/ *a.* strong; (*grand*) big; (*pluie*) heavy; (*bruit*) loud; (*pente*) steep; (*élève*) clever. ● *adv.* (*frapper*) hard; (*parler*) loud; (*très*) very; (*beaucoup*) very much. ● *n.m.* strong point. **au plus ~ de,** at the height of. **c'est une ~e tête,** she/he's headstrong.

fort² /fɔr/ *n.m.* (*mil.*) fort.

forteresse /fɔrtərɛs/ *n.f.* fortress.

fortifiant /fɔrtifjɑ̃/ *n.m.* tonic.

fortif|ier /fɔrtifje/ *v.t.* fortify. **~ication** *n.f.* fortification.

fortiori /fɔrsjɔri/ **a ~,** even more so.

fortuit, ~e /fɔrtɥi, -t/ *a.* fortuitous.

fortune /fɔrtyn/ *n.f.* fortune. **de ~,** (*improvisé*) makeshift. **faire ~,** make one's fortune.

fortuné /fɔrtyne/ *a.* wealthy.

fosse /fos/ *n.f.* pit; (*tombe*) grave. **~ d'aisances,** cesspool. **~ d'orchestre,** orchestral pit. **~ septique,** septic tank.

fossé /fose/ *n.m.* ditch; (*fig.*) gulf.

fossette /fosɛt/ *n.f.* dimple.

fossile /fosil/ *n.m.* fossil.

fossoyeur /foswajœr/ *n.m.* gravedigger.

fou *ou* **fol*, folle** /fu, fɔl/ *a.* mad; (*course, regard*) wild; (*énorme: fam.*) tremendous. **~ de,** crazy about. ● *n.m.* madman; (*bouffon*) jester. ● *n.f.* madwoman; (*fam.*) gay. **le ~ rire,** the giggles.

foudre /fudr/ *n.f.* lightning.

foudroy|er /fudrwaje/ *v.t.* strike by lightning; (*maladie etc.*) strike down; (*atterrer*) stagger. **~ant,** **~ante** *a.* staggering; (*mort, maladie*) violent.

fouet /fwɛ/ *n.m.* whip; (*culin.*) whisk.

fouetter /fwete/ *v.t.* whip; (*crème etc.*) whisk.

fougère /fuʒɛr/ *n.f.* fern.

fougu|e /fug/ *n.f.* ardour. **~eux, ~euse** *a.* ardent.

fouill|e /fuj/ *n.f.* search; (*archéol.*) excavation. **~er** *v.t./i.* search; (*creuser*) dig. **~er dans,** (*tiroir*) rummage through.

fouillis /fuji/ *n.m.* jumble.

fouine /fwin/ *n.f.* beech-marten.

fouiner /fwine/ *v.i.* nose about.

foulard /fular/ *n.m.* scarf.

foule /ful/ *n.f.* crowd. **une ~ de,** (*fig.*) a mass of.

foulée /fule/ *n.f.* stride. **il l'a fait dans la ~,** he did it while he was at it.

fouler /fule/ *v.t.* press; (*sol*) tread. **se ~ le poignet/le pied** sprain one's wrist/foot. **ne pas se ~,** (*fam.*) not strain o.s.

foulure /fulyr/ *n.f.* sprain.

four /fur/ *n.m.* oven; (*de potier*) kiln; (*théâtre*) flop. **~ à micro-ondes,** microwave oven. **~ crématoire,** crematorium.

fourbe /furb/ *a.* deceitful.

fourbu /furby/ *a.* exhausted.

fourche /furʃ/ *n.f.* fork; (*à foin*) pitchfork.

fourchette /furʃɛt/ *n.f.* fork; (*comm.*) margin.

fourchu /furʃy/ *a.* forked.

fourgon /furgɔ̃/ *n.m.* van; (*wagon*) wagon. **~ mortuaire,** hearse.

fourgonnette /furgɔnɛt/ *n.f.* (small) van.

fourmi /furmi/ *n.f.* ant. **avoir des ~s,** have pins and needles.

fourmiller /furmije/ *v.i.* swarm (**de,** with).

fournaise /furnɛz/ *n.f.* (*feu, endroit*) furnace.

fourneau (*pl.* ~x) /furno/ *n.m.* stove.

fournée /furne/ *n.f.* batch.

fourni /furni/ *a.* (*épais*) thick.

fourn|ir /furnir/ *v.t.* supply, provide; (*client*) supply; (*effort*) put in. ~**ir à qn.,** supply s.o. with. **se ~ir chez,** shop at. ~**isseur** *n.m.* supplier. ~**iture** *n.f.* supply.

fourrage /furaʒ/ *n.m.* fodder.

fourré [1] /fure/ *n.m.* thicket.

fourré [2] /fure/ *a.* (*vêtement*) fur-lined; (*gâteau etc.*) filled (*with jam, cream, etc.*).

fourreau (*pl.* ~x) /furo/ *n.m.* sheath.

fourr|er /fure/ *v.t.* (*mettre: fam.*) stick. ~**e-tout** *n.m. invar.* (*sac*) holdall.

fourreur /furœr/ *n.m.* furrier.

fourrière /furjɛr/ *n.f.* (*lieu*) pound.

fourrure /furyr/ *n.f.* fur.

fourvoyer (se) /(sə)furvwaje/ *v. pr.* go astray.

foutaise /futɛz/ *n.f.* (*argot*) rubbish.

foutre /futr/ *v.t.* (*argot*) = **ficher** [2].

foutu, ~**e** /futy/ *a.* (*argot*) = **fichu.**

foyer /fwaje/ *n.m.* home; (*âtre*) hearth; (*club*) club; (*d'étudiants*) hostel; (*théâtre*) foyer; (*photo.*) focus; (*centre*) centre.

fracas /fraka/ *n.m.* din; (*de train*) roar; (*d'objet qui tombe*) crash.

fracass|er /frakase/ *v.t.,* **se ~er** *v. pr.* smash. ~**ant,** ~**ante** *a.* (*bruyant, violent*) shattering.

fraction /fraksjɔ̃/ *n.f.* fraction. ~**ner** /-jɔne/ *v.t.,* **se ~er** *v. pr.* split (up).

fractur|e /fraktyr/ *n.f.* fracture. ~**er** *v.t.* (*os*) fracture; (*porte etc.*) break open.

fragil|e /fraʒil/ *a.* fragile. ~**ité** *n.f.* fragility.

fragment /fragmɑ̃/ *n.m.* bit, fragment. ~**aire** /-tɛr/ *a.* fragmentary. ~**er** /-te/ *v.t.* split, fragment.

fraîche /frɛʃ/ *voir* **frais** [1].

fraîchement /frɛʃmɑ̃/ *adv.* (*récemment*) freshly; (*avec froideur*) coolly.

fraîcheur /frɛʃœr/ *n.f.* coolness; (*nouveauté*) freshness.

fraîchir /freʃir/ *v.i.* freshen.

frais [1]**, fraîche** /frɛ, -ʃ/ *a.* fresh; (*temps, accueil*) cool; (*peinture*) wet. ● *adv.* (*récemment*) newly. ● *n.m.* **mettre au ~,** put in a cool

place. **prendre le ~,** take a breath of cool air. ~ **et dispos,** fresh. **il fait ~,** it is cool.

frais [2] /frɛ/ *n.m. pl.* expenses; (*droits*) fees. ~ **généraux,** (*comm.*) overheads, running expenses. ~ **de scolarité,** school fees.

frais|e /frɛz/ *n.f.* strawberry. ~**ier** *n.m.* strawberry plant.

frambois|e /frɑ̃bwaz/ *n.f.* raspberry. ~**ier** *n.m.* raspberry bush.

fran|c [1]**, ~che** /frɑ̃, -ʃ/ *a.* frank; (*regard*) open; (*net*) clear; (*cassure*) clean; (*libre*) free; (*véritable*) downright. ~**c-maçon** (*pl.* ~**cs-maçons**) *n.m.* Freemason. ~**c-maçonnerie** *n.f.* Freemasonry. ~**parler** *n.m. inv.* outspokenness.

franc [2] /frɑ̃/ *n.m.* franc.

français, ~**e** /frɑ̃sɛ, -z/ *a.* French. ● *n.m.,* f. Frenchman, Frenchwoman. ● *n.m.* (*lang.*) French.

France /frɑ̃s/ *n.f.* France.

franche /frɑ̃ʃ/ *voir* **franc** [1].

franchement /frɑ̃ʃmɑ̃/ *adv.* frankly; (*nettement*) clearly; (*tout à fait*) really.

franchir /frɑ̃ʃir/ *v.t.* (*obstacle*) get over; (*traverser*) cross; (*distance*) cover; (*limite*) exceed.

franchise /frɑ̃ʃiz/ *n.f.* frankness; (*douanière*) exemption (from duties).

franco /frɑ̃ko/ *adv.* postage paid.

franco- /frɑ̃ko/ *préf.* Franco-.

francophone /frɑ̃kɔfɔn/ *a.* French-speaking. ● *n.m./f.* French speaker.

frange /frɑ̃ʒ/ *n.f.* fringe.

franquette (à la bonne) /(alabɔn)frɑ̃kɛt/ *adv.* informally.

frappant, ~**e** /frapɑ̃, -t/ *a.* striking.

frappe /frap/ *n.f.* (*de courrier etc.*) typing; (*de dactylo*) touch.

frappé, ~**e** /frape/ *a.* chilled.

frapp|er /frape/ *v.t./i.* strike; (*battre*) hit, strike; (*monnaie*) mint; (*à la porte*) knock, bang. ~**é de panique,** panic-stricken.

frasque /frask/ *n.f.* escapade.

fratern|el, ~**elle** /fratɛrnɛl/ *a.* brotherly. ~**iser** *v.i.* fraternize. ~**ité** *n.f.* brotherhood.

fraude /frod/ *n.f.* fraud; (*à un examen*) cheating.

frauder /frode/ *v.t./i.* cheat.

frauduleu|x, ~**se** /frodylø, -z/ *a.* fraudulent.

frayer /freje/ *v.t.* open up. **se ~ un passage**, force one's way (**dans**, through).

frayeur /frɛjœr/ *n.f.* fright.

fredonner /frədɔne/ *v.t.* hum.

free-lance /frilɑ̃s/ *a. & n.m./f.* free-lance.

freezer /frizœr/ *n.m.* freezer.

frégate /fregat/ *n.f.* frigate.

frein /frɛ̃/ *n.m.* brake. **mettre un ~ à**, curb. **~ à main**, hand brake.

frein|er /frene/ *v.t.* slow down; (*modérer*, *enrayer*) curb. ● *v.i.* (*auto.*) brake. **~age** /frɛnaʒ/ *n.m.* braking.

frelaté /frəlate/ *a.* adulterated.

frêle /frɛl/ *a.* frail.

frelon /frəlɔ̃/ *n.m.* hornet.

freluquet /frəlyke/ *n.m.* (*fam.*) weed.

frémir /fremir/ *v.i.* shudder, shake; (*feuille*, *eau*) quiver.

frêne /frɛn/ *n.m.* ash.

fréné|sie /frenezi/ *n.f.* frenzy. **~tique** *a.* frenzied.

fréqu|ent, ~ente /frekɑ̃, -t/ *a.* frequent. **~emment** /-amɑ̃/ *adv.* frequently. **~ence** *n.f.* frequency.

fréquenté /frekɑ̃te/ *a.* crowded.

fréquent|er /frekɑ̃te/ *v.t.* frequent; (*école*) attend; (*personne*) see. **~ation** *n.f.* frequenting. **~ations** *n.f. pl.* acquaintances.

frère /frɛr/ *n.m.* brother.

fresque /frɛsk/ *n.f.* fresco.

fret /frɛt/ *n.m.* freight.

frétiller /fretije/ *v.i.* wriggle.

fretin /frətɛ̃/ *n.m.* **menu ~**, small fry.

friable /frijabl/ *a.* crumbly.

friand, ~e /frijɑ̃, -d/ *a.* **~ de**, fond of.

friandise /frijɑ̃diz/ *n.f.* sweet; (*Amer.*) candy; (*gâteau*) cake.

fric /frik/ *n.m.* (*fam.*) money.

fricassée /frikase/ *n.f.* casserole.

friche (en) /(ɑ̃)friʃ/ *adv.* fallow. **être en ~**, lie fallow.

friction /friksjɔ̃/ *n.f.* friction; (*massage*) rub-down. **~ner** /-jɔne/ *v.t.* rub (down).

frigidaire /friʒidɛr/ *n.m.* (P.) refrigerator.

frigid|e /friʒid/ *a.* frigid. **~ité** *n.f.* frigidity.

frigo /frigo/ *n.m.* (*fam.*) fridge.

frigorif|ier /frigɔrifje/ *v.t.* refrigerate. **~ique** *a.* (*vitrine etc.*) refrigerated.

frileu|x, ~se /frilø, -z/ *a.* sensitive to cold.

frime /frim/ *n.f.* (*fam.*) show off. **~r** *v.i.* (*fam.*) putting on a show.

frimousse /frimus/ *n.f.* (sweet) face.

fringale /frɛ̃gal/ *n.f.* (*fam.*) ravenous appetite.

fringant, ~e /frɛ̃gɑ̃, -t/ *a.* dashing.

fringues /frɛ̃g/ *n.f. pl.* (*fam.*) togs.

friper /fripe/ *v.t.*, **se ~** *v. pr.* crumple.

fripon, ~ne /fripɔ̃, -ɔn/ *n.m.*, *f.* rascal. ● *a.* rascally.

fripouille /fripuj/ *n.f.* rogue.

frire /frir/ *v.t./i.* fry. **faire ~**, fry.

frise /friz/ *n.f.* frieze.

fris|er /frize/ *v.t./i.* (*cheveux*) curl; (*personne*) curl the hair of. **~é** *a.* curly.

frisquet /friske/ *a.m.* (*fam.*) chilly.

frisson /frisɔ̃/ *n.m.* (*de froid*) shiver; (*de peur*) shudder. **~ner** /-ɔne/ *v.i.* shiver; shudder.

frit, ~e /fri, -t/ *a.* fried. ● *n.f.* chip. **avoir la ~e**, (*fam.*) feel good.

friteuse /fritøz/ *n.f.* (deep)fryer.

friture /frityr/ *n.f.* fried fish; (*huile*) (frying) oil *ou* fat.

frivol|e /frivɔl/ *a.* frivolous. **~ité** *n.f.* frivolity.

froid, ~e /frwa, -d/ *a. & n.m.* cold. **avoir/prendre ~**, be/catch cold. **il fait ~**, it is cold. **~ement** /-dmɑ̃/ *adv.* coldly; (*calculer*) coolly. **~eur** /-dœr/ *n.f.* coldness.

froisser /frwase/ *v.t.* crumple; (*fig.*) offend. **se ~** *v. pr.* crumple; (*fig.*) take offence. **se ~ un muscle**, strain a muscle.

frôler /frole/ *v.t.* brush against, skim; (*fig.*) come close to.

fromag|e /frɔmaʒ/ *n.m.* cheese. **~er, ~ère** *a.* cheese; *n.m.*, *f.* cheese maker; (*marchand*) cheesemonger.

froment /frɔmɑ̃/ *n.m.* wheat.

froncer /frɔ̃se/ *v.t.* gather. **~ les sourcils**, frown.

fronde /frɔ̃d/ *n.f.* sling; (*fig.*) revolt.

front /frɔ̃/ *n.m.* forehead; (*mil.*, *pol.*) front. **de ~**, at the same time; (*de face*) head-on; (*côte à côte*) abreast. **faire ~ à**, face up to. **~al** (*m. pl.* **~aux**) /-tal, -to/ *a.* frontal.

frontali|er, ère /frɔ̃talje, -ɛr/ *a.* border. **(travailleur) ~er**, commuter from across the border.

frontière /frɔ̃tjɛr/ *n.f.* border, frontier.

frott|er /frɔte/ *v.t./i.* rub; (*allumette*) strike. **~ement** *n.m.* rubbing.

frottis /frɔti/ *n.m.* **~ vaginal**, smear test.

frouss|e /frus/ *n.f.* (*fam.*) fear. **avoir la ~e**, (*fam.*) be scared. **~ard, ~arde** *n.m., f.* (*fam.*) coward.

fructifier /fryktifje/ *v.i.* **faire ~**, put to work.

fructueu|x, ~se /fryktɥø, -z/ *a.* fruitful.

frug|al (*m. pl.* **~aux**) /frygal, -o/ *a.* frugal. **~alité** *n.f.* frugality.

fruit /frɥi/ *n.m.* fruit. **des ~s,** (some) fruit. **~s de mer,** seafood. **~é** /-te/ *a.* fruity. **~ier, ~ière** /-tje, -tjɛr/ *a.* fruit; *n.m., f.* fruiterer.

fruste /fryst/ *a.* coarse.

frustr|er /frystre/ *v.t.* frustrate. **~ant, ~ante** *a.* frustrating. **~ation** *n.f.* frustration.

fuel /fjul/ *n.m.* fuel oil.

fugiti|f, ~ve /fyʒitif, -v/ *a.* (*passager*) fleeting. ● *n.m., f.* fugitive.

fugue /fyg/ *n.f.* (*mus.*) fugue. **faire une ~,** run away.

fuir† /fɥir/ *v.i.* flee, run away; (*eau, robinet, etc.*) leak. ● *v.t.* (*éviter*) shun.

fuite /fɥit/ *n.f.* flight; (*de liquide, d'une nouvelle*) leak. **en ~,** on the run. **mettre en ~,** put to flight. **prendre la ~,** take (to) flight.

fulgurant, ~e /fylgyrã, -t/ *a.* (*vitesse*) lightning.

fumée /fyme/ *n.f.* smoke; (*vapeur*) steam.

fum|er /fyme/ *v.t./i.* smoke. **~e-cigarette** *n.m. invar.* cigarette-holder. **~é** *a.* (*poisson, verre*) smoked. **~eur, ~euse** *n.m., f.* smoker.

fumet /fymɛ/ *n.m.* aroma.

fumeu|x, ~se /fymø, -z/ *a.* (*confus*) hazy.

fumier /fymje/ *n.m.* manure.

fumiste /fymist/ *n.m./f.* (*fam.*) shirker.

funambule /fynãbyl/ *n.m./f.* tightrope walker.

funèbre /fynɛbr/ *a.* funeral; (*fig.*) gloomy.

funérailles /fyneraj/ *n.f. pl.* funeral.

funéraire /fynerɛr/ *a.* funeral.

funeste /fynɛst/ *a.* fatal.

funiculaire /fynikylɛr/ *n.m.* funicular.

fur /fyr/ *n.m.* **au ~ et à mesure,** as one goes along, progressively. **au ~ et à mesure que,** as.

furet /fyrɛ/ *n.m.* ferret.

fureter /fyrte/ *v.i.* nose (about).

fureur /fyrœr/ *n.f.* fury; (*passion*) passion. **avec ~,** furiously; passionately. **mettre en ~,** infuriate. **faire ~,** be all the rage.

furibond, ~e /furibõ, -d/ *a.* furious.

furie /fyri/ *n.f.* fury; (*femme*) shrew.

furieu|x, ~se /fyrjø, -z/ *a.* furious.

furoncle /fyrõkl/ *n.m.* boil.

furti|f, ~ve /fyrtif, -v/ *a.* furtive.

fusain /fyzɛ̃/ *n.m.* (*crayon*) charcoal; (*arbre*) spindle-tree.

fuseau (*pl.* **~x**) /fyzo/ *n.m.* ski trousers; (*pour filer*) spindle. **~ horaire,** time zone.

fusée /fyze/ *n.f.* rocket.

fuselage /fyzlaʒ/ *n.m.* fuselage.

fuselé /fyzle/ *a.* slender.

fusible /fyzibl/ *n.m.* fuse.

fuser /fyze/ *v.i.* issue forth.

fusil /fyzi/ *n.m.* rifle, gun; (*de chasse*) shotgun. **~ mitrailleur,** machine-gun.

fusill|er /fyzije/ *v.t.* shoot. **~ade** *n.f.* shooting.

fusion /fyzjõ/ *n.f.* fusion; (*comm.*) merger. **~ner** /-jɔne/ *v.t./i.* merge.

fut /fy/ *voir* être.

fût /fy/ *n.m.* (*tonneau*) barrel; (*d'arbre*) trunk.

futé /fyte/ *a.* cunning.

futil|e /fytil/ *a.* futile. **~ité** *n.f.* futility.

futur /fytyr/ *a. & n.m.* future. **~e femme/maman,** wife-/mother-to-be.

fuyant, ~e /fɥijã, -t/ *a.* (*front, ligne*) receding; (*personne*) evasive.

fuyard, ~e /fɥijar, -d/ *n.m., f.* runaway.

G

gabardine /gabardin/ *n.f.* gabardine; raincoat.

gabarit /gabari/ *n.m.* dimension; (*patron*) template; (*fig.*) calibre.

gâcher /gaʃe/ *v.t.* (*gâter*) spoil; (*gaspiller*) waste.

gâchette /gaʃɛt/ *n.f.* trigger.

gâchis /gaʃi/ *n.m.* waste.

gadoue /gadu/ *n.f.* sludge.

gaff|e /gaf/ *n.f.* blunder. **faire ~e,** (*fam.*) be careful (**à,** of). **~er** *v.i.* blunder.

gag /gag/ *n.m.* gag.

gage /gaʒ/ *n.m.* pledge; (*de jeu*) forfeit. **~s,** (*salaire*) wages. **en ~**

de, as a token of. **mettre en ~,** pawn.

gageure /gaʒyr/ *n.f.* wager (against all the odds).

gagn|er /gaɲe/ *v.t.* (*match, prix, etc.*) win; (*argent, pain*) earn; (*temps, terrain*) gain; (*atteindre*) reach; (*convaincre*) win over. ● *v.i.* win; (*fig.*) gain. **~er sa vie,** earn one's living. **~ant, ~ante,** *a.* winning; *n.m., f.* winner. **~e-pain** *n.m. invar.* job.

gai /ge/ *a.* cheerful; (*ivre*) merry. **~ement** *adv.* cheerfully. **~eté** *n.f.* cheerfulness. **~etés** *n.f. pl.* delights.

gaillard, ~e /gajar, -d/ *a.* hale and hearty; (*grivois*) coarse. ● *n.m.* hale and hearty fellow; (*type: fam.*) fellow.

gain /gɛ̃/ *n.m.* (*salaire*) earnings; (*avantage*) gain; (*économie*) saving. **~s,** (*comm.*) profits; (*au jeu*) winnings.

gaine /gɛn/ *n.f.* (*corset*) girdle; (*étui*) sheath.

gala /gala/ *n.m.* gala.

galant, ~e /galɑ̃, -t/ *a.* courteous; (*scène, humeur*) romantic.

galaxie /galaksi/ *n.f.* galaxy.

galb|e /galb/ *n.m.* curve. **~é** *a.* shapely.

gale /gal/ *n.f.* (*de chat etc.*) mange.

galéjade /galeʒad/ *n.f.* (*fam.*) tall tale.

galère /galɛr/ *n.f.* (*navire*) galley. **c'est la ~!,** (*fam.*) what an ordeal!

galérer /galere/ *v.i.* (*fam.*) have a hard time.

galerie /galri/ *n.f.* gallery; (*théâtre*) circle; (*de voiture*) roof- rack.

galet /galɛ/ *n.m.* pebble.

galette /galɛt/ *n.f.* flat cake.

galeu|x, ~se /galø, -z/ *a.* (*animal*) mangy.

galipette /galipɛt/ *n.f.* somersault.

Galles /gal/ *n.f. pl.* **le pays de ~,** Wales.

gallois, ~e /galwa, -z/ *a.* Welsh. ● *n.m., f.* Welshman, Welshwoman. ● *n.m.* (*lang.*) Welsh.

galon /galɔ̃/ *n.m.* braid; (*mil.*) stripe. **prendre du ~,** be promoted.

galop /galo/ *n.m.* gallop. **aller au ~,** gallop. **~ d'essai,** trial run. **~er** /-ɔpe/ *v.i.* (*cheval*) gallop; (*personne*) run.

galopade /galɔpad/ *n.f.* wild rush.

galopin /galɔpɛ̃/ *n.m.* (*fam.*) rascal.

galvaudé /galvode/ *a.* worthless.

gambad|e /gɑ̃bad/ *n.f.* leap. **~er** *v.i.* leap about.

gamelle /gamɛl/ *n.f.* (*de soldat*) mess bowl *ou* tin; (*d'ouvrier*) food-box.

gamin, ~e /gamɛ̃, -in/ *a.* playful. ● *n.m., f.* (*fam.*) kid.

gamme /gam/ *n.f.* (*mus.*) scale; (*série*) range. **haut de ~,** up-market, top of the range. **bas de ~,** down-market, bottom of the range.

gang /gɑ̃g/ *n.m.* gang.

ganglion /gɑ̃glijɔ̃/ *n.m.* swelling.

gangrène /gɑ̃grɛn/ *n.f.* gangrene.

gangster /gɑ̃gstɛr/ *n.m.* gangster; (*escroc*) crook.

gant /gɑ̃/ *n.m.* glove. **~ de toilette,** face-flannel, face-cloth. **~é** /gɑ̃te/ *a.* (*personne*) wearing gloves.

garag|e /garaʒ/ *n.m.* garage. **~iste** *n.m.* garage owner; (*employé*) garage mechanic.

garant, ~e /garɑ̃, -t/ *n.m., f.* guarantor. ● *n.m.* guarantee. **se porter ~ de,** guarantee, vouch for.

garant|ie /garɑ̃ti/ *n.f.* guarantee; (*protection*) safeguard. **~ies,** (*de police d'assurance*) cover. **~ir** *v.t.* guarantee; (*protéger*) protect (**de, from**).

garce /gars/ *n.f.* (*fam.*) bitch.

garçon /garsɔ̃/ *n.m.* boy; (*célibataire*) bachelor. **~ (de café),** waiter. **~ d'honneur,** best man.

garçonnière /garsɔnjɛr/ *n.f.* bachelor flat.

garde ¹ /gard/ *n.f.* guard; (*d'enfants, de bagages*) care; (*service*) guard (duty); (*infirmière*) nurse. **de ~,** on duty. **~ à vue,** (*police*) custody. **mettre en ~,** warn. **prendre ~,** be careful (**à, of**). **(droit de) ~,** custody (**de, of**).

garde ² /gard/ *n.m.* (*personne*) guard; (*de propriété, parc*) warden. **~ champêtre,** village policeman. **~ du corps,** bodyguard.

gard|er /garde/ *v.t.* (*conserver, maintenir*) keep; (*vêtement*) keep on; (*surveiller*) look after; (*défendre*) guard. **se ~er** *v. pr.* (*denrée*) keep. **~er le lit,** stay in bed. **se ~er de faire,** be careful not to do. **~e-à-vous** *int.* (*mil.*) attention. **~e-boue** *n.m. invar.* mudguard. **~e-chasse** (*pl.* **~es-chasses**) *n.m.* gamekeeper. **~e-fou** *n.m. invar.* railing. **~e-manger** *n.m. invar.* (food) safe; (*placard*) larder. **~e-robe** *n.f.* wardrobe.

garderie /gardəri/ *n.f.* crèche.

gardien, ~**ne** /gardjɛ̃, -jɛn/ n.m., f. (*de prison, réserve*) warden; (*d'immeuble*) caretaker; (*de musée*) attendant; (*garde*) guard. ~ **de but,** goalkeeper. ~ **de la paix,** policeman. ~ **de nuit,** night watchman. ~**ne d'enfants,** childminder.

gare[1] /gar/ n.f. (*rail.*) station. ~ **routière,** coach station; (*Amer.*) bus station.

gare[2] /gar/ int. ~ **(à toi),** watch out!

garer /gare/ v.t., **se** ~ v. pr. park.

gargariser (se) /(sə)gargarize/ v. pr. gargle.

gargarisme /gargarism/ n.m. gargle.

gargouille /garguj/ n.f. (water)-spout; (*sculptée*) gargoyle.

gargouiller /garguje/ v.i. gurgle.

garnement /garnəmɑ̃/ n.m. rascal.

garn|ir /garnir/ v.t. fill; (*décorer*) decorate; (*couvrir*) cover; (*doubler*) line; (*culin.*) garnish. ~**i** a. (*plat*) served with vegetables. **bien** ~**i,** (*rempli*) well-filled.

garnison /garnizɔ̃/ n.f. garrison.

garniture /garnityr/ n.f. (*légumes*) vegetables; (*ornement*) trimming; (*de voiture*) trim.

garrot /garo/ n.m. (*méd.*) tourniquet.

gars /ɡɑ/ n.m. (*fam.*) fellow.

gas-oil /gazɔjl/ n.m. diesel oil.

gaspill|er /gaspije/ v.t. waste. ~**age** n.m. waste.

gastrique /gastrik/ a. gastric.

gastronom|e /gastrɔnɔm/ n.m./f. gourmet. ~**ie** n.f. gastronomy.

gâteau (*pl.* ~**x**) /gato/ n.m. cake. ~ **sec,** biscuit; (*Amer.*) cookie. **un papa** ~, a doting dad.

gâter /gate/ v.t. spoil. **se** ~ v. pr. (*dent, viande*) go bad; (*temps*) get worse.

gâterie /gatri/ n.f. little treat.

gâteu|x, ~**se** /gatø, -z/ a. senile.

gauch|e[1] /goʃ/ a. left. **à** ~**e,** on the left; (*direction*) (to the) left. **la** ~**e,** the left (side); (*pol.*) the left (wing). ~**er,** ~**ère** a. & n.m., f. left-handed (person). ~**iste** a. & n.m./f. (*pol.*) leftist.

gauche[2] /goʃ/ a. (*maladroit*) awkward. ~**rie** n.f. awkwardness.

gaufre /gofr/ n.f. waffle.

gaufrette /gofrɛt/ n.f. wafer.

gaulois, ~**e** /golwa, -z/ a. Gallic; (*fig.*) bawdy. ● n.m., f. Gaul.

gausser (se) /(sə)gose/ v. pr. **se** ~ **de,** deride, scoff at.

gaver /gave/ v.t. force-feed; (*fig.*) cram. **se** ~ **de,** gorge o.s. with.

gaz /gaz/ n.m. invar. gas. ~ **lacrymogène,** tear-gas.

gaze /gaz/ n.f. gauze.

gazelle /gazɛl/ n.f. gazelle.

gaz|er /gaze/ v.i. (*fam.*) **ça** ~**e,** it's going all right.

gazette /gazɛt/ n.f. newspaper.

gazeu|x, ~**se** /gazø, -z/ a. (*boisson*) fizzy.

gazoduc /gazɔdyk/ n.m. gas pipeline.

gazomètre /gazɔmɛtr/ n.m. gasometer.

gazon /gazɔ̃/ n.m. lawn, grass.

gazouiller /gazuje/ v.i. (*oiseau*) chirp; (*bébé*) babble.

geai /ʒɛ/ n.m. jay.

géant, ~**e** /ʒeɑ̃, -t/ a. & n.m., f. giant.

geindre /ʒɛ̃dr/ v.i. groan.

gel /ʒɛl/ n.m. frost; (*pâte*) gel; (*comm.*) freezing.

gélatine /ʒelatin/ n.f. gelatine.

gel|er /ʒəle/ v.t./i. freeze. **on gèle,** it's freezing. ~**é** a. frozen; (*membre abîmé*) frost-bitten. ~**ée** n.f. frost; (*culin.*) jelly. ~**ée blanche,** hoarfrost.

gélule /ʒelyl/ n.f. (*méd.*) capsule.

Gémeaux /ʒemo/ n.m. pl. Gemini.

gém|ir /ʒemir/ v.i. groan. ~**issement** n.m. groan(ing).

gênant, ~**e** /ʒɛnɑ̃, -t/ a. embarrassing; (*irritant*) annoying.

gencive /ʒɑ̃siv/ n.f. gum.

gendarme /ʒɑ̃darm/ n.m. policeman, gendarme. ~**rie** /-əri/ n.f. police force; (*local*) police station.

gendre /ʒɑ̃dr/ n.m. son-in-law.

gène /ʒɛn/ n.m. gene.

gêne /ʒɛn/ n.f. discomfort; (*confusion*) embarrassment; (*dérangement*) trouble. **dans la** ~, in financial straits.

généalogie /ʒenealɔʒi/ n.f. genealogy.

gên|er /ʒene/ v.t. bother, disturb; (*troubler*) embarrass; (*encombrer*) hamper; (*bloquer*) block. ~**é** a. embarrassed.

génér|al (*m. pl.* ~**aux**) /ʒeneral, -o/ a. general. ● n.m. (*pl.* ~**aux**) general. **en** ~**al,** in general. ~**alement** adv. generally.

généralis|er /ʒeneralize/ v.t./i. generalize. **se** ~**er** v. pr. become general. ~**ation** n.f. generalization.

généraliste /ʒeneralist/ n.m./f. general practitioner, GP.

généralité /ʒeneralite/ n.f. majority. ~s, general points.

génération /ʒenerɑsjɔ̃/ n.f. generation.

génératrice /ʒeneratris/ n.f. generator.

généreu|x, ~se /ʒenerø, -z/ a. generous. ~sement adv. generously.

générique /ʒenerik/ n.m. (cinéma) credits. ● a. generic.

générosité /ʒenerozite/ n.f. generosity.

genêt /ʒənɛ/ n.m. (plante) broom.

génétique /ʒenetik/ a. genetic. ● n.f. genetics.

Genève /ʒənɛv/ n.m./f. Geneva.

gén|ial (m. pl. ~iaux) /ʒenjal, -jo/ a. brilliant; (fam.) fantastic.

génie /ʒeni/ n.m. genius. ~ civil, civil engineering.

genièvre /ʒənjɛvr/ n.m. juniper.

génisse /ʒenis/ n.f. heifer.

génit|al (m. pl. ~aux) /ʒenital, -o/ a. genital.

génocide /ʒenɔsid/ n.m. genocide.

génoise /ʒenwaz/ n.f. sponge (cake).

genou (pl. ~x) /ʒnu/ n.m. knee. à ~x, kneeling. se mettre à ~x, kneel.

genre /ʒɑ̃r/ n.m. sort, kind; (attitude) manner; (gram.) gender. ~ de vie, life-style.

gens /ʒɑ̃/ n.m./f. pl. people.

genti|l, ~lle /ʒɑ̃ti, -j/ a. kind, nice; (agréable) nice; (sage) good. ~llesse /-jɛs/ n.f. kindness. ~ment adv. kindly.

géograph|ie /ʒeɔgrafi/ n.f. geography. ~e n.m./f. geographer. ~ique a. geographical.

geôl|ier, ~ière /ʒolje, -jɛr/ n.m., f. gaoler, jailer.

géolog|ie /ʒeɔlɔʒi/ n.f. geology. ~ique a. geological. ~gue n.m./f. geologist.

géomètre /ʒeɔmɛtr/ n.m. surveyor.

géométr|ie /ʒeɔmetri/ n.f. geometry. ~ique a. geometric.

géranium /ʒeranjɔm/ n.m. geranium.

géran|t, ~te /ʒerɑ̃, -t/ n.m., f. manager, manageress. ~t d'immeuble, landlord's agent. ~ce n.f. management.

gerbe /ʒɛrb/ n.f. (de fleurs, d'eau) spray; (de blé) sheaf.

gercé /ʒɛrse/ a. chapped.

ger|cer /ʒɛrse/ v.t./i., se ~cer v. pr. chap. ~çure n.f. chap.

gérer /ʒere/ v.t. manage.

germain, ~e /ʒɛrmɛ̃, -ɛn/ a. cousin ~, first cousin.

germanique /ʒɛrmanik/ a. Germanic.

germ|e /ʒɛrm/ n.m. germ. ~er v.i. germinate.

gésier /ʒezje/ n.m. gizzard.

gestation /ʒɛstasjɔ̃/ n.f. gestation.

geste /ʒɛst/ n.m. gesture.

gesticul|er /ʒɛstikyle/ v.i. gesticulate. ~ation n.f. gesticulation.

gestion /ʒɛstjɔ̃/ n.f. management.

geyser /ʒɛzɛr/ n.m. geyser.

ghetto /gɛto/ n.m. ghetto.

gibecière /ʒibsjɛr/ n.f. shoulder-bag.

gibet /ʒibɛ/ n.m. gallows.

gibier /ʒibje/ n.m. (animaux) game.

giboulée /ʒibule/ n.f. shower.

gicl|er /ʒikle/ v.i. squirt. faire ~er, squirt. ~ée n.f. squirt.

gifl|e /ʒifl/ n.f. slap (in the face). ~er v.t. slap.

gigantesque /ʒigɑ̃tɛsk/ a. gigantic.

gigot /ʒigo/ n.m. leg (of lamb).

gigoter /ʒigɔte/ v.i. (fam.) wriggle.

gilet /ʒilɛ/ n.m. waistcoat; (cardigan) cardigan. ~ de sauvetage, life-jacket.

gin /dʒin/ n.m. gin.

gingembre /ʒɛ̃ʒɑ̃br/ n.m. ginger.

gingivite /ʒɛ̃ʒivit/ n.f. gum infection.

girafe /ʒiraf/ n.f. giraffe.

giratoire /ʒiratwar/ a. sens ~, roundabout.

giroflée /ʒirɔfle/ n.f. wallflower.

girouette /ʒirwɛt/ n.f. weathercock, weather-vane.

gisement /ʒizmɑ̃/ n.m. deposit.

gitan, ~e /ʒitɑ̃, -an/ n.m., f. gypsy.

gîte /ʒit/ n.m. (maison) home; (abri) shelter. ~ rural, holiday cottage.

givr|e /ʒivr/ n.m. (hoar-)frost. ~er v.t., se ~er v. pr. frost (up).

givré /ʒivre/ a. (fam.) nuts.

glace /glas/ n.f. ice; (crème) ice-cream; (vitre) window; (miroir) mirror; (verre) glass.

glac|er /glase/ v.t. freeze; (gâteau, boisson) ice; (papier) glaze; (pétrifier) chill. se ~er v. pr. freeze. ~é a. (vent, accueil) icy.

glac|ial (m. pl. ~iaux) /glasjal, -jo/ a. icy.

glacier /glasje/ n.m. (géog.) glacier; (vendeur) ice-cream man.

glacière /glasjɛr/ *n.f.* icebox.

glaçon /glasɔ̃/ *n.m.* (*pour boisson*) ice-cube; (*péj.*) cold fish.

glaïeul /glajœl/ *n.m.* gladiolus.

glaise /glɛz/ *n.f.* clay.

gland /glɑ̃/ *n.m.* acorn; (*ornement*) tassel.

glande /glɑ̃d/ *n.f.* gland.

glander /glɑ̃de/ *v.i.* (*fam.*) laze around.

glaner /glane/ *v.t.* glean.

glapir /glapir/ *v.i.* yelp.

glas /glɑ/ *n.m.* knell.

glauque /glok/ *a.* (*fig.*) gloomy.

glissant, ~e /glisɑ̃, -t/ *a.* slippery.

gliss|er /glise/ *v.i.* slide; (*sur l'eau*) glide; (*déraper*) slip; (*véhicule*) skid. ● *v.t.*, **se ~er** *v. pr.* slip (**dans**, into). **~ade** *n.f.* sliding; (*endroit*) slide. **~ement** *n.m.* sliding; gliding; (*fig.*) shift. **~ement de terrain**, landslide.

glissière /glisjɛr/ *n.f.* groove. **à ~,** (*porte, système*) sliding.

glob|al (*m. pl.* **~aux**) /glɔbal, -o/ *a.* (*entier, général*) overall. **~alement** *adv.* as a whole.

globe /glɔb/ *n.m.* globe. **~ oculaire,** eyeball. **~ terrestre,** globe.

globule /glɔbyl/ *n.m.* (*du sang*) corpuscle.

gloire /glwar/ *n.f.* glory.

glorieu|x, ~se /glɔrjø, -z/ *a.* glorious. **~sement** *adv.* gloriously.

glorifier /glɔrifje/ *v.t.* glorify.

glose /gloz/ *n.f.* gloss.

glossaire /glɔsɛr/ *n.m.* glossary.

glouss|er /gluse/ *v.i.* chuckle; (*poule*) cluck. **~ement** *n.m.* chuckle; cluck.

glouton, ~ne /glutɔ̃, -ɔn/ *a.* gluttonous. ● *n.m., f.* glutton.

gluant, ~e /glyɑ̃, -t/ *a.* sticky.

glucose /glykoz/ *n.m.* glucose.

glycérine /gliserin/ *n.f.* glycerine.

glycine /glisin/ *n.f.* wisteria.

gnome /gnom/ *n.m.* gnome.

go /go/ **tout de go,** straight out.

GO (*abrév. grandes ondes*) long wave.

goal /gol/ *n.m.* goalkeeper.

gobelet /gɔblɛ/ *n.m.* tumbler, mug.

gober /gɔbe/ *v.t.* swallow (whole). **je ne peux pas le ~,** (*fam.*) I can't stand him.

godasse /gɔdas/ *n.f.* (*fam.*) shoe.

godet /gɔdɛ/ *n.m.* (small) pot.

goéland /gɔelɑ̃/ *n.m.* (sea)gull.

goélette /gɔelɛt/ *n.f.* schooner.

gogo (à) /(a)gɔgo/ *adv.* (*fam.*) galore, in abundance.

goguenard, ~e /gɔgnar, -d/ *a.* mocking.

goguette (en) /(ɑ̃)gɔgɛt/ *adv.* (*fam.*) having a binge *ou* spree.

goinfr|e /gwɛ̃fr/ *n.m.* (*glouton: fam.*) pig. **se ~er** *v. pr.* (*fam.*) stuff o.s. like a pig (**de**, with).

golf /gɔlf/ *n.m.* golf; golf course.

golfe /gɔlf/ *n.m.* gulf.

gomm|e /gɔm/ *n.f.* rubber; (*Amer.*) eraser; (*résine*) gum. **~er** *v.t.* rub out.

gond /gɔ̃/ *n.m.* hinge. **sortir de ses ~s,** go mad.

gondol|e /gɔ̃dɔl/ *n.f.* gondola. **~ier** *n.m.* gondolier.

gondoler (se) /(sə)gɔ̃dɔle/ *v. pr.* warp; (*rire: fam.*) split one's sides.

gonfl|er /gɔ̃fle/ *v.t./i.* swell; (*ballon, pneu*) pump up, blow up; (*exagérer*) inflate. **se ~er** *v. pr.* swell. **~é** *a.* swollen. **il est ~é,** (*fam.*) he's got a nerve. **~ement** *n.m.* swelling.

gorge /gɔrʒ/ *n.f.* throat; (*poitrine*) breast; (*vallée*) gorge.

gorgée /gɔrʒe/ *n.f.* sip, gulp.

gorg|er /gɔrʒe/ *v.t.* fill (**de**, with). **se ~er** *v. pr.* gorge o.s. (**de**, with). **~é de,** full of.

gorille /gɔrij/ *n.m.* gorilla; (*garde: fam.*) bodyguard.

gosier /gozje/ *n.m.* throat.

gosse /gɔs/ *n.m./f.* (*fam.*) kid.

gothique /gɔtik/ *a.* Gothic.

goudron /gudrɔ̃/ *n.m.* tar. **~ner** /-ɔne/ *v.t.* tar; (*route*) surface. **à faible teneur en ~,** low tar.

gouffre /gufr/ *n.m.* gulf, abyss.

goujat /guʒa/ *n.m.* lout, boor.

goulot /gulo/ *n.m.* neck. **boire au ~,** drink from the bottle.

goulu, ~e /guly/ *a.* gluttonous. ● *n.m., f.* glutton.

gourde /gurd/ *n.f.* (*à eau*) flask; (*idiot: fam.*) chump.

gourdin /gurdɛ̃/ *n.m.* club, cudgel.

gourer (se) /(sə)gure/ *v. pr.* (*fam.*) make a mistake.

gourmand, ~e /gurmɑ̃, -d/ *a.* greedy. ● *n.m., f.* glutton. **~ise** /-diz/ *n.f.* greed; (*mets*) delicacy.

gourmet /gurmɛ/ *n.m.* gourmet.

gourmette /gurmɛt/ *n.f.* chain bracelet.

gousse /gus/ *n.f.* **~ d'ail,** clove of garlic.

goût /gu/ *n.m.* taste.

goûter /gute/ *v.t.* taste; (*apprécier*) enjoy. ● *v.i.* have tea. ● *n.m.* tea, snack. **~ à** ou **de,** taste.

goutt|e /gut/ *n.f.* drop; (*méd.*) gout. **~er** *v.i.* drip.

goutte-à-goutte /gutagut/ *n.m.* drip.

gouttelette /gutlɛt/ *n.f.* droplet.

gouttière /gutjɛr/ *n.f.* gutter.

gouvernail /guvɛrnaj/ *n.m.* rudder; (*barre*) helm.

gouvernante /guvɛrnɑ̃t/ *n.f.* governess.

gouvernement /guvɛrnəmɑ̃/ *n.m.* government. **~al** (*m. pl.* **~aux**) /-tal, -to/ *a.* governmental.

gouvern|er /guvɛrne/ *v.t./i.* govern. **~eur** *n.m.* governor.

grâce /grɑs/ *n.f.* (*charme*) grace; (*faveur*) favour; (*jurid.*) pardon; (*relig.*) grace. **~ à,** thanks to.

gracier /grasje/ *v.t.* pardon.

gracieu|x, ~se /grasjø, -z/ *a.* graceful; (*gratuit*) free. **~sement** *adv.* gracefully; free (of charge).

gradation /gradasjɔ̃/ *n.f.* gradation.

grade /grad/ *n.m.* rank. **monter en ~,** be promoted.

gradé /grade/ *n.m.* non-commissioned officer.

gradin /gradɛ̃/ *n.m.* tier, step. **en ~s,** terraced.

gradué /gradɥe/ *a.* graded, graduated.

graduel, ~le /gradɥɛl/ *a.* gradual.

grad|uer /gradɥe/ *v.t.* increase gradually. **~uation** *n.f.* graduation.

graffiti /grafiti/ *n.m. pl.* graffiti.

grain /grɛ̃/ *n.m.* grain; (*naut.*) squall; (*de café*) bean; (*de poivre*) pepper corn. **~ de beauté,** beauty spot. **~ de raisin,** grape.

graine /grɛn/ *n.f.* seed.

graissage /grɛsaʒ/ *n.m.* lubrication.

graiss|e /grɛs/ *n.f.* fat; (*lubrifiant*) grease. **~er** *v.t.* grease. **~eux, ~euse** *a.* greasy.

gramm|aire /gramɛr/ *n.f.* grammar. **~atical** (*m. pl.* **~aticaux**) *a.* grammatical.

gramme /gram/ *n.m.* gram.

grand, ~e /grɑ̃, -d/ *a.* big, large; (*haut*) tall; (*mérite, distance, ami*) great; (*bruit*) loud; (*plus âgé*) big. ● *adv.* (*ouvrir*) wide. **~ ouvert,** wide open. **voir ~,** think big. ● *n.m., f.* (*adulte*) grown-up; (*enfant*) older child. **au ~ air,** in the open air. **au ~ jour,** in broad day-light; (*fig.*) in the open. **de ~e envergure,** large-scale. **en ~e partie,** largely. **~-angle,** *n.m.* wide angle. **~e banlieue,** outer suburbs. **G~e-Bretagne** *n.f.* Great Britain. **pas ~-chose,** not much. **~ ensemble,** housing estate. **~es lignes,** (*rail.*) main lines. **~ magasin,** department store. **~-mère** (*pl.* **~s-mères**) *n.f.* grandmother. **~s-parents** *n.m. pl.* grandparents. **~-père** (*pl.* **~s-pères**) *n.m.* grandfather. **~e personne,** grown-up. **~ public,** general public. **~-rue** *n.f.* high street. **~e surface,** hypermarket. **~es vacances,** summer holidays.

grandeur /grɑ̃dœr/ *n.f.* greatness; (*dimension*) size. **folie des ~s,** delusions of grandeur.

grandiose /grɑ̃djoz/ *a.* grandiose.

grandir /grɑ̃dir/ *v.i.* grow; (*bruit*) grow louder. ● *v.t.* make taller.

grange /grɑ̃ʒ/ *n.f.* barn.

granit /granit/ *n.m.* granite.

granulé /granyle/ *n.m.* granule.

graphique /grafik/ *a.* graphic. ● *n.m.* graph.

graphologie /grafɔlɔʒi/ *n.f.* graphology.

grappe /grap/ *n.f.* cluster. **~ de raisin,** bunch of grapes.

grappin /grapɛ̃/ *n.m.* **mettre le ~ sur,** get one's claws into.

gras, ~se /grɑ, -s/ *a.* fat; (*aliment*) fatty; (*surface*) greasy; (*épais*) thick; (*caractères*) bold. ● *n.m.* (*culin.*) fat. **faire la ~se matinée,** sleep late. **~sement payé,** highly paid.

gratification /gratifikasjɔ̃/ *n.f.* bonus, satisfaction.

gratifi|er /gratifje/ *v.t.* favour, reward (**de,** with). **~ant, ~ante** *a.* rewarding.

gratin /gratɛ̃/ *n.m.* baked dish with cheese topping; (*élite: fam.*) upper crust.

gratis /gratis/ *adv.* free.

gratitude /gratityd/ *n.f.* gratitude.

gratt|er /grate/ *v.t./i.* scratch; (*avec un outil*) scrape. **se ~er** *v. pr.* scratch o.s. **ça me ~e,** (*fam.*) it itches. **~e-ciel** *n.m. invar.* skyscraper. **~-papier** *n.m. invar.* (*péj.*) pen pusher.

gratuit, ~e /gratɥi, -t/ *a.* free; (*acte*) gratuitous. **~ement** /-tmɑ̃/ *adv.* free (of charge).

gravats /grava/ *n.m. pl.* rubble.

grave /grav/ a. serious; (*solennel*) grave; (*voix*) deep; (*accent*) grave. **~ment** adv. seriously; gravely.

grav|er /grave/ v.t. engrave; (*sur bois*) carve. **~eur** n.m. engraver.

gravier /gravje/ n.m. gravel.

gravir /gravir/ v.t. climb.

gravitation /gravitasjɔ̃/ n.f. gravitation.

gravité /gravite/ n.f. gravity.

graviter /gravite/ v.i. revolve.

gravure /gravyr/ n.f. engraving; (*de tableau, photo*) print, plate.

gré /gre/ n.m. (*volonté*) will; (*goût*) taste. **à son ~,** (*agir*) as one likes. **de bon ~,** willingly. **bon ~ mal gré,** like it or not. **je vous en saurais ~,** I'll be grateful for that.

grec, ~que /grɛk/ a. & n.m., f. Greek. ● n.m. (*lang.*) Greek.

Grèce /grɛs/ n.f. Greece.

greff|e /grɛf/ n.f. graft; (*d'organe*) transplant. **~er** /grefe/ v.t. graft; transplant.

greffier /grefje/ n.m. clerk of the court.

grégaire /gregɛr/ a. gregarious.

grêle[1] /grɛl/ a. (*maigre*) spindly; (*voix*) shrill.

grêl|e[2] /grɛl/ n.f. hail. **~er** /grele/ v.i. hail. **~on** n.m. hailstone.

grelot /grəlo/ n.m. (little) bell.

grelotter /grəlɔte/ v.i. shiver.

grenade[1] /grənad/ n.f. (*fruit*) pomegranate.

grenade[2] /grənad/ n.f. (*explosif*) grenade.

grenat /grəna/ a. invar. dark red.

grenier /grənje/ n.m. attic; (*pour grain*) loft.

grenouille /grənuj/ n.f. frog.

grès /grɛ/ n.m. sandstone; (*poterie*) stoneware.

grésiller /grezije/ v.i. sizzle; (*radio*) crackle.

grève[1] /grɛv/ n.f. strike. **se mettre en ~,** go on strike. **~ du zèle,** work-to-rule; (*Amer.*) rule-book slowdown. **~ de la faim,** hunger strike. **~ sauvage,** wildcat strike.

grève[2] /grɛv/ n.f. (*rivage*) shore.

gréviste /grevist/ n.m./f. striker.

gribouill|er /gribuje/ v.t./i. scribble. **~is** /-ji/ n.m. scribble.

grief /grijɛf/ n.m. grievance.

grièvement /grijɛvmɑ̃/ adv. seriously.

griff|e /grif/ n.f. claw; (*de couturier*) label. **~er** v.t. scratch, claw.

griffonner /grifɔne/ v.t./i. scrawl.

grignoter /griɲɔte/ v.t./i. nibble.

gril /gril/ n.m. grill, grid(iron).

grillade /grijad/ n.f. (*viande*) grill.

grillage /grijaʒ/ n.m. wire netting.

grille /grij/ n.f. railings; (*portail*) (metal) gate; (*de fenêtre*) bars; (*de cheminée*) grate; (*fig.*) grid.

grill|er /grije/ v.t./i. burn; (*ampoule*) blow; (*feu rouge*) go through. **(faire) ~er,** (*pain*) toast; (*viande*) grill; (*café*) roast. **~e-pain** n.m. invar. toaster.

grillon /grijɔ̃/ n.m. cricket.

grimace /grimas/ n.f. (funny) face; (*de douleur, dégoût*) grimace.

grimer /grime/ v.t., **se ~** v. pr. make up.

grimper /grɛ̃pe/ v.t./i. climb.

grinc|er /grɛ̃se/ v.i. creak. **~er des dents,** grind one's teeth. **~ement** n.m. creak(ing).

grincheu|x, ~se /grɛ̃ʃø, -z/ a. grumpy.

gripp|e /grip/ n.f. influenza, flu. **être ~é,** have (the) flu; (*mécanisme*) be seized up *ou* jammed.

gris, ~e /gri, -z/ a. grey; (*saoul*) tipsy.

grisaille /grizaj/ n.f. greyness, gloom.

grisonner /grizɔne/ v.i. go grey.

grisou /grizu/ n.m. **coup de ~,** firedamp explosion.

grive /griv/ n.f. (*oiseau*) thrush.

grivois, ~e /grivwa, -z/ a. bawdy.

grog /grɔg/ n.m. grog.

grogn|er /grɔɲe/ v.i. growl; (*fig.*) grumble. **~ement** n.m. growl; grumble.

grognon, ~ne /grɔɲɔ̃, -ɔn/ a. grumpy.

groin /grwɛ̃/ n.m. snout.

grommeler /grɔmle/ v.t./i. mutter.

grond|er /grɔ̃de/ v.i. rumble; (*chien*) growl; (*conflit etc.*) be brewing. ● v.t. scold. **~ement** n.m. rumbling; growling.

groom /grum/ n.m. page(-boy).

gros, ~se /gro, -s/ a. big, large; (*gras*) fat; (*important*) great; (*épais*) thick; (*lourd*) heavy. ● n.m., f. fat man, fat woman. ● n.m. **le ~ de,** the bulk of. **de ~,** (*comm.*) wholesale. **en ~,** roughly; (*comm.*) wholesale. **~ bonnet,** (*fam.*) bigwig. **~ lot,** jackpot. **~ mot,** rude word. **~ plan,** close-up. **~ titre,** headline. **~se caisse,** big drum.

groseille /grozεj/ *n.f.* (red *ou* white) currant. **~ à maquereau,** gooseberry.

grosse /gros/ *voir* gros.

grossesse /grosεs/ *n.f.* pregnancy.

grosseur /grosœr/ *n.f.* (*volume*) size; (*enflure*) lump.

gross|ier, ~ière /grosje, -jεr/ *a.* coarse, rough; (*imitation, instrument*) crude; (*vulgaire*) coarse; (*insolent*) rude; (*erreur*) gross. **~ièrement** *adv.* (*sommairement*) roughly; (*vulgairement*) coarsely. **~ièreté** *n.f.* coarseness; crudeness; rudeness; (*mot*) rude word.

grossir /grosir/ *v.t./i.* swell; (*personne*) put on weight; (*au microscope*) magnify; (*augmenter*) grow; (*exagérer*) magnify.

grossiste /grosist/ *n.m./f.* wholesaler.

grosso modo /grosomodo/ *adv.* roughly.

grotesque /grotεsk/ *a.* grotesque; (*ridicule*) ludicrous.

grotte /grot/ *n.f.* cave, grotto.

grouill|er /gruje/ *v.i.* be swarming (**de,** with). **~ant, ~ante** *a.* swarming.

groupe /grup/ *n.m.* group; (*mus.*) band. **~ électrogène,** generating set. **~ scolaire,** school block.

group|er /grupe/ *v.t.,* **se ~er** *v. pr.* group (together). **~ement** *n.m.* grouping.

grue /gry/ *n.f.* (*machine, oiseau*) crane.

grumeau (*pl.* **~x**) /grymo/ *n.m.* lump.

gruyère /gryjεr/ *n.m.* gruyère (cheese).

gué /ge/ *n.m.* ford. **passer** *ou* **traverser à ~,** ford.

guenon /gənõ/ *n.f.* female monkey.

guépard /gepar/ *n.m.* cheetah.

guêp|e /gεp/ *n.f.* wasp. **~ier** /gepje/ *n.m.* wasp's nest; (*fig.*) trap.

guère /gεr/ *adv.* (**ne**) **~,** hardly. **il n'y a ~ d'espoir,** there is no hope.

guéridon /geridõ/ *n.m.* pedestal table.

guérill|a /gerija/ *n.f.* guerrilla warfare. **~ero** /-jero/ *n.m.* guerrilla.

guér|ir /gerir/ *v.t.* (*personne, maladie, mal*) cure (**de,** of); (*plaie, membre*) heal. ● *v.i.* get better; (*blessure*) heal. **~ir de,** recover from. **~ison** *n.f.* curing; healing; (*de personne*)

recovery. **~isseur, ~isseuse** *n.m., f.* healer.

guérite /gerit/ *n.f.* (*mil.*) sentry-box.

guerre /gεr/ *n.f.* war. **en ~,** at war. **faire la ~,** wage war (**à,** against). **~ civile,** civil war. **~ d'usure,** war of attrition.

guerr|ier, ~ière /gεrje, -jεr/ *a.* warlike. ● *n.m.,* f. warrior.

guet /gε/ *n.m.* watch. **faire le ~,** be on the watch. **~-apens** /gεtapã/ *n.m. invar.* ambush.

guetter /gete/ *v.t.* watch; (*attendre*) watch out for.

gueule /gœl/ *n.f.* mouth; (*figure: fam.*) face. **ta ~!,** (*fam.*) shut up!

gueuler /gœle/ *v.i.* (*fam.*) bawl.

gueuleton /gœltõ/ *n.m.* (*repas: fam.*) blow-out, slap-up meal.

gui /gi/ *n.m.* mistletoe.

guichet /giʃε/ *n.m.* window, counter; (*de gare*) ticket-office (window); (*de théâtre*) box-office (window).

guide /gid/ *n.m.* guide. ● *n.f.* (*fille scout*) girl guide. **~s** *n.f. pl.* (*rênes*) reins.

guider /gide/ *v.t.* guide.

guidon /gidõ/ *n.m.* handlebars.

guignol /giɲɔl/ *n.m.* puppet; (*personne*) clown; (*spectacle*) puppet-show.

guili-guili /giligili/ *n.m.* (*fam.*) tickle. **faire ~ à,** tickle.

guillemets /gijmε/ *n.m. pl.* quotation marks, inverted commas. **entre ~,** in inverted commas.

guilleret, ~te /gijrε, -t/ *a.* sprightly, jaunty.

guillotin|e /gijɔtin/ *n.f.* guillotine. **~er** *v.t.* guillotine.

guimauve /gimov/ *n.f.* marshmallow. **c'est de la ~,** (*fam.*) it's mush.

guindé /gɛ̃de/ *a.* stilted.

guirlande /girlãd/ *n.f.* garland.

guise /giz/ *n.f.* **à sa ~,** as one pleases. **en ~ de,** by way of.

guitar|e /gitar/ *n.f.* guitar. **~iste** *n.m./f.* guitarist.

gus /gys/ *n.m.* (*fam.*) bloke.

guttur|al (*m. pl.* **~aux**) /gytyral, -o/ *a.* guttural.

gym /ʒim/ *n.f.* gym.

gymnas|e /ʒimnaz/ *n.m.* gym (nasium). **~te** /-ast/ *n.m./f.* gymnast. **~tique** /-astik/ *n.f.* gymnastics.

gynécolo|gie /ʒinekɔlɔʒi/ *n.f.* gynaecology. **~gique** *a.* gynaeco-

logical. **~gue** *n.m./f.* gynaecologist.
gypse /ʒips/ *n.m.* gypsum.

H

habile /abil/ *a.* skilful, clever. **~té**
n.f. skill.

habilité /abilite/ *a.* **~ à faire,** entitled to do.

habill|er /abije/ *v.t.* dress (**de,** in);
(*équiper*) clothe; (*recouvrir*) cover
(**de,** with). **s'~er** *v. pr.* dress (o.s.),
get dressed; (*se déguiser*) dress up.
~é *a.* (*costume*) dressy. **~ement**
n.m. clothing.

habit /abi/ *n.m.* dress, outfit; (*de
cérémonie*) tails. **~s,** clothes.

habitable /abitabl/ *a.* (in)habitable.

habitant, ~e /abitã, -t/ *n.m.,* *f.* (*de
maison*) occupant; (*de pays*) inhabitant.

habitat /abita/ *n.m.* housing conditions; (*d'animal*) habitat.

habitation /abitasjɔ̃/ *n.f.* living; (*logement*) house.

habit|er /abite/ *v.i.* live. ● *v.t.* live in;
(*planète, zone*) inhabit. **~é a.** (*terre*)
inhabited.

habitude /abityd/ *n.f.* habit. **avoir
l'~ de faire,** be used to doing. **d'~,**
usually. **comme d'~,** as usual.

habitué, ~e /abitye/ *n.m., f.* regular
visitor; (*client*) regular.

habituel, ~le /abitɥɛl/ *a.* usual.
~lement *adv.* usually.

habituer /abitye/ *v.t.* **~ à,** accustom
to. **s'~ à,** get used to.

hache /'aʃ/ *n.f.* axe.

haché /'aʃe/ *a.* (*viande*) minced;
(*phrases*) jerky.

hacher /'aʃe/ *v.t.* mince; (*au couteau*)
chop.

hachette /'aʃɛt/ *n.f.* hatchet.

hachis /'aʃi/ *n.m.* minced meat;
(*Amer.*) ground meat.

hachisch /'aʃiʃ/ *n.m.* hashish.

hachoir /'aʃwar/ *n.m.* (*appareil*)
mincer; (*couteau*) chopper;
(*planche*) chopping board.

hagard, ~e /'agar, -d/ *a.* wild(-look-
ing).

haie /'ɛ/ *n.f.* hedge; (*rangée*) row.
course de ~s, hurdle race.

haillon /'ajɔ̃/ *n.m.* rag.

hain|e /'ɛn/ *n.f.* hatred. **~eux, ~euse**
a. full of hatred.

haïr /'air/ *v.t.* hate.

hâl|e /'ɑl/ *n.m.* (sun-)tan. **~é** *a.*
(sun-)tanned.

haleine /alɛn/ *n.f.* breath. **hors d'~,**
out of breath. **travail de longue ~,**
long job.

hal|er /'ale/ *v.t.* tow. **~age** *n.m.* tow-
ing.

haleter /'alte/ *v.i.* pant.

hall /'ol/ *n.m.* hall; (*de gare*) concourse.

halle /'al/ *n.f.* (covered) market. **~s,**
(main) food market.

hallucination /alysinɑsjɔ̃/ *n.f.* hallucination.

halo /'alo/ *n.m.* halo.

halte /'alt/ *n.f.* stop; (*repos*) break;
(*escale*) stopping place. ● *int.* stop;
(*mil.*) halt. **faire ~,** stop.

halt|ère /altɛr/ *n.m.* dumb-bell.
~érophilie *n.f.* weight-lifting.

hamac /'amak/ *n.m.* hammock.

hamburger /'ɑburgœr/ *n.m.* hamburger.

hameau (*pl.* **~x**) /'amo/ *n.m.* hamlet.

hameçon /amsɔ̃/ *n.m.* (fish-)hook.

hanche /'ɑ̃ʃ/ *n.f.* hip.

hand-ball /'ɑ̃dbal/ *n.m.* handball.

handicap /'ɑ̃dikap/ *n.m.* handicap.
~é, ~ée *a.* & *n.m., f.* handicapped
(person). **~er** *v.t.* handicap.

hangar /'ɑ̃gar/ *n.m.* shed; (*pour
avions*) hangar.

hanneton /'antɔ̃/ *n.m.* May-bug.

hanter /'ɑ̃te/ *v.t.* haunt.

hantise /'ɑ̃tiz/ *n.f.* obsession (**de,**
with).

happer /'ape/ *v.t.* snatch, catch.

haras /'arɑ/ *n.m.* stud-farm.

harasser /'arase/ *v.t.* exhaust.

harcèlement /'arsɛlmɑ̃/ *n.m.* **~
sexuel,** sexual harassment.

harceler /'arsəle/ *v.t.* harass.

hardi /'ardi/ *a.* bold. **~esse** /-djɛs/ *n.f.*
boldness. **~ment** *adv.* boldly.

hareng /'arɑ̃/ *n.m.* herring.

hargn|e /'arɲ/ *n.f.* (aggressive) bad
temper. **~eux, ~euse** *a.* bad-
tempered.

haricot /'ariko/ *n.m.* bean. **~ vert,**
French *ou* string bean; (*Amer.*)
green bean.

harmonica /armɔnika/ *n.m.* harmonica.

harmon|ie /armɔni/ *n.f.* harmony.
~ieux, ~ieuse *a.* harmonious.

harmoniser /armɔnize/ v.t., s'~ v. pr. harmonize.

harnacher /'arnaʃe/ v.t. harness.

harnais /'arnɛ/ n.m. harness.

harp|e /'arp/ n.f. harp. **~iste** n.m./f. harpist.

harpon /'arpɔ̃/ n.m. harpoon. **~ner** /-ɔne/ v.t. harpoon; (arrêter: fam.) detain.

hasard /'azar/ n.m. chance; (coïncidence) coincidence. **~s**, (risques) hazards. **au ~**, (choisir etc.) at random; (flâner) aimlessly. **~eux**, **~euse** /-dø, -z/ a. risky.

hasarder /'azarde/ v.t. risk; (remarque) venture. **se ~ dans**, risk going into. **se ~ à faire**, risk doing.

hâte /'at/ n.f. haste. **à la ~, en ~**, hurriedly. **avoir ~ de**, be eager to.

hâter /'ate/ v.t. hasten. **se ~** v. pr. hurry (**de**, to).

hâti|f, **~ve** /'atif, -v/ a. hasty; (précoce) early.

hauss|e /'os/ n.f. rise (**de**, in). **~e des prix**, price rises. **en ~e**, rising. **~er** v.t. raise; (épaules) shrug. **se ~er** v. pr. stand up, raise o.s. up.

haut, **~e** /'o, 'ot/ a. high; (de taille) tall. ● adv. high; (parler) loud(ly); (lire) aloud. ● n.m. top. **à ~e voix**, aloud. **des ~s et des bas**, ups and downs. **en ~**, (regarder, jeter) up; (dans une maison) upstairs. **en ~ (de)**, at the top (of). **~ en couleur**, colourful. **plus ~**, further up, higher up; (dans un texte) above. **en ~ lieu**, in high places. **~-de-forme** (pl. **~s-de-forme**) n.m. top hat. **~-fourneau** (pl. **~s-fourneaux**) n.m. blast-furnace. **~-le-cœur** n.m. invar. nausea. **~-parleur** n.m. loudspeaker.

hautain, **~e** /'otɛ̃, -ɛn/ a. haughty.

hautbois /'obwa/ n.m. oboe.

hautement /'otmã/ adv. highly.

hauteur /'otœr/ n.f. height; (colline) hill; (arrogance) haughtiness. **à la ~**, (fam.) up to it. **à la ~ de**, level with; (tâche, situation) equal to.

hâve /'av/ a. gaunt.

havre /'avr/ n.m. haven.

Haye (La) /(la)'ɛ/ n.f. The Hague.

hayon /'ajɔ̃/ n.m. (auto.) rear opening, tail-gate.

hebdo /ɛbdo/ n.m. (fam.) weekly.

hebdomadaire /ɛbdɔmadɛr/ a. & n.m. weekly.

héberg|er /ebɛrʒe/ v.t. accommodate, take in. **~ement** n.m. accommodation.

hébété /ebete/ a. dazed.

hébraïque /ebraik/ a. Hebrew.

hébreu (pl. **~x**) /ebrø/ a.m. Hebrew. ● n.m. (lang.) Hebrew. **c'est de l'~!**, it's double Dutch.

hécatombe /ekatɔ̃b/ n.f. slaughter.

hectare /ɛktar/ n.m. hectare (=10,000 square metres).

hégémonie /eʒemɔni/ n.f. hegemony.

hein /'ɛ̃/ int. (fam.) eh.

hélas /'elas/ int. alas. ● adv. sadly.

héler /'ele/ v.t. hail.

hélice /elis/ n.f. propeller.

hélicoptère /elikɔptɛr/ n.m. helicopter.

helvétique /ɛlvetik/ a. Swiss.

hématome /ematom/ n.m. bruise.

hémisphère /emisfɛr/ n.m. hemisphere.

hémorragie /emɔraʒi/ n.f. haemorrhage.

hémorroïdes /emɔrɔid/ n.f. pl. piles, haemorrhoids.

henn|ir /'enir/ v.i. neigh. **~issement** n.m. neigh.

hépatite /epatit/ n.f. hepatitis.

herbage /ɛrbaʒ/ n.m. pasture.

herb|e /ɛrb/ n.f. grass; (méd., culin.) herb. **en ~e**, green; (fig.) budding. **~eux**, **~euse** a. grassy.

herbicide /ɛrbisid/ n.m. weed-killer.

hérédit|é /eredite/ n.f. heredity. **~aire** a. hereditary.

héré|sie /erezi/ n.f. heresy. **~tique** a. heretical; n.m./f. heretic.

hériss|er /'erise/ v.t., **se ~er** v. pr. bristle. **~er de qch.**, ruffle s.o. **~é a**. bristling (**de**, with).

hérisson /'erisɔ̃/ n.m. hedgehog.

héritage /eritaʒ/ n.m. inheritance; (spirituel etc.) heritage.

hérit|er /erite/ v.t./i. inherit (**de**, from). **~er de qch.**, inherit sth. **~ier**, **~ière** n.m., f. heir, heiress.

hermétique /ɛrmetik/ a. airtight; (fig.) unfathomable. **~ment** adv. hermetically.

hermine /ɛrmin/ n.f. ermine.

hernie /'ɛrni/ n.f. hernia.

héroïne¹ /erɔin/ n.f. (femme) heroine.

héroïne² /erɔin/ n.f. (drogue) heroin.

héroï|que /erɔik/ a. heroic. **~sme** n.m. heroism.

héron /'erɔ̃/ n.m. heron.

héros /'ero/ n.m. hero.

hésit|er /ezite/ v.i. hesitate (**à,** to). **en ~ant,** hesitantly. **~ant, ~ante** a. hesitant. **~ation** n.f. hesitation.

hétéro /eterɔ/ n.m. & a. (fam.) straight.

hétéroclite /eterɔklit/ a. heterogeneous.

hétérogène /eterɔʒɛn/ a. heterogeneous.

hétérosexuel, ~le /eterɔseksyɛl/ n.m., f. & a. heterosexual.

hêtre /'ɛtr/ n.m. beech.

heure /œr/ n.f. time; (mesure de durée) hour; (scol.) period. **quelle ~ est-il?,** what time is it? **il est dix/** etc. **~s,** it is ten/etc. o'clock. **à l'~,** (venir, être) on time. **d'~ en heure,** hourly. **~ avancée,** late hour. **~ d'affluence, ~ de pointe,** rush-hour. **~ indue,** ungodly hour. **~s creuses,** off-peak periods. **~s supplémentaires,** overtime.

heureusement /œrøzmɑ̃/ adv. fortunately, luckily.

heureu|x, ~se /œrø, -z/ a. happy; (chanceux) lucky, fortunate.

heurt /'œr/ n.m. collision; (conflit) clash.

heurter /'œrte/ v.t. (cogner) hit; (mur etc.) bump into, hit; (choquer) offend. **se ~ à,** bump into, hit; (fig.) come up against.

hexagone /ɛgzagɔn/ n.m. hexagon. **l'~,** France.

hiberner /iberne/ v.i. hibernate.

hibou (pl. **~x**) /'ibu/ n.m. owl.

hideu|x, ~se /'idø, -z/ a. hideous.

hier /jɛr/ adv. yesterday. **~ soir,** last night, yesterday evening.

hiérarch|ie /'jerarʃi/ n.f. hierarchy. **~ique** a. hierarchical.

hi-fi† /'ifi/ a. invar. & n.f. (fam.) hi-fi.

hilare /ilar/ a. merry.

hilarité /ilarite/ n.f. laughter.

hindou, ~e /ɛ̃du/ a. & n.m., f. Hindu.

hippi|que /ipik/ a. horse, equestrian. **~sme** n.m. horse-riding.

hippodrome /ipodrom/ n.m. racecourse.

hippopotame /ipopotam/ n.m. hippopotamus.

hirondelle /irɔ̃dɛl/ n.f. swallow.

hirsute /irsyt/ a. shaggy.

hisser /'ise/ v.t. hoist, haul. **se ~** v. pr. raise o.s.

histoire /istwar/ n.f. (récit, mensonge) story; (étude) history; (affaire) business. **~(s),** (chichis) fuss. **~s,** (ennuis) trouble.

historien, ~ne /istɔrjɛ̃, -jɛn/ n.m., f. historian.

historique /istɔrik/ a. historical.

hiver /ivɛr/ n.m. winter. **~nal** (m. pl. **~naux**) a. winter; (glacial) wintry. **~ner** v.i. winter.

H.L.M. /'aʃɛlɛm/ n.m./f. (=habitation à loyer modéré) block of council flats; (Amer.) (government-sponsored) low-cost apartment building.

hocher /'ɔʃe/ v.t. **~ la tête,** (pour dire oui) nod; (pour dire non) shake one's head.

hochet /'ɔʃɛ/ n.m. rattle.

hockey /'ɔkɛ/ n.m. hockey. **~ sur glace,** ice hockey.

hold-up /'ɔldœp/ n.m. invar. (attaque) hold-up.

hollandais, ~e /'ɔlɑ̃dɛ, -z/ a. Dutch. ● n.m., f. Dutchman, Dutchwoman. ● n.m. (lang.) Dutch.

Hollande /'ɔlɑ̃d/ n.f. Holland.

hologramme /ɔlɔgram/ n.m. hologram.

homard /'ɔmar/ n.m. lobster.

homéopathie /ɔmeɔpati/ n.f. homeopathy.

homicide /ɔmisid/ n.m. homicide. **~ involontaire,** manslaughter.

hommage /ɔmaʒ/ n.m. tribute. **~s,** (salutations) respects. **rendre ~ à,** pay tribute.

homme /ɔm/ n.m. man; (espèce) man(kind). **~ d'affaires,** businessman. **~ de la rue,** man in the street. **~ d'État,** statesman. **~ de paille,** stooge. **~-grenouille** (pl. **~s-grenouilles**) n.m. frogman. **~ politique,** politician.

homog|ène /ɔmɔʒɛn/ a. homogeneous. **~énéité** n.f. homogeneity.

homologue /ɔmɔlɔg/ n.m./f. counterpart.

homologué /ɔmɔlɔge/ a. (record) officially recognized; (tarif) official.

homologuer /ɔmɔlɔge/ v.t. recognize (officially), validate.

homonyme /ɔmɔnim/ n.m. (personne) namesake.

homosex|uel, ~uelle /ɔmɔsɛksyɛl/ a. & n.m., f. homosexual. **~ualité** n.f. homosexuality.

Hongrie /'ɔ̃gri/ n.f. Hungary.

hongrois, ~e /'ɔ̃grwa, -z/ a. & n.m., f. Hungarian.

honnête /ɔnɛt/ a. honest; (satisfaisant) fair. ~ment adv. honestly; fairly. ~té n.f. honesty.

honneur /ɔnœr/ n.m. honour; (mérite) credit. d'~, (invité, place) of honour; (membre) honorary. en l'~ de, in honour of. en quel ~?, (fam.) why? faire ~ à, (équipe, famille) bring credit to.

honorable /ɔnɔrabl/ a. honourable; (convenable) respectable. ~ment /-əmɑ̃/ adv. honourably; respectably.

honoraire /ɔnɔrɛr/ a. honorary. ~s n.m. pl. fees.

honorer /ɔnɔre/ v.t. honour; (faire honneur à) do credit to. s'~ de, pride o.s. on.

honorifique /ɔnɔrifik/ a. honorary.

hont|e /'ɔ̃t/ n.f. shame. avoir ~e, be ashamed (de, of). faire ~e à, make ashamed. ~eux, ~euse a. (personne) ashamed (de, of); (action) shameful. ~eusement adv. shamefully.

hôpit|al (pl. ~aux) /ɔpital, -o/ n.m. hospital.

hoquet /'ɔkɛ/ n.m. hiccup. le ~, (the) hiccups.

horaire /ɔrɛr/ a. hourly. ● n.m. timetable. ~ flexible, flexitime.

horizon /ɔrizɔ̃/ n.m. horizon; (perspective) view.

horizont|al (m. pl. ~aux) /ɔrizɔ̃tal, -o/ a. horizontal. ~alement adv. horizontally.

horloge /ɔrlɔʒ/ n.f. clock.

horlog|er, ~ère /ɔrlɔʒe, -ɛr/ n.m., f. watchmaker.

hormis /'ɔrmi/ prép. save.

hormon|al (m. pl. ~aux) /ɔrmɔnal, -no/ a. hormonal, hormone.

hormone /ɔrmɔn/ n.f. hormone.

horoscope /ɔrɔskɔp/ n.m. horoscope.

horreur /ɔrœr/ n.f. horror. avoir ~ de, detest.

horrible /ɔribl/ a. horrible. ~ment /-əmɑ̃/ adv. horribly.

horrifier /ɔrifje/ v.t. horrify.

hors /'ɔr/ prép. ~ de, out of; (à l'extérieur de) outside. ~-bord n.m. invar. speedboat. ~ d'atteinte, out of reach. ~ d'haleine, out of breath. ~-d'œuvre n.m. invar. hors-d'œuvre. ~ de prix, exorbitant. ~ de soi, beside o.s. ~-jeu a. invar. offside. ~-la-loi n.m. invar. outlaw.

~ pair, outstanding. ~-taxe a. invar. duty-free.

hortensia /ɔrtɑ̃sja/ n.m. hydrangea.

horticulture /ɔrtikyltyr/ n.f. horticulture.

hospice /ɔspis/ n.m. home.

hospital|ier, ~ière¹ /ɔspitalje, -jɛr/ a. hospitable. ~ité n.f. hospitality.

hospital|ier, ~ière² /ɔspitalje, -jɛr/ a. (méd.) hospital. ~iser v.t. take to hospital.

hostie /ɔsti/ n.f. (relig.) host.

hostil|e /ɔstil/ a. hostile. ~ité n.f. hostility.

hosto /ɔstɔ/ n.m. (fam.) hospital.

hôte /ot/ n.m. (maître) host; (invité) guest.

hôtel /otɛl/ n.m. hotel. ~ (particulier), (private) mansion. ~ de ville, town hall. ~ier, ~ière /otəlje, -jɛr/ a. hotel; n.m., f. hotelier. ~lerie n.f. hotel business; (auberge) country hotel.

hôtesse /otɛs/ n.f. hostess. ~ de l'air, air hostess.

hotte /'ɔt/ n.f. basket; (de cuisinière) hood.

houblon /'ublɔ̃/ n.m. le ~, hops.

houill|e /'uj/ n.f. coal. ~e blanche, hydroelectric power. ~er, ~ère a. coal; n.f. coalmine.

houl|e /'ul/ n.f. (de mer) swell. ~eux, ~euse a. stormy.

houligan /uligan/ n.m. hooligan.

houpette /'upɛt/ n.f. powder-puff.

hourra /'ura/ n.m. & int. hurrah.

housse /'us/ n.f. dust-cover.

houx /'u/ n.m. holly.

hovercraft /ɔvɛrkraft/ n.m. hovercraft.

hublot /'yblo/ n.m. porthole.

huche /'yʃ/ n.f. ~ à pain, breadbin.

huer /'ɥe/ v.t. boo. huées n.f. pl. boos.

huil|e /'ɥil/ n.f. oil; (personne: fam.) bigwig. ~er v.t. oil. ~eux, ~euse a. oily.

huis /'ɥi/ n.m. à ~ clos, in camera.

huissier /ɥisje/ n.m. (appariteur) usher; (jurid.) bailiff.

huit /'ɥi(t)/ a. eight. ● n.m. eight. ~ jours, a week. lundi en ~, a week on Monday. ~aine /'ɥitɛn/ n.f. (semaine) week. ~ième /'ɥitjɛm/ a. & n.m./f. eighth.

huître /ɥitr/ n.f. oyster.

humain, ~e /ymɛ̃, ymɛn/ a. human; (compatissant) humane. ~ement /ymɛnmɑ̃/ adv. humanly; humanely.

humanitaire /ymanitɛr/ *a.* humanitarian.

humanité /ymanite/ *n.f.* humanity.

humble /œ̃bl/ *a.* humble.

humecter /ymɛkte/ *v.t.* moisten.

humer /'yme/ *v.t.* smell.

humeur /ymœr/ *n.f.* mood; (*tempérament*) temper. **de bonne/mauvaise ~,** in a good/bad mood.

humid|e /ymid/ *a.* damp; (*chaleur, climat*) humid; (*lèvres, yeux*) moist. **~ité** *n.f.* humidity.

humil|ier /ymilje/ *v.t.* humiliate. **~iation** *n.f.* humiliation.

humilité /ymilite/ *n.f.* humility.

humorist|e /ymɔrist/ *n.m./f.* humorist. **~ique** *a.* humorous.

humour /ymur/ *n.m.* humour; (*sens*) sense of humour.

huppé /'ype/ *a.* (*fam.*) high-class.

hurl|er /'yrle/ *v.t./i.* howl. **~ement** *n.m.* howl(ing).

hurluberlu /yrlybɛrly/ *n.m.* scatterbrain.

hutte /'yt/ *n.f.* hut.

hybride /ibrid/ *a. & n.m.* hybrid.

hydratant, ~e /idratɑ̃, -t/ *a.* (*lotion*) moisturizing.

hydrate /idrat/ *n.m.* **~ de carbone,** carbohydrate.

hydraulique /idrolik/ *a.* hydraulic.

hydravion /idravjɔ̃/ *n.m.* seaplane.

hydro-electrique /idrɔelɛktrik/ *a.* hydroelectric.

hydrogène /idrɔʒɛn/ *n.m.* hydrogen.

hyène /'jɛn/ *n.f.* hyena.

hygi|ène /iʒjɛn/ *n.f.* hygiene. **~iénique** /iʒjenik/ *a.* hygienic.

hymne /imn/ *n.m.* hymn. **~ national,** national anthem.

hyper- /ipɛr/ *préf.* hyper-.

hypermarché /ipɛrmarʃe/ *n.m.* (*supermarché*) hypermarket.

hypermétrope /ipɛrmetrɔp/ *a.* long-sighted.

hypertension /ipɛrtɑ̃sjɔ̃/ *n.f.* high blood-pressure.

hypno|se /ipnoz/ *n.f.* hypnosis. **~tique** /-ɔtik/ *a.* hypnotic. **~tisme** /-ɔtism/ *n.m.* hypnotism.

hypnotis|er /ipnɔtize/ *v.t.* hypnotize. **~eur** *n.m.* hypnotist.

hypocrisie /ipɔkrizi/ *n.f.* hypocrisy.

hypocrite /ipɔkrit/ *a.* hypocritical. **●** *n.m./f.* hypocrite.

hypoth|èque /ipɔtɛk/ *n.f.* mortgage. **~équer** *v.t.* mortgage.

hypoth|èse /ipɔtɛz/ *n.f.* hypothesis. **~étique** *a.* hypothetical.

hystér|ie /isteri/ *n.f.* hysteria. **~ique** *a.* hysterical.

I

iceberg /isbɛrg/ *n.m.* iceberg.

ici /isi/ *adv.* (*espace*) here; (*temps*) now. **d'~ demain,** by tomorrow. **d'~ là,** in the meantime. **d'~ peu,** shortly. **~ même,** in this very place.

icône /ikon/ *n.f.* icon.

idé|al (*m. pl.* **~aux**) /ideal, -o/ *a.* ideal. **●** *n.m.* (*pl.* **~aux**) ideal. **~aliser** *v.t.* idealize.

idéalis|te /idealist/ *a.* idealistic. **●** *n.m./f.* idealist. **~me** *n.m.* idealism.

idée /ide/ *n.f.* idea; (*esprit*) mind. **~ fixe,** obsession. **~ reçue,** conventional opinion.

identif|ier /idɑ̃tifje/ *v.t.*, **s'~ier** *v. pr.* identify (**à,** with). **~ication** *n.f.* identification.

identique /idɑ̃tik/ *a.* identical.

identité /idɑ̃tite/ *n.f.* identity.

idéolog|ie /ideɔlɔʒi/ *n.f.* ideology. **~ique** *a.* ideological.

idiom|e /idjom/ *n.m.* idiom. **~atique** /idjɔmatik/ *a.* idiomatic.

idiot, ~e /idjo, idjɔt/ *a.* idiotic. **●** *n.m.,* *f.* idiot. **~ie** /idjɔsi/ *n.f.* idiocy; (*acte, parole*) idiotic thing.

idiotisme /idjɔtism/ *n.m.* idiom.

idolâtrer /idɔlatre/ *v.t.* idolize.

idole /idɔl/ *n.f.* idol.

idyll|e /idil/ *n.f.* idyll. **~ique** *a.* idyllic.

if /if/ *n.m.* (*arbre*) yew.

igloo /iglu/ *n.m.* igloo.

ignare /iɲar/ *a.* ignorant. **●** *n.m./f.* ignoramus.

ignifugé /iɲifyʒe/ *a.* fireproof.

ignoble /iɲɔbl/ *a.* vile.

ignoran|t, ~te /iɲɔrɑ̃, -t/ *a.* ignorant. **●** *n.m.,* *f.* ignoramus. **~ce** *n.f.* ignorance.

ignorer /iɲɔre/ *v.t.* not know; (*personne*) ignore.

il /il/ *pron.* he; (*chose*) it. **il est vrai/etc. que,** it is true/*etc.* that. **il neige/pleut/***etc.*, it is snowing/raining/*etc.* **Il y a,** there is; (*pluriel*) there are; (*temps*) ago; (*durée*) for. **il y a 2 ans,** 2 years ago. **il y a plus d'une heure que j'attends,** I've been waiting for over an hour.

île /il/ *n.f.* island. **~ déserte,** desert island. **~s anglo-normandes,** Channel Islands. **~s Britanniques,** British Isles.

illég|al (*m. pl.* **~aux**) /ilegal, -o/ *a.* illegal. **~alité** *n.f.* illegality.

illégitim|e /ileʒitim/ *a.* illegitimate. **~ité** *n.f.* illegitimacy.

illettré, ~e /iletre/ *a. & n.m.,* f. illiterate.

illicite /ilisit/ *a.* illicit.

illimité /ilimite/ *a.* unlimited.

illisible /ilizibl/ *a.* illegible; (*livre*) unreadable.

illogique /ilɔʒik/ *a.* illogical.

illumin|er /ilymine/ *v.t.,* **s'~er** *v. pr.* light up. **~ation** *n.f.* illumination. **~é** *a.* (*monument*) floodlit.

illusion /ilyzjõ/ *n.f.* illusion. **se faire des ~s,** delude o.s. **~ner** /-jɔne/ *v.t.* delude. **~niste** /-jɔnist/ *n.m./f.* conjuror.

illusoire /ilyzwar/ *a.* illusory.

illustre /ilystr/ *a.* illustrious.

illustr|er /ilystre/ *v.t.* illustrate. **s'~er** *v. pr.* become famous. **~ation** *n.f.* illustration. **~é** *a.* illustrated; *n.m.* illustrated magazine.

îlot /ilo/ *n.m.* island; (*de maisons*) block.

ils /il/ *pron.* they.

imag|e /imaʒ/ *n.f.* picture; (*métaphore*) image; (*reflet*) reflection. **~é** *a.* full of imagery.

imaginaire /imaʒinɛr/ *a.* imaginary.

imaginati|f, ~ve /imaʒinatif, -v/ *a.* imaginative.

imagin|er /imaʒine/ *v.t.* imagine; (*inventer*) think up. **s'~er** *v. pr.* imagine (**que,** that). **~ation** *n.f.* imagination.

imbattable /ɛbatabl/ *a.* unbeatable.

imbécil|e /ɛbesil/ *a.* idiotic. ● *n.m./f.* idiot. **~lité** *n.f.* idiocy; (*action*) idiotic thing.

imbib|er /ɛbibe/ *v.t.* soak (**de,** with). **être ~é,** (*fam.*) be sozzled. **s'~er** *v. pr.* become soaked.

imbriqué /ɛbrike/ *a.* (*lié*) linked.

imbroglio /ɛbrɔglio/ *n.m.* imbroglio.

imbu /ɛby/ *a.* **~ de,** full of.

imbuvable /ɛbyvabl/ *a.* undrinkable; (*personne: fam.*) insufferable.

imit|er /imite/ *v.t.* imitate; (*personnage*) impersonate; (*faire comme*) do the same as; (*document*) copy. **~ateur, ~atrice** *n.m.,* f. imitator; impersonator. **~ation** *n.f.* imitation; impersonation.

immaculé /imakyle/ *a.* spotless.

immangeable /ɛmãʒabl/ *a.* inedible.

immatricul|er /imatrikyle/ *v.t.* register. **(se) faire ~er,** register. **~ation** *n.f.* registration.

immature /imatyr/ *a.* immature.

immédiat, ~e /imedja, -t/ *a.* immediate. ● *n.m.* **dans l'~,** for the moment. **~ement** /-tmã/ *adv.* immediately.

immens|e /imãs/ *a.* immense. **~ément** *adv.* immensely. **~ité** *n.f.* immensity.

immer|ger /imɛrʒe/ *v.t.* immerse. **s'~ger** *v. pr.* submerge. **~sion** *n.f.* immersion.

immeuble /imœbl/ *n.m.* block of flats, building. **~ (de bureaux),** (office) building *ou* block.

immigr|er /imigre/ *v.i.* immigrate. **~ant, ~ante** *a. & n.m.,* f. immigrant. **~ation** *n.f.* immigration. **~é, ~ée** *a. & n.m.,* f. immigrant.

imminen|t, ~te /iminã, -t/ *a.* imminent. **~ce** *n.f.* imminence.

immiscer (s') /(s)imise/ *v. pr.* interfere (**dans,** in).

immobil|e /imɔbil/ *a.* still, motionless. **~ité** *n.f.* stillness; (*inaction*) immobility.

immobil|ier, ~ière /imɔbilje, -jɛr/ *a.* property. **agence ~ière,** estate agent's office; (*Amer.*) real estate office. **agent ~ier,** estate agent; (*Amer.*) real estate agent. **l'~ier,** property; (*Amer.*) real estate.

immobilis|er /imɔbilize/ *v.t.* immobilize; (*stopper*) stop. **s'~er** *v. pr.* stop. **~ation** *n.f.* immobilization.

immodéré /imɔdere/ *a.* immoderate.

immoler /imɔle/ *v.t.* sacrifice.

immonde /imõd/ *a.* filthy.

immondices /imõdis/ *n.f. pl.* refuse.

immor|al (*m. pl.* **~aux**) /imɔral, -o/ *a.* immoral. **~alité** *n.f.* immorality.

immortaliser /imɔrtalize/ *v.t.* immortalize.

immort|el, ~elle /imɔrtɛl/ *a.* immortal. **~alité** *n.f.* immortality.

immuable /imɥabl/ *a.* unchanging.

immunis|er /imynize/ *v.t.* immunize. **~é contre,** (*à l'abri de*) immune to.

immunité /imynite/ *n.f.* immunity.

impact /ɛpakt/ *n.m.* impact.

impair[1] /ɛpɛr/ *a.* (*numéro*) odd.

impair[2] /ɛpɛr/ *n.m.* blunder.

impardonnable /ɛpardɔnabl/ *a.* unforgivable.

imparfait, ~e /ɛparfɛ, -t/ *a. & n.m.* imperfect.

impart|ial (*m. pl.* ~iaux) /ɛparsjal, -jo/ *a.* impartial. ~ialité *n.f.* impartiality.

impasse /ɛpɑs/ *n.f.* (*rue*) dead end; (*situation*) deadlock.

impassible /ɛpasibl/ *a.* impassive.

impat|ient, ~iente /ɛpasjɑ̃, -t/ *a.* impatient. ~iemment /-jamɑ̃/ *adv.* impatiently. ~ience *n.f.* impatience.

impatienter /ɛpasjɑ̃te/ *v.t.* annoy. **s'**~ *v. pr.* lose patience (**contre,** with).

impayable /ɛpɛjabl/ *a.* (killingly) funny, hilarious.

impayé /ɛpeje/ *a.* unpaid.

impeccable /ɛpekabl/ *a.* impeccable.

impénétrable /ɛpenetrabl/ *a.* impenetrable.

impensable /ɛpɑ̃sabl/ *a.* unthinkable.

impérati|f, ~ve /ɛperatif, -v/ *a.* imperative. ● *n.m.* requirement; (*gram.*) imperative.

impératrice /ɛperatris/ *n.f.* empress.

imperceptible /ɛpɛrsɛptibl/ *a.* imperceptible.

imperfection /ɛpɛrfɛksjɔ̃/ *n.f.* imperfection.

impér|ial (*m. pl.* ~iaux) /ɛperjal, -jo/ *a.* imperial. ~ialisme *n.m.* imperialism.

impériale /ɛperjal/ *n.f.* upper deck.

impérieu|x, ~se /ɛperjø, -z/ *a.* imperious; (*pressant*) pressing.

impérissable /ɛperisabl/ *a.* undying.

imperméable /ɛpɛrmeabl/ *a.* impervious (**à,** to); (*manteau, tissu*) waterproof. ● *n.m.* raincoat.

impersonnel, ~le /ɛpɛrsɔnɛl/ *a.* impersonal.

impertinen|t, ~te /ɛpɛrtinɑ̃, -t/ *a.* impertinent. ~ce *n.f.* impertinence.

imperturbable /ɛpɛrtyrbabl/ *a.* unshakeable.

impét|ueux, ~ueuse /ɛpetɥø, -z/ *a.* impetuous. ~uosité *n.f.* impetuosity.

impitoyable /ɛpitwajabl/ *a.* merciless.

implacable /ɛplakabl/ *a.* implacable.

implant /ɛplɑ̃/ *n.m.* implant.

implant|er /ɛplɑ̃te/ *v.t.* establish. **s'**~er *v. pr.* become established. ~ation *n.f.* establishment.

implication /ɛplikasjɔ̃/ *n.f.* implication.

implicite /ɛplisit/ *a.* implicit.

impliquer /ɛplike/ *v.t.* imply (**que,** that). ~ **dans,** implicate in.

implorer /ɛplɔre/ *v.t.* implore.

impoli /ɛpɔli/ *a.* impolite. ~tesse *n.f.* impoliteness; (*remarque*) impolite remark.

impondérable /ɛpɔ̃derabl/ *a. & n.m.* imponderable.

impopulaire /ɛpɔpylɛr/ *a.* unpopular.

importance /ɛpɔrtɑ̃s/ *n.f.* importance; (*taille*) size; (*ampleur*) extent. **sans** ~, unimportant.

important, ~e /ɛpɔrtɑ̃, -t/ *a.* important; (*en quantité*) considerable, sizeable, big. ● *n.m.* l'~, the important thing.

import|er [1] /ɛpɔrte/ *v.t.* (*comm.*) import. ~ateur, ~atrice *n.m.. f.* importer. *a.* importing. ~ation *n.f.* import.

import|er [2] /ɛpɔrte/ *v.i.* matter, be important (**à,** to). **Il** ~e **que,** it is important that. **n'**~e, **peu** ~e, it does not matter. **n'**~e **comment,** anyhow. **n'**~e **où,** anywhere. **n'**~e **qui,** anybody. **n'**~e **quoi,** anything.

importun, ~e /ɛpɔrtœ̃, -yn/ *a.* troublesome. ● *n.m., f.* nuisance. ~er /-yne/ *v.t.* trouble.

imposant, ~e /ɛpozɑ̃, -t/ *a.* imposing.

imposer /ɛpoze/ *v.t.* impose (**à,** on); (*taxer*) tax. **s'**~ *v. pr.* (*action*) be essential; (*se faire reconnaître*) stand out. **en** ~ **à qn.,** impress s.o.

imposition /ɛpozisjɔ̃/ *n.f.* taxation. ~ **des mains,** laying-on of hands.

impossibilité /ɛposibilite/ *n.f.* impossibility. **dans l'**~ **de,** unable to.

impossible /ɛposibl/ *a. & n.m.* impossible. **faire l'**~, do the impossible.

impost|eur /ɛpostœr/ *n.m.* impostor. ~ure *n.f.* imposture.

impôt /ɛpo/ *n.m.* tax. ~s, (*contributions*) tax(ation), taxes. ~ **sur le revenu,** income tax.

impotent, ~e /ɛpotɑ̃, -t/ *a.* crippled. ● *n.m., f.* cripple.

impraticable /ɛpratikabl/ *a.* (*route*) impassable.

imprécis, ~e /ɛpresi, -z/ *a.* imprecise. ~ion /-zjɔ̃/ *n.f.* imprecision.

imprégner /ɛpreɲe/ *v.t.* fill (**de,** with); (*imbiber*) impregnate (**de,** with). **s'** ~ **de,** become filled with;

(*s'imbiber*) become impregnated with.

imprenable /ɛprənabl/ *a.* impregnable.

impresario /ɛpresarjo/ *n.m.* manager.

impression /ɛpresjɔ̃/ *n.f.* impression; (*de livre*) printing.

impressionn|er /ɛpresjone/ *v.t.* impress. **~able** *a.* impressionable. **~ant, ~ante** *a.* impressive.

imprévisible /ɛprevizibl/ *a.* unpredictable.

imprévoyant, ~e /ɛprevwajɑ̃, -t/ *a.* improvident.

imprévu /ɛprevy/ *a.* unexpected. ● *n.m.* unexpected incident.

imprim|er /ɛprime/ *v.t.* print; (*marquer*) imprint; (*transmettre*) impart. **~ante** *n.f.* (*d'un ordinateur*) printer. **~é** *a.* printed; *n.m.* (*formulaire*) printed form. **~erie** *n.f.* (*art*) printing; (*lieu*) printing works. **~eur** *n.m.* printer.

improbable /ɛprɔbabl/ *a.* unlikely, improbable.

impromptu /ɛprɔ̃pty/ *a.* & *adv.* impromptu.

impropr|e /ɛprɔpr/ *a.* incorrect. **~e à**, unfit for. **~iété,** *n.f.* incorrectness; (*erreur*) error.

improvis|er /ɛprɔvize/ *v.t./i.* improvise. **~ation** *n.f.* improvisation.

improviste (à l') /(al)ɛprɔvist/ *adv.* unexpectedly.

imprud|ent, ~ente /ɛprydɑ̃, -t/ *a.* careless. **il est ~ent de**, it is unwise to. **~emment** /-amɑ̃/ *adv.* carelessly. **~ence** *n.f.* carelessness; (*acte*) careless action.

impuden|t, ~te /ɛpydɑ̃, -t/ *a.* impudent. **~ce** *n.f.* impudence.

impudique /ɛpydik/ *a.* immodest.

impuissan|t, ~te /ɛpɥisɑ̃, -t/ *a.* helpless; (*méd.*) impotent. **~t à**, powerless to. **~ce** *n.f.* helplessness; (*méd.*) impotence.

impulsi|f, ~ve /ɛpylsif, -v/ *a.* impulsive.

impulsion /ɛpylsjɔ̃/ *n.f.* (*poussée, influence*) impetus; (*instinct, mouvement*) impulse.

impunément /ɛpynemɑ̃/ *adv.* with impunity.

impuni /ɛpyni/ *a.* unpunished.

impunité /ɛpynite/ *n.f.* impunity.

impur /ɛpyr/ *a.* impure. **~eté** *n.f.* impurity.

imput|er /ɛpyte/ *v.t.* **~er à**, impute to. **~able** *a.* ascribable (**à**, to).

inabordable /inabɔrdabl/ *a.* (*prix*) prohibitive.

inacceptable /inaksɛptabl/ *a.* unacceptable; (*scandaleux*) outrageous.

inaccessible /inaksesibl/ *a.* inaccessible.

inaccoutumé /inakutyme/ *a.* unaccustomed.

inachevé /inaʃve/ *a.* unfinished.

inacti|f, ~ve /inaktif, -v/ *a.* inactive.

inaction /inaksjɔ̃/ *n.f.* inactivity.

inadapté, ~e /inadapte/ *n.m.*, *f.* (*psych.*) maladjusted person.

inadéquat, ~e /inadekwa, -t/ *a.* inadequate.

inadmissible /inadmisibl/ *a.* unacceptable.

inadvertance /inadvɛrtɑ̃s/ *n.f.* **par ~**, by mistake.

inaltérable /inalterabl/ *a.* stable, that does not deteriorate; (*sentiment*) unfailing.

inanimé /inanime/ *a.* (*évanoui*) unconscious; (*mort*) lifeless; (*matière*) inanimate.

inaperçu /inapɛrsy/ *a.* unnoticed.

inappréciable /inapresjabl/ *a.* invaluable.

inapte /inapt/ *a.* unsuited (**à**, to). **~ à faire**, incapable of doing.

inarticulé /inartikyle/ *a.* inarticulate.

inassouvi /inasuvi/ *a.* unsatisfied.

inattendu /inatɑ̃dy/ *a.* unexpected.

inattenti|f, ~ve /inatɑ̃tif, -v/ *a.* inattentive (**à**, to).

inattention /inatɑ̃sjɔ̃/ *n.f.* inattention.

inaugur|er /inɔgyre/ *v.t.* inaugurate. **~ation** *n.f.* inauguration.

inaugur|al (*m. pl.* **~aux**) /inɔgyral, -o/ *a.* inaugural.

incalculable /ɛkalkylabl/ *a.* incalculable.

incapable /ɛkapabl/ *a.* incapable (**de qch.**, of sth.). **~ de faire**, unable to do, incapable of doing. ● *n.m./f.* incompetent.

incapacité /ɛkapasite/ *n.f.* incapacity. **dans l' ~ de**, unable to.

incarcérer /ɛkarsere/ *v.t.* incarcerate.

incarn|er /ɛkarne/ *v.t.* embody. **~ation** *n.f.* embodiment, incarnation. **~é a.** (*ongle*) ingrowing.

incartade /ɛ̃kartad/ n.f. indiscretion, misdeed, prank.

incassable /ɛ̃kɑsabl/ a. unbreakable.

incendiaire /ɛ̃sɑ̃djɛr/ a. incendiary, (*propos*) inflammatory. ● n.m./f. arsonist.

incend|ie /ɛ̃sɑ̃di/ n.m. fire. ~**ie criminel**, arson. ~**ier** v.t. set fire to.

incert|ain, ~**aine** /ɛ̃sɛrtɛ̃, -ɛn/ a. uncertain; (*contour*) vague. ~**itude** n.f. uncertainty.

incessamment /ɛ̃sɛsamɑ̃/ adv. shortly.

incessant, ~**e** /ɛ̃sɛsɑ̃, -t/ a. incessant.

incest|e /ɛ̃sɛst/ n.m. incest. ~**ueux,** ~**ueuse** a. incestuous.

inchangé /ɛ̃ʃɑ̃ʒe/ a. unchanged.

incidence /ɛ̃sidɑ̃s/ n.f. effect.

incident /ɛ̃sidɑ̃/ n.m. incident. ~ **technique,** technical hitch.

incinér|er /ɛ̃sinere/ v.t. incinerate; (*mort*) cremate. ~**ateur** n.m. incinerator.

incis|er /ɛ̃size/ v.t. (*abcès etc.*) lance. ~**ion** n.f. lancing; (*entaille*) incision.

incisi|f, ~**ve** /ɛ̃sizif, -v/ a. incisive.

incit|er /ɛ̃site/ v.t. incite (**à,** to). ~**ation** n.f. incitement.

inclinaison /ɛ̃klinɛzõ/ n.f. incline; (*de la tête*) tilt.

inclination¹ /ɛ̃klinasjõ/ n.f. (*penchant*) inclination.

inclin|er /ɛ̃kline/ v.t. tilt, lean; (*courber*) bend; (*inciter*) encourage (**à,** to). ● v.i. ~**er à,** be inclined to. **s'~er** v. pr. (*se courber*) bow down; (*céder*) give in; (*chemin*) slope. ~**er la tête,** (*approuver*) nod; (*révérence*) bow. ~**ation²** n.f. (*de la tête*) nod; (*du buste*) bow.

incl|ure /ɛ̃klyr/ v.t. include; (*enfermer*) enclose. **jusqu'au lundi** ~**us,** up to and including Monday. ~**usion** n.f. inclusion.

incognito /ɛ̃kɔɲito/ adv. incognito.

incohéren|t, ~**te** /ɛ̃kɔerɑ̃, -t/ a. incoherent. ~**ce** n.f. incoherence.

incollable /ɛ̃kɔlabl/ a. **il est** ~, he can't be stumped.

incolore /ɛ̃kɔlɔr/ a. colourless; (*crème, verre*) clear.

incomber /ɛ̃kõbe/ v.i. **il vous/etc. incombe de,** it is your/etc. responsibility to.

incombustible /ɛ̃kõbystibl/ a. incombustible.

incommode /ɛ̃kɔmɔd/ a. awkward.

incommoder /ɛ̃kɔmɔde/ v.t. inconvenience.

incomparable /ɛ̃kõparabl/ a. incomparable.

incompatib|le /ɛ̃kõpatibl/ a. incompatible. ~**ilité** n.f. incompatibility.

incompéten|t, ~**te** /ɛ̃kõpetɑ̃, -t/ a. incompetent. ~**ce** n.f. incompetence.

incompl|et, ~**ète** /ɛ̃kõplɛ, -t/ a. incomplete.

incompréhensible /ɛ̃kõpreɑ̃sibl/ a. incomprehensible.

incompréhension /ɛ̃kõpreɑ̃sjõ/ n.f. lack of understanding.

incompris, ~**e** /ɛ̃kõpri, -z/ a. misunderstood.

inconcevable /ɛ̃kõsvabl/ a. inconceivable.

inconciliable /ɛ̃kõsiljabl/ a. irreconcilable.

inconditionnel, ~**le** /ɛ̃kõdisjɔnɛl/ a. unconditional.

inconduite /ɛ̃kõdɥit/ n.f. loose behaviour.

inconfort /ɛ̃kõfɔr/ n.m. discomfort. ~**able** /-tabl/ a. uncomfortable.

incongru /ɛ̃kõgry/ a. unseemly.

inconnu, ~**e** /ɛ̃kɔny/ a. unknown (**à,** to). ● n.m., f. stranger. ● n.m. **l'**~, the unknown. ● n.f. unknown (quantity).

inconsc|ient, ~**iente** /ɛ̃kõsjɑ̃, -t/ a. unconscious (**de,** of); (*fou*) mad. ● n.m. (psych.) subconscious. ~**iemment** /-jamɑ̃/ adv. unconsciously. ~**ience** n.f. unconsciousness; (*folie*) madness.

inconsidéré /ɛ̃kõsidere/ a. thoughtless.

inconsistant, ~**e** /ɛ̃kõsistɑ̃, -t/ a. (*fig.*) flimsy.

inconsolable /ɛ̃kõsɔlabl/ a. inconsolable.

inconstan|t, ~**te** /ɛ̃kõstɑ̃, -t/ a. fickle. ~**ce** n.f. fickleness.

incontest|able /ɛ̃kõtɛstabl/ a. indisputable. ~**é** a. undisputed.

incontinen|t, ~**te** /ɛ̃kõtinɑ̃, -t/ a. incontinent. ~**ce** n.f. incontinence.

incontrôlable /ɛ̃kõtrolabl/ a. unverifiable.

inconvenan|t, ~**te** /ɛ̃kõvnɑ̃, t/ a. improper. ~**ce** n.f. impropriety.

inconvénient /ɛ̃kõvenjɑ̃/ n.m. disadvantage; (*risque*) risk; (*objection*) objection.

incorpor|er /ɛkɔrpɔre/ *v.t.* incorporate; (*mil.*) enlist. **~ation** *n.f.* incorporation; (*mil.*) enlistment.

incorrect /ɛkɔrɛkt/ *a.* (*faux*) incorrect; (*malséant*) improper; (*impoli*) impolite.

incorrigible /ɛkɔriʒibl/ *a.* incorrigible.

incrédul|e /ɛkredyl/ *a.* incredulous. **~ité** *n.f.* incredulity.

increvable /ɛkrəvabl/ *a.* (*fam.*) tireless.

incriminer /ɛkrimine/ *v.t.* incriminate.

incroyable /ɛkrwajabl/ *a.* incredible.

incroyant, ~e /ɛkrwajɑ̃, -t/ *n.m., f.* non-believer.

incrust|er /ɛkryste/ *v.t.* (*décorer*) inlay (**de,** with). **s'~er** (*invité: péj.*) take root. **~ation** *n.f.* inlay.

incubateur /ɛkybatœr/ *n.m.* incubator.

inculp|er /ɛkylpe/ *v.t.* charge (**de,** with). **~ation** *n.f.* charge. **~é, ~ée** *n.m., f.* accused.

inculquer /ɛkylke/ *v.t.* instil (**à,** into).

inculte /ɛkylt/ *a.* uncultivated; (*personne*) uneducated.

incurable /ɛkyrabl/ *a.* incurable.

incursion /ɛkyrsjɔ̃/ *n.f.* incursion.

incurver /ɛkyrve/ *v.t.,* **s'~** *v. pr.* curve.

Inde /ɛ̃d/ *n.f.* India.

indécen|t, ~te /ɛ̃desɑ̃, -t/ *a.* indecent. **~ce** *n.f.* indecency.

indéchiffrable /ɛ̃deʃifrabl/ *a.* indecipherable.

indécis, ~e /ɛ̃desi, -z/ *a.* indecisive; (*qui n'a pas encore pris de décision*) undecided. **~ion** /-izjɔ̃/ *n.f.* indecision.

indéfendable /ɛ̃defɑ̃dabl/ *a.* indefensible.

indéfini /ɛ̃defini/ *a.* indefinite; (*vague*) undefined. **~ment** *adv.* indefinitely. **~ssable** *a.* indefinable.

indélébile /ɛ̃delebil/ *a.* indelible.

indélicat, ~e /ɛ̃delika, -t/ *a.* (*malhonnête*) unscrupulous.

indemne /ɛ̃dɛmn/ *a.* unharmed.

indemniser /ɛ̃dɛmnize/ *v.t.* compensate (**de,** for).

indemnité /ɛ̃dɛmnite/ *n.f.* indemnity; (*allocation*) allowance. **~s de licenciement,** redundancy payment.

indéniable /ɛ̃denjabl/ *a.* undeniable.

indépend|ant, ~ante /ɛ̃depɑ̃dɑ̃, -t/ *a.* independent. **~amment** *adv.*

independently. **~amment de,** apart from. **~ance** *n.f.* independence.

indescriptible /ɛ̃dɛskriptibl/ *a.* indescribable.

indésirable /ɛ̃dezirabl/ *a. & n.m./f.* undesirable.

indestructible /ɛ̃dɛstryktibl/ *a.* indestructible.

indétermination /ɛ̃detɛrminasjɔ̃/ *n.f.* indecision.

indéterminé /ɛ̃detɛrmine/ *a.* unspecified.

index /ɛ̃dɛks/ *n.m.* forefinger; (*liste*) index. **~er** *v.t.* index.

indic /ɛ̃dik/ (*fam.*) grass.

indica|teur, ~trice /ɛ̃dikatœr, -tris/ *n.m., f.* (police) informer. ● *n.m.* (*livre*) guide; (*techn.*) indicator. **~teur des chemins de fer,** railway timetable. **~teur des rues,** street directory.

indicati|f, ~ve /ɛ̃dikatif, -v/ *a.* indicative (**de,** of). ● *n.m.* (*radio*) signature tune; (*téléphonique*) dialling code; (*gram.*) indicative.

indication /ɛ̃dikasjɔ̃/ *n.f.* indication; (*renseignement*) information; (*directive*) instruction.

indice /ɛ̃dis/ *n.m.* sign; (*dans une enquête*) clue; (*des prix*) index; (*de salaire*) rating.

indien, ~ne /ɛ̃djɛ̃, -jɛn/ *a. & n.m., f.* Indian.

indifféremment /ɛ̃diferamɑ̃/ *adv.* equally.

indifféren|t, ~te /ɛ̃diferɑ̃, -t/ *a.* indifferent (**à,** to). **ça m'est ~t,** it makes no difference to me. **~ce** *n.f.* indifference.

indigène /ɛ̃diʒɛn/ *a. & n.m./f.* native.

indigen|t, ~te /ɛ̃diʒɑ̃, -t/ *a.* poor **~ce** *n.f.* poverty.

indigest|e /ɛ̃diʒɛst/ *a.* indigestible. **~ion** *n.f.* indigestion.

indignation /ɛ̃diɲasjɔ̃/ *n.f.* indignation.

indign|e /ɛ̃diɲ/ *a.* unworthy (**de,** of); (*acte*) vile. **~ité** *n.f.* unworthiness; (*acte*) vile act.

indigner /ɛ̃diɲe/ **s'~** *v. pr.* become indignant (**de,** at).

indiqu|er /ɛ̃dike/ *v.t.* show, indicate; (*renseigner sur*) point out, tell; (*déterminer*) give, state, appoint. **~er du doigt,** point to *ou* out *ou* at. **~é** *a.* (*heure*) appointed; (*opportun*) appropriate; (*conseillé*) recommended.

indirect /ɛ̃dirɛkt/ *a.* indirect.

indiscipliné /ɛ̃disipline/ *a.* unruly.

indiscr|et, **~ète** /ɛ̃diskrɛ, -t/ a. inquisitive. **~étion** n.f. indiscretion; inquisitiveness.

indiscutable /ɛ̃diskytabl/ a. unquestionable.

indispensable /ɛ̃dispɑ̃sabl/ a. indispensable. **il est ~ qu'il vienne**, it is essential that he comes.

indispos|er /ɛ̃dispoze/ v.t. make unwell. **~er** (*mécontenter*) antagonize. **~é** a. unwell. **~ition** n.f. indisposition.

indistinct, **~e** /ɛ̃distɛ̃(kt), -ɛkt/ a. indistinct. **~ement** /-ɛktəmɑ̃/ adv. indistinctly; (*également*) without distinction.

individ|u /ɛ̃dividy/ n.m. individual. **~ualiste** n.m./f. individualist.

individuel, **~le** /ɛ̃dividɥɛl/ a. individual; (*opinion*) personal. **chambre ~le**, single room. **maison ~le**, private house. **~lement** adv. individually.

indivisible /ɛ̃divizibl/ a. indivisible.

indolen|t, **~te** /ɛ̃dɔlɑ̃, -t/ a. indolent. **~ce** n.f. indolence.

indolore /ɛ̃dɔlɔr/ a. painless.

Indonésie /ɛ̃dɔnezi/ n.f. Indonesia.

Indonésien, **~ne** /ɛ̃dɔnezjɛ̃, -jɛn/ a. & n.m., f. Indonesian.

indu, **~e** /ɛ̃dy/ a. **à une heure ~e**, at some ungodly hour.

induire /ɛ̃dɥir/ v.t. infer (**de**, from). **~ en erreur**, mislead.

indulgen|t, **~te** /ɛ̃dylʒɑ̃, -t/ a. indulgent; (*clément*) lenient. **~ce** n.f. indulgence; leniency.

industr|ie /ɛ̃dystri/ n.f. industry. **~ialisé** a. industrialized.

industriel, **~le** /ɛ̃dystrijɛl/ a. industrial. ● n.m. industrialist. **~lement** adv. industrially.

inébranlable /inebrɑ̃labl/ a. unshakeable.

inédit, **~e** /inedi, -t/ a. unpublished; (*fig.*) original.

inefficace /inefikas/ a. ineffective.

inég|al (*m. pl.* **~aux**) /inegal, -o/ a. unequal; (*irrégulier*) uneven. **~alé** a. unequalled. **~alable** a. matchless. **~alité** n.f. (*injustice*) inequality; (*irrégularité*) unevenness; (*différence*) difference (**de**, between).

inéluctable /inelyktabl/ a. inescapable.

inept|e /inɛpt/ a. inept, absurd. **~ie** /inɛpsi/ n.f. ineptitude.

inépuisable /inepɥizabl/ a. inexhaustible.

inert|e /inɛrt/ a. inert; (*mort*) lifeless. **~ie** /inɛrsi/ n.f. inertia.

inespéré /inɛspere/ a. unhoped for.

inestimable /inɛstimabl/ a. priceless.

inévitable /inevitabl/ a. inevitable.

inexact, **~e** /inɛgza(kt), -akt/ a. (*imprécis*) inaccurate; (*incorrect*) incorrect.

inexcusable /inɛkskyzabl/ a. unforgivable.

inexistant, **~e** /inɛgzistɑ̃, -t/ a. nonexistent.

inexorable /inɛgzɔrabl/ a. inexorable.

inexpérience /inɛksperjɑ̃s/ n.f. inexperience.

inexpli|cable /inɛksplikabl/ a. inexplicable. **~qué** a. unexplained.

in extremis /inɛkstremis/ adv. & a. (*par nécessité*) (taken/done etc.) as a last resort; (*au dernier moment*) (at the) last minute.

inextricable /inɛkstrikabl/ a. inextricable.

infaillible /ɛ̃fajibl/ a. infallible.

infâme /ɛ̃fɑm/ a. vile.

infamie /ɛ̃fami/ n.f. infamy; (*action*) vile action.

infanterie /ɛ̃fɑ̃tri/ n.f. infantry.

infantile /ɛ̃fɑ̃til/ a. infantile.

infantilisme /ɛ̃fɑ̃tilism/ n.m. infantilism. **faire de l'~**, be childish.

infarctus /ɛ̃farktys/ n.m. coronary (thrombosis).

infatigable /ɛ̃fatigabl/ a. tireless.

infatué /ɛ̃fatɥe/ a. **~ de sa personne**, full of himself.

infect /ɛ̃fɛkt/ a. revolting.

infect|er /ɛ̃fɛkte/ v.t. infect. **s'~er** v. pr. become infected. **~ion** /-ksjɔ̃/ n.f. infection.

infectieu|x, **~se** /ɛ̃fɛksjø, -z/ a. infectious.

inférieur, **~e** /ɛ̃ferjœr/ a. (*plus bas*) lower; (*moins bon*) inferior (**à**, to). ● n.m., f. inferior. **~ à**, (*plus petit que*) smaller than.

infériorité /ɛ̃ferjorite/ n.f. inferiority.

infern|al (*m. pl.* **~aux**) /ɛ̃fɛrnal, -o/ a. infernal.

infester /ɛ̃fɛste/ v.t. infest.

infid|èle /ɛ̃fidɛl/ a. unfaithful. **~élité** n.f. unfaithfulness; (*acte*) infidelity.

infiltr|er (**s'**) /(s)ɛ̃filtre/ v. pr. **s'~er (dans)**, (*personnes, idées, etc.*) infiltrate; (*liquide*) percolate. **~ation** *n.f.* infiltration.

infime /ɛ̃fim/ *a.* tiny, minute.

infini /ɛ̃fini/ *a.* infinite. ● *n.m.* infinity. **à l'~**, endlessly. **~ment** *adv.* infinitely.

infinité /ɛ̃finite/ *n.f.* **une ~ de**, an infinite amount of.

infinitésimal /ɛ̃finitezimal/ *a.* infinitesimal.

infinitif /ɛ̃finitif/ *n.m.* infinitive.

infirm|e /ɛ̃firm/ *a. & n.m./f.* disabled (person). **~ité** *n.f.* disability.

infirmer /ɛ̃firme/ *v.t.* invalidate.

infirm|erie /ɛ̃firmǝri/ *n.f.* sickbay, infirmary. **~ier** *n.m.* (male) nurse. **~ière** *n.f.* nurse. **~ière-chef**, sister.

inflammable /ɛ̃flamabl/ *a.* (in)flammable.

inflammation /ɛ̃flamɑsjɔ̃/ *n.f.* inflammation.

inflation /ɛ̃flɑsjɔ̃/ *n.f.* inflation.

inflexible /ɛ̃flɛksibl/ *a.* inflexible.

inflexion /ɛ̃flɛksjɔ̃/ *n.f.* inflexion.

infliger /ɛ̃fliʒe/ *v.t.* inflict; (*sanction*) impose.

influen|ce /ɛ̃flyɑ̃s/ *n.f.* influence. **~çable** *a.* easily influenced. **~cer** *v.t.* influence.

influent, ~e /ɛ̃flyɑ̃, -t/ *a.* influential.

influer /ɛ̃flye/ *v.i.* **~ sur**, influence.

info /ɛ̃fo/ *n.f.* (some) news. **les ~s**, the news.

informa|teur, ~trice /ɛ̃fɔrmatœr, -tris/ *n.m., f.* informant.

informaticien, ~ne /ɛ̃fɔrmatisjɛ̃, -jɛn/ *n.m., f.* computer scientist.

information /ɛ̃fɔrmɑsjɔ̃/ *n.f.* information; (*jurid.*) inquiry. **une ~**, (some) information; (*nouvelle*) (some) news. **les ~s**, the news.

informati|que /ɛ̃fɔrmatik/ *n.f.* computer science; (*techniques*) data processing. **~ser** *v.t.* computerize.

informe /ɛ̃fɔrm/ *a.* shapeless.

informer /ɛ̃fɔrme/ *v.t.* inform (de, about, of). **s'~** *v. pr.* enquire (de, about).

infortune /ɛ̃fɔrtyn/ *n.f.* misfortune.

infraction /ɛ̃fraksjɔ̃/ *n.f.* offence. **~ à**, breach of.

infranchissable /ɛ̃frɑ̃ʃisabl/ *a.* impassable; (*fig.*) insuperable.

infrarouge /ɛ̃fraruʒ/ *a.* infra-red.

infrastructure /ɛ̃frastryktyr/ *n.f.* infrastructure.

infructueu|x, ~se /ɛ̃fryktɥø, -z/ *a.* fruitless.

infus|er /ɛ̃fyze/ *v.t./i.* infuse, brew. **~ion** *n.f.* herb-tea, infusion.

ingénier (s') /(s)ɛ̃ʒenje/ *v. pr.* **s'~ à**, strive to.

ingénieur /ɛ̃ʒenjœr/ *n.m.* engineer.

ingén|ieux, ~ieuse /ɛ̃ʒenjø, -z/ *a.* ingenious. **~iosité** *n.f.* ingenuity.

ingénu /ɛ̃ʒeny/ *a.* naïve.

ingér|er (s') /(s)ɛ̃ʒere/ *v. pr.* **s'~er dans**, interfere in. **~ence** *n.f.* interference.

ingrat, ~e /ɛ̃gra, -t/ *a.* ungrateful; (*pénible*) thankless; (*disgracieux*) unattractive. **~itude** /-tityd/ *n.f.* ingratitude.

ingrédient /ɛ̃gredjɑ̃/ *n.m.* ingredient.

ingurgiter /ɛ̃gyrʒite/ *v.t.* swallow.

inhabité /inabite/ *a.* uninhabited.

inhabituel, ~le /inabitɥɛl/ *a.* unusual.

inhalation /inalɑsjɔ̃/ *n.f.* inhaling.

inhérent, ~e /inerɑ̃, -t/ *a.* inherent (à, in).

inhibition /inibisjɔ̃/ *n.f.* inhibition.

inhospital|ier, ~ière /inɔspitalje, -jɛr/ *a.* inhospitable.

inhumain, ~e /inymɛ̃, -ɛn/ *a.* inhuman.

inhum|er /inyme/ *v.t.* bury. **~ation** *n.f.* burial.

inimaginable /inimaʒinabl/ *a.* unimaginable.

inimitié /inimitje/ *n.f.* enmity.

ininterrompu /inɛ̃tɛrɔ̃py/ *a.* continuous, uninterrupted.

iniqu|e /inik/ *a.* iniquitous. **~ité** *n.f.* iniquity.

init|ial (m. pl. ~iaux) /inisjal, -jo/ *a.* initial. **~ialement** *adv.* initially.

initiale /inisjal/ *n.f.* initial.

initialis|er /inisjalize/ (*comput.*) format. **~ation** *n.f.* formatting.

initiative /inisjativ/ *n.f.* initiative.

init|ier /inisje/ *v.t.* initiate (à, into). **s'~ier** *v. pr.* become initiated (à, into). **~iateur, ~iatrice** *n.m., f.* initiator. **~iation** *n.f.* initiation.

inject|er /ɛ̃ʒɛkte/ *v.t.* inject. **~é de sang**, bloodshot. **~ion** /-ksjɔ̃/ *n.f.* injection.

injur|e /ɛ̃ʒyr/ *n.f.* insult. **~ier** *v.t.* insult. **~ieux, ~ieuse** *a.* insulting.

injust|e /ɛ̃ʒyst/ *a.* unjust, unfair. **~ice** *n.f.* injustice.

inlassable /ɛ̃lɑsabl/ *a.* tireless.

inné /ine/ *a.* innate, inborn.

innocen|t, ~te /inɔsɑ̃, -t/ *a. & n.m., f.* innocent. **~ce** *n.f.* innocence.

innocenter /inɔsɑ̃te/ v.t. (disculper) clear, prove innocent.

innombrable /inɔ̃brabl/ a. countless.

innov|er /inɔve/ v.i. innovate. **~ateur, ~atrice** n.m., f. innovator. **~ation** n.f. innovation.

inoccupé /inɔkype/ a. unoccupied.

inoculer /inɔkyle/ v.t. inoculate.

inodore /inɔdɔr/ a. odourless.

inoffensi|f, ~ve /inɔfɑ̃sif, -v/ a. harmless.

inond|er /inɔ̃de/ v.t. flood; (mouiller) soak; (envahir) inundate (de, with). **~é de soleil**, bathed in sunlight. **~ation** n.f. flood; (action) flooding.

inopérant, ~e /inɔperɑ̃, -t/ a. inoperative.

inopiné /inɔpine/ a. unexpected.

inopportun, ~e /inɔpɔrtœ̃, -yn/ a. inopportune.

inoubliable /inublijabl/ a. unforgettable.

inouï /inwi/ a. incredible.

inox /inɔks/ n.m. (P.) stainless steel.

inoxydable /inɔksidabl/ a. **acier ~**, stainless steel.

inqualifiable /ɛ̃kalifjabl/ a. unspeakable.

inqu|iet, ~iète /ɛ̃kjɛ, -jɛt/ a. worried. ● n.m., f. worrier.

inquiét|er /ɛ̃kjete/ v.t. worry. **s'~er** worry (de, about). **~ant, ~ante** a. worrying.

inquiétude /ɛ̃kjetyd/ n.f. anxiety, worry.

inquisition /ɛ̃kizisjɔ̃/ n.f. inquisition.

insaisissable /ɛ̃sezizabl/ a. indefinable.

insalubre /ɛ̃salybr/ a. unhealthy.

insanité /ɛ̃sanite/ n.f. insanity.

insatiable /ɛ̃sasjabl/ a. insatiable.

insatisfaisant, ~e /ɛ̃satisfəzɑ̃, -t/ a. unsatisfactory.

insatisfait, ~e /ɛ̃satisfɛ, -t/ a. (mécontent) dissatisfied; (frustré) unfulfilled.

inscription /ɛ̃skripsjɔ̃/ n.f. inscription; (immatriculation) enrolment.

inscrire† /ɛ̃skrir/ v.t. write (down); (graver, tracer) inscribe; (personne) enrol; (sur une liste) put down. **s'~** v. pr. put one's name down. **s'~ à**, (école) enrol at; (club, parti) join; (examen) enter for. **s'~ dans le cadre de**, come within the framework of.

insecte /ɛ̃sɛkt/ n.m. insect.

insecticide /ɛ̃sɛktisid/ n.m. insecticide.

insécurité /ɛ̃sekyrite/ n.f. insecurity.

insensé /ɛ̃sɑ̃se/ a. mad.

insensib|le /ɛ̃sɑ̃sibl/ a. insensitive (à, to); (graduel) imperceptible. **~ilité** n.f. insensitivity.

inséparable /ɛ̃separabl/ a. inseparable.

insérer /ɛ̃sere/ v.t. insert. **s'~ dans**, be part of.

insidieu|x, ~se /ɛ̃sidjø, -z/ a. insidious.

insigne /ɛ̃siɲ/ n.m. badge. **~(s)**, (d'une fonction) insignia.

insignifian|t, ~te /ɛ̃siɲifjɑ̃, -t/ a. insignificant. **~ce** n.f. insignificance.

insinuation /ɛ̃sinɥasjɔ̃/ n.f. insinuation.

insinuer /ɛ̃sinɥe/ v.t. insinuate. **s'~ dans**, penetrate.

insipide /ɛ̃sipid/ a. insipid.

insistan|t, ~te /ɛ̃sistɑ̃, -t/ a. insistent. **~ce** n.f. insistence.

insister /ɛ̃siste/ v.i. insist (pour faire, on doing). **~ sur**, stress.

insolation /ɛ̃sɔlasjɔ̃/ n.f. (méd.) sunstroke.

insolen|t, ~te /ɛ̃sɔlɑ̃, -t/ a. insolent. **~ce** n.f. insolence.

insolite /ɛ̃sɔlit/ a. unusual.

insoluble /ɛ̃sɔlybl/ a. insoluble.

insolvable /ɛ̃sɔlvabl/ a. insolvent.

insomnie /ɛ̃sɔmni/ n.f. insomnia.

insonoriser /ɛ̃sɔnɔrize/ v.t. soundproof.

insoucian|t, ~te /ɛ̃susjɑ̃, -t/ a. carefree. **~ce** n.f. unconcern.

insoumission /ɛ̃sumisjɔ̃/ n.f. rebelliousness.

insoupçonnable /ɛ̃supsɔnabl/ a. undetectable.

insoutenable /ɛ̃sutnabl/ a. unbearable; (argument) untenable.

inspec|ter /ɛ̃spɛkte/ v.t. inspect. **~teur, ~trice** n.m., f. inspector. **~tion** /-ksjɔ̃/ n.f. inspection.

inspir|er /ɛ̃spire/ v.t. inspire. ● v.i. breathe in. **~er à qn.**, inspire s.o. with. **s'~er de**, be inspired by. **~ation** n.f. inspiration; (respiration) breath.

instab|le /ɛ̃stabl/ a. unstable; (temps) unsettled; (meuble, equilibre) unsteady. **~ilité** n.f. instability; unsteadiness.

install|er /ɛ̃stale/ v.t. install; (gaz, meuble) put in; (étagère) put up;

(*équiper*) fit out. **s'~er** *v. pr.* settle (down); (*emménager*) settle in. **s'~er comme**, set o.s. up as. **~ation** *n.f.* installation; (*de local*) fitting out; (*de locataire*) settling in. **~ations** *n.f. pl.* (*appareils*) fittings.

instance /ɛ̃stɑ̃s/ *n.f.* authority; (*prière*) entreaty. **avec ~**, with insistence. **en ~**, pending. **en ~ de**, in the course of, on the point of.

instant /ɛ̃stɑ̃/ *n.m.* moment, instant. **à l'~**, this instant.

instantané /ɛ̃stɑ̃tane/ *a.* instantaneous; (*café*) instant.

instar /ɛ̃star/ *n.m.* **à l'~ de**, like.

instaur|er /ɛ̃stɔre/ *v.t.* institute. **~ation** *n.f.* institution.

instiga|teur, ~trice /ɛ̃stigatœr, -tris/ *n.m., f.* instigator. **~tion** /-asjɔ̃/ *n.f.* instigation.

instinct /ɛ̃stɛ̃/ *n.m.* instinct. **d'~**, instinctively.

instincti|f, ~ve /ɛ̃stɛ̃ktif, -v/ *a.* instinctive. **~vement** *adv.* instinctively.

instit /ɛ̃stit/ *n.m./f.* (*fam.*) teacher.

instituer /ɛ̃stitɥe/ *v.t.* establish.

institut /ɛ̃stity/ *n.m.* institute. **~ de beauté**, beauty parlour. **~ universitaire de technologie**, polytechnic, technical college.

institu|teur, ~trice /ɛ̃stitytœr, -tris/ *n.m., f.* primary-school teacher.

institution /ɛ̃stitysjɔ̃/ *n.f.* institution; (*école*) private school.

instructi|f, ~ve /ɛ̃stryktif, -v/ *a.* instructive.

instruction /ɛ̃stryksjɔ̃/ *n.f.* education; (*document*) directive. **~s**, (*ordres, mode d'emploi*) instructions.

instruire† /ɛ̃strɥir/ *v.t.* teach, educate. **~ de**, inform of. **s'~** *v. pr.* educate o.s. **s'~ de**, enquire about.

instruit, ~e /ɛ̃strɥi, -t/ *a.* educated.

instrument /ɛ̃strymɑ̃/ *n.m.* instrument; (*outil*) implement.

insu /ɛ̃sy/ *n.m.* **à l'~ de**, without the knowledge of.

insubordination /ɛ̃sybɔrdinasjɔ̃/ *n.f.* insubordination.

insuffisan|t, ~te /ɛ̃syfizɑ̃, -t/ *a.* inadequate; (*en nombre*) insufficient. **~ce** *n.f.* inadequacy.

insulaire /ɛ̃sylɛr/ *a.* island. ● *n.m./f.* islander.

insuline /ɛ̃sylin/ *n.f.* insulin.

insult|e /ɛ̃sylt/ *n.f.* insult. **~er** *v.t.* insult.

insupportable /ɛ̃sypɔrtabl/ *a.* unbearable.

insurg|er (s') /(s)ɛ̃syrʒe/ *v. pr.* rebel. **~é, ~ée** *a. & n.m., f.* rebel.

insurmontable /ɛ̃syrmɔ̃tabl/ *a.* insurmountable.

insurrection /ɛ̃syrɛksjɔ̃/ *n.f.* insurrection.

intact /ɛ̃takt/ *a.* intact.

intangible /ɛ̃tɑ̃ʒibl/ *a.* intangible.

intarissable /ɛ̃tarisabl/ *a.* inexhaustible.

intégr|al (*m. pl.* **~aux**) /ɛ̃tegral, -o/ *a.* complete; (*édition*) unabridged. **~alement** *adv.* in full. **~alité** *n.f.* whole. **dans son ~alité**, in full.

intégrant, ~e /ɛ̃tegrɑ̃, -t/ *a.* **faire partie ~e de**, be part and parcel of.

intègre /ɛ̃tegr/ *a.* upright.

intégr|er /ɛ̃tegre/ *v.t.*, **s'~er** *v. pr.* integrate. **~ation** *n.f.* integration.

intégri|ste /ɛ̃tegrist/ *a.* fundamentalist. **~sme** /-sm/ *n.m.* fundamentalism.

intégrité /ɛ̃tegrite/ *n.f.* integrity.

intellect /ɛ̃telɛkt/ *n.m.* intellect. **~uel, ~uelle** *a. & n.m., f.* intellectual.

intelligence /ɛ̃teliʒɑ̃s/ *n.f.* intelligence; (*compréhension*) understanding; (*complicité*) complicity.

intellig|ent, ~ente /ɛ̃teliʒɑ̃, -t/ *a.* intelligent. **~emment** /-amɑ̃/ *adv.* intelligently.

intelligible /ɛ̃teliʒibl/ *a.* intelligible.

intempéries /ɛ̃tɑ̃peri/ *n.f. pl.* severe weather.

intempesti|f, ~ve /ɛ̃tɑ̃pɛstif, -v/ *a.* untimely.

intenable /ɛ̃tnabl/ *a.* unbearable; (*enfant*) impossible.

intendan|t, ~te /ɛ̃tɑ̃dɑ̃, -t/ *n.m.* (*mil.*) quartermaster. ● *n.m., f.* (*scol.*) bursar. **~ce** *n.f.* (*scol.*) bursar's office.

intens|e /ɛ̃tɑ̃s/ *a.* intense; (*circulation*) heavy. **~ément** *adv.* intensely. **~ifier** *v.t.*, **s'~ifier** *v. pr.* intensify. **~ité** *n.f.* intensity.

intensi|f, ~ve /ɛ̃tɑ̃sif, -v/ *a.* intensive.

intenter /ɛ̃tɑ̃te/ *v.t.* **~ un procès** *ou* **une action**, institute proceedings (**à**, **contre**, against).

intention /ɛ̃tɑ̃sjɔ̃/ *n.f.* intention (**de faire**, of doing). **à l'~ de qn.**, for s.o. **~né** /-jɔne/ *a.* **bien/mal ~né**, well-/ill-intentioned.

intentionnel, ~le /ɛ̃tɑ̃sjɔnɛl/ *a.* intentional.

inter- /ɛ̃tɛr/ *préf.* inter-.

interaction /ɛ̃tɛraksjɔ̃/ *n.f.* interaction.

intercaler /ɛ̃tɛrkale/ *v.t.* insert.

intercéder /ɛ̃tɛrsede/ *v.i.* intercede **(en faveur de,** on behalf of).

intercept|er /ɛ̃tɛrsɛpte/ *v.t.* intercept. **~ion** /-psjɔ̃/ *n.f.* interception.

interchangeable /ɛ̃tɛrʃɑ̃ʒabl/ *a.* interchangeable.

interdiction /ɛ̃tɛrdiksjɔ̃/ *n.f.* ban. **~ de fumer,** no smoking.

interdire† /ɛ̃tɛrdir/ *v.t.* forbid; (*officiellement*) ban, prohibit. **~ à qn. de faire,** forbid s.o. to do.

interdit, ~e /ɛ̃tɛrdi, -t/ *a.* (*étonné*) nonplussed.

intéressant, ~e /ɛ̃terɛsɑ̃, -t/ *a.* interesting; (*avantageux*) attractive.

intéressé, ~e /ɛ̃terese/ *a.* (*en cause*) concerned; (*pour profiter*) self-interested. ● *n.m., f.* person concerned.

intéresser /ɛ̃terese/ *v.t.* interest; (*concerner*) concern. **s'~ à,** be interested in.

intérêt /ɛ̃terɛ/ *n.m.* interest; (*égoïsme*) self-interest. **~(s),** (*comm.*) interest. **vous avez ~ à,** it is in your interest to.

interférence /ɛ̃tɛrferɑ̃s/ *n.f.* interference.

intérieur /ɛ̃terjœr/ *a.* inner, inside; (*vol, politique*) domestic; (*vie, calme*) inner. ● *n.m.* interior; (*de boîte, tiroir*) inside. **à l'~ (de),** inside; (*fig.*) within. **~ement** *adv.* inwardly.

intérim /ɛ̃terim/ *n.m.* interim. **assurer l'~,** deputize (**de,** for). **par ~,** acting. **faire de l'~,** temp. **~aire** *a.* temporary, interim.

interjection /ɛ̃tɛrʒɛksjɔ̃/ *n.f.* interjection.

interlocu|teur, ~trice /ɛ̃tɛrlɔkytœr, -tris/ *n.m., f.* **son ~teur,** the person one is speaking to.

interloqué /ɛ̃tɛrlɔke/ *a.* **être ~,** be taken aback.

intermède /ɛ̃tɛrmɛd/ *n.m.* interlude.

intermédiaire /ɛ̃tɛrmedjɛr/ *a.* intermediate. ● *n.m./f.* intermediary.

interminable /ɛ̃tɛrminabl/ *a.* endless.

intermittence /ɛ̃tɛrmitɑ̃s/ *n.f.* **par ~,** intermittently.

intermittent, ~e /ɛ̃tɛrmitɑ̃, -t/ *a.* intermittent.

internat /ɛ̃tɛrna/ *n.m.* boarding-school.

internation|al (*m. pl.* **~aux**) /ɛ̃tɛrnasjɔnal, -o/ *a.* international.

interne /ɛ̃tɛrn/ *a.* internal. ● *n.m./f.* (*scol.*) boarder.

intern|er /ɛ̃tɛrne/ *v.t.* (*pol.*) intern; (*méd.*) confine. **~ement** *n.m.* (*pol.*) internment.

interpell|er /ɛ̃tɛrpɔle/ *v.t.* shout to; (*apostropher*) shout at; (*interroger*) question. **~ation** *n.f.* (*pol.*) questioning.

interphone /ɛ̃tɛrfɔn/ *n.m.* intercom.

interposer (s') /(s)ɛ̃tɛrpoze/ *v. pr.* intervene.

interpr|ète /ɛ̃tɛrprɛt/ *n.m./f.* interpreter; (*artiste*) performer. **~étariat** *n.m.* interpreting.

interprét|er /ɛ̃tɛrprete/ *v.t.* interpret; (*jouer*) play; (*chanter*) sing. **~ation** *n.f.* interpretation; (*d'artiste*) performance.

interroga|teur, ~trice /ɛ̃tɛrɔgatœr, -tris/ *a.* questioning.

interrogati|f, ~ve /ɛ̃tɛrɔgatif, -v/ *a.* interrogative.

interrogatoire /ɛ̃terɔgatwar/ *n.m.* interrogation.

interro|ger /ɛ̃tɛrɔʒe/ *v.t.* question; (*élève*) test. **~gateur, ~gatrice** *a.* questioning. **~gation** *n.f.* question; (*action*) questioning; (*épreuve*) test.

interr|ompre† /ɛ̃terɔ̃pr/ *v.t.* break off, interrupt; (*personne*) interrupt. **s'~ompre** *v. pr.* break off. **~upteur** *n.m.* switch. **~uption** *n.f.* interruption; (*arrêt*) break.

intersection /ɛ̃tɛrsɛksjɔ̃/ *n.f.* intersection.

interstice /ɛ̃tɛrstis/ *n.m.* crack.

interurbain /ɛ̃tɛryrbɛ̃/ *n.m.* long-distance telephone service.

intervalle /ɛ̃tɛrval/ *n.m.* space; (*temps*) interval. **dans l'~,** in the meantime.

interven|ir† /ɛ̃tɛrvənir/ *v.i.* intervene; (*survenir*) occur; (*méd.*) operate. **~tion** /-vɑ̃sjɔ̃/ *n.f.* intervention; (*méd.*) operation.

intervertir /ɛ̃tɛrvɛrtir/ *v.t.* invert.

interview /ɛ̃tɛrvju/ *n.f.* interview. **~er** /-ve/ *v.t.* interview.

intestin /ɛ̃tɛstɛ̃/ *n.m.* intestine.

intim|e /ɛ̃tim/ *a.* intimate; (*fête, vie*) private; (*dîner*) quiet. ● *n.m./f.* intimate friend. **~ement** *adv.*

intimately. **~ité** *n.f.* intimacy; (*vie privée*) privacy.

intimid|er /ɛ̃timide/ *v.t.* intimidate. **~ation** *n.f.* intimidation.

intituler /ɛ̃tityle/ *v.t.* entitle. **s'~** *v. pr.* be entitled.

intolérable /ɛ̃tɔlerabl/ *a.* intolerable.

intoléran|t, ~te /ɛ̃tɔlerɑ̃, -t/ *a.* intolerant. **~ce** *n.f.* intolerance.

intonation /ɛ̃tɔnasjɔ̃/ *n.f.* intonation.

intox /ɛ̃tɔks/ *n.f.* (*fam.*) brainwashing.

intoxi|quer /ɛ̃tɔsike/ *v.t.* poison; (*pol.*) brainwash. **~cation** *n.f.* poisoning; (*pol.*) brainwashing.

intraduisible /ɛ̃traduizibl/ *a.* untranslatable.

intraitable /ɛ̃trɛtabl/ *a.* inflexible.

intransigean|t, ~te /ɛ̃trɑ̃siʒɑ̃, -t/ *a.* intransigent. **~ce** *n.f.* intransigence.

intransiti|f, ~ve /ɛ̃trɑ̃zitif, -v/ *a.* intransitive.

intraveineu|x, ~se /ɛ̃travɛnø, -z/ *a.* intravenous.

intrépide /ɛ̃trepid/ *a.* fearless.

intrigu|e /ɛ̃trig/ *n.f.* intrigue; (*théâtre*) plot. **~er** *v.t./i.* intrigue.

intrinsèque /ɛ̃trɛ̃sɛk/ *a.* intrinsic.

introduction /ɛ̃trɔdyksjɔ̃/ *n.f.* introduction.

introduire† /ɛ̃trɔdɥir/ *v.t.* introduce, bring in; (*insérer*) put in, insert. **~ qn.,** show s.o. in. **s'~ dans,** get into, enter.

introspecti|f, ~ve /ɛ̃trɔspɛktif, -v/ *a.* introspective.

introuvable /ɛ̃truvabl/ *a.* that cannot be found.

introverti, ~e /ɛ̃trɔvɛrti/ *n.m., f.* introvert. ● *a.* introverted.

intrus, ~e /ɛ̃try, -z/ *n.m., f.* intruder. **~ion** /-zjɔ̃/ *n.f.* intrusion.

intuiti|f, ~ve /ɛ̃tɥitif, -v/ *a.* intuitive.

intuition /ɛ̃tɥisjɔ̃/ *n.f.* intuition.

inusable /inyzabl/ *a.* hard-wearing.

inusité /inyzite/ *a.* little used.

inutil|e /inytil/ *a.* useless; (*vain*) needless. **~ement** *adv.* needlessly. **~ité** *n.f.* uselessness.

inutilisable /inytilizabl/ *a.* unusable.

invalid|e /ɛ̃valid/ *a. & n.m./f.* disabled (person). **~ité** *n.f.* disablement.

invariable /ɛ̃varjabl/ *a.* invariable.

invasion /ɛ̃vazjɔ̃/ *n.f.* invasion.

invectiv|e /ɛ̃vɛktiv/ *n.f.* invective. **~er** *v.t.* abuse.

invend|able /ɛ̃vɑ̃dabl/ *a.* unsaleable. **~u** *a.* unsold.

inventaire /ɛ̃vɑ̃tɛr/ *n.m.* inventory. **faire l'~ de,** take stock of.

invent|er /ɛ̃vɑ̃te/ *v.t.* invent. **~eur** *n.m.* inventor. **~ion** /ɛ̃vɑ̃sjɔ̃/ *n.f.* invention.

inventi|f, ~ve /ɛ̃vɑ̃tif, -v/ *a.* inventive.

inverse /ɛ̃vɛrs/ *a.* opposite; (*ordre*) reverse. ● *n.m.* reverse. **~ment** /-əmɑ̃/ *adv.* conversely.

invers|er /ɛ̃vɛrse/ *v.t.* reverse, invert. **~ion** *n.f.* inversion.

investigation /ɛ̃vɛstigasjɔ̃/ *n.f.* investigation.

invest|ir /ɛ̃vɛstir/ *v.t.* invest. **~issement** *n.m.* (*comm.*) investment.

investiture /ɛ̃vɛstityr/ *n.f.* nomination.

invétéré /ɛ̃vetere/ *a.* inveterate.

invincible /ɛ̃vɛ̃sibl/ *a.* invincible.

invisible /ɛ̃vizibl/ *a.* invisible.

invit|er /ɛ̃vite/ *v.t.* invite (**à,** to). **~ation** *n.f.* invitation. **~é, ~ée** *n.m., f.* guest.

invivable /ɛ̃vivabl/ *a.* unbearable.

involontaire /ɛ̃vɔlɔ̃tɛr/ *a.* involuntary.

invoquer /ɛ̃vɔke/ *v.t.* call upon, invoke; (*alléguer*) plead.

invraisembl|able /ɛ̃vrɛsɑ̃blabl/ *a.* improbable; (*incroyable*) incredible. **~ance** *n.f.* improbability.

invulnérable /ɛ̃vylnerabl/ *a.* invulnerable.

iode /jɔd/ *n.m.* iodine.

ion /jɔ̃/ *n.m.* ion.

ira, irait /ira, irɛ/ *voir* aller[1].

Irak /irak/ *n.m.* Iraq. **~ien, ~ienne** *a. & n.m., f.* Iraqi.

Iran /irɑ̃/ *n.m.* Iran. **~ien, ~ienne** /iranjɛ̃, -jɛn/ *a. & n.m., f.* Iranian.

irascible /irasibl/ *a.* irascible.

iris /iris/ *n.m.* iris.

irlandais, ~e /irlɑ̃dɛ, -z/ *a.* Irish. ● *n.m., f.* Irishman, Irishwoman.

Irlande /irlɑ̃d/ *n.f.* Ireland.

iron|ie /irɔni/ *n.f.* irony. **~ique** *a.* ironic(al).

irraisonné /irɛzɔne/ *a.* irrational.

irrationnel, ~le /irasjɔnɛl/ *a.* irrational.

irréalisable /irealizabl/ *a.* (*projet*) unworkable.

irrécupérable /irekyperabl/ *a.* irretrievable, beyond recall.

irréel, ~le /ireɛl/ *a.* unreal.

irréfléchi /irefleʃi/ a. thoughtless.
irréfutable /irefytabl/ a. irrefutable.
irrégul|ier, ~ière /iregylje, -jɛr/ a. irregular. **~arité** n.f. irregularity.
irrémédiable /iremedjabl/ a. irreparable.
irremplaçable /irɑ̃plasabl/ a. irreplaceable.
irréparable /ireparabl/ a. beyond repair.
irréprochable /ireprɔʃabl/ a. flawless.
irrésistible /irezistibl/ a. irresistible; (drôle) hilarious.
irrésolu /irezɔly/ a. indecisive.
irrespirable /irɛspirabl/ a. stifling.
irresponsable /irɛspɔ̃sabl/ a. irresponsible.
irréversible /irevɛrsibl/ a. irreversible.
irrévocable /irevɔkabl/ a. irrevocable.
irrigation /irigasjɔ̃/ n.f. irrigation.
irriguer /irige/ v.t. irrigate.
irrit|er /irite/ v.t. irritate. **s'~er de,** be annoyed at. **~able** a. irritable. **~ation** n.f. irritation.
irruption /irypsjɔ̃/ n.f. **faire ~ dans,** burst into.
Islam /islam/ n.m. Islam.
islamique /islamik/ a. Islamic.
islandais, ~e /islɑ̃dɛ, -z/ a. Icelandic. ● n.m., f. Icelander. ● n.m. (lang.) Icelandic.
Islande /islɑ̃d/ n.f. Iceland.
isolé /izɔle/ a. isolated. **~ment** adv. in isolation.
isol|er /izɔle/ v.t. isolate; (électr.) insulate. **s'~er** v. pr. isolate o.s. **~ant** n.m. insulating material. **~ation** n.f. insulation. **~ement** n.m. isolation.
isoloir /izɔlwar/ n.m. polling booth.
isorel /izɔrɛl/ n.m. (P.) hardboard.
isotope /izɔtɔp/ n.m. isotope.
Israël /israɛl/ n.m. Israel.
israélien, ~ne /israeljɛ̃, -jɛn/ a. & n.m., f. Israeli.
israélite /israelit/ a. Jewish. ● n.m./f. Jew, Jewess.
issu /isy/ a. **être ~ de,** come from.
issue /isy/ n.f. exit; (résultat) outcome; (fig.) solution. **à l'~ de,** at the conclusion of. **rue ou voie sans ~,** dead end.
isthme /ism/ n.m. isthmus.
Italie /itali/ n.f. Italy.
italien, ~ne /italjɛ̃, -jɛn/ a. & n.m., f. Italian. ● n.m. (lang.) Italian.

italique /italik/ n.m. italics.
itinéraire /itinerɛr/ n.m. itinerary, route.
itinérant, ~e /itinerɑ̃, -t/ a. itinerant.
I.U.T. /iyte/ n.m. (abrév.) polytechnic.
I.V.G. /iveʒe/ n.f. (abrév.) abortion.
ivoire /ivwar/ n.m. ivory.
ivr|e /ivr/ a. drunk. **~esse** n.f. drunkenness. **~ogne** n.m. drunk(ard).

J

j' /ʒ/ voir je.
jacasser /ʒakase/ v.i. chatter.
jachère (en) /(ɑ̃)ʒaʃɛr/ adv. fallow.
jacinthe /ʒasɛ̃t/ n.f. hyacinth.
jade /ʒad/ n.m. jade.
jadis /ʒadis/ adv. long ago.
jaillir /ʒajir/ v.i. (liquide) spurt (out); (lumière) stream out; (apparaître, fuser) burst forth.
jais /ʒɛ/ n.m. **(noir) de ~,** jet-black.
jalon /ʒalɔ̃/ n.m. (piquet) marker. **~ner** /-ɔne/ v.t. mark (out).
jalou|x, ~se /ʒalu, -z/ a. jealous. **~ser** v.t. be jealous of. **~sie** n.f. jealousy; (store) (venetian) blind.
jamais /ʒamɛ/ adv. ever. **(ne) ~,** never. **il ne boit ~,** he never drinks. **à ~,** for ever. **si ~,** if ever.
jambe /ʒɑ̃b/ n.f. leg.
jambon /ʒɑ̃bɔ̃/ n.m. ham. **~neau** (pl. ~neaux) /-ɔno/ n.m. knuckle of ham.
jante /ʒɑ̃t/ n.f. rim.
janvier /ʒɑ̃vje/ n.m. January.
Japon /ʒapɔ̃/ n.m. Japan.
japonais, ~e /ʒapɔnɛ, -z/ a. & n.m., f. Japanese. ● n.m. (lang.) Japanese.
japper /ʒape/ v.i. yelp.
jaquette /ʒakɛt/ n.f. (de livre, femme) jacket; (d'homme) morning coat.
jardin /ʒardɛ̃/ n.m. garden. **~ d'enfants,** nursery (school). **~ public,** public park.
jardin|er /ʒardine/ v.i. garden. **~age** n.m. gardening. **~ier, ~ière** n.m., f. gardener; n.f. (meuble) plant-stand. **~ière de légumes,** mixed vegetables.
jargon /ʒargɔ̃/ n.m. jargon.
jarret /ʒarɛ/ n.m. back of the knee.

jarretelle /ʒartɛl/ n.f. suspender; (*Amer.*) garter.

jarretière /ʒartjɛr/ n.f. garter.

jaser /ʒaze/ v.i. jabber.

jasmin /ʒasmɛ̃/ n.m. jasmine.

jatte /ʒat/ n.f. bowl.

jaug|e /ʒoʒ/ n.f. capacity; (*de navire*) tonnage; (*compteur*) gauge. **~er** v.t. gauge.

jaun|e /ʒon/ a. & n.m. yellow; (*péj.*) scab. **~e d'œuf,** (egg) yolk. **rire ~e,** laugh on the other side of one's face. **~ir** v.t./i. turn yellow.

jaunisse /ʒonis/ n.f. jaundice.

javelot /ʒavlo/ n.m. javelin.

jazz /dʒaz/ n.m. jazz.

J.C. /ʒezykri/ n.m. (*abrév.*) **500 avant/ après ~,** 500 B.C./A.D.

je, j'* /ʒə, ʒ/ pron. I.

jean /dʒin/ n.m. jeans.

jeep /(d)ʒip/ n.f. jeep.

jerrycan /ʒerikan/ n.m. jerrycan.

jersey /ʒɛrze/ n.m. jersey.

Jersey /ʒɛrze/ n.f. Jersey.

Jésus /ʒezykri/ n.m. Jesus.

jet[1] /ʒɛ/ n.m. throw; (*de liquide, vapeur*) jet. **~ d'eau,** fountain.

jet[2] /dʒɛt/ n.m. (*avion*) jet.

jetable /ʒətabl/ a. disposable.

jetée /ʒte/ n.f. pier.

jeter /ʒte/ v.t. throw; (*au rebut*) throw away; (*regard, ancre, lumière*) cast; (*cri*) utter; (*bases*) lay. **~ un coup d'œil,** have *ou* take a look (à, at). **se ~ contre,** (*heurter*) bash into. **se ~ dans,** (*fleuve*) flow into. **se ~ sur,** (*se ruer sur*) rush at.

jeton /ʒtɔ̃/ n.m. token; (*pour compter*) counter.

jeu (*pl.* **~x**) /ʒø/ n.m. game; (*amusement*) play; (*au casino etc.*) gambling; (*théâtre*) acting; (*série*) set; (*de lumière, ressort*) play. **en ~,** (*honneur*) at stake; (*forces*) at work. **~ de cartes,** (*paquet*) pack of cards. **~ d'échecs,** (*boîte*) chess set. **~ de mots,** pun. **~ télévisé,** television quiz.

jeudi /ʒødi/ n.m. Thursday.

jeun (à) /(a)ʒœ̃/ adv. **être/rester à ~,** be/stay without food; **comprimé à prendre à ~,** tablet to be taken on an empty stomach.

jeune /ʒœn/ a. young. ● n.m./f. young person. **~ fille,** girl. **~s mariés,** newlyweds. **les ~s,** young people.

jeûn|e /ʒøn/ n.m. fast. **~er** v.i. fast.

jeunesse /ʒœnɛs/ n.f. youth; (*apparence*) youthfulness. **la ~,** (*jeunes*) the young.

joaill|ier, ~ière /ʒɔalje, -jɛr/ n.m., f. jeweller. **~erie** n.f. jewellery; (*magasin*) jeweller's shop.

job /dʒɔb/ n.m. (*fam.*) job.

jockey /ʒɔkɛ/ n.m. jockey.

joie /ʒwa/ n.f. joy.

joindre† /ʒwɛ̃dr/ v.t. join (à, to); (*contacter*) contact; (*mains, pieds*) put together; (*efforts*) combine; (*dans une enveloppe*) enclose. **se ~ à,** join.

joint, ~e /ʒwɛ̃, -t/ a. (*efforts*) joint; (*pieds*) together. ● n.m. joint; (*ligne*) join; (*de robinet*) washer. **~ure** /-tyr/ n.f. joint; (*ligne*) join.

joker /ʒɔkɛr/ n.m. (*carte*) joker.

joli /ʒɔli/ a. pretty, nice; (*somme, profit*) nice. **c'est du ~!,** (*ironique*) charming! **c'est bien ~ mais,** that is all very well but. **~ment** adv. prettily; (*très: fam.*) awfully.

jonc /ʒɔ̃/ n.m. (bul)rush.

jonch|er /ʒɔ̃ʃe/ v.t., **~é de,** littered with.

jonction /ʒɔ̃ksjɔ̃/ n.f. junction.

jongl|er /ʒɔ̃gle/ v.i. juggle. **~eur, ~euse** n.m., f. juggler.

jonquille /ʒɔ̃kij/ n.f. daffodil.

Jordanie /ʒɔrdani/ n.f. Jordan.

joue /ʒu/ n.f. cheek.

jou|er /ʒwe/ v.t./i. play; (*théâtre*) act; (*au casino etc.*) gamble; (*fonctionner*) work; (*film, pièce*) put on; (*cheval*) back; (*être important*) count. **~er à ou de,** play. **~er la comédie,** put on an act. **bien ~é!,** well done!

jouet /ʒwɛ/ n.m. toy; (*personne, fig.*) plaything; (*victime*) victim.

joueu|r, ~se /ʒwœr, -øz/ n.m., f. player; (*parieur*) gambler.

joufflu /ʒufly/ a. chubby-cheeked; (*visage*) chubby.

joug /ʒu/ n.m. yoke.

jouir /ʒwir/ v.i. (*sexe*) come. **~ de,** enjoy.

jouissance /ʒwisɑ̃s/ n.f. pleasure; (*usage*) use (**de qch.,** of sth.).

joujou (*pl.* **~x**) /ʒuʒu/ n.m. (*fam.*) toy.

jour /ʒur/ n.m. day; (*opposé à nuit*) day(time); (*lumière*) daylight; (*aspect*) light; (*ouverture*) gap. **de nos ~s,** nowadays. **du ~ au lendemain,** overnight. **il fait ~,** it is (day)light. **~ chômé ou férié,** public holiday. **~ de fête,** holiday. **~ ouvrable, ~**

de travail, working day. **mettre à ~,** update. **mettre au ~,** uncover. **au grand ~,** in the open. **donner le ~,** give birth. **voir le ~,** be born. **vivre au ~ le jour,** live from day to day.

journ|al (*pl.* **~aux**) /ʒurnal, -o/ *n.m.* (news)paper; (*spécialisé*) journal; (*intime*) diary; (*radio*) news. **~al de bord**) log-book.

journal|ier, ~ière /ʒurnalje, -jɛr/ *a.* daily.

journalis|te /ʒurnalist/ *n.m./f.* journalist. **~me** *n.m.* journalism.

journée /ʒurne/ *n.f.* day.

journellement /ʒurnɛlmɑ̃/ *adv.* daily.

jov|ial (*m. pl.* **~iaux**) /ʒɔvjal, -jo/ *a.* jovial.

joyau (*pl.* **~x**) /ʒwajo/ *n.m.* gem.

joyeu|x, ~se /ʒwajø, -z/ *a.* merry, joyful. **~x anniversaire,** happy birthday. **~sement** *adv.* merrily.

jubilé /ʒybile/ *n.m.* jubilee.

jubil|er /ʒybile/ *v.i.* be jubilant. **~ation** *n.f.* jubilation.

jucher /ʒyʃe/ *v.t.,* **se ~** *v. pr.* perch.

judaïque /ʒydaik/ *a.* Jewish. **~sme** *n.m.* Judaism.

judas /ʒyda/ *n.m.* peep-hole.

judiciaire /ʒydisjɛr/ *a.* judicial.

judicieu|x, ~se /ʒydisjø, -z/ *a.* judicious.

judo /ʒydo/ *n.m.* judo.

juge /ʒyʒ/ *n.m.* judge; (*arbitre*) referee. **~ de paix,** Justice of the Peace. **~ de touche,** linesman.

jugé (au) /(o)ʒyʒe/ *adv.* by guess-work.

jugement /ʒyʒmɑ̃/ *n.m.* judgement; (*criminel*) sentence.

jugeote /ʒyʒɔt/ *n.f.* (*fam.*) gumption, common sense.

juger /ʒyʒe/ *v.t./i.* judge; (*estimer*) consider (**que,** that). **~ de,** judge.

juguler /ʒygyle/ *v.t.* stifle, check.

jui|f, ~ve /ʒɥif, -v/ *a.* Jewish. **●** *n.m., f.* Jew, Jewess.

juillet /ʒɥijɛ/ *n.m.* July.

juin /ʒɥɛ̃/ *n.m.* June.

jules /ʒyl/ *n.m.* (*fam.*) guy.

jum|eau, ~elle (*m. pl.* **~eaux**) /ʒymo, -ɛl/ *a. & n.m., f.* twin. **~elage** *n.m.* twinning. **~eler** *v.t.* (*villes*) twin.

jumelles /ʒymɛl/ *n.f. pl.* binoculars.

jument /ʒymɑ̃/ *n.f.* mare.

jungle /ʒœ̃gl/ *n.f.* jungle.

junior /ʒynjɔr/ *n.m./f. & a.* junior.

junte /ʒœ̃t/ *n.f.* junta.

jupe /ʒyp/ *n.f.* skirt.

jupon /ʒypɔ̃/ *n.m.* slip, petticoat.

juré, ~e /ʒyre/ *n.m., f.* juror. **●** *a.* sworn.

jurer /ʒyre/ *v.t.* swear (**que,** that). **●** *v.i.* (*pester*) swear; (*contraster*) clash (**avec,** with). **~ de qch./de faire,** swear to sth./to do.

juridiction /ʒyridiksjɔ̃/ *n.f.* jurisdiction; (*tribunal*) court of law.

juridique /ʒyridik/ *a.* legal.

juriste /ʒyrist/ *n.m./f.* legal expert.

juron /ʒyrɔ̃/ *n.m.* swear-word.

jury /ʒyri/ *n.m.* jury.

jus /ʒy/ *n.m.* juice; (*de viande*) gravy. **~ de fruit,** fruit juice.

jusque /ʒysk(ə)/ *prép.* **jusqu'à,** (up) to, as far as; (*temps*) until, till; (*limite*) up to; (*y compris*) even. **jusqu'à ce que,** until. **jusqu'à présent,** until now. **jusqu'en,** until. **jusqu'où?,** how far? **~ dans, ~ sur,** as far as.

juste /ʒyst/ *a.* fair, just; (*légitime*) just; (*correct, exact*) right; (*vrai*) true; (*vêtement*) tight; (*quantité*) on the short side. **le ~ milieu,** the happy medium. **●** *adv.* rightly, correctly; (*chanter*) in tune; (*seulement, exactement*) just. **(un peu) ~,** (*calculer, mesurer*) a bit fine *ou* close. **au ~,** exactly. **c'était ~,** (*presque raté*) it was a close thing.

justement /ʒystəmɑ̃/ *adv.* just; (*avec justice ou justesse*) justly.

justesse /ʒystɛs/ *n.f.* accuracy. **de ~,** just, narrowly.

justice /ʒystis/ *n.f.* justice; (*autorités*) law; (*tribunal*) court.

justif|ier /ʒystifje/ *v.t.* justify. **●** *v.i.* **~ier de,** prove. **se ~ier** *v. pr.* justify o.s. **~iable** *a.* justifiable. **~ication** *n.f.* justification.

juteu|x, ~se /ʒytø, -z/ *a.* juicy.

juvénile /ʒyvenil/ *a.* youthful.

juxtaposer /ʒykstapoze/ *v.t.* juxtapose.

K

kaki /kaki/ *a. invar. & n.m.* khaki.

kaléidoscope /kaleidɔskɔp/ *n.m.* kaleidoscope.

kangourou /kɑ̃guru/ *n.m.* kangaroo.

karaté /karate/ *n.m.* karate.

kart /kart/ *n.m.* go-cart.

kascher /kaʃɛr/ *a. invar.* kosher.

képi /kepi/ *n.m.* kepi.

kermesse /kɛrmɛs/ *n.f.* fair; (*de charité*) fête.

kérosène /kerozɛn/ *n.m.* kerosene, aviation fuel.

kibboutz /kibuts/ *n.m.* kibbutz.

kidnapp|er /kidnape/ *v.t.* kidnap. **~eur**, **~euse** *n.m.*, *f.* kidnapper.

kilo /kilo/ *n.m.* kilo.

kilogramme /kilɔgram/ *n.m.* kilogram.

kilohertz /kilɔɛrts/ *n.m.* kilohertz.

kilom|ètre /kilɔmɛtr/ *n.m.* kilometre. **~étrage** *n.m.* (*approx.*) mileage.

kilowatt /kilɔwat/ *n.m.* kilowatt.

kinésithérapie /kineziterapi/ *n.f.* physiotherapy.

kiosque /kjɔsk/ *n.m.* kiosk. **~ à musique**, bandstand.

kit /kit/ *n.m.* **meubles en ~**, flat-pack furniture.

kiwi /kiwi/ *n.m.* (*fruit*, *bird*) kiwi.

klaxon /klaksɔn/ *n.m.* (P.) (*auto.*) horn. **~ner** /-e/ *v.i.* sound one's horn.

knock-out /nɔkaut/ *n.m.* knock-out.

ko /kao/ *n.m.* (*comput.*) k.

K.O. /kao/ *a. invar.* (knocked) out.

k-way /kawe/ *n.m. invar.* (P.) cagoule.

kyste /kist/ *n.m.* cyst.

L

l', **la** /l, la/ *voir* le.

là /la/ *adv.* there; (*ici*) here; (*chez soi*) in; (*temps*) then. **c'est là que**, this is where. **là où**, where. **là-bas** *adv.* over there. **là-dedans** *adv.* inside, in there. **là-dessous** *adv.* underneath, under there. **là-dessus** *adv.* on there. **là-haut** *adv.* up there; (*à l'étage*) upstairs.

-là /la/ *adv.* (*après un nom précédé de ce, cette, etc.*) **cet homme-là**, that man. **ces maisons-là**, those houses.

label /labɛl/ *n.m.* (*comm.*) seal.

labeur /labœr/ *n.m.* toil.

labo /labo/ *n.m.* (*fam.*) lab.

laboratoire /labɔratwar/ *n.m.* laboratory.

laborieu|x, **~se** /labɔrjø, -z/ *a.* laborious; (*personne*) industrious; (*dur*) heavy going. **classes/masses ~ses**, working classes/masses.

labour /labur/ *n.m.* ploughing; (*Amer.*) plowing. **~er** *v.t./i.* plough; (*Amer.*) plow; (*déchirer*) rip at. **~eur** *n.m.* ploughman; (*Amer.*) plowman.

labyrinthe /labirɛ̃t/ *n.m.* maze.

lac /lak/ *n.m.* lake.

lacer /lase/ *v.t.* lace up.

lacérer /lasere/ *v.t.* tear (up).

lacet /lasɛ/ *n.m.* (shoe-)lace; (*de route*) sharp bend, zigzag.

lâche /lɑʃ/ *a.* cowardly; (*détendu*) loose. ● *n.m./f.* coward. **~ment** *adv.* in a cowardly way.

lâcher /lɑʃe/ *v.t.* let go of; (*abandonner*) give up; (*laisser*) leave; (*libérer*) release; (*parole*) utter; (*desserrer*) loosen. ● *v.i.* give way. **~ prise**, let go.

lâcheté /lɑʃte/ *n.f.* cowardice.

laconique /lakɔnik/ *a.* laconic.

lacrymogène /lakrimɔʒɛn/ *a.* **gaz ~**, tear gas. **grenade ~**, tear gas grenade.

lacté /lakte/ *a.* milk.

lacune /lakyn/ *n.f.* gap.

ladite /ladit/ *voir* ledit.

lagune /lagyn/ *n.f.* lagoon.

laïc /laik/ *n.m.* layman.

laid, **~e** /lɛ, lɛd/ *a.* ugly; (*action*) vile. **~eur** /lɛdœr/ *n.f.* ugliness.

lain|e /lɛn/ *n.f.* wool. **de ~e**, woollen. **~age** *n.m.* woollen garment.

laïque /laik/ *a.* secular; (*habit, personne*) lay. ● *n.m./f.* layman, laywoman.

laisse /lɛs/ *n.f.* lead, leash.

laisser /lese/ *v.t.* leave. **~ qn. faire**, let s.o. do. **~ qch. à qn.**, let s.o. have sth., leave s.o. sth. **~ tomber**, drop. **se ~ aller**, let o.s. go. **~-aller** *n.m. invar.* carelessness. **laissez-passer** *n.m. invar.* pass.

lait /lɛ/ *n.m.* milk. **frère/sœur de ~**, foster-brother/-sister. **~age** /lɛtaʒ/ *n.m.* milk product. **~eux**, **~euse** /lɛtø, -z/ *a.* milky.

lait|ier, **~ière** /letje, lɛtjɛr/ *a.* dairy. ● *n.m.*, *f.* dairyman, dairywoman. ● *n.m.* (*livreur*) milkman. **~erie** /lɛtri/ *n.f.* dairy.

laiton /lɛtɔ̃/ *n.m.* brass.

laitue /lety/ *n.f.* lettuce.

laïus /lajys/ *n.m.* (*péj.*) big speech.

lama /lama/ *n.m.* llama.

lambeau (*pl.* **~x**) /lɑ̃bo/ *n.m.* shred. **en ~x**, in shreds.

lambris /lɑ̃bri/ *n.m.* panelling.

lame /lam/ *n.f.* blade; (*lamelle*) strip; (*vague*) wave. **~ de fond,** ground swell.

lamelle /lamɛl/ *n.f.* (thin) strip.

lamentable /lamɑ̃tabl/ *a.* deplorable.

lament|er (se) /(sə)lamɑ̃te/ *v. pr.* moan. **~ation(s)** *n.f.* (*pl.*) moaning.

laminé /lamine/ *a.* laminated.

lampadaire /lɑ̃padɛr/ *n.m.* standard lamp; (*de rue*) street lamp.

lampe /lɑ̃p/ *n.f.* lamp; (*de radio*) valve; (*Amer.*) vacuum tube. **~ (de poche),** torch; (*Amer.*) flashlight. **~ de chevet,** bedside lamp.

lampion /lɑ̃pjɔ̃/ *n.m.* (Chinese) lantern.

lance /lɑ̃s/ *n.f.* spear; (*de tournoi*) lance; (*tuyau*) hose. **~ d'incendie,** fire hose.

lancée /lɑ̃se/ *n.f.* **continuer sur sa ~,** keep going.

lanc|er /lɑ̃se/ *v.t.* throw; (*avec force*) hurl; (*navire, idée, personne*) launch; (*émettre*) give out; (*regard*) cast; (*moteur*) start. **se ~er** *v. pr.* (*sport*) gain momentum; (*se précipiter*) rush. **se ~er dans,** launch into. ● *n.m.* throw; (*action*) throwing. **~ement** *n.m.* throwing; (*de navire*) launching. **~e-missiles** *n.m. invar.* missile launcher. **~e-pierres** *n.m. invar.* catapult.

lancinant, ~e /lɑ̃sinɑ̃, -t/ *a.* haunting; (*douleur*) throbbing.

landau /lɑ̃do/ *n.m.* pram; (*Amer.*) baby carriage.

lande /lɑ̃d/ *n.f.* heath, moor.

langage /lɑ̃gaʒ/ *n.m.* language.

langoureu|x, ~se /lɑ̃gurø, -z/ *a.* languid.

langoust|e /lɑ̃gust/ *n.f.* (spiny) lobster. **~ine** *n.f.* (Norway) lobster.

langue /lɑ̃g/ *n.f.* tongue; (*idiome*) language. **il m'a tiré la ~,** he stuck out his tongue out at me. **de ~ anglaise/française,** English-/French-speaking. **~ maternelle,** mother tongue.

languette /lɑ̃gɛt/ *n.f.* tongue.

langueur /lɑ̃gœr/ *n.f.* languor.

langu|ir /lɑ̃gir/ *v.i.* languish; (*conversation*) flag. **faire ~ir qn.,** keep s.o. waiting. **se ~ir de,** miss. **~issant** *a.* languid.

lanière /lanjɛr/ *n.f.* strap.

lanterne /lɑ̃tɛrn/ *n.f.* lantern; (*électrique*) lamp; (*de voiture*) sidelight.

laper /lape/ *v.t./i.* lap.

lapider /lapide/ *v.t.* stone.

lapin /lapɛ̃/ *n.m.* rabbit. **poser un ~ à qn.,** stand s.o. up.

laps /laps/ *n.m.* **~ de temps,** lapse of time.

lapsus /lapsys/ *n.m.* slip (of the tongue).

laquais /lakɛ/ *n.m.* lackey.

laqu|e /lak/ *n.f.* lacquer. **~er** *v.t.* lacquer.

laquelle /lakɛl/ *voir* lequel.

larcin /larsɛ̃/ *n.m.* theft.

lard /lar/ *n.m.* (pig's) fat; (*viande*) bacon.

large /larʒ/ *a.* wide, broad; (*grand*) large; (*non borné*) broad; (*généreux*) generous. ● *adv.* (*mesurer*) broadly; (*voir*) big. ● *n.m.* **de ~,** (*mesure*) wide. **le ~,** (*mer*) the open sea. **au ~ de,** (*en face de: naut.*) off. **~ d'esprit,** broad-minded. **~ment** /-əmɑ̃/ *adv.* widely; (*ouvrir*) wide; (*amplement*) amply; (*généreusement*) generously; (*au moins*) easily.

largesse /larʒɛs/ *n.f.* generosity.

largeur /larʒœr/ *n.f.* width, breadth; (*fig.*) breadth.

larguer /large/ *v.t.* drop. **~ les amarres,** cast off.

larme /larm/ *n.f.* tear; (*goutte: fam.*) drop.

larmoyant, ~e /larmwajɑ̃, -t/ *a.* tearful.

larron /larɔ̃/ *n.m.* thief.

larve /larv/ *n.f.* larva.

larvé /larve/ *a.* latent.

laryngite /larɛ̃ʒit/ *n.f.* laryngitis.

larynx /larɛ̃ks/ *n.m.* larynx.

las, ~se /lɑ, lɑs/ *a.* weary.

lasagnes /lazaɲ/ *n.f. pl.* lasagne.

lasci|f, ~ve /lasif, -v/ *a.* lascivious.

laser /lazɛr/ *n.m.* laser.

lasse /lɑs/ *voir* las.

lasser /lɑse/ *v.t.* weary. **se ~** *v. pr.* weary (**de,** of).

lassitude /lɑsityd/ *n.f.* weariness.

lasso /laso/ *n.m.* lasso.

latent, ~e /latɑ̃, -t/ *a.* latent.

latér|al (*m. pl.* **~aux**) /lateral, -o/ *a.* lateral.

latex /latɛks/ *n.m.* latex.

latin, ~e /latɛ̃, -in/ *a. & n.m.,* *f.* Latin. ● *n.m.* (*lang.*) Latin.

latitude /latityd/ *n.f.* latitude.

latrines /latrin/ *n.f. pl.* latrine(s).

latte /lat/ *n.f.* lath; (*de plancher*) board.

lauréat, ~e /lɔrea, -t/ *a.* prize-winning. ● *n.m., f.* prize-winner.

laurier /lɔrje/ *n.m.* laurel; (*culin.*) bay-leaves.

lavable /lavabl/ *a.* washable.

lavabo /lavabo/ *n.m.* wash-basin. **~s**, toilet(s).

lavage /lavaʒ/ *n.m.* washing. **~ de cerveau**, brainwashing.

lavande /lavɑ̃d/ *n.f.* lavender.

lave /lav/ *n.f.* lava.

lav|er /lave/ *v.t.* wash; (*injure etc.*) avenge. **se ~er** *v. pr.* wash (o.s.). **(se) ~er de**, clear (o.s.) of. **~e-glace** *n.m.* windscreen washer. **~eur de carreaux**, window-cleaner. **~e-vaisselle** *n.m. invar.* dishwasher.

laverie /lavri/ *n.f.* **~ (automatique)**, launderette; (*Amer.*) laundromat.

lavette /lavɛt/ *n.f.* dishcloth; (*péj.*) wimp.

lavoir /lavwar/ *n.m.* wash-house.

laxati|f, **~ve** /laksatif, -v/ *a. & n.m.* laxative.

laxisme /laksism/ *n.m.* laxity.

layette /lɛjɛt/ *n.f.* baby clothes.

le *ou* **l'***, **la** *ou* **l'*** (*pl.* **les**) /lə, l/, /la, le/ *article* the; (*mesure*) a, per. ● *pron.* (*homme*) him; (*femme*) her; (*chose, animal*) it. **les** *pron.* them. **aimer le thé/la France**, like tea/France. **le matin**, in the morning. **il sort le mardi**, he goes out on Tuesdays. **levez le bras**, raise your arm. **je le connais**, I know him. **je le sais**, I know (it).

lécher /leʃe/ *v.t.* lick.

lèche-vitrines /lɛʃvitrin/ *n.m.* **faire du ~**, go window-shopping.

leçon /ləsɔ̃/ *n.f.* lesson. **faire la ~ à**, lecture.

lec|teur, **~trice** /lɛktœr, -tris/ *n.m.,f.* reader; (*univ.*) foreign language assistant. **~teur de cassettes**, cassette player. **~teur de disquettes**, (disk) drive.

lecture /lɛktyr/ *n.f.* reading.

ledit, **ladite** (*pl.* **lesdit(e)s**) /lədi, ladit, ledi(t)/ *a.* the aforesaid.

lég|al (*m. pl.* **~aux**) /legal, -o/ *a.* legal. **~alement** *adv.* legally. **~aliser** *v.t.* legalize. **~alité** *n.f.* legality; (*loi*) law.

légation /legɑsjɔ̃/ *n.f.* legation.

légend|e /leʒɑ̃d/ *n.f.* (*histoire, inscription*) legend. **~aire** *a.* legendary.

lég|er, **~ère** /leʒe, -ɛr/ *a.* light; (*bruit, faute, maladie*) slight; (*café, argument*) weak; (*imprudent*) thoughtless; (*frivole*) fickle. **à la**

~ère, thoughtlessly. **~èrement** /-ɛrmɑ̃/ *adv.* lightly; (*agir*) thoughtlessly; (*un peu*) slightly. **~èreté** /-ɛrte/ *n.f.* lightness; thoughtlessness.

légion /leʒjɔ̃/ *n.f.* legion. **une ~ de**, a crowd of. **~naire** /-jɔnɛr/ *n.m.* (*mil.*) legionnaire.

législati|f, **~ve** /leʒislatif, -v/ *a.* legislative.

législation /leʒislasjɔ̃/ *n.f.* legislation.

législature /leʒislatyr/ *n.f.* term of office.

légitim|e /leʒitim/ *a.* legitimate. **en état de ~ de défense**, acting in self-defence. **~ité** *n.f.* legitimacy.

legs /lɛg/ *n.m.* legacy.

léguer /lege/ *v.t.* bequeath.

légume /legym/ *n.m.* vegetable.

lendemain /lɑ̃dmɛ̃/ *n.m.* **le ~**, the next day, the day after; (*fig.*) the future. **le ~ de**, the day after. **le ~ matin/soir**, the next morning/evening.

lent, **~e** /lɑ̃, lɑ̃t/ *a.* slow. **~ement** /lɑ̃tmɑ̃/ *adv.* slowly. **~eur** /lɑ̃tœr/ *n.f.* slowness.

lentille[1] /lɑ̃tij/ *n.f.* (*plante*) lentil.

lentille[2] /lɑ̃tij/ *n.f.* (*verre*) lens; **~s de contact**, (contact) lenses.

léopard /leɔpar/ *n.m.* leopard.

lèpre /lɛpr/ *n.f.* leprosy.

lequel, **laquelle** (*pl.* **lesquel(le)s**) /ləkɛl, lakɛl, lekɛl/ *pron.* (*à + lequel = auquel*, *à + lesquel(le)s = auxquel(le)s*; *de + lequel = duquel*, *de + lesquel(le)s = desquel(le)s*) which; (*interrogatif*) which (one); (*personne*) who; (*complément indirect*) whom.

les /le/ *voir* le.

lesbienne /lɛsbjɛn/ *n.f.* lesbian.

léser /leze/ *v.t.* wrong.

lésiner /lezine/ *v.i.* **ne pas ~ sur**, not stint on.

lésion /lezjɔ̃/ *n.f.* lesion.

lesquels, **lesquelles** /lekɛl/ *voir* lequel.

lessive /lesiv/ *n.f.* washing-powder; (*linge, action*) washing.

lest /lɛst/ *n.m.* ballast. **jeter du ~**, (*fig.*) climb down. **~er** *v.t.* ballast.

leste /lɛst/ *a.* nimble; (*grivois*) coarse.

léthargi|e /letarʒi/ *n.f.* lethargy. **~ique** *a.* lethargic.

lettre /lɛtr/ *n.f.* letter. **à la ~**, literally. **en toutes ~s**, in full. **~**

exprès, express letter. **les ∼s**, (*univ.*) (the) arts.
lettré /letre/ *a.* well-read.
leucémie /løsemi/ *n.f.* leukaemia.
leur /lœr/ *a.* (*f. invar.*) their. ● *pron.* (to) them. **le ∼, la ∼, les ∼s**, theirs.
leurr|e /lœr/ *n.m.* illusion; (*duperie*) deception. **∼er** *v.t.* delude.
levain /ləvɛ̃/ *n.m.* leaven.
levé /ləve/ *a.* (*debout*) up.
levée /ləve/ *n.f.* lifting; (*de courrier*) collection; (*de troupes, d'impôts*) levying.
lever /ləve/ *v.t.* lift (up), raise; (*interdiction*) lift; (*séance*) close; (*armée, impôts*) levy. ● *v.i.* (*pâte*) rise. **se ∼** *v. pr.* get up; (*soleil, rideau*) rise; (*jour*) break. ● *n.m.* **au ∼**, on getting up. **∼ du jour**, daybreak. **∼ du rideau**, (*théâtre*) curtain (up). **∼ du soleil**, sunrise.
levier /ləvje/ *n.m.* lever.
lèvre /lɛvr/ *n.f.* lip.
lévrier /levrije/ *n.m.* greyhound.
levure /ləvyr/ *n.f.* yeast. **∼ alsacienne** *ou* **chimique**, baking powder.
lexicographie /lɛksikɔgrafi/ *n.f.* lexicography.
lexique /lɛksik/ *n.m.* vocabulary; (*glossaire*) lexicon.
lézard /lezar/ *n.m.* lizard.
lézard|e /lezard/ *n.f.* crack. **se ∼er** *v. pr.* crack.
liaison /ljɛzɔ̃/ *n.f.* connection; (*transport*) link; (*contact*) contact; (*gram., mil.*) liaison; (*amoureuse*) affair.
liane /ljan/ *n.f.* creeper.
liasse /ljas/ *n.f.* bundle, wad.
Liban /libɑ̃/ *n.m.* Lebanon.
libanais, ∼e /libanɛ, -z/ *a. & n.m., f.* Lebanese.
libell|er /libele/ *v.t.* (*chèque*) write; (*lettre*) draw up. **∼é à l'ordre de**, made out to.
libellule /libelyl/ *n.f.* dragonfly.
libér|al (*m. pl.* **∼aux**) /liberal, -o/ *a.* liberal. **les professions ∼ales** the professions. **∼alement** *adv.* liberally. **∼alisme** *n.m.* liberalism. **∼alité** *n.f.* liberality.
libér|er /libere/ *v.t.* (*personne*) free, release; (*pays*) liberate, free. **se ∼er** *v. pr.* free o.s. **∼ateur, ∼atrice** *a.* liberating; *n.m., f.* liberator. **∼ation** *n.f.* release; (*de pays*) liberation.
liberté /libɛrte/ *n.f.* freedom, liberty; (*loisir*) free time. **en ∼ provisoire**,

on bail. **être/mettre en ∼**, be/set free.
libertin, ∼e /libɛrtɛ̃, -in/ *a. & n.m., f.* libertine.
librair|e /librɛr/ *n.m./f.* bookseller. **∼ie** /-eri/ *n.f.* bookshop.
libre /libr/ *a.* free; (*place, pièce*) vacant, free; (*passage*) clear; (*école*) private (*usually religious*). **∼ de qch./de faire**, free from sth./to do. **∼-échange** *n.m.* free trade. **∼ment** /-əmɑ̃/ *adv.* freely. **∼-service** (*pl.* **∼s-services**) *n.m.* self-service.
Libye /libi/ *n.f.* Libya.
libyen, ∼ne /libjɛ̃, -jɛn/ *a. & n.m., f.* Libyan.
licence /lisɑ̃s/ *n.f.* licence; (*univ.*) degree.
licencié, ∼e /lisɑ̃sje/ *n.m., f.* **∼ ès lettres/sciences**, Bachelor of Arts/Science.
licenc|ier /lisɑ̃sje/ *v.t.* make redundant, (*pour faute*) dismiss. **∼iements** *n.m. pl.* redundancies.
licencieu|x, ∼se /lisɑ̃sjø, -z/ *a.* licentious, lascivious.
lichen /likɛn/ *n.m.* lichen.
licite /lisit/ *a.* lawful.
licorne /likɔrn/ *n.f.* unicorn.
lie /li/ *n.f.* dregs.
liège /ljɛʒ/ *n.m.* cork.
lien /ljɛ̃/ *n.m.* (*rapport*) link; (*attache*) bond, tie; (*corde*) rope.
lier /lje/ *v.t.* tie (up), bind; (*relier*) link; (*engager, unir*) bind. **∼ conversation**, strike up a conversation. **se ∼ avec**, make friends with. **ils sont très liés**, they are very close.
lierre /ljɛr/ *n.m.* ivy.
lieu (*pl.* **∼x**) /ljø/ *n.m.* place. **∼x**, (*locaux*) premises; (*d'un accident*) scene. **au ∼ de**, instead of. **avoir ∼**, take place. **tenir ∼ de**, serve as. **en premier ∼**, firstly. **en dernier ∼**, lastly. **∼ commun**, commonplace.
lieutenant /ljøtnɑ̃/ *n.m.* lieutenant.
lièvre /ljɛvr/ *n.m.* hare.
ligament /ligamɑ̃/ *n.m.* ligament.
ligne /liɲ/ *n.f.* line; (*trajet*) route; (*formes*) lines; (*de femme*) figure. **en ∼**, (*joueurs etc.*) lined up; (*personne au téléphone*) on the phone.
lignée /liɲe/ *n.f.* ancestry, line.
ligoter /ligɔte/ *v.t.* tie up.
ligu|e /lig/ *n.f.* league. **se ∼er** *v. pr.* form a league (**contre**, against).
lilas /lila/ *n.m. & a. invar.* lilac.
limace /limas/ *n.f.* slug.
limande /limɑ̃d/ *n.f.* (*poisson*) dab.

lim|e /lim/ *n.f.* file. **~e à ongles,** nail file. **~er** *v.t.* file.

limier /limje/ *n.m.* bloodhound; (*policier*) sleuth.

limitation /limitasjɔ̃/ *n.f.* limitation. **~ de vitesse,** speed limit.

limit|e /limit/ *n.f.* limit; (*de jardin, champ*) boundary. **~** *a.* (*vitesse, âge*) maximum. **cas ~e,** borderline case. **date ~e,** deadline. **~er** *v.t.* limit; (*délimiter*) form the border of.

limoger /limɔʒe/ *v.t.* dismiss.

limon /limɔ̃/ *n.m.* stilt.

limonade /limɔnad/ *n.f.* lemonade.

limpid|e /lɛ̃pid/ *a.* limpid, clear. **~ité** *n.f.* clearness.

lin /lɛ̃/ *n.m.* (*tissu*) linen.

linceul /lɛ̃sœl/ *n.m.* shroud.

linéaire /lineɛr/ *a.* linear.

linge /lɛ̃ʒ/ *n.m.* linen; (*lessive*) washing; (*torchon*) cloth. **~** (**de corps**), underwear. **~rie** *n.f.* underwear.

lingot /lɛ̃go/ *n.m.* ingot.

linguiste /lɛ̃gɥist/ *n.m./f.* linguist.

linguistique /lɛ̃gɥistik/ *a.* linguistic. ● *n.f.* linguistics.

lino /lino/ *n.m.* lino.

linoléum /linɔleɔm/ *n.m.* linoleum.

lion, ~ne /ljɔ̃, ljɔn/ *n.m., f.* lion, lioness. **le L~,** Leo.

lionceau (*pl.* **~x**) /liɔ̃so/ *n.m.* lion cub.

liquéfier /likefje/ *v.t.*, **se ~** *v. pr.* liquefy.

liqueur /likœr/ *n.f.* liqueur.

liquide /likid/ *a. & n.m.* liquid. (*argent*) **~,** ready money. **payer en ~,** pay cash.

liquid|er /likide/ *v.t.* liquidate; (*vendre*) sell. **~ation** *n.f.* liquidation; (*vente*) (clearance) sale.

lire†¹ /lir/ *v.t./i.* read.

lire² /lir/ *n.f.* lira.

lis¹ /li/ *voir* lire¹.

lis² /lis/ *n.m.* (*fleur*) lily.

lisible /lizibl/ *a.* legible; (*roman etc.*) readable.

lisière /lizjɛr/ *n.f.* edge.

liss|e /lis/ *a.* smooth. **~er** *v.t.* smooth.

liste /list/ *n.f.* list. **~ électorale,** register of voters.

listing /listiŋ/ *n.m.* printout.

lit¹ /li/ *voir* lire¹.

lit² /li/ *n.m.* (*de personne, fleuve*) bed. **se mettre au ~,** get into bed. **~ de camp,** camp-bed. **~ d'enfant,** cot. **~ d'une personne,** single bed.

litanie /litani/ *n.f.* litany.

litchi /litʃi/ *n.m.* litchi.

literie /litri/ *n.f.* bedding.

litière /litjɛr/ *n.f.* (*paille*) litter.

litige /litiʒ/ *n.m.* dispute.

litre /litr/ *n.m.* litre.

littéraire /literɛr/ *a.* literary.

littér|al (*m. pl.* **~aux**) /literal, -o/ *a.* literal. **~alement** *adv.* literally.

littérature /literatyr/ *n.f.* literature.

littor|al (*pl.* **~aux**) /litɔral, -o/ *n.m.* coast.

liturg|ie /lityrʒi/ *n.f.* liturgy. **~ique** *a.* liturgical.

livide /livid/ *a.* (*blême*) pallid.

livraison /livrɛzɔ̃/ *n.f.* delivery.

livre¹ /livr/ *n.m.* book. **~ de bord,** log-book. **~ de compte,** books. **~ de poche,** paperback.

livre² /livr/ *n.f.* (*monnaie, poids*) pound.

livrée /livre/ *n.f.* livery.

livr|er /livre/ *v.t.* deliver; (*abandonner*) give over (**à,** to); (*secret*) give away. **~é à soi-même,** left to o.s. **se ~er à,** give o.s. over to; (*actes, boisson*) indulge in; (*se confier à*) confide in; (*effectuer*) carry out.

livret /livrɛ/ *n.m.* book; (*mus.*) libretto. **~ scolaire,** school report (book).

livreu|r, ~se /livrœr, -øz/ *n.m., f.* delivery boy *ou* girl.

lobe /lɔb/ *n.m.* lobe.

loc|al¹ (*m. pl.* **~aux**) /lɔkal, -o/ *a.* local. **~alement** *adv.* locally.

loc|al² (*pl.* **~aux**) /lɔkal, -o/ *n.m.* premises. **~aux,** premises.

localisé /lɔkalize/ *a.* localized.

localité /lɔkalite/ *n.f.* locality.

locataire /lɔkatɛr/ *n.m./f.* tenant; (*de chambre, d'hôtel*) lodger.

location /lɔkasjɔ̃/ *n.f.* (*de maison*) renting; (*de voiture*) hiring, renting; (*de place*) booking, reservation; (*guichet*) booking office; (*théâtre*) box office; (*par propriétaire*) renting out; hiring out. **en ~,** (*voiture*) on hire, rented.

lock-out /lɔkaut/ *n.m. invar.* lockout.

locomotion /lɔkɔmosjɔ̃/ *n.f.* locomotion.

locomotive /lɔkɔmɔtiv/ *n.f.* engine, locomotive.

locution /lɔkysjɔ̃/ *n.f.* phrase.

logarithme /lɔgaritm/ *n.m.* logarithm.

loge /lɔʒ/ *n.f.* (*de concierge*) lodge; (*d'acteur*) dressing-room; (*de spectateur*) box.

logement /lɔʒmɑ̃/ *n.m.* accommodation; (*appartement*) flat; (*habitat*) housing.

log|er /lɔʒe/ *v.t.* accommodate. ● *v.i.*, **se ~er** *v. pr.* live. **trouver à se ~er**, find accommodation. **être ~é**, live. **se ~er dans**, further. **il revient de ~**, (*fig.*) he had a close shave.

logeu|r, ~se /lɔʒœr, -øz/ *n.m., f.* landlord, landlady.

logiciel /lɔʒisjɛl/ *n.m.* software.

logique /lɔʒik/ *a.* logical. ● *n.f.* logic. **~ment** *adv.* logically.

logis /lɔʒi/ *n.m.* dwelling.

logistique /lɔʒistik/ *n.f.* logistics.

logo /lɔgo/ *n.m.* logo.

loi /lwa/ *n.f.* law.

loin /lwɛ̃/ *adv.* far (away). **au ~**, far away. **de ~**, from far away; (*de beaucoup*) by far. **~ de là**, far from it. **plus ~**, further. **il revient de ~**, (*fig.*) he had a close shave.

lointain, ~e /lwɛ̃tɛ̃, -ɛn/ *a.* distant. ● *n.m.* distance.

loir /lwar/ *n.m.* dormouse.

loisir /lwazir/ *n.m.* (spare) time. **~s**, spare time; (*distractions*) spare time activities. **à ~**, at one's leisure.

londonien, ~ne /lɔ̃dɔnjɛ̃, -jɛn/ *a.* London. ● *n.m., f.* Londoner.

Londres /lɔ̃dr/ *n.m./f.* London.

long, ~ue /lɔ̃, lɔ̃g/ *a.* long. ● *n.m.* **de ~**, (*mesure*) long. **à la ~ue**, in the end. **à ~ terme**, long-term. **de ~ en large**, back and forth. **~ à faire**, a long time doing. **(tout) le ~ de**, (all) along.

longer /lɔ̃ʒe/ *v.t.* go along; (*limiter*) border.

longévité /lɔ̃ʒevite/ *n.f.* longevity.

longiligne /lɔ̃ʒiliɲ/ *a.* tall and slender.

longitude /lɔ̃ʒityd/ *n.f.* longitude.

longtemps /lɔ̃tɑ̃/ *adv.* a long time. **avant ~**, before long. **trop ~**, too long. **ça prendra ~**, it will take a long time.

longue /lɔ̃g/ *voir* long.

longuement /lɔ̃gmɑ̃/ *adv.* at length.

longueur /lɔ̃gœr/ *n.f.* length. **~s**, (*de texte etc.*) over-long parts. **à ~ de journée**, all day long. **~ d'onde**, wavelength.

longue-vue /lɔ̃gvy/ *n.f.* telescope.

look /luk/ *n.m.* (*fam.*) look, image.

lopin /lɔpɛ̃/ *n.m.* **~ de terre**, patch of land.

loquace /lɔkas/ *a.* talkative.

loque /lɔk/ *n.f.* **~s**, rags. **~ (humaine)**, (human) wreck.

loquet /lɔkɛ/ *n.m.* latch.

lorgner /lɔrɲe/ *v.t.* eye.

lors de /lɔrdə/ *prép.* at the time of.

lorsque /lɔrsk(ə)/ *conj.* when.

losange /lɔzɑ̃ʒ/ *n.m.* diamond.

lot /lo/ *n.m.* prize; (*portion, destin*) lot.

loterie /lɔtri/ *n.f.* lottery.

lotion /lɔsjɔ̃/ *n.f.* lotion.

lotissement /lɔtismɑ̃/ *n.m.* (*à construire*) building plot; (*construit*) (housing) development.

louable /lwabl/ *a.* praiseworthy.

louange /lwɑ̃ʒ/ *n.f.* praise.

louche[1] /luʃ/ *a.* shady, dubious.

louche[2] /luʃ/ *n.f.* ladle.

loucher /luʃe/ *v.i.* squint.

louer[1] /lwe/ *v.t.* (*maison*) rent; (*voiture*) hire, rent; (*place*) book, reserve; (*propriétaire*) rent out; hire out. **à ~**, to let, for rent (*Amer.*).

louer[2] /lwe/ *v.t.* (*approuver*) praise (**de**, for). **se ~ de**, congratulate o.s. on.

loufoque /lufɔk/ *a.* (*fam.*) crazy.

loup /lu/ *n.m.* wolf.

loupe /lup/ *n.f.* magnifying glass.

louper /lupe/ *v.t.* (*fam.*) miss.

lourd, ~e /lur, -d/ *a.* heavy; (*chaleur*) close; (*faute*) gross. **~ de conséquences**, with dire consequences. **~ement** /-dəmɑ̃/ *adv.* heavily. **~eur** /-dœr/ *n.f.* heaviness.

lourdaud, ~e /lurdo, -d/ *a.* loutish. ● *n.m., f.* lout, oaf.

loutre /lutr/ *n.f.* otter.

louve /luv/ *n.f.* she-wolf.

louveteau (*pl.* **~x**) /luvto/ *n.m.* wolf cub; (*scout*) Cub (Scout).

louvoyer /luvwaje/ *v.i.* (*fig.*) sidestep the issue; (*naut.*) tack.

loy|al (*m. pl.* **~aux**) /lwajal, -o/ *a.* loyal; (*honnête*) fair. **~alement** *adv.* loyally; fairly. **~auté** *n.f.* loyalty; fairness.

loyer /lwaje/ *n.m.* rent.

lu /ly/ *voir* lire[1].

lubie /lybi/ *n.f.* whim.

lubrifi|er /lybrifje/ *v.t.* lubricate. **~iant** *n.m.* lubricant.

lubrique /lybrik/ *a.* lewd.

lucarne /lykarn/ *n.f.* skylight.

lucid|e /lysid/ *a.* lucid. **~ité** *n.f.* lucidity.

lucrati|f, ~ve /lykratif, -v/ *a.* lucrative. **à but non ~f**, non-profit-making.

lueur /lɥœr/ *n.f.* (faint) light, glimmer; (*fig.*) glimmer, gleam.

luge /lyʒ/ *n.f.* toboggan.

lugubre /lygybr/ *a.* gloomy.

lui /lɥi/ *pron.* him; (*sujet*) he; (*chose*) it; (*objet indirect*) (to) him; (*femme*) (to) her; (*chose*) (to) it. **~-même** *pron.* himself; itself.

luire† /lɥir/ *v.i.* shine; (*reflet humide*) glisten; (*reflet chaud, faible*) glow.

lumbago /lɔ̃bago/ *n.m.* lumbago.

lumière /lymjɛr/ *n.f.* light. **~s,** (*connaissances*) knowledge. **faire (toute) la ~ sur,** clear up.

luminaire /lyminɛr/ *n.m.* lamp.

lumineu|x, ~se /lyminø, -z/ *a.* luminous; (*éclairé*) illuminated; (*source, rayon*) (of) light; (*vif*) bright.

lunaire /lynɛr/ *a.* lunar.

lunatique /lynatik/ *a.* temperamental.

lunch /lœnʃ/ *n.m.* buffet lunch.

lundi /lœdi/ *n.m.* Monday.

lune /lyn/ *n.f.* moon. **~ de miel,** honeymoon.

lunette /lynɛt/ *n.f.* **~s,** glasses; (*de protection*) goggles. **~ arrière,** (*auto.*) rear window. **~s de soleil,** sun-glasses.

luron /lyrɔ̃/ *n.m.* **gai** *ou* **joyeux ~,** (*fam.*) quite a lad.

lustre /lystr/ *n.m.* (*éclat*) lustre; (*objet*) chandelier.

lustré /lystre/ *a.* shiny.

luth /lyt/ *n.m.* lute.

lutin /lytɛ̃/ *n.m.* goblin.

lutrin /lytrɛ̃/ *n.m.* lectern.

lutt|e /lyt/ *n.f.* fight, struggle; (*sport*) wrestling. **~er** *v.i.* fight, struggle; (*sport*) wrestle. **~eur, ~euse** *n.m.*, *f.* fighter; (*sport*) wrestler.

luxe /lyks/ *n.m.* luxury. **de ~,** luxury; (*produit*) de luxe.

Luxembourg /lyksãbur/ *n.m.* Luxemburg.

lux|er /lykse/ *v.t.* **se ~er le genou,** dislocate one's knee. **~ation** *n.f.* dislocation.

luxueu|x, ~se /lyksɥø, -z/ *a.* luxurious.

luxure /lyksyr/ *n.f.* lust.

luxuriant, ~e /lyksyrjã, -t/ *a.* luxuriant.

luzerne /lyzɛrn/ *n.f.* (*plante*) lucerne, alfalfa.

lycée /lise/ *n.m.* (secondary) school. **~n, ~nne** /-ɛ̃, -ɛn/ *n.m.*, *f.* pupil (at secondary school).

lynch|er /lɛ̃ʃe/ *v.t.* lynch. **~age** *n.m.* lynching.

lynx /lɛ̃ks/ *n.m.* lynx.

lyophilis|er /ljɔfilize/ *v.t.* freeze-dry. **~é** *a.* freeze-dried.

lyre /lir/ *n.f.* lyre.

lyri|que /lirik/ *a.* (*poésie*) lyric; (*passionné*) lyrical. **artiste/théâtre ~que,** opera singer/-house. **~sme** *n.m.* lyricism.

lys /lis/ *n.m.* lily.

M

m' /m/ *voir* me.

ma /ma/ *voir* mon.

maboul /mabul/ *a.* (*fam.*) mad.

macabre /makabr/ *a.* gruesome, macabre.

macadam /makadam/ *n.m.* (*goudronné*) Tarmac (P.).

macaron /makarɔ̃/ *n.m.* (*gâteau*) macaroon; (*insigne*) badge.

macaronis /makarɔni/ *n.m. pl.* macaroni.

macédoine /masedwan/ *n.f.* mixed vegetables. **~ de fruits,** fruit salad.

macérer /masere/ *v.t./i.* soak; (*dans du vinaigre*) pickle.

mâchefer /maʃfɛr/ *n.m.* clinker.

mâcher /maʃe/ *v.t.* chew. **ne pas ~ ses mots,** not mince one's words.

machiavélique /makjavelik/ *a.* machiavellian.

machin /maʃɛ̃/ *n.m.* (*chose: fam.*) thing; (*personne: fam.*) what's-his-name.

machin|al (*m. pl.* **~aux**) /maʃinal, -o/ *a.* automatic. **~alement** *adv.* automatically.

machinations /maʃinasjɔ̃/ *n.f. pl.* machinations.

machine /maʃin/ *n.f.* machine; (*d'un train, navire*) engine. **~ à écrire,** typewriter. **~ à laver/coudre,** washing-/sewing-machine. **~ à sous,** fruit machine; (*Amer.*) slot-machine. **~-outil** (*pl.* **~s-outils**) *n.f.* machine tool. **~rie** *n.f.* machinery.

machiner /maʃine/ *v.t.* plot.

machiniste /maʃinist/ *n.m.* (*théâtre*) stage-hand; (*conducteur*) driver.

macho /ma(t)ʃo/ *n.m.* (*fam.*) macho.

mâchoire /maʃwar/ *n.f.* jaw.

mâchonner /maʃɔne/ *v.t.* chew at.

maçon /masɔ̃/ *n.m.* builder; (*poseur de briques*) bricklayer. **~nerie** /-ɔnri/ *n.f.* brickwork; (*pierres*) stonework, masonry.

maçonnique /masɔnik/ *a.* Masonic.

macrobiotique /makrɔbjɔtik/ *a.* macrobiotic.

maculer /makyle/ *v.t.* stain.

Madagascar /madagaskar/ *n.f.* Madagascar.

madame (*pl.* **mesdames**) /madam, medam/ *n.f.* madam. **M~** *ou* **Mme Dupont,** Mrs Dupont. **bonsoir, mesdames,** good evening, ladies.

madeleine /madlɛn/ *n.f.* madeleine (*small shell-shaped sponge-cake*).

mademoiselle (*pl.* **mesdemoiselles**) /madmwazɛl, medmwazɛl/ *n.f.* miss. **M~** *ou* **Mlle Dupont,** Miss Dupont. **bonsoir, mesdemoiselles,** good evening, ladies.

madère /madɛr/ *n.m.* (*vin*) Madeira.

madone /madɔn/ *n.f.* madonna.

madrig|al (*pl.* **~aux**) /madrigal, -o/ *n.m.* madrigal.

maestro /maɛstro/ *n.m.* maestro.

maf(f)ia /mafja/ *n.f.* Mafia.

magasin /magazɛ̃/ *n.m.* shop, store; (*entrepôt*) warehouse; (*d'une arme etc.*) magazine.

magazine /magazin/ *n.m.* magazine; (*émission*) programme.

Maghreb /magrɛb/ *n.m.* North Africa. **~in, ~ine** *a.* & *n.m.*, *f.* North African.

magicien, ~ne /maʒisjɛ̃, -jɛn/ *n.m.*, *f.* magician.

magie /maʒi/ *n.f.* magic.

magique /maʒik/ *a.* magic; (*mystérieux*) magical.

magistr|al (*m. pl.* **~aux**) /maʒistral, -o/ *a.* masterly; (*grand: hum.*) colossal. **~alement** *adv.* in a masterly fashion.

magistrat /maʒistra/ *n.m.* magistrate.

magistrature /maʒistratyr/ *n.f.* judiciary.

magnanim|e /maɲanim/ *a.* magnanimous. **~ité** *n.f.* magnanimity.

magnat /magna/ *n.m.* tycoon, magnate.

magner (se) /(sə)maɲe/ *v. pr.* (*argot*) hurry.

magnésie /maɲezi/ *n.f.* magnesia.

magnéti|que /maɲetik/ *a.* magnetic. **~ser** *v.t.* magnetize. **~sme** *n.m.* magnetism.

magnétophone /maɲetɔfɔn/ *n.m.* tape recorder. **~ à cassettes,** cassette recorder.

magnétoscope /maɲetɔskɔp/ *n.m.* video-recorder.

magnifi|que /maɲifik/ *a.* magnificent. **~cence** *n.f.* magnificence.

magnolia /maɲɔlja/ *n.m.* magnolia.

magot /mago/ *n.m.* (*fam.*) hoard (of money).

magouill|er /maguje/ *v.i.* (*fam.*) scheming. **~eur, ~euse** *n.m.*, *f.* (*fam.*) schemer. **~e** *n.f.* (*fam.*) scheming.

magret /magrɛ/ *n.m.* **~ de canard,** steaklet of duck.

mai /mɛ/ *n.m.* May.

maigr|e /mɛgr/ *a.* thin; (*viande*) lean; (*yaourt*) low-fat; (*fig.*) poor, meagre. **faire ~e,** abstain from meat. **~ement** *adv.* poorly. **~eur** *n.f.* thinness; leanness; (*fig.*) meagreness.

maigrir /megrir/ *v.i.* get thin(ner); (*en suivant un régime*) slim. ● *v.t.* make thin(ner).

maille /mɑj/ *n.f.* stitch; (*de filet*) mesh. **~ filée,** ladder, run.

maillet /majɛ/ *n.m.* mallet.

maillon /majɔ̃/ *n.m.* link.

maillot /majo/ *n.m.* (*de sport*) jersey. **~ (de corps),** vest. **~ (de bain),** (swimming) costume.

main /mɛ̃/ *n.f.* hand. **avoir la ~ heureuse,** be lucky. **donner la ~ à qn.,** hold s.o.'s hand. **en ~s propres,** in person. **en bonnes ~,** in good hands. **~ courante,** handrail. **~-d'œuvre** (*pl.* **~s- d'œuvre**) *n.f.* labour; (*ensemble d'ouvriers*) labour force. **~-forte** *n.f. invar.* assistance. **se faire la ~,** get the hang of it. **perdre la ~,** lose one's touch. **sous la ~,** to hand. **vol/attaque à ~ armée,** armed robbery/attack.

mainmise /mɛ̃miz/ *n.f.* **~ sur,** complete hold on.

maint, ~e /mɛ̃, mɛ̃t/ *a.* many a. **~s,** many. **à ~es reprises,** on many occasions.

maintenant /mɛ̃tnɑ̃/ *adv.* now; (*de nos jours*) nowadays.

maintenir† /mɛ̃tnir/ *v.t.* keep, maintain; (*soutenir*) hold up; (*affirmer*) maintain. **se ~** *v. pr.* (*continuer*) persist; (*rester*) remain.

maintien /mɛ̃tjɛ̃/ *n.m.* (*attitude*) bearing; (*conservation*) maintenance.

maire /mɛr/ *n.m.* mayor.

mairie /meri/ *n.f.* town hall; (*administration*) town council.

mais /mɛ/ *conj.* but. ~ **oui**, ~ **si**, of course. ~ **non**, definitely not.

maïs /mais/ *n.m.* (*à cultiver*) maize; (*culin.*) sweetcorn; (*Amer.*) corn.

maison /mɛzɔ̃/ *n.f.* house; (*foyer*) home; (*immeuble*) building. ~ (**de commerce**), firm. ● *a. invar.* (*culin.*) home-made. **à la** ~, at home. **rentrer** *ou* **aller à la** ~, go home. ~ **des jeunes**, youth centre. ~ **de repos**, ~ **de convalescence**, convalescent home. ~ **de retraite**, old people's home. ~ **mère**, parent company.

maisonnée /mɛzɔne/ *n.f.* household.

maisonnette /mɛzɔnɛt/ *n.f.* small house, cottage.

maître /mɛtr/ *n.m.* master. ~ (**d'école**), schoolmaster. ~ **de**, in control of. **se rendre** ~ **de**, gain control of; (*incendie*) bring under control. ~ **assistant/de conférences**, junior/senior lecturer. ~ **chanteur**, blackmailer. ~ **d'hôtel**, head waiter; (*domestique*) butler. ~ **nageur**, swimming instructor.

maîtresse /mɛtrɛs/ *n.f.* mistress. ~ (**d'école**), schoolmistress. ● *a.f.* (*idée, poutre, qualité*) main. ~ **de**, in control of.

maîtris|e /metriz/ *n.f.* mastery; (*univ.*) master's degree. ~**e** (**de soi**), self-control. ~**er** *v.t.* master; (*incendie*) control; (*personne*) subdue. **se** ~**er** *v. pr.* control o.s.

maïzena /maizena/ *n.f.* (P.) cornflour.

majesté /maʒɛste/ *n.f.* majesty.

majestueu|x, ~**se** /maʒɛstɥø, -z/ *a.* majestic. ~**sement** *adv.* majestically.

majeur /maʒœr/ *a.* major; (*jurid.*) of age. ● *n.m.* middle finger. **en** ~**e partie**, mostly. **la** ~**e partie de**, most of.

major|er /maʒɔre/ *v.t.* increase. ~**ation** *n.f.* increase (**de**, in).

majorit|é /maʒɔrite/ *n.f.* majority. **en** ~**é**, chiefly. ~**aire** *a.* majority. **être** ~**aire**, be in the majority.

Majorque /maʒɔrk/ *n.f.* Majorca.

majuscule /maʒyskyl/ *a.* capital. ● *n.f.* capital letter.

mal¹ /mal/ *adv.* badly; (*incorrectement*) wrong(ly). ~ (**à l'aise**), uncomfortable. **aller** ~, (*malade*) be bad. **c'est** ~ **de**, it is wrong *ou* bad to. ~ **entendre/comprendre**, not hear/understand properly. ~ **famé**, of ill repute. ~ **fichu**, (*personne: fam.*) feeling lousy. ~ **en point**, in a bad state. **pas** ~, not bad; quite a lot.

mal² (*pl.* **maux**) /mal, mo/ *n.m.* evil; (*douleur*) pain, ache; (*maladie*) disease; (*effort*) trouble; (*dommage*) harm; (*malheur*) misfortune. **avoir** ~ **à la tête/aux dents/à la gorge**, have a headache/a toothache/a sore throat. **avoir** ~ **le** ~ **de mer/du pays**, be seasick/homesick. **faire du** ~ **à**, hurt, harm. **se donner du** ~ **pour faire qch.**, go to a lot of trouble to do sth.

malade /malad/ *a.* sick, ill; (*bras, gorge*) bad; (*plante*) diseased. **tu es complètement** ~!, (*fam.*) you're mad. ● *n.m./f.* sick person; (*d'un médecin*) patient.

maladie /maladi/ *n.f.* illness, disease.

maladi|f, ~**ve** /maladif, -v/ *a.* sickly; (*peur*) morbid.

maladresse /maladrɛs/ *n.f.* clumsiness; (*erreur*) blunder.

maladroit, ~**e** /maladrwa, -t/ *a. & n.m., f.* clumsy (person).

malais, ~**e¹** /malɛ, -z/ *a. & n.m., f.* Malay.

malaise² /malɛz/ *n.m.* feeling of faintness *ou* dizziness; (*fig.*) uneasiness, malaise.

malaisé /maleze/ *a.* difficult.

malaria /malarja/ *n.f.* malaria.

Malaysia /malɛzja/ *n.f.* Malaysia.

malaxer /malakse/ *v.t.* (*pétrir*) knead; (*mêler*) mix.

malchanc|e /malʃɑ̃s/ *n.f.* misfortune. ~**eux**, ~**euse** *a.* unlucky.

malcommode /malkɔmɔd/ *a.* awkward.

mâle /mɑl/ *a.* male; (*viril*) manly. ● *n.m.* male.

malédiction /malediksjɔ̃/ *n.f.* curse.

maléfice /malefis/ *n.m.* evil spell.

maléfique /malefik/ *a.* evil.

malencontreu|x, ~**se** /malɑ̃kɔ̃trø, -z/ *a.* unfortunate.

malentendant, ~**e** *a. & n.m., f.* hard of hearing.

malentendu /malɑ̃tɑ̃dy/ *n.m.* misunderstanding.

malfaçon /malfasɔ̃/ *n.f.* fault.

malfaisant, ~e /malfəzɑ̃, -t/ *a.*
harmful.

malfaiteur /malfɛtœr/ *n.m.* criminal.

malformation /malfɔrmɑsjɔ̃/ *n.f.*
malformation.

malgache /malgaʃ/ *a. & n.m./f.* Ma-
lagasy.

malgré /malgre/ *prép.* in spite of,
despite. **~ tout,** after all.

malhabile /malabil/ *a.* clumsy.

malheur /malœr/ *n.m.* misfortune;
(*accident*) accident. **faire un ~,** be a
big hit.

malheureu|x, ~se /malœrø, -z/ *a.*
unhappy; (*regrettable*) unfortunate;
(*sans succès*) unlucky; (*insignifiant*)
wretched. ● *n.m., f.* (poor) wretch.
~sement *adv.* unfortunately.

malhonnête /malɔnɛt/ *a.* dishonest.
~té *n.f.* dishonesty; (*action*) dishonest action.

malic|e /malis/ *n.f.* mischievousness;
(*méchanceté*) malice. **~ieux,
~ieuse** *a.* mischievous.

mal|in, ~igne /malɛ̃, -iɲ/ *a.* clever,
smart; (*méchant*) malicious; (*tumeur*) malignant; (*difficile: fam.*)
difficult. **~ignité** *n.f.* malignancy.

malingre /malɛ̃gr/ *a.* puny.

malintentionné /malɛ̃tɑ̃sjɔne/ *a.*
malicious.

malle /mal/ *n.f.* (*valise*) trunk;
(*auto.*) boot; (*auto., Amer.*) trunk.

malléable /maleabl/ *a.* malleable.

mallette /malɛt/ *n.f.* (small) suitcase.

malmener /malməne/ *v.t.* manhandle, handle roughly.

malnutrition /malnytrisjɔ̃/ *n.f.* malnutrition.

malodorant, ~e /malɔdɔrɑ̃, -t/ *a.*
smelly, foul-smelling.

malotru /malɔtry/ *n.m.* boor.

malpoli /malpɔli/ *a.* impolite.

malpropre /malprɔpr/ *a.* dirty. **~té**
/-əte/ *n.f.* dirtiness.

malsain, ~e /malsɛ̃, -ɛn/ *a.* unhealthy.

malt /malt/ *n.m.* malt.

maltais, ~e /maltɛ, -z/ *a. & n.m., f.*
Maltese.

Malte /malt/ *n.f.* Malta.

maltraiter /maltrete/ *v.t.* ill-treat.

malveillan|t, ~te /malvejɑ̃, -t/ *a.*
malevolent. **~ce** *n.f.* malevolence.

maman /mamɑ̃/ *n.f.* mum(my),
mother.

mamelle /mamɛl/ *n.f.* teat.

mamelon /mamlɔ̃/ *n.m.* (*anat.*) nipple; (*colline*) hillock.

mamie /mami/ *n.f.* (*fam.*) granny.

mammifère /mamifɛr/ *n.m.* mammal.

mammouth /mamut/ *n.m.* mammoth.

manche[1] /mɑ̃ʃ/ *n.f.* sleeve; (*sport,
pol.*) round. **la M~,** the Channel.

manche[2] /mɑ̃ʃ/ *n.m.* (*d'un instrument*) handle. **~ à balai,** broomstick.

manchette /mɑ̃ʃɛt/ *n.f.* cuff; (*de
journal*) headline.

manchot[1]**, ~e** /mɑ̃ʃo, -ɔt/ *a. & n.m.,
f.* one-armed (person); (*sans bras*)
armless (person).

manchot[2] /mɑ̃ʃo/ *n.m.* (*oiseau*) penguin.

mandarin /mɑ̃darɛ̃/ *n.m.* (*fonctionnaire*) mandarin.

mandarine /mɑ̃darin/ *n.f.* tangerine,
mandarin (orange).

mandat /mɑ̃da/ *n.m.* (*postal*) money
order; (*pol.*) mandate; (*procuration*)
proxy; (*de police*) warrant. **~aire**
/-tɛr/ *n.m.* (*représentant*) representative. **~er** /-te/ *v.t.* (*pol.*)
delegate.

manège /manɛʒ/ *n.m.* riding-school;
(*à la foire*) merry-go-round; (*manœuvre*) wiles, ploy.

manette /manɛt/ *n.f.* lever; (*comput.*) joystick.

mangeable /mɑ̃ʒabl/ *a.* edible.

mangeoire /mɑ̃ʒwar/ *n.f.* trough.

mang|er /mɑ̃ʒe/ *v.t./i.* eat; (*fortune*)
go through; (*ronger*) eat into.
● *n.m.* food. **donner à ~er à,** feed.
~eur, ~euse *n.m., f.* eater.

mangue /mɑ̃g/ *n.f.* mango.

maniable /manjabl/ *a.* easy to handle.

maniaque /manjak/ *a.* fussy.
● *n.m./f.* fuss-pot; (*fou*) maniac. **un
~ de,** a maniac for.

manie /mani/ *n.f.* habit; obsession.

man|ier /manje/ *v.t.* handle.
~iement *n.m.* handling.

manière /manjɛr/ *n.f.* way, manner.
~s, (*politesse*) manners; (*chichis*)
fuss. **de cette ~,** in this way. **de ~
à,** so as to. **de toute ~,** anyway, in
any case.

maniéré /manjere/ *a.* affected.

manif /manif/ *n.f.* (*fam.*) demo.

manifestant, ~e /manifɛstɑ̃, -t/
n.m., f. demonstrator.

manifeste /manifɛst/ *a.* obvious.
● *n.m.* manifesto.

manifest|er [1] /manifɛste/ *v.t.* show, manifest. **se ~er** *v. pr.* (*sentiment*) show itself; (*apparaître*) appear. **~ation** [1] *n.f.* expression, demonstration, manifestation; (*de maladie*) appearance.

manifest|er [2] /manifɛste/ *v.i.* (*pol.*) demonstrate. **~ation** [2] *n.f.* (*pol.*) demonstration; (*événement*) event.

maniganc|e /manigɑ̃s/ *n.f.* little plot. **~er** *v.t.* plot.

manipul|er /manipyle/ *v.t.* handle; (*péj.*) manipulate. **~ation** *n.f.* handling; (*péj.*) manipulation.

manivelle /manivɛl/ *n.f.* crank.

manne /man/ *n.f.* (*aubaine*) godsend.

mannequin /mankɛ̃/ *n.m.* (*personne*) model; (*statue*) dummy.

manœuvr|e [1] /manœvr/ *n.f.* manœuvre. **~er** *v.t./i.* manœuvre; (*machine*) operate.

manœuvre [2] /manœvr/ *n.m.* (*ouvrier*) labourer.

manoir /manwar/ *n.m.* manor.

manque /mɑ̃k/ *n.m.* lack (**de**, of); (*vide*) gap. **~s**, (*défauts*) faults. **~ à gagner**, loss of profit. **en (état de) ~**, having withdrawal symptoms.

manqué /mɑ̃ke/ *a.* (*écrivain etc.*) failed. **garçon ~**, tomboy.

manquement /mɑ̃kmɑ̃/ *n.m.* **~ à**, breach of.

manquer /mɑ̃ke/ *v.t.* miss; (*gâcher*) spoil; (*examen*) fail. ● *v.i.* be short *ou* lacking; (*absent*) be absent; (*en moins, disparu*) be missing; (*échouer*) fail. **~ à**, (*devoir*) fail in. **~ de**, be short of, lack. **il/ça lui manque**, he misses him/it. **~ (de) faire**, (*faillir*) nearly do. **ne pas ~ de**, not fail to.

mansarde /mɑ̃sard/ *n.f.* attic.

manteau (*pl.* **~x**) /mɑ̃to/ *n.m.* coat.

manucur|e /manykyr/ *n.m./f.* manicurist. **~er** *v.t.* manicure.

manuel, ~le /manɥɛl/ *a.* manual. ● *n.m.* (*livre*) manual. **~lement** *adv.* manually.

manufactur|e /manyfaktyr/ *n.f.* factory. **~é** *a.* manufactured.

manuscrit, ~e /manyskri, -t/ *a.* handwritten. ● *n.m.* manuscript.

manutention /manytɑ̃sjɔ̃/ *n.f.* handling.

mappemonde /mapmɔ̃d/ *n.f.* world map; (*sphère*) globe.

maquereau (*pl.* **~x**) /makro/ *n.m.* (*poisson*) mackerel; (*fam.*) pimp.

maquette /makɛt/ *n.f.* (scale) model; (*mise en page*) paste-up.

maquill|er /makije/ *v.t.* make up; (*truquer*) fake. **se ~er** *v. pr.* make (o.s.) up. **~age** *n.m.* make-up.

maquis /maki/ *n.m.* (*paysage*) scrub; (*mil.*) Maquis, underground.

maraîch|er, ~ère /mareʃe, -ɛʃɛr/ *n.m., f.* market gardener; (*Amer.*) truck farmer. **cultures ~ères**, market gardening.

marais /marɛ/ *n.m.* marsh.

marasme /marasm/ *n.m.* slump.

marathon /maratɔ̃/ *n.m.* marathon.

marbre /marbr/ *n.m.* marble.

marc /mar/ *n.m.* (*eau-de-vie*) marc. **~ de café**, coffee-grounds.

marchand, ~e /marʃɑ̃, -d/ *n.m., f.* trader; (*de charbon, vins*) merchant. ● *a.* (*valeur*) market. **~ de couleurs**, ironmonger; (*Amer.*) hardware merchant. **~ de journaux**, newsagent. **~ de légumes**, greengrocer. **~ de poissons**, fishmonger.

marchand|er /marʃɑ̃de/ *v.t.* haggle over. ● *v.i.* haggle. **~age** *n.m.* haggling.

marchandise /marʃɑ̃diz/ *n.f.* goods.

marche /marʃ/ *n.f.* (*démarche, trajet*) walk; (*rythme*) pace; (*mil., mus.*) march; (*d'escalier*) step; (*sport*) walking; (*de machine*) working; (*de véhicule*) running. **en ~**, (*train etc.*) moving. **faire ~ arrière**, (*véhicule*) reverse. **mettre en ~**, start (up). **se mettre en ~**, start moving.

marché /marʃe/ *n.m.* market; (*contrat*) deal. **faire son ~**, do one's shopping. **~ aux puces**, flea market. **M~ commun**, Common Market. **~ noir**, black market.

marchepied /marʃəpje/ *n.m.* (*de train, camion*) step.

march|er /marʃe/ *v.i.* walk; (*aller*) go; (*fonctionner*) work, run; (*prospérer*) go well; (*consentir: fam.*) agree. **~er (au pas)**, (*mil.*) march. **faire ~er qn.**, pull s.o.'s leg. **~eur, ~euse** *n.m., f.* walker.

mardi /mardi/ *n.m.* Tuesday. **M~ gras**, Shrove Tuesday.

mare /mar/ *n.f.* (*étang*) pond; (*flaque*) pool.

marécag|e /marekaʒ/ *n.m.* marsh. **~eux, ~euse** *a.* marshy.

maréch|al (*pl.* **~aux**) /mareʃal, -o/ *n.m.* marshal. **~al-ferrant** (*pl.* **~aux-ferrants**) blacksmith.

marée /mare/ *n.f.* tide; (*poissons*) fresh fish. **~ haute/basse,** high/low tide. **~ noire,** oil-slick.

marelle /marɛl/ *n.f.* hopscotch.

margarine /margarin/ *n.f.* margarine.

marge /marʒ/ *n.f.* margin. **en ~ de,** (*à l'écart de*) on the fringe(s) of. **~ bénéficiaire,** profit margin.

margin|al, ~ale (*m. pl.* **~aux**) /marʒinal, -o/ *a.* marginal. ● *n.m., f.* drop-out.

marguerite /margərit/ *n.f.* daisy; (*qui imprime*) daisy-wheel.

mari /mari/ *n.m.* husband.

mariage /marjaʒ/ *n.m.* marriage; (*cérémonie*) wedding.

marié, ~e /marje/ *a.* married. ● *n.m.* (bride)groom. ● *n.f.* bride. **les ~s,** the bride and groom.

marier /marje/ *v.t.* marry. **se ~** *v. pr.* get married, marry. **se ~ avec,** marry, get married to.

marin, ~e /marɛ̃, -in/ *a.* sea. ● *n.m.* sailor. ● *n.f.* navy. **~e marchande,** merchant navy.

mariner /marine/ *v.t./i.* marinate. **faire ~,** (*fam.*) keep hanging around.

marionnette /marjɔnɛt/ *n.f.* puppet; (*à fils*) marionette.

maritalement /maritalmɑ̃/ *adv.* as husband and wife.

maritime /maritim/ *a.* maritime, coastal; (*droit, agent*) shipping.

mark /mark/ *n.m.* mark.

marmaille /marmaj/ *n.f.* (*enfants: fam.*) brats.

marmelade /marməlad/ *n.f.* stewed fruit. **~ (d'oranges),** marmelade.

marmite /marmit/ *n.f.* (cooking-)pot.

marmonner /marmɔne/ *v.t./i.* mumble.

marmot /marmo/ *n.m.* (*fam.*) kid.

marmotter /marmɔte/ *v.t./i.* mumble.

Maroc /marɔk/ *n.m.* Morocco.

marocain, ~e /marɔkɛ̃, -ɛn/ *a. & n.m., f.* Moroccan.

maroquinerie /marɔkinri/ *n.f.* (*magasin*) leather goods shop.

marotte /marɔt/ *n.f.* fad, craze.

marquant, ~e /markɑ̃, -t/ *a.* (*remarquable*) outstanding; (*qu'on n'oublie pas*) significant.

marque /mark/ *n.f.* mark; (*de produits*) brand, make. **à vos ~s!,** (*sport*) on your marks! **de ~,** (*comm.*) brand-name; (*fig.*) important. **~ de fabrique,** trade mark. **~ déposée,** registered trade mark.

marqué /marke/ *a.* marked.

marquer /marke/ *v.t.* mark; (*indiquer*) show; (*écrire*) note down; (*point, but*) score; (*joueur*) mark; (*animal*) brand. ● *v.i.* (*trace*) leave a mark; (*événement*) stand out.

marqueterie /markɛtri/ *n.f.* marquetry.

marquis, ~e¹ /marki, -z/ *n.m., f.* marquis, marchioness.

marquise² /markiz/ *n.f.* (*auvent*) glass awning.

marraine /marɛn/ *n.f.* godmother.

marrant, ~e /marɑ̃, -t/ *a.* (*fam.*) funny.

marre /mar/ *adv.* **en avoir ~,** (*fam.*) be fed up (**de,** with).

marrer (se) /(sə)mare/ *v. pr.* (*fam.*) laugh, have a (good) laugh.

marron /marɔ̃/ *n.m.* chestnut; (*couleur*) brown; (*coup: fam.*) thump. ● *a. invar.* brown. **~ d'Inde,** horse-chestnut.

mars /mars/ *n.m.* March.

marsouin /marswɛ̃/ *n.m.* porpoise.

marteau (*pl.* **~x**) /marto/ *n.m.* hammer. **~ (de porte),** (door) knocker. **~ piqueur** *ou* **pneumatique,** pneumatic drill. **être ~,** (*fam.*) mad.

marteler /martəle/ *v.t.* hammer.

mart|ial (*m. pl.* **~iaux**) /marsjal, -jo/ *a.* martial.

martien, ~ne /marsjɛ̃, -jɛn/ *a. & n.m., f.* Martian.

martyr, ~e¹ /martir/ *n.m., f.* martyr. ● *a.* martyred. **~iser** *v.t.* martyr, (*fig.*) batter.

martyre² /martir/ *n.m.* (*souffrance*) martyrdom.

marxis|te /marksist/ *a. & n.m./f.* Marxist. **~me** *n.m.* Marxism.

mascara /maskara/ *n.m.* mascara.

mascarade /maskarad/ *n.f.* masquerade.

mascotte /maskɔt/ *n.f.* mascot.

masculin, ~e /maskylɛ̃, -in/ *a.* masculine; (*sexe*) male; (*mode, équipe*) men's. ● *n.m.* masculine. **~ité** /-inite/ *n.f.* masculinity.

maso /mazo/ *n.m./f.* (*fam.*) masochist. ● *a. invar.* masochistic.

masochis|te /mazɔsist/ *n.m./f.* masochist. ● *a.* masochistic. **~me** *n.m.* masochism.

masqu|e /mask/ *n.m.* mask. **~er** *v.t.* (*cacher*) hide, conceal (**à**, from); (*lumière*) block (off).

massacr|e /masakr/ *n.m.* massacre. **~er** *v.t.* massacre; (*abîmer*: *fam.*) spoil.

massage /masaʒ/ *n.m.* massage.

masse /mas/ *n.f.* (*volume*) mass; (*gros morceau*) lump, mass; (*outil*) sledge-hammer. **en ~,** (*vendre*) in bulk; (*venir*) in force; (*production*) mass. **la ~,** (*foule*) the masses. **une ~ de,** (*fam.*) masses of.

masser[1] /mase/ *v.t.*, **se ~** *v. pr.* (*gens, foule*) mass.

mass|er[2] /mase/ *v.t.* (*pétrir*) massage. **~eur, ~euse** *n.m.*, *f.* masseur, masseuse.

massi|f, ~ve /masif, -v/ *a.* massive; (*or, argent*) solid. ● *n.m.* (*de fleurs*) clump; (*géog.*) massif. **~vement** *adv.* (*en masse*) in large numbers.

massue /masy/ *n.f.* club, bludgeon.

mastic /mastik/ *n.m.* putty.

mastiquer /mastike/ *v.t.* (*mâcher*) chew.

masturb|er (se) /(sə)mastyrbe/ *v. pr.* masturbate. **~ation** *n.f.* masturbation.

masure /mazyr/ *n.f.* hovel.

mat /mat/ *a.* (*couleur*) matt; (*bruit*) dull. **être ~,** (*aux échecs*) be checkmate.

mât /mɑ/ *n.m.* mast; (*pylône*) pole.

match /matʃ/ *n.m.* match; (*Amer.*) game. **(faire) ~ nul,** tie, draw. **~ aller,** first leg. **~ retour,** return match.

matelas /matla/ *n.m.* mattress. **~ pneumatique,** air mattress.

matelassé /matlase/ *a.* padded; (*tissu*) quilted.

matelot /matlo/ *n.m.* sailor.

mater /mate/ *v.t.* (*personne*) subdue; (*réprimer*) stifle.

matérialiser (se) /(sə)materjalize/ *v. pr.* materialize.

matérialiste /materjalist/ *a.* materialistic. ● *n.m./f.* materialist.

matériaux /materjo/ *n.m. pl.* materials.

matériel, ~le /materjɛl/ *a.* material. ● *n.m.* equipment, materials; (*d'un ordinateur*) hardware.

maternel, ~le /matɛrnɛl/ *a.* motherly, maternal; (*rapport de parenté*) maternal. ● *n.f.* nursery school.

maternité /matɛrnite/ *n.f.* maternity hospital; (*état de mère*) motherhood.

mathémati|que /matematik/ *a.* mathematical. ● *n.f. pl.* mathematics. **~cien, ~cienne** *n.m.*, *f.* mathematician.

maths /mat/ *n.f. pl.* (*fam.*) maths.

matière /matjɛr/ *n.f.* matter; (*produit*) material; (*sujet*) subject. **en ~ de,** as regards. **~ plastique,** plastic. **~s grasses,** fat. **à 0% de ~s grasses,** fat free. **~s premières,** raw materials.

matin /matɛ̃/ *n.m.* morning. **de bon ~,** early in the morning.

matin|al (*m. pl.* **~aux**) /matinal, -o/ *a.* morning; (*de bonne heure*) early. **être ~,** be up early.

matinée /matine/ *n.f.* morning; (*spectacle*) matinée.

matou /matu/ *n.m.* tom-cat.

matraqu|e /matrak/ *n.f.* (*de police*) truncheon; (*Amer.*) billy (club). **~er** *v.t.* club, beat; (*message*) plug.

matrice /matris/ *n.f.* (*techn.*) matrix.

matrimon|ial (*m. pl.* **~iaux**) /matrimonjal, -jo/ *a.* matrimonial.

maturité /matyrite/ *n.f.* maturity.

maudire† /modir/ *v.t.* curse.

maudit, ~e /modi, -t/ *a.* (*fam.*) damned.

maugréer /mogree/ *v.i.* grumble.

mausolée /mozole/ *n.m.* mausoleum.

maussade /mosad/ *a.* gloomy.

mauvais, ~e /mɔvɛ, -z/ *a.* bad; (*erroné*) wrong; (*malveillant*) evil; (*désagréable*) nasty, bad; (*mer*) rough. ● *n.m.* **il fait ~,** the weather is bad. **le ~ moment,** the wrong time. **~e herbe,** weed. **~e langue,** gossip. **~e passe,** tight spot. **~ traitements,** ill-treatment.

mauve /mov/ *a. & n.m.* mauve.

mauviette /movjɛt/ *n.f.* weakling.

maux /mo/ *voir* mal[2].

maxim|al (*m. pl.* **~aux**) /maksimal, -o/ *a.* maximum.

maxime /maksim/ *n.f.* maxim.

maximum /maksimɔm/ *a. & n.m.* maximum. **au ~,** as much as possible; (*tout au plus*) at most.

mayonnaise /majɔnɛz/ *n.f.* mayonnaise.

mazout /mazut/ *n.m.* (fuel) oil.

me, m'* /mə, m/ *pron.* me; (*indirect*) (to) me; (*réfléchi*) myself.

méandre /meɑ̃dr/ *n.m.* meander.

mec /mɛk/ *n.m.* (*fam.*) bloke, guy.

mécanicien /mekanisjẽ/ *n.m.* mechanic; (*rail.*) train driver.

mécani|que /mekanik/ *a.* mechanical; (*jouet*) clockwork. **problème ~que**, engine trouble. ● *n.f.* mechanics; (*mécanisme*) mechanism. **~ser** *v.t.* mechanize.

mécanisme /mekanism/ *n.m.* mechanism.

méch|ant, ~ante /meʃã, -t/ *a.* (*cruel*) wicked; (*désagréable*) nasty; (*enfant*) naughty; (*chien*) vicious; (*sensationnel: fam.*) terrific. ● *n.m.,* *f.* (*enfant*) naughty child. **~amment** *adv.* wickedly. **~anceté** *n.f.* wickedness; (*action*) wicked action.

mèche /mɛʃ/ *n.f.* (*de cheveux*) lock; (*de bougie*) wick; (*d'explosif*) fuse. **de ~ avec**, in league with.

méconnaissable /mekɔnɛsabl/ *a.* unrecognizable.

méconn|aître /mekɔnɛtr/ *v.t.* be ignorant of; (*mésestimer*) underestimate. **~aissance** *n.f.* ignorance. **~u** *a.* unrecognized.

mécontent, ~e /mekõtã, -t/ *a.* dissatisfied (**de**, with); (*irrité*) annoyed (**de**, at, with). **~ement** /-tmã/ *n.m.* dissatisfaction; annoyance. **~er** /-te/ *v.t.* dissatisfy; (*irriter*) annoy.

médaill|e /medaj/ *n.f.* medal; (*insigne*) badge; (*bijou*) medallion. **~é, ~ée** *n.m., f.* medal holder.

médaillon /medajõ/ *n.m.* medallion; (*bijou*) locket.

médecin /medsẽ/ *n.m.* doctor.

médecine /medsin/ *n.f.* medicine.

média /medja/ *n.m.* medium. **les ~s**, the media.

média|teur, ~trice /medjatœr, -tris/ *n.m., f.* mediator.

médiation /medjasjõ/ *n.f.* mediation.

médiatique /medjatik/ *a.* **événement/personnalité ~**, media event/personality.

médic|al (*m. pl.* **~aux**) /medikal, -o/ *a.* medical.

médicament /medikamã/ *n.m.* medicine.

médicin|al (*m. pl.* **~aux**) /medisinal, -o/ *a.* medicinal.

médico-lég|al (*m. pl.* **~aux**) /medikolegal, -o/ *a.* forensic.

médiév|al (*m. pl.* **~aux**) /medjeval, -o/ *a.* medieval.

médiocr|e /medjɔkr/ *a.* mediocre, poor. **~ement** *adv.* (*peu*) not very;

(*mal*) in a mediocre way. **~ité** *n.f.* mediocrity.

médire /medir/ *v.i.* **~ de**, speak ill of.

médisance /medizãs/ *n.f.* **~(s)**, malicious gossip.

méditati|f, ~ve /meditatif, -v/ *a.* (*pensif*) thoughtful.

médit|er /medite/ *v.t./i.* meditate. **~er de**, plan to. **~ation** *n.f.* meditation.

Méditerranée /mediterane/ *n.f.* **la ~**, the Mediterranean.

méditerranéen, ~ne /mediteraneẽ, -ɛn/ *a.* Mediterranean.

médium /medjɔm/ *n.m.* (*personne*) medium.

méduse /medyz/ *n.f.* jellyfish.

meeting /mitiŋ/ *n.m.* meeting.

méfait /mefɛ/ *n.m.* misdeed. **les ~s de**, (*conséquences*) the ravages of.

méfian|t, ~te /mefjã, -t/ *a.* distrustful. **~ce** *n.f.* distrust.

méfier (se) /(sə)mefje/ *v. pr.* be wary *ou* careful. **se ~ de**, distrust, be wary of.

mégarde (par) /(par)megard/ *adv.* by accident, accidentally.

mégère /meʒɛr/ *n.f.* (*femme*) shrew.

mégot /mego/ *n.m.* (*fam.*) cigarette-end.

meilleur, ~e /mɛjœr/ *a. & adv.* better (**que**, than). **le ~ livre**/*etc.*, the best book/*etc.* **mon ~ ami**/*etc.*, my best friend/*etc.* **~ marché**, cheaper. ● *n.m., f.* **le ~/la ~e**, the best (one).

mélancol|ie /melãkɔli/ *n.f.* melancholy. **~ique** *a.* melancholy.

mélang|e /melãʒ/ *n.m.* mixture, blend. **~er** *v.t.*, **se ~er** *v. pr.* mix, blend; (*embrouiller*) mix up.

mélasse /melas/ *n.f.* treacle; (*Amer.*) molasses.

mêlée /mele/ *n.f.* scuffle; (*rugby*) scrum.

mêler /mele/ *v.t.* mix (**à**, with); (*qualités*) combine; (*embrouiller*) mix up. **~ à**, (*impliquer dans*) involve in. **se ~** *v. pr.* mix; combine. **se ~ à**, (*se joindre à*) join. **se ~ de**, meddle in. **mêle-toi de ce qui te regarde**, mind your own business.

méli-mélo /melimelo/ *n.m.* (*pl.* **mélis-mélos**) jumble.

mélo /melo/ (*fam.*) *n.m.* melodrama. ● *a. invar.* melodramatic.

mélod|ie /melɔdi/ *n.f.* melody. **~ieux, ~ieuse** *a.* melodious. **~ique** *a.* melodic.

mélodram|e /melɔdram/ *n.m.* me-
lodrama. **~atique** *a.* melodramatic.

mélomane /melɔman/ *n.m./f.* music
lover.

melon /mlɔ̃/ *n.m.* melon. **(chapeau)**
~, bowler (hat).

membrane /mɑ̃bran/ *n.f.* membrane.

membre[1] /mɑ̃br/ *n.m.* limb.

membre[2] /mɑ̃br/ *n.m.* (*adhérent*)
member.

même /mɛm/ *a.* same. **ce livre/***etc.*
~, this very book/*etc.* **la bonté/***etc.*
~, kindness/*etc.* itself. ● *pron.* le
~/la ~, the same (one). ● *adv.*
even. **à ~,** (*sur*) directly on. **à ~**
de, in a position to. **de ~,** (*aussi*)
too; (*de la même façon*) likewise. **de**
~ que, just as. **en ~ temps,** at the
same time.

mémé /meme/ *n.f.* (*fam.*) granny.

mémo /memo/ *n.m.* memo.

mémoire /memwar/ *n.f.* memory.
● *n.m.* (*requête*) memorandum;
(*univ.*) dissertation. **~s,** (*souvenirs*
écrits) memoirs. **à la ~ de,** to the
memory of. **de ~,** from memory. **~**
morte/vive, (*comput.*) ROM/RAM.

mémorable /memɔrabl/ *a.* memorable.

mémorandum /memɔrɑ̃dɔm/ *n.m.*
memorandum.

menac|e /mənas/ *n.f.* threat. **~er** *v.t.*
threaten (**de faire,** to do).

ménage /menaʒ/ *n.m.* (married) couple; (*travail*) housework. **se mettre**
en ~, set up house. **scène de ~,**
scene. **dépenses du ~,** household
expenditure.

ménagement /menaʒmɑ̃/ *n.m.* care
and consideration.

ménag|er[1]**, ~ère** /menaʒe, -ɛr/ *a.*
household, domestic. **travaux ~ers,**
housework. ● *n.f.* housewife.

ménager[2] /menaʒe/ *v.t.* treat with
tact; (*utiliser*) be sparing in the use
of; (*organiser*) prepare (carefully).

ménagerie /menaʒri/ *n.f.* menagerie.

mendiant, ~e /mɑ̃djɑ̃, -t/ *n.m.,* *f.*
beggar.

mendicité /mɑ̃disite/ *n.f.* begging.

mendier /mɑ̃dje/ *v.t.* beg for. ● *v.i.*
beg.

menées /məne/ *n.f. pl.* schemings.

mener /məne/ *v.t.* lead; (*entreprise,*
pays) run. ● *v.i.* lead. **~ à,** (*accom-*
pagner à) take to. **~ à bien,** see
through.

meneur /mənœr/ *n.m.* (*chef*)
(ring)leader. **~ de jeu,** compère;
(*Amer.*) master of ceremonies.

méningite /menɛ̃ʒit/ *n.f.* meningitis.

ménopause /menɔpoz/ *n.f.* menopause.

menotte /mənɔt/ *n.f.* (*fam.*) hand.
~s, handcuffs.

mensong|e /mɑ̃sɔ̃ʒ/ *n.m.* lie; (*action*)
lying. **~er, ~ère** *a.* untrue.

menstruation /mɑ̃stryasjɔ̃/ *n.f.* menstruation.

mensualité /mɑ̃sɥalite/ *n.f.* monthly
payment.

mensuel, ~le /mɑ̃sɥɛl/ *a. & n.m.*
monthly. **~lement** *adv.* monthly.

mensurations /mɑ̃syrasjɔ̃/ *n.f. pl.*
measurements.

ment|al (*m. pl.* **~aux**) /mɑ̃tal, -o/ *a.*
mental.

mentalité /mɑ̃talite/ *n.f.* mentality.

menteu|r, ~se /mɑ̃tœr, -øz/ *n.m., f.*
liar. ● *a.* untruthful.

menthe /mɑ̃t/ *n.f.* mint.

mention /mɑ̃sjɔ̃/ *n.f.* mention; (*an-*
notation) note; (*scol.*) grade. **~ bien,**
(*scol.*) distinction. **~ner** /-jɔne/ *v.t.*
mention.

mentir† /mɑ̃tir/ *v.i.* lie.

menton /mɑ̃tɔ̃/ *n.m.* chin.

mentor /mɛ̃tɔr/ *n.m.* mentor.

menu[1] /məny/ *n.m.* (*carte*) menu;
(*repas*) meal.

menu[2] /məny/ *a.* (*petit*) tiny; (*fin*)
fine; (*insignifiant*) minor. ● *adv.*
(*couper*) fine.

menuis|ier /mənɥizje/ *n.m.* carpen-
ter, joiner. **~erie** *n.f.* carpentry,
joinery.

méprendre (se) /(sə)meprɑ̃dr/ *v. pr.*
se ~ sur, be mistaken about.

mépris /mepri/ *n.m.* contempt, scorn
(**de,** for). **au ~ de,** in defiance of.

méprisable /meprizabl/ *a.* despicable.

méprise /mepriz/ *n.f.* mistake.

mépris|er /meprize/ *v.t.* scorn,
despise. **~ant, ~ante** *a.* scornful.

mer /mɛr/ *n.f.* sea; (*marée*) tide. **en**
haute ~, on the open sea.

mercenaire /mɛrsənɛr/ *n.m. & a.*
mercenary.

merci /mɛrsi/ *int.* thank you, thanks
(**de, pour,** for). ● *n.f.* mercy. **~**
beaucoup, ~ bien, thank you very
much.

merc|ier, ~ière /mɛrsje, -jɛr/ *n.m., f.*
haberdasher; (*Amer.*) notions

merchant. **~erie** n.f. haberdashery; (*Amer.*) notions store.

mercredi /mɛrkrədi/ n.m. Wednesday. **~ des Cendres,** Ash Wednesday.

mercure /mɛrkyr/ n.m. mercury.

merde /mɛrd/ n.f. (*fam.*) shit. **être dans la ~,** be in a mess.

mère /mɛr/ n.f. mother. **~ de famille,** mother.

méridien /meridjɛ̃/ n.m. meridian.

méridion|al, ~ale (*m. pl. ~aux*) /meridjɔnal, -o/ a. southern. ● n.m., f. southerner.

meringue /mərɛ̃g/ n.f. meringue.

mérite /merit/ n.m. merit. **il n'a aucun ~,** that's as it should be. **il a du ~,** it's very much to his credit.

mérit|er /merite/ v.t. deserve. **~ant, ~ante** a. deserving.

méritoire /meritwar/ a. commendable.

merlan /mɛrlɑ̃/ n.m. whiting.

merle /mɛrl/ n.m. blackbird.

merveille /mɛrvɛj/ n.f. wonder, marvel. **à ~,** wonderfully. **faire des ~s,** work wonders.

merveilleu|x, ~se /mɛrvɛjø, -z/ a. wonderful, marvellous. **~sement** adv. wonderfully.

mes /me/ voir mon.

mésange /mezɑ̃ʒ/ n.f. tit(mouse).

mésaventure /mezavɑ̃tyr/ n.f. misadventure.

mesdames /medam/ voir madame.

mesdemoiselles /medmwazɛl/ voir mademoiselle.

mésentente /mezɑ̃tɑ̃t/ n.f. disagreement.

mesquin, ~e /mɛskɛ̃, -in/ a. mean. **~erie** /-inri/ n.f. meanness.

mess /mɛs/ n.m. (*mil.*) mess.

messag|e /mesaʒ/ n.m. message. **~er, ~ère** n.m., f. messenger.

messe /mɛs/ n.f. (*relig.*) mass.

Messie /mesi/ n.m. Messiah.

messieurs /mesjø/ voir monsieur.

mesure /məzyr/ n.f. measurement; (*quantité, étalon*) measure; (*disposition*) measure, step; (*cadence*) time; (*modération*) moderation. **à ~ que,** as. **dans la ~ où,** in so far as. **dans une certaine ~,** to some extent. **en ~ de,** in a position to.

mesuré /məzyre/ a. measured; (*personne*) moderate.

mesurer /məzyre/ v.t. measure; (*juger*) assess; (*argent, temps*) ration. **se ~ avec,** pit o.s. against.

met /mɛ/ voir mettre.

métabolisme /metabɔlism/ n.m. metabolism.

mét|al (*pl. ~aux*) /metal, -o/ n.m. metal. **~allique** a. (*objet*) metal; (*éclat etc.*) metallic.

métallurg|ie /metalyrʒi/ n.f. (*industrie*) steel ou metal industry. **~iste** n.m. steel ou metal worker.

métamorphos|e /metamɔrfoz/ n.f. metamorphosis. **~er** v.t., **se ~er** v. pr. transform.

métaphor|e /metafɔr/ n.f. metaphor. **~ique** a. metaphorical.

météo /meteo/ n.f. (*bulletin*) weather forecast.

météore /meteɔr/ n.m. meteor.

météorolog|ie /meteɔrɔlɔʒi/ n.f. meteorology; (*service*) weather bureau. **~ique** a. weather; (*études etc.*) meteorological.

méthod|e /metɔd/ n.f. method; (*ouvrage*) course, manual. **~ique** a. methodical.

méticuleu|x, ~se /metikylø, -z/ a. meticulous.

métier /metje/ n.m. job; (*manuel*) trade; (*intellectuel*) profession; (*expérience*) skill. **~ (à tisser),** loom. **remettre sur le ~,** keep going back to the drawing-board.

métis, ~se /metis/ a. & n.m., f. half-caste.

métrage /metraʒ/ n.m. length. **court ~,** short film. **long ~,** full-length film.

mètre /mɛtr/ n.m. metre; (*règle*) rule. **~ ruban,** tape-measure.

métreur /metrœr/ n.m. quantity surveyor.

métrique /metrik/ a. metric.

métro /metro/ n.m. underground; (*à Paris*) Métro.

métropol|e /metrɔpɔl/ n.f. metropolis; (*pays*) mother country. **~itain, ~itaine** a. metropolitan.

mets ¹ /mɛ/ n.m. dish.

mets ² /mɛ/ voir mettre.

mettable /metabl/ a. wearable.

metteur /metœr/ n.m. **~ en scène,** (*théâtre*) producer; (*cinéma*) director.

mettre† /mɛtr/ v.t. put; (*vêtement*) put on; (*radio, chauffage, etc.*) put ou switch on; (*table*) lay; (*pendule*) set; (*temps*) take; (*installer*) put in; (*supposer*) suppose. **se ~** v. pr. put o.s.; (*objet*) go; (*porter*) wear. **~ bas,** give birth. **~ qn. en boîte,** pull s.o.'s

leg. **~ en cause** *ou* **en question,**
question. **~ en colère,** make angry.
~ en valeur, highlight. (*un bien*)
exploit. **se ~ à,** (*entrer dans*) get *ou*
go into. **se ~ à faire,** start doing.
~ à l'aise, make o.s. comfortable. **se
~ à table,** sit down at the table. **se
~ au travail,** set to work. **(se) ~ en
ligne,** line up. **se ~ dans tous ses
états,** get into a state. **se ~ du sable
dans les yeux,** get sand in one's
eyes.

meuble /mœbl/ *n.m.* piece of
furniture. **~s,** furniture.

meublé /møble/ *n.m.* furnished flat-
let.

meubler /møble/ *v.t.* furnish; (*fig.*)
fill. **se ~** *v. pr.* buy furniture.

meugl|er /møgle/ *v.i.* moo. **~e-
ment(s)** *n.m.* (*pl.*) mooing.

meule /møl/ *n.f.* (*de foin*) haystack;
(*à moudre*) millstone.

meun|ier, ~ière /mønje, -jɛr/ *n.m.,
f.* miller.

meurs, meurt /mœr/ *voir* mourir.

meurtr|e /mœrtr/ *n.m.* murder. **~ier,
~ière** *a.* deadly; *n.m.* murderer; *n.f.*
murderess.

meurtr|ir /mœrtrir/ *v.t.* bruise.
~issure *n.f.* bruise.

meute /møt/ *n.f.* (*troupe*) pack.

mexicain, ~e /mɛksikɛ̃, -ɛn/ *a. &
n.m., f.* Mexican.

Mexique /mɛksik/ *n.m.* Mexico.

mi- /mi/ *préf.* mid-, half-. **à mi-chemin,** half-way. **à mi-côte,** half-way
up the hill. **la mi-juin**/*etc.*, mid-
June/*etc.*

miaou /mjau/ *n.m.* mew.

miaul|er /mjole/ *v.i.* mew. **~ement**
n.m. mew.

miche /miʃ/ *n.f.* round loaf.

micro /mikro/ *n.m.* microphone,
mike; (*comput.*) micro.

micro- /mikro/ *préf.* micro-.

microbe /mikrɔb/ *n.m.* germ.

microfilm /mikrɔfilm/ *n.m.* micro-
film.

micro-onde /mikrɔõd/ *n.f.* microwave. **un (four à) ~s,** microwave
(oven).

microphone /mikrɔfɔn/ *n.m.* microphone.

microplaquette /mikrɔplakɛt/ *n.f.*
(micro)chip.

microprocesseur /mikrɔprɔsɛsœr/
n.m. microprocess.

microscop|e /mikrɔskɔp/ *n.m.*
microscope. **~ique** *a.* microscopic.

microsillon /mikrɔsijõ/ *n.m.* long-
playing record.

midi /midi/ *n.m.* twelve o'clock, midday, noon; (*déjeuner*) lunch-time;
(*sud*) south. **le M~,** the South of
France.

mie /mi/ *n.f.* soft part (of the loaf). **un
pain de ~,** a sandwich loaf.

miel /mjɛl/ *n.m.* honey.

mielleu|x, ~se /mjɛlø, -z/ *a.* unctu-
ous.

mien, ~ne /mjɛ̃, mjɛn/ *pron.* **le ~, la
~ne, les ~(ne)s,** mine.

miette /mjɛt/ *n.f.* crumb; (*fig.*) scrap.
en ~s, in pieces.

mieux /mjø/ *adv. & a. invar.* better
(**que,** than). **le** *ou* **la** *ou* **les ~,** (the)
best. ● *n.m.* best; (*progrès*) im-
provement. **faire de son ~,** do one's
best. **tu ferais ~ de faire,** you
would be better off doing. **le ~
serait de,** the best thing would be to.

mièvre /mjɛvr/ *a.* genteel and insipid.

mignon, ~ne /miɲõ, -ɔn/ *a.* pretty.

migraine /migrɛn/ *n.f.* headache.

migration /migrasjõ/ *n.f.* migration.

mijoter /miʒote/ *v.t./i.* simmer;
(*tramer*: *fam.*) cook up.

mil /mil/ *n.m.* a thousand.

milic|e /milis/ *n.f.* militia. **~ien** *n.m.*
militiaman.

milieu (*pl.* **~x**) /miljø/ *n.m.* middle;
(*environnement*) environment;
(*groupe*) circle; (*voie*) middle way;
(*criminel*) underworld. **au ~ de,** in
the middle of. **en plein** *ou* **au beau
~ de,** right in the middle (of).

militaire /militɛr/ *a.* military.
● *n.m.* soldier.

milit|er /milite/ *v.i.* be a militant.
~er pour, militate in favour of.
~ant, ~ante *n.m., f.* militant.

milk-shake /milkʃɛk/ *n.m.* milk
shake.

mille[1] /mil/ *a. & n.m. invar.* a
thousand. **deux ~,** two thousand.
dans le ~, bang on target.

mille[2] /mil/ *n.m.* **~ (marin),** (nautical) mile.

millénaire /milenɛr/ *n.m.* millennium.

mille-pattes /milpat/ *n.m. invar.*
centipede.

millésime /milezim/ *n.m.* year.

millésimé /milezime/ *a.* **vin ~,** vintage wine.

millet /mijɛ/ *n.m.* millet.

milliard /miljar/ *n.m.* thousand million, billion. **~aire** /-dɛr/ *n.m./f.* multimillionaire.

millier /milje/ *n.m.* thousand. **un ~ (de)**, about a thousand.

millimètre /milimɛtr/ *n.m.* millimetre.

million /miljɔ̃/ *n.m.* million. **deux ~s (de)**, two million. **~naire** /-jɔnɛr/ *n.m./f.* millionaire.

mim|e /mim/ *n.m./f.* (*personne*) mime. ● *n.m.* (*art*) mime. **~er** *v.t.* mime; (*singer*) mimic.

mimique /mimik/ *n.f.* (expressive) gestures.

mimosa /mimoza/ *n.m.* mimosa.

minable /minabl/ *a.* shabby.

minaret /minarɛ/ *n.m.* minaret.

minauder /minode/ *v.i.* simper.

minc|e /mɛ̃s/ *a.* thin; (*svelte, insignifiant*) slim. ● *int.* dash (it). **~ir** *v.i.* get slimmer. **ça te ~it**, it makes you look slimmer. **~eur** *n.f.* thinness; slimness.

mine [1] /min/ *n.f.* expression; (*allure*) appearance. **avoir bonne ~**, look well. **faire ~ de**, make as if to.

mine [2] /min/ *n.f.* (*exploitation, explosif*) mine; (*de crayon*) lead. **~ de charbon**, coal-mine.

miner /mine/ *v.t.* (*saper*) undermine; (*garnir d'explosifs*) mine.

minerai /minrɛ/ *n.m.* ore.

minér|al (*m. pl.* **~aux**) /mineral, -o/ *a.* mineral. ● *n.m.* (*pl.* **~aux**) mineral.

minéralogique /mineralɔʒik/ *a.* **plaque ~**, number/license (*Amer.*) plate.

minet, ~te /minɛ, -t/ *n.m., f.* (*chat: fam.*) puss(y).

mineur [1], **~e** /minœr/ *a.* minor; (*jurid.*) under age. ● *n.m., f.* (*jurid.*) minor.

mineur [2] /minœr/ *n.m.* (*ouvrier*) miner.

mini- /mini/ *préf.* mini-.

miniature /minjatyr/ *n.f.* & *a.* miniature.

minibus /minibys/ *n.m.* minibus.

min|ier, ~ière /minje, -jɛr/ *a.* mining.

minim|al (*m. pl.* **~aux**) /minimal, -o/ *a.* minimum.

minime /minim/ *a.* minor. ● *n.m./f.* (*sport*) junior.

minimiser /minimize/ *v.t.* minimize.

minimum /minimɔm/ *a.* & *n.m.* minimum. **au ~**, (*pour le moins*) at the very least.

mini-ordinateur /miniɔrdinatœr/ *n.m.* minicomputer.

minist|ère /ministɛr/ *n.m.* ministry; (*gouvernement*) government. **~ère de l'Intérieur**, Home Office; (*Amer.*) Department of the Interior. **~ériel**, **~érielle** *a.* ministerial, government.

ministre /ministr/ *n.m.* minister. **~ de l'Intérieur**, Home Secretary; (*Amer.*) Secretary of the Interior.

Minitel /minitɛl/ *n.m.* (P.) Minitel (*telephone videotext system*).

minorer /minɔre/ *v.t.* reduce.

minorit|é /minɔrite/ *n.f.* minority. **~aire** *a.* minority. **être ~aire**, be in the minority.

minuit /minɥi/ *n.m.* midnight.

minuscule /minyskyl/ *a.* minute. ● *n.f.* (**lettre**) **~**, small letter.

minut|e /minyt/ *n.f.* minute. **~er** *v.t.* time (to the minute).

minuterie /minytri/ *n.f.* time-switch.

minutie /minysi/ *n.f.* meticulousness.

minutieu|x, ~se /minysjø, -z/ *a.* meticulous. **~sement** *adv.* meticulously.

mioche /mjɔʃ/ *n.m., f.* (*fam.*) youngster, kid.

mirabelle /mirabɛl/ *n.f.* (mirabelle) plum.

miracle /mirɑkl/ *n.m.* miracle.

miraculeu|x, ~se /mirakylø, -z/ *a.* miraculous. **~sement** *adv.* miraculously.

mirage /miraʒ/ *n.m.* mirage.

mire /mir/ *n.f.* (*fig.*) centre of attraction; (TV) test card.

miro /miro/ *a.* *invar.* (*fam.*) short-sighted.

mirobolant, ~e /mirɔbɔlɑ̃, -t/ *a.* (*fam.*) marvellous.

miroir /mirwar/ *n.m.* mirror.

miroiter /mirwate/ *v.i.* gleam, shimmer.

mis, ~e [1] /mi, miz/ *voir* mettre. ● *a.* **bien ~**, well-dressed.

misanthrope /mizɑ̃trɔp/ *n.m.* misanthropist. ● *a.* misanthropic.

mise [2] /miz/ *n.f.* (*argent*) stake; (*tenue*) attire. **~ à feu**, blast-off. **~ au point**, adjustment; (*fig.*) clarification; **~ de fonds**, capital outlay. **~ en garde**, warning. **~ en scène**, (*théâtre*) production; (*cinéma*) direction.

miser /mize/ v.t. (argent) bet, stake (**sur,** on). **~ sur,** (compter sur: fam.) bank on.

misérable /mizerabl/ a. miserable, wretched; (indigent) poverty-stricken; (minable) seedy. ● n.m./f. wretch.

mis|ère /mizɛr/ n.f. (grinding) poverty; (malheur) misery. **~éreux, ~éreuse** n.m., f. pauper.

miséricorde /mizerikɔrd/ n.f. mercy.

missel /misɛl/ n.m. missal.

missile /misil/ n.m. missile.

mission /misjɔ̃/ n.m. mission. **~naire** /-jɔnɛr/ n.m./f. missionary.

missive /misiv/ n.f. missive.

mistral /mistral/ n.m. invar. (vent) mistral.

mitaine /mitɛn/ n.f. mitten.

mit|e /mit/ n.f. (clothes-)moth. **~é** a. moth-eaten.

mi-temps /mitɑ̃/ n.f. invar. (repos: sport) half-time; (période: sport) half. **à ~,** part time.

miteu|x, ~se /mitø, -z/ a. shabby.

mitigé /mitiʒe/ a. (modéré) lukewarm.

mitonner /mitɔne/ v.t. cook slowly with care; (fig.) cook up.

mitoyen, ~ne /mitwajɛ̃, -ɛn/ a. **mur ~,** party wall.

mitrailler /mitraje/ v.t. machine-gun; (fig.) bombard.

mitrailllette /mitrajɛt/ n.f. sub-machine-gun. **~euse** n.f. machine-gun.

mi-voix (à) /(a)mivwa/ adv. in an undertone.

mixeur /miksœr/ n.m. liquidizer, blender.

mixte /mikst/ a. mixed; (usage) dual; (tribunal) joint; (école) co-educational.

mixture /mikstyr/ n.f. (péj.) mixture.

mobile [1] /mɔbil/ a. mobile; (pièce) moving; (feuillet) loose. ● n.m. (art) mobile.

mobile [2] /mɔbil/ n.m. (raison) motive.

mobilier /mɔbilje/ n.m. furniture.

mobilis|er /mɔbilize/ v.t. mobilize. **~ation** n.f. mobilization.

mobilité /mɔbilite/ n.f. mobility.

mobylette /mɔbilɛt/ n.f. (P.) moped.

mocassin /mɔkasɛ̃/ n.m. moccasin.

moche /mɔʃ/ a. (laid: fam.) ugly; (mauvais: fam.) lousy.

modalité /mɔdalite/ n.f. mode.

mode [1] /mɔd/ n.f. fashion; (coutume) custom. **à la ~,** fashionable.

mode [2] /mɔd/ n.m. method, mode; (genre) way. **~ d'emploi,** directions (for use).

modèle /mɔdɛl/ n.m. & a. model. **~ réduit,** (small-scale) model.

modeler /mɔdle/ v.t. model (**sur,** on). **se ~ sur,** model o.s. on.

modem /mɔdɛm/ n.m. modem.

modéré, ~e /mɔdere/ a. & n.m., f. moderate. **~ment** adv. moderately.

modér|er /mɔdere/ v.t. moderate. **se ~er** v. pr. restrain o.s. **~ateur, ~atrice** a. moderating. **~ation** n.f. moderation.

modern|e /mɔdɛrn/ a. modern. ● n.m. modern style. **~iser** v.t. modernize.

modest|e /mɔdɛst/ a. modest. **~ement** adv. modestly. **~ie** n.f. modesty.

modif|ier /mɔdifje/ v.t. modify. **se ~ier** v. pr. alter. **~ication** n.f. modification.

modique /mɔdik/ a. low.

modiste /mɔdist/ n.f. milliner.

module /mɔdyl/ n.m. module.

modul|er /mɔdyle/ v.t./i. modulate. **~ation** n.f. modulation.

moelle /mwal/ n.f. marrow. **~ épinière,** spinal cord.

moelleu|x, ~se /mwalø, -z/ a. soft; (onctueux) smooth.

mœurs /mœr(s)/ n.f. pl. (morale) morals; (habitudes) customs; (manières) ways.

moi /mwa/ pron. me; (indirect) (to) me; (sujet) I. ● n.m. self. **~-même** pron. myself.

moignon /mwaɲɔ̃/ n.m. stump.

moindre /mwɛ̃dr/ a. (moins grand) less(er). **le** ou **la ~, les ~s,** the slightest, the least.

moine /mwan/ n.m. monk.

moineau (pl. **~x**) /mwano/ n.m. sparrow.

moins /mwɛ̃/ adv. less (**que,** than). ● prép. (soustraction) minus. **~ de,** (quantité) less, not so much (**que,** as); (objets, personnes) fewer, not so many (**que,** as). **~ de dix francs/ d'une heure/**etc., less than ten francs/one pound/etc. **le** ou **la** ou **les ~,** the least. **le ~ grand/haut,** the smallest/lowest. **au ~, du ~,** at least. **de ~,** less. **en ~,** less; (manquant) missing. **une heure ~ dix,** ten to one. **à ~ que,** unless. **de ~ en moins,** less and less.

mois /mwa/ n.m. month.

moïse /mɔiz/ *n.m.* moses basket.
mois|i /mwazi/ *a.* mouldy. ● *n.m.*
mould. **de ~i**, (*odeur, goût*) musty.
~ir *v.i.* go mouldy. **~issure** *n.f.*
mould.
moisson /mwasɔ̃/ *n.f.* harvest.
moissonn|er /mwasɔne/ *v.t.* harvest,
reap. **~eur**, **~euse** *n.m.*, *f.*
harvester. **~euse-batteuse** (*pl.*
~euses-batteuses) *n.f.* combine
harvester.
moit|e /mwat/ *a.* sticky, clammy.
~eur *n.f.* stickiness.
moitié /mwatje/ *n.f.* half; (*milieu*)
half-way mark. **à ~**, half-way. **à ~
vide/fermé**/*etc.*, half empty/closed/
etc. **à ~ prix**, (at) half-price. **la ~ de**,
half (of). **~ moitié**, half-and-half.
moka /mɔka/ *n.m.* (*gâteau*) coffee
cream cake.
mol /mɔl/ *voir* mou.
molaire /mɔlɛr/ *n.f.* molar.
molécule /mɔlekyl/ *n.f.* molecule.
molester /mɔlɛste/ *v.t.* manhandle,
rough up.
molle /mɔl/ *voir* mou.
moll|ement /mɔlmɑ̃/ *adv.* softly; (*fai-
blement*) feebly. **~esse** *n.f.* softness;
(*faiblesse, indolence*) feebleness.
mollet /mɔlɛ/ *n.m.* (*de jambe*) calf.
molletonné /mɔltɔne/ *a.* (fleece-)
lined.
mollir /mɔlir/ *v.i.* soften; (*céder*)
yield.
mollusque /mɔlysk/ *n.m.* mollusc.
môme /mom/ *n.m./f.* (*fam.*) kid.
moment /mɔmɑ̃/ *n.m.* moment; (*période*) time. **(petit) ~**, short while.
au ~ où, when. **par ~s**, now and
then. **du ~ ou ou que**, seeing that.
en ce ~, at the moment.
momentané /mɔmɑ̃tane/ *a.* mo-
mentary. **~ment** *adv.* momentarily;
(*en ce moment*) at present.
momie /mɔmi/ *n.f.* mummy.
mon, ma *ou* **mon*** (*pl.* **mes**) /mɔ̃,
ma, mɔ̃, me/ *a.* my.
Monaco /mɔnako/ *n.f.* Monaco.
monarchie /mɔnarʃi/ *n.f.* monarchy.
monarque /mɔnark/ *n.m.* monarque.
monastère /mɔnastɛr/ *n.m.* monastery.
monceau (*pl.* **~x**) /mɔ̃so/ *n.m.* heap,
pile
mondain, ~e /mɔ̃dɛ̃, -ɛn/ *a.* society,
social.
monde /mɔ̃d/ *n.m.* world. **du ~**, (a lot
of) people; (*quelqu'un*) somebody. **le
(grand) ~**, (high) society. **se faire**

un ~ de qch., make a great deal of
fuss about sth.
mond|ial (*m. pl.* **~iaux**) /mɔ̃djal, -jo/
a. world; (*influence*) worldwide.
~ialement *adv.* the world over.
monégasque /mɔnegask/ *a. & n.m./
f.* Monegasque.
monétaire /mɔnetɛr/ *a.* monetary.
moni|teur, ~trice /mɔnitœr, -tris/
n.m., *f.* instructor, instructress; (*de
colonie de vacances*) supervisor;
(*Amer.*) (camp) counselor.
monnaie /mɔnɛ/ *n.f.* currency;
(*pièce*) coin; (*appoint*) change. **faire
la ~ de**, get change for. **faire à qn.
la ~ de**, give s.o. change for. **menue
ou petite ~**, small change.
monnayer /mɔneje/ *v.t.* convert into
cash.
mono /mɔno/ *a. invar.* mono.
monocle /mɔnɔkl/ *n.m.* monocle.
monocorde /mɔnɔkɔrd/ *a.* monoto-
nous.
monogramme /mɔnɔgram/ *n.m.*
monogram.
monologue /mɔnɔlɔg/ *n.m.* monologue.
monopol|e /mɔnɔpɔl/ *n.m.* mono-
poly. **~iser** *v.t.* monopolize.
monosyllabe /mɔnɔsilab/ *n.m.*
monosyllable.
monoton|e /mɔnɔtɔn/ *a.* mono-
tonous. **~ie** *n.f.* monotony.
monseigneur /mɔ̃sɛɲœr/ *n.m.* Your
ou His Grace.
monsieur (*pl.* **messieurs**) /məsjø,
mesjø/ *n.m.* gentleman. **M~** *ou* **M.
Dupont**, Mr Dupont. **Messieurs** *ou*
MM. Dupont, Messrs Dupont. **oui
~**, yes; (*avec déférence*) yes, sir.
monstre /mɔ̃str/ *n.m.* monster. ● *a.*
(*fam.*) colossal.
monstr|ueux, ~ueuse /mɔ̃stryø, -z/
a. monstrous. **~uosité** *n.f.* monstrosity.
mont /mɔ̃/ *n.m.* mount. **par ~s et
par vaux**, up hill and down dale.
montage /mɔ̃taʒ/ *n.m.* (*assemblage*)
assembly; (*cinéma*) editing.
montagn|e /mɔ̃taɲ/ *n.f.* mountain;
(*région*) mountains. **~es russes**,
roller-coaster. **~ard, ~arde** *n.m.*, *f.*
mountain dweller. **~eux, ~euse** *a.*
mountainous.
montant[1]**, ~e** /mɔ̃tɑ̃, -t/ *a.* rising;
(*col*) high-necked.
montant[2] /mɔ̃tɑ̃/ *n.m.* amount;
(*pièce de bois*) upright.

mont-de-piété (*pl.* **monts-de-piété**) /mõdpjete/ *n.m.* pawnshop.

monte-charge /mõtʃarʒ/ *n.m. invar.* service lift; (*Amer.*) dumb waiter.

montée /mõte/ *n.f.* ascent, climb; (*de prix*) rise; (*côte*) hill. **au milieu de la ~,** halfway up. **à la ~ de lait,** when the milk comes.

monter /mõte/ *v.i.* (*aux. être*) go *ou* come up; (*grimper*) climb; (*prix, mer*) rise. **~ à,** (*cheval*) mount. **~ dans,** (*train, avion*) get on to; (*voiture*) get into. **~ sur,** (*colline*) climb up; (*trône*) ascend. ● *v.t.* (*aux. avoir*) go *ou* come up; (*objet*) take *ou* bring up; (*cheval, garde*) mount; (*société*) start up. **~ à cheval,** (*sport*) ride. **~ en flèche,** soar. **~ en graine,** go to seed.

monteu|r, ~se /mõtœr, -øz/ *n.m., f.* (*techn.*) fitter; (*cinéma*) editor.

monticule /mõtikyl/ *n.m.* mound.

montre /mõtr/ *n.f.* watch. **~-bracelet** (*pl.* **~s-bracelets**) *n.f.* wristwatch. **faire ~ de,** show.

montrer /mõtre/ *v.t.* show (à, to). **se ~** *v. pr.* show o.s.; (*être*) be; (*s'avérer*) prove to be. **~ du doigt,** point to.

monture /mõtyr/ *n.f.* (*cheval*) mount; (*de lunettes*) frame; (*de bijou*) setting.

monument /monymã/ *n.m.* monument. **~ aux morts,** war memorial. **~al** (*m. pl.* **~aux**) /-tal, -to/ *a.* monumental.

moqu|er (se) /(sə)mɔke/ *v. pr.* se **~er de,** make fun of. **je m'en ~e,** (*fam.*) I couldn't care less. **~erie** *n.f.* mockery. **~eur, ~euse** *a.* mocking.

moquette /mɔkɛt/ *n.f.* fitted carpet; (*Amer.*) wall-to-wall carpeting.

mor|al, ~ale (*m. pl.* **~aux**) /mɔral, -o/ *a.* moral. ● *n.m.* (*pl.* **~aux**) morale. ● *n.f.* moral code; (*mœurs*) morals; (*de fable*) moral. **avoir le ~al,** be on form. **ça m'a remonté le ~al,** it gave me a boost. **faire la ~ale à,** lecture. **~alement** *adv.* morally. **~alité** *n.f.* morality; (*de fable*) moral.

moralisa|teur, ~trice /mɔralizatœr, -tris/ *a.* moralizing.

morbide /mɔrbid/ *a.* morbid.

morceau (*pl.* **~x**) /mɔrso/ *n.m.* piece, bit; (*de sucre*) lump; (*de viande*) cut; (*passage*) passage. **manger un ~,** have a bite to eat. **mettre en ~x,** smash *ou* tear *etc.* to bits.

morceler /mɔrsəle/ *v.t.* fragment.

mordant, ~e /mɔrdã, -t/ *a.* scathing; (*froid*) biting. ● *n.m.* (*énergie*) vigour, punch.

mordiller /mɔrdije/ *v.t.* nibble at.

mord|re /mɔrdr/ *v.t./i.* bite. **~re sur,** overlap into. **~re à l'hameçon,** bite. **~u, ~ue** *n.m., f.* (*fam.*) fan; *a.* bitten. **~u de,** (*fam.*) crazy about.

morfondre (se) /(sə)mɔrfõdr/ *v. pr.* mope, wait anxiously.

morgue [1] /mɔrg/ *n.f.* morgue, mortuary.

morgue [2] /mɔrg/ *n.f.* (*attitude*) haughtiness.

moribond, ~e /mɔribõ, -d/ *a.* dying.

morne /mɔrn/ *a.* dull.

morose /mɔroz/ *a.* morose.

morphine /mɔrfin/ *n.f.* morphine.

mors /mɔr/ *n.m.* (*de cheval*) bit.

morse [1] /mɔrs/ *n.m.* walrus.

morse [2] /mɔrs/ *n.m.* (*code*) Morse code.

morsure /mɔrsyr/ *n.f.* bite.

mort [1] /mɔr/ *n.f.* death.

mort [2], **~e** /mɔr, -t/ *a.* dead. ● *n.m., f.* dead man, dead woman. **les ~s,** the dead. **de fatigue,** dead tired. **~-né** *a.* stillborn.

mortadelle /mɔrtadɛl/ *n.f.* mortadella.

mortalité /mɔrtalite/ *n.f.* death rate.

mortel, ~le /mɔrtɛl/ *a.* mortal; (*accident*) fatal; (*poison, silence*) deadly. ● *n.m., f.* mortal. **~lement** *adv.* mortally.

mortier /mɔrtje/ *n.m.* mortar.

mortifié /mɔrtifje/ *a.* mortified.

mortuaire /mɔrtɥɛr/ *a.* (*cérémonie*) funeral; (*avis*) death.

morue /mɔry/ *n.f.* cod.

mosaïque /mɔzaik/ *n.f.* mosaic.

Moscou /mɔsku/ *n.m./f.* Moscow.

mosquée /mɔske/ *n.f.* mosque.

mot /mo/ *n.m.* word; (*lettre, message*) line, note. **~ d'ordre,** watchword. **~ de passe,** password. **~s croisés,** crossword (puzzle).

motard /mɔtar/ *n.m.* biker; (*policier*) police motorcyclist.

motel /mɔtɛl/ *n.m.* motel.

moteur [1] /mɔtœr/ *n.m.* engine, motor. **barque à ~,** motor launch.

mo|teur [2], **~trice** /mɔtœr, -tris/ *a.* (*nerf*) motor; (*force*) driving. **à 4 roues motrices,** 4-wheel drive.

motif /mɔtif/ *n.m.* reason; (*jurid.*) motive; (*dessin*) pattern.

motion /mosjõ/ *n.f.* motion.

motiv|er /mɔtive/ *v.t.* motivate; (*justifier*) justify. **~ation** *n.f.* motivation.

moto /mɔto/ *n.f.* motor cycle. **~cycliste** *n.m./f.* motorcyclist.

motorisé /mɔtɔrize/ *a.* motorized.

motrice /mɔtris/ *voir* moteur².

motte /mɔt/ *n.f.* lump; (*de beurre*) slab; (*de terre*) clod. **~ de gazon,** turf.

mou *ou* **mol*, molle** /mu, mɔl/ *a.* soft; (*péj.*) flabby; (*faible, indolent*) feeble. ● *n.m.* **du ~,** slack. **avoir du ~,** be slack.

mouchard, ~e /muʃar, -d/ *n.m.*, *f.* informer; (*scol.*) sneak. **~er** /-de/ *v.t.* (*fam.*) inform on.

mouche /muʃ/ *n.f.* fly.

moucher (se) /(sə)muʃe/ *v. pr.* blow one's nose.

moucheron /muʃrɔ̃/ *n.m.* midge.

moucheté /muʃte/ *a.* speckled.

mouchoir /muʃwar/ *n.m.* hanky; handkerchief; (*en papier*) tissue.

moudre /mudr/ *v.t.* grind.

moue /mu/ *n.f.* long face. **faire la ~,** pull a long face.

mouette /mwɛt/ *n.f.* (sea)gull.

moufle /mufl/ *n.f.* (*gant*) mitten.

mouill|er /muje/ *v.t.* wet, make wet. **se ~er** *v. pr.* get (o.s.) wet. **~er (l'ancre),** anchor. **~é a.** wet.

moulage /mulaʒ/ *n.m.* cast.

moul|e¹ /mul/ *n.m.* mould. **~er** *v.t.* mould; (*statue*) cast. **~e à gâteau,** cake tin. **~e à tarte,** flan dish.

moule² /mul/ *n.f.* (*coquillage*) mussel.

moulin /mulɛ̃/ *n.m.* mill; (*moteur*: *fam.*) engine. **~ à vent,** windmill.

moulinet /mulinɛ/ *n.m.* (*de canne à pêche*) reel. **faire des ~s avec qch.,** twirl sth. around.

moulinette /mulinɛt/ *n.f.* (P.) purée maker.

moulu /muly/ *a.* ground; (*fatigué*: *fam.*) dead beat.

moulure /mulyr/ *n.f.* moulding.

mourant, ~e /murã, -t/ *a.* dying. ● *n.m.*, *f.* dying person.

mourir† /murir/ *v.i.* (*aux. être*) die. **~ d'envie de,** be dying to. **~ de faim,** be starving. **~ d'ennui,** be dead bored.

mousquetaire /muskətɛr/ *n.m.* musketeer.

mousse¹ /mus/ *n.f.* moss; (*écume*) froth, foam; (*de savon*) lather; (*des-*

sert) mousse. **~ à raser,** shaving cream.

mousse² /mus/ *n.m.* ship's boy.

mousseline /muslin/ *n.f.* muslin; (*de soie*) chiffon.

mousser /muse/ *v.i.* froth, foam; (*savon*) lather.

mousseu|x, ~se /musø, -z/ *a.* frothy. ● *n.m.* sparkling wine.

mousson /musɔ̃/ *n.f.* monsoon.

moustach|e /mustaʃ/ *n.f.* moustache. **~es,** (*d'animal*) whiskers. **~u** *a.* wearing a moustache.

moustiquaire /mustikɛr/ *n.f.* mosquito-net.

moustique /mustik/ *n.m.* mosquito.

moutarde /mutard/ *n.f.* mustard.

mouton /mutɔ̃/ *n.m.* sheep; (*peau*) sheepskin; (*viande*) mutton.

mouvant, ~e /muvã, -t/ *a.* changing; (*terrain*) shifting.

mouvement /muvmã/ *n.m.* movement; (*agitation*) bustle; (*en gymnastique*) exercise; (*impulsion*) impulse; (*tendance*) tendency. **en ~,** in motion.

mouvementé /muvmãte/ *a.* eventful.

mouvoir† /muvwar/ *v.t.* (*membre*) move. **se ~** *v. pr.* move.

moyen¹**, ~ne** /mwajɛ̃, -jɛn/ *a.* average; (*médiocre*) poor. ● *n.f.* average; (*scol.*) pass-mark. **de taille ~ne,** medium-sized. **~ âge,** Middle Ages. **~ne d'âge,** average age. **M~-Orient** *n.m.* Middle East. **~nement** /- jɛnmã/ *adv.* moderately.

moyen² /mwajɛ̃/ *n.m.* means, way. **~s,** means; (*dons*) abilities. **au ~ de,** by means of. **il n'y a pas ~ de,** it is not possible to.

moyennant /mwajɛnã/ *prép.* (*pour*) for; (*grâce à*) with.

moyeu (*pl.* **~x**) /mwajø/ *n.m.* hub.

mû, mue¹ /my/ *a.* driven (**par,** by).

mucoviscidose /mykɔvisidoz/ *n.f.* cystic fibrosis.

mue² /my/ *n.f.* moulting; (*de voix*) breaking of the voice.

muer /mɥe/ *v.i.* moult; (*voix*) break. **se ~ en,** change into.

muesli /mysli/ *n.m.* muesli.

muet, ~te /mɥɛ, -t/ *a.* (*personne*) dumb; (*fig.*) speechless (**de,** with); (*silencieux*) silent. ● *n.m.*, *f.* dumb person.

mufle /myfl/ *n.m.* nose, muzzle; (*personne*: *fam.*) boor, lout.

mugir /myʒir/ v.i. (vache) moo; (bœuf) bellow; (fig.) howl.

muguet /mygɛ/ n.m. lily of the valley.

mule /myl/ n.f. (she-)mule; (pantoufle) mule.

mulet /mylɛ/ n.m. (he-)mule.

multi- /mylti/ préf. multi-.

multicolore /myltikɔlɔr/ a. multicoloured.

multination|al, ~ale (m. pl. ~aux) /myltinasjɔnal, -o/ a. & n.f. multinational.

multiple /myltipl/ a. & n.m. multiple.

multiplicité /myltiplisite/ n.f. multiplicity, abundance.

multipl|ier /myltiplije/ v.t., **se ~ier** v. pr. multiply. **~ication** n.f. multiplication.

multitude /myltityd/ n.f. multitude, mass.

municip|al (m. pl. ~aux) /mynisipal, -o/ a. municipal; (conseil) town. **~alité** n.f. (ville) municipality; (conseil) town council.

munir /mynir/ v.t. **~ de**, provide with. **se ~ de**, provide o.s. with.

munitions /mynisjɔ̃/ n.f. pl. ammunition.

mur /myr/ n.m. wall. **~ du son**, sound barrier.

mûr /myr/ a. ripe; (personne) mature.

muraille /myrɑj/ n.f. (high) wall.

mur|al (m. pl. ~aux) /myral, -o/ a. wall; (tableau) mural.

mûre /myr/ n.f. blackberry.

muret /myrɛ/ n.m. low wall.

mûrir /myrir/ v.t./i. ripen; (abcès) come to a head; (personne, projet) mature.

murmur|e /myrmyr/ n.m. murmur. **~er** v.t./i. murmur.

musc /mysk/ n.m. musk.

muscade /myskad/ n.f. **noix (de) ~**, nutmeg.

muscl|e /myskl/ n.m. muscle. **~é** a. muscular, brawny.

muscul|aire /myskylɛr/ a. muscular. **~ature** n.f. muscles.

museau (pl. ~x) /myzo/ n.m. muzzle; (de porc) snout.

musée /myze/ n.m. museum; (de peinture) art gallery.

museler /myzle/ v.t. muzzle.

muselière /myzəljɛr/ n.f. muzzle.

musette /myzɛt/ n.f. haversack.

muséum /myzeɔm/ n.m. (natural history) museum.

music|al (m. pl. ~aux) /myzikal, -o/ a. musical.

music-hall /myzikol/ n.m. variety theatre.

musicien, ~ne /myzisjɛ̃, -jɛn/ a. musical. ● n.m., f. musician.

musique /myzik/ n.f. music; (orchestre) band.

musulman, ~e /myzylmɑ̃, -an/ a. n.m., f. Muslim.

mutation /mytɑsjɔ̃/ n.f. change; (biologique) mutation.

muter /myte/ v.t. transfer.

mutil|er /mytile/ v.t. mutilate. **~ation** n.f. mutilation. **~é, ée** a. & n.m., f. disabled (person).

mutin, ~e /mytɛ̃, -in/ a. saucy. ● n.m., f. rebel.

mutin|er (se) /(sə)mytine/ v. pr. mutiny. **~é** a. mutinous. **~erie** n.f. mutiny.

mutisme /mytism/ n.m. silence.

mutuel, ~le /mytɥɛl/ a. mutual. ● n.f. Friendly Society; (Amer.) benefit society. **~lement** adv. mutually; (l'un l'autre) each other.

myop|e /mjɔp/ a. short-sighted. **~ie** n.f. short-sightedness.

myosotis /mjozotis/ n.m. forget-me-not.

myriade /mirjad/ n.f. myriad.

myrtille /mirtij/ n.f. bilberry; (Amer.) blueberry.

mystère /mistɛr/ n.m. mystery.

mystérieu|x, ~se /misterjø, -z/ a. mysterious.

mystif|ier /mistifje/ v.t. deceive, hoax. **~ication** n.f. hoax.

mysti|que /mistik/ a. mystic(al). ● n.m./f. mystic. ● n.f. (puissance) mystique. **~cisme** n.m. mysticism.

myth|e /mit/ n.m. myth. **~ique** a. mythical.

mytholog|ie /mitɔlɔʒi/ n.f. mythology. **~ique** a. mythological.

mythomane /mitɔman/ n.m./f. compulsive liar (and fantasizer).

N

n' /n/ voir ne.

nacr|e /nakr/ n.f. mother-of-pearl. **~é** a. pearly.

nage /naʒ/ n.f. swimming; (manière) (swimming) stroke. **à la ~,** by swimming. **traverser à la ~,** swim across. **en ~,** sweating.

nageoire /naʒwar/ n.f. fin.

nag|er /naʒe/ v.t./i. swim. **~eur, ~euse** n.m., f. swimmer.

naguère /nagɛr/ adv. some time ago.

naï|f, ~ve /naif, -v/ a. naïve.

nain, ~e /nɛ̃, nɛn/ n.m., f. & a. dwarf.

naissance /nɛsɑ̃s/ n.f. birth. **donner ~ à,** give birth to, (fig.) give rise to.

naître† /nɛtr/ v.i. be born; (résulter) arise (**de,** from). **faire ~,** (susciter) give rise to.

naïveté /naivte/ n.f. naïvety.

nana /nana/ n.f. (fam.) girl.

nanti /nɑ̃ti/ n.m. **les ~s,** the affluent.

nantir /nɑ̃tir/ v.t. **~ de,** provide with.

naphtaline /naftalin/ n.f. mothballs.

nappe /nap/ n.f. table-cloth; (de pétrole, gaz) layer. **~ phréatique,** ground water.

napperon /naprɔ̃/ n.m. (cloth) table-mat.

narcotique /narkɔtik/ a. & n.m. narcotic.

narguer /narge/ v.t. mock.

narine /narin/ n.f. nostril.

narquois, ~e /narkwa, -z/ a. derisive.

narr|er /nare/ v.t. narrate. **~ateur, ~atrice** n.m., f. narrator. **~ation** n.f. narrative; (action) narration; (scol.) composition.

nas|al (m. pl. **~aux**) /nazal, -o/ a. nasal.

naseau (pl. **~x**) /nazo/ n.m. nostril.

nasiller /nazije/ v.i. have a nasal twang.

nat|al (m. pl. **~als**) /natal/ a. native.

natalité /natalite/ n.f. birth rate.

natation /natasjɔ̃/ n.f. swimming.

nati|f, ~ve /natif, -v/ a. native.

nation /nasjɔ̃/ n.f. nation.

nation|al, ~ale (m. pl. **~aux**) /nasjɔnal, -o/ a. national. ● n.f. A road; (Amer.) highway. **~aliser** v.t. nationalize. **~alisme** n.m. nationalism.

nationalité /nasjɔnalite/ n.f. nationality.

Nativité /nativite/ n.f. **la ~,** the Nativity.

natte /nat/ n.f. (de cheveux) plait; (tapis de paille) mat.

naturaliser /natyralize/ v.t. naturalize.

nature /natyr/ n.f. nature. ● a. invar. (eau, omelette, etc.) plain. **de ~**

à, likely to. **payer en ~,** pay in kind. **~ morte,** still life.

naturel, ~le /natyrɛl/ a. natural. ● n.m. nature; (simplicité) naturalness. **~lement** adv. naturally.

naufrag|e /nofraʒ/ n.m. (ship-)wreck. **faire ~e,** be shipwrecked; (bateau) be wrecked. **~é, ~ée** a. & n.m., f. shipwrecked (person).

nauséabond, ~e /nozeabɔ̃, -d/ a. nauseating.

nausée /noze/ n.f. nausea.

nautique /notik/ a. nautical; (sports) aquatic.

naval (m. pl. **~s**) /naval/ a. naval.

navet /navɛ/ n.m. turnip; (film, tableau) dud.

navette /navɛt/ n.f. shuttle (service). **faire la ~,** shuttle back and forth.

navigable /navigabl/ a. navigable.

navig|uer /navige/ v.i. sail; (piloter) navigate. **~ateur** n.m. seafarer; (d'avion) navigator. **~ation** n.f. navigation; (trafic) shipping.

navire /navir/ n.m. ship.

navré /navre/ a. sorry (**de,** to).

navrer /navre/ v.t. upset.

ne, n'* /nə, n/ adv. **ne pas,** not. **ne jamais,** never. **ne plus,** (temps) no longer, not any more. **ne que,** only. **je crains qu'il ne parte,** (sans valeur négative) I am afraid he will leave.

né, née /ne/ voir naître. ● a. & n.m., f. born. **il est né,** he was born. **premier-/dernier-né,** first-/last-born. **née Martin,** née Martin.

néanmoins /neɑ̃mwɛ̃/ adv. nevertheless.

néant /neɑ̃/ n.m. nothingness; (aucun) none.

nébuleu|x, ~se /nebylø, -z/ a. nebulous.

nécessaire /nesesɛr/ a. necessary. ● n.m. (sac) bag; (trousse) kit. **le ~,** (l'indispensable) the necessities. **faire le ~,** do what is necessary. **~ment** adv. necessarily.

nécessité /nesesite/ n.f. necessity.

nécessiter /nesesite/ v.t. necessitate.

nécrologie /nekrɔlɔʒi/ n.f. obituary.

néerlandais, ~e /neɛrlɑ̃dɛ, -z/ a. Dutch. ● n.m., f. Dutchman, Dutchwoman. ● n.m. (lang.) Dutch.

nef /nɛf/ n.f. nave.

néfaste /nefast/ a. harmful (**à,** to); (funeste) ill-fated.

négati|f, **~ve** /negatif, -v/ a. & n.m., f. negative.

négation /negɑsjɔ̃/ n.f. negation.

négligé /negliʒe/ a. (tenue, travail) slovenly. ● n.m. (tenue) négligé.

négligeable /negliʒabl/ a. negligible, insignificant.

négligen|t, **~te** /negliʒɑ̃, -t/ a. careless, negligent. **~ce** n.f. carelessness, negligence; (erreur) omission.

négliger /negliʒe/ v.t. neglect; (ne pas tenir compte de) disregard. **se ~** v. pr. neglect o.s.

négoc|e /negɔs/ n.m. business. **~iant**, **~iante** n.m., f. merchant.

négoc|ier /negɔsje/ v.t./i. negotiate. **~iable** a. negotiable. **~iateur**, **~iatrice** n.m., f. negotiator. **~iation** n.f. negotiation.

nègre[1] /nɛgr/ a. (musique etc.) Negro.

nègre[2] /nɛgr/ n.m. (écrivain) ghost writer.

neig|e /nɛʒ/ n.f. snow. **~eux**, **~euse** a. snowy.

neiger /neʒe/ v.i. snow.

nénuphar /nenyfar/ n.m. waterlily.

néologisme /neɔlɔʒism/ n.m. neologism.

néon /neɔ̃/ n.m. neon.

néo-zélandais, **~e** /neɔzelɑ̃dɛ, -z/ a. New Zealand. ● n.m., f. New Zealander.

nerf /nɛr/ n.m. nerve; (vigueur: fam.) stamina.

nerv|eux, **~euse** /nɛrvø, -z/ a. nervous; (irritable) nervy; (centre, cellule) nerve-; (voiture) responsive. **~eusement** adv. nervously. **~osité** n.f. nervousness; (irritabilité) touchiness.

nervure /nɛrvyr/ n.f. (bot.) vein.

net, **~te** /nɛt/ a. (clair, distinct) clear; (propre) clean; (soigné) neat; (prix, poids) net. ● adv. (s'arrêter) dead; (refuser) flatly; (parler) plainly; (se casser) clean. **~tement** adv. clearly; (certainement) definitely.

netteté /nɛtte/ n.f. clearness.

nettoy|er /nɛtwaje/ v.t. clean. **~age** n.m. cleaning. **~age à sec,** dry-cleaning.

neuf[1] /nœf/ (/nœv/ before heures, ans) a. & n.m. nine.

neu|f[2], **~ve** /nœf, -v/ a. & n.m. new. **remettre à ~f,** brighten up. **du ~f,** (fait nouveau) some new development.

neutr|e /nøtr/ a. neutral; (gram.) neuter. ● n.m. (gram.) neuter. **~alité** n.f. neutrality.

neutron /nøtrɔ̃/ n.m. neutron.

neuve /nœv/ voir neuf[2].

neuvième /nœvjɛm/ a. & n.m./f. ninth.

neveu (pl. **~x**) /nəvø/ n.m. nephew.

névros|e /nevroz/ n.f. neurosis. **~é, ~ée** a. & n.m., f. neurotic.

nez /ne/ n.m. nose. **~ à nez,** face to face. **~ épaté,** flat nose. **~ retroussé,** turned-up nose. **avoir du ~,** have flair.

ni /ni/ conj. neither, nor. **ni grand ni petit,** neither big nor small. **ni l'un ni l'autre ne fument,** neither (one nor the other) smokes.

niais, **~e** /njɛ, -z/ a. silly. ● n.m., f. simpleton. **~erie** /-zri/ n.f. silliness.

niche /niʃ/ n.f. (de chien) kennel; (cavité) niche; (farce) trick.

nichée /niʃe/ n.f. brood.

nicher /niʃe/ v.i. nest. **se ~** v. pr. nest; (se cacher) hide.

nickel /nikɛl/ n.m. nickel. **c'est ~!,** (fam.) it's spotless.

nicotine /nikɔtin/ n.f. nicotine.

nid /ni/ n.m. nest. **~ de poule,** pothole.

nièce /njɛs/ n.f. niece.

nier /nje/ v.t. deny.

nigaud, **~e** /nigo, -d/ a. silly. ● n.m., f. silly idiot.

nippon, **~e** /nipɔ̃, -ɔn/ a. & n.m., f. Japanese.

niveau (pl. **~x**) /nivo/ n.m. level; (compétence) standard. **au ~,** up to standard. **~ à bulle,** spirit-level. **~ de vie,** standard of living.

nivel|er /nivle/ v.t. level. **~lement** /-ɛlmɑ̃/ n.m. levelling.

noble /nɔbl/ a. noble. ● n.m./f. nobleman, noblewoman.

noblesse /nɔblɛs/ n.f. nobility.

noce /nɔs/ n.f. wedding; (personnes) wedding guests. **~s,** wedding. **faire la ~,** (fam.) make merry.

noci|f, **~ve** /nɔsif, -v/ a. harmful.

noctambule /nɔktɑ̃byl/ n.m./f. night-owl, late-night reveller.

nocturne /nɔktyrn/ a. nocturnal.

Noël /nɔɛl/ n.m. Christmas.

nœud[1] /nø/ n.m. knot; (ornemental) bow. **~s,** (fig.) ties. **~ coulant,** noose. **~ papillon,** bow-tie.

nœud[2] /nø/ n.m. (naut.) knot.

noir, **~e** /nwar/ a. black; (obscur, sombre) dark; (triste) gloomy.

● *n.m.* black; (*obscurité*) dark. **travail au ~,** moonlighting. ● *n.m., f.* (*personne*) Black. ● *n.f.* (*mus.*) crotchet. **~ceur** *n.f.* blackness; (*indignité*) vileness.

noircir /nwarsir/ *v.t./i.,* **se ~** *v. pr.* blacken.

nois|ette /nwazɛt/ *n.f.* hazel-nut; (*de beurre*) knob. **~etier** *n.m.* hazel tree.

noix /nwa/ *n.f.* nut; (*du noyer*) walnut; (*de beurre*) knob. **~ de cajou,** cashew nut. **~ de coco,** coconut. **à la ~,** (*fam.*) useless.

nom /nɔ̃/ *n.m.* name; (*gram.*) noun. **au ~ de,** on behalf of. **~ de famille,** surname. **~ de jeune fille,** maiden name. **~ propre,** proper noun.

nomade /nɔmad/ *a.* nomadic. ● *n.m./f.* nomad.

no man's land /nɔmanslɑ̃d/ *n.m. invar.* no man's land.

nombre /nɔ̃br/ *n.m.* number. **au ~ de,** (*parmi*) among; (*l'un de*) one of. **en (grand) ~,** in large numbers.

nombreu|x, ~se /nɔ̃brø, -z/ *a.* numerous; (*important*) large.

nombril /nɔ̃bri/ *n.m.* navel.

nomin|al (*m. pl.* **~aux**) /nɔminal, -o/ *a.* nominal.

nomination /nɔminasjɔ̃/ *n.f.* appointment.

nommément /nɔmemɑ̃/ *adv.* by name.

nommer /nɔme/ *v.t.* name; (*élire*) appoint. **se ~** *v. pr.* (*s'appeler*) be called.

non /nɔ̃/ *adv.* no; (*pas*) not. ● *n.m. invar.* no. **~ (pas) que,** not that. **il vient, ~?,** he is coming, isn't he? **moi ~ plus,** neither am, do, can, *etc.* I.

non- /nɔ̃/ *préf.* non-. **~-fumeur,** non-smoker.

nonante /nɔnɑ̃t/ *a. & n.m.* ninety.

nonchalance /nɔ̃ʃalɑ̃s/ *n.f.* nonchalance.

non-sens /nɔ̃sɑ̃s/ *n.m.* absurdity.

non-stop /nɔnstɔp/ *a. invar.* non-stop.

nord /nɔr/ *n.m.* north. ● *a. invar.* north; (*partie*) northern; (*direction*) northerly. **au ~ de,** to the north of. **~-africain, ~-africaine** *a. & n.m., f.* North African. **~-est** *n.m.* north-east. **~-ouest** *n.m.* north-west.

nordique /nɔrdik/ *a. & n.m./f.* Scandinavian.

norm|al, ~ale (*m. pl.* **~aux**) /nɔrmal, -o/ *a.* normal. ● *n.f.* normality; (*norme*) norm; (*moyenne*) average. **~alement** *adv.* normally.

normand, ~e /nɔrmɑ̃, -d/ *a. & n.m., f.* Norman.

Normandie /nɔrmɑ̃di/ *n.f.* Normandy.

norme /nɔrm/ *n.f.* norm; (*de production*) standard.

Norvège /nɔrvɛʒ/ *n.f.* Norway.

norvégien, ~ne /nɔrveʒjɛ̃, -jɛn/ *a. & n.m., f.* Norwegian.

nos /no/ *voir* notre.

nostalg|ie /nɔstalʒi/ *n.f.* nostalgia. **~ique** *a.* nostalgic.

notable /nɔtabl/ *a. & n.m.* notable.

notaire /nɔtɛr/ *n.m.* notary.

notamment /nɔtamɑ̃/ *adv.* notably.

notation /nɔtasjɔ̃/ *n.f.* notation; (*remarque*) remark.

note /nɔt/ *n.f.* (*remarque*) note; (*chiffrée*) mark; (*facture*) bill; (*mus.*) note. **~ (de service),** memorandum. **prendre ~ de,** take note of.

not|er /nɔte/ *v.t.* note, notice; (*écrire*) note (down); (*devoir*) mark. **bien/mal ~é,** (*employé etc.*) highly/poorly rated.

notice /nɔtis/ *n.f.* note; (*mode d'emploi*) directions.

notif|ier /nɔtifje/ *v.t.* notify (**à,** to). **~ication** *n.f.* notification.

notion /nosjɔ̃/ *n.f.* notion.

notoire /nɔtwar/ *a.* well-known; (*criminel*) notorious.

notre (*pl.* **nos**) /nɔtr, no/ *a.* our.

nôtre /notr/ *pron.* **le** *ou* **la ~, les ~s,** ours.

nouer /nwe/ *v.t.* tie, knot; (*relations*) strike up.

noueu|x, ~se /nwø, -z/ *a.* gnarled.

nougat /nuga/ *n.m.* nougat.

nouille /nuj/ *n.f.* (*idiot: fam.*) idiot.

nouilles /nuj/ *n.f. pl.* noodles.

nounours /nunurs/ *n.m.* teddy bear.

nourri /nuri/ *a.* (*fig.*) intense. **logé ~,** bed and board. **~ au sein,** breastfed.

nourrice /nuris/ *n.f.* child-minder; (*qui allaite*) wet-nurse.

nourr|ir /nurir/ *v.t.* feed; (*faire vivre*) feed, provide for; (*sentiment: fig.*) nourish. ● *v.i.* be nourishing. **se ~ir** *v. pr.* eat. **se ~ir de,** feed on. **~issant, ~issante** *a.* nourishing.

nourrisson /nurisɔ̃/ *n.m.* infant.

nourriture /nurityr/ *n.f.* food.

nous /nu/ *pron.* we; (*complément*) us; (*indirect*) (to) us; (*réfléchi*) ourselves; (*l'un l'autre*) each other. **~mêmes** *pron.* ourselves.

nouveau *ou* **nouvel*, nouvelle**[1] (*m. pl.* **~x**) /nuvo, nuvɛl/ *a.* & *n.m.* new. ● *n.m., f.* (*élève*) new boy, new girl. **de ~, à ~,** again. **du ~,** (*fait nouveau*) some new development. **nouvel an,** new year. **~x mariés,** newly-weds. **~-né, ~-née** *a.* newborn; *n.m., f.* newborn baby. **~ venu, nouvelle venue,** newcomer. **Nouvelle Zélande,** New Zealand.

nouveauté /nuvote/ *n.f.* novelty; (*chose*) new thing.

nouvelle[2] /nuvɛl/ *n.f.* (piece of) news; (*récit*) short story. **~s,** news.

nouvellement /nuvɛlmã/ *adv.* newly, recently.

novembre /nɔvãbr/ *n.m.* November.

novice /nɔvis/ *a.* inexperienced. ● *n.m./f.* novice.

noyade /nwajad/ *n.f.* drowning.

noyau (*pl.* **~x**) /nwajo/ *n.m.* (*de fruit*) stone; (*de cellule*) nucleus; (*groupe*) group; (*centre: fig.*) core.

noyauter /nwajote/ *v.t.* (*organisation*) infiltrate.

noy|er[1] /nwaje/ *v.t.* drown; (*inonder*) flood. **se ~er** *v. pr.* drown; (*volontairement*) drown o.s. **se ~er dans un verre d'eau,** make a mountain out of a molehill. **~é, ~ée** *n.m., f.* drowning person; (*mort*) drowned person.

noyer[2] /nwaje/ *n.m.* (*arbre*) walnut-tree.

nu /ny/ *a.* naked; (*mains, mur, fil*) bare. ● *n.m.* nude. **se mettre à nu,** (*fig.*) bare one's heart. **mettre à nu,** lay bare. **nu-pieds** *adv.* barefoot; *n.m. pl.* beach shoes. **nu-tête** *adv.* bareheaded. **à l'œil nu,** to the naked eye.

nuag|e /nyaʒ/ *n.m.* cloud. **~eux, ~euse** *a.* cloudy.

nuance /nyãs/ *n.f.* shade; (*de sens*) nuance; (*différence*) difference.

nuancer /nyãse/ *v.t.* (*opinion*) qualify.

nucléaire /nykleɛr/ *a.* nuclear.

nudis|te /nydist/ *n.m./f.* nudist. **~me** *n.m.* nudism.

nudité /nydite/ *n.f.* (*de personne*) nudity; (*de chambre etc.*) bareness.

nuée /nɥe/ *n.f.* (*foule*) host.

nues /ny/ *n.f. pl.* **tomber des ~,** be amazed. **porter aux ~,** extol.

nuire† /nɥir/ *v.i.* **~ à,** harm.

nuisible /nɥizibl/ *a.* harmful.

nuit /nɥi/ *n.f.* night. **cette ~,** tonight; (*hier*) last night. **il fait ~,** it is dark. **~ blanche,** sleepless night. **la ~, de ~,** at night. **~ de noces,** wedding night.

nul, ~le /nyl/ *a.* (*aucun*) no; (*zéro*) nil; (*qui ne vaut rien*) useless; (*non valable*) null. **match ~,** draw. **~ en,** no good at. ● *pron.* no one. **~ autre,** no one else. **~le part,** nowhere. **~lement** *adv.* not at all. **~lité** *n.f.* uselessness; (*personne*) useless person.

numéraire /nymerɛr/ *n.m.* cash.

numér|al (*pl.* **~aux**) /nymeral, -o/ *n.m.* numeral.

numérique /nymerik/ *a.* numerical; (*montre, horloge*) digital.

numéro /nymero/ *n.m.* number; (*de journal*) issue; (*spectacle*) act. **~ter** /-ɔte/ *v.t.* number.

nuque /nyk/ *n.f.* nape (of the neck).

nurse /nœrs/ *n.f.* (children's) nurse.

nutriti|f, ~ve /nytritif, -v/ *a.* nutritious; (*valeur*) nutritional.

nutrition /nytrisjɔ̃/ *n.f.* nutrition.

nylon /nilɔ̃/ *n.m.* nylon.

nymphe /nɛ̃f/ *n.f.* nymph.

O

oasis /ɔazis/ *n.f.* oasis.

obéir /ɔbeir/ *v.i.* obey. **~ à,** obey. **être obéi,** be obeyed.

obéissan|t, ~te /ɔbeisã, -t/ *a.* obedient. **~ce** *n.f.* obedience.

obèse /ɔbɛz/ *a.* obese.

obésité /ɔbezite/ *n.f.* obesity.

object|er /ɔbʒɛkte/ *v.t.* put forward (as an excuse). **~er que,** object that. **~ion** /-ksjɔ̃/ *n.f.* objection.

objecteur /ɔbʒɛktœr/ *n.m.* **~ de conscience,** conscientious objector.

objecti|f, ~ve /ɔbʒɛktif, -v/ *a.* objective. ● *n.m.* objective; (*photo.*) lens. **~vement** *adv.* objectively. **~vité** *n.f.* objectivity.

objet /ɔbʒɛ/ *n.m.* object; (*sujet*) subject. **être** *ou* **faire l'~ de,** be the subject of; (*recevoir*) receive. **~ d'art,** objet d'art. **~s de toilette,** toilet requisites. **~s trouvés,** lost property; (*Amer.*) lost and found.

obligation /ɔbligasjɔ̃/ *n.f.* obligation; (*comm.*) bond. **être dans l'~ de,** be under obligation to.

obligatoire /ɔbligatwar/ *a.* compulsory. **~ment** *adv.* of necessity; (*fam.*) inevitably.

obligean|t, ~te /ɔbliʒɑ̃, -t/ *a.* obliging, kind. **~ce** *n.f.* kindness.

oblig|er /ɔbliʒe/ *v.t.* compel, oblige (à **faire,** to do); (*aider*) oblige. **être ~é de,** have to. **~é à qn.,** obliged to s.o. (**de,** for).

oblique /ɔblik/ *a.* oblique. **regard ~,** sidelong glance. **en ~,** at an angle.

obliquer /ɔblike/ *v.i.* turn off (**vers,** towards).

oblitérer /ɔblitere/ *v.t.* (*timbre*) cancel.

oblong, ~ue /ɔblɔ̃, -g/ *a.* oblong.

obnubilé, ~e /ɔbnybile/ *a.* obsessed.

obsc|ène /ɔpsɛn/ *a.* obscene. **~énité** *n.f.* obscenity.

obscur /ɔpskyr/ *a.* dark; (*confus, humble*) obscure.

obscurantisme /ɔpskyrɑ̃tism/ *n.m.* obscurantism.

obscurcir /ɔpskyrsir/ *v.t.* darken; (*fig.*) obscure. **s'~** *v. pr.* (*ciel etc.*) darken.

obscurité /ɔpskyrite/ *n.f.* dark(-ness); (*passage, situation*) obscurity.

obséd|er /ɔpsede/ *v.t.* obsess. **~ant, ~ante** *a.* obsessive. **~é, ~ée** *n.m., f.* maniac.

obsèques /ɔpsɛk/ *n.f. pl.* funeral.

observation /ɔpsɛrvasjɔ̃/ *n.f.* observation; (*reproche*) criticism; (*obéissance*) observance. **en ~,** under observation.

observatoire /ɔpsɛrvatwar/ *n.m.* observatory; (*mil.*) observation post.

observ|er /ɔpsɛrve/ *v.t.* observe; (*surveiller*) watch, observe. **faire ~er qch.,** point sth. out (**à,** to). **~ateur, ~atrice** *a.* observant; *n.m., f.* observer.

obsession /ɔpsesjɔ̃/ *n.f.* obsession.

obstacle /ɔpstakl/ *n.m.* obstacle; (*cheval*) jump; (*athlète*) hurdle. **faire ~ à,** stand in the way of.

obstétrique /ɔpstetrik/ *n.f.* obstetrics.

obstin|é /ɔpstine/ *a.* obstinate. **~ation** *n.f.* obstinacy.

obstiner (s') /(s)ɔpstine/ *v. pr.* persist (**à,** in).

obstruction /ɔpstryksjɔ̃/ *n.f.* obstruction. **faire de l'~,** obstruct.

obstruer /ɔpstrye/ *v.t.* obstruct.

obten|ir† /ɔptənir/ *v.t.* get, obtain. **~tion** /-ɑ̃sjɔ̃/ *n.f.* obtaining.

obturateur /ɔptyratœr/ *n.m.* (*photo.*) shutter.

obtus, ~e /ɔpty, -z/ *a.* obtuse.

obus /ɔby/ *n.m.* shell.

occasion /ɔkazjɔ̃/ *n.f.* opportunity (**de faire,** of doing); (*circonstance*) occasion; (*achat*) bargain; (*article non neuf*) second-hand buy. **à l'~,** sometimes. **d'~,** second-hand. **~nel, ~nelle** /-jɔnɛl/ *a.* occasional.

occasionner /ɔkazjone/ *v.t.* cause.

occident /ɔksidɑ̃/ *n.m.* west. **~al, ~ale** (*m. pl.* **~aux**) /-tal, -to/ *a.* western. ● *n.m., f.* westerner.

occulte /ɔkylt/ *a.* occult.

occupant, ~e /ɔkypɑ̃, -t/ *n.m., f.* occupant. ● *n.m.* (*mil.*) forces of occupation.

occupation /ɔkypasjɔ̃/ *n.f.* occupation.

occupé /ɔkype/ *a.* busy; (*place, pays*) occupied; (*téléphone*) engaged; (*Amer.*) busy.

occuper /ɔkype/ *v.t.* occupy; (*poste*) hold. **s'~** *v. pr.* (*s'affairer*) keep busy (**à faire,** doing). **s'~ de,** (*personne, problème*) take care of; (*bureau, firme*) be in charge of.

occurrence (en l') /(ɑ̃l)ɔkyrɑ̃s/ *adv.* in this case.

océan /ɔseɑ̃/ *n.m.* ocean.

ocre /ɔkr/ *a. invar.* ochre.

octane /ɔktan/ *n.m.* octane.

octante /ɔktɑ̃t/ *a.* (*régional*) eighty.

octave /ɔktav/ *n.f.* (*mus.*) octave.

octet /ɔktɛ/ *n.m.* byte.

octobre /ɔktɔbr/ *n.m.* October.

octogone /ɔktɔgɔn/ *n.m.* octagon.

octroyer /ɔktrwaje/ *v.t.* grant.

oculaire /ɔkylɛr/ *a.* ocular.

oculiste /ɔkylist/ *n.m./f.* eye-specialist.

ode /ɔd/ *n.f.* ode.

odeur /ɔdœr/ *n.f.* smell.

odieu|x, ~se /ɔdjø, -z/ *a.* odious.

odorant, ~e /ɔdɔrɑ̃, -t/ *a.* sweet-smelling.

odorat /ɔdɔra/ *n.m.* (sense of) smell.

œcuménique /ekymenik/ *a.* ecumenical.

œil (*pl.* **yeux**) /œj, jø/ *n.m.* eye. **à l'~,** (*fam.*) free. **à mes yeux,** in my view. **faire de l'~ à,** make eyes at. **faire les gros yeux à,** scowl at. **ouvrir l'~,** keep one's eye open. **fermer l'~,** shut one's eyes. **~ poché,** black eye. **yeux bridés,** slit eyes.

œillade /œjad/ *n.f.* wink.

œillères /œjɛr/ *n.f. pl.* blinkers.

œillet /œjɛ/ *n.m.* (*plante*) carnation; (*trou*) eyelet.

œuf (*pl.* ~**s**) /œf, ø/ *n.m.* egg. ~ **à la coque/dur/sur le plat,** boiled/hard-boiled/fried egg.

œuvre /œvr/ *n.f.* (*ouvrage, travail*) work. ~ **d'art,** work of art. ~ (**de bienfaisance**), charity. **être à l'~,** be at work. **mettre en ~,** (*moyens*) implement.

œuvrer /œvre/ *v.i.* work.

off /ɔf/ *a. invar.* **voix ~,** voice off.

offense /ɔfɑ̃s/ *n.f.* insult; (*péché*) offence.

offens|er /ɔfɑ̃se/ *v.t.* offend. **s'~er de,** take offence at. ~**ant,** ~**ante** *a.* offensive.

offensi|f, ~ve /ɔfɑ̃sif, -v/ *a. & n.f.* offensive.

offert, ~e /ɔfɛr, -t/ *voir* offrir.

office /ɔfis/ *n.m.* office; (*relig.*) service; (*de cuisine*) pantry. **d'~,** automatically.

officiel, ~le /ɔfisjɛl/ *a. & n.m.,* *f.* official. ~**lement** *adv.* officially.

officier [1] /ɔfisje/ *n.m.* officer.

officier [2] /ɔfisje/ *v.i.* (*relig.*) officiate.

officieu|x, ~se /ɔfisjø, -z/ *a.* unofficial. ~**sement** *adv.* unofficially.

offrande /ɔfrɑ̃d/ *n.f.* offering.

offrant /ɔfrɑ̃/ *n.m.* **au plus ~,** to the highest bidder.

offre /ɔfr/ *n.f.* offer; (*aux enchères*) bid. **l'~ et la demande,** supply and demand. ~**s d'emploi,** jobs advertised, (*rubrique*) situations vacant.

offrir† /ɔfrir/ *v.t.* offer (**de faire,** to do); (*cadeau*) give; (*acheter*) buy. **s'~** *v. pr.* offer o.s. (**comme,** as); (*spectacle*) present itself; (*s'acheter*) treat o.s. to. ~ **à boire à,** (*chez soi*) give a drink to; (*au café*) buy a drink for.

offusquer /ɔfyske/ *v.t.* offend.

ogive /ɔʒiv/ *n.f.* (*atomique etc.*) warhead.

ogre /ɔgr/ *n.m.* ogre.

oh /o/ *int.* oh.

oie /wa/ *n.f.* goose.

oignon /ɔɲɔ̃/ *n.m.* (*légume*) onion; (*de tulipe etc.*) bulb.

oiseau (*pl.* ~**x**) /wazo/ *n.m.* bird.

oisi|f, ~ve /wazif, -v/ *a.* idle. ~**veté** *n.f.* idleness.

O.K. /ɔke/ *int.* O.K.

oléoduc /ɔleɔdyk/ *n.m.* oil pipeline.

oliv|e /ɔliv/ *n.f. & a. invar.* olive. ~**ier** *n.m.* olive-tree.

olympique /ɔlɛ̃pik/ *a.* Olympic.

ombrag|e /ɔ̃braʒ/ *n.m.* shade. **prendre ~e de,** take offence at. ~**é** *a.* shady. ~**eux, ~euse** *a.* easily offended.

ombre /ɔ̃br/ *n.f.* (*pénombre*) shade; (*contour*) shadow; (*soupçon: fig.*) hint, shadow. **dans l'~,** (*secret*) in the dark. **faire de l'~ à qn.,** be in s.o.'s light.

ombrelle /ɔ̃brɛl/ *n.f.* parasol.

omelette /ɔmlɛt/ *n.f.* omelette.

omettre† /ɔmɛtr/ *v.t.* omit.

omission /ɔmisjɔ̃/ *n.f.* omission.

omnibus /ɔmnibys/ *n.m.* stopping train.

omoplate /ɔmɔplat/ *n.f.* shoulder-blade.

on /ɔ̃/ *pron.* we, you, one; (*les gens*) people, they; (*quelqu'un*) someone. **on dit,** people say, they say, it is said (**que,** that).

once /ɔ̃s/ *n.f.* ounce.

oncle /ɔ̃kl/ *n.m.* uncle.

onctueu|x, ~se /ɔktɥø, -z/ *a.* smooth.

onde /ɔ̃d/ *n.f.* wave. ~**s courtes/longues,** short/long wave. **sur les ~s,** on the radio.

ondée /ɔ̃de/ *n.f.* shower.

on-dit /ɔ̃di/ *n.m. invar.* **les ~,** rumour.

ondul|er /ɔ̃dyle/ *v.i.* undulate; (*cheveux*) be wavy. ~**ation** *n.f.* wave, undulation. ~**é** *a.* (*chevelure*) wavy.

onéreu|x, ~se /ɔnerø, -z/ *a.* costly.

ongle /ɔ̃gl/ *n.m.* (finger-)nail. **se faire les ~s,** do one's nails.

ont /ɔ̃/ *voir* avoir.

ONU *abrév.* (*Organisation des nations unies*) UN.

onyx /ɔniks/ *n.m.* onyx.

onz|e /ɔ̃z/ *a. & n.m.* eleven. ~**ième** *a. & n.m./f.* eleventh.

opale /ɔpal/ *n.f.* opal.

opa|que /ɔpak/ *a.* opaque. ~**cité** *n.f.* opaqueness.

open /ɔpɛn/ *n.m.* open (championship).

opéra /ɔpera/ *n.m.* opera; (*édifice*) opera-house. ~**-comique** (*pl.* ~**s-comiques**) *n.m.* light opera.

opérateur /ɔperatœr/ *n.m.* (*caméraman*) cameraman.

opération /ɔperasjɔ̃/ *n.f.* operation; (*comm.*) deal.

opérationnel, ~le /ɔperasjɔnɛl/ *a.* operational.

opératoire /ɔperatwar/ *a.* (*méd.*) surgical. **bloc ~,** operating suite.

opérer /ɔpere/ *v.t.* (*personne*) operate on; (*kyste etc.*) remove; (*exécuter*) carry out, make. **se faire ~,** have an operation. ● *v.i.* (*méd.*) operate; (*faire effet*) work. **s'~** *v. pr.* (*se produire*) occur.

opérette /ɔperɛt/ *n.f.* operetta.

opiner /ɔpine/ *v.i.* nod.

opiniâtre /ɔpinjɑtr/ *a.* obstinate.

opinion /ɔpinjɔ̃/ *n.f.* opinion.

opium /ɔpjɔm/ *n.m.* opium.

opportun, ~e /ɔpɔrtœ̃, -yn/ *a.* opportune. **~ité** /-ynite/ *n.f.* opportuneness.

opposant, ~e /ɔpozɑ̃, -t/ *n.m., f.* opponent.

opposé /ɔpoze/ *a.* (*sens, angle, etc.*) opposite; (*factions*) opposing; (*intérêts*) conflicting. ● *n.m.* opposite. **à l'~,** (*opinion etc.*) contrary (**de,** to). **être ~ à,** be opposed to.

opposer /ɔpoze/ *v.t.* (*objets*) place opposite each other; (*personnes*) oppose; (*contraster*) contrast; (*résistance, argument*) put up. **s'~** *v. pr.* (*personnes*) confront each other; (*styles*) contrast. **s'~ à,** oppose.

opposition /ɔpozisjɔ̃/ *n.f.* opposition. **par ~ à,** in contrast with. **entrer en ~ avec,** come into conflict with. **faire ~ à un chèque,** stop a cheque.

oppress|er /ɔprese/ *v.t.* oppress. **~ant, ~ante** *a.* oppressive. **~eur** *n.m.* oppressor. **~ion** *n.f.* oppression.

opprimer /ɔprime/ *v.t.* oppress.

opter /ɔpte/ *v.i.* **~ pour,** opt for.

opticien, ~ne /ɔptisjɛ̃, -jɛn/ *n.m., f.* optician.

optimis|te /ɔptimist/ *n.m./f.* optimist. ● *a.* optimistic. **~me** *n.m.* optimism.

optimum /ɔptimɔm/ *a. & n.m.* optimum.

option /ɔpsjɔ̃/ *n.f.* option.

optique /ɔptik/ *a.* (*verre*) optical. ● *n.f.* (*perspective*) perspective.

opulen|t, ~te /ɔpylɑ̃, -t/ *a.* opulent **~ce** *n.f.* opulence.

or[1] /ɔr/ *n.m.* gold. **d'~,** golden. **en ~,** gold; (*occasion*) golden.

or[2] /ɔr/ *conj.* now, well.

oracle /ɔrakl/ *n.m.* oracle.

orag|e /ɔraʒ/ *n.m.* (thunder)storm. **~eux, ~euse** *a.* stormy.

oraison /ɔrɛzɔ̃/ *n.f.* prayer.

or|al (*m. pl.* **~aux**) /ɔral, -o/ *a.* oral. ● *n.m.* (*pl.* **~aux**) oral.

orang|e /ɔrɑ̃ʒ/ *n.f. & a. invar.* orange. **~é** *a.* orange-coloured. **~er** *n.m.* orange-tree.

orangeade /ɔrɑ̃ʒad/ *n.f.* orangeade.

orateur /ɔratœr/ *n.m.* speaker.

oratorio /ɔratɔrjo/ *n.m.* oratorio.

orbite /ɔrbit/ *n.f.* orbit; (*d'œil*) socket.

orchestr|e /ɔrkɛstr/ *n.m.* orchestra; (*de jazz*) band; (*parterre*) stalls. **~er** *v.t.* orchestrate.

orchidée /ɔrkide/ *n.f.* orchid.

ordinaire /ɔrdinɛr/ *a.* ordinary; (*habituel*) usual; (*qualité*) standard. ● *n.m.* **l'~,** the ordinary; (*nourriture*) the standard fare. **d'~, à l'~,** usually. **~ment** *adv.* usually.

ordinateur /ɔrdinatœr/ *n.m.* computer.

ordination /ɔrdinasjɔ̃/ *n.f.* (*relig.*) ordination.

ordonnance /ɔrdɔnɑ̃s/ *n.f.* (*ordre, décret*) order; (*de médecin*) prescription; (*soldat*) orderly.

ordonné /ɔrdɔne/ *a.* tidy.

ordonner /ɔrdɔne/ *v.t.* order (**à qn. de,** s.o. to); (*agencer*) arrange; (*méd.*) prescribe; (*prêtre*) ordain.

ordre /ɔrdr/ *n.m.* order; (*propreté*) tidiness. **aux ~s de qn.,** at s.o.'s disposal. **avoir de l'~,** be tidy. **de premier ~,** first-rate. **l'~ du jour,** (*programme*) agenda. **mettre en ~,** tidy (up). **de premier ~,** first rate. **jusqu'à nouvel ~,** until further notice. **un ~ de grandeur,** an approximate idea.

ordure /ɔrdyr/ *n.f.* filth. **~s,** (*détritus*) rubbish; (*Amer.*) garbage. **~s ménagères,** household refuse.

oreille /ɔrɛj/ *n.f.* ear.

oreiller /ɔreje/ *n.m.* pillow.

oreillons /ɔrɛjɔ̃/ *n.m. pl.* mumps.

orfèvr|e /ɔrfɛvr/ *n.m.* goldsmith, silversmith. **~erie** *n.f.* goldsmith's *ou* silversmith's trade.

organe /ɔrgan/ *n.m.* organ; (*porte-parole*) mouthpiece.

organigramme /ɔrganigram/ *n.m.* flow chart.

organique /ɔrganik/ *a.* organic.

organisation /ɔrganizasjɔ̃/ *n.f.* organization.

organis|er /ɔrganize/ v.t. organize. **s'~er** v. pr. organize o.s. **~ateur, ~atrice** n.m., f. organizer.

organisme /ɔrganism/ n.m. body, organism.

organiste /ɔrganist/ n.m./f. organist.

orgasme /ɔrgasm/ n.m. orgasm.

orge /ɔrʒ/ n.f. barley.

orgelet /ɔrʒəlɛ/ n.m. (furoncle) sty.

orgie /ɔrʒi/ n.f. orgy.

orgue /ɔrg/ n.m. organ. **~s** n.f. pl. organ. **~ de Barbarie,** barrel-organ.

orgueil /ɔrgœj/ n.m. pride.

orgueilleu|x, ~se /ɔrgœjø, -z/ a. proud.

Orient /ɔrjɑ̃/ n.m. **l'~,** the Orient.

orientable /ɔrjɑ̃tabl/ a. adjustable.

orient|al, ~ale (m. pl. **~aux**) /ɔrjɑ̃tal, -o/ a. eastern; (de l'Orient) oriental. ● n.m., f. Oriental.

orientation /ɔrjɑ̃tasjɔ̃/ n.f. direction; (d'une politique) course; (de maison) aspect. **~ professionnelle,** careers advisory service.

orienté /ɔrjɑ̃te/ a. (partial) slanted, tendentious.

orienter /ɔrjɑ̃te/ v.t. position; (personne) direct. **s'~** v. pr. (se repérer) find one's bearings. **s'~ vers,** turn towards.

orifice /ɔrifis/ n.m. orifice.

origan /ɔrigɑ̃/ n.m. oregano.

originaire /ɔriʒinɛr/ a. **être ~ de,** be a native of.

origin|al, ~ale (m. pl. **~aux**) /ɔriʒinal, -o/ a. original; (curieux) eccentric. ● n.m., f. original. ● n.m., f. eccentric. **~alité** n.f. originality; eccentricity.

origine /ɔriʒin/ n.f. origin. **à l'~,** originally. **d'~,** (pièce, pneu) original.

originel, ~le /ɔriʒinɛl/ a. original.

orme /ɔrm/ n.m. elm.

ornement /ɔrnəmɑ̃/ n.m. ornament. **~al** (m. pl. **~aux**) /-tal, -to/ a. ornamental.

orner /ɔrne/ v.t. decorate.

ornière /ɔrnjɛr/ n.f. rut.

ornithologie /ɔrnitɔlɔʒi/ n.f. ornithology.

orphelin, ~e /ɔrfəlɛ̃, -in/ n.m., f. orphan. ● a. orphaned. **~at** /-ina/ n.m. orphanage.

orteil /ɔrtɛj/ n.m. toe.

orthodox|e /ɔrtɔdɔks/ a. orthodox. **~ie** n.f. orthodoxy.

orthograph|e /ɔrtɔgraf/ n.f. spelling. **~ier** v.t. spell.

orthopédique /ɔrtɔpedik/ a. orthopaedic.

ortie /ɔrti/ n.f. nettle.

os (pl. **os**) /ɔs, o/ n.m. bone.

OS abrév. voir ouvrier spécialisé.

oscar /ɔskar/ n.m. award; (au cinéma) oscar.

oscill|er /ɔsile/ v.i. sway; (techn.) oscillate; (hésiter) waver, fluctuate. **~ation** n.f. (techn.) oscillation; (variation) fluctuation.

oseille /ozɛj/ n.f. (plante) sorrel.

os|er /oze/ v.t./i. dare. **~é** a. daring.

osier /ozje/ n.m. wicker.

ossature /osatyr/ n.f. frame.

ossements /ɔsmɑ̃/ n.m. pl. bones.

osseu|x, ~se /ɔsø, -z/ a. bony; (tissu) bone.

ostensible /ɔstɑ̃sibl/ a. conspicuous, obvious.

ostentation /ɔstɑ̃tasjɔ̃/ n.f. ostentation.

ostéopathe /ɔsteopat/ n.m./f. osteopath.

otage /ɔtaʒ/ n.m. hostage.

otarie /ɔtari/ n.f. sea-lion.

ôter /ote/ v.t. remove (à qn., from s.o.); (déduire) take away.

otite /ɔtit/ n.f. ear infection.

ou /u/ conj. or. **ou bien,** or else. **vous ou moi,** either you or me.

où /u/ adv. & pron. where; (dans lequel) in which; (sur lequel) on which; (auquel) at which. **d'où,** from which; (pour cette raison) hence. **d'où?,** from where? **par où,** through which. **par où?,** which way? **où qu'il soit,** wherever he may be. **au prix où c'est,** at those prices. **le jour où,** the day when.

ouate /wat/ n.f. cotton wool; (Amer.) absorbent cotton.

oubli /ubli/ n.m. forgetfulness; (trou de mémoire) lapse of memory; (négligence) oversight. **l'~,** (tomber dans, sauver de) oblivion.

oublier /ublije/ v.t. forget. **s'~** v. pr. forget o.s.; (chose) be forgotten.

oublieu|x, ~se /ublijø, -z/ a. forgetful (de, of).

ouest /wɛst/ n.m. west. ● a. invar. west; (partie) western; (direction) westerly.

ouf /uf/ int. phew.

oui /wi/ adv. yes.

ouï-dire (par) /(par)widir/ adv. by hearsay.

ouïe /wi/ n.f. hearing.

ouïes /wi/ n.f. pl. gills.

ouille /uj/ *int.* ouch.

ouïr /wir/ *v.t.* hear.

ouragan /uragã/ *n.m.* hurricane.

ourler /urle/ *v.t.* hem.

ourlet /urlɛ/ *n.m.* hem.

ours /urs/ *n.m.* bear. ~ **blanc,** polar bear. ~ **en peluche,** teddy bear. ~ **mal léché,** boor.

ouste /ust/ *int.* (*fam.*) scram.

outil /uti/ *n.m.* tool.

outillage /utijaʒ/ *n.m.* tools; (*d'une usine*) equipment.

outiller /utije/ *v.t.* equip.

outrage /utraʒ/ *n.m.* (grave) insult.

outrag|er /utraʒe/ *v.t.* offend. ~**eant,** ~**eante** *a.* offensive.

outranc|e /utrãs/ *n.f.* excess. **à** ~**e,** to excess; (*guerre*) all-out. ~**ier,** ~**ière** *a.* excessive.

outre /utr/ *prép.* besides. **en** ~, besides. ~**-mer** *adv.* overseas. ~ **mesure,** excessively.

outrepasser /utrəpase/ *v.t.* exceed.

outrer /utre/ *v.t.* exaggerate; (*indigner*) incense.

outsider /utsajdœr/ *n.m.* outsider.

ouvert, ~**e** /uvɛr, -t/ *voir* ouvrir. ● *a.* open; (*gaz, radio, etc.*) on. ~**ement** /-təmã/ *adv.* openly.

ouverture /uvɛrtyr/ *n.f.* opening; (*mus.*) overture; (*photo.*) aperture. ~**s,** (*offres*) overtures. ~ **d'esprit,** open-mindedness.

ouvrable /uvrabl/ *a.* **jour** ~, working day.

ouvrag|e /uvraʒ/ *n.m.* (*travail, livre*) work; (*couture*) needlework. ~**é** *a.* finely worked.

ouvreuse /uvrøz/ *n.f.* usherette.

ouvr|ier, ~**ière** /uvrije, -jɛr/ *n.m., f.* worker. ● *a.* working-class; (*conflit*) industrial; (*syndicat*) workers'. ~**ier qualifié/spécialisé,** skilled/ unskilled worker.

ouvr|ir† /uvrir/ *v.t.* open (up); (*gaz, robinet, etc.*) turn *ou* switch on. ● *v.i.* open (up). **s'**~*v. pr.* open (up). **s'**~**ir à qn.,** open one's heart to s.o. ~**e-boîte(s)** *n.m.* tin-opener. ~**e-bouteille(s)** *n.m.* bottle-opener.

ovaire /ɔvɛr/ *n.m.* ovary.

ovale /ɔval/ *a. & n.m.* oval.

ovation /ɔvasjõ/ *n.f.* ovation.

overdose /ɔvɛrdoz/ *n.f.* overdose

ovni /ɔvni/ *n.m.* (*abrév.*) UFO.

ovule /ɔvyl/ *n.m.* (*à féconder*) egg; (*gynécologique*) pessary.

oxyder (s') /(s)ɔkside/ *v. pr.* become oxidized.

oxygène /ɔksiʒɛn/ *n.m.* oxygen.

oxygéner (s') /(s)ɔksiʒene/ *v. pr.* (*fam.*) get some fresh air.

ozone /ozon/ *n.f.* ozone. **la couche d'**~, the ozone layer.

P

pacemaker /pesmekœr/ *n.m.* pacemaker.

pachyderme /paʃidɛrm/ *n.m.* elephant.

pacifier /pasifje/ *v.t.* pacify.

pacifique /pasifik/ *a.* peaceful; (*personne*) peaceable; (*géog.*) Pacific. ● *n.m.* **P**~, Pacific (Ocean).

pacifiste /pasifist/ *n.m./f.* pacifist.

pacotille /pakɔtij/ *n.f.* trash.

pacte /pakt/ *n.m.* pact.

pactiser /paktize/ *v.i.* ~ **avec,** be in league *ou* agreement with.

paddock /padɔk/ *n.m.* paddock.

pag|aie /pagɛ/ *n.f.* paddle. ~**ayer** *v.i.* paddle.

pagaille /pagaj/ *n.f.* mess, shambles.

page /paʒ/ *n.f.* page. **être à la** ~, be up to date.

pagode /pagɔd/ *n.f.* pagoda.

paie /pɛ/ *n.f.* pay.

paiement /pɛmã/ *n.m.* payment.

païen, ~**ne** /pajɛ̃, -jɛn/ *a. & n.m., f.* pagan.

paillasse /pajas/ *n.f.* straw mattress; (*dans un laboratoire*) draining-board.

paillasson /pajasõ/ *n.m.* doormat.

paille /pɑj/ *n.f.* straw; (*défaut*) flaw.

paillette /pajɛt/ *n.f.* (*sur robe*) sequin; (*de savon*) flake. ~**s d'or,** gold-dust.

pain /pɛ̃/ *n.m.* bread: (*unité*) loaf (of bread); (*de savon etc.*) bar. ~ **d'épice,** gingerbread. ~ **grillé,** toast.

pair [1] /pɛr/ *a.* (*nombre*) even.

pair [2] /pɛr/ *n.m.* (*personne*) peer. **au** ~, (*jeune fille etc.*) au pair. **aller de** ~, go together (**avec,** with).

paire /pɛr/ *n.f.* pair.

paisible /pezibl/ *a.* peaceful.

paître /pɛtr/ *v.i.* (*brouter*) graze.

paix /pɛ/ *n.f.* peace; (*traité*) peace treaty.

Pakistan /pakistã/ *n.m.* Pakistan.

pakistanais, ~**e** /pakistanɛ, -z/ *a. & n.m., f.* Pakistani.

palace /palas/ *n.m.* luxury hotel.
palais[1] /palɛ/ *n.m.* palace. **P~ de Justice,** Law Courts. **~ des sports,** sports stadium.
palais[2] /palɛ/ *n.m.* (*anat.*) palate.
palan /palɑ̃/ *n.m.* hoist.
pâle /pɑl/ *a.* pale.
Palestine /palɛstin/ *n.f.* Palestine.
palestinien, ~ne /palɛstinjɛ̃, -jɛn/ *a. & n.m., f.* Palestinian.
palet /palɛ/ *n.m.* (*hockey*) puck.
paletot /palto/ *n.m.* thick jacket.
palette /palɛt/ *n.f.* palette.
pâleur /pɑlœr/ *n.f.* paleness.
palier /palje/ *n.m.* (*d'escalier*) landing; (*étape*) stage; (*de route*) level stretch.
pâlir /pɑlir/ *v.t./i.* (turn) pale.
palissade /palisad/ *n.f.* fence.
pallier /palje/ *v.t.* alleviate.
palmarès /palmarɛs/ *n.m.* list of prize-winners.
palm|e /palm/ *n.f.* palm leaf; (*symbole*) palm; (*de nageur*) flipper. **~ier** *n.m.* palm(-tree).
palmé /palme/ *a.* (*patte*) webbed.
pâlot, ~te /pɑlo, -ɔt/ *a.* pale.
palourde /palurd/ *n.f.* clam.
palper /palpe/ *v.t.* feel.
palpit|er /palpite/ *v.i.* (*battre*) pound, palpitate; (*frémir*) quiver. **~ations** *n.f. pl.* palpitations. **~ant, ~ante** *a.* thrilling.
paludisme /palydism/ *n.m.* malaria.
pâmer (se) /(sə)pɑme/ *v. pr.* swoon.
pamphlet /pɑ̃flɛ/ *n.m.* satirical pamphlet.
pamplemousse /pɑ̃pləmus/ *n.m.* grapefruit.
pan[1] /pɑ̃/ *n.m.* piece; (*de chemise*) tail.
pan[2] /pɑ̃/ *int.* bang.
panacée /panase/ *n.f.* panacea.
panache /panaʃ/ *n.m.* plume; (*bravoure*) gallantry; (*allure*) panache.
panaché /panaʃe/ *a.* (*bariolé, mélangé*) motley. **glace ~e,** mixed-flavour ice cream. ● *n.m.* shandy. **bière ~e, demi ~,** shandy.
pancarte /pɑ̃kart/ *n.f.* sign; (*de manifestant*) placard.
pancréas /pɑ̃kreas/ *n.m.* pancreas.
pané /pane/ *a.* breaded.
panier /panje/ *n.m.* basket. **~ à provisions,** shopping basket. **~ à salade,** (*fam.*) police van.
paniqu|e /panik/ *n.f.* panic. (*fam.*) **~er** *v.i.* panic.

panne /pan/ *n.f.* breakdown. **être en ~,** have broken down. **être en ~ sèche,** have run out of petrol *ou* gas (*Amer.*). **~ d'électricité** *ou* **de courant,** power failure.
panneau (*pl.* **~x**) /pano/ *n.m.* sign; (*publicitaire*) hoarding; (*de porte etc.*) panel. **~ (d'affichage),** notice-board. **~ (de signalisation),** road sign.
panoplie /panɔpli/ *n.f.* (*jouet*) outfit; (*gamme*) range.
panoram|a /panɔrama/ *n.m.* panorama. **~ique** *a.* panoramic.
panse /pɑ̃s/ *n.f.* paunch.
pans|er /pɑ̃se/ *v.t.* (*plaie*) dress; (*personne*) dress the wound(s) of; (*cheval*) groom. **~ement** *n.m.* dressing. **~ement adhésif,** sticking-plaster.
pantalon /pɑ̃talɔ̃/ *n.m.* (pair of) trousers. **~s,** trousers.
panthère /pɑ̃tɛr/ *n.f.* panther.
pantin /pɑ̃tɛ̃/ *n.m.* puppet.
pantomime /pɑ̃tɔmim/ *n.f.* mime; (*spectacle*) mime show.
pantoufle /pɑ̃tufl/ *n.f.* slipper.
paon /pɑ̃/ *n.m.* peacock.
papa /papa/ *n.m.* dad(dy). **de ~,** (*fam.*) old-time.
papauté /papote/ *n.f.* papacy.
pape /pap/ *n.m.* pope.
paperass|e /papras/ *n.f.* **~e(s),** (*péj.*) papers. **~erie** *n.f.* (*péj.*) papers; (*tracasserie*) red tape.
papet|ier, ~ière /paptje, -jɛr/ *n.m., f.* stationer. **~erie** /papetri/ *n.f.* (*magasin*) stationer's shop.
papier /papje/ *n.m.* paper; (*formulaire*) form. **~s (d'identité),** (identity) papers. **~ à lettres,** writing-paper. **~ aluminium,** tin foil. **~ buvard,** blotting-paper. **~ calque,** tracing-paper. **~ carbone,** carbon paper. **~ collant,** sticky paper. **~ de verre,** sandpaper. **~ hygiénique,** toilet-paper. **~ journal,** newspaper. **~ mâché,** papier mâché. **~ peint,** wallpaper.
papillon /papijɔ̃/ *n.m.* butterfly; (*contravention*) parking-ticket. **~ (de nuit),** moth.
papot|er /papote/ *v.i.* prattle. **~age** *n.m.* prattle.
paprika /paprika/ *n.m.* paprika.
Pâque /pak/ *n.f.* Passover.
paquebot /pakbo/ *n.m.* liner.
pâquerette /pakrɛt/ *n.f.* daisy.
Pâques /pak/ *n.f. pl. & n.m.* Easter.

paquet /pakɛ/ *n.m.* packet; (*de cartes*) pack; (*colis*) parcel. **un ~ de**, (*tas*) a mass of.

par /par/ *prép.* by; (*à travers*) through; (*motif*) out of, from; (*provenance*) from. **commencer/finir qch.**, begin/end with sth. **commencer/finir ~ faire**, begin by/end up (by) doing. **~ an/mois/***etc.*, a *ou* per year/month/*etc.* **~ avion**, (*lettre*) (by) airmail. **~-ci, par-là,** here and there. **~ contre**, on the other hand. **~ hasard,** by chance. **~ ici/là,** this/that way. **~ inadvertance,** inadvertently. **~ intermittence,** intermittently. **~ l'intermédiaire de**, through. **~ jour,** a day. **~ malheur** *ou* **malchance,** unfortunately. **~ miracle,** miraculously. **~ moments,** at times. **~ opposition à**, as opposed to. **~ personne,** each, per person.

parabole /parabɔl/ *n.f.* (*relig.*) parable; (*maths*) parabola.

paracétamol /parasetamɔl/ *n.m.* paracetamol.

parachever /paraʃve/ *v.t.* perfect.

parachut|e /paraʃyt/ *n.m.* parachute. **~er** *v.t.* parachute. **~iste** *n.m./f.* parachutist; (*mil.*) paratrooper.

parad|e /parad/ *n.f.* parade; (*sport*) parry; (*réplique*) reply. **~er** *v.i.* show off.

paradis /paradi/ *n.m.* paradise. **~ fiscal,** tax haven.

paradox|e /paradɔks/ *n.m.* paradox. **~al** (*m. pl.* **~aux**) *a.* paradoxical.

paraffine /parafin/ *n.f.* paraffin wax.

parages /paraʒ/ *n.m. pl.* area, vicinity.

paragraphe /paragraf/ *n.m.* paragraph.

paraître† /parɛtr/ *v.i.* appear; (*sembler*) seem, appear; (*ouvrage*) be published, come out. **faire ~**, (*ouvrage*) bring out.

parallèle /paralɛl/ *a.* parallel; (*illégal*) unofficial. ● *n.m.* parallel. **faire un ~ entre**, draw a parallel between. **faire le ~**, make a connection. ● *n.f.* parallel (line). **~ment** *adv.* parallel (**à**, to).

paraly|ser /paralize/ *v.t.* paralyse. **~sie** *n.f.* paralysis. **~tique** *a. & n.m./f.* paralytic.

paramètre /paramɛtr/ *n.m.* parameter.

paranoïa /paranɔja/ *n.f.* paranoia.

parapet /parapɛ/ *n.m.* parapet.

paraphe /paraf/ *n.m.* signature.

paraphrase /parafraz/ *n.f.* paraphrase.

parapluie /paraplɥi/ *n.m.* umbrella.

parasite /parazit/ *n.m.* parasite. **~s,** (*radio*) interference.

parasol /parasɔl/ *n.m.* sunshade.

paratonnerre /paratɔnɛr/ *n.m.* lightning-conductor *ou* -rod.

paravent /paravɑ̃/ *n.m.* screen.

parc /park/ *n.m.* park; (*de bétail*) pen; (*de bébé*) play-pen; (*entrepôt*) dépot. **~ de stationnement,** car- park.

parcelle /parsɛl/ *n.f.* fragment; (*de terre*) plot.

parce que /parsk(ə)/ *conj.* because.

parchemin /parʃəmɛ̃/ *n.m.* parchment.

parcimon|ie /parsimɔni/ *n.f.* **avec ~ie,** parsimoniously. **~ieux, ~ieuse** *a.* parsimonious.

parcmètre /parkmɛtr/ *n.m.* parking-meter.

parcourir† /parkurir/ *v.t.* travel *ou* go through; (*distance*) travel; (*des yeux*) glance *ou* run over.

parcours /parkur/ *n.m.* route; (*voyage*) journey.

par-delà /pardəla/ *prép. & adv.* beyond.

par-derrière /pardɛrjɛr/ *prép. & adv.* behind, at the back *ou* rear (of).

par-dessous /pardsu/ *prép. & adv.* under(neath).

pardessus /pardəsy/ *n.m.* overcoat.

par-dessus /pardsy/ *prép. & adv.* over. **~ bord,** overboard. **~ le marché,** into the bargain. **~ tout,** above all.

par-devant /pardəvɑ̃/ *adv.* at *ou* from the front, in front.

pardon /pardɔ̃/ *n.m.* forgiveness. **(je vous demande) ~!,** (I am) sorry!; (*pour demander qch.*) excuse me!

pardonn|er /pardɔne/ *v.t.* forgive. **~er qch. à qn.,** forgive s.o. for sth. **~able** *a.* forgivable.

paré /pare/ *a.* ready.

pare-balles /parbal/ *a. invar.* bulletproof.

pare-brise /parbriz/ *n.m. invar.* windscreen; (*Amer.*) windshield.

pare-chocs /parʃɔk/ *n.m. invar.* bumper.

pareil, ~le /parɛj/ *a.* similar (**à** to); (*tel*) such (a). ● *n.m., f.* equal. ● *adv.* (*fam.*) the same. **c'est ~,** it is the same. **vos ~s,** (*péj.*) those of

your type, those like you. **~lement**
adv. the same.
parement /paʀmã/ *n.m.* facing.
parent, ~e /paʀã, -t/ *a.* related (**de,
to**). ● *n.m., f.* relative, relation. **~s**
(*père et mère*) *n.m. pl.* parents. **~
seul,** single parent.
parenté /paʀãte/ *n.f.* relationship.
parenthèse /paʀãtɛz/ *n.f.* bracket,
parenthesis; (*fig.*) digression.
parer¹ /paʀe/ *v.t.* (*coup*) parry. ● *v.i.*
~ à, deal with. **~ au plus pressé,**
tackle the most urgent things first.
parer² /paʀe/ *v.t.* (*orner*) adorn.
paress|e /paʀɛs/ *n.f.* laziness. **~er**
/-ese/ *v.i.* laze (about). **~eux, ~euse**
a. lazy; *n.m., f.* lazybones.
parfaire /paʀfɛʀ/ *v.t.* perfect.
parfait, ~e /paʀfɛ, -t/ *a.* perfect.
~ement /-tmã/ *adv.* perfectly; (*bien
sûr*) certainly.
parfois /paʀfwa/ *adv.* sometimes.
parfum /paʀfœ̃/ *n.m.* scent; (*substance*) perfume, scent; (*goût*) flavour.
parfum|er /paʀfyme/ *v.t.* perfume;
(*gâteau*) flavour. **se ~er** *v. pr.* put
on one's perfume. **~é** *a.* fragrant;
(*savon*) scented. **~erie** *n.f.* (*produits*) perfumes; (*boutique*) perfume
shop.
pari /paʀi/ *n.m.* bet.
par|ier /paʀje/ *v.t.* bet. **~ieur, ~ieuse**
n.m., f. punter, better.
Paris /paʀi/ *n.m./f.* Paris.
parisien, ~ne /paʀizjɛ̃, -jɛn/ *a.* Paris,
Parisian. ● *n.m., f.* Parisian.
parit|é /paʀite/ *n.f.* parity. **~aire** *a.*
(*commission*) joint.
parjur|e /paʀʒyʀ/ *n.m.* perjury.
● *n.m./f.* perjurer. **se ~er** *v. pr.*
perjure o.s.
parking /paʀkiŋ/ *n.m.* car-park;
(*Amer.*) parking-lot; (*stationnement*)
parking.
parlement /paʀləmã/ *n.m.* parliament. **~aire** /-tɛʀ/ *a.* parliamen-
tary; *n.m./f.* Member of Parliament;
(*fig.*) negotiator. **~er** /-te/ *v.i.* ne-
gotiate.
parl|er /paʀle/ *v.i.* talk, speak (**à,** to).
● *v.t.* (*langue*) speak; (*politique,
affaires, etc.*) talk. **se ~er** *v. pr.*
(*langue*) be spoken. ● *n.m.* speech;
(*dialecte*) dialect. **~ant, ~ante** *a.*
(*film*) talking; (*fig.*) eloquent. **~eur,
~euse** *n.m., f.* talker.
parloir /paʀlwaʀ/ *n.m.* visiting room.
parmi /paʀmi/ *prép.* among(st).

parod|ie /paʀɔdi/ *n.f.* parody. **~ier**
v.t. parody.
paroi /paʀwa/ *n.f.* wall; (*cloison*)
partition (wall). **~ rocheuse,** rock
face.
paroiss|e /paʀwas/ *n.f.* parish. **~ial**
(*m. pl.* **~iaux**) *a.* parish. **~ien,
~ienne** *n.m., f.* parishioner.
parole /paʀɔl/ *n.f.* (*mot, promesse*)
word; (*langage*) speech. **demander
la ~,** ask to speak. **prendre la ~,**
(begin to) speak. **tenir ~,** keep one's
word. **croire qn. sur ~,** take s.o.'s
word for it.
paroxysme /paʀɔksism/ *n.m.* height,
highest point.
parquer /paʀke/ *v.t.,* **se ~** *v. pr.*
(*auto.*) park. **~ des réfugiés,** pen
up refugees.
parquet /paʀkɛ/ *n.m.* floor; (*jurid.*)
public prosecutor's department.
parrain /paʀɛ̃/ *n.m.* godfather; (*fig.*)
sponsor. **~er** /-ene/ *v.t.* sponsor.
pars, part¹ /paʀ/ *voir* partir.
parsemer /paʀsəme/ *v.t.* strew (**de,**
with).
part² /paʀ/ *n.f.* share, part. **à ~,** (*de
côté*) aside; (*séparément*) apart; (*excepté*) apart from. **d'autre ~,** on the
other hand; (*de plus*) moreover. **de
la ~ de,** from. **de toutes ~s,** from
all sides. **de ~ et d'autre,** on both
sides. **d'une ~,** on the one hand.
faire ~ à qn., inform s.o. (**de,** of).
faire la ~ des choses, make
allowances. **prendre ~ à,** take part
in; (*joie, douleur*) share. **pour ma ~,**
as for me.
partag|e /paʀtaʒ/ *n.m.* dividing; shar-
ing out; (*part*) share. **~er** *v.t.* divide;
(*distribuer*) share out; (*avoir en
commun*) share. **se ~er qch.,** share
sth.
partance (en) /(ã)paʀtãs/ *adv.* about
to depart.
partant /paʀtã/ *n.m.* (*sport*) starter.
partenaire /paʀtənɛʀ/ *n.m./f.* partner.
parterre /paʀtɛʀ/ *n.m.* flower-bed;
(*théâtre*) stalls.
parti /paʀti/ *n.m.* (*pol.*) party; (*en
mariage*) match; (*décision*) decision.
~ pris, prejudice. **prendre ~ pour,**
side with. **j'en prends mon ~,** I've
come to terms with that.
part|ial (*m. pl.* **~iaux**) /paʀsjal, -jo/ *a.*
biased. **~ialité** *n.f.* bias.
participe /paʀtisip/ *n.m.* (*gram.*)
participle.

particip|er /partisipe/ *v.i.* ~er à,
take part in, participate in;
(*profits*, *frais*) share; (*spectacle*)
appear in. ~ant, ~ante *n.m.*, *f.*
participant (à, in); (*à un concours*)
entrant. ~ation *n.f.* participation;
sharing; (*comm.*) interest. (*d'un artiste*) appearance.

particularité /partikylarite/ *n.f.* par-
ticularity.

particule /partikyl/ *n.f.* particle.

particul|ier, ~ière /partikylje, -jɛr/
a. (*spécifique*) particular; (*bizarre*)
peculiar; (*privé*) private. ● *n.m.*
private individual. **en** ~ier, in particular; (*en privé*) in private. ~ier à,
peculiar to. ~ièrement *adv.* parti-
cularly.

partie /parti/ *n.f.* part; (*cartes*, *sport*)
game; (*jurid.*) party; (*sortie*) outing,
party. **une** ~ **de pêche,** a fishing
trip. **en** ~, partly. **faire** ~ **de,** be
part of; (*adhérer à*) belong to. **en
grande** ~, largely. ~ **intégrante,**
integral part.

partiel, ~**le** /parsjɛl/ *a.* partial.
● *n.m.* (*univ.*) class examination.
~**lement** *adv.* partially, partly.

partir† /partir/ *v.i.* (*aux. être*) go;
(*quitter un lieu*) leave, go; (*tache*)
come out; (*bouton*) come off; (*coup
de feu*) go off; (*commencer*) start. **à**
~ **de,** from.

partisan, ~**e** /partizã, -an/ *n.m.*, *f.*
supporter. ● *n.m.* (*mil.*) partisan.
être ~ **de,** be in favour of.

partition /partisjɔ̃/ *n.f.* (*mus.*) score.

partout /partu/ *adv.* everywhere. ~
où, wherever.

paru /pary/ *voir* paraître.

parure /paryr/ *n.f.* adornment; (*bijoux*) jewellery; (*de draps*) set.

parution /parysjɔ̃/ *n.f.* publication.

parvenir† /parvənir/ *v.i.* (*aux. être*)
~ **à,** reach; (*résultat*) achieve. ~ **à
faire,** manage to do. **faire** ~, send.

parvenu, ~**e** /parvəny/ *n.m.*, *f.*
upstart.

parvis /parvi/ *n.m.* (*place*) square.

pas [1] /pɑ/ *adv.* not. (**ne**) ~, not. **je ne
sais** ~, I do not know. ~ **de sucre/
livres/***etc.***,** no sugar/books/*etc.* ~
du tout, not at all. ~ **encore,** not
yet ~ **mal,** not bad; (*beaucoup*)
quite a lot (**de,** of). ~ **vrai?,** (*fam.*)
isn't that so?

pas [2] /pɑ/ *n.m.* step; (*bruit*) footstep;
(*trace*) footprint; (*vitesse*) pace; (*de
vis*) thread. **à deux** ~ **(de),** close by.

au ~, at a walking pace; (*véhicule*)
very slowly. **au** ~ **(cadencé),** in
step. **à** ~ **de loup,** stealthily. **faire
les cent** ~, walk up and down. **faire
les premiers** ~, take the first steps.
sur le ~ **de la porte,** on the doorstep.

passable /pɑsabl/ *a.* tolerable. **mention** ~, pass mark.

passage /pɑsaʒ/ *n.m.* passing, passage; (*traversée*) crossing; (*visite*)
visit; (*chemin*) way, passage; (*d'une
œuvre*) passage. **de** ~, (*voyageur*)
visiting; (*amant*) casual. ~ **à niveau,** level crossing. ~ **clouté,** pedestrian crossing. ~ **interdit,**
(*panneau*) no thoroughfare. ~ **souterrain,** subway; (*Amer.*) underpass.

passag|er, ~**ère** /pɑsaʒe, -ɛr/ *a.*
temporary. ● *n.m.*, *f.* passenger.
~**er clandestin,** stowaway.

passant, ~**e** /pɑsã, -t/ *a.* (*rue*) busy.
● *n.m.*, *f.* passer-by. ● *n.m.* (*anneau*) loop.

passe /pɑs/ *n.f.* pass. **bonne/mau-
vaise** ~, good/bad patch. **en** ~ **de,**
on the road to. ~**-droit,** *n.m.* special
privilege. ~**-montagne** *n.m.* Balaclava. ~**-partout** *n.m.* *invar.*
master-key; *a. invar.* for all occasions. ~**-temps** *n.m. invar.* pastime.

passé /pɑse/ *a.* (*révolu*) past; (*dernier*) last; (*fini*) over; (*fané*) faded.
● *prép.* after. ● *n.m.* past. ~ **de
mode,** out of fashion.

passeport /pɑspɔr/ *n.m.* passport.

passer /pɑse/ *v.i.* (*aux. être ou avoir*)
pass; (*aller*) go; (*venir*) come;
(*temps*) pass (by), go by; (*film*) be
shown; (*couleur*) fade. ● *v.t.* (*aux.
avoir*) pass, cross; (*donner*) pass,
hand; (*mettre*) put; (*oublier*) overlook; (*enfiler*) slip on; (*dépasser*) go
beyond; (*temps*) spend, pass; (*film*)
show; (*examen*) take; (*commande*)
place; (*soupe*) strain. **se** ~ *v. pr.*
happen, take place. **laisser** ~, let
through; (*occasion*) miss. ~ **à tabac,**
(*fam.*) beat up. ~ **devant,** (*édifice*)
go past. ~ **en fraude,** smuggle. ~
outre, take no notice (**à,** of). ~ **par,**
go through. ~ **pour,** (*riche etc.*) be
taken to be. ~ **sur,** (*détail*) pass
over. ~ **l'aspirateur,** hoover,
vacuum. ~ **un coup de fil à qn.,**
give s.o. a ring. **je vous passe Mme
X,** (*par le standard*) I'm putting you
through to Mrs X; (*en donnant*

l'appareil) I'll hand you over to Mrs X. **se ~ de**, go *ou* do without.

passerelle /pɑsrɛl/ *n.f.* footbridge; (*pour accéder à un avion, à un navire*) gangway.

pass|eur, ~euse /pɑsœr, œz/ *n.m., f.* smuggler.

passible /pasibl/ *a.* **~ de**, liable to.

passi|f, ~ve /pasif, -v/ *a.* passive. ● *n.m.* (*comm.*) liabilities. **~vité** *n.f.* passiveness.

passion /pɑsjɔ̃/ *n.f.* passion.

passionn|er /pɑsjɔne/ *v.t.* fascinate. **se ~er pour**, have a passion for. **~é** *a.* passionate. **être ~é de**, have a passion for. **~ément** *adv.* passionately.

passoire /pɑswar/ *n.f.* (*à thé*) strainer; (*à légumes*) colander.

pastel /pastɛl/ *n.m. & a. invar.* pastel.

pastèque /pastɛk/ *n.f.* watermelon.

pasteur /pastœr/ *n.m.* (*relig.*) minister.

pasteurisé /pastœrize/ *a.* pasteurized.

pastiche /pastiʃ/ *n.m.* pastiche.

pastille /pastij/ *n.f.* (*bonbon*) pastille, lozenge.

pastis /pastis/ *n.m.* aniseed liqueur.

patate /patat/ *n.f.* (*fam.*) potato. **~ (douce)**, sweet potato.

patauger /patoʒe/ *v.i.* splash about.

pâte /pɑt/ *n.f.* paste; (*farine*) dough; (*à tarte*) pastry; (*à frire*) batter. **~s (alimentaires)**, pasta. **~ à modeler**, Plasticine (P.). **~ dentifrice**, toothpaste.

pâté /pɑte/ *n.m.* (*culin.*) pâté; (*d'encre*) ink-blot. **~ de maisons**, block of houses; (*de sable*) sand-pie. **~ en croûte**, meat pie.

pâtée /pɑte/ *n.f.* feed, mash.

patelin /patlɛ̃/ *n.m.* (*fam.*) village.

patent, ~e[1] /patɑ̃, -t/ *a.* patent.

patent|e[2] /patɑ̃t/ *n.f.* trade licence. **~é** *a.* licensed.

patère /patɛr/ *n.f.* (*coat*) peg.

patern|el, ~elle /patɛrnɛl/ *a.* paternal. **~ité** *n.f.* paternity.

pâteu|x, ~se /patø, -z/ *a.* pasty; (*langue*) coated.

pathétique /patetik/ *a.* moving. ● *n.m.* pathos.

patholog|ie /patɔlɔʒi/ *n.f.* pathology. **~ique** *a.* pathological.

pat|ient, ~iente /pasjɑ̃, -t/ *a. & n.m., f.* patient. **~iemment** /-jamɑ̃/ *adv.* patiently. **~ience** *n.f.* patience.

patienter /pasjɑ̃te/ *v.i.* wait.

patin /patɛ̃/ *n.m.* skate. **~ à roulettes**, roller-skate.

patin|er /patine/ *v.i.* skate; (*voiture*) spin. **~age** *n.m.* skating. **~eur, ~euse** *n.m., f.* skater.

patinoire /patinwar/ *n.f.* skating-rink.

pâtir /pɑtir/ *v.i.* suffer (**de**, from).

pâtiss|ier, ~ière /pɑtisje, -jɛr/ *n.m., f.* pastry-cook, cake shop owner. **~erie** *n.f.* cake shop; (*gâteau*) pastry; (*art*) cake making.

patois /patwa/ *n.m.* patois.

patraque /patrak/ *a.* (*fam.*) peaky, out of sorts.

patrie /patri/ *n.f.* homeland.

patrimoine /patrimwan/ *n.m.* heritage.

patriot|e /patrijɔt/ *a.* patriotic. ● *n.m./f.* patriot. **~ique** *a.* patriotic. **~isme** *n.m.* patriotism.

patron[1]**, ~ne** /patrɔ̃, -ɔn/ *n.m., f.* employer; boss; (*propriétaire*) owner, boss; (*saint*) patron saint. **~al** (*m. pl.* **~aux**) /-ɔnal, -o/ *a.* employers'. **~at** /-ɔna/ *n.m.* employers.

patron[2] /patrɔ̃/ *n.m.* (*couture*) pattern.

patronage /patrɔnaʒ/ *n.m.* patronage; (*foyer*) youth club.

patronner /patrɔne/ *v.t.* support.

patrouill|e /patruj/ *n.f.* patrol. **~er** *v.i.* patrol.

patte /pat/ *n.f.* leg; (*pied*) foot; (*de chat*) paw. **~s**, (*favoris*) sideburns.

pâturage /pɑtyraʒ/ *n.m.* pasture.

pâture /pɑtyr/ *n.f.* food.

paume /pom/ *n.f.* (*de main*) palm.

paumé, ~e /pome/ *n.m., f.* (*fam.*) wretch, loser.

paumer /pome/ *v.t.* (*fam.*) lose.

paupière /popjɛr/ *n.f.* eyelid.

pause /poz/ *n.f.* pause; (*halte*) break.

pauvre /povr/ *a.* poor. ● *n.m./f.* poor man, poor woman. **~ment** /-əmɑ̃/ *adv.* poorly. **~té** /-əte/ *n.f.* poverty.

pavaner (se) /(sə)pavane/ *v. pr.* strut.

pav|er /pave/ *v.t.* pave; (*chaussée*) cobble. **~é** *n.m.* paving-stone; cobble(-stone).

pavillon[1] /pavijɔ̃/ *n.m.* house; (*de gardien*) lodge.

pavillon[2] /pavijɔ̃/ *n.m.* (*drapeau*) flag.

pavoiser /pavwaze/ *v.t.* deck with flags. ● *v.i.* put out the flags.

pavot /pavo/ *n.m.* poppy.

payant, ~e /pɛjɑ̃, -t/ *a.* (*billet*) for which a charge is made; (*spectateur*) (fee-)paying; (*rentable*) profitable.

payer /peje/ *v.t./i.* pay; (*service, travail, etc.*) pay for; (*acheter*) buy (à, for). **se ~** *v. pr.* (*s'acheter*) buy o.s. **faire ~ à qn.,** (*cent francs etc.*) charge s.o. (**pour,** for). **se ~ la tête de,** make fun of. **il me le paiera!,** he'll pay for this.

pays /pei/ *n.m.* country; (*région*) region; (*village*) village. **du ~,** local. **les P~-Bas,** the Netherlands. **le ~ de Galles,** Wales.

paysage /peizaʒ/ *n.m.* landscape.

paysan, ~ne /peizɑ̃, -an/ *n.m.,* *f.* farmer, country person; (*péj.*) peasant. ● *a.* (*agricole*) farming; (*rural*) country.

PCV (en) /(ɑ̃)peseve/ *adv.* **appeler** *ou* **téléphoner en ~,** reverse the charges; (*Amer.*) call collect.

PDG *abrév. voir* président directeur général.

péage /peaʒ/ *n.m.* toll; (*lieu*) toll-gate.

peau (*pl.* **~x**) /po/ *n.f.* skin; (*cuir*) hide. **~ de chamois,** chamois (-leather). **~ de mouton,** sheep-skin. **être bien/mal dans sa ~,** be/ not be at ease with oneself.

pêche[1] /pɛʃ/ *n.f.* peach.

pêche[2] /pɛʃ/ *n.f.* (*activité*) fishing; (*poissons*) catch. **~ à la ligne,** angling.

péché /peʃe/ *n.m.* sin.

péch|er /peʃe/ *v.i.* sin. **~er par timidité/**etc.**,** be too timid/*etc.* **~eur, ~eresse** *n.m., f.* sinner.

pêch|er /peʃe/ *v.t.* (*poisson*) catch; (*dénicher: fam.*) dig up. ● *v.i.* fish. **~eur** *n.m.* fisherman; (*à la ligne*) angler.

pécule /pekyl/ *n.m.* (*économies*) sav-ings.

pécuniaire /pekynjɛr/ *a.* financial.

pédago|gie /pedagɔʒi/ *n.f.* edu-cation. **~gique** *a.* educational. **~gue** *n.m./f.* teacher.

pédal|e /pedal/ *n.f.* pedal. **~er** *v.i.* pedal.

pédalo /pedalo/ *n.m.* pedal boat.

pédant, ~e /pedɑ̃, -t/ *a.* pedantic.

pédé /pede/ *n.m.* (*argot*) queer, fag (*Amer.*).

pédestre /pedɛstr/ *a.* **faire de la randonnée ~,** go walking *ou* hik-ing.

pédiatre /pedjatr/ *n.m./f.* paediatri-cian.

pédicure /pedikyr/ *n.m./f.* chiropo-dist.

pedigree /pedigre/ *n.m.* pedigree.

pègre /pɛgr/ *n.f.* underworld.

peign|e /pɛɲ/ *n.m.* comb. **~er** /peɲe/ *v.t.* comb; (*personne*) comb the hair of. **se ~er** *v. pr.* comb one's hair.

peignoir /pɛɲwar/ *n.m.* dressing-gown.

peindre† /pɛ̃dr/ *v.t.* paint.

peine /pɛn/ *n.f.* sadness, sorrow; (*effort, difficulté*) trouble; (*punition*) punishment; (*jurid.*) sentence. **avoir de la ~,** feel sad. **faire de la ~ à,** hurt. **ce n'est pas la ~ de faire,** it is not worth (while) doing. **se donner** *ou* **prendre la ~ de faire,** go to the trouble of doing. **~ de mort** death penalty.

peine (à) /(a)pɛn/ *adv.* hardly.

peiner /pene/ *v.i.* struggle. ● *v.t.* sadden.

peintre /pɛ̃tr/ *n.m.* painter. **~ en bâtiment,** house painter.

peinture /pɛ̃tyr/ *n.f.* painting; (*ma-tière*) paint. **~ à l'huile,** oil-paint-ing.

péjorati|f, ~ve /peʒɔratif, -v/ *a.* pejorative.

pelage /pəlaʒ/ *n.m.* coat, fur.

pêle-mêle /pɛlmɛl/ *adv.* in a jumble.

peler /pəle/ *v.t./i.* peel.

pèlerin /pɛlrɛ̃/ *n.m.* pilgrim. **~age** /-inaʒ/ *n.m.* pilgrimage.

pèlerine /pɛlrin/ *n.f.* cape.

pélican /pelikɑ̃/ *n.m.* pelican.

pelle /pɛl/ *n.f.* shovel; (*d'enfant*) spade. **~tée** *n.f.* shovelful.

pellicule /pelikyl/ *n.f.* film. **~s,** (*che-veux*) dandruff.

pelote /pəlɔt/ *n.f.* ball; (*d'épingles*) pincushion.

peloton /plɔtɔ̃/ *n.m.* troop, squad; (*sport*) pack. **~ d'exécution,** fir-ing-squad.

pelotonner (se) /(sə)plɔtɔne/ *v. pr.* curl up.

pelouse /pluz/ *n.f.* lawn.

peluche /plyʃ/ *n.f.* (*tissu*) plush; (*jouet*) cuddly toy. **en ~,** (*lapin, chien*) fluffy, furry.

pelure /plyr/ *n.f.* peeling.

pén|al (*m. pl.* **~aux**) /penal, -o/ *a.* penal. **~aliser** *v.t.* penalize. **~alité** *n.f.* penalty.

penalt|y (*pl.* **~ies**) /penalti/ *n.m.* penalty (kick).

penaud, ~e /pəno, -d/ *a.* sheepish.

penchant /pãʃã/ n.m. inclination; (goût) liking (**pour**, for).

pench|er /pãʃe/ v.t. tilt. ● v.i. lean (over), tilt. **se ~er** v. pr. lean (forward). **~er pour**, favour. **se ~er sur**, (problème etc.) examine.

pendaison /pãdɛzõ/ n.f. hanging.

pendant[1] /pãdã/ prép. (au cours de) during; (durée) for. **~ que**, while.

pendant[2], **~e** /pãdã, -t/ a. hanging; (question etc.) pending. ● n.m. (contrepartie) matching piece (**de**, to). **faire ~ à**, match. **~ d'oreille**, drop ear-ring.

pendentif /pãdãtif/ n.m. pendant.

penderie /pãdri/ n.f. wardrobe.

pend|re /pãdr/ v.t./i. hang. **se ~re** v. pr. hang (**à**, from); (se tuer) hang o.s. **~re la crémaillère**, have a house-warming. **~u, ~ue** a. hanging (**à**, from); n.m., f. hanged man, hanged woman.

pendul|e /pãdyl/ n.f. clock. ● n.m. pendulum. **~ette** n.f. (travelling) clock.

pénétr|er /penetre/ v.i. **~er (dans)**, enter. ● v.t. penetrate. **se ~er de**, become convinced of. **~ant, ~ante** a. penetrating.

pénible /penibl/ a. difficult; (douloureux) painful; (fatigant) tiresome. **~ment** /-əmã/ adv. with difficulty; (cruellement) painfully.

péniche /peniʃ/ n.f. barge.

pénicilline /penisilin/ n.f. penicillin.

péninsule /penɛ̃syl/ n.f. peninsula.

pénis /penis/ n.m. penis.

pénitence /penitãs/ n.f. (peine) penance; (regret) penitence; (fig.) punishment. **faire ~**, repent.

péniten|cier /penitãsje/ n.m. penitentiary. **~tiaire** /-sjɛr/ a. prison.

pénombre /penõbr/ n.f. half-light.

pensée[1] /pãse/ n.f. thought.

pensée[2] /pãse/ n.f. (fleur) pansy.

pens|er /pãse/ v.t./i. think. **~er à**, (réfléchir à) think about; (se souvenir de, prévoir) think of. **~er faire**, think of doing. **faire ~er à**, remind one of. **~eur** n.m. thinker.

pensi|f, ~ve /pãsif, -v/ a. pensive.

pension /pãsjõ/ n.f. (scol.) boarding-school; (repas, somme) board; (allocation) pension. **~ (de famille)**, guest-house. **~ alimentaire**, (jurid.) alimony. **~naire** /-jɔnɛr/ n.m./f. boarder; (d'hôtel) guest. **~nat** /-jɔna/ n.m. boarding-school.

pente /pãt/ n.f. slope. **en ~**, sloping.

Pentecôte /pãtkot/ n.f. **la ~**, Whitsun.

pénurie /penyri/ n.f. shortage.

pépé /pepe/ n.m. (fam.) grandad.

pépier /pepje/ v.i. chirp.

pépin /pepɛ̃/ n.m. (graine) pip; (ennui: fam.) hitch; (parapluie: fam.) brolly.

pépinière /pepinjɛr/ n.f. (tree) nursery.

perçant, ~e /pɛrsã, -t/ a. (froid) piercing; (regard) keen.

percée /pɛrse/ n.f. opening; (attaque) breakthrough.

perce-neige /pɛrsənɛʒ/ n.m./f. invar. snowdrop.

percepteur /pɛrsɛptœr/ n.m. tax-collector.

perceptible /pɛrsɛptibl/ a. perceptible.

perception /pɛrsɛpsjõ/ n.f. perception; (d'impôts) collection.

percer /pɛrse/ v.t. pierce; (avec perceuse) drill; (mystère) penetrate. ● v.i. break through; (dent) come through.

perceuse /pɛrsøz/ n.f. drill.

percevoir† /pɛrsəvwar/ v.t. perceive; (impôt) collect.

perche /pɛrʃ/ n.f. (bâton) pole.

perch|er /pɛrʃe/ v.t., **se ~er** v. pr. perch. **~oir** n.m. perch.

percolateur /pɛrkɔlatœr/ n.m. percolator.

percussion /pɛrkysjõ/ n.f. percussion.

percuter /pɛrkyte/ v.t. strike; (véhicule) crash into.

perd|re /pɛrdr/ v.t./i. lose; (gaspiller) waste; (ruiner) ruin. **se ~re** v. pr. get lost; (rester inutilisé) go to waste. **~ant, ~ante** a. losing; n.m., f. loser. **~u a.** (endroit) isolated; (moments) spare; (malade) finished.

perdreau (pl. **~x**) /pɛrdro/ n.m. (young) partridge.

perdrix /pɛrdri/ n.f. partridge.

père /pɛr/ n.m. father. **~ de famille**, father, family man. **~ spirituel**, father figure. **le ~ Noël**, Father Christmas, Santa Claus.

péremptoire /perãptwar/ a. peremptory.

perfection /pɛrfɛksjõ/ n.f. perfection.

perfectionn|er /pɛrfɛksjɔne/ v.t. improve. **se ~er en anglais**/etc., improve one's English/etc. **~é a.**

sophisticated. **~ement** *n.m.* improvement.

perfectionniste /pɛrfɛksjɔnist/ *n.m./f.* perfectionist.

perfid|e /pɛrfid/ *a.* perfidious, treacherous. **~ie** *n.f.* perfidy.

perfor|er /pɛrfɔre/ *v.t.* perforate; (*billet, bande*) punch. **~ateur** *n.m.* (*appareil*) punch. **~ation** *n.f.* perforation; (*trou*) hole.

performan|ce /pɛrfɔrmɑ̃s/ *n.f.* performance. **~t, ~te** *a.* high-performance, successful.

perfusion /pɛrfysjɔ̃/ *n.f.* drip. **mettre qn. sous ~,** put s.o. on a drip.

péricliter /periklite/ *v.i.* decline, be in rapid decline.

péridural /peridyral/ *a.* **(anesthésie) ~e,** epidural.

péril /peril/ *n.m.* peril.

périlleu|x, ~se /perijø, -z/ *a.* perilous.

périmé /perime/ *a.* expired; (*désuet*) outdated.

périmètre /perimɛtr/ *n.m.* perimeter.

périod|e /perjɔd/ *n.f.* period. **~ique** *a.* periodic(al); *n.m.* (*journal*) periodical.

péripétie /peripesi/ *n.f.* (unexpected) event, adventure.

périphér|ie /periferi/ *n.f.* periphery; (*banlieue*) outskirts. **~ique** *a.* peripheral; *n.m.* **(boulevard) ~ique,** ring road.

périple /peripl/ *n.m.* journey.

pér|ir /perir/ *v.i.* perish, die. **~issable** *a.* perishable.

périscope /periskɔp/ *n.m.* periscope.

perle /pɛrl/ *n.f.* (*bijou*) pearl; (*boule, de sueur*) bead.

permanence /pɛrmanɑ̃s/ *n.f.* permanence; (*bureau*) duty office; (*scol.*) study room. **de ~,** on duty. **en ~,** permanently. **assurer une ~,** keep the office open.

permanent, ~e /pɛrmanɑ̃, -t/ *a.* permanent; (*spectacle*) continuous; (*comité*) standing. ● *n.f.* (*coiffure*) perm.

perméable /pɛrmeabl/ *a.* permeable; (*personne*) susceptible (**à,** to).

permettre† /pɛrmɛtr/ *v.t.* allow, permit. **~ à qn. de,** allow *ou* permit s.o. to. **se ~ de,** take the liberty to.

permis, ~e /pɛrmi, -z/ *a.* allowed. ● *n.m.* licence, permit. **~ (de conduire),** driving-licence.

permission /pɛrmisjɔ̃/ *n.f.* permission. **en ~,** (*mil.*) on leave.

permut|er /pɛrmyte/ *v.t.* change round. **~ation** *n.f.* permutation.

pernicieu|x, ~se /pɛrnisjø, -z/ *a.* pernicious.

Pérou /peru/ *n.m.* Peru.

perpendiculaire /pɛrpɑ̃dikylɛr/ *a.* & *n.f.* perpendicular.

perpétrer /pɛrpetre/ *v.t.* perpetrate.

perpétuel, ~le /pɛrpetɥɛl/ *a.* perpetual.

perpétuer /pɛrpetɥe/ *v.t.* perpetuate.

perpétuité (à) /(a)pɛrpetɥite/ *adv.* for life.

perplex|e /pɛrplɛks/ *a.* perplexed. **~ité** *n.f.* perplexity.

perquisition /pɛrkizisjɔ̃/ *n.f.* (police) search. **~ner** /-jɔne/ *v.t./i.* search.

perron /pɛrɔ̃/ *n.m.* (front) steps.

perroquet /pɛrɔkɛ/ *n.m.* parrot.

perruche /perʃ/ *n.f.* budgerigar.

perruque /peryk/ *n.f.* wig.

persan, ~e /pɛrsɑ̃, -an/ *a.* & *n.m.* (*lang.*) Persian.

persécut|er /pɛrsekyte/ *v.t.* persecute. **~ion** /-ysjɔ̃/ *n.f.* persecution.

persévér|er /pɛrsevere/ *v.i.* persevere. **~ance** *n.f.* perseverance.

persienne /pɛrsjɛn/ *n.f.* (outside) shutter.

persil /pɛrsi/ *n.m.* parsley.

persistan|t, ~te /pɛrsistɑ̃, -t/ *a.* persistent; (*feuillage*) evergreen. **~ce** *n.f.* persistence.

persister /pɛrsiste/ *v.i.* persist (**à faire,** in doing).

personnage /pɛrsɔnaʒ/ *n.m.* character; (*important*) personality.

personnalité /pɛrsɔnalite/ *n.f.* personality.

personne /pɛrsɔn/ *n.f.* person. **~s,** people. ● *pron.* (*quelqu'un*) anybody. **(ne) ~,** nobody.

personnel, ~le /pɛrsɔnɛl/ *a.* personal; (*égoïste*) selfish. ● *n.m.* staff. **~lement** *adv.* personally.

personnifier /pɛrsɔnifje/ *v.t.* personify.

perspective /pɛrspɛktiv/ *n.f.* (*art*) perspective; (*vue*) view; (*possibilité*) prospect; (*point de vue*) viewpoint, perspective.

perspicac|e /pɛrspikas/ *a.* shrewd. **~ité** *n.f.* shrewdness.

persua|der /pɛrsɥade/ *v.t.* persuade (**de faire,** to do). **~sion** /-ɥazjɔ̃/ *n.f.* persuasion.

persuasi|f, **~ve** /pɛrsɥazif, -v/ *a.*
persuasive.

perte /pɛrt/ *n.f.* loss; (*ruine*) ruin. **à
~ de vue**, as far as the eye can see.
~ de, (*temps, argent*) waste of. **~
sèche**, total loss. **~s**, (*méd.*) discharge.

pertinen|t, **~te** /pɛrtinɑ̃, -t/ *a.* perti-
nent; (*esprit*) judicious. **~ce** *n.f.*
pertinence.

perturb|er /pɛrtyrbe/ *v.t.* disrupt;
(*personne*) perturb. **~ateur**,
~atrice *a.* disruptive; *n.m.*, *f.* disruptive element. **~ation** *n.f.* disrup-
tion.

pervenche /pɛrvɑ̃ʃ/ *n.f.* periwinkle;
(*fam.*) traffic warden.

pervers, **~e** /pɛrvɛr, -s/ *a.* perverse;
(*dépravé*) perverted. **~ion** /-sjɔ̃/ *n.f.*
perversion.

pervert|ir /pɛrvɛrtir/ *v.t.* pervert. **~i,
~ie** *n.m.*, *f.* pervert.

pes|ant, **~ante** /pəzɑ̃, -t/ *a.* heavy.
~amment *adv.* heavily. **~anteur**
n.f. heaviness. **la ~anteur**, (*force*)
gravity.

pèse-personne /pɛzpɛrsɔn/ *n.m.*
(bathroom) scales.

pes|er /pəze/ *v.t./i.* weigh. **~er sur**,
bear upon. **~ée** *n.f.* weighing; (*effort*) pressure.

peseta /pezeta/ *n.f.* peseta.

pessimis|te /pesimist/ *a.* pess-
imistic. ● *n.m.* pessimist. **~me** *n.m.*
pessimism.

peste /pɛst/ *n.f.* plague; (*personne*)
pest.

pester /pɛste/ *v.i.* **~ (contre)**, curse.

pestilentiel, **~le** /pɛstilɑ̃sjɛl/ *a.* fetid, stinking.

pet /pɛ/ *n.m.* fart.

pétale /petal/ *n.m.* petal.

pétanque /petɑ̃k/ *n.f.* bowls.

pétarader /petarade/ *v.i.* backfire.

pétard /petar/ *n.m.* banger.

péter /pete/ *v.i.* fart; (*fam.*) go bang;
(*casser: fam.*) snap.

pétill|er /petije/ *v.i.* (*feu*) crackle;
(*champagne, yeux*) sparkle. **~er
d'intelligence**, sparkle with intelligence. **~ant**, **~ante** *a.* (*gazeux*)
fizzy.

petit, **~e** /pti, -t/ *a.* small; (*avec
nuance affective*) little; (*jeune*)
young, small; (*faible*) slight; (*mesquin*) petty. ● *n.m.*, *f.* little child;
(*scol.*) junior. **~s**, (*de chat*) kittens;
(*de chien*) pups. **en ~**, in miniature.
~ ami, boy-friend. **~e amie**, girl-

friend. **~ à petit**, little by little. **~es
annonces**, small ads. **~e cuiller**,
teaspoon. **~ déjeuner**, breakfast. **le
~ écran**, the small screen,
television. **~-enfant** (*pl.* **~s-
enfants**) *n.m.* grandchild. **~e-fille**
(*pl.* **~es-filles**) *n.f.* granddaughter.
~-fils (*pl.* **~s-fils**) *n.m.* grandson.
~ pain, roll. **~-pois** (*pl.* **~s-pois**)
n.m. garden pea.

petitesse /ptitɛs/ *n.f.* smallness;
(*péj.*) meanness.

pétition /petisjɔ̃/ *n.f.* petition.

pétrifier /petrifje/ *v.t.* petrify.

pétrin /petrɛ̃/ *n.m.* (*situation: fam.*)
dans le ~, in a fix.

pétrir /petrir/ *v.t.* knead.

pétrol|e /petrɔl/ *n.m.* (*brut*) oil;
(*pour lampe etc.*) paraffin. **lampe à
~e**, oil lamp. **~ier**, **~ière** *a.* oil; *n.m.*
(*navire*) oil-tanker.

pétulant, **~e** /petylɑ̃, -t/ *a.* exuberant, full of high spirits.

peu /pø/ *adv.* **~ (de)**, (*quantité*) little,
not much; (*nombre*) few, not many.
~ intéressant/*etc.*, not very inter-
esting/*etc.* ● *pron.* little. **~** little.
un ~ (de), a little. **à ~ près**, more or
less. **de ~**, only just. **~ à peu**,
gradually. **~ après/avant**, shortly
after/before. **~ de chose**, not much.
~ nombreux, few. **~ souvent**,
seldom. **pour ~ que**, as long as.

peuplade /pœplad/ *n.f.* tribe.

peuple /pœpl/ *n.m.* people.

peupler /pœple/ *v.t.* populate.

peuplier /pøplije/ *n.m.* poplar.

peur /pœr/ *n.f.* fear. **avoir ~**, be
afraid (**de**, of). **de ~ de**, for fear of.
faire ~ à, frighten. **~eux**, **~euse** *a.*
fearful, timid.

peut /pø/ *voir* pouvoir[1].

peut-être /pøtɛtr/ *adv.* perhaps,
maybe. **~ que**, perhaps, maybe.

peux /pø/ *voir* pouvoir[1].

pèze /pɛz/ *n.m.* (*fam.*) **du ~**, money,
dough.

phallique /falik/ *a.* phallic.

phantasme /fɑ̃tasm/ *n.m.* fantasy.

phare /far/ *n.m.* (*tour*) lighthouse;
(*de véhicule*) headlight. **~ anti-
brouillard**, fog lamp.

pharmaceutique /farmasøtik/ *a.*
pharmaceutical.

pharmac|ie /farmasi/ *n.f.* (*magasin*)
chemist's (shop); (*Amer.*) pharmacy;
(*science*) pharmacy; (*armoire*) medicine cabinet. **~ien**, **~ienne** *n.m.*, *f.*
chemist, pharmacist.

pharyngite /farɛ̃ʒit/ *n.f.* pharyngitis.

phase /fɑz/ *n.f.* phase.

phénomène /fenɔmɛn/ *n.m.* phenomenon; (*original*: *fam.*) eccentric.

philanthrop|e /filɑ̃trɔp/ *n.m./f.* philanthropist. **~ique** *a.* philanthropic.

philatél|ie /filateli/ *n.f.* philately. **~iste** *n.m./f.* philatelist.

philharmonique /filarmɔnik/ *a.* philharmonic.

Philippines /filipin/ *n.f. pl.* **les ~,** the Philippines.

philosoph|e /filɔzɔf/ *n.m./f.* philosopher. ● *a.* philosophical. **~ie** *n.f.* philosophy. **~ique** *a.* philosophical.

phobie /fɔbi/ *n.f.* phobia.

phonétique /fɔnetik/ *a.* phonetic.

phoque /fɔk/ *n.m.* (*animal*) seal.

phosphate /fɔsfat/ *n.m.* phosphate.

phosphore /fɔsfɔr/ *n.m.* phosphorus.

photo /fɔto/ *n.f.* photo; (*art*) photography. **prendre en ~,** take a photo of. **~ d'identité,** passport photograph.

photocop|ie /fɔtɔkɔpi/ *n.f.* photocopy. **~ier** *v.t.* photocopy. **~ieuse** *n.f.* photocopier.

photogénique /fɔtɔʒenik/ *a.* photogenic.

photograph|e /fɔtɔgraf/ *n.m./f.* photographer. **~ie** *n.f.* photograph; (*art*) photography. **~ier** *v.t.* take a photo of. **~ique** *a.* photographic.

phrase /frɑz/ *n.f.* sentence.

physicien, ~ne /fizisjɛ̃, -jɛn/ *n.m., f.* physicist.

physiologie /fizjɔlɔʒi/ *n.f.* physiology.

physionomie /fizjɔnɔmi/ *n.f.* face.

physique [1] /fizik/ *a.* physical. ● *n.m.* physique. **au ~,** physically. **~ment** *adv.* physically.

physique [2] /fizik/ *n.f.* physics.

piailler /pjaje/ *v.i.* squeal, squawk.

pian|o /pjano/ *n.m.* piano. **~iste** *n.m./f.* pianist.

pianoter /pjanɔte/ *v.t.* (*air*) tap out. ● *v.i.* (**sur,** on) (*ordinateur*) tap away; (*table*) tap one's fingers.

pic /pik/ *n.m.* (*outil*) pickaxe; (*sommet*) peak; (*oiseau*) woodpecker. **à ~,** (*verticalement*) sheer; (*couler*) straight to the bottom; (*arriver*) just at the right time.

pichenette /piʃnɛt/ *n.f.* flick.

pichet /piʃɛ/ *n.m.* jug.

pickpocket /pikpɔkɛt/ *n.m.* pickpocket.

pick-up /pikœp/ *n.m. invar.* record-player.

picorer /pikɔre/ *v.t./i.* peck.

picot|er /pikɔte/ *v.t.* prick; (*yeux*) make smart. **~ement** *n.m.* pricking; smarting.

pie /pi/ *n.f.* magpie.

pièce /pjɛs/ *n.f.* piece; (*chambre*) room; (*pour raccommoder*) patch; (*écrit*) document. **~ (de monnaie),** coin. **~ (de théâtre),** play. **dix francs/etc. (la) ~,** ten francs/*etc.* each. **~ de rechange,** spare part. **~ détachée,** part. **~ d'identité,** identity paper. **~ montée,** tiered cake. **~s justificatives,** supporting documents. **deux/trois etc. ~s,** two-/three-/*etc.* room flat *ou* apartment (*Amer.*).

pied /pje/ *n.m.* foot; (*de meuble*) leg; (*de lampe*) base; (*de salade*) plant. **à ~,** on foot. **au ~ de la lettre,** literally. **avoir ~,** have a footing. **avoir les ~s plats,** have flat feet. **comme un ~,** (*fam.*) terribly. **mettre sur ~,** set up. **~ bot,** club-foot. **sur un ~ d'égalité,** on an equal footing. **mettre les ~s dans le plat,** put one's foot in it. **c'est le ~!,** (*fam.*) it's great!

piédest|al (*pl.* **~aux**) /pjedɛstal, -o/ *n.m.* pedestal.

plège /pjɛʒ/ *n.m.* trap.

piég|er /pjeʒe/ *v.t.* trap; (*avec explosifs*) booby-trap. **lettre/voiture ~ée,** letter-/car-bomb.

pierr|e /pjɛr/ *n.f.* stone. **~e d'achoppement,** stumbling-block. **~e de touche,** touchstone. **~e précieuse,** precious stone. **~e tombale,** tombstone. **~eux, ~euse** *a.* stony.

piété /pjete/ *n.f.* piety.

piétiner /pjetine/ *v.i.* stamp one's feet; (*ne pas avancer*: *fig.*) mark time. ● *v.t.* trample (on).

piéton /pjetɔ̃/ *n.m.* pedestrian. **~nier, ~nière** /-ɔnje, -jɛr/ *a.* pedestrian.

piètre /pjɛtr/ *a.* wretched.

pieu (*pl.* **~x**) /pjø/ *n.m.* post, stake.

pieuvre /pjœvr/ *n.f.* octopus.

pieu|x, ~se /pjø, -z/ *a.* pious.

pif /pif/ *n.m.* (*fam.*) nose.

pigeon /piʒɔ̃/ *n.m.* pigeon.

piger /piʒe/ *v.t./i.* (*fam.*) understand, get (it).

pigment /pigmã/ *n.m.* pigment.
pignon /piɲɔ̃/ *n.m.* (*de maison*) gable.
pile /pil/ *n.f.* (*tas, pilier*) pile; (*électr.*) battery; (*atomique*) pile. ● *adv.* (*s'arrêter*: *fam.*) dead. **à dix heures ~,** (*fam.*) at ten on the dot. **~ ou face?,** heads or tails?
piler /pile/ *v.t.* pound.
pilier /pilje/ *n.m.* pillar.
pill|er /pije/ *v.t.* loot. **~age** *n.m.* looting. **~ard, ~arde** *n.m., f.* looter.
pilonner /pilɔne/ *v.t.* pound.
pilori /pilɔri/ *n.m.* **mettre** *ou* **clouer au ~,** pillory.
pilot|e /pilɔt/ *n.m.* pilot; (*auto.*) driver. ● *a.* pilot. **~er** *v.t.* (*aviat., naut.*) pilot; (*auto.*) drive; (*fig.*) guide.
pilule /pilyl/ *n.f.* pill. **la ~,** the pill.
piment /pimã/ *n.m.* pepper, pimento; (*fig.*) spice. **~é** /-te/ *a.* spicy.
pimpant, ~e /pɛ̃pã, -t/ *a.* spruce.
pin /pɛ̃/ *n.m.* pine.
pinard /pinar/ *n.m.* (*vin*: *fam.*) plonk, cheap wine.
pince /pɛ̃s/ *n.f.* (*outil*) pliers; (*levier*) crowbar; (*de crabe*) pincer; (*à sucre*) tongs. **~ (à épiler),** tweezers. **~ (à linge),** (clothes-)peg.
pinceau (*pl.* **~x**) /pɛ̃so/ *n.m.* paintbrush.
pinc|er /pɛ̃se/ *v.t.* pinch; (*arrêter*: *fam.*) pinch. **se ~er le doigt,** catch one's finger. **~é** *a.* (*ton, air*) stiff. **~ée** *n.f.* pinch (**de,** of).
pince-sans-rire /pɛ̃sãrir/ *a. invar.* po-faced. **c'est un ~,** he's po-faced.
pincettes /pɛ̃sɛt/ *n.f. pl.* (fire) tongs.
pinède /pinɛd/ *n.f.* pine forest.
pingouin /pɛ̃gwɛ̃/ *n.m.* penguin.
ping-pong /piŋpɔ̃g/ *n.m.* table tennis, ping-pong.
pingre /pɛ̃gr/ *a.* miserly.
pinson /pɛ̃sɔ̃/ *n.m.* chaffinch.
pintade /pɛ̃tad/ *n.f.* guinea-fowl.
pioch|e /pjɔʃ/ *n.f.* pick(axe). **~er** *v.t./i.* dig; (*étudier*: *fam.*) study hard, slog away (at).
pion /pjɔ̃/ *n.m.* (*de jeu*) piece; (*échecs*) pawn; (*scol., fam.*) supervisor.
pionnier /pjɔnje/ *n.m.* pioneer.
pipe /pip/ *n.f.* pipe. **fumer la ~,** smoke a pipe.
pipe-line /piplin/ *n.m.* pipeline.
piquant, ~e /pikã, -t/ *a.* (*barbe etc.*) prickly; (*goût*) pungent; (*détail etc.*) spicy. ● *n.m.* prickle; (*de hérisson*) spine, prickle; (*fig.*) piquancy.

pique [1] /pik/ *n.f.* (*arme*) pike.
pique [2] /pik/ *n.m.* (*cartes*) spades.
pique-niqu|e /piknik/ *n.m.* picnic. **~er** *v.i.* picnic.
piquer /pike/ *v.t.* prick; (*langue*) burn, sting; (*abeille etc.*) sting; (*serpent etc.*) bite; (*enfoncer*) stick; (*coudre*) (machine-)stitch; (*curiosité*) excite; (*crise*) have; (*voler*: *fam.*) pinch. ● *v.i.* (*avion*) dive; (*goût*) be hot. **~ une tête,** plunge headlong. **se ~ de,** pride o.s. on.
piquet /pikɛ/ *n.m.* stake; (*de tente*) peg. **au ~,** (*scol.*) in the corner. **~ de grève,** (strike) picket.
piqûre /pikyr/ *n.f.* prick; (*d'abeille etc.*) sting; (*de serpent etc.*) bite; (*point*) stitch; (*méd.*) injection, shot (*Amer.*) **faire une ~ à qn.,** give s.o. an injection.
pirate /pirat/ *n.m.* pirate. **~ de l'air,** hijacker. **~rie** *n.f.* piracy.
pire /pir/ *a.* worse (**que,** than). **le ~ livre**/*etc.*, the worst book/*etc.* ● *n.m.* **le ~,** the worst (thing). **au ~,** at worst.
pirogue /pirɔg/ *n.f.* canoe, dug-out.
pirouette /pirwɛt/ *n.f.* pirouette.
pis [1] /pi/ *n.m.* (*de vache*) udder.
pis [2] /pi/ *a. invar.* & *adv.* worse. **aller de mal en ~,** go from bad to worse.
pis-aller /pizale/ *n.m. invar.* stopgap, temporary expedient.
piscine /pisin/ *n.f.* swimming-pool. **~ couverte,** indoor swimming-pool.
pissenlit /pisãli/ *n.m.* dandelion.
pistache /pistaʃ/ *n.f.* pistachio.
piste /pist/ *n.f.* track; (*de personne, d'animal*) track, trail; (*aviat.*) runway; (*de cirque*) ring; (*de ski*) run; (*de patinage*) rink; (*de danse*) floor; (*sport*) race-track. **~ cyclable,** cycle-track; (*Amer.*) bicycle path.
pistolet /pistɔlɛ/ *n.m.* gun, pistol; (*de peintre*) spray-gun.
piston /pistɔ̃/ *n.m.* (*techn.*) piston. **il a un ~,** (*fam.*) somebody is pulling strings for him.
pistonner /pistɔne/ *v.t.* (*fam.*) recommend, pull strings for.
piteu|x, ~se /pitø, -z/ *a.* pitiful.
pitié /pitje/ *n.f.* pity. **il me fait ~, j'ai ~ de lui,** I pity him.
piton /pitɔ̃/ *n.m.* (*à crochet*) hook; (*sommet pointu*) peak.
pitoyable /pitwajabl/ *a.* pitiful.
pitre /pitr/ *n.m.* clown. **faire le ~,** clown around.

pittoresque /pitɔrɛsk/ *a.* pictur-esque.

pivot /pivo/ *n.m.* pivot. **~er** /-ɔte/ *v.i.* revolve; (*personne*) swing round.

pizza /pidza/ *n.f.* pizza.

placage /plakaʒ/ *n.m.* (*en bois*) ve-neer; (*sur un mur*) facing.

placard /plakar/ *n.m.* cupboard; (*af-fiche*) poster. **~er** /-de/ *v.t.* (*affiche*) post up; (*mur*) cover with posters.

place /plas/ *n.f.* place; (*espace libre*) room, space; (*siège*) seat, place; (*prix d'un trajet*) fare; (*esplanade*) square; (*emploi*) position; (*de park-ing*) space. **à la ~ de**, instead of. **en ~, à sa ~,** in its place. **faire ~ à,** give way to. **sur ~,** on the spot. **remettre qn. à sa ~,** put s.o. in his place. **ça prend de la ~,** it takes up a lot of room. **se mettre à la ~ de qn.** put oneself in s.o.'s shoes *ou* place.

placebo /plasebo/ *n.m.* placebo.

placenta /plasɛ̃ta/ *n.m.* placenta.

plac|er /plase/ *v.t.* place; (*invité, spec-tateur*) seat; (*argent*) invest. **se ~er** *v. pr.* (*personne*) take up a position; (*troisième etc.: sport*) come (in); (*à un endroit*) to go and stand (**à,** in). **~é** *a.* (*sport*) placed. **bien ~é pour,** in a position to. **~ement** *n.m.* (*d'ar-gent*) investment.

placide /plasid/ *a.* placid.

plafond /plafɔ̃/ *n.m.* ceiling.

plage /plaʒ/ *n.f.* beach; (*station*) (sea-side) resort; (*aire*) area.

plagiat /plaʒja/ *n.m.* plagiarism.

plaid /plɛd/ *n.m.* travelling-rug.

plaider /plede/ *v.t./i.* plead.

plaid|oirie /plɛdwari/ *n.f.* (defence) speech. **~oyer** *n.m.* plea.

plaie /plɛ/ *n.f.* wound; (*personne*: *fam.*) nuisance.

plaignant, ~e /plɛɲɑ̃, -t/ *n.m., f.* plaintiff.

plaindre† /plɛ̃dr/ *v.t.* pity. **se ~** *v. pr.* complain (**de,** about). **se ~ de,** (*souffrir de*) complain of.

plaine /plɛn/ *n.f.* plain.

plaint|e /plɛ̃t/ *n.f.* complaint; (*gémis-sement*) groan. **~if, ~ive** *a.* plain-tive.

plaire† /plɛr/ *v.i.* **~ à,** please. **ça lui plaît,** he likes it. **elle lui plaît,** he likes her. **ça me plaît de faire,** I like *ou* enjoy doing. **s'il vous plaît,** please. **se ~** *v. pr.* (*à Londres etc.*) like *ou* enjoy it.

plaisance /plɛzɑ̃s/ *n.f.* **la (navigation de) ~,** yachting.

plaisant, ~e /plɛzɑ̃, -t/ *a.* pleasant; (*drôle*) amusing.

plaisant|er /plɛzɑ̃te/ *v.i.* joke. **~erie** *n.f.* joke. **~in** *n.m.* joker.

plaisir /plezir/ *n.m.* pleasure. **faire ~ à,** please. **pour le ~,** for fun *ou* pleasure.

plan¹ /plɑ̃/ *n.m.* plan; (*de ville*) map; (*surface, niveau*) plane. **~ d'eau,** expanse of water. **premier ~,** foreground. **dernier ~,** background.

plan², ~e /plɑ̃, -an/ *a.* flat.

planche /plɑ̃ʃ/ *n.f.* board, plank; (*gravure*) plate; (*de potager*) bed. **~ à repasser,** ironing-board. **~ à voile,** sailboard; (*sport*) windsurf-ing.

plancher /plɑ̃ʃe/ *n.m.* floor.

plancton /plɑ̃ktɔ̃/ *n.m.* plankton.

plan|er /plane/ *v.i.* glide. **~er sur,** (*mystère, danger*) hang over. **~eur** *n.m.* (*avion*) glider.

planète /planɛt/ *n.f.* planet.

planif|ier /planifje/ *v.t.* plan. **~ication** *n.f.* planning.

planqu|e /plɑ̃k/ *n.f.* (*fam.*) hideout; (*emploi: fam.*) cushy job. **~er** *v.t.,* **se ~er** *v. pr.* hide.

plant /plɑ̃/ *n.m.* seedling; (*de lé-gumes*) bed.

plante /plɑ̃t/ *n.f.* plant. **~ des pieds,** sole (of the foot).

plant|er /plɑ̃te/ *v.t.* (*plante etc.*) plant; (*enfoncer*) drive in; (*installer*) put up; (*mettre*) put. **rester ~é,** stand still, remain standing. **~ation** *n.f.* planting; (*de tabac etc.*) plantation.

plantureu|x, ~se /plɑ̃tyrø, -z/ *a.* abundant; (*femme*) buxom.

plaque /plak/ *n.f.* plate; (*de marbre*) slab; (*insigne*) badge; (*commémora-tive*) plaque. **~ chauffante,** hot-plate. **~ minéralogique,** number-plate.

plaqu|er /plake/ *v.t.* (*bois*) veneer; (*aplatir*) flatten; (*rugby*) tackle; (*abandonner: fam.*) ditch. **~er qch. sur** *ou* **contre,** make sth. stick to. **~age** *n.m.* (*rugby*) tackle.

plasma /plasma/ *n.m.* plasma.

plastic /plastik/ *n.m.* plastic explo-sive.

plastique /plastik/ *a. & n.m.* plastic. **en ~,** plastic.

plastiquer /plastike/ *v.t.* blow up.

plat¹, **~e** /pla, -t/ a. flat. ● n.m. (de
la main) flat. **à ~** adv. (poser) flat; a.
(batterie, pneu) flat. **à ~ ventre,** flat
on one's face.

plat² /pla/ n.m. (culin.) dish; (partie
de repas) course.

platane /platan/ n.m. plane(-tree).

plateau (pl. **~x**) /plato/ n.m. tray;
(d'électrophone) turntable, deck; (de
balance) pan; (géog.) plateau. **~ de
fromages,** cheeseboard.

plateau-repas (pl. **plateaux-repas**)
n.m. tray meal.

plate-bande (pl. **plates-bandes**)
/platbɑ̃d/ n.f. flower-bed.

plate-forme (pl. **plates-formes**)
/platfɔrm/ n.f. platform.

platine¹ /platin/ n.m. platinum.

platine² /platin/ n.f. (de tourne-
disque) turntable.

platitude /platityd/ n.f. platitude.

platonique /platɔnik/ a. platonic.

plâtr|e /platr/ n.m. plaster; (méd.)
(plaster) cast. **~er** v.t. plaster; (membre) put in plaster.

plausible /plozibl/ a. plausible.

plébiscite /plebisit/ n.m. plebiscite.

plein, **~e** /plɛ̃, plɛn/ a. full (**de,** of);
(total) complete. ● n.m. **faire le ~
(d'essence),** fill up (the tank). **à ~,**
to the full. **à ~ temps,** full-time. **en
~ air,** in the open air. **en ~ milieu/
visage,** right in the middle/the face.
en ~e nuit/etc., in the middle of the
night/etc. **~ les mains,** all over
one's hands.

pleinement /plɛnmɑ̃/ adv. fully.

pléthore /pletɔr/ n.f. over-abun-
dance, plethora.

pleurer /plœre/ v.i. cry, weep (**sur,**
over); (yeux) water. ● v.t. mourn.

pleurésie /plœrezi/ n.f. pleurisy.

pleurnicher /plœrniʃe/ v.i. (fam.)
snivel.

pleurs (en) /(ɑ̃)plœr/ adv. in tears.

pleuvoir† /plœvwar/ v.i. rain; (fig.)
rain ou shower down. **il pleut,** it is
raining. **il pleut à verse** ou **à
torrents,** it is pouring.

pli /pli/ n.m. fold; (de jupe) pleat; (de
pantalon) crease; (enveloppe) cover;
(habitude) habit. **(faux) ~,** crease.

pliant, **~e** /plijɑ̃, -t/ a. folding;
(parapluie) telescopic. ● n.m. folding stool, camp-stool.

plier /plije/ v.t. fold; (courber) bend;
(personne) submit (**à,** to). ● v.i.
bend; (personne) submit. **se ~** v.
pr. fold. **se ~ à,** submit to.

plinthe /plɛ̃t/ n.f. skirting-board;
(Amer.) baseboard.

plisser /plise/ v.t. crease; (yeux)
screw up; (jupe) pleat.

plomb /plɔ̃/ n.m. lead; (fusible) fuse.
~s, (de chasse) lead shot. **de** ou **en
~,** lead. **de ~,** (ciel) leaden.

plomb|er /plɔ̃be/ v.t. (dent) fill.
~age n.m. filling.

plomb|ier /plɔ̃bje/ n.m. plumber.
~erie n.f. plumbing.

plongeant, **~e** /plɔ̃ʒɑ̃, -t/ a. (vue)
from above; (décolleté) plunging.

plongeoir /plɔ̃ʒwar/ n.m. diving-
board.

plongeon /plɔ̃ʒɔ̃/ n.m. dive.

plong|er /plɔ̃ʒe/ v.i. dive; (route)
plunge. ● v.t. plunge. **se ~er** v. pr.
plunge (**dans,** into). **~é dans,** (lecture) immersed in. **~ée** n.f. diving.
en ~ée (sous-marin) submerged.
~eur, **~euse** n.m., f. diver; (employé) dishwasher.

plouf /pluf/ n.m. & int. splash.

ployer /plwaje/ v.t./i. bend.

plu /ply/ voir plaire, pleuvoir.

pluie /plɥi/ n.f. rain; (averse) shower.
~ battante/diluvienne, driving/
torrential rain.

plumage /plymaʒ/ n.m. plumage.

plume /plym/ n.f. feather; (stylo)
pen; (pointe) nib.

plumeau (pl. **~x**) /plymo/ n.m.
feather duster.

plumer /plyme/ v.t. pluck.

plumier /plymje/ n.m. pencil box.

plupart /plypar/ n.f. most. **la ~ des,**
(gens, cas, etc.) most. **la ~ du
temps,** most of the time. **pour la
~,** for the most part.

pluriel, **~le** /plyrjɛl/ a. & n.m.
plural. **au ~,** (nom) plural.

plus¹ /ply/ adv. de négation. **(ne) ~,**
(temps) no longer, not any more.
(ne) ~ de, (quantité) no more. **je
n'y vais ~,** I do not go there any
longer ou any more. **(il n'y a) ~ de
pain,** (there is) no more bread.

plus² /ply/ (/plyz/ before vowel, /plys/
in final position) adv. more (**que,**
than). **~ âgé/tard**/etc., older/later/
etc. **~ beau**/etc., more beautiful/etc.
le ~, the most. **le ~ beau**/etc., the
most beautiful; (de deux) the more
beautiful. **le ~ de,** (gens etc.) most.
~ de, (pain etc.) more; (dix jours
etc.) more than. **il est ~ de huit
heures**/etc. it is after eight/etc.
o'clock. **de ~,** more (**que,** than);

(*en outre*) moreover. **(âgés) de ~ de**
(*huit ans etc.*) over, more than. **de ~
en plus,** more and more. **en ~,**
extra. **en ~ de,** in addition to. **~
ou moins,** more or less.

plus³ /plys/ *conj.* plus.

plusieurs /plyzjœr/ *a. & pron.* several.

plus-value /plyvaly/ *n.f.* (*bénéfice*) profit.

plutôt /plyto/ *adv.* rather (**que,** than).

pluvieu|x, ~se /plyvjø, -z/ *a.* rainy.

pneu (*pl. ~s*) /pnø/ *n.m.* tyre; (*lettre*) express letter. **~matique** *a.* inflatable.

pneumonie /pnømɔni/ *n.f.* pneumonia.

poche /pɔʃ/ *n.f.* pocket; (*sac*) bag. **~s,** (*sous les yeux*) bags.

pocher /pɔʃe/ *v.t.* (*œuf*) poach.

pochette /pɔʃɛt/ *n.f.* pack(et), envelope; (*sac*) bag, pouch; (*d'allumettes*) book; (*de disque*) sleeve; (*mouchoir*) pocket handkerchief. **~ surprise,** lucky bag.

podium /pɔdjɔm/ *n.m.* rostrum.

poêle¹ /pwal/ *n.f.* **~ (à frire),** frying-pan.

poêle² /pwal/ *n.m.* stove.

poème /pɔɛm/ *n.m.* poem.

poésie /pɔezi/ *n.f.* poetry; (*poème*) poem.

poète /pɔɛt/ *n.m.* poet.

poétique /pɔetik/ *a.* poetic.

poids /pwa/ *n.m.* weight. **~ coq/lourd/plume,** bantam weight/heavyweight/featherweight. **~ lourd,** (*camion*) lorry, juggernaut; (*Amer.*) truck.

poignant, ~e /pwaɲɑ̃, -t/ *a.* poignant.

poignard /pwaɲar/ *n.m.* dagger. **~er** /-de/ *v.t.* stab.

poigne /pwaɲ/ *n.f.* grip. **avoir de la ~,** have an iron fist.

poignée /pwaɲe/ *n.f.* handle; (*quantité*) handful. **~ de main,** handshake.

poignet /pwaɲɛ/ *n.m.* wrist; (*de chemise*) cuff.

poil /pwal/ *n.m.* hair; (*pelage*) fur; (*de brosse*) bristle. **~s,** (*de tapis*) pile. **à ~,** (*fam.*) naked. **~u** *a.* hairy.

poinçon /pwɛ̃sɔ̃/ *n.m.* awl; (*marque*) hallmark. **~ner** /-ɔne/ *v.t.* (*billet*) punch. **~neuse** /-ɔnøz/ *n.f.* punch.

poing /pwɛ̃/ *n.m.* fist.

point¹ /pwɛ̃/ *n.m.* point; (*note: scol.*) mark; (*tache*) spot, dot; (*de couture*) stitch. **~ (final),** full stop, period. **à ~,** (*culin.*) medium; (*arriver*) at the right time. **faire le ~,** take stock. **mettre au ~,** (*photo.*) focus; (*technique*) perfect; (*fig.*) clear up. **deux ~s,** colon. **~ culminant,** peak. **~ de repère,** landmark. **~s de suspension,** suspension points. **~ de suture,** (*méd.*) stitch. **~ de vente,** retail outlet. **~ de vue,** point of view. **~ d'interrogation/d'exclamation,** question/exclamation mark. **~ du jour,** daybreak. **~ mort,** (*auto.*) neutral. **~ virgule,** semicolon. **sur le ~ de,** about to.

point² /pwɛ̃/ *adv.* (**ne**) **~,** not

pointe /pwɛ̃t/ *n.f.* point, tip; (*clou*) tack; (*de grille*) spike; (*fig.*) touch (**de,** of). **de ~,** (*industrie*) highly advanced. **en ~,** pointed. **heure de ~,** peak hour. **sur la ~ des pieds,** on tiptoe.

pointer¹ /pwɛ̃te/ *v.t.* (*cocher*) tick off. ● *v.i.* (*employé*) clock in *ou* out. **se ~** *v. pr.* (*fam.*) turn up.

pointer² /pwɛ̃te/ *v.t.* (*diriger*) point, aim.

pointillé /pwɛ̃tije/ *n.m.* dotted line. ● *a.* dotted.

pointilleu|x, ~se /pwɛ̃tijø, -z/ *a.* fastidious, particular.

pointu /pwɛ̃ty/ *a.* pointed; (*aiguisé*) sharp.

pointure /pwɛ̃tyr/ *n.f.* size.

poire /pwar/ *n.f.* pear.

poireau (*pl. ~x*) /pwaro/ *n.m.* leek.

poireauter /pwarote/ *v.i.* (*fam.*) hang about.

poirier /pwarje/ *n.m.* pear-tree.

pois /pwa/ *n.m.* pea; (*dessin*) dot.

poison /pwazɔ̃/ *n.m.* poison.

poisseu|x, ~se /pwasø, -z/ *a.* sticky.

poisson /pwasɔ̃/ *n.m.* fish. **~ rouge,** goldfish. **~ d'avril,** April fool. **les P~s,** Pisces.

poissonn|ier, ~ière /pwasɔnje, -jɛr/ *n.m., f.* fishmonger. **~erie** *n.f.* fish shop.

poitrail /pwatraj/ *n.m.* breast.

poitrine /pwatrin/ *n.f.* chest; (*seins*) bosom; (*culin.*) breast.

poivr|e /pwavr/ *n.m.* pepper. **~é** *a.* peppery. **~ière** *n.f.* pepper-pot.

poivron /pwavrɔ̃/ *n.m.* pepper, capsicum.

poivrot, **~e** /pwavro, -ɔt/ *n.m.*, *f.* (*fam.*) drunkard.

poker /pɔkɛr/ *n.m.* poker.

polaire /pɔlɛr/ *a.* polar.

polariser /pɔlarize/ *v.t.* polarize.

polaroïd /pɔlarɔid/ *n.m.* (P.) Polaroid (P.).

pôle /pol/ *n.m.* pole.

polémique /pɔlemik/ *n.f.* argument. ● *a.* controversial.

poli /pɔli/ *a.* (*personne*) polite. **~ment** *adv.* politely.

polic|e[1] /pɔlis/ *n.f.* police; (*discipline*) (law and) order. **~ier**, **~ière** *a.* police; (*roman*) detective; *n.m.* policeman.

police[2] /pɔlis/ *n.f.* (*d'assurance*) policy.

polio(myélite) /pɔljɔ(mjelit)/ *n.f.* polio(myelitis).

polir /pɔlir/ *v.t.* polish.

polisson, **~ne** /pɔlisɔ̃, -ɔn/ *a.* naughty. ● *n.m.*, *f.* rascal.

politesse /pɔlitɛs/ *n.f.* politeness; (*parole*) polite remark.

politicien, **~ne** /pɔlitisjɛ̃, -jɛn/ *n.m.*, *f.* (*péj.*) politician.

politi|que /pɔlitik/ *a.* political. ● *n.f.* politics; (*ligne de conduite*) policy. **~ser** *v.t.* politicize.

pollen /pɔlɛn/ *n.m.* pollen.

polluant, **~e** /pɔlɥɑ̃, -t/ *a.* polluting. ● *n.m.* pollutant.

poll|uer /pɔlɥe/ *v.t.* pollute. **~ution** *n.f.* pollution.

polo /pɔlo/ *n.m.* polo; (*vêtement*) sports shirt, tennis shirt.

Pologne /pɔlɔɲ/ *n.f.* Poland.

polonais, **~e** /pɔlɔnɛ, -z/ *a.* Polish. ● *n.m.*, *f.* Pole. ● *n.m.* (*lang.*) Polish.

poltron, **~ne** /pɔltrɔ̃, -ɔn/ *a.* cowardly. ● *n.m.*, *f.* coward.

polycopier /pɔlikɔpje/ *v.t.* duplicate, stencil.

polygamie /pɔligami/ *n.f.* polygamy.

polyglotte /pɔliglɔt/ *n.m./f.* polyglot.

polyvalent, **~e** /pɔlivalɑ̃, -t/ *a.* varied; (*personne*) versatile.

pommade /pɔmad/ *n.f.* ointment.

pomme /pɔm/ *n.f.* apple; (*d'arrosoir*) rose. **~ d'Adam**, Adam's apple. **~ de pin**, pine cone. **~ de terre**, potato. **~s frites**, chips; (*Amer.*) French fries. **tomber dans les ~s**, (*fam.*) pass out.

pommeau (*pl.* **~x**) /pɔmo/ *n.m.* (*de canne*) knob.

pommette /pɔmɛt/ *n.f.* cheek-bone.

pommier /pɔmje/ *n.m.* apple-tree.

pompe /pɔ̃p/ *n.f.* pump; (*splendeur*) pomp. **~ à incendie**, fire-engine. **~s funèbres**, undertaker's.

pomper /pɔ̃pe/ *v.t.* pump; (*copier*: *fam.*) copy, crib. **~ l'air à qn.**, (*fam.*) get on s.o.'s nerves.

pompeu|x, **~se** /pɔ̃pø, -z/ *a.* pompous.

pompier /pɔ̃pje/ *n.m.* fireman.

pompiste /pɔ̃pist/ *n.m./f.* petrol pump attendant; (*Amer.*) gas station attendant.

pompon /pɔ̃pɔ̃/ *n.m.* pompon.

pomponner /pɔ̃pɔne/ *v.t.* deck out.

poncer /pɔ̃se/ *v.t.* rub down.

ponctuation /pɔ̃ktɥasjɔ̃/ *n.f.* punctuation.

ponct|uel, **~uelle** /pɔ̃ktɥɛl/ *a.* punctual. **~ualité** *n.f.* punctuality.

ponctuer /pɔ̃ktɥe/ *v.t.* punctuate.

pondéré /pɔ̃dere/ *a.* level-headed.

pondre /pɔ̃dr/ *v.t./i.* lay.

poney /pɔnɛ/ *n.m.* pony.

pont /pɔ̃/ *n.m.* bridge; (*de navire*) deck; (*de graissage*) ramp. **faire le ~**, take the extra day(s) off (*between holidays*). **~ aérien**, airlift. **~-levis** (*pl.* **~s-levis**) *n.m.* drawbridge.

ponte /pɔ̃t/ *n.f.* laying (of eggs).

pontife /pɔ̃tif/ *n.m.* (**souverain**) **~**, pope.

pontific|al (*m. pl.* **~aux**) /pɔ̃tifikal, -o/ *a.* papal.

pop /pɔp/ *n.m. & a. invar.* (*mus.*) pop.

popote /pɔpɔt/ *n.f.* (*fam.*) cooking.

populace /pɔpylas/ *n.f.* (*péj.*) rabble.

popul|aire /pɔpylɛr/ *a.* popular; (*expression*) colloquial; (*quartier*, *origine*) working-class. **~arité** *n.f.* popularity.

population /pɔpylasjɔ̃/ *n.f.* population.

populeu|x, **~se** /pɔpylø, -z/ *a.* populous.

porc /pɔr/ *n.m.* pig; (*viande*) pork.

porcelaine /pɔrsəlɛn/ *n.f.* china, porcelain.

porc-épic (*pl.* **porcs-épics**) /pɔrkepik/ *n.m.* porcupine.

porche /pɔrʃ/ *n.m.* porch.

porcherie /pɔrʃəri/ *n.f.* pigsty.

por|e /pɔr/ *n.m.* pore. **~eux**, **~euse** *a.* porous.

pornograph|ie /pɔrnɔgrafi/ *n.f.* pornography. **~ique** *a.* pornographic.

port[1] /pɔr/ *n.m.* port, harbour. **à bon ~**, safely. **~ maritime**, seaport.

port[2] /pɔr/ *n.m.* (*transport*) carriage; (*d'armes*) carrying; (*de barbe*) wearing.

portail /pɔrtaj/ *n.m.* portal.

portant, ~e /pɔrtɑ̃, -t/ *a.* **bien/mal ~,** in good/bad health.

portati|f, ~ve /pɔrtatif, -v/ *a.* portable.

porte /pɔrt/ *n.f.* door; (*passage*) doorway; (*de jardin, d'embarquement*) gate. **mettre à la ~,** throw out. **~ d'entrée,** front door. **~- fenêtre** (*pl. ~s-fenêtres*) *n.f.* French window.

porté /pɔrte/ *a.* **~ à,** inclined to. **~ sur,** fond of.

portée /pɔrte/ *n.f.* (*d'une arme*) range; (*de voûte*) span; (*d'animaux*) litter; (*impact*) significance; (*mus.*) stave. **à ~ de,** within reach of. **à ~ de (la) main,** within (arm's) reach. **hors de ~ (de),** out of reach (of). **à la ~ de qn.** at s.o.'s level.

portefeuille /pɔrtəfœj/ *n.m.* wallet; (*de ministre*) portfolio.

portemanteau (*pl. ~x*) /pɔrtmɑ̃to/ *n.m.* coat *ou* hat stand.

port|er /pɔrte/ *v.t.* carry; (*vêtement, bague*) wear; (*fruits, responsabilité, nom*) bear; (*coup*) strike; (*amener*) bring; (*inscrire*) enter. ● *v.i.* (*bruit*) carry; (*coup*) hit home. **~er sur,** rest on; (*concerner*) bear on. **se ~er bien,** be *ou* feel well. **se ~er candidat,** stand as a candidate. **~er aux nues,** praise to the skies. **~e-avions** *n.m. invar.* aircraft-carrier. **~e-bagages** *n.m. invar.* luggage rack. **~e-bonheur** *n.m. invar.* (*objet*) charm. **~e-clefs** *n.m. invar.* keyring. **~e-documents** *n.m. invar.* attaché case, document wallet. **~e-monnaie** *n.m. invar.* purse. **~e-parole** *n.m. invar.* spokesman. **~e-voix** *n.m. invar.* megaphone.

porteu|r, ~se /pɔrtœr, -øz/ *n.m., f.* (*de nouvelles*) bearer; (*méd.*) carrier. ● *n.m.* (*rail.*) porter.

portier /pɔrtje/ *n.m.* door-man.

portière /pɔrtjɛr/ *n.f.* door.

portillon /pɔrtijɔ̃/ *n.m.* gate.

portion /pɔrsjɔ̃/ *n.f.* portion.

portique /pɔrtik/ *n.m.* portico; (*sport*) crossbar.

porto /pɔrto/ *n.m.* port (wine).

portrait /pɔrtrɛ/ *n.m.* portrait. **~-robot** (*pl. ~s-robots*) *n.m.* identikit, photofit.

portuaire /pɔrtɥɛr/ *a.* port.

portugais, ~e /pɔrtygɛ, -z/ *a. & n.m., f.* Portuguese. ● *n.m.* (*lang.*) Portuguese.

Portugal /pɔrtygal/ *n.m.* Portugal.

pose /poz/ *n.f.* installation; (*attitude*) pose; (*photo.*) exposure.

posé /poze/ *a.* calm, serious.

poser /poze/ *v.t.* put (down); (*installer*) install, put in; (*fondations*) lay; (*question*) ask; (*problème*) pose. ● *v.i.* (*modèle*) pose. **se ~** *v. pr.* (*avion, oiseau*) land; (*regard*) alight; (*se présenter*) arise. **~ sa candidature,** apply (à, for).

positi|f, ~ve /pozitif, -v/ *a.* positive.

position /pozisjɔ̃/ *n.f.* position; (*banque*) balance (of account). **prendre ~,** take a stand.

posologie /pozɔlɔʒi/ *n.f.* directions for use.

poss|éder /posede/ *v.t.* possess; (*propriété*) own, possess. **~esseur** *n.m.* possessor; owner.

possessi|f, ~ve /posesif, -v/ *a.* possessive.

possession /posesjɔ̃/ *n.f.* possession. **prendre ~ de,** take possession of.

possibilité /posibilite/ *n.f.* possibility.

possible /posibl/ *a.* possible. ● *n.m.* **le ~,** what is possible. **dès que ~,** as soon as possible. **faire son ~,** do one's utmost. **le plus tard/etc. ~,** as late/etc. as possible. **pas ~,** impossible; (*int.*) really!

post- /pɔst/ *préf.* post- .

post|al (*m. pl. ~aux*) /pɔstal, -o/ *a.* postal.

poste[1] /pɔst/ *n.f.* (*service*) post; (*bureau*) post office. **~ aérienne,** airmail. **mettre à la ~,** post. **~ restante,** poste restante.

poste[2] /pɔst/ *n.m.* (*lieu, emploi*) post; (*de radio, télévision*) set; (*téléphone*) extension (number). **~ d'essence,** petrol *ou* gas (*Amer.*) station. **~ d'incendie,** fire point. **~ de pilotage,** cockpit. **~ de police,** police station. **~ de secours,** first-aid post.

poster[1] /pɔste/ *v.t.* (*lettre, personne*) post.

poster[2] /pɔstɛr/ *n.m.* poster.

postérieur /pɔsterjœr/ *a.* later; (*partie*) back. **~ à,** after. ● *n.m.* (*fam.*) posterior.

postérité /pɔsterite/ *n.f.* posterity.

posthume /pɔstym/ *a.* posthumous.

postiche /pɔstiʃ/ *a.* false.

post|ier, ~ière /pɔstje, -jɛr/ *n.m., f.* postal worker.

post-scriptum /pɔstskriptɔm/ *n.m. invar.* postscript.

postul|er /pɔstyle/ *v.t./i.* apply (**à** *ou* **pour,** for); (*principe*) postulate. **~ant, ~ante** *n.m., f.* applicant.

posture /pɔstyr/ *n.f.* posture.

pot /po/ *n.m.* pot; (*en carton*) carton; (*en verre*) jar; (*chance: fam.*) luck; (*boisson: fam.*) drink. **~-au-feu** /pɔtofø/ *n.m. invar.* (*plat*) stew. **~ d'échappement,** exhaust-pipe. **~-de-vin** (*pl.* **~s-de-vin**) *n.m.* bribe. **~-pourri,** (*pl.* **~s-pourris**) *n.m.* pot pourri.

potable /pɔtabl/ *a.* drinkable. **eau ~,** drinking water.

potage /pɔtaʒ/ *n.m.* soup.

potag|er, ~ère /pɔtaʒe, -ɛr/ *a.* vegetable. ● *n.m.* vegetable garden.

pote /pɔt/ *n.m.* (*fam.*) chum.

poteau (*pl.* **~x**) /pɔto/ *n.m.* post; (*télégraphique*) pole. **~ indicateur,** signpost.

potelé /pɔtle/ *a.* plump.

potence /pɔtɑ̃s/ *n.f.* gallows.

potentiel, ~le /pɔtɑ̃sjɛl/ *a. & n.m.* potential.

pot|erie /pɔtri/ *n.f.* pottery; (*objet*) piece of pottery. **~ier** *n.m.* potter.

potins /pɔtɛ̃/ *n.m. pl.* gossip.

potion /posjɔ̃/ *n.f.* potion.

potiron /pɔtirɔ̃/ *n.m.* pumpkin.

pou (*pl.* **~x**) /pu/ *n.m.* louse.

poubelle /pubɛl/ *n.f.* dustbin; (*Amer.*) garbage can.

pouce /pus/ *n.m.* thumb; (*de pied*) big toe; (*mesure*) inch.

poudr|e /pudr/ *n.f.* powder. **~e** (**à canon**), gunpowder. **en ~e,** (*lait*) powdered; (*chocolat*) drinking. **~er** *v.t.* powder. **~eux, ~euse** *a.* powdery.

poudrier /pudrije/ *n.m.* (powder) compact.

poudrière /pudrijɛr/ *n.f.* (*région: fig.*) powder-keg.

pouf /puf/ *n.m.* pouffe.

pouffer /pufe/ *v.i.* guffaw.

pouilleu|x, ~se /pujø, -z/ *a.* filthy.

poulailler /pulɑje/ *n.m.* (hen-)coop.

poulain /pulɛ̃/ *n.m.* foal; (*protégé*) protégé.

poule /pul/ *n.f.* hen; (*culin.*) fowl; (*femme: fam.*) tart; (*rugby*) group.

poulet /pulɛ/ *n.m.* chicken.

pouliche /puliʃ/ *n.f.* filly.

poulie /puli/ *n.f.* pulley.

pouls /pu/ *n.m.* pulse.

poumon /pumɔ̃/ *n.m.* lung.

poupe /pup/ *n.f.* stern.

poupée /pupe/ *n.f.* doll.

poupon /pupɔ̃/ *n.m.* baby. **~nière** /-ɔnjɛr/ *n.f.* crèche, day nursery.

pour /pur/ *prép.* for; (*envers*) to; (*à la place de*) on behalf of; (*comme*) as. **~ cela,** for that reason. **~ cent,** per cent. **~ de bon,** for good. **~ faire,** (in order) to do. **~ que,** so that. **~ moi,** as for me. **~ petit/etc. qu'il soit,** however small/etc. he may be. **trop poli/etc. ~,** too polite/etc. to. **le ~ et le contre,** the pros and cons. **~ ce qui est de,** as for.

pourboire /purbwar/ *n.m.* tip.

pourcentage /pursɑ̃taʒ/ *n.m.* percentage.

pourchasser /purʃase/ *v.t.* pursue.

pourparlers /purparle/ *n.m. pl.* talks.

pourpre /purpr/ *a. & n.m.* crimson; (*violet*) purple.

pourquoi /purkwa/ *conj. & adv.* why. ● *n.m. invar.* reason.

pourra, pourrait /pura, purɛ/ *voir* pouvoir[1].

pourr|ir /purir/ *v.t./i.* rot. **~i a** *a.* rotten. **~iture** *n.f.* rot.

poursuite /pursɥit/ *n.f.* pursuit (**de,** of). **~s,** (*jurid.*) legal action.

poursuiv|re† /pursɥivr/ *v.t.* pursue; (*continuer*) continue (with). **~re (en justice),** (*au criminel*) prosecute; (*au civil*) sue. ● *v.i.,* **se ~re** *v. pr.* continue. **~ant, ~ante** *n.m., f.* pursuer.

pourtant /purtɑ̃/ *adv.* yet.

pourtour /purtur/ *n.m.* perimeter.

pourv|oir† /purvwar/ *v.t.* **~oir de,** provide with. ● *v.i.* **~oir à,** provide for. **~u de,** supplied with. ● *v. pr.* **se ~oir de** (*argent*) provide o.s. with. **~oyeur, ~oyeuse** *n.m., f.* supplier.

pourvu que /purvyk(ə)/ *conj.* (*condition*) provided (that); (*souhait*) let us hope (that). **pourvu qu'il ne soit rien arrivé,** I hope nothing's happened.

pousse /pus/ *n.f.* growth; (*bourgeon*) shoot.

poussé /puse/ *a.* (*études*) advanced.

poussée /puse/ *n.f.* pressure; (*coup*) push; (*de prix*) upsurge; (*méd.*) outbreak.

pousser /puse/ *v.t.* push; (*du coude*) nudge; (*cri*) let out; (*soupir*) heave; (*continuer*) continue; (*exhorter*) urge (**à**, to); (*forcer*) drive (**à**, to); (*amener*) bring (**à**, to). ● *v.i.* push; (*grandir*) grow. **faire ~** (*cheveux*) let grow; (*plante*) grow. **se ~** *v. pr.* move over *ou* up.

poussette /pusɛt/ *n.f.* push-chair; (*Amer.*) (baby) stroller.

pouss|ière /pusjɛr/ *n.f.* dust. **~iéreux, ~iéreuse** *a.* dusty.

poussi|f, ~ve /pusif, -v/ *a.* short-winded, wheezing.

poussin /pusɛ̃/ *n.m.* chick.

poutre /putr/ *n.f.* beam: (*en métal*) girder.

pouvoir[1]† /puvwar/ *v. aux.* (*possibilité*) can, be able; (*permission, éventualité*) may, can. **il peut/pouvait/ pourrait venir**, he can/could/might come. **je n'ai pas pu**, I could not. **j'ai pu faire**, (*réussi à*) I managed to do. **je n'en peux plus**, I am exhausted. **il se peut que**, it may be that.

pouvoir[2] /puvwar/ *n.m.* power; (*gouvernement*) government. **au ~**, in power. **~s publics**, authorities.

prairie /preri/ *n.f.* meadow.

praline /pralin/ *n.f.* sugared almond.

praticable /pratikabl/ *a.* practicable.

praticien, ~ne /pratisjɛ̃, -jɛn/ *n.m., f.* practitioner.

pratiquant, ~e /pratikã, -t/ *a.* practising. ● *n.m., f.* churchgoer.

pratique /pratik/ *a.* practical. ● *n.f.* practice; (*expérience*) experience. **la ~ du golf/du cheval**, golfing/ riding. **~ment** *adv.* in practice; (*presque*) practically.

pratiquer /pratike/ *v.t./i.* practise; (*sport*) play; (*faire*) make.

pré /pre/ *n.m.* meadow.

pré- /pre/ *préf.* pre-.

préalable /prealabl/ *a.* preliminary, prior. ● *n.m.* precondition. **au ~**, first.

préambule /preãbyl/ *n.m.* preamble.

préau (*pl.* **~x**) /preo/ *n.m.* (*scol.*) playground shelter.

préavis /preavi/ *n.m.* (advance) notice.

précaire /prekɛr/ *a.* precarious.

précaution /prekosjɔ̃/ *n.f.* (*mesure*) precaution; (*prudence*) caution.

précéd|ent, ~ente /presedã, -t/ *a.* previous. ● *n.m* precedent. **~emment** /-amã/ *adv.* previously.

précéder /presede/ *v.t./i.* precede.

précepte /presɛpt/ *n.m.* precept.

précep|teur, ~trice /preseptœr, -tris/ *n.m., f.* tutor.

prêcher /preʃe/ *v.t./i.* preach.

précieu|x, ~se /presjø, -z/ *a.* precious.

précipice /presipis/ *n.m.* abyss, chasm.

précipit|é /presipite/ *a.* hasty. **~amment** *adv.* hastily. **~ation** *n.f.* haste.

précipiter /presipite/ *v.t.* throw, precipitate; (*hâter*) hasten. **se ~** *v. pr.* rush (**sur**, at, on to); (*se jeter*) throw o.s; (*s'accélérer*) speed up.

précis, ~e /presi, -z/ *a.* precise; (*mécanisme*) accurate. ● *n.m.* summary. **dix heures/etc. ~es**, ten o'clock/etc. sharp. **~ément** /-zemã/ *adv.* precisely.

préciser /presize/ *v.t./i.* specify; (*pensée*) be more specific about. **se ~** *v. pr.* become clear(er).

précision /presizjɔ̃/ *n.f.* precision; (*détail*) detail.

précoc|e /prekɔs/ *a.* early; (*enfant*) precocious. **~ité** *n.f.* earliness; precociousness.

préconçu /prekɔ̃sy/ *a.* preconceived.

préconiser /prekɔnize/ *v.t.* advocate.

précurseur /prekyrsœr/ *n.m.* forerunner.

prédécesseur /predesesœr/ *n.m.* predecessor.

prédicateur /predikatœr/ *n.m.* preacher.

prédilection /predilɛksjɔ̃/ *n.f.* preference.

préd|ire† /predir/ *v.t.* predict. **~iction** *n.f.* prediction.

prédisposer /predispoze/ *v.t.* predispose.

prédominant, ~e /predɔminã, -t/ *a.* predominant.

prédominer /predɔmine/ *v.i.* predominate.

préfabriqué /prefabrike/ *a.* prefabricated.

préface /prefas/ *n.f.* preface.

préfecture /prefɛktyr/ *n.f.* prefecture. **~ de police,** police headquarters.

préférence /preferãs/ *n.f.* preference. **de ~**, preferably. **de ~ à**, in preference to.

préférentiel, ~le /preferãsjɛl/ *a.* preferential.

préfér|er /prefere/ *v.t.* prefer (**à**, to). **je ne préfère pas**, I'd rather not. **~er faire**, prefer to do. **~able** *a.* preferable. **~é, ~ée** *a. & n.m., f.* favourite.

préfet /prefɛ/ *n.m.* prefect. **~ de police,** prefect *ou* chief of police.

préfixe /prefiks/ *n.m.* prefix.

préhistorique /preistɔrik/ *a.* prehistoric.

préjudic|e /preʒydis/ *n.m.* harm, prejudice. **porter ~e à,** harm. **~iable** *a.* harmful.

préjugé /preʒyʒe/ *n.m.* prejudice. **avoir un ~ contre,** be prejudiced against. **sans ~s,** without prejudices.

préjuger /preʒyʒe/ *v.i.* **~ de,** prejudge.

prélasser (se) /(sə)prelɑse/ *v. pr.* loll (about).

prél|ever /prelve/ *v.t.* deduct (**sur,** from); (*sang*) take. **~èvement** *n.m.* deduction. **~èvement de sang,** blood sample.

préliminaire /preliminɛr/ *a. & n.m.* preliminary. **~s,** (*sexuels*) foreplay.

prélude /prelyd/ *n.m.* prelude.

prématuré /prematyre/ *a.* premature. ● *n.m.* premature baby.

prémédit|er /premedite/ *v.t.* premeditate. **~ation** *n.f.* premeditation.

prem|ier, ~ière /prəmje, -jɛr/ *a.* first; (*rang*) front, first; (*enfance*) early; (*nécessité, souci*) prime; (*qualité*) top, prime; (*état*) original. ● *n.m., f.* first (one). ● *n.m.* (*date*) first; (*étage*) first floor. ● *n.f.* (*rail.*) first class; (*exploit jamais vu*) first; (*cinéma, théâtre*) première. **de ~ier ordre,** first-rate. **en ~ier,** first. **~ier jet,** first draft. **~ier ministre,** Prime Minister.

premièrement /prəmjɛrmã/ *adv.* firstly.

prémisse /premis/ *n.f.* premiss.

prémonition /premɔnisjɔ̃/ *n.f.* premonition.

prémunir /premynir/ *v.t.* protect (**contre,** against).

prenant, ~e /prənã, -t/ *a.* (*activité*) engrossing; (*enfant*) demanding.

prénatal (*m. pl.* **~s**) /prenatal/ *a.* antenatal; (*Amer.*) prenatal.

prendre† /prãdr/ *v.t.* take; (*attraper*) catch, get; (*acheter*) get; (*repas*) have; (*engager, adopter*) take on; (*poids*) put on; (*chercher*) pick up; (*panique, colère*) take hold of. ● *v.i.* (*liquide*) set; (*feu*) catch; (*vaccin*) take. **se ~ pour,** think one is. **s'en ~ à,** attack; (*rendre responsable*) blame. **s'y ~,** set about (it).

preneu|r, ~se /prənœr, -øz/ *n.m., f.* buyer. **être ~r,** be willing to buy. **trouver ~r,** find a buyer.

prénom /prenɔ̃/ *n.m.* first name. **~mer** /-ɔme/ *v.t.* call. **se ~mer** *v. pr.* be called.

préoccup|er /preɔkype/ *v.t.* worry; (*absorber*) preoccupy. **se ~er de,** be worried about; be preoccupied about. **~ation** *n.f.* worry; (*idée fixe*) preoccupation.

préparatifs /preparatif/ *n.m. pl.* preparations.

préparatoire /preparatwar/ *a.* preparatory.

prépar|er /prepare/ *v.t.* prepare; (*repas, café*) make. **se ~er** *v. pr.* prepare o.s.; (*être proche*) be brewing. **~er à qn.,** (*surprise*) have (got) in store for s.o. **~ation** *n.f.* preparation.

prépondéran|t, ~te /prepɔ̃derã, -t/ *a.* dominant. **~ce** *n.f.* dominance.

prépos|er /prepoze/ *v.t.* put in charge (**à,** of). **~é, ~ée** *n.m., f.* employee; (*des postes*) postman, postwoman.

préposition /prepozisjɔ̃/ *n.f.* preposition.

préretraite /prerətrɛt/ *n.f.* early retirement.

prérogative /prerɔgativ/ *n.f.* prerogative.

près /prɛ/ *adv.* near, close. **~ de,** near (to), close to; (*presque*) nearly. **à cela ~,** apart from that. **de ~,** closely.

présag|e /prezaʒ/ *n.m.* foreboding, omen. **~er** *v.t.* forebode.

presbyte /prɛsbit/ *a.* long-sighted, far-sighted.

presbytère /prɛsbitɛr/ *n.m.* presbytery.

prescr|ire† /prɛskrir/ *v.t.* prescribe. **~iption** *n.f.* prescription.

préséance /preseãs/ *n.f.* precedence.

présence /prezãs/ *n.f.* presence; (*scol.*) attendance.

présent, ~e /prezã, -t/ *a.* present. ● *n.m.* (*temps, cadeau*) present. **à ~,** now.

présent|er /prezãte/ *v.t.* present; (*personne*) introduce (**à,** to); (*montrer*) show. **se ~er** *v. pr.* introduce o.s. (**à,** to); (*aller*) go; (*apparaître*) appear; (*candidat*) come forward; (*occasion etc.*) arise. **~er bien,** have a pleasing appearance. **se ~er à,** (*examen*) sit for; (*élection*) stand for. **se ~er bien,** look good. **~able** *a.* presentable. **~ateur, ~atrice** *n.m.,* *f.* presenter. **~ation** *n.f.* presentation; introduction.

préservatif /prezɛrvatif/ *n.m.* condom.

préserv|er /prezɛrve/ *v.t.* protect. **~ation** *n.f.* protection, preservation.

présiden|t, ~te /prezidã, -t/ *n.m., f.* president; (*de firme, comité*) chairman, chairwoman. **~t directeur général,** managing director. **~ce** *n.f.* presidency; chairmanship.

présidentiel, ~le /prezidãsjɛl/ *a.* presidential.

présider /prezide/ *v.t.* preside over. ● *v.i.* preside.

présomption /prezɔpsjɔ̃/ *n.f.* presumption.

présomptueu|x, ~se /prezɔptɥø, -z/ *a.* presumptuous.

presque /prɛsk(ə)/ *adv.* almost, nearly. **~ jamais,** hardly ever. **~ rien,** hardly anything. **~ pas (de),** hardly any.

presqu'île /prɛskil/ *n.f.* peninsula.

pressant, ~e /prɛsã, -t/ *a.* pressing, urgent.

presse /prɛs/ *n.f.* (*journaux, appareil*) press.

pressent|ir /presãtir/ *v.t.* sense. **~iment** *n.m.* presentiment.

press|er /prese/ *v.t.* squeeze, press; (*appuyer sur, harceler*) press; (*hâter*) hasten; (*inciter*) urge (**de,** to). ● *v.i.* (*temps*) press; (*affaire*) be pressing. **se ~er** *v. pr.* (*se hâter*) hurry; (*se grouper*) crowd. **~é** *a.* in a hurry; (*orange, citron*) freshly squeezed. **~e-papiers** *n.m. invar.* paperweight.

pressing /presiŋ/ *n.m.* (*magasin*) dry-cleaner's.

pression /presjɔ̃/ *n.f.* pressure. ● *n.m./f.* (*bouton*) press-stud; (*Amer.*) snap.

pressoir /prɛswar/ *n.m.* press.

pressuriser /presyrize/ *v.t.* pressurize.

prestance /prɛstãs/ *n.f.* (imposing) presence.

prestation /prɛstasjɔ̃/ *n.f.* allowance; (*d'artiste etc.*) performance.

prestidigita|teur, ~trice /prɛstidiʒitatœr, -tris/ *n.m., f.* conjuror. **~tion** /-asjɔ̃/ *n.f.* conjuring.

prestig|e /prɛstiʒ/ *n.m.* prestige. **~ieux, ~ieuse** *a.* prestigious.

présumer /prezyme/ *v.t.* presume. **~ que,** assume that. **~ de,** overrate.

prêt[1], **~e** /prɛ, -t/ *a.* ready (**à qch.,** for sth., **à faire,** to do). **~-à-porter** /prɛ(t)aporte/ *n.m. invar.* ready-to-wear clothes.

prêt[2] /prɛ/ *n.m.* loan.

prétendant /pretãdã/ *n.m.* (*amoureux*) suitor.

prétend|re /pretãdr/ *v.t.* claim (**que,** that); (*vouloir*) intend. **~re qn. riche/etc.,** claim that s.o. is rich/*etc.* **~u** *a.* so-called. **~ument** *adv.* supposedly, allegedly.

prétent|ieux, ~ieuse /pretãsjø, -z/ *a.* pretentious. **~ion** *n.f.* pretentiousness; (*exigence*) claim.

prêt|er /prete/ *v.t.* lend (**à,** to); (*attribuer*) attribute. ● *v.i.* **~er à,** lead to. **~er attention,** pay attention. **~er serment,** take an oath. **~eur, ~euse** /prɛtœr, -øz/ *n.m., f.* (money-)lender. **~eur sur gages,** pawnbroker.

prétext|e /pretɛkst/ *n.m.* pretext, excuse. **~er** *v.t.* plead.

prêtre /prɛtr/ *n.m.* priest.

prêtrise /pretriz/ *n.f.* priesthood.

preuve /prœv/ *n.f.* proof. **faire ~ de,** show. **faire ses ~s,** prove one's *ou* its worth.

prévaloir /prevalwar/ *v.i.* prevail.

prévenan|t, ~te /prɛvnã, -t/ *a.* thoughtful. **~ce(s)** *n.f.* (*pl.*) thoughtfulness.

prévenir† /prɛvnir/ *v.t.* (*menacer*) warn; (*informer*) tell; (*éviter, anticiper*) forestall.

préventi|f, ~ve /prevãtif, -v/ *a.* preventive.

prévention /prevãsjɔ̃/ *n.f.* prevention; (*préjuge*) prejudice. **~ routière,** road safety.

prévenu, ~e /prɛvny/ *n.m., f.* defendant.

prév|oir† /prevwar/ *v.t.* foresee; (*temps*) forecast; (*organiser*) plan (for), provide for; (*envisager*) allow (for). **~u pour,** (*jouet etc.*) designed for. **~isible** *a.* foreseeable. **~ision** *n.f.* prediction; (*météorologique*) forecast.

prévoyan|t, ~te /prevwajã, -t/ *a.* showing foresight **~ce** *n.f.* foresight.

prier /prije/ *v.i.* pray. ● *v.t.* pray to; (*implorer*) beg (**de,** to); (*demander à*) ask (**de,** to). **je vous en prie,**

please; (*il n'y a pas de quoi*) don't mention it.

prière /prijɛr/ *n.f.* prayer; (*demande*) request. **~ de,** (*vous êtes prié de*) will you please.

primaire /primɛr/ *a.* primary.

primauté /primote/ *n.f.* primacy.

prime /prim/ *n.f.* free gift; (*d'employé*) bonus; (*subvention*) subsidy; (*d'assurance*) premium.

primé /prime/ *a.* prize-winning.

primer /prime/ *v.t./i.* excel.

primeurs /primœr/ *n.f. pl.* early fruit and vegetables.

primevère /primvɛr/ *n.f.* primrose.

primiti|f, **~ve** /primitif, -v/ *a.* primitive; (*originel*) original. ● *n.m.*, *f.* primitive.

primord|ial (*m. pl.* **~iaux**) /primɔrdjal, -jo/ *a.* essential.

princ|e /prɛ̃s/ *n.m.* prince. **~esse** *n.f.* princess. **~ier,** **~ière** *a.* princely.

princip|al (*m. pl.* **~aux**) /prɛ̃sipal, -o/ *a.* main, principal. ● *n.m.* (*pl.* **~aux**) headmaster; (*chose*) main thing. **~alement** *adv.* mainly.

principauté /prɛ̃sipote/ *n.f.* principality.

principe /prɛ̃sip/ *n.m.* principle. **en ~,** theoretically; (*d'habitude*) as a rule.

printan|ier, **~ière** /prɛ̃tanje, -jɛr/ *a.* spring(-like).

printemps /prɛ̃tɑ̃/ *n.m.* spring.

priorit|é /prijɔrite/ *n.f.* priority; (*auto.*) right of way. **~aire** *a.* priority. **être ~aire,** have priority.

pris, **~e** *see* **prendre**[^1] /pri, -z/ *voir* prendre. ● *a.* (*place*) taken; (*personne, journée*) busy; (*gorge*) infected. **~ de,** (*peur, fièvre, etc.*) stricken with. **~ de panique,** panic-stricken.

prise[^2] /priz/ *n.f.* hold, grip; (*animal etc. attrapé*) catch; (*mil.*) capture. **~ (de courant),** (*mâle*) plug; (*femelle*) socket. **aux ~s avec,** at grips with. **~ de conscience,** awareness. **~ de contact,** first contact, initial meeting. **~ de position,** stand. **~ de sang,** blood test.

priser /prize/ *v.t.* (*estimer*) prize.

prisme /prism/ *n.m.* prism.

prison /prizɔ̃/ *n.f.* prison, gaol, jail; (*réclusion*) imprisonment. **~nier,** **~nière** /-ɔnje, -jɛr/ *n.m.*, *f.* prisoner.

privé /prive/ *a.* private. ● *n.m.* (*comm.*) private sector. **en ~,** **dans le ~,** in private.

priv|er /prive/ *v.t.* **~er de,** deprive of. **se ~er de,** go without. **~ation** *n.f.* deprivation; (*sacrifice*) hardship.

privil|ège /privilɛʒ/ *n.m.* privilege. **~égié,** **~égiée** *a.* & *n.m.*, *f.* privileged (person).

prix /pri/ *n.m.* price; (*récompense*) prize. **à tout ~,** at all costs. **au ~ de,** (*fig.*) at the expense of. **~ coûtant, ~ de revient,** cost price. **à ~ fixe,** set price.

pro- /pro/ *préf.* pro-.

probab|le /prɔbabl/ *a.* probable, likely. **~ilité** *n.f.* probability. **~lement** *adv.* probably.

probant, **~e** /prɔbɑ̃, -t/ *a.* convincing, conclusive.

probité /prɔbite/ *n.f.* integrity.

problème /prɔblɛm/ *n.m.* problem.

procéd|er /prɔsede/ *v.i.* proceed. **~er à,** carry out. **~é** *n.m.* process; (*conduite*) behaviour.

procédure /prɔsedyr/ *n.f.* procedure.

procès /prɔsɛ/ *n.m.* (*criminel*) trial; (*civil*) lawsuit, proceedings. **~-verbal** (*pl.* **~-verbaux**) *n.m.* report; (*contravention*) ticket.

procession /prɔsesjɔ̃/ *n.f.* procession.

processus /prɔsesys/ *n.m.* process.

prochain, **~e** /prɔʃɛ̃, -ɛn/ *a.* (*suivant*) next; (*proche*) imminent; (*avenir*) near. **je descends à la ~e,** I'm getting off at the next stop. ● *n.m.* fellow. **~ement** /-ɛnmɑ̃/ *adv.* soon.

proche /prɔʃ/ *a.* near, close; (*avoisinant*) neighbouring; (*parent, ami*) close. **~ de,** close *ou* near to. **de ~ en proche,** gradually. **dans un ~ avenir,** in the near future. **être ~,** (*imminent*) be approaching. **~s** *n.m. pl.* close relations. **P~-Orient** *n.m.* Near East.

proclam|er /prɔklame/ *v.t.* declare, proclaim. **~ation** *n.f.* declaration, proclamation.

procréation /prɔkreasjɔ̃/ *n.f.* procreation.

procuration /prɔkyrasjɔ̃/ *n.f.* proxy.

procurer /prɔkyre/ *v.t.* bring (**à,** to). **se ~** *v. pr.* obtain.

procureur /prɔkyrœr/ *n.m.* public prosecutor.

prodig|e /prɔdiʒ/ *n.m.* marvel; (*personne*) prodigy. **enfant/musicien ~e,** child/musical prodigy. **~ieux,** **~ieuse** *a.* tremendous, prodigious.

prodigu|e /prɔdig/ *a.* wasteful. **fils ~e,** prodigal son. **~er** *v.t.* **~er à,** lavish on.

[^1]: prendre
[^2]: prise

promoteur /prɔmɔtœr/ *n.m.* (*immo-bilier*) property developer.

prom|ouvoir /prɔmuvwar/ *v.t.* promote. **être ~u,** be promoted. **~otion** *n.f.* promotion; (*univ.*) year; (*comm.*) special offer.

prompt, ~e /prɔ̃, -t/ *a.* swift.

prôner /prone/ *v.t.* extol; (*préconiser*) preach, advocate.

pronom /prɔnɔ̃/ *n.m.* pronoun. **~inal** (*m. pl.* **~inaux**) /-ɔminal, -o/ *a.* pronominal.

prononc|er /prɔnɔ̃se/ *v.t.* pronounce; (*discours*) make. **se ~er** *v. pr.* (*mot*) be pronounced; (*personne*) make a decision (**pour,** in favour of). **~é** *a.* pronounced. **~iation** *n.f.* pronuncia-tion.

pronosti|c /prɔnɔstik/ *n.m.* forecast; (*méd.*) prognosis. **~quer** *v.t.* fore-cast.

propagande /prɔpagɑ̃d/ *n.f.* propa-ganda.

propag|er /prɔpaʒe/ *v.t., se ~er* *v. pr.* spread. **~ation** /-gasjɔ̃/ *n.f.* spread (-ing).

proph|ète /prɔfɛt/ *n.m.* prophet. **~étie** /-esi/ *n.f.* prophecy. **~étique** *a.* prophetic. **~étiser** *v.t./i.* pro-phesy.

propice /prɔpis/ *a.* favourable.

proportion /prɔpɔrsjɔ̃/ *n.f.* propor-tion; (*en mathématiques*) ratio. **toutes ~s gardées,** making appro-priate allowances. **~né** /-jɔne/ *a.* proportionate (**à,** to). **~nel, ~nelle** /-jɔnɛl/ *a.* proportional. **~ner** /-jɔne/ *v.t.* proportion.

propos /prɔpo/ *n.m.* intention; (*su-jet*) subject. ● *n.m. pl.* (*paroles*) remarks. **à ~,** at the right time; (*dans un dialogue*) by the way. **à ~ de,** about. **à tout ~,** at every possible occasion.

propos|er /prɔpoze/ *v.t.* propose; (*of-frir*) offer. **se ~er** *v. pr.* volunteer (**pour,** to); (*but*) set o.s. **se ~er de faire,** propose to do. **~ition** *n.f.* proposal; (*affirmation*) proposition; (*gram.*) clause.

propre[1] /prɔpr/ *a.* clean; (*soigné*) neat; (*honnête*) decent. **mettre au ~,** write out again neatly. **c'est du ~!** (*ironique*) well done! **~ment**[1] /-əmɑ̃/ *adv.* cleanly; neatly; decently.

propre[2] /prɔpr/ *a.* (*à soi*) own; (*sens*) literal. **~ à,** (*qui convient*) suited to; (*spécifique*) peculiar to. **~-à-rien** *n.m./f.* good-for-nothing. **~ment**[2]

/-əmɑ̃/ *adv.* strictly. **le bureau**/*etc.* **~ment dit,** the office/*etc.* itself.

propreté /prɔprəte/ *n.f.* cleanliness; (*netteté*) neatness.

propriétaire /prɔprijetɛr/ *n.m./f.* owner; (*comm.*) proprietor; (*qui loue*) landlord, landlady.

propriété /prɔprijete/ *n.f.* property; (*droit*) ownership.

propuls|er /prɔpylse/ *v.t.* propel. **~ion** *n.f.* propulsion.

prorata /prɔrata/ *n.m. invar.* **au ~ de,** in proportion to.

proroger /prɔrɔʒe/ *v.t.* (*contrat*) de-fer; (*passeport*) extend.

prosaïque /prɔzaik/ *a.* prosaic.

proscr|ire /prɔskrir/ *v.t.* proscribe. **~it, ~ite** *a.* proscribed; *n.m., f.* (*exilé*) exile.

prose /proz/ *n.f.* prose.

prospec|ter /prɔspɛkte/ *v.t.* prospect. **~teur, ~trice** *n.m., f.* prospector. **~tion** /-ksjɔ̃/ *n.f.* prospecting.

prospectus /prɔspɛktys/ *n.m.* leaflet.

prosp|ère /prɔspɛr/ *a.* flourishing, thriving. **~érer** *v.i.* thrive, prosper. **~érité** *n.f.* prosperity.

prostern|er (se) /(sə)prɔstɛrne/ *v. pr.* bow down. **~é** *a.* prostrate.

prostit|uée /prɔstitɥe/ *n.f.* pros-titute. **~ution** *n.f.* prostitution.

prostré /prɔstre/ *a.* prostrate.

protagoniste /prɔtagɔnist/ *n.m.* pro-tagonist.

protec|teur, ~trice /prɔtɛktœr, -tris/ *n.m., f.* protector. ● *a.* protec-tive.

protection /prɔtɛksjɔ̃/ *n.f.* protec-tion; (*fig.*) patronage.

protég|er /prɔteʒe/ *v.t.* protect; (*fig.*) patronize. **se ~er** *v. pr.* protect o.s. **~é** *n.m.* protégé. **~ée** *n.f.* protégée.

protéine /prɔtein/ *n.f.* protein.

protestant, ~e /prɔtɛstɑ̃, -t/ *a. & n.m., f.* Protestant.

protest|er /prɔtɛste/ *v.t./i.* protest. **~ation** *n.f.* protest.

protocole /prɔtɔkɔl/ *n.m.* protocol.

prototype /prɔtɔtip/ *n.m.* prototype.

protubéran|t, ~te /prɔtyberɑ̃, -t/ *a.* bulging. **~ce,** *n.f.* protuberance.

proue /pru/ *n.f.* bow, prow.

prouesse /prus/ *n.f.* feat, exploit.

prouver /pruve/ *v.t.* prove.

provenance /prɔvnɑ̃s/ *n.f.* origin. **en ~ de,** from.

provençal, ~ale (*m. pl.* **~aux**) /prɔvɑ̃sal, -o/ *a. & n.m., f.* Provençal.

Provence /prɔvɑ̃s/ *n.f.* Provence.

provenir† /prɔvnir/ *v.i.* ~ **de,** come from.

proverb|e /prɔvɛrb/ *n.m.* proverb. ~**ial** (*m. pl.* ~**iaux**) *a.* proverbial.

providence /prɔvidɑ̃s/ *n.f.* providence.

provinc|e /prɔvɛ̃s/ *n.f.* province. **de** ~**e,** provincial. **la** ~**e,** the provinces. ~**ial,** ~**iale** (*m. pl.* ~**iaux**) *a. & n.m., f.* provincial.

proviseur /prɔvizœr/ *n.m.* headmaster, principal.

provision /prɔvizjɔ̃/ *n.f.* supply, store; (*dans un compte*) funds; (*acompte*) deposit. ~**s,** (*vivres*) provisions. **panier à** ~**s,** shopping basket.

provisoire /prɔvizwar/ *a.* temporary. ~**ment** *adv.* temporarily.

provo|quer /prɔvɔke/ *v.t.* cause; (*exciter*) arouse; (*défier*) provoke. ~**cant,** ~**cante** *a.* provocative. ~**cation** *n.f.* provocation.

proximité /prɔksimite/ *n.f.* proximity. **à** ~ **de,** close to.

prude /pryd/ *a.* prudish. ● *n.f.* prude.

prud|ent, ~**ente** /prydɑ̃, -t/ *a.* cautious; (*sage*) wise. **soyez** ~**ent,** be careful. ~**emment** /-amɑ̃/ *adv.* cautiously; wisely. ~**ence** *n.f.* caution; wisdom.

prune /pryn/ *n.f.* plum.

pruneau (*pl.* ~**x**) /pryno/ *n.m.* prune.

prunelle[1] /prynɛl/ *n.f.* (*pupille*) pupil.

prunelle[2] /prynɛl/ *n.f.* (*fruit*) sloe.

psaume /psom/ *n.m.* psalm.

pseudo- /psødɔ/ *préf.* pseudo-.

pseudonyme /psødɔnim/ *n.m.* pseudonym.

psychanalys|e /psikanaliz/ *n.f.* psychoanalysis. ~**er** *v.t.* psychoanalyse. ~**te** /-st/ *n.m./f.* psychoanalyst.

psychiatr|e /psikjatr/ *n.m./f.* psychiatrist. ~**ie** *n.f.* psychiatry. ~**ique** *a.* psychiatric.

psychique /psiʃik/ *a.* mental, psychological.

psycholo|gie /psikɔlɔʒi/ *n.f.* psychology. ~**gique** *a.* psychological. ~**gue** *n.m./f.* psychologist.

psychosomatique /psikɔsɔmatik/ *a.* psychosomatic.

psychothérapie /psikɔterapi/ *n.f.* psychotherapy.

PTT *abrév.* (*Postes, Télécommunications et Télédiffusion*) Post Office.

pu /py/ *voir* pouvoir[1].

puant, ~**e** /pɥɑ̃, -t/ *a.* stinking. ~**eur** /-tœr/ *n.f.* stink.

pub /pyb/ *n.f.* **la** ~, advertising. **une** ~, an advert.

puberté /pybɛrte/ *n.f.* puberty.

publi|c, ~**que** /pyblik/ *a.* public. ● *n.m.* public; (*assistance*) audience. **en** ~**c,** in public.

publicit|é /pyblisite/ *n.f.* publicity, advertising; (*annonce*) advertisement. ~**aire** *a.* publicity.

publ|ier /pyblije/ *v.t.* publish. ~**ication** *n.f.* publication.

publiquement /pyblikmɑ̃/ *adv.* publicly.

puce[1] /pys/ *n.f.* flea. **marché aux** ~**s,** flea market.

puce[2] /pys/ *n.f.* (*électronique*) chip.

pud|eur /pydœr/ *n.f.* modesty. ~**ique** *a.* modest.

pudibond, ~**e** /pydibɔ̃, -d/ *a.* prudish.

puer /pɥe/ *v.i.* stink. ● *v.t.* stink of.

puéricultrice /pɥerikyltris/ *n.f.* children's nurse.

puéril /pɥeril/ *a.* puerile.

pugilat /pyʒila/ *n.m.* fight.

puis /pɥi/ *adv.* then.

puiser /pɥize/ *v.t.* draw (**qch. dans,** sth. from). ● *v.i.* ~ **dans qch.,** dip into sth.

puisque /pɥisk(ə)/ *conj.* since, as.

puissance /pɥisɑ̃s/ *n.f.* power. **en** ~ *a.* potential; *adv.* potentially.

puiss|ant, ~**ante** /pɥisɑ̃, -t/ *a.* powerful. ~**amment** *adv.* powerfully.

puits /pɥi/ *n.m.* well; (*de mine*) shaft.

pull(-over) /pyl(ɔvɛr)/ *n.m.* pullover, jumper.

pulpe /pylp/ *n.f.* pulp.

pulsation /pylsɑsjɔ̃/ *n.f.* (heart-)beat.

pulvéris|er /pylverize/ *v.t.* pulverize; (*liquide*) spray. ~**ateur** *n.m.* spray.

punaise /pynɛz/ *n.f.* (*insecte*) bug; (*clou*) drawing-pin; (*Amer.*) thumbtack.

punch[1] /pɔ̃ʃ/ *n.m.* punch.

punch[2] /pœnʃ/ *n.m.* **avoir du** ~, have drive.

pun|ir /pynir/ *v.t.* punish. ~**ition** *n.f.* punishment.

punk /pœnk/ *a. invar.* punk.

pupille[1] /pypij/ *n.f.* (*de l'œil*) pupil.

pupille[2] /pypij/ *n.m./f.* (*enfant*) ward.

pupitre /pypitr/ *n.m.* (*scol.*) desk. ~ à musique, music stand.

pur /pyr/ *a.* pure; (*whisky*) neat. ~ement *adv.* purely. ~eté *n.f.* purity. ~-sang *n.m. invar.* (*cheval*) thoroughbred.

purée /pyre/ *n.f.* purée; (*de pommes de terre*) mashed potatoes.

purgatoire /pyrgatwar/ *n.m.* purgatory.

purg|e /pyrʒ/ *n.f.* purge. ~er *v.t.* (*pol., méd.*) purge; (*peine: jurid.*) serve.

purif|ier /pyrifje/ *v.t.* purify. ~ication *n.f.* purification.

purin /pyrɛ̃/ *n.m.* (liquid) manure.

puritain, -e /pyritɛ̃, -ɛn/ *n.m., f.* puritan. ● *a.* puritanical.

pus /py/ *n.m.* pus.

pustule /pystyl/ *n.f.* pimple.

putain /pytɛ̃/ *n.f.* (*fam.*) whore.

putréfier (se) /(sə)pytrefje/ *v. pr.* putrefy.

putsch /putʃ/ *n.m.* putsch.

puzzle /pœzl/ *n.m.* jigsaw (puzzle).

P-V *abrév.* (*procès-verbal*) ticket, traffic fine.

pygmée /pigme/ *n.m.* pygmy.

pyjama /piʒama/ *n.m.* pyjamas. **un ~**, a pair of pyjamas.

pylône /pilon/ *n.m.* pylon.

pyramide /piramid/ *n.f.* pyramid.

Pyrénées /pirene/ *n.f. pl.* **les ~**, the Pyrenees.

pyromane /pirɔman/ *n.m./f.* arsonist.

Q

QG *abrév.* (quartier général) HQ.

QI *abrév.* (*quotient intellectuel*) IQ.

qu' /k/ *voir* que.

quadrill|er /kadrije/ *v.t.* (*zone*) comb, control. ~age *n.m.* (*mil.*) control. ~é *a.* (*papier*) squared.

quadrupède /kadrypɛd/ *n.m.* quadruped.

quadrupl|e /kadrypl/ *a. & n.m.* quadruple. ~er *v.t./i.* quadruple. ~és, ~ées *n.m., f. pl.* quadruplets.

quai /ke/ *n.m.* (*de gare*) platform; (*de port*) quay; (*de rivière*) embankment.

qualificatif /kalifikatif/ *n.m.* (*épithète*) term.

qualif|ier /kalifje/ *v.t.* qualify; (*décrire*) describe (de, as). **se ~ier** *v. pr.* qualify (**pour**, for). ~ication *n.f.* qualification; description. ~ié *a.* qualified; (*main d'œuvre*) skilled.

qualit|é /kalite/ *n.f.* quality; (*titre*) occupation. **en ~é de**, in one's capacity as. ~atif, ~ative *a.* qualitative.

quand /kɑ̃/ *conj. & adv.* when. ~ **même**, all the same. ~ (**bien**) **même**, even if.

quant (à) /kɑ̃t(a)/ *prép.* as for.

quant-à-soi /kɑ̃taswa/ *n.m.* **rester sur son ~**, stand aloof.

quantit|é /kɑ̃tite/ *n.f.* quantity. **une ~é de**, a lot of. **des ~és**, masses. ~atif, ~ative *a.* quantitative.

quarantaine /karɑ̃tɛn/ *n.f.* (*méd.*) quarantine. **une ~ (de)**, about forty.

quarant|e /karɑ̃t/ *a. & n.m.* forty. ~ième *a. & n.m./f.* fortieth.

quart /kar/ *n.m.* quarter; (*naut.*) watch. ~ (**de litre**), quarter litre. ~ **de finale**, quarter-final. ~ **d'heure**, quarter of an hour.

quartier /kartje/ *n.m.* neighbourhood, district; (*de lune, bœuf*) quarter; (*de fruit*) segment. ~s, (*mil.*) quarters. **de ~, du ~**, local. ~ **général**, headquarters. **avoir ~ libre**, be free.

quartz /kwarts/ *n.m.* quartz.

quasi- /kazi/ *préf.* quasi-.

quasiment /kazimɑ̃/ *adv.* almost.

quatorz|e /katɔrz/ *a. & n.m.* fourteen. ~ième *a. & n.m./f.* fourteenth.

quatre /katr(ə)/ *a. & n.m.* four. ~-vingt(s) *a. & n.m.* eighty. ~-vingt-dix *a. & n.m.* ninety.

quatrième /katrijɛm/ *a. & n.m./f.* fourth. ~ment *adv.* fourthly.

quatuor /kwatɥɔr/ *n.m.* quartet.

que, qu'* /kə, k/ *conj.* that; (*comparaison*) than. **qu'il vienne**, let him come. **qu'il vienne ou non**, whether he comes or not. **ne faire ~ demander**/*etc.*, only ask/*etc.* ● *adv.* (**ce**) ~ **tu es bête, qu'est-ce ~ tu es bête**, how silly you are. ~ **de**, what a lot of. ● *pron. rel.* (*personne*) that, whom; (*chose*) that, which; (*temps, moment*) when; (*interrogatif*) what. **un jour**/*etc.* ~, one day/*etc.* when. ~ **faites-vous?, qu'est-ce ~ vous faites?**, what are you doing?

Québec /kebɛk/ *n.m.* Quebec.

quel, ~le /kɛl/ *a.* what; (*interrogatif*) which, what; (*qui*) who. ● *pron.*

which. **~ dommage,** what a pity. **~ qu'il soit,** (*chose*) whatever *ou* whichever it may be; (*personne*) whoever he may be.

quelconque /kɛlkɔ̃k/ *a.* any, some; (*banal*) ordinary; (*médiocre*) poor.

quelque /kɛlkə/ *a.* some. **~s,** a few, some. ● *adv.* (*environ*) some. **et ~,** (*fam.*) and a bit. **~ chose,** something; (*interrogation*) anything. **~ part,** somewhere. **~ peu,** somewhat.

quelquefois /kɛlkəfwa/ *adv.* sometimes.

quelques|-uns, ~-unes /kɛlkəzœ̃, -yn/ *pron.* some, a few.

quelqu'un /kɛlkœ̃/ *pron.* someone, somebody; (*interrogation*) anyone, anybody.

quémander /kemɑ̃de/ *v.t.* beg for.

qu'en-dira-t-on /kɑ̃diratɔ̃/ *n.m. invar.* **le ~,** gossip.

querell|e /kərɛl/ *n.f.* quarrel. **~eur, ~euse** *a.* quarrelsome.

quereller (se) /(sə)kərele/ *v. pr.* quarrel.

question /kɛstjɔ̃/ *n.f.* question; (*affaire*) matter, question. **en ~,** in question; (*en jeu*) at stake. **il est ~ de,** (*cela concerne*) it is about; (*on parle de*) there is talk of. **il n'en est pas ~,** it is out of the question. **~ner** /-jɔne/ *v.t.* question.

questionnaire /kɛstjɔnɛr/ *n.m.* questionnaire.

quêt|e /kɛt/ *n.f.* (*relig.*) collection. **en ~e de,** in search of. **~er** /kete/ *v.i.* collect money; *v.t.* seek.

quetsche /kwɛtʃ/ *n.f.* (sort of dark red) plum.

queue /kø/ *n.f.* tail; (*de poêle*) handle; (*de fruit*) stalk; (*de fleur*) stem; (*file*) queue; (*file: Amer.*) line; (*de train*) rear. **faire la ~,** queue (up); (*Amer.*) line up. **~ de cheval,** pony-tail.

qui /ki/ *pron. rel.* (*personne*) who; (*chose*) which, that; (*interrogatif*) who; (*après prép.*) whom; (*quiconque*) whoever. **à ~ est ce stylo**/*etc.*?, whose pen/*etc.* is this? **qu'est-ce ~?,** what? **~ est-ce qui?,** who? **~ que ce soit,** anyone.

quiche /kiʃ/ *n.f.* quiche.

quiconque /kikɔ̃k/ *pron.* whoever; (*n'importe qui*) anyone.

quiétude /kjetyd/ *n.f.* quiet.

quignon /kiɲɔ̃/ *n.m.* **~ de pain,** chunk of bread.

quille [1] /kij/ *n.f.* (*de bateau*) keel.

quille [2] /kij/ *n.f.* (*jouet*) skittle.

quincaill|ier, ~ière /kɛ̃kaje, -jɛr/ *n.m.,* *f.* hardware dealer. **~erie** *n.f.* hardware; (*magasin*) hardware shop.

quinine /kinin/ *n.f.* quinine.

quinquenn|al (*m. pl.* **~aux**) /kɛ̃kenal, -o/ *a.* five-year.

quint|al (*pl.* **~aux**) /kɛ̃tal, -o/ *n.m.* quintal (= *100 kg.*).

quinte /kɛ̃t/ *n.f.* **~ de toux,** coughing fit.

quintette /kɛ̃tɛt/ *n.m.* quintet.

quintupl|e /kɛ̃typl/ *a.* fivefold. ● *n.m.* quintuple. **~er** *v.t./i.* increase fivefold. **~és, ~ées,** *n.m., f. pl.* quintuplets.

quinzaine /kɛ̃zɛn/ *n.f.* **une ~ (de),** about fifteen.

quinz|e /kɛ̃z/ *a. & n.m.* fifteen. **~e jours,** two weeks. **~ième** *a. & n.m./ f.* fifteenth.

quiproquo /kiprɔko/ *n.m.* misunderstanding.

quittance /kitɑ̃s/ *n.f.* receipt.

quitte /kit/ *a.* quits (**envers,** with). **~ à faire,** even if it means doing.

quitter /kite/ *v.t.* leave; (*vêtement*) take off. **se ~** *v. pr.* part.

quoi /kwa/ *pron.* what; (*après prép.*) which. **de ~ vivre/manger**/*etc.*, (*assez*) enough to live on/to eat/*etc.* **de ~ écrire,** sth. to write with, what is necessary to write with. **~ que,** whatever. **~ que ce soit,** anything.

quoique /kwak(ə)/ *conj.* (al)though.

quolibet /kɔlibɛ/ *n.m.* gibe.

quorum /kɔrɔm/ *n.m.* quorum.

quota /kɔta/ *n.m.* quota.

quote-part (*pl.* **quotes-parts**) /kɔtpar/ *n.f.* share.

quotidien, ~ne /kɔtidjɛ̃, -jɛn/ *a.* daily; (*banal*) everyday. ● *n.m.* daily (paper). **~nement** /-jɛnmɑ̃/ *adv.* daily.

quotient /kɔsjɑ̃/ *n.m.* quotient.

R

rab /rab/ *n.m.* (*fam.*) extra. **il y en a en ~,** there's some over.

rabâcher /rabaʃe/ *v.t.* keep repeating.

rabais /rabɛ/ *n.m.* (price) reduction.

rabaisser /rabese/ *v.t.* (*déprécier*) belittle; (*réduire*) reduce.

rabat /raba/ *n.m.* flap. **~-joie** *n.m. invar.* killjoy.

rabattre /rabatr/ *v.t.* pull *ou* put down; (*diminuer*) reduce; (*déduire*) take off. **se ~** *v. pr.* (*se refermer*) close; (*véhicule*) cut in, turn sharply. **se ~ sur**, fall back on.

rabbin /rabɛ̃/ *n.m.* rabbi.

rabibocher /rabiboʃe/ *v.t.* (*fam.*) reconcile.

rabiot /rabjo/ *n.m.* (*fam.*) = **rab.**

râblé /rɑble/ *a.* stocky, sturdy.

rabot /rabo/ *n.m.* plane. **~er** /-ɔte/ *v.t.* plane.

raboteu|x, ~se /rabotø, -z/ *a.* uneven.

rabougri /rabugri/ *a.* stunted.

rabrouer /rabrue/ *v.t.* snub.

racaille /rakɑj/ *n.f.* rabble.

raccommoder /rakɔmɔde/ *v.t.* mend; (*personnes: fam.*) reconcile.

raccompagner /rakɔ̃paɲe/ *v.t.* see *ou* take back (home).

raccord /rakɔr/ *n.m.* link; (*de papier peint*) join. **~ (de peinture)**, touch-up.

raccord|er /rakɔrde/ *v.t.* connect, join. **~ement** *n.m.* connection.

raccourci /rakursi/ *n.m.* short cut. **en ~**, in brief.

raccourcir /rakursir/ *v.t.* shorten. ● *v.i.* get shorter.

raccrocher /rakrɔʃe/ *v.t.* hang back up; (*personne*) grab hold of; (*relier*) connect. **~ (le récepteur)**, hang up. **se ~ à**, cling to; (*se relier à*) be connected to *ou* with.

rac|e /ras/ *n.f.* race; (*animale*) breed. **de ~e**, pure-bred. **~ial** (*m. pl. ~iaux*) *a.* racial.

rachat /raʃa/ *n.m.* buying (back); (*de pécheur*) redemption.

racheter /raʃte/ *v.t.* buy (back); (*davantage*) buy more; (*nouvel objet*) buy another; (*pécheur*) redeem. **se ~** *v. pr.* make amends.

racine /rasin/ *n.f.* root. **~ carrée/ cubique**, square/cube root.

racis|te /rasist/ *a. & n.m./f.* racist. **~me** *n.m.* racism.

racket /rakɛt/ *n.m.* racketeering.

raclée /rɑkle/ *n.f.* (*fam.*) thrashing.

racler /rɑkle/ *v.t.* scrape. **se ~ la gorge**, clear one's throat.

racol|er /rakɔle/ *v.t.* solicit; (*marchand, parti*) drum up. **~age** *n.m.* soliciting.

racontars /rakɔ̃tar/ *n.m. pl.* (*fam.*) gossip, stories.

raconter /rakɔ̃te/ *v.t.* (*histoire*) tell, relate; (*vacances etc.*) tell about. **~ à qn. que**, tell s.o. that, say to s.o. that.

racorni /rakɔrni/ *a.* hard(ened).

radar /radar/ *n.m.* radar.

rade /rad/ *n.f.* harbour. **en ~**, (*personne: fam.*) stranded, behind.

radeau (*pl. ~x*) /rado/ *n.m.* raft.

radiateur /radjatœr/ *n.m.* radiator; (*électrique*) heater.

radiation /radjɑsjɔ̃/ *n.f.* (*énergie*) radiation.

radic|al (*m. pl. ~aux*) /radikal, -o/ *a.* radical. ● *n.m.* (*pl. ~aux*) radical.

radier /radje/ *v.t.* cross off.

radieu|x, ~se /radjø, -z/ *a.* radiant.

radin, ~e /radɛ̃, -in/ *a.* (*fam.*) stingy.

radio /radjo/ *n.f.* radio; (*radiographie*) X-ray.

radioacti|f, ~ve /radjoaktif, -v/ *a.* radioactive. **~vité** *n.f.* radioactivity.

radiocassette /radjokasɛt/ *n.f.* radio-cassette-player.

radiodiffus|er /radjodifyze/ *v.t.* broadcast. **~ion** *n.f.* broadcasting.

radiograph|ie /radjografi/ *n.f.* (*photographie*) X-ray. **~ier** *v.t.* X-ray. **~ique** *a.* X-ray.

radiologue /radjolɔg/ *n.m./f.* radiographer.

radiophonique /radjofɔnik/ *a.* radio.

radis /radi/ *n.m.* radish. **ne pas avoir un ~**, be broke.

radoter /radɔte/ *v.i.* (*fam.*) talk drivel.

radoucir (se) /(sə)radusir/ *v. pr.* calm down; (*temps*) become milder.

rafale /rafal/ *n.f.* (*de vent*) gust; (*tir*) burst of gunfire.

raffermir /rafɛrmir/ *v.t.* strengthen. **se ~** *v. pr.* become stronger.

raffin|é /rafine/ *a.* refined. **~ement** *n.m.* refinement.

raffin|er /rafine/ *v.t.* refine. **~age** *n.m.* refining. **~erie** *n.f.* refinery.

raffoler /rafɔle/ *v.i.* **~ de**, be extremely fond of.

raffut /rafy/ *n.m.* (*fam.*) din.

rafiot /rafjo/ *n.m.* (*fam.*) boat.

rafistoler /rafistɔle/ *v.t.* (*fam.*) patch up.

rafle /rɑfl/ *n.f.* (police) raid.

rafler /rɑfle/ *v.t.* grab, swipe.

rafraîch|ir /rafreʃir/ *v.t.* cool (down); (*raviver*) brighten up; (*personne, mémoire*) refresh. **se ~ir** *v. pr.* (*se laver*) freshen up; (*boire*) refresh o.s.; (*temps*) get cooler. **~issant, ~issante** *a.* refreshing.

rafraîchissement /rafreʃismɑ̃/ *n.m.* (*boisson*) cold drink. **~s,** (*fruits etc.*) refreshments.

ragaillardir /ragajardir/ *v.t.* (*fam.*) buck up. **se ~** *v. pr.* buck up.

rag|e /raʒ/ *n.f.* rage; (*maladie*) rabies. **faire ~e,** rage. **~e de dents,** raging toothache. **~er** *v.i.* rage. **~eur, ~euse** *a.* ill-tempered. **~eant, ~eante** *a.* maddening.

ragot(s) /rago/ *n.m.* (*pl.*) (*fam.*) gossip.

ragoût /ragu/ *n.m.* stew.

raid /rɛd/ *n.m.* (*mil.*) raid; (*sport*) rally.

raid|e /rɛd/ *a.* stiff; (*côte*) steep; (*corde*) tight; (*cheveux*) straight. ● *adv.* (*en pente*) steeply. **~eur** *n.f.* stiffness; steepness.

raidir /redir/ *v.t.,* **se ~** *v. pr.* stiffen; (*position*) harden; (*corde*) tighten.

raie [1] /rɛ/ *n.f.* line; (*bande*) strip; (*de cheveux*) parting.

raie [2] /rɛ/ *n.f.* (*poisson*) skate.

raifort /rɛfɔr/ *n.m.* horse-radish.

rail /raj/ *n.m.* (*barre*) rail. **le ~,** (*transport*) rail.

raill|er /raje/ *v.t.* mock (at). **~erie** *n.f.* mocking remark. **~eur, ~euse** *a.* mocking.

rainure /renyr/ *n.f.* groove.

raisin /rɛzɛ̃/ *n.m.* **~(s),** grapes. **~ sec,** raisin.

raison /rɛzɔ̃/ *n.f.* reason. **à ~ de,** at the rate of. **avec ~,** rightly. **avoir ~,** be right (**de faire,** to do). **avoir ~ de qn.,** get the better of s.o. **donner ~ à,** prove right. **en ~ de,** (*cause*) because of. **~ de plus,** all the more reason. **perdre la ~,** lose one's mind.

raisonnable /rɛzɔnabl/ *a.* reasonable, sensible.

raisonn|er /rɛzɔne/ *v.i.* reason. ● *v.t.* (*personne*) reason with. **~ement** *n.m.* reasoning; (*propositions*) argument.

rajeunir /raʒœnir/ *v.t.* make (look) younger; (*moderniser*) modernize; (*méd.*) rejuvenate. ● *v.i.* look younger.

rajout /raʒu/ *n.m.* addition. **~er** /-te/ *v.t.* add.

rajust|er /raʒyste/ *v.t.* straighten; (*salaires*) (re)adjust. **~ement** *n.m.* (re)adjustment.

râl|e /rɑl/ *n.m.* (*de blessé*) groan. **~er** *v.i.* groan; (*protester: fam.*) moan.

ralent|ir /ralɑ̃tir/ *v.t./i.,* **se ~ir** *v. pr.* slow down. **~i** *a.* slow; *n.m.* (*cinéma*) slow motion. **être** *ou* **tourner au ~i,** tick over, idle.

rall|ier /ralje/ *v.t.* rally; (*rejoindre*) rejoin. **se ~ier** *v. pr.* rally. **se ~ier à,** (*avis*) come over to. **~iement** *n.m.* rallying.

rallonge /ralɔ̃ʒ/ *n.f.* (*de table*) extension. **~ de,** (*supplément de*) extra.

rallonger /ralɔ̃ʒe/ *v.t.* lengthen.

rallumer /ralyme/ *v.t.* light (up) again; (*lampe*) switch on again; (*ranimer: fig.*) revive.

rallye /rali/ *n.m.* rally.

ramadan /ramadɑ̃/ *n.m.* Ramadan.

ramassé /ramɑse/ *a.* squat; (*concis*) concise.

ramass|er /ramɑse/ *v.t.* pick up; (*récolter*) gather; (*recueillir*) collect. **se ~er** *v. pr.* draw o.s. together, curl up. **~age** *n.m.* (*cueillette*) gathering. **~age scolaire,** school bus service.

rambarde /rɑ̃bard/ *n.f.* guardrail.

rame /ram/ *n.f.* (*aviron*) oar; (*train*) train; (*perche*) stake.

rameau (*pl.* **~x**) /ramo/ *n.m.* branch.

ramener /ramne/ *v.t.* bring back. **~ à,** (*réduire à*) reduce to. **se ~** *v. pr.* (*fam.*) turn up. **se ~ à,** (*problème*) come down to.

ram|er /rame/ *v.i.* row. **~eur, ~euse** *n.m., f.* rower.

ramif|ier (se) /(sə)ramifje/ *v. pr.* ramify. **~ication** *n.f.* ramification.

ramollir /ramɔlir/ *v.t.,* **se ~** *v. pr.* soften.

ramon|er /ramɔne/ *v.t.* sweep. **~eur** *n.m.* (chimney-)sweep.

rampe /rɑ̃p/ *n.f.* banisters; (*pente*) ramp. **~ de lancement,** launching pad.

ramper /rɑ̃pe/ *v.i.* crawl.

rancard /rɑ̃kar/ *n.m.* (*fam.*) appointment.

rancart /rɑ̃kar/ *n.m.* **mettre** *ou* **jeter au ~,** (*fam.*) scrap.

ranc|e /rɑ̃s/ *a.* rancid. **~ir** *v.i.* go *ou* turn rancid.

rancœur /rɑ̃kœr/ *n.f.* resentment.

rançon /rɑ̃sɔ̃/ *n.f.* ransom. **~ner** /-ɔne/ *v.t.* hold to ransom.

rancun|e /rɑ̃kyn/ *n.f.* grudge. **sans ~!,** no hard feelings. **~ier, ~ière** *a.* vindictive.

randonnée /rɑ̃dɔne/ *n.f.* walk; (*en auto*, *vélo*) ride.

rang /rɑ̃/ *n.m.* row; (*hiérarchie*, *condition*) rank. **se mettre en ~**, line up. **au premier ~**, in the first row; (*fig.*) at the forefront. **de second ~**, (*péj.*) second-rate.

rangée /rɑ̃ʒe/ *n.f.* row.

rang|er /rɑ̃ʒe/ *v.t.* put away; (*chambre etc.*) tidy (up); (*disposer*) place; (*véhicule*) park. **se ~er** *v. pr.* (*véhicule*) park; (*s'écarter*) stand aside; (*s'assagir*) settle down. **se ~er à**, (*avis*) accept. **~ement** *n.m.* (*de chambre*) tidying (up); (*espace*) storage space.

ranimer /ranime/ *v.t.*, **se ~** *v. pr.* revive.

rapace¹ /rapas/ *n.m.* bird of prey.

rapace² /rapas/ *a.* grasping.

rapatr|ier /rapatrije/ *v.t.* repatriate. **~iement** *n.m.* repatriation.

râp|e /rɑp/ *n.f.* (*culin.*) grater; (*lime*) rasp. **~er** *v.t.* grate; (*bois*) rasp.

râpé /rɑpe/ *a.* threadbare. **c'est ~!**, (*fam.*) that's right out!

rapetisser /raptise/ *v.t.* make smaller. ● *v.i.* get smaller.

râpeu|x, ~se /rɑpø, -z/ *a.* rough.

rapid|e /rapid/ *a.* fast, rapid. ● *n.m.* (*train*) express (train); (*cours d'eau*) rapids *pl.* **~ement** *adv.* fast, rapidly. **~ité** *n.f.* speed.

rapiécer /rapjese/ *v.t.* patch.

rappel /rapɛl/ *n.m.* recall; (*deuxième avis*) reminder; (*de salaire*) back pay; (*méd.*) booster.

rappeler /raple/ *v.t.* call back; (*diplomate*, *réserviste*) recall; (*évoquer*) remind, recall. **~ qch. à qn.**, (*redire*) remind s.o. of sth. **se ~** *v. pr.* remember, recall.

rapport /rapɔr/ *n.m.* connection; (*compte rendu*) report; (*profit*) yield. **~s**, (*relations*) relations. **en ~ avec**, (*accord*) in keeping with. **mettre/se mettre en ~ avec**, put/get in touch with. **par ~ à**, in relation to. **~s (sexuels)**, intercourse.

rapport|er /rapɔrte/ *v.t.* bring back; (*profit*) bring in; (*dire*, *répéter*) report. ● *v.i.* (*comm.*) bring in a good return; (*mouchard*: *fam.*) tell. **se ~er à**, relate to. **s'en ~er à**, rely on. **~eur, ~euse** *n.m., f.* (*mouchard*) tell-tale; *n.m.* (*instrument*) protractor.

rapproch|er /raprɔʃe/ *v.t.* bring closer (**de**, to); (*réconcilier*) bring together; (*comparer*) compare. **se ~er** *v. pr.* get near *ou* come closer (**de**, to); (*personnes*, *pays*) come together; (*s'apparenter*) be close (**de**, to). **~é** *a.* close. **~ement** *n.m.* reconciliation; (*rapport*) connection; (*comparaison*) parallel.

rapt /rapt/ *n.m.* abduction.

raquette /rakɛt/ *n.f.* (*de tennis*) racket; (*de ping-pong*) bat.

rare /rar/ *a.* rare; (*insuffisant*) scarce. **~ment** *adv.* rarely, seldom. **~té** *n.f.* rarity; scarcity; (*objet*) rarity.

raréfier (se) /(sə)rarefje/ *v. pr.* (*nourriture etc.*) become scarce.

ras, ~e /rɑ, rɑz/ *a.* (*herbe*, *poil*) short. **à ~ de**, very close to. **en avoir ~ le bol**, (*fam.*) be really fed up. **~e campagne**, open country. **coupé à ~**, cut short. **à ~ bord**, to the brim. **pull ~ du cou**, round-neck pull-over. **~-le-bol** *n.m.* (*fam.*) anger.

ras|er /rɑze/ *v.t.* shave; (*cheveux*, *barbe*) shave off; (*frôler*) skim; (*abattre*) raze; (*ennuyer*: *fam.*) bore. **se ~er** *v. pr.* shave. **~age** *n.m.* shaving. **~eur, ~euse** *n.m., f.* (*fam.*) bore.

rasoir /rɑzwar/ *n.m.* razor.

rassas|ier /rasazje/ *v.t.* satisfy. **être ~ié de**, have had enough of.

rassembl|er /rasɑ̃ble/ *v.t.* gather; (*courage*) muster. **se ~er** *v. pr.* gather. **~ement** *n.m.* gathering.

rasseoir (se) /(sə)raswar/ *v. pr.* sit down again.

rass|is, ~ise *ou* **~ie** /rasi, -z/ *a.* (*pain*) stale.

rassurer /rasyre/ *v.t.* reassure.

rat /ra/ *n.m.* rat.

ratatiner (se) /(sə)ratatine/ *v. pr.* shrivel up.

rate /rat/ *n.f.* spleen.

râteau (*pl.* **~x**) /rɑto/ *n.m.* rake.

râtelier /rɑtəlje/ *n.m.* (*stable-*)rack; (*fam.*) dentures.

rat|er /rate/ *v.t./i.* miss; (*gâcher*) spoil; (*échouer*) fail. **c'est ~é**, that's right out. **~é, ~ée** *n.m., f.* (*personne*) failure. **avoir des ~és**, (*auto.*) backfire.

ratif|ier /ratifje/ *v.t.* ratify. **~ication** *n.f.* ratification.

ratio /rasjo/ *n.m.* ratio.

ration /rasjɔ̃/ *n.f.* ration.

rationaliser /rasjɔnalize/ *v.t.* rationalize.

rationnel, ~le /rasjɔnɛl/ *a.* rational.

rationn|er /rasjɔne/ *v.t.* ration. **~ement** *n.m.* rationing.

ratisser /ratise/ *v.t.* rake; (*fouiller*) comb.

rattacher /rataʃe/ *v.t.* tie up again; (*relier*) link; (*incorporer*) join.

rattrapage /ratrapaʒ/ *n.m.* **~ scolaire,** remedial classes.

rattraper /ratrape/ *v.t.* catch; (*rejoindre*) catch up with; (*retard, erreur*) make up for. **se ~** *v. pr.* catch up; (*se dédommager*) make up for it. **se ~ à,** catch hold of.

ratur|e /ratyr/ *n.f.* deletion. **~er** *v.t.* delete.

rauque /rok/ *a.* raucous, harsh.

ravager /ravaʒe/ *v.t.* devastate, ravage.

ravages /ravaʒ/ *n.m. pl.* **faire des ~,** wreak havoc.

raval|er /ravale/ *v.t.* (*façade etc.*) clean; (*humilier*) lower (**à,** down to). **~ement** *n.m.* cleaning.

ravi /ravi/ *a.* delighted (**que,** that).

ravier /ravje/ *n.m.* hors-d'œuvre dish.

ravigoter /ravigɔte/ *v.t.* (*fam.*) buck up.

ravin /ravɛ̃/ *n.m.* ravine.

ravioli /ravjɔli/ *n.m. pl.* ravioli.

ravir /ravir/ *v.t.* delight. **~ à qn.,** (*enlever*) rob s.o. of.

raviser (se) /(sə)ravize/ *v. pr.* change one's mind.

ravissant, ~e /ravisã, -t/ *a.* beautiful.

ravisseu|r, ~se /ravisœr, -øz/ *n.m., f.* kidnapper.

ravitaill|er /ravitaje/ *v.t.* provide with supplies; (*avion*) refuel. **se ~er** *v. pr.* stock up. **~ement** *n.m.* provision of supplies (**de,** to), refuelling; (*denrées*) supplies.

raviver /ravive/ *v.t.* revive.

rayé /reje/ *a.* striped.

rayer /reje/ *v.t.* scratch; (*biffer*) cross out.

rayon /rejɔ̃/ *n.m.* ray; (*planche*) shelf; (*de magasin*) department; (*de roue*) spoke; (*de cercle*) radius. **~ d'action,** range. **~ de miel,** honeycomb. **~ X,** X-ray. **en connaître un ~,** (*fam.*) know one's stuff.

rayonn|er /rejɔne/ *v.i.* radiate; (*de joie*) beam; (*se déplacer*) tour around (*from a central point*). **~ement** *n.m.* (*éclat*) radiance; (*in-*

fluence) influence; (*radiations*) radiation.

rayure /rejyr/ *n.f.* scratch; (*dessin*) stripe. **à ~s,** striped.

raz-de-marée /radmare/ *n.m. invar.* tidal wave. **~ électoral,** landslide.

re- /rə/ *préf.* re-.

ré- /re/ *préf.* re-.

réacteur /reaktœr/ *n.m.* jet engine; (*nucléaire*) reactor.

réaction /reaksjɔ̃/ *n.f.* reaction. **~ en chaîne,** chain reaction. **~naire** /-jɔnɛr/ *a. & n.m./f.* reactionary.

réadapter /readapte/ *v.t.,* **se ~** *v. pr.* readjust (**à,** to).

réaffirmer /reafirme/ *v.t.* reaffirm.

réagir /reaʒir/ *v.i.* react.

réalis|er /realize/ *v.t.* carry out; (*effort, bénéfice, achat*) make; (*rêve*) fulfil; (*film*) produce, direct; (*capital*) realize; (*se rendre compte de*) realize. **se ~er** *v. pr.* materialize. **~ateur, ~atrice** *n.m., f.* (*cinéma*) director; (*TV*) producer. **~ation** *n.f.* realization; (*œuvre*) achievement.

réalis|te /realist/ *a.* realistic. ● *n.m./f.* realist. **~me** *n.m.* realism.

réalité /realite/ *n.f.* reality.

réanim|er /reanime/ *v.t.* resuscitate. **~ation** *n.f.* resuscitation. **service de ~ation,** intensive care.

réapparaître /reaparetr/ *v.i.* reappear.

réarm|er (se) /(sə)rearme/ *v. pr.* rearm. **~ement** *n.m.* rearmament.

rébarbati|f, ~ve /rebarbatif, -v/ *a.* forbidding, off-putting.

rebâtir /rəbatir/ *v.t.* rebuild.

rebelle /rəbɛl/ *a.* rebellious; (*soldat*) rebel. ● *n.m./f.* rebel.

rebeller (se) /(sə)rəbele/ *v. pr.* rebel, hit back defiantly.

rébellion /rebeljɔ̃/ *n.f.* rebellion.

rebiffer (se) /(sə)rəbife/ *v. pr.* (*fam.*) rebel.

rebond /rəbɔ̃/ *n.m.* bounce; (*par ricochet*) rebound. **~ir** /-ɔ̃dir/ *v.i.* bounce; rebound.

rebondi /rəbɔ̃di/ *a.* chubby.

rebondissement /rəbɔ̃dismã/ *n.m.* (new) development.

rebord /rəbɔr/ *n.m.* edge. **~ de la fenêtre,** window-ledge.

rebours (à) /(a)rəbur/ *adv.* the wrong way.

rebrousse-poil (à) /(a)rəbruspwal/ *adv.* (*fig.*) **prendre qn. ~,** rub s.o. up the wrong way.

rebrousser /rəbruse/ v.t. ~ chemin, turn back.

rebuffade /rəbyfad/ n.f. rebuff.

rébus /rebys/ n.m. rebus.

rebut /rəby/ n.m. **mettre** ou **jeter au ~,** scrap.

rebut|er /rəbyte/ v.t. put off. **~ant, ~ante** a. off-putting.

récalcitrant, ~e /rekalsitrɑ̃, -t/ a. stubborn.

recal|er /rəkale/ v.t. (fam.) fail. **se faire ~er** ou **être ~é,** fail.

récapitul|er /rekapityle/ v.t./i. recapitulate. **~ation** n.f. recapitulation.

recel /rəsɛl/ n.m. receiving. **~er** /rəs(ə)le/ v.t. (objet volé) receive; (cacher) conceal.

récemment /resamɑ̃/ adv. recently.

recens|er /rəsɑ̃se/ v.t. (population) take a census of; (objets) list. **~ement** n.m. census; list.

récent, ~e /resɑ̃, -t/ a. recent.

récépissé /resepise/ n.m. receipt.

récepteur /resɛptœr/ n.m. receiver.

récepti|f, ~ve /resɛptif, -v/ a. receptive.

réception /resɛpsjɔ̃/ n.f. reception. **~ de,** (lettre etc.) receipt of. **~niste** /-jɔnist/ n.m./f. receptionist.

récession /resesjɔ̃/ n.f. recession.

recette /rəsɛt/ n.f. (culin.) recipe; (argent) takings. **~s,** (comm.) receipts.

receveu|r, ~se /rəsvœr, -øz/ n.m., f. (des impôts) tax collector.

recevoir† /rəsvwar/ v.t. receive; (client, malade) see; (obtenir) get, receive. **être reçu (à),** pass. ● v.i. (médecin) receive patients. **se ~** v. pr. (tomber) land.

rechange (de) /(də)rəʃɑ̃ʒ/ a. (roue, vêtements, etc.) spare; (solution etc.) alternative.

réchapper /reʃape/ v.i. ~ **de** ou **à,** come through, survive.

recharg|e /rəʃarʒ/ n.f. (de stylo) refill. **~er** v.t. refill; (batterie) recharge.

réchaud /reʃo/ n.m. stove.

réchauff|er /reʃofe/ v.t. warm up. **se ~er** v. pr. warm o.s. up; (temps) get warmer. **~ement** n.m. (de température) rise (de, in).

rêche /rɛʃ/ a. rough.

recherche /rəʃɛrʃ/ n.f. search (de, for); (raffinement) elegance. **~(s),** (univ.) research. **~s,** (enquête) investigations.

recherch|er /rəʃɛrʃe/ v.t. search for. **~é** a. in great demand; (élégant) elegant. **~é pour meurtre,** wanted for murder.

rechigner /rəʃiɲe/ v.i. ~ **à,** balk at.

rechut|e /rəʃyt/ n.f. (méd.) relapse. **~er** v.i. relapse.

récidiv|e /residiv/ n.f. second offence. **~er** v.i. commit a second offence.

récif /resif/ n.m. reef.

récipient /resipjɑ̃/ n.m. container.

réciproque /resiprɔk/ a. mutual, reciprocal. **~ment** adv. each other; (inversement) conversely.

récit /resi/ n.m. (compte rendu) account, story; (histoire) story.

récital (pl. **~s**) /resital/ n.m. recital.

récit|er /resite/ v.t. recite. **~ation** n.f. recitation.

réclame /reklam/ n.f. **faire de la ~,** advertise. **en ~,** on offer.

réclam|er /reklame/ v.t. call for, demand; (revendiquer) claim. ● v.i. complain. **~ation** n.f. complaint.

reclus, ~e /rəkly, -z/ n.m., f. recluse. ● a. cloistered.

réclusion /reklyzjɔ̃/ n.f. imprisonment.

recoin /rəkwɛ̃/ n.m. nook.

récolt|e /rekɔlt/ n.f. (action) harvest; (produits) crop, harvest; (fig.) crop. **~er** v.t. harvest, gather; (fig.) collect.

recommand|er /rəkɔmɑ̃de/ v.t. recommend; (lettre) register. **envoyer en ~é,** send registered. **~ation** n.f. recommendation.

recommencer /rəkɔmɑ̃se/ v.t./i. (reprendre) begin ou start again; (refaire) repeat. **ne recommence pas,** don't do it again.

récompens|e /rekɔ̃pɑ̃s/ n.f. reward; (prix) award. **~er** v.t. reward (de, for).

réconcil|ier /rekɔ̃silje/ v.t. reconcile. **se ~ier** v. pr. become reconciled (avec, with). **~iation** n.f. reconciliation.

reconduire† /rəkɔ̃dɥir/ v.t. see home; (à la porte) show out; (renouveler) renew.

réconfort /rekɔ̃fɔr/ n.m. comfort. **~er** /-te/ v.t. comfort.

reconnaissable /rəkɔnɛsabl/ a. recognizable.

reconnaissan|t, ~te /rəkɔnɛsɑ̃, -t/ a. grateful (de, for). **~ce** n.f. gratitude; (fait de reconnaître) recognition; (mil.) reconnaissance.

reconnaître† /rəkɔnɛtr/ *v.t.* recognize; (*admettre*) admit (**que,** that); (*mil.*) reconnoitre; (*enfant, tort*) acknowledge.

reconstituant /rəkɔ̃stituɑ̃/ *n.m.* tonic.

reconstituer /rəkɔ̃stitɥe/ *v.t.* reconstitute; (*crime*) reconstruct.

reconstr|uire† /rəkɔ̃strɥir/ *v.t.* rebuild. **~uction** *n.f.* rebuilding.

reconversion /rəkɔ̃vɛrsjɔ̃/ *n.f.* (*de main-d'œuvre*) redeployment.

recopier /rəkɔpje/ *v.t.* copy out.

record /rəkɔr/ *n.m. & a. invar.* record.

recoupe|r /rəkupe/ *v.t.* confirm. **se ~** *v. pr.* check, tally, match up. **par ~ment,** by making connections.

recourbé /rəkurbe/ *a.* curved; (*nez*) hooked.

recourir /rəkurir/ *v.i.* **~ à,** resort to.

recours /rəkur/ *n.m.* resort. **avoir ~ à,** have recourse to, resort to.

recouvrer /rəkuvre/ *v.t.* recover.

recouvrir† /rəkuvrir/ *v.t.* cover.

récréation /rekreasjɔ̃/ *n.f.* recreation; (*scol.*) playtime.

récrier (se) /(sə)rekrije/ *v. pr.* cry out.

récrimination /rekriminasjɔ̃/ *n.f.* recrimination.

recroqueviller (se) /(sə)rəkrɔkvije/ *v. pr.* curl up.

recrudescence /rəkrydesɑ̃s/ *n.f.* new outbreak.

recrue /rəkry/ *n.f.* recruit.

recrut|er /rəkryte/ *v.t.* recruit. **~ement** *n.m.* recruitment.

rectang|le /rɛktɑ̃gl/ *n.m.* rectangle. **~ulaire** *a.* rectangular.

rectif|ier /rɛktifje/ *v.t.* correct, rectify. **~ication** *n.f.* correction.

recto /rɛkto/ *n.m.* front of the page.

reçu /rəsy/ *voir* recevoir. ● *n.m.* receipt. ● *a.* accepted; (*candidat*) successful.

recueil /rəkœj/ *n.m.* collection.

recueill|ir† /rəkœjir/ *v.t.* collect; (*prendre chez soi*) take in. **se ~ir** *v. pr.* meditate. **~ement** *n.m.* meditation. **~i** *a.* meditative.

recul /rəkyl/ *n.m.* retreat; (*éloignement*) distance; (*déclin*) decline. **(mouvement de) ~,** backward movement. **~ade** *n.f.* retreat.

reculé /rəkyle/ *a.* (*région*) remote.

reculer /rəkyle/ *v.t./i.* move back; (*véhicule*) reverse; (*armée*) retreat; (*diminuer*) decline; (*différer*) postpone. **~ devant,** (*fig.*) shrink from.

reculons (à) /(a)rəkylɔ̃/ *adv.* backwards.

récupér|er /rekypere/ *v.t./i.* recover; (*vieux objets*) salvage. **~ation** *n.f.* recovery; salvage.

récurer /rekyre/ *v.t.* scour. **poudre à ~,** scouring powder.

récuser /rekyze/ *v.t.* challenge. **se ~** *v. pr.* state that one is not qualified to judge.

recycl|er /rəsikle/ *v.t.* (*personne*) retrain; (*chose*) recycle. **se ~er** *v. pr.* retrain. **~age** *n.m.* retraining; recycling.

rédac|teur, ~trice /redaktœr, -tris/ *n.m., f.* writer, editor. **le ~teur en chef,** the editor (in chief).

rédaction /redaksjɔ̃/ *n.f.* writing; (*scol.*) composition; (*personnel*) editorial staff.

reddition /redisjɔ̃/ *n.f.* surrender.

redemander /rədmɑ̃de/ *v.t.* ask again for; ask for more of.

redevable /rədvabl/ *a.* **être ~ à qn. de,** (*argent*) owe sb; (*fig.*) be indebted to s.o. for.

redevance /rədvɑ̃s/ *n.f.* (*de télévision*) licence fee.

rédiger /rediʒe/ *v.t.* write; (*contrat*) draw up.

redire† /rədir/ *v.t.* repeat. **avoir** *ou* **trouver à ~ à,** find fault with.

redondant, ~e /rədɔ̃dɑ̃, -t/ *a.* superfluous.

redonner /rədɔne/ *v.t.* give back; (*davantage*) give more.

redoubl|er /rəduble/ *v.t./i.* increase; (*classe: scol.*) repeat. **~er de prudence/***etc.*, be more careful/*etc.* **~ement** *n.m.* (*accroissement*) increase (**de,** in).

redout|er /rədute/ *v.t.* dread. **~able** *a.* formidable.

redoux /rədu/ *n.m.* milder weather.

redress|er /rədrese/ *v.t.* straighten (out *ou* up); (*situation*) right, redress. **se ~er** *v. pr.* (*personne*) straighten (o.s.) up; (*se remettre debout*) stand up; (*pays, économie*) recover. **~ement** /rədrɛsmɑ̃/ *n.m.* (*relèvement*) recovery.

réduction /redyksjɔ̃/ *n.f.* reduction.

réd|uire† /redɥir/ *v.t.* reduce (**à,** to). **se ~ à,** (*revenir à*) come down to.

réduit¹, **~e** /redɥi, -t/ *a.* (*objet*) small-scale; (*limité*) limited.

réduit² /redɥi/ *n.m.* recess.

réédu|quer /reedyke/ v.t. (personne) rehabilitate; (membre) re-educate. **~cation** n.f. rehabilitation; re-education.

réel, ~le /reɛl/ a. real. ● n.m. reality. **~lement** adv. really.

réexpédier /reɛkspedje/ v.t. forward; (retourner) send back.

refaire† /rəfɛr/ v.t. do again; (erreur, voyage) make again; (réparer) do up, redo.

réfection /refɛksjɔ̃/ n.f. repair.

réfectoire /refɛktwar/ n.m. refectory.

référence /referãs/ n.f. reference.

référendum /referɛ̃dɔm/ n.m. referendum.

référer /refere/ v.i. en ~ à, refer the matter to. **se ~ à,** refer to.

refermer /rəfɛrme/ v.t., **se ~,** v. pr. close (again).

refiler /rəfile/ v.t. (fam.) palm off (à, on).

réfléch|ir /refleʃir/ v.i. think (à, about). ● v.t. reflect. **se ~ir** v. pr. be reflected. **~i** a. (personne) thoughtful; (verbe) reflexive.

refl|et /rəflɛ/ n.m. reflection; (lumière) light. **~éter** /-ete/ v.t. reflect. **se ~éter** v. pr. be reflected.

réflexe /reflɛks/ a. & n.m. reflex.

réflexion /reflɛksjɔ̃/ n.f. reflection; (pensée) thought, reflection. **à la ~,** on second thoughts.

refluer /rəflye/ v.i. flow back; (foule) retreat.

reflux /rəfly/ n.m. (de marée) ebb.

refondre /rəfɔ̃dr/ v.t. recast.

réform|e /refɔrm/ n.f. reform. **~atrice** n.m., f. reformer. **~er** v.t. reform; (soldat) invalid (out of the army).

refoul|er /rəfule/ v.t. (larmes) force back; (désir) repress. **~é** a. repressed. **~ement** n.m. repression.

réfractaire /refraktɛr/ a. **être ~ à,** resist.

refrain /rəfrɛ̃/ n.m. chorus. **le même ~,** the same old story.

refréner /rəfrene/ v.t. curb, check.

réfrigér|er /refriʒere/ v.t. refrigerate. **~ateur** n.m. refrigerator.

refroid|ir /rəfrwadir/ v.t./i. cool (down). **se ~ir** v. pr. (personne, temps) get cold; (ardeur) cool (off). **~issement** n.m. cooling; (rhume) chill.

refuge /rəfyʒ/ n.m. refuge; (chalet) mountain hut.

réfug|ier (se) /(sə)refyʒje/ v. pr. take refuge. **~ié, ~iée** n.m., f. refugee.

refus /rəfy/ n.m. refusal. **ce n'est pas de ~,** I wouldn't say no. **~er** /-ze/ v.t. refuse (de, to); (recaler) fail. **se ~er à,** (évidence etc.) reject.

réfuter /refyte/ v.t. refute.

regagner /rəgaɲe/ v.t. regain; (revenir à) get back to.

regain /rəgɛ̃/ n.m. **~ de,** renewal of.

régal (pl. ~s) /regal/ n.m. treat. **~er** v.t. treat (de, to). **se ~er** v. pr. treat o.s. (de, to).

regard /rəgar/ n.m. (expression, coup d'œil) look; (fixe) stare; (vue, œil) eye. **au ~ de,** in regard to. **en ~ de,** compared with.

regardant, ~e /rəgardã, -t/ a. careful (with money). **peu ~ (sur),** not fussy (about).

regarder /rəgarde/ v.t. look at; (observer) watch; (considérer) consider; (concerner) concern. **~ (fixement),** stare at. ● v.i. look. **~ à,** (qualité etc.) pay attention to. **~ vers,** (maison) face. **se ~** v. pr. (personnes) look at each other.

régates /regat/ n.f. pl. regatta.

régénérer /reʒenere/ v.t. regenerate.

régen|t, ~te /reʒã, -t/ n.m., f. regent. **~ce** n.f. regency.

régenter /reʒãte/ v.t. rule.

reggae /rege/ n.m. reggae.

régie /reʒi/ n.f. (entreprise) public corporation; (radio, TV) control room; (cinéma, théâtre) production.

regimber /rəʒɛ̃be/ v.i. balk.

régime /reʒim/ n.m. (organisation) system; (pol.) regime; (méd.) diet; (de moteur) speed; (de bananes) bunch. **se mettre au ~,** go on a diet.

régiment /reʒimã/ n.m. regiment.

région /reʒjɔ̃/ n.f. region. **~al** (m. pl. ~aux) /-jɔnal, -o/ a. regional.

régir /reʒir/ v.t. govern.

régisseur /reʒisœr/ n.m. (théâtre) stage-manager; (cinéma, TV) assistant director.

registre /rəʒistr/ n.m. register.

réglage /reglaʒ/ n.m. adjustment.

règle /rɛgl/ n.f. rule; (instrument) ruler. **~s,** (de femme) period. **en ~,** in order. **à ~ à calculer,** slide-rule.

réglé /regle/ a. (vie) ordered; (arrangé) settled.

règlement /rɛgləmã/ n.m. regulation; (règles) regulations; (solution, paiement) settlement. **~aire** /-tɛr/ a. (uniforme) regulation.

réglement|er /rɛglǝmãte/ v.t. regulate. **~ation** n.f. regulation.

régler /regle/ v.t. settle; (*machine*) adjust; (*programmer*) set; (*facture*) settle; (*personne*) settle up with; (*papier*) rule. **~ son compte à,** settle a score with.

réglisse /reglis/ n.f. liquorice.

règne /rɛɲ/ n.m. reign; (*végétal, animal, minéral*) kingdom.

régner /reɲe/ v.i. reign.

regorger /rǝgɔrʒe/ v.i. **~ de,** be overflowing with.

regret /rǝgrɛ/ n.m. regret. **à ~,** with regret.

regrett|er /rǝgrete/ v.t. regret; (*personne*) miss. **~able** a. regrettable.

regrouper /rǝgrupe/ v.t., group together. **se ~** v. pr. gather (together).

régulariser /regylarize/ v.t. regularize.

régulation /regylɑsjɔ̃/ n.f. regulation.

régul|ier, ~ière /regylje, -jɛr/ a. regular; (*qualité, vitesse*) steady, even; (*ligne, paysage*) even; (*légal*) legal; (*honnête*) honest. **~arité** n.f. regularity; steadiness; evenness. **~ièrement** adv. regularly; (*d'ordinaire*) normally.

réhabilit|er /reabilite/ n.f. rehabilitate. **~ation** n.f. rehabilitation.

rehausser /rǝose/ v.t. raise; (*faire valoir*) enhance.

rein /rɛ̃/ n.m. kidney. **~s,** (*dos*) back.

réincarnation /reɛ̃karnɑsjɔ̃/ n.f. reincarnation.

reine /rɛn/ n.f. queen. **~-claude** n.f. greengage.

réinsertion /reɛ̃sɛrsjɔ̃/ n.f. reintegration, rehabilitation.

réintégrer /reɛ̃tegre/ v.t. (*lieu*) return to; (*jurid.*) reinstate.

réitérer /reitere/ v.t. repeat.

rejaillir /rǝʒajir/ v.i. **~ sur,** rebound on.

rejet /rǝʒɛ/ n.m. rejection.

rejeter /rǝʒte/ v.t. throw back; (*refuser*) reject; (*vomir*) bring up; (*déverser*) discharge. **~ une faute/etc. sur qn.,** shift the blame for a mistake/*etc.* on to s.o.

rejeton(s) /rǝʒtɔ̃/ n.m. (pl.) (*fam.*) offspring.

rejoindre† /rǝʒwɛ̃dr/ v.t. go back to, rejoin; (*rattraper*) catch up with; (*rencontrer*) join, meet. **se ~** v. pr.

(*personnes*) meet; (*routes*) join, meet.

réjoui /reʒwi/ a. joyful.

réjou|ir /reʒwir/ v.t. delight. **se ~ir** v. pr. be delighted (**de qch.,** at sth.). **~issances** n.f. pl. festivities. **~issant, ~issante** a. cheering.

relâche /rǝlɑʃ/ n.m. (*repos*) respite. **faire ~,** (*théâtre*) close.

relâché /rǝlɑʃe/ a. lax.

relâch|er /rǝlɑʃe/ v.t. slacken; (*personne*) release; (*discipline*) relax. **se ~er** v. pr. slacken. **~ement** n.m. slackening.

relais /rǝlɛ/ n.m. relay. **~ (routier),** roadside café.

relanc|e /rǝlãs/ n.f. boost. **~er** v.t. boost, revive; (*renvoyer*) throw back.

relati|f, ~ve /rǝlatif, -v/ a. relative.

relation /rǝlɑsjɔ̃/ n.f. relation(ship); (*ami*) acquaintance; (*récit*) account. **~s,** relation. **en ~ avec qn.,** in touch with s.o.

relativement /rǝlativmã/ adv. relatively. **~ à,** in relation to.

relativité /rǝlativite/ n.f. relativity.

relax|er (se) /(sǝ)rǝlakse/ v. pr. relax. **~ation** n.f. relaxation. **~e** a. (*fam.*) laid-back.

relayer /rǝleje/ v.t. relieve; (*émission*) relay. **se ~** v. pr. take over from one another.

reléguer /rǝlege/ v.t. relegate.

relent /rǝlã/ n.m. stink.

relève /rǝlɛv/ n.f. relief. **prendre** ou **assurer la ~,** take over (**de,** from).

relevé /rǝlve/ n.m. list; (*de compte*) statement; (*de compteur*) reading. ● a. spicy.

relever /rǝlve/ v.t. pick up; (*personne tombée*) help up; (*remonter*) raise; (*col*) turn up; (*manches*) roll up; (*sauce*) season; (*goût*) bring out; (*compteur*) read; (*défi*) accept; (*relayer*) relieve; (*remarquer, noter*) note; (*rebâtir*) rebuild. ● v.i. **~ de,** (*dépendre de*) be the concern of; (*méd.*) recover from. **se ~** v. pr. (*personne*) get up (again); (*pays, économie*) recover.

relief /rǝljɛf/ n.m. relief. **mettre en ~,** highlight.

relier /rǝlje/ v.t. link (**à,** to); (*ensemble*) link together; (*livre*) bind.

religieu|x, ~se /rǝliʒjø, -z/ a. religious. ● n.m. monk. ● n.f. nun; (*culin.*) choux bun.

religion /rǝliʒjɔ̃/ n.f. religion.

reliquat /rəlika/ *n.m.* residue.

relique /rəlik/ *n.f.* relic.

reliure /rəljyr/ *n.f.* binding.

reluire /rəluir/ *v.i.* shine. **faire ~,** shine.

reluisant, ~e /rəluizã, -t/ *a.* peu *ou* pas **~,** not brilliant.

reman|ier /rəmanje/ *v.t.* revise; (*ministère*) reshuffle. **~iement** *n.m.* revision; reshuffle.

remarier (se) /(sə)rəmarje/ *v. pr.* remarry.

remarquable /rəmarkabl/ *a.* remarkable.

remarque /rəmark/ *n.f.* remark; (*par écrit*) note.

remarquer /rəmarke/ *v.t.* notice; (*dire*) say. **faire ~,** point out (**à,** to). **se faire ~,** attract attention. **remarque(z),** mind you.

remblai /rãblɛ/ *n.m.* embankment.

rembourrer /rãbure/ *v.t.* pad.

rembours|er /rãburse/ *v.t.* repay; (*billet, frais*) refund. **~ement** *n.m.* repayment; refund.

remède /rəmɛd/ *n.m.* remedy; (*médicament*) medicine.

remédier /rəmedje/ *v.i.* ~ **à,** remedy.

remémorer (se) /(sə)rəmemɔre/ *v. pr.* recall.

remerc|ier /rəmɛrsje/ *v.t.* thank (**de,** for); (*licencier*) dismiss. **~iements** *n.m. pl.* thanks.

remettre† /rəmɛtr/ *v.t.* put back; (*vêtement*) put back on; (*donner*) hand (over); (*devoir, démission*) hand in; (*restituer*) give back; (*différer*) put off; (*ajouter*) add; (*se rappeler*) remember; (*peine*) remit. **se ~** *v. pr.* (*guérir*) recover. **se ~ à,** go back to. **se ~ à faire,** start doing again. **s'en ~ à,** leave it to. **~ en cause** *ou* **en question,** call into question.

réminiscence /reminisãs/ *n.f.* reminiscence.

remise[1] /rəmiz/ *n.f.* (*abri*) shed.

remise[2] /rəmiz/ *n.f.* (*rabais*) discount; (*livraison*) delivery; (*ajournement*) postponement. **~ en cause** *ou* **en question,** calling into question.

remiser /rəmize/ *v.t.* put away.

rémission /remisjɔ̃/ *n.f.* remission.

remontant /rəmɔ̃tã/ *n.m.* tonic.

remontée /rəmɔ̃te/ *n.f.* ascent; (*d'eau, de prix*) rise. **~ mécanique,** ski-lift.

remont|er /rəmɔ̃te/ *v.i.* go *ou* come (back) up; (*prix, niveau*) rise (again); (*revenir*) go back. ● *v.t.* (*rue etc.*) go *ou* come (back) up; (*relever*) raise; (*montre*) wind up; (*objet démonté*) put together again; (*personne*) buck up. **~e-pente** *n.m.* ski-lift.

remontoir /rəmɔ̃twar/ *n.m.* winder.

remontrer /rəmɔ̃tre/ *v.t.* show again. **en ~ à qn.,** go one up on s.o.

remords /rəmɔr/ *n.m.* remorse. **avoir un** *ou* **des ~,** feel remorse.

remorqu|e /rəmɔrk/ *n.f.* (*véhicule*) trailer. **en ~,** on tow. **~er** *v.t.* tow.

remorqueur /rəmɔrkœr/ *n.m.* tug.

remous /rəmu/ *n.m.* eddy; (*de bateau*) backwash; (*fig.*) turmoil.

rempart /rãpar/ *n.m.* rampart.

remplaçant, ~e /rãplasã, -t/ *n.m., f.* replacement; (*joueur*) reserve.

remplac|er /rãplase/ *v.t.* replace. **~ement** *n.m.* replacement.

rempli /rãpli/ *a.* full (**de,** of).

rempl|ir /rãplir/ *v.t.* fill (up); (*formulaire*) fill (in *ou* out); (*tâche, condition*) fulfil. **se ~ir** *v. pr.* fill (up). **~issage** *n.m.* filling; (*de texte*) padding.

remporter /rãpɔrte/ *v.t.* take back; (*victoire*) win.

remuant, ~e /rəmɥã, -t/ *a.* restless.

remue-ménage /rəmymenaʒ/ *n.m. invar.* commotion, bustle.

remuer /rəmɥe/ *v.t./i.* move; (*thé, café*) stir; (*gigoter*) fidget. **se ~** *v. pr.* move.

rémunér|er /remynere/ *v.t.* pay. **~ation** *n.f.* payment.

renâcler /rənakle/ *v.i.* snort. **~ à,** balk at, jib at.

ren|aître /rənɛtr/ *v.i.* be reborn; (*sentiment*) be revived. **~aissance** *n.f.* rebirth.

renard /rənar/ *n.m.* fox.

renchérir /rãʃerir/ *v.i.* become dearer. **~ sur,** go one better than.

rencontr|e /rãkɔ̃tr/ *n.f.* meeting; (*de routes*) junction; (*mil.*) encounter; (*match*) match; (*Amer.*) game. **~er** *v.t.* meet; (*heurter*) strike; (*trouver*) find. **se ~er** *v. pr.* meet.

rendement /rãdmã/ *n.m.* yield; (*travail*) output.

rendez-vous /rãdevu/ *n.m.* appointment; (*d'amoureux*) date; (*lieu*) meeting-place. **prendre ~ (avec),** make an appointment (with).

rendormir (se) /(sə)rãdɔrmir/ *v. pr.* go back to sleep.

rendre /rãdr/ *v.t.* give back, return; (*donner en retour*) return; (*monnaie*) give; (*hommage*) pay; (*justice*) dispense; (*jugement*) pronounce. **~ heureux/possible/***etc.*, make happy/possible/ *etc.* ● *v.i.* (*terres*) yield; (*vomir*) vomit. **se ~** *v. pr.* (*capituler*) surrender; (*aller*) go (**à,** to); (*ridicule, utile, etc.*) make o.s. **~ compte de,** report on. **~ des comptes à,** be accountable to. **~ justice à qn.,** do s.o. justice. **~ service (à),** help. **~ visite à,** visit. **se ~ compte de,** realize.

rendu /rãdy/ *a.* **être ~,** (*arrivé*) have arrived.

rêne /rɛn/ *n.f.* rein.

renégat, ~e /renega, -t/ *n.m., f.* renegade.

renfermé /rãfɛrme/ *n.m.* stale smell. **sentir le ~,** smell stale. ● *a.* withdrawn.

renfermer /rãfɛrme/ *v.t.* contain. **se ~ (en soi-même),** withdraw (into o.s.).

renfl|é /rãfle/ *a.* bulging. **~ement** *n.m.* bulge.

renflouer /rãflue/ *v.t.* refloat.

renfoncement /rãfɔ̃smã/ *n.m.* recess.

renforcer /rãfɔrse/ *v.t.* reinforce.

renfort /rãfɔr/ *n.m.* reinforcement. **de ~,** (*armée, personnel*) back-up. **à grand ~ de,** with a great deal of.

renfrogn|er (se) /(sə)rãfrɔɲe/ *v. pr.* scowl. **~é** *a.* surly, sullen.

rengaine /rãgɛn/ *n.f.* (*péj.*) **la même ~,** the same old story.

renier /rənje/ *v.t.* (*personne, pays*) disown, deny; (*foi*) renounce.

renifler /rənifle/ *v.t./i.* sniff.

renne /rɛn/ *n.m.* reindeer.

renom /rənɔ̃/ *n.m.* renown; (*réputation*) reputation. **~mé** /-ɔme/ *a.* famous. **~mée** /-ɔme/ *n.f.* fame; reputation.

renonc|er /rənɔ̃se/ *v.i.* **~er à,** (*habitude, ami, etc.*) give up, renounce. **~er à faire,** give up (all thought of) doing. **~ement** *n.m.,* **~iation** *n.f.* renunciation.

renouer /rənwe/ *v.t.* tie up (again); (*reprendre*) renew. ● *v.i.* **~ avec,** start up again with.

renouveau (*pl.* **~x**) /rənuvo/ *n.m.* revival.

renouvel|er /rənuvle/ *v.t.* renew; (*réitérer*) repeat. **se ~er** *v. pr.* be

renewed; be repeated. **~lement** /-vɛlmã/ *n.m.* renewal.

rénov|er /renɔve/ *v.t.* (*édifice*) renovate; (*institution*) reform. **~ation** *n.f.* renovation; reform.

renseignement /rãsɛɲmã/ *n.m.* **~(s),** information. **(bureau des) ~s,** information desk.

renseigner /rãsɛɲe/ *v.t.* inform, give information to. **se ~** *v. pr.* enquire, make enquiries, find out.

rentab|le /rãtabl/ *a.* profitable. **~ilité** *n.f.* profitability.

rent|e /rãt/ *n.f.* (private) income; (*pension*) pension, annuity. **~ier, ~ière** *n.m., f.* person of private means.

rentrée /rãtre/ *n.f.* return; **la ~ parlementaire,** the reopening of Parliament; (*scol.*) start of the new year.

rentrer /rãtre/ (*aux. être*) *v.i.* go *ou* come back home, return home; (*entrer*) go *ou* come in; (*entrer à nouveau*) go *ou* come back in; (*revenu*) come in; (*élèves*) go back. **~ dans,** (*heurter*) smash into. ● *v.t.* (*aux. avoir*) bring in; (*griffes*) draw in; (*vêtement*) tuck in **~ dans l'ordre,** be back to normal. **~ dans ses frais,** break even.

renverse (à la) /(ala)rãvɛrs/ *adv.* backwards.

renvers|er /rãvɛrse/ *v.t.* knock over *ou* down; (*piéton*) knock down; (*liquide*) upset, spill; (*mettre à l'envers*) turn upside down; (*gouvernement*) overturn; (*inverser*) reverse. **se ~er** *v. pr.* (*véhicule*) overturn; (*verre, vase*) fall over. **~ement** *n.m.* (*pol.*) overthrow.

renv|oi /rãvwa/ *n.m.* return; dismissal; expulsion; postponement; reference; (*rot*) belch. **~oyer†** *v.t.* send back, return; (*employé*) dismiss; (*élève*) expel; (*ajourner*) 1postpone; (*référer*) refer; (*réfléchir*) reflect.

réorganiser /reɔrganize/ *v.t.* reorganize.

réouverture /reuvɛrtyr/ *n.f.* reopening.

repaire /rəpɛr/ *n.m.* den.

répandre /repãdr/ *v.t.* (*liquide*) spill; (*étendre, diffuser*) spread; (*lumière, sang*) shed; (*odeur*) give off. **se ~** *v. pr.* spread; (*liquide*) spill. **se ~ en,** (*injures etc.*) pour forth, launch forth into.

répandu /repɑ̃dy/ *a.* (*courant*) wide-spread.

répar|er /repare/ *v.t.* repair, mend; (*faute*) make amends for; (*remédier à*) put right. **~ateur** *n.m.* repairer. **~ation** *n.f.* repair; (*compensation*) compensation.

repartie /rəparti/ *n.f.* retort. **avoir (le sens) de la ~**, be good at repartee.

repartir† /rəpartir/ *v.i.* start (up) again; (*voyageur*) set off again; (*s'en retourner*) go back.

répart|ir /repartir/ *v.t.* distribute; (*partager*) share out; (*étaler*) spread. **~ition** *n.f.* distribution.

repas /rəpɑ/ *n.m.* meal.

repass|er /rəpase/ *v.i.* come *ou* go back. ● *v.t.* (*linge*) iron; (*leçon*) go over; (*examen*) retake, (*film*) show again. **~age** *n.m.* ironing.

repêcher /rəpeʃe/ *v.t.* fish out; (*candidat*) allow to pass.

repentir /rəpɑ̃tir/ *n.m.* repentance. **se ~** *v. pr.* (*relig.*) repent (**de**, of). **se ~ de**, (*regretter*) regret.

répercu|ter /repɛrkyte/ *v.t.* (*bruit*) echo. **se ~ter** *v. pr.* echo. **se ~ter sur**, have repercussions on. **~ssion** *n.f.* repercussion.

repère /rəpɛr/ *n.m.* mark; (*jalon*) marker; (*fig.*) landmark.

repér|er /rəpere/ *v.t.* locate, spot. **se ~** *v. pr.* find one's bearings.

répert|oire /repɛrtwar/ *n.m.* index; (*artistique*) repertoire. **~orier** *v.t.* index.

répéter /repete/ *v.t.* repeat. ● *v.t./i.* (*théâtre*) rehearse. **se ~** *v. pr.* be repeated; (*personne*) repeat o.s.

répétition /repetisjɔ̃/ *n.f.* repetition; (*théâtre*) rehearsal.

repiquer /rəpike/ *v.t.* (*plante*) plant out.

répit /repi/ *n.m.* rest, respite.

replacer /rəplase/ *v.t.* replace.

repl|i /rəpli/ *n.m.* fold; (*retrait*) withdrawal. **~ier** *v.t.* fold (up); (*ailes, jambes*) tuck in. **se ~ier** *v. pr.* withdraw (**sur soi-même**, into o.s.).

répliqu|e /replik/ *n.f.* reply; (*riposte*) retort; (*discussion*) objection; (*théâtre*) line(s); (*copie*) replica. **~er** *v.t./i.* reply; (*riposter*) retort; (*objecter*) answer back.

répond|ant, ~e /repɔ̃dɑ̃, -t/ *n.m., f.* guarantor. **avoir du ~**, have money behind one.

répondeur /repɔ̃dœr/ *n.m.* answering machine.

répondre /repɔ̃dr/ *v.t.* (*remarque etc.*) reply with. **~ que**, answer *ou* reply that. ● *v.i.* answer, reply; (*être insolent*) answer back; (*réagir*) respond (**à**, to). **~ à**, answer. **~ de**, answer for.

réponse /repɔ̃s/ *n.f.* answer, reply; (*fig.*) response.

report /rəpɔr/ *n.m.* (*transcription*) transfer; (*renvoi*) postponement.

reportage /rəpɔrtaʒ/ *n.m.* report; (*en direct*) commentary, (*par écrit*) article.

reporter[1] /rəpɔrte/ *v.t.* take back; (*ajourner*) put off; (*transcrire*) transfer. **se ~ à**, refer to.

reporter[2] /rəpɔrtɛr/ *n.m.* reporter.

repos /rəpo/ *n.m.* rest; (*paix*) peace; (*tranquillité*) peace and quiet; (*moral*) peace of mind.

repos|er /rəpoze/ *v.t.* put down again; (*délasser*) rest. ● *v.i.* rest (**sur**, on). **se ~** *v. pr.* rest. **se ~ sur**, rely on. **~ant, ~ante** *a.* restful. **laisser ~er**, (*pâte*) leave to stand.

repoussant, ~e /rəpusɑ̃, -t/ *a.* repulsive.

repousser /rəpuse/ *v.t.* push back; (*écarter*) push away; (*dégoûter*) repel; (*décliner*) reject; (*ajourner*) put back. ● *v.i.* grow again.

répréhensible /repreɑ̃sibl/ *a.* blame-worthy.

reprendre† /rəprɑ̃dr/ *v.t.* take back; (*retrouver*) regain; (*souffle*) get back; (*évadé*) recapture; (*recommencer*) resume; (*redire*) repeat; (*modifier*) alter; (*blâmer*) reprimand. **~ du pain/etc.**, take some more bread/ etc. ● *v.i.* (*recommencer*) resume; (*affaires*) pick up. **se ~** *v. pr.* (*se ressaisir*) pull o.s. together; (*se corriger*) correct o.s. **on ne m'y reprendra pas**, I won't be caught out again.

représailles /rəprezaj/ *n.f. pl.* reprisals.

représentati|f, ~ve /rəprezɑ̃tatif, -v/ *a.* representative.

représent|er /rəprezɑ̃te/ *v.t.* represent; (*théâtre*) perform. **se ~er** *v. pr.* (*s'imaginer*) imagine. **~ant, ~ante** *n.m., f.* representative. **~ation** *n.f.* representation; (*théâtre*) performance.

réprimand|e /reprimɑ̃d/ *n.f.* reprimand. **~er** *v.t.* reprimand.

répr|imer /reprime/ *v.t.* (*peuple*) re-press (*sentiment*) suppress. **~ession** *n.f.* repression.

repris /rəpri/ *n.m.* **~ de justice**, ex-convict.

reprise /rəpriz/ *n.f.* resumption; (*théâtre*) revival; (*télévision*) repeat; (*de tissu*) darn, mend; (*essor*) recovery; (*comm.*) part-exchange, trade-in. **à plusieurs ~s**, on several occasions.

repriser /rəprize/ *v.t.* darn, mend.

réprobation /reprɔbasjɔ̃/ *n.f.* condemnation.

reproch|e /rəprɔʃ/ *n.m.* reproach, blame. **~er** *v.t.* **~er qch. à qn.**, reproach *ou* blame s.o. for sth.

reprod|uire† /rəprɔdɥir/ *v.t.* reproduce. **se ~uire** *v. pr.* reproduce; (*arriver*) recur. **~ucteur, ~uctrice** *a.* reproductive. **~uction** *n.f.* reproduction.

réprouver /repruve/ *v.t.* condemn.

reptile /rɛptil/ *n.m.* reptile.

repu /rəpy/ *a.* satiated.

républi|que /repyblik/ *n.f.* republic. **~que populaire**, people's republic. **~cain, ~caine** *a. & n.m.*, *f.* republican.

répudier /repydje/ *v.t.* repudiate.

répugnance /repyɲɑ̃s/ *n.f.* repugnance; (*hésitation*) reluctance.

répugn|er /repyɲe/ *v.i.* **~er à**, be repugnant to. **~er à faire**, be reluctant to do. **~ant, ~ante** *a.* repulsive.

répulsion /repylsjɔ̃/ *n.f.* repulsion.

réputation /repytasjɔ̃/ *n.f.* reputation.

réputé /repyte/ *a.* renowned (**pour**, for). **~ pour être**, reputed to be.

requérir /rəkerir/ *v.t.* require, demand.

requête /rəkɛt/ *n.f.* request; (*jurid.*) petition.

requiem /rekɥijɛm/ *n.m. invar.* requiem.

requin /rəkɛ̃/ *n.m.* shark.

requis, ~e /rəki, -z/ *a.* required.

réquisition /rekizisjɔ̃/ *n.f.* requisition. **~ner** /-jɔne/ *v.t.* requisition.

rescapé, ~e /rɛskape/ *n.m.*, *f.* survivor. ● *a.* surviving.

rescousse /rɛskus/ *n.f.* **à la ~**, to the rescue.

réseau (*pl.* **~x**) /rezo/ *n.m.* network.

réservation /rezɛrvasjɔ̃/ *n.f.* reservation. **bureau de ~**, booking office.

réserve /rezɛrv/ *n.f.* reserve; (*restriction*) reservation, reserve; (*indienne*) reservation; (*entrepôt*) store-room. **en ~**, in reserve. **les ~s**, (*mil.*) the reserves.

réserv|er /rezɛrve/ *v.t.* reserve; (*place*) book, reserve. **se ~er le droit de**, reserve the right to. **~é** *a.* (*personne, place*) reserved.

réserviste /rezɛrvist/ *n.m.* reservist.

réservoir /rezɛrvwar/ *n.m.* tank; (*lac*) reservoir.

résidence /rezidɑ̃s/ *n.f.* residence.

résident, ~e /rezidɑ̃, -t/ *n.m.*, *f.* resident foreigner. **~iel, ~ielle** /-sjɛl/ *a.* residential.

résider /rezide/ *v.i.* reside.

résidu /rezidy/ *n.m.* residue.

résign|er (se) /(sə)reziɲe/ *v. pr.* **se ~er à faire**, resign o.s. to doing. **~ation** *n.f.* resignation.

résilier /rezilje/ *v.t.* terminate.

résille /rezij/ *n.f.* (hair-)net.

résine /rezin/ *n.f.* resin.

résistance /rezistɑ̃s/ *n.f.* resistance; (*fil électrique*) element.

résistant, ~e /rezistɑ̃, -t/ *a.* tough.

résister /reziste/ *v.i.* resist. **~ à**, resist; (*examen, chaleur*) stand up to.

résolu /rezɔly/ *voir* **résoudre**. ● *a.* resolute. **~ à**, resolved to. **~ment** *adv.* resolutely.

résolution /rezɔlysjɔ̃/ *n.f.* (*fermeté*) resolution; (*d'un problème*) solving.

résonance /rezɔnɑ̃s/ *n.f.* resonance.

résonner /rezɔne/ *v.i.* resound.

résor|ber /rezɔrbe/ *v.t.* reduce. **se ~ber** *v. pr.* be reduced. **~ption** *n.f.* reduction.

résoudre† /rezudr/ *v.t.* solve; (*décider*) decide on. **se ~ à**, resolve to.

respect /rɛspɛ/ *n.m.* respect.

respectab|le /rɛspɛktabl/ *a.* respectable. **~ilité** *n.f.* respectability.

respecter /rɛspɛkte/ *v.t.* respect. **faire ~**, (*loi, décision*) enforce.

respecti|f, ~ve /rɛspɛktif, -v/ *a.* respective. **~vement** *adv.* respectively.

respectueu|x, ~se /rɛspɛktɥø, -z/ *a.* respectful.

respir|er /rɛspire/ *v.i.* breathe; (*se reposer*) get one's breath. ● *v.t.* breathe; (*exprimer*) radiate.

~**ation** *n.f.* breathing; (*haleine*) breath. ~**atoire** *a.* breathing.

resplend|ir /rɛsplɑ̃dir/ *v.i.* shine (**de**, with). ~**issant**, ~**issante** *a.* radiant.

responsabilité /rɛspɔ̃sabilite/ *n.f.* responsibility; (*légale*) liability.

responsable /rɛspɔ̃sabl/ *a.* responsible (**de**, for). ~ **de**, (*chargé de*) in charge of. ● *n.m./f.* person in charge; (*coupable*) person responsible.

resquiller /rɛskije/ *v.i.* (*fam.*) get in without paying; (*dans la queue*) jump the queue.

ressaisir (se) /(sə)rəsezir/ *v. pr.* pull o.s. together.

ressasser /rəsase/ *v.t.* keep going over.

ressembl|er /rəsɑ̃ble/ *v.i.* ~**er à**, resemble, look like. **se** ~**er** *v. pr.* look alike. ~**ance** *n.f.* resemblance. ~**ant**, ~**ante** *a.* (*portrait*) true to life; (*pareil*) alike.

ressemeler /rəsəmle/ *v.t.* sole.

ressentiment /rəsɑ̃timɑ̃/ *n.m.* resentment.

ressentir /rəsɑ̃tir/ *v.t.* feel. **se** ~ **de**, feel the effects of.

resserre /rəsɛr/ *n.f.* shed.

resserrer /rəsere/ *v.t.* tighten; (*contracter*) contract. **se** ~ *v. pr.* tighten; contract; (*route etc.*) narrow.

resservir /rəsɛrvir/ *v.i.* come in useful (again).

ressort /rəsɔr/ *n.m.* (*objet*) spring; (*fig.*) energy. **du** ~ **de**, within the jurisdiction *ou* scope of. **en dernier** ~, in the last resort.

ressortir† /rəsɔrtir/ *v.i.* go *ou* come back out; (*se voir*) stand out. **faire** ~, bring out. ~ **de**, (*résulter*) result *ou* emerge from.

ressortissant, ~**e** /rəsɔrtisɑ̃, -t/ *n.m.*, *f.* national.

ressource /rəsurs/ *n.f.* resource. ~**s**, resources.

ressusciter /resysite/ *v.i.* come back to life.

restant, ~**e** /rɛstɑ̃, -t/ *a.* remaining. ● *n.m.* remainder.

restaur|ant /rɛstɔrɑ̃/ *n.m.* restaurant. ~**ateur**, ~**atrice** *n.m.*, *f.* restaurant owner.

restaur|er /rɛstɔre/ *v.t.* restore. **se** ~**er** *v. pr.* eat. ~**ation** *n.f.* restoration; (*hôtellerie*) catering.

reste /rɛst/ *n.m.* rest; (*d'une soustraction*) remainder. ~**s**, remains (**de**, of); (*nourriture*) leftovers. **un** ~ **de**

pain/*etc.*, some left-over bread/*etc.* **au** ~, **du** ~, moreover, besides.

rest|er /rɛste/ *v.i.* (*aux. être*) stay, remain; (*subsister*) be left, remain. **il** ~**e du pain**/*etc.*, there is some bread/*etc.* left (over). **il me** ~**e du pain**, I have some bread left (over). **il me** ~**e à**, it remains for me to. **en** ~**er à**, go no further than. **en** ~**er là**, stop there.

restitu|er /rɛstitɥe/ *v.t.* (*rendre*) return, restore; (*son*) reproduce. ~**ution** *n.f.* return.

restreindre† /rɛstrɛ̃dr/ *v.t.* restrict. **se** ~ *v. pr.* (*dans les dépenses*) cut down.

restricti|f, ~**ve** /rɛstriktif, -v/ *a.* restrictive.

restriction /rɛstriksjɔ̃/ *n.f.* restriction.

résultat /rezylta/ *n.m.* result.

résulter /rezylte/ *v.i.* ~ **de**, result from.

résum|er /rezyme/ *v.t.*, **se** ~**er** *v. pr.* summarize. ~**é** *n.m.* summary. **en** ~**é**, in short.

résurrection /rezyrɛksjɔ̃/ *n.f.* resurrection; (*renouveau*) revival.

rétabl|ir /retablir/ *v.t.* restore; (*personne*) restore to health. **se** ~**ir** *v. pr.* be restored; (*guérir*) recover. ~**issement** *n.m.* restoring; (*méd.*) recovery.

retaper /rətape/ *v.t.* (*maison etc.*) do up. **se** ~ *v. pr.* (*guérir*) get back on one's feet.

retard /rətar/ *n.m.* lateness; (*sur un programme*) delay; (*infériorité*) backwardness. **avoir du** ~, be late; (*montre*) be slow. **en** ~, late; (*retardé*) backward. **en** ~ **sur**, behind. **rattraper** *ou* **combler son** ~, catch up.

retardataire /rətardatɛr/ *n.m./f.* latecomer. ● *a.* (*arrivant*) late.

retardé /rətarde/ *a.* backward.

retardement (à) /(a)rətardəmɑ̃/ *a.* (*bombe etc.*) delayed-action.

retarder /rətarde/ *v.t.* delay; (*sur un programme*) set back; (*montre*) put back. ● *v.i.* (*montre*) be slow; (*fam.*) be out of touch.

retenir† /rətnir/ *v.t.* hold back; (*souffle, attention, prisonnier*) hold; (*eau, chaleur*) retain, hold; (*larmes*) hold back; (*garder*) keep; (*retarder*) detain; (*réserver*) book; (*se rappeler*) remember; (*déduire*) deduct; (*accepter*) accept. **se** ~ *v. pr.* (*se contenir*) restrain o.s. **se ~ à,** hold on to. **se ~ de,** stop o.s. from.

rétention /retɑ̃sjɔ̃/ *n.f.* retention.

retent|ir /rətɑ̃tir/ *v.i.* ring out **(de,** with). **~issant, ~issante** *a.* resounding. **~issement** *n.m.* (*effet, répercussion*) effect.

retenue /rətny/ *n.f.* restraint; (*somme*) deduction; (*scol.*) detention.

réticen|t, ~te /retisɑ̃, -t/ *a.* (*hésitant*) reluctant; (*réservé*) reticent. **~ce** *n.f.* reluctance; reticence.

rétif, ~ve /retif, -v/ *a.* restive, recalcitrant.

rétine /retin/ *n.f.* retina.

retiré /rətire/ *a.* (*vie*) secluded; (*lieu*) remote.

retirer /rətire/ *v.t.* (*sortir*) take out; (*ôter*) take off; (*argent, candidature*) withdraw; (*avantage*) derive. **~ à qn.,** take away from s.o. **se ~** *v. pr.* withdraw, retire.

retombées /rətɔ̃be/ *n.f. pl.* fall-out.

retomber /rətɔ̃be/ *v.i.* fall; (*à nouveau*) fall again. **~ dans,** (*erreur etc.*) fall back into.

rétorquer /retɔrke/ *v.t.* retort.

rétorsion /retɔrsjɔ̃/ *n.f.* **mesures de ~,** retaliation.

retouch|e /rətuʃ/ *n.f.* touch-up; alteration. **~er** *v.t.* touch up; (*vêtement*) alter.

retour /rətur/ *n.m.* return. **être de ~,** be back **(de,** from). **~ en arrière,** flashback. **par ~ du courrier,** by return of post. **en ~,** in return.

retourner /rəturne/ *v.t.* (*aux. avoir*) turn over; (*vêtement*) turn inside out; (*lettre, compliment*) return; (*émouvoir: fam.*) upset. ● *v.i.* (*aux. être*) go back, return. **se ~** *v. pr.* turn round; (*dans son lit*) twist and turn. **s'en ~,** go back. **se ~ contre,** turn against.

retracer /rətrase/ *v.t.* retrace.

rétracter /retrakte/ *v.t.,* **se ~** *v. pr.* retract.

retrait /rətrɛ/ *n.m.* withdrawal; (*des eaux*) ebb, receding. **être (situé) en ~,** be set back.

retraite /rətrɛt/ *n.f.* retirement; (*pension*) (retirement) pension; (*fuite, refuge*) retreat. **mettre à la ~,** pension off. **prendre sa ~,** retire.

retraité, ~e /rətrete/ *a.* retired. ● *n.m., f.* (old-age) pensioner, senior citizen.

retrancher /rətrɑ̃ʃe/ *v.t.* remove; (*soustraire*) deduct. **se ~** *v. pr.* (*mil.*) entrench o.s. **se ~ derrière/dans,** take refuge behind/in.

retransm|ettre /rətrɑ̃smɛtr/ *v.t.* broadcast. **~ission** *n.f.* broadcast.

rétrécir /retresir/ *v.t.* narrow; (*vêtement*) take in. ● *v.i.* (*tissu*) shrink. **se ~,** (*rue*) narrow.

rétrib|uer /retribɥe/ *v.t.* pay. **~ution** *n.f.* payment.

rétroacti|f, ~ve /retrɔaktif, -v/ *a.* retrospective. **augmentation à effet ~f,** backdated pay rise.

rétrograd|e /retrɔgrad/ *a.* retrograde. **~er** *v.i.* (*reculer*) fall back, recede; *v.t.* demote.

rétrospectivement /retrɔspɛktivmɑ̃/ *adv.* in retrospect.

retrousser /rətruse/ *v.t.* pull up.

retrouvailles /rətruvɑj/ *n.f. pl.* reunion.

retrouver /rətruve/ *v.t.* find (again); (*rejoindre*) meet (again); (*forces, calme*) regain; (*se rappeler*) remember. **se ~** *v. pr.* find o.s. (back); (*se réunir*) meet (again). **s'y ~,** (*s'orienter, comprendre*) find one's way; (*rentrer dans ses frais*) break even.

rétroviseur /retrɔvizœr/ *n.m.* (*auto.*) (rear-view) mirror.

réunion /reynjɔ̃/ *n.f.* meeting; (*d'objets*) collection.

réunir /reynir/ *v.t.* gather, collect; (*rapprocher*) bring together; (*convoquer*) call together; (*raccorder*) join; (*qualités*) combine. **se ~** *v. pr.* meet.

réussi /reysi/ *a.* successful.

réussir /reysir/ *v.i.* succeed, be successful (**à faire,** in doing). **~ à qn.,** work well for s.o.; (*climat etc.*) agree with s.o. ● *v.t.* make a success of.

réussite /reysit/ *n.f.* success; (*jeu*) patience.

revaloir /rəvalwar/ *v.t.* **je vous revaudrai cela,** (*en mal*) I'll pay you back for this; (*en bien*) I'll repay you some day.

revaloriser /rəvalɔrize/ *v.t.* (*monnaie*) revalue; (*salaires*) raise.

revanche /rəvɑ̃ʃ/ *n.f.* revenge; (*sport*) return *ou* revenge match. **en ~,** on the other hand.

rêvasser /rɛvase/ *v.i.* day-dream.

rêve /rɛv/ *n.m.* dream. **faire un ~,** have a dream.

revêche /rəvɛʃ/ *a.* ill-tempered.

réveil /revɛj/ *n.m.* waking up, (*fig.*) awakening; (*pendule*) alarm-clock.

réveill|er /reveje/ *v.t.*, **se ~er** *v. pr.* wake (up); (*fig.*) awaken. **~é** *a.* awake. **~e-matin** *n.m. invar.* alarm-clock.

réveillon /revɛjɔ̃/ *n.m.* (*Noël*) Christmas Eve; (*nouvel an*) New Year's Eve. **~ner** /-jɔne/ *v.i.* celebrate the *réveillon*.

révél|er /revele/ *v.t.* reveal. **se ~er** *v. pr.* be revealed. **se ~er facile**/*etc.*, prove easy/*etc.* **~ateur, ~atrice** *a.* revealing. ● *n.m.* (*photo*) developer. **~ation** *n.f.* revelation.

revenant /rəvnɑ̃/ *n.m.* ghost.

revendi|quer /rəvɑ̃dike/ *v.t.* claim. **~catif, ~cative** *a.* (*mouvement etc.*) in support of one's claims. **~cation** *n.f.* claim; (*action*) claiming.

revend|re /rəvɑ̃dr/ *v.t.* sell (again). **~eur, ~euse** *n.m.*, *f.* dealer.

revenir† /rəvnir/ *v.i.* (*aux. être*) come back, return (**à**, to). **~à**, (*activité*) go back to; (*se résumer à*) come down to; (*échoir à*) fall to; (*coûter*) cost. **~ de**, (*maladie, surprise*) get over. **~ sur ses pas**, retrace one's steps. **faire ~**, (*culin.*) brown. **ça me revient**, it comes back to me.

revente /rəvɑ̃t/ *n.f.* resale.

revenu /rəvny/ *n.m.* income; (*d'un état*) revenue.

rêver /reve/ *v.t./i.* dream (**à** *ou* **de**, of).

réverbération /reverberasjɔ̃/ *n.f.* reflection, reverberation.

réverbère /reverbɛr/ *n.m.* street lamp.

révérenc|e /reverɑ̃s/ *n.f.* reverence; (*salut d'homme*) bow; (*salut de femme*) curtsy. **~ieux, ~ieuse** *a.* reverent.

révérend, ~e /reverɑ̃, -d/ *a. & n.m.* reverend.

rêverie /revri/ *n.f.* day-dream; (*activité*) day-dreaming.

revers /rəver/ *n.m.* reverse; (*de main*) back; (*d'étoffe*) wrong side; (*de veste*) lapel; (*tennis*) backhand; (*fig.*) set-back.

réversible /reversibl/ *a.* reversible.

revêt|ir /rəvetir/ *v.t.* cover; (*habit*) put on; (*prendre, avoir*) assume. **~ement** /-vɛtmɑ̃/ *n.m.* covering; (*de route*) surface.

rêveu|r, ~se /revœr, -øz/ *a.* dreamy. ● *n.m.*, *f.* dreamer.

revigorer /rəvigɔre/ *v.t.* revive.

revirement /rəvirmɑ̃/ *n.m.* sudden change.

révis|er /revize/ *v.t.* revise; (*véhicule*) overhaul. **~ion** *n.f.* revision; overhaul.

revivre† /rəvivr/ *v.i.* live again. ● *v.t.* relive. **faire ~**, revive.

révocation /revɔkasjɔ̃/ *n.f.* repeal; (*d'un fonctionnaire*) dismissal.

revoir† /rəvwar/ *v.t.* see (again); (*réviser*) revise. **au ~**, goodbye.

révolte /revɔlt/ *n.f.* revolt.

révolt|er /revɔlte/ *v.t.*, **se ~er** *v. pr.* revolt. **~ant, ~ante** *a.* revolting. **~é, ~ée** *n.m.*, *f.* rebel.

révolu /revɔly/ *a.* past.

révolution /revɔlysjɔ̃/ *n.f.* revolution. **~naire** /-jɔnɛr/ *a. & n.m./f.* revolutionary. **~ner** /- jɔne/ *v.t.* revolutionize.

revolver /revɔlvɛr/ *n.m.* revolver, gun.

révoquer /revɔke/ *v.t.* repeal; (*fonctionnaire*) dismiss.

revue /rəvy/ *n.f.* (*examen, défilé*) review; (*magazine*) magazine; (*spectacle*) variety show.

rez-de-chaussée /redʃose/ *n.m. invar.* ground floor; (*Amer.*) first floor.

RF *abrév.* (*République Française*) French Republic.

rhabiller (se) /(sə)rabije/ *v. pr.* get dressed (again), dress (again).

rhapsodie /rapsɔdi/ *n.f.* rhapsody.

rhétorique /retɔrik/ *n.f.* rhetoric. ● *a.* rhetorical.

rhinocéros /rinɔserɔs/ *n.m.* rhinoceros.

rhubarbe /rybarb/ *n.f.* rhubarb.

rhum /rɔm/ *n.m.* rum.

rhumatis|me /rymatism/ *n.m.* rheumatism. **~ant, ~ante** /-zɑ̃, -t/ *a.* rheumatic.

rhume /rym/ *n.m.* cold. **~ des foins**, hay fever.

ri /ri/ *voir* rire.

riant, ~e /rjɑ̃, -t/ *a.* cheerful.

ricaner /rikane/ *v.i.* snigger, giggle.

riche /riʃ/ *a.* rich (**en**, in). ● *n.m./f.* rich person. **~ment** *adv.* richly.

richesse /riʃɛs/ *n.f.* wealth; (*de sol, décor*) richness. **~s**, wealth.

ricoch|er /rikɔʃe/ *v.i.* rebound, ricochet. **~et** *n.m.* rebound, ricochet. **par ~er**, indirectly.

rictus /riktys/ *n.m.* grin, grimace.

rid|e /rid/ *n.f.* wrinkle; (*sur l'eau*) ripple. **~er** *v.t.* wrinkle; (*eau*) ripple.

producti|f, ~ve /prɔdyktif, -v/ *a.*
productive. **~vité** *n.f.* productivity.

prod|uire† /prɔdɥir/ *v.t.* produce. **se
~uire** *v. pr.* (*survenir*) happen;
(*acteur*) perform. **~ucteur,
~uctrice** *a.* producing; *n.m.*, *f.*
producer. **~uction** *n.f.* production;
(*produit*) product.

produit /prɔdɥi/ *n.m.* product. **~s,**
(*de la terre*) produce. **~ chimique,**
chemical. **~s alimentaires,** foodstuffs. **~ de consommation,** consumer goods. **~ national brut,** gross
national product.

proéminent, ~e /prɔeminɑ̃, -t/ *a.*
prominent.

prof /prɔf/ *n.m.* (*fam.*) teacher.

profane /prɔfan/ *a.* secular. ● *n.m./
f.* lay person.

profaner /prɔfane/ *v.t.* desecrate.

proférer /prɔfere/ *v.t.* utter.

professer [1] /prɔfese/ *v.t.* (*déclarer*)
profess.

professer [2] /prɔfese/ *v.t./i.* (*enseigner*) teach.

professeur /prɔfesœr/ *n.m.* teacher;
(*univ.*) lecturer; (*avec chaire*) professor.

profession /prɔfesjɔ̃/ *n.f.* occupation;
(*intellectuelle*) profession. **~nel,
~nelle** /-jɔnɛl/ *a.* professional;
(*école*) vocational; *n.m.*, *f.* professional.

professorat /prɔfesɔra/ *n.m.* teaching.

profil /prɔfil/ *n.m.* profile.

profiler (se) /(sə)prɔfile/ *v. pr.* be
outlined.

profit /prɔfi/ *n.m.* profit. **au ~ de,** in
aid of. **~able** /-tabl/ *a.* profitable.

profiter /prɔfite/ *v.i.* **~ à,** benefit. **~
de,** take advantage of.

profond, ~e /prɔfɔ̃, -d/ *a.* deep;
(*sentiment, intérêt*) profound;
(*causes*) underlying. **au plus ~ de,**
in the depths of. **~ément** /-demɑ̃/
adv. deeply; (*différent, triste*) pro-
foundly; (*dormir*) soundly. **~eur**
/-dœr/ *n.f.* depth.

profusion /prɔfyzjɔ̃/ *n.f.* profusion.

progéniture /prɔʒenityr/ *n.f.* offspring.

programmation /prɔgramasjɔ̃/ *n.f.*
programming.

programm|e /prɔgram/ *n.m.* pro-
gramme; (*matières: scol.*) syllabus;
(*informatique*) program. **~e
(d'études),** curriculum. **~er** *v.t.*
(*ordinateur, appareil*) program;

(*émission*) schedule. **~eur, ~euse**
n.m., *f.* computer programmer.

progrès /prɔgrɛ/ *n.m. & n.m. pl.*
progress. **faire des ~,** make progress.

progress|er /prɔgrese/ *v.i.* progress.
~ion /-ɛsjɔ̃/ *n.f.* progression.

progressi|f, ~ve /prɔgresif, -v/ *a.*
progressive. **~vement** *adv.* progressively.

progressiste /prɔgresist/ *a.* progressive.

prohib|er /prɔibe/ *v.t.* prohibit.
~ition *n.f.* prohibition.

prohibiti|f, ~ve /prɔibitif, -v/ *a.*
prohibitive.

proie /prwa/ *n.f.* prey. **en ~ à,**
tormented by.

projecteur /prɔʒɛktœr/ *n.m.* floodlight; (*mil.*) searchlight; (*cinéma*)
projector.

projectile /prɔʒɛktil/ *n.m.* missile.

projection /prɔʒɛksjɔ̃/ *n.f.* projection; (*séance*) show.

projet /prɔʒɛ/ *n.m.* plan; (*ébauche*)
draft. **~ de loi,** bill.

projeter /prɔʒte/ *v.t.* plan (**de,** to);
(*film*) project, show; (*jeter*) hurl,
project.

prolét|aire /prɔletɛr/ *n.m./f.* pro-
letarian. **~ariat** *n.m.* proletariat.
~arien, ~arienne *a.* proletarian.

prolifér|er /prɔlifere/ *v.i.* proliferate.
~ation *n.f.* proliferation.

prolifique /prɔlifik/ *a.* prolific.

prologue /prɔlɔg/ *n.m.* prologue.

prolongation /prɔlɔ̃gasjɔ̃/ *n.f.*
extension. **~s,** (*football*) extra time.

prolong|er /prɔlɔ̃ʒe/ *v.t.* prolong. **se
~er** *v. pr.* continue, extend. **~é** *a.*
prolonged. **~ement** *n.m.* extension.

promenade /prɔmnad/ *n.f.* walk; (*à
bicyclette, à cheval*) ride; (*en auto*)
drive, ride. **faire une ~,** go for a
walk.

promen|er /prɔmne/ *v.t.* take for a
walk. **~er sur qch.,** (*main, regard*)
run over sth. **se ~er** *v. pr.* walk.
(aller) se ~er, go for a walk. **~eur,
~euse** *n.m.*, *f.* walker.

promesse /prɔmɛs/ *n.f.* promise.

promett|re† /prɔmɛtr/ *v.t./i.* prom-
ise. **~re (beaucoup),** be promising.
se ~re de, resolve to. **~eur, ~euse**
a. promising.

promontoire /prɔmɔ̃twar/ *n.m.*
headland.

rideau (*pl.* **~x**) /rido/ *n.m.* curtain; (*métallique*) shutter; (*fig.*) screen. **~ de fer**, (*pol.*) Iron Curtain.

ridicul|e /ridikyl/ *a.* ridiculous. ● *n.m.* absurdity. **le ~e**, ridicule. **~iser** *v.t.* ridicule.

rien /rjɛ̃/ *pron.* **(ne) ~**, nothing. ● *n.m.* trifle. **de ~!**, don't mention it! **~ d'autre/de plus**, nothing else/more. **~ du tout**, nothing at all. **~ que**, just, only. **trois fois ~**, next to nothing. **il n'y est pour ~**, he has nothing to do with it. **en un ~ de temps**, in next to no time. **~ à faire**, it's no good!

rieu|r, **~se** /rjœr, rjøz/ *a.* merry.

rigid|e /riʒid/ *a.* rigid; (*muscle*) stiff. **~ité** *n.f.* rigidity; stiffness.

rIgole /rigɔl/ *n.f.* channel.

rigol|er /rigɔle/ *v.i.* laugh; (*s'amuser*) have some fun; (*plaisanter*) joke. **~ade** *n.f.* fun.

rigolo, **~te** /rigɔlo, -ɔt/ *a.* (*fam.*) funny. ● *n.m.*, *f.* (*fam.*) joker.

rigoureu|x, **~se** /rigurø, -z/ *a.* rigorous; (*hiver*) harsh. **~sement** *adv.* rigorously.

rigueur /rigœr/ *n.f.* rigour. **à la ~**, at a pinch. **être de ~**, be the rule. **tenir ~ à qn. de qch.**, hold sth. against s.o.

rim|e /rim/ *n.f.* rhyme. **~er** *v.i.* rhyme (**avec**, with). **cela ne ~e à rien**, it makes no sense.

rin|cer /rɛ̃se/ *v.t.* rinse. **~çage** *n.m.* rinse; (*action*) rinsing. **~ce-doigts** *n.m. invar.* finger-bowl.

ring /riŋ/ *n.m.* boxing ring.

ripost|e /ripɔst/ *n.f.* retort; (*mil.*) reprisal. **~er** *v.i.* retaliate; *v.t.* retort (**que**, that). **~er à**, (*attaque*) counter; (*insulte etc.*) reply to.

rire† /rir/ *v.i.* laugh (**de**, at); (*plaisanter*) joke; (*s'amuser*) have fun. **c'était pour ~**, it was a joke. ● *n.m.* laugh. **~s, le ~**, laughter.

risée /rize/ *n.f.* **la ~ de**, the laughing-stock of.

risible /rizibl/ *a.* laughable.

risqu|e /risk/ *n.m.* risk. **~é á** risky; (*osé*) daring. **~er** *v.t.* risk. **~er de faire**, stand a good chance of doing. **se ~er à/dans**, venture into/to.

rissoler /risɔle/ *v.t./i.* brown. **(faire) ~**, brown.

ristourne /risturn/ *n.f.* discount.

rite /rit/ *n.m.* rite; (*habitude*) ritual.

rituel, **~le** /rituɛl/ *a.* & *n.m.* ritual.

rivage /rivaʒ/ *n.m.* shore.

riv|al, **~ale** (*m. pl.* **~aux**) /rival, -o/ *n.m.*, *f.* rival. ● *a.* rival. **~aliser** *v.i.* compete (**avec**, with). **~alité** *n.f.* rivalry.

rive /riv/ *n.f.* (*de fleuve*) bank; (*de lac*) shore.

riv|er /rive/ *v.t.* rivet. **~er son clou à qn.**, shut s.o. up. **~et** *n.m.* rivet.

riverain, **~e** /rivrɛ̃, -ɛn/ *a.* riverside. ● *n.m.*, *f.* riverside resident; (*d'une rue*) resident.

rivière /rivjɛr/ *n.f.* river.

rixe /riks/ *n.f.* brawl.

riz /ri/ *n.m.* rice. **~ière** /rizjɛr/ *n.f.* paddy(-field), rice field.

robe /rɔb/ *n.f.* (*de femme*) dress; (*de juge*) robe; (*de cheval*) coat. **~ de chambre**, dressing-gown.

robinet /rɔbinɛ/ *n.m.* tap; (*Amer.*) faucet.

robot /rɔbo/ *n.m.* robot.

robuste /rɔbyst/ *a.* robust. **~sse** /-ɛs/ *n.f.* robustness.

roc /rɔk/ *n.m.* rock.

rocaill|e /rɔkɑj/ *n.f.* rocky ground; (*de jardin*) rockery. **~eux**, **~euse** *a.* (*terrain*) rocky.

roch|e /rɔʃ/ *n.f.* rock. **~eux**, **~euse** *a.* rocky.

rocher /rɔʃe/ *n.m.* rock.

rock /rɔk/ *n.m.* (*mus.*) rock.

rod|er /rɔde/ *v.t.* (*auto.*) run in; (*auto., Amer.*) break in. **être ~é**, (*personne*) be broken in. **~age** *n.m.* running in; breaking in.

rôd|er /rɔde/ *v.i.* roam; (*suspect*) prowl. **~eur**, **~euse** *n.m.*, *f.* prowler.

rogne /rɔɲ/ *n.f.* (*fam.*) anger.

rogner /rɔɲe/ *v.t.* trim; (*réduire*) cut. **~ sur**, cut down on.

rognon /rɔɲɔ̃/ *n.m.* (*culin.*) kidney.

rognures /rɔɲyr/ *n.f. pl.* scraps.

roi /rwa/ *n.m.* king. **les Rois mages**, the Magi. **la fête des Rois**, Twelfth Night.

roitelet /rwatlɛ/ *n.m.* wren.

rôle /rol/ *n.m.* role, part.

romain, **~e** /rɔmɛ̃, -ɛn/ *a.* & *n.m.*, *f.* Roman. ● *n.f.* (*laitue*) cos.

roman /rɔmɑ̃/ *n.m.* novel; (*fig.*) story; (*genre*) fiction.

romance /rɔmɑ̃s/ *n.f.* sentimental ballad.

romanc|ier, **~ière** /rɔmɑ̃sje, -jɛr/ *n.m.*, *f.* novelist.

romanesque /rɔmanɛsk/ *a.* romantic; (*fantastique*) fantastic. **œuvres ~s**, novels, fiction.

romanichel, ~le /rɔmaniʃɛl/ *n.m.*, *f.* gypsy.

romanti|que /rɔmɑ̃tik/ *a. & n.m./f.* romantic. **~sme** *n.m.* romanticism.

rompre† /rɔ̃pr/ *v.t./i.* break; (*relations*) break off; (*fiancés*) break it off. **se ~** *v. pr.* break.

rompu /rɔ̃py/ *a.* (*exténué*) exhausted.

ronces /rɔ̃s/ *n.f. pl.* brambles.

ronchonner /rɔ̃ʃɔne/ *v.i.* (*fam.*) grumble.

rond, ~e [1] /rɔ̃, rɔ̃d/ *a.* round; (*gras*) plump; (*ivre: fam.*) tight. ● *n.m.* (*cercle*) ring; (*tranche*) slice. **il n'a pas un ~,** (*fam.*) he hasn't got a penny. **en ~,** in a circle. **~ement** /rɔ̃dmɑ̃/ *adv.* briskly; (*franchement*) straight. **~eur** /rɔ̃dœr/ *n.f.* roundness; (*franchise*) frankness; (*embonpoint*) plumpness. **~-point** (*pl.* **~s-points**) *n.m.* roundabout; (*Amer.*) traffic circle.

ronde [2] /rɔ̃d/ *n.f.* round(s); (*de policier*) beat; (*mus.*) semibreve.

rondelet, ~te /rɔ̃dlɛ, -t/ *a.* chubby.

rondelle /rɔ̃dɛl/ *n.f.* (*techn.*) washer; (*tranche*) slice.

rondin /rɔ̃dɛ̃/ *n.m.* log.

ronfl|er /rɔ̃fle/ *v.i.* snore; (*moteur*) hum. **~ement(s)** *n.m.* (*pl.*) snoring; humming.

rong|er /rɔ̃ʒe/ *v.t.* gnaw (at); (*vers, acide*) eat into; (*personne: fig.*) consume. **se ~er les ongles,** bite one's nails. **~eur** *n.m.* rodent.

ronronn|er /rɔ̃rɔne/ *v.i.* purr. **~ement** *n.m.* purr(ing).

roquette /rɔkɛt/ *n.f.* rocket.

rosace /rɔzas/ *n.f.* (*d'église*) rose window.

rosaire /rɔzɛr/ *n.m.* rosary.

rosbif /rɔsbif/ *n.m.* roast beef.

rose /roz/ *n.f.* rose. ● *a.* pink; (*situation, teint*) rosy. ● *n.m.* pink.

rosé /roze/ *a.* pinkish; (*vin*) rosé. ● *n.m.* rosé.

roseau (*pl.* **~x**) /rozo/ *n.m.* reed.

rosée /roze/ *n.f.* dew.

roseraie /rozrɛ/ *n.f.* rose garden.

rosette /rozɛt/ *n.f.* rosette.

rosier /rozje/ *n.m.* rose-bush, rose tree.

rosse /rɔs/ *a.* (*fam.*) nasty.

rosser /rɔse/ *v.t.* thrash.

rossignol /rɔsiɲɔl/ *n.m.* nightingale.

rot /ro/ *n.m.* (*fam.*) burp.

rotati|f, ~ve /rɔtatif, -v/ *a.* rotary.

rotation /rɔtɑsjɔ̃/ *n.f.* rotation.

roter /rɔte/ *v.i.* (*fam.*) burp.

rotin /rɔtɛ̃/ *n.m.* (rattan) cane.

rôt|ir /rotir/ *v.t./i.*, **se ~ir** *v. pr.* roast. **~i** *n.m.* roasting meat; (*cuit*) roast. **~i de porc,** roast pork.

rôtisserie /rotisri/ *n.f.* grill-room.

rôtissoire /rotiswar/ *n.f.* (roasting) spit.

rotule /rɔtyl/ *n.f.* kneecap.

roturi|er, ère /rɔtyrje, -ɛr/ *n.m.*, *f.* commoner.

rouage /rwaʒ/ *n.m.* (*techn.*) (working) part. **~s,** (*d'une organisation*: *fig.*) wheels.

roucouler /rukule/ *v.i.* coo.

roue /ru/ *n.f.* wheel. **~ (dentée),** cog(-wheel). **~ de secours,** spare wheel.

roué /rwe/ *a.* wily, calculating.

rouer /rwe/ *v.t.* **~ de coups,** thrash.

rouet /rwɛ/ *n.m.* spinning-wheel.

rouge /ruʒ/ *a.* red; (*fer*) red-hot. ● *n.m.* red; (*vin*) red wine; (*fard*) rouge. **~ (à lèvres),** lipstick. ● *n.m./f.* (*pol.*) red. **~-gorge** (*pl.* **~s-gorges**) *n.m.* robin.

rougeole /ruʒɔl/ *n.f.* measles.

rougeoyer /ruʒwaje/ *v.i.* glow (red).

rouget /ruʒɛ/ *n.m.* red mullet.

rougeur /ruʒœr/ *n.f.* redness; (*tache*) red blotch; (*gêne, honte*) red face.

rougir /ruʒir/ *v.t./i.* turn red; (*de honte*) blush.

rouill|e /ruj/ *n.f.* rust. **~é** *a.* rusty. **~er** *v.i.*, **se ~er** *v. pr.* get rusty, rust.

roulant, ~e /rulɑ̃, -t/ *a.* (*meuble*) on wheels; (*escalier*) moving.

rouleau (*pl.* **~x**) /rulo/ *n.m.* roll; (*outil, vague*) roller. **~ à pâtisserie,** rolling-pin. **~ compresseur,** steam-roller.

roulement /rulmɑ̃/ *n.m.* rotation; (*bruit*) rumble; (*succession de personnes*) turnover; (*de tambour*) roll. **~ à billes,** ball-bearing. **par ~,** in rotation.

rouler /rule/ *v.t./i.* roll; (*ficelle, manches*) roll up; (*duper: fam.*) cheat; (*véhicule, train*) go, travel; (*conducteur*) drive. **se ~ dans** *v. pr.* roll (over) in.

roulette /rulɛt/ *n.f.* (*de meuble*) castor; (*de dentiste*) drill; (*jeu*) roulette. **comme sur des ~s,** very smoothly.

roulis /ruli/ *n.m.* rolling.

roulotte /rulɔt/ *n.f.* caravan.

roumain, ~e /rumɛ̃, -ɛn/ *a. & n.m.*, *f.* Romanian.

Roumanie /rumani/ *n.f.* Romania.

roupiller /rupije/ *v.i.* (*fam.*) sleep.

rouquin, **~e** /rukɛ̃, -in/ a. (*fam.*) red-haired. ● *n.m.*, *f.* (*fam.*) redhead.

rouspéter /ruspete/ *v.i.* (*fam.*) grumble, moan, complain.

rousse /rus/ *voir* roux.

roussir /rusir/ *v.t.* scorch. ● *v.i.* turn brown.

route /rut/ *n.f.* road; (*naut., aviat.*) route; (*direction*) way; (*voyage*) journey; (*chemin: fig.*) path. **en ~**, on the way. **en ~!**, let's go! **mettre en ~**, start. **~ nationale**, trunk road, main road. **se mettre en ~**, set out.

rout|ier, **~ière** /rutje, -jɛr/ a. road. ● *n.m.* long-distance lorry driver *ou* truck driver (*Amer.*); (*restaurant*) roadside café.

routine /rutin/ *n.f.* routine.

rouvrir /ruvrir/ *v.t.*, **se ~ir** *v. pr.* reopen, open again.

rou|x, **~sse** /ru, rus/ a. red, reddish-brown; (*personne*) red-haired. ● *n.m.*, *f.* redhead.

roy|al (*m. pl.* **~aux**) /rwajal, -jo/ a. royal; (*total: fam.*) thorough. **~alement** *adv.* royally.

royaume /rwajom/ *n.m.* kingdom. **R~-Uni** *n.m.* United Kingdom.

royauté /rwajote/ *n.f.* royalty.

ruade /ryad, rɥad/ *n.f.* kick.

ruban /rybɑ̃/ *n.m.* ribbon; (*de magnétophone*) tape; (*de chapeau*) band. **~ adhésif**, sticky tape.

rubéole /rybeɔl/ *n.f.* German measles.

rubis /rybi/ *n.m.* ruby; (*de montre*) jewel.

rubrique /rybrik/ *n.f.* heading; (*article*) column.

ruche /ryʃ/ *n.f.* beehive.

rude /ryd/ a. rough; (*pénible*) tough; (*grossier*) crude; (*fameux: fam.*) tremendous. **~ment** *adv.* (*frapper etc.*) hard; (*traiter*) harshly; (*très: fam.*) awfully.

rudiment|s /rydimɑ̃/ *n.m. pl.* rudiments. **~aire** /-tɛr/ a. rudimentary.

rudoyer /rydwaje/ *v.t.* treat harshly.

rue /ry/ *n.f.* street.

ruée /rɥe/ *n.f.* rush.

ruelle /rɥɛl/ *n.f.* alley.

ruer /rɥe/ *v.i.* (*cheval*) kick. **se ~ dans/vers**, rush into/towards. **se ~ sur**, pounce on.

rugby /rygbi/ *n.m.* Rugby.

rugby|man (*pl.* **~men**) /rygbiman, -mɛn/ *n.m.* Rugby player.

rug|ir /ryʒir/ *v.i.* roar. **~issement** *n.m.* roar.

rugueu|x, **~se** /rygø, -z/ a. rough.

ruin|e /rɥin/ *n.f.* ruin. **en ~e(s)**, in ruins. **~er** *v.t.* ruin.

ruineu|x, **~se** /rɥinø, -z/ a. ruinous.

ruisseau (*pl.* **~x**) /rɥiso/ *n.m.* stream; (*rigole*) gutter.

ruisseler /rɥisle/ *v.i.* stream.

rumeur /rymœr/ *n.f.* (*nouvelle*) rumour; (*son*) murmur, hum; (*protestation*) rumblings.

ruminer /rymine/ *v.t./i.* (*herbe*) ruminate; (*méditer*) meditate.

rupture /ryptyr/ *n.f.* break; (*action*) breaking; (*de contrat*) breach; (*de pourparlers*) breakdown.

rur|al (*m. pl.* **~aux**) /ryral, -o/ a. rural.

ruse /ryz/ *n.f.* cunning; (*perfidie*) trickery. **une ~e**, a trick, a ruse. **~é** a. cunning.

russe /rys/ a. & *n.m./f.* Russian. ● *n.m.* (*lang.*) Russian.

Russie /rysi/ *n.f.* Russia.

rustique /rystik/ a. rustic.

rustre /rystr/ *n.m.* lout, boor.

rutilant, **~e** /rytilɑ̃, -t/ a. sparkling, gleaming.

rythm|e /ritm/ *n.m.* rhythm; (*vitesse*) rate; (*de la vie*) pace. **~é, ~ique** *adjs.* rhythmical.

S

s' /s/ *voir* se.

sa /sa/ *voir* son[1].

SA *abrév.* (*société anonyme*) PLC.

sabbat /saba/ *n.m.* sabbath. **~ique** a. **année ~ique**, sabbatical year.

sabl|e /sabl/ *n.m.* sand. **~es mouvants**, quicksands. **~er** *v.t.* sand. **~er le champagne**, drink champagne. **~eux, ~euse, ~onneux, ~onneuse** *adjs.* sandy.

sablier /sablije/ *n.m.* (*culin.*) eggtimer.

saborder /saborde/ *v.t.* (*navire, projet*) scuttle.

sabot /sabo/ *n.m.* (*de cheval etc.*) hoof; (*chaussure*) clog; (*de frein*) shoe. **~ de Denver**, (wheel) clamp.

sabot|er /sabote/ *v.t.* sabotage; (*bâcler*) botch. **~age** *n.m.* sabotage; (*acte*) act of sabotage. **~eur, ~euse** *n.m.*, *f.* saboteur.

sabre /sɑbr/ *n.m.* sabre.

sac /sak/ *n.m.* bag; (*grand, en toile*) sack. **mettre à ~,** (*maison*) ransack; (*ville*) sack. **~ à dos,** rucksack. **~ à main,** handbag. **~ de couchage,** sleeping-bag. **mettre dans le même ~,** lump together.

saccad|e /sakad/ *n.f.* jerk. **~é** *a.* jerky.

saccager /sakaʒe/ *v.t.* (*ville, pays*) sack; (*maison*) ransack; (*ravager*) wreck.

saccharine /sakarin/ *n.f.* saccharin.

sacerdoce /sasɛrdɔs/ *n.m.* priesthood; (*fig.*) vocation.

sachet /saʃɛ/ *n.m.* (small) bag; (*de médicament etc.*) sachet. **~ de thé,** tea-bag.

sacoche /sakɔʃ/ *n.f.* bag; (*d'élève*) satchel; (*de moto*) saddle-bag.

sacquer /sake/ *v.t.* (*fam.*) sack. **je ne peux pas le ~,** I can't stand him.

sacr|e /sakr/ *n.m.* (*de roi*) coronation; (*d'évêque*) consecration. **~er** *v.t.* crown; consecrate.

sacré /sakre/ *a.* sacred; (*maudit: fam.*) damned.

sacrement /sakrəmɑ̃/ *n.m.* sacrament.

sacrifice /sakrifis/ *n.m.* sacrifice.

sacrifier /sakrifje/ *v.t.* sacrifice. **~ à,** conform to. **se ~** *v. pr.* sacrifice o.s.

sacrilège /sakrilɛʒ/ *n.m.* sacrilege. ● *a.* sacrilegious.

sacristain /sakristɛ̃/ *n.m.* sexton.

sacristie /sakristi/ *n.f.* (*protestante*) vestry; (*catholique*) sacristy.

sacro-saint, ~e /sakrosɛ̃, -t/ *a.* sacrosanct.

sadi|que /sadik/ *a.* sadistic. ● *n.m./f.* sadist. **~sme** *n.m.* sadism.

safari /safari/ *n.m.* safari.

sagace /sagas/ *a.* shrewd.

sage /saʒ/ *a.* wise; (*docile*) good. ● *n.m.* wise man. **~-femme** (*pl.* **~s-femmes**) *n.f.* midwife. **~ment** *adv.* wisely; (*docilement*) quietly. **~sse** /-ɛs/ *n.f.* wisdom.

Sagittaire /saʒitɛr/ *n.m.* **le ~,** Sagittarius.

Sahara /saara/ *n.m.* **le ~,** the Sahara (desert).

saignant, ~e /sɛɲɑ̃, -t/ *a.* (*culin.*) rare.

saign|er /seɲe/ *v.t./i.* bleed. **~er du nez,** have a nosebleed. **~ée** *n.f.* bleeding. **~ement** *n.m.* bleeding. **~ement de nez,** nosebleed.

saill|ie /saji/ *n.f.* projection. **faire ~ie,** project. **~ant, ~ante** *a.* projecting; (*remarquable*) salient.

sain, ~e /sɛ̃, sɛn/ *a.* healthy; (*moralement*) sane. **~ et sauf,** safe and sound. **~ement** /sɛnmɑ̃/ *adv.* healthily; (*juger*) sanely.

saindoux /sɛ̃du/ *n.m.* lard.

saint, ~e /sɛ̃, sɛt/ *a.* holy; (*bon, juste*) saintly. ● *n.m., f.* saint. **S~e-Esprit** *n.m.* Holy Spirit. **S~-Siège** *n.m.* Holy See. **S~-Sylvestre** *n.f.* New Year's Eve. **S~e Vierge,** Blessed Virgin.

sainteté /sɛ̃tte/ *n.f.* holiness; (*d'un lieu*) sanctity.

sais /sɛ/ *voir* savoir.

saisie /sezi/ *n.f.* (*jurid.*) seizure; (*comput.*) keyboarding. **~ de données,** data capture.

sais|ir /sezir/ *v.t.* grab (hold of), seize; (*occasion, biens*) seize; (*comprendre*) grasp; (*frapper*) strike; (*comput.*) keyboard, capture. **~i de,** (*peur*) stricken by, overcome by. **se ~ir de,** seize. **~issant, ~issante** *a.* (*spectacle*) gripping.

saison /sɛzɔ̃/ *n.f.* season. **la morte ~,** the off season. **~nier, ~nière** /-ɔnje, -jɛr/ *a.* seasonal.

sait /sɛ/ *voir* savoir.

salad|e /salad/ *n.f.* salad; (*laitue*) lettuce; (*désordre: fam.*) mess. **~ier** *n.m.* salad bowl.

salaire /salɛr/ *n.m.* wages, salary.

salami /salami/ *n.m.* salami.

salarié, ~e /salarje/ *a.* wage-earning. ● *n.m., f.* wage-earner.

salaud /salo/ *n.m.* (*argot*) bastard.

sale /sal/ *a.* dirty, filthy; (*mauvais*) nasty.

sal|er /sale/ *v.t.* salt. **~é** *a.* (*goût*) salty; (*plat*) salted; (*viande, poisson*) salt; (*grivois: fam.*) spicy; (*excessif: fam.*) steep.

saleté /salte/ *n.f.* dirtiness; (*crasse*) dirt; (*action*) dirty trick; (*obscénité*) obscenity. **~(s),** (*camelote*) rubbish. **~s,** (*détritus*) mess.

salière /saljɛr/ *n.f.* salt-cellar.

salin, ~e /salɛ̃, -in/ *a.* saline.

sal|ir /salir/ *v.t.* (make) dirty; (*réputation*) tarnish. **se ~ir** *v. pr.* get dirty. **~issant, ~issante** *a.* dirty; (*étoffe*) easily dirtied.

salive /saliv/ *n.f.* saliva.

salle /sal/ *n.f.* room; (*grande, publique*) hall; (*d'hôpital*) ward; (*théâtre, cinéma*) auditorium. **~ à manger,**

dining-room. **~ d'attente,** waiting-room. **~ de bains,** bathroom. **~ de séjour,** living-room. **~ de classe,** classroom. **~ d'embarquement,** departure lounge. **~ d'opération,** operating theatre. **~ des ventes,** saleroom.

salon /salɔ̃/ *n.m.* lounge; (*de coiffure, beauté*) salon; (*exposition*) show. **~ de thé,** tea-room.

salope /salɔp/ *n.f.* (*argot*) bitch.

saloperie /salɔpri/ *n.f.* (*fam.*) (*action*) dirty trick; (*chose de mauvaise qualité*) rubbish.

salopette /salɔpɛt/ *n.f.* dungarees; (*d'ouvrier*) overalls.

salsifis /salsifi/ *n.m.* salsify.

saltimbanque /saltɛ̃bɑ̃k/ *n.m./f.* (street *ou* fairground) acrobat.

salubre /salybr/ *a.* healthy.

saluer /salɥe/ *v.t.* greet; (*en partant*) take one's leave of; (*de la tête*) nod to; (*de la main*) wave to; (*mil.*) salute.

salut /saly/ *n.m.* greeting; (*de la tête*) nod; (*de la main*) wave; (*mil.*) salute; (*sauvegarde, rachat*) salvation. ● *int.* (*bonjour*: *fam.*) hallo; (*au revoir*: *fam.*) bye-bye.

salutaire /salytɛr/ *a.* salutary.

salutation /salytɑsjɔ̃/ *n.f.* greeting. **veuillez agréer, Monsieur, mes ~s distingués,** yours faithfully.

salve /salv/ *n.f.* salvo.

samedi /samdi/ *n.m.* Saturday.

sanatorium /sanatɔrjɔm/ *n.m.* sanatorium.

sanctifier /sɑ̃ktifje/ *v.t.* sanctify.

sanction /sɑ̃ksjɔ̃/ *n.f.* sanction. **~ner** /-jɔne/ *v.t.* sanction; (*punir*) punish.

sanctuaire /sɑ̃ktɥɛr/ *n.m.* sanctuary.

sandale /sɑ̃dal/ *n.f.* sandal.

sandwich /sɑ̃dwitʃ/ *n.m.* sandwich.

sang /sɑ̃/ *n.m.* blood. **~-froid** *n.m. invar.* calm, self-control. **se faire du mauvais ~** *ou* **un ~ d'encre** be worried stiff.

sanglant, ~e /sɑ̃glɑ̃, -t/ *a.* bloody.

sangl|e /sɑ̃gl/ *n.f.* strap. **~er** *v.t.* strap.

sanglier /sɑ̃glije/ *n.m.* wild boar.

sanglot /sɑ̃glo/ *n.m.* sob. **~er** /-ɔte/ *v.i.* sob.

sangsue /sɑ̃sy/ *n.f.* leech.

sanguin, ~e /sɑ̃gɛ̃, -in/ *a.* (*groupe etc.*) blood; (*caractère*) fiery.

sanguinaire /sɑ̃ginɛr/ *a.* blood-thirsty.

sanitaire /sanitɛr/ *a.* health; (*conditions*) sanitary; (*appareils, installations*) bathroom, sanitary. **~s** *n.m. pl.* bathroom.

sans /sɑ̃/ *prép.* without. **~ que vous le sachiez,** without your knowing. **~-abri** /sɑ̃zabri/ *n.m./f. invar.* homeless person. **~ ça,** **~ quoi,** otherwise. **~ arrêt,** nonstop. **~ encombre/faute/ tarder,** without incident/fail/delay. **~ fin/goût/limite,** endless/tasteless/limitless. **~-gêne** *a. invar.* inconsiderate, thoughtless; *n.m. invar.* thoughtlessness. **~ importance/pareil/précédent/travail,** unimportant/unparalleled/unprecedented/unemployed. **~ plus,** but no more than that, but nothing more.

santé /sɑ̃te/ *n.f.* health. **à ta** *ou* **votre santé,** cheers!

saoul, ~e /su, sul/ *voir* soûl.

saper /sape/ *v.t.* undermine.

sapeur /sapœr/ *n.m.* (*mil.*) sapper. **~-pompier** (*pl.* **~s-pompiers**) *n.m.* fireman.

saphir /safir/ *n.m.* sapphire.

sapin /sapɛ̃/ *n.m.* fir(-tree). **~ de Noël,** Christmas tree.

sarbacane /sarbakan/ *n.f.* (*jouet*) pea-shooter.

sarcas|me /sarkasm/ *n.m.* sarcasm. **~tique** *a.* sarcastic.

sarcler /sarkle/ *v.t.* weed.

sardine /sardin/ *n.f.* sardine.

sardonique /sardɔnik/ *a.* sardonic.

sarment /sarmɑ̃/ *n.m.* vine shoot.

sas /sɑs/ *n.m.* (*naut., aviat.*) airlock.

satané /satane/ *a.* (*fam.*) blasted.

satanique /satanik/ *a.* satanic.

satellite /satelit/ *n.m.* satellite.

satin /satɛ̃/ *n.m.* satin.

satir|e /satir/ *n.f.* satire. **~ique** *a.* satirical.

satisfaction /satisfaksjɔ̃/ *n.f.* satisfaction.

satis|faire† /satisfɛr/ *v.t.* satisfy. ● *v.i.* **~faire à,** satisfy. **~faisant, ~faisante** *a.* (*acceptable*) satisfactory. **~fait, ~faite** *a.* satisfied (**de,** with).

satur|er /satyre/ *v.t.* saturate. **~ation** *n.f.* saturation.

sauc|e /sos/ *n.f.* sauce; (*jus de viande*) gravy. **~er** *v.t.* (*plat*) wipe. **se faire ~er** (*fam.*) get soaked. **~e tartare,** tartar sauce. **~ière** *n.f.* sauce-boat.

saucisse /sosis/ *n.f.* sausage.

saucisson /sosisɔ̃/ *n.m.* (slicing) sausage.

sauf[1] /sof/ *prép.* except. **~ erreur/ imprévu,** barring error/the unforeseen. **~ avis contraire,** unless you hear otherwise.

sau|f[2], **~ve** /sof, sov/ *a.* safe, unharmed. **~f-conduit** *n.m.* safe conduct.

sauge /soʒ/ *n.f.* (*culin.*) sage.

saugrenu /sogrəny/ *a.* preposterous, ludicrous.

saule /sol/ *n.m.* willow. **~ pleureur,** weeping willow.

saumon /somɔ̃/ *n.m.* salmon. ● *a. invar.* salmon-pink.

saumure /somyr/ *n.f.* brine.

sauna /sona/ *n.m.* sauna.

saupoudrer /supudre/ *v.t.* sprinkle (de, with).

saut /so/ *n.m.* jump, leap. **faire un ~ chez qn.,** pop round to s.o.'s (place). **le ~,** (*sport*) jumping. **~ en hauteur/longueur,** high/long jump. **~ périlleux,** somersault. **au ~ du lit,** on getting up.

sauté /sote/ *a. & n.m.* (*culin.*) sauté.

saut|er /sote/ *v.i.* jump, leap; (*exploser*) blow up; (*fusible*) blow; (*se détacher*) come off. ● *v.t.* jump (over); (*page, classe*) skip. **faire ~er,** (*détruire*) blow up; (*fusible*) blow; (*casser*) break; (*culin.*) sauté; (*renvoyer: fam.*) kick out. **~er à la corde,** skip. **~er aux yeux,** be obvious. **~e-mouton** *n.m.* leapfrog. **~er au cou de qn.,** fling one's arms round s.o. **~er sur une occasion,** jump at an opportunity.

sauterelle /sotrɛl/ *n.f.* grasshopper.

sautiller /sotije/ *v.i.* hop.

sauvage /sovaʒ/ *a.* wild; (*primitif, cruel*) savage; (*farouche*) unsociable; (*illégal*) unauthorized. ● *n.m./f.* unsociable person; (*brute*) savage. **~rie** *n.f.* savagery.

sauve /sov/ *voir* sauf[2].

sauvegard|e /sovgard/ *n.f.* safeguard; (*comput.*) backup. **~er** *v.t.* safeguard; (*comput.*) save.

sauv|er /sove/ *v.t.* save; (*d'un danger*) rescue, save; (*matériel*) salvage. **se ~er** *v. pr.* (*fuir*) run away; (*partir: fam.*) be off. **~e-qui-peut** *n.m. invar.* stampede. **~etage** *n.m.* rescue; salvage. **~eteur** *n.m.* rescuer. **~eur** *n.m.* saviour.

sauvette (à la) /(ala)sovɛt/ *adv.* hastily; (*vendre*) illicitly.

savamment /savamɑ̃/ *adv.* learnedly; (*avec habileté*) skilfully.

savan|t, ~e /savɑ̃, -t/ *a.* learned; (*habile*) skilful. ● *n.m.* scientist.

saveur /savœr/ *n.f.* flavour; (*fig.*) savour.

savoir† /savwar/ *v.t.* know; (*apprendre*) hear. **elle sait conduire/ nager,** she can drive/swim. ● *n.m.* learning. **à ~,** namely. **faire ~ à qn. que,** inform s.o. that. **je ne saurais pas,** I could not, I cannot. **(pas) que je sache,** (not) as far as I know.

savon /savɔ̃/ *n.m.* soap. **passer un ~ à qn.,** (*fam.*) give s.o. a dressing down. **~ner** /-ɔne/ *v.t.* soap. **~nette** /-ɔnɛt/ *n.f.* bar of soap. **~neux, ~neuse** /-ɔnø, -z/ *a.* soapy.

savour|er /savure/ *v.t.* savour. **~eux, ~euse** *a.* tasty; (*fig.*) spicy.

saxo(phone) /saksɔ(fɔn)/ *n.m.* sax(ophone).

scabreu|x, ~se /skabrø, -z/ *a.* risky; (*indécent*) obscene.

scandal|e /skɑ̃dal/ *n.m.* scandal; (*tapage*) uproar; (*en public*) noisy scene. **faire ~e,** shock people. **faire un ~e,** make a scene. **~eux, ~euse** *a.* scandalous. **~iser** *v.t.* scandalize, shock.

scander /skɑ̃de/ *v.t.* (*vers*) scan; (*slogan*) chant.

scandinave /skɑ̃dinav/ *a. & n.m./f.* Scandinavian.

Scandinavie /skɑ̃dinavi/ *n.f.* Scandinavia.

scarabée /skarabe/ *n.m.* beetle.

scarlatine /skarlatin/ *n.f.* scarlet fever.

scarole /skarɔl/ *n.f.* endive.

sceau (*pl.* **~x**) /so/ *n.m.* seal.

scélérat /selera/ *n.m.* scoundrel.

scell|er /sele/ *v.t.* seal; (*fixer*) cement. **~és** *n.m. pl.* seals.

scénario /senarjo/ *n.m.* scenario.

scène /sɛn/ *n.f.* scene; (*estrade, art dramatique*) stage. **mettre en ~,** (*pièce*) stage. **~ de ménage,** domestic scene.

scepti|que /sɛptik/ *a.* sceptical. ● *n.m./f.* sceptic. **~cisme** *n.m.* scepticism.

sceptre /sɛptr/ *n.m.* sceptre.

schéma /ʃema/ *n.m.* diagram. **~tique** *a.* diagrammatic; (*sommaire*) sketchy.

schisme /ʃism/ *n.m.* schism.

schizophrène /skizɔfrɛn/ *a. & n.m./f.* schizophrenic.

sciatique /sjatik/ *n.f.* sciatica.

scie /si/ *n.f.* saw.

sciemment /sjamã/ *adv.* knowingly.

scien|ce /sjãs/ *n.f.* science; (*savoir*) knowledge. **~ce-fiction** *n.f.* science fiction. **~tifique** *a.* scientific; *n.m./f.* scientist.

scier /sje/ *v.t.* saw.

scinder /sɛ̃de/ *v.t.*, **se ~** *v. pr.* split.

scintill|er /sɛ̃tije/ *v.i.* glitter; (*étoile*) twinkle. **~ement** *n.m.* glittering; twinkling.

scission /sisjɔ̃/ *n.f.* split.

sciure /sjyr/ *n.f.* sawdust.

sclérose /skleroz/ *n.f.* sclerosis. **~ en plaques,** multiple sclerosis.

scol|aire /skɔlɛr/ *a.* school. **~arisation** *n.f.*, **~arité** *n.f.* schooling. **~arisé** *a.* provided with schooling.

scorbut /skɔrbyt/ *n.m.* scurvy.

score /skɔr/ *n.m.* score.

scories /skɔri/ *n.f. pl.* slag.

scorpion /skɔrpjɔ̃/ *n.m.* scorpion. **le S~,** Scorpio.

scotch[1] /skɔtʃ/ *n.m.* (*boisson*) Scotch (whisky).

scotch[2] /skɔtʃ/ *n.m.* (P.) Sellotape (P.); (*Amer.*) Scotch (tape) (P.).

scout, ~e /skut/ *n.m. & a.* scout.

script /skript/ *n.m.* (*cinéma*) script; (*écriture*) printing. **~-girl,** continuity girl.

scrupul|e /skrypyl/ *n.m.* scruple. **~eusement** *adv.* scrupulously. **~eux, ~euse** *a.* scrupulous.

scruter /skryte/ *v.t.* examine, scrutinize.

scrutin /skrytɛ̃/ *n.m.* (*vote*) ballot; (*opération électorale*) poll.

sculpt|er /skylte/ *v.t.* sculpture; (*bois*) carve (**dans,** out of). **~eur** *n.m.* sculptor. **~ure** *n.f.* sculpture.

se, s'* /sə, s/ *pron.* himself; (*femelle*) herself; (*indéfini*) oneself; (*non humain*) itself; (*pl.*) themselves; (*réciproque*) each other, one another. **se parler,** (*à soi-même*) talk to o.s.; (*réciproque*) talk to each other. **se faire,** (*passif*) be done. **se laver les mains,** (*possessif*) wash one's hands.

séance /seãs/ *n.f.* session; (*cinéma, théâtre*) show. **~ de pose,** sitting. **~ tenante,** forthwith.

seau (*pl.* **~x**) /so/ *n.m.* bucket, pail.

sec, sèche /sɛk, sɛʃ/ *a.* dry; (*fruits*) dried; (*coup, bruit*) sharp; (*cœur*) hard; (*whisky*) neat; (*Amer.*) straight. ● *n.m.* **à ~,** (*sans eau*)

dry; (*sans argent*) broke. **au ~,** in a dry place. ● *n.f.* (*fam.*) (*cigarette*) fag.

sécateur /sekatœr/ *n.m.* (*pour les haies*) shears; (*petit*) secateurs.

sécession /sesesjɔ̃/ *n.f.* secession. **faire ~,** secede.

sèche /sɛʃ/ *voir* **sec. ~ment** *adv.* drily.

sèche-cheveux /sɛʃʃəvø/ *n.m. invar.* hair-drier.

sécher /seʃe/ *v.t./i.* dry; (*cours: fam.*) skip; (*ne pas savoir: fam.*) be stumped. **se ~** *v. pr.* dry o.s.

sécheresse /seʃrɛs/ *n.f.* dryness; (*temps sec*) drought.

séchoir /seʃwar/ *n.m.* drier.

second, ~e[1] /sgɔ̃, -d/ *a. & n.m.,* second. ● *n.m.* (*adjoint*) second in command; (*étage*) second floor, (*Amer.*) third floor. ● *n.f.* (*transport*) second class.

secondaire /sgɔ̃dɛr/ *a.* secondary.

seconde[2] /sgɔ̃d/ *n.f.* (*instant*) second.

seconder /sgɔ̃de/ *v.t.* assist.

secouer /skwe/ *v.t.* shake; (*poussière, torpeur*) shake off. **se ~,** (*fam.*) (*se dépêcher*) get a move on; (*réagir*) shake o.s. up.

secour|ir /skurir/ *v.t.* assist, help. **~able** *a.* helpful. **~iste** *n.m./f.* first-aid worker.

secours /skur/ *n.m.* assistance, help. ● *n.m. pl.* (*méd.*) first aid. **au ~!,** help! **de ~,** emergency; (*équipe, opération*) rescue.

secousse /skus/ *n.f.* jolt, jerk; (*électrique*) shock; (*séisme*) tremor.

secr|et, ~ète /səkrɛ, -t/ *a.* secret. ● *n.m.* secret; (*discrétion*) secrecy. **le ~et professionnel,** professional secrecy. **~et de Polichinelle,** open secret. **en ~et,** in secret, secretly.

secrétaire /skretɛr/ *n.m./f.* secretary. **~ de direction,** executive secretary. ● *n.m.* (*meuble*) writing-desk. **~ d'État,** junior minister.

secrétariat /skretarja/ *n.m.* secretarial work; (*bureau*) secretary's office; (*d'un organisme*) secretariat.

sécrét|er /sekrete/ *v.t.* secrete. **~ion** /-sjɔ̃/ *n.f.* secretion.

sect|e /sɛkt/ *n.f.* sect. **~aire** *a.* sectarian.

secteur /sɛktœr/ *n.m.* area; (*mil., comm.*) sector; (*circuit: électr.*) mains. **~ primaire/secondaire/ter-**

tiaire, primary/secondary/tertiary industry.

section /sɛksjɔ̃/ *n.f.* section; (*transports publics*) fare stage; (*mil.*) platoon. **~ner** /-jɔne/ *v.t.* sever.

sécu /seky/ *n.f.* (*fam.*) **la ~,** the social security services.

séculaire /sekylɛr/ *a.* age-old.

sécul|ier, ~ière /sekylje, -jɛr/ *a.* secular.

sécuriser /sekyrize/ *v.t.* reassure.

sécurité /sekyrite/ *n.f.* security; (*absence de danger*) safety. **en ~,** safe, secure. **S~ sociale,** social services, social security services.

sédatif /sedatif/ *n.m.* sedative.

sédentaire /sedɑ̃tɛr/ *a.* sedentary.

sédiment /sedimɑ̃/ *n.m.* sediment.

séditieu|x, ~se /sedisjø, -z/ *a.* seditious.

sédition /sedisjɔ̃/ *n.f.* sedition.

séd|uire† /sedɥir/ *v.t.* charm; (*plaire à*) appeal to; (*abuser de*) seduce. **~ucteur, ~uctrice** *a.* seductive; *n.m.*, *f.* seducer. **~uction** *n.f.* seduction; (*charme*) charm. **~uisant, ~uisante** *a.* attractive.

segment /sɛgmɑ̃/ *n.m.* segment.

ségrégation /segregasjɔ̃/ *n.f.* segregation.

seigle /sɛgl/ *n.m.* rye.

seigneur /sɛɲœr/ *n.m.* lord. **le S~,** the Lord.

sein /sɛ̃/ *n.m.* breast; (*fig.*) bosom. **au ~ de,** in the midst of.

Seine /sɛn/ *n.f.* Seine.

séisme /seism/ *n.m.* earthquake.

seiz|e /sɛz/ *a. & n.m.* sixteen. **~ième** *a. & n.m./f.* sixteenth.

séjour /seʒur/ *n.m.* stay; (*pièce*) living-room. **~ner** *v.i.* stay.

sel /sɛl/ *n.m.* salt; (*piquant*) spice.

sélect /selɛkt/ *a.* select.

sélecti|f, ~ve /selɛktif, -v/ *a.* selective.

sélection /selɛksjɔ̃/ *n.f.* selection. **~ner** /-jɔne/ *v.t.* select.

self(-service) /sɛlf(sɛrvis)/ *n.m.* self-service.

selle /sɛl/ *n.f.* saddle.

seller /sele/ *v.t.* saddle.

sellette /selɛt/ *n.f.* **sur la ~,** (*question*) under examination; (*personne*) in the hot seat.

selon /slɔ̃/ *prép.* according to (**que,** whether).

semaine /smɛn/ *n.f.* week. **en ~,** in the week.

sémantique /semɑ̃tik/ *a.* semantic. ● *n.f.* semantics.

sémaphore /semafɔr/ *n.m.* (*appareil*) semaphore.

semblable /sɑ̃blabl/ *a.* similar (**à,** to). **de ~s propos**/*etc.,* (*tels*) such remarks/*etc.* ● *n.m.* fellow (creature).

semblant /sɑ̃blɑ̃/ *n.m.* **faire ~ de,** pretend to. **un ~ de,** a semblance of.

sembl|er /sɑ̃ble/ *v.i.* seem (**à,** to; **que,** that). **il me ~e que,** it seems to me that.

semelle /smɛl/ *n.f.* sole.

semence /smɑ̃s/ *n.f.* seed; (*clou*) tack. **~s,** (*graines*) seed.

sem|er /sme/ *v.t.* sow; (*jeter, parsemer*) strew; (*répandre*) spread; (*personne*: *fam.*) lose. **~eur, ~euse** *n.m.,* *f.* sower.

semestr|e /smɛstr/ *n.m.* half-year; (*univ.*) semester. **~iel, ~ielle** *a.* half-yearly.

semi- /səmi/ *préf.* semi-.

séminaire /seminɛr/ *n.m.* (*relig.*) seminary; (*univ.*) seminar.

semi-remorque /səmirəmɔrk/ *n.m.* articulated lorry; (*Amer.*) semi(-trailer).

semis /smi/ *n.m.* (*terrain*) seed-bed; (*plant*) seedling.

sémit|e /semit/ *a.* Semitic. ● *n.m./f.* Semite. **~ique** *a.* Semitic.

semonce /səmɔ̃s/ *n.f.* reprimand. **coup de ~,** warning shot.

semoule /səmul/ *n.f.* semolina.

sénat /sena/ *n.m.* senate. **~eur** /-tœr/ *n.m.* senator.

sénil|e /senil/ *a.* senile. **~ité** *n.f.* senility.

sens /sɑ̃s/ *n.m.* sense; (*signification*) meaning, sense; (*direction*) direction. **à mon ~,** to my mind. **à ~ unique,** (*rue etc.*) one-way. **ça n'a pas de ~,** that does not make sense. **~ commun,** common sense. **~ giratoire,** roundabout; (*Amer.*) rotary. **~ interdit,** no entry; (*rue*) one-way street. **dans le ~ des aiguilles d'une montre,** clockwise. **~ dessus dessous,** upside down.

sensation /sɑ̃sasjɔ̃/ *n.f.* feeling, sensation. **faire ~,** create a sensation. **~nel, ~nelle** /-jɔnɛl/ *a.* sensational.

sensé /sɑ̃se/ *a.* sensible.

sensibiliser /sɑ̃sibilize/ *v.t.* **~ à,** make sensitive to.

sensib|le /sɑ̃sibl/ *a.* sensitive (**à,** to); (*appréciable*) noticeable. **~ilité** *n.f.*

sensitivity. **~lement** *adv.* noticeably; (*à peu prés*) more or less.

sensoriel, ~le /sɑ̃sɔrjɛl/ *a.* sensory.

sens|uel, ~uelle /sɑ̃sɥɛl/ *a.* sensuous; (*sexuel*) sensual. **~ualité** *n.f.* sensuousness; sensuality.

sentenc|e /sɑ̃tɑ̃s/ *n.f.* sentence. **~ieux, ~ieuse** *a.* sententious.

senteur /sɑ̃tœr/ *n.f.* scent.

sentier /sɑ̃tje/ *n.m.* path.

sentiment /sɑ̃timɑ̃/ *n.m.* feeling. **avoir le ~ de,** be aware of.

sentiment|al (*m. pl.* **~aux**) /sɑ̃timɑ̃tal, -o/ *a.* sentimental. **~alité** *n.f.* sentimentality.

sentinelle /sɑ̃tinɛl/ *n.f.* sentry.

sentir† /sɑ̃tir/ *v.t.* feel; (*odeur*) smell; (*goût*) taste; (*pressentir*) sense. **~ la lavande**/*etc.*, smell of lavender/*etc.* ● *v.i.* smell. **je ne peux pas le ~,** (*fam.*) I can't stand him. **se ~ fier/ mieux**/*etc.*, feel proud/better/*etc.*

séparatiste /separatist/ *a. & n.m./f.* separatist.

séparé /separe/ *a.* separate; (*conjoints*) separated. **~ment** *adv.* separately.

sépar|er /separe/ *v.t.* separate; (*en deux*) split. **se ~er** *v. pr.* separate, part (**de,** from); (*se détacher*) split. **se ~er de,** (*se défaire de*) part with. **~ation** *n.f.* separation.

sept /sɛt/ *a. & n.m.* seven.

septante /sɛptɑ̃t/ *a. & n.m.* (*en Belgique, Suisse*) seventy.

septembre /sɛptɑ̃br/ *n.m.* September.

septentrion|al (*m. pl.* **~aux**) /sɛptɑ̃trijɔnal, -o/ *a.* northern.

septième /sɛtjɛm/ *a. & n.m./f.* seventh.

sépulcre /sepylkr/ *n.m.* (*relig.*) sepulchre.

sépulture /sepyltyr/ *n.f.* burial; (*lieu*) burial place.

séquelles /sekɛl/ *n.f. pl.* (*maladie*) after-effects; (*fig.*) aftermath.

séquence /sekɑ̃s/ *n.f.* sequence.

séquestrer /sekɛstre/ *v.t.* confine (illegally); (*biens*) impound.

sera, serait /sra, srɛ/ *voir* être.

serein, ~e /sərɛ̃, -ɛn/ *a.* serene.

sérénade /serenad/ *n.f.* serenade.

sérénité /serenite/ *n.f.* serenity.

sergent /sɛrʒɑ̃/ *n.m.* sergeant.

série /seri/ *n.f.* series; (*d'objets*) set. **de ~,** (*véhicule etc.*) standard. **fabrication** *ou* **production en ~,** mass production.

sérieu|x, ~se /serjø, -z/ *a.* serious; (*digne de foi*) reliable; (*chances, raison*) good. ● *n.m.* seriousness. **garder/perdre son ~x,** keep/be unable to keep a straight face. **prendre au ~x,** take seriously. **~sement** *adv.* seriously.

serin /srɛ̃/ *n.m.* canary.

seringue /srɛ̃g/ *n.f.* syringe.

serment /sɛrmɑ̃/ *n.m.* oath; (*promesse*) pledge.

sermon /sɛrmɔ̃/ *n.m.* sermon. **~ner** /-ɔne/ *v.t.* (*fam.*) lecture.

séropositi|f, ~ve /seropozitif, -v/ *a.* HIV-positive.

serpe /sɛrp/ *n.f.* bill(hook).

serpent /sɛrpɑ̃/ *n.m.* snake. **~ à sonnettes,** rattlesnake.

serpenter /sɛrpɑ̃te/ *v.i.* meander.

serpentin /sɛrpɑ̃tɛ̃/ *n.m.* streamer.

serpillière /sɛrpijɛr/ *n.f.* floor-cloth.

serre¹ /sɛr/ *n.f.* (*local*) greenhouse.

serre² /sɛr/ *n.f.* (*griffe*) claw.

serré /sere/ *a.* (*habit, nœud, programme*) tight; (*personnes*) packed, crowded; (*lutte, mailles*) close; (*cœur*) heavy.

serrer /sere/ *v.t.* (*saisir*) grip; (*presser*) squeeze; (*vis, corde, ceinture*) tighten; (*poing, dents*) clench; (*pieds*) pinch. **~ qn. dans ses bras,** hug. **~ les rangs,** close ranks. **~ qn.,** (*vêtement*) be tight on s.o. ● *v.i.* **~ à droite,** keep over to the right. **se ~** *v. pr.* (*se rapprocher*) squeeze (up) (**contre,** against). **~ de près,** follow closely. **~ la main à,** shake hands with.

serrur|e /seryr/ *n.f.* lock. **~ier** *n.m.* locksmith.

sertir /sɛrtir/ *v.t.* (*bijou*) set.

sérum /serɔm/ *n.m.* serum.

servante /sɛrvɑ̃t/ *n.f.* (maid)servant.

serveu|r, ~se /sɛrvœr, -øz/ *n.m., f.* waiter, waitress; (*au bar*) barman, barmaid.

serviable /sɛrvjabl/ *a.* helpful.

service /sɛrvis/ *n.m.* service; (*fonction, temps de travail*) duty; (*pourboire*) service (charge). **~ (non) compris,** service (not) included. **être de ~,** be on duty. **pendant le ~,** (when) on duty. **rendre un ~/mauvais ~ à qn.,** do s.o. a favour/disservice. **~ (policiers*) police. **~ après-vente,** after-sales service. **~ militaire,** military service.

serviette /sɛrvjɛt/ *n.f.* (*de toilette*) towel; (*sac*) briefcase. **~ (de table)**, serviette; (*Amer.*) napkin. **~ hygiénique,** sanitary towel.

servile /sɛrvil/ *a.* servile.

servir† /sɛrvir/ *v.t./i.* serve; (*être utile*) be of use, serve. **~ qn. (à table)**, wait on s.o. **ça sert à,** (*outil, récipient, etc.*) it is used for. **ça me sert à/de,** I use it for/as. **~ de,** serve as, be used as. **~ à qn. de guide**/*etc.*, act as a guide/*etc.* for s.o. **se ~** *v. pr.* (*à table*) help o.s. (**de,** to). **se ~ de,** use.

serviteur /sɛrvitœr/ *n.m.* servant.

servitude /sɛrvityd/ *n.f.* servitude.

ses /se/ *voir* son¹.

session /sesjɔ̃/ *n.f.* session.

seuil /sœj/ *n.m.* doorstep; (*entrée*) doorway; (*fig.*) threshold.

seul, ~e /sœl/ *a.* alone, on one's own; (*unique*) only. **un ~ travail**/*etc.*, only one job/*etc.* **pas un ~ ami**/ *etc.*, not a single friend/*etc.* **parler tout ~,** talk to o.s. **faire qch. tout ~,** do sth. on one's own. ● *n.m., f.* **le ~, la ~e,** the only one. **un ~, une ~e,** only one. **pas un ~,** not (a single) one.

seulement /sœlmɑ̃/ *adv.* only.

sève /sɛv/ *n.f.* sap.

sév|ère /sevɛr/ *a.* severe. **~èrement** *adv.* severely. **~érité** /-erite/ *n.f.* severity.

sévices /sevis/ *n.m. pl.* cruelty.

sévir /sevir/ *v.i.* (*fléau*) rage. **~ contre,** punish.

sevrer /səvre/ *v.t.* wean.

sex|e /sɛks/ *n.m.* sex; (*organes*) sex organs. **~isme** *n.m.* sexism. **~iste** *a.* sexist.

sex|uel, ~uelle /sɛksɥɛl/ *a.* sexual. **~ualité** *n.f.* sexuality.

seyant, ~e /sɛjɑ̃, -t/ *a.* becoming.

shampooing /ʃɑ̃pwɛ̃/ *n.m.* shampoo.

shérif /ʃerif/ *n.m.* sheriff.

short /ʃɔrt/ *n.m.* (pair of) shorts.

si¹ (**s'** before il, ils) /si, s/ *conj.* if; (*interrogation indirecte*) if, whether. **si on partait?,** (*suggestion*) what about going? **s'il vous** *ou* **te plaît,** please. **si oui,** if so. **si seulement,** if only.

si² /si/ *adv.* (*tellement*) so; (*oui*) yes. **un si bon repas,** such a good meal. **pas si riche que,** not as rich as. **si habile qu'il soit,** however skilful he may be. **si bien que,** with the result that.

siamois, ~e /sjamwa, -z/ *a.* Siamese.

Sicile /sisil/ *n.f.* Sicily.

sida /sida/ *n.m.* (*méd.*) AIDS.

sidéré /sidere/ *a.* staggered.

sidérurgie /sideryrʒi/ *n.f.* iron and steel industry.

siècle /sjɛkl/ *n.m.* century; (*époque*) age.

siège /sjɛʒ/ *n.m.* seat; (*mil.*) siege. **~ éjectable,** ejector seat. **~ social,** head office, headquarters.

siéger /sjeʒe/ *v.i.* (*assemblée*) sit.

sien, ~ne /sjɛ̃, sjɛn/ *pron.* **le ~, la ~ne, les ~(ne)s,** his; (*femme*) hers; (*chose*) its. **les ~s,** (*famille*) one's family.

sieste /sjɛst/ *n.f.* nap; (*en Espagne*) siesta. **faire la ~,** have an afternoon nap.

siffl|er /sifle/ *v.i.* whistle; (*avec un sifflet*) blow one's whistle; (*serpent, gaz*) hiss. ● *v.t.* (*air*) whistle; (*chien*) whistle to *ou* for; (*acteur*) hiss; (*signaler*) blow one's whistle for. **~ement** *n.m.* whistling. **un ~ement,** a whistle.

sifflet /siflɛ/ *n.m.* whistle. **~s,** (*huées*) boos.

siffloter /siflɔte/ *v.t./i.* whistle.

sigle /sigl/ *n.m.* abbreviation, acronym.

sign|al (*pl.* **~aux**) /siɲal, -o/ *n.m.* signal. **~aux lumineux,** (*auto.*) traffic signals.

signal|er /siɲale/ *v.t.* indicate; (*par une sonnerie, un écriteau*) signal; (*dénoncer, mentionner*) report; (*faire remarquer*) point out. **se ~er par,** distinguish o.s. by. **~ement** *n.m.* description.

signalisation /siɲalizasjɔ̃/ *n.f.* signalling, signposting; (*signaux*) signals.

signataire /siɲatɛr/ *n.m./f.* signatory.

signature /siɲatyr/ *n.f.* signature; (*action*) signing.

signe /siɲ/ *n.m.* sign; (*de ponctuation*) mark. **faire ~ à,** beckon (**de,** to); (*contacter*) contact. **faire ~ que non,** shake one's head. **faire ~ que oui,** nod.

signer /siɲe/ *v.t.* sign. **se ~** *v. pr.* (*relig.*) cross o.s.

signet /siɲɛ/ *m.* bookmark.

significati|f, ~ve /siɲifikatif, -v/ *a.* significant.

signification /siɲifikasjɔ̃/ *n.f.* meaning.

signifier /siɲifje/ v.t. mean, signify; (faire connaître) make known (à, to).

silenc|e /silɑ̃s/ n.m. silence; (mus.) rest. **garder le ~e,** keep silent. **~ieux, ~ieuse** a. silent; n.m. (auto.) silencer; (auto., Amer.) muffler.

silex /silɛks/ n.m. flint.

silhouette /silwɛt/ n.f. outline, silhouette.

silicium /silisjɔm/ n.m. silicon.

sillage /sijaʒ/ n.m. (trace d'eau) wake.

sillon /sijɔ̃/ n.m. furrow; (de disque) groove.

sillonner /sijɔne/ v.t. criss-cross.

silo /silo/ n.m. silo.

simagrées /simagre/ n.f. pl. fuss, pretence.

simil|aire /similɛr/ a. similar. **~itude** n.f. similarity.

simple /sɛ̃pl/ a. simple; (non double) single. ● n.m. (tennis) singles. **~ d'esprit** n.m./f. simpleton. **~ soldat,** private. **~ment** /-əmɑ̃/ adv. simply.

simplicité /sɛ̃plisite/ n.f. simplicity; (naïveté) simpleness.

simplif|ier /sɛ̃plifje/ v.t. simplify. **~ication** n.f. simplification.

simpliste /sɛ̃plist/ a. simplistic.

simulacre /simylakr/ n.m. pretence, sham.

simul|er /simyle/ v.t. simulate. **~ateur** m. (appareil) simulator. **~ation** n.f. simulation.

simultané /simyltane/ a. simultaneous. **~ment** adv. simultaneously.

sinc|ère /sɛ̃sɛr/ a. sincere. **~èrement** adv. sincerely. **~érité** n.f. sincerity.

singe /sɛ̃ʒ/ n.m. monkey, ape.

singer /sɛ̃ʒe/ v.t. mimic, ape.

singeries /sɛ̃ʒri/ n.f. pl. antics.

singulariser (se) /(sə)sɛ̃gylarize/ v. pr. make o.s. conspicuous.

singul|ier, ~ière /sɛ̃gylje, -jɛr/ a. peculiar, remarkable; (gram.) singular. ● n.m. (gram.) singular. **~arité** n.f. peculiarity. **~ièrement** adv. peculiarly; (beaucoup) remarkably.

sinistre[1] /sinistr/ a. sinister.

sinistr|e[2] /sinistr/ n.m. disaster; (incendie) blaze; (dommages) damage. **~é** a. disaster-stricken; n.m., f. disaster victim.

sinon /sinɔ̃/ conj. (autrement) otherwise; (sauf) except (que, that); (si ce n'est) if not.

sinueu|x, ~se /sinɥø, -z/ a. winding; (fig.) tortuous.

sinus /sinys/ n.m. (anat.) sinus.

sionisme /sjɔnism/ n.m. Zionism.

siphon /sifɔ̃/ n.m. siphon; (de WC) U-bend.

sirène[1] /sirɛn/ n.f. (appareil) siren.

sirène[2] /sirɛn/ n.f. (femme) mermaid.

sirop /siro/ n.m. syrup; (boisson) cordial.

siroter /sirɔte/ v.t. sip.

sirupeu|x, ~se /sirypø, -z/ a. syrupy.

sis, ~e /si, siz/ a. situated.

sismique /sismik/ a. seismic.

site /sit/ n.m. setting; (pittoresque) beauty spot; (emplacement) site; (monument etc.) place of interest.

sitôt /sito/ adv. ~ **entré**/etc., immediately after coming in/etc. ~ **que,** as soon as. **pas de ~,** not for a while.

situation /sitɥasjɔ̃/ n.f. situation, position. ~ **de famille,** marital status.

situ|er /sitɥe/ v.t. situate, locate. **se ~er** v. pr. (se trouver) be situated. **~é** a. situated.

six /sis/ (/si/ before consonant, /siz/ before vowel) a. & n.m. six. **~ième** /sizjɛm/ a. & n.m./f. sixth.

sketch (pl. **~es**) /skɛtʃ/ n.m. (théâtre) sketch.

ski /ski/ n.m. (patin) ski; (sport) skiing. **faire du ~,** ski. ~ **de fond,** cross-country skiing. ~ **nautique,** water-skiing.

sk|ier /skje/ v.i. ski. **~ieur, ~ieuse** n.m., f. skier.

slalom /slalɔm/ n.m. slalom.

slave /slav/ a. Slav; (lang.) Slavonic. ● n.m./f. Slav.

slip /slip/ n.m. (d'homme) (under)pants; (de femme) knickers; (Amer.) panties. ~ **de bain,** (swimming) trunks; (du bikini) briefs.

slogan /slɔgɑ̃/ n.m. slogan.

smoking /smɔkiŋ/ n.m. evening ou dinner suit, dinner-jacket.

snack(-bar) /snak(bar)/ n.m. snack-bar.

snob /snɔb/ n.m./f. snob. ● a. snobbish. **~isme** n.m. snobbery.

sobr|e /sɔbr/ a. sober. **~iété** n.f. sobriety.

sobriquet /sɔbrikɛ/ n.m. nickname.

sociable /sɔsjabl/ a. sociable.

soc|ial (*m. pl.* **~iaux**) /sɔsjal, -jo/ *a.* social.

socialis|te /sɔsjalist/ *n.m./f.* socialist. **~me** *n.m.* socialism.

société /sɔsjete/ *n.f.* society; (*compagnie, firme*) company.

sociolo|gie /sɔsjɔlɔʒi/ *n.f.* sociology. **~gique** *a.* sociological. **~gue** *n.m./f.* sociologist.

socle /sɔkl/ *n.m.* (*de colonne, statue*) plinth; (*de lampe*) base.

socquette /sɔkɛt/ *n.f.* ankle sock.

soda /sɔda/ *n.m.* (fizzy) drink.

sodium /sɔdjɔm/ *n.m.* sodium.

sœur /sœr/ *n.f.* sister.

sofa /sofa/ *n.m.* sofa.

soi /swa/ *pron.* oneself. **en ~,** in itself. **~-disant** *a. invar.* so-called; (*qui se veut tel*) self-styled; *adv.* supposedly.

soie /swa/ *n.f.* silk.

soif /swaf/ *n.f.* thirst. **avoir ~,** be thirsty. **donner ~ à,** make thirsty.

soigné /swaɲe/ *a.* tidy, neat; (*bien fait*) careful.

soigner /swaɲe/ *v.t.* look after, take care of; (*tenue, style*) take care over; (*maladie*) treat. **se ~** *v. pr.* look after o.s.

soigneu|x, ~se /swaɲø, -z/ *a.* careful (**de,** about); (*ordonné*) tidy. **~sement** *adv.* carefully.

soi-même /swamɛm/ *pron.* oneself.

soin /swɛ̃/ *n.m.* care; (*ordre*) tidiness. **~s,** care; (*méd.*) treatment. **avoir ou prendre ~ de qn./de faire,** take care of s.o./to do. **premiers ~s,** first aid.

soir /swar/ *n.m.* evening.

soirée /sware/ *n.f.* evening; (*réception*) party. **~ dansante,** dance.

soit /swa/ *voir* être. ● *conj.* (*à savoir*) that is to say. **~ . . . soit,** either . . . or.

soixantaine /swasãtɛn/ *n.f.* **une ~ (de),** about sixty.

soixant|e /swasãt/ *a. & n.m.* sixty. **~e-dix** *a. & n.m.* seventy. **~e-dixième** *a. & n.m./f.* seventieth. **~ième** *a. & n.m./f.* sixtieth.

soja /sɔʒa/ *n.m.* (*graines*) soya beans; (*plante*) soya.

sol /sɔl/ *n.m.* ground; (*de maison*) floor; (*terrain agricole*) soil.

solaire /sɔlɛr/ *a.* solar; (*huile, filtre*) sun. **les rayons ~s,** the sun's rays.

soldat /sɔlda/ *n.m.* soldier.

solde[1] /sɔld/ *n.f.* (*salaire*) pay.

solde[2] /sɔld/ *n.m.* (*comm.*) balance. **~s,** (*articles*) sale goods. **en ~,**

(*acheter etc.*) at sale price. **les ~s,** the sales.

solder /sɔlde/ *v.t.* reduce; (*liquider*) sell off at sale price; (*compte*) settle. **se ~ par,** (*aboutir à*) end in.

sole /sɔl/ *n.f.* (*poisson*) sole.

soleil /sɔlɛj/ *n.m.* sun; (*chaleur*) sunshine; (*fleur*) sunflower. **il y a du ~,** it is sunny.

solennel, ~le /sɔlanɛl/ *a.* solemn.

solennité /sɔlanite/ *n.f.* solemnity.

solex /sɔleks/ *n.m.* (P.) moped.

solfège /sɔlfɛʒ/ *n.m.* elementary musical theory.

solid|aire /sɔlidɛr/ *a.* (*mécanismes*) interdependent; (*couple*) (mutually) supportive; (*ouvriers*) who show solidarity. **~arité** *n.f.* solidarity.

solidariser (se) /(sə)sɔlidarize/ *v. pr.* show solidarity (**avec,** with).

solid|e /sɔlid/ *a.* solid. ● *n.m.* (*objet*) solid; (*corps*) sturdy. **~ement** *adv.* solidly. **~ité** *n.f.* solidity.

solidifier /sɔlidifje/ *v.t.,* **se ~** *v. pr.* solidify.

soliste /sɔlist/ *n.m./f.* soloist.

solitaire /sɔlitɛr/ *a.* solitary. ● *n.m./f.* (*ermite*) hermit; (*personne insociable*) loner.

solitude /sɔlityd/ *n.f.* solitude.

solive /sɔliv/ *n.f.* joist.

sollicit|er /sɔlisite/ *v.t.* request; (*attirer, pousser*) prompt; (*tenter*) tempt; (*faire travailler*) make demands on. **~ation** *n.f.* earnest request.

sollicitude /sɔlisityd/ *n.f.* concern.

solo /sɔlo/ *n.m. & a. invar.* (*mus.*) solo.

solstice /sɔlstis/ *n.m.* solstice.

soluble /sɔlybl/ *a.* soluble.

solution /sɔlysjɔ̃/ *n.f.* solution.

solvable /sɔlvabl/ *a.* solvent.

solvant /sɔlvã/ *n.m.* solvent.

sombre /sɔ̃br/ *a.* dark; (*triste*) sombre.

sombrer /sɔ̃bre/ *v.i.* sink (**dans,** into).

sommaire /sɔmɛr/ *a.* summary; (*tenue, repas*) scant. ● *n.m.* summary.

sommation /sɔmasjɔ̃/ *n.f.* (*mil.*) warning; (*jurid.*) summons.

somme[1] /sɔm/ *n.f.* sum. **en ~, ~ toute,** in short. **faire la ~ de,** add (up), total (up).

somme[2] /sɔm/ *n.m.* (*sommeil*) nap.

sommeil /sɔmɛj/ *n.m.* sleep; (*besoin de dormir*) drowsiness. **avoir ~,** be *ou* feel sleepy. **~ler** /-meje/ *v.i.* doze; (*fig.*) lie dormant.

sommelier /sɔməlje/ *n.m.* wine waiter.

sommer /sɔme/ *v.t.* summon.

sommes /sɔm/ *voir* être.

sommet /sɔmɛ/ *n.m.* top; (*de montagne*) summit; (*de triangle*) apex; (*gloire*) height.

sommier /sɔmje/ *n.m.* base (of bed).

somnambule /sɔmnãbyl/ *n.m.* sleepwalker.

somnifère /sɔmnifɛr/ *n.m.* sleeping-pill.

somnolen|t, ~te /sɔmnɔlã, -t/ *a.* drowsy. **~ce** *n.f.* drowsiness.

somnoler /sɔmnɔle/ *v.i.* doze.

sompt|ueux, ~ueuse /sõptɥø, -z/ *a.* sumptuous. **~uosité** *n.f.* sumptuousness.

son [1] **, sa** *ou* **son*** (*pl.* **ses**) /sõ, sa, sõn, se/ *a.* his; (*femme*) her; (*chose*) its; (*indéfini*) one's.

son [2] /sõ/ *n.m.* (*bruit*) sound.

son [3] /sõ/ *n.m.* (*de blé*) bran.

sonar /sɔnar/ *n.m.* Sonar.

sonate /sɔnat/ *n.f.* sonata.

sonde /sõd/ *n.f.* (*pour les forages*) drill; (*méd.*) probe.

sond|er /sõde/ *v.t.* sound; (*terrain*) drill; (*personne*) sound out. **~age** *n.m.* sounding; drilling. **~age** (**d'opinion**), (opinion) poll.

song|e /sõʒ/ *n.m.* dream. **~er** *v.i.* dream; *v.t.* **~er que**, think that. **~er à**, think about. **~eur, ~euse** *a.* pensive.

sonnantes /sɔnãt/ *a.f. pl.* **à six**/*etc.* **heures ~**, on the stroke of six/*etc.*

sonné /sɔne/ *a.* (*fam.*) crazy; (*fatigué*) knocked out.

sonn|er /sɔne/ *v.t./i.* ring; (*clairon, glas*) sound; (*heure*) strike; (*domestique*) ring for. **midi ~é**, well past noon. **~er de**, (*clairon etc.*) sound, blow.

sonnerie /sɔnri/ *n.f.* ringing; (*de clairon*) sound; (*mécanisme*) bell.

sonnet /sɔnɛ/ *n.m.* sonnet.

sonnette /sɔnɛt/ *n.f.* bell.

sonor|e /sɔnɔr/ *a.* resonant; (*onde, effets, etc.*) sound. **~ité** *n.f.* resonance; (*d'un instrument*) tone.

sonoris|er /sɔnɔrize/ *v.t.* (*salle*) wire for sound. **~ation** *n.f.* (*matériel*) sound equipment.

sont /sõ/ *voir* être.

sophistiqué /sɔfistike/ *a.* sophisticated.

soporifique /sɔpɔrifik/ *a.* soporific.

sorbet /sɔrbɛ/ *n.m.* sorbet.

sorcellerie /sɔrsɛlri/ *n.f.* witchcraft.

sorc|ier /sɔrsje/ *n.m.* sorcerer. **~ière** *n.f.* witch.

sordide /sɔrdid/ *a.* sordid; (*lieu*) squalid.

sort /sɔr/ *n.m.* (*destin, hasard*) fate; (*condition*) lot; (*maléfice*) spell. **tirer** (**qch.**) **au ~**, draw lots (for sth.).

sortant, ~e /sɔrtã, -t/ *a.* (*président etc.*) outgoing.

sorte /sɔrt/ *n.f.* sort, kind. **de ~ que**, so that. **en quelque ~**, in a way. **faire en ~ que**, see to it that.

sortie /sɔrti/ *n.f.* departure, exit; (*porte*) exit; (*promenade, dîner*) outing; (*invective*) outburst; (*parution*) appearance; (*de disque, gaz*) release; (*d'un ordinateur*) output. **~s**, (*argent*) outgoings.

sortilège /sɔrtilɛʒ/ *n.m.* (magic) spell.

sortir† /sɔrtir/ *v.i.* (*aux. être*) go out, leave; (*venir*) come out; (*aller au spectacle etc.*) go out; (*livre, film*) come out; (*plante*) come up. **~ de**, (*pièce*) leave; (*milieu social*) come from; (*limites*) go beyond. ● *v.t.* (*aux. avoir*) take out; (*livre, modèle*) bring out; (*dire: fam.*) come out with. **~ d'affaire, (s')en ~**, get out of an awkward situation. **~ du commun** *ou* **de l'ordinaire**, be out of the ordinary.

sosie /sɔzi/ *n.m.* double.

sot, ~te /so, sɔt/ *a.* foolish.

sottise /sɔtiz/ *n.f.* foolishness; (*action, remarque*) foolish thing.

sou /su/ *n.m.* **~s**, money. **pas un ~**, not a penny. **sans le ~**, without a penny. **près de ses ~s**, tight-fisted.

soubresaut /subrəso/ *n.m.* (sudden) start.

souche /suʃ/ *n.f.* (*d'arbre*) stump; (*de famille, vigne*) stock; (*de carnet*) counterfoil. **planté comme une ~**, standing like an idiot.

souci [1] /susi/ *n.m.* (*inquiétude*) worry; (*préoccupation*) concern. **se faire du ~**, worry.

souci [2] /susi/ *n.m.* (*plante*) marigold.

soucier (se) /(sə)susje/ *v. pr.* **se ~ de**, be concerned about.

soucieu|x, ~se /susjø, -z/ *a.* concerned (**de**, about).

soucoupe /sukup/ *n.f.* saucer. **~ volante**, flying saucer.

soudain, ~e /sudɛ̃, -ɛn/ *a.* sudden. ● *adv.* suddenly. **~ement** /-ɛnmã/

adv. suddenly. **~eté** /-ɛnte/ *n.f.* suddenness.

soude /sud/ *n.f.* soda.

soud|er /sude/ *v.t.* solder, (*à la flamme*) weld. **se ~er** *v. pr.* (*os*) knit (together). **~ure** *n.f.* soldering, welding; (*substance*) solder.

soudoyer /sudwaje/ *v.t.* bribe.

souffle /sufl/ *n.m.* blow, puff; (*haleine*) breath; (*respiration*) breathing; (*explosion*) blast; (*vent*) breath of air.

soufflé /sufle/ *n.m.* (*culin.*) soufflé.

souffl|er /sufle/ *v.i.* blow; (*haleter*) puff. ● *v.t.* (*bougie*) blow out; (*poussière, fumée*) blow; (*par explosion*) destroy; (*chuchoter*) whisper. **~er son rôle à,** prompt. **~eur, ~euse** *n.m., f.* (*théâtre*) prompter.

soufflet /suflɛ/ *n.m.* (*instrument*) bellows.

souffrance /sufrɑ̃s/ *n.f.* suffering. **en ~,** (*affaire*) pending.

souffr|ir† /sufrir/ *v.i.* suffer (**de,** from). ● *v.t.* (*endurer*) suffer; (*admettre*) admit of. **il ne peut pas le ~ir,** he cannot stand *ou* bear him. **~ant, ~ante** *a.* unwell.

soufre /sufr/ *n.m.* sulphur.

souhait /swɛ/ *n.m.* wish. **nos ~s de,** (*vœux*) good wishes for. **à vos ~s!,** bless you!

souhait|er /swete/ *v.t.* (*bonheur etc.*) wish for. **~er qch. à qn.,** wish s.o. sth. **~er que/faire,** hope that/to do. **~able** /swɛtabl/ *a.* desirable.

souiller /suje/ *v.t.* soil.

soûl, ~e /su, sul/ *a.* drunk. ● *n.m.* **tout son ~,** as much as one can.

soulag|er /sulaʒe/ *v.t.* relieve. **~ement** *n.m.* relief.

soûler /sule/ *v.t.* make drunk. **se ~** *v. pr.* get drunk.

soulèvement /sulɛvmɑ̃/ *n.m.* uprising.

soulever /sulve/ *v.t.* lift, raise; (*exciter*) stir; (*question, poussière*) raise. **se ~** *v. pr.* lift *ou* raise o.s. up; (*se révolter*) rise up.

soulier /sulje/ *n.m.* shoe.

souligner /suliɲe/ *v.t.* underline; (*taille, yeux*) emphasize.

soum|ettre† /sumɛtr/ *v.t.* (*dompter, assujettir*) subject (**à,** to); (*présenter*) submit (**à,** to). **se ~ettre** *v. pr.* submit (**à,** to). **~is, ~ise** *a.* submissive. **~ission** *n.f.* submission.

soupape /supap/ *n.f.* valve.

soupçon /supsɔ̃/ *n.m.* suspicion. **un ~ de,** (*fig.*) a touch of. **~ner** /-ɔne/ *v.t.* suspect. **~neux, ~neuse** /-ɔnø, -z/ *a.* suspicious.

soupe /sup/ *n.f.* soup.

souper /supe/ *n.m.* supper. ● *v.i.* have supper.

soupeser /supəze/ *v.t.* judge the weight of; (*fig.*) weigh up.

soupière /supjɛr/ *n.f.* (soup) tureen.

soupir /supir/ *n.m.* sigh. **pousser un ~,** heave a sigh. **~er** *v.i.* sigh.

soupir|ail (*pl.* **~aux**) /supiraj, -o/ *n.m.* small basement window.

soupirant /supirɑ̃/ *n.m.* suitor.

souple /supl/ *a.* supple; (*règlement, caractère*) flexible. **~sse** /-ɛs/ *n.f.* suppleness; flexibility.

source /surs/ *n.f.* source; (*eau*) spring. **de ~ sûre,** from a reliable source. **~ thermale,** hot springs.

sourcil /sursi/ *n.m.* eyebrow.

sourciller /sursije/ *v.i.* **sans ~,** without batting an eyelid.

sourd, ~e /sur, -d/ *a.* deaf; (*bruit, douleur*) dull; (*inquiétude, conflit*) silent, hidden. ● *n.m., f.* deaf person. **faire la ~e oreille,** turn a deaf ear. **~-muet** (*pl.* **~s-muets**), **~e-muette** (*pl.* **~es-muettes**) *a.* deaf and dumb; *n.m., f.* deaf mute.

sourdine /surdin/ *n.f.* (*mus.*) mute. **en ~,** quietly.

souricière /surisjɛr/ *n.f.* mousetrap; (*fig.*) trap.

sourire /surir/ *n.m.* smile. **garder le ~,** keep smiling. ● *v.i.* smile (**à,** at). **~ à,** (*fortune*) smile on.

souris /suri/ *n.f.* mouse.

sournois, ~e /surnwa, -z/ *a.* sly, underhand. **~ement** /-zmɑ̃/ *adv.* slyly.

sous /su/ *prép.* under, beneath. **~ la main,** handy. **~ la pluie,** in the rain. **~ peu,** shortly. **~ terre,** underground.

sous- /su/ *préf.* (*subordination*) sub-; (*insuffisance*) under-.

sous-alimenté /suzalimɑ̃te/ *a.* undernourished.

sous-bois /subwa/ *n.m. invar.* undergrowth.

souscr|ire /suskrir/ *v.i.* **~ire à,** subscribe to. **~iption** *n.f.* subscription.

sous-direct|eur, ~rice /sudirɛktœr, -ris/ *n.m., f.* assistant manager.

sous-entend|re /suzɑ̃tɑ̃dr/ *v.t.* imply. **~u** *n.m.* insinuation.

sous-estimer /suzɛstime/ *v.t.* underestimate.

sous-jacent, ~e /suʒasã, -t/ *a.* underlying.

sous-marin, ~e /sumarɛ̃, -in/ *a.* underwater. ● *n.m.* submarine.

sous-officier /suzɔfisje/ *n.m.* non-commissioned officer.

sous-préfecture /suprefɛktyr/ *n.f.* sub-prefecture.

sous-produit /suprɔdɥi/ *n.m.* by-product.

sous-programme /suprɔgram/ *n.m.* subroutine.

soussigné, ~e /susiɲe/ *a. & n.m., f.* undersigned.

sous-sol /susɔl/ *n.m.* (*cave*) basement.

sous-titr|e /sutitr/ *n.m.* subtitle. **~er** *v.t.* subtitle.

soustr|aire† /sustrɛr/ *v.t.* remove; (*déduire*) subtract. **se ~aire à,** escape from. **~action** *n.f.* (*déduction*) subtraction.

sous-trait|er /sutrete/ *v.t.* subcontract. **~ant** *n.m.* subcontractor.

sous-verre /suvɛr/ *n.m. invar.* picture frame, glass mount.

sous-vêtement /suvetmã/ *n.m.* undergarment. **~s,** underwear.

soutane /sutan/ *n.f.* cassock.

soute /sut/ *n.f.* (*de bateau*) hold. **~ à charbon,** coal-bunker.

soutenir† /sutnir/ *v.t.* support; (*fortifier, faire durer*) sustain; (*résister à*) withstand. **~ que,** maintain that. **se ~** *v. pr.* (*se tenir debout*) support o.s.

soutenu /sutny/ *a.* (*constant*) sustained; (*style*) lofty.

souterrain, ~e /suterɛ̃, -ɛn/ *a.* underground. ● *n.m.* underground passage, subway.

soutien /sutjɛ̃/ *n.m.* support. **~-gorge** (*pl.* **~s-gorge**) *n.m.* bra.

soutirer /sutire/ *v.t.* **~ à qn.,** extract from s.o.

souvenir[1] /suvnir/ *n.m.* memory, recollection; (*objet*) memento; (*cadeau*) souvenir. **en ~ de,** in memory of.

souvenir[2]† **(se)** /(sə)suvnir/ *v. pr.* **se ~ de,** remember. **se ~ que,** remember that.

souvent /suvã/ *adv.* often.

souverain, ~e /suvrɛ̃, -ɛn/ *a.* sovereign; (*extrême: péj.*) supreme.

● *n.m., f.* sovereign. **~eté** /-ɛnte/ *n.f.* sovereignty.

soviétique /sɔvjetik/ *a.* Soviet. ● *n.m./f.* Soviet citizen.

soyeu|x, ~se /swajø, -z/ *a.* silky.

spacieu|x, ~se /spasjø, -z/ *a.* spacious.

spaghetti /spageti/ *n.m. pl.* spaghetti.

sparadrap /sparadra/ *n.m.* sticking-plaster; (*Amer.*) adhesive tape *ou* bandage.

spasm|e /spasm/ *n.m.* spasm. **~odique** *a.* spasmodic.

spat|ial (*m. pl.* **~iaux**) /spasjal, -jo/ *a.* space.

spatule /spatyl/ *n.f.* spatula.

speaker, ~ine /spikœr, -rin/ *n.m., f.* announcer.

spéc|ial (*m. pl.* **~iaux**) /spesjal, -jo/ *a.* special; (*singulier*) peculiar. **~ialement** *adv.* especially; (*exprès*) specially.

spécialis|er (se) /(sə)spesjalize/ *v. pr.* specialize (**dans,** in). **~ation** *n.f.* specialization.

spécialiste /spesjalist/ *n.m./f.* specialist.

spécialité /spesjalite/ *n.f.* speciality; (*Amer.*) specialty.

spécif|ier /spesifje/ *v.t.* specify. **~ication** *n.f.* specification.

spécifique /spesifik/ *a.* specific.

spécimen /spesimɛn/ *n.m.* specimen.

spectacle /spɛktakl/ *n.m.* sight, spectacle; (*représentation*) show.

spectaculaire /spɛktakylɛr/ *a.* spectacular.

specta|teur, ~trice /spɛktatœr, -tris/ *n.m., f.* onlooker; (*sport*) spectator. **les ~teurs,** (*théâtre*) the audience.

spectre /spɛktr/ *n.m.* (*revenant*) spectre; (*images*) spectrum.

spécul|er /spekyle/ *v.i.* speculate. **~ateur, ~atrice** *n.m., f.* speculator. **~ation** *n.f.* speculation.

spéléologie /speleɔlɔʒi/ *n.f.* cave exploration, pot-holing; (*Amer.*) spelunking.

sperme /spɛrm/ *n.m.* sperm.

sph|ère /sfɛr/ *n.f.* sphere. **~érique** *a.* spherical.

sphinx /sfɛ̃ks/ *n.m.* sphinx.

spirale /spiral/ *n.f.* spiral.

spirite /spirit/ *n.m./f.* spiritualist.

spirituel, ~le /spiritɥel/ *a.* spiritual; (*amusant*) witty.

spiritueux /spirityø/ *n.m.* (*alcool*) spirit.

splend|ide /splãdid/ *a.* splendid. **~eur** *n.f.* splendour.

spongieu|x, ~se /spɔ̃ʒjø, -z/ *a.* spongy.

sponsor /spɔ̃sɔr/ *n.m.* sponsor. **~iser** *v.t.* sponsor.

spontané /spɔ̃tane/ *a.* spontaneous. **~ité** *n.f.* spontaneity. **~ment** *adv.* spontaneously.

sporadique /spɔradik/ *a.* sporadic.

sport /spɔr/ *n.m.* sport. ● *a. invar.* (*vêtements*) casual. **veste/voiture de ~,** sports jacket/car.

sporti|f, ~ve /spɔrtif, -v/ *a.* sporting; (*physique*) athletic; (*résultats*) sports. ● *n.m.* sportsman. ● *n.f.* sportswoman.

spot /spɔt/ *n.m.* spotlight; (*publicitaire*) ad.

spray /spre/ *n.m.* spray; (*méd.*) inhaler.

sprint /sprint/ *n.m.* sprint. **~er** *v.i.* sprint; *n.m.* /-œr/ sprinter.

square /skwar/ *n.m.* (public) garden.

squash /skwaʃ/ *n.m.* squash.

squatter /skwatœr/ *n.m.* squatter. **~iser** *v.t.* squat in.

squelett|e /skəlɛt/ *n.m.* skeleton. **~ique** /-etik/ *a.* skeletal; (*maigre*) all skin and bone.

stabiliser /stabilize/ *v.t.* stabilize.

stab|le /stabl/ *a.* stable. **~ilité** *n.f.* stability.

stade[1] /stad/ *n.m.* (*sport*) stadium.

stade[2] /stad/ *n.m.* (*phase*) stage.

stag|e /staʒ/ *n.m.* course. **~iaire** *a. & n.m./f.* course member; (*apprenti*) trainee.

stagn|er /stagne/ *v.i.* stagnate. **~ant, ~ante** *a.* stagnant. **~ation** *n.f.* stagnation.

stand /stãd/ *n.m.* stand, stall. **~ de tir,** (shooting-)range.

standard[1] /stãdar/ *n.m.* switchboard. **~iste** /-dist/ *n.m./f.* switchboard operator.

standard[2] /stãdar/ *a. invar.* standard. **~iser** /-dize/ *v.t.* standardize.

standing /stãdiŋ/ *n.m.* status, standing. **de ~,** (*hôtel etc.*) luxury.

star /star/ *n.f.* (*actrice*) star.

starter /starter/ *n.m.* (*auto.*) choke.

station /stasjɔ̃/ *n.f.* station; (*halte*) stop. **~ balnéaire,** seaside resort. **~ debout,** standing position. **~ de taxis,** taxi rank; (*Amer.*) taxi stand.

~-service (*pl.* **~s-service**) *n.f.* service station. **~ thermale,** spa.

stationnaire /stasjɔnɛr/ *a.* stationary.

stationn|er /stasjɔne/ *v.i.* park. **~ement** *n.m.* parking.

statique /statik/ *a.* static.

statistique /statistik/ *n.f.* statistic; (*science*) statistics. ● *a.* statistical.

statue /staty/ *n.f.* statue.

statuer /statɥe/ *v.i.* **~ sur,** rule on.

statu quo /statykwo/ *n.m.* status quo.

stature /statyr/ *n.f.* stature.

statut /staty/ *n.m.* status. **~s,** (*règles*) statutes. **~aire** /-tɛr/ *a.* statutory.

steak /stɛk/ *n.m.* steak.

stencil /stɛnsil/ *n.m.* stencil.

sténo /steno/ *n.f.* (*personne*) stenographer; (*sténographie*) shorthand.

sténodactylo /stenɔdaktilo/ *n.f.* shorthand typist; (*Amer.*) stenographer.

sténographie /stenɔgrafi/ *n.f.* shorthand.

stéréo /stereo/ *n.f. & a. invar.* stereo. **~phonique** /-eɔfɔnik/ *a.* stereophonic.

stéréotyp|e /stereɔtip/ *n.m.* stereotype. **~é** *a.* stereotyped.

stéril|e /steril/ *a.* sterile. **~ité** *n.f.* sterility.

stérilet /sterilɛ/ *n.m.* coil, IUD.

stérilis|er /sterilize/ *v.t.* sterilize. **~ation** *n.f.* sterilization.

stéroïde /steroid/ *a. & n.m.* steroid.

stéthoscope /stetɔskɔp/ *n.m.* stethoscope.

stigmat|e /stigmat/ *n.m.* mark, stigma. **~iser** *v.t.* stigmatize.

stimul|er /stimyle/ *v.t.* stimulate. **~ant** *n.m.* stimulus; (*médicament*) stimulant. **~ateur cardiaque,** pacemaker. **~ation** *n.f.* stimulation.

stipul|er /stipyle/ *v.t.* stipulate. **~ation** *n.f.* stipulation.

stock /stɔk/ *n.m.* stock. **~er** *v.t.* stock. **~iste** *n.m.* stockist; (*Amer.*) dealer.

stoïque /stɔik/ *a.* stoical. ● *n.m./f.* stoic.

stop /stɔp/ *int.* stop. ● *n.m.* stop sign; (*feu arrière*) brake light. **faire du ~,** (*fam.*) hitch-hike.

stopper /stɔpe/ *v.t./i.* stop; (*vêtement*) mend, reweave.

store /stɔr/ *n.m.* blind; (*Amer.*) shade; (*de magasin*) awning.

strabisme /strabism/ *n.m.* squint.

strapontin /strapɔ̃tɛ̃/ *n.m.* folding seat, jump seat.

stratagème /strataʒɛm/ *n.m.* stratagem.

stratég|ie /strateʒi/ *n.f.* strategy. **~ique** *a.* strategic.

stress /stres/ *n.* stress, **~ant** *a.* stressful. **~er** *v.t.* put under stress.

strict /strikt/ *a.* strict; (*tenue, vérité*) plain. **le ~ minimum,** the absolute minimum. **~ement** *adv.* strictly.

strident, ~e /stridã, -t/ *a.* shrill.

str|ie /stri/ *n.f.* streak. **~ier** *v.t.* streak.

strip-tease /striptiz/ *n.m.* strip-tease.

strophe /strɔf/ *n.f.* stanza, verse.

structur|e /stryktyr/ *n.f.* structure. **~al** (*m. pl.* **~aux**) *a.* structural. **~er** *v.t.* structure.

studieu|x, ~se /stydjø, -z/ *a.* studious; (*période*) devoted to study.

studio /stydjo/ *n.m.* (*d'artiste, de télévision, etc.*) studio; (*logement*) studio flat, bed-sitter.

stupéf|ait, ~aite /stypefɛ, -t/ *a.* amazed. **~action** *n.f.* amazement.

stupéf|ier /stypefje/ *v.t.* amaze. **~iant, ~iante** *a.* amazing; *n.m.* drug, narcotic.

stupeur /stypœr/ *n.f.* amazement; (*méd.*) stupor.

stupid|e /stypid/ *a.* stupid. **~ité** *n.f.* stupidity.

styl|e /stil/ *n.m.* style. **~isé** *a.* stylized.

stylé /stile/ *a.* well-trained.

styliste /stilist/ *n.m./f.* fashion designer.

stylo /stilo/ *n.m.* pen. **~ (à) bille,** ball-point pen. **~ (à) encre,** fountain-pen.

su /sy/ *voir* savoir.

suave /sɥav/ *a.* sweet.

subalterne /sybaltɛrn/ *a.* & *n.m./f.* subordinate.

subconscient, ~e /sypkɔ̃sjã, -t/ *a.* & *n.m.* subconscious.

subdiviser /sybdivize/ *v.t.* subdivide.

subir /sybir/ *v.t.* suffer; (*traitement, expériences*) undergo.

subit, ~e /sybi, -t/ *a.* sudden. **~ement** /-tmã/ *adv.* suddenly.

subjecti|f, ~ve /sybʒɛktif, -v/ *a.* subjective. **~vité** *n.f.* subjectivity.

subjonctif /sybʒɔ̃ktif/ *a.* & *n.m.* subjunctive.

subjuguer /sybʒyge/ *v.t.* (*charmer*) captivate.

sublime /syblim/ *a.* sublime.

submer|ger /sybmɛrʒe/ *v.t.* submerge, (*fig.*) overwhelm. **~sion** *n.f.* submersion.

subordonné, ~e /sybɔrdɔne/ *a.* & *n.m., f.* subordinate.

subord|onner /sybɔrdɔne/ *v.t.* subordinate (**à,** to). **~ination** *n.f.* subordination.

subreptice /sybrɛptis/ *a.* surreptitious.

subside /sybzid/ *n.m.* grant.

subsidiare /sypsidjɛr/ *a.* subsidiary.

subsist|er /sybziste/ *v.i.* subsist; (*durer, persister*) exist. **~ance** *n.f.* subsistence.

substance /sypstãs/ *n.f.* substance.

substantiel, ~le /sypstãsjɛl/ *a.* substantial.

substantif /sypstãtif/ *n.m.* noun.

substit|uer /sypstitɥe/ *v.t.* substitute (**à,** for). **se ~uer à,** (*remplacer*) substitute for; (*évincer*) take over from. **~ut** *n.m.* substitute; (*jurid.*) deputy public prosecutor. **~ution** *n.f.* substitution.

subterfuge /syptɛrfyʒ/ *n.m.* subterfuge.

subtil /syptil/ *a.* subtle. **~ité** *n.f.* subtlety.

subtiliser /syptilize/ *v.t.* **~ qch. (à qn.),** spirit sth. away (from s.o.).

subvenir /sybvønir/ *v.i.* **~ à,** provide for.

subvention /sybvãsjɔ̃/ *n.f.* subsidy. **~ner** /-jɔne/ *v.t.* subsidize.

subversi|f, ~ve /sybvɛrsif, -v/ *a.* subversive.

subversion /sybvɛrsjɔ̃/ *n.f.* subversion.

suc /syk/ *n.m.* juice.

succédané /syksedane/ *n.m.* substitute (**de,** for).

succéder /syksede/ *v.i.* **~ à,** succeed. **se ~** *v. pr.* succeed one another.

succès /syksɛ/ *n.m.* success. **à ~,** (*film, livre, etc.*) successful. **avoir du ~,** be a success.

successeur /syksesœr/ *n.m.* successor.

successi|f, ~ve /syksesif, -v/ *a.* successive. **~vement** *adv.* successively.

succession /syksesjɔ̃/ *n.f.* succession; (*jurid.*) inheritance.

succinct, ~e /syksɛ̃, -t/ *a.* succinct.

succomber /sykɔ̃be/ *v.i.* die. **~ à,** succumb to.

succulent, ~e /sykylã, -t/ *a.* succulent.

succursale /sykyrsal/ *n.f.* (*comm.*) branch.

sucer /syse/ *v.t.* suck.

sucette /sysɛt/ *n.f.* (*bonbon*) lollipop; (*tétine*) dummy; (*Amer.*) pacifier.

sucr|e /sykr/ *n.m.* sugar. **~e d'orge,** barley sugar. **~e en poudre,** caster sugar; (*Amer.*) finely ground sugar. **~e glace,** icing sugar. **~e roux,** brown sugar. **~ier, ~ière** *a.* sugar; *n.m.* (*récipient*) sugar-bowl.

sucr|er /sykre/ *v.t.* sugar, sweeten. **~é** *a.* sweet; (*additionné de sucre*) sweetened.

sucreries /sykrəri/ *n.f. pl.* sweets.

sud /syd/ *n.m.* south. ● *a. invar.* south; (*partie*) southern; (*direction*) southerly. **~-africain, ~-africaine** *a. & n.m., f.* South African. **~-est** *n.m.* south-east. **~-ouest** *n.m.* south-west.

Suède /sɥɛd/ *n.f.* Sweden.

suédois, ~e /sɥedwa, -z/ *a.* Swedish. ● *n.m., f.* Swede. ● *n.m.* (*lang.*) Swedish.

suer /sɥe/ *v.t./i.* sweat. **faire ~ qn.,** (*fam.*) get on s.o.'s nerves.

sueur /sɥœr/ *n.f.* sweat. **en ~,** sweating.

suff|ire† /syfir/ *v.i.* be enough (**à qn.,** for s.o.). **il ~it de faire,** one only has to do. **il ~it d'une goutte pour,** a drop is enough to. **~ire à,** (*besoin*) satisfy. **se ~ire à soi-même,** be self-sufficient.

suffis|ant, ~ante /syfizɑ̃, -t/ *a.* sufficient; (*vaniteux*) conceited. **~amment** *adv.* sufficiently. **~amment de,** sufficient. **~ance** *n.f.* (*vanité*) conceit.

suffixe /syfiks/ *n.m.* suffix.

suffoquer /syfɔke/ *v.t./i.* choke, suffocate.

suffrage /syfraʒ/ *n.m.* (*voix: pol.*) vote; (*modalité*) suffrage.

sugg|érer /sygʒere/ *v.t.* suggest. **~estion** /-ʒɛstjɔ̃/ *n.f.* suggestion.

suggesti|f, ~ve /sygʒɛstif, -v/ *a.* suggestive.

suicid|e /sɥisid/ *n.m.* suicide. **~aire** *a.* suicidal.

suicid|er (se) /(sə)sɥiside/ *v. pr.* commit suicide. **~é, ~ée** *n.m., f.* suicide.

suie /sɥi/ *n.f.* soot.

suint|er /sɥɛ̃te/ *v.i.* ooze. **~ement** *n.m.* oozing.

suis /sɥi/ *voir* être, suivre.

Suisse /sɥis/ *n.f.* Switzerland.

suisse /sɥis/ *a. & n.m.* Swiss. **~sse** /-ɛs/ *n.f.* Swiss (woman).

suite /sɥit/ *n.f.* continuation, rest; (*d'un film*) sequel; (*série*) series; (*appartement, escorte*) suite; (*résultat*) consequence; (*cohérence*) order. **~s,** (*de maladie*) after-effects. **à la ~, de ~,** (*successivement*) in succession. **à la ~ de,** (*derrière*) behind. **à la ~ de, par ~ de,** as a result of. **faire ~ (à),** follow. **par la ~,** afterwards. **~ à votre lettre du,** further to your letter of the.

suivant¹, ~e /sɥivɑ̃, -t/ *a.* following, next. ● *n.m., f.* following *ou* next person.

suivant² /sɥivɑ̃/ *prép.* (*selon*) according to.

suivi /sɥivi/ *a.* steady, sustained; (*cohérent*) consistent. **peu/très ~,** (*cours*) poorly-/well-attended.

suivre† /sɥivr/ *v.t./i.* follow; (*comprendre*) keep up (with), follow. **se ~** *v. pr.* follow each other. **faire ~,** (*courrier etc.*) forward.

sujet¹, ~te /syʒɛ, -t/ *a.* **~ à,** liable *ou* subject to. ● *n.m., f.* (*gouverné*) subject.

sujet² /syʒɛ/ *n.m.* (*matière, individu*) subject; (*motif*) cause; (*gram.*) subject. **au ~ de,** about.

sulfurique /sylfyrik/ *a.* sulphuric.

sultan /syltɑ̃/ *n.m.* sultan.

summum /sɔmɔm/ *n.m.* height.

super /sypɛr/ *n.m.* (*essence*) four-star, premium (*Amer.*). ● *a. invar.* (*fam.*) great. ● *adv.* (*fam.*) ultra, fantastically.

superbe /sypɛrb/ *a.* superb.

supercherie /sypɛrʃəri/ *n.f.* trickery.

supérette /sypɛrɛt/ *n.f.* minimarket.

superficie /sypɛrfisi/ *n.f.* area.

superficiel, ~le /sypɛrfisjɛl/ *a.* superficial.

superflu /sypɛrfly/ *a.* superfluous. ● *n.m.* (*excédent*) surplus.

supérieur, ~e /syperjœr/ *a.* (*plus haut*) upper; (*quantité, nombre*) greater (**à,** than); (*études, principe*) higher (**à,** than); (*meilleur, hautain*) superior (**à,** to). ● *n.m., f.* superior.

supériorité /syperjɔrite/ *n.f.* superiority.

superlati|f, ~ve /sypɛrlatif, -v/ *a. & n.m.* superlative.

supermarché /sypɛrmarʃe/ *n.m.* supermarket.

superposer /sypɛrpoze/ v.t. super-impose.

superproduction /sypɛrprɔdyksjɔ̃/ n.f. (film) spectacular.

superpuissance /sypɛrpɥisɑ̃s/ n.f. superpower.

supersonique /sypɛrsɔnik/ a. super-sonic.

superstit|ion /sypɛrstisjɔ̃/ n.f. superstition. **~ieux, ~ieuse** a. superstitious.

superviser /sypɛrvize/ v.t. supervise.

supplanter /syplɑ̃te/ v.t. supplant.

suppléan|t, ~te /sypleɑ̃, -t/ n.m., f. & a. **(professeur) ~t,** supply teacher; **(juge) ~t,** deputy (judge). **~ce** n.f. (fonction) temporary appointment.

suppléer /syplee/ v.t. (remplacer) replace; (ajouter) supply. ● v.i. **~ à,** (compenser) make up for.

supplément /syplemɑ̃/ n.m. (argent) extra charge; (de frites, légumes) extra portion. **en ~,** extra. **un ~ de,** (travail etc.) extra. **payer pour un ~ de bagages,** pay extra for excess luggage. **~aire** /-tɛr/ a. extra, additional.

supplic|e /syplis/ n.m. torture. **~ier** v.t. torture.

supplier /syplije/ v.t. beg, beseech **(de,** to).

support /sypɔr/ n.m. support; (publicitaire: fig.) medium.

support|er[1] /sypɔrte/ v.t. (endurer) bear; (subir) suffer; (soutenir) support; (résister à) withstand. **~able** a. bearable.

supporter[2] /sypɔrtɛr/ n.m. (sport) supporter.

suppos|er /sypoze/ v.t. suppose; (impliquer) imply. **à ~er que,** supposing that. **~ition** n.f. supposition.

suppositoire /sypozitwar/ n.m. suppository.

suppr|imer /syprime/ v.t. get rid of, remove; (annuler) cancel; (mot) delete. **~imer à qn.,** (enlever) take away from s.o. **~ession** n.f. removal; cancellation; deletion.

suprématie /sypremasi/ n.f. supremacy.

suprême /syprɛm/ a. supreme.

sur /syr/ prép. on, upon; (par-dessus) over; (au sujet de) about, on; (pro portion) out of; (mesure) by. **aller/tourner/etc. ~,** go/turn/etc. towards. **mettre/jeter/etc. ~,** put/throw/etc. on to. **~-le-champ** adv.

immediately. **~ le qui-vive,** on the alert. **~ mesure,** made to measure. **~ place,** on the spot. **~ ce,** hereupon.

sur- /syr/ préf. over-.

sûr /syr/ a. certain, sure; (sans danger) safe; (digne de confiance) reliable; (main) steady; (jugement) sound.

surabondance /syrabɔ̃dɑ̃s/ n.f. superabundance.

suranné /syrane/ a. outmoded.

surcharg|e /syrʃarʒ/ n.f. overloading; (poids) extra load. **~er** v.t. overload; (texte) alter.

surchauffer /syrʃofe/ v.t. overheat.

surchoix /syrʃwa/ a. invar. of finest quality.

surclasser /syrklase/ v.t. outclass.

surcroît /syrkrwa/ n.m. increase **(de,** in), additional amount **(de,** of). **de ~,** in addition.

surdité /syrdite/ n.f. deafness.

sureau (pl. **~x)** /syro/ n.m. (arbre) elder.

surélever /syrelve/ v.t. raise.

sûrement /syrmɑ̃/ adv. certainly; (sans danger) safely.

surench|ère /syrɑ̃ʃɛr/ n.f. higher bid. **~érir** v.i. bid higher **(sur,** than).

surestimer /syrɛstime/ v.t. overestimate.

sûreté /syrte/ n.f. safety; (garantie) surety; (d'un geste) steadiness. **être en ~,** be safe. **S~ (nationale),** division of French Ministère de l'Intérieur in charge of police.

surexcité /syrɛksite/ a. very excited.

surf /syrf/ n.m. surfing.

surface /syrfas/ n.f. surface. **faire ~,** (sous-marin etc.) surface. **en ~,** (fig.) superficially.

surfait, ~e /syrfɛ, -t/ a. overrated.

surgelé /syrʒəle/ a. (deep-)frozen. **(aliments) ~s,** frozen food.

surgir /syrʒir/ v.i. appear (suddenly); (difficulté) arise.

surhomme /syrɔm/ n.m. superman.

surhumain, ~e /syrymɛ̃, -ɛn/ a. superhuman.

surlendemain /syrlɑ̃dmɛ̃/ n.m. **le ~,** two days later. **le ~ de,** two days after.

surligneur /syrliɲœr/ n.m. highlighter (pen).

surmen|er /syrməne/ v.t., **se ~er** v. pr. overwork. **~age** n.m. overworking; (méd.) overwork.

surmonter /syrmɔ̃te/ v.t. (vaincre) overcome, surmount; (être au-dessus de) surmount, top.

surnager /syrnaʒe/ v.i. float.

surnaturel, ~le /syrnatyrɛl/ a. supernatural.

surnom /syrnɔ̃/ n.m. nickname. **~mer** /-ɔme/ v.t. nickname.

surnombre (en) /(ɑ̃)syrnɔ̃br/ adv. too many. **il est en ~,** he is one too many.

surpasser /syrpase/ v.t. surpass.

surpeuplé /syrpœple/ a. overpopulated.

surplomb /syrplɔ̃/ n.m. **en ~,** overhanging. **~er** /-be/ v.t./i. overhang.

surplus /syrply/ n.m. surplus.

surpr|endre† /syrprɑ̃dr/ v.t. (étonner) surprise; (prendre au dépourvu) catch, surprise; (entendre) overhear. **~enant, ~enante** a. surprising. **~is, ~ise** a. surprised (**de,** at).

surprise /syrpriz/ n.f. surprise: **~partie** (pl. **~s-parties**) n.f. party.

surréalisme /syrrealism/ n.m. surrealism.

sursaut /syrso/ n.m. start, jump. **en ~,** with a start. **~ de,** (regain) burst of. **~er** /-te/ v.i. start, jump.

sursis /syrsi/ n.m. reprieve; (mil.) deferment. **deux ans (de prison) avec ~,** a two-year suspended sentence.

surtaxe /syrtaks/ n.f. surcharge.

surtout /syrtu/ adv. especially, mainly; (avant tout) above all. **~ pas,** certainly not.

surveillant, ~e /syrvɛjɑ̃, -t/ n.m., f. (de prison) warder; (au lycée) supervisor (in charge of discipline).

surveill|er /syrveje/ v.t. watch; (travaux, élèves) supervise. **~ance** n.f. watch; supervision; (de la police) surveillance.

survenir /syrvənir/ v.i. occur, come about; (personne) turn up; (événement) take place.

survêtement /syrvɛtmɑ̃/ n.m. (sport) track suit.

survie /syrvi/ n.f. survival.

survivance /syrvivɑ̃s/ n.f. survival.

surviv|re† /syrvivr/ v.i. survive. **~re à,** (conflit etc.) survive; (personne) outlive. **~ant, ~ante,** a. surviving; n.m., f. survivor.

survol /syrvɔl/ n.m. **le ~ de,** flying over. **~er** v.t. fly over; (livre) skim through.

survolté /syrvɔlte/ a. (surexcité) worked up.

susceptib|le /sysɛptibl/ a. touchy. **~le de faire,** (possibilité) liable to do; (capacité) able to do. **~lité** n.f. susceptibility.

susciter /sysite/ v.t. (éveiller) arouse; (occasionner) create.

suspect, ~e /syspɛ, -ɛkt/ a. (témoignage) suspect; (individu) suspicious. **~ de,** suspected of. ● n.m., f. suspect. **~er** /-ɛkte/ v.t. suspect.

suspend|re /syspɑ̃dr/ v.t. (arrêter, différer, destituer) suspend; (accrocher) hang (up). **se ~re à,** hang from. **~u à,** hanging from.

suspens (en) /(ɑ̃)syspɑ̃/ adv. (affaire) in abeyance; (dans l'indécision) in suspense.

suspense /syspɛns/ n.m. suspense.

suspension /syspɑ̃sjɔ̃/ n.f. suspension; (lustre) chandelier.

suspicion /syspisjɔ̃/ n.f. suspicion.

susurrer /sysyre/ v.t./i. murmur.

suture /sytyr/ n.f. **point de ~,** stitch.

svelte /svɛlt/ a. slender.

S.V.P. abrév. voir s'il vous plaît.

sweat-shirt /switʃœrt/ n.m. sweatshirt.

syllabe /silab/ n.f. syllable.

symbol|e /sɛ̃bɔl/ n.m. symbol. **~ique** a. symbolic(al). **~iser** v.t. symbolize.

symétr|ie /simetri/ n.f. symmetry. **~ique** a. symmetrical.

sympa /sɛ̃pa/ a. invar. (fam.) nice. **sois ~,** be a pal.

sympath|ie /sɛ̃pati/ n.f. (goût) liking; (affinité) affinity; (condoléances) sympathy. **~ique** a. nice, pleasant.

sympathis|er /sɛ̃patize/ v.i. get on well (**avec,** with). **~ant, ~ante** n.m., f. sympathizer.

symphon|ie /sɛ̃fɔni/ n.f. symphony. **~ique** a. symphonic; (orchestre) symphony.

symposium /sɛ̃pozjɔm/ n.m. symposium.

sympt|ôme /sɛ̃ptom/ n.m. symptom. **~omatique** /-ɔmatik/ a. symptomatic.

synagogue /sinagɔg/ n.f. synagogue.

synchroniser /sɛ̃krɔnize/ v.t. synchronize.

syncope /sɛ̃kɔp/ *n.f.* (*méd.*) black-out.

syncoper /sɛ̃kɔpe/ *v.t.* syncopate.

syndic /sɛ̃dik/ *n.m.* ~ **(d'immeuble),** managing agent.

syndic|at /sɛ̃dika/ *n.m.* (trade) union. ~**at d'initiative,** tourist office. ~**al** (*m. pl.* ~**aux**) *a.* (trade-)union. ~**aliste** *n.m./f.* trade-unionist; *a.* (trade-)union.

syndiqué, ~**e** /sɛ̃dike/ *n.m.*, *f.* (trade-)union member.

syndrome /sɛ̃drom/ *n.m.* syndrome.

synonyme /sinɔnim/ *a.* synonymous. ● *n.m.* synonym.

syntaxe /sɛ̃taks/ *n.f.* syntax.

synthèse /sɛ̃tez/ *n.f.* synthesis.

synthétique /sɛ̃tetik/ *a.* synthetic.

synthé(tiseur) /sɛ̃te(tizœr)/ *n.m.* synthesizer.

syphilis /sifilis/ *n.f.* syphilis.

Syrie /siri/ *n.f.* Syria.

syrien, ~**ne** /sirjɛ̃, -jɛn/ *a. & n.m.,f.* Syrian.

systématique /sistematik/ *a.* systematic. ~**ment** *adv.* systematically.

système /sistɛm/ *n.m.* system. **le ~ D,** coping with problems.

T

t' /t/ *voir* te.

ta /ta/ *voir* ton[1].

tabac /taba/ *n.m.* tobacco; (*magasin*) tobacconist's shop. ● *a. invar.* buff. ~ **à priser,** snuff.

tabasser /tabase/ *v.t.* (*fam.*) beat up.

table /tabl/ *n.f.* table. **à ~!,** come and eat! **faire ~ rase,** make a clean sweep (**de,** of). ~ **de nuit,** bedside table. ~ **des matières,** table of contents. ~ **roulante,** (tea-)trolley; (*Amer.*) (serving) cart.

tableau (*pl.* ~**x**) /tablo/ *n.m.* picture; (*peinture*) painting; (*panneau*) board; (*graphique*) chart; (*liste*) list. ~ **(noir),** blackboard. ~ **d'affichage,** notice-board. ~ **de bord,** dashboard.

tabler /table/ *v.i.* ~ **sur,** count on.

tablette /tablɛt/ *n.f.* shelf. ~ **de chocolat,** bar of chocolate.

tablier /tablije/ *n.m.* apron; (*de pont*) platform; (*de magasin*) shutter.

tabloïd(e) /tablɔid/ *a. & n.m.* tabloïd.

tabou /tabu/ *n.m. & a.* taboo.

tabouret /taburɛ/ *n.m.* stool.

tabulateur /tabylatœr/ *n.m.* tabulator.

tac /tak/ *n.m.* **du ~ au tac,** tit for tat.

tache /taʃ/ *n.f.* mark, spot; (*salissure*) stain. **faire ~ d'huile,** spread. ~ **de rousseur,** freckle.

tâche /taʃ/ *n.f.* task, job.

tacher /taʃe/ *v.t.* stain. **se ~** *v. pr.* (*personne*) get stains on one's clothes.

tâcher /taʃe/ *v.i.* ~ **de faire,** try to do.

tacheté /taʃte/ *a.* spotted.

tacite /tasit/ *a.* tacit.

taciturne /tasityrn/ *a.* taciturn.

tact /takt/ *n.m.* tact.

tactile /taktil/ *a.* tactile.

tactique /taktik/ *a.* tactical. ● *n.f.* tactics. **une ~,** a tactic.

taie /tɛ/ *n.f.* ~ **d'oreiller,** pillowcase.

taillader /tɑjade/ *v.t.* gash, slash.

taille[1] /tɑj/ *n.f.* (*milieu du corps*) waist; (*hauteur*) height; (*grandeur*) size. **de ~,** sizeable. **être de ~ à faire,** be up to doing.

taill|e[2] /tɑj/ *n.f.* cutting; pruning; (*forme*) cut. ~**er** *v.t.* cut; (*arbre*) prune; (*crayon*) sharpen; (*vêtement*) cut out. **se ~er** *v. pr.* (*argot*) clear off. ~**e-crayon(s)** *n.m. invar.* pencil-sharpener.

tailleur /tɑjœr/ *n.m.* tailor; (*costume*) lady's suit. **en ~,** cross-legged.

taillis /tɑji/ *n.m.* copse.

taire† /tɛr/ *v.t.* say nothing about. **se ~** *v. pr.* be silent *ou* quiet; (*devenir silencieux*) fall silent. **faire ~,** silence.

talc /talk/ *n.m.* talcum powder.

talent /talɑ̃/ *n.m.* talent. ~**ueux,** ~**ueuse** /-tɥø, -z/ *a.* talented.

taloche /talɔʃ/ *n.f.* (*fam.*) slap.

talon /talɔ̃/ *n.m.* heel; (*de chèque*) stub.

talonner /talɔne/ *v.t.* follow hard on the heels of.

talus /taly/ *n.m.* embankment.

tambour /tɑ̃bur/ *n.m.* drum; (*personne*) drummer; (*porte*) revolving door.

tambourin /tɑ̃burɛ̃/ *n.m.* tambourine.

tambouriner /tɑ̃burine/ *v.t./i.* drum (**sur,** on).

tamis /tami/ *n.m.* sieve. ~**er** /-ze/ *v.t.* sieve.

Tamise /tamiz/ *n.f.* Thames.

tamisé /tamize/ a. (*lumière*) subdued.

tampon /tɑ̃pɔ̃/ n.m. (*pour boucher*) plug; (*ouate*) wad, pad; (*timbre*) stamp; (*de train*) buffer. **~ (hygiénique)**, tampon.

tamponner /tɑ̃pɔne/ v.t. crash into; (*timbrer*) stamp; (*plaie*) dab; (*mur*) plug. **se ~** v. pr. (*véhicules*) crash into each other.

tandem /tɑ̃dɛm/ n.m. (*bicyclette*) tandem; (*personnes: fig.*) duo.

tandis que /tɑ̃dik(ə)/ conj. while.

tangage /tɑ̃gaʒ/ n.m. pitching.

tangente /tɑ̃ʒɑ̃t/ n.f. tangent.

tangible /tɑ̃ʒibl/ a. tangible.

tango /tɑ̃go/ n.m. tango.

tanguer /tɑ̃ge/ v.i. pitch.

tanière /tanjɛr/ n.f. den.

tank /tɑ̃k/ n.m. tank.

tann|er /tane/ v.t. tan. **~é** a. (*visage*) tanned, weather-beaten.

tant /tɑ̃/ adv. (*travailler, manger, etc.*) so much. **~ (de)**, (*quantité*) so much; (*nombre*) so many. **~ que**, as long as; (*autant que*) as much as. **en ~ que**, (*comme*) as. **~ mieux!**, fine!, all the better! **~ pis!**, too bad!

tante /tɑ̃t/ n.f. aunt.

tantôt /tɑ̃to/ adv. sometimes; (*cet après-midi*) this afternoon.

tapag|e /tapaʒ/ n.m. din. **~eur, ~euse** a. rowdy; (*tape-à-l'œil*) flashy.

tapant, ~e /tapɑ̃, -t/ a. **à deux/trois/** etc. **heures ~es** at exactly two/three/*etc.* o'clock.

tape /tap/ n.f. slap. **~-à-l'œil** a. invar. flashy, tawdry.

taper /tape/ v.t. bang; (*enfant*) slap; (*emprunter: fam.*) touch for money. **~ (à la machine)**, type. ● v.i. (*cogner*) bang; (*soleil*) beat down. **~ dans**, (*puiser dans*) dig into. **~ sur**, thump; (*critiquer: fam.*) knock. **se ~** v. pr. (*repas: fam.*) put away; (*corvée: fam.*) do.

tap|ir (se) /(sə)tapir/ v. pr. crouch. **~i** a. crouching.

tapis /tapi/ n.m. carpet; (*petit*) rug; (*aux cartes*) baize. **~ de bain**, bath mat. **~-brosse** n.m. doormat. **~ de sol**, groundsheet. **~ roulant**, (*pour objets*) conveyor belt.

tapiss|er /tapise/ v.t. (wall)paper; (*fig.*) cover (**de**, with). **~erie** n.f. tapestry; (*papier peint*) wallpaper. **~ier, ~ière** n.m., f. (*décorateur*)

interior decorator; (*qui recouvre un siège*) upholsterer.

tapoter /tapɔte/ v.t. tap, pat.

taquin, ~e /takɛ̃, -in/ a. fond of teasing. ● n.m., f. tease(r). **~er** /-ine/ v.t. tease. **~erie(s)** /-inri/ n.f. (pl.) teasing.

tarabiscoté /tarabiskɔte/ a. overelaborate.

tard /tar/ adv. late. **au plus ~**, at the latest. **plus ~**, later. **sur le ~**, late in life.

tard|er /tarde/ v.i. (*être lent à venir*) be a long time coming. **~er (à faire)**, take a long time (doing), delay (doing). **sans (plus) ~er**, without (further) delay. **il me tarde de**, I long to.

tardi|f, ~ve /tardif, -v/ a. late; (*regrets*) belated.

tare /tar/ n.f. (*défaut*) defect.

taré /tare/ a. cretin.

targette /tarʒɛt/ n.f. bolt.

targuer (se) /(sə)targe/ v. pr. **se ~ de**, boast about.

tarif /tarif/ n.m. tariff; (*de train, taxi*) fare. **~s postaux**, postage ou postal rates. **~aire** a. tariff.

tarir /tarir/ v.t./i., **se ~** v. pr. dry up.

tartare /tartar/ a. (*culin.*) tartar.

tarte /tart/ n.f. tart; (*Amer.*) (open) pie. ● a. invar. (*sot: fam.*) stupid; (*laid: fam.*) ugly.

tartin|e /tartin/ n.f. slice of bread. **~e beurrée**, slice of bread and butter. **~er** v.t. spread.

tartre /tartr/ n.m. (*bouilloire*) fur, calcium deposit; (*dents*) tartar.

tas /tɑ/ n.m. pile, heap. **un ou des ~ de**, (*fam.*) lots of.

tasse /tɑs/ n.f. cup. **~ à thé**, teacup.

tasser /tɑse/ v.t. pack, squeeze; (*terre*) pack (down). **se ~** v. pr. (*terrain*) sink; (*se serrer*) squeeze up.

tâter /tɑte/ v.t. feel; (*fig.*) sound out. ● v.i. **~ de**, try out.

tatillon, ~ne /tatijɔ̃, -jɔn/ a. finicky.

tâtonn|er /tɑtɔne/ v.i. grope about. **~ements** n.m. pl. (*essais*) trial and error.

tâtons (à) /(a)tɑtɔ̃/ adv. **avancer** ou **marcher à ~**, grope one's way along.

tatou|er /tatwe/ v.t. tattoo. **~age** n.m. (*dessin*) tattoo.

taudis /todi/ n.m. hovel.

taule /tol/ n.f. (*fam.*) prison.

taup|e /top/ n.f. mole. **~inière** n.f. molehill.

taureau (*pl.* **~x**) /tɔro/ *n.m.* bull. **le T~,** Taurus.

taux /to/ *n.m.* rate.

taverne /tavɛrn/ *n.f.* tavern.

tax|e /taks/ *n.f.* tax. **~e sur la valeur ajoutée,** value added tax. **~er** *v.t.* tax; (*produit*) fix the price of. **~er qn. de,** accuse s.o. of.

taxi /taksi/ *n.m.* taxi(-cab); (*personne*: *fam.*) taxi-driver.

taxiphone /taksifɔn/ *n.m.* pay phone.

Tchécoslovaquie /tʃekɔslɔvaki/ *n.f.* Czechoslovakia.

tchèque /tʃɛk/ *a.* & *n.m./f.* Czech.

te, t' /tə, t/ *pron.* you; (*indirect*) (to) you; (*réfléchi*) yourself.

technicien, ~ne /tɛknisjɛ̃, -jɛn/ *n.m., f.* technician.

technique /tɛknik/ *a.* technical. ● *n.f.* technique. **~ment** *adv.* technically.

technolog|ie /tɛknɔlɔʒi/ *n.f.* technology. **~ique** *a.* technological.

teck /tɛk/ *n.m.* teak.

tee-shirt /tiʃœrt/ *n.m.* tee-shirt.

teindre† /tɛ̃dr/ *v.t.* dye. **se ~ les cheveux** *v. pr.* dye one's hair.

teint /tɛ̃/ *n.m.* complexion.

teint|e /tɛ̃t/ *n.f.* shade, tint. **une ~e de,** (*fig.*) a tinge of. **~er** *v.t.* (*papier, verre, etc.*) tint; (*bois*) stain.

teintur|e /tɛ̃tyr/ *n.f.* dyeing; (*produit*) dye. **~erie** *n.f.* (*boutique*) dry-cleaner's. **~ier, ~ière** *n.m., f.* dry-cleaner.

tel, ~le /tɛl/ *a.* such. **un ~ livre**/*etc.*, such a book/*etc.* **un ~ chagrin**/*etc.*, such sorrow/*etc.* **~ que,** such as, like; (*ainsi que*) (just) as. **~ ou tel,** such-and-such. **~ quel,** (just) as it is.

télé /tele/ *n.f.* (*fam.*) TV.

télécommande /telekɔmɑ̃d/ *n.f.* remote control.

télécommunications /telekɔmynikɑsjɔ̃/ *n.f. pl.* telecommunications.

télécopi|e /telekɔpi/ *n.f.* tele(fax). **~eur** *n.m.* fax machine.

téléfilm /telefilm/ *n.m.* (tele)film.

télégramme /telegram/ *n.m.* telegram.

télégraph|e /telegraf/ *n.m.* telegraph. **~ier** *v.t./i.* **~ier (à),** cable. **~ique** *a.* telegraphic; (*fil, poteau*) telegraph.

téléguid|er /telegide/ *v.t.* control by radio. **~é** *a.* radio-controlled.

télématique /telematik/ *n.f.* computer communications.

télépathe /telepat/ *a.* & *n.m., f.* psychic.

télépathie /telepati/ *n.f.* telepathy.

téléphérique /teleferik/ *n.m.* cable-car.

téléphon|e /telefɔn/ *n.m.* (tele)phone. **~e rouge,** (*pol.*) hot line. **~er** *v.t./i.* **~er (à),** (tele)phone. **~ique** *a.* (tele)phone. **~iste** *n.m./f.* operator.

télescop|e /telɛskɔp/ *n.m.* telescope. **~ique** *a.* telescopic.

télescoper /telɛskɔpe/ *v.t.* smash into. **se ~** *v. pr.* (*véhicules*) smash into each other.

télésiège /telesjɛʒ/ *n.m.* chair-lift.

téléski /teleski/ *n.m.* ski tow.

téléspecta|teur, ~trice /telespɛktatœr, -tris/ *n.m., f.* (television) viewer.

télévente /televɑ̃t/ *n.f.* telesales.

télévis|é /televize/ *a.* **émission ~ée,** television programme. **~eur** *n.m.* television set.

télévision /televizjɔ̃/ *n.f.* television.

télex /telɛks/ *n.m.* telex.

télexer /telɛkse/ *v.t.* telex.

telle /tɛl/ *voir* tel.

tellement /tɛlmɑ̃/ *adv.* (*tant*) so much; (*si*) so. **~ de,** (*quantité*) so much; (*nombre*) so many.

témér|aire /temerɛr/ *a.* rash. **~ité** *n.f.* rashness.

témoignage /temwaɲaʒ/ *n.m.* testimony, evidence; (*récit*) account. **~ de,** (*sentiment*) token of.

témoigner /temwaɲe/ *v.i.* testify (**de,** to). ● *v.t.* show. **~ que,** testify that.

témoin /temwɛ̃/ *n.m.* witness; (*sport*) baton. **être ~ de,** witness. **~ oculaire,** eyewitness.

tempe /tɑ̃p/ *n.f.* (*anat.*) temple.

tempérament /tɑ̃peramɑ̃/ *n.m.* temperament; (*physique*) constitution. **à ~,** (*acheter*) on hire-purchase; (*Amer.*) on the instalment plan.

température /tɑ̃peratyr/ *n.f.* temperature.

tempér|er /tɑ̃pere/ *v.t.* temper. **~é** *a.* (*climat*) temperate.

tempête /tɑ̃pɛt/ *n.f.* storm. **~ de neige,** snowstorm.

tempêter /tɑ̃pete/ *v.i.* (*crier*) rage.

temple /tɑ̃pl/ *n.m.* temple; (*protestant*) church.

temporaire /tɑ̃pɔrɛr/ *a.* temporary. **~ment** *adv.* temporarily.

temporel, ~le /tɑ̃pɔrɛl/ *a.* temporal.

temporiser /tɑ̃pɔrize/ *v.i.* play for time.

temps¹ /tɑ̃/ *n.m.* time; (*gram.*) tense; (*étape*) stage. **à ~ partiel/plein,** part-/full-time. **ces derniers ~,** lately. **dans le ~,** at one time. **dans quelque ~,** in a while. **de ~ en temps,** from time to time. **~ d'ar-rêt,** pause. **avoir tout son ~,** have plenty of time.

temps² /tɑ̃/ *n.m.* (*atmosphère*) weather. **~ de chien,** filthy weather. **quel ~ fait-il?,** what's the weather like?

tenace /tənas/ *a.* stubborn.

ténacité /tenasite/ *n.f.* stubbornness.

tenaille(s) /tənɑj/ *n.f.* (*pl.*) pincers.

tenanc|ier, ~ière /tənɑ̃sje, -jɛr/ *n.m., f.* keeper (**de,** of).

tenant /tənɑ̃/ *n.m.* (*partisan*) sup-porter; (*d'un titre*) holder.

tendance /tɑ̃dɑ̃s/ *n.f.* tendency; (*opi-nions*) leanings; (*évolution*) trend. **avoir ~ à,** have a tendency to, tend to.

tendon /tɑ̃dɔ̃/ *n.m.* tendon.

tendre¹ /tɑ̃dr/ *v.t.* stretch; (*piège*) set; (*bras*) stretch out; (*main*) hold out; (*cou*) crane; (*tapisserie*) hang. **~ à qn.,** hold out to s.o. ● *v.i.* **~ à,** tend to. **~ l'oreille,** prick up one's ears.

tendre² /tɑ̃dr/ *a.* tender; (*couleur, bois*) soft. **~ment** /-əmɑ̃/ *adv.* tenderly. **~sse** /-ɛs/ *n.f.* tenderness.

tendu /tɑ̃dy/ *a.* (*corde*) tight; (*personne, situation*) tense; (*main*) outstretched.

tén|èbres /tenɛbr/ *n.f. pl.* darkness. **~ébreux, ~ébreuse** *a.* dark.

teneur /tənœr/ *n.f.* content.

tenir† /tənir/ *v.t.* hold; (*pari, promesse, hôtel*) keep; (*place*) take up; (*propos*) utter; (*rôle*) play. **~ de,** (*avoir reçu de*) have got from. **~ pour,** regard as. **~ propre/chaud/ etc.,** keep clean/warm/*etc.* ● *v.i.* hold. **~ à,** be attached to. **~ à faire,** be anxious to do. **~ dans,** fit into. **~ de qn.,** take after s.o. **se ~** *v. pr.* (*rester*) remain; (*debout*) stand; (*avoir lieu*) be held. **se ~ à,** hold on to. **se ~ bien,** behave o.s. **s'en ~ à,** (*se limiter à*) confine o.s. to. **~ bon,** stand firm. **~ compte de,** take into account. **~ le coup,** hold out. **~ tête à,** stand up to. **tiens!,** (*sur-prise*) hey!

tennis /tenis/ *n.m.* tennis; (*terrain*) tennis-court. ● *n.m. pl.* (*chaus-sures*) sneakers. **~ de table,** table tennis.

ténor /tenɔr/ *n.m.* tenor.

tension /tɑ̃sjɔ̃/ *n.f.* tension. **avoir de la ~,** have high blood-pressure.

tentacule /tɑ̃takyl/ *n.m.* tentacle.

tentative /tɑ̃tativ/ *n.f.* attempt.

tente /tɑ̃t/ *n.f.* tent.

tenter¹ /tɑ̃te/ *v.t.* try (**de faire,** to do).

tent|er² /tɑ̃te/ *v.t.* (*allécher*) tempt. **~é de,** tempted to. **~ation** *n.f.* temptation.

tenture /tɑ̃tyr/ *n.f.* (wall) hanging. **~s,** drapery.

tenu /təny/ *voir* **tenir.** ● *a.* **bien ~,** well-kept. **~ de,** obliged to.

ténu /teny/ *a.* (*fil etc.*) fine; (*cause, nuance*) tenuous.

tenue /təny/ *n.f.* (*habillement*) dress; (*de sport*) clothes; (*de maison*) up-keep; (*conduite*) (good) behaviour; (*maintien*) posture. **~ de soirée,** evening dress.

ter /tɛr/ *a. invar.* (*numéro*) B, b.

térébenthine /terebɑ̃tin/ *n.f.* turpen-tine.

tergiverser /tɛrʒivɛrse/ *v.i.* procras-tinate.

terme /tɛrm/ *n.m.* (*mot*) term; (*date limite*) time-limit; (*fin*) end; (*date de loyer*) term. **à long/court ~,** long-/ short-term. **en bons ~s,** on good terms (**avec,** with).

termin|al, ~ale (*m. pl. ~aux*) /tɛrminal, -o/ *a.* terminal. **(classe) ~ale,** sixth form; (*Amer.*) twelfth grade. ● *n.m.* (*pl. ~aux*) terminal.

termin|er /tɛrmine/ *v.t./i.* finish; (*soirée, débat*) end, finish. **se ~er** *v. pr.* end (**par,** with). **~aison** *n.f.* (*gram.*) ending.

terminologie /tɛrminɔlɔʒi/ *n.f.* ter-minology.

terminus /tɛrminys/ *n.m.* terminus.

terne /tɛrn/ *a.* dull, drab.

ternir /tɛrnir/ *v.t./i.,* **se ~** *v. pr.* tarnish.

terrain /tɛrɛ̃/ *n.m.* ground; (*parcelle*) piece of land; (*à bâtir*) plot. **~ d'aviation,** airfield. **~ de camping,** campsite. **~ de golf,** golf-course. **~ de jeu,** playground. **~ vague,** waste ground; (*Amer.*) vacant lot.

terrasse /tɛras/ *n.f.* terrace; (*de café*) pavement area.

terrassement /tɛrasmɑ̃/ *n.m.* exca-vation.

terrasser /tɛrase/ *v.t.* (*adversaire*) floor; (*maladie*) strike down.

terrassier /tɛrasje/ *n.m.* navvy, labourer, ditch-digger.

terre /tɛr/ *n.f.* (*planète, matière*) earth; (*étendue, pays*) land; (*sol*) ground; (*domaine*) estate. **à ~,** (*naut.*) ashore. **par ~,** (*tomber, jeter*) to the ground; (*s'asseoir, poser*) on the ground. **~** (*cuite*), terracotta. **~-à-terre** *a. invar.* matter-of-fact, down-to-earth. **~-plein** *n.m.* platform, (*auto.*) central reservation. **la ~ ferme,** dry land. **~ glaise,** clay.

terreau (*m. pl.* **~x**) /tɛro/ *n.m.* compost.

terrer (se) /(sə)tɛre/ *v. pr.* hide o.s., dig o.s. in.

terrestre /tɛrɛstr/ *a.* land; (*de notre planète*) earth's; (*fig.*) earthly.

terreur /tɛrœr/ *n.f.* terror.

terreu|x, ~se /tɛrø, -z/ *a.* earthy; (*sale*) grubby.

terrible /tɛribl/ *a.* terrible; (*formidable*: *fam.*) terrific.

terrien, ~ne /tɛrjɛ̃, -jɛn/ *n.m., f.* earth-dweller.

terrier /tɛrje/ *n.m.* (*trou de lapin etc.*) burrow; (*chien*) terrier.

terrifier /tɛrifje/ *v.t.* terrify.

terrine /tɛrin/ *n.f.* (*culin.*) terrine.

territ|oire /tɛritwar/ *n.m.* territory. **~orial** (*m. pl.* **~oriaux**) *a.* territorial.

terroir /tɛrwar/ *n.m.* (*sol*) soil; (*région*) region. **du ~,** country.

terroriser /tɛrɔrize/ *v.t.* terrorize.

terroris|te /tɛrɔrist/ *n.m./f.* terrorist. **~me** *n.m.* terrorism.

tertre /tɛrtr/ *n.m.* mound.

tes /te/ *voir* ton [1].

tesson /tɛsɔ̃/ *n.m.* **~ de bouteille,** piece of broken bottle.

test /tɛst/ *n.m.* test. **~er** *v.t.* test.

testament /tɛstamɑ̃/ *n.m.* (*jurid.*) will; (*politique, artistique*) testament. **Ancien/Nouveau T~,** Old/New Testament.

testicule /tɛstikyl/ *n.m.* testicle.

tétanos /tetanos/ *n.m.* tetanus.

têtard /tɛtar/ *n.m.* tadpole.

tête /tɛt/ *n.f.* head; (*figure*) face; (*cheveux*) hair; (*cerveau*) brain. **à la ~ de,** at the head of. **à ~ reposée,** in a leisurely moment. **de ~,** (*calculer*) in one's head. **en ~,** (*sport*) in the lead. **faire la ~,** sulk. **faire une ~,** (*football*) head the ball. **tenir ~ à qn.,** stand up to s.o. **une forte ~,** a

rebel. **la ~ la première,** head first. **il n'en fait qu'à sa ~,** he does just as he pleases. **de la ~ aux pieds,** from head to toe. **~-à-queue** *n.m. invar.* (*auto.*) spin. **~-à-tête** *n.m. invar.* tête-à-tête. **en ~-à-tête,** in private.

tétée /tete/ *n.f.* feed.

téter /tete/ *v.t./i.* suck.

tétine /tetin/ *n.f.* (*de biberon*) teat; (*sucette*) dummy; (*Amer.*) pacifier.

têtu /tety/ *a.* stubborn.

texte /tɛkst/ *n.m.* text; (*de leçon*) subject; (*morceau choisi*) passage.

textile /tɛkstil/ *n.m. & a.* textile.

textuel, ~le /tɛkstɥɛl/ *a.* literal.

texture /tɛkstyr/ *n.f.* texture.

thaïlandais, ~e /tailɑ̃dɛ, -z/ *a. & n.m., f.* Thai.

Thaïlande /tailɑ̃d/ *n.f.* Thailand.

thé /te/ *n.m.* tea.

théâtr|al (*m. pl.* **~aux**) /teatral, -o/ *a.* theatrical.

théâtre /teatr/ *n.m.* theatre; (*jeu forcé*) play-acting; (*d'un crime*) scene. **faire du ~,** act.

théière /tejɛr/ *n.f.* teapot.

thème /tɛm/ *n.m.* theme; (*traduction*: *scol.*) prose.

théolog|ie /teɔlɔʒi/ *n.f.* theology. **~ien** *n.m.* theologian. **~ique** *a.* theological.

théorème /teɔrɛm/ *n.m.* theorem.

théor|ie /teɔri/ *n.f.* theory. **~icien, ~icienne** *n.m., f.* theorist. **~ique** *a.* theoretical. **~iquement,** *adv.* theoretically.

thérap|ie /terapi/ *n.f.* therapy. **~eutique** *a.* therapeutic.

thermique /tɛrmik/ *a.* thermal.

thermomètre /tɛrmɔmɛtr/ *n.m.* thermometer.

thermonucléaire /tɛrmɔnykleɛr/ *a.* thermonuclear.

thermos /tɛrmos/ *n.m./f.* (P.) Thermos (P.) (flask).

thermostat /tɛrmɔsta/ *n.m.* thermostat.

thésauriser /tezɔrize/ *v.t./i.* hoard.

thèse /tɛz/ *n.f.* thesis.

thon /tɔ̃/ *n.m.* (*poisson*) tuna.

thrombose /trɔ̃boz/ *n.f.* thrombosis.

thym /tɛ̃/ *n.m.* thyme.

thyroïde /tirɔid/ *n.f.* thyroid.

tibia /tibja/ *n.m.* shin-bone.

tic /tik/ *n.m.* (*contraction*) twitch; (*manie*) mannerism.

ticket /tikɛ/ *n.m.* ticket.

tic-tac /tiktak/ *n.m. invar.* (*de pendule*) ticking. **faire ~,** go tick tock.

tiède /tjɛd/ *a.* lukewarm; (*atmosphère*) mild. **tiédeur** /tjedœr/ *n.f.* lukewarmness; mildness.

tiédir /tjedir/ *v.t./i.* **(faire)** ~, warm slightly.

tien, ~ne /tjɛ̃, tjɛn/ *pron.* **le ~, la ~ne, les ~(ne)s,** yours. **à la ~ne!,** cheers!

tiens, tient /tjɛ̃/ *voir* tenir.

tiercé /tjɛrse/ *n.m.* place-betting.

tier|s, ~ce /tjɛr, -s/ *a.* third. ● *n.m.* (*fraction*) third; (*personne*) third party. **T~s-Monde** *n.m.* Third World.

tifs /tif/ *n.m. pl.* (*fam.*) hair.

tige /tiʒ/ *n.f.* (*bot.*) stem, stalk; (*en métal*) shaft.

tignasse /tiɲas/ *n.f.* mop of hair.

tigre /tigr/ *n.m.* tiger. **~sse** /-ɛs/ *n.f.* tigress.

tigré /tigre/ *a.* (*rayé*) striped; (*chat*) tabby.

tilleul /tijœl/ *n.m.* lime(-tree), linden (-tree); (*infusion*) lime tea.

timbale /tɛ̃bal/ *n.f.* (*gobelet*) (metal) tumbler.

timbr|e /tɛ̃br/ *n.m.* stamp; (*sonnette*) bell; (*de voix*) tone. **~e-poste** (*pl.* **~es-poste**) *n.m.* postage stamp. **~er** *v.t.* stamp.

timbré /tɛ̃bre/ *a.* (*fam.*) crazy.

timid|e /timid/ *a.* timid. **~ité** *n.f.* timidity.

timoré /timɔre/ *a.* timorous.

tintamarre /tɛ̃tamar/ *n.m.* din.

tint|er /tɛ̃te/ *v.i.* ring; (*clefs*) jingle. **~ement** *n.m.* ringing; jingling.

tique /tik/ *n.f.* (*insecte*) tick.

tir /tir/ *n.m.* (*sport*) shooting; (*action de tirer*) firing; (*feu, rafale*) fire. **~ à l'arc,** archery. **~ forain,** shooting-gallery.

tirade /tirad/ *n.f.* soliloquy.

tirage /tiraʒ/ *n.m.* (*de photo*) printing; (*de journal*) circulation; (*de livre*) edition; (*de loterie*) draw; (*de cheminée*) draught. **~ au sort,** drawing lots.

tiraill|er /tiraje/ *v.t.* pull (away) at; (*harceler*) plague. **~é entre,** (*possibilités etc.*) torn between. **~ement** *n.m.* (*douleur*) gnawing pain; (*conflit*) conflict.

tiré /tire/ *a.* (*traits*) drawn.

tire-bouchon /tirbuʃɔ̃/ *n.m.* corkscrew.

tire-lait /tirlɛ/ *n.m.* breastpump.

tirelire /tirlir/ *n.f.* money-box; (*Amer.*) coin-bank.

tirer /tire/ *v.t.* pull; (*navire*) tow, tug; (*langue*) stick out; (*conclusion, trait, rideaux*) draw; (*coup de feu*) fire; (*gibier*) shoot; (*photo*) print. **~ de,** (*sortir*) take *ou* get out of; (*extraire*) extract from; (*plaisir, nom*) derive from. ● *v.i.* shoot, fire (**sur,** at). **~ sur,** (*couleur*) verge on; (*corde*) pull at. **se ~** *v. pr.* (*fam.*) clear off. **se ~ de,** get out of. **s'en ~,** (*en réchapper*) pull through; (*réussir: fam.*) cope. **~ à sa fin,** be drawing to a close. **~ au clair,** clarify. **~ au sort,** draw lots (for). **~ parti de,** take advantage of. **~ profit de,** profit from.

tiret /tirɛ/ *n.m.* dash.

tireur /tirœr/ *n.m.* gunman. **~ d'élite,** marksman. **~ isolé,** sniper.

tiroir /tirwar/ *n.m.* drawer. **~-caisse** (*pl.* **~s-caisses**) *n.m.* till.

tisane /tizan/ *n.f.* herb-tea.

tison /tizɔ̃/ *n.m.* ember.

tisonnier /tizɔnje/ *n.m.* poker.

tiss|er /tise/ *v.t.* weave. **~age** *n.m.* weaving. **~erand** /tisrɑ̃/ *n.m.* weaver.

tissu /tisy/ *n.m.* fabric, material; (*biologique*) tissue. **un ~ de,** (*fig.*) a web of. **~-éponge** (*pl.* **~s-éponge**) *n.m.* towelling.

titre /titr/ *n.m.* title; (*diplôme*) qualification; (*comm.*) bond. **~s,** (*droits*) claims. **(gros) ~s,** headlines. **à ce ~,** (*pour cette qualité*) as such. **à ~ d'exemple,** as an example. **à juste ~,** rightly. **à ~ privé,** in a private capacity. **~ de propriété,** title-deed.

titré /titre/ *a.* titled.

titrer /titre/ *v.t.* (*journal*) give as a headline.

tituber /titybe/ *v.i.* stagger.

titul|aire /titylɛr/ *a.* **être ~aire,** have tenure. **être ~aire de,** hold. ● *n.m./f.* (*de permis etc.*) holder. **~ariser** *v.t.* give tenure to.

toast /tost/ *n.m.* piece of toast; (*allocution*) toast.

toboggan /tɔbɔgɑ̃/ *n.m.* (*traîneau*) toboggan; (*glissière*) slide; (*auto.*) flyover; (*auto., Amer.*) overpass.

toc /tɔk/ *int.* **~ toc!** knock knock!

tocsin /tɔksɛ̃/ *n.m.* alarm (bell).

toge /tɔʒ/ *n.f.* (*de juge etc.*) gown.

tohu-bohu /tɔyboy/ *n.m.* hubbub.

toi /twa/ *pron.* you; (*réfléchi*) yourself. **lève-~,** stand up.

toile /twal/ *n.f.* cloth; (*sac, tableau*) canvas; (*coton*) cotton. **~ d'arai-**

gnée, (spider's) web; (*délabrée*) cobweb. **~ de fond,** backdrop, backcloth.

toilette /twalɛt/ *n.f.* washing; (*habillement*) clothes, dress. **~s,** (*cabinets*) toilet(s). **de ~,** (*articles, savon, etc.*) toilet. **faire sa ~,** wash (and get ready).

toi-même /twamɛm/ *pron.* yourself.

toiser /twaze/ *v.t.* **~ qn.,** look s.o. up and down.

toison /twazɔ̃/ *n.f.* (*laine*) fleece.

toit /twa/ *n.m.* roof. **~ ouvrant,** (*auto.*) sun-roof.

toiture /twatyr/ *n.f.* roof.

tôle /tol/ *n.f.* (*plaque*) iron sheet. **~ ondulée,** corrugated iron.

tolérable /tɔlerabl/ *a.* tolerable.

toléran|t, **~te** /tɔlerɑ̃, -t/ *a.* tolerant. **~ce** *n.f.* tolerance; (*importations*: *comm.*) allowance.

tolérer /tɔlere/ *v.t.* tolerate; (*importations*: *comm.*) allow.

tollé /tɔle/ *n.m.* hue and cry.

tomate /tɔmat/ *n.f.* tomato.

tombe /tɔ̃b/ *n.f.* grave; (*avec monument*) tomb.

tombeau (*pl.* **~x**) /tɔ̃bo/ *n.m.* tomb.

tombée /tɔ̃be/ *n.f.* **~ de la nuit,** nightfall.

tomber /tɔ̃be/ *v.i.* (*aux. être*) fall; (*fièvre, vent*) drop; (*enthousiasme*) die down. **faire ~,** knock over; (*gouvernement*) bring down. **laisser ~,** drop; (*abandonner*) let down. **laisse ~!,** forget it! **~ à l'eau,** (*projet*) fall through. **~ bien** *ou* **à point,** come at the right time. **~ en panne,** break down. **~ en syncope,** faint. **~ sur,** (*trouver*) run across.

tombola /tɔ̃bɔla/ *n.f.* tombola; (*Amer.*) lottery.

tome /tɔm/ *n.m.* volume.

ton[1], **ta** *ou* **ton*** (*pl.* **tes**) /tɔ̃, ta, tɔ̃, te/ *a.* your.

ton[2] /tɔ̃/ *n.m.* tone; (*gamme*: *mus.*) key; (*hauteur de la voix*) pitch. **de bon ~,** in good taste.

tonalité /tɔnalite/ *n.f.* tone; (*téléphone*) dialling tone; (*téléphone*: *Amer.*) dial tone.

tond|re /tɔ̃dr/ *v.t.* (*herbe*) mow; (*mouton*) shear; (*cheveux*) clip. **~euse** *n.f.* shears; clippers. **~euse (à gazon),** (lawn-)mower.

tongs /tɔ̃g/ *n.f. pl.* flip-flops.

tonifier /tɔnifje/ *v.t.* tone up.

tonique /tɔnik/ *a. & n.m.* tonic.

tonne /tɔn/ *n.f.* ton(ne).

tonneau (*pl.* **~x**) /tɔno/ *n.m.* (*récipient*) barrel; (*naut.*) ton; (*culbute*) somersault.

tonnelle /tɔnɛl/ *n.f.* bower.

tonner /tɔne/ *v.i.* thunder.

tonnerre /tɔnɛr/ *n.m.* thunder.

tonte /tɔ̃t/ *n.f.* (*de gazon*) mowing; (*de moutons*) shearing.

tonton /tɔ̃tɔ̃/ *n.m.* (*fam.*) uncle.

tonus /tɔnys/ *n.m.* energy.

top /tɔp/ *n.m.* (*signal pour marquer un instant précis*) stroke.

topo /tɔpo/ *n.m.* (*fam.*) talk, oral report.

toquade /tɔkad/ *n.f.* craze; (*pour une personne*) infatuation.

toque /tɔk/ *n.f.* (fur) hat; (*de jockey*) cap; (*de cuisinier*) hat.

toqué /tɔke/ *a.* (*fam.*) crazy.

torche /tɔrʃ/ *n.f.* torch.

torcher /tɔrʃe/ *v.t.* (*fam.*) wipe.

torchon /tɔrʃɔ̃/ *n.m.* cloth, duster; (*pour la vaisselle*) tea-towel; (*Amer.*) dish-towel.

tordre /tɔrdr/ *v.t.* twist; (*linge*) wring. **se ~** *v. pr.* twist, bend; (*de douleur*) writhe. **se ~ (de rire),** split one's sides.

tordu /tɔrdy/ *a.* twisted, bent; (*esprit*) warped.

tornade /tɔrnad/ *n.f.* tornado.

torpeur /tɔrpœr/ *n.f.* lethargy.

torpill|e /tɔrpij/ *n.f.* torpedo. **~er** *v.t.* torpedo.

torréfier /tɔrefje/ *v.t.* roast.

torrent /tɔrɑ̃/ *n.m.* torrent. **~iel,** **~ielle** /-sjɛl/ *a.* torrential.

torride /tɔrid/ *a.* torrid.

torsade /tɔrsad/ *n.f.* twist.

torse /tɔrs/ *n.m.* chest; (*sculpture*) torso.

tort /tɔr/ *n.m.* wrong. **à ~,** wrongly. **à ~ et à travers,** without thinking. **avoir ~,** be wrong (de faire, to do). **donner ~ à,** prove wrong. **être dans son ~,** be in the wrong. **faire (du) ~ à,** harm.

torticolis /tɔrtikɔli/ *n.m.* stiff neck.

tortiller /tɔrtije/ *v.t.* twist, twirl. **se ~** *v. pr.* wriggle, wiggle.

tortionnaire /tɔrsjɔnɛr/ *n.m.* torturer.

tortue /tɔrty/ *n.f.* tortoise; (*de mer*) turtle.

tortueu|x, **~se** /tɔrtɥø, -z/ *a.* (*explication*) tortuous; (*chemin*) twisting.

tortur|e(s) /tɔrtyr/ *n.f.* (*pl.*) torture. **~er** *v.t.* torture.

tôt /to/ adv. early. **plus ~**, earlier. **au plus ~**, at the earliest. **le plus ~ possible**, as soon as possible. **~ ou tard**, sooner or later.

tot|al (m. pl. **~aux**) /total, -o/ a. total. ● n.m. (pl. **~aux**) total. ● adv. (fam.) to conclude, in short. **au ~al**, all in all. **~alement** adv. totally. **~aliser** v.t. total.

totalitaire /totaliter/ a. totalitarian.

totalité /totalite/ n.f. entirety. **la ~ de**, all of.

toubib /tubib/ n.m. (fam.) doctor.

touchant, ~e /tuʃã, -t/ a. (émouvant) touching.

touche /tuʃ/ n.f. (de piano) key; (de peintre) touch. **(ligne de) ~**, touchline. **une ~ de**, a touch of.

toucher¹ /tuʃe/ v.t. touch; (émouvoir) move, touch; (contacter) get in touch with; (cible) hit; (argent) draw; (chèque) cash; (concerner) affect. ● v.i. **~ à**, touch; (question) touch on; (fin, but) approach. **je vais lui en ~ un mot**, I'll talk to him about it. **se ~** v. pr. (lignes) touch.

toucher² /tuʃe/ n.m. (sens) touch.

touffe /tuf/ n.f. (de poils, d'herbe) tuft; (de plantes) clump.

touffu /tufy/ a. thick, bushy; (fig.) complex.

toujours /tuʒur/ adv. always; (encore) still; (en tout cas) anyhow. **pour ~**, for ever.

toupet /tupɛ/ n.m. (culot: fam.) cheek, nerve.

toupie /tupi/ n.f. (jouet) top.

tour¹ /tur/ n.f. tower; (immeuble) tower block; (échecs) rook. **~ de contrôle**, control tower.

tour² /tur/ n.m. (mouvement, succession, tournure) turn; (excursion) trip; (à pied) walk; (en auto) drive; (artifice) trick; (circonférence) circumference; (techn.) lathe. **~ (de piste)**, lap. **à ~ de rôle**, in turn. **à mon/etc. ~**, when it is my/etc. turn. **c'est mon/etc. ~ de**, it is my/etc. turn to. **faire le ~ de**, go round; (question) survey. **~ d'horizon**, survey. **~ de passe-passe**, sleight of hand. **~ de taille**, waist measurement; (ligne) waistline.

tourbe /turb/ n.f. peat.

tourbillon /turbijõ/ n.m. whirlwind; (d'eau) whirlpool; (fig.) whirl, swirl. **~ner** /-jone/ v.i. whirl, swirl.

tourelle /turɛl/ n.f. turret.

tourisme /turism/ n.m. tourism. **faire du ~**, do some sightseeing.

tourist|e /turist/ n.m./f. tourist. **~ique** a. tourist; (route) scenic.

tourment /turmã/ n.m. torment. **~er** /-te/ v.t. torment. **se ~er** v. pr. worry.

tournage /turnaʒ/ n.m. (cinéma) shooting.

tournant¹, ~e /turnã, -t/ a. (qui pivote) revolving.

tournant² /turnã/ n.m. bend; (fig.) turning-point.

tourne-disque /turnədisk/ n.m. record-player.

tournée /turne/ n.f. (voyage, consommations) round; (théâtre) tour. **faire la ~**, make the rounds (de, of). **je paye** ou **j'offre la ~**, I'll buy this round.

tourner /turne/ v.t. turn; (film) shoot, make. ● v.i. turn; (toupie, tête) spin; (moteur, usine) run. **se ~** v. pr. turn. **~ au froid**, turn cold. **~ autour de**, go round; (personne, maison) hang around; (terre) revolve round; (question) centre on. **~ de l'œil**, (fam.) faint. **~ en dérision**, mock. **~ en ridicule**, ridicule. **~ le dos à**, turn one's back on. **~ mal**, turn out badly.

tournesol /turnəsol/ n.m. sunflower.

tournevis /turnəvis/ n.m. screwdriver.

tourniquet /turnikɛ/ n.m. (barrière) turnstile.

tournoi /turnwa/ n.m. tournament.

tournoyer /turnwaje/ v.i. whirl.

tournure /turnyr/ n.f. turn; (locution) turn of phrase.

tourte /turt/ n.f. pie.

tourterelle /turtərɛl/ n.f. turtle-dove.

Toussaint /tusɛ̃/ n.f. **la ~**, All Saints' Day.

tousser /tuse/ v.i. cough.

tout¹, ~e (pl. **tous, toutes** /tu, tut/) a. all; (n'importe quel) any; (tout à fait) entirely. **~ le pays/etc.**, the whole country/etc., all the country/etc. **~e la nuit/journée**, the whole night/day. **~ un paquet**, a whole pack. **tous les jours/mois/etc.**, every day/month/etc. ● pron. everything, all. **tous** /tus/, **toutes**, all. **prendre ~**, take everything, take it all. **~ ce que**, all that. **~ le monde**, everyone. **tous les deux, toutes les deux**, both of them. **tous les trois**, all three (of them). ● adv.

(*très*) very; (*tout à fait*) quite. ~ **au bout/début/***etc.*, right at the end/ beginning/*etc.* **le ~ premier,** the very first. ~ **en chantant/marchant/***etc.*, while singing/walking/ *etc.* ~ **à coup,** all of a sudden. ~ **à fait,** quite, completely. ~ **à l'heure,** in a moment; (*passé*) a moment ago. ~ **au** *ou* **le long de,** throughout. ~ **au plus/moins,** at most/least. ~ **de même,** all the same. ~ **de suite,** straight away. ~ **entier,** whole. ~ **le contraire,** quite the opposite. ~ **neuf,** brand-new. ~ **nu,** stark naked. ~ **près,** nearby. ~**puissant,** ~**e-puissante** *a.* omnipotent. ~ **seul,** alone. ~ **terrain** *a. invar.* all terrain. **pas du** ~**!,** not at all!

tout[2] /tu/ *n.m.* (*ensemble*) whole. **en** ~, in all. **pas du** ~**!,** not at all!

tout-à-l'égout /tutalegu/ *n.m.* main drainage.

toutefois /tutfwa/ *adv.* however.

toux /tu/ *n.f.* cough.

toxicomane /tɔksikɔman/ *n.m./f.* drug addict.

toxine /tɔksin/ *n.f.* toxin.

toxique /tɔksik/ *a.* toxic.

trac /trak/ *n.m.* **le** ~, nerves; (*théâtre*) stage fright.

tracas /traka/ *n.m.* worry. ~**ser** /-se/ *v.t.,* **se** ~**ser** *v. pr.* worry.

trace /tras/ *n.f.* trace, mark; (*d'animal, de pneu*) tracks; (*vestige*) trace. **sur la** ~ **de,** on the track of. ~**s de pas,** footprints.

tracé /trase/ *n.m.* (*ligne*) line; (*plan*) layout.

tracer /trase/ *v.t.* draw, trace; (*écrire*) write; (*route*) mark out.

trachée(-artère) /traʃe(artɛr)/ *n.f.* windpipe.

tract /trakt/ *n.m.* leaflet.

tractations /traktɑsjɔ̃/ *n.f. pl.* dealings.

tracteur /traktœr/ *n.m.* tractor.

traction /traksjɔ̃/ *n.f.* (*sport*) press-up, push-up.

tradition /tradisjɔ̃/ *n.f.* tradition. ~**nel,** ~**nelle** /-jɔnɛl/ *a.* traditional.

trad|uire† /tradɥir/ *v.t.* translate; (*sentiment*) express. ~**uire en justice,** take to court. ~**ucteur,** ~**uctrice** *n.m.,* *f.* translator. ~**uction** *n.f.* translation.

trafic /trafik/ *n.m.* (*commerce, circulation*) traffic.

trafiqu|er /trafike/ *v.i.* traffic. ● *v.t.* (*fam.*) (*vin*) doctor; (*moteur*) fiddle

with. ~**ant,** ~**ante** *n.m.,* *f.* trafficker; (*d'armes, de drogues*) dealer.

tragédie /traʒedi/ *n.f.* tragedy.

tragique /traʒik/ *a.* tragic. ~**ment** *adv.* tragically.

trah|ir /trair/ *v.t.* betray. ~**ison** *n.f.* betrayal; (*crime*) treason.

train /trɛ̃/ *n.m.* (*rail.*) train; (*allure*) pace. **en** ~, (*en forme*) in shape. **en** ~ **de faire,** (busy) doing. **mettre en** ~, start up. ~ **d'atterrissage,** undercarriage. ~ **électrique,** (*jouet*) electric train set. ~ **de vie,** lifestyle.

traînard, ~**e** /trɛnar, -d/ *n.m.,* *f.* slowcoach; (*Amer.*) slowpoke; (*en marchant*) straggler.

traîne /trɛn/ *n.f.* (*de robe*) train. **à la** ~, lagging behind; (*en remorque*) in tow.

traîneau (*pl.* ~**x**) /trɛno/ *n.m.* sledge.

traînée /trene/ *n.f.* (*trace*) trail; (*bande*) streak; (*femme: péj.*) slut.

traîner /trene/ *v.t.* drag (along); (*véhicule*) pull. ● *v.i.* (*pendre*) trail; (*rester en arrière*) trail behind; (*flâner*) hang about; (*papiers, affaires*) lie around. ~ (**en longueur**)**,** drag on. **se** ~ *v. pr.* (*par terre*) crawl. (**faire**) ~ **en longueur,** drag out. ~ **les pieds,** drag one's feet. **ça n'a pas traîné!,** that didn't take long.

train-train /trɛ̃trɛ̃/ *n.m.* routine.

traire† /trɛr/ *v.t.* milk.

trait /trɛ/ *n.m.* line; (*en dessinant*) stroke; (*caractéristique*) feature, trait; (*acte*) act. ~**s,** (*du visage*) features. **avoir** ~ **à,** relate to. **d'un** ~, (*boire*) in one gulp. ~ **d'union,** hyphen; (*fig.*) link.

traite /trɛt/ *n.f.* (*de vache*) milking; (*comm.*) draft. **d'une (seule)** ~, in one go, at a stretch.

traité /trete/ *n.m.* (*pacte*) treaty; (*ouvrage*) treatise.

traitement /trɛtmɑ̃/ *n.m.* treatment; (*salaire*) salary. ~ **de données,** data processing. ~ **de texte,** word processing.

traiter /trete/ *v.t.* treat; (*affaire*) deal with; (*données, produit*) process. ~ **qn. de lâche/***etc.*, call s.o. a coward/ *etc.* ● *v.i.* deal (**avec,** with). ~ **de,** (*sujet*) deal with.

traiteur /trɛtœr/ *n.m.* caterer; (*boutique*) delicatessen.

traître, ~**sse** /trɛtr, -ɛs/ *a.* treacherous. ● *n.m./f.* traitor.

trajectoire /traʒɛktwar/ *n.f.* path.

trajet /traʒɛ/ *n.m.* (*à parcourir*) distance; (*voyage*) journey; (*itinéraire*) route.

trame /tram/ *n.f.* (*de tissu*) weft; (*de récit etc.*) framework. **usé jusqu'à la ~,** threadbare.

tramer /trame/ *v.t.* plot; (*complot*) hatch. **qu'est-ce qui se trame?,** what's brewing?

tramway /tramwɛ/ *n.m.* tram; (*Amer.*) streetcar.

tranchant, ~e /trɑ̃ʃɑ̃, -t/ *a.* sharp; (*fig.*) cutting. ● *n.m.* cutting edge. **à double ~,** two-edged.

tranche /trɑ̃ʃ/ *n.f.* (*rondelle*) slice; (*bord*) edge; (*partie*) portion.

tranchée /trɑ̃ʃe/ *n.f.* trench.

tranch|er [1] /trɑ̃ʃe/ *v.t.* cut; (*question*) decide. ● *v.i.* (*décider*) decide. **~é a.** (*net*) clear-cut.

trancher [2] /trɑ̃ʃe/ *v.i.* (*contraster*) contrast (**sur,** with).

tranquill|e /trɑ̃kil/ *a.* quiet; (*esprit*) at rest; (*conscience*) clear. **être/laisser ~e,** be/leave in peace. **~ement** *adv.* quietly. **~ité** *n.f.* (peace and) quiet; (*d'esprit*) peace of mind.

tranquillisant /trɑ̃kilizɑ̃/ *n.m.* tranquillizer.

tranquilliser /trɑ̃kilize/ *v.t.* reassure.

transaction /trɑ̃zaksjɔ̃/ *n.f.* transaction.

transat /trɑ̃zat/ *n.m.* (*fam.*) deckchair.

transatlantique /trɑ̃zatlɑ̃tik/ *n.m.* transatlantic liner. ● *a.* transatlantic.

transborder /trɑ̃sbɔrde/ *v.t.* transfer, transship.

transcend|er /trɑ̃sɑ̃de/ *v.t.* transcend. **~ant, ~ante** *a.* transcendent.

transcr|ire /trɑ̃skrir/ *v.t.* transcribe. **~iption** *n.f.* transcription; (*copie*) transcript.

transe /trɑ̃s/ *n.f.* **en ~,** in a trance; (*fig.*) very excited.

transférer /trɑ̃sfere/ *v.t.* transfer.

transfert /trɑ̃sfɛr/ *n.m.* transfer.

transform|er /trɑ̃sfɔrme/ *v.t.* change; (*radicalement*) transform; (*vêtement*) alter. **se ~er** *v. pr.* change; be transformed. **(se) ~er en,** turn into. **~ateur** *n.m.* transformer. **~ation** *n.f.* change; transformation.

transfuge /trɑ̃sfyʒ/ *n.m.* renegade.

transfusion /trɑ̃sfyzjɔ̃/ *n.f.* transfusion.

transgresser /trɑ̃sgrese/ *v.t.* disobey.

transiger /trɑ̃ziʒe/ *v.i.* compromise. **ne pas ~ sur,** not compromise on.

transi /trɑ̃zi/ *a.* chilled to the bone.

transistor /trɑ̃zistɔr/ *n.m.* (*dispositif, poste de radio*) transistor.

transit /trɑ̃zit/ *n.m.* transit. **~er** *v.t./i.* pass in transit.

transiti|f, ~ve /trɑ̃zitif, -v/ *a.* transitive.

transi|tion /trɑ̃zisjɔ̃/ *n.f.* transition. **~toire** *a.* (*provisoire*) transitional.

translucide /trɑ̃slysid/ *a.* translucent.

transm|ettre† /trɑ̃smɛtr/ *v.t.* pass on; (*techn.*) transmit; (*radio*) broadcast. **~ission** *n.f.* transmission; (*radio*) broadcasting.

transparaître /trɑ̃sparɛtr/ *v.i.* show (through).

transparen|t, ~te /trɑ̃sparɑ̃, -t/ *a.* transparent. **~ce** *n.f.* transparency.

transpercer /trɑ̃spɛrse/ *v.t.* pierce.

transpir|er /trɑ̃spire/ *v.i.* perspire. **~ation** *n.f.* perspiration.

transplant|er /trɑ̃splɑ̃te/ *v.t.* (*bot., méd.*) transplant. **~ation** *n.f.* (*bot.*) transplantation; (*méd.*) transplant.

transport /trɑ̃spɔr/ *n.m.* transport(ation); (*sentiment*) rapture. **les ~s,** transport. **les ~s en commun,** public transport.

transport|er /trɑ̃spɔrte/ *v.t.* transport; (*à la main*) carry. **se ~er** *v. pr.* take o.s. (**à,** to). **~eur** *n.m.* haulier; (*Amer.*) trucker.

transposer /trɑ̃spoze/ *v.t.* transpose.

transvaser /trɑ̃svaze/ *v.t.* decant.

transvers|al (*m. pl.* **~aux**) /trɑ̃sversal, -o/ *a.* cross, transverse.

trap|èze /trapɛz/ *n.m.* (*sport*) trapeze. **~éziste** /-ezist/ *n.m./f.* trapeze artist.

trappe /trap/ *n.f.* trapdoor.

trappeur /trapœr/ *n.m.* trapper.

trapu /trapy/ *a.* stocky.

traquenard /traknar/ *n.m.* trap.

traquer /trake/ *v.t.* track down.

traumatis|me /tromatism/ *n.m.* trauma. **~ant, ~ante** /-zɑ̃, -t/ *a.* traumatic. **~er** /-ze/ *v.t.* traumatize.

trav|ail (*pl.* **~aux**) /travaj, -o/ *n.m.* work; (*emploi, poste*) job; (*façonnage*) working. **~aux,** work. **en ~ail,** (*femme*) in labour. **~ail à la chaîne,** production line work. **~ail à la pièce** *ou* **à la tâche,** piece-work. **~ail au noir,** (*fam.*) moonlighting. **~aux forcés,** hard labour. **~aux**

manuels, handicrafts. **~aux ména-gers,** housework.
travaill|er /travaje/ v.i. work; (se déformer) warp. **~er à,** (livre etc.) work on. ● v.t. (façonner) work; (étudier) work at ou on; (tourmenter) worry. **~eur, ~euse** n.m., f. worker; a. hardworking.
travailliste /travajist/ a. Labour. ● n.m./f. Labour party member.
travers /travɛr/ n.m. (défaut) failing. **à ~,** through. **au ~ (de),** through. **de ~,** (chapeau, nez) crooked; (mal) badly, the wrong way; (regarder) askance. **en ~ (de),** across.
traverse /travɛrs/ n.f. (rail.) sleeper; (rail., Amer.) tie.
traversée /travɛrse/ n.f. crossing.
traverser /travɛrse/ v.t. cross; (transpercer) go (right) through; (période, forêt) go ou pass through.
traversin /travɛrsɛ̃/ n.m. bolster.
travesti /travɛsti/ n.m. transvestite.
travestir /travɛstir/ v.t. disguise; (vérité) misrepresent.
trébucher /trebyʃe/ v.i. stumble, trip (over). **faire ~,** trip (up).
trèfle /trɛfl/ n.m. (plante) clover; (cartes) clubs.
treillage /trɛjaʒ/ n.m. trellis.
treillis[1] /trɛji/ n.m. trellis; (en métal) wire mesh.
treillis[2] /trɛji/ n.m. (tenue militaire) combat uniform.
treiz|e /trɛz/ a. & n.m. thirteen. **~ième** a. & n.m./f. thirteenth.
tréma /trema/ n.m. diaeresis.
trembl|er /trãble/ v.i. shake, tremble; (lumière, voix) quiver. **~ement** n.m. shaking; (frisson) shiver. **~ement de terre,** earthquake.
trembloter /trãblote/ v.i. quiver.
trémousser (se) /(sə)tremuse/ v. pr. wriggle, wiggle.
trempe /trãp/ n.f. (caractère) calibre.
tremper /trãpe/ v.t./i. soak; (plonger) dip; (acier) temper. **mettre à ~ ou faire ~,** soak. **~ dans,** (fig.) be involved in. **se ~** v. pr. (se baigner) have a dip.
trempette /trãpɛt/ n.f. **faire ~,** have a little dip.
tremplin /trãplɛ̃/ n.m. springboard.
trentaine /trãtɛn/ n.f. **une ~ (de),** about thirty. **il a la ~,** he's about thirty.
trent|e /trãt/ a. & n.m. thirty. **~ième** a. & n.m./f. thirtieth. **se mettre sur son ~e et un,** put on one's Sunday

best. **tous les ~e-six du mois,** once in a blue moon.
trépider /trepide/ v.i. vibrate.
trépied /trepje/ n.m. tripod.
trépigner /trepiɲe/ v.i. stamp one's feet.
très /trɛ/ (/trɛz/ before vowel) adv. very. **~ aimé/estimé,** much liked/esteemed.
trésor /trezɔr/ n.m. treasure; (ressources: comm.) finances. **le T~,** the revenue department.
trésorerie /trezɔrri/ n.f. (bureaux) accounts department; (du Trésor) revenue office; (argent) finances; (gestion) accounts.
trésor|ier, ~ière /trezɔrje, -jɛr/ n.m., f. treasurer.
tressaill|ir /tresajir/ v.i. shake, quiver; (sursauter) start. **~ement** n.m. quiver; start.
tressauter /tresote/ v.i. (sursauter) start, jump.
tresse /trɛs/ n.f. braid, plait.
tresser /trese/ v.t. braid, plait.
tréteau (pl. **~x**) /treto/ n.m. trestle. **~x,** (théâtre) stage.
treuil /trœj/ n.m. winch.
trêve /trɛv/ n.f. truce; (fig.) respite. **~ de plaisanteries,** enough of this joking.
tri /tri/ n.m. (classement) sorting; (sélection) selection. **faire le ~ de,** sort; select. **~age** /-jaʒ/ n.m. sorting.
triang|le /trijãgl/ n.m. triangle. **~ulaire** a. triangular.
trib|al (m. pl. **~aux**) /tribal, -o/ a. tribal.
tribord /tribɔr/ n.m. starboard.
tribu /triby/ n.f. tribe.
tribulations /tribylasjõ/ n.f. pl. tribulations.
tribun|al (m. pl. **~aux**) /tribynal, -o/ n.m. court. **~al d'instance,** magistrates' court.
tribune /tribyn/ n.f. (public) gallery; (dans un stade) grandstand; (d'orateur) rostrum; (débat) forum.
tribut /triby/ n.m. tribute.
tributaire /tribytɛr/ a. **~ de,** dependent on.
trich|er /triʃe/ v.i. cheat. **~erie** n.f. cheating. **une ~erie,** piece of trickery. **~eur, ~euse** n.m., f. cheat.
tricolore /trikɔlɔr/ a. three-coloured; (français) red, white and blue; (français: fig.) French.
tricot /triko/ n.m. knitting; (pull) sweater. **en ~,** knitted. **~ de corps,**

vest; (*Amer.*) undershirt. **~er** /-ɔte/
v.t./i. knit.
trictrac /triktrak/ *n.m.* backgammon.
tricycle /trisikl/ *n.m.* tricycle.
trier /trije/ *v.t.* (*classer*) sort; (*choisir*) select.
trilogie /trilɔʒi/ *n.f.* trilogy.
trimbaler /trɛ̃bale/ *v.t.*, **se ~** *v. pr.*
(*fam.*) trail around.
trimer /trime/ *v.i.* (*fam.*) slave.
trimestr|e /trimɛstr/ *n.m.* quarter;
(*scol.*) term. **~iel**, **~ielle** *a.* quar-
terly; (*bulletin*) end-of-term.
tringle /trɛ̃gl/ *n.f.* rod.
Trinité /trinite/ *n.f.* **la ~**, (*dogme*) the
Trinity; (*fête*) Trinity.
trinquer /trɛ̃ke/ *v.i.* clink glasses.
trio /trijo/ *n.m.* trio.
triomph|e /trijɔ̃f/ *n.m.* triumph. **~al**
(*m. pl.* **~aux**) *a.* triumphant.
triomph|er /trijɔ̃fe/ *v.i.* triumph (**de**,
over); (*jubiler*) be triumphant.
~ant, **~ante** *a.* triumphant.
trip|es /trip/ *n.f. pl.* (*mets*) tripe;
(*entrailles*: *fam.*) guts.
triple /tripl/ *a.* triple, treble. ● *n.m.*
le ~, three times as much (**de**, as).
~ment /-əmɑ̃/ *adv.* trebly.
tripl|er /triple/ *v.t./i.* triple, treble.
~és, **~ées** /-e/ *n.m., f. pl.* triplets.
tripot /tripo/ *n.m.* gambling den.
tripoter /tripɔte/ *v.t.* (*fam.*) fiddle
with. ● *v.i.* (*fam.*) fiddle about.
trique /trik/ *n.f.* cudgel.
trisomique /trizɔmik/ *a.* **enfant ~**,
Down's (syndrome) child.
triste /trist/ *a.* sad; (*rue, temps,
couleur*) gloomy; (*lamentable*)
wretched, dreadful. **~ment** /- əmɑ̃/
adv. sadly. **~sse** /-ɛs/ *n.f.* sadness;
gloominess.
triv|ial (*m. pl.* **~iaux**) /trivjal, -jo/ *a.*
coarse. **~ialité** *n.f.* coarseness.
troc /trɔk/ *n.m.* exchange; (*comm.*)
barter.
troène /trɔɛn/ *n.m.* (*bot.*) privet.
trognon /trɔɲɔ̃/ *n.m.* (*de pomme*)
core.
trois /trwɑ/ *a. & n.m.* three. **hôtel ~-
étoiles**, three-star hotel. **~ième**
/-zjɛm/ *a. & n.m./f.* third.
~ièmement /-zjɛmmɑ̃/ *adv.* thirdly.
trombe /trɔ̃b/ *n.f.* **~ d'eau**, downpour.
trombone /trɔ̃bɔn/ *n.m.* (*mus.*)
trombone; (*agrafe*) paper-clip.
trompe /trɔ̃p/ *n.f.* (*d'éléphant*) trunk;
(*mus.*) horn.

tromp|er /trɔ̃pe/ *v.t.* deceive, mis-
lead; (*déjouer*) elude. **se ~er** *v. pr.*
be mistaken. **se ~er de route/
train/etc.**, take the wrong road/
train/etc. **~erie** *n.f.* deception.
~eur, **~euse** *a.* (*personne*) deceitful; (*chose*) deceptive.
trompette /trɔ̃pɛt/ *n.f.* trumpet.
tronc /trɔ̃/ *n.m.* trunk; (*boîte*) collection box.
tronçon /trɔ̃sɔ̃/ *n.m.* section. **~ner**
/-ɔne/ *v.t.* cut into sections.
trôn|e /tron/ *n.m.* throne. **~er** *v.i.*
occupy the place of honour.
tronquer /trɔ̃ke/ *v.t.* truncate.
trop /tro/ *adv.* (*grand, loin, etc.*) too;
(*boire, marcher, etc.*) too much. **~
(de)**, (*quantité*) too much; (*nombre*)
too many. **c'est ~ chauffé**, it's
overheated. **de ~, en ~**, too much;
too many. **il a bu un verre de ~**,
he's had one too many. **de ~**,
(*intrus*) in the way. **~-plein** *n.m.*
excess; (*dispositif*) overflow.
trophée /trɔfe/ *n.m.* trophy.
tropic|al (*m. pl.* **~aux**) /trɔpikal, -o/
a. tropical.
tropique /trɔpik/ *n.m.* tropic. **~s**,
tropics.
troquer /trɔke/ *v.t.* exchange;
(*comm.*) barter (**contre**, for).
trot /tro/ *n.m.* trot. **aller au ~**, trot.
au ~, (*fam.*) on the double.
trotter /trɔte/ *v.i.* trot.
trotteuse /trɔtøz/ *n.f.* (*aiguille de
montre*) second hand.
trottiner /trɔtine/ *v.i.* patter along.
trottinette /trɔtinɛt/ *n.f.* (*jouet*)
scooter.
trottoir /trɔtwar/ *n.m.* pavement;
(*Amer.*) sidewalk. **~ roulant**, moving walkway.
trou /tru/ *n.m.* hole; (*moment*) gap;
(*lieu*: *péj.*) dump. **~ (de mémoire)**,
lapse (of memory). **~ de la serrure**,
keyhole. **faire son ~**, carve one's
niche.
trouble /trubl/ *a.* (*eau, image*) un-
clear; (*louche*) shady. ● *n.m.*
agitation. **~s**, (*pol.*) disturbances;
(*méd.*) trouble.
troubl|er /truble/ *v.t.* disturb; (*eau*)
make cloudy; (*inquiéter*) trouble.
~ant, **~ante** *a.* disturbing. **se ~er**
v. pr. (*personne*) become flustered.
~e-fête *n.m./ f. invar.* killjoy.
trouée /true/ *n.f.* gap, open space;
(*mil.*) breach (**dans**, in).

trouer /true/ v.t. make a hole ou holes in. **mes chaussures se sont trouées,** my shoes have got holes in them.

trouille /truj/ n.f. **avoir la ~,** (fam.) be scared.

troupe /trup/ n.f. troop; (d'acteurs) troupe. **~s,** (mil.) troops.

troupeau (pl. **~x**) /trupo/ n.m. herd; (de moutons) flock.

trousse /trus/ n.f. case, bag; (de réparations) kit. **aux ~s de,** on the tail of. **~ de toilette,** toilet bag.

trousseau (pl. **~x**) /truso/ n.m. (de clefs) bunch; (de mariée) trousseau.

trouvaille /truvɑj/ n.f. find.

trouver /truve/ v.t. find; (penser) think. **aller/venir ~,** (rendre visite à) go/come and see. **se ~** v. pr. find o.s.; (être) be; (se sentir) feel. **il se trouve que,** it happens that. **se ~ mal,** faint.

truand /tryɑ̃/ n.m. gangster.

truc /tryk/ n.m. (moyen) way; (artifice) trick; (chose: fam.) thing. **~age** n.m. = **truquage.**

truchement /tryʃmɑ̃/ n.m. **par le ~ de,** through.

truculent, ~e /trykylɑ̃, -t/ a. colourful.

truelle /tryɛl/ n.f. trowel.

truffe /tryf/ n.f. (champignon, chocolat) truffle; (nez) nose.

truffer /tryfe/ v.t. (fam.) fill, pack (**de,** with).

truie /trɥi/ n.f. (animal) sow.

truite /trɥit/ n.f. trout.

truqu|er /tryke/ v.t. fix, rig; (photo, texte) fake. **~age** n.m. fixing; faking; (cinéma) special effect.

trust /trœst/ n.m. (comm.) trust.

tsar /tsar/ n.m. tsar, czar.

tsigane /tsigan/ a. & n.m./f. (Hungarian) gypsy.

tu [1] /ty/ pron. (parent, ami, enfant, etc.) you.

tu [2] /ty/ voir taire.

tuba /tyba/ n.m. (mus.) tuba; (sport) snorkel.

tube /tyb/ n.m. tube.

tubercul|eux, ~euse /tybɛrkylø, -z/ a. **être ~eux,** have tuberculosis. **~ose** n.f. tuberculosis.

tubulaire /tybylɛr/ a. tubular.

tubulure /tybylyr/ n.f. tubing.

tu|er /tɥe/ v.t. kill; (d'une balle) shoot, kill; (épuiser) exhaust. **se ~er** v. pr. kill o.s.; (accident) be killed. **~ant, ~ante,** a. exhausting.

~é, ~ée n.m., f. person killed. **~eur, ~euse** n.m., f. killer.

tuerie /tyri/ n.f. slaughter.

tue-tête (à) /(a)tytɛt/ adv. at the top of one's voice.

tuile /tɥil/ n.f. tile; (malchance: fam.) (stroke of) bad luck.

tulipe /tylip/ n.f. tulip.

tuméfié /tymefje/ a. swollen.

tumeur /tymœr/ n.f. tumour.

tumult|e /tymylt/ n.m. commotion; (désordre) turmoil. **~ueux, ~ueuse** a. turbulent.

tunique /tynik/ n.f. tunic.

Tunisie /tynizi/ n.f. Tunisia.

tunisien, ~ne /tynizjɛ̃, -jɛn/ a. & n.m., f. Tunisian.

tunnel /tynɛl/ n.m. tunnel.

turban /tyrbɑ̃/ n.m. turban.

turbine /tyrbin/ n.f. turbine.

turbo /tyrbo/ a. turbo. n.f. (voiture) turbo.

turbulen|t, ~te /tyrbylɑ̃, -t/ a. boisterous, turbulent. **~ce** n.f. turbulence.

tur|c, ~que /tyrk/ a. Turkish. ● n.m., f. Turk. ● n.m. (lang.) Turkish.

turf /tyrf/ n.m. **le ~,** the turf. **~iste** n.m./f. racegoer.

Turquie /tyrki/ n.f. Turkey.

turquoise /tyrkwaz/ a. invar. turquoise.

tutelle /tytɛl/ n.f. (jurid.) guardianship; (fig.) protection.

tu|teur, ~trice /tytœr, -tris/ n.m., f. (jurid.) guardian. ● n.m. (bâton) stake.

tut|oyer /tytwaje/ v.t. address familiarly (using tu). **~oiement** n.m. use of (familiar) tu.

tuyau (pl. **~x**) /tɥijo/ n.m. pipe; (conseil: fam.) tip. **~ d'arrosage,** hose-pipe. **~ter** v.t. (fam.) give a tip to. **~terie** n.f. piping.

TVA abrév. (taxe sur la valeur ajoutée) VAT.

tympan /tɛ̃pɑ̃/ n.m. ear-drum.

type /tip/ n.m. (modèle) type; (traits) features; (individu: fam.) bloke, guy. ● a. invar. typical. **le ~ même de,** a classic example of.

typhoïde /tifɔid/ n.f. typhoid (fever).

typhon /tifɔ̃/ n.m. typhoon.

typhus /tifys/ n.m. typhus.

typique /tipik/ a. typical. **~ment** adv. typically.

tyran /tirɑ̃/ n.m. tyrant.

tyrann|ie /tirani/ *n.f.* tyranny. **~ique** *a.* tyrannical. **~iser** *v.t.* oppress, tyrannize.

U

ulcère /ylsɛr/ *n.m.* ulcer.

ulcérer /ylsere/ *v.t.* (*vexer*) embitter, gall.

ULM *abrév. m.* (*ultraléger motorisé*) microlight.

ultérieur /ylterjœr/ *a.*, **~ement** *adv.* later.

ultimatum /yltimatɔm/ *n.m.* ultimatum.

ultime /yltim/ *a.* final.

ultra /yltra/ *n.m./f.* hardliner.

ultra- /yltra/ *préf.* ultra-.

un, une /œ̃, yn/ *a.* one; (*indéfini*) a, an. **un enfant**, /œ̃nɑ̃fɑ̃/ a child. ● *pron. & n.m./f.* one. **l'un**, one. **les uns**, some. **l'un et l'autre**, both. **l'un l'autre, les uns les autres**, each other. **l'un ou l'autre**, either. **la une**, (*de journal*) front page. **un autre**, another. **un par un**, one by one.

unanim|e /ynanim/ *a.* unanimous. **~ité** *n.f.* unanimity. **à l'~ité**, unanimously.

uni /yni/ *a.* united; (*couple*) close; (*surface*) smooth; (*sans dessins*) plain.

unième /ynjɛm/ *a.* -first. **vingt et ~**, twenty-first. **cent ~**, one hundred and first.

unif|ier /ynifje/ *v.t.* unify. **~ication** *n.f.* unification.

uniform|e /ynifɔrm/ *n.m.* uniform. ● *a.* uniform. **~ément** *adv.* uniformly. **~iser** *v.t.* standardize. **~ité** *n.f.* uniformity.

unilatér|al (*m. pl.* **~aux**) /ynilateral, -o/ *a.* unilateral.

union /ynjɔ̃/ *n.f.* union. **l'U~ soviétique**, the Soviet Union.

unique /ynik/ *a.* (*seul*) only; (*prix, voie*) one; (*incomparable*) unique. **enfant ~**, only child. **sens ~**, one-way street. **~ment** *adv.* only, solely.

unir /ynir/ *v.t.*, **s'~** *v. pr.* unite, join.

unisson (à l') /(a)ynisɔ̃/ *adv.* in unison.

unité /ynite/ *n.f.* unit; (*harmonie*) unity.

univers /ynivɛr/ *n.m.* universe.

universel, ~le /ynivɛrsɛl/ *a.* universal.

universit|é /ynivɛrsite/ *n.f.* university. **~aire** *a.* university; *n.m./f.* academic.

uranium /yranjɔm/ *n.m.* uranium.

urbain, ~e /yrbɛ̃, -ɛn/ *a.* urban.

urbanisme /yrbanism/ *n.m.* town planning; (*Amer.*) city planning.

urgence /yrʒɑ̃s/ *n.f.* (*cas*) emergency; (*de situation, tâche, etc.*) urgency. **d'~** *a.* emergency; *adv.* urgently.

urgent, ~e /yrʒɑ̃, -t/ *a.* urgent.

urger /yrʒe/ *v.i.* **ça urge!**, (*fam.*) it's getting urgent.

urin|e /yrin/ *n.f.* urine. **~er** *v.i.* urinate.

urinoir /yrinwar/ *n.m.* urinal.

urne /yrn/ *n.f.* (*électorale*) ballot-box; (*vase*) urn. **aller aux ~s**, go to the polls.

URSS *abrév.* (*Union des Républiques Socialistes Soviétiques*) USSR.

urticaire /yrtikɛr/ *n.f.* **une crise d' ~**, nettle rash.

us /ys/ *n.m. pl.* **les us et coutumes**, habits and customs.

usage /yzaʒ/ *n.m.* use; (*coutume*) custom; (*de langage*) usage. **à l'~ de**, for. **d'~**, (*habituel*) customary. **faire ~ de**, make use of.

usagé /yzaʒe/ *a.* worn.

usager /yzaʒe/ *n.m.* user.

usé /yze/ *a.* worn (out); (*banal*) trite.

user /yze/ *v.t.* wear (out); (*consommer*) use (up). ● *v.i.* **~ de**, use. **s'~** *v. pr.* (*tissu etc.*) wear (out).

usine /yzin/ *n.f.* factory; (*de métallurgie*) works.

usité /yzite/ *a.* common.

ustensile /ystɑ̃sil/ *n.m.* utensil.

usuel, ~le /yzɥɛl/ *a.* ordinary, everyday.

usufruit /yzyfrɥi/ *n.m.* usufruct.

usure /yzyr/ *n.f.* (*détérioration*) wear (and tear).

usurper /yzyrpe/ *v.t.* usurp.

utérus /yterys/ *n.m.* womb, uterus.

utile /ytil/ *a.* useful. **~ment** *adv.* usefully.

utilis|er /ytilize/ *v.t.* use. **~able** *a.* usable. **~ation** *n.f.* use.

utilitaire /ytilitɛr/ *a.* utilitarian.

utilité /ytilite/ *n.f.* use(fulness).

utop|ie /ytɔpi/ *n.f.* Utopia; (*idée*) Utopian idea. **~ique** *a.* Utopian.

UV *abrév. f.* (*unité de valeur*) (*scol.*) credit.

V

va /va/ *voir* aller[1].

vacanc|e /vakɑ̃s/ *n.f.* (*poste*) vacancy. **~es,** holiday(s); (*Amer.*) vacation. **en ~es,** on holiday. **~ier, ~ière** *n.m.,* *f.* holiday-maker; (*Amer.*) vacationer.

vacant, ~e /vakɑ̃, -t/ *a.* vacant.

vacarme /vakarm/ *n.m.* uproar.

vaccin /vaksɛ̃/ *n.m.* vaccine; (*inoculation*) vaccination.

vaccin|er /vaksine/ *v.t.* vaccinate. **~ation** *n.f.* vaccination.

vache /vaʃ/ *n.f.* cow. ● *a.* (*méchant: fam.*) nasty. **~ment** *adv.* (*très: fam.*) damned; (*pleuvoir, manger, etc.: fam.*) a hell of a lot. **~rie** *n.f.* (*fam.*) nastiness; (*chose: fam.*) nasty thing.

vacill|er /vasije/ *v.i.* sway, wobble; (*lumière*) flicker; (*fig.*) falter. **~ant, ~ante** *a.* (*mémoire, démarche*) shaky.

vadrouiller /vadruje/ *v.i.* (*fam.*) wander about.

va-et-vient /vaevjɛ̃/ *n.m. invar.* to and fro (motion); (*de personnes*) comings and goings.

vagabond, ~e /vagabɔ̃, -d/ *n.m., f.* (*péj.*) vagrant, vagabond. **~er** /-de/ *v.i.* wander.

vagin /vaʒɛ̃/ *n.m.* vagina.

vagir /vaʒir/ *v.i.* cry.

vague[1] /vag/ *a.* vague. ● *n.m.* vagueness. **il est resté dans le ~,** he was vague about it. **~ment** *adv.* vaguely.

vague[2] /vag/ *n.f.* wave. **~ de fond,** ground swell. **~ de froid,** cold spell. **~ de chaleur,** hot spell.

vaill|ant, ~ante /vajɑ̃, -t/ *a.* brave; (*vigoureux*) healthy. **~amment** /-amɑ̃/ *adv.* bravely.

vaille /vaj/ *voir* valoir.

vain, ~e /vɛ̃, vɛn/ *a.* vain. **en ~,** in vain. **~ement** /vɛnmɑ̃/ *adv.* vainly.

vain|cre† /vɛ̃kr/ *v.t.* defeat; (*surmonter*) overcome. **~cu, ~cue** *n.m., f.* (*sport*) loser. **~queur** *n.m.* victor; (*sport*) winner.

vais /vɛ/ *voir* aller[1].

vaisseau (*pl.* **~x**) /vɛso/ *n.m.* ship; (*veine*) vessel. **~ spatial,** space-ship.

vaisselle /vɛsɛl/ *n.f.* crockery; (*à laver*) dishes. **faire la ~,** do the washing-up, wash the dishes. **produit pour la ~,** washing-up liquid.

val (*pl.* **~s** *ou* **vaux**) /val, vo/ *n.m.* valley.

valable /valabl/ *a.* valid; (*de qualité*) worthwhile.

valet /valɛ/ *n.m.* (*cartes*) jack. **~ (de chambre),** manservant. **~ de ferme,** farm-hand.

valeur /valœr/ *n.f.* value; (*mérite*) worth, value. **~s,** (*comm.*) stocks and shares. **avoir de la ~,** be valuable.

valid|e /valid/ *a.* (*personne*) fit; (*billet*) valid. **~er** *v.t.* validate. **~ité** *n.f.* validity.

valise /valiz/ *n.f.* (suit)case. **faire ses ~s,** pack (one's bags).

vallée /vale/ *n.f.* valley.

vallon /valɔ̃/ *n.m.* (small) valley. **~né** /-ɔne/ *a.* undulating.

valoir† /valwar/ *v.i.* be worth; (*s'appliquer*) apply. **~ qch.,** be worth sth.; (*être aussi bon que*) be as good as sth. ● *v.t.* **~ qch. à qn.,** bring s.o. sth. **se ~** *v. pr.* (*être équivalents*) be as good as each other. **faire ~,** put forward to advantage; (*droit*) assert. **~ la peine, ~ le coup,** be worth it. **ça ne vaut rien,** it is no good. **il vaudrait mieux faire,** we'd better do. **ça ne me dit rien qui vaille,** I don't think much of it.

valoriser /valɔrize/ *v.t.* add value to. **se sentir valorisé,** feel valued.

vals|e /vals/ *n.f.* waltz. **~er** *v.i.* waltz.

valve /valv/ *n.f.* valve.

vampire /vɑ̃pir/ *n.m.* vampire.

van /vɑ̃/ *n.m.* van.

vandal|e /vɑ̃dal/ *n.m./f.* vandal. **~isme** *n.m.* vandalism.

vanille /vanij/ *n.f.* vanilla.

vanit|é /vanite/ *n.f.* vanity. **~eux, ~euse** *a.* vain, conceited.

vanne /van/ *n.f.* (*d'écluse*) sluice (-gate); (*fam.*) joke.

vant|ail (*pl.* **~aux**) /vɑ̃taj, -o/ *n.m.* door, flap.

vantard, ~e /vɑ̃tar, -d/ *a.* boastful; *n.m., f.* boaster. **~ise** /-diz/ *n.f.* boastfulness; (*acte*) boast.

vanter /vɑ̃te/ *v.t.* praise. **se ~** *v. pr.* boast (**de,** about).

va-nu-pieds /vanypje/ *n.m./f. invar.* vagabond, beggar.

vapeur[1] /vapœr/ *n.f.* (*eau*) steam; (*brume, émanation*) vapour.

vapeur[2] /vapœr/ *n.m.* (*bateau*) steamer.

vaporeu|x, **~se** /vapɔrø, -z/ *a.* hazy; (*léger*) filmy, flimsy.

vaporis|er /vapɔrize/ *v.t.* spray. **~ateur** *n.m.* spray.

vaquer /vake/ *v.i.* **~ à,** attend to.

varappe /varap/ *n.f.* rock climbing.

vareuse /varøz/ *n.f.* (*d'uniforme*) tunic.

variable /varjabl/ *a.* variable; (*temps*) changeable.

variante /varjãt/ *n.f.* variant.

varicelle /varisɛl/ *n.f.* chicken-pox.

varices /varis/ *n.f. pl.* varicose veins.

var|ier /varje/ *v.t./i.* vary. **~iation** *n.f.* variation. **~ié** *a.* (*non monotone, étendu*) varied; (*divers*) various.

variété /varjete/ *n.f.* variety. **~s,** (*spectacle*) variety.

variole /varjɔl/ *n.f.* smallpox.

vase [1] /vɑz/ *n.m.* vase.

vase [2] /vɑz/ *n.f.* (*boue*) silt, mud.

vaseu|x, **~se** /vɑzø, -z/ *a.* (*confus: fam.*) woolly, hazy.

vasistas /vazistas/ *n.m.* fanlight, hinged panel (*in door or window*).

vaste /vast/ *a.* vast, huge.

vaudeville /vodvil/ *n.m.* vaudeville, light comedy.

vau-l'eau (à) /(a)volo/ *adv.* downhill.

vaurien, **~ne** /vorjɛ̃, -jɛn/ *n.m., f.* good-for-nothing.

vautour /votur/ *n.m.* vulture.

vautrer (se) /(sə)votre/ *v. pr.* sprawl. **se ~ dans,** (*vice, boue*) wallow in.

va-vite (à la) /(ala)vavit/ *adv.* (*fam.*) in a hurry.

veau (*pl.* **~x**) /vo/ *n.m.* calf; (*viande*) veal; (*cuir*) calfskin.

vécu /veky/ *voir* vivre. ● *a.* (*réel*) true, real.

vedette [1] /vədɛt/ *n.f.* (*artiste*) star. **en ~,** (*objet*) in a prominent position; (*personne*) in the limelight.

vedette [2] /vədɛt/ *n.f.* (*bateau*) launch.

végét|al (*m. pl.* **~aux**) /veʒetal, -o/ *a.* plant. ● *n.m.* (*pl.* **~aux**) plant.

végétalien, **~ne** /veʒetaljɛ̃, -jɛn/ *a. & n.m., f.* vegan.

végétarien, **~ne** /veʒetarjɛ̃, -jɛn/ *a. & n.m., f.* vegetarian.

végétation /veʒetasjɔ̃/ *n.f.* vegetation. **~s,** (*méd.*) adenoids.

végéter /veʒete/ *v.i.* vegetate.

véhémen|t, **~te** /veemã, -t/ *a.* vehement. **~ce** *n.f.* vehemence.

véhicul|e /veikyl/ *n.m.* vehicle. **~er** *v.t.* convey.

veille [1] /vɛj/ *n.f.* **la ~ (de),** the day before. **la ~ de Noël,** Christmas Eve. **à la ~ de,** on the eve of.

veille [2] /vɛj/ *n.f.* (*état*) wakefulness.

veillée /veje/ *n.f.* evening (gathering); (*mortuaire*) vigil, wake.

veiller /veje/ *v.i.* stay up *ou* awake. **~ à,** attend to. **~ sur,** watch over. ● *v.t.* (*malade*) watch over.

veilleur /vɛjœr/ *n.m.* **~ de nuit,** night-watchman.

veilleuse /vɛjøz/ *n.f.* night-light; (*de véhicule*) sidelight; (*de réchaud*) pilot-light. **mettre qch. en ~,** put sth. on the back burner.

veinard, **~e** /vɛnar, -d/ *n.m., f.* (*fam.*) lucky devil.

veine [1] /vɛn/ *n.f.* (*anat.*) vein; (*nervure, filon*) vein.

veine [2] /vɛn/ *n.f.* (*chance: fam.*) luck. **avoir de la ~,** (*fam.*) be lucky.

velcro /vɛlkrɔ/ *n.m.* (P.) velcro.

véliplanchiste /veliplãʃist/ *n.m./f.* windsurfer.

vélo /velo/ *n.m.* bicycle, bike; (*activité*) cycling.

vélodrome /velodrɔm/ *n.m.* velodrome, cycle-racing track.

vélomoteur /velomɔtœr/ *n.m.* moped.

velours /vlur/ *n.m.* velvet. **~ côtelé,** **~ à côtes,** corduroy.

velouté /velute/ *a.* smooth. ● *n.m.* smoothness.

velu /vəly/ *a.* hairy.

venaison /vənɛzɔ̃/ *n.f.* venison.

vendang|es /vãdãʒ/ *n.f. pl.* grape harvest. **~er** *v.i.* pick the grapes. **~eur,** **~euse** *n.m., f.* grape-picker.

vendetta /vãdeta/ *n.f.* vendetta.

vendeu|r, **~se** /vãdœr, -øz/ *n.m., f.* shop assistant; (*marchand*) salesman, saleswoman; (*jurid.*) vendor, seller.

vendre /vãdr/ *v.t.,* **se ~** *v. pr.* sell. **à ~,** for sale.

vendredi /vãdrədi/ *n.m.* Friday. **V~ saint,** Good Friday.

vénéneu|x, **~se** /venenø, -z/ *a.* poisonous.

vénérable /venerabl/ *a.* venerable.

vénérer /venere/ *v.t.* revere.

vénérien, **~ne** /venerjɛ̃, -jɛn/ *a.* venereal.

vengeance /vãʒãs/ *n.f.* revenge, vengeance.

veng|er /vãʒe/ *v.t.* avenge. **se ~er** *v. pr.* take (one's) revenge (**de,** for).

~eur, ~eresse a. vengeful; n.m., f. avenger.

ven|in /vənɛ̃/ n.m. venom. **~imeux, ~imeuse** a. poisonous, venomous.

venir† /vənir/ v.i. (aux. être) come (de, from). **~ faire,** come to do. **venez faire,** come and do. **~ de faire,** to have just done. **il vient/ venait d'arriver,** he has/had just arrived. **en ~ à,** (question, conclusion, etc.) come to. **en ~ aux mains,** come to blows. **faire ~,** send for. **il m'est venu à l'esprit** ou **à l'idée que,** it occurred to me that.

vent /vɑ̃/ n.m. wind. **être dans le ~,** (fam.) be with it. **il fait du ~,** it is windy.

vente /vɑ̃t/ n.f. sale. **~ (aux enchères),** auction. **en ~,** on ou for sale. **~ de charité,** (charity) bazaar.

ventil|er /vɑ̃tile/ v.t. ventilate. **~ateur** n.m. fan, ventilator. **~ation** n.f. ventilation.

ventouse /vɑ̃tuz/ n.f. (dispositif) suction pad; (pour déboucher l'évier etc.) plunger.

ventre /vɑ̃tr/ n.m. belly, stomach; (utérus) womb. **avoir/prendre du ~,** have/develop a paunch.

ventriloque /vɑ̃trilɔk/ n.m./f. ventriloquist.

ventru /vɑ̃try/ a. pot-bellied.

venu /vəny/ voir venir. ● a. **bien ~,** (à propos) timely. **mal ~,** untimely. **être mal ~ de faire,** have no grounds for doing.

venue /vəny/ n.f. coming.

vêpres /vɛpr/ n.f. pl. vespers.

ver /vɛr/ n.m. worm; (des fruits, de la viande) maggot; (du bois) woodworm. **~ luisant,** glow-worm. **~ à soie,** silkworm. **~ solitaire,** tapeworm. **~ de terre,** earthworm.

véranda /verɑ̃da/ n.f. veranda.

verb|e /vɛrb/ n.m. (gram.) verb. **~al** (m. pl. **~aux**) a. verbal.

verdâtre /vɛrdɑtr/ a. greenish.

verdict /vɛrdikt/ n.m. verdict.

verdir /vɛrdir/ v.i. turn green.

verdoyant, ~e /vɛrdwajɑ̃, -t/ a. green, verdant.

verdure /vɛrdyr/ n.f. greenery.

véreu|x, ~se /verø, -z/ a. maggoty, wormy; (malhonnête: fig.) shady.

verger /vɛrʒe/ n.m. orchard.

vergla|s /vɛrgla/ n.m. (black) ice; (Amer.) sleet. **~cé** a. icy.

vergogne (sans) /(sɑ̃)vɛrgɔɲ/ a. shameless. ● adv. shamelessly.

véridique /veridik/ a. truthful.

vérif|ier /verifje/ v.t. check, verify; (compte) audit; (confirmer) confirm. **~ication** n.f. check(ing), verification.

véritable /veritabl/ a. true, real; (authentique) real. **~ment** /- əmɑ̃/ adv. really.

vérité /verite/ n.f. truth; (de tableau, roman) trueness to life. **en ~,** in fact.

vermeil, ~le /vɛrmɛj/ a. bright red.

vermicelle(s) /vɛrmisɛl/ n.m. (pl.) vermicelli.

vermine /vɛrmin/ n.f. vermin.

vermoulu /vɛrmuly/ a. wormeaten.

vermouth /vɛrmut/ n.m. (apéritif) vermouth.

verni /vɛrni/ a. (fam.) lucky. **chaussures ~es,** patent (leather) shoes.

vernir /vɛrnir/ v.t. varnish.

vernis /vɛrni/ n.m. varnish; (de poterie) glaze. **~ à ongles,** nail polish ou varnish.

vernissage /vɛrnisaʒ/ n.m. (exposition) preview.

vernisser /vɛrnise/ v.t. glaze.

verra, verrait /vɛra, vɛrɛ/ voir voir.

verre /vɛr/ n.m. glass. **prendre** ou **boire un ~,** have a drink. **~ de contact,** contact lens. **~ dépoli/ grossissant,** frosted/magnifying glass. **~rie** n.f. (objets) glassware.

verrière /vɛrjɛr/ n.f. (toit) glass roof; (paroi) glass wall.

verrou /vɛru/ n.m. bolt. **sous les ~s,** behind bars.

verrouiller /vɛruje/ v.t. bolt.

verrue /vɛry/ n.f. wart.

vers[1] /vɛr/ prép. towards; (temps) about.

vers[2] /vɛr/ n.m. (ligne) line. **les ~,** (poésie) verse.

versant /vɛrsɑ̃/ n.m. slope, side.

versatile /vɛrsatil/ a. fickle.

verse (à) /(a)vɛrs/ adv. in torrents.

versé /vɛrse/ a. **~ dans,** versed in.

Verseau /vɛrso/ n.m. **le ~,** Aquarius.

vers|er /vɛrse/ v.t./i. pour; (larmes, sang) shed; (basculer) overturn; (payer) pay. **~ement** n.m. payment.

verset /vɛrsɛ/ n.m. (relig.) verse.

version /vɛrsjɔ̃/ n.f. version; (traduction) translation.

verso /vɛrso/ n.m. back (of the page).

vert, ~e /vɛr, -t/ a. green; (vieillard) sprightly. ● a. green.

vertèbre /vɛrtɛbr/ n.f. vertebra.

vertement /vɛrtəmɑ̃/ adv. sharply.
vertic|al, ~ale (m. pl. **~aux**) /vɛr-
tikal, -o/ a. & n.f. vertical. **à la ~ale,**
~alement adv. vertically.
vertig|e /vɛrtiʒ/ n.m. dizziness. **~es,**
dizzy spells. **avoir le** ou **un ~e,** feel
dizzy. **~ineux, ~ineuse** a. dizzy;
(très grand) staggering.
vertu /vɛrty/ n.f. virtue. **en ~ de,** by
virtue of. **~eux, ~euse** /-tɥø, -z/ a.
virtuous.
verve /vɛrv/ n.f. spirit, wit.
verveine /vɛrvɛn/ n.f. verbena.
vésicule /vezikyl/ n.f. **~ biliaire,**
gall-bladder.
vessie /vesi/ n.f. bladder.
veste /vɛst/ n.f. jacket.
vestiaire /vɛstjɛr/ n.m. cloakroom;
(sport) changing-room.
vestibule /vɛstibyl/ n.m. hall.
vestige /vɛstiʒ/ n.m. (objet) relic;
(trace) vestige.
veston /vɛstɔ̃/ n.m. jacket.
vêtement /vɛtmɑ̃/ n.m. article of
clothing. **~s,** clothes.
vétéran /veterɑ̃/ n.m. veteran.
vétérinaire /veterinɛr/ n.m./f. vet,
veterinary surgeon, (Amer.) veter-
inarian.
vétille /vetij/ n.f. trifle.
vêt|ir /vetir/ v.t., se **~ir** v. pr. dress.
~u a. dressed (**de,** in).
veto /veto/ n.m. invar. veto.
vétuste /vetyst/ a. dilapidated.
veu|f, ~ve /vœf, -v/ a. widowed.
● n.m. widower. ● n.f. widow.
veuille /vœj/ voir vouloir.
veule /vøl/ a. feeble.
veut, veux /vø/ voir vouloir.
vexation /vɛksɑsjɔ̃/ n.f. humiliation.
vex|er /vɛkse/ v.t. upset, hurt. se **~er**
v. pr. be upset, be hurt. **~ant,**
~ante a. upsetting.
via /vja/ prép. via.
viable /vjabl/ a. viable.
viaduc /vjadyk/ n.m. viaduct.
viande /vjɑ̃d/ n.f. meat.
vibr|er /vibre/ v.i. vibrate; (être ému)
thrill. **~ant, ~ante** a. (émouvant)
vibrant. **~ation** n.f. vibration.
vicaire /vikɛr/ n.m. curate.
vice /vis/ n.m. (moral) vice; (défec-
tuosité) defect.
vice- /vis/ préf. vice-.
vice versa /vis(e)vɛrsa/ adv. vice
versa.
vicier /visje/ v.t. taint.
vicieu|x, ~se /visjø, -z/ a. depraved.
● n.m., f. pervert.

vicin|al (pl. **~aux**) /visinal, -o/ a.m.
chemin ~al, by-road, minor road.
vicomte /vikɔ̃t/ n.m. viscount.
victime /viktim/ n.f. victim; (d'un
accident) casualty.
vict|oire /viktwar/ n.f. victory;
(sport) win. **~orieux, ~orieuse** a.
victorious; (équipe) winning.
victuailles /viktɥɑj/ n.f. pl. provisions.
vidang|e /vidɑ̃ʒ/ n.f. emptying;
(auto.) oil change; (dispositif) waste
pipe. **~er** v.t. empty.
vide /vid/ a. empty. ● n.m. empti-
ness, void; (trou, manque) gap;
(espace sans air) vacuum. **à ~,**
empty.
vidéo /video/ a. invar. video. **jeu**
~, video game. **~cassette** n.f.
video(tape). **~thèque** n.f. video library.
vide-ordures /vidɔrdyr/ n.m. invar.
(rubbish) chute.
vider /vide/ v.t. empty; (poisson) gut;
(expulser: fam.) throw out. **~ les**
lieux, vacate the premises. se **~** v.
pr. empty.
videur /vidœr/ n.m. bouncer.
vie /vi/ n.f. life; (durée) lifetime. **à ~,**
pour la ~, for life. **donner la ~ à,**
give birth to. **en ~,** alive. **~ chère,**
high cost of living.
vieil /vjɛj/ voir vieux.
vieillard /vjɛjar/ n.m. old man.
vieille /vjɛj/ voir vieux.
vieillesse /vjɛjɛs/ n.f. old age.
vieill|ir /vjɛjir/ v.i. grow old, age;
(mot, idée) become old-fashioned.
● v.t. age. **~issement** n.m. ageing.
viens, vient /vjɛ̃/ voir venir.
vierge /vjɛrʒ/ n.f. virgin. **la V~,**
Virgo. ● a. virgin; (feuille, film)
blank.
vieux ou **vieil*, vieille** (m. pl. **vieux**)
/vjø, vjɛj/ a. old. ● n.m. old man.
● n.f. old woman. **les ~,** old people.
mon ~, (fam.) old man ou boy. **ma**
vieille, (fam.) old girl, dear. **vieille**
fille, (péj.) spinster. **~ garçon,**
bachelor. **~ jeu** a. invar. old-fashioned.
vif, vive /vif, viv/ a. lively; (émotion,
vent) keen; (froid) biting; (lumière)
bright; (douleur, parole) sharp;
(souvenir, style, teint) vivid; (succès,
impatience) great. **brûler/enterrer**
~, burn/bury alive. **de vive voix,**

personally. **avoir les nerfs à ~,** be on edge.

vigie /viʒi/ *n.f.* look-out.

vigilan|t, ~te /viʒilɑ̃, -t/ *a.* vigilant. **~ce** *n.f.* vigilance.

vigne /viɲ/ *n.f.* (*plante*) vine; (*vignoble*) vineyard.

vigneron, ~ne /viɲrɔ̃, -ɔn/ *n.m., f.* wine-grower.

vignette /viɲɛt/ *n.f.* (*étiquette*) label; (*auto.*) road tax sticker.

vignoble /viɲɔbl/ *n.m.* vineyard.

vigoureu|x, ~se /vigurø, -z/ *a.* vigorous, sturdy.

vigueur /vigœr/ *n.f.* vigour. **être/ entrer en ~,** (*loi*) be/come into force. **en ~,** (*terme*) in use.

VIH *abrév.* (*virus d'immunodéficience humaine*) HIV.

vil /vil/ *a.* vile, base.

vilain, ~e /vilɛ̃, -ɛn/ *a.* (*mauvais*) nasty; (*laid*) ugly.

villa /villa/ *n.f.* (detached) house.

village /vilaʒ/ *n.m.* village.

villageois, ~e /vilaʒwa, -z/ *a.* village. ● *n.m., f.* villager.

ville /vil/ *n.f.* town; (*importante*) city. **~ d'eaux,** spa.

vin /vɛ̃/ *n.m.* wine. **~ d'honneur,** reception. **~ ordinaire,** table wine.

vinaigre /vinɛgr/ *n.m.* vinegar.

vinaigrette /vinɛgrɛt/ *n.f.* oil and vinegar dressing, vinaigrette.

vindicati|f, ~ve /vɛ̃dikatif, -v/ *a.* vindictive.

vingt /vɛ̃/ (/vɛ̃t/ *before vowel and in numbers 22-29*) *a. & n.m.* twenty. **~ième** *a. & n.m./f.* twentieth.

vingtaine /vɛ̃tɛn/ *n.f.* **une ~ (de),** about twenty.

vinicole /vinikɔl/ *a.* wine(-growing).

vinyle /vinil/ *n.m.* vinyl.

viol /vjɔl/ *n.m.* (*de femme*) rape; (*de lieu, loi*) violation.

violacé /vjɔlase/ *a.* purplish.

viol|ent, ~ente /vjɔlɑ̃, -t/ *a.* violent. **~emment** /-amɑ̃/ *adv.* violently. **~ence** *n.f.* violence; (*acte*) act of violence.

viol|er /vjɔle/ *v.t.* rape; (*lieu, loi*) violate. **~ation** *n.f.* violation.

violet, ~te /vjɔlɛ, -t/ *a. & n.m.* purple. ● *n.f.* violet.

violon /vjɔlɔ̃/ *n.m.* violin. **~iste** /-ɔnist/ *n.m./f.* violinist. **~ d'ingres,** hobby.

violoncell|e /vjɔlɔ̃sɛl/ *n.m.* cello. **~iste** /-elist/ *n.m./f.* cellist.

vipère /vipɛr/ *n.f.* viper, adder.

virage /viraʒ/ *n.m.* bend; (*de véhicule*) turn; (*changement d'attitude:* *fig.*) change of course.

virée /vire/ *n.f.* (*fam.*) trip, outing.

vir|er /vire/ *v.i.* turn. **~er de bord,** tack. **~er au rouge/***etc.,* turn red/ *etc.* ● *v.t.* (*argent*) transfer; (*expulser: fam.*) throw out. **~ement** *n.m.* (*comm.*) (credit) transfer.

virevolter /virvɔlte/ *v.i.* spin round, swing round.

virginité /virʒinite/ *n.f.* virginity.

virgule /virgyl/ *n.f.* comma; (*dans un nombre*) (decimal) point.

viril /viril/ *a.* manly, virile. **~ité** *n.f.* manliness, virility.

virtuel, ~le /virtɥɛl/ *a.* virtual. **~lement** *adv.* virtually.

virtuos|e /virtɥoz/ *n.m./f.* virtuoso. **~ité** *n.f.* virtuosity.

virulen|t, ~te /virylɑ̃, -t/ *a.* virulent. **~ce** *n.f.* virulence.

virus /virys/ *n.m.* virus.

vis [1] /vi/ *voir* vivre, voir.

vis [2] /vis/ *n.f.* screw.

visa /viza/ *n.m.* visa.

visage /vizaʒ/ *n.m.* face.

vis-à-vis /vizavi/ *adv.* face to face, opposite. **~ de,** opposite; (*à l'égard de*) with respect to. ● *n.m. invar.* (*personne*) person opposite.

viscères /visɛr/ *n.m. pl.* intestines.

visées /vize/ *n.f. pl.* aim. **avoir des ~ sur,** have designs on.

viser /vize/ *v.t.* aim at; (*concerner*) be aimed at; (*timbrer*) stamp. ● *v.i.* aim. **~ à,** aim at; (*mesure, propos*) be aimed at.

visib|le /vizibl/ *a.* visible. **~ilité** *n.f.* visibility. **~lement** *adv.* visibly.

visière /vizjɛr/ *n.f.* (*de casquette*) peak; (*de casque*) visor.

vision /vizjɔ̃/ *n.f.* vision.

visionnaire /vizjɔnɛr/ *a. & n.m./f.* visionary.

visionn|er /vizjɔne/ *v.t.* view. **~euse** *n.f.* (*appareil*) viewer.

visite /vizit/ *n.f.* visit; (*examen*) examination; (*personne*) visitor. **heures de ~,** visiting hours. **~ guidée,** guided tour. **rendre ~ à,** visit. **être en ~ (chez qn.),** be visiting (s.o.).

visit|er /vizite/ *v.t.* visit; (*examiner*) examine. **~eur, ~euse** *n.m., f.* visitor.

vison /vizɔ̃/ *n.m.* mink.

visqueu|x, ~se /viskø, -z/ *a.* viscous.

visser /vise/ *v.t.* screw (on).
visuel, ~le /vizyɛl/ *a.* visual.
vit /vi/ *voir* vivre, voir.
vit|al (*m. pl.* **~aux**) /vital, -o/ *a.* vital.
~alité *n.f.* vitality.
vitamine /vitamin/ *n.f.* vitamin.
vite /vit/ *adv.* fast, quickly; (*tôt*) soon.
~!, quick! **faire ~,** be quick.
vitesse /vitɛs/ *n.f.* speed; (*régime*: *auto.*) gear. **à toute ~,** at top speed. **en ~,** in a hurry, quickly.
vitic|ole /vitikɔl/ *a.* wine. **~ulteur** *n.m.* wine-grower. **~ulture** *n.f.* wine-growing.
vitrage /vitraʒ/ *n.m.* (*vitres*) windows. **double-~,** double glazing.
vitr|ail (*pl.* **~aux**) /vitraj, -o/ *n.m.* stained-glass window.
vitr|e /vitr/ *n.f.* (window) pane; (*de véhicule*) window. **~é** *a.* glass, glazed. **~er** *v.t.* glaze.
vitrine /vitrin/ *n.f.* (shop) window; (*meuble*) display cabinet.
vivable /vivabl/ *a.* **ce n'est pas ~,** it's unbearable.
vivace /vivas/ *a.* (*plante, sentiment*) perennial.
vivacité /vivasite/ *n.f.* liveliness; (*agilité*) quickness; (*d'émotion, de l'air*) keenness; (*de souvenir, style, teint*) vividness.
vivant, ~e /vivã, -t/ *a.* (*doué de vie, en usage*) living; (*en vie*) alive, living; (*actif, vif*) lively. ● *n.m.* **un bon ~,** a bon viveur. **de son ~,** in one's lifetime. **les ~s,** the living.
vivats /viva/ *n.m. pl.* cheers.
vive¹ /viv/ *voir* vif.
vive² /viv/ *int.* **~ le roi/président/ etc.!,** long live the king/president/ etc.!
vivement /vivmã/ *adv.* (*vite, sèchement*) sharply; (*avec éclat*) vividly; (*beaucoup*) greatly. **~ la fin!,** roll on the end, I'll be glad when it's the end!
vivier /vivje/ *n.m.* fish-pond.
vivifier /vivifje/ *v.t.* invigorate.
vivisection /viviseksjɔ̃/ *n.f.* vivisection.
vivoter /vivɔte/ *v.i.* plod on, get by.
vivre† /vivr/ *v.i.* live. **~ de,** (*nourriture*) live on. ● *v.t.* (*vie*) live; (*période, aventure*) live through. **~s** *n.m. pl.* supplies. **faire ~,** (*famille etc.*) support. **~ encore,** be still alive.
vlan /vlã/ *int.* bang.
vocabulaire /vɔkabylɛr/ *n.m.* vocabulary.

voc|al (*m. pl.* **~aux**) /vɔkal, -o/ *a.* vocal.
vocalise /vɔkaliz/ *n.f.* voice exercise.
vocation /vɔkasjɔ̃/ *n.f.* vocation.
vociférer /vɔsifere/ *v.t./i.* scream.
vodka /vɔdka/ *n.f.* vodka.
vœu (*pl.* **~x**) /vø/ *n.m.* (*souhait*) wish; (*promesse*) vow.
vogue /vɔg/ *n.f.* fashion, vogue.
voguer /vɔge/ *v.i.* sail.
voici /vwasi/ *prép.* here is, this is; (*au pluriel*) here are, these are. **me ~,** here I am. **~ un an,** (*temps passé*) a year ago. **~ un an que,** it is a year since.
voie /vwa/ *n.f.* (*route*) road; (*chemin*) way; (*moyen*) means, way; (*partie de route*) lane; (*rails*) track; (*quai*) platform. **en ~ de,** in the process of. **en ~ de développement,** (*pays*) developing. **par la ~ des airs,** by air. **~ de dégagement,** slip-road. **~ ferrée,** railway; (*Amer.*) railroad. **~ lactée,** Milky Way. **~ navigable,** waterway. **~ publique,** public highway. **~ sans issue,** cul-de-sac, dead end. **sur la bonne ~,** (*fig.*) well under way. **mettre sur une ~ de garage,** (*fig.*) sideline.
voilà /vwala/ *prép.* there is, that is; (*au pluriel*) there are, those are; (*voici*) here are, these are. **le ~,** there he is. **~!,** right!; (*en offrant qch.*) there you are! **~ un an,** (*temps passé*) a year ago. **~ un an que,** it is a year since.
voilage /vwalaʒ/ *n.m.* net curtain.
voile¹ /vwal/ *n.f.* (*de bateau*) sail; (*sport*) sailing.
voile² /vwal/ *n.m.* veil; (*tissu léger et fin*) net.
voil|er¹ /vwale/ *v.t.* veil. **se ~er** *v. pr.* (*devenir flou*) become hazy. **~é** *a.* (*terme, femme*) veiled; (*flou*) hazy.
voiler² /vwale/ *v.t.,* **se ~** *v. pr.* (*roue etc.*) buckle.
voilier /vwalje/ *n.m.* sailing-ship.
voilure /vwalyr/ *n.f.* sails.
voir† /vwar/ *v.t./i.* see. **se ~** *v. pr.* (*être visible*) show; (*se produire*) be seen; (*se trouver*) find o.s.; (*se fréquenter*) see each other. **ça n'a rien à ~ avec,** that has nothing to do with. **faire ~, laisser ~,** show. **je ne peux pas le ~,** (*fam.*) I cannot stand him. **~ trouble,** have blurred vision. **voyons!,** (*irritation*) come on!
voire /vwar/ *adv.* indeed.

voirie /vwari/ *n.f.* (*service*) highway maintenance. **travaux de ~,** roadworks.

voisin, **~e** /vwazẽ, -in/ *a.* (*proche*) neighbouring; (*adjacent*) next (**de,** to); (*semblable*) similar (**de,** to). ● *n.m., f.* neighbour. **le ~,** the man next door.

voisinage /vwazinaʒ/ *n.m.* neighbourhood; (*proximité*) proximity.

voiture /vwatyr/ *n.f.* (motor) car; (*wagon*) coach, carriage. **en ~!,** all aboard! **~ à cheval,** horse-drawn carriage. **~ de course,** racing-car. **~ d'enfant,** pram; (*Amer.*) baby carriage. **~ de tourisme,** private car.

voix /vwa/ *n.f.* voice; (*suffrage*) vote. **à ~ basse,** in a whisper.

vol [1] /vɔl/ *n.m.* (*d'avion, d'oiseau*) flight; (*groupe d'oiseaux etc.*) flock, flight. **à ~ d'oiseau,** as the crow flies. **~ libre,** hang-gliding. **~ plané,** gliding.

vol [2] /vɔl/ *n.m.* (*délit*) theft; (*hold-up*) robbery. **~ à la tire,** pickpocketing.

volage /vɔlaʒ/ *a.* fickle.

volaille /vɔlaj/ *n.f.* **la ~,** (*poules etc.*) poultry. **une ~,** a fowl.

volant /vɔlã/ *n.m.* (steering-)wheel; (*de jupe*) flounce.

volcan /vɔlkã/ *n.m.* volcano. **~ique** /-anik/ *a.* volcanic.

volée /vɔle/ *n.f.* flight; (*oiseaux*) flight, flock; (*de coups, d'obus*) volley. **à toute ~,** with full force. **de ~, à la ~,** in flight.

voler [1] /vɔle/ *v.i.* (*oiseau etc.*) fly.

vol|er [2] /vɔle/ *v.t./i.* steal (**à,** from). **il ne l'a pas ~é,** he deserved it. **~er qn.,** rob s.o. **~eur, ~euse** *n.m., f.* thief; *a.* thieving.

volet /vɔle/ *n.m.* (*de fenêtre*) shutter; (*de document*) (folded *ou* tear-off) section. **trié sur le ~,** hand-picked.

voleter /vɔlte/ *v.i.* flutter.

volière /vɔljɛr/ *n.f.* aviary.

volontaire /vɔlɔ̃tɛr/ *a.* voluntary; (*personne*) determined. ● *n.m./f.* volunteer. **~ment** *adv.* voluntarily; (*exprès*) intentionally.

volonté /vɔlɔ̃te/ *n.f.* (*faculté, intention*) will; (*souhait*) wish; (*énergie*) will-power. **à ~** (*à son gré*) at will. **bonne ~,** goodwill. **mauvaise ~,** ill will. **faire ses quatre ~s,** do exactly as one pleases.

volontiers /vɔlɔ̃tje/ *adv.* (*de bon gré*) with pleasure, willingly, gladly; (*ordinairement*) readily.

volt /vɔlt/ *n.m.* volt. **~age** *n.m.* voltage.

volte-face /vɔltafas/ *n.f. invar.* about-face. **faire ~,** turn round.

voltige /vɔltiʒ/ *n.f.* acrobatics.

voltiger /vɔltiʒe/ *v.i.* flutter.

volubile /vɔlybil/ *a.* voluble.

volume /vɔlym/ *n.m.* volume.

volumineu|x, ~se /vɔlyminø, -z/ *a.* bulky.

volupt|é /vɔlypte/ *n.f.* sensual pleasure. **~ueux, ~ueuse** *a.* voluptuous.

vom|ir /vɔmir/ *v.t./i.* vomit. **~i** *n.m.* vomit. **~issement(s)** *n.m.* (*pl.*) vomiting.

vont /vɔ̃/ *voir* aller [1].

vorace /vɔras/ *a.* voracious.

vos /vo/ *voir* votre.

vote /vɔt/ *n.m.* (*action*) voting; (*d'une loi*) passing; (*suffrage*) vote.

vot|er /vɔte/ *v.i.* vote. ● *v.t.* vote for; (*adopter*) pass; (*crédits*) vote. **~ant, ~ante** *n.m., f.* voter.

votre (*pl.* **vos**) /vɔtr, vo/ *a.* your.

vôtre /votr/ *pron.* **le** *ou* **la ~, les ~s,** yours.

vou|er /vwe/ *v.t.* dedicate (**à,** to); (*promettre*) vow. **~é à l'échec,** doomed to failure.

vouloir† /vulwar/ *v.t.* want (**faire,** to do). **ça ne veut pas bouger**/*etc.*, it will not move/*etc.* **je voudrais/vou- drais bien venir**/*etc.*, I should *ou* would like/really like to come/*etc.* **je veux bien venir**/*etc.*, I am happy to come/*etc.* **voulez-vous attendre**/ *etc.*?, will you wait/*etc.*? **veuillez attendre**/*etc.*, kindly wait/*etc.* **~ absolument faire,** insist on doing. **comme** *ou* **si vous voulez,** if you like *ou* wish. **en ~ à qn.,** have a grudge against s.o.; (*être en colère contre*) be annoyed with s.o. **qu'est- ce qu'il me veut?,** what does he want with me? **ne pas ~ de qch./ qn.,** not want sth./s.o. **~ dire,** mean. **~ du bien à,** wish well.

voulu /vuly/ *a.* (*délibéré*) intentional; (*requis*) required.

vous /vu/ *pron.* (*sujet, complément*) you; (*indirect*) (to) you; (*réfléchi*) yourself; (*pl.*) yourselves; (*l'un à l'au- tre*) each other. **~-même** *pron.* yourself. **~-mêmes** *pron.* your- selves.

voûte /vut/ *n.f.* (*plafond*) vault; (*porche*) archway.

voûté /vute/ *a.* bent, stooped. **il a le dos ~,** he's stooped.

vouv|oyer /vuvwaje/ *v.t.* address politely (using *vous*). **~oiement** *n.m.* use of (polite) *vous*.

voyage /vwajaʒ/ *n.m.* journey, trip; (*par mer*) voyage. **~(s),** (*action*) travelling. **~ d'affaires,** business trip. **~ de noces,** honeymoon. **~ organisé,** (package) tour.

voyag|er /vwajaʒe/ *v.i.* travel. **~eur, ~euse** *n.m., f.* traveller.

voyant¹, ~e /vwajã, -t/ *a.* gaudy. ● *n.f.* (*femme*) clairvoyant.

voyant² /vwajã/ *n.m.* (*signal*) (warning) light.

voyelle /vwajɛl/ *n.f.* vowel.

voyeur /vwajœr/ *n.m.* voyeur.

voyou /vwaju/ *n.m.* hooligan.

vrac (en) /(ã)vrak/ *adv.* in disorder; (*sans emballage, au poids*) loose, in bulk.

vrai /vrɛ/ *a.* true; (*réel*) real. ● *n.m.* truth. **à ~ dire,** to tell the truth.

vraiment /vrɛmã/ *adv.* really.

vraisembl|able /vrɛsãblabl/ *a.* likely. **~ablement** *adv.* very likely. **~ance** *n.f.* likelihood, plausibility.

vrille /vrij/ *n.f.* (*aviat.*) spin.

vromb|ir /vrɔ̃bir/ *v.i.* hum. **~issement** *n.m.* humming.

VRP *abrév. m.* (*voyageur représentant placier*) rep.

vu /vy/ *voir* voir. ● *a.* **bien/mal ~,** well/not well thought of. ● *prép.* in view of. **~ que,** seeing that.

vue /vy/ *n.f.* (*spectacle*) sight; (*sens*) (eye)sight; (*panorama, idée*) view. **avoir en ~,** have in mind. **à ~,** (*tirer, payable*) at sight. **de ~,** by sight. **perdre de ~,** lose sight of. **en ~,** (*proche*) in sight; (*célèbre*) in the public eye. **en ~ de faire,** with a view to doing.

vulg|aire /vylgɛr/ *a.* (*grossier*) vulgar; (*ordinaire*) common. **~arité** *n.f.* vulgarity.

vulgariser /vylgarize/ *v.t.* popularize.

vulnérab|le /vylnerabl/ *a.* vulnerable. **~ilité** *n.f.* vulnerability.

vulve /vylv/ *n.f.* vulva.

W

wagon /vagɔ̃/ *n.m.* (*de voyageurs*) carriage; (*Amer.*) car; (*de marchandises*) wagon; (*Amer.*) freight car. **~-lit** (*pl.* **~s-lits**) *n.m.* sleeping-car, sleeper. **~-restaurant** (*pl.* **~s-restaurants**) *n.m.* dining-car.

walkman /wokman/ *n.m.* (P.) walkman.

wallon, ~ne /walɔ̃, -ɔn/ *a. & n.m., f.* Walloon.

waters /watɛr/ *n.m. pl.* toilet.

watt /wat/ *n.m.* watt.

w.-c. /(dubla)vese/ *n.m. pl.* toilet.

week-end /wikɛnd/ *n.m.* weekend.

western /wɛstɛrn/ *n.m.* western.

whisk|y (*pl.* **~ies**) /wiski/ *n.m.* whisky.

X

xénophob|e /ksenɔfɔb/ *a.* xenophobic. ● *n.m./f.* xenophobe. **~ie** *n.f.* xenophobia.

xérès /kserɛs/ *n.m.* sherry.

xylophone /ksilɔfɔn/ *n.m.* xylophone.

Y

y /i/ *adv. & pron.* there; (*dessus*) on it; (*pl.*) on them; (*dedans*) in it; (*pl.*) in them. **s'y habituer,** (*à cela*) get used to it. **s'y attendre,** expect it. **y penser,** think of it. **il y entra,** (*dans cela*) he entered it. **j'y vais,** I'm on my way. **ça y est,** that is it. **y être pour qch.,** have sth. to do with it.

yacht /jɔt/ *n.m.* yacht.

yaourt /jaur(t)/ *n.m.* yoghurt. **~ière** /-tjɛr/ *n.f.* yoghurt maker.

yeux /jø/ *voir* œil.

yiddish /(j)idiʃ/ *n.m.* Yiddish.

yoga /jɔga/ *n.m.* yoga.

yougoslave /jugɔslav/ *a. & n.m./f.* Yugoslav.

Yougoslavie /jugɔslavi/ *n.f.* Yugoslavia.

yo-yo /jojo/ *n.m. invar.* (P.) yo-yo (P.).

yuppie /jœpi/ *n.m./f.* yuppie.

Z

zèbre /zɛbr/ *n.m.* zebra.
zébré /zebre/ *a.* striped.
zèle /zɛl/ *n.m.* zeal.
zélé /zele/ *a.* zealous.
zénith /zenit/ *n.m.* zenith.
zéro /zero/ *n.m.* nought, zero; (*température*) zero; (*dans un numéro*) 0; (*football*) nil; (*football: Amer.*) zero; (*personne*) nonentity. **(re)partir de ~,** start from scratch.
zeste /zɛst/ *n.m.* peel. **un ~ de,** (*fig.*) a pinch of.
zézayer /zezeje/ *v.i.* lisp.
zigzag /zigzag/ *n.m.* zigzag. **en ~,** zigzag. **~uer** /-e/ *v.i.* zigzag.
zinc /zɛ̃g/ *n.m.* (*métal*) zinc; (*comptoir: fam.*) bar.
zizanie /zizani/ *n.f.* **semer la ~,** put the cat among the pigeons.
zizi /zizi/ *n.m.* (*fam.*) willy.
zodiaque /zɔdjak/ *n.m.* zodiac.
zona /zona/ *n.m.* (*méd.*) shingles.
zone /zon/ *n.f.* zone, area; (*faubourgs*) shanty town. **~ bleue,** restricted parking zone.
zoo /zo(o)/ *n.m.* zoo.
zoolog|ie /zɔɔlɔʒi/ *n.f.* zoology. **~ique** *a.* zoological. **~iste** *n.m./f.* zoologist.
zoom /zum/ *n.m.* zoom lens.
zut /zyt/ *int.* blast (it), (oh) hell.

ANGLAIS-FRANÇAIS
ENGLISH-FRENCH

A

a /eɪ, *unstressed* ə/ *a.* (*before vowel* **an** /æn, ən/) un(e). **I'm a painter,** je suis peintre. **ten pence a kilo,** dix pence le kilo. **once a year,** une fois par an.

aback /ə'bæk/ *adv.* **taken ~,** déconcerté, interdit.

abandon /ə'bændən/ *v.t.* abandonner. ● *n.* désinvolture *f.* **~ed** *a.* (*behaviour*) débauché. **~ment** *n.* abandon *m.*

abashed /ə'bæʃt/ *a.* confus.

abate /ə'beɪt/ *v.i.* se calmer. ● *v.t.* diminuer. **~ment** *n.* diminution *f.*

abattoir /'æbətwɑ:(r)/ *n.* abattoir *m.*

abbey /'æbɪ/ *n.* abbaye *f.*

abb|ot /'æbət/ *n.* abbé *m.* **~ess** *n.* abbesse *f.*

abbreviat|e /ə'bri:vɪeɪt/ *v.t.* abréger. **~ion** /-'eɪʃn/ *n.* abréviation *f.*

abdicat|e /'æbdɪkeɪt/ *v.t./i.* abdiquer. **~ion** /-'keɪʃn/ *n.* abdication *f.*

abdom|en /'æbdəmən/ *n.* abdomen *m.* **~inal** /-'dɒmɪnl/ *a.* abdominal.

abduct /æb'dʌkt/ *v.t.* enlever. **~ion** /-kʃn/ *n.* rapt *m.* **~or** *n.* ravisseu|r, -se *m., f.*

aberration /æbə'reɪʃn/ *n.* aberration *f.*

abet /ə'bet/ *v.t.* (*p.t.* **abetted**) (*jurid.*) encourager.

abeyance /ə'beɪəns/ *n.* **in ~,** (*matter*) en suspens; (*custom*) en désuétude.

abhor /əb'hɔ:(r)/ *v.t.* (*p.t.* **abhorred**) exécrer. **~rence** /-'hɒrəns/ *n.* horreur *f.* **~rent** /-'hɒrənt/ *a.* exécrable.

abide /ə'baɪd/ *v.t.* supporter. **~ by,** respecter.

abiding /ə'baɪdɪŋ/ *a.* éternel.

ability /ə'bɪlətɪ/ *n.* aptitude *f.* (**to do,** à faire); (*talent*) talent *m.*

abject /'æbdʒekt/ *a.* abject.

ablaze /ə'bleɪz/ *a.* en feu. **~ with,** (*anger etc.: fig.*) enflammé de.

abl|e /'eɪbl/ *a.* (**-er, -est**) capable (**to, de**). **be ~e,** pouvoir; (*know how to*) savoir. **~y** *adv.* habilement.

ablutions /ə'blu:ʃnz/ *n. pl.* ablutions *f. pl.*

abnormal /æb'nɔ:ml/ *a.* anormal. **~ity** /-'mælətɪ/ *n.* anomalie *f.* **~ly** *adv.* (*unusually*) exceptionnellement.

aboard /ə'bɔ:d/ *adv.* à bord. ● *prep.* à bord de.

abode /ə'bəʊd/ (*old use*) demeure *f.* **of no fixed ~,** sans domicile fixe.

aboli|sh /ə'bɒlɪʃ/ *v.t.* supprimer, abolir. **~tion** /æbə'lɪʃn/ *n.* suppression *f.*, abolition *f.*

abominable /ə'bɒmɪnəbl/ *a.* abominable.

abominat|e /ə'bɒmɪneɪt/ *v.t.* exécrer. **~ion** /-'neɪʃn/ *n.* abomination *f.*

aboriginal /æbə'rɪdʒənl/ *a. & n.* aborigène (*m.*).

aborigines /æbə'rɪdʒəni:z/ *n. pl.* aborigènes *m. pl.*

abort /ə'bɔ:t/ *v.t.* faire avorter. ● *v.i.* avorter. **~ive** *a.* (*attempt etc.*) manqué.

abortion /ə'bɔ:ʃn/ *n.* avortement *m.* **have an ~,** se faire avorter.

abound /ə'baʊnd/ *v.i.* abonder (**in, en**).

about /ə'baʊt/ *adv.* (*approximately*) environ; (*here and there*) çà et là; (*all round*) partout, autour; (*nearby*) dans les parages; (*of rumour*) en circulation. ● *prep.* au sujet de; (*round*) autour de; (*somewhere in*) dans. **~-face, ~-turn** *ns.* (*fig.*) volteface *f. invar.* **~ here,** par ici. **be ~ to do,** être sur le point de faire. **how** *or* **what ~ leaving,** si on partait. **what's the film ~?,** quel est le sujet du film? **talk ~,** parler de.

above /ə'bʌv/ *adv.* au-dessus; (*on page*) au-dessus. ● *prep.* au-dessus de. **he is not ~ lying,** il n'est pas incapable de mentir. **~ all,** pardessus tout. **~-board** *a.* honnête. **~-mentioned** *a.* mentionné ci-dessus.

abrasion /ə'breɪʒn/ n. frottement m.; (injury) écorchure f.

abrasive /ə'breɪsɪv/ a. abrasif; (manner) brusque. ● n. abrasif m.

abreast /ə'brest/ adv. de front. **keep ~ of**, se tenir au courant de.

abridge /ə'brɪdʒ/ v.t. abréger. **~ment** n. abrégement m., réduction f.; (abridged text) abrégé m.

abroad /ə'brɔːd/ adv. à l'étranger; (far and wide) de tous côtés.

abrupt /ə'brʌpt/ a. (sudden, curt) brusque; (steep) abrupt. **~ly** adv. (suddenly) brusquement; (curtly, rudely) avec brusquerie. **~ness** n. brusquerie f.

abscess /'æbses/ n. abcès m.

abscond /əb'skɒnd/ v.i. s'enfuir.

abseil /'æbseɪl/ v.i. descendre en rappel.

absen|t[1] /'æbsənt/ a. absent; (look etc.) distrait. **~ce** n. absence f.; (lack) manque m. **in the ~ce of**, à défaut de. **~tly** adv. distraitement. **~t-minded** a. distrait. **~t-mindedness** n. distraction f.

absent[2] /əb'sent/ v. pr. **~ o.s.**, s'absenter.

absentee /æbsən'tiː/ n. absent(e) m. (f.). **~ism** n. absentéisme m.

absolute /'æbsəluːt/ a. absolu; (coward etc.: fam.) véritable. **~ly** adv. absolument.

absolution /æbsə'luːʃn/ n. absolution f.

absolve /əb'zɒlv/ v.t. (from sin) absoudre (**from**, de); (from vow etc.) délier (**from**, de).

absor|b /əb'sɔːb/ v.t. absorber. **~ption** n. absorption f.

absorbent /əb'sɔːbənt/ a. absorbant. **~ cotton**, (Amer.) coton hydrophile m.

abst|ain /əb'stem/ v.i. s'abstenir (**from**, de). **~ention** /-'stenʃn/ n. abstention f.; (from drink) abstinence f.

abstemious /əb'stiːmɪəs/ a. sobre.

abstinen|ce /'æbstɪnəns/ n. abstinence f. **~t** a. sobre.

abstract[1] /'æbstrækt/ a. abstrait. ● n. (quality) abstrait m.; (summary) résumé m.

abstract[2] /əb'strækt/ v.t. retirer, extraire. **~ion** /-kʃn/ n. extraction f.; (idea) abstraction f.

abstruse /əb'struːs/ a. obscur.

absurd /əb'sɜːd/ a. absurde. **~ity** n. absurdité f.

abundan|t /ə'bʌndənt/ a. abondant. **~ce** n. abondance f. **~tly** adv. (entirely) tout à fait.

abuse[1] /ə'bjuːz/ v.t. (misuse) abuser de; (ill-treat) maltraiter; (insult) injurier.

abus|e[2] /ə'bjuːs/ n. (misuse) abus m. (**of**, de); (insults) injures f. pl. **~ive** a. injurieux. **get ~ive**, devenir grossier.

abut /ə'bʌt/ v.i. (p.t. **abutted**) être contigu (**on**, à).

abysmal /ə'bɪzməl/ a. (great) profond; (bad: fam.) exécrable.

abyss /ə'bɪs/ n. abîme m.

academic /ækə'demɪk/ a. universitaire; (scholarly) intellectuel; (pej.) théorique. ● n. universitaire m./f. **~ally** /-lɪ/ adv. intellectuellement.

academ|y /ə'kædəmɪ/ n. (school) école f. **A~y**, (society) Académie f. **~ician** /-'mɪʃn/ n. académicien(ne) m. (f.).

accede /ək'siːd/ v.i. **~ to**, (request, post, throne) accéder à.

accelerat|e /ək'seləreɪt/ v.t. accélérer. ● v.i. (speed up) s'accélérer; (auto.) accélérer. **~ion** /-'reɪʃn/ n. accélération f.

accelerator /ək'seləreɪtə(r)/ n. (auto.) accélérateur m.

accent[1] /'æksənt/ n. accent m.

accent[2] /æk'sent/ v.t. accentuer.

accentuat|e /ək'sentʃueɪt/ v.t. accentuer. **~ion** /-'eɪʃn/ n. accentuation f.

accept /ək'sept/ v.t. accepter. **~able** a. acceptable. **~ance** n. acceptation f.; (approval, favour) approbation f.

access /'ækses/ n. accès m. (**to sth.**, à qch.; **to s.o.**, auprès de qn.). **~ible** /ək'sesəbl/ a. accessible. **~ road**, route d'accès f.

accession /æk'seʃn/ n. accession f.; (thing added) nouvelle acquisition f.

accessory /ək'sesərɪ/ a. accessoire. ● n. accessoire m.; (person: jurid.) complice m./f.

accident /'æksɪdənt/ n. accident m.; (chance) hasard m. **~al** /-'dentl/ a. accidentel, fortuit. **~ally** /-'dentlɪ/ adv. involontairement. **~-prone**, qui attire les accidents.

acclaim /ə'kleɪm/ v.t. acclamer. ● n. acclamation(s) f. (pl.).

acclimat|e /'æklɪmeɪt/ v.t./i. (Amer.) (s')acclimater. **~ion** /-'meɪʃn/ n. (Amer.) acclimatation f.

acclimatiz|e /ə'klaɪmətaɪz/ v.t./i. (s')acclimater. **~ation** /-'zeɪʃn/ n. acclimatation f.

accommodat|e /ə'kɒmədeɪt/ v.t. loger, avoir de la place pour; (adapt) adapter; (supply) fournir; (oblige) obliger. **~ing** a. obligeant. **~ion** /-'deɪʃn/ n. (living premises) logement m.; (rented rooms) chambres f. pl.

accompan|y /ə'kʌmpənɪ/ v.t. accompagner. **~iment** n. accompagnement m. **~ist** n. accompagnateur, -trice m., f.

accomplice /ə'kʌmplɪs/ n. complice m./f.

accomplish /ə'kʌmplɪʃ/ v.t. (perform) accomplir; (achieve) réaliser. **~ed** a. accompli. **~ment** n. accomplissement m. **~ments** n. pl. (abilities) talents m. pl.

accord /ə'kɔ:d/ v.i. concorder. ● v.t. accorder. ● n. accord m. **of one's own ~,** de sa propre initiative. **~ance** n. **in ~ance with,** conformément à.

according /ə'kɔ:dɪŋ/ adv. **~ to,** selon, suivant. **~ly** adv. en conséquence.

accordion /ə'kɔ:dɪən/ n. accordéon m.

accost /ə'kɒst/ v.t. aborder.

account /ə'kaʊnt/ n. (comm.) compte m.; (description) compte rendu m.; (importance) importance f. ● v.t. considérer. **~ for,** rendre compte de, expliquer. **on ~ of,** à cause de. **on no ~,** en aucun cas. **take into ~,** tenir compte de. **~able** a. responsable (for, de; to, envers). **~ability** /-ə'bɪlətɪ/ n. responsabilité f.

accountan|t /ə'kaʊntənt/ n. comptable m./f., expert-comptable m. **~cy** n. comptabilité f.

accredited /ə'kredɪtɪd/ a. accrédité.

accrue /ə'kru:/ v.i. s'accumuler. **~ to,** (come to) revenir à.

accumulat|e /ə'kju:mjʊleɪt/ v.t./i. (s')accumuler. **~ion** /-'leɪʃn/ n. accumulation f.

accumulator /ə'kju:mjʊleɪtə(r)/ n. (battery) accumulateur m.

accura|te /'ækjərət/ a. exact, précis. **~cy** n. cxactitude f., précision f. **~tely** adv. exactement, avec précision.

accus|e /ə'kju:z/ v.t. accuser. **the ~ed,** l'accusé(e) m.(f.). **~ation** /ækju:'zeɪʃn/ n. accusation f.

accustom /ə'kʌstəm/ v.t. accoutumer. **~ed** a. accoutumé. **become ~ed to,** s'accoutumer à.

ace /eɪs/ n. (card, person) as m.

ache /eɪk/ n. douleur f., mal m. ● v.i. faire mal. **my leg ~s,** ma jambe me fait mal, j'ai mal à la jambe.

achieve /ə'tʃi:v/ v.t. réaliser, accomplir; (success) obtenir. **~ment** n. réalisation f. (of, de); (feat) exploit m., réussite f.

acid /'æsɪd/ a. & n. acide (m.). **~ity** /ə'sɪdətɪ/ n. acidité f. **~ rain,** pluies acides f. pl.

acknowledge /ək'nɒlɪdʒ/ v.t. reconnaître. **~ (receipt of),** accuser réception de. **~ment** n. reconnaissance f.; accusé de réception m.

acme /'ækmɪ/ n. sommet m.

acne /'æknɪ/ n. acné f.

acorn /'eɪkɔ:n/ n. (bot.) gland m.

acoustic /ə'ku:stɪk/ a. acoustique. **~s** n. pl. acoustique f.

acquaint /ə'kweɪnt/ v.t. **~ s.o. with sth.,** mettre qn. au courant de qch. **be ~ed with,** (person) connaître; (fact) savoir. **~ance** n. (knowledge, person) connaissance f.

acquiesce /ækwɪ'es/ v.i. consentir. **~nce** n. consentement m.

acqui|re /ə'kwaɪə(r)/ v.t. acquérir; (habit) prendre. **~sition** /ækwɪ'zɪʃn/ n. acquisition f. **~sitive** /ə'kwɪzətɪv/ a. avide, âpre au gain.

acquit /ə'kwɪt/ v.t. (p.t. acquitted) acquitter. **~ o.s. well,** bien s'en tirer. **~tal** n. acquittement m.

acre /'eɪkə(r)/ n. (approx.) demi-hectare m. **~age** n. superficie f.

acrid /'ækrɪd/ a. âcre.

acrimon|ious /ækrɪ'məʊnɪəs/ a. acerbe, acrimonieux. **~y** /'ækrɪmənɪ/ n. acrimonie f.

acrobat /'ækrəbæt/ n. acrobate m./f. **~ic** /-'bætɪk/ a. acrobatique. **~ics** /-'bætɪks/ n. pl. acrobatie f.

acronym /'ækrənɪm/ n. sigle m.

across /ə'krɒs/ adv. & prep. (side to side) d'un côté à l'autre (de); (on other side) de l'autre côté (from, de); (crosswise) en travers (de), à travers. **go or walk ~,** traverser.

acrylic /ə'krɪlɪk/ a. & n. acrylique (m.).

act /ækt/ n. (deed, theatre) acte m.; (in variety show) numéro m.; (decree) loi f. ● v.i. agir; (theatre) jouer; (function) marcher; (pretend) jouer la comédie. ● v.t. (part, role)

jouer. **~ as,** servir de. **~ing** *a.*
(*temporary*) intérimaire; *n.* (*theatre*) jeu *m.*

action /'ækʃn/ *n.* action *f.*; (*mil.*)
combat *m.* **out of ~,** hors service.
take ~, agir.

activate /'æktveɪt/ *v.t.* (*machine*)
actionner; (*reaction*) activer.

activ|e /'æktɪv/ *a.* actif; (*interest*) vif;
(*volcano*) en activité. **~ism** *n.*
activisme *m.* **~ist** *n.* activiste *m./f.*
~ity /-'tɪvətɪ/ *n.* activité *f.*

ac|tor /'æektə(r)/ *n.* acteur *m.* **~tress**
n. actrice *f.*

actual /'æktʃʊəl/ *a.* réel; (*example*)
concret. **the ~ pen which,** le stylo
même que. **in the ~ house,** (*the
house itself*) dans la maison elle-
même. **no ~ promise,** pas de promesse en tant que telle. **~ity**
/-'ælətɪ/ *n.* réalité *f.* **~ly** *adv.*
(*in fact*) en réalité, réellement.

actuary /'æktʃʊərɪ/ *n.* actuaire *m./f.*

acumen /'ækjumən, *Amer.* ə'kju:-
mən/ *n.* perspicacité *f.*

acupunctur|e /'ækjʊpʌŋktʃə(r)/ *n.*
acupuncture *f.* **~ist** *n.* acupuncteur
m.

acute /ə'kju:t/ *a.* aigu; (*mind*) pénétrant; (*emotion*) intense, vif; (*shortage*) grave. **~ly** *adv.* vivement.
~ness *n.* intensité *f.*

ad /æd/ *n.* (*fam.*) annonce *f.*

AD *abbr.* après J.-C.

adamant /'ædəmənt/ *a.* inflexible.

Adam's apple /'ædəmz'æpl/ *n.*
pomme d'Adam *f.*

adapt /ə'dæpt/ *v.t./i.* (s')adapter.
~ation /-'teɪʃn/ *n.* adaptation *f.*
~or *n.* (*electr.*) adaptateur *m.*; (*for
two plugs*) prise multiple *f.*

adaptab|le /ə'dæptəbl/ *a.* souple;
(*techn.*) adaptable. **~ility** /-'bɪlətɪ/
n. souplesse *f.*

add /æd/ *v.t./i.* ajouter. **~ (up),**
(*total*) additionner. **~ up to,** (*total*)
s'élever à. **~ing machine,** machine
à calculer *f.*

adder /'ædə(r)/ *n.* vipère *f.*

addict /'ædɪkt/ *n.* intoxiqué(e) *m.* (*f.*);
(*fig.*) fanatique *m./f.*

addict|ed /ə'dɪktɪd/ *a.* **~ed to,**
(*drink*) adonné à. **be ~ed to,** (*fig.*)
être un fanatique de. **~ion** /-kʃn/ *n.*
(*med.*) dépendance *f.*; (*fig.*) manie *f.*
~ive *a.* (*drug etc.*) qui crée une
dépendance.

addition /ə'dɪʃn/ *n.* addition *f.* **in ~,**
en outre. **~al** /-ʃənl/ *a.* supplémentaire.

additive /'ædɪtɪv/ *n.* additif *m.*

address /ə'dres/ *n.* adresse *f.*;
(*speech*) allocution *f.* ● *v.t.* adresser; (*speak to*) s'adresser à. **~ee**
/ædre'si:/ *n.* destinataire *m./f.*

adenoids /'ædɪnɔɪdz/ *n. pl.* végéta-
tions (adénoïdes) *f. pl.*

adept /'ædept, *Amer.* ə'dept/ *a.* & *n.*
expert (**at,** en) (*m.*).

adequa|te /'ædɪkwət/ *a.* suffisant;
(*satisfactory*) satisfaisant. **~cy** *n.*
quantité suffisante *f.*; (*of person*)
compétence *f.* **~tely** *adv.* suffisamment.

adhere /əd'hɪə(r)/ *v.i.* adhérer (**to,** à).
~ to, (*fig.*) respecter. **~nce** /-rəns/
n. adhésion *f.*

adhesion /əd'hi:ʒn/ *n.* (*grip*) adhé-
rence *f.*; (*support: fig.*) adhésion *f.*

adhesive /əd'hi:sɪv/ *a.* & *n.* adhésif
(*m.*).

ad infinitum /ædɪnfɪ'naɪtəm/ *adv.* à
l'infini.

adjacent /ə'dʒeɪsnt/ *a.* contigu (**to,** à).

adjective /'ædʒɪktɪv/ *n.* adjectif *m.*

adjoin /ə'dʒɔɪn/ *v.t.* être contigu à.

adjourn /ə'dʒɜ:n/ *v.t.* ajourner.
● *v.t./i.* **~ (the meeting),** suspendre la séance. **~ to,** (*go*) se
retirer à.

adjudicate /ə'dʒu:dɪkeɪt/ *v.t./i.* juger.

adjust /ə'dʒʌst/ *v.t.* (*machine*) régler;
(*prices*) (r)ajuster; (*arrange*) rajuster, arranger. ● *v.t./i.* **~ (o.s.) to,**
s'adapter à. **~able** *a.* réglable.
~ment *n.* (*techn.*) réglage *m.*; (*of
person*) adaptation *f.*

ad lib /æd'lɪb/ *v.i.* (*p.t.* **ad libbed**)
(*fam.*) improviser.

administer /əd'mɪnɪstə(r)/ *v.t.* ad-
ministrer.

administration /ədmɪnɪ'streɪʃn/ *n.*
administration *f.*

administrative /əd'mɪnɪstrətɪv/ *a.*
administratif.

administrator /əd'mɪnɪstreɪtə(r)/ *n.*
administra|teur, -trice *m.*, *f.*

admirable /'ædmərəbl/ *a.* admirable.

admiral /'ædmərəl/ *n.* amiral *m.*

admir|e /əd'maɪə(r)/ *v.t.* admirer.
~ation /ædmə'reɪʃn/ *n.* admiration
f. **~er** *n.* admira|teur, -trice *m.*, *f.*

admissible /əd'mɪsəbl/ *a.* admissible.

admission /əd'mɪʃn/ *n.* (*to museum,
theatre, etc.*) entrée *f.*;
(*confession*) aveu *m.*

admit /əd'mɪt/ *v.t.* (*p.t.* **admitted**) laisser entrer; (*acknowledge*) reconnaître, admettre. ~ **to**, avouer. ~**tance** *n.* entrée *f.* ~**tedly** *adv.* il est vrai (que).

admonish /əd'mɒnɪʃ/ *v.t.* réprimander.

ado /ə'duː/ *n.* **without more** ~, sans plus de cérémonies.

adolescen|t /ædə'lesnt/ *n. & a.* adolescent(e) (*m. (f.)*). ~**ce** *n.* adolescence *f.*

adopt /ə'dɒpt/ *v.t.* adopter. ~**ed** *a.* (*child*) adoptif. ~**ion** /-pʃn/ *n.* adoption *f.*

adoptive /ə'dɒptɪv/ *a.* adoptif.

ador|e /ə'dɔː(r)/ *v.t.* adorer. ~**able** *a.* adorable. ~**ation** /ædə'reɪʃn/ *n.* adoration *f.*

adorn /ə'dɔːn/ *v.t.* orner. ~**ment** *n.* ornement *m.*

adrift /ə'drɪft/ *a. & adv.* à la dérive.

adroit /ə'drɔɪt/ *a.* adroit.

adulation /ædju'leɪʃn/ *n.* adulation *f.*

adult /'ædʌlt/ *a. & n.* adulte (*m./f.*). ~**hood** *n.* condition d'adulte *f.*

adulterate /ə'dʌltəreɪt/ *v.t.* falsifier, frelater, altérer.

adulter|y /ə'dʌltərɪ/ *n.* adultère *m.* ~**er**, ~**ess** *ns.* épou|x, -se adultère *m., f.* ~**ous** *a.* adultère.

advance /əd'vɑːns/ *v.t.* avancer. ● *v.i.* (s')avancer; (*progress*) avancer. ● *n.* avance *f.* ● *a.* (*payment*) anticipé. **in** ~, à l'avance. ~**d** *a.* avancé; (*studies*) supérieur. ~**ment** *n.* avancement *m.*

advantage /əd'vɑːntɪdʒ/ *n.* avantage *m.* **take** ~ **of**, profiter de; (*person*) exploiter. ~**ous** /ædvən'teɪdʒəs/ *a.* avantageux.

advent /'ædvənt/ *n.* arrivée *f.*

Advent /'ædvənt/ *n.* Avent *m.*

adventur|e /əd'ventʃə(r)/ *n.* aventure *f.* ~**er** *n.* explora|teur, -trice *m., f.*; (*pej.*) aventur|ier, -ière *m., f.* ~**ous** *a.* aventureux.

adverb /'ædvɜːb/ *n.* adverbe *m.*

adversary /'ædvəsərɪ/ *n.* adversaire *m./f.*

advers|e /'ædvɜːs/ *a.* défavorable. ~**ity** /əd'vɜːsətɪ/ *n.* adversité *f.*

advert /'ædvɜːt/ *n.* (*fam.*) annonce *f.*; (*TV*) pub *f.*, publicité *f.* ~**isement** /əd'vɜːtɪsmənt/ *n.* publicité *f.*; (*in paper etc.*) annonce *f.*

advertis|e /'ædvətaɪz/ *v.t./i.* faire de la publicité (pour); (*sell*) mettre une annonce (pour vendre). ~ **for**, (*seek*) chercher (par voie d'annonce). ~**ing** *n.* publicité *f.* ~**er** /-ə(r)/ *n.* annonceur *m.*

advice /əd'vaɪs/ *n.* conseil(s) *m.* (*pl.*); (*comm.*) avis *m.* **some** ~, **a piece of** ~, un conseil.

advis|e /əd'vaɪz/ *v.t.* conseiller; (*inform*) aviser. ~**e against**, déconseiller. ~**able** *a.* conseillé, prudent (**to**, de). ~**er** *n.* conseill|er, -ère *m., f.* ~**ory** *a.* consultatif.

advocate[1] /'ædvəkət/ *n.* (*jurid.*) avocat *m.* ~**s of**, les défenseurs de.

advocate[2] /'ædvəkeɪt/ *v.t.* recommander.

aegis /'iːdʒɪs/ *n.* **under the** ~ **of**, sous l'égide de *f.*

aeon /'iːən/ *n.* éternité *f.*

aerial /'eərɪəl/ *a.* aérien. ● *n.* antenne *f.*

aerobatics /eərə'bætɪks/ *n. pl.* acrobatie aérienne *f.*

aerobics /eə'rəʊbɪks/ *n.* aérobic *m.*

aerodrome /'eərədrəʊm/ *n.* aérodrome *m.*

aerodynamic /eərəʊdaɪ'næmɪk/ *a.* aérodynamique.

aeroplane /'eərəpleɪn/ *n.* avion *m.*

aerosol /'eərəsɒl/ *n.* atomiseur *m.*

aesthetic /iːs'θetɪk, *Amer.* es'θetɪk/ *a.* esthétique.

afar /ə'fɑː(r)/ *adv.* **from** ~, de loin.

affable /'æfəbl/ *a.* affable.

affair /ə'feə(r)/ *n.* (*matter*) affaire *f.*; (*romance*) liaison *f.*

affect /ə'fekt/ *v.t.* affecter. ~**ation** /æfek'teɪʃn/ *n.* affectation *f.* ~**ed** *a.* affecté.

affection /ə'fekʃn/ *n.* affection *f.*

affectionate /ə'fekʃənət/ *a.* affectueux.

affiliat|e /ə'fɪlɪeɪt/ *v.t.* affilier. ~**ed company**, filiale *f.* ~**ion** /-'eɪʃn/ *n.* affiliation *f.*

affinity /ə'fɪnətɪ/ *n.* affinité *f.*

affirm /ə'fɜːm/ *v.t.* affirmer. ~**ation** /æfə'meɪʃn/ *n.* affirmation *f.*

affirmative /ə'fɜːmətɪv/ *a.* affirmatif. ● *n.* affirmative *f.*

affix /ə'fɪks/ *v.t.* apposer.

afflict /ə'flɪkt/ *v.t.* affliger. ~**ion** /-kʃn/ *n.* affliction *f.*, détresse *f.*

affluen|t /'æfluənt/ *a.* riche. ~**ce** *n.* richesse *f.*

afford /ə'fɔːd/ *v.t.* avoir les moyens d'acheter; (*provide*) fournir. ~ **to do**, avoir les moyens de faire; (*be able*) se permettre de faire. **can you** ~ **the time?**, avez-vous le temps?

affray /ə'freɪ/ n. rixe f.

affront /ə'frʌnt/ n. affront m. ● v.t. insulter.

afield /ə'fiːld/ adv. **far ~**, loin.

afloat /ə'fləʊt/ adv. à flot.

afoot /ə'fʊt/ adv. **sth. is ~**, il se trame or se prépare qch.

aforesaid /ə'fɔːsed/ a. susdit.

afraid /ə'freɪd/ a. **be ~**, avoir peur (**of**, **to**, de; **that**, que); (be sorry) regretter. **I am ~ that**, (regret to say) je regrette de dire que.

afresh /ə'freʃ/ adv. de nouveau.

Africa /'æfrɪkə/ n. Afrique f. **~n** a. & n. africain(e) (m. (f.)).

after /'ɑːftə(r)/ adv. & prep. après. ● conj. après que. **~ doing**, après avoir fait. **~ all** après tout. **~-effect** n. suite f. **~-sales service**, service après-vente m. **~ the manner of**, d'après. **be ~**, (seek) chercher.

aftermath /'ɑːftəmɑːθ/ n. suites f. pl.

afternoon /ɑːftə'nuːn/ n. après-midi m./f. invar.

afters /'ɑːftəz/ n. pl. (fam.) dessert m.

aftershave /'ɑːftəʃeɪv/ n. lotion après-rasage f.

afterthought /'ɑːftəθɔːt/ n. réflexion après coup f. **as an ~**, en y repensant.

afterwards /'ɑːftəwədz/ adv. après, par la suite.

again /ə'gen/ adv. de nouveau, encore une fois; (besides) en outre. **do ~**, **see ~**/etc., refaire, revoir/etc.

against /ə'genst/ prep. contre. **~ the law**, illégal.

age /eɪdʒ/ n. âge m. ● v.t./i. (pres. p. **ageing**) vieillir. **~ group**, tranche d'âge f. **~ limit**, limite d'âge. **for ~s**, (fam.) une éternité. **of ~**, (jurid.) majeur. **ten years of ~**, âgé de dix ans. **~less** a. toujours jeune.

aged¹ /eɪdʒd/ a. **~ six**, âgé de six ans.

aged² /'eɪdʒɪd/ a. âgé, vieux.

agen|cy /'eɪdʒənsɪ/ n. agence f.; (means) entremise f. **~t** n. agent m.

agenda /ə'dʒendə/ n. ordre du jour m.

agglomeration /əglɒmə'reɪʃn/ n. agglomération f.

aggravat|e /'ægrəveɪt/ v.t. (make worse) aggraver; (annoy: fam.) exaspérer. **~ion** /-'veɪʃn/ n. aggravation f.; exaspération f.; (trouble: fam.) ennuis m. pl.

aggregate /'ægrɪgət/ a. & n. total (m.).

aggress|ive /ə'gresɪv/ a. agressif. **~ion** /-ʃn/ n. agression f. **~iveness** n. agressivité f. **~or** n. agresseur m.

aggrieved /ə'griːvd/ a. peiné.

aghast /ə'gɑːst/ a. horrifié.

agil|e /'ædʒaɪl, Amer. 'ædʒl/ a. agile. **~ity** /ə'dʒɪlətɪ/ n. agilité f.

agitat|e /'ædʒɪteɪt/ v.t. agiter. **~ion** /-'teɪʃn/ n. agitation f. **~or** n. agita|teur, -trice m., f.

agnostic /æg'nɒstɪk/ a. & n. agnostique (m./f.).

ago /ə'gəʊ/ adv. il y a. **a month ~**, il y a un mois. **long ~**, il y a longtemps. **how long ~?**, il y a combien de temps?

agog /ə'gɒg/ a. impatient, en émoi.

agon|y /'ægənɪ/ n. grande souffrance f.; (mental) angoisse f. **~ize** v.i. souffrir. **~ize over**, se torturer l'esprit pour. **~ized** a. angoissé. **~izing** a. angoissant.

agree /ə'griː/ v.i. être or se mettre d'accord (**on**, sur); (of figures) concorder. ● v.t. (date) convenir de. **~ that**, reconnaître que. **~ to do**, accepter de faire. **~ to sth.**, accepter qch. **onions don't ~ with me**, je ne digère pas les oignons. **~d** a. (time, place) convenu. **be ~d**, être d'accord.

agreeable /ə'griːəbl/ a. agréable. **be ~**, (willing) être d'accord.

agreement /ə'griːmənt/ n. accord m. **in ~**, d'accord.

agricultur|e /'ægrɪkʌltʃə(r)/ n. agriculture f. **~al** /-'kʌltʃərəl/ a. agricole.

aground /ə'graʊnd/ adv. **run ~**, (of ship) (s')échouer.

ahead /ə'hed/ adv. (in front) en avant, devant; (in advance) à l'avance. **~ of s.o.**, devant qn.; en avance sur qn. **~ of time**, en avance. **straight ~**, tout droit.

aid /eɪd/ v.t. aider. ● n. aide f. **in ~ of**, au profit de.

aide /eɪd/ n. aide m./f.

AIDS /eɪdz/ n. (med.) sida m.

ail /eɪl/ v.t. **what ~s you?**, qu'avez-vous? **~ing** a. souffrant. **~ment** n. maladie f.

aim /eɪm/ v.t. diriger; (gun) braquer (**at**, sur); (remark) destiner. ● v.i. viser. ● n. but m. **~ at**, viser. **~ to**, avoir l'intention de. **take ~**, viser. **~less** a., **~lessly** adv. sans but.

air /eə(r)/ n. air m. ● v.t. aérer; (views) exposer librement. ● a.

(*base etc.*) aérien. **~-bed** *n.* matelas pneumatique *m.* **~-conditioned** *a.* climatisé. **~-conditioning** *n.* climatisation *f.* **~ force/hostess,** armée/hôtesse de l'air *f.* **~ letter,** aérogramme *m.* **~mail,** poste aérienne *f.* **by ~mail,** par avion. **~ raid,** attaque aérienne *f.* **~ terminal,** aérogare *f.* **~ traffic controller,** aiguilleur du ciel *m.* **by ~,** par avion. **in the ~,** (*rumour*) répandu; (*plan*) incertain. **on the ~,** à l'antenne.

airborne /'eəbɔ:n/ *a.* en (cours de) vol; (*troops*) aéroporté.

aircraft /'eəkrɑ:ft/ *n. invar.* avion *m.* **~-carrier** *n.* porte-avions *m. invar.*

airfield /'eəfi:ld/ *n.* terrain d'aviation *m.*

airgun /'eəgʌn/ *n.* carabine à air comprimé *f.*

airlift /'eəlɪft/ *n.* pont aérien *m.* ● *v.t.* transporter par pont aérien.

airline /'eəlaɪn/ *n.* ligne aérienne *f.* **~r** /-ə(r)/ *n.* avion de ligne *m.*

airlock /'eəlɒk/ *n.* (*in pipe*) bulle d'air *f.*; (*chamber: techn.*) sas *m.*

airman /'eəmən/ *n.* (*pl.* **-men**) aviateur *m.*

airplane /'eəpleɪn/ *n.* (*Amer.*) avion *m.*

airport /'eəpɔ:t/ *n.* aéroport *m.*

airsickness /'eəsɪknɪs/ *n.* mal de l'air *m.*

airtight /'eətaɪt/ *a.* hermétique.

airways /'eəweɪz/ *n. pl.* compagnie d'aviation *f.*

airworthy /'eəwɜ:ðɪ/ *a.* en état de navigation.

airy /'eərɪ/ *a.* (**-ier, -iest**) bien aéré; (*manner*) désinvolte.

aisle /aɪl/ *n.* (*of church*) nef latérale *f.*; (*gangway*) couloir *m.*

ajar /ə'dʒɑ:(r)/ *adv. & a.* entrouvert.

akin /ə'kɪn/ *a.* **~ to,** apparenté à.

alabaster /'æləbɑ:stə(r)/ *n.* albâtre *m.*

à la carte /ɑ:lɑ:'kɑ:t/ *adv. & a.* (*culin.*) à la carte.

alacrity /ə'lækrətɪ/ *n.* empressement *m.*

alarm /ə'lɑ:m/ *n.* alarme *f.*; (*clock*) réveil *m.* ● *v.t.* alarmer. **~-clock** *n.* réveil *m.*, réveille-matin *m. invar.* **~ist** *n.* alarmiste *m./f.*

alas /ə'læs/ *int.* hélas.

albatross /'ælbətrɒs/ *n.* albatros *m.*

album /'ælbəm/ *n.* album *m.*

alcohol /'ælkəhɒl/ *n.* alcool *m.* **~ic** /-'hɒlɪk/ *a.* alcoolique; (*drink*) alcoo-

lisé; *n.* alcoolique *m./f.* **~ism** *n.* alcoolisme *m.*

alcove /'ælkəʊv/ *n.* alcôve *f.*

ale /eɪl/ *n.* bière *f.*

alert /ə'lɜ:t/ *a.* (*lively*) vif; (*watchful*) vigilant. ● *n.* alerte *f.* ● *v.t.* alerter. **~ s.o. to,** prévenir qn. de. **on the ~,** sur le qui-vive. **~ness** *n.* vivacité *f.*; vigilance *f.*

A-level /'eɪlevl/ *n.* baccalauréat *m.*

algebra /'ældʒɪbrə/ *n.* algèbre *f.* **~ic** /-'breɪk/ *a.* algébrique.

Algeria /æl'dʒɪərɪə/ *n.* Algérie *f.* **~n** *a. & n.* algérien(ne) (*m. (f.)*).

algorithm /'ælgərɪðm/ *n.* algorithme *m.*

alias /'eɪlɪəs/ *n.* (*pl.* **-ases**) faux nom *m.* ● *adv.* alias.

alibi /'ælɪbaɪ/ *n.* (*pl.* **-is**) alibi *m.*

alien /'eɪlɪən/ *n. & a.* étrang|er, -ère (*m., f.*) (**to**, à).

alienat|e /'eɪlɪəneɪt/ *v.t.* aliéner. **~e one's friends/***etc.***,** s'aliéner ses amis/*etc.* **~ion** /-'neɪʃn/ *n.* aliénation *f.*

alight¹ /ə'laɪt/ *v.i.* (*person*) descendre; (*bird*) se poser.

alight² /ə'laɪt/ *a.* en feu, allumé.

align /ə'laɪn/ *v.t.* aligner. **~ment** *n.* alignement *m.*

alike /ə'laɪk/ *a.* semblable. ● *adv.* de la même façon. **look** *or* **be ~,** se ressembler.

alimony /'ælɪmənɪ, *Amer.* -məʊnɪ/ *n.* pension alimentaire *f.*

alive /ə'laɪv/ *a.* vivant. **~ to,** sensible à, sensibilisé à. **~ with,** grouillant de.

alkali /'ælkəlaɪ/ *n.* (*pl.* **-is**) alcali *m.*

all /ɔ:l/ *a.* tout(e), tous, toutes. ● *pron.* tous, toutes; (*everything*) tout. ● *adv.* tout. **~ (the) men,** tous les hommes. **~ of it,** (le) tout. **~ of us,** nous tous. **~ but,** presque. **~ for sth.,** à fond pour qch. **~ in,** (*exhausted*) épuisé. **~-in** *a.* tout compris. **~-in wrestling,** catch *m.* **~ out,** à fond. **~-out** *a.* (*effort*) maximum. **~ over,** partout (sur *or* dans); (*finished*) fini. **~ right,** bien; (*agreeing*) bon! **~ round,** dans tous les domaines; (*for all*) pour tous. **~-round** *a.* général. **~ there,** (*alert*) éveillé. **~ the better,** tant mieux. **~ the same,** tout de même. **the best of ~,** le meilleur.

allay /ə'leɪ/ *v.t.* calmer.

allegation /ælɪ'geɪʃn/ *n.* allégation *f.*

allege /ə'ledʒ/ v.t. prétendre. **~dly** /-ɪdlɪ/ adv. d'après ce qu'on dit.

allegiance /ə'liːdʒəns/ n. fidélité f.

allerg|y /'ælədʒɪ/ n. allergie f. **~ic** /ə'lɜːdʒɪk/ a. allergique (**to**, à).

alleviate /ə'liːvɪeɪt/ v.t. alléger.

alley /'ælɪ/ n. (street) ruelle f.

alliance /ə'laɪəns/ n. alliance f.

allied /'ælaɪd/ a. allié.

alligator /'ælɪgeɪtə(r)/ n. alligator m.

allocat|e /'æləkeɪt/ v.t. (assign) attribuer; (share out) distribuer. **~ion** /-'keɪʃn/ n. allocation f.

allot /ə'lɒt/ v.t. (p.t. **allotted**) attribuer. **~ment** n. attribution f.; (share) partage m.; (land) parcelle de terre f. (louée pour la culture).

allow /ə'laʊ/ v.t. permettre; (grant) accorder; (reckon on) prévoir; (agree) reconnaître. **~ s.o. to,** permettre à qn. de. **~ for,** tenir compte de.

allowance /ə'laʊəns/ n. allocation f., indemnité f. **make ~s for,** être indulgent envers; (take into account) tenir compte de.

alloy /'ælɔɪ/ n. alliage m.

allude /ə'luːd/ v.i. **~ to,** faire allusion à.

allure /ə'lʊə(r)/ v.t. attirer.

allusion /ə'luːʒn/ n. allusion f.

ally [1] /'ælaɪ/ n. allié(e) m. (f.).

ally [2] /ə'laɪ/ v.t. allier. **~ o.s. with,** s'allier à or avec.

almanac /'ɔːlmənæk/ n. almanach m.

almighty /ɔːl'maɪtɪ/ a. tout-puissant; (very great. fam.) sacré, formidable.

almond /'ɑːmənd/ n. amande f.

almost /'ɔːlməʊst/ adv. presque.

alms /ɑːmz/ n. aumône f.

alone /ə'ləʊn/ a. & adv. seul.

along /ə'lɒŋ/ prep. le long de. ● adv. **come ~,** venir. **go** or **walk ~,** passer. **all ~,** (time) tout le temps, depuis le début. **~ with,** avec.

alongside /əlɒŋ'saɪd/ adv. (naut.) bord à bord. **come ~,** accoster. ● prep. le long de.

aloof /ə'luːf/ adv. à l'écart. ● a. distant. **~ness** n. réserve f.

aloud /ə'laʊd/ adv. à haute voix.

alphabet /'ælfəbet/ n. alphabet m. **~ical** /-'betɪkl/ a. alphabétique.

alpine /'ælpaɪn/ a. (landscape) alpestre; (climate) alpin.

Alpine /'ælpaɪn/ a. des Alpes.

Alps /ælps/ n. pl. **the ~,** les Alpes f. pl.

already /ɔːl'redɪ/ adv. déjà.

alright /ɔːl'raɪt/ a. & adv. = **all right**.

Alsatian /æl'seɪʃn/ n. (dog) berger allemand m.

also /'ɔːlsəʊ/ adv. aussi.

altar /'ɔːltə(r)/ n. autel m.

alter /'ɔːltə(r)/ v.t./i. changer. **~ation** /-'reɪʃn/ n. changement m.; (to garment) retouche f.

alternate [1] /ɔːl'tɜːnət/ a. alterné, alternatif; (Amer.) = **alternative. on ~ days/**etc., (first one then the other) tous les deux jours/etc. **~ly** adv. tour à tour.

alternate [2] /'ɔːltɜːneɪt/ v.i. alterner. ● v.t. faire alterner.

alternative /ɔːl'tɜːnətɪv/ a. autre; (policy) de rechange. ● n. alternative f., choix m. **~ly** adv. comme alternative. **or ~ly,** ou alors.

alternator /'ɔːltɜːneɪtə(r)/ n. alternateur m.

although /ɔːl'ðəʊ/ conj. bien que.

altitude /'æltɪtjuːd/ n. altitude f.

altogether /ɔːltə'geðə(r)/ adv. (completely) tout à fait; (on the whole) à tout prendre.

aluminium /æljʊ'mɪnɪəm/ (Amer. **aluminum** /ə'luːmɪnəm/) n. aluminium m.

always /'ɔːlweɪz/ adv. toujours.

am /æm/ see be.

a.m. /er'em/ adv. du matin.

amalgamate /ə'mælgəmeɪt/ v.t./i. (s')amalgamer; (comm.) fusionner.

amass /ə'mæs/ v.t. amasser.

amateur /'æmətə(r)/ n. amateur m. ● a. (musician etc.) amateur invar. **~ish** a. (pej.) d'amateur. **~ishly** adv. en amateur.

amaz|e /ə'meɪz/ v.t. étonner. **~ed** a. étonné. **~ement** n. étonnement m. **~ingly** adv. étonnamment.

ambassador /æm'bæsədə(r)/ n. ambassadeur m.

amber /'æmbə(r)/ n. ambre m.; (auto.) feu orange m.

ambigu|ous /æm'bɪgjʊəs/ a. ambigu. **~ity** /-'gjuːətɪ/ n. ambiguïté f.

ambiti|on /æm'bɪʃn/ n. ambition f. **~ous** a. ambitieux.

ambivalent /æm'bɪvələnt/ a. ambigu, ambivalent.

amble /'æmbl/ v.i. marcher sans se presser, s'avancer lentement.

ambulance /'æmbjʊləns/ n. ambulance f.

ambush /'æmbʊʃ/ n. embuscade f. ● v.t. tendre une embuscade à.

amenable /ə'miːnəbl/ *a.* obligeant. **~ to**, (*responsive*) sensible à.

amend /ə'mend/ *v.t.* modifier, corriger. **~ment** *n.* (*to rule*) amendement *m.*

amends /ə'mendz/ *n. pl.* **make ~**, réparer son erreur.

amenities /ə'miːnətɪz/ *n. pl.* (*pleasant features*) attraits *m. pl.*; (*facilities*) aménagements *m. pl.*

America /ə'merɪkə/ *n.* Amérique *f.* **~n** *a. & n.* américain(e) (*m.* (*f.*)).

amiable /'eɪmɪəbl/ *a.* aimable.

amicable /'æmɪkəbl/ *a.* amical.

amid(st) /ə'mɪd(st)/ *prep.* au milieu de.

amiss /ə'mɪs/ *a. & adv.* mal. **sth. ~**, qch. qui ne va pas. **take sth. ~**, être offensé par qch.

ammonia /ə'məʊnɪə/ *n.* (*gas*) ammoniac *m.*; (*water*) ammoniaque *f.*

ammunition /æmjʊ'nɪʃn/ *n.* munitions *f. pl.*

amnesia /æm'niːzɪə/ *n.* amnésie *f.*

amnesty /'æmnəstɪ/ *n.* amnistie *f.*

amok /ə'mɒk/ *adv.* **run ~**, devenir fou furieux; (*crowd*) se déchaîner.

among(st) /ə'mʌŋ(st)/ *prep.* parmi, entre. **~ the crowd**, (*in the middle of*) parmi la foule. **~ the English/** *etc.*, (*race, group*) chez les Anglais/ *etc.* **~ ourselves/***etc.*, entre nous/*etc.*

amoral /eɪ'mɒrəl/ *a.* amoral.

amorous /'æmərəs/ *a.* amoureux.

amorphous /ə'mɔːfəs/ *a.* amorphe.

amount /ə'maʊnt/ *n.* quantité *f.*; (*total*) montant *m.*; (*sum of money*) somme *f.* ● *v.i.* **~ to**, (*add up to*) s'élever à; (*be equivalent to*) revenir à.

amp /æmp/ *n.* (*fam.*) ampère *m.*

ampere /'æmpeə(r)/ *n.* ampère *m.*

amphibi|an /æm'fɪbɪən/ *n.* amphibie *m.* **~ous** *a.* amphibie.

ampl|e /'æmpl/ *a.* (**-er, -est**) (*enough*) (bien) assez de; (*large, roomy*) ample. **~y** *adv.* amplement.

amplif|y /'æmplɪfaɪ/ *v.t.* amplifier. **~ier** *n.* amplificateur *m.*

amputat|e /'æmpjʊteɪt/ *v.t.* amputer. **~ion** /-'teɪʃn/ *n.* amputation *f.*

amuck /ə'mʌk/ *see* amok.

amuse /ə'mjuːz/ *v.t.* amuser. **~ment** *n.* amusement *m.*, divertissement *m.* **~ment arcade**, salle de jeux *f.*

an /æn, *unstressed* ən/ *see* a.

anachronism /ə'nækrənɪzəm/ *n.* anachronisme *m.*

anaem|ia /ə'niːmɪə/ *n.* anémie *f.* **~ic** *a.* anémique.

anaesthetic /ænɪs'θetɪk/ *n.* anesthésique *m.* **give an ~**, faire une anesthésie (**to**, à).

analogue, analog /'ænəlɒg/ *a.* analogique.

analogy /ə'nælədʒɪ/ *n.* analogie *f.*

analys|e (*Amer.* **analyze**) /'ænəlaɪz/ *v.t.* analyser. **~t** /-ɪst/ *n.* analyste *m.*/ *f.*

analysis /ə'næləsɪs/ *n.* (*pl.* **-yses** /-əsiːz/) analyse *f.*

analytic(al) /ænə'lɪtɪk(l)/ *a.* analytique.

anarch|y /'ænəkɪ/ *n.* anarchie *f.* **~ist** *n.* anarchiste *m.*/*f.*

anathema /ə'næθəmə/ *n.* **that is ~ to me**, j'ai cela en abomination.

anatom|y /ə'nætəmɪ/ *n.* anatomie *f.* **~ical** /ænə'tɒmɪkl/ *a.* anatomique.

ancest|or /'ænsestə(r)/ *n.* ancêtre *m.* **~ral** /-'sestrəl/ *a.* ancestral.

anchor /'æŋkə(r)/ *n.* ancre *f.* ● *v.t.* mettre à l'ancre. ● *v.i.* jeter l'ancre.

anchovy /'æntʃəvɪ/ *n.* anchois *m.*

ancient /'eɪnʃənt/ *a.* ancien.

ancillary /æn'sɪlərɪ/ *a.* auxiliaire.

and /ænd, *unstressed* ən(d)/ *conj.* et. **go ~ see him**, allez le voir. **richer ~ richer**, de plus en plus riche.

anecdote /'ænɪkdəʊt/ *n.* anecdote *f.*

anemia /ə'niːmɪə/ *n.* (*Amer.*) = **anaemia**.

anesthetic /ænɪs'θetɪk/ (*Amer.*) = **anaesthetic**.

anew /ə'njuː/ *adv.* de *or* à nouveau.

angel /'eɪndʒl/ *n.* ange *m.* **~ic** /æn'dʒelɪk/ *a.* angélique.

anger /'æŋgə(r)/ *n.* colère *f.* ● *v.t.* mettre en colère, fâcher.

angle[1] /'æŋgl/ *n.* angle *m.*

angle[2] /'æŋgl/ *v.i.* pêcher (à la ligne). **~ for**, (*fig.*) quêter. **~r** /-ə(r)/ *n.* pêcheu|r, -se *m.*, *f.*

Anglican /'æŋglɪkən/ *a. & n.* anglican(e) (*m.* (*f.*)).

Anglo- /'æŋgləʊ/ *pref.* anglo- .

Anglo-Saxon /'æŋgləʊ'sæksn/ *a. & n.* anglo-saxon(ne) (*m.* (*f.*)).

angr|y /'æŋgrɪ/ *a.* (**-ier, -iest**) fâché, en colère. **get ~y**, se fâcher, se mettre en colère (**with**, contre). **make s.o. ~y**, mettre qn. en colère. **~ily** *adv.* en colère.

anguish /'æŋgwɪʃ/ *n.* angoisse *f.*

angular /'æŋgjʊlə(r)/ *a.* (*features*) anguleux.

animal /'ænɪml/ *n. & a.* animal (*m.*).

animate [^1] /'ænɪmət/ a. animé.

animat|e [^2] /'ænɪmeɪt/ v.t. animer.
~ion /-'meɪʃn/ n. animation f.

animosity /ænɪ'mɒsəti/ n. animosité f.

aniseed /'ænɪsi:d/ n. anis m.

ankle /'æŋkl/ n. cheville f. **~ sock,** socquette f.

annex /ə'neks/ v.t. annexer. **~ation** /ænek'seɪʃn/ n. annexion f.

annexe /'æneks/ n. annexe f.

annihilate /ə'naɪəleɪt/ v.t. anéantir.

anniversary /ænɪ'vɜːsərɪ/ n. anniversaire m.

announce /ə'naʊns/ v.t. annoncer. **~ment** n. annonce f. **~r** /-ə(r)/ n. (radio, TV) speaker(ine) m. (f.).

annoy /ə'nɔɪ/ v.t. agacer, ennuyer. **~ance** n. contrariété f. **~ed** a. fâché (**with,** contre). **get ~ed,** se fâcher. **~ing** a. ennuyeux.

annual /'ænjʊəl/ a. annuel. ● n. publication annuelle f. **~ly** adv. annuellement.

annuity /ə'nju:ətɪ/ n. rente (viagère) f.

annul /ə'nʌl/ v.t. (p.t. **annulled**) annuler. **~ment** n. annulation f.

anomal|y /ə'nɒməlɪ/ n. anomalie f. **~ous** a. anormal.

anonym|ous /ə'nɒnɪməs/ a. anonyme. **~ity** /ænə'nɪmətɪ/ n. anonymat m.

anorak /'ænəræk/ n. anorak m.

another /ə'nʌðə(r)/ a. & pron. un(e) autre. **~ coffee,** (one more) encore un café. **~ ten minutes,** encore dix minutes, dix minutes de plus.

answer /'ɑːnsə(r)/ n. réponse f.; (solution) solution f. ● v.t. répondre à; (prayer) exaucer. ● v.i. répondre. **~ the door,** ouvrir la porte. **~ back,** répondre. **~ for,** répondre de. **~ to,** (superior) dépendre de; (description) répondre à **~able** a. responsable (**for,** de; **to,** devant). **~ing machine,** répondeur m.

ant /ænt/ n. fourmi f.

antagonis|m /æn'tægənɪzəm/ n. antagonisme m. **~tic** /-'nɪstɪk/ a. antagoniste.

antagonize /æn'tægənaɪz/ v.t. provoquer l'hostilité de.

Antarctic /æn'tɑːktɪk/ a. & n. antarctique (m.).

ante- /'æntɪ/ pref. anti-, anté-.

antelope /'æntɪləʊp/ n. antilope f.

antenatal /'æntɪneɪtl/ a. prénatal.

antenna /æn'tenə/ n. (pl. **-ae** /-iː/) (of insect) antenne f.; (pl. **-as**; aerial: Amer.) antenne f.

anthem /'ænθəm/ n. (relig.) motet m.; (of country) hymne national m.

anthology /æn'θɒlədʒɪ/ n. anthologie f.

anthropolog|y /ænθrə'pɒlədʒɪ/ n. anthropologie f. **~ist** n. anthropologue m./f.

anti- /'æntɪ/ pref. anti-. **~-aircraft** a. antiaérien.

antibiotic /æntɪbaɪ'ɒtɪk/ n. antibiotique m.

antibody /'æntɪbɒdɪ/ n. anticorps m.

antic /'æntɪk/ n. bouffonnerie f.

anticipat|e /æn'tɪsɪpeɪt/ v.t. (foresee, expect) prévoir, s'attendre à; (forestall) devancer. **~ion** /-'peɪʃn/ n. attente f. **in ~ion of,** en prévision or attente de.

anticlimax /æntɪ'klaɪmæks/ n. (letdown) déception f. **it was an ~,** ça n'a pas répondu à l'attente.

anticlockwise /æntɪ'klɒkwaɪz/ adv. & a. dans le sens inverse des aiguilles d'une montre.

anticyclone /æntɪ'saɪkləʊn/ n. anticyclone m.

antidote /'æntɪdəʊt/ n. antidote m.

antifreeze /'æntɪfriːz/ n. antigel m.

antihistamine /æntɪ'hɪstəmiːn/ n. antihistaminique m.

antipathy /æn'tɪpəθɪ/ n. antipathie f.

antiquated /'æntɪkweɪtɪd/ a. vieillot, suranné.

antique /æn'tiːk/ a. (old) ancien; (from antiquity) antique. ● n. objet ancien m., antiquité f. **~ dealer,** antiquaire m./f. **~ shop,** magasin d'antiquités m.

antiquity /æn'tɪkwətɪ/ n. antiquité f.

anti-Semiti|c /æntɪsɪ'mɪtɪk/ a. antisémite. **~sm** /-'semɪtɪzəm/ n. antisémitisme m.

antiseptic /æntɪ'septɪk/ a. & n. antiseptique (m.).

antisocial /æntɪ'səʊʃl/ a. asocial, antisocial; (unsociable) insociable.

antithesis /æn'tɪθəsɪs/ n. (pl. **-eses** /-əsiːz/) antithèse f.

antlers /'æntləz/ n. pl. bois m. pl.

anus /'eɪnəs/ n. anus m.

anvil /'ænvɪl/ n. enclume f.

anxiety /æŋ'zaɪətɪ/ n. (worry) anxiété f.; (eagerness) impatience f.

anxious /'æŋkʃəs/ a. (troubled) anxieux; (eager) impatient (**to,** de).

~ly *adv.* anxieusement; impatiement.

any /'enɪ/ *a.* (*some*) du, de l', de la, des; (*after negative*) de, d'; (*every*) tout; (*no matter which*) n'importe quel. **at ~ moment**, à tout moment. **have you ~ water?**, avez-vous de l'eau? ● *pron.* (*no matter which one*) n'importe lequel; (*someone*) quelqu'un; (*any amount of it or them*) en. **I do not have ~**, je n'en ai pas. **did you see ~ of them?**, en avez-vous vu? ● *adv.* (*a little*) un peu. **do you have ~ more?**, en avez-vous encore? **do you have ~ more tea?**, avez-vous encore du thé? **not ~**, nullement. **I don't do it ~ more**, je ne le fais plus.

anybody /'enɪbɒdɪ/ *pron.* n'importe qui; (*somebody*) quelqu'un; (*after negative*) personne. **he did not see ~**, il n'a vu personne.

anyhow /'enɪhaʊ/ *adv.* de toute façon; (*badly*) n'importe comment.

anyone /'enɪwʌn/ *pron.* **= anybody**.

anything /'enɪθɪŋ/ *pron.* n'importe quoi; (*something*) quelque chose; (*after negative*) rien. **he did not see ~**, il n'a rien vu. **~ but**, (*cheap etc.*) nullement. **~ you do**, tout ce que tu fais.

anyway /'enɪweɪ/ *adv.* de toute façon.

anywhere /'enɪweə(r)/ *adv.* n'importe où; (*somewhere*) quelque part; (*after negative*) nulle part. **he does not go ~**, il ne va nulle part. **~ you go**, partout où tu vas, où que tu ailles. **~ else**, partout ailleurs.

apart /ə'pɑ:t/ *adv.* (*on or to one side*) à part; (*separated*) séparé; (*into pieces*) en pièces. **~ from**, à part, excepté. **ten metres ~**, (*distant*) à dix mètres l'un de l'autre. **come ~**, (*break*) tomber en morceaux; (*machine*) se démonter. **legs ~**, les jambes écartées. **keep ~**, séparer. **take ~**, démonter.

apartment /ə'pɑ:tmənt/ *n.* (*Amer.*) appartement *m.* **~s**, logement *m.*

apath|y /'æpəθɪ/ *n.* apathie *f.* **~etic** /-'θetɪk/ *a.* apathique.

ape /eɪp/ *n.* singe *m.* ● *v.t.* singer.

aperitif /ə'perətɪf/ *n.* apéritif *m.*

aperture /'æpətʃə(r)/ *n.* ouverture *f.*

apex /'eɪpeks/ *n.* sommet *m.*

apiece /ə'pi:s/ *adv.* chacun.

apologetic /əpɒlə'dʒetɪk/ *a.* (*tone etc.*) d'excuse. **be ~**, s'excuser. **~ally** /-lɪ/ *adv.* en s'excusant.

apologize /ə'pɒlədʒaɪz/ *v.i.* s'excuser (**for**, de; **to**, auprès de).

apology /ə'pɒlədʒɪ/ *n.* excuses *f. pl.*; (*defence of belief*) apologie *f.*

Apostle /ə'pɒsl/ *n.* apôtre *m.*

apostrophe /ə'pɒstrəfɪ/ *n.* apostrophe *f.*

appal /ə'pɔ:l/ *v.t.* (*p.t.* **appalled**) épouvanter. **~ling** *a.* épouvantable.

apparatus /æpə'reɪtəs/ *n.* (*machine & anat.*) appareil *m.*

apparel /ə'pærəl/ *n.* habillement *m.*

apparent /ə'pærənt/ *a.* apparent. **~ly** *adv.* apparemment.

appeal /ə'pi:l/ *n.* appel *m.*; (*attractiveness*) attrait *m.*, charme *m.* ● *v.i.* (*jurid.*) faire appel. **~ to s.o.**, (*beg*) faire appel à qn.; (*attract*) plaire à qn. **~ to s.o. for sth.**, demander qch. à qn. **~ing** *a.* (*attractive*) attirant.

appear /ə'pɪə(r)/ *v.i.* apparaître; (*arrive*) se présenter; (*seem, be published*) paraître; (*theatre*) jouer. **~ on TV**, passer à la télé. **~ance** *n.* apparition *f.*; (*aspect*) apparence *f.*

appease /ə'pi:z/ *v.t.* apaiser.

appendicitis /əpendɪ'saɪtɪs/ *n.* appendicite *f.*

appendix /ə'pendɪks/ *n.* (*pl.* **-ices** /-ɪsi:z/) appendice *m.*

appetite /'æpɪtaɪt/ *n.* appétit *m.*

appetizer /'æpɪtaɪzə(r)/ *n.* (*snack*) amuse-gueule *m. invar.*; (*drink*) apéritif *m.*

appetizing /'æpɪtaɪzɪŋ/ *a.* appétissant.

applau|d /ə'plɔ:d/ *v.t./i.* applaudir; (*decision*) applaudir à. **~se** *n.* applaudissements *m. pl.*

apple /'æpl/ *n.* pomme *f.* **~-tree** *n.* pommier *m.*

appliance /ə'plaɪəns/ *n.* appareil *m.*

applicable /'æplɪkəbl/ *a.* applicable.

applicant /'æplɪkənt/ *n.* candidat(e) *m. (f.)* (**for**, à).

application /æplɪ'keɪʃn/ *n.* application *f.*; (*request, form*) demande *f.*; (*for job*) candidature *f.*

apply /ə'plaɪ/ *v.t.* appliquer. ● *v.i.* **~ to**, (*refer*) s'appliquer à; (*ask*) s'adresser à. **~ for**, (*job*) postuler pour; (*grant*) demander. **~ o.s. to**, s'appliquer à. **applied** *a.* appliqué.

appoint /ə'pɔɪnt/ *v.t.* (*to post*) nommer; (*fix*) désigner. **well-~ed** *a.* bien équipé. **~ment** *n.* nomination *f.*; (*meeting*) rendez-vous *m. invar.*;

(*job*) poste *m*. **make an ~ment**, prendre rendez-vous (**with**, avec).

apportion /əˈpɔːʃn/ *v.t*. répartir.

apprais|e /əˈpreɪz/ *v.t*. évaluer. **~al** *n*. évaluation *f*.

appreciable /əˈpriːʃəbl/ *a*. appréciable.

appreciat|e /əˈpriːʃɪeɪt/ *v.t*. (*like*) apprécier; (*understand*) comprendre; (*be grateful for*). être reconnaissant de. ● *v.i*. prendre de la valeur. **~ion** /-ˈeɪʃn/ *n*. appréciation *f*.; (*gratitude*) reconnaissance *f*.; (*rise*) augmentation *f*. **~ive** / əˈpriːʃɪətɪv/ *a*. reconnaissant; (*audience*) enthousiaste.

apprehen|d /æprɪˈhend/ *v.t*. (*arrest, fear*) appréhender; (*understand*) comprendre. **~sion** *n*. appréhension *f*.

apprehensive /æprɪˈhensɪv/ *a*. inquiet. **be ~ of**, craindre.

apprentice /əˈprentɪs/ *n*. apprenti *m*. ● *v.t*. mettre en apprentissage. **~ship** *n*. apprentissage *m*.

approach /əˈprəʊtʃ/ *v.t*. (s')approcher de; (*accost*) aborder; (*with request*) s'adresser à. ● *v.i*. (s')approcher. ● *n*. approche *f*. **an ~ to**, (*problem*) une façon d'aborder; (*person*) une démarche auprès de. **~able** *a*. accessible; (*person*) abordable.

appropriate [1] /əˈprəʊprɪət/ *a*. approprié, propre. **~ly** *adv*. à propos.

appropriate [2] /əˈprəʊprɪeɪt/ *v.t*. s'approprier.

approval /əˈpruːvl/ *n*. approbation *f*. **on ~**, à *or* sous condition.

approv|e /əˈpruːv/ *v.t./i*. approuver. **~e of**, approuver. **~ingly** *adv*. d'un air *or* d'un ton approbateur.

approximate [1] /əˈprɒksɪmət/ *a*. approximatif. **~ly** *adv*. approximativement.

approximat|e [2] /əˈprɒksɪmeɪt/ *v.i*. **~e to**, se rapprocher de. **~ion** /-ˈmeɪʃn/ *n*. approximation *f*.

apricot /ˈeɪprɪkɒt/ *n*. abricot *m*.

April /ˈeɪprəl/ *n*. avril *m*. **make an ~ fool of**, faire un poisson d'avril à.

apron /ˈeɪprən/ *n*. tablier *m*.

apse /æps/ *n*. (*of church*) abside *f*.

apt /æpt/ *a*. (*suitable*) approprié; (*pupil*) doué. **be ~ to**, avoir tendance à. **~ly** *adv*. à propos.

aptitude /ˈæptɪtjuːd/ *n*. aptitude *f*.

aqualung /ˈækwəlʌŋ/ *n*. scaphandre autonome *m*.

aquarium /əˈkweərɪəm/ *n*. (*pl*. **-ums**) aquarium *m*.

Aquarius /əˈkweərɪəs/ *n*. le Verseau.

aquatic /əˈkwætɪk/ *a*. aquatique; (*sport*) nautique.

aqueduct /ˈækwɪdʌkt/ *n*. aqueduc *m*.

Arab /ˈærəb/ *n*. & *a*. arabe (*m*./*f*.). **~ic** *a*. & *n*. (*lang*.) arabe (*m*.). **~ic numerals**, chiffres arabes *m. pl*.

Arabian /əˈreɪbɪən/ *a*. arabe.

arable /ˈærəbl/ *a*. arable.

arbiter /ˈɑːbɪtə(r)/ *n*. arbitre *m*.

arbitrary /ˈɑːbɪtrərɪ/ *a*. arbitraire.

arbitrat|e /ˈɑːbɪtreɪt/ *v.i*. arbitrer. **~ion** /-ˈtreɪʃn/ *n*. arbitrage *m*. **~or** *n*. arbitre *m*.

arc /ɑːk/ *n*. arc *m*.

arcade /ɑːˈkeɪd/ *n*. (*shops*) galerie *f*.; (*arches*) arcades *f. pl*.

arch [1] /ɑːtʃ/ *n*. arche *f*.; (*in church etc*.) arc *m*.; (*of foot*) voûte plantaire *f*. ● *v.t./i*. (s')arquer.

arch [2] /ɑːtʃ/ *a*. (*playful*) malicieux.

arch- /ɑːtʃ/ *pref*. (*hypocrite etc*.) grand, achevé.

archaeolog|y /ɑːkɪˈɒlədʒɪ/ *n*. archéologie *f*. **~ical** /-əˈlɒdʒɪkl/ *a*. archéologique. **~ist** *n*. archéologue *m*./*f*.

archaic /ɑːˈkeɪɪk/ *a*. archaïque.

archbishop /ɑːtʃˈbɪʃəp/ *n*. archevêque *m*.

archeology /ɑːkɪˈɒlədʒɪ/ *n*. (*Amer*.) = **archaeology**.

archer /ˈɑːtʃə(r)/ *n*. archer *m*. **~y** *n*. tir à l'arc *m*.

archetype /ˈɑːkɪtaɪp/ *n*. archétype *m*., modèle *m*.

archipelago /ɑːkɪˈpeləgəʊ/ *n*. (*pl*. **-os**) archipel *m*.

architect /ˈɑːkɪtekt/ *n*. architecte *m*.

architectur|e /ˈɑːkɪtektʃə(r)/ *n*. architecture *f*. **~al** /-ˈtektʃərəl/ *a*. architectural.

archiv|es /ˈɑːkaɪvz/ *n. pl*. archives *f. pl*. **~ist** /-ɪvɪst/ *n*. archiviste *m*./*f*.

archway /ˈɑːtʃweɪ/ *n*. voûte *f*.

Arctic /ˈɑːktɪk/ *a*. & *n*. arctique (*m*.). **arctic** *a*. glacial.

ardent /ˈɑːdnt/ *a*. ardent. **~ly** *adv*. ardemment.

ardour /ˈɑːdə(r)/ *n*. ardeur *f*.

arduous /ˈɑːdjʊəs/ *a*. ardu.

are /ɑː(r)/ *see* **be**.

area /ˈeərɪə/ *n*. (*surface*) superficie *f*.; (*region*) région *f*.; (*district*) quartier *m*.; (*fig*.) domaine *m*. **parking/picnic ~**, aire de parking/de pique-nique *f*.

arena /əˈriːnə/ *n*. arène *f*.

aren't /ɑ:nt/ = are not.

Argentin|a /ɑ:dʒən'ti:nə/ n. Argentine f. **~e** /'ɑ:dʒəntaɪn/, **~ian** /-'tɪnɪən/ a. & n. argentin(e) (m. (f.)).

argu|e /'ɑ:gju:/ v.i. (quarrel) se disputer; (reason) argumenter. ● v.t. (debate) discuter. **~e that,** alléguer que. **~able** /-'ʊəbl/ a. le cas selon certains. **~ably** adv. selon certains.

argument /'ɑ:gjʊmənt/ n. dispute f.; (reasoning) argument m.; (discussion) débat m. **~ative** /-'mentətɪv/ a. raisonneur, contrariant.

arid /'ærɪd/ a. aride.

Aries /'eəri:z/ n. le Bélier.

arise /ə'raɪz/ v.i. (p.t. **arose,** p.p. **arisen**) se présenter; (old use) se lever. **~ from,** résulter de.

aristocracy /ærɪ'stɒkrəsɪ/ n. aristocratie f.

aristocrat /'ærɪstəkræt, Amer. ə'rɪstəkræt/ n. aristocrate m./f. **~ic** /-'krætɪk/ a. aristocratique.

arithmetic /ə'rɪθmətɪk/ n. arithmétique f.

ark /ɑ:k/ n. (relig.) arche f.

arm[1] /ɑ:m/ n. bras m. **~ in arm,** bras dessus bras dessous. **~-band** n. brassard m.

arm[2] /ɑ:m/ v.t. armer. **~ed robbery,** vol à main armée m.

armament /'ɑ:məmənt/ n. armement m.

armchair /'ɑ:mtʃeə(r)/ n. fauteuil m.

armistice /'ɑ:mɪstɪs/ n. armistice m.

armour /'ɑ:mə(r)/ n. armure f.; (on tanks etc.) blindage m. **~-clad, ~ed** adjs. blindé.

armoury /'ɑ:mərɪ/ n. arsenal m.

armpit /'ɑ:mpɪt/ n. aisselle f.

arms /ɑ:mz/ n. pl. (weapons) armes f. pl. **~ dealer,** trafiquant d'armes m.

army /'ɑ:mɪ/ n. armée f.

aroma /ə'rəʊmə/ n. arôme m. **~tic** /ærə'mætɪk/ a. aromatique.

arose /ə'rəʊz/ see arise.

around /ə'raʊnd/ adv. (tout) autour; (here and there) çà et là. ● prep. autour de. **~ here,** par ici.

arouse /ə'raʊz/ v.t. (awaken, cause) éveiller; (excite) exciter.

arrange /ə'reɪndʒ/ v.t. arranger; (time, date) fixer. **~ to,** s'arranger pour. **~ment** n. arrangement m. **make ~ments,** prendre des dispositions.

array /ə'reɪ/ v.t. (mil.) déployer; (dress) vêtir. ● n. **an ~ of,** (display) un étalage impressionnant de.

arrears /ə'rɪəz/ n. pl. arriéré m. **in ~,** (rent) arriéré. **he is in ~,** il a des paiements en retard.

arrest /ə'rest/ v.t. arrêter; (attention) retenir. ● n. arrestation f. **under ~,** en état d'arrestation.

arrival /ə'raɪvl/ n. arrivée f. **new ~,** nouveau venu m., nouvelle venue f.

arrive /ə'raɪv/ v.i. arriver.

arrogan|t /'ærəgənt/ a. arrogant. **~ce** n. arrogance f. **~tly** adv. avec arrogance.

arrow /'ærəʊ/ n. flèche f.

arse /ɑ:s/ n. (sl.) cul m. (sl.)

arsenal /'ɑ:sənl/ n. arsenal m.

arsenic /'ɑ:snɪk/ n. arsenic m.

arson /'ɑ:sn/ n. incendie criminel m. **~ist** n. incendiaire m./f.

art /ɑ:t/ n. art m.; (fine arts) beaux-arts m. pl. **~s,** (univ.) lettres f. pl. **~ gallery,** (public) musée (d'art) m.; (private) galerie (d'art) f. **~ school,** école des beaux-arts f.

artefact /'ɑ:tɪfækt/ n. objet fabriqué m.

arter|y /'ɑ:tərɪ/ n. artère f. **~ial** /-'tɪərɪəl/ a. artériel. **~ial road,** route principale f.

artful /'ɑ:tfl/ a. astucieux, rusé. **~ness** n. astuce f.

arthriti|s /ɑ:'θraɪtɪs/ n. arthrite f. **~c** /-ɪtɪk/ a. arthritique.

artichoke /'ɑ:tɪtʃəʊk/ n. artichaut m.

article /'ɑ:tɪkl/ n. article m. **~ of clothing,** vêtement m. **~d** a. (jurid.) en stage.

articulate[1] /ɑ:'tɪkjʊlət/ a. (person) capable de s'exprimer clairement; (speech) distinct.

articulat|e[2] /ɑ:'tɪkjʊleɪt/ v.t./i. articuler. **~ed lorry,** semi-remorque m. **~ion** /-'leɪʃn/ n. articulation f.

artifice /'ɑ:tɪfɪs/ n. artifice m.

artificial /ɑ:tɪ'fɪʃl/ a. artificiel. **~ity** /-ʃɪ'ælətɪ/ n. manque de naturel m.

artillery /ɑ:'tɪlərɪ/ n. artillerie f.

artisan /ɑ:tɪ'zæn/ n. artisan m.

artist /'ɑ:tɪst/ n. artiste m./f. **~ic** /-'tɪstɪk/ a. artistique. **~ry** n. art m.

artiste /ɑ:'ti:st/ n. (entertainer) artiste m./f.

artless /'ɑ:tlɪs/ a. ingénu, naïf.

artwork /'ɑ:twɜ:k/ n. (of book) illustrations f. pl.

as /æz, unstressed əz/ adv. & conj. comme; (while) pendant que. **as you get older,** en vieillissant. **as she came in,** en entrant. **as a mother,** en tant que mère. **as a gift,** en cadeau.

as from Monday, à partir de lundi.
as tall as, aussi grand que. **~ for, as
to,** quant à. **~ if,** comme si. **you
look as if you're tired,** vous avez
l'air (d'être) fatigué. **as much, as
many,** autant (**as,** que). **as soon as,**
aussitôt que. **as well,** aussi (**as,** bien
que). **as wide as possible,** aussi
large que possible.

asbestos /æz'bestɒs/ *n.* amiante *f.*

ascend /ə'send/ *v.t.* gravir; (*throne*)
monter sur. ● *v.i.* monter. **~ant** *n.*
be in the ~ant, monter.

ascent /ə'sent/ *n.* (*climbing*) ascension *f.*; (*slope*) côte *f.*

ascertain /æsə'teɪn/ *v.t.* s'assurer de.
~ that, s'assurer que.

ascetic /ə'setɪk/ *a.* ascétique. ● *n.*
ascète *m./f.*

ascribe /ə'skraɪb/ *v.t.* attribuer.

ash¹ /æʃ/ *n.* **~(-tree),** frêne *m.*

ash² /æʃ/ *n.* cendre *f.* **Ash Wednesday,** Mercredi des Cendres *m.* **~en**
a. cendreux.

ashamed /ə'ʃeɪmd/ *a.* **be ~,** avoir
honte (**of,** de).

ashore /ə'ʃɔː(r)/ *adv.* à terre.

ashtray /'æʃtreɪ/ *n.* cendrier *m.*

Asia /'eɪʃə, *Amer.* 'eɪʒə/ *n.* Asie *f.* **~n**
a. & n. asiatique (*m./f.*). **the ~n
community,** la communauté indo-
pakistanaise. **~tic** /-ɪ'ætɪk/ *a.* asiatique.

aside /ə'saɪd/ *adv.* de côté. ● *n.*
aparté *m.* **~ from,** à part.

ask /ɑːsk/ *v.t./i.* demander; (*a question*) poser; (*invite*) inviter. **~ s.o.
sth.,** demander qch. à qn. **~ s.o. to
do,** demander à qn. de faire. **~
about,** (*thing*) se renseigner sur;
(*person*) demander des nouvelles
de. **~ for,** demander.

askance /ə'skæns/ *adv.* **look ~ at,**
regarder avec méfiance.

askew /ə'skjuː/ *adv. & a.* de travers.

asleep /ə'sliːp/ *a.* endormi; (*numb*)
engourdi. ● *adv.* **fall ~,** s'endormir.

asparagus /ə'spærəgəs/ *n.* (*plant*)
asperge *f.*; (*culin.*) asperges *f. pl.*

aspect /'æspekt/ *n.* aspect *m.*; (*direction*) orientation *f.*

aspersions /ə'spɜːʃnz/ *n. pl.* **cast ~
on,** calomnier.

asphalt /'æsfælt, *Amer.* 'æsfɔːlt/ *n.*
asphalte *m.* ● *v.t.* asphalter.

asphyxiat|e /əs'fɪksɪeɪt/ *v.t./i.*
(s')asphyxier. **~ion** /-'eɪʃn/ *n.* asphyxie *f.*

aspir|e /əs'paɪə(r)/ *v.i.* **~e to,** aspirer
à. **~ation** /æspə'reɪʃn/ *n.* aspiration
f.

aspirin /'æsprɪn/ *n.* aspirine *f.*

ass /æs/ *n.* âne *m.*; (*person: fam.*)
idiot(e) *m.* (*f.*).

assail /ə'seɪl/ *v.t.* assaillir. **~ant** *n.*
agresseur *m.*

assassin /ə'sæsɪn/ *n.* assassin *m.*

assassinat|e /ə'sæsɪneɪt/ *v.t.* as-
sassiner. **~ion** /-'neɪʃn/ *n.* assassi-
nat *m.*

assault /ə'sɔːlt/ *n.* (*mil.*) assaut *m.*;
(*jurid.*) agression *f.* ● *v.t.* (*person:
jurid.*) agresser.

assembl|e /ə'sembl/ *v.t.* (*things*) as-
sembler; (*people*) rassembler. ● *v.i.*
s'assembler, se rassembler. **~age** *n.*
assemblage *m.*

assembly /ə'semblɪ/ *n.* assemblée *f.*
~ line, chaîne de montage *f.*

assent /ə'sent/ *n.* assentiment *m.*
● *v.i.* consentir.

assert /ə'sɜːt/ *v.t.* affirmer; (*one's
rights*) revendiquer. **~ion** /-ʃn/ *n.*
affirmation *f.* **~ive** *a.* affirmatif,
péremptoire.

assess /ə'ses/ *v.t.* évaluer; (*payment*)
déterminer le montant de. **~ment** *n.*
évaluation *f.* **~or** *n.* (*valuer*) expert
m.

asset /'æset/ *n.* (*advantage*) atout *m.*
~s, (*comm.*) actif *m.*

assiduous /ə'sɪdjʊəs/ *a.* assidu.

assign /ə'saɪn/ *v.t.* (*allot*) assigner. **~
s.o. to,** (*appoint*) affecter qn. à.

assignment /ə'saɪnmənt/ *n.* (*task*)
mission *f.*, tâche *f.*; (*schol.*) rapport
m.

assimilat|e /ə'sɪməleɪt/ *v.t./i.* (s')as-
similer. **~ion** /-'leɪʃn/ *n.* assimila-
tion *f.*

assist /ə'sɪst/ *v.t./i.* aider. **~ance** *n.*
aide *f.*

assistant /ə'sɪstənt/ *n.* aide *m./f.*; (*in
shop*) vendeu|r, -se *m., f.* ● *a.* (*man-
ager etc.*) adjoint.

associat|e¹ /ə'səʊʃɪeɪt/ *v.t.* associer.
● *v.i.* **~e with,** fréquenter. **~ion**
/-'eɪʃn/ *n.* association *f.*

associate² /ə'səʊʃɪət/ *n. & a.* asso-
cié(e) (*m.* (*f.*)).

assort|ed /ə'sɔːtɪd/ *a.* divers; (*foods*)
assortis. **~ment** *n.* assortiment *m.*
an ~ment of guests/*etc.***,** des in-
vités/*etc.* divers.

assume /ə'sjuːm/ *v.t.* supposer, présumer; (*power, attitude*) prendre;
(*role, burden*) assumer.

assumption /əˈsʌmpʃn/ n. (sth. supposed) supposition f.
assurance /əˈʃʊərəns/ n. assurance f.
assure /əˈʃʊə(r)/ v.t. assurer. ~d a. assuré. ~dly /-rɪdlɪ/ adv. assurément.
asterisk /ˈæstərɪsk/ n. astérisque m.
astern /əˈstɜːn/ adv. à l'arrière.
asthma /ˈæsmə/ n. asthme m. ~tic /-ˈmætɪk/ a. & n. asthmatique (m./f.).
astonish /əˈstɒnɪʃ/ v.t. étonner. ~ingly adv. étonnamment. ~ment n. étonnement m.
astound /əˈstaʊnd/ v.t. stupéfier.
astray /əˈstreɪ/ adv. & a. go ~, s'égarer. lead ~, égarer.
astride /əˈstraɪd/ adv. & prep. à califourchon (sur).
astrolog|y /əˈstrɒlədʒɪ/ n. astrologie f. ~er n. astrologue m.
astronaut /ˈæstrənɔːt/ n. astronaute m./f.
astronom|y /əˈstrɒnəmɪ/ n. astronomie f. ~er n. astronome m. ~ical /æstrəˈnɒmɪkl/ a. astronomique.
astute /əˈstjuːt/ a. astucieux. ~ness n. astuce f.
asylum /əˈsaɪləm/ n. asile m.
at /æt, unstressed ət/ prep. à. at the doctor's/etc., chez le médecin/etc. surprised at, (cause) étonné de. angry at, fâché contre. not at all, pas du tout. no wind/etc. at all, (of any kind) pas le moindre vent/etc. at night, la nuit. at once, tout de suite; (simultaneously) à la fois. ~ sea, en mer. at times, parfois.
ate /et/ see eat.
atheis|t /ˈeɪθɪɪst/ n. athée m./f. ~m /-zəm/ n. athéisme m.
athlet|e /ˈæθliːt/ n. athlète m./f. ~ic /-ˈletɪk/ a. athlétique. ~ics /-ˈletɪks/ n. pl. athlétisme m.
Atlantic /ətˈlæntɪk/ a. atlantique. ● n. ~ (Ocean), Atlantique m.
atlas /ˈætləs/ n. atlas m.
atmospher|e /ˈætməsfɪə(r)/ n. atmosphère f. ~ic /-ˈferɪk/ a. atmosphérique.
atoll /ˈætɒl/ n. atoll m.
atom /ˈætəm/ n. atome m. ~ic /əˈtɒmɪk/ a. atomique. ~(ic) bomb, bombe atomique f.
atomize /ˈætəmaɪz/ v.t. atomiser. ~r /-ə(r)/ n. atomiseur m.
atone /əˈtəʊn/ v.i. ~ for, expier. ~ment n. expiation f.
atrocious /əˈtrəʊʃəs/ a. atroce.

atrocity /əˈtrɒsətɪ/ n. atrocité f.
atrophy /ˈætrəfɪ/ n. atrophie f. ● v.t./i. (s')atrophier.
attach /əˈtætʃ/ v.t./i. (s')attacher; (letter) joindre (to, à). ~ed a. be ~ed to, (like) être attaché à. the ~ed letter, la lettre ci-jointe. ~ment n. (accessory) accessoire m.; (affection) attachement m.
attaché /əˈtæʃeɪ/ n. (pol.) attaché(e) m. (f.). ~ case, mallette f.
attack /əˈtæk/ n. attaque f.; (med.) crise f. ● v.t. attaquer. ~er n. agresseur m., attaquant(e) m. (f.).
attain /əˈteɪn/ v.t. atteindre (à); (gain) acquérir. ~able a. accessible. ~ment n. acquisition f. (of, de). ~ments, réussites f. pl.
attempt /əˈtempt/ v.t. tenter. ● n. tentative f. an ~ on s.o.'s life, un attentat contre qn.
attend /əˈtend/ v.t. assister à; (class) suivre; (school, church) aller à; (escort) accompagner. ● v.i. assister. ~ (to), (look after) s'occuper de. ~ance n. présence f.; (people) assistance f.
attendant /əˈtendənt/ n. employé(e) m. (f.); (servant) serviteur m. ● a. concomitant.
attention /əˈtenʃn/ n. attention f.; ~!, (mil.) garde-à-vous! pay ~, faire or prêter attention (to, à).
attentive /əˈtentɪv/ a. attentif; (considerate) attentionné. ~ly adv. attentivement. ~ness n. attention f.
attenuate /əˈtenjʊeɪt/ v.t. atténuer.
attest /əˈtest/ v.t./i. ~ (to), attester. ~ation /æteˈsteɪʃn/ n. attestation f.
attic /ˈætɪk/ n. grenier m.
attitude /ˈætɪtjuːd/ n. attitude f.
attorney /əˈtɜːnɪ/ n. mandataire m.; (Amer.) avocat m.
attract /əˈtrækt/ v.t. attirer. ~ion /-kʃn/ n. attraction f.; (charm) attrait m.
attractive /əˈtræktɪv/ a. attrayant, séduisant. ~ly adv. agréablement. ~ness n. attrait m., beauté f.
attribute[1] /əˈtrɪbjuːt/ v.t. ~ to, attribuer à.
attribute[2] /ˈætrɪbjuːt/ n. attribut m.
attrition /əˈtrɪʃn/ n. war of ~, guerre d'usure f.
aubergine /ˈəʊbəʒiːn/ n. aubergine f.
auburn /ˈɔːbən/ a. châtain roux invar.
auction /ˈɔːkʃn/ n. vente aux enchères f. ● v.t. vendre aux

enchères. **~eer** /-ə'nıə(r)/ *n.* commissaire-priseur *m.*

audaci|ous /ɔː'deɪʃəs/ *a.* audacieux. **~ty** /-æsətɪ/ *n.* audace *f.*

audible /'ɔːdəbl/ *a.* audible.

audience /'ɔːdɪəns/ *n.* auditoire *m.*; (*theatre, radio*) public *m.*; (*interview*) audience *f.*

audio typist /'ɔːdɪəʊ'taɪpɪst/ *n.* audio-typiste *m./f.*

audio-visual /ɔːdɪəʊ'vɪʒʊəl/ *a.* audio-visuel.

audit /'ɔːdɪt/ *n.* vérification des comptes *f.* ● *v.t.* vérifier.

audition /ɔː'dɪʃn/ *n.* audition *f.* ● *v.t./i.* auditionner.

auditor /'ɔːdɪtə(r)/ *n.* commissaire aux comptes *m.*

auditorium /ɔːdɪ'tɔːrɪəm/ *n.* (*of theatre etc.*) salle *f.*

augur /'ɔːgə(r)/ *v.i.* **~ well/ill**, être de bon/mauvais augure.

August /'ɔːgəst/ *n.* août *m.*

aunt /ɑːnt/ *n.* tante *f.*

au pair /əʊ'peə(r)/ *n.* jeune fille au pair *f.*

aura /'ɔːrə/ *n.* atmosphère *f.*

auspices /'ɔːspɪsɪz/ *n. pl.* auspices *m. pl.*, égide *f.*

auspicious /ɔː'spɪʃəs/ *a.* favorable.

auster|e /ɔː'stɪə(r)/ *a.* austère. **~ity** /-erətɪ/ *n.* austérité *f.*

Australia /ɒ'streɪlɪə/ *n.* Australie *f.* **~n** *a. & n.* australien(ne) (*m. (f.)*).

Austria /'ɒstrɪə/ *n.* Autriche *f.* **~n** *a. & n.* autrichien(ne) (*m. (f.)*).

authentic /ɔː'θentɪk/ *a.* authentique. **~ity** /-ən'tɪsətɪ/ *n.* authenticité *f.*

authenticate /ɔː'θentɪkeɪt/ *v.t.* authentifier.

author /'ɔːθə(r)/ *n.* auteur *m.* **~ship** *n.* (*origin*) paternité *f.*

authoritarian /ɔːθɒrɪ'teərɪən/ *a.* autoritaire.

authorit|y /ɔː'θɒrətɪ/ *n.* autorité *f.*; (*permission*) autorisation *f.* **~ative** /-ɪtətɪv/ *a.* (*credible*) qui fait autorité; (*trusted*) autorisé; (*manner*) autoritaire.

authoriz|e /'ɔːθəraɪz/ *v.t.* autoriser. **~ation** /-'zeɪʃn/ *n.* autorisation *f.*

autistic /ɔː'tɪstɪk/ *a.* autistique.

autobiography /ɔːtəbaɪ'ɒgrəfɪ/ *n.* autobiographie *f.*

autocrat /'ɔːtəkræt/ *n.* autocrate *m.* **~ic** /-'krætɪk/ *a.* autocratique.

autograph /'ɔːtəgrɑːf/ *n.* autographe *m.* ● *v.t.* signer, dédicacer.

auto-immune /ɔːtəʊɪ'mjuːn/ *a.* auto-immune.

automat|e /'ɔːtəmeɪt/ *v.t.* automatiser. **~ion** /-'meɪʃn/ *n.* automatisation *f.*

automatic /ɔːtə'mætɪk/ *a.* automatique. ● *n.* (*auto.*) voiture automatique *f.* **~ally** /-klɪ/ *adv.* automatiquement.

automobile /'ɔːtəməbiːl/ *n.* (*Amer.*) auto(mobile) *f.*

autonom|y /ɔː'tɒnəmɪ/ *n.* autonomie *f.* **~ous** *a.* autonome.

autopsy /'ɔːtɒpsɪ/ *n.* autopsie *f.*

autumn /'ɔːtəm/ *n.* automne *m.* **~al** /-'tʌmnəl/ *a.* automnal.

auxiliary /ɔːg'zɪlɪərɪ/ *a. & n.* auxiliaire (*m./f.*). **~ (verb)**, auxiliaire *m.*

avail /ə'veɪl/ *v.t.* **~ o.s. of**, profiter de. ● *n.* **of no ~**, inutile. **to no ~**, sans résultat.

availab|le /ə'veɪləbl/ *a.* disponible. **~ility** /-'bɪlətɪ/ *n.* disponibilité *f.*

avalanche /'ævəlɑːnʃ/ *n.* avalanche *f.*

avant-garde /ævɑ̃'gɑːd/ *a.* d'avant-garde.

avaric|e /'ævərɪs/ *n.* avarice *f.* **~ious** /-'rɪʃəs/ *a.* avare.

avenge /ə'vendʒ/ *v.t.* venger. **~ o.s.**, se venger (**on**, de).

avenue /'ævənjuː/ *n.* avenue *f.*; (*line of approach: fig.*) voie *f.*

average /'ævərɪdʒ/ *n.* moyenne *f.* ● *a.* moyen. ● *v.t./i.* faire la moyenne de; (*produce, do*) faire en moyenne. **on ~**, en moyenne.

avers|e /ə'vɜːs/ *a.* **be ~e to**, répugner à. **~ion** /-ʃn/ *n.* aversion *f.*

avert /ə'vɜːt/ *v.t.* (*turn away*) détourner; (*ward off*) éviter.

aviary /'eɪvɪərɪ/ *n.* volière *f.*

aviation /eɪvɪ'eɪʃn/ *n.* aviation *f.*

avid /'ævɪd/ *a.* avide.

avocado /ævə'kɑːdəʊ/ *n.* (*pl.* **-os**) avocat *m.*

avoid /ə'vɔɪd/ *v.t.* éviter. **~able** *a.* évitable. **~ance** *n.* **the ~ance of s.o./sth. is . . .**, éviter qn./qch., c'est . . .

await /ə'weɪt/ *v.t.* attendre.

awake /ə'weɪk/ *v.t./i.* (*p.t.* **awoke**, *p.p.* **awoken**) (s')éveiller. ● *a.* **be ~**, ne pas dormir, être (r)éveillé.

awaken /ə'weɪkən/ *v.t./i.* (s')éveiller.

award /ə'wɔːd/ *v.t.* attribuer. ● *n.* récompense *f.*, prix *m.*; (*scholarship*) bourse *f.* **pay ~**, augmentation (de salaire) *f.*

aware /ə'weə(r)/ *a.* averti. **be ~ of,** (*danger*) être conscient de; (*fact*) savoir. **become ~ of,** prendre conscience de. **~ness** *n.* conscience *f.*

awash /ə'wɒʃ/ *a.* inondé (**with,** de).

away /ə'weɪ/ *adv.* (*far*) (au) loin; (*absent*) absent, parti; (*persistently*) sans arrêt; (*entirely*) complètement. **~ from,** loin de. **move ~,** s'écarter; (*to new home*) déménager. **six kilometres ~,** à six kilomètres (de distance). **take ~,** emporter. ● *a. & n.* **~ (match),** match à l'extérieur *m.*

awe /ɔ:/ *n.* crainte (révérencielle) *f.* **~-inspiring, ~some** *adjs.* terrifiant; (*sight*) imposant. **~struck** *a.* terrifié.

awful /'ɔ:fl/ *a.* affreux. **~ly** /'ɔ:flɪ/ *adv.* (*badly*) affreusement; (*very: fam.*) rudement.

awhile /ə'waɪl/ *adv.* quelque temps.

awkward /'ɔ:kwəd/ *a.* difficile; (*inconvenient*) inopportun; (*clumsy*) maladroit; (*embarrassing*) gênant; (*embarrassed*) gêné. **~ly** *adv.* maladroitement; avec gêne. **~ness** *n.* maladresse *f.*; (*discomfort*) gêne *f.*

awning /'ɔ:nɪŋ/ *n.* auvent *m.*; (*of shop*) store *m.*

awoke, awoken /ə'wəʊk, ə'wəʊkən/ *see* awake.

awry /ə'raɪ/ *adv.* **go ~,** mal tourner. **sth. is ~,** qch. ne va pas.

axe, (*Amer.*) **ax** /æks/ *n.* hache *f.* ● *v.t.* (*pres. p.* **axing**) (*eliminate*) supprimer; (*employee*) renvoyer.

axiom /'æksɪəm/ *n.* axiome *m.*

axis /'æksɪs/ *n.* (*pl.* **axes** /-si:z/) axe *m.*

axle /'æksl/ *n.* essieu *m.*

ay(e) /aɪ/ *adv. & n.* oui (*m. invar.*).

B

BA *abbr. see* Bachelor of Arts.

babble /'bæbl/ *v.i.* babiller; (*stream*) gazouiller. ● *n.* babillage *m.*

baboon /bə'bu:n/ *n.* babouin *m.*

baby /'beɪbɪ/ *n.* bébé *m.* **~ carriage,** (*Amer.*) voiture d'enfant *f.* **~-sit** *v.i.* garder les enfants. **~-sitter** *n.* baby-sitter *m./f.*

babyish /'beɪbɪɪʃ/ *a.* enfantin.

bachelor /'bætʃələ(r)/ *n.* célibataire *m.* **B~ of Arts/Science,** licencié(e) ès lettres/sciences *m.* (*f.*).

back /bæk/ *n.* (*of person, hand, page, etc.*) dos *m.*; (*of house*) derrière *m.*; (*of vehicle*) arrière *m.*; (*of room*) fond *m.*; (*of chair*) dossier *m.*; (*football*) arrière *m.* ● *a.* de derrière, arrière *invar.*; (*taxes*) arriéré. ● *adv.* en arrière; (*returned*) de retour, rentré. ● *v.t.* (*support*) appuyer; (*bet on*) miser sur; (*vehicle*) faire reculer. ● *v.i.* (*of person, vehicle*) reculer. **at the ~ of beyond,** au diable. **at the ~ of the book,** à la fin du livre. **come ~,** revenir. **give ~,** rendre. **take ~,** reprendre. **I want it ~,** je veux le récupérer. **in ~ of,** (*Amer.*) derrière. **~-bencher** *n.* (*pol.*) membre sans portefeuille *m.* **~ down,** abandonner, se dégonfler. **~ number,** vieux numéro *m.* **~ out,** se dégager, se dégonfler; (*auto.*) sortir en reculant. **~-pedal** *v.i.* pédaler en arrière; (*fig.*) faire machine arrière (**on,** à propos de). **~ up,** (*support*) appuyer. **~-up** *n.* appui *m.*; (*Amer., fam.*) embouteillage *m.*; (*comput.*) sauvegarde *f.*; *a.* de réserve; (*comput.*) de sauvegarde.

backache /'bækeɪk/ *n.* mal de reins *m.*, mal aux reins *m.*

backbiting /'bækbaɪtɪŋ/ *n.* médisance *f.*

backbone /'bækbəʊn/ *n.* colonne vertébrale *f.*

backdate /bæk'deɪt/ *v.t.* antidater; (*arrangement*) rendre rétroactif.

backer /'bækə(r)/ *n.* partisan *m.*; (*comm.*) bailleur de fonds *m.*

backfire /bæk'faɪə(r)/ *v.i.* (*auto.*) pétarader; (*fig.*) mal tourner.

backgammon /bæk'gæmən/ *n.* trictrac *m.*

background /'bækgraʊnd/ *n.* fond *m.*, arrière-plan *m.*; (*context*) contexte *m.*; (*environment*) milieu *m.*; (*experience*) formation *f.* ● *a.* (*music, noise*) de fond.

backhand /'bækhænd/ *n.* revers *m.* **~ed** *a.* équivoque. **~ed stroke,** revers *m.* **~er** *n.* revers *m.*; (*bribe: sl.*) pot de vin *m.*

backing /'bækɪŋ/ *n.* appui *m.*

backlash /'bæklæʃ/ *n.* choc en retour *m.*, répercussions *f. pl.*

backlog /'bæklɒg/ *n.* accumulation (de travail) *f.*

backpack /'bækpæk/ *n.* sac à dos *m.*

backside /'bæksaɪd/ n. (*buttocks*: *fam.*) derrière m.

backstage /bæk'steɪdʒ/ a. & adv. dans les coulisses.

backstroke /'bækstrəʊk/ n. dos crawlé m.

backtrack /'bæktræk/ v.i. rebrousser chemin; (*change one's opinion*) faire marche arrière.

backward /'bækwəd/ a. (*step etc.*) en arrière; (*retarded*) arriéré.

backwards /'bækwədz/ adv. en arrière; (*walk*) à reculons; (*read*) à l'envers; (*fall*) à la renverse. **go ~ and forwards**, aller et venir.

backwater /'bækwɔːtə(r)/ n. (*pej.*) trou perdu m.

bacon /'beɪkən/ n. lard m.; (*in rashers*) bacon m.

bacteria /bæk'tɪərɪə/ n. pl. bactéries f. pl. **~l** a. bactérien.

bad /bæd/ a. (**worse, worst**) mauvais; (*wicked*) méchant; (*ill*) malade; (*accident*) grave; (*food*) gâté. **feel ~**, se sentir mal. **go ~**, se gâter. **~ language**, gros mots m. pl. **~-mannered** a. mal élevé. **~-tempered** a. grincheux. **~ly** adv. mal; (*hurt*) grièvement. **too ~!**, tant pis; (*I'm sorry*) dommage! **want ~ly**, avoir grande envie de.

badge /bædʒ/ n. insigne m.; (*of identity*) plaque f.

badger /'bædʒə(r)/ n. blaireau m. ● v.t. harceler.

badminton /'bædmɪntən/ n. badminton m.

baffle /'bæfl/ v.t. déconcerter.

bag /bæg/ n. sac m. **~s**, (*luggage*) bagages m.pl.; (*under eyes*) poches f. pl. ● v.t. (p.t. **bagged**) mettre en sac; (*take*: *fam.*) s'adjuger. **~s of**, (*fam.*) beaucoup de.

baggage /'bægɪdʒ/ n. bagages m. pl. **~ reclaim**, livraison des bagages f.

baggy /'bægɪ/ a. trop grand.

bagpipes /'bægpaɪps/ n. pl. cornemuse f.

Bahamas /bə'hɑːməz/ n. pl. **the ~,** les Bahamas f. pl.

bail [1] /beɪl/ n. caution f. **on ~,** sous caution. ● v.t. mettre en liberté (provisoire) sous caution. **~ out,** (*fig.*) sortir d'affaire.

bail [2] /beɪl/ n. (*cricket*) bâtonnet m.

bail [3] /beɪl/ v.t. (*naut.*) écoper.

bailiff /'beɪlɪf/ n. huissier m.

bait /beɪt/ n. appât m. ● v.t. appâter; (*fig.*) tourmenter.

bak|e /beɪk/ v.t. (faire) cuire (au four). ● v.i. cuire (au four); (*person*) faire du pain or des gâteaux. **~ed beans,** haricots blancs à la tomate m.pl. **~ed potato,** pomme de terre en robe des champs f. **~er** n. boulang|er, -ère m., f. **~ing** n. cuisson f. **~ing-powder** n. levure f.

bakery /'beɪkərɪ/ n. boulangerie f.

Balaclava /bælə'klɑːvə/ n. **~ (helmet),** passe-montagne m.

balance /'bæləns/ n. équilibre m.; (*scales*) balance f.; (*outstanding sum*: *comm.*) solde m.; (*of payments, of trade*) balance f.; (*remainder*) reste m.; (*money in account*) position f. ● v.t. tenir en équilibre; (*weigh up & comm.*) balancer; (*budget*) équilibrer; (*to compensate*) contrebalancer. ● v. i. être en équilibre. **~d** a. équilibré.

balcony /'bælkənɪ/ n. balcon m.

bald /bɔːld/ a. (-er, -est) chauve; (*tyre*) lisse; (*fig.*) simple. **~ing** a. **be ~,** perdre ses cheveux. **~ness** n. calvitie f.

bale [1] /beɪl/ n. (*of cotton*) balle f.; (*of straw*) botte f.

bale [2] /beɪl/ v.i. **~ out,** sauter en parachute.

baleful /'beɪlfʊl/ a. sinistre.

balk /bɔːk/ v.t. contrecarrer. ● v.i. **~ at,** reculer devant.

ball [1] /bɔːl/ n. (*golf, tennis, etc.*) balle f.; (*football*) ballon m.; (*croquet, billiards, etc.*) boule f.; (*of wool*) pelote f.; (*sphere*) boule f. **~-bearing** n. roulement à billes m. **~-cock** n. robinet à flotteur m. **~-point** n. stylo à bille m.

ball [2] /bɔːl/ n. (*dance*) bal m.

ballad /'bæləd/ n. ballade f.

ballast /'bæləst/ n. lest m.

ballerina /bælə'riːnə/ n. ballerine f.

ballet /'bæleɪ/ n. ballet m.

ballistic /bə'lɪstɪk/ a. **~ missile,** engin balistique m.

balloon /bə'luːn/ n. ballon m.

ballot /'bælət/ n. scrutin m. **~-(paper),** bulletin de vote m. **~-box** n. urne f. ● v.i. (p.t. **balloted**) (*pol.*) voter. ● v.t. (*members*) consulter par voie de scrutin.

ballroom /'bɔːlruːm/ n. salle de bal f.

ballyhoo /bælɪ'huː/ n. (*publicity*) battage m.; (*uproar*) tapage m.

balm /bɑːm/ n. baume m. **~y** a. (*fragrant*) embaumé; (*mild*) doux; (*crazy*: *sl.*) dingue.

baloney /bə'ləʊnɪ/ n. (sl.) idioties f. pl., calembredaines f. pl.

balustrade /bælə'streɪd/ n. balustrade f.

bamboo /bæm'buː/ n. bambou m.

ban /bæn/ v.t. (p.t. **banned**) interdire. **~ from**, exclure de. ● n. interdiction f.

banal /bə'nɑːl, Amer. 'beɪnl/ a. banal. **~ity** /-ælətɪ/ n. banalité f.

banana /bə'nɑːnə/ n. banane f.

band /bænd/ n. (strip, group of people) bande f.; (mus.) orchestre m.; (pop group) groupe m. (mil.) fanfare f. ● v.i. **~ together**, se liguer.

bandage /'bændɪdʒ/ n. pansement m. ● v.t. bander, panser.

bandit /'bændɪt/ n. bandit m.

bandstand /'bændstænd/ n. kiosque à musique m.

bandwagon /'bændwægən/ n. **climb on the ~**, prendre le train en marche.

bandy[1] /'bændɪ/ v.t. **~ about**, (rumours, ideas, etc.) faire circuler.

bandy[2] /'bændɪ/ a. (-ier, -iest) qui a les jambes arquées.

bang /bæŋ/ n. (blow, noise) coup (violent) m.; (explosion) détonation f.; (of door) claquement m. ● v.t./i. frapper; (door) claquer. ● int. vlan. ● adv. (fam.) exactement. **~ in the middle**, en plein milieu. **~ one's head**, se cogner la tête. **~s**, frange f.

banger /'bæŋə(r)/ n. (firework) pétard m.; (culin., sl.) saucisse f. (old) **~**, (car. sl.) guimbarde f.

bangle /'bæŋgl/ n. bracelet m.

banish /'bænɪʃ/ v.t. bannir.

banisters /'bænɪstəz/ n. pl. rampe (d'escalier) f.

banjo /'bændʒəʊ/ (pl. -os) banjo m.

bank[1] /bæŋk/ n. (of river) rive f.; (of earth) talus m.; (of sand) banc m. ● v.t. (earth) amonceler; (fire) couvrir. ● v.i. (aviat.) virer.

bank[2] /bæŋk/ n. banque f. ● v.t. mettre en banque. ● v.i. **~ with**, avoir un compte à. **~ account**, compte en banque m. **~ card**, carte bancaire f. **~ holiday**, jour férié m. **~ on**, compter sur. **~ statement**, relevé de compte m.

bank|ing /'bæŋkɪŋ/ n. opérations bancaires f. pl.; (as career) la banque. **~er** n. banquier m.

banknote /'bæŋknəʊt/ n. billet de banque m.

bankrupt /'bæŋkrʌpt/ a. **be ~**, être en faillite. **go ~**, faire faillite. ● n. failli(e) m. (f.). ● v.t. mettre en faillite. **~cy** n. faillite f.

banner /'bænə(r)/ n. bannière f.

banns /bænz/ n. pl. bans m. pl.

banquet /'bæŋkwɪt/ n. banquet m.

banter /'bæntə(r)/ n. plaisanterie f. ● v.i. plaisanter.

bap /bæp/ n. petit pain m.

baptism /'bæptɪzəm/ n. baptême m.

Baptist /'bæptɪst/ n. baptiste m./f.

baptize /bæp'taɪz/ v.t. baptiser.

bar /bɑː(r)/ n. (of metal) barre f.; (on window & jurid.) barreau m.; (of chocolate) tablette f.; (pub) bar m.; (counter) comptoir m., bar m.; (division: mus.) mesure f.; (fig.) obstacle m. ● v.t. (p.t. **barred**) (obstruct) barrer; (prohibit) interdire; (exclude) exclure. ● prep. sauf. **~ code**, code-barres m. invar. **~ of soap**, savonnette f.

Barbados /bɑː'beɪdɒs/ n. Barbade f.

barbarian /bɑː'beərɪən/ n. barbare m./f.

barbari|c /bɑː'bærɪk/ a. barbare. **~ty** /-ətɪ/ n. barbarie f.

barbarous /'bɑːbərəs/ a. barbare.

barbecue /'bɑːbɪkjuː/ n. barbecue m. ● v.t. griller, rôtir (au barbecue).

barbed /bɑːbd/ a. **~ wire**, fil de fer barbelé m.

barber /'bɑːbə(r)/ n. coiffeur m. (pour hommes).

barbiturate /bɑː'bɪtjʊrət/ n. barbiturique m.

bare /beə(r)/ a. (-er, -est) (not covered or adorned) nu; (cupboard) vide; (mere) simple. ● v.t. mettre à nu.

barefaced /'beəfeɪst/ a. éhonté.

barefoot /'beəfʊt/ a. nu-pieds invar., pieds nus.

barely /'beəlɪ/ adv. à peine.

bargain /'bɑːgɪn/ n. (deal) marché m.; (cheap thing) occasion f. ● v.i. négocier; (haggle) marchander. **not ~ for**, ne pas s'attendre à.

barge /bɑːdʒ/ n. chaland m. ● v.i. **~ in**, interrompre; (into room) faire irruption.

baritone /'bærɪtəʊn/ n. baryton m.

bark[1] /bɑːk/ n. (of tree) écorce f.

bark[2] /bɑːk/ n. (of dog) aboiement m. ● v.i. aboyer.

barley /'bɑːlɪ/ n. orge f. **~ sugar**, sucre d'orge m.

barmaid /'bɑːmeɪd/ n. serveuse f.

barman /'bɑːmən/ n. (pl. **-men**) barman m.

barmy /'bɑːmɪ/ a. (sl.) dingue.

barn /bɑːn/ n. grange f.

barometer /bə'rɒmɪtə(r)/ n. baromètre m.

baron /'bærən/ n. baron m. ~ess n. baronne f.

baroque /bə'rɒk, Amer. bə'rəʊk/ a. & n. baroque (m.).

barracks /'bærəks/ n. pl. caserne f.

barrage /'bærɑːʒ, Amer. bə'rɑːʒ/ n. (barrier) barrage m.; (mil.) tir de barrage m.; (of complaints) série f.

barrel /'bærəl/ n. tonneau m.; (of oil) baril m.; (of gun) canon m. ~-organ n. orgue de Barbarie (m.).

barren /'bærən/ a. stérile.

barricade /bærɪ'keɪd/ n. barricade f. ● v.t. barricader.

barrier /'bærɪə(r)/ n. barrière f.

barring /'bɑːrɪŋ/ prep. sauf.

barrister /'bærɪstə(r)/ n. avocat m.

barrow /'bærəʊ/ n. charrette à bras f.; (wheelbarrow) brouette f.

bartender /'bɑːtendə(r)/ n. (Amer.) barman m.

barter /'bɑːtə(r)/ n. troc m., échange m. ● v.t. troquer, échanger (for, contre).

base /beɪs/ n. base f. ● v.t. baser (on, sur; in, à). ● a. bas, ignoble. ~less a. sans fondement.

baseball /'beɪsbɔːl/ n. base-ball m.

baseboard /'beɪsbɔːd/ n. (Amer.) plinthe f.

basement /'beɪsmənt/ n. sous-sol m.

bash /bæʃ/ v.t. cogner. ● n. coup (violent) m. **have a ~ at**, (sl.) s'essayer à. ~ed in, enfoncé.

bashful /'bæʃfl/ a. timide.

basic /'beɪsɪk/ a. fondamental, élémentaire. **the ~s**, les éléments de base m. pl. ~ally /-klɪ/ adv. au fond.

basil /'bæzɪl, Amer. 'beɪzl/ n. basilic m.

basin /'beɪsn/ n. (for liquids) cuvette f.; (for food) bol m.; (for washing) lavabo m.; (of river) bassin m.

basis /'beɪsɪs/ n. (pl. **bases** /-siːz/) base f.

bask /bɑːsk/ v.i. se chauffer.

basket /'bɑːskɪt/ n. corbeille f.; (with handle) panier m.

basketball /'bɑːskɪtbɔːl/ n. basket (-ball) m.

Basque /bɑːsk/ a. & n. basque (m./f.).

bass [1] /beɪs/ a. (mus.) bas, grave. ● n. (pl. **basses**) basse f.

bass [2] /bæs/ n. invar. (freshwater fish) perche f.; (sea) bar m.

bassoon /bə'suːn/ n. basson m.

bastard /'bɑːstəd/ n. bâtard(e) m. (f.); (sl.) sal|aud, -ope m., f.

baste [1] /beɪst/ v.t. (sew) bâtir.

baste [2] /beɪst/ v.t. (culin.) arroser.

bastion /'bæstɪən/ n. bastion m.

bat [1] /bæt/ n. (cricket etc.) batte f.; (table tennis) raquette f. ● v.t. (p.t. **batted**) (ball) frapper. **not ~ an eyelid**, ne pas sourciller.

bat [2] /bæt/ n. (animal) chauve-souris f.

batch /bætʃ/ n. (of people) fournée f.; (of papers) paquet m.; (of goods) lot m.

bated /'beɪtɪd/ a. **with ~ breath**, en retenant son souffle.

bath /bɑːθ/ n. (pl. **-s** /bɑːðz/) bain m.; (tub) baignoire f. (**swimming**) **~s**, piscine f. ● v.t. donner un bain à ● a. de bain. **have a ~**, prendre un bain. **~ mat**, tapis de bain m.

bathe /beɪð/ v.t. baigner. ● v.i. se baigner; (Amer.) prendre un bain. ● n. bain (de mer) m. ~**r** /-ə(r)/ n. baigneu|r, -se m., f.

bathing /'beɪðɪŋ/ n. baignade f. ~-costume n. maillot de bain m.

bathrobe /'bæθrəʊb/ m. (Amer.) robe de chambre f.

bathroom /'bɑːθrʊm/ n. salle de bains f.

baton /'bætən/ n. (mil.) bâton m.; (mus.) baguette f.

battalion /bə'tæljən/ n. bataillon m.

batter /'bætə(r)/ v.t. (strike) battre; (ill-treat) maltraiter. ● n. (culin.) pâte (à frire) f. ~**ed** a. (pan, car) cabossé; (face) meurtri. ~**ing** n. **take a ~ing**, subir des coups.

battery /'bætərɪ/ n. (mil., auto.) batterie f.; (of torch, radio) pile f.

battle /'bætl/ n. bataille f.; (fig.) lutte f. ● v.i. se battre.

battlefield /'bætlfiːld/ n. champ de bataille m.

battlements /'bætlmənts/ n. pl. (crenellations) créneaux m. pl.; (wall) remparts m. pl.

battleship /'bætlʃɪp/ n. cuirassé m.

baulk /bɔːk/ v.t./i. = **balk**.

bawdy /'bɔːdɪ/ a. (-ier, -iest) paillard. ~**iness** n. paillardise f.

bawl /bɔːl/ v.t./i. brailler.

bay ¹ /beɪ/ n. (bot.) laurier m. ~-leaf n. feuille de laurier f.

bay ² /beɪ/ n. (geog., archit.) baie f.; (area) aire f. ~ **window,** fenêtre en saillie f.

bay ³ /beɪ/ n. (bark) aboiement m. ● v.i. aboyer. **at** ~, aux abois. **keep** or **hold at** ~, tenir à distance.

bayonet /'beɪənɪt/ n. baïonnette f.

bazaar /bə'zɑ:(r)/ n. (shop, market) bazar m.; (sale) vente f.

BC abbr. (before Christ) avant J.-C.

be /bi:/ v.i. (present tense am, are, is; p.t. was, were; p.p. been) être. **be hot/right**/etc., avoir chaud/ raison/ etc. **he is 30,** (age) il a 30 ans. **it is fine/cold**/etc., (weather) il fait beau/froid/etc. **I'm a painter** ● je suis peintre ● **how are you?,** (health) comment allez-vous? **he is to leave,** (must) il doit partir; (will) il va partir, il est prévu qu'il parte. **how much is it?,** (cost) ça fait or c'est combien? **be reading/walking**/etc., (aux.) lire/ marcher/etc. **the child was found,** l'enfant a été retrouvé, on a retrouvé l'enfant. **have been to,** avoir été à, être allé à.

beach /bi:tʃ/ n. plage f.

beacon /'bi:kən/ n. (lighthouse) phare m.; (marker) balise f.

bead /bi:d/ n. perle f.

beak /bi:k/ n. bec m.

beaker /'bi:kə(r)/ n. gobelet m.

beam /bi:m/ n. (timber) poutre f.; (of light) rayon m.; (of torch) faisceau m. ● v.i. (radiate) rayonner. ● v.t. (broadcast) diffuser. ~ing a. radieux.

bean /bi:n/ n. haricot m.; (of coffee) grain m.

bear ¹ /beə(r)/ n. ours m.

bear ² /beə(r)/ v.t. (p.t. bore, p.p. borne) (carry, show, feel) porter; (endure, sustain) supporter; (child) mettre au monde. ● v.i. ~ **left**/etc., (go) prendre à gauche/etc. ~ **in mind,** tenir compte de. ~ **on,** se rapporter à. ~ **out,** corroborer. ~ **up!,** courage! ~**able** a. supportable. ~**er** n. porteu|r, -se m., f.

beard /bɪəd/ n. barbe f. ~**ed** a. barbu.

bearing /'beərɪŋ/ n. (behaviour) maintien m.; (relevance) rapport m. **get one's** ~**s,** s'orienter.

beast /bi:st/ n. bête f.; (person) brute f.

beastly /'bi:stlɪ/ a. (-ier, -iest) (fam.) détestable.

beat /bi:t/ v.t./i. (p.t. beat, p.p. beaten) battre. ● n. (of drum, heart) battement m.; (mus.) mesure f.; (of policeman) ronde f. ~ **a retreat,** battre en retraite. ~ **it!,** dégage! ~ **s.o. down,** faire baisser son prix à qn. ~ **off the competition,** éliminer la concurrence. ~ **up,** tabasser. **it** ~**s me,** (fam.) ça me dépasse. ~**er** n. batteur m. ~**ing** n. raclée f.

beautician /bju:'tɪʃn/ n. esthétici|en(ne) m. (f.).

beautiful /'bju:tɪfl/ a. beau. ~**ly** /-flɪ/ adv. merveilleusement.

beautify /'bju:tɪfaɪ/ v.t. embellir.

beauty /'bju:tɪ/ n. beauté f. ~ **parlour,** institut de beauté m. ~ **spot,** grain de beauté m.; (fig.) site pittoresque m.

beaver /'bi:və(r)/ n. castor m.

became /bɪ'keɪm/ see become.

because /bɪ'kɒz/ conj. parce que. ~ **of,** à cause de.

beck /bek/ n. **at the** ~ **and call of,** aux ordres de.

beckon /'bekən/ v.t./i. ~ **(to),** faire signe à.

become /bɪ'kʌm/ v.t./i. (p.t. became, p.p. become) devenir; (befit) convenir à. **what has** ~ **of her?,** qu'est-elle devenue?

becoming /bɪ'kʌmɪŋ/ a. (seemly) bienséant; (clothes) seyant.

bed /bed/ n. lit m.; (layer) couche f.; (of sea) fond m.; (of flowers) parterre m. **go to** ~, (aller) se coucher. ● v.i. (p.t. bedded) ~ **down,** se coucher. ~**ding** n. literie f.

bedbug /'bedbʌg/ n. punaise f.

bedclothes /'bedkləʊðz/ n. pl. couvertures f. pl. et draps m. pl.

bedevil /bɪ'devl/ v.t. (p.t. bedevilled) (confuse) embrouiller; (plague) tourmenter.

bedlam /'bedləm/ n. chahut m.

bedraggled /bɪ'drægld/ a. (untidy) débraillé.

bedridden /'bedrɪdn/ a. cloué au lit.

bedroom /'bedrʊm/ n. chambre (à coucher) f.

bedside /'bedsaɪd/ n. chevet m. ~ **book,** livre de chevet m.

bedsit, bedsitter /'bedsɪt, -'sɪtə(r)/ ns. (fam.) n. chambre meublée f., studio m.

bedspread /'bedspred/ n. dessus-de-lit m. invar.

bedtime /'bedtaɪm/ n. heure du coucher f.

bee /bi:/ *n.* abeille *f.* **make a ~-line for,** aller tout droit vers.

beech /bi:tʃ/ *n.* hêtre *m.*

beef /bi:f/ *n.* bœuf *m.* ● *v.i.* (*grumble: sl.*) rouspéter.

beefburger /'bi:fb3:gə(r)/ *n.* hamburger *m.*

beefeater /'bi:fi:tə(r)/ *n.* hallebardier *m.*

beefy /'bi:fɪ/ *a.* (**-ier, -iest**) musclé.

beehive /'bi:haɪv/ *n.* ruche *f.*

been /bi:n/ *see* be.

beer /bɪə(r)/ *n.* bière *f.*

beet /bi:t/ *n.* (*plant*) betterave *f.*

beetle /'bi:tl/ *n.* scarabée *m.*

beetroot /'bi:tru:t/ *n. invar.* (*culin.*) betterave *f.*

befall /bɪ'fɔ:l/ *v.t.* (*p.t.* **befell,** *p.p.* **befallen**) arriver à.

befit /bɪ'fɪt/ (*v.t.* (*p.t.* **befitted**) convenir à, seoir à.

before /bɪ'fɔ:(r)/ *prep.* (*time*) avant; (*place*) devant. ● *adv.* avant; (*already*) déjà. ● *conj.* ~ **leaving,** avant de partir. ~ **he leaves,** avant qu'il (ne) parte. **the day ~,** la veille. **two days ~,** deux jours avant.

beforehand /bɪ'fɔ:bænd/ *adv.* à l'avance, avant.

befriend /bɪ'frend/ *v.t.* offrir son amitié à, aider.

beg /beg/ *v.t.* (*p.t.* **begged**) (*entreat*) supplier (**to do,** de faire). ~ **(for),** (*money, food*) mendier; (*request*) solliciter, demander. ● *v.i.* ~ **(for alms),** mendier. **it is going ~ging,** personne n'en veut.

began /bɪ'gæn/ *see* begin.

beggar /'begə(r)/ *n.* mendiant(e) *m.* (*f.*); (*sl.*) individu *m.*

begin /bɪ'gɪn/ *v.t./i.* (*p.t.* **began,** *p.p.* **begun,** *pres. p.* **beginning**) commencer (**to do,** à faire). ~**ner** *n.* débutant(e) *m.* (*f.*). ~**ning** *n.* commencement *m.,* début *m.*

begrudge /bɪ'grʌdʒ/ *v.t.* (*envy*) envier; (*give unwillingly*) donner à contrecœur. ~ **doing,** faire à contrecœur.

beguile /bɪ'gaɪl/ *v.t.* tromper.

begun /bɪ'gʌn/ *see* begin.

behalf /bɪ'hɑ:f/ *n.* **on ~ of,** pour; (*as representative*) au nom de, pour (le compte de).

behave /bɪ'heɪv/ *v.i.* se conduire. ~ **(o.s.),** se conduire bien.

behaviour, (*Amer.*) **behavior** /bɪ'heɪvjə(r)/ *n.* conduite *f.,* comportement *m.*

behead /bɪ'hed/ *v.t.* décapiter.

behind /bɪ'haɪnd/ *prep.* derrière; (*in time*) en retard sur. ● *adv.* derrière; (*late*) en retard. ● *n.* (*buttocks*) derrière *m.* **leave ~,** oublier.

behold /bɪ'həʊld/ *v.t.* (*p.t.* **beheld**) (*old use*) voir.

beige /beɪʒ/ *a.* & *n.* beige (*m.*).

being /'bi:ɪŋ/ *n.* (*person*) être *m.* **bring into ~,** créer. **come into ~,** prendre naissance.

belated /bɪ'leɪtɪd/ *a.* tardif.

belch /beltʃ/ *v.i.* faire un renvoi. ● *v.t.* ~ **out,** (*smoke*) vomir. ● *n.* renvoi *m.*

belfry /'belfrɪ/ *n.* beffroi *m.*

Belg|ium /'beldʒəm/ *n.* Belgique *f.* ~**an** *a.* & *n.* belge (*m./f.*).

belie /bɪ'laɪ/ *v.t.* démentir.

belief /bɪ'li:f/ *n.* croyance *f.*; (*trust*) confiance *f.*; (*faith: relig.*) foi *f.*

believ|e /bɪ'li:v/ *v.t./i.* croire. ~**e in,** croire à; (*deity*) croire en. ~**able** *a.* croyable. ~**er** *n.* croyant(e) *m.* (*f.*).

belittle /bɪ'lɪtl/ *v.t.* déprécier.

bell /bel/ *n.* cloche *f.*; (*small*) clochette *f.*; (*on door*) sonnette *f.*; (*of phone*) sonnerie *f.*

belligerent /bɪ'lɪdʒərənt/ *a.* & *n.* belligérant(e) (*m.* (*f.*)).

bellow /'beləʊ/ *v.t./i.* beugler.

bellows /'beləʊz/ *n. pl.* soufflet *m.*

belly /'belɪ/ *n.* ventre *m.* ~**-ache** *n.* mal au ventre *m.*

bellyful /'belɪfʊl/ *n.* **have a ~,** en avoir plein le dos.

belong /bɪ'lɒŋ/ *v.i.* ~ **to,** appartenir à; (*club*) être membre de.

belongings /bɪ'lɒŋɪŋz/ *n. pl.* affaires *f. pl.*

beloved /bɪ'lʌvɪd/ *a.* & *n.* bienaimé(e) (*m.* (*f.*)).

below /bɪ'ləʊ/ *prep.* au-dessous de; (*fig.*) indigne de. ● *adv.* en dessous; (*on page*) ci-dessous.

belt /belt/ *n.* ceinture *f.*; (*techn.*) courroie *f.*; (*fig.*) région *f.* ● *v.t.* (*hit: sl.*) rosser. ● *v.i.* (*rush: sl.*) filer à toute allure.

beltway /'beltweɪ/ *n.* (*Amer.*) périphérique *m.*

bemused /bɪ'mju:zd/ *a.* (*confused*) stupéfié; (*thoughtful*) pensif.

bench /bentʃ/ *n.* banc *m.*; (*working-table*) établi *m.* **the ~,** (*jurid.*) la magistrature (assise). ~**-mark** *n.* repère *m.*

bend /bend/ *v.t./i.* (*p.t.* **bent**) (se) courber; (*arm, leg*) plier. ● *n.*

courbe *f.*; (*in road*) virage *m.*; (*of arm, knee*) pli *m.* ~ **down** *or* **over,** se pencher.

beneath /br'ni:θ/ *prep.* sous, au-dessous de; (*fig.*) indigne de. ● *adv.* (au-)dessous.

benefactor /'benɪfæktə(r)/ *n.* bien-fai|teur, -trice *m.*, *f.*

beneficial /benɪ'fɪʃl/ *a.* avantageux, favorable.

benefit /'benɪfɪt/ *n.* avantage *m.*; (*allowance*) allocation *f.* ● *v.t.* (*p.t.* **benefited,** *pres. p.* **benefiting**) (*be useful to*) profiter à; (*do good to*) faire du bien à. ~ **from,** tirer profit de.

benevolen|t /br'nevələnt/ *a.* bienveillant. ~**ce** *n.* bienveillance *f.*

benign /br'nam/ *a.* (*kindly*) bienveillant; (*med.*) bénin.

bent /bent/ *see* **bend.** ● *n.* (*talent*) aptitude *f.*; (*inclination*) penchant *m.* ● *a.* tordu; (*sl.*) corrompu. ~ **on doing,** décidé à faire.

bequeath /br'kwi:ð/ *v.t.* léguer.

bequest /br'kwest/ *n.* legs *m.*

bereave|d /br'ri:vd/ *a.* the ~d **wife/** *etc.*, la femme/*etc.* du disparu. ~**ment** *n.* deuil *m.*

beret /'bereɪ/ *n.* béret *m.*

Bermuda /bə'mju:də/ *n.* Bermudes *f. pl.*

berry /'berɪ/ *n.* baie *f.*

berserk /bə's3:k/ *a.* **go ~,** devenir fou furieux.

berth /b3:θ/ *n.* (*in train, ship*) couchette *f.*; (*anchorage*) mouillage *m.* ● *v.i.* mouiller. **give a wide ~ to,** éviter.

beseech /br'si:tʃ/ *v.t.* (*p.t.* **besought**) implorer, supplier.

beset /br'set/ *v.t.* (*p.t.* **beset,** *pres. p.* **besetting**) (*attack*) assaillir; (*surround*) entourer.

beside /br'saɪd/ *prep.* à côté de. ~ **o.s.,** hors de soi. ~ **the point,** sans rapport.

besides /br'saɪdz/ *prep.* en plus de; (*except*) excepté. ● *adv.* en plus.

besiege /br'si:dʒ/ *v.t.* assiéger.

best /best/ *a.* meilleur. **the ~ book/** *etc.*, le meilleur livre/*etc.* ● *adv.* (**the**) ~, (*sing etc.*) le mieux. ● *n.* **the ~, (one),** le meilleur, la meilleure. ~ **man,** garçon d'honneur *m.* **the ~ part of,** la plus grande partie de. **the ~ thing is to . . .,** le mieux est de . . . **do one's ~,**

faire de son mieux. **make the ~ of,** s'accommoder de.

bestow /br'stəʊ/ *v.t.* accorder.

best-seller /best'selə(r)/ *n.* best-seller *m.*, succès de librairie *m.*

bet /bet/ *n.* pari *m.* ● *v.t./i.* (*p.t.* **bet** *or* **betted,** *pres. p.* **betting**) parier.

betray /br'treɪ/ *v.t.* trahir. ~**al** *n.* trahison *f.*

better /'betə(r)/ *a.* meilleur. ● *adv.* mieux. ● *v.t.* (*improve*) améliorer; (*do better than*) surpasser. ~ **one's ~s,** ses supérieurs *m. pl.* **be ~ off,** (*financially*) avoir plus d'argent. **he's ~ off at home,** il est mieux chez lui. **I had ~ go,** je ferais mieux de partir. **the ~ part of,** la plus grande partie de. **get ~,** s'améliorer; (*recover*) se remettre. **get the ~ of,** l'emporter sur. **so much the ~,** tant mieux.

betting-shop /'betɪŋʃɒp/ *n.* bureau de P.M.U. *m.*

between /br'twi:n/ *prep.* entre. ● *adv.* **in ~,** au milieu.

beverage /'bevərɪdʒ/ *n.* boisson *f.*

bevy /'bevɪ/ *n.* essaim *m.*

beware /br'weə(r)/ *v.i.* prendre garde (**of, à**).

bewilder /br'wɪldə(r)/ *v.t.* désorienter, embarrasser. ~**ment** *n.* désorientation *f.*

bewitch /br'wɪtʃ/ *v.t.* enchanter.

beyond /br'jɒnd/ *prep.* au-delà de; (*doubt, reach*) hors de; (*besides*) excepté. ● *adv.* au-delà. **it is ~ me,** ça me dépasse.

bias /'baɪəs/ *n.* (*inclination*) penchant *m.*; (*prejudice*) préjugé *m.* ● *v.t.* (*p.t.* **biased**) influencer. ~**ed** *a.* partial.

bib /bɪb/ *n.* bavoir *m.*

Bible /'baɪbl/ *n.* Bible *f.*

biblical /'bɪblɪkl/ *a.* biblique.

bicarbonate /baɪ'kɑ:bənət/ *n.* bicarbonate *m.*

biceps /'baɪseps/ *n.* biceps *m.*

bicker /'bɪkə(r)/ *v.i.* se chamailler.

bicycle /'baɪsɪkl/ *n.* bicyclette *f.* ● *v.i.* faire de la bicyclette.

bid¹ /bɪd/ *n.* (*at auction*) offre *f.*, enchère *f.*; (*attempt*) tentative *f.* ● *v.t./i.* (*p.t. & p.p.* **bid,** *pres. p.* **bidding**) (*offer*) faire une offre *or* une enchère (de). **the highest ~der,** le plus offrant.

bid² /bɪd/ *v.t.* (*p.t.* **bade** /bæd/, *p.p.* **bidden** *or* **bid,** *pres. p.* **bidding**) ordonner; (*say*) dire. **~ding** *n.* ordre *m.*

bide /baɪd/ *v.t.* **~ one's time,** attendre le bon moment.

biennial /baɪˈenɪəl/ *a.* biennal.

bifocals /baɪˈfəʊklz/ *n. pl.* lunettes bifocales *f. pl.*

big /bɪg/ *a.* (**bigger, biggest**) grand; (*in bulk*) gros; (*generous: sl.*) généreux; ● *adv.* (*fam.*) en grand; (*earn: fam.*) gros. **~ business,** les grandes affaires. **~-headed** *a.* prétentieux. **~ shot,** (*sl.*) huile *f.* **think ~,** (*fam.*) voir grand.

bigam|y /ˈbɪgəmɪ/ *n.* bigamie *f.* **~ist** *n.* bigame *m./f.* **~ous** *a.* bigame.

bigot /ˈbɪgət/ *n.* fanatique *m./f.* **~ed** *a.* fanatique. **~ry** *n.* fanatisme *m.*

bike /baɪk/ *n.* (*fam.*) vélo *m.*

bikini /bɪˈkiːnɪ/ *n.* (*pl.* **-is**) bikini *m.*

bilberry /ˈbɪlbərɪ/ *n.* myrtille *f.*

bile /baɪl/ *n.* bile *f.*

bilingual /baɪˈlɪŋgwəl/ *a.* bilingue.

bilious /ˈbɪlɪəs/ *a.* bilieux.

bill [1] /bɪl/ *n.* (*invoice*) facture *f.*; (*in hotel, for gas, etc.*) note *f.*; (*in restaurant*) addition *f.*; (*of sale*) acte *m.*; (*pol.*) projet de loi *m.*; (*banknote: Amer.*) billet de banque *m.* ● *v.t.* (*person: comm.*) envoyer la facture à. (*theatre*) **on the ~,** à l'affiche.

bill [2] /bɪl/ *n.* (*of bird*) bec *m.*

billboard /ˈbɪlbɔːd/ *n.* panneau d'affichage *m.*

billet /ˈbɪlɪt/ *n.* cantonnement *m.* ● *v.t.* (*p.t.* **billeted**) cantonner (**on,** chez).

billfold /ˈbɪlfəʊld/ *n.* (*Amer.*) portefeuille *m.*

billiards /ˈbɪljədz/ *n.* billard *m.*

billion /ˈbɪljən/ *n.* billion *m.*; (*Amer.*) milliard *m.*

billy-goat /ˈbɪlɪgəʊt/ *n.* bouc *m.*

bin /bɪn/ *n.* (*for rubbish, litter*) boîte (à ordures) *f.*, poubelle *f.*; (*for bread*) huche *f.*, coffre *m.*

binary /ˈbaɪnərɪ/ *a.* binaire.

bind /baɪnd/ *v.t.* (*p.t.* **bound**) lier; (*book*) relier; (*jurid.*) obliger. ● *n.* (*bore: sl.*) plaie *f.* **be ~ing on,** être obligatoire pour.

binding /ˈbaɪndɪŋ/ *n.* reliure *f.*

binge /bɪndʒ/ *n.* **go on a ~,** (*spree: sl.*) faire la bringue.

bingo /ˈbɪŋgəʊ/ *n.* loto *m.*

binoculars /bɪˈnɒkjʊləz/ *n. pl.* jumelles *f. pl.*

biochemistry /baɪəʊˈkemɪstrɪ/ *n.* biochimie *f.*

biodegradable /baɪəʊdɪˈgreɪdəbl/ *a.* biodégradable.

biograph|y /baɪˈɒgrəfɪ/ *n.* biographie *f.* **~er** *n.* biographe *m./f.*

biolog|y /baɪˈɒlədʒɪ/ *n.* biologie *f.* **~ical** /-əˈlɒdʒɪkl/ *a.* biologique. **~ist** *n.* biologiste *m./f.*

biorhythm /ˈbaɪəʊrɪðəm/ *n.* biorythme *m.*

birch /bɜːtʃ/ *n.* (*tree*) bouleau *m.*; (*whip*) verge *f.*, fouet *m.*

bird /bɜːd/ *n.* oiseau *m.*; (*fam.*) individu *m.*; (*girl: sl.*) poule *f.*

Biro /ˈbaɪərəʊ/ *n.* (*pl.* **-os**) (P.) stylo à bille *m.*, Bic *m.* (P.).

birth /bɜːθ/ *n.* naissance *f.* **give ~,** accoucher. **~ certificate,** acte de naissance *m.* **~-control** *n.* contrôle des naissances *m.* **~-rate** *n.* natalité *f.*

birthday /ˈbɜːθdeɪ/ *n.* anniversaire *m.*

birthmark /ˈbɜːθmɑːk/ *n.* tache de vin *f.*, envie *f.*

biscuit /ˈbɪskɪt/ *n.* biscuit *m.*; (*Amer.*) petit pain (au lait) *m.*

bisect /baɪˈsekt/ *v.t.* couper en deux.

bishop /ˈbɪʃəp/ *n.* évêque *m.*

bit [1] /bɪt/ *n.* morceau *m.*; (*of horse*) mors *m.*; (*of tool*) mèche *f.* **a ~,** (*a little*) un peu.

bit [2] /bɪt/ *see* bite.

bit [3] /bɪt/ *n.* (*comput.*) bit *m.*, élement binaire *m.*

bitch /bɪtʃ/ *n.* chienne *f.*; (*woman: fam.*) garce *f.* ● *v.i.* (*grumble: fam.*) râler. **~y** *a.* (*fam.*) vache.

bite /baɪt/ *v.t./i.* (*p.t.* **bit,** *p.p.* **bitten**) mordre. ● *n.* morsure *f.*; (*by insect*) piqûre *f.*; (*mouthful*) bouchée *f.* **~ one's nails,** se ronger les ongles. **have a ~,** manger un morceau.

biting /ˈbaɪtɪŋ/ *a.* mordant.

bitter /ˈbɪtə(r)/ *a.* amer; (*weather*) glacial, âpre. ● *n.* bière anglaise *f.* **~ly** *adv.* amèrement. **it is ~ly cold,** il fait un temps glacial. **~ness** *n.* amertume *f.*

bitty /ˈbɪtɪ/ *a.* décousu.

bizarre /bɪˈzɑː(r)/ *a.* bizarre.

blab /blæb/ *v.i.* (*p.t.* **blabbed**) jaser.

black /blæk/ *a.* (**-er, -est**) noir. ● *n.* (*colour*) noir *m.* **B~,** (*person*) Noir(e) *m.* (*f.*). ● *v.t.* noircir; (*goods*) boycotter. **~ and blue,** couvert de bleus. **~ eye,** œil poché *m.* **~ ice,** verglas *m.* **~ list,** liste noire *f.* **~ market,** marché noir *m.* **~ sheep,** brebis galeuse *f.* **~ spot,** point noir *m.*

blackberry /'blækbərɪ/ n. mûre f.
blackbird /'blækbɜ:d/ n. merle m.
blackboard /'blækbɔ:d/ n. tableau noir m.
blackcurrant /'blækkʌrənt/ n. cassis m.
blacken /'blækən/ v.t./i. noircir.
blackhead /'blækhed/ n. point noir m.
blackleg /'blækleg/ n. jaune m.
blacklist /'blæklɪst/ v.t. mettre sur la liste noire or à l'index.
blackmail /'blækmeɪl/ n. chantage m. ● v.t. faire chanter. ~er n. maître-chanteur m.
blackout /'blækaʊt/ n. panne d'électricité f.; (med.) syncope f.
blacksmith /'blæksmɪθ/ n. forgeron m.
bladder /'blædə(r)/ n. vessie f.
blade /bleɪd/ n. (of knife etc.) lame f.; (of propeller, oar) pale f. ~ of grass, brin d'herbe m.
blame /bleɪm/ v.t. accuser. ● n. faute f. ~ s.o. for sth., reprocher qch. à qn. he is to ~, il est responsable (for, de). ~less a. irréprochable.
bland /blænd/ a. (-er, -est) (gentle) doux; (insipid) fade.
blank /blæŋk/ a. blanc; (look) vide; (cheque) en blanc. ● n. blanc m. ~ (cartridge), cartouche à blanc f.
blanket /'blæŋkɪt/ n. couverture f.; (layer: fig.) couche f. ● v.t (p.t. blanketed) recouvrir.
blare /bleə(r)/ v.t./i. beugler. ● n. vacarme n., beuglement m.
blarney /'blɑ:nɪ/ n. boniment m.
blasé /'blɑ:zeɪ/ a. blasé.
blasphem|y /'blæsfəmɪ/ n. blasphème m. ~ous a. blasphématoire; (person) blasphémateur.
blast /blɑ:st/ n. explosion f.; (wave of air) souffle m.; (of wind) rafale f.; (noise from siren etc.) coup m. ● v.t. (blow up) faire sauter. ● a. (fam.) maudit, fichu. ~-furnace n. haut fourneau m. ~ off, être mis à feu. ~-off n. mise à feu f.
blatant /'bleɪtnt/ a. (obvious) flagrant; (shameless) éhonté.
blaze[1] /bleɪz/ n. flamme f.; (conflagration) incendie m.; (fig.) éclat m. ● v.i. (fire) flamber; (sky, eyes, etc.) flamboyer.
blaze[2] /bleɪz/ v.t. ~ a trail, montrer or marquer la voie.
blazer /'bleɪzə(r)/ n. blazer m.

bleach /bli:tʃ/ n. décolorant m.; (for domestic use) eau de Javel f. ● v.t.i. blanchir; (hair) décolorer.
bleak /bli:k/ a. (-er, -est) morne.
bleary /'blɪərɪ/ a. (eyes) voilé.
bleat /bli:t/ n. bêlement m. ● v.i. bêler.
bleed /bli:d/ v.t./i. (p.t. bled) saigner.
bleep /bli:p/ n. bip m. ~er n. bip m.
blemish /'blemɪʃ/ n. tare f., défaut m.; (on reputation) tache f. ● v.t. entacher.
blend /blend/ v.t./i. (se) mélanger. ● n. mélange m. ~er n. mixer n.
bless /bles/ v.t. bénir. be ~ed with, avoir le bonheur de posséder. ~ing n. bénédiction f.; (benefit) avantage m.; (stroke of luck) chance f.
blessed /'blesɪd/ a. (holy) saint; (damned: fam.) sacré.
blew /blu:/ see blow[1].
blight /blaɪt/ n. (disease: bot.) rouille f.; (fig.) fléau m.
blind /blaɪnd/ a. aveugle. ● v.t. aveugler. ● n. (on window) store m.; (deception) feinte f. be ~ to, ne pas voir. ~ alley, impasse f. ~ corner, virage sans visibilité m. ~ man, aveugle m. ~ spot, (auto.) angle mort m. ~ers n. pl. (Amer.) œillères f. pl. ~ly adv. aveuglément. ~ness n. cécité f.
blindfold /'blaɪndfəʊld/ a. & adv. les yeux bandés. ● n. bandeau m. ● v.t. bander les yeux à.
blink /blɪŋk/ v.i. cligner des yeux; (of light) clignoter.
blinkers /'blɪŋkəz/ n. pl. œillères f. pl.
bliss /blɪs/ n. félicité f. ~ful a. bienheureux. ~fully adv. joyeusement, merveilleusement.
blister /'blɪstə(r)/ n. ampoule f. (on paint) cloque f. ● v.i. se couvrir d'ampoules; cloquer.
blithe /blaɪð/ a. joyeux.
blitz /blɪts/ n. (aviat.) raid éclair m. ● v.t. bombarder.
blizzard /'blɪzəd/ n. tempête de neige f.
bloated /'bləʊtɪd/ a. gonflé.
bloater /'bləʊtə(r)/ n. hareng saur m.
blob /blɒb/ n. (drop) (grosse) goutte f.; (stain) tache f.
bloc /blɒk/ n. bloc m.
block /blɒk/ n. bloc m.; (buildings) pâté de maisons m.; (in pipe) obstruction f. ~ (of flats), immeuble m. ● v.t. bloquer. ~ letters, majus-

cules *f. pl.* ~**age** *n.* obstruction *f.* ~-**buster** *n.* gros succès *m.*

blockade /blɒˈkeɪd/ *n.* blocus *m.* ● *v.t.* bloquer.

bloke /bləʊk/ *n.* (*fam.*) type *m.*

blond /blɒnd/ *a. & n.* blond (*m.*).

blonde /blɒnd/ *a. & n.* blonde (*f.*).

blood /blʌd/ *n.* sang *m.* ● *a.* (*donor, bath, etc.*) de sang; (*bank, poisoning, etc.*) du sang; (*group, vessel*) sanguin. ~-**curdling** *a.* à tourner le sang. ~**less** *a.* (*fig.*) pacifique. ~-**pressure** *n.* tension artérielle *f.* ~**test**, prise de sang *f.*

bloodhound /ˈblʌdhaʊnd/ *n.* limier *m.*

bloodshed /ˈblʌdʃed/ *n.* effusion de sang *f.*

bloodshot /ˈblʌdʃɒt/ *a.* injecté de sang.

bloodstream /ˈblʌdstriːm/ *n.* sang *m.*

bloodthirsty /ˈblʌdθɜːstɪ/ *a.* sanguinaire.

bloody /ˈblʌdɪ/ *a.* (-**ier, -iest**) sanglant; (*sl.*) sacré. ● *adv.* (*sl.*) vachement. ~-**minded** *a.* (*fam.*) hargneux, obstiné.

bloom /bluːm/ *n.* fleur *f.* ● *v.i.* fleurir; (*fig.*) s'épanouir.

bloomer /ˈbluːmə(r)/ *n.* (*sl.*) gaffe *f.*

blossom /ˈblɒsəm/ *n.* fleur(s) *f.* (*pl.*). ● *v.i.* fleurir; (*person: fig.*) s'épanouir.

blot /blɒt/ *n.* tache *f.* ● *v.t.* (*p.t.* **blotted**) tacher; (*dry*) sécher. ~ **out**, effacer. ~**ter**, ~**ting-paper** *ns.* buvard *m.*

blotch /blɒtʃ/ *n.* tache *f.* ~**y** *a.* couvert de taches.

blouse /blaʊz/ *n.* chemisier *m.*

blow [1] /bləʊ/ *v.t./i.* (*p.t.* **blew**, *p.p.* **blown**) souffler; (*fuse*) (faire) sauter; (*squander: sl.*) claquer; (*opportunity*) rater. ~ **one's nose**, se moucher. ~ **a whistle**, siffler. ~ **away** *or* **off**, emporter. ~-**dry** *v.t.* sécher; *n.* brushing *m.* ~ **out**, (*candle*) souffler. ~-**out** *n.* (*of tyre*) éclatement *m.* ~ **over**, passer. ~ **up**, (faire) sauter; (*tyre*) gonfler; (*photo.*) agrandir.

blow [2] /bləʊ/ *n.* coup *m.*

blowlamp /ˈbləʊlæmp/ *n.* chalumeau *m.*

blown /bləʊn/ *see* blow [1].

blowtorch /ˈbləʊtɔːtʃ/ *n.* (*Amer.*) chalumeau *m.*

blowy /ˈbləʊɪ/ *a.* **it is** ~, il y a du vent.

bludgeon /ˈblʌdʒən/ *n.* gourdin *m.* ● *v.t.* matraquer.

blue /bluː/ *a.* (-**er, -est**) bleu; (*film*) porno. ● *n.* bleu *m.* **come out of the** ~, être inattendu. **have the** ~**s**, avoir le cafard.

bluebell /ˈbluːbel/ *n.* jacinthe des bois *f.*

bluebottle /ˈbluːbɒtl/ *n.* mouche à viande *f.*

blueprint /ˈbluːprɪnt/ *n.* plan *m.*

bluff [1] /blʌf/ *v.t./i.* bluffer. ● *n.* bluff *m.* **call. s.o.'s** ~, dire chiche à qn.

bluff [2] /blʌf/ *a.* (*person*) brusque.

blunder /ˈblʌndə(r)/ *v.i.* faire une gaffe; (*move*) avancer à tâtons. ● *n.* gaffe *f.*

blunt /blʌnt/ *a.* (*knife*) émoussé; (*person*) brusque. ● *v.t.* émousser. ~**ly** *adv.* carrément. ~**ness** *n.* brusquerie *f.*

blur /blɜː(r)/ *n.* tache floue *f.* ● *v.t.* (*p.t.* **blurred**) rendre flou.

blurb /blɜːb/ *n.* résumé publicitaire *m.*

blurt /blɜːt/ *v.t.* ~ **out**, lâcher, dire.

blush /blʌʃ/ *v.i.* rougir. ● *n.* rougeur *f.* ~**er** *n.* blush *m.*

bluster /ˈblʌstə(r)/ *v.i.* (*wind*) faire rage; (*swagger*) fanfaronner. ~**y** *a.* à bourrasques.

boar /bɔː(r)/ *n.* sanglier *m.*

board /bɔːd/ *n.* planche *f.*; (*for notices*) tableau *m.*; (*food*) pension *f.*; (*committee*) conseil *m.* ● *v.t./i.* (*bus, train*) monter dans; (*naut.*) monter à bord (de). ~ **of directors**, conseil d'administration *m.* **go by the** ~, passer à l'as. **full** ~, pension complète *f.* **half** ~, demi-pension *f.* **on** ~, à bord. ~ **up**, boucher. ~ **with**, être en pension chez. ~**er** *n.* pensionnaire *m./f.* ~**ing-house** *n.* pension (de famille) *f.* ~**ing-school** *n.* pensionnat *m.*, pension *f.*

boast /bəʊst/ *v.i.* se vanter (**about**, de). ● *v.t.* s'enorgueillir de. ● *n.* vantardise *f.* ~**er** *n.* vantard(e) *m.* (*f.*). ~**ful** *a.* vantard. ~**fully** *adv.* en se vantant.

boat /bəʊt/ *n.* bateau *m.*; (*small*) canot *m.* **in the same** ~, logé à la même enseigne. ~**ing** *n.* canotage *m.*

boatswain /ˈbəʊsn/ *n.* maître d'équipage *m.*

bob [1] /bɒb/ *v.i.* (*p.t.* **bobbed**). ~ **up and down**, monter et descendre.

bob [2] /bɒb/ *n. invar.* (*sl.*) shilling *m.*

bobby /ˈbɒbɪ/ *n.* (*fam.*) flic *m.*

bobsleigh /'bɒbsleɪ/ *n.* bob-(sleigh) *m.*

bode /bəʊd/ *v.i.* ~ **well/ill**, être de bon/mauvais augure.

bodily /'bɒdɪlɪ/ *a.* physique, corporel. ● *adv.* physiquement; (*in person*) en personne.

body /'bɒdɪ/ *n.* corps *m.*; (*mass*) masse *f.*; (*organization*) organisme *m.* ~**(work)**, (*auto.*) carrosserie *f.* **the main ~ of**, le gros de. ~**builder** *n.* culturiste *m./f.* ~**building** *n.* culturisme *m.*

bodyguard /'bɒdɪgɑːd/ *n.* garde du corps *m.*

bog /bɒg/ *n.* marécage *m.* ● *v.t.* (*p.t.* **bogged**). **get ~ged down**, s'embourber.

boggle /'bɒgl/ *v.i.* **the mind ~s**, on est stupéfait.

bogus /'bəʊgəs/ *a.* faux.

bogy /'bəʊgɪ/ *n.* (*annoyance*) embêtement *m.* ~**(man)**, croquemitaine *m.*

boil [1] /bɔɪl/ *n.* furoncle *m.*

boil [2] /bɔɪl/ *v.t./i.* (faire) bouillir. **bring to the ~**, porter à ébullition. **~ down to**, se ramener à. **~ over**, déborder. **~ing hot**, bouillant. **~ing point**, point d'ébullition *m.* **~ed** *a.* (*egg*) à la coque; (*potatoes*) à l'eau.

boiler /'bɔɪlə(r)/ *n.* chaudière *f.* **~ suit**, bleu (de travail) *m.*

boisterous /'bɔɪstərəs/ *a.* tapageur.

bold /bəʊld/ *a.* (**-er, -est**) hardi; (*cheeky*) effronté; (*type*) gras. **~ness** *n.* hardiesse *f.*

Bolivia /bə'lɪvɪə/ *n.* Bolivie *f.* **~n** *a.* & *n.* bolivien(ne) (*m.* (*f.*)).

bollard /'bɒləd/ *n.* (*on road*) borne *f.*

bolster /'bəʊlstə(r)/ *n.* traversin *m.* ● *v.t.* soutenir.

bolt /bəʊlt/ *n.* verrou *m.*; (*for nut*) boulon *m.*; (*lightning*) éclair *m.* ● *v.t.* (*door etc.*) verrouiller; (*food*) engouffrer. ● *v.i.* se sauver. **~ upright**, tout droit.

bomb /bɒm/ *n.* bombe *f.* ● *v.t.* bombarder. **~ scare**, alerte à la bombe *f.* **~er** *n.* (*aircraft*) bombardier *m.*; (*person*) plastiqueur *m.*

bombard /bɒm'bɑːd/ *v.t.* bombarder.

bombastic /bɒm'bæstɪk/ *a.* grandiloquent.

bombshell /'bɒmʃel/ *n.* **be a ~**, tomber comme une bombe.

bona fide /bəʊnə'faɪdɪ/ *a.* de bonne foi.

bond /bɒnd/ *n.* (*agreement*) engagement *m.*; (*link*) lien *m.*; (*comm.*) obligation *f.*, bon *m.* **in ~**, (*entreposé*) en douane.

bondage /'bɒndɪdʒ/ *n.* esclavage *m.*

bone /bəʊn/ *n.* os *m.*; (*of fish*) arête *f.* ● *v.t.* désosser. **~-dry** *a.* tout à fait sec. **~ idle**, paresseux comme une couleuvre.

bonfire /'bɒnfaɪə(r)/ *n.* feu *m.*; (*for celebration*) feu de joie *m.*

bonnet /'bɒnɪt/ *n.* (*hat*) bonnet *m.*; (*of vehicle*) capot *m.*

bonus /'bəʊnəs/ *n.* prime *f.*

bony /'bəʊnɪ/ *a.* (**-ier, -iest**) (*thin*) osseux; (*meat*) plein d'os; (*fish*) plein d'arêtes.

boo /buː/ *int.* hou. ● *v.t./i.* huer. ● *n.* huée *f.*

boob /buːb/ *n.* (*blunder*: *sl.*) gaffe *f.* ● *v.i.* (*sl.*) gaffer.

booby-trap /'buːbɪtræp/ *n.* engin piégé *m.* ● *v.t.* (*p.t.* **-trapped**) piéger.

book /bʊk/ *n.* livre *m.*; (*of tickets etc.*) carnet *m.*, **~s**, (*comm.*) comptes *m. pl.* ● *v.t.* (*reserve*) réserver; (*driver*) dresser un P.V. à; (*player*) prendre le nom de; (*write down*) inscrire. ● *v.i.* retenir des places. **~able** *a.* qu'on peut retenir. **(fully) ~ed**, complet. **~ing office**, guichet *m.*

bookcase /'bʊkkeɪs/ *n.* bibliothèque *f.*

bookkeeping /'bʊkkiːpɪŋ/ *n.* comptabilité *f.*

booklet /'bʊklɪt/ *n.* brochure *f.*

bookmaker /'bʊkmeɪkə(r)/ *n.* bookmaker *m.*

bookseller /'bʊkselə(r)/ *n.* libraire *m./f.*

bookshop /'bʊkʃɒp/ *n.* librairie *f.*

bookstall /'bʊkstɔːl/ *n.* kiosque (à journaux) *m.*

boom /buːm/ *v.i.* (*gun, wind, etc.*) gronder; (*trade*) prospérer. ● *n.* grondement *m.*; (*comm.*) boom *m.*, prospérité *f.*

boon /buːn/ *n.* (*benefit*) aubaine *f.*

boost /buːst/ *v.t.* stimuler; (*morale*) remonter; (*price*) augmenter; (*publicize*) faire de la réclame pour. ● *n.* **give a ~ to**, = boost.

boot /buːt/ *n.* (*knee-length*); botte *f.*; (*ankle-length*) chaussure (montante) *f.*; (*for walking*) chaussure de marche *f.*; (*sport*) chaussure de sport *f.*; (*of vehicle*) coffre *m.*

● *v.t./i.* **~ up,** (*comput.*) démarrer, lancer (le programme). **get the ~,** (*sl.*) être mis à la porte.

booth /buːð/ *n.* (*for telephone*) cabine *f.*; (*at fair*) baraque *f.*

booty /'buːtɪ/ *n.* butin *m.*

booze /buːz/ *v.i.* (*fam.*) boire (beaucoup). ● *n.* (*fam.*) alcool *m.*; (*spree*) beuverie *f.*

border /'bɔːdə(r)/ *n.* (*edge*) bord *m.*; (*frontier*) frontière *f.*; (*in garden*) bordure *f.* ● *v.i.* **~ on,** (*be next to, come close to*) être voisin de, avoisiner.

borderline /'bɔːdəlaɪn/ *n.* ligne de démarcation *f.* **~ case,** cas limite *m.*

bore¹ /bɔː(r)/ *see* **bear²**.

bore² /bɔː(r)/ *v.t./i.* (*techn.*) forer.

bore³ /bɔː(r)/ *v.t.* ennuyer. ● *n.* raseu|r, -se *m.*, *f.*; (*thing*) ennui *m.* **be ~d,** s'ennuyer. **~dom** *n.* ennui *m.* **boring** *a.* ennuyeux.

born /bɔːn/ *a.* né. **be ~,** naître.

borne /bɔːn/ *see* **bear²**.

borough /'bʌrə/ *n.* municipalité *f.*

borrow /'bɒrəʊ/ *v.t.* emprunter (**from,** à). **~ing** *n.* emprunt *m.*

bosom /'bʊzəm/ *n.* sein *m.* **~ friend,** ami(e) intime *m.* (*f.*).

boss /bɒs/ *n.* (*fam.*) patron(ne) *m.* (*f.*) ● *v.t.* **~ (about),** (*fam.*) donner des ordres à, régenter.

bossy /'bɒsɪ/ *a.* autoritaire.

botan|y /'bɒtənɪ/ *n.* botanique *f.* **~ical** /bə'tænɪkl/ *a.* botanique. **~ist** *n.* botaniste *m./f.*

botch /bɒtʃ/ *v.t.* bâcler, saboter.

both /bəʊθ/ *a.* les deux. ● *pron.* tous *or* toutes (les) deux, l'un(e) et l'autre. ● *adv.* à la fois. **~ the books,** les deux livres. **we ~ agree,** nous sommes tous les deux d'accord. **I bought ~ (of them),** j'ai acheté les deux. **I saw ~ of you,** je vous ai vus tous les deux. **~ Paul and Anne,** (et) Paul et Anne.

bother /'bɒðə(r)/ *v.t.* (*annoy, worry*) ennuyer; (*disturb*) déranger. ● *v.i.* se déranger. ● *n.* ennui *m.*; (*effort*) peine *f.* **don't ~** (*calling*), ce n'est pas la peine (d'appeler). **don't ~ about us,** ne t'inquiète pas pour nous. **I can't be ~ed,** j'ai la flemme. **it's no ~,** ce n'est rien.

bottle /'bɒtl/ *n.* bouteille *f.*; (*for baby*) biberon *m.* ● *v.t.* mettre en bouteille(s). **~ bank,** collecteur (de verre usagé) *m.* **~-opener** *n.* ouvre-bouteille(s) *m.* **~ up,** contenir.

bottleneck /'bɒtlnek/ *n.* (*traffic jam*) bouchon *m.*

bottom /'bɒtəm/ *n.* fond *m.*; (*of hill, page, etc.*) bas *m.*; (*buttocks*) derrière *m.* ● *a.* inférieur, du bas. **~less** *a.* insondable.

bough /baʊ/ *n.* rameau *m.*

bought /bɔːt/ *see* **buy.**

boulder /'bəʊldə(r)/ *n.* rocher *m.*

boulevard /'buːləvɑːd/ *n.* boulevard *m.*

bounce /baʊns/ *v.i.* rebondir; (*person*) faire des bonds, bondir; (*cheques: sl.*) être refusé. ● *v.t.* faire rebondir. ● *n.* rebond *m.*

bouncer /'baʊnsə(r)/ *n.* videur *m.*

bound¹ /baʊnd/ *v.i.* (*leap*) bondir. ● *n.* bond *m.*

bound² /baʊnd/ *see* **bind.** ● *a.* **be ~ for,** être en route pour, aller. vers. **~ to,** (*obliged*) obligé de; (*certain*) sûr de.

boundary /'baʊndrɪ/ *n.* limite *f.*

bound|s /baʊndz/ *n. pl.* limites *f. pl.* **out of ~s,** interdit. **~ed by,** limité par. **~less** *a.* sans bornes.

bouquet /bʊ'keɪ/ *n.* bouquet *m.*

bout /baʊt/ *n.* période *f.*; (*med.*) accès *m.*; (*boxing*) combat *m.*

boutique /buː'tiːk/ *n.* boutique (de mode) *f.*

bow¹ /bəʊ/ *n.* (*weapon*) arc *m.*; (*mus.*) archet *m.*; (*knot*) nœud *m.* **~-legged** *a.* aux jambes arquées. **~-tie** *n.* nœud papillon *m.*

bow² /baʊ/ *n.* (*with head*) salut *m.*; (*with body*) révérence *f.* ● *v.t./i.* (s')incliner.

bow³ /baʊ/ *n.* (*naut.*) proue *f.*

bowels /'baʊəlz/ *n. pl.* intestins *m. pl.*; (*fig.*) entrailles *f. pl.*

bowl¹ /bəʊl/ *n.* cuvette *f.*; (*for food*) bol *m.*; (*for soup etc.*) assiette creuse *f.*

bowl² /bəʊl/ *n.* (*ball*) boule *f.* ● *v.t./i.* (*cricket*) lancer. **~ over,** bouleverser. **~ing** *n.* jeu de boules *m.* **~ing-alley** *n.* bowling *m.*

bowler¹ /'bəʊlə(r)/ *n.* (*cricket*) lanceur *m.*

bowler² /'bəʊlə(r)/ *n.* **~ (hat),** (chapeau) melon *m.*

box¹ /bɒks/ *n.* boîte *f.*; (*cardboard*) carton *m.*; (*theatre*) loge *f.* ● *v.t.* mettre en boîte. **the ~,** (*fam.*) la télé. **~ in,** enfermer. **~-office** *n.* bureau de location *m.* **Boxing Day,** le lendemain de Noël.

box 285 **break**

box² /bɒks/ v.t./i. (sport) boxer. ~ s.o.'s ears, gifler qn. ~ing n. boxe f.; a. de boxe.

boy /bɔɪ/ n. garçon m. ~-friend n. (petit) ami m. ~hood n. enfance f. ~ish a. enfantin, de garçon.

boycott /'bɔɪkɒt/ v.t. boycotter. ● n. boycottage m.

bra /brɑː/ n. soutien-gorge m.

brace /breɪs/ n. (fastener) attache f.; (dental) appareil m.; (for bit) vilbrequin m. ~s, (for trousers) bretelles f. pl. ● v.t. soutenir. ~ o.s., rassembler ses forces.

bracelet /'breɪslɪt/ n. bracelet m.

bracing /'breɪsɪŋ/ a. vivifiant.

bracken /'brækən/ n. fougère f.

bracket /'brækɪt/ n. (for shelf etc.) tasseau m., support m.; (group) tranche f. **(round)** ~, (printing sign) parenthèse f. **(square)** ~, crochet m. ● v.t. (p.t. **bracketed**) mettre entre parenthèses or crochets.

brag /bræg/ v.i. (p.t. **bragged**) se vanter.

braid /breɪd/ n. (trimming) galon m.; (of hair) tresse f.

Braille /breɪl/ n. braille m.

brain /breɪn/ n. cerveau m. ~s, (fig.) intelligence f. ● v.t. assommer. ~-child n. invention personnelle f. ~-drain n. exode des cerveaux m. ~less a. stupide.

brainwash /'breɪnwɒʃ/ v.t. faire un lavage de cerveau à.

brainwave /'breɪnweɪv/ n. idée géniale f., trouvaille f.

brainy /'breɪnɪ/ a. (-ier, -iest) intelligent.

braise /breɪz/ v.t. braiser.

brake /breɪk/ n. (auto & fig.) frein m. ● v.t./i. freiner. ~ fluid, liquide de frein m. ~ light, feu de stop m. ~ lining, garniture de frein f.

bramble /'bræmbl/ n. ronce f.

bran /bræn/ n. (husks) son m.

branch /brɑːntʃ/ n. branche f.; (of road) embranchement m.; (comm.) succursale f.; (of bank) agence f. ● v.i. ~ **(off),** bifurquer.

brand /brænd/ n. marque f. ● v.t. ~ s.o. as, donner à qn. la réputation de. ~-new a. tout neuf.

brandish /'brændɪʃ/ v.t. brandir.

brandy /'brændɪ/ n. cognac m.

brash /bræʃ/ a. effronté.

brass /brɑːs/ n. cuivre m. **get down to** ~ **tacks,** en venir aux choses sérieuses. **the** ~, (mus.) les cuivres m. pl. **top** ~, (sl.) gros bonnets m. pl.

brassière /'bræsɪə(r), Amer. brə'zɪər/ n. soutien-gorge m.

brat /bræt/ n. (child: pej.) môme m./ f.; (ill-behaved) garnement m.

bravado /brə'vɑːdəʊ/ n. bravade f.

brave /breɪv/ a. (-er, -est) courageux, brave. ● n. (American Indian) brave m. ● v.t. braver. ~ry /-ərɪ/ n. courage m.

bravo /'brɑːvəʊ/ int. bravo.

brawl /brɔːl/ n. bagarre f. ● v.i. se bagarrer.

brawn /brɔːn/ n. muscles m. pl. ~y a. musclé.

bray /breɪ/ n. braiment m. ● v.i. braire.

brazen /'breɪzn/ a. effronté.

brazier /'breɪzɪə(r)/ n. brasero m.

Brazil /brə'zɪl/ n. Brésil m. ~ian a. & n. brésilien(ne) (m. (f.)).

breach /briːtʃ/ n. violation f.; (of contract) rupture f.; (gap) brèche f. ● v.t. ouvrir une brèche dans.

bread /bred/ n. pain m. ~ **and butter,** tartine f. ~-**bin,** (Amer.) ~-**box** ns. boîte à pain f. ~-**winner** n. soutien de famille m.

breadcrumbs /'bredkrʌmz/ n. pl. (culin.) chapelure f.

breadline /'bredlaɪn/ n. **on the** ~, dans l'indigence.

breadth /bretθ/ n. largeur f.

break /breɪk/ v.t. (p.t. **broke,** p.p. **broken**) casser; (smash into pieces) briser; (vow, silence, rank, etc.) rompre; (law) violer; (a record) battre; (news) révéler; (journey) interrompre; (heart, strike, ice) briser. ● v.i. (se) casser; se briser. ● n. cassure f., rupture f.; (in relationship, continuity) rupture f.; (interval) interruption f.; (at school) récréation f., récré f.; (for coffee) pause f.; (luck: fam.) chance f. ~ **one's arm,** se casser le bras. ~ **away from,** quitter. ~ **down** v.i. (collapse) s'effondrer; (fail) échouer; (machine) tomber en panne; v.t. (door) enfoncer; (analyse) analyser. ~ **even,** rentrer dans ses frais. ~-**in** n. cambriolage m. ~ **into,** cambrioler. ~ **off,** (se) détacher; (suspend) rompre; (stop talking) s'interrompre. ~ **out,** (fire, war, etc.) éclater. ~ **up,** (end) (faire) cesser; (couple) rompre; (marriage) (se) briser; (*crowd*) (se) disperser; (*schools*) entrer en vacances. **~able** *a.* cassable. **~age** *n.* casse *f.*

breakdown /'breɪkdaʊn/ *n.* (*techn.*) panne *f.*; (*med.*) dépression *f.*; (*of figures*) analyse *f.* ● *a.* (*auto.*) de dépannage.

breaker /'breɪkə(r)/ *n.* (*wave*) brisant *m.*

breakfast /'brekfəst/ *n.* petit déjeuner *m.*

breakthrough /'breɪkθruː/ *n.* percée *f.*

breakwater /'breɪkwɔːtə(r)/ *n.* brise-lames *m. invar.*

breast /brest/ *n.* sein *m.*; (*chest*) poitrine *f.* **~-feed** *v.t.* (*p.t.* **-fed**) allaiter. **~-stroke** *n.* brasse *f.*

breath /breθ/ *n.* souffle *m.*, haleine *f.* **out of ~,** essoufflé. **under one's ~,** tout bas. **~less** *a.* essoufflé.

breathalyser /'breθəlaɪzə(r)/ *n.* alcootest *m.*

breath|e /briːð/ *v.t./i.* respirer. **~ in,** inspirer. **~ out,** expirer. **~ing** *n.* respiration *f.*

breather /'briːðə(r)/ *n.* moment de repos *m.*

breathtaking /'breθteɪkɪŋ/ *a.* à vous couper le souffle.

bred /bred/ *see* breed.

breeches /'brɪtʃɪz/ *n. pl.* culotte *f.*

breed /briːd/ *v.t.* (*p.t.* **bred**) élever; (*give rise to*) engendrer. ● *v.i.* se reproduire. ● *n.* race *f.* **~er** *n.* éleveur *m.* **~ing** *n.* élevage *m.*; (*fig.*) éducation *f.*

breez|e /briːz/ *n.* brise *f.* **~y** *a.* (*weather*) frais; (*cheerful*) jovial; (*casual*) désinvolte.

Breton /'bretn/ *a. & n.* breton(ne) (*m.* (*f.*)).

brevity /'brevətɪ/ *n.* brièveté *f.*

brew /bruː/ *v.t.* (*beer*) brasser; (*tea*) faire infuser. ● *v.i.* fermenter; infuser; (*fig.*) se préparer. ● *n.* décoction *f.* **~er** *n.* brasseur *m.* **~ery** *n.* brasserie *f.*

bribe /braɪb/ *n.* pot-de-vin *m.* ● *v.t.* soudoyer, acheter. **~ry** /-ərɪ/ *n.* corruption *f.*

brick /brɪk/ *n.* brique *f.*

bricklayer /'brɪkleɪə(r)/ *n.* maçon *m.*

bridal /'braɪdl/ *a.* nuptial.

bride /braɪd/ *n.* mariée *f.*

bridegroom /'braɪdɡrʊm/ *n.* marié *m.*

bridesmaid /'braɪdzmeɪd/ *n.* demoiselle d'honneur *f.*

bridge[1] /brɪdʒ/ *n.* pont *m.*; (*naut.*) passerelle *f.*; (*of nose*) arête *f.* ● *v.t.* **~ a gap,** combler une lacune.

bridge[2] /brɪdʒ/ *n.* (*cards*) bridge *m.*

bridle /'braɪdl/ *n.* bride *f.* ● *v.t.* brider. **~-path** *n.* allée cavalière *f.*

brief[1] /briːf/ *a.* (**-er, -est**) bref. **~ly** *adv.* brièvement. **~ness** *n.* brièveté *f.*

brief[2] /briːf/ *n.* instructions *f. pl.*; (*jurid.*) dossier *m.* ● *v.t.* donner des instructions à. **~ing** *n.* briefing *m.*

briefcase /'briːfkeɪs/ *n.* serviette *f.*

briefs /briːfs/ *n. pl.* slip *m.*

brigad|e /brɪ'ɡeɪd/ *n.* brigade *f.* **~ier** /-ə'dɪə(r)/ *n.* général de brigade *m.*

bright /braɪt/ *a.* (**-er, -est**) brillant, vif; (*day, room*) clair; (*cheerful*) gai; (*clever*) intelligent. **~ly** *adv.* brillamment. **~ness** *n.* éclat *m.*

brighten /'braɪtn/ *v.t.* égayer. ● *v.i.* (*weather*) s'éclaircir; (*of face*) s'éclairer.

brillian|t /'brɪljənt/ *a.* brillant; (*light*) éclatant; (*very good: fam.*) super. **~ce** *n.* éclat *m.*

brim /brɪm/ *n.* bord *m.* ● *v.i.* (*p.t.* **brimmed**). **~ over,** déborder.

brine /braɪn/ *n.* saumure *f.*

bring /brɪŋ/ *v.t.* (*p.t.* **brought**) (*thing*) apporter; (*person, vehicle*) amener. **~ about,** provoquer. **~ back,** rapporter; ramener. **~ down,** faire tomber; (*shoot down, knock down*) abattre. **~ forward,** avancer. **~ off,** réussir. **~ out,** (*take out*) sortir; (*show*) faire ressortir; (*book*) publier. **~ round** *or* **to,** ranimer. **~ to bear,** (*pressure etc.*) exercer. **~ up,** élever; (*med.*) vomir; (*question*) soulever.

brink /brɪŋk/ *n.* bord *m.*

brisk /brɪsk/ *a.* (**-er, -est**) vif. **~ness** *n.* vivacité *f.*

bristl|e /'brɪsl/ *n.* poil *m.* ● *v.i.* se hérisser. **~ing with,** hérissé de.

Britain /'brɪtn/ *n.* Grande-Bretagne *f.*

British /'brɪtɪʃ/ *a.* britannique. **the ~,** les Britanniques *m. pl.*

Briton /'brɪtn/ *n.* Britannique *m./f.*

Brittany /'brɪtənɪ/ *n.* Bretagne *f.*

brittle /'brɪtl/ *a.* fragile.

broach /brəʊtʃ/ *v.t.* entamer.

broad /brɔːd/ *a.* (**-er, -est**) large; (*daylight, outline*) grand. **~ bean,** fève *f.* **~-minded** *a.* large d'esprit. **~ly** *adv.* en gros.

broadcast /'brɔːdkɑːst/ *v.t./i.* (*p.t.* **broadcast**) diffuser; (*person*) parler à la télévision *or* à la radio. ● *n.* émission *f.*

broaden /'brɔːdn/ *v.t./i.* (s')élargir.

broccoli /'brɒkəlɪ/ *n. invar.* brocoli *m.*

brochure /'brəʊʃə(r)/ *n.* brochure *f.*

broke /brəʊk/ *see* break. ● *a.* (*penniless*: *sl.*) fauché.

broken /'brəʊkən/ *see* break. ● *a.* ~ **English,** mauvais anglais *m.* ~-**hearted** *a.* au cœur brisé.

broker /'brəʊkə(r)/ *n.* courtier *m.*

brolly /'brɒlɪ/ *n.* (*fam.*) pépin *m.*

bronchitis /brɒŋ'kaɪtɪs/ *n.* bronchite *f.*

bronze /brɒnz/ *n.* bronze *m.* ● *v.t./i.* (se) bronzer.

brooch /brəʊtʃ/ *n.* broche *f.*

brood /bruːd/ *n.* nichée *f.*, couvée *f.* ● *v.i.* couver; (*fig.*) méditer tristement. ~**y** *a.* mélancolique.

brook[1] /brʊk/ *n.* ruisseau *m.*

brook[2] /brʊk/ *v.t.* souffrir.

broom /bruːm/ *n.* balai *m.*

broomstick /'bruːmstɪk/ *n.* manche à balai *m.*

broth /brɒθ/ *n.* bouillon *m.*

brothel /'brɒθl/ *n.* maison close *f.*

brother /'brʌðə(r)/ *n.* frère *m.* ~**hood** *n.* fraternité *f.* ~-**in-law** *n.* (*pl.* ~**s-in-law**) beau-frère *m.* ~**ly** *a.* fraternel.

brought /brɔːt/ *see* bring.

brow /braʊ/ *n.* front *m.*; (*of hill*) sommet *m.*

browbeat /'braʊbiːt/ *v.t.* (*p.t.* -**beat,** *p.p.* -**beaten**) intimider.

brown /braʊn/ *a.* (**-er, -est**) marron (*invar.*); (*cheveux*) brun. ● *n.* marron *m.*; brun *m.* ● *v.t./i.* brunir; (*culin.*) (faire) dorer. **be ~ed off,** (*sl.*) en avoir ras le bol. ~ **bread,** pain bis *m.* ~ **sugar,** cassonade *f.*

Brownie /'braʊnɪ/ *n.* jeannette *f.*

browse /braʊz/ *v.i.* feuilleter; (*animal*) brouter.

bruise /bruːz/ *n.* bleu *m.* ● *v.t.* (*hurt*) faire un bleu à; (*fruit*) abîmer. ~**d** *a.* couvert de bleus.

brunch /brʌntʃ/ *n.* petit déjeuner copieux *m.* (*pris comme déjeuner*).

brunette /bruː'net/ *n.* brunette *f.*

brunt /brʌnt/ *n.* **the ~ of,** le plus fort de.

brush /brʌʃ/ *n.* brosse *f.*; (*skirmish*) accrochage *m.*; (*bushes*) broussailles *f. pl.* ● *v.t.* brosser. ~ **against,** effleurer. ~ **aside,** écarter. **give s.o. the ~-off,** (*reject*: *fam.*) en-

voyer promener qn. ~ **up (on),** remettre à.

Brussels /'brʌslz/ *n.* Bruxelles *m./f.* ~ **sprouts,** choux de Bruxelles *m. pl.*

brutal /'bruːtl/ *a.* brutal. ~**ity** /-'tælətɪ/ *n.* brutalité *f.*

brute /bruːt/ *n.* brute *f.* **by ~ force,** par la force.

B.Sc. *abbr. see* Bachelor of Science.

bubble /'bʌbl/ *n.* bulle *f.* ● *v.i.* bouillonner. ~ **bath,** bain moussant *m.* ~ **over,** déborder.

buck[1] /bʌk/ *n.* mâle *m.* ● *v.i.* ruer. ~ **up,** (*sl.*) prendre courage; (*hurry*: *sl.*) se grouiller.

buck[2] /bʌk/ *n.* (*Amer., sl.*) dollar *m.*

buck[3] /bʌk/ *n.* **pass the ~,** rejeter la responsabilité (**to,** sur).

bucket /'bʌkɪt/ *n.* seau *m.* ~ **shop,** agence de charters *f.*

buckle /'bʌkl/ *n.* boucle *f.* ● *v.t./i.* (*fasten*) (se) boucler; (*bend*) voiler. ~ **down to,** s'atteler à.

bud /bʌd/ *n.* bourgeon *m.* ● *v.i.* (*p.t.* **budded**) bourgeonner.

Buddhis|t /'bʊdɪst/ *a. & n.* bouddhiste (*m./f.*) ~**m** /-ɪzəm/ *n.* bouddhisme *m.*

budding /'bʌdɪŋ/ *a.* (*talent etc.*) naissant; (*film star etc.*) en herbe.

buddy /'bʌdɪ/ *n.* (*fam.*) copain *m.*

budge /bʌdʒ/ *v.t./i.* (faire) bouger.

budgerigar /'bʌdʒərɪgɑː(r)/ *n.* perruche *f.*

budget /'bʌdʒɪt/ *n.* budget *m.* ● *v.i.* (*p.t.* **budgeted**). ~ **for,** prévoir (dans son budget).

buff /bʌf/ *n.* (*colour*) chamois *m.*; (*fam.*) fanatique *m./f.*

buffalo /'bʌfələʊ/ *n.* (*pl.* **-oes** *or* **-o**) buffle *m.*; (*Amer.*) bison *m.*

buffer /'bʌfə(r)/ *n.* tampon *m.* ~ **zone,** zone tampon *f.*

buffet[1] /'bʊfeɪ/ *n.* (*meal, counter*) buffet *m.* ~ **car,** buffet *m.*

buffet[2] /'bʌfɪt/ *n.* (*blow*) soufflet *m.* ● *v.t.* (*p.t.* **buffeted**) souffleter.

buffoon /bə'fuːn/ *n.* bouffon *m.*

bug /bʌg/ *n.* (*insect*) punaise *f.*; (*any small insect*) bestiole *f.*; (*germ*: *sl.*) microbe *m.*; (*device*: *sl.*) micro *m.*; (*defect*: *sl.*) défaut *m.* ● *v.t.* (*p.t.* **bugged**) mettre des micros dans; (*Amer., sl.*) embêter.

buggy /'bʌgɪ/ *n.* (*child's*) poussette *f.*

bugle /'bjuːgl/ *n.* clairon *m.*

build /bɪld/ *v.t./i.* (*p.t.* **built**) bâtir, construire. ● *n.* carrure *f.* ~ **up,** (*increase*) augmenter, monter; (*ac-*

cumulate) (s')accumuler. **~-up** *n.* accumulation *f.*; (*fig.*) publicité *f.* **~er** *n.* entrepreneur *m.*; (*workman*) ouvrier *m.*

building /'bɪldɪŋ/ *n.* bâtiment *m.*; (*dwelling*) immeuble *m.* **~ society,** caisse d'épargne-logement *f.*

built /bɪlt/ *see* build. **~-in** *a.* encastré. **~-up area,** agglomération *f.*, zone urbanisée *f.*

bulb /bʌlb/ *n.* oignon *m.*; (*electr.*) ampoule *f.* **~ous** *a.* bulbeux.

Bulgaria /bʌl'geərɪə/ *n.* Bulgarie *f.* **~n** *a. & n.* bulgare (*m./f.*).

bulg|e /bʌldʒ/ *n.* renflement *m.* ● *v.i.* se renfler, être renflé. **be ~ing with,** être gonflé *or* bourré de.

bulimia /bjuː'lɪmɪə/ *n.* boulimie *f.*

bulk /bʌlk/ *n.* grosseur *f.* **in ~,** en gros; (*loose*) en vrac. **the ~ of,** la majeure partie de. **~y** *a.* gros.

bull /bʊl/ *n.* taureau *m.* **~'s-eye** *n.* centre (de la cible) *m.*

bulldog /'bʊldɒg/ *n.* bouledogue *m.*

bulldoz|e /'bʊldəʊz/ *v.t.* raser au bulldozer. **~r** /-ə(r)/ *n.* bulldozer *m.*

bullet /'bʊlɪt/ *n.* balle *f.* **~-proof** *a.* pare-balles *invar.*; (*vehicle*) blindé.

bulletin /'bʊlətɪn/ *n.* bulletin *m.*

bullfight /'bʊlfaɪt/ *n.* corrida *f.* **~er** *n.* torero *m.*

bullion /'bʊljən/ *n.* or *or* argent en lingots *m.*

bullring /'bʊlrɪŋ/ *n.* arène *f.*

bully /'bʊlɪ/ *n.* brute *f.*; tyran *m.* ● *v.t.* (*treat badly*) brutaliser; (*persecute*) tyranniser; (*coerce*) forcer (**into,** à).

bum[1] /bʌm/ *n.* (*sl.*) derrière *m.*

bum[2] /bʌm/ *n.* (*Amer., sl.*) vagabond(e) *m.* (*f.*).

bumble-bee /'bʌmblbiː/ *n.* bourdon *m.*

bump /bʌmp/ *n.* choc *m.*; (*swelling*) bosse *f.* ● *v.t./i.* cogner, heurter. **~ along,** cahoter. **~ into,** (*hit*) rentrer dans; (*meet*) tomber sur. **~y** *a.* cahoteux.

bumper /'bʌmpə(r)/ *n.* pare-chocs *m. invar.* ● *a.* exceptionnel.

bumptious /'bʌmpʃəs/ *a.* prétentieux.

bun /bʌn/ *n.* (*cake*) petit pain au lait *m.*; (*hair*) chignon *m.*

bunch /bʌntʃ/ *n.* (*of flowers*) bouquet *m.*; (*of keys*) trousseau *m.*; (*of people*) groupe *m.*; (*of bananas*) régime *m.* **~ of grapes,** grappe de raisin *f.*

bundle /'bʌndl/ *n.* paquet *m.* ● *v.t.* mettre en paquet; (*push*) pousser.

bung /bʌŋ/ *n.* bonde *f.* ● *v.t.* boucher; (*throw: sl.*) flanquer.

bungalow /'bʌŋgələʊ/ *n.* bungalow *m.*

bungle /'bʌŋgl/ *v.t.* gâcher.

bunion /'bʌnjən/ *n.* (*med.*) oignon *m.*

bunk[1] /bʌŋk/ *n.* couchette *f.* **~-beds** *n. pl.* lits superposés *m. pl.*

bunk[2] /bʌŋk/ *n.* (*nonsense: sl.*) foutaise(s) *f.* (*pl.*).

bunker /'bʌŋkə(r)/ *n.* (*mil.*) bunker *m.*

bunny /'bʌnɪ/ *n.* (*children's use*) (Jeannot) lapin *m.*

buoy /bɔɪ/ *n.* bouée *f.* ● *v.t.* **~ up,** (*hearten*) soutenir, encourager.

buoyan|t /'bɔɪənt/ *a.* (*cheerful*) gai. **~cy** *n.* gaieté *f.*

burden /'bɜːdn/ *n.* fardeau *m.* ● *v.t.* accabler. **~some** *a.* lourd.

bureau /'bjʊərəʊ/ *n.* (*pl.* **-eaux** /-əʊz/) bureau *m.*

bureaucracy /bjʊə'rɒkrəsɪ/ *n.* bureaucratie *f.*

bureaucrat /'bjʊərəkræt/ *n.* bureaucrate *m./f.* **~ic** /-'krætɪk/ *a.* bureaucratique.

burglar /'bɜːglə(r)/ *n.* cambrioleur *m.* **~ize** *v.t.* (*Amer.*) cambrioler. **~ alarm,** alarme *f.* **~y** *n.* cambriolage *m.*

burgle /'bɜːgl/ *v.t.* cambrioler.

Burgundy /'bɜːgəndɪ/ *n.* (*wine*) bourgogne *m.*

burial /'berɪəl/ *n.* enterrement *m.*

burlesque /bɜː'lesk/ *n.* (*imitation*) parodie *f.*

burly /'bɜːlɪ/ *a.* (**-ier, -iest**) costaud, solidement charpenté.

Burm|a /'bɜːmə/ *n.* Birmanie *f.* **~ese** /-'miːz/ *a. & n.* birman(e) (*m.* (*f.*)).

burn /bɜːn/ *v.t./i.* (*p.t.* **burned** *or* **burnt**) brûler. ● *n.* brûlure *f.* **~ down** *or* **be ~ed down,** être réduit en cendres. **~er** *n.* brûleur *m.* **~ing** *a.* (*fig.*) brûlant.

burnish /'bɜːnɪʃ/ *v.t.* polir.

burnt /bɜːnt/ *see* burn.

burp /bɜːp/ *n.* (*fam.*) rot *m.* ● *v.i.* (*fam.*) roter.

burrow /'bʌrəʊ/ *n.* terrier *m.* ● *v.t.* creuser.

bursar /'bɜːsə(r)/ *n.* économe *m./f.*

bursary /'bɜːsərɪ/ *n.* bourse *f.*

burst /bɜːst/ *v.t./i.* (*p.t.* **burst**) crever, (faire) éclater. ● *n.* explosion *f.*; (*of laughter*) éclat *m.*; (*surge*) élan *m.*

be ~ing with, déborder de. **~ into,** faire irruption dans. **~ into tears,** fondre en larmes. **~ out laughing,** éclater de rire. **~ pipe,** conduite qui a éclaté *f.*

bury /'berɪ/ *v.t.* (*person etc.*) enterrer; (*hide, cover*) enfouir; (*engross, thrust*) plonger.

bus /bʌs/ *n.* (*pl.* **buses**) (auto)bus *m.* ● *v.t.* transporter en bus. ● *v.i.* (*p.t.* **bussed**) prendre l'autobus. **~-stop** *n.* arrêt d'autobus *m.*

bush /bʊʃ/ *n.* buisson *m.*; (*land*) brousse *f.* **~y** *a.* broussailleux.

business /'bɪznɪs/ *n.* (*task, concern*) affaire *f.*; (*commerce*) affaires *f. pl.*; (*line of work*) métier *m.*; (*shop*) commerce *m.* **he has no ~ to,** il n'a pas le droit de. **mean ~,** être sérieux. **that's none of your ~!,** ça ne vous regarde pas! **~man,** homme d'affaires *m.*

businesslike /'bɪznɪslaɪk/ *a.* sérieux.

busker /'bʌskə(r)/ *n.* musicien(ne) des rues *m.* (*f.*).

bust¹ /bʌst/ *n.* buste *m.*; (*bosom*) poitrine *f.*

bust² /bʌst/ *v.t./i.* (*p.t.* **busted** or **bust**) (*burst*: *sl.*) crever; (*break*: *sl.*) (se) casser. ● *a.* (*broken, finished*: *sl.*) fichu. **~-up** *n.* (*sl.*) engueulade *f.* **go ~,** (*sl.*) faire faillite.

bustl|e /'bʌsl/ *v.i.* s'affairer. ● *n.* affairement *m.*, remue-ménage *m.* **~ing** *a.* (*place*) bruyant, animé.

bus|y /'bɪzɪ/ *a.* (**-ier, -iest**) occupé; (*street*) animé; (*day*) chargé. ● *v.t.* **~y o.s. with,** s'occuper à. **~ily** *adv.* activement.

busybody /'bɪzɪbɒdɪ/ *n.* **be a ~,** faire la mouche du coche.

but /bʌt, *unstressed* bət/ *conj.* mais. ● *prep.* sauf. ● *adv.* (*only*) seulement. **~ for,** sans. **nobody ~,** personne d'autre que. **nothing ~,** rien que.

butane /'bjuːtem/ *n.* butane *m.*

butcher /'bʊtʃə(r)/ *n.* boucher *m.* ● *v.t.* massacrer. **~y** *n.* boucherie *f.*, massacre *m.*

butler /'bʌtlə(r)/ *n.* maître d'hôtel *m.*

butt /bʌt/ *n.* (*of gun*) crosse *f.*; (*of cigarette*) mégot *m.*; (*target*) cible *f.*; (*barrel*) tonneau; (*Amer., fam.*) derrière *m.* ● *v.i.* **~ in,** interrompre.

butter /'bʌtə(r)/ *n.* beurre *m.* ● *v.t.* beurrer. **~-bean** *n.* haricot blanc *m.* **~-fingers** *n.* maladroit(e) *m.* (*f.*).

buttercup /'bʌtəkʌp/ *n.* bouton-d'or *m.*

butterfly /'bʌtəflaɪ/ *n.* papillon *m.*

buttock /'bʌtək/ *n.* fesse *f.*

button /'bʌtn/ *n.* bouton *m.* ● *v.t./i.* **~ (up),** (se) boutonner.

buttonhole /'bʌtnhəʊl/ *n.* boutonnière *f.* ● *v.t.* accrocher.

buttress /'bʌtrɪs/ *n.* contrefort *m.* ● *v.t.* soutenir.

buxom /'bʌksəm/ *a.* bien en chair.

buy /baɪ/ *v.t.* (*p.t.* **bought**) acheter (**from,** à); (*believe*: *sl.*) croire, avaler. ● *n.* achat *m.* **~ sth for s.o.** acheter qch. à qn., prendre qch. pour qn. **~er** *n.* acheteu|r, -se *m.*, *f.*

buzz /bʌz/ *n.* bourdonnement *m.* ● *v.i.* bourdonner. **~ off,** (*sl.*) ficher le camp. **~er** *n.* sonnerie *f.*

by /baɪ/ *prep.* par, de; (*near*) à côté de; (*before*) avant; (*means*) en, à, par. **by bike,** à vélo. **by car,** en auto. **by day,** de jour. **by the kilo,** au kilo. **by running**/*etc.*, en courant/*etc.* **by sea,** par mer. **by that time,** à ce moment-là. **~ the way,** à propos. ● *adv.* (*near*) tout près. **by and large,** dans l'ensemble. **by-election** *n.* élection partielle *f.* **~-law** *n.* arrêté *m.*; (*of club etc.*) statut *m.* **by o.s.,** tout seul. **~-product** *n.* sous-produit *m.*; (*fig.*) conséquence *f.* **by-road** *n.* chemin de traverse *m.*

bye(-bye) /baɪ('baɪ)/ *int.* (*fam.*) au revoir, salut.

bypass /'baɪpɑːs/ *n.* (*auto.*) route qui contourne *f.*; (*med.*) pontage *m.* ● *v.t.* contourner.

bystander /'baɪstændə(r)/ *n.* specta|teur, -trice *m.*, *f.*

byte /baɪt/ *n.* octet *m.*

byword /'baɪwɜːd/ *n.* **be a ~ for,** être connu pour.

C

cab /kæb/ *n.* taxi *m.*; (*of lorry, train*) cabine *f.*

cabaret /'kæbəreɪ/ *n.* spectacle (de cabaret) *m.*

cabbage /'kæbɪdʒ/ *n.* chou *m.*

cabin /'kæbɪn/ *n.* (*hut*) cabane *f.*; (*in ship, aircraft*) cabine *f.*

cabinet /'kæbɪnɪt/ *n.* (petite) armoire *f.*, meuble de rangement *m.*; (*for* *filing*) classeur *m*. **C~**, (*pol.*) cabinet *m*. **~-maker** *n*. ébéniste *m*.

cable /'keɪbl/ *n*. câble *m*. ● *v.t.* câbler. **~-car** *n*. téléphérique *m*. **~ railway**, funiculaire *m*.

caboose /kə'buːs/ *n*. (*rail., Amer.*) fourgon *m*.

cache /kæʃ/ *n*. (*place*) cachette *f*. **a ~ of arms**, des armes cachées.

cackle /'kækl/ *n*. caquet *m*. ● *v.i.* caqueter.

cactus /'kæktəs/ *n*. (*pl.* **-ti** /-taɪ/ *or* **-tuses**) cactus *m*.

caddie /'kædɪ/ *n*. (*golf*) caddie *m*.

caddy /'kædɪ/ *n*. boîte à thé *f*.

cadence /'keɪdns/ *n*. cadence *f*.

cadet /kə'det/ *n*. élève officier *m*.

cadge /kædʒ/ *v.t.* se fairer payer, écornifler. ● *v.i.* quémander. **~ money from**, taper. **~r** /-ə(r)/ *n*. écornifleu|r, -se *m., f*.

Caesarean /sɪ'zeərɪən/ *a*. **~ (section)**, césarienne *f*.

café /'kæfeɪ/ *n*. café(-restaurant) *m*.

cafeteria /kæf'tɪərɪə/ *n*. cafétéria *f*.

caffeine /'kæfiːn/ *n*. caféine *f*.

cage /keɪdʒ/ *n*. cage *f*. ● *v.t.* mettre en cage.

cagey /'keɪdʒɪ/ *a*. (*secretive: fam.*) peu communicatif.

cagoule /kə'guːl/ *n*. K-way *m*. (P.).

Cairo /'kaɪərəʊ/ *n*. le Caire *m*.

cajole /kə'dʒəʊl/ *v.t.* **~ s.o. into doing**, faire l'enjoleur pour que qn. fasse.

cake /keɪk/ *n*. gâteau *m*. **~d** *a*. durci. **~d with**, raidi par.

calamit|y /kə'læmətɪ/ *n*. calamité *f*. **~ous** *a*. désastreux.

calcium /'kælsɪəm/ *n*. calcium *m*.

calculat|e /'kælkjʊleɪt/ *v.t./i.* calculer; (*Amer.*) supposer. **~ed** *a*. (*action*) délibéré. **~ing** *a*. calculateur. **~ion** /-'leɪʃn/ *n*. calcul *m*. **~or** *n*. calculatrice *f*.

calculus /'kælkjʊləs/ *n*. (*pl.* **-li** /-laɪ/ *or* **-luses**) calcul *m*.

calendar /'kælmdə(r)/ *n*. calendrier *m*.

calf[1] /kɑːf/ *n*. (*pl.* **calves**) (*young cow or bull*) veau *m*.

calf[2] /kɑːf/ *n*. (*pl.* **calves**) (*of leg*) mollet *m*.

calibre /'kælɪbə(r)/ *n*. calibre *m*.

calico /'kælɪkəʊ/ *n*. calicot *m*.

call /kɔːl/ *v.t./i.* appeler. **~ (in or round)**, (*visit*) passer. ● *n*. appel *m*.; (*of bird*) cri *m*.; visite *f*. **be ~ed**, (*named*) s'appeler. **be on ~**, être de garde. **~ back**, rappeler; (*visit*) repasser. **~-box** *n*. cabine téléphonique *f*. **~ for**, (*require*) demander; (*fetch*) passer prendre. **~-girl** *n*. callgirl *f*. **~ off**, annuler. **~ out (to)**, appeler. **~ on**, (*visit*) passer chez; (*appeal to*) faire appel à. **~ up**, appeler (au téléphone); (*mil.*) mobiliser, appeler. **~er** *n*. visiteu|r, -se *m., f*.; (*on phone*) personne qui appelle *f*. **~ing** *n*. vocation *f*.

callous /'kæləs/ *a*., **~ly** *adv*. sans pitié. **~ness** *n*. manque de pitié *m*.

callow /'kæləʊ/ *a*. (**-er, -est**) inexpérimenté.

calm /kɑːm/ *a*. (**-er, -est**) calme. ● *n*. calme *m*. ● *v.t./i.* **~ (down)**, (se) calmer. **~ness** *n*. calme *m*.

calorie /'kælərɪ/ *n*. calorie *f*.

camber /'kæmbə(r)/ *n*. (*of road*) bombement *m*.

camcorder /'kæmkɔːdə(r)/ *n*. caméscope *m*.

came /keɪm/ *see* come.

camel /'kæml/ *n*. chameau *m*.

cameo /'kæmɪəʊ/ *n*. (*pl.* **-os**) camée *m*.

camera /'kæmərə/ *n*. appareil (-photo) *m*.; (*for moving pictures*) caméra *f*. **in ~**, à huis clos. **~man** *n*. (*pl.* **-men**) caméraman *m*.

camouflage /'kæməflɑːʒ/ *n*. camouflage *m*. ● *v.t.* camoufler.

camp[1] /kæmp/ *n*. camp *m*. ● *v.i.* camper. **~-bed** *n*. lit de camp *m*. **~er** *n*. campeu|r, -se *m., f*. **~er (-van)**, camping-car *m*. **~ing** *n*. camping *m*.

camp[2] /kæmp/ *a*. (*mannered*) affecté; (*vulgar*) de mauvais goût.

campaign /kæm'peɪn/ *n*. campagne *f*. ● *v.i.* faire campagne.

campsite /'kæmpsaɪt/ *n*. (*for holidaymakers*) camping *m*.

campus /'kæmpəs/ *n*. (*pl.* **-puses**) campus *m*.

can[1] /kæn/ *n*. bidon *m*.; (*sealed container for food*) boîte *f*. ● *v.t.* (*p.t.* **canned**) mettre en boîte. **~ it!**, (*Amer., sl.*) ferme-la! **~ned music**, musique de fond enregistrée *f*. **~-opener** *n*. ouvre-boîte(s) *m*.

can[2] /kæn, *unstressed* kən/ *v. aux.* (*be able to*) pouvoir; (*know how to*) savoir.

Canad|a /'kænədə/ *n*. Canada *m*. **~ian** /kə'neɪdɪən/ *a. & n*. canadien(ne) (*m. (f.)*).

canal /kə'næl/ *n*. canal *m*.

canary /kə'neərɪ/ n. canari m.

cancel /'kænsl/ v.t./i. (p.t. **cancelled**) (call off, revoke) annuler; (cross out) barrer; (a stamp) oblitérer. ~ **out**, (se) neutraliser. ~**lation** /-ə'leɪʃn/ n. annulation f.; oblitération f.

cancer /'kænsə(r)/ n. cancer m. ~**ous** a. cancéreux.

Cancer /'kænsə(r)/ n. le Cancer.

candid /'kændɪd/ a. franc. ~**ness** n. franchise f.

candida|te /'kændɪdeɪt/ n. candidat(e) m. (f.). ~**cy** /-əsɪ/ n. candidature f.

candle /'kændl/ n. bougie f., chandelle f.; (in church) cierge m.

candlestick /'kændlstɪk/ n. bougeoir m., chandelier m.

candour, (Amer.) **candor** /'kændə(r)/ n. franchise f.

candy /'kændɪ/ n. (Amer.) bonbon(s) m. (pl.). ~-**floss** n. barbe à papa f.

cane /keɪn/ n. canne f.; (for baskets) rotin m.; (for punishment: schol.) baguette f., bâton m. ● v.t. donner des coups de baguette or de bâton à, fustiger.

canine /'keɪnaɪn/ a. canin.

canister /'kænɪstə(r)/ n. boîte f.

cannabis /'kænəbɪs/ n. cannabis m.

cannibal /'kænɪbl/ n. cannibale m./f. ~**ism** n. cannibalisme m.

cannon /'kænən/ n. (pl. ~ or ~s) canon m. ~-**ball** n. boulet de canon m.

cannot /'kænət/ = **can not**.

canny /'kænɪ/ a. rusé, madré.

canoe /kə'nu:/ n. (sport) canoë m., kayak m. ● v.i. faire du canoë or du kayak. ~**ist** n. canoéiste m./f.

canon /'kænən/ n. (clergyman) chanoine m.; (rule) canon m.

canonize /'kænənaɪz/ v.t. canoniser.

canopy /'kænəpɪ/ n. dais m.; (over doorway) marquise f.

can't /kɑ:nt/ = **can not**.

cantankerous /kæn'tæŋkərəs/ a. acariâtre, grincheux.

canteen /kæn'ti:n/ n. (restaurant) cantine f.; (flask) bidon m.

canter /'kæntə(r)/ n. petit galop m. ● v.i. aller au petit galop.

canvas /'kænvəs/ n. toile f.

canvass /'kænvəs/ v.t./i. (comm., pol.) solliciter des commandes or des voix (de). ~**ing** n. (comm.) démarchage m.; (pol.) démarchage électoral m. ~ **opinion**, sonder l'opinion.

canyon /'kænjən/ n. cañon m.

cap /kæp/ n. (hat) casquette f.; (of bottle, tube) bouchon m.; (of beer or milk bottle) capsule f.; (of pen) capuchon m.; (for toy gun) amorce f. ● v.t. (p.t. **capped**) (bottle) capsuler; (outdo) surpasser. ~**ped with**, coiffé de.

capab|le /'keɪpəbl/ a. (person) capable (of, de), compétent. **be** ~**le of**, (of situation, text, etc.) être susceptible de. ~**ility** /-'bɪlətɪ/ n. capacité f. ~**ly** adv. avec compétence.

capacity /kə'pæsətɪ/ n. capacité f. **in one's** ~ **as**, en sa qualité de.

cape[1] /keɪp/ n. (cloak) cape f.

cape[2] /keɪp/ n. (geog.) cap m.

caper[1] /'keɪpə(r)/ v.i. gambader. ● n. (prank) farce f.; (activity: sl.) affaire f.

caper[2] /'keɪpə(r)/ n. (culin.) câpre f.

capital /'kæpɪtl/ a. capital. ● n. (town) capitale f.; (money) capital m. ~ **(letter)**, majuscule f.

capitalis|t /'kæpɪtəlɪst/ a. & n. capitaliste (m./f.). ~**m** /-zəm/ n. capitalisme m.

capitalize /'kæpɪtəlaɪz/ v.i. ~ **on**, tirer profit de.

capitulat|e /kə'pɪtʃuleɪt/ v.i. capituler. ~**ion** /-'leɪʃn/ n. capitulation f.

capricious /kə'prɪʃəs/ a. capricieux.

Capricorn /'kæprɪkɔːn/ n. le Capricorne.

capsize /kæp'saɪz/ v.t./i. (faire) chavirer.

capsule /'kæpsjuːl/ n. capsule f.

captain /'kæptɪn/ n. capitaine m.

caption /'kæpʃn/ n. (for illustration) légende f.; (heading) sous-titre m.

captivate /'kæptɪveɪt/ v.t. captiver.

captiv|e /'kæptɪv/ a. & n. capti|f, -ve (m., f.). ~**ity** /-'tɪvətɪ/ n. captivité f.

capture /'kæptʃə(r)/ v.t. (person, animal) prendre, capturer; (attention) retenir. ● n. capture f.

car /kɑ:(r)/ n. voiture f. ~ **ferry**, ferry m. ~-**park** n. parking m. ~ **phone**, téléphone de voiture m. ~-**wash** n. station de lavage f., lave-auto m.

carafe /kə'ræf/ n. carafe f.

caramel /'kærəmel/ n. caramel m.

carat /'kærət/ n. carat m.

caravan /'kærəvæn/ n. caravane f.

carbohydrate /kɑ:bəʊ'haɪdreɪt/ n. hydrate de carbone m.

carbon /'kɑ:bən/ n. carbone m. ~ **copy**, ~ **paper**, carbone m.

carburettor, (*Amer.*) **carburetor** /kɑːbjʊˈretə(r)/ n. carburateur m.

carcass /ˈkɑːkəs/ n. carcasse f.

card /kɑːd/ n. carte f. ~-index n. fichier m.

cardboard /ˈkɑːdbɔːd/ n. carton m.

cardiac /ˈkɑːdɪæk/ a. cardiaque.

cardigan /ˈkɑːdɪgən/ n. cardigan m.

cardinal /ˈkɑːdɪml/ a. cardinal. ● n. (*relig.*) cardinal m.

care /keə(r)/ n. (*attention*) soin m., attention f.; (*worry*) souci m.; (*protection*) garde f. ● v.i. ~ **about**, s'intéresser à. ~ **for**, s'occuper de; (*invalid*) soigner. ~ **to** or **for**, aimer, vouloir. **I don't** ~, ça m'est égal. **take** ~ **of**, s'occuper de. **take** ~ **(of yourself)**, prends soin de toi. **take** ~ **to do sth.**, faire bien attention à faire qch.

career /kəˈrɪə(r)/ n. carrière f. ● v.i. aller à toute vitesse.

carefree /ˈkeəfriː/ a. insouciant.

careful /ˈkeəfl/ a. soigneux; (*cautious*) prudent. **(be)** ~!, (fais) attention! ~**ly** adv. avec soin.

careless /ˈkeəlɪs/ a. négligent; (*work*) peu soigné. ~ **about**, peu soucieux de. ~**ly** adv. négligemment. ~**ness** n. négligence f.

caress /kəˈres/ n. caresse f. ● v.t. caresser.

caretaker /ˈkeəteɪkə(r)/ n. gardien(ne) m. (f.). ● a. (*president*) par intérim.

cargo /ˈkɑːgəʊ/ n. (*pl.* -oes) cargaison f. ~ **boat**, cargo m.

Caribbean /kærɪˈbiːən/ a. caraïbe. ● n. **the** ~, (*sea*) la mer des Caraïbes; (*islands*) les Antilles f. pl.

caricature /ˈkærɪkətʊə(r)/ n. caricature f. ● v.t. caricaturer.

caring /ˈkeərɪŋ/ a. (*mother, son, etc.*) aimant. ● n. affection f.

carnage /ˈkɑːnɪdʒ/ n. carnage m.

carnal /ˈkɑːnl/ a. charnel.

carnation /kɑːˈneɪʃn/ n. œillet m.

carnival /ˈkɑːnɪvl/ n. carnaval m.

carol /ˈkærəl/ n. chant (de Noël) m.

carp[1] /kɑːp/ n. invar. carpe f.

carp[2] /kɑːp/ v.i. ~ **(at)**, critiquer.

carpenter /ˈkɑːpəntə(r)/ n. charpentier m.; (*for light woodwork, furniture*) menuisier m. ~**ry** n. charpenterie f.; menuiserie f.

carpet /ˈkɑːpɪt/ n. tapis m. ● v.t. (*p.t.* **carpeted**) recouvrir d'un tapis. ~-**sweeper** n. balai mécanique m. **on the** ~, (*fam.*) sur la sellette.

carriage /ˈkærɪdʒ/ n. (*rail & horse-drawn*) voiture f.; (*of goods*) transport m.; (*cost*) port m.

carriageway /ˈkærɪdʒweɪ/ n. chaussée f.

carrier /ˈkærɪə(r)/ n. transporteur m.; (*med.*) porteu|r, -se m., f. ~ **(bag)**, sac en plastique m.

carrot /ˈkærət/ n. carotte f.

carry /ˈkærɪ/ v.t./i. porter; (*goods*) transporter; (*involve*) comporter; (*motion*) voter. **be carried away**, s'emballer. ~-**cot** n. porte-bébé m. ~ **off**, enlever; (*prize*) remporter. ~ **on**, continuer; (*behave: fam.*) se conduire (mal). ~ **out**, (*an order, plan*) exécuter; (*duty*) accomplir; (*task*) effectuer.

cart /kɑːt/ n. charrette f. ● v.t. transporter; (*heavy object: sl.*) trimballer.

cartilage /ˈkɑːtɪlɪdʒ/ n. cartilage m.

carton /ˈkɑːtn/ n. (*box*) carton m.; (*of yoghurt, cream*) pot m.; (*of cigarettes*) cartouche f.

cartoon /kɑːˈtuːn/ n. dessin (humoristique) m.; (*cinema*) dessin animé m. ~**ist** n. dessina|teur, -trice m., f.

cartridge /ˈkɑːtrɪdʒ/ n. cartouche f.

carve /kɑːv/ v.t. tailler; (*meat*) découper.

cascade /kæsˈkeɪd/ n. cascade f. ● v.i. tomber en cascade.

case[1] /keɪs/ n. cas m.; (*jurid.*) affaire f.; (*phil.*) arguments m. pl. **in** ~ **he comes**, au cas où il viendrait. **in** ~ **of fire**, en cas d'incendie. **in** ~ **of any problems**, au cas où il y aurait un problème. **in that** ~, à ce moment-là.

case[2] /keɪs/ n. (*crate*) caisse f.; (*for camera, cigarettes, spectacles, etc.*) étui m.; (*suitcase*) valise f.

cash /kæʃ/ n. argent m. ● a. (*price etc.*) (au) comptant. ● v.t. encaisser. ~ **a cheque**, (*person*) encaisser un chèque; (*bank*) payer un chèque. **pay** ~, payer comptant. **in** ~, en espèces. ~ **desk**, caisse f. ~ **dispenser**, distributeur de billets m. ~-**flow** n. cash-flow m. ~ **in (on)**, profiter (de). ~ **register**, caisse enregistreuse f.

cashew /ˈkæʃuː/ n. noix de cajou f.

cashier /kæˈʃɪə(r)/ n. caiss|ier, -ière m., f.

cashmere /ˈkæʃmɪə(r)/ n. cachemire m.

casino /kəˈsiːnəʊ/ n. (*pl.* -os) casino m.

cask /kɑ:sk/ *n.* tonneau *m.*

casket /'kɑ:skɪt/ *n.* (*box*) coffret *m.*; (*coffin: Amer.*) cercueil *m.*

casserole /'kæsərəʊl/ *n.* (*utensil*) cocotte *f.*; (*stew*) daube *f.*

cassette /kə'set/ *n.* cassette *f.*

cast /kɑ:st/ *v.t.* (*p.t.* **cast**) (*throw*) jeter; (*glance, look*) jeter; (*shadow*) projeter; (*vote*) donner; (*metal*) couler. **~ (off),** (*shed*) se dépouiller de. ● *n.* (*theatre*) distribution *f.*; (*of dice*) coup *m.*; (*mould*) moule *m.*; (*med.*) plâtre *m.* **~ iron,** fonte *f.* **~-iron** *a.* de fonte; (*fig.*) solide. **~-offs** *n. pl.* vieux vêtements *m. pl.*

castanets /kæstə'nets/ *n. pl.* castagnettes *f. pl.*

castaway /'kɑ:stəweɪ/ *n.* naufragé(e) *m.* (*f.*).

caste /kɑ:st/ *n.* caste *f.*

castle /'kɑ:sl/ *n.* château *m.*; (*chess*) tour *f.*

castor /'kɑ:stə(r)/ *n.* (*wheel*) roulette *f.* **~ sugar,** sucre en poudre *m.*

castrat|e /kæ'streɪt/ *v.t.* châtrer. **~ion** /-ʃn/ *n.* castration *f.*

casual /'kæʒʊəl/ *a.* (*remark*) fait au hasard; (*meeting*) fortuit; (*attitude*) désinvolte; (*work*) temporaire; (*clothes*) sport *invar.* **~ly** *adv.* par hasard; (*carelessly*) avec désinvolture.

casualty /'kæʒʊəltɪ/ *n.* (*dead*) mort(e) *m.* (*f.*); (*injured*) blessé(e) *m.* (*f.*); (*accident victim*) accidenté(e) *m.* (*f.*).

cat /kæt/ *n.* chat *m.* **C~'s-eyes** *n. pl.* (P.) catadioptres *m. pl.*

catalogue /'kætəlɒg/ *n.* catalogue *m.* ● *v.t.* cataloguer.

catalyst /'kætəlɪst/ *n.* catalyseur *m.*

catapult /'kætəpʌlt/ *n.* lance-pierres *m. invar.* ● *v.t.* catapulter.

cataract /'kætərækt/ *n.* (*waterfall & med.*) cataracte *f.*

catarrh /kə'tɑ:(r)/ *n.* rhume *m.*, catarrhe *m.*

catastroph|e /kə'tæstrəfɪ/ *n.* catastrophe *f.* **~ic** /kætə'strɒfɪk/ *a.* catastrophique.

catch /kætʃ/ *v.t.* (*p.t.* **caught**) attraper; (*grab*) prendre, saisir; (*catch unawares*) surprendre; (*jam, trap*) prendre; (*understand*) saisir. ● *v.i.* prendre; (*get stuck*) se prendre (**in,** dans). ● *n.* capture *f.*, prise *f.*; (*on door*) loquet *m.*; (*fig.*) piège *m.* **~ fire,** prendre feu. **~ on,** (*fam.*) prendre, devenir populaire. **~ out,** prendre en faute. **~-phrase** *n.* slo-

gan *m.* **~ sight of,** apercevoir. **~ s.o.'s eye,** attirer l'attention de qn. **~ up,** se rattraper. **~ up (with),** rattraper.

catching /'kætʃɪŋ/ *a.* contagieux.

catchment /'kætʃmənt/ *n.* **~ area,** région desservie *f.*

catchy /'kætʃɪ/ *a.* facile à retenir.

categorical /kætɪ'gɒrɪkl/ *a.* catégorique.

category /'kætɪgərɪ/ *n.* catégorie *f.*

cater /'keɪtə(r)/ *v.i.* s'occuper de la nourriture. **~ for,** (*pander to*) satisfaire; (*of magazine etc.*) s'adresser à. **~er** *n.* traiteur *m.*

caterpillar /'kætəpɪlə(r)/ *n.* chenille *f.*

cathedral /kə'θi:drəl/ *n.* cathédrale *f.*

catholic /'kæθəlɪk/ *a.* universel. **C~** *a.* & *n.* catholique (*m./f.*). **C~ism** /kə'θɒlɪsɪzəm/ *n.* catholicisme *m.*

cattle /'kætl/ *n. pl.* bétail *m.*

catty /'kætɪ/ *a.* méchant.

caucus /'kɔ:kəs/ *n.* comité électoral *m.*

caught /kɔ:t/ *see* catch.

cauliflower /'kɒlɪflaʊə(r)/ *n.* choufleur *m.*

cause /kɔ:z/ *n.* cause *f.*; (*reason*) raison *f.*, motif *m.* ● *v.t.* causer. **~ sth. to grow/move/***etc.***,** faire pousser/bouger/*etc.* qch.

causeway /'kɔ:zweɪ/ *n.* chaussée *f.*

cauti|on /'kɔ:ʃn/ *n.* prudence *f.*; (*warning*) avertissement *m.* ● *v.t.* avertir. **~ous** *a.* prudent. **~ously** *adv.* prudemment.

cavalier /kævə'lɪə(r)/ *a.* cavalier.

cavalry /'kævəlrɪ/ *n.* cavalerie *f.*

cave /keɪv/ *n.* caverne *f.*, grotte *f.* ● *v.i.* **~ in,** s'effondrer; (*agree*) céder.

caveman /'keɪvmæn/ *n.* (*pl.* **-men**) homme des cavernes *m.*

cavern /'kævən/ *n.* caverne *f.*

caviare, *Amer.* **caviar** /'kævɪɑ:(r)/ *n.* caviar *m.*

caving /'keɪvɪŋ/ *n.* spéléologie *f.*

cavity /'kævɪtɪ/ *n.* cavité *f.*

cavort /kə'vɔ:t/ *v.i.* gambader.

CD /si:'di:/ *n.* compact disc *m.*

cease /si:s/ *v.t./i.* cesser. **~-fire** *n.* cessez-le-feu *m. invar.* **~less** *a.* incessant.

cedar /'si:də(r)/ *n.* cèdre *m.*

cede /si:d/ *v.t.* céder.

cedilla /sɪ'dɪlə/ *n.* cédille *f.*

ceiling /'si:lɪŋ/ *n.* plafond *m.*

celebrat|e /'selɪbreɪt/ *v.t.* (*perform, glorify*) célébrer; (*event*) fêter, célébrer. ● *v.i.* **we shall ~e**, on va fêter ça. **~ion** /-'breɪʃn/ *n.* fête *f.*

celebrated /'selɪbreɪtɪd/ *a.* célèbre.

celebrity /sɪ'lebrətɪ/ *n.* célébrité *f.*

celery /'selərɪ/ *n.* céleri *m.*

cell /sel/ *n.* cellule *f.*; (*electr.*) élément *m.*

cellar /'selə(r)/ *n.* cave *f.*

cell|o /'tʃeləʊ/ *n.* (*pl.* **-os**) violoncelle *m.* **~ist** *n.* violoncelliste *m./f.*

Cellophane /'seləfeɪn/ *n.* (P.) cellophane *f.* (P.).

Celt /kelt/ *n.* Celte *m./f.* **~ic** *a.* celtique, celte.

cement /sɪ'ment/ *n.* ciment *m.* ● *v.t.* cimenter. **~-mixer** *n.* bétonnière *f.*

cemetery /'semətrɪ/ *n.* cimetière *m.*

censor /'sensə(r)/ *n.* censeur *m.* ● *v.t.* censurer. **the ~**, la censure. **~ship** *n.* censure *f.*

censure /'senʃə(r)/ *n.* blâme *m.* ● *v.t.* blâmer.

census /'sensəs/ *n.* recensement *m.*

cent /sent/ *n.* (*coin*) cent *m.*

centenary /sen'ti:nərɪ, *Amer.* 'sentənərɪ/ *n.* centenaire *m.*

centigrade /'sentɪgreɪd/ *a.* centigrade.

centilitre, *Amer.* **centiliter** /'sentɪli:tə(r)/ *n.* centilitre *m.*

centimetre, *Amer.* **centimeter** /'sentɪmi:tə(r)/ *n.* centimètre *m.*

centipede /'sentɪpi:d/ *n.* millepattes *m. invar.*

central /'sentrəl/ *a.* central. **~ heating**, chauffage central *m.* **~ize** *v.t.* centraliser. **~ly** *adv.* (*situated*) au centre.

centre /'sentə(r)/ *n.* centre *m.* ● *v.t.* (*p.t.* **centred**) centrer. ● *v.i.* **~ on**, tourner autour de.

centrifugal /sen'trɪfjʊgl/ *a.* centrifuge.

century /'sentʃərɪ/ *n.* siècle *m.*

ceramic /sɪ'ræmɪk/ *a.* (*art*) céramique; (*object*) en céramique.

cereal /'sɪərɪəl/ *n.* céréale *f.*

cerebral /'serɪbrəl, *Amer.* sə'ri:brəl/ *a.* cérébral.

ceremonial /serɪ'məʊnɪəl/ *a.* de cérémonie. ● *n.* cérémonial *m.*

ceremon|y /'serɪmənɪ/ *n.* cérémonie *f.* **~ious** /-'məʊnɪəs/ *a.* solennel.

certain /'sɜ:tn/ *a.* certain. **for ~**, avec certitude. **make ~ of**, s'assurer de. **~ly** *adv.* certainement. **~ty** *n.* certitude *f.*

certificate /sə'tɪfɪkət/ *n.* certificat *m.*

certify /'sɜ:tɪfaɪ/ *v.t.* certifier.

cervical /sɜ:'vaɪkl/ *a.* cervical.

cessation /se'seɪʃn/ *n.* cessation *f.*

cesspit, cesspool /'sespɪt, 'sespu:l/ *ns.* fosse d'aisances *f.*

chafe /tʃeɪf/ *v.t.* frotter (contre).

chaff /tʃɑ:f/ *v.t.* taquiner.

chaffinch /'tʃæfɪntʃ/ *n.* pinson *m.*

chagrin /'ʃægrɪn/ *n.* vif dépit *m.*

chain /tʃeɪn/ *n.* chaîne *f.* ● *v.t.* enchaîner. **~ reaction**, réaction en chaîne *f.* **~-smoke** *v.i.* fumer de manière ininterrompue. **~ store**, magasin à succursales multiples *m.*

chair /tʃeə(r)/ *n.* chaise *f.*; (*armchair*) fauteuil *m.*; (*univ.*) chaire *f.* ● *v.t.* (*preside over*) présider.

chairman /'tʃeəmən/ *n.* (*pl.* **-men**) président(e) *m.* (*f.*).

chalet /'ʃæleɪ/ *n.* chalet *m.*

chalk /tʃɔ:k/ *n.* craie *f.* **~y** *a.* crayeux.

challeng|e /'tʃælɪndʒ/ *n.* défi *m.*; (*task*) gageure *f.* ● *v.t.* (*summon*) défier (**to do**, de faire); (*question truth of*) contester. **~er** *n.* (*sport*) challenger *m.* **~ing** *a.* stimulant.

chamber /'tʃeɪmbə(r)/ *n.* (*old use*) chambre *f.* **~ music**, musique de chambre *f.* **~-pot** *n.* pot de chambre *m.*

chambermaid /'tʃeɪmbəmeɪd/ *n.* femme de chambre *f.*

chamois /'ʃæmɪ/ *n.* **~(-leather)**, peau de chamois *f.*

champagne /ʃæm'peɪn/ *n.* champagne *m.*

champion /'tʃæmpɪən/ *n.* champion(ne) *m.* (*f.*). ● *v.t.* défendre. **~ship** *n.* championnat *m.*

chance /tʃɑ:ns/ *n.* (*luck*) hasard *m.*; (*opportunity*) occasion *f.*; (*likelihood*) chances *f. pl.*; (*risk*) risque *m.* ● *a.* fortuit. ● *v.t.* **~ doing**, prendre le risque de faire. **~ it**, risquer le coup. **by ~**, par hasard. **by any ~**, par hasard. **~s are that**, il est probable que.

chancellor /'tʃɑ:nsələ(r)/ *n.* chancelier *m.* **C~ of the Exchequer**, Chancelier de l'Échiquier.

chancy /'tʃɑ:nsɪ/ *a.* risqué.

chandelier /ʃændə'lɪə(r)/ *n.* lustre *m.*

change /tʃeɪndʒ/ *v.t.* (*alter*) changer; (*exchange*) échanger (**for**, contre); (*money*) changer. **~ trains/one's dress**/*etc.*, (*by substitution*) changer de train/de robe/*etc.* ● *v.i.* changer; (*change clothes*) se changer. ● *n.* changement *m.*; (*money*) monnaie *f.* **a ~ for the better**, une amélioration. **a ~ for the worse,** un changement en pire. **~ into,** se transformer en; (*clothes*) mettre. **a ~ of clothes,** des vêtements de rechange. **~ one's mind,** changer d'avis. **~ over,** passer (**to,** à). **for a ~,** pour changer. **~-over** *n.* passage *m.* **~able** *a.* changeant; (*weather*) variable. **~ing** *a.* changeant. **~-ing room,** (*in shop*) cabine d'essayage *f.*; (*sport.*) vestiaire *m.*

channel /'tʃænl/ *n.* chenal *m.*; (*TV*) chaîne*f.*; (*medium, agency*) canal *m.*; (*groove*) rainure *f.* ● *v.t.* (*p.t.* **chan-nelled**) (*direct*) canaliser. **the (English) C~,** la Manche. **the C~ Islands,** les îles anglo-normandes *f. pl.*

chant /tʃɑ:nt/ *n.* (*relig.*) psalmodie *f.*; (*of demonstrators*) chant (scandé) *m.* ● *v.t./i.* psalmodier; scander (des slogans).

chao|s /'keɪɒs/ *n.* chaos *m.* **~tic** /-'ɒtɪk/ *a.* chaotique.

chap /tʃæp/ *n.* (*man: fam.*) type *m.*

chapel /'tʃæpl/ *n.* chapelle *f.*; (*Non-conformist*) église (non-conformiste) *f.*

chaperon /'ʃæpərəʊn/ *n.* chaperon *m.* ● *v.t.* chaperonner.

chaplain /'tʃæplɪn/ *n.* aumônier *m.*

chapped /tʃæpt/ *a.* gercé.

chapter /'tʃæptə(r)/ *n.* chapitre *m.*

char¹ /tʃɑ:(r)/ *n.* (*fam.*) femme de ménage *f.*

char² /tʃɑ:(r)/ *v.t.* (*p.t.* **charred**) car-boniser.

character /'kærəktə(r)/ *n.* caractère *m.*; (*in novel, play*) personnage *m.* **of good ~,** de bonne réputation. **~ize** *v.t.* caractériser.

characteristic /kærəktə'rɪstɪk/ *a.* & *n.* caractéristique (*f.*). **~ally** *adv.* typiquement.

charade /ʃə'rɑ:d/ *n.* charade *f.*

charcoal /'tʃɑ:kəʊl/ *n.* charbon (de bois) *m.*

charge /tʃɑ:dʒ/ *n.* prix *m.*; (*mil.*) charge *f.*; (*jurid.*) inculpation *f.*, accusation *f.*; (*task, custody*) charge *f.* **~s,** frais *m. pl.* ● *v.t.* faire payer; (*ask*) demander (**for,** pour); (*enemy, gun*) charger; (*jurid.*) inculper, ac-cuser (**with,** de). ● *v.i.* foncer, se précipiter. **~ card,** carte d'achat *f.* **~ it to my account,** mettez-le sur mon compte. **in ~ of,** responsable de. **take ~ of,** prendre en charge, se

charger de. **~able to,** (*comm.*) aux frais de.

charisma /kə'rɪzmə/ *n.* magnétisme *m.* **~tic** /kærɪz'mætɪk/ *a.* charisma-tique.

charit|y /'tʃærətɪ/ *n.* charité *f.*; (*society*) fondation charitable *f.* **~able** *a.* charitable.

charlatan /'ʃɑ:lətən/ *n.* charlatan *m.*

charm /tʃɑ:m/ *n.* charme *m.*; (*trinket*) amulette *f.* ● *v.t.* charmer. **~ing** *a.* charmant.

chart /tʃɑ:t/ *n.* (*naut.*) carte (marine) *f.*; (*table*) tableau *m.*, graphique *m.* ● *v.t.* (*route*) porter sur la carte.

charter /'tʃɑ:tə(r)/ *n.* charte *f.* **~ (flight),** charter *m.* ● *v.t.* affréter. **~ed accountant,** expert-comptable *m.*

charwoman /'tʃɑ:wʊmən/ *n.* (*pl.* -**women**) femme de ménage *f.*

chase /tʃeɪs/ *v.t.* poursuivre. ● *v.i.* courir (**after,** après). ● *n.* chasse *f.* **~ away** *or* **off,** chasser.

chasm /'kæzəm/ *n.* abîme *m.*

chassis /'ʃæsɪ/ *n.* châssis *m.*

chaste /tʃeɪst/ *a.* chaste.

chastise /tʃæ'staɪz/ *v.t.* châtier.

chastity /'tʃæstətɪ/ *n.* chasteté *f.*

chat /tʃæt/ *n.* causette *f.* ● *v.i.* (*p.t.* **chatted**) bavarder. **have a ~,** bavarder. **~ show,** talk-show *m.* **~ up,** (*fam.*) draguer. **~ty** *a.* bavard.

chatter /'tʃætə(r)/ *n.* bavardage *m.* ● *v.i.* bavarder. **his teeth are ~ing,** il claque des dents.

chatterbox /'tʃætəbɒks/ *n.* bavard(e) *m.* (*f.*).

chauffeur /'ʃəʊfə(r)/ *n.* chauffeur (de particulier) *m.*

chauvinis|t /'ʃəʊvɪnɪst/ *n.* chauvin(e) *m.* (*f.*). **male ~t,** (*pej.*) phallocrate *m.* **~m** /-zəm/ *n.* chauvinisme *m.*

cheap /tʃi:p/ *a.* (**-er, -est**) bon marché *invar.*; (*fare, rate*) réduit; (*worth-less*) sans valeur. **~er,** meilleur marché *invar.* **~(ly)** *adv.* à bon marché. **~ness** *n.* bas prix *m.*

cheapen /'tʃi:pən/ *v.t.* déprécier.

cheat /tʃi:t/ *v.i.* tricher; (*by fraud*) frauder. ● *v.t.* (*defraud*) frauder; (*deceive*) tromper. ● *n.* escroc *m.*

check¹ /tʃek/ *v.t./i.* vérifier; (*tickets*) contrôler; (*stop*) enrayer, arrêter; (*restrain*) contenir; (*rebuke*) répri-mander; (*tick off: Amer.*) cocher. ● *n.* vérification *f.*; contrôle *m.*; (*curb*) frein *m.*; (*chess*) échec *m.*; (*bill: Amer.*) addition *f.*; (*cheque:*

Amer.) chèque *m.* **~ in,** signer le registre; (*at airport*) passer à l'enregistrement. **~-in** *n.* enregistrement *m.* **~-list** *n.* liste récapitulative *f.* **~ out,** régler sa note. **~-out** *n.* caisse *f.* **~-point** *n.* contrôle *m.* **~ up,** verifier. **~ up on,** (*detail*) vérifier; (*situation*) s'informer sur. **~-up** *n.* examen médical *m.*

check² /tʃek/ *n.* (*pattern*) carreaux *m. pl.* **~ed** *a.* à carreaux.

checking /ˈtʃekɪŋ/ *a.* **~ account,** (*Amer.*) compte courant *m.*

checkmate /ˈtʃekmeɪt/ *n.* échec et mat *m.*

checkroom /ˈtʃekrʊm/ *n.* (*Amer.*) vestiaire *m.*

cheek /tʃiːk/ *n.* joue *f.*; (*impudence*) culot *m.* **~y** *a.* effronté.

cheer /tʃɪə(r)/ *n.* gaieté *f.* **~s,** acclamations *f. pl.*; (*when drinking*) à votre santé. ● *v.t.* acclamer, applaudir. **~ (up),** (*gladden*) remonter le moral à. **~ up,** prendre courage. **~ful** à gai. **~fulness** *n.* gaieté *f.*

cheerio /tʃɪərɪˈəʊ/ *int.* (*fam.*) salut.

cheese /tʃiːz/ *n.* fromage *m.*

cheetah /ˈtʃiːtə/ *n.* guépard *m.*

chef /ʃef/ *n.* (*cook*) chef *m.*

chemical /ˈkemɪkl/ *a.* chimique. ● *n.* produit chimique *m.*

chemist /ˈkemɪst/ *n.* pharmacien(ne) *m.* (*f.*); (*scientist*) chimiste *m./f.* **~'s shop,** pharmacie *f.* **~ry** *n.* chimie *f.*

cheque /tʃek/ *n.* chèque *m.* **~-book** *n.* chéquier *m.* **~ card,** carte bancaire *f.*

chequered /ˈtʃekəd/ *a.* (*pattern*) à carreaux; (*fig.*) mouvementé.

cherish /ˈtʃerɪʃ/ *v.t.* chérir; (*hope*) nourrir, caresser.

cherry /ˈtʃerɪ/ *n.* cerise *f.*

chess /tʃes/ *n.* échecs *m. pl.* **~-board** *n.* échiquier *m.*

chest /tʃest/ *n.* (*anat.*) poitrine *f.*; (*box*) coffre *m.* **~ of drawers,** commode *f.*

chestnut /ˈtʃesnʌt/ *n.* châtaigne *f.*; (*edible*) marron *m.*, châtaigne *f.*

chew /tʃuː/ *v.t.* mâcher. **~ing-gum** *n.* chewing-gum *m.*

chic /ʃiːk/ *a.* chic *invar.*

chick /tʃɪk/ *n.* poussin *m.*

chicken /ˈtʃɪkɪn/ *n.* poulet *m.* ● *a.* (*sl.*) froussard. ● *v.i.* **~ out,** (*sl.*) se dégonfler. **~-pox** *n.* varicelle *f.*

chick-pea /ˈtʃɪkpiː/ *n.* pois chiche *m.*

chicory /ˈtʃɪkərɪ/ *n.* (*for salad*) endive *f.*; (*in coffee*) chicorée *f.*

chief /tʃiːf/ *n.* chef *m.* ● *a.* principal. **~ly** *adv.* principalement.

chilblain /ˈtʃɪlbleɪn/ *n.* engelure *f.*

child /tʃaɪld/ *n.* (*pl.* **children** /ˈtʃɪldrən/) enfant *m./f.* **~hood** *n.* enfance *f.* **~ish** *a.* enfantin. **~less** *a.* sans enfants. **~like** *a.* innocent, candide. **~-minder** *n.* nourrice *f.*

childbirth /ˈtʃaɪldbɜːθ/ *n.* accouchement *m.*

Chile /ˈtʃɪlɪ/ *n.* Chili *m.* **~an** *a.* & *n.* chilien(ne) (*m.* (*f.*)).

chill /tʃɪl/ *n.* froid *m.*; (*med.*) refroidissement *m.* ● *a.* froid. ● *v.t.* (*person*) donner froid à; (*wine*) rafraîchir; (*food*) mettre au frais. **~y** *a.* froid; (*sensitive to cold*) frileux. **be** *or* **feel ~y,** avoir froid.

chilli /ˈtʃɪlɪ/ *n.* (*pl.* **-ies**) piment *m.*

chime /tʃaɪm/ *n.* carillon *m.* ● *v.t./i.* carillonner.

chimney /ˈtʃɪmnɪ/ *n.* cheminée *f.* **~-sweep** *n.* ramoneur *m.*

chimpanzee /tʃɪmpænˈziː/ *n.* chimpanzé *m.*

chin /tʃɪn/ *n.* menton *m.*

china /ˈtʃaɪnə/ *n.* porcelaine *f.*

China /ˈtʃaɪnə/ *n.* Chine *f.* **~ese** /-ˈniːz/ *a.* & *n.* chinois(e) (*m.* (*f.*)).

chink¹ /tʃɪŋk/ *n.* (*slit*) fente *f.*

chink² /tʃɪŋk/ *n.* tintement *m.* ● *v.t./ i.* (faire) tinter.

chip /tʃɪp/ *n.* (*on plate etc.*) ébréchure *f.*; (*piece*) éclat *m.*; (*of wood*) copeau *m.*; (*culin.*) frite *f.*; (*microchip*) microplaquette *f.*, puce *f.* ● *v.t./i.* (*p.t.* **chipped**) (s')ébrécher. **~ in,** (*fam.*) dire son mot; (*with money: fam.*) contribuer. **(potato) ~s,** (*Amer.*) chips *f. pl.*

chipboard /ˈtʃɪpbɔːd/ *n.* aggloméré *m.*

chiropodist /kɪˈrɒpədɪst/ *n.* pédicure *m./f.*

chirp /tʃɜːp/ *n.* pépiement *m.* ● *v.i.* pépier.

chirpy /ˈtʃɜːpɪ/ *a.* gai.

chisel /ˈtʃɪzl/ *n.* ciseau *m.* ● *v.t.* (*p.t.* **chiselled**) ciseler.

chit /tʃɪt/ *n.* note *f.*, mot *m.*

chit-chat /ˈtʃɪttʃæt/ *n.* bavardage *m.*

chivalr|y /ˈʃɪvlrɪ/ *n.* galanterie *f.* **~ous** *a.* chevaleresque.

chives /tʃaɪvz/ *n. pl.* ciboulette *f.*

chlorine /ˈklɔːriːn/ *n.* chlore *m.*

choc-ice /ˈtʃɒkaɪs/ *n.* esquimau *m.*

chock /tʃɒk/ n. cale f. **~-a-block, ~-full** adjs. archiplein.

chocolate /'tʃɒklət/ n. chocolat m.

choice /tʃɔɪs/ n. choix m. ● a. de choix.

choir /'kwaɪə(r)/ n. chœur m.

choirboy /'kwaɪəbɔɪ/ n. jeune choriste m.

choke /tʃəʊk/ v.t./i. (s')étrangler. ● n. starter m. **~ (up),** boucher.

cholera /'kɒlərə/ n. choléra m.

cholesterol /kə'lestərɒl/ n. cholestérol m.

choose /tʃuːz/ v.t./i. (p.t. **chose,** p.p. **chosen**) choisir. **~ to do,** décider de faire.

choosy /'tʃuːzɪ/ a. (fam.) exigeant.

chop /tʃɒp/ v.t./i. (p.t. **chopped**) (wood) couper (à la hache); (food) hacher. ● n. (meat) côtelette f. **~ down,** abattre. **~per** n. hachoir m.; (sl.) hélicoptère m. **~ping-board** n. planche à découper f.

choppy /'tʃɒpɪ/ a. (sea) agité.

chopstick /'tʃɒpstɪk/ n. baguette f.

choral /'kɔːrəl/ a. choral.

chord /kɔːd/ n. (mus.) accord m.

chore /tʃɔː(r)/ n. travail (routinier) m.; (unpleasant task) corvée f.

choreography /kɒrɪ'ɒgrəfɪ/ n. chorégraphie f.

chortle /'tʃɔːtl/ n. gloussement m. ● v.i. glousser.

chorus /'kɔːrəs/ n. chœur m.; (of song) refrain m.

chose, chosen /tʃəʊz, 'tʃəʊzn/ see choose.

Christ /kraɪst/ n. le Christ.

christen /'krɪsn/ v.t. baptiser. **~ing** n. baptême m.

Christian /'krɪstʃən/ a. & n. chrétien(ne) (m. (f.)). **~ name,** prénom m. **~ity** /-stɪ'ænətɪ/ n. christianisme m.

Christmas /'krɪsməs/ n. Noël m. ● a. (card, tree, etc.) de Noël. **~-box** n. étrennes f. pl. **~ Day/Eve,** le jour/la veille de Noël.

chrome /krəʊm/ n. chrome m.

chromium /'krəʊmɪəm/ n. chrome m.

chromosome /'krəʊməsəʊm/ n. chromosome m.

chronic /'krɒnɪk/ a. (situation, disease) chronique; (bad: fam.) affreux.

chronicle /'krɒnɪkl/ n. chronique f.

chronolog|y /krə'nɒlədʒɪ/ n. chronologie f. **~ical** /krɒnə'lɒdʒɪkl/ a. chronologique.

chrysanthemum /krɪ'sænθəməm/ n.

chrysanthème m.

chubby /'tʃʌbɪ/ a. (-ier, -iest) dodu, potelé.

chuck /tʃʌk/ v.t. (fam.) lancer. **~ away** or **out,** (fam.) balancer.

chuckle /'tʃʌkl/ n. gloussement m. ● v.i. glousser, rire.

chuffed /tʃʌft/ a. (sl.) bien content.

chum /tʃʌm/ n. cop|ain, -ine m., f. **~my** a. amical. **~my with,** copain avec.

chunk /tʃʌŋk/ n. (gros) morceau m.

chunky /'tʃʌŋkɪ/ a. trapu.

church /tʃɜːtʃ/ n. église f.

churchyard /'tʃɜːtʃjɑːd/ n. cimetière m.

churlish /'tʃɜːlɪʃ/ a. grossier.

churn /tʃɜːn/ n. baratte f.; (milk-can) bidon m. ● v.t. baratter. **~ out,** produire (en série).

chute /ʃuːt/ n. glissière f.; (for rubbish) vide-ordures m. invar.

chutney /'tʃʌtnɪ/ n. condiment (de fruits) m.

cider /'saɪdə(r)/ n. cidre m.

cigar /sɪ'gɑː(r)/ n. cigare m.

cigarette /sɪgə'ret/ n. cigarette f. **~ end,** mégot m. **~-holder** n. fume-cigarette m. invar.

cinder /'sɪndə(r)/ n. cendre f.

cine-camera /'sɪnɪkæmərə/ n. caméra f.

cinema /'sɪnəmə/ n. cinéma m.

cinnamon /'sɪnəmən/ n. cannelle f.

cipher /'saɪfə(r)/ n. (numeral, code) chiffre m.; (person) nullité f.

circle /'sɜːkl/ n. cercle m.; (theatre) balcon m. ● v.t. (go round) faire le tour de; (word, error, etc.) entourer d'un cercle. ● v.i. décrire des cercles.

circuit /'sɜːkɪt/ n. circuit m. **~-breaker** n. disjoncteur m.

circuitous /sɜː'kjuːɪtəs/ a. indirect.

circular /'sɜːkjʊlə(r)/ a. & n. circulaire (f.).

circulat|e /'sɜːkjʊleɪt/ v.t./i. (faire) circuler. **~ion** /-'leɪʃn/ n. circulation f.; (of newspaper) tirage m.

circumcis|e /'sɜːkəmsaɪz/ v.t. circoncire. **~ion** /-'sɪʒn/ n. circoncision f.

circumference /sɜː'kʌmfərəns/ n. circonférence f.

circumflex /'sɜːkəmfleks/ n. circonflexe m.

circumspect /'sɜːkəmspekt/ a. circonspect.

circumstance /'sɜːkəmstəns/ *n.* circonstance *f.* **~s,** (*financial*) situation financière *f.*

circus /'sɜːkəs/ *n.* cirque *m.*

cistern /'sɪstən/ *n.* réservoir *m.*

citadel /'sɪtədel/ *n.* citadelle *f.*

cit|e /saɪt/ *v.t.* citer. **~ation** /-'teɪʃn/ *n.* citation *f.*

citizen /'sɪtɪzn/ *n.* citoyen(ne) *m.* (*f.*); (*of town*) habitant(e) *m.* (*f.*). **~ship** *n.* citoyenneté *f.*

citrus /'sɪtrəs/ *a.* **~ fruit(s),** agrumes *m. pl.*

city /'sɪtɪ/ *n.* (grande) ville *f.* **the C~,** la Cité de Londres.

civic /'sɪvɪk/ *a.* civique. **~ centre,** centre administratif *m.* **~s** *n. pl.* instruction civique *f.*

civil /'sɪvl/ *a.* civil; (*rights*) civique; (*defence*) passif. **~ engineer,** ingénieur civil *m.* **C~ Servant,** fonctionnaire *m./f.* **C~ Service,** fonction publique *f.* **~ war,** guerre civile *f.* **~ity** /sɪ'vɪlətɪ/ *n.* civilité *f.*

civilian /sɪ'vɪliən/ *a. & n.* civil(e) (*m.* (*f.*)).

civiliz|e /'sɪvəlaɪz/ *v.t.* civiliser. **~ation** /-'zeɪʃn/ *n.* civilisation *f.*

civvies /'sɪvɪz/ *n. pl.* **in ~,** (*sl.*) en civil.

clad /klæd/ *a.* **~ in,** vêtu de.

claim /kleɪm/ *v.t.* revendiquer, réclamer; (*assert*) prétendre. ● *n.* revendication *f.*, prétention *f.*; (*assertion*) affirmation *f.*; (*for insurance*) réclamation *f.*; (*right*) droit *m.*

claimant /'kleɪmənt/ *n.* (*of social benefits*) demandeur *m.*

clairvoyant /kleə'vɔɪənt/ *n.* voyant(e) *m.* (*f.*).

clam /klæm/ *n.* palourde *f.*

clamber /'klæmbə(r)/ *v.i.* grimper.

clammy /'klæmɪ/ *a.* (**-ier, -iest**) moite.

clamour /'klæmə(r)/ *n.* clameur *f.*, cris *m. pl.* ● *v.i.* **~ for,** demander à grands cris.

clamp /klæmp/ *n.* agrafe *f.*; (*large*) crampon *m.*; (*for carpentry*) serre-joint(s) *m.*; (*for car*) sabot de Denver *m.* ● *v.t.* serrer; (*car*) mettre un sabot de Denver à. **~ down on,** sévir contre.

clan /klæn/ *n.* clan *m.*

clandestine /klæn'destɪn/ *a.* clandestin.

clang /klæŋ/ *n.* son métallique *m.*

clanger /'klæŋə(r)/ *n.* (*sl.*) bévue *f.*

clap /klæp/ *v.t./i.* (*p.t.* **clapped**) applaudir; (*put forcibly*) mettre. ● *n.*

applaudissement *m.*; (*of thunder*) coup *m.* **~ one's hands,** battre des mains.

claptrap /'klæptræp/ *n.* baratin *m.*

claret /'klærət/ *n.* bordeaux rouge *m.*

clarif|y /'klærɪfaɪ/ *v.t./i.* (se) clarifier. **~ication** /-ɪ'keɪʃn/ *n.* clarification *f.*

clarinet /klærɪ'net/ *n.* clarinette *f.*

clarity /'klærətɪ/ *n.* clarté *f.*

clash /klæʃ/ *n.* choc *m.*; (*fig.*) conflit *m.* ● *v.i.* (*metal objects*) s'entrechoquer; (*fig.*) se heurter.

clasp /klɑːsp/ *n.* (*fastener*) fermoir *m.*, agrafe *f.* ● *v.t.* serrer.

class /klɑːs/ *n.* classe *f.* ● *v.t.* classer.

classic /'klæsɪk/ *a. & n.* classique (*m.*). **~s,** (*univ.*) les humanités *f. pl.* **~al** *a.* classique.

classif|y /'klæsɪfaɪ/ *v.t.* classifier. **~ication** /-ɪ'keɪʃn/ *n.* classification *f.* **~ied** *a.* (*information etc.*) secret. **~ied advertisement,** petite annonce *f.*

classroom /'klɑːsrʊm/ *n.* salle de classe *f.*

classy /'klɑːsɪ/ *a.* (*sl.*) chic *invar.*

clatter /'klætə(r)/ *n.* cliquetis *m.* ● *v.i.* cliqueter.

clause /klɔːz/ *n.* clause *f.*; (*gram.*) proposition *f.*

claustrophob|ia /klɔːstrə'fəʊbɪə/ *n.* claustrophobie *f.* **~ic** *a. & n.* claustrophobe (*m./f.*).

claw /klɔː/ *n.* (*of animal, small bird*) griffe *f.*; (*of bird of prey*) serre *f.*; (*of lobster*) pince *f.* ● *v.t.* griffer.

clay /kleɪ/ *n.* argile *f.*

clean /kliːn/ *a.* (**-er, -est**) propre; (*shape, stroke, etc.*) net. ● *adv.* complètement. ● *v.t.* nettoyer. ● *v.i.* **~ up,** faire le nettoyage. **~ one's teeth,** se brosser les dents. **~-shaven** *a.* glabre. **~er** *n.* (*at home*) femme de ménage *f.*; (*industrial*) agent de nettoyage *m./f.*; (*of clothes*) teintur|ier, -ière *m.*, *f.* **~ly** *adv.* proprement; (*sharply*) nettement.

cleanliness /'klenlɪnɪs/ *n.* propreté *f.*

cleans|e /klenz/ *v.t.* nettoyer; (*fig.*) purifier. **~ing cream,** crème démaquillante *f.*

clear /klɪə(r)/ *a.* (**-er, -est**) clair; (*glass*) transparent; (*profit*) net; (*road*) dégagé. ● *adv.* complètement. ● *v.t.* (*free*) dégager (**of,** de); (*table*) débarrasser; (*building*) évacuer; (*cheque*) encaisser; (*jump over*) franchir; (*debt*) liquider; (*jurid.*) disculper. **~ (away or**

off), (*remove*) enlever. ● *v.i.* (*fog*) se dissiper. **~ of,** (*away from*) à l'écart de. **~ off** *or* **out,** (*sl.*) décamper. **~ out,** (*clean*) nettoyer. **~ up,** (*tidy*) ranger; (*mystery*) éclaircir; (*of weather*) s'éclaircir. **make sth. ~,** être très clair sur qch. **~-cut** *a.* net. **~ly** *adv.* clairement.

clearance /'klɪərəns/ *n.* (*permission*) autorisation *f.*; (*space*) dégagement *m.* **~ sale,** liquidation *f.*

clearing /'klɪərɪŋ/ *n.* clairière *f.*

clearway /'klɪəweɪ/ *n.* route à stationnement interdit *f.*

cleavage /'kli:vɪdʒ/ *n.* clivage *m.*; (*breasts*) décolleté *m.*

clef /klef/ *n.* (*mus.*) clé *f.*

cleft /kleft/ *n.* fissure *f.*

clemen|t /'klemənt/ *a.* clément. **~cy** *n.* clémence *f.*

clench /klentʃ/ *v.t.* serrer.

clergy /'klɜ:dʒɪ/ *n.* clergé *m.* **~man** *n.* (*pl.* **-men**) ecclésiastique *m.*

cleric /'klerɪk/ *n.* clerc *m.* **~al** *a.* (*relig.*) clérical; (*of clerks*) de bureau, d'employé.

clerk /klɑ:k, *Amer.* klɜ:k/ *n.* employé(e) de bureau *m.* (*f.*). (*Amer.*) (*sales*) **~,** vendeu|r, -se *m.*, *f.*

clever /'klevə(r)/ *a.* (**-er, -est**) intelligent; (*skilful*) habile. **~ly** *adv.* intelligemment; habilement. **~ness** *n.* intelligence *f.*

cliché /'kli:ʃeɪ/ *n.* cliché *m.*

click /klɪk/ *n.* déclic *m.* ● *v.i.* faire un déclic; (*people: sl.*) s'entendre, se plaire. ● *v.t.* (*heels, tongue*) faire claquer.

client /'klaɪənt/ *n.* client(e) *m.* (*f.*).

clientele /kli:ən'tel/ *n.* clientèle *f.*

cliff /klɪf/ *n.* falaise *f.*

climat|e /'klaɪmɪt/ *n.* climat *m.* **~ic** /-'mætɪk/ *a.* climatique.

climax /'klaɪmæks/ *n.* point culminant *m.*; (*sexual*) orgasme *m.*

climb /klaɪm/ *v.t.* (*stairs*) monter, grimper; (*tree, ladder*) monter *or* grimper à; (*mountain*) faire l'ascension de. ● *v.i.* monter, grimper. ● *n.* montée *f.* **~ down,** (*fig.*) reculer. **~-down,** *n.* recul *m.* **~er** *n.* (*sport*) alpiniste *m./f.*

clinch /klɪntʃ/ *v.t.* (*a deal*) conclure.

cling /klɪŋ/ *v.i.* (*p.t.* **clung**) se cramponner (**to,** à); (*stick*) coller. **~-film** *n.* (P.) film adhésif *m.*

clinic /'klɪnɪk/ *n.* centre médical *m.*; (*private*) clinique *f.*

clinical /'klɪnɪkl/ *a.* clinique.

clink /klɪŋk/ *n.* tintement *m.* ● *v.t./i.* (faire) tinter.

clinker /'klɪŋkə(r)/ *n.* mâchefer *m.*

clip¹ /klɪp/ *n.* (*for paper*) trombone *m.*; (*for hair*) barrette *f.*; (*for tube*) collier *m.* ● *v.t.* (*p.t.* **clipped**) attacher (**to,** à).

clip² /klɪp/ *v.t.* (*p.t.* **clipped**) (*cut*) couper. ● *n.* coupe *f.*; (*of film*) extrait *m.*; (*blow: fam.*) taloche *f.* **~ping** *n.* coupure *f.*

clippers /'klɪpəz/ *n. pl.* tondeuse *f.*; (*for nails*) coupe-ongles *m.*

clique /kli:k/ *n.* clique *f.*

cloak /kləʊk/ *n.* (grande) cape *f.*, manteau ample *m.*

cloakroom /'kləʊkrʊm/ *n.* vestiaire *m.*; (*toilet*) toilettes *f. pl.*

clobber /'klɒbə(r)/ *n.* (*sl.*) affaires *f. pl.* ● *v.t.* (*hit: sl.*) rosser.

clock /klɒk/ *n.* pendule *f.*; (*large*) horloge *f.* ● *v.i.* **~ in** *or* **out,** pointer. **~ up,** (*miles etc.: fam.*) faire. **~-tower** *n.* clocher *m.*

clockwise /'klɒkwaɪz/ *a. & adv.* dans le sens des aiguilles d'une montre.

clockwork /'klɒkwɜ:k/ *n.* mécanisme *m.* ● *a.* mécanique.

clog /klɒg/ *n.* sabot *m.* ● *v.t./i.* (*p.t.* **clogged**) se boucher.

cloister /'klɔɪstə(r)/ *n.* cloître *m.*

close¹ /kləʊs/ *a.* (**-er, -est**) (*near*) proche (**to,** de); (*link, collaboration*) étroit; (*examination*) attentif; (*friend*) intime; (*order, match*) serré; (*weather*) lourd. **~ together,** (*crowded*) serrés. ● *adv.* (tout) près. ● *n.* (*street*) impasse *f.* **~ by, ~ at hand,** tout près. **~-up** *n.* gros plan *m.* **have a ~ shave,** l'échapper belle. **keep a ~ watch on,** surveiller de près. **~ly** *adv.* (*follow*) de près. **~ness** *n.* proximité *f.*

close² /kləʊz/ *v.t.* fermer. ● *v.i.* se fermer; (*of shop etc.*) fermer; (*end*) (se) terminer. ● *n.* fin *f.* **~d shop,** organisation qui exclut les travailleurs non syndiqués *f.*

closet /'klɒzɪt/ *n.* (*Amer.*) placard *m.*

closure /'kləʊʒə(r)/ *n.* fermeture *f.*

clot /klɒt/ *n.* (*of blood*) caillot *m.*; (*in sauce*) grumeau *m.* ● *v.t./i.* (*p.t.* **clotted**) (se) conguler.

cloth /klɒθ/ *n.* tissu *m.*; (*duster*) linge *m.*; (*table-cloth*) nappe *f.*

cloth|e /kləʊð/ *v.t.* vêtir. **~ing** *n.* vêtements *m. pl.*

clothes /kləʊðz/ n. pl. vêtements m. pl., habits m. pl. ~-brush n. brosse à habits f. ~-hanger n. cintre m. ~-line n. corde à linge f. ~-peg, (Amer.) ~-pin ns. pince à linge f.

cloud /klaʊd/ n. nuage m. ● v.i. se couvrir (de nuages); (become gloomy) s'assombrir. ~y a. (sky) couvert; (liquid) trouble.

cloudburst /'klaʊdbɜːst/ n. trombe d'eau f.

clout /klaʊt/ n. (blow) coup de poing m.; (power: fam.) pouvoir effectif m. ● v.t. frapper.

clove /kləʊv/ n. clou de girofle m. ~ of garlic, gousse d'ail f.

clover /'kləʊvə(r)/ n. trèfle m.

clown /klaʊn/ n. clown m. ● v.i. faire le clown.

cloy /klɔɪ/ v.t. écœurer.

club /klʌb/ n. (group) club m.; (weapon) massue f. ~s, (cards) trèfle m. ● v.t./i. (p.t. clubbed) matraquer. (golf) ~, club (de golf) m. ~ together, (share costs) se cotiser.

cluck /klʌk/ v.i. glousser.

clue /kluː/ n. indice m.; (in crossword) définition f. I haven't a ~, (fam.) je n'en ai pas la moindre idée.

clump /klʌmp/ n. massif m.

clums|y /'klʌmzɪ/ a. (-ier, -iest) maladroit; (tool) peu commode. ~iness n. maladresse f.

clung /klʌŋ/ see cling.

cluster /'klʌstə(r)/ n. (petit) groupe m. ● v.i. se grouper.

clutch /klʌtʃ/ v.t. (hold) serrer fort; (grasp) saisir. ● v.i. ~ at, (try to grasp) essayer de saisir. ● n. étreinte f.; (auto.) embrayage m.

clutter /'klʌtə(r)/ n. désordre m., fouillis m. ● v.t. encombrer.

coach /kəʊtʃ/ n. autocar m.; (of train) wagon m.; (horse-drawn) carrosse m.; (sport) entraîneu|r, -se m., f. ● v.t. donner des leçons (particulières) à; (sport) entraîner.

coagulate /kəʊ'ægjʊleɪt/ v.t./i. (se) coaguler.

coal /kəʊl/ n. charbon m. ~-mine n. mine de charbon f.

coalfield /'kəʊlfiːld/ n. bassin houiller m.

coalition /kəʊə'lɪʃn/ n. coalition f.

coarse /kɔːs/ a. (-er, -est) grossier. ~ness n. caractère grossier m.

coast /kəʊst/ n. côte f. ● v.i. (car, bicycle) descendre en roue libre. ~al a. côtier.

coaster /'kəʊstə(r)/ n. (ship) caboteur m.; (mat) dessous de verre m.

coastguard /'kəʊstgɑːd/ n. gardecôte m.

coastline /'kəʊstlaɪn/ n. littoral m.

coat /kəʊt/ n. manteau m.; (of animal) pelage m.; (of paint) couche f. ● v.t. enduire, couvrir; (with chocolate) enrober (with, de). ~-hanger n. cintre m. ~ of arms, armoiries f. pl. ~ing n. couche f.

coax /kəʊks/ v.t. amadouer.

cob /kɒb/ n. (of corn) épi m.

cobble [1] /'kɒbl/ n. pavé m. ~-stone n. pavé m.

cobble [2] /'kɒbl/ v.t. rapetasser.

cobbler /'kɒblə(r)/ n. (old use) cordonnier m.

cobweb /'kɒbweb/ n. toile d'araignée f.

cocaine /kəʊ'keɪn/ n. cocaïne f.

cock /kɒk/ n. (oiseau) mâle m.; (rooster) coq m. ● v.t. (gun) armer; (ears) dresser. ~-and-bull story, histoire à dormir debout f. ~-eyed a. (askew: sl.) de travers. ~-up n. (sl.) pagaille f.

cockerel /'kɒkərəl/ n. jeune coq m.

cockle /'kɒkl/ n. (culin.) coque f.

cockney /'kɒknɪ/ n. Cockney m./f.

cockpit /'kɒkpɪt/ n. poste de pilotage m.

cockroach /'kɒkrəʊtʃ/ n. cafard m.

cocksure /kɒk'ʃʊə(r)/ a. sûr de soi.

cocktail /'kɒkteɪl/ n. cocktail m. ~ party, cocktail m. fruit ~, macédoine (de fruits) f.

cocky /'kɒkɪ/ a. (-ier, -iest) trop sûr de soi, arrogant.

cocoa /'kəʊkəʊ/ n. cacao m.

coconut /'kəʊkənʌt/ n. noix de coco f.

cocoon /kə'kuːn/ n. cocon m.

COD abbr. (cash on delivery) paiement à la livraison m.

cod /kɒd/ n. invar. morue f. ~-liver oil, huile de foie de morue f.

coddle /'kɒdl/ v.t. dorloter.

code /kəʊd/ n. code m. ● v.t. coder.

codify /'kəʊdɪfaɪ/ v.t. codifier.

coeducational /kəʊedʒʊ'keɪʃənl/ a. (school, teaching) mixte.

coerc|e /kəʊ'ɜːs/ v.t. contraindre. ~ion /-ʃn/ n. contrainte f.

coexist /kəʊɪg'zɪst/ v.i. coexister. ~ence n. coexistence f.

coffee /'kɒfɪ/ n. café m. ~ **bar,** café m., cafétéria f. ~-**pot** n. cafetière f. ~-**table** n. table basse f.

coffer /'kɒfə(r)/ n. coffre m.

coffin /'kɒfɪn/ n. cercueil m.

cog /kɒɡ/ n. dent f.; (fig.) rouage m.

cogent /'kəʊdʒənt/ a. convaincant; (relevant) pertinent.

cognac /'kɒnjæk/ n. cognac m.

cohabit /kəʊ'hæbɪt/ v.i. vivre en concubinage.

coherent /kəʊ'hɪərənt/ a. cohérent.

coil /kɔɪl/ v.t./i. (s')enrouler. ● n. rouleau m.; (one ring) spire f.; (contraceptive) stérilet m.

coin /kɔɪn/ n. pièce (de monnaie) f. ● v.t. (word) inventer. ~**age** n. monnaie f.; (fig.) invention f. ~-**box** n. téléphone public m.

coincide /kəʊn'saɪd/ v.i. coïncider.

coinciden|ce /kəʊ'ɪnsɪdəns/ n. coïncidence f. ~**tal** /-'dentl/ a. dû à une coïncidence.

coke /kəʊk/ n. coke m.

colander /'kʌləndə(r)/ n. passoire f.

cold /kəʊld/ a. (-er, -est) froid. be or **feel** ~, avoir froid. **it is** ~, il fait froid. ● n. froid m.; (med.) rhume m. ~-**blooded** a. sans pitié. ~ **cream,** crème de beauté f. **get** ~ **feet,** se dégonfler. ~-**shoulder** v.t. snober. ~ **sore,** bouton de fièvre m. ~**ness** n. froideur f.

coleslaw /'kəʊlslɔ:/ n. salade de chou cru f.

colic /'kɒlɪk/ n. coliques f. pl.

collaborat|e /kə'læbəreɪt/ v.i. collaborer. ~**ion** /-'reɪʃn/ n. collaboration f. ~**or** n. collabora|teur, -trice m., f.

collage /'kɒlɑ:ʒ/ n. collage m.

collapse /kə'læps/ v.i. s'effondrer; (med.) avoir un malaise. ● n. effondrement m.

collapsible /kə'læpsəbl/ a. pliant.

collar /'kɒlə(r)/ n. col m.; (of dog) collier m. ● v.t. (take: sl.) piquer. ~-**bone** n. clavicule f.

collateral /kə'lætərəl/ n. nantissement m.

colleague /'kɒli:ɡ/ n. collègue m./f.

collect /kə'lekt/ v.t. rassembler; (pick up) ramasser; (call for) passer prendre; (money, rent) encaisser; (taxes) percevoir; (as hobby) collectionner. ● v.i. se rassembler; (dust) s'amasser. ● adv. **call** ~, (Amer.) téléphoner en PCV. ~**ion** /-kʃn/ n. collection f.; (in church)

quête f.; (of mail) levée f. ~**or** n. (as hobby) collectionneu|r, -se m., f.

collective /kə'lektɪv/ a. collectif.

college /'kɒlɪdʒ/ n. (for higher education) institut m., école f.; (within university) collège m. **be at** ~, être en faculté.

collide /kə'laɪd/ v.i. entrer en collision (**with,** avec).

colliery /'kɒlɪərɪ/ n. houillère f.

collision /kə'lɪʒn/ n. collision f.

colloquial /kə'ləʊkwɪəl/ a. familier. ~**ism** n. expression familière f.

collusion /kə'lu:ʒn/ n. collusion f.

colon /'kəʊlən/ n. (gram.) deux-points m. invar.; (anat.) côlon m.

colonel /'kɜ:nl/ n. colonel m.

colonize /'kɒlənaɪz/ v.t. coloniser.

colon|y /'kɒlənɪ/ n. colonie f. ~**ial** /kə'ləʊnɪəl/ a. & n. colonial(e) (m. (f.)).

colossal /kə'lɒsl/ a. colossal.

colour /'kʌlə(r)/ n. couleur f. ● a. (photo etc.) en couleur; (TV set) couleur invar. ● v.t. colorer; (with crayon) colorier. ~-**blind** a. daltonien. ~-**fast** a. grand teint. invar. ~**ful** a. coloré; (person) haut en couleur. ~**ing** n. (of skin) teint m.; (in food) colorant m.

coloured /'kʌləd/ a. (person, pencil) de couleur. ● n. personne de couleur f.

colt /kəʊlt/ n. poulain m.

column /'kɒləm/ n. colonne f.

columnist /'kɒləmnɪst/ n. journaliste chroniqueur m.

coma /'kəʊmə/ n. coma m.

comb /kəʊm/ n. peigne m. ● v.t. peigner; (search) ratisser. ~ **one's hair,** se peigner.

combat /'kɒmbæt/ n. combat m. ● v.t. (p.t. **combated**) combattre. ~**ant** /-ətənt/ n. combattant(e) m. (f.).

combination /kɒmbɪ'neɪʃn/ n. combinaison f.

combine[1] /kəm'baɪn/ v.t./i. (se) combiner, (s')unir.

combine[2] /'kɒmbaɪn/ n. (comm.) trust m., cartel m. ~ **harvester,** moissonneuse-batteuse f.

combustion /kəm'bʌstʃən/ n. combustion f.

come /kʌm/ v.i. (p.t. **came,** p.p. **come**) venir; (occur) arriver; (sexually) jouir. ~ **about,** arriver. ~ **across,** rencontrer or trouver par hasard. ~ **away** or **off,** se détacher,

partir. ~ **back,** revenir. ~**-back** *n.*
rentrée *f.*; (*retort*) réplique *f.* ~ **by,**
obtenir. ~ **down,** descendre; (*price*)
baisser. ~**-down** *n.* humiliation *f.* ~
forward, se présenter. ~ **from,** être
de. ~ **in,** entrer. ~ **in for,** recevoir.
~ **into,** (*money*) hériter de. ~ **off,**
(*succeed*) réussir; (*fare*) s'en tirer. ~
on, (*actor*) entrer en scène; (*light*)
s'allumer; (*improve*) faire des
progrès. ~ **on!,** allez! ~ **out,**
sortir. ~ **round** *or* **to,** revenir à
soi. ~ **through,** s'en tirer (indemne
de). ~ **to,** (*amount*) revenir à;
(*decision, conclusion*) arriver à. ~
up, monter; (*fig.*) se présenter. ~ **up
against,** rencontrer. **get one's** ~-
uppance *n.* (*fam.*) finir par recevoir
ce qu'on mérite. ~ **up with,** (*find*)
trouver; (*produce*) produire.

comedian /kə'miːdiən/ *n.* comique
m.

comedy /'kɒmədɪ/ *n.* comédie *f.*

comely /'kʌmlɪ/ *a.* (**-ier, -iest**) (*old
use*) avenant, beau.

comet /'kɒmɪt/ *n.* comète *f.*

comfort /'kʌmfət/ *n.* confort *m.*;
(*consolation*) réconfort *m.* ● *v.t.*
consoler. **one's** ~**s,** ses aises.
~**able** *a.* (*chair, car, etc.*) confortable; (*person*) à l'aise, bien; (*wealthy*)
aisé.

comforter /'kʌmfətə(r)/ *n.* (*baby's
dummy*) sucette *f.*; (*quilt*: *Amer.*)
édredon *m.*

comfy /'kʌmfɪ/ *a.* (*fam.*) = **comfortable.**

comic /'kɒmɪk/ *a.* comique. ● *n.*
(*person*) comique *m.*; (*periodical*)
comic *m.* ~ **strip,** bande dessinée *f.*
~**al** *a.* comique.

coming /'kʌmɪŋ/ *n.* arrivée *f.* ● *a.* à
venir. ~**s and goings,** allées et
venues *f. pl.*

comma /'kɒmə/ *n.* virgule *f.*

command /kə'mɑːnd/ *n.* (*authority*)
commandement *m.*; (*order*) ordre
m.; (*mastery*) maîtrise *f.* ● *v.t.* commander (**s.o. to,** à qn. de); (*be able to
use*) disposer de; (*require*) nécessiter; (*respect*) inspirer. ~**er** *n.* commandant *m.* ~**ing** *a.* imposant.

commandeer /kɒmən'dɪə(r)/ *v.t.* réquisitionner.

commandment /kə'mɑːndmənt/ *n.*
commandement *m.*

commando /kə'mɑːndəʊ/ *n.* (*pl.* **-os**)
commando *m.*

commemorat|e /kə'meməreɪt/ *v.t.*
commémorer. ~**ion** /-'reɪʃn/ *n.* com-
mémoration *f.* ~**ive** /-ətɪv/ *a.* commémoratif.

commence /kə'mens/ *v.t./i.*
commencer. ~**ment** *n.* commencement *m.*; (*univ., Amer.*) cérémonie
de distribution des diplômes *f.*

commend /kə'mend/ *v.t.* (*praise*)
louer; (*entrust*) confier. ~**able** *a.*
louable. ~**ation** /kɒmen'deɪʃn/ *n.*
éloge *m.*

commensurate /kə'menʃərət/ *a.*
proportionné.

comment /'kɒment/ *n.* commentaire
m. ● *v.i.* faire des commentaires. ~
on, commenter.

commentary /'kɒməntrɪ/ *n.* commentaire *m.*; (*radio, TV*) reportage
m.

commentat|e /'kɒmənteɪt/ *v.i.* faire
un reportage. ~**or** *n.* commenta-
teur, -trice *m., f.*

commerce /'kɒmɜːs/ *n.* commerce *m.*

commercial /kə'mɜːʃl/ *a.* commercial; (*traveller*) de commerce. ● *n.*
publicité *f.* ~**ize** *v.t.* commercialiser.

commiserat|e /kə'mɪzəreɪt/ *v.i.* com-
patir (**with,** avec). ~**ion** /-'reɪʃn/ *n.*
commisération *f.*

commission /kə'mɪʃn/ *n.* commission *f.*; (*order for work*) commande
f. ● *v.t.* (*order*) commander; (*mil.*)
nommer officier. ~ **to do,** charger
de faire. **out of** ~, hors service. ~**er**
n. préfet (de police) *m.*; (*in E.C.*)
commissaire *m.*

commissionaire /kəmɪʃə'neə(r)/ *n.*
commissionnaire *m.*

commit /kə'mɪt/ *v.t.* (*p.t.* **committed**) commettre; (*entrust*)
confier. ~ **o.s.,** s'engager. ~ **perjury,** se parjurer. ~ **suicide,** se
suicider. ~ **to memory,** apprendre
par cœur. ~**ment** *n.* engagement *m.*

committee /kə'mɪtɪ/ *n.* comité *m.*

commodity /kə'mɒdɪtɪ/ *n.* produit
m., article *m.*

common /'kɒmən/ *a.* (**-er, -est**)
(*shared by all*) commun; (*usual*)
courant, commun; (*vulgar*) vulgaire, commun. ● *n.* terrain communal *m.* ~ **law,** droit coutumier *m.*
C~ Market, Marché Commun *m.* ~
room *n.* (*school.*) salle commune *f.* ~
sense, bon sens *m.* **House of C~s,**
Chambre des Communes *f.* **in** ~, en
commun. ~**ly** *adv.* communément.

commoner /'kɒmənə(r)/ n. rotur|ier, -ière m., f.

commonplace /'kɒmənpleɪs/ a. banal. ● n. banalité f.

Commonwealth /'kɒmənwelθ/ n. **the ~**, le Commonwealth m.

commotion /kə'məʊʃn/ n. agitation f., remue-ménage m. invar.

communal /'kɒmjʊnl/ a. (shared) commun; (life) collectif.

commune /'kɒmju:n/ n. (group) communauté f.

communicat|e /kə'mju:nɪkeɪt/ v.t./i. communiquer. **~ion**/-'keɪʃn/ n. communication f. **~ive** /-ətɪv/ a. communicatif.

communion /kə'mju:nɪən/ n. communion f.

communiqué /kə'mju:nɪkeɪ/ n. communiqué m.

Communis|t /'kɒmjʊnɪst/ a. & n. communiste (m./f.) **~m** /-zəm/ n. communisme m.

community /kə'mju:nətɪ/ n. communauté f.

commutation /kɒmju:'teɪʃn/ n. **~ ticket**, carte d'abonnement f.

commute /kə'mju:t/ v.i. faire la navette. ● v.t. (jurid.) commuer. **~r** /-ə(r)/ n. banlieusard(e) m. (f.).

compact[1] /kəm'pækt/ a. compact. **~ 'kɒmpækt**/ disc, (disque) compact m.

compact[2] /'kɒmpækt/ n. (lady's case) poudrier m.

companion /kəm'pænjən/ n. compagnon, -agne m., f. **~ship** n. camaraderie f.

company /'kʌmpənɪ/ n. (companionship, firm) compagnie f.; (guests) invité(e)s m. (f.) pl.

comparable /'kɒmpərəbl/ a. comparable.

compar|e /kəm'peə(r)/ v.t. comparer (with, to, à). **~ed with** or **to**, en comparaison de. ● v.i. être comparable. **~ative** /-'pærətɪv/ a. (study, form) comparatif; (comfort etc.) relatif. **~atively** /-'pærətɪvlɪ/ adv. relativement.

comparison /kəm'pærɪsn/ n. comparaison f.

compartment /kəm'pɑ:tmənt/ n. compartiment m.

compass /'kʌmpəs/ n. (for direction) boussole f.; (scope) portée f. **~(es)**, (for drawing) compas m.

compassion /kəm'pæʃn/ n. compassion f. **~ate** a. compatissant.

compatib|le /kəm'pætəbl/ a. compatible. **~ility** /-'bɪlətɪ/ n. compatibilité f.

compatriot /kəm'pætrɪət/ n. compatriote m./f.

compel /kəm'pel/ v.t. (p.t. **compelled**) contraindre. **~ling** a. irrésistible.

compendium /kəm'pendɪəm/ n. abrégé m., résumé m.

compensat|e /'kɒmpənseɪt/ v.t./i. (financially) dédommager (for, de). **~e for sth.**, compenser qch. **~ion** /-'seɪʃn/ n. compensation f.; (financial) dédommagement m.

compete /kəm'pi:t/ v.i. concourir. **~ with**, rivaliser avec.

competen|t /'kɒmpɪtənt/ a. compétent. **~ce** n. compétence f.

competition /kɒmpə'tɪʃn/ n. (contest) concours m.; (sport) compétition f.; (comm.) concurrence f.

competitive /kəm'petətɪv/ a. (prices) concurrentiel, compétitif. **~ examination**, concours m.

competitor /kəm'petɪtə(r)/ n. concurrent(e) m. (f.).

compile /kəm'paɪl/ v.t. (list) dresser; (book) rédiger. **~r** /-ə(r)/ n. rédac|teur, -trice m., f.

complacen|t /kəm'pleɪsnt/ a. content de soi. **~cy** contentement de soi m.

complain /kəm'pleɪn/ v.i. se plaindre (about, of, de).

complaint /kəm'pleɪnt/ n. plainte f.; (in shop etc.) réclamation f.; (illness) maladie f.

complement /'kɒmplɪmənt/ n. complément m. ● v.t. compléter. **~ary** /-'mentrɪ/ a. complémentaire.

complet|e /kəm'pli:t/ a. complet; (finished) achevé; (downright) parfait. ● v.t. achever; (a form) remplir. **~ely** adv. complètement. **~ion** /-ʃn/ n. achèvement m.

complex /'kɒmpleks/ a. complexe. ● n. (psych., archit.) complexe m. **~ity** /kəm'pleksətɪ/ n. complexité f.

complexion /kəm'plekʃn/ n. (of face) teint m.; (fig.) caractère m.

compliance /kəm'plaɪəns/ n. (agreement) conformité f.

complicat|e /'kɒmplɪkeɪt/ v.t. compliquer. **~ed** a. compliqué. **~ion** /-'keɪʃn/ n. complication f.

complicity /kəm'plɪsətɪ/ n. complicité f.

compliment /'kɒmplɪmənt/ n. compliment m. ● v.t. /'kɒmplɪment/ complimenter.

complimentary /kɒmplɪ'mentrɪ/ a. (offert) à titre gracieux; (praising) flatteur.

comply /kəm'plaɪ/ v.i. ~ with, se conformer à, obéir à.

component /kəm'pəʊnənt/ n. (of machine etc.) pièce f.; (chemical substance) composant m.; (element: fig.) composante f. ● a. constituant.

compose /kəm'pəʊz/ v.t. composer. ~ o.s., se calmer. ~d a. calme. ~r /-ə(r)/ n. (mus.) compositeur m.

composition /kɒmpə'zɪʃn/ n. composition f.

compost /'kɒmpɒst, Amer. 'kɒmpəʊst/ n. compost m.

composure /kəm'pəʊʒə(r)/ n. calme m.

compound[1] /'kɒmpaʊnd/ n. (substance, word) composé m.; (enclosure) enclos m. ● a. composé.

compound[2] /kəm'paʊnd/ v.t. (problem etc.) aggraver.

comprehen|d /kɒmprɪ'hend/ v.t. comprendre. ~sion n. compréhension f.

comprehensive /kɒmprɪ'hensɪv/ a. étendu, complet; (insurance) tousrisques invar. ~ school, collège d'enseignement secondaire m.

compress /kəm'pres/ v.t. comprimer. ~ion /-ʃn/ n. compression f.

comprise /kəm'praɪz/ v.t. comprendre, inclure.

compromise /'kɒmprəmaɪz/ n. compromis m. ● v.t. compromettre. ● v.i. transiger, trouver un compromis. **not ~ on,** ne pas transiger sur.

compulsion /kəm'pʌlʃn/ n. contrainte f.

compulsive /kəm'pʌlsɪv/ a. (psych.) compulsif; (liar, smoker) invétéré.

compulsory /kəm'pʌlsərɪ/ a. obligatoire.

compunction /kəm'pʌŋkʃn/ n. scrupule m.

computer /kəm'pjuːtə(r)/ n. ordinateur m. ~ **science,** informatique f. ~**ize** v.t. informatiser.

comrade /'kɒmr(e)ɪd/ n. camarade m./f. ~**ship** n. camaraderie f.

con[1] /kɒn/ v.t. (p.t. conned) (sl.) rouler, escroquer (**out of,** de). ● n. (sl.) escroquerie f. ~ **s.o. into**

doing, arnaquer qn. en lui faisant faire. ~ **man,** (sl.) escroc m.

con[2] /kɒn/ see pro.

concave /'kɒnkeɪv/ a. concave.

conceal /kən'siːl/ v.t. dissimuler. ~**ment** n. dissimulation f.

concede /kən'siːd/ v.t. concéder. ● v.i. céder.

conceit /kən'siːt/ n. suffisance f. ~**ed** a. suffisant.

conceivabl|e /kən'siːvəbl/ a. concevable. ~**y** adv. **this may ~y be done,** il est concevable que cela puisse se faire.

conceive /kən'siːv/ v.t./i. concevoir. ~ **of,** concevoir.

concentrat|e /'kɒnsntreɪt/ v.t./i. (se) concentrer. ~**ion** /-'treɪʃn/ n. concentration f.

concept /'kɒnsept/ n. concept m. ~**ual** /kən'septʃʊəl/ a. notionnel.

conception /kən'sepʃn/ n. conception f.

concern /kən'sɜːn/ n. (interest, business) affaire f.; (worry) inquiétude f.; (firm: comm.) entreprise f., affaire f. ● v.t. concerner. ~ **o.s. with, be** ~**ed with,** s'occuper de. ~**ing** prep. en ce qui concerne.

concerned /kən'sɜːnd/ a. inquiet.

concert /'kɒnsət/ n. concert m. **in ~,** ensemble.

concerted /kən'sɜːtɪd/ a. concerté.

concertina /kɒnsə'tiːnə/ n. concertina m.

concerto /kən'tʃeətəʊ/ n. (pl. -os) concerto m.

concession /kən'seʃn/ n. concession f.

conciliation /kənsɪlɪ'eɪʃn/ n. conciliation f.

concise /kən'saɪs/ a. concis. ~**ly** adv. avec concision. ~**ness** n. concision f.

conclu|de /kən'kluːd/ v.t. conclure. ● v.i. se terminer. ~**ding** a. final. ~**sion** n. conclusion f.

conclusive /kən'kluːsɪv/ a. concluant. ~**ly** adv. de manière concluante.

concoct /kən'kɒkt/ v.t. confectionner; (invent: fig.) fabriquer. ~**ion** /-kʃn/ n. mélange m.

concourse /'kɒnkɔːs/ n. (rail.) hall m.

concrete /'kɒŋkriːt/ n. béton m. ● a. concret. ● v.t. bétonner. ~**-mixer** n. bétonnière f.

concur /kən'kɜ:(r)/ *v.i.* (*p.t.* **concurred**) être d'accord.

concurrently /kən'kʌrəntlɪ/ *adv.* simultanément.

concussion /kən'kʌʃn/ *n.* commotion (cérébrale) *f.*

condemn /kən'dem/ *v.t.* condamner. **~ation** /kɒndem'neɪʃn/ *n.* condamnation *f.*

condens|e /kən'dens/ *v.t./i.* (se) condenser. **~ation** /kɒnden'seɪʃn/ *n.* condensation *f.*; (*mist*) buée *f.*

condescend /kɒndɪ'send/ *v.i.* condescendre.

condiment /'kɒndɪmənt/ *n.* condiment *m.*

condition /kən'dɪʃn/ *n.* condition *f.* ● *v.t.* conditionner. **on ~ that,** à condition que. **~al** *a.* conditionnel. **be ~al upon,** dépendre de. **~er** *n.* après-shampooing *m.*

condolences /kən'dəʊlənsɪz/ *n. pl.* condoléances *f. pl.*

condom /'kɒndɒm/ *n.* préservatif *m.*

condominium /kɒndə'mɪnɪəm/ *n.* (*Amer.*) copropriété *f.*

condone /kən'dəʊn/ *v.t.* pardonner, fermer les yeux sur.

conducive /kən'dju:sɪv/ *a.* **~ to,** favorable à.

conduct¹ /kən'dʌkt/ *v.t.* conduire; (*orchestra*) diriger.

conduct² /'kɒndʌkt/ *n.* conduite *f.*

conduct|or /kən'dʌktə(r)/ *n.* chef d'orchestre *m.*; (*of bus*) receveur *m.*; (*on train: Amer.*) chef de train *m.*; (*electr.*) conducteur *m.* **~ress** *n.* receveuse *f.*

cone /kəʊn/ *n.* cône *m.*; (*of ice-cream*) cornet *m.*

confectioner /kən'fekʃənə(r)/ *n.* confiseu|r, -se *m., f.* **~y** *n.* confiserie *f.*

confederation /kənfedə'reɪʃn/ *n.* confédération *f.*

confer /kən'fɜ:(r)/ *v.t./i.* (*p.t.* **conferred**) conférer.

conference /'kɒnfərəns/ *n.* conférence *f.*

confess /kən'fes/ *v.t./i.* avouer; (*relig.*) (se) confesser. **~ion** /-ʃn/ *n.* confession *f.*; (*of crime*) aveu *m.*

confessional /kən'feʃənl/ *n.* confessionnal *m.*

confetti /kən'fetɪ/ *n.* confettis *m. pl.*

confide /kən'faɪd/ *v.t.* confier. ● *v.i.* **~ in,** se confier à.

confiden|t /'kɒnfɪdənt/ *a.* sûr. **~ce** *n.* (*trust*) confiance *f.*; (*boldness*) confiance en soi *f.*; (*secret*) confidence *f.*

~ce trick, escroquerie *f.* **in ~ce,** en confidence.

confidential /kɒnfɪ'denʃl/ *a.* confidentiel.

configure /kən'fɪɡə(r)/ *v.t.* (*comput.*) configurer.

confine /kən'faɪn/ *v.t.* enfermer; (*limit*) limiter. **~d space,** espace réduit *m.* **~d to,** limité à. **~ment** *n.* détention *f.*; (*med.*) couches *f. pl.*

confines /'kɒnfaɪnz/ *n. pl.* confins *m. pl.*

confirm /kən'fɜ:m/ *v.t.* confirmer. **~ation** /kɒnfə'meɪʃn/ *n.* confirmation *f.* **~ed** *a.* (*bachelor*) endurci; (*smoker*) invétéré.

confiscat|e /'kɒnfɪskeɪt/ *v.t.* confisquer. **~ion** /-'keɪʃn/ *n.* confiscation *f.*

conflagration /kɒnflə'ɡreɪʃn/ *n.* incendie *m.*

conflict¹ /'kɒnflɪkt/ *n.* conflit *m.*

conflict² /kən'flɪkt/ *v.i.* (*statements, views*) être en contradiction (**with,** avec); (*appointments*) tomber en même temps (**with,** que). **~ing** *a.* contradictoire.

conform /kən'fɔ:m/ *v.t./i.* (se) conformer. **~ist** *n.* conformiste *m./f.*

confound /kən'faʊnd/ *v.t.* confondre. **~ed** *a.* (*fam.*) sacré.

confront /kən'frʌnt/ *v.t.* affronter. **~ with,** confronter avec. **~ation** /kɒnfrʌn'teɪʃn/ *n.* confrontation *f.*

confus|e /kən'fju:z/ *v.t.* embrouiller; (*mistake, confound*) confondre. **become ~ed,** s'embrouiller. **I am ~ed,** je m'y perds. **~ing** *a.* déroutant. **~ion** /-ʒn/ *n.* confusion *f.*

congeal /kən'dʒi:l/ *v.t./i.* (se) figer.

congenial /kən'dʒi:nɪəl/ *a.* sympathique.

congenital /kən'dʒenɪtl/ *a.* congénital.

congest|ed /kən'dʒestɪd/ *a.* encombré; (*med.*) congestionné. **~ion** /-stʃən/ *n.* (*traffic*) encombrement(s) *m.* (*pl.*); (*med.*) congestion *f.*

conglomerate /kən'ɡlɒmərət/ *n.* (*comm.*) conglomérat *m.*

congratulat|e /kən'ɡrætjʊleɪt/ *v.t.* féliciter (**on,** de). **~ions** /-'leɪʃnz/ *n. pl.* félicitations *f. pl.*

congregat|e /'kɒnɡrɪɡeɪt/ *v.i.* se rassembler. **~ion** /-'ɡeɪʃn/ *n.* assemblée *f.*

congress /'kɒnɡres/ *n.* congrès *m.* **C~,** (*Amer.*) le Congrès.

conic(al) /'kɒnɪk(l)/ *a.* conique.

conifer /'kɒnɪfə(r)/ n. conifère m.

conjecture /kən'dʒektʃə(r)/ n. conjecture f. ● v.t./i. conjecturer.

conjugal /'kɒndʒʊgl/ a. conjugal.

conjugat|e /'kɒndʒʊgeɪt/ v.t. conjuguer. ~ion /-'geɪʃn/ n. conjugaison f.

conjunction /kən'dʒʌŋkʃn/ n. conjonction f. **in ~ with,** conjointement avec.

conjunctivitis /kɒndʒʌŋktɪ'vaɪtɪs/ n. conjonctivite f.

conjur|e /'kʌndʒə(r)/ v.i. faire des tours de passe-passe. ● v.t. **~e up,** faire apparaître. **~or** n. prestidigita|teur, -trice m., f.

conk /kɒŋk/ v.i. **~ out,** (sl.) tomber en panne.

conker /'kɒŋkə(r)/ n. (horse-chestnut fruit: fam.) marron m.

connect /kə'nekt/ v.t./i. (se) relier; (in mind) faire le rapport entre; (install, wire up to mains) brancher. **~ with,** (of train) assurer la correspondance avec. **~ed** a. lié. **be ~ed with,** avoir rapport à; (deal with) avoir des rapports avec.

connection /kə'nekʃn/ n. rapport m.; (rail.) correspondance f.; (phone call) communication f.; (electr.) contact m.; (joining piece) raccord m. **~s,** (comm.) relations f. pl.

conniv|e /kə'naɪv/ v.i. **~e at,** se faire le complice de. **~ance** n. connivence f.

connoisseur /kɒnə'sɜː(r)/ n. connaisseur m.

connot|e /kə'nəʊt/ v.t. connoter. **~ation** /kɒnə'teɪʃn/ n. connotation f.

conquer /'kɒŋkə(r)/ v.t. vaincre; (country) conquérir. **~or** n. conquérant m.

conquest /'kɒŋkwest/ n. conquête f.

conscience /'kɒnʃəns/ n. conscience f.

conscientious /kɒnʃɪ'enʃəs/ a. consciencieux.

conscious /'kɒnʃəs/ a. conscient; (deliberate) voulu. **~ly** adv. consciemment. **~ness** n. conscience f.; (med.) connaissance f.

conscript[1] /kən'skrɪpt/ v.t. recruter par conscription. **~ion** /-pʃn/ n. conscription f.

conscript[2] /'kɒnskrɪpt/ n. conscrit m.

consecrate /'kɒnsɪkreɪt/ v.t. consacrer.

consecutive /kən'sekjʊtɪv/ a. consécutif. **~ly** adv. consécutivement.

consensus /kən'sensəs/ n. consensus m.

consent /kən'sent/ v.i. consentir (**to, à**). ● n. consentement m.

consequence /'kɒnsɪkwəns/ n. conséquence f.

consequent /'kɒnsɪkwənt/ a. résultant. **~ly** adv. par conséquent.

conservation /kɒnsə'veɪʃn/ n. préservation f. **~ area,** zone classée f.

conservationist /kɒnsə'veɪʃənɪst/ n. défenseur de l'environnement m.

conservative /kən'sɜːvətɪv/ a. conservateur; (estimate) modeste. **C~** a. & n. conserva|teur, -trice (m. (f.)).

conservatory /kən'sɜːvətrɪ/ n. (greenhouse) serre f.; (room) véranda f.

conserve /kən'sɜːv/ v.t. conserver; (energy) économiser.

consider /kən'sɪdə(r)/ v.t. considérer; (allow for) tenir compte de; (possibility) envisager (**doing,** de faire). **~ation** /-'reɪʃn/ n. considération f.; (respect) égard(s) m. (pl.). **~ing** prep. compte tenu de.

considerabl|e /kən'sɪdərəbl/ a. considérable; (much) beaucoup de. **~y** adv. beaucoup, considérablement.

considerate /kən'sɪdərət/ a. prévenant, attentionné.

consign /kən'saɪn/ v.t. (entrust) confier; (send) expédier. **~ment** n. envoi m.

consist /kən'sɪst/ v.i. consister (**of,** en; **in doing,** à faire).

consisten|t /kən'sɪstənt/ a. cohérent. **~t with,** conforme à. **~cy** n. (of liquids) consistance f.; (of argument) cohérence f. **~tly** adv. régulièrement.

consol|e /kən'səʊl/ v.t. consoler. **~ation** /kɒnsə'leɪʃn/ n. consolation f.

consolidat|e /kən'sɒlɪdeɪt/ v.t./i. (se) consolider. **~ion** /-'deɪʃn/ n. consolidation f.

consonant /'kɒnsənənt/ n. consonne f.

consort[1] /'kɒnsɔːt/ n. époux m., épouse f.

consort[2] /kən'sɔːt/ v.i. **~ with,** fréquenter.

consortium /kən'sɔːtɪəm/ n. (pl. **-tia**) consortium m.

conspicuous /kən'spɪkjʊəs/ *a.* (*easily seen*) en évidence; (*showy*) voyant; (*noteworthy*) remarquable.

conspiracy /kən'spɪrəsɪ/ *n.* conspiration *f.*

conspire /kən'spaɪə(r)/ *v.i.* (*person*) comploter (**to do,** de faire), conspirer; (*events*) conspirer (**to do,** à faire).

constable /'kʌnstəbl/ *n.* agent de police *m.*, gendarme *m.*

constant /'kɒnstənt/ *a.* incessant; (*unchanging*) constant; (*friend*) fidèle. ● *n.* constante *f.* ~**ly** *adv.* constamment.

constellation /kɒnstə'leɪʃn/ *n.* constellation *f.*

consternation /kɒnstə'neɪʃn/ *n.* consternation *f.*

constipat|e /'kɒnstɪpeɪt/ *v.t.* constiper. ~**ion** /-'peɪʃn/ *n.* constipation *f.*

constituency /kən'stɪtjʊənsɪ/ *n.* circonscription électorale *f.*

constituent /kən'stɪtjʊənt/ *a.* constitutif. ● *n.* élément constitutif *m.*; (*pol.*) élec|teur, -trice *m., f.*

constitut|e /'kɒnstɪtjuːt/ *v.t.* constituer. ~**ion** /-'tjuːʃn/ *n.* constitution *f.* ~**ional** /-'tjuːʃənl/ *a.* constitutionnel; *n.* promenade *f.*

constrain /kən'streɪn/ *v.t.* contraindre.

constraint /kən'streɪnt/ *n.* contrainte *f.*

constrict /kən'strɪkt/ *v.t.* resserrer; (*movement*) gêner. ~**ion** /-kʃn/ *n.* resserrement *m.*

construct /kən'strʌkt/ *v.t.* construire. ~**ion** /-kʃn/ *n.* construction *f.* ~**ion worker,** ouvrier du bâtiment *m.*

constructive /kən'strʌktɪv/ *a.* constructif.

construe /kən'struː/ *v.t.* interpréter.

consul /'kɒnsl/ *n.* consul *m.* ~**ar** /-jʊlə(r)/ *a.* consulaire.

consulate /'kɒnsjʊlət/ *n.* consulat *m.*

consult /kən'sʌlt/ *v.t.* consulter. ● *v.i.* ~ **with,** conférer avec. ~**ation** /kɒnsl'teɪʃn/ *n.* consultation *f.*

consultant /kən'sʌltənt/ *n.* conseil|ler, -ère *m., f.*; (*med.*) spécialiste *m./f.*

consume /kən'sjuːm/ *v.t.* consommer; (*destroy*) consumer. ~**r** /-ə(r)/ *n.* consomma|teur, -trice *m., f. a.* (*society*) de consommation.

consumerism /kən'sjuːmərɪzəm/ *n.* protection des consommateurs *f.*

consummate /'kɒnsəmeɪt/ *v.t.* consommer.

consumption /kən'sʌmpʃn/ *n.* consommation *f.*; (*med.*) phtisie *f.*

contact /'kɒntækt/ *n.* contact *m.*; (*person*) relation *f.* ● *v.t.* contacter. ~ **lenses,** lentilles (de contact) *f. pl.*

contagious /kən'teɪdʒəs/ *a.* contagieux.

contain /kən'teɪn/ *v.t.* contenir. ~ **o.s.,** se contenir. ~**er** *n.* récipient *m.*; (*for transport*) container *m.*

contaminat|e /kən'tæmɪneɪt/ *v.t.* contaminer. ~**ion** /-'neɪʃn/ *n.* contamination *f.*

contemplat|e /'kɒntempleɪt/ *v.t.* (*gaze at*) contempler; (*think about*) envisager. ~**ion** /-'pleɪʃn/ *n.* contemplation *f.*

contemporary /kən'temprərɪ/ *a. & n.* contemporain(e) (*m. (f.)*).

contempt /kən'tempt/ *n.* mépris *m.* ~**ible** *a.* méprisable. ~**uous** /-tʃʊəs/ *a.* méprisant.

contend /kən'tend/ *v.t.* soutenir. ● *v.i.* ~ **with,** (*compete*) rivaliser avec; (*face*) faire face à. ~**er** *n.* adversaire *m./f.*

content¹ /kən'tent/ *a.* satisfait. ● *v.t.* contenter. ~**ed** *a.* satisfait. ~**ment** *n.* contentement *m.*

content² /'kɒntent/ *n.* (*of letter*) contenu *m.*; (*amount*) teneur *f.* ~**s,** contenu *m.*

contention /kən'tenʃn/ *n.* dispute *f.*; (*claim*) affirmation *f.*

contest¹ /'kɒntest/ *n.* (*competition*) concours *m.*; (*fight*) combat *m.*

contest² /kən'test/ *v.t.* contester; (*compete for or in*) disputer. ~**ant** *n.* concurrent(e) *m. (f.)*.

context /'kɒntekst/ *n.* contexte *m.*

continent /'kɒntɪnənt/ *n.* continent *m.* **the C~,** l'Europe (continentale) *f.* ~**al** /-'nentl/ *a.* continental; européen. ~**al quilt,** couette *f.*

contingen|t /kən'tɪndʒənt/ *a.* **be ~t upon,** dépendre de. ● *n.* (*mil.*) contingent *m.* ~**cy** *n.* éventualité *f.* ~**cy plan,** plan d'urgence *m.*

continual /kən'tɪnjʊəl/ *a.* continuel. ~**ly** *adv.* continuellement.

continu|e /kən'tɪnjuː/ *v.t./i.* continuer; (*resume*) reprendre. ~**ance** *n.* continuation *f.* ~**ation** /-ʊ'eɪʃn/ *n.* continuation *f.*; (*after interrup*-

tion) reprise *f*.; (*new episode*) suite *f*. **~ed** *a*. continu.

continuity /kɒntɪ'nju:ətɪ/ *n*. continuité *f*.

continuous /kən'tɪnjʊəs/ *a*. continu. **~ stationery,** papier continu *m*. **~ly** *adv*. sans interruption, continûment.

contort /kən'tɔ:t/ *v.t*. tordre. **~ o.s.,** se contorsionner. **~ion** /-ʃn/ *n*. torsion *f*.; contorsion *f*. **~ionist** /-ʃənɪst/ *n*. contorsionniste *m*./*f*.

contour /'kɒntʊə(r)/ *n*. contour *m*.

contraband /'kɒntrəbænd/ *n*. contrebande *f*.

contraception /kɒntrə'sepʃn/ *n*. contraception *f*.

contraceptive /kɒntrə'septɪv/ *a. & n*. contraceptif (*m*.).

contract[1] /'kɒntrækt/ *n*. contrat *m*.

contract[2] /kən'trækt/ *v.t./i*. (se) contracter. **~ion** /-kʃn/ *n*. contraction *f*.

contractor /kən'træktə(r)/ *n*. entrepreneur *m*.

contradict /kɒntrə'dɪkt/ *v.t*. contredire. **~ion** /-kʃn/ *n*. contradiction *f*. **~ory** *a*. contradictoire.

contralto /kən'træltəʊ/ *n*. (*pl*. **-os**) contralto *m*.

contraption /kən'træpʃn/ *n*. (*fam*.) engin *m*., truc *m*.

contrary[1] /'kɒntrərɪ/ *a*. contraire (**to,** à). ● *n*. contraire *m*. ● *adv*. **~ to,** contrairement à. **on the ~,** au contraire.

contrary[2] /kən'treərɪ/ *a*. entêté.

contrast[1] /'kɒntrɑ:st/ *n*. contraste *m*.

contrast[2] /kən'trɑ:st/ *v.t./i*. contraster. **~ing** *a*. contrasté.

contraven|e /kɒntrə'vi:n/ *v.t*. enfreindre. **~tion** /-'venʃn/ *n*. infraction *f*.

contribut|e /kən'trɪbju:t/ *v.t*. donner. ● *v.i*. **~e to,** contribuer à; (*take part*) participer à; (*newspaper*) collaborer à. **~ion** /kɒntrɪ'bju:ʃn/ *n*. contribution *f*. **~or** *n*. collabora|teur, -trice *m*.,*f*.

contrivance /kən'traɪvəns/ *n*. (*device*) appareil *m*., truc *m*.

contrive /kən'traɪv/ *v.t*. imaginer. **~ to do,** trouver moyen de faire. **~d** *a*. tortueux.

control /kən'trəʊl/ *v.t*. (*p.t*. **controlled**) (*a firm etc*.) diriger; (*check*) contrôler; (*restrain*) maîtriser. ● *n*. contrôle *m*.; (*mastery*) maîtrise *f*. **~s,** commandes *f. pl*.; (*knobs*) bou-

tons *m. pl*. **~ tower,** tour de contrôle *f*. **have under ~,** (*event*) avoir en main. **in ~ of,** maître de.

controversial /kɒntrə'vɜ:ʃl/ *a*. discutable, discuté.

controversy /'kɒntrəvɜ:sɪ/ *n*. controverse *f*.

conurbation /kɒnɜ:'beɪʃn/ *n*. agglomération *f*., conurbation *f*.

convalesce /kɒnvə'les/ *v.i*. être en convalescence. **~nce** *n*. convalescence *f*. **~nt** *a. & n*. convalescent(e) (*m. (f.)*). **~nt home,** maison de convalescence *f*.

convector /kən'vektə(r)/ *n*. convecteur *m*.

convene /kən'vi:n/ *v.t*. convoquer. ● *v.i*. se réunir.

convenience /kən'vi:nɪəns/ *n*. commodité *f*. **~s,** toilettes *f. pl*. **all modern ~s,** tout le confort moderne. **at your ~,** quand cela vous conviendra, à votre convenance. **~ foods,** plats tout préparés *m. pl*.

convenient /kən'vi:nɪənt/ *a*. commode, pratique; (*time*) bien choisi. **be ~ for,** convenir à. **~ly** *adv*. (*arrive*) à propos. **~ly situated,** bien situé.

convent /'kɒnvənt/ *n*. couvent *m*.

convention /kən'venʃn/ *n*. (*assembly, agreement*) convention *f*.; (*custom*) usage *m*. **~al** *a*. conventionnel.

converge /kən'vɜ:dʒ/ *v.i*. converger.

conversant /kən'vɜ:snt/ *a*. **be ~ with,** connaître; (*fact*) savoir; (*machinery*) s'y connaître en.

conversation /kɒnvə'seɪʃn/ *n*. conversation *f*. **~al** *a*. (*tone etc*.) de la conversation; (*French etc*.) de tous les jours. **~alist** *n*. causeu|r, -se *m*.,*f*.

converse[1] /kən'vɜ:s/ *v.i*. s'entretenir, converser (**with,** avec).

converse[2] /'kɒnvɜ:s/ *a. & n*. inverse (*m*.). **~ly** *adv*. inversement.

conver|t[1] /kən'vɜ:t/ *v.t*. convertir; (*house*) aménager. ● *v.i*. **~t into,** se transformer en. **~sion** /-ʃn/ *n*. conversion *f*. **~tible** *a*. convertible. ● *n*. (*car*) décapotable *f*.

convert[2] /'kɒnvɜ:t/ *n*. converti(e) *m*. (*f*.).

convex /'kɒnveks/ *a*. convexe.

convey /kən'veɪ/ *v.t*. (*wishes, order*) transmettre; (*goods, people*) transporter; (*idea, feeling*) communiquer.

~ance *n.* transport *m.* **~or belt,** tapis roulant *m.*

convict¹ /kən'vɪkt/ *v.t.* déclarer coupable. **~ion** /-kʃn/ *n.* condamnation *f.*; (*opinion*) conviction *f.*

convict² /'kɒnvɪkt/ *n.* prisonni|er, -ère *m.*, *f.*

convinc|e /kən'vɪns/ *v.t.* convaincre. **~ing** *a.* convaincant.

convivial /kən'vɪvɪəl/ *a.* joyeux.

convoke /kən'vəʊk/ *v.t.* convoquer.

convoluted /'kɒnvəluːtɪd/ *a.* (*argument etc.*) compliqué.

convoy /'kɒnvɔɪ/ *n.* convoi *m.*

convuls|e /kən'vʌls/ *v.t.* convulser; (*fig.*) bouleverser. **be ~ed with laughter,** se tordre de rire. **~ion** /-ʃn/ *n.* convulsion *f.*

coo /kuː/ *v.i.* roucouler.

cook /kʊk/ *v.t./i.* (faire) cuire; (*of person*) faire la cuisine. ● *n.* cuisin|ier, -ière *m.*, *f.* **~ up,** (*fam.*) fabriquer. **~ing** *n.* cuisine *f.*; *a.* de cuisine.

cooker /'kʊkə(r)/ *n.* (*stove*) cuisinière *f.*; (*apple*) pomme à cuire *f.*

cookery /'kʊkərɪ/ *n.* cuisine *f.* **~ book,** livre de cuisine *m.*

cookie /'kʊkɪ/ *n.* (*Amer.*) biscuit *m.*

cool /kuːl/ *a.* (**-er, -est**) frais; (*calm*) calme; (*unfriendly*) froid. ● *n.* fraîcheur *f.*; (*calmness: sl.*) sang-froid *m.* ● *v.t./i.* rafraîchir. **in the ~,** au frais. **~ box,** glacière *f.* **~er** *n.* (*for food*) glacière *f.*; **~ly** *adv.* calmement; froidement. **~ness** *n.* fraîcheur *f.*; froideur *f.*

coop /kuːp/ *n.* poulailler *m.* ● *v.t.* **~ up,** enfermer.

co-operat|e /kəʊ'ɒpəreɪt/ *v.i.* coopérer. **~ion** /-'reɪʃn/ *n.* coopération *f.*

co-operative /kəʊ'ɒpərətɪv/ *a.* coopératif. ● *n.* coopérative *f.*

co-opt /kəʊ'ɒpt/ *v.t.* coopter.

co-ordinat|e /kəʊ'ɔːdmeɪt/ *v.t.* coordonner. **~ion** /-'neɪʃn/ *n.* coordination *f.*

cop /kɒp/ *v.t.* (*p.t.* **copped**) (*sl.*) piquer. ● *n.* (*policeman: sl.*) flic *m.* **~ out,** (*sl.*) se dérober. **~-out** *n.* (*sl.*) dérobade *f.*

cope /kəʊp/ *v.i.* assurer. **~ with,** s'en sortir avec.

copious /'kəʊpɪəs/ *a.* copieux.

copper¹ /'kɒpə(r)/ *n.* cuivre *m.*; (*coin*) sou *m.* *a.* de cuivre.

copper² /'kɒpə(r)/ *n.* (*sl.*) flic *m.*

coppice, copse /'kɒpɪs, kɒps/ *ns.* taillis *m.*

copulat|e /'kɒpjʊleɪt/ *v.i.* s'accoupler. **~ion** /-'leɪʃn/ *n.* copulation *f.*

copy /'kɒpɪ/ *n.* copie *f.*; (*of book, newspaper*) exemplaire *m.*; (*print, photo.*) épreuve *f.* ● *v.t./i.* copier. **~-writer** *n.* rédacteur-concepteur *m.*, rédactrice-conceptrice *f.*

copyright /'kɒpɪraɪt/ *n.* droit d'auteur *m.*, copyright *m.*

coral /'kɒrəl/ *n.* corail *m.*

cord /kɔːd/ *n.* (petite) corde *f.*; (*of curtain, pyjamas, etc.*) cordon *m.*; (*electr.*) cordon électrique *m.*; (*fabric*) velours côtelé *m.*

cordial /'kɔːdɪəl/ *a.* cordial. ● *n.* (*fruit-flavoured drink*) sirop *m.*

cordon /'kɔːdn/ *n.* cordon *m.* ● *v.t.* **~ off,** mettre un cordon autour de.

corduroy /'kɔːdərɔɪ/ *n.* velours côtelé *m.*, velours à côtes *m.*

core /kɔː(r)/ *n.* (*of apple*) trognon *m.*; (*of problem*) cœur *m.*; (*techn.*) noyau *m.* ● *v.t.* vider.

cork /kɔːk/ *n.* liège *m.*; (*for bottle*) bouchon *m.* ● *v.t.* boucher.

corkscrew /'kɔːkskruː/ *n.* tire-bouchon *m.*

corn¹ /kɔːn/ *n.* blé *m.*; (*maize: Amer.*) maïs *m.*; (*seed*) grain *m.* **~-cob** *n.* épi de maïs *m.*

corn² /kɔːn/ *n.* (*hard skin*) cor *m.*

cornea /'kɔːnɪə/ *n.* cornée *f.*

corned /kɔːnd/ *a.* **~ beef,** corned-beef *m.*

corner /'kɔːnə(r)/ *n.* coin *m.*; (*bend in road*) virage *m.*; (*football*) corner *m.* ● *v.t.* coincer, acculer; (*comm.*) accaparer. ● *v.i.* prendre un virage. **~-stone** *n.* pierre angulaire *f.*

cornet /'kɔːnɪt/ *n.* cornet *m.*

cornflakes /'kɔːnfleɪks/ *n. pl.* corn flakes *m. pl.*

cornflour /'kɔːnflaʊə(r)/ *n.* farine de maïs *f.*

cornice /'kɔːnɪs/ *n.* corniche *f.*

cornstarch /kɔːnstɑːtʃ/ *n. Amer.* = **cornflour**

cornucopia /kɔːnjʊ'kəʊpɪə/ *n.* corne d'abondance *f.*

Corn|wall /'kɔːnwəl/ *n.* Cornouailles *f.* **~ish** *a.* de Cornouailles.

corny /'kɔːnɪ/ *a.* (**-ier, -iest**) (*trite: fam.*) rebattu; (*mawkish: fam.*) à l'eau de rose.

corollary /kə'rɒlərɪ, *Amer.* 'kɒrələrɪ/ *n.* corollaire *m.*

coronary /'kɒrənərɪ/ n. infarctus m.

coronation /kɒrə'neɪʃn/ n. couronnement m.

coroner /'kɒrənə(r)/ n. coroner m.

corporal[1] /'kɔːpərəl/ n. caporal m.

corporal[2] /'kɔːpərəl/ a. ~ **punishment**, châtiment corporel m.

corporate /'kɔːpərət/ a. en commun; (body) constitué.

corporation /kɔːpə'reɪʃn/ n. (comm.) société f.; (of town) municipalité f.

corps /kɔː(r)/ n. (pl. **corps** /kɔːz/) corps m.

corpse /kɔːps/ n. cadavre m.

corpulent /'kɔːpjʊlənt/ a. corpulent.

corpuscle /'kɔːpʌsl/ n. globule m.

corral /kə'rɑːl/ n. (Amer.) corral m.

correct /kə'rekt/ a. (right) exact, juste, correct; (proper) correct. **you are ~,** vous avez raison. ● v.t. corriger. **~ion** /-kʃn/ n. correction f.

correlat|e /'kɒrəleɪt/ v.t./i. (faire) correspondre. **~ion** /-'leɪʃn/ n. corrélation f.

correspond /kɒrɪ'spɒnd/ v.i. correspondre. **~ence** n. correspondance f. **~ence course,** cours par correspondance m. **~ent** n. correspondant(e) m.(f.).

corridor /'kɒrɪdɔː(r)/ n. couloir m.

corroborate /kə'rɒbəreɪt/ v.t. corroborer.

corro|de /kə'rəʊd/ v.t./i. (se) corroder. **~sion** n. corrosion f.

corrosive /kə'rəʊsɪv/ a. corrosif.

corrugated /'kɒrəgeɪtɪd/ a. ondulé. **~ iron,** tôle ondulée f.

corrupt /kə'rʌpt/ a. corrompu. ● v.t. corrompre. **~ion** /-pʃn/ n. corruption f.

corset /'kɔːsɪt/ n. (boned) corset m.; (elasticated) gaine f.

Corsica /'kɔːsɪkə/ n. Corse f.

cortisone /'kɔːtɪzəʊn/ n. cortisone f.

cos /kɒs/ n. laitue romaine f.

cosh /kɒʃ/ n. matraque f. ● v.t. matraquer.

cosmetic /kɒz'metɪk/ n. produit de beauté m. ● a. cosmétique; (fig., pej.) superficiel.

cosmic /'kɒzmɪk/ a. cosmique.

cosmonaut /'kɒzmənɔːt/ n. cosmonaute m./f.

cosmopolitan /kɒzmə'pɒlɪt(ə)n/ a. & n. cosmopolite (m./f.).

cosmos /'kɒzmɒs/ n. cosmos m.

Cossack /'kɒsæk/ n. cosaque m.

cosset /'kɒsɪt/ v.t. (p.t. **cosseted**) dorloter.

cost /kɒst/ v.t. (p.t. **cost**) coûter; (p.t. **costed**) établir le prix de. ● n. coût m. **~s,** (jurid.) dépens m. pl. **at all ~s,** à tout prix. **to one's ~,** à ses dépens. **~-effective** a. rentable. **~-effectiveness** n. rentabilité f. **~-price,** prix de revient m. **~ of living,** coût de la vie m.

co-star /'kəʊstɑː(r)/ n. partenaire m./f.

costly /'kɒstlɪ/ a. (-ier, -iest) coûteux; (valuable) précieux.

costume /'kɒstjuːm/ n. costume m.; (for swimming) maillot m. **~ jewellery,** bijoux de fantaisie m. pl.

cos|y /'kəʊzɪ/ a. (-ier, -iest) confortable, intime. ● n. couvre–théière m. **~iness** n. confort m.

cot /kɒt/ n. lit d'enfant m.; (camp-bed: Amer.) lit de camp m.

cottage /'kɒtɪdʒ/ n. petite maison de campagne f.; (thatched) chaumière f. **~ cheese,** fromage blanc (maigre) m. **~ industry,** activité artisanale f. **~ pie,** hachis Parmentier m.

cotton /'kɒtn/ n. coton m.; (for sewing) fil (à coudre) m. ● v.i. ~ **on,** (sl.) piger. **~ candy,** (Amer.) barbe à papa f. **~ wool,** coton hydrophile m.

couch /kaʊtʃ/ n. divan m. ● v.t. (express) formuler.

couchette /kuːʃet/ n. couchette f.

cough /kɒf/ v.i. tousser. ● n. toux f. **~ up,** (sl.) cracher, payer.

could /kʊd, unstressed kəd/ p.t. of **can**[2].

couldn't /'kʊdnt/ = **could not**.

council /'kaʊnsl/ n. conseil m. **~ house,** maison construite par la municipalité f., (approx.) H.L.M. m./f.

councillor /'kaʊnsələ(r)/ n. conseill|er, -ère municipal(e) m., f.

counsel /'kaʊnsl/ n. conseil m. ● n. invar. (jurid.) avocat(e) m. (f.). **~lor** n. conseill|er, -ère m., f.

count[1] /kaʊnt/ v.t./i. compter. ● n. compte m. **~ on,** compter sur.

count[2] /kaʊnt/ n. (nobleman) comte m.

countdown /'kaʊntdaʊn/ n. compte à rebours m.

countenance /'kaʊntɪnəns/ n. mine f. ● v.t. admettre, approuver.

counter[1] /'kaʊntə(r)/ n. comptoir m.; (in bank etc.) guichet m.; (token) jeton m.

counter 311 **cox**

counter ² /ˈkaʊntə(r)/ *adv.* **~ to,** à l'encontre de. ● *a.* opposé. ● *v.t.* opposer; (*blow*) parer. ● *v.i.* riposter.

counter- /ˈkaʊntə(r)/ *pref.* contre-.

counteract /kaʊntərˈækt/ *v.t.* neutraliser.

counter-attack /ˈkaʊntərətæk/ *n.* contre-attaque *f.* ● *v.t./i.* contre-attaquer.

counterbalance /ˈkaʊntəbæləns/ *n.* contrepoids *m.* ● *v.t.* contrebalancer.

counter-clockwise /kaʊntəˈklɒkwaɪz/ *a.* & *adv.* (*Amer.*) dans le sens inverse des aiguilles d'une montre.

counterfeit /ˈkaʊntəfɪt/ *a.* & *n.* faux (*m.*). ● *v.t.* contrefaire.

counterfoil /ˈkaʊntəfɔɪl/ *n.* souche *f.*

countermand /kaʊntəˈmaːnd/ *v.t.* annuler.

counterpart /ˈkaʊntəpaːt/ *n.* équivalent *m.*; (*person*) homologue *m./f.*

counter-productive /kaʊntəprəˈdʌktɪv/ *a.* (*measure*) qui produit l'effet contraire.

countersign /ˈkaʊntəsam/ *v.t.* contresigner.

counter-tenor /ˈkaʊntətenə(r)/ *n.* haute-contre *m.*

countess /ˈkaʊntɪs/ *n.* comtesse *f.*

countless /ˈkaʊntlɪs/ *a.* innombrable.

countrified /ˈkʌntrɪfaɪd/ *a.* rustique.

country /ˈkʌntrɪ/ *n.* (*land, region*) pays *m.*; (*homeland*) patrie *f.*; (*countryside*) campagne *f.* **~ dance,** danse folklorique *f.*

countryman /ˈkʌntrɪmən/ *n.* (*pl.* -men) campagnard *m.*; (*fellow citizen*) compatriote *m.*

countryside /ˈkʌntrɪsaɪd/ *n.* campagne *f.*

county /ˈkaʊntɪ/ *n.* comté *m.*

coup /kuː/ *n.* (*achievement*) joli coup *m.*; (*pol.*) coup d'état *m.*

coupé /ˈkuːpeɪ/ *n.* (*car*) coupé *m.*

couple /ˈkʌpl/ *n.* (*people, animals*) couple *m.* ● *v.t./i.* (s')accoupler. **a ~ (of),** (*two or three*) deux ou trois.

coupon /ˈkuːpɒn/ *n.* coupon *m.*; (*for shopping*) bon *or* coupon de réduction *m.*

courage /ˈkʌrɪdʒ/ *n.* courage *m.* **~ous** /kəˈreɪdʒəs/ *a.* courageux.

courgette /kʊəˈʒet/ *n.* courgette *f.*

courier /ˈkʊrɪə(r)/ *n.* messager, -ère *m.*, *f.*; (*for tourists*) guide *m.*

course /kɔːs/ *n.* cours *m.*; (*for training*) stage *m.*; (*series*) série *f.*; (*culin.*) plat *m.*; (*for golf*) terrain *m.*; (*at sea*) itinéraire *m.* **change ~,** changer de cap. **~ (of action),** façon de faire *f.* **during the ~ of,** pendant. **in due ~,** en temps utile. **of ~,** bien sûr.

court /kɔːt/ *n.* cour *f.*; (*tennis*) court *m.* ● *v.t.* faire la cour à; (*danger*) rechercher. **~ martial,** (*pl.* **courts martial**) conseil de guerre *m.* **~-martial** *v.t.* (*p.t.* **-martialled**) faire passer en conseil de guerre. **~-house** *n.* (*Amer.*) palais de justice *m.* **~ shoe,** escarpin *m.* **go to ~,** aller devant les tribunaux.

courteous /ˈkɜːtɪəs/ *a.* courtois.

courtesy /ˈkɜːtəsɪ/ *n.* courtoisie *f.* **by ~ of,** avec la permission de.

courtier /ˈkɔːtɪə(r)/ *n.* (*old use*) courtisan *m.*

courtroom /ˈkɔːtrʊm/ *n.* salle de tribunal *f.*

courtyard /ˈkɔːtjaːd/ *n.* cour *f.*

cousin /ˈkʌzn/ *n.* cousin(e) *m.* (*f.*). **first ~,** cousin(e) germain(e) *m.* (*f.*).

cove /kəʊv/ *n.* anse *f.*, crique *f.*

covenant /ˈkʌvənənt/ *n.* convention *f.*

Coventry /ˈkɒvntrɪ/ *n.* **send to ~,** mettre en quarantaine.

cover /ˈkʌvə(r)/ *v.t.* couvrir. ● *n.* (*for bed, book, etc.*) couverture *f.*; (*lid*) couvercle *m.*; (*for furniture*) housse *f.*; (*shelter*) abri *m.* **~ charge,** couvert *m.* **~ up,** cacher; (*crime*) couvrir. **~ up for,** couvrir. **~-up** *n.* tentative pour cacher la vérité *f.* **take ~,** se mettre à l'abri. **~ing** *n.* enveloppe *f.* **~ing letter,** lettre *f.* (*jointe à un document*).

coverage /ˈkʌvərɪdʒ/ *n.* reportage *m.*

coveralls /ˈkʌvərɔːlz/ (*Amer.*) bleu de travail *m.*

covert /ˈkʌvət, Amer. /ˈkəʊvɜːrt/ *a.* (*activity*) secret; (*threat*) voilé (*look*) dérobé.

covet /ˈkʌvɪt/ *v.t.* convoiter.

cow /kaʊ/ *n.* vache *f.*

coward /ˈkaʊəd/ *n.* lâche *m./f.* **~ly** *a.* lâche.

cowardice /ˈkaʊədɪs/ *n.* lâcheté *f.*

cowboy /ˈkaʊbɔɪ/ *n.* cow-boy *m.*

cower /ˈkaʊə(r)/ *v.t.* se recroqueviller (sous l'effet de la peur).

cowshed /ˈkaʊʃed/ *n.* étable *f.*

cox /kɒks/ *n.* barreur *m.* ● *v.t.* barrer.

coxswain /'kɒksn/ n. barreur m.

coy /kɔɪ/ a. (**-er, -est**) (faussement) timide, qui fait le or la timide.

cozy /'kəʊzɪ/ Amer. = **cosy**.

crab /kræb/ n. crabe m. ● v.i. (p.t. **crabbed**) rouspéter. **~-apple** n. pomme sauvage f.

crack /kræk/ n. fente f.; (in glass) fêlure f.; (noise) craquement m.; (joke: sl.) plaisanterie f. ● a. (fam.) d'élite, ● v.t./i. (break partially) (se) fêler; (split) (se) fendre; (nut) casser; (joke) raconter; (problem) résoudre. **~ down on,** (fam.) sévir contre. **~ up,** (fam.) craquer. **get ~ing,** (fam.) s'y mettre.

cracked /krækt/ a. (sl.) cinglé.

cracker /'krækə(r)/ n. pétard m.; (culin.) biscuit (salé) m.

crackers /'krækəz/ a. (sl.) cinglé.

crackle /'krækl/ v.i. crépiter. ● n. crépitement m.

crackpot /'krækpɒt/ n. (sl.) cinglé(e) m. (f.).

cradle /'kreɪdl/ n. berceau m. ● v.t. bercer.

craft[1] /krɑːft/ n. métier artisanal m.; (technique) art m.; (cunning) ruse f.

craft[2] /krɑːft/ n. invar. (boat) bateau m.

craftsman /'krɑːftsmən/ n. (pl. -men) artisan m. **~ship** n. art m.

crafty /'krɑːftɪ/ a. (-ier, -iest) rusé.

crag /kræg/ n. rocher à pic m. **~gy** a. à pic; (face) rude.

cram /kræm/ v.t./i. (p.t. **crammed**). **~ (for an exam),** bachoter. **~ into,** (pack) (s')entasser dans. **~ with,** (fill) bourrer de.

cramp /kræmp/ n. crampe f.

cramped /kræmpt/ a. à l'étroit.

cranberry /'krænbərɪ/ n. canneberge f.

crane /kreɪn/ n. grue f. ● v.t. (neck) tendre.

crank[1] /kræŋk/ n. (techn.) manivelle f.

crank[2] /kræŋk/ n. excentrique m./f. **~y** a. excentrique; (Amer.) grincheux.

cranny /'krænɪ/ n. fissure f.

craps /kræps/ n. **shoot ~,** (Amer.) jouer aux dés.

crash /kræʃ/ n. accident m.; (noise) fracas m.; (of thunder) coup m.; (of firm) faillite f. ● v.t./i. avoir un accident (avec); (of plane) s'écraser; (two vehicles) se percuter. ● a. (course) intensif. **~-helmet** n. cas-

que (anti-choc) m. **~ into,** rentrer dans. **~-land** v.i. atterrir en catastrophe.

crass /kræs/ a. grossier.

crate /kreɪt/ n. cageot m.

crater /'kreɪtə(r)/ n. cratère m.

cravat /krə'væt/ n. foulard m.

crav|e /kreɪv/ v.t./i. **~e (for),** désirer ardemment. **~ing** n. envie irrésistible f.

crawl /krɔːl/ v.i. ramper; (vehicle) se traîner. ● n. (pace) pas m.; (swimming) crawl m. **be ~ing with,** grouiller de.

crayfish /'kreɪfɪʃ/ n. invar. écrevisse f.

crayon /'kreɪən/ n. crayon m.

craze /kreɪz/ n. engouement m.

crazed /kreɪzd/ a. affolé.

craz|y /'kreɪzɪ/ a. (-ier, -iest) fou. **~y about,** (person) fou de; (thing) fana or fou de. **~iness** n. folie f. **~y paving,** dallage irrégulier m.

creak /kriːk/ n. grincement m. ● v.i. grincer. **~y** a. grinçant.

cream /kriːm/ n. crème f. ● a. crème invar. ● v.t. écrémer. **~ cheese,** fromage frais m. **~ off,** se servir en prenant. **~y** a. crémeux.

crease /kriːs/ n. pli m. ● v.t./i. (se) froisser.

creat|e /kriː'eɪt/ v.t. créer. **~ion** /-ʃn/ n. création f. **~ive** a. créateur. **~or** n. créa|teur, -trice m.,f.

creature /'kriːtʃə(r)/ n. créature f.

crèche /kreʃ/ n. garderie f.

credence /'kriːdns/ n. **give ~ to,** ajouter foi à.

credentials /krɪ'denʃlz/ n. pl. (identity) pièces d'identité f. pl.; (competence) références f. pl.

credib|le /'kredəbl/ a. (excuse etc.) croyable, plausible. **~ility** /-'bɪlətɪ/ n. crédibilité f.

credit /'kredɪt/ n. crédit m.; (honour) honneur m. **in ~,** créditeur. **~s,** (cinema) générique m. ● a. (balance) créditeur. ● v.t. (p.t. **credited**) croire; (comm.) créditer. **~ card,** carte de crédit f. **~ note,** avoir m. **~ s.o. with,** attribuer à qn. **~worthy** a. solvable. **~or** n. créan|cier, -ière m.,f.

creditable /'kredɪtəbl/ a. méritoire, honorable.

credulous /'kredjʊləs/ a. crédule.

creed /kriːd/ n. credo m.

creek /kriːk/ *n.* crique *f.*; (*Amer.*) ruisseau *m.* **up the ~,** (*sl.*) dans le pétrin.

creep /kriːp/ *v.i.* (*p.t.* **crept**) ramper; (*fig.*) se glisser. ● *n.* (*person: sl.*) pauvre type *m.* **give s.o. the ~s,** faire frissonner qn. **~er** *n.* liane *f.* **~y** *a.* qui fait frissonner.

cremat|e /krɪˈmeɪt/ *v.t.* incinérer. **~ion** /-ʃn/ *n.* incinération *f.*

crematorium /kremɪˈtɔːrɪəm/ *n.* (*pl.* **-ia**) crématorium *m.*

Creole /ˈkriːəʊl/ *n.* créole *m./f.*

crêpe /kreɪp/ *n.* crêpe *m.* **~ paper,** papier crêpon *m.*

crept /krept/ *see* creep.

crescendo /krɪˈʃendəʊ/ *n.* (*pl.* **-os**) crescendo *m.*

crescent /ˈkresnt/ *n.* croissant *m.*; (*fig.*) rue en demi-lune *f.*

cress /kres/ *n.* cresson *m.*

crest /krest/ *n.* crête *f.*; (*coat of arms*) armoiries *f. pl.*

Crete /kriːt/ *n.* Crète *f.*

cretin /ˈkretɪn, *Amer.* ˈkriːtn/ *n.* crétin(e) *m.* (*f.*). **~ous** *a.* crétin.

crevasse /krɪˈvæs/ *n.* crevasse *f.*

crevice /ˈkrevɪs/ *n.* fente *f.*

crew /kruː/ *n.* équipage *m.*; (*gang*) équipe *f.* **~ cut,** coupe en brosse *f.* **~ neck,** (col) ras du cou *m.*

crib[1] /krɪb/ *n.* lit d'enfant *m.*

crib[2] /krɪb/ *v.t./i.* (*p.t.* **cribbed**) copier. ● *n.* (*schol.*, *fam.*) traduction *f.*, aide-mémoire *m. invar.*

crick /krɪk/ *n.* (*in neck*) torticolis *m.*

cricket[1] /ˈkrɪkɪt/ *n.* (*sport*) cricket *m.* **~er** *n.* joueur de cricket *m.*

cricket[2] /ˈkrɪkɪt/ *n.* (*insect*) grillon *m.*

crime /kraɪm/ *n.* crime *m.*; (*minor*) délit *m.*; (*acts*) criminalité *f.*

criminal /ˈkrɪmɪnl/ *a. & n.* criminel(le) *m.* (*f.*).

crimp /krɪmp/ *v.t.* (*hair*) friser.

crimson /ˈkrɪmzn/ *a. & n.* cramoisi (*m.*).

cring|e /krɪndʒ/ *v.i.* reculer; (*fig.*) s'humilier. **~ing** *a.* servile.

crinkle /ˈkrɪŋkl/ *v.t./i.* (se) froisser. ● *n.* pli *m.*

cripple /ˈkrɪpl/ *n.* infirme *m./f.* ● *v.t.* estropier; (*fig.*) paralyser.

crisis /ˈkraɪsɪs/ *n.* (*pl.* **crises** /-siːz/) crise *f.*

crisp /krɪsp/ *a.* (**-er**, **-est**) (*culin.*) croquant; (*air*, *reply*) vif. **~s** *n. pl.* chips *f. pl.*

criss-cross /ˈkrɪskrɒs/ *a.* entrecroisé. ● *v.t./i.* (s')entrecroiser.

criterion /kraɪˈtɪərɪən/ *n.* (*pl.* **-ia**) critère *m.*

critic /ˈkrɪtɪk/ *n.* critique *m.* **~al** *a.* critique. **~ally** *adv.* d'une manière critique; (*ill*) gravement.

criticism /ˈkrɪtɪsɪzəm/ *n.* critique *f.*

criticize /ˈkrɪtɪsaɪz/ *v.t./i.* critiquer.

croak /krəʊk/ *n.* (*bird*) coassement *m.*; (*frog*) coassement *m.* ● *v.i.* croasser; coasser.

crochet /ˈkrəʊʃeɪ/ *n.* crochet *m.* ● *v.t.* faire au crochet.

crockery /ˈkrɒkərɪ/ *n.* vaisselle *f.*

crocodile /ˈkrɒkədaɪl/ *n.* crocodile *m.*

crocus /ˈkrəʊkəs/ *n.* (*pl.* **-uses**) crocus *m.*

crony /ˈkrəʊnɪ/ *n.* cop|ain, -ine *m.*, *f.*

crook /krʊk/ *n.* (*criminal: fam.*) escroc *m.*; (*stick*) houlette *f.*

crooked /ˈkrʊkɪd/ *a.* tordu; (*winding*) tortueux; (*askew*) de travers; (*dishonest*: *fig.*) malhonnête. **~ly** *adv.* de travers.

croon /kruːn/ *v.t./i.* chantonner.

crop /krɒp/ *n.* récolte *f.*; (*fig.*) quantité *f.* ● *v.t.* (*p.t.* **cropped**) couper. ● *v.i.* **~ up,** se présenter.

croquet /ˈkrəʊkeɪ/ *n.* croquet *m.*

croquette /krəʊˈket/ *n.* croquette *f.*

cross /krɒs/ *n.* croix *f.*; (*hybrid*) hybride *m.* ● *v.t./i.* traverser; (*legs*, *animals*) croiser; (*cheque*) barrer; (*paths*) se croiser. ● *a.* en colère, fâché (**with,** contre). **~-check** *v.t.* vérifier (pour confirmer). **~-country (running),** cross *m.* **~ off** *or* **out,** rayer. **~ s.o.'s mind,** venir à l'esprit de qn. **talk at ~ purposes,** parler sans se comprendre. **~ly** *adv.* avec colère.

crossbar /ˈkrɒsbɑː(r)/ *n.* barre transversale *f.*

cross-examine /krɒsɪɡˈzæmɪn/ *v.t.* faire subir un contre-interrogatoire à.

cross-eyed /ˈkrɒsaɪd/ *a.* **be ~,** loucher.

crossfire /ˈkrɒsfaɪə(r)/ *n.* feux croisés *m. pl.*

crossing /ˈkrɒsɪŋ/ *n.* (*by boat*) traversée *f.*; (*on road*) passage clouté *m.*

cross-reference /krɒsˈrefrəns/ *n.* renvoi *m.*

crossroads /ˈkrɒsrəʊdz/ *n.* carrefour *m.*

cross-section /krɒsˈsekʃn/ *n.* coupe transversale *f.*; (*sample*: *fig.*) échantillon *m.*

cross-wind /'krɒswɪnd/ *n.* vent de travers *m.*

crosswise /'krɒswaɪz/ *adv.* en travers.

crossword /'krɒswɜːd/ *n.* mots croisés *m. pl.*

crotch /krɒtʃ/ *n.* (*of garment*) entrejambes *m. invar.*

crotchet /'krɒtʃɪt/ *n.* (*mus.*) noire *f.*

crotchety /'krɒtʃɪtɪ/ *a.* grincheux.

crouch /krautʃ/ *v.i.* s'accroupir.

crow /krəʊ/ *n.* corbeau *m.* ● *v.i.* (*of cock*) (*p.t.* **crew**) chanter; (*fig.*) jubiler. **as the ~ flies,** à vol d'oiseau. **~'s feet,** pattes d'oie *f. pl.*

crowbar /'krəʊbɑː(r)/ *n.* pied-de-biche *m.*

crowd /kraud/ *n.* foule *f.* ● *v.i.* affluer. ● *v.t.* remplir. **~ into,** (s')entasser dans. **~ed** *a.* plein.

crown /kraun/ *n.* couronne *f.*; (*top part*) sommet *m.* ● *v.t.* couronner. **C~ Court,** Cour d'assises *f.* **C~ prince,** prince héritier *m.*

crucial /'kruːʃl/ *a.* crucial.

crucifix /'kruːsɪfɪks/ *n.* crucifix *m.*

crucif|y /'kruːsɪfaɪ/ *v.t.* crucifier. **~ixion** /-'fɪkʃn/ *n.* crucifixion *f.*

crude /kruːd/ *a.* (**-er, -est**) (*raw*) brut; (*rough, vulgar*) grossier.

cruel /krʊəl/ *a.* (**crueller, cruellest**) cruel. **~ty** *n.* cruauté *f.*

cruet /'kruːɪt/ *n.* huilier *m.*

cruis|e /kruːz/ *n.* croisière *f.* ● *v.i.* (*ship*) croiser; (*tourists*) faire une croisière; (*vehicle*) rouler. **~er** *n.* croiseur *m.* **~ing speed,** vitesse de croisière *f.*

crumb /krʌm/ *n.* miette *f.*

crumble /'krʌmbl/ *v.t./i.* (s')effriter; (*bread*) (s')émietter; (*collapse*) s'écrouler.

crummy /'krʌmɪ/ *a.* (**-ier, -iest**) (*sl.*) moche, minable.

crumpet /'krʌmpɪt/ *n.* (*culin.*) petite crêpe (grillée) *f.*

crumple /'krʌmpl/ *v.t./i.* (se) froisser.

crunch /krʌntʃ/ *v.t.* croquer. ● *n.* (*event*) moment critique *m.* **when it comes to the ~,** quand ça devient sérieux.

crusade /kruːˈseɪd/ *n.* croisade *f.* **~r** /-ə(r)/ *n.* (*knight*) croisé *m.*; (*fig.*) militant(e) *m. (f.).*

crush /krʌʃ/ *v.t.* écraser; (*clothes*) froisser. ● *n.* (*crowd*) presse *f.* **a ~ on,** (*sl.*) le béguin pour.

crust /krʌst/ *n.* croûte *f.* **~y** *a.* croustillant.

crutch /krʌtʃ/ *n.* béquille *f.*; (*crotch*) entrejambes *m. invar.*

crux /krʌks/ *n.* **the ~ of,** (*problem etc.*) le nœud de.

cry /kraɪ/ *n.* cri *m.* ● *v.i.* (*weep*) pleurer; (*call out*) crier. **~-baby** *n.* pleurnicheu|r, -se *m., f.* **~ off,** abandonner.

crying /'kraɪɪŋ/ *a.* (*evil etc.*) flagrant. **a ~ shame,** une vraie honte.

crypt /krɪpt/ *n.* crypte *f.*

cryptic /'krɪptɪk/ *a.* énigmatique.

crystal /'krɪstl/ *n.* cristal *m.* **~-clear** *a.* parfaitement clair. **~lize** *v.t./i.* (se) cristalliser.

cub /kʌb/ *n.* petit *m.* **Cub (Scout),** louveteau *m.*

Cuba /'kjuːbə/ *n.* Cuba *m.* **~n** *a. & n.* cubain(e) (*m. (f.)*).

cubby-hole /'kʌbɪhəʊl/ *n.* cagibi *m.*

cub|e /kjuːb/ *n.* cube *m.* **~ic** *a.* cubique; (*metre etc.*) cube.

cubicle /'kjuːbɪkl/ *n.* (*in room, hospital, etc.*) box *m.*; (*at swimming-pool*) cabine *f.*

cuckoo /'kʊkuː/ *n.* coucou *m.*

cucumber /'kjuːkʌmbə(r)/ *n.* concombre *m.*

cuddl|e /'kʌdl/ *v.t.* câliner. ● *v.i.* (**kiss and**) **~e,** s'embrasser. ● *n.* caresse *f.* **~y** *a.* câlin, caressant.

cudgel /'kʌdʒl/ *n.* gourdin *m.*

cue¹ /kjuː/ *n.* signal *m.*; (*theatre*) réplique *f.*

cue² /kjuː/ *n.* (*billiards*) queue *f.*

cuff /kʌf/ *n.* manchette *f.*; (*Amer.*) revers *m.* ● *v.t.* gifler. **~-link** *n.* bouton de manchette *m.* **off the ~,** impromptu.

cul-de-sac /'kʌldəsæk/ *n.* (*pl.* **culs-de-sac**) impasse *f.*

culinary /'kʌlɪnərɪ/ *a.* culinaire.

cull /kʌl/ *v.t.* (*select*) choisir; (*kill*) abattre sélectivement.

culminat|e /'kʌlmɪneɪt/ *v.i.* **~e in,** se terminer par. **~ion** /-'neɪʃn/ *n.* point culminant *m.*

culprit /'kʌlprɪt/ *n.* coupable *m./f.*

cult /kʌlt/ *n.* culte *m.* **~ movie,** film culte.

cultivat|e /'kʌltɪveɪt/ *v.t.* cultiver. **~ion** /-'veɪʃn/ *n.* culture *f.*

cultural /'kʌltʃərəl/ *a.* culturel.

culture /'kʌltʃə(r)/ *n.* culture *f.* **~d** *a.* cultivé.

cumbersome /'kʌmbəsəm/ *a.* encombrant.

cumulative /'kjuːmjʊlətɪv/ *a.* cumulatif.

cunning /'kʌnɪŋ/ a. rusé. ● n. astuce f., ruse f.

cup /kʌp/ n. tasse f.; (prize) coupe f. **Cup final**, finale de la coupe f. ~ **size**, profondeur de bonnet f. ~-**tie** n. match de coupe m.

cupboard /'kʌbəd/ n. placard m., armoire f.

cupful /'kʌpfʊl/ n. tasse f.

Cupid /'kju:pɪd/ n. Cupidon m.

curable /'kjʊərəbl/ a. guérissable.

curate /'kjʊərət/ n. vicaire m.

curator /kjʊə'reɪtə(r)/ n. (of museum) conservateur m.

curb[1] /kɜ:b/ n. (restraint) frein m. ● v.t. (desires etc.) refréner; (price increase etc.) freiner.

curb[2] (Amer.) **kerb** /kɜ:b/ n. bord du trottoir m.

curdle /'kɜ:dl/ v.t./i. (se) cailler.

curds /kɜ:dz/ n. pl. lait caillé m.

cure[1] /kjʊə(r)/ v.t. guérir; (fig.) éliminer. ● n. (recovery) guérison f.; (remedy) remède m.

cure[2] /kjʊə(r)/ v.t. (culin.) fumer; (in brine) saler.

curfew /'kɜ:fju:/ n. couvre-feu m.

curio /'kjʊərɪəʊ/ n. (pl. -os) curiosité f., bibelot m.

curi|ous /'kjʊərɪəs/ a. curieux. ~**osity** /-'ɒsətɪ/ n. curiosité f.

curl /kɜ:l/ v.t./i. (hair) boucler. ● n. boucle f. ~ **up**, se pelotonner; (shrivel) se racornir.

curler /'kɜ:lə(r)/ n. bigoudi m.

curly /'kɜ:lɪ/ a. (-ier, -iest) bouclé.

currant /'kʌrənt/ n. raisin de Corinthe m.; (berry) groseille f.

currency /'kʌrənsɪ/ n. (money) monnaie f.; (acceptance) cours m. **foreign** ~, devises étrangères f. pl.

current /'kʌrənt/ a. (common) courant; (topical) actuel; (year etc.) en cours. ● n. courant m. ~ **account**, compte courant m. ~ **events**, l'actualité f. ~**ly** adv. actuellement.

curriculum /kə'rɪkjʊləm/ n. (pl. -la) programme scolaire m. ~ **vitae**, curriculum vitae m.

curry[1] /'kʌrɪ/ n. curry m., cari m.

curry[2] /'kʌrɪ/ v.t. ~ **favour with**, chercher les bonnes grâces de.

curse /kɜ:s/ n. malédiction f.; (oath) juron m. ● v.t. maudire. ● v.i. (swear) jurer.

cursor /'kɜ:sə(r)/ n. curseur m.

cursory /'kɜ:sərɪ/ a. (trop) rapide.

curt /kɜ:t/ a. brusque.

curtail /kɜ:'teɪl/ v.t. écourter, raccourcir; (expenses etc.) réduire.

curtain /'kɜ:tn/ n. rideau m.

curtsy /'kɜ:tsɪ/ n. révérence f. ● v.i. faire une révérence.

curve /kɜ:v/ n. courbe f. ● v.t./i. (se) courber; (of road) tourner.

cushion /'kʊʃn/ n. coussin m. ● v.t. (a blow) amortir; (fig.) protéger.

cushy /'kʊʃɪ/ a. (-ier, -iest) (job etc.: fam.) pépère.

custard /'kʌstəd/ n. crème anglaise f.; (set) crème renversée f.

custodian /kʌ'stəʊdɪən/ n. gardien(ne) m. (f.).

custody /'kʌstədɪ/ n. garde f.; (jurid.) détention préventive f.

custom /'kʌstəm/ n. coutume f.; (patronage: comm.) clientèle f. ~-**built**, ~-**made** adjs. fait etc. sur commande. ~**ary** a. d'usage.

customer /'kʌstəmə(r)/ n. client(e) m. (f.); (fam.) **an odd/a difficult** ~, un individu curieux/difficile.

customize /'kʌstəmaɪz/ v.t. personnaliser.

customs /'kʌstəmz/ n. pl. douane f. ● a. douanier. ~ **officer**, douanier m.

cut /kʌt/ v.t./i. (p.t. **cut**, pres. p. **cutting**) couper; (hedge, jewel) tailler; (prices etc.) réduire. ● n. coupure f.; (of clothes) coupe f.; (piece) morceau m.; réduction f. ~ **back** or **down (on)**, réduire. ~-**back** n. réduction f. ~ **in**, (auto.) se rabattre. ~ **off**, couper; (fig.) isoler. ~ **out**, découper; (leave out) supprimer. ~-**price** a. à prix réduit. ~ **short**, (visit) écourter. ~ **up**, couper; (carve) découper. ~ **up about**, démoralisé par.

cute /kju:t/ a. (-er, -est) (fam.) astucieux; (Amer.) mignon.

cuticle /'kju:tɪkl/ n. petites peaux f. pl. (de l'ongle).

cutlery /'kʌtlərɪ/ n. couverts m. pl.

cutlet /'kʌtlɪt/ n. côtelette f.

cutting /'kʌtɪŋ/ a. cinglant. ● n. (from newspaper) coupure f.; (plant) bouture f. ~ **edge**, tranchant m.

CV abbr. see curriculum vitae.

cyanide /'saɪənaɪd/ n. cyanure m.

cybernetics /saɪbə'netɪks/ n. cybernétique f.

cycl|e /'saɪkl/ n. cycle m.; (bicycle) vélo m. ● v.i. aller à vélo. ~**ing** n. cyclisme m. ~**ist** n. cycliste m./f.

cyclic(al) /'saɪklɪk(l)/ a. cyclique.

cyclone /'saɪkləʊn/ n. cyclone m.

cylind|er /'sɪlmdə(r)/ n. cylindre m.
~rical /-'lmdrɪkl/ a. cylindrique.

cymbal /'sɪmbl/ n. cymbale f.

cynic /'sɪnɪk/ n. cynique m./f. **~al** a.
cynique. **~ism** /-sɪzəm/ n. cynisme
m.

cypress /'saɪprəs/ n. cyprès m.

Cypr|us /'saɪprəs/ n. Chypre f. **~iot**
/'sɪprɪət/ a. & n. cypriote (m./f.).

cyst /sɪst/ n. kyste m. **~ic fibrosis,**
mucoviscidose f.

cystitis /sɪst'aɪtɪs/ n. cystite f.

czar /zɑː(r)/ n. tsar m.

Czech /tʃek/ a. & n. tchèque (m./f.).

Czechoslovak /tʃekə'sləʊvæk/ a. &
n. tchécoslovaque (m./f.). **~ia**
/-slə'vækɪə/ n. Tchécoslovaquie f.

D

dab /dæb/ v.t. (p.t. **dabbed**)
tamponner. ● n. a **~ of,** un petit
coup de; (fam.) be a **~ hand at,**
avoir le coup de main pour. **~ sth.
on,** appliquer qch. à petits coups sur.

dabble /'dæbl/ v.i. **~ in,** se mêler un
peu de. **~r** /-ə(r)/ n. amateur m.

dad /dæd/ n. (fam.) papa m. **~dy** n.
(children's use) papa m.

daffodil /'dæfədɪl/ n. jonquille f.

daft /dɑːft/ a. (-er, -est) idiot.

dagger /'dægə(r)/ n. poignard m.

dahlia /'deɪlɪə/ n. dahlia m.

daily /'deɪlɪ/ a. quotidien. ● adv.
tous les jours. ● n. (newspaper)
quotidien m.; (charwoman: fam.)
femme de ménage f.

dainty /'deɪntɪ/ a. (-ier, -iest) délicat.

dairy /'deərɪ/ n. (on farm) laiterie f.;
(shop) crémerie f. ● a. laitier.

daisy /'deɪzɪ/ n. pâquerette f. **~
wheel,** marguerite f.

dale /deɪl/ n. vallée f.

dam /dæm/ n. barrage m. ● v.t. (p.t.
dammed) endiguer.

damag|e /'dæmɪdʒ/ n. dégâts m. pl.,
dommages m. pl.; (harm: fig.) préjudice m. **~es,** (jurid.) dommages et
intérêts m. pl. ● v.t. abîmer; (fig.)
nuire à. **~ing** a. nuisible.

dame /deɪm/ n. (old use) dame f.;
(Amer., sl.) fille f.

damn /dæm/ v.t. (relig.) damner;
(swear at) maudire; (condemn: fig.)
condamner. ● int. zut, merde. ● n.

not care a **~,** s'en foutre. ● a.
sacré. ● adv. rudement. **~ation**
/-'neɪʃn/ n. damnation f.

damp /dæmp/ n. humidité f. ● a.
(-er, -est) humide. ● v.t. humecter;
(fig.) refroidir. **~en** v.t. = **damp.**
~ness n. humidité f.

dance /dɑːns/ v.t./i. danser. ● n.
danse f.; (gathering) bal m. **~ hall,**
dancing m., salle de danse f. **~r**
/-ə(r)/ n. danseu|r, -se m., f.

dandelion /'dændɪlaɪən/ n. pissenlit
m.

dandruff /'dændrʌf/ n. pellicules f.
pl.

dandy /'dændɪ/ n. dandy m.

Dane /deɪn/ n. Danois(e) m. (f.).

danger /'deɪndʒə(r)/ n. danger m.;
(risk) risque m. be in **~ of,** risquer
de. **~ous** a. dangereux.

dangle /'dæŋgl/ v.t./i. (se) balancer,
(laisser) pendre. **~ sth. in front of
s.o.,** (fig.) faire miroiter qch. à qn.

Danish /'deɪnɪʃ/ a. danois. ● n.
(lang.) danois m.

dank /dæŋk/ a. (-er, -est) humide et
froid.

dapper /'dæpə(r)/ a. élégant.

dare /deə(r)/ v.t. **~ (to) do,** oser faire.
~ s.o. to do, défier qn. de faire.
● n. défi m. **I ~ say,** je suppose
(that, que).

daredevil /'deədevl/ n. casse-cou m.
invar.

daring /'deərɪŋ/ a. audacieux.

dark /dɑːk/ a. (-er, -est) obscur,
sombre, noir; (colour) foncé, sombre; (skin) brun, foncé; (gloomy)
sombre. ● n. noir m.; (nightfall)
tombée de la nuit f. **~ horse,**
individu aux talents inconnus m.
~-room n. chambre noire f. in the
~, (fig.) dans l'ignorance (about,
de). **~ness** n. obscurité f.

darken /'dɑːkən/ v.t./i. (s')assombrir.

darling /'dɑːlɪŋ/ a. & n. chéri(e) (m.
(f.)).

darn /dɑːn/ v.t. repriser.

dart /dɑːt/ n. fléchette f. **~s,** (game)
fléchettes f. pl. ● v.i. s'élancer.

dartboard /'dɑːtbɔːd/ n. cible f.

dash /dæʃ/ v.i. (hurry) se dépêcher;
(forward etc.) se précipiter. ● v.t.
jeter (avec violence); (hopes) briser.
● n. ruée f.; (stroke) tiret m. a **~ of,**
un peu de. **~ off,** (leave) partir en
vitesse.

dashboard /'dæʃbɔːd/ n. tableau de
bord m.

dashing /'dæʃɪŋ/ a. fringant.

data /'deɪtə/ n. pl. données f. pl. ~ **processing,** traitement des données m.

database /'deɪtəbeɪs/ n. base de données f.

date [1] /deɪt/ n. date f.; (*meeting: fam.*) rendez-vous m. ● v.t./i. dater; (*go out with: fam.*) sortir avec. ~ **from,** dater de. **out of** ~, (*old-fashioned*) démodé; (*passport*) périmé. **to** ~, à ce jour. **up to** ~, (*modern*) moderne; (*list*) à jour. ~**d** /-ɪd/ a. démodé.

date [2] /deɪt/ n. (*fruit*) datte f.

daub /dɔːb/ v.t. barbouiller.

daughter /'dɔːtə(r)/ n. fille f. ~**-in-law** n. (pl. ~**s-in-law**) belle-fille f.

daunt /dɔːnt/ v.t. décourager.

dauntless /'dɔːntlɪs/ a. intrépide.

dawdle /'dɔːdl/ v.i. lambiner. ~**r** /-ə(r)/ n. lambin(e) m. (f.).

dawn /dɔːn/ n. aube f. ● v.i. poindre; (*fig.*) naître. **it** ~**ed on me,** je m'en suis rendu compte.

day /deɪ/ n. jour m.; (*whole day*) journée f.; (*period*) époque f. ~**-break** n. point du jour m. ~**-dream** n. rêverie f.; v.i. rêvasser. **the** ~ **before,** la veille. **the following** or **next** ~, le lendemain.

daylight /'deɪlaɪt/ n. jour m.

daytime /'deɪtaɪm/ n. jour m., journée f.

daze /deɪz/ v.t. étourdir; (*with drugs*) hébéter. ● n. **in a** ~, étourdi; hébété.

dazzle /'dæzl/ v.t. éblouir.

deacon /'diːkən/ n. diacre m.

dead /ded/ a. mort; (*numb*) engourdi. ● adv. complètement. ● n. **in the** ~ **of,** au cœur de. **the** ~, les morts. ~ **beat,** éreinté. ~ **end,** impasse f. ~**-end job,** travail sans avenir m. **a** ~ **loss,** (*thing*) une perte de temps; (*person*) une catastrophe. ~**-pan** a. impassible. **in** ~ **centre,** au beau milieu. **stop** ~, s'arrêter net. **the race was a** ~ **heat,** ils ont été classés ex aequo.

deaden /'dedn/ v.t. (*sound, blow*) amortir; (*pain*) calmer.

deadline /'dedlaɪn/ n. date limite f.

deadlock /'dedlɒk/ n. impasse f.

deadly /'dedlɪ/ a. (-**ier,** -**iest**) mortel; (*weapon*) meurtrier.

deaf /def/ a. (-**er,** -**est**) sourd. **the** ~ **and dumb,** les sourds-muets. ~**-aid** n. appareil acoustique m. ~**ness** n. surdité f.

deafen /'defn/ v.t. assourdir.

deal /diːl/ v.t. (p.t. **dealt**) donner; (*a blow*) porter. ● v.i. (*trade*) commercer. ● n. affaire f.; (*cards*) donne f. **a great** or **good** ~, beaucoup (**of,** de). ~ **in,** faire le commerce de. ~ **with,** (*handle, manage*) s'occuper de; (*be about*) traiter de. ~**er** n. marchand(e) m. (f.); (*agent*) concessionnaire m./f.

dealings /'diːlɪŋz/ n. pl. relations f. pl.

dean /diːn/ n. doyen m.

dear /dɪə(r)/ a. (-**er,** -**est**) cher. ● n. (**my**) ~, mon cher, ma chère; (*darling*) (**mon**) chéri, (**ma**) chérie. ● adv. cher. ● int. **oh** ~**!,** oh mon Dieu! ~**ly** adv. tendrement; (*pay*) cher.

dearth /dɜːθ/ n. pénurie f.

death /deθ/ n. mort f. ~ **certificate,** acte de décès m. ~ **duty,** droits de succession m. pl. ~ **penalty,** peine de mort f. **it is a** ~**-trap,** (*place, vehicle*) il y a danger de mort. ~**ly** a. de mort, mortel.

debar /dɪ'bɑː(r)/ v.t. (p.t. **debarred**) exclure.

debase /dɪ'beɪs/ v.t. avilir.

debat|e /dɪ'beɪt/ n. discussion f., débat m. ● v.t. discuter. ~**e whether,** se demander si. ~**able** a. discutable.

debauch /dɪ'bɔːtʃ/ v.t. débaucher. ~**ery** n. débauche f.

debilitate /dɪ'bɪlɪteɪt/ v.t. débiliter.

debility /dɪ'bɪlətɪ/ n. débilité f.

debit /'debɪt/ n. débit m. **in** ~, débiteur. ● a. (*balance*) débiteur. ● v.t. (p.t. **debited**) débiter.

debris /'deɪbriː/ n. débris m. pl.

debt /det/ n. dette f. **in** ~, endetté. ~**or** n. débi|teur, -trice m., f.

debunk /diː'bʌŋk/ v.t. (*fam.*) démythifier.

decade /'dekeɪd/ n. décennie f.

decaden|t /'dekədənt/ a. décadent. ~**ce** n. décadence f.

decaffeinated /diː'kæfɪneɪtɪd/ a. décaféiné.

decanter /dɪ'kæntə(r)/ n. carafe f.

decathlon /dɪ'kæθlən/ n. décathlon m.

decay /dɪ'keɪ/ v.i. se gâter, pourrir; (*fig.*) décliner. ● n. pourriture f.; (*of tooth*) carie f.; (*fig.*) déclin m.

deceased /dɪ'siːst/ a. décédé. ● n. défunt(e) m. (f.).

deceit /dɪ'siːt/ n. tromperie f. **~ful** a. trompeur. **~fully** adv. d'une manière trompeuse.

deceive /dɪ'siːv/ v.t. tromper.

December /dɪ'sembə(r)/ n. décembre m.

decen|t /'diːsnt/ a. décent, convenable; (good: fam.) (assez) bon; (kind: fam.) gentil. **~cy** n. décence f. **~tly** adv. décemment.

decentralize /diː'sentrəlaɪz/ v.t. décentraliser.

decept|ive /dɪ'septɪv/ a. trompeur. **~ion** /-pʃn/ n. tromperie f.

decibel /'desɪbel/ n. décibel m.

decide /dɪ'saɪd/ v.t./i. décider; (question) régler. **~ on**, se décider pour. **~ to do**, décider de faire. **~d** /-ɪd/ a. (firm) résolu; (clear) net. **~dly** /-ɪdlɪ/ adv. résolument; nettement.

deciduous /dɪ'sɪdjʊəs/ a. à feuillage caduc.

decimal /'desɪml/ a. décimal. ● n. décimale f. **~ point**, virgule f.

decimate /'desɪmeɪt/ v.t. décimer.

decipher /dɪ'saɪfə(r)/ v.t. déchiffrer.

decision /dɪ'sɪʒn/ n. décision f.

decisive /dɪ'saɪsɪv/ a. (conclusive) décisif; (firm) décidé. **~ly** adv. d'une façon décidée.

deck /dek/ n. pont m.; (of cards: Amer.) jeu m. **~-chair** n. chaise longue f. **top ~**, (of bus) impériale f.

declar|e /dɪ'kleə(r)/ v.t. déclarer. **~ation** /deklə'reɪʃn/ n. déclaration f.

decline /dɪ'klaɪn/ v.t./i. refuser (poliment); (deteriorate) décliner; (fall) baisser. ● n. déclin m.; baisse f.

decode /diː'kəʊd/ v.t. décoder.

decompos|e /diːkəm'pəʊz/ v.t./i. (se) décomposer. **~ition** /-ɒmpə'zɪʃn/ n. décomposition f.

décor /'deɪkɔː(r)/ n. décor m.

decorat|e /'dekəreɪt/ v.t. décorer; (room) peindre or tapisser. **~ion** /-'reɪʃn/ n. décoration f. **~ive** /-ətɪv/ a. décoratif.

decorator /'dekəreɪtə(r)/ n. peintre en bâtiment m. **(interior) ~**, décora|teur, -trice d'appartements m., f.

decorum /dɪ'kɔːrəm/ n. décorum m.

decoy¹ /'diːkɔɪ/ n. (bird) appeau m.; (trap) piège m., leurre m.

decoy² /dɪ'kɔɪ/ v.t. attirer, appâter.

decrease /dɪ'kriːs/ v.t./i. diminuer. ● n. /'diːkriːs/ diminution f.

decree /dɪ'kriː/ n. (pol., relig.) décret m.; (jurid.) jugement m. ● v.t. (p.t. decreed) décréter.

decrepit /dɪ'krepɪt/ a. (building) délabré; (person) décrépit.

decry /dɪ'kraɪ/ v.t. dénigrer.

dedicat|e /'dedɪkeɪt/ v.t. dédier. **~e o.s. to**, se consacrer à. **~ed** a. dévoué. **~ion** /-'keɪʃn/ n. dévouement m.; (in book) dédicace f.

deduce /dɪ'djuːs/ v.t. déduire.

deduct /dɪ'dʌkt/ v.t. déduire; (from wages) retenir. **~ion** /-kʃn/ n. déduction f.; retenue f.

deed /diːd/ n. acte m.

deem /diːm/ v.t. juger.

deep /diːp/ a. (-er, -est) profond. ● adv. profondément. **~ in thought**, absorbé dans ses pensées. **~ into the night**, tard dans la nuit. **~-freeze** n. congélateur m.; v.t. congeler. **~-fry**, frire. **~ly** adv. profondément.

deepen /'diːpən/ v.t. approfondir. ● v.i. devenir plus profond; (mystery, night) s'épaissir.

deer /dɪə(r)/ n. invar. cerf m.; (doe) biche f.

deface /dɪ'feɪs/ v.t. dégrader.

defamation /defə'meɪʃn/ n. diffamation f.

default /dɪ'fɔːlt/ v.i. (jurid.) faire défaut. ● n. **by ~**, (jurid.) par défaut. **win by ~**, gagner par forfait. ● a. (comput.) par défaut.

defeat /dɪ'fiːt/ v.t. vaincre; (thwart) faire échouer. ● n. défaite f.; (of plan etc.) échec m.

defect¹ /'diːfekt/ n. défaut m. **~ive** /dɪ'fektɪv/ a. défectueux.

defect² /dɪ'fekt/ v.i. faire défection. **~ to**, passer à. **~or** n. transfuge m./f.

defence /dɪ'fens/ n. défense f. **~less** a. sans défense.

defend /dɪ'fend/ v.t. défendre. **~ant** n. (jurid.) accusé(e) m. (f.). **~er**, défenseur m.

defense /dɪ'fens/ n. Amer. = **defence**.

defensive /dɪ'fensɪv/ a. défensif. ● n. défensive f.

defer /dɪ'fɜː(r)/ v.t. (p.t. deferred) (postpone) différer, remettre.

deferen|ce /'defərəns/ n. déférence f. **~tial** /-'renʃl/ a. déférent.

defian|ce /dɪ'faɪəns/ n. défi m. **in ~ce of**, au mépris de. **~t** a. de défi. **~tly** adv. d'un air de défi.

deficien|t /dɪˈfɪʃnt/ a. insuffisant. **be ~t in,** manquer de. **~cy** n. insuffisance f.; (*fault*) défaut m.

deficit /ˈdefɪsɪt/ n. déficit m.

defile /dɪˈfaɪl/ v.t. souiller.

define /dɪˈfaɪn/ v.t. définir.

definite /ˈdefɪnɪt/ a. précis; (*obvious*) net; (*firm*) catégorique; (*certain*) certain. **~ly** adv. certainement; (*clearly*) nettement.

definition /defɪˈnɪʃn/ n. définition f.

definitive /dɪˈfɪnətɪv/ a. définitif.

deflat|e /dɪˈfleɪt/ v.t. dégonfler. **~ion** /-ʃn/ n. dégonflement m.; (*comm.*) déflation f.

deflect /dɪˈflekt/ v.t./i. (faire) dévier.

deforestation /diːˌfɒrɪˈsteɪʃn/ n. déforestation f.

deform /dɪˈfɔːm/ v.t. déformer. **~ed** a. difforme. **~ity** n. difformité f.

defraud /dɪˈfrɔːd/ v.t. (*state, customs*) frauder. **~ s.o. of sth.,** escroquer qch. à qn.

defray /dɪˈfreɪ/ v.t. payer.

defrost /diːˈfrɒst/ v.t. dégivrer.

deft /deft/ a. (**-er, -est**) adroit. **~ness** n. adresse f.

defunct /dɪˈfʌŋkt/ a. défunt.

defuse /diːˈfjuːz/ v.t. désamorcer.

defy /dɪˈfaɪ/ v.t. défier; (*attempts*) résister à.

degenerate [1] /dɪˈdʒenəreɪt/ v.i. dégénérer (**into,** en).

degenerate [2] /dɪˈdʒenərət/ a. & n. dégénéré(e) (m. (f.)).

degrad|e /dɪˈɡreɪd/ v.t. dégrader. **~ation** /degrəˈdeɪʃn/ n. dégradation f.; (*state*) déchéance f.

degree /dɪˈɡriː/ n. degré m.; (*univ.*) diplôme universitaire m.; (*Bachelor's degree*) licence f. **higher ~,** (*univ.*) maîtrise f. or doctorat m. **to such a ~ that,** à tel point que.

dehydrate /diːˈhaɪdreɪt/ v.t./i. (se) déshydrater.

de-ice /diːˈaɪs/ v.t. dégivrer.

deign /deɪn/ v.t. **~ to do,** daigner faire.

deity /ˈdiːɪtɪ/ n. divinité f.

deject|ed /dɪˈdʒektɪd/ a. abattu. **~ion** /-kʃn/ n. abattement m.

delay /dɪˈleɪ/ v.t. retarder. ● v.i. tarder. ● n. (*lateness, time overdue*) retard m.; (*waiting*) délai m. **~ doing,** attendre pour faire.

delectable /dɪˈlektəbl/ a. délectable, très agréable.

delegate [1] /ˈdelɪɡət/ n. délégué(e) m. (f.).

delegat|e [2] /ˈdelɪɡeɪt/ v.t. déléguer. **~ion** /-ˈɡeɪʃn/ n. délégation f.

delet|e /dɪˈliːt/ v.t. effacer; (*with line*) barrer. **~ion** /-ʃn/ n. suppression f.; (*with line*) rature f.

deliberate [1] /dɪˈlɪbərət/ a. délibéré; (*steps, manner*) mesuré. **~ly** adv. exprès, délibérément.

deliberat|e [2] /dɪˈlɪbəreɪt/ v.i. délibérer. ● v.t. considérer. **~ion** /-ˈreɪʃn/ n. délibération f.

delica|te /ˈdelɪkət/ a. délicat. **~cy** n. délicatesse f.; (*food*) mets délicat or raffiné m.

delicatessen /delɪkəˈtesn/ n. épicerie fine f., charcuterie f.

delicious /dɪˈlɪʃəs/ a. délicieux.

delight /dɪˈlaɪt/ n. grand plaisir m., joie f., délice m. (f. in pl.); (*thing*) délice m. (f. in pl.). ● v.t. réjouir. ● v.i. **~ in,** prendre plaisir à. **~ed** a. ravi. **~ful** a. charmant, très agréable.

delinquen|t /dɪˈlɪŋkwənt/ a. & n. délinquant(e) (m. (f.)) **~cy** n. délinquance f.

deliri|ous /dɪˈlɪrɪəs/ a. **be ~ous,** délirer. **~um** n. délire m.

deliver /dɪˈlɪvə(r)/ v.t. (*message*) remettre; (*goods*) livrer; (*letters*) distribuer; (*free*) délivrer; (*utter*) prononcer; (*med.*) accoucher; (*a blow*) porter. **~ance** n. délivrance f. **~y** n. livraison f.; distribution f.; accouchement m.

delta /ˈdeltə/ n. delta m.

delu|de /dɪˈluːd/ v.t. tromper. **~de o.s.,** se faire des illusions. **~sion** /-ʒn/ n. illusion f.

deluge /ˈdeljuːdʒ/ n. déluge m. ● v.t. inonder (**with,** de).

de luxe /dəˈlʌks/ a. de luxe.

delve /delv/ v.i. fouiller.

demagogue /ˈdeməɡɒɡ/ n. démagogue m./f.

demand /dɪˈmɑːnd/ v.t. exiger; (*in negotiations*) réclamer. ● n. exigence f.; (*claim*) revendication f.; (*comm.*) demande f. **in ~,** recherché. **on ~,** à la demande. **~ing** a. exigeant.

demarcation /diːmɑːˈkeɪʃn/ n. démarcation f.

demean /dɪˈmiːn/ v.t. **~ o.s.,** s'abaisser, s'avilir.

demeanour, (*Amer.*) **demeanor** /dɪˈmiːnə(r)/ n. comportement m.

demented /dɪˈmentɪd/ a. dément.

demerara /demə'reərə/ n. (*brown sugar*) cassonade f.

demise /dr'maɪz/ n. décès m.

demo /'deməʊ/ n. (pl. **-os**) (*demonstration*: *fam.*) manif f.

demobilize /diː'məʊbəlaɪz/ v.t. démobiliser.

democracy /dr'mɒkrəsɪ/ n. démocratie f.

democrat /'deməkræt/ n. démocrate m./f. **~ic** /-'krætɪk/ a. démocratique.

demoli|sh /dr'mɒlɪʃ/ v.t. démolir. **~tion** /demə'lɪʃn/ n. démolition f.

demon /'diːmən/ n. démon m.

demonstrat|e /'demənstreɪt/ v.t. démontrer. ● v.i. (*pol.*) manifester. **~ion** /-'streɪʃn/ n. démonstration f.; (*pol.*) manifestation f. **~or** n. manifestant(e) m. (f.).

demonstrative /dr'mɒnstrətɪv/ a. démonstratif.

demoralize /dr'mɒrəlaɪz/ v.t. démoraliser.

demote /dr'məʊt/ v.t. rétrograder.

demure /dr'mjʊə(r)/ a. modeste.

den /den/ n. antre m.

denial /dr'naɪəl/ n. dénégation f.; (*statement*) démenti m.

denigrate /'denɪgreɪt/ v.t. dénigrer.

denim /'denɪm/ n. toile de coton f. **~s**, (*jeans*) blue-jeans m. pl.

Denmark /'denmɑːk/ n. Danemark m.

denomination /dɪnɒmɪ'neɪʃn/ n. (*relig.*) confession f.; (*money*) valeur f.

denote /dr'nəʊt/ v.t. dénoter.

denounce /dr'naʊns/ v.t. dénoncer.

dens|e /dens/ a. (**-er, -est**) dense; (*person*) obtus. **~ely** adv. (*packed etc.*) très. **~ity** n. densité f.

dent /dent/ n. bosse f. ● v.t. cabosser. **there is a ~ in the car door,** la portière est cabossée.

dental /'dentl/ a. dentaire. **~ floss,** fil dentaire m. **~ surgeon,** dentiste m./f.

dentist /'dentɪst/ n. dentiste m./f. **~ry** n. art dentaire m.

dentures /'dentʃəz/ n. pl. dentier m.

denude /dr'njuːd/ v.t. dénuder.

denunciation /dɪnʌnsɪ'eɪʃn/ n. dénonciation f.

deny /dr'naɪ/ v.t. nier (**that,** que); (*rumour*) démentir; (*disown*) renier; (*refuse*) refuser.

deodorant /diː'əʊdərənt/ n. & a. déodorant (m.).

depart /dr'pɑːt/ v.i. partir. **~ from,** (*deviate*) s'écarter de.

department /dr'pɑːtmənt/ n. département m.; (*in shop*) rayon m.; (*in office*) service m. **D~ of Health,** ministère de la santé m. **~ store,** grand magasin m.

departure /dr'pɑːtʃə(r)/ n. départ m. **a ~ from,** (*custom, diet, etc.*) une entorse à.

depend /dr'pend/ v.i. dépendre (**on,** de). **it (all) ~s,** ça dépend. **~ on,** (*rely on*) compter sur. **~ing on the weather,** selon le temps qu'il fera. **~able** a. sûr. **~ence** n. dépendance f. **~ent** a. dépendant. **be ~ent on,** dépendre de.

dependant /dr'pendənt/ n. personne à charge f.

depict /dr'pɪkt/ v.t. (*describe*) dépeindre; (*in picture*) représenter.

deplete /dr'pliːt/ v.t. (*reduce*) réduire; (*use up*) épuiser.

deplor|e /dr'plɔː(r)/ v.t. déplorer. **~able** a. déplorable.

deploy /dr'plɔɪ/ v.t. déployer.

depopulate /diː'pɒpjʊleɪt/ v.t. dépeupler.

deport /dr'pɔːt/ v.t. expulser. **~ation** /diːpɔː'teɪʃn/ n. expulsion f.

depose /dr'pəʊz/ v.t. déposer.

deposit /dr'pɒzɪt/ v.t. (p.t. **deposited**) déposer. ● n. dépôt m.; (*of payment*) acompte m.; (*to reserve*) arrhes f. pl.; (*against damage*) caution f.; (*on bottle etc.*) consigne f.; (*of mineral*) gisement m. **~ account,** compte de dépôt m. **~or** n. (*comm.*) déposant(e) m. (f.), épargnant(e) m. (f.).

depot /'depəʊ, *Amer.* 'diːpəʊ/ n. dépôt m.; (*Amer.*) gare (routière) f.

deprav|e /dr'preɪv/ v.t. dépraver. **~ity** /-'prævətɪ/ n. dépravation f.

deprecate /'deprəkeɪt/ v.t. désapprouver.

depreciat|e /dr'priːʃɪeɪt/ v.t./i. (se) déprécier. **~ion** /-'eɪʃn/ n. dépréciation f.

depress /dr'pres/ v.t. (*sadden*) déprimer; (*push down*) appuyer sur. **become ~ed,** déprimer. **~ing** a. déprimant. **~ion** /-ʃn/ n. dépression f.

deprivation /deprɪ'veɪʃn/ n. privation f.

deprive /dr'praɪv/ v.t. **~ of,** priver de. **~d** a. (*child etc.*) déshérité.

depth /depθ/ n. profondeur f. **be out of one's ~,** perdre pied; (*fig.*) être perdu. **in the ~s of,** au plus profond de.

deputation /depjʊˈteɪʃn/ n. députation f.

deputize /ˈdepjʊtaɪz/ v.i. assurer l'intérim (**for,** de). ● v.t. (Amer.) déléguer, nommer.

deputy /ˈdepjʊtɪ/ n. suppléant(e) m. (f.) ● a. adjoint. ~ **chairman,** vice-président m.

derail /dɪˈreɪl/ v.t. faire dérailler. **be** ~**ed,** dérailler. ~**ment** n. déraillement m.

deranged /dɪˈreɪndʒd/ a. (mind) dérangé.

derelict /ˈderəlɪkt/ a. abandonné.

deri|de /dɪˈraɪd/ v.t. railler. ~**sion** /-ˈrɪʒn/ n. dérision f. ~**sive** a. (laughter, person) railleur.

derisory /dɪˈraɪsərɪ/ a. (scoffing) railleur; (offer etc.) dérisoire.

derivative /dɪˈrɪvətɪv/ a. & n. dérivé (m.).

deriv|e /dɪˈraɪv/ v.t. ~**e from,** tirer de. ● v.i. ~**e from,** dériver de. ~**ation** /derɪˈveɪʃn/ n. dérivation f.

derogatory /dɪˈrɒgətrɪ/ a. (word) péjoratif; (remark) désobligeant.

derv /dɜːv/ n. gas-oil m., gazole m.

descend /dɪˈsend/ v.t./i. descendre. **be** ~**ed from,** descendre de. ~**ant** n. descendant(e) m. (f.).

descent /dɪˈsent/ n. descente f.; (lineage) origine f.

descri|be /dɪˈskraɪb/ v.t. décrire. ~**ption** /-ˈskrɪpʃn/ n. description f. ~**ptive** /-ˈskrɪptɪv/ a. descriptif.

desecrat|e /ˈdesɪkreɪt/ v.t. profaner. ~**ion** /-ˈkreɪʃn/ n. profanation f.

desert[1] /ˈdezət/ n. désert m. ● a. désertique. ~ **island,** île déserte f.

desert[2] /dɪˈzɜːt/ v.t./i. déserter. ~**ed** a. désert. ~**er** n. déserteur m. ~**ion** /-ʃn/ n. désertion f.

deserts /dɪˈzɜːts/ n. pl. **one's** ~, ce qu'on mérite.

deserv|e /dɪˈzɜːv/ v.t. mériter (**to,** de). ~**edly** /-ɪdlɪ/ adv. à juste titre. ~**ing** a. (person) méritant; (action) méritoire.

design /dɪˈzaɪn/ n. (sketch) dessin m., plan m.; (construction) conception f.; (pattern) motif m.; (style of dress) modèle m.; (aim) dessein m. ● v.t. (sketch) dessiner; (devise, intend) concevoir. ~**er** n. dessina|teur, -trice m., f.; (of fashion) styliste m./f.

designat|e /ˈdezɪgneɪt/ v.t. désigner. ~**ion** /-ˈneɪʃn/ n. désignation f.

desir|e /dɪˈzaɪə(r)/ n. désir m. ● v.t. désirer. ~**able** a. désirable. ~**ability** /-əˈbɪlətɪ/ n. attrait m.

desk /desk/ n. bureau m.; (of pupil) pupitre m.; (in hotel) réception f.; (in bank) caisse f.

desolat|e /ˈdesələt/ a. (place) désolé; (bleak: fig.) morne. ~**ion** /-ˈleɪʃn/ n. désolation f.

despair /dɪˈspeə(r)/ n. désespoir m. ● v.i. désespérer (**of,** de).

despatch /dɪˈspætʃ/ v.t. = dispatch.

desperate /ˈdespərət/ a. désespéré; (criminal) prêt à tout. **be** ~ **for,** avoir une envie folle de. ~**ly** adv. désespérément; (worried) terriblement; (ill) gravement.

desperation /despəˈreɪʃn/ n. désespoir m. **in** or **out of** ~, en désespoir de cause.

despicable /dɪˈspɪkəbl/ a. méprisable, infâme.

despise /dɪˈspaɪz/ v.t. mépriser.

despite /dɪˈspaɪt/ prep. malgré.

desponden|t /dɪˈspɒndənt/ a. découragé. ~**cy** n. découragement m.

despot /ˈdespɒt/ n. despote m.

dessert /dɪˈzɜːt/ n. dessert m. ~**spoon** n. cuiller à dessert f. ~**spoonful** n. cuillerée à soupe f.

destination /destɪˈneɪʃn/ n. destination f.

destine /ˈdestɪn/ v.t. destiner.

destiny /ˈdestɪnɪ/ n. destin m.

destitute /ˈdestɪtjuːt/ a. indigent. ~ **of,** dénué de.

destr|oy /dɪˈstrɔɪ/ v.t. détruire; (animal) abattre. ~**uction** n. destruction f. ~**uctive** a. destructeur.

destroyer /dɪˈstrɔɪə(r)/ n. (warship) contre-torpilleur m.

detach /dɪˈtætʃ/ v.t. détacher. ~**able** a. détachable. ~**ed** a. détaché. ~**ed house,** maison individuelle f.

detachment /dɪˈtætʃmənt/ n. détachement m.

detail /ˈdiːteɪl/ n. détail m. ● v.t. exposer en détail; (troops) détacher. **go into** ~, entrer dans le détail. ~**ed** a. détaillé.

detain /dɪˈteɪn/ v.t. retenir; (in prison) détenir. ~**ee** /diːteɪˈniː/ n. détenu(e) m. (f.).

detect /dɪˈtekt/ v.t. découvrir; (perceive) distinguer; (tumour) dépister; (mine) détecter. ~**ion** /-kʃn/ n. découverte f.; dépistage m.; détection f. ~**or** n. détecteur m.

detective /dɪ'tektɪv/ *n.* policier *m.*; (*private*) détective *m.*

detention /dɪ'tenʃn/ *n.* détention *f.*; (*schol.*) retenue *f.*

deter /dɪ'tɜ:(r)/ *v.t.* (*p.t.* **deterred**) dissuader (**from,** de).

detergent /dɪ'tɜ:dʒənt/ *a.* & *n.* détergent (*m.*).

deteriorat|e /dɪ'tɪərɪəreɪt/ *v.i.* se détériorer. **~ion** /-'reɪʃn/ *n.* détérioration *f.*

determin|e /dɪ'tɜ:mɪn/ *v.t.* déterminer. **~e to do,** décider de faire. **~ation** /-'neɪʃn/ *n.* détermination *f.* **~ed** *a.* déterminé. **~ed to do,** décidé à faire.

deterrent /dɪ'terənt, *Amer.* dɪ'tɜ:rənt/ *n.* force de dissuasion *f.*

detest /dɪ'test/ *v.t.* détester. **~able** *a.* détestable.

detonat|e /'detəneɪt/ *v.t./i.* (faire) détoner. **~ion** /-'neɪʃn/ *n.* détonation *f.* **~or** *n.* détonateur *m.*

detour /'di:tʊə(r)/ *n.* détour *m.*

detract /dɪ'trækt/ *v.i.* **~ from,** (*lessen*) diminuer.

detriment /'detrɪmənt/ *n.* détriment *m.* **~al** /-'mentl/ *a.* préjudiciable (**to,** à).

devalu|e /di:'vælju:/ *v.t.* dévaluer. **~ation** /-jʊ'eɪʃn/ *n.* dévaluation *f.*

devastat|e /'devəsteɪt/ *v.t.* dévaster; (*overwhelm: fig.*) accabler. **~ing** *a.* accablant.

develop /dɪ'veləp/ *v.t./i.* (*p.t.* **developed**) (se) développer; (*contract*) contracter; (*build on, transform*) exploiter, aménager; (*change*) évoluer; (*appear*) se manifester. **~ into,** devenir. **~ing country,** pays en voie de développement *m.* **~ment** *n.* développement *m.* (**housing**) **~,** lotissement *m.* (**new**) **~ment,** fait nouveau *m.*

deviant /'di:vɪənt/ *a.* anormal. ● *n.* (*psych.*) déviant *m.*

deviat|e /'di:vɪeɪt/ *v.i.* dévier. **~e from,** (*norm*) s'écarter de. **~ion** /-'eɪʃn/ *n.* déviation *f.*

device /dɪ'vaɪs/ *n.* appareil *m.*; (*scheme*) procédé *m.*

devil /'devl/ *n.* diable *m.* **~ish** *a.* diabolique.

devious /'di:vɪəs/ *a.* tortueux. **he is ~,** il a l'esprit tortueux.

devise /dɪ'vaɪz/ *v.t.* inventer; (*plan, means*) combiner, imaginer.

devoid /dɪ'vɔɪd/ *a.* **~ of,** dénué de.

devolution /di:və'lu:ʃn/ *n.* décentralisation *f.*; (*of authority, power*) délégation *f.* (**to,** à).

devot|e /dɪ'vəʊt/ *v.t.* consacrer. **~ed** *a.* dévoué. **~edly** *adv.* avec dévouement. **~ion** /-ʃn/ *n.* dévouement *m.*; (*relig.*) dévotion *f.* **~ions,** (*relig.*) dévotions *f. pl.*

devotee /devə'ti:/ *n.* **~ of,** passionné(e) de *m.* (*f.*).

devour /dɪ'vaʊə(r)/ *v.t.* dévorer.

devout /dɪ'vaʊt/ *a.* fervent.

dew /dju:/ *n.* rosée *f.*

dexterity /dek'sterətɪ/ *n.* dextérité *f.*

diabet|es /daɪə'bi:ti:z/ *n.* diabète *m.* **~ic** /-'betɪk/ *a.* & *n.* diabétique (*m./f.*).

diabolical /daɪə'bɒlɪkl/ *a.* diabolique; (*bad: fam.*) atroce.

diagnose /'daɪəgnəʊz/ *v.t.* diagnostiquer.

diagnosis /daɪəg'nəʊsɪs/ *n.* (*pl.* **-oses**) /-si:z/) diagnostic *m.*

diagonal /daɪ'ægənl/ *a.* diagonal. ● *n.* diagonale *f.* **~ly** *adv.* en diagonale.

diagram /'daɪəgræm/ *n.* schéma *m.*

dial /'daɪəl/ *n.* cadran *m.* ● *v.t.* (*p.t.* **dialled**) (*number*) faire; (*person*) appeler. **~ling code,** (*Amer.*) **~ code,** indicatif *m.* **~ling tone,** (*Amer.*) **~ tone,** tonalité *f.*

dialect /'daɪəlekt/ *n.* dialecte *m.*

dialogue /'daɪəlɒg/ *n.* dialogue *m.*

diameter /daɪ'æmɪtə(r)/ *n.* diamètre *m.*

diamond /'daɪəmənd/ *n.* diamant *m.*; (*shape*) losange *m.*; (*baseball*) terrain *m.* **~s,** (*cards*) carreau *m.*

diaper /'daɪəpə(r)/ *n.* (*baby's nappy: Amer.*) couche *f.*

diaphragm /'daɪəfræm/ *n.* diaphragme *m.*

diarrhoea, (*Amer.*) **diarrhea** /daɪə'rɪə/ *n.* diarrhée *f.*

diary /'daɪərɪ/ *n.* (*for appointments etc.*) agenda *m.*; (*appointments*) emploi du temps *m.* (*for private thoughts*) journal intime *m.*

dice /daɪs/ *n. invar.* dé *m.* ● *v.t.* (*food*) couper en dés.

dicey /'daɪsɪ/ *a.* (*fam.*) risqué.

dictat|e /dɪk'teɪt/ *v.t./i.* dicter. **~ion** /-ʃn/ *n.* dictée *f.*

dictates /'dɪkteɪts/ *n. pl.* préceptes *m. pl.*

dictator /dɪk'teɪtə(r)/ *n.* dictateur *m.* **~ship** *n.* dictature *f.*

dictatorial /dɪktəˈtɔːrɪəl/ a. dictatorial.

diction /ˈdɪkʃn/ n. diction f.

dictionary /ˈdɪkʃənrɪ/ n. dictionnaire m.

did /dɪd/ see do.

diddle /ˈdɪdl/ v.t. (sl.) escroquer.

didn't /ˈdɪdnt/ = did not.

die [1] /daɪ/ v.i. (pres. p. dying) mourir. ~ **down**, diminuer. ~ **out**, disparaître. **be dying to do/for**, mourir d'envie de faire/de.

die [2] /daɪ/ n. (metal mould) matrice f., étampe f.

die-hard /ˈdaɪhɑːd/ n. réactionnaire m./f.

diesel /ˈdiːzl/ n. diesel m. ~ **engine**, moteur diesel m.

diet /ˈdaɪət/ n. (habitual food) alimentation f.; (restricted) régime m. ● v.i. suivre un régime.

diet|etic /daɪəˈtetɪk/ a. diététique. ~**ician** n. diététicien(ne) m. (f.).

differ /ˈdɪfə(r)/ v.i. différer (**from**, de); (disagree) ne pas être d'accord.

differen|t /ˈdɪfrənt/ a. différent. ~**ce** n. différence f.; (disagreement) différend m. ~**tly** adv. différemment (**from**, de).

differential /dɪfəˈrenʃl/ a. & n. différentiel (m.).

differentiate /dɪfəˈrenʃɪeɪt/ v.t. différencier. ● v.i. faire la différence (**between**, entre).

difficult /ˈdɪfɪkəlt/ a. difficile. ~**y** n. difficulté f.

diffiden|t /ˈdɪfɪdənt/ a. qui manque d'assurance. ~**ce** n. manque d'assurance m.

diffuse [1] /dɪˈfjuːs/ a. diffus.

diffus|e [2] /dɪˈfjuːz/ v.t. diffuser. ~**ion** /-ʒn/ n. diffusion f.

dig /dɪg/ v.t./i. (p.t. dug, pres. p. digging) creuser; (thrust) enfoncer. ● n. (poke) coup de coude m.; (remark) coup de patte m.; (archaeol.) fouilles f. pl. ~**s**, (lodgings: fam.) chambre meublée f. ~ (**over**), bêcher. ~ **up**, déterrer.

digest [1] /dɪˈdʒest/ v.t./i. digérer. ~**ible** a. digestible. ~**ion** /-stʃən/ n. digestion f.

digest [2] /ˈdaɪdʒest/ n. sommaire m.

digestive /dɪˈdʒestɪv/ a. digestif.

digger /ˈdɪgə(r)/ n. (techn.) pelleteuse f., excavateur m.

digit /ˈdɪdʒɪt/ n. chiffre m.

digital /ˈdɪdʒɪtl/ a. (clock) numérique, à affichage numérique; (recording) numérique.

dignif|y /ˈdɪgnɪfaɪ/ v.t. donner de la dignité à. ~**ied** a. digne.

dignitary /ˈdɪgnɪtərɪ/ n. dignitaire m.

dignity /ˈdɪgnɪtɪ/ n. dignité f.

digress /daɪˈgres/ v.i. faire une digression. ~ **from**, s'écarter de. ~**ion** /-ʃn/ n. digression f.

dike /daɪk/ n. digue f.

dilapidated /dɪˈlæpɪdeɪtɪd/ a. délabré.

dilat|e /daɪˈleɪt/ v.t./i. (se) dilater. ~**ion** /-ʃn/ n. dilatation f.

dilatory /ˈdɪlətərɪ/ a. dilatoire.

dilemma /dɪˈlemə/ n. dilemme m.

dilettante /dɪlɪˈtæntɪ/ n. dilettante m./f.

diligen|t /ˈdɪlɪdʒənt/ a. assidu. ~**ce** n. assiduité f.

dilly-dally /ˈdɪlɪdælɪ/ v.i. (fam.) lanterner.

dilute /daɪˈljuːt/ v.t. diluer.

dim /dɪm/ a. (**dimmer, dimmest**) (weak) faible; (dark) sombre; (indistinct) vague; (fam.) stupide. ● v.t./i. (p.t. **dimmed**) (light) (s')atténuer. ~**ly** adv. (shine) faiblement; (remember) vaguement. ~**mer** n. ~ (**switch**), variateur d'intensité m. ~**ness** n. faiblesse f.; (of room etc.) obscurité f.

dime /daɪm/ n. (in USA, Canada) pièce de dix cents f.

dimension /daɪˈmenʃn/ n. dimension f.

diminish /dɪˈmɪnɪʃ/ v.t./i. diminuer.

diminutive /dɪˈmɪnjʊtɪv/ a. minuscule. ● n. diminutif m.

dimple /ˈdɪmpl/ n. fossette f.

din /dɪn/ n. vacarme m.

dine /daɪn/ v.i. dîner. ~**r** /-ə(r)/ n. dîneu|r, -se m., f.; (rail.) wagon-restaurant m.; (Amer.) restaurant à service rapide m.

dinghy /ˈdɪŋgɪ/ n. canot m.; (inflatable) canot pneumatique m.

ding|y /ˈdɪndʒɪ/ a. (**-ier, -iest**) miteux, minable. ~**iness** n. aspect miteux or minable m.

dining-room /ˈdaɪnɪŋrʊm/ n. salle à manger f.

dinner /ˈdɪnə(r)/ n. (evening meal) dîner m.; (lunch) déjeuner m. ~-**jacket** n. smoking m. ~ **party**, dîner m.

dinosaur /ˈdaɪnəsɔː(r)/ n. dinosaure m.

dint /dɪnt/ n. **by ~ of,** à force de.

diocese /'daɪəsɪs/ n. diocèse m.

dip /dɪp/ v.t./i. (p.t. **dipped**) plonger.
● n. (slope) déclivité f.; (in sea) bain
rapide m. **~ into,** (book) feuilleter;
(savings) puiser dans. **~ one's
headlights,** se mettre en code.

diphtheria /dɪf'θɪərɪə/ n. diphtérie f.

diphthong /'dɪfθɒŋ/ n. diphtongue f.

diploma /dɪ'pləʊmə/ n. diplôme m.

diplomacy /dɪ'pləʊməsɪ/ n. diplo-
matie f.

diplomat /'dɪpləmæt/ n. diplomate
m./f. **~ic** /-'mætɪk/ a. (pol.) diplo-
matique; (tactful) diplomate.

dire /daɪə(r)/ a. (-er, -est) affreux;
(need, poverty) extrême.

direct /dɪ'rekt/ a. direct. ● adv.
directement. ● v.t. diriger; (letter,
remark) adresser; (a play) mettre en
scène. **~ s.o. to,** indiquer à qn. le
chemin de; (order) signifier à qn. de.
~ness n. franchise f.

direction /dɪ'rekʃn/ n. direction f.;
(theatre) mise en scène f. **~s,** in-
dications f. pl. **ask ~s,** demander le
chemin. **~s for use,** mode d'emploi
m.

directly /dɪ'rektlɪ/ adv. directement;
(at once) tout de suite. ● conj. dès
que.

director /dɪ'rektə(r)/ n. direc|teur,
-trice m., f.; (theatre) metteur en
scène m.

directory /dɪ'rektərɪ/ n. (phone book)
annuaire m.

dirt /dɜːt/ n. saleté f.; (earth) terre f.
~ cheap, (sl.) très bon marché
invar. **~-track** n. (sport) cendrée f.

dirty /'dɜːtɪ/ a. (-ier, -iest) sale;
(word) grossier. **get ~,** se salir.
● v.t./i. (se) salir.

disability /dɪsə'bɪlətɪ/ n. handicap m.

disable /dɪs'eɪbl/ v.t. rendre infirme.
~d a. handicapé.

disadvantage /dɪsəd'vɑːntɪdʒ/ n. dé-
savantage m. **~d** a. déshérité.

disagree /dɪsə'griː/ v.i. ne pas être
d'accord (with, avec). **~ with s.o.,**
(food, climate) ne pas convenir à qn.
~ment n. désaccord m.; (quarrel)
différend m.

disagreeable /dɪsə'griːəbl/ a. désagréable.

disappear /dɪsə'pɪə(r)/ v.i. disparaître. **~ance** n. disparition f.

disappoint /dɪsə'pɔɪnt/ v.t. décevoir.
~ing a. décevant. **~ed** a. déçu.
~ment n. déception f.

disapprov|e /dɪsə'pruːv/ v.i. **~e (of),**
désapprouver. **~al** n. désapproba-
tion f.

disarm /dɪs'ɑːm/ v.t./i. désarmer.
~ament n. désarmement m.

disarray /dɪsə'reɪ/ n. désordre m.

disassociate /dɪsə'səʊʃɪeɪt/ v.t. = **dissociate.**

disast|er /dɪ'zɑːstə(r)/ n. désastre m.
~rous a. désastreux.

disband /dɪs'bænd/ v.t./i. (se) disperser.

disbelief /dɪsbɪ'liːf/ n. incrédulité f.

disc /dɪsk/ n. disque m.; (comput.) =
disk. ~ brake, frein à disque m. **~
jockey,** disc-jockey m., animateur m.

discard /dɪ'skɑːd/ v.t. se débarrasser
de; (beliefs etc.) abandonner.

discern /dɪ'sɜːn/ v.t. discerner. **~ible**
a. perceptible. **~ing** a. perspicace.

discharge[1] /dɪs'tʃɑːdʒ/ v.t. (unload)
décharger; (liquid) déverser; (duty)
remplir; (dismiss) renvoyer; (prisoner) libérer. ● v.i. (of pus) s'écouler.

discharge[2] /'dɪstʃɑːdʒ/ n. (med.)
écoulement m.; (dismissal) renvoi
m.; (electr.) décharge m.

disciple /dɪ'saɪpl/ n. disciple m.

disciplin|e /'dɪsɪplɪn/ n. discipline f.
● v.t. discipliner; (punish) punir.
~ary a. disciplinaire.

disclaim /dɪs'kleɪm/ v.t. désavouer.
~er n. correctif m., précision f.

disclos|e /dɪs'kləʊz/ v.t. révéler.
~ure /-ʒə(r)/ n. révélation f.

disco /'dɪskəʊ/ n. (pl. -os) (club. fam.)
discothèque f., disco m.

discolour /dɪs'kʌlə(r)/ v.t./i. (se)
décolorer. **~oration** /-'reɪʃn/ n. dé-
coloration f.

discomfort /dɪs'kʌmfət/ n. gêne f.

disconcert /dɪskən'sɜːt/ v.t. déconcerter.

disconnect /dɪskə'nekt/ v.t. détacher;
(unplug) débrancher; (cut off) couper.

discontent /dɪskən'tent/ n. mécon-
tentement m. **~ed** a. mécontent.

discontinue /dɪskən'tɪnjuː/ v.t. interrompre, cesser.

discord /'dɪskɔːd/ n. discorde f.;
(mus.) dissonance f. **~ant** /-'skɔːdə-
nt/ a. discordant.

discothèque /'dɪskətek/ n. discothèque f.

discount[1] /'dɪskaʊnt/ n. rabais m.

discount[2] /dɪs'kaʊnt/ v.t. ne pas
tenir compte de.

discourage /dɪˈskʌrɪdʒ/ v.t. décourager.

discourse /ˈdɪskɔːs/ n. discours m.

discourteous /dɪsˈkɜːtɪəs/ a. impoli, peu courtois.

discover /dɪˈskʌvə(r)/ v.t. découvrir. **~y** n. découverte f.

discredit /dɪsˈkredɪt/ v.t. (p.t. **discredited**) discréditer. ● n. discrédit m.

discreet /dɪˈskriːt/ a. discret. **~ly** adv. discrètement.

discrepancy /dɪˈskrepənsɪ/ n. contradiction f., incohérence f.

discretion /dɪˈskreʃn/ n. discrétion f.

discriminat|e /dɪˈskrɪmɪneɪt/ v.t./i. distinguer. **~e against**, faire de la discrimination contre. **~ing** a. (person) qui a du discernement. **~ion** /-ˈneɪʃn/ n. discernement m.; (bias) discrimination f.

discus /ˈdɪskəs/ n. disque m.

discuss /dɪˈskʌs/ v.t. (talk about) discuter de; (argue about, examine critically) discuter. **~ion** /-ʃn/ n. discussion f.

disdain /dɪsˈdeɪn/ n. dédain m. **~ful** a. dédaigneux.

disease /dɪˈziːz/ n. maladie f. **~d** a. malade.

disembark /dɪsɪmˈbɑːk/ v.t./i. débarquer.

disembodied /dɪsɪmˈbɒdɪd/ a. désincarné.

disenchant /dɪsɪnˈtʃɑːnt/ v.t. désenchanter. **~ment** n. désenchantement m.

disengage /dɪsɪnˈgeɪdʒ/ v.t. dégager; (mil.) retirer. ● v.i. (mil.) retirer. (auto.) débrayer. **~ment** n. dégagement m.

disentangle /dɪsɪnˈtæŋgl/ v.t. démêler.

disfavour, (Amer.) **disfavor** /dɪsˈfeɪvə(r)/ n. défaveur f.

disfigure /dɪsˈfɪgə(r)/ v.t. défigurer.

disgrace /dɪsˈgreɪs/ n. (shame) honte f.; (disfavour) disgrâce f. ● v.t. déshonorer. **~d** a. (in disfavour) disgracié. **~ful** a. honteux.

disgruntled /dɪsˈgrʌntld/ a. mécontent.

disguise /dɪsˈgaɪz/ v.t. déguiser. ● n. déguisement m. **in ~**, déguisé.

disgust /dɪsˈgʌst/ n. dégoût m. ● v.t. dégoûter. **~ing** a. dégoûtant.

dish /dɪʃ/ n. plat m. ● v.t. **~ out**, (fam.) distribuer. **~ up**, servir. **the ~es**, (crockery) la vaisselle.

dishcloth /ˈdɪʃklɒθ/ n. lavette f.; (for drying) torchon m.

dishearten /dɪsˈhɑːtn/ v.t. décourager.

dishevelled /dɪˈʃevld/ a. échevelé.

dishonest /dɪsˈɒnɪst/ a. malhonnête. **~y** n. malhonnêteté f.

dishonour, (Amer.) **dishonor** /dɪsˈɒnə(r)/ n. déshonneur m. ● v.t. déshonorer. **~able** a. déshonorant. **~ably** adv. avec déshonneur.

dishwasher /ˈdɪʃwɒʃə(r)/ n. lave-vaisselle m. invar.

disillusion /dɪsɪˈluːʒn/ v.t. désillusionner. **~ment** n. désillusion f.

disincentive /dɪsɪnˈsentɪv/ n. **be a ~ to**, décourager.

disinclined /dɪsɪnˈklaɪnd/ a. **~ to**, peu disposé à.

disinfect /dɪsɪnˈfekt/ v.t. désinfecter. **~ant** n. désinfectant m.

disinherit /dɪsɪnˈherɪt/ v.t. déshériter.

disintegrate /dɪsˈɪntɪgreɪt/ v.t./i. (se) désintégrer.

disinterested /dɪsˈɪntrəstɪd/ a. désintéressé.

disjointed /dɪsˈdʒɔɪntɪd/ a. (talk) décousu.

disk /dɪsk/ n. (Amer.) = **disc**; (comput.) disque m. **~ drive**, drive m., lecteur de disquettes m.

diskette /dɪˈsket/ n. disquette f.

dislike /dɪsˈlaɪk/ n. aversion f. ● v.t. ne pas aimer.

dislocat|e /ˈdɪsləkeɪt/ v.t. (limb) disloquer. **~ion** /-ˈkeɪʃn/ n. dislocation f.

dislodge /dɪsˈlɒdʒ/ v.t. (move) déplacer; (drive out) déloger.

disloyal /dɪsˈlɔɪəl/ a. déloyal. **~ty** n. déloyauté f.

dismal /ˈdɪzməl/ a. morne, triste.

dismantle /dɪsˈmæntl/ v.t. démonter, défaire.

dismay /dɪsˈmeɪ/ n. consternation f. ● v.t. consterner.

dismiss /dɪsˈmɪs/ v.t. renvoyer; (appeal) rejeter; (from mind) écarter. **~al** n. renvoi m.

dismount /dɪsˈmaʊnt/ v.i. descendre, mettre pied à terre.

disobedien|t /dɪsəˈbiːdɪənt/ a. désobéissant. **~ce** n. désobéissance f.

disobey /dɪsəˈbeɪ/ v.t. désobéir à ● v.i. désobéir.

disorder /dɪsˈɔːdə(r)/ n. désordre m.; (ailment) trouble(s) m. (pl.). ~ly a. désordonné.

disorganize /dɪsˈɔːɡənaɪz/ v.t. désorganiser.

disorientate /dɪsˈɔːrɪənteɪt/ v.t. désorienter.

disown /dɪsˈəʊn/ v.t. renier.

disparaging /dɪˈspærɪdʒɪŋ/ a. désobligeant. ~ly adv. de façon désobligeante.

disparity /dɪˈspærətɪ/ n. disparité f., écart m.

dispassionate /dɪˈspæʃənət/ a. impartial; (unemotional) calme.

dispatch /dɪˈspætʃ/ v.t. (send, complete) expédier; (troops) envoyer. ● n. expédition f.; envoi m.; (report) dépêche f. ~-rider n. estafette f.

dispel /dɪˈspel/ v.t. (p.t. **dispelled**) dissiper.

dispensary /dɪˈspensərɪ/ n. pharmacie f., officine f.

dispense /dɪˈspens/ v.t. distribuer; (medicine) préparer. ● v.i. ~ with, se passer de. ~r /-ə(r)/ n. (container) distributeur m.

dispers|e /dɪˈspɜːs/ v.t./i. (se) disperser. ~al n. dispersion f.

dispirited /dɪˈspɪrɪtɪd/ a. découragé, abattu.

displace /dɪsˈpleɪs/ v.t. déplacer.

display /dɪˈspleɪ/ v.t. montrer, exposer; (feelings) manifester. ● n. exposition f.; manifestation f.; (comm.) étalage m.; (of computer) visuel m.

displeas|e /dɪsˈpliːz/ v.t. déplaire à. ~ed with, mécontent de. ~ure /-ˈpleʒə(r)/ n. mécontentement m.

disposable /dɪˈspəʊzəbl/ a. à jeter.

dispos|e /dɪˈspəʊz/ v.t. disposer. ● v.i. ~e of, se débarrasser de. well ~ed to, bien disposé envers. ~al n. (of waste) évacuation f. at s.o.'s ~al, à la disposition de qn.

disposition /dɪspəˈzɪʃn/ n. disposition f.; (character) naturel m.

disproportionate /dɪsprəˈpɔːʃənət/ a. disproportionné.

disprove /dɪsˈpruːv/ v.t. réfuter.

dispute /dɪˈspjuːt/ v.t. contester. ● n. discussion f.; (pol.) conflit m. in ~, contesté.

disqualif|y /dɪsˈkwɒlɪfaɪ/ v.t. rendre inapte; (sport) disqualifier. ~y from driving, retirer le permis à. ~ication /-ɪˈkeɪʃn/ n. disqualification f.

disquiet /dɪsˈkwaɪət/ n. inquiétude f. ~ing a. inquiétant.

disregard /dɪsrɪˈɡɑːd/ v.t. ne pas tenir compte de. ● n. indifférence f. (for, à).

disrepair /dɪsrɪˈpeə(r)/ n. mauvais état m., délabrement m.

disreputable /dɪsˈrepjʊtəbl/ a. peu recommendable.

disrepute /dɪsrɪˈpjuːt/ n. discrédit m.

disrespect /dɪsrɪˈspekt/ n. manque de respect m. ~ful a. irrespectueux.

disrupt /dɪsˈrʌpt/ v.t. (disturb, break up) perturber; (plans) déranger. ~ion /-pʃn/ n. perturbation f. ~ive a. perturbateur.

dissatisf|ied /dɪsˈsætɪsfaɪd/ a. mécontent. ~action /dɪsætɪsˈfækʃn/ n. mécontentement m.

dissect /dɪˈsekt/ v.t. disséquer. ~ion /-kʃn/ n. dissection f.

disseminate /dɪˈsemɪneɪt/ v.t. disséminer.

dissent /dɪˈsent/ v.i. différer (from, de). ● n. dissentiment m.

dissertation /dɪsəˈteɪʃn/ n. (univ.) mémoire m.

disservice /dɪsˈsɜːvɪs/ n. mauvais service m.

dissident /ˈdɪsɪdənt/ a. & n. dissident(e) (m. (f.)).

dissimilar /dɪˈsɪmɪlə(r)/ a. dissemblable, différent.

dissipate /ˈdɪsɪpeɪt/ v.t./i. (se) dissiper; (efforts) gaspiller. ~d /-ɪd/ a. (person) débauché.

dissociate /dɪˈsəʊʃɪeɪt/ v.t. dissocier. ~ o.s. from, se désolidariser de.

dissolute /ˈdɪsəljuːt/ a. dissolu.

dissolution /dɪsəˈluːʃn/ n. dissolution f.

dissolve /dɪˈzɒlv/ v.t./i. (se) dissoudre.

dissuade /dɪˈsweɪd/ v.t. dissuader.

distance /ˈdɪstəns/ n. distance f. from a ~, de loin. in the ~, au loin.

distant /ˈdɪstənt/ a. éloigné, lointain; (relative) éloigné; (aloof) distant.

distaste /dɪsˈteɪst/ n. dégoût m. ~ful a. désagréable.

distemper /dɪˈstempə(r)/ n. (paint) badigeon m.; (animal disease) maladie f. ● v.t. badigeonner.

distend /dɪˈstend/ v.t./i. (se) distendre.

distil /dɪˈstɪl/ v.t. (p.t. **distilled**) distiller. ~lation /-ˈleɪʃn/ n. distillation f.

distillery /dɪˈstɪlərɪ/ n. distillerie f.
distinct /dɪˈstɪŋkt/ a. distinct;
(*marked*) net. **as ~ from**, par opposition à. **~ion** /-kʃn/ n. distinction f.;
(*in exam*) mention très bien f. **~ive**
a. distinctif. **~ly** adv. (*see*) distinctement; (*forbid*) expressément; (*markedly*) nettement.
distinguish /dɪˈstɪŋgwɪʃ/ v.t./i.
distinguer. **~ed** a. distingué.
distort /dɪˈstɔːt/ v.t. déformer. **~ion**
/-ʃn/ n. distorsion f.; (*of facts*) déformation f.
distract /dɪˈstrækt/ v.t. distraire.
~ed a. (*distraught*) éperdu. **~ing**
a. gênant. **~ion** /-kʃn/ n. (*lack of
attention, entertainment*) distraction
f.
distraught /dɪˈstrɔːt/ a. éperdu.
distress /dɪˈstres/ n. douleur f.;
(*poverty, danger*) détresse f. ● v.t.
peiner. **~ing** a. pénible.
distribut|e /dɪˈstrɪbjuːt/ v.t. distribuer. **~ion** /-ˈbjuːʃn/ n. distribution f. **~or** n. distributeur m.
district /ˈdɪstrɪkt/ n. région f.; (*of
town*) quartier m.
distrust /dɪsˈtrʌst/ n. méfiance f.
● v.t. se méfier de.
disturb /dɪsˈtɜːb/ v.t. déranger;
(*alarm, worry*) troubler. **~ance** n.
dérangement m. (**of**, de); (*noise*)
tapage m. **~ances** n. pl. (*pol.*) troubles m. pl. **~ed** a. troublé; (*psychologically*) perturbé. **~ing** a.
troublant.
disused /dɪsˈjuːzd/ a. désaffecté.
ditch /dɪtʃ/ n. fossé m. ● v.t. (*sl.*)
abandonner.
dither /ˈdɪðə(r)/ v.i. hésiter.
ditto /ˈdɪtəʊ/ adv. idem.
divan /dɪˈvæn/ n. divan m.
div|e /daɪv/ v.i. plonger; (*rush*) se
précipiter. ● n. plongeon m.; (*of
plane*) piqué m.; (*place: sl.*) bouge
m. **~er** n. plongeu|r, -se m., f. **~ing-
board** n. plongeoir m. **~ing-suit** n.
tenue de plongée f.
diverge /daɪˈvɜːdʒ/ v.i. diverger.
divergent /daɪˈvɜːdʒənt/ a. divergent.
diverse /daɪˈvɜːs/ a. divers.
diversify /daɪˈvɜːsɪfaɪ/ v.t. diversifier.
diversity /daɪˈvɜːsətɪ/ n. diversité f.
diver|t /daɪˈvɜːt/ v.t. détourner; (*traf-
fic*) dévier. **~sion** /-ʃn/ n. détournement m.; (*distraction*) diversion f.;
(*of traffic*) déviation f.
divest /daɪˈvest/ v.t. **~ of**, (*strip of*)
priver de, déposséder de.

divide /dɪˈvaɪd/ v.t./i. (se) diviser.
dividend /ˈdɪvɪdend/ n. dividende m.
divine /dɪˈvaɪn/ a. divin.
divinity /dɪˈvɪnətɪ/ n. divinité f.
division /dɪˈvɪʒn/ n. division f.
divorce /dɪˈvɔːs/ n. divorce m. (**from**,
d'avec). ● v.t./i. divorcer (d'avec).
~d a. divorcé.
divorcee /dɪvɔːˈsiː, *Amer*. dɪvɔːˈseɪ/ n.
divorcé(e) m. (f.).
divulge /daɪˈvʌldʒ/ v.t. divulguer.
DIY abbr. see **do-it-yourself**.
dizz|y /ˈdɪzɪ/ a. (**-ier, -iest**) vertigineux. **be** or **feel ~y**, avoir le
vertige. **~iness** n. vertige m.
do /duː/ v.t./i. (*3 sing. present tense*
does; *p.t.* did; *p.p.*, done) faire;
(*progress, be suitable*) aller; (*be
enough*) suffire; (*swindle: sl.*) avoir.
do well/badly, se débrouiller bien/
mal. **do the house**, peindre *ou*
nettoyer *etc.* la maison. **well done!**,
bravo! **well done**, (*culin.*) bien cuit.
done for, (*fam.*) fichu. ● v. aux.
do you see?, voyez-vous? **do you
live here?**, est-ce que vous habitez
ici? **I do live here**, si, j'habite ici. **I
do not smoke**, je ne fume pas. **don't
you?, doesn't he?**, *etc.*, n'est-ce pas?
● n. (*pl.* dos or do's) soirée f., fête f.
dos and don'ts, choses à faire et à
ne pas faire. **do away with**,
supprimer. **do in**, (*sl.*) tuer. **do-it-
yourself** n. bricolage m.; a. (*shop,
book*) de bricolage. **do out**, (*clean*)
nettoyer. **do up**, (*fasten*) fermer;
(*house*) refaire. **it's to ~ with the
house**, c'est à propos de la maison.
it's nothing to do with me, ça n'a
rien à voir avec moi. **I could do with
a holiday**, j'aurais bien besoin de
vacances. **~ without**, se passer de.
docile /ˈdəʊsaɪl/ a. docile.
dock[1] /dɒk/ n. dock m. ● v.t./i. (se)
mettre à quai. **~er** n. docker m.
dock[2] /dɒk/ n. (*jurid.*) banc des
accusés m.
dock[3] /dɒk/ v.t. (*money*) retrancher.
dockyard /ˈdɒkjɑːd/ n. chantier naval
m.
doctor /ˈdɒktə(r)/ n. médecin m.,
docteur m.; (*univ.*) docteur m.
● v.t. (*cat*) châtrer; (*fig.*) altérer.
doctorate /ˈdɒktərət/ n. doctorat m.
doctrine /ˈdɒktrɪn/ n. doctrine f.
document /ˈdɒkjʊmənt/ n. document
m. **~ary** /-ˈmentrɪ/ a. & n. documen-

taire (*m.*). **~ation** /-'eɪʃn/ *n.* documentation *f.*

doddering /'dɒdərɪŋ/ *a.* gâteux.

dodge /dɒdʒ/ *v.t.* esquiver. ● *v.i.* faire un saut de côté. ● *n.* (*fam.*) truc *m.*

dodgems /'dɒdʒəmz/ *n. pl.* autos tamponneuses *f. pl.*

dodgy /'dɒdʒɪ/ *a.* (**-ier, -iest**) (*fam.*: *difficult*) épineux, délicat; (*dangerous*) douteux.

doe /dəʊ/ *n.* (*deer*) biche *f.*

does /dʌz/ *see* do.

doesn't /'dʌznt/ = does not.

dog /dɒg/ *n.* chien *m.* ● *v.t.* (*p.t.* **dogged**) poursuivre. **~-collar** *n.* (*fam.*) (faux) col d'ecclésiastique *m.* **~-eared** *a.* écorné.

dogged /'dɒgɪd/ *a.* obstiné.

dogma /'dɒgmə/ *n.* dogme *m.* **~tic** /-'mætɪk/ *a.* dogmatique.

dogsbody /'dɒgzbɒdɪ/ *n.* factotum *m.*, bonne à tout faire *f.*

doily /'dɔɪlɪ/ *n.* napperon *m.*

doings /'duːɪŋz/ *n. pl.* (*fam.*) activités *f. pl.*, occupations *f. pl.*

doldrums /'dɒldrəmz/ *n. pl.* **be in the ~**, (*person*) avoir le cafard.

dole /dəʊl/ *v.t.* **~ out**, distribuer. ● *n.* (*fam.*) indemnité de chômage *f.* **on the ~**, (*fam.*) au chômage.

doleful /'dəʊlfl/ *a.* triste, morne.

doll /dɒl/ *n.* poupée *f.* ● *v.t.* **~ up**, (*fam.*) bichonner.

dollar /'dɒlə(r)/ *n.* dollar *m.*

dollop /'dɒləp/ *n.* (*of food etc.*: *fam.*) gros morceau *m.*

dolphin /'dɒlfɪn/ *n.* dauphin *m.*

domain /də'meɪn/ *n.* domaine *m.*

dome /dəʊm/ *n.* dôme *m.*

domestic /də'mestɪk/ *a.* familial; (*trade, flights, etc.*) intérieur; (*animal*) domestique. **~ science**, arts ménagers *m. pl.* **~ated** *a.* (*animal*) domestiqué.

domesticity /dɒme'stɪsətɪ/ *n.* vie de famille *f.*

dominant /'dɒmɪnənt/ *a.* dominant.

dominat|e /'dɒmɪneɪt/ *v.t./i.* dominer. **~ion** /-'neɪʃn/ *n.* domination *f.*

domineering /dɒmɪ'nɪərɪŋ/ *a.* dominateur, autoritaire.

dominion /də'mɪnjən/ *n.* (*British pol.*) dominion *m.*

domino /'dɒmɪnəʊ/ *n.* (*pl.* **-oes**) domino *m.* **~es**, (*game*) dominos *m. pl.*

don [1] /dɒn/ *v.t.* (*p.t.* **donned**) revêtir, endosser.

don [2] /dɒn/ *n.* professeur d'université *m.*

donat|e /dəʊ'neɪt/ *v.t.* faire don de. **~ion** /-ʃn/ *n.* don *m.*

done /dʌn/ *see* do.

donkey /'dɒŋkɪ/ *n.* âne *m.* **the ~-work** le sale boulot.

donor /'dəʊnə(r)/ *n.* dona|teur, -trice *m.,f.*; (*of blood*) donneu|r, -se *m.,f.*

don't /dəʊnt/ = do not.

doodle /'duːdl/ *v.i.* griffonner.

doom /duːm/ *n.* (*ruin*) ruine *f.*; (*fate*) destin *m.* ● *v.t.* **be ~ed to**, être destiné *or* condamné à. **~ed (to failure)**, voué à l'échec.

door /dɔː(r)/ *n.* porte *f.*; (*of vehicle*) portière *f.*, porte *f.*

doorbell /'dɔːbel/ *n.* sonnette *f.*

doorman /'dɔːmən/ *n.* (*pl.* **-men**) portier *m.*

doormat /'dɔːmæt/ *n.* paillasson *m.*

doorstep /'dɔːstep/ *n.* pas de (la) porte *m.*, seuil *m.*

doorway /'dɔːweɪ/ *n.* porte *f.*

dope /dəʊp/ *n.* (*fam.*) drogue *f.*; (*idiot*: *sl.*) imbécile *m./f.* ● *v.t.* doper. **~y** *a.* (*foolish*: *sl.*) imbécile.

dormant /'dɔːmənt/ *a.* en sommeil.

dormitory /'dɔːmɪtrɪ, *Amer.* 'dɔːmɪtɔːrɪ/ *n.* dortoir *m.*; (*univ.*, *Amer.*) résidence *f.*

dormouse /'dɔːmaʊs/ *n.* (*pl.* **-mice**) loir *m.*

dos|e /dəʊs/ *n.* dose *f.* **~age** *n.* dose *f.*; (*on label*) posologie *f.*

doss /dɒs/ *v.i.* (*sl.*) roupiller. **~-house** *n.* asile de nuit *m.*

dossier /'dɒsɪə(r)/ *n.* dossier *m.*

dot /dɒt/ *n.* point *m.* **on the ~**, (*fam.*) à l'heure pile. **~-matrix** *a.* (*printer*) matriciel.

dote /dəʊt/ *v.i.* **~ on**, être gaga de.

dotted /'dɒtɪd/ *a.* (*fabric*) à pois. **~ line**, ligne en pointillés *f.* **~ with**, parsemé de.

dotty /'dɒtɪ/ *a.* (**-ier, -iest**) (*fam.*) cinglé, dingue.

double /'dʌbl/ *a.* double; (*room, bed*) pour deux personnes. ● *adv.* deux fois. ● *n.* double *m.*; (*stuntman*) doublure *f.* **~s**, (*tennis*) double *m.* ● *v.t./i.* doubler; (*fold*) plier en deux. **at** *or* **on the ~**, au pas de course. **~ the size**, deux fois plus grand: **pay ~**, payer le double. **~-bass** *n.* (*mus.*) contrebasse *f.* **~-breasted** *a.* croisé. **~-check** *v.t.* revérifier. **~ chin**, double menton *m.* **~-cross** *v.t.* tromper. **~-dealing** *n.* double jeu

m. **~-decker** *n.* autobus à impériale *m.* **~ Dutch,** de l'hébreu *m.*
doubly /'dʌblɪ/ *adv.* doublement.
doubt /daʊt/ *n.* doute *m.* ● *v.t.* douter de. **~ if** *or* **that,** douter que. **~ful** *a.* incertain, douteux; (*person*) qui a des doutes. **~less** *adv.* sans doute.
dough /dəʊ/ *n.* pâte *f.*; (*money: sl.*) fric *m.*
doughnut /'dəʊnʌt/ *n.* beignet *m.*
douse /daʊs/ *v.t.* arroser; (*light, fire*) éteindre.
dove /dʌv/ *n.* colombe *f.*
Dover /'dəʊvə(r)/ *n.* Douvres *m./f.*
dovetail /'dʌvteɪl/ *v.t./i.* (s')ajuster.
dowdy /'daʊdɪ/ *a.* (**-ier, -iest**) (*clothes*) sans chic, monotone.
down¹ /daʊn/ *n.* (*fluff*) duvet *m.*
down² /daʊn/ *adv.* en bas; (*of sun*) couché; (*lower*) plus bas. ● *prep.* en bas de; (*along*) le long de. ● *v.t.* (*knock down, shoot down*) abattre; (*drink*) vider. **come** *or* **go ~,** descendre. **go ~ to the post office,** aller à la poste. **~-and-out** *n.* clochard(e) *m.* (*f.*). **~-hearted** *a.* découragé. **~-market** *a.* bas de gamme. **~ payment,** acompte *m.* **~-to-earth** *a.* terre-à-terre *invar.* **~ under,** aux antipodes. **~ with,** à bas.
downcast /'daʊnkɑːst/ *a.* démoralisé.
downfall /'daʊnfɔːl/ *n.* chute *f.*
downgrade /daʊn'greɪd/ *v.t.* déclasser.
downhill /daʊn'hɪl/ *adv.* **go ~,** descendre; (*pej.*) baisser.
downpour /'daʊnpɔː(r)/ *n.* grosse averse *f.*
downright /'daʊnraɪt/ *a.* (*utter*) véritable; (*honest*) franc. ● *adv.* carrément.
downs /daʊnz/ *n. pl.* région de collines *f.*
downstairs /daʊn'steəz/ *adv.* en bas. ● *a.* d'en bas.
downstream /'daʊnstriːm/ *adv.* en aval.
downtown /'daʊntaʊn/ *a.* (*Amer.*) du centre de la ville. **~ Boston**/*etc.*, le centre de Boston/*etc.*
downtrodden /'daʊntrɒdn/ *a.* opprimé.
downward /'daʊnwəd/ *a. & adv.*, **~s** *adv.* vers le bas.
dowry /'daʊərɪ/ *n.* dot *f.*
doze /dəʊz/ *v.i.* sommeiller. **~ off,** s'assoupir. ● *n.* somme *m.*

dozen /'dʌzn/ *n.* douzaine *f.* **a ~ eggs,** une douzaine d'œufs. **~s of,** (*fam.*) des dizaines de.
Dr *abbr.* (*Doctor*) Docteur.
drab /dræb/ *a.* terne.
draft¹ /drɑːft/ *n.* (*outline*) brouillon *m.*; (*comm.*) traite *f.* ● *v.t.* faire le brouillon de; (*draw up*) rédiger. **the ~,** (*mil., Amer.*) la conscription. **a ~ treaty,** un projet de traité.
draft² /drɑːft/ *n.* (*Amer.*) = **draught.**
drag /dræg/ *v.t./i.* (*p.t.* **dragged**) traîner; (*river*) draguer; (*pull away*) arracher. ● *n.* (*task: fam.*) corvée *f.*; (*person: fam.*) raseu|r, -se *m.*, *f.* **in ~,** en travesti. **~ on,** s'éterniser.
dragon /'drægən/ *n.* dragon *m.*
dragon-fly /'drægənflaɪ/ *n.* libellule *f.*
drain /dreɪn/ *v.t.* (*land*) drainer; (*vegetables*) égoutter; (*tank, glass*) vider; (*use up*) épuiser. **~ (off),** (*liquid*) faire écouler. ● *v.i.* **~ (off),** (*of liquid*) s'écouler. ● *n.* (*sewer*) égout *m.* **~-(pipe),** tuyau d'écoulement *m.* **be a ~ on,** pomper. **~ing-board** *n.* égouttoir *m.*
drama /'drɑːmə/ *n.* art dramatique *m.*, théâtre *m.*; (*play, event*) drame *m.* **~tic** /drə'mætɪk/ *a.* (*situation*) dramatique; (*increase*) spectaculaire. **~tist** /'dræmətɪst/ *n.* dramaturge *m.* **~tize** /'dræmətaɪz/ *v.t.* adapter pour la scène; (*fig.*) dramatiser.
drank /dræŋk/ *see* drink.
drape /dreɪp/ *v.t.* draper. **~s** *n. pl.* (*Amer.*) rideaux *m. pl.*
drastic /'dræstɪk/ *a.* sévère.
draught /drɑːft/ *n.* courant d'air *m.* **~s,** (*game*) dames *f. pl.* **~ beer,** bière (à la) pression *f.* **~y** *a.* plein de courants d'air.
draughtsman /'drɑːftsmən/ *n.* (*pl.* -**men**) dessina|teur, -trice industriel(le) *m.*, *f.*
draw /drɔː/ *v.t.* (*p.t.* **drew**, *p.p.* **drawn**) (*pull*) tirer; (*attract*) attirer; (*pass*) passer; (*picture*) dessiner; (*line*) tracer. ● *v.i.* dessiner; (*sport*) faire match nul; (*come, move*) venir. ● *n.* (*sport*) match nul *m.*; (*in lottery*) tirage au sort *m.* **~ back,** (*recoil*) reculer. **~ in,** (*days*) diminuer. **~ near,** (s')approcher (**to,** de). **~ out,** (*money*) retirer. **~ up** *v.i.* (*stop*) s'arrêter;

v.t. (*document*) dresser; (*chair*) approcher.

drawback /'drɔːbæk/ *n.* inconvénient *m.*

drawbridge /'drɔːbrɪdʒ/ *n.* pont-levis *m.*

drawer /drɔː(r)/ *n.* tiroir *m.*

drawers /drɔːz/ *n. pl.* culotte *f.*

drawing /'drɔːɪŋ/ *n.* dessin *m.* **~-board** *n.* planche à dessin *f.* **~-pin** *n.* punaise *f.* **~-room** *n.* salon *m.*

drawl /drɔːl/ *n.* voix traînante *f.*

drawn /drɔːn/ *see* draw. ● *a.* (*features*) tiré; (*match*) nul.

dread /dred/ *n.* terreur *f.*, crainte *f.* ● *v.t.* redouter.

dreadful /'dredfl/ *a.* épouvantable, affreux. **~ly** *adv.* terriblement.

dream /driːm/ *n.* rêve *m.* ● *v.t./i.* (*p.t.* **dreamed** *or* **dreamt**) rêver. ● *a.* (*ideal*) de ses rêves. **~ up,** imaginer. **~er** *n.* rêveu|r, -se *m., f.* **~y** *a.* rêveur.

drear|y /'drɪərɪ/ *a.* (**-ier, -iest**) triste; (*boring*) monotone. **~iness** *n.* tristesse *f.*; monotonie *f.*

dredge /dredʒ/ *n.* drague *f.* ● *v.t./i.* draguer. **~r** /-ə(r)/ *n.* dragueur *m.*

dregs /dregz/ *n. pl.* lie *f.*

drench /drentʃ/ *v.t.* tremper.

dress /dres/ *n.* robe *f.*; (*clothing*) tenue *f.* ● *v.t./i.* (s')habiller; (*food*) assaisonner; (*wound*) panser. **~ circle,** premier balcon *m.* **~ rehearsal,** répétition générale *f.* **~ up as,** se déguiser en. **get ~ed,** s'habiller.

dresser /'dresə(r)/ *n.* buffet *m.*; (*actor's*) habilleu|r, -se *m., f.*

dressing /'dresɪŋ/ *n.* (*sauce*) assaisonnement *m.*; (*bandage*) pansement *m.* **~-gown** *n.* robe de chambre *f.* **~-room** *n.* (*sport*) vestiaire *m.*; (*theatre*) loge *f.* **~-table** *n.* coiffeuse *f.*

dressmak|er /'dresmeɪkə(r)/ *n.* couturière *f.* **~ing** *n.* couture *f.*

dressy /'dresɪ/ *a.* (**-ier, -iest**) chic *invar.*

drew /druː/ *see* draw.

dribble /'drɪbl/ *v.i.* couler goutte à goutte; (*person*) baver; (*football*) dribbler.

dribs and drabs /drɪbznˈdræbz/ *n. pl.* petites quantités *f. pl.*

dried /draɪd/ *a.* (*fruit etc.*) sec.

drier /'draɪə(r)/ *n.* séchoir *m.*

drift /drɪft/ *v.i.* aller à la dérive; (*pile up*) s'amonceler. ● *n.* dérive *f.*; amoncellement *m.*; (*of events*) tour-

nure *f.*; (*meaning*) sens *m.* **~ towards,** glisser vers. (**snow**) **~,** congère *f.* **~er** *n.* personne sans but dans la vie *f.*

driftwood /'drɪftwʊd/ *n.* bois flotté *m.*

drill /drɪl/ *n.* (*tool*) perceuse *f.*; (*for teeth*) roulette *f.*; (*training*) exercice *m.*; (*procedure*: *fam.*) marche à suivre *f.* (**pneumatic**) **~,** marteau piqueur *m.* ● *v.t.* percer; (*train*) entraîner. ● *v.i.* être à l'exercice.

drily /'draɪlɪ/ *adv.* sèchement.

drink /drɪŋk/ *v.t./i.* (*p.t.* **drank,** *p.p.* **drunk**) boire. ● *n.* (*liquid*) boisson *f.*; (*glass of alcohol*) verre *m.* **a ~ of water,** un verre d'eau. **~able** *a.* (*not unhealthy*) potable; (*palatable*) buvable. **~er** *n.* buveu|r, -se *m., f.* **~ing water,** eau potable *f.*

drip /drɪp/ *v.i.* (*p.t.* **dripped**) (é)goutter; (*washing*) s'égoutter. ● *n.* goutte *f.*; (*person*: *sl.*) lavette *f.* **~-dry** *v.t.* laisser égoutter; *a.* sans repassage.

dripping /'drɪpɪŋ/ *n.* (*Amer.* **~s**) graisse de rôti *f.*

drive /draɪv/ *v.t.* (*p.t.* **drove,** *p.p.* **driven**) chasser, pousser; (*vehicle*) conduire; (*machine*) actionner. ● *v.i.* conduire. ● *n.* promenade en voiture *f.*; (*private road*) allée *f.*; (*fig.*) énergie *f.*; (*psych.*) instinct *m.*; (*pol.*) campagne *f.*; (*auto.*) traction *f.*; (*golf, comput.*) drive *m.* **it's a two-hour ~,** c'est deux heures en voiture. **~ at,** en venir à. **~ away,** (*of car*) partir. **~ in,** (*force in*) enfoncer. **~ mad,** rendre fou. **lefthand ~,** conduite à gauche *f.*

drivel /'drɪvl/ *n.* radotage *m.*

driver /'draɪvə(r)/ *n.* conduc|teur, -trice *m., f.*, chauffeur *m.* **~'s license** (*Amer.*), permis de conduire *m.*

driving /'draɪvɪŋ/ *n.* conduite *f.* **~ licence,** permis de conduire *m.* **~ rain,** pluie battante *f.* **~ school,** auto-école *f.* **take one's ~ test,** passer son permis.

drizzle /'drɪzl/ *n.* bruine *f.* ● *v.i.* bruiner.

dromedary /'drɒmədərɪ, (*Amer.*) 'drɒmədərɪ/ *n.* dromadaire *m.*

drone /drəʊn/ *n.* (*noise*) bourdonnement *m.*; (*bee*) faux bourdon *m.* ● *v.i.* bourdonner; (*fig.*) parler d'une voix monotone.

drool /druːl/ *v.i.* baver (**over,** sur).

droop /druːp/ *v.i.* pencher, tomber.

drop /drɒp/ n. goutte f.; (fall, lowering) chute f. ● v.t./i. (p.t. **dropped**) (laisser) tomber; (decrease, lower) baisser. ~ (off), (person from car) déposer. ~ a line, écrire un mot (to, à). ~ in, passer (on, chez). ~ off, (doze) s'assoupir. ~ out, se retirer (of, de); (of student) abandonner. ~-out n. marginal(e) m. (f.), raté(e) m. (f.).

droppings /'drɒpɪŋz/ n. pl. crottes f. pl.

dross /drɒs/ n. déchets m. pl.

drought /draʊt/ n. sécheresse f.

drove /drəʊv/ see drive.

droves /drəʊvz/ n. pl. foule(s) f. (pl.).

drown /draʊn/ v.t./i. (se) noyer.

drowsy /'draʊzɪ/ a. somnolent. be or feel ~, avoir envie de dormir.

drudge /drʌdʒ/ n. esclave du travail m. ~ry /-ərɪ/ n. travail pénible et ingrat m.

drug /drʌg/ n. drogue f.; (med.) médicament m. ● v.t. (p.t. **drugged**) droguer. ~ addict, drogué(e) m. (f.). ~gist n. pharmacien (-ne) m. (f.).

drugstore /'drʌgstɔː(r)/ n. (Amer.) drugstore m.

drum /drʌm/ n. tambour m.; (for oil) bidon m. ~s, batterie f. ● v.i. (p.t. **drummed**) tambouriner. ● v.t. ~ into s.o., répéter sans cesse à qn. ~ up, (support) susciter; (business) créer. ~mer n. tambour m.; (in pop group) batteur m.

drumstick /'drʌmstɪk/ n. baguette de tambour f.; (of chicken) pilon m.

drunk /drʌŋk/ see drink. ● a. ivre. get ~, s'enivrer. ● n., ~ard n. ivrogne(sse) m. (f.). ~en a. ivre; (habitually) ivrogne. ~enness n. ivresse f.

dry /draɪ/ a. (**drier, driest**) sec; (day) sans pluie. ● v.t./i. (faire) sécher. be or feel ~, avoir soif. ~-clean v.t. nettoyer à sec. ~-cleaner n. teinturier m. ~ run, galop d'essai m. ~ up, (dry dishes) essuyer la vaisselle; (of supplies) (se) tarir; (be silent: fam.) se taire. ~ness n. sécheresse f.

dual /'djuːəl/ a. double. ~ carriageway, route à quatre voies f. ~-purpose a. qui fait double emploi.

dub /dʌb/ v.t. (p.t. **dubbed**) (film) doubler; (nickname) surnommer.

dubious /'djuːbɪəs/ a. (pej.) douteux. be ~ about sth., (person) avoir des doutes sur qch.

duchess /'dʌtʃɪs/ n. duchesse f.

duck /dʌk/ n. canard m. ● v.i. se baisser subitement. ● v.t. (head) baisser; (person) plonger dans l'eau. ~ling n. caneton m.

duct /dʌkt/ n. conduit m.

dud /dʌd/ a. (tool etc.: sl.) mal fichu; (coin: sl.) faux; (cheque: sl.) sans provision. ● n. be a ~, (not work: sl.) ne pas marcher.

dude /duːd/ n. (Amer.) dandy m.

due /djuː/ a. (owing) dû; (expected) attendu; (proper) qui convient. ● adv. ~ east/etc., droit vers l'est/etc. ● n. dû m. ~s, droits m. pl.; (of club) cotisation f. ~ to, à cause de; (caused by) dû à. she's ~ to leave now, c'est prévu qu'elle parte maintenant. in ~ course, (eventually) avec le temps; (at the right time) en temps et lieu.

duel /'djuːəl/ n. duel m.

duet /djuː'et/ n. duo m.

duffle /'dʌfl/ a. ~ bag, sac de marin m. ~ coat, duffel-coat m.

dug /dʌg/ see dig.

duke /djuːk/ n. duc m.

dull /dʌl/ a. (-er, -est) ennuyeux; (colour) terne; (weather) morne; (sound) sourd; (stupid) bête; (blunt) émoussé. ● v.t. (pain) amortir; (mind) engourdir.

duly /'djuːlɪ/ adv. comme il convient; (in due time) en temps voulu.

dumb /dʌm/ a. (-er, -est) muet; (stupid: fam.) bête.

dumbfound /dʌm'faʊnd/ v.t. sidérer, ahurir.

dummy /'dʌmɪ/ n. (comm.) article factice m.; (of tailor) mannequin m.; (of baby) sucette f. ● a. factice. ~ run, galop d'essai m.

dump /dʌmp/ v.t. déposer; (abandon: fam.) se débarrasser de; (comm.) dumper. ● n. tas d'ordures m.; (refuse tip) décharge f.; (mil.) dépôt m.; (dull place: fam.) trou m. be in the ~s, (fam.) avoir le cafard.

dumpling /'dʌmplɪŋ/ n. boulette de pâte f.

dumpy /'dʌmpɪ/ a. (-ier, -iest) boulot, rondelet.

dunce /dʌns/ n. cancre m., âne m.

dune /djuːn/ n. dune f.

dung /dʌŋ/ n. (excrement) bouse f., crotte f.; (manure) fumier m.

dungarees /dʌŋgə'riːz/ n. pl. (overalls) salopette f.; (jeans: Amer.) jean m.

dungeon /ˈdʌndʒən/ n. cachot m.

dunk /dʌŋk/ v.t. tremper.

dupe /djuːp/ v.t. duper. ● n. dupe f.

duplex /ˈdjuːpleks/ n. duplex m.

duplicate¹ /ˈdjuːplɪkət/ n. double m.
● a. identique.

duplicat|e² /ˈdjuːplɪkeɪt/ v.t. faire un
double de; (on machine) polycopier.
~or n. duplicateur m.

duplicity /djuːˈplɪsəti/ n. duplicité f.

durable /ˈdjʊərəbl/ a. (tough) résistant; (enduring) durable.

duration /djʊˈreɪʃn/ n. durée f.

duress /djʊˈres/ n. contrainte f.

during /ˈdjʊərɪŋ/ prep. pendant.

dusk /dʌsk/ n. crépuscule m.

dusky /ˈdʌskɪ/ a. (-ier, -iest) foncé.

dust /dʌst/ n. poussière f. ● v.t.
épousseter; (sprinkle) saupoudrer
(with, de). ~-jacket n. jaquette f.

dustbin /ˈdʌstbɪn/ n. poubelle f.

duster /ˈdʌstə(r)/ n. chiffon m.

dustman /ˈdʌstmən/ n. (pl. -men)
éboueur m.

dustpan /ˈdʌstpæn/ n. pelle à poussière f.

dusty /ˈdʌstɪ/ a. (-ier, -iest) poussiéreux.

Dutch /dʌtʃ/ a. hollandais. ● n.
(lang.) hollandais m. **go** ~, partager
les frais. ~man n. Hollandais m.
~woman n. Hollandaise f.

dutiful /ˈdjuːtɪfl/ a. obéissant.

dut|y /ˈdjuːtɪ/ n. devoir m.; (tax) droit
m. ~ies, (of official etc.) fonctions f.
pl. ~y-free a. hors-taxe. **on** ~y, de
service.

duvet /ˈduːveɪ/ n. couette f.

dwarf /dwɔːf/ n. (pl. -fs) nain(e) m.
(f.). ● v.t. rapetisser.

dwell /dwel/ v.i. (p.t. **dwelt**)
demeurer. ~ **on**, s'étendre sur.
~er n. habitant(e) m. (f.). ~ing n.
habitation f.

dwindle /ˈdwɪndl/ v.i. diminuer.

dye /daɪ/ v.t. (pres. p. **dyeing**)
teindre. ● n. teinture f.

dying /ˈdaɪɪŋ/ a. mourant; (art) qui
se perd.

dynamic /daɪˈnæmɪk/ a. dynamique.

dynamism /ˈdaɪnəmɪzəm/ n. dynamisme m.

dynamite /ˈdaɪnəmaɪt/ n. dynamite
f. ● v.t. dynamiter.

dynamo /ˈdaɪnəməʊ/ n. (pl. -os)
dynamo f.

dynasty /ˈdɪnəstɪ, Amer. ˈdaɪnəstɪ/ n.
dynastie f.

dysentery /ˈdɪsəntrɪ/ n. dysenterie f.

dyslexi|a /dɪsˈleksɪə/ n. dyslexie f. ~c
a. & n. dyslexique (m./f.).

E

each /iːtʃ/ a. chaque. ● pron.
chacun(e). ~ **one**, chacun(e). ~
other, l'un(e) l'autre, les un(e)s les
autres. **know** ~ **other**, se connaître.
love ~ **other**, s'aimer. **a pound** ~,
(get) une livre chacun; (cost) une
livre chaque.

eager /ˈiːgə(r)/ a. impatient (**to**, de);
(supporter, desire) ardent. **be** ~ **to**,
(want) avoir envie de. ~ **for**, avide
de. ~ly adv. avec impatience or
ardeur. ~ness n. impatience f.,
désir m., ardeur f.

eagle /ˈiːgl/ n. aigle m.

ear¹ /ɪə(r)/ n. oreille f. ~-drum n.
tympan m. ~-ring n. boucle d'oreille
f.

ear² /ɪə(r)/ n. (of corn) épi m.

earache /ˈɪəreɪk/ n. mal à l'oreille m.,
mal d'oreille m.

earl /ɜːl/ n. comte m.

earlier /ˈɜːlɪə(r)/ a. (in series) précédent; (in history) plus ancien, antérieur; (in future) plus avancé.
● adv. précédemment; antérieurement; avant.

early /ˈɜːlɪ/ (-ier, -iest) adv. tôt, de
bonne heure. (ahead of time) en
avance. ● a. premier; (hour) matinal; (fruit) précoce; (retirement)
anticipé. **have an** ~ **dinner**, dîner
tôt. **in** ~ **summer**, au début de l'été.

earmark /ˈɪəmɑːk/ v.t. destiner, réserver (**for**, à).

earn /ɜːn/ v.t. gagner; (interest:
comm.) rapporter. ~ **s.o. sth.**,
(bring) valoir qch. à qn.

earnest /ˈɜːnɪst/ a. sérieux. **in** ~,
sérieusement.

earnings /ˈɜːnɪŋz/ n. pl. salaire m.;
(profits) bénéfices m. pl.

earphone /ˈɪəfəʊn/ n. écouteur m.

earshot /ˈɪəʃɒt/ n. **within** ~, à portée
de voix.

earth /ɜːθ/ n. terre f. ● v.t. (electr.)
mettre à la terre. **why/how/where
on** ~ . . . ?, pourquoi/comment/où
diable . . . ? ~ly a. terrestre.

earthenware /ˈɜːθnweə(r)/ n. faïence
f.

earthquake /'ɜːθkweɪk/ *n.* tremblement de terre *m.*

earthy /'ɜːθɪ/ *a.* (*of earth*) terreux; (*coarse*) grossier.

earwig /'ɪəwɪg/ *n.* perce-oreille *m.*

ease /iːz/ *n.* aisance *f.*, facilité *f.*; (*comfort*) bien-être *m.* ● *v.t./i.* (*se*) calmer; (*relax*) (se) détendre; (*slow down*) ralentir; (*slide*) glisser. **at ~**, à l'aise; (*mil.*) au repos. **with ~**, aisément.

easel /'iːzl/ *n.* chevalet *m.*

east /iːst/ *n.* est *m.* ● *a.* d'est. ● *adv.* vers l'est. **the E~**, (*Orient*) l'Orient *m.* **~erly** *a.* d'est. **~ern** *a.* de l'est, oriental. **~ward** *a.* à l'est. **~wards** *adv.* vers l'est.

Easter /'iːstə(r)/ *n.* Pâques *f. pl.* (*or m. sing.*). **~ egg**, œuf de Pâques *m.*

easy /'iːzɪ/ *a.* (**-ier, -iest**) facile; (*relaxed*) aisé. **~ chair**, fauteuil *m.* **go ~ with**, (*fam.*) y aller doucement avec. **take it ~**, ne pas se fatiguer.

easily *adv.* facilement.

easygoing /iːzɪ'gəʊɪŋ/ *a.* (*with people*) accommodant; (*relaxed*) décontracté.

eat /iːt/ *v.t./i.* (*p.t.* **ate**, *p.p.* **eaten**) manger. **~ into**, ronger. **~able** *a.* mangeable. **~er** *n.* mangeu|r, -se *m., f.*

eau-de-Cologne /əʊdəkə'ləʊn/ *n.* eau de Cologne *f.*

eaves /iːvz/ *n. pl.* avant-toit *m.*

eavesdrop /'iːvzdrɒp/ *v.i.* (*p.t.* **dropped**). **~ (on)**, écouter en cachette.

ebb /eb/ *n.* reflux *m.* ● *v.i.* refluer; (*fig.*) décliner.

ebony /'ebənɪ/ *n.* ébène *f.*

ebullient /ɪ'bʌlɪənt/ *a.* exubérant.

EC *abbr.* (*European Community*) CE.

eccentric /ɪk'sentrɪk/ *a. & n.* excentrique (*m./f.*). **~ity** /eksen'trɪsətɪ/ *n.* excentricité *f.*

ecclesiastical /ɪkliːzɪ'æstɪkl/ *a.* ecclésiastique.

echo /'ekəʊ/ *n.* (*pl.* **-oes**) écho *m.* ● *v.t./i.* (*p.t.* **echoed**, *pres. p.* **echoing**) (se) répercuter; (*fig.*) répéter.

eclipse /ɪ'klɪps/ *n.* éclipse *f.* ● *v.t.* éclipser.

ecolog|y /iː'kɒlədʒɪ/ *n.* écologie *f.* **~ical** /iːkə'lɒdʒɪkl/ *a.* écologique.

economic /iːkə'nɒmɪk/ *a.* économique; (*profitable*) rentable. **~al** *a.* économique; (*person*) économe. **~s** *n.* économie politique *f.*

economist /ɪ'kɒnəmɪst/ *n.* économiste *m./f.*

econom|y /ɪ'kɒnəmɪ/ *n.* économie *f.* **~ize** *v.i.* **~ (on)**, économiser.

ecosystem /'iːkəʊsɪstəm/ *n.* écosystème *m.*

ecstasy /'ekstəsɪ/ *n.* extase *f.*

ECU /'eɪkjuː/ *n.* ÉCU *m.*

eczema /'eksɪmə/ *n.* eczéma *m.*

eddy /'edɪ/ *n.* tourbillon *m.*

edge /edʒ/ *n.* bord *m.*; (*of town*) abords *m. pl.*; (*of knife*) tranchant *m.* ● *v.t.* border. ● *v.i.* (*move*) se glisser. **have the ~ on**, (*fam.*) l'emporter sur. **on ~**, énervé.

edgeways /'edʒweɪz/ *adv.* de côté. **I can't get a word in ~**, je ne peux pas placer un mot.

edging /'edʒɪŋ/ *n.* bordure *f.*

edgy /'edʒɪ/ *a.* énervé.

edible /'edɪbl/ *a.* mangeable; (*not poisonous*) comestible.

edict /'iːdɪkt/ *n.* décret *m.*

edifice /'edɪfɪs/ *n.* édifice *m.*

edify /'edɪfaɪ/ *v.t.* édifier.

edit /'edɪt/ *v.t.* (*p.t.* **edited**) (*newspaper*) diriger; (*prepare text of*) mettre au point, préparer; (*write*) rédiger; (*cut*) couper.

edition /ɪ'dɪʃn/ *n.* édition *f.*

editor /'edɪtə(r)/ *n.* (*writer*) rédac|teur, -trice *m., f.*; (*annotator*) édi|teur, -trice *m., f.* **the ~ (in chief)**, le rédacteur en chef. **~ial** /-'tɔːrɪəl/ *a.* de la rédaction; *n.* éditorial *m.*

educat|e /'edʒʊkeɪt/ *v.t.* instruire; (*mind, public*) éduquer. **~ed** *a.* instruit. **~ion** /-'keɪʃn/ *n.* éducation *f.*; (*schooling*) enseignement *m.* **~ional** /-'keɪʃənl/ *a.* pédagogique, éducatif.

EEC *abbr.* (*European Economic Community*) CEE *f.*

eel /iːl/ *n.* anguille *f.*

eerie /'ɪərɪ/ *a.* (**-ier, -iest**) sinistre.

effect /ɪ'fekt/ *n.* effet *m.* ● *v.t.* effectuer. **come into ~**, entrer en vigueur. **in ~**, effectivement. **take ~**, agir.

effective /ɪ'fektɪv/ *a.* efficace; (*striking*) frappant; (*actual*) effectif. **~ly** *adv.* efficacement; de manière frappante; effectivement. **~ness** *n.* efficacité *f.*

effeminate /ɪ'femɪnət/ *a.* efféminé.

effervescent /efə'vesnt/ *a.* effervescent.

efficien|t /ɪ'fɪʃnt/ a. efficace; (*person*) compétent. **~cy** n. efficacité f.; compétence f. **~tly** adv. efficacement.

effigy /'efɪdʒɪ/ n. effigie f.

effort /'efət/ n. effort m. **~less** a. facile.

effrontery /ɪ'frʌntərɪ/ n. effronterie f.

effusive /ɪ'fjuːsɪv/ a. expansif.

e.g. /iː'dʒiː/ abbr. par exemple.

egalitarian /ɪɡælɪ'teərɪən/ a. égalitaire. ● n. égalitariste m./f.

egg [1] /eɡ/ n. œuf m. **~-cup** n. coquetier m. **~-plant** n. aubergine f.

egg [2] /eɡ/ v.t. **~ on**, (fam.) inciter.

eggshell /'eɡʃel/ n. coquille d'œuf f.

ego /'iːɡəʊ/ n. (pl. **-os**) moi m. **~(t)ism** n. égoïsme m. **~(t)ist** n. égoïste m./f.

Egypt /'iːdʒɪpt/ n. Égypte f. **~ian** /ɪ'dʒɪpʃn/ a. & n. égyptien(ne) (m. (f.)).

eh /eɪ/ int. (fam.) hein.

eiderdown /'aɪdədaʊn/ n. édredon m.

eight /eɪt/ a. & n. huit (m.). **eighth** /eɪtθ/ a. & n. huitième (m./f.).

eighteen /eɪ'tiːn/ a. & n. dix-huit (m.). **~th** a. & n. dix-huitième (m./f.).

eight|y /'eɪtɪ/ a. & n. quatre-vingts (m.) **~ieth** a. & n. quatre-vingtième (m./f.).

either /'aɪðə(r)/ a. & pron. l'un(e) ou l'autre; (*with negative*) ni l'un(e) ni l'autre; (*each*) chaque. ● adv. non plus. ● conj. **~ . . . or**, ou (bien) . . . ou (bien); (*with negative*) ni . . . ni.

eject /ɪ'dʒekt/ v.t. éjecter. **~or seat**, siège éjectable m.

eke /iːk/ v.t. **~ out**, faire durer; (*living*) gagner difficilement.

elaborate [1] /ɪ'læbərət/ a. compliqué, recherché.

elaborate [2] /ɪ'læbəreɪt/ v.t. élaborer. ● v.i. préciser. **~ on**, s'étendre sur.

elapse /ɪ'læps/ v.i. s'écouler.

elastic /ɪ'læstɪk/ a. & n. élastique (m.). **~ band**, élastique m. **~ity** /elæ'stɪsətɪ/ n. élasticité f.

elated /ɪ'leɪtɪd/ a. fou de joie.

elbow /'elbəʊ/ n. coude m. **~ room**, possibilité de manœuvrer f.

elder [1] /'eldə(r)/ a. & n. aîné(e) (m. (f.)).

elder [2] /'eldə(r)/ n. (*tree*) sureau m.

elderly /'eldəlɪ/ a. (assez) âgé.

eldest /'eldɪst/ a. & n. aîné(e) (m. (f.)).

elect /ɪ'lekt/ v.t. élire. ● a. (*president etc.*) futur. **~ to do**, choisir de faire. **~ion** /-kʃn/ n. élection f.

elector /ɪ'lektə(r)/ n. élec|teur, -trice m., f. **~al** a. électoral. **~ate** n. électorat m.

electric /ɪ'lektrɪk/ a. électrique. **~ blanket**, couverture chauffante f. **~al** a. électrique.

electrician /ɪlek'trɪʃn/ n. électricien m.

electricity /ɪlek'trɪsətɪ/ n. électricité f.

electrify /ɪ'lektrɪfaɪ/ v.t. électrifier; (*excite*) électriser.

electrocute /ɪ'lektrəkjuːt/ v.t. électrocuter.

electron /ɪ'lektrɒn/ n. électron m.

electronic /ɪlek'trɒnɪk/ a. électronique. **~s** n. électronique f.

elegan|t /'elɪɡənt/ a. élégant. **~ce** n. élégance f. **~tly** adv. élégamment.

element /'elɪmənt/ n. élément m.; (*of heater etc.*) résistance f. **~ary** /-'mentrɪ/ a. élémentaire.

elephant /'elɪfənt/ n. éléphant m.

elevat|e /'elɪveɪt/ v.t. élever. **~ion** /-'veɪʃn/ n. élévation f.

elevator /'elɪveɪtə(r)/ n. (*Amer.*) ascenseur m.

eleven /ɪ'levn/ a. & n. onze (m.). **~th** a. & n. onzième (m./f.).

elf /elf/ (pl. **elves**) lutin m.

elicit /ɪ'lɪsɪt/ v.t. obtenir (**from**, de).

eligible /'elɪdʒəbl/ a. admissible (**for**, à). **be ~ for**, (*entitled to*) avoir droit à.

eliminat|e /ɪ'lɪmɪneɪt/ v.t. éliminer. **~ion** /-'neɪʃn/ n. élimination f.

élit|e /eɪ'liːt/ n. élite f. **~ist** a. & n. élitiste (m./f.).

ellip|se /ɪ'lɪps/ n. ellipse f. **~tical** a. elliptique.

elm /elm/ n. orme m.

elocution /elə'kjuːʃn/ n. élocution f.

elongate /'iːlɒŋɡeɪt/ v.t. allonger.

elope /ɪ'ləʊp/ v.i. s'enfuir. **~ment** n. fugue (amoureuse) f.

eloquen|t /'eləkwənt/ a. éloquent. **~ce** n. éloquence f. **~tly** adv. avec éloquence.

else /els/ adv. d'autre. **everybody ~**, tous les autres. **nobody ~**, personne d'autre. **nothing ~**, rien d'autre. **or ~**, ou bien. **somewhere ~**, autre part. **~where** adv. ailleurs.

elucidate /ɪ'luːsɪdeɪt/ v.t. élucider.

elude /ɪ'luːd/ v.t. échapper à; (*question*) éluder.

elusive /ɪ'lu:sɪv/ a. insaisissable.
emaciated /ɪ'meɪʃɪeɪtɪd/ a. émacié.
emanate /'emǝneɪt/ v.i. émaner.
emancipat|e /ɪ'mænsɪpeɪt/ v.t.
émanciper. **~ion** /-'peɪʃn/ n. éman-
cipation f.
embalm /ɪm'bɑ:m/ v.t. embaumer.
embankment /ɪm'bæŋkmǝnt/ n. (of
river) quai m.; (of railway) remblai
m., talus m.
embargo /ɪm'bɑ:gǝʊ/ n. (pl. -oes)
embargo m.
embark /ɪm'bɑ:k/ v.t./i. (s')em-
barquer. **~ on**, (business etc.) se
lancer dans; (journey) commencer.
~ation /emba:'keɪʃn/ n. embarquement m.
embarrass /ɪm'bærǝs/ v.t. embarrasser, gêner. **~ment** n. embarras m.,
gêne f.
embassy /'embǝsɪ/ n. ambassade f.
embed /ɪm'bed/ v.t. (p.t. **embedded**)
encastrer.
embellish /ɪm'belɪʃ/ v.t. embellir.
~ment n. enjolivement m.
embers /'embǝz/ n. pl. braise f.
embezzle /ɪm'bezl/ v.t. détourner.
~ment n. détournement de fonds
m. **~r** /-ǝ(r)/ n. escroc m.
embitter /ɪm'bɪtǝ(r)/ v.t. (person)
aigrir; (situation) envenimer.
emblem /'emblǝm/ n. emblème m.
embod|y /ɪm'bɒdɪ/ v.t. incarner, ex-
primer; (include) contenir. **~iment**
n. incarnation f.
emboss /ɪm'bɒs/ v.t. (metal) repousser; (paper) gaufrer.
embrace /ɪm'breɪs/ v.t./i. (s')em-
brasser. ● n. étreinte f.
embroider /ɪm'brɔɪdǝ(r)/ v.t. broder.
~y n. broderie f.
embroil /ɪm'brɔɪl/ v.t. mêler (in, à).
embryo /'embrɪǝʊ/ n. (pl. -os) embryon m. **~nic** /-'ɒnɪk/ a. embryon-
naire.
emend /ɪ'mend/ v.t. corriger.
emerald /'emǝrǝld/ n. émeraude f.
emerge /ɪ'mɜ:dʒ/ v.i. apparaître.
~nce /-ǝns/ n. apparition f.
emergency /ɪ'mɜ:dʒǝnsɪ/ n. (crisis)
crise f.; (urgent case: med.) urgence
f. ● a. d'urgence. **~ exit**, sortie de
secours f. **~ landing**, atterrissage
forcé m. **in an ~**, en cas d'urgence.
emery /'emǝrɪ/ n. émeri m.
emigrant /'emɪgrǝnt/ n. émigrant(e)
m. (f.).
emigrat|e /'emɪgreɪt/ v.i. émigrer.
~ion /-'greɪʃn/ n. émigration f.

eminen|t /'emɪnǝnt/ a. éminent. **~ce**
n. éminence f. **~tly** adv. éminem-
ment, parfaitement.
emissary /'emɪsǝrɪ/ n. émissaire m.
emi|t /ɪ'mɪt/ v.t. (p.t. **emitted**)
émettre. **~ssion** n. émission f.
emotion /ɪ'mǝʊʃn/ n. émotion f. **~al**
a. (person, shock) émotif; (speech,
scene) émouvant.
emotive /ɪ'mǝʊtɪv/ a. émotif.
emperor /'empǝrǝ(r)/ n. empereur m.
emphasis /'emfǝsɪs/ n. (on word)
accent m. **lay ~ on**, mettre l'accent
sur.
emphasize /'emfǝsaɪz/ v.t. souligner;
(syllable) insister sur.
emphatic /ɪm'fætɪk/ a. catégorique;
(manner) énergique.
empire /'empaɪǝ(r)/ n. empire m.
employ /ɪm'plɔɪ/ v.t. employer. **~er**
n. employeu|r, -se m., f. **~ment** n.
emploi m. **~ment agency**, agence
de placement f.
employee /emplɔɪ'i:/ n. employé(e)
m. (f.).
empower /ɪm'paʊǝ(r)/ v.t. autoriser
(to do, à faire).
empress /'emprɪs/ n. impératrice f.
empt|y /'emptɪ/ a. (-ier, -est) vide;
(promise) vain. ● v.t./i. (se) vider.
~y-handed a. les mains vides. **on
an ~y stomach**, à jeun. **~ies** n. pl.
bouteilles vides f. pl. **~iness** n. vide
m.
emulat|e /'emjʊleɪt/ v.t. imiter. **~ion**
/-'leɪʃn/ n. (comput.) émulation f.
emulsion /ɪ'mʌlʃn/ n. émulsion f. **~
(paint)**, peinture-émulsion f.
enable /ɪ'neɪbl/ v.t. **~ s.o. to**, permettre à qn. de.
enact /ɪ'nækt/ v.t. (law) promulguer;
(scene) représenter.
enamel /ɪ'næml/ n. émail m. ● v.t.
(p.t. **enamelled**) émailler.
enamoured /ɪ'næmǝd/ a. **be ~ of**,
aimer beaucoup, être épris de.
encampment /ɪn'kæmpmǝnt/ n.
campement m.
encase /ɪn'keɪs/ v.t. (cover) recouvrir
(in, de); (enclose) enfermer (in,
dans).
enchant /ɪn'tʃɑ:nt/ v.t. enchanter.
~ing a. enchanteur. **~ment** n. en-
chantement m.
encircle /ɪn'sɜ:kl/ v.t. encercler.
enclave /'enkleɪv/ n. enclave f.
enclose /ɪn'klǝʊz/ v.t. (land) clô-
turer; (with letter) joindre. **~d** a.

(*space*) clos; (*market*) couvert; (*with letter*) ci-joint.

enclosure /ɪn'kləʊʒə(r)/ *n.* enceinte *f.*; (*comm.*) pièce jointe *f.*

encompass /ɪn'kʌmpəs/ *v.t.* (*include*) inclure.

encore /'ɒŋkɔː(r)/ *int.* & *n.* bis (*m.*).

encounter /ɪn'kaʊntə(r)/ *v.t.* rencontrer. ● *n.* rencontre *f.*

encourage /ɪn'kʌrɪdʒ/ *v.t.* encourager. **~ment** *n.* encouragement *m.*

encroach /ɪn'krəʊtʃ/ *v.i.* ~ **upon**, empiéter sur.

encumber /ɪn'kʌmbə(r)/ *v.t.* encombrer.

encyclical /ɪn'sɪklɪkl/ *n.* encyclique *f.*

encyclopaed|ia, encycloped|ia /ɪnsaɪklə'piːdɪə/ *n.* encyclopédie *f.* **~ic** *a.* encyclopédique.

end /end/ *n.* fin *f.*; (*farthest part*) bout *m.* ● *v.t./i.* (se) terminer. ~ **up doing**, finir par faire. **come to an** ~, prendre fin. **~-product**, produit fini *m.* **in the** ~, finalement. **no** ~ **of**, (*fam.*) énormément de. **on** ~, (*upright*) debout; (*in a row*) de suite. **put an** ~ **to**, mettre fin à.

endanger /ɪn'deɪndʒə(r)/ *v.t.* mettre en danger.

endear|ing /ɪn'dɪərɪŋ/ *a.* attachant. **~ment** *n.* parole tendre *f.*

endeavour, (*Amer.*) **endeavor** /ɪn'devə(r)/ *n.* effort *m.* ● *v.i.* s'efforcer (**to**, de).

ending /'endɪŋ/ *n.* fin *f.*

endive /'endɪv/ *n.* chicorée *f.*

endless /'endlɪs/ *a.* interminable; (*times*) innombrable; (*patience*) infini.

endorse /ɪn'dɔːs/ *v.t.* (*document*) endosser; (*action*) approuver. **~ment** *n.* (*auto.*) contravention *f.*

endow /ɪn'daʊ/ *v.t.* doter. **~ed with**, doté de. **~ment** *n.* dotation *f.* (**of**, de).

endur|e /ɪn'djʊə(r)/ *v.t.* supporter. ● *v.i.* durer. **~able** *a.* supportable. **~ance** *n.* endurance *f.* **~ing** *a.* durable.

enemy /'enəmɪ/ *n.* & *a.* ennemi(e) (*m.* (*f.*)).

energetic /enə'dʒetɪk/ *a.* énergique.

energy /'enədʒɪ/ *n.* énergie *f.*

enforce /ɪn'fɔːs/ *v.t.* appliquer, faire respecter; (*impose*) imposer (**on**, à). **~d** *a.* forcé.

engage /ɪn'geɪdʒ/ *v.t.* engager. ● *v.i.* ~ **in**, prendre part à. **~d** *a.* fiancé;

(*busy*) occupé. **get** ~**d**, se fiancer. **~ment** *n.* fiançailles *f. pl.*; (*meeting*) rendez-vous *m.*; (*undertaking*) engagement *m.*

engaging /ɪn'geɪdʒɪŋ/ *a.* engageant, séduisant.

engender /ɪn'dʒendə(r)/ *v.t.* engendrer.

engine /'endʒɪn/ *n.* moteur *m.*; (*of train*) locomotive *f.*; (*of ship*) machine *f.* **~-driver** *n.* mécanicien *m.*

engineer /endʒɪ'nɪə(r)/ *n.* ingénieur *m.*; (*appliance repairman*) dépanneur *m.* ● *v.t.* (*contrive*: *fam.*) machiner. **~ing** *n.* (*mechanical*) mécanique *f.*; (*road-building etc.*) génie *m.*

England /'ɪŋglənd/ *n.* Angleterre *f.*

English /'ɪŋglɪʃ/ *a.* anglais. ● *n.* (*lang.*) anglais *m.* **~-speaking** *a.* anglophone. **the** ~, les Anglais *m. pl.* **~man** *n.* Anglais *m.* **~woman** *n.* Anglaise *f.*

engrav|e /ɪn'greɪv/ *v.t.* graver. **~ing** *n.* gravure *f.*

engrossed /ɪn'grəʊst/ *a.* absorbé (**in**, par).

engulf /ɪn'gʌlf/ *v.t.* engouffrer.

enhance /ɪn'hɑːns/ *v.t.* rehausser; (*price, value*) augmenter.

enigma /ɪ'nɪgmə/ *n.* énigme *f.* **~tic** /enɪg'mætɪk/ *a.* énigmatique.

enjoy /ɪn'dʒɔɪ/ *v.t.* aimer (*doing*, faire); (*benefit from*) jouir de. ~ **o.s.**, s'amuser. ~ **your meal**, bon appétit! **~able** *a.* agréable. **~ment** *n.* plaisir *m.*

enlarge /ɪn'lɑːdʒ/ *v.t./i.* (s')agrandir. ~ **upon**, s'étendre sur. **~ment** *n.* agrandissement *m.*

enlighten /ɪn'laɪtn/ *v.t.* éclairer. **~ment** *n.* édification *f.*; (*information*) éclaircissements *m. pl.*

enlist /ɪn'lɪst/ *v.t.* (*person*) recruter; (*fig.*) obtenir. ● *v.i.* s'engager.

enliven /ɪn'laɪvn/ *v.t.* animer.

enmity /'enmətɪ/ *n.* inimitié *f.*

enormity /ɪ'nɔːmətɪ/ *n.* énormité *f.*

enormous /ɪ'nɔːməs/ *a.* énorme. **~ly** *adv.* énormément.

enough /ɪ'nʌf/ *adv.* & *n.* assez. ● *a.* assez de. ~ **glasses/time/** *etc.*, assez de verres/de temps/ *etc.* **have** ~ **of**, en avoir assez de.

enquir|e /ɪn'kwaɪə(r)/ *v.t./i.* demander. **~e about**, se renseigner sur. **~y** *n.* demande de renseignements *f.*

enrage /ɪn'reɪdʒ/ v.t. mettre en rage, rendre furieux.

enrich /ɪn'rɪtʃ/ v.t. enrichir.

enrol, (*Amer.*) **enroll** /ɪn'rəʊl/ v.t./i. (*p.t.* **enrolled**) (s')inscrire. ~**ment** n. inscription f.

ensconce /ɪn'skɒns/ v.t. ~ **o.s.**, bien s'installer.

ensemble /ɒn'sɒmbl/ n. (*clothing & mus.*) ensemble m.

ensign /'ensən, 'ensaɪn/ n. (*flag*) pavillon m.

enslave /ɪn'sleɪv/ v.t. asservir.

ensue /ɪn'sju:/ v.i. s'ensuivre.

ensure /ɪn'ʃʊə(r)/ v.t. assurer. ~ **that**, (*ascertain*) s'assurer que.

entail /ɪn'teɪl/ v.t. entraîner.

entangle /ɪn'tæŋgl/ v.t. emmêler.

enter /'entə(r)/ v.t. (*room, club, race, etc.*) entrer dans; (*note down, register*) inscrire; (*data*) entrer, saisir. ● v.i. entrer (**into**, dans). ~ **for**, s'inscrire à.

enterprise /'entəpraɪz/ n. entreprise f.; (*boldness*) initiative f.

enterprising /'entəpraɪzɪŋ/ a. entreprenant.

entertain /entə'teɪn/ v.t. amuser, divertir; (*guests*) recevoir; (*ideas*) considérer. ~**er** n. artiste m./f. ~**ing** a. divertissant. ~**ment** n. amusement m., divertissement m.; (*performance*) spectacle m.

enthral, (*Amer.*) **enthrall** /ɪn'θrɔ:l/ v.t. (*p.t.* **enthralled**) captiver.

enthuse /ɪn'θju:z/ v.i. ~ **over**, s'enthousiasmer pour.

enthusiasm /ɪn'θju:zɪæzəm/ n. enthousiasme m.

enthusiast /ɪn'θju:zɪæst/ n. fervent(e) m. (f.), passionné(e) m. (f.) (**for**, de). ~**ic** /-'æstɪk/ a. (*supporter*) enthousiaste. **be ~ic about**, être enthousiasmé par. ~**ically** adv. /-'æstɪklɪ/ adv. avec enthousiasme.

entice /ɪn'taɪs/ v.t. attirer. ~ **to do**, entraîner à faire. ~**ment** n. (*attraction*) attrait m.

entire /ɪn'taɪə(r)/ a. entier. ~**ly** adv. entièrement.

entirety /ɪn'taɪərətɪ/ n. **in its ~**, en entier.

entitle /ɪn'taɪtl/ v.t. donner droit à (**to sth.**, à qch.; **to do**, de faire). ~**d** a. (*book*) intitulé. **be ~d to sth.**, avoir droit à qch. ~**ment** n. droit m.

entity /'entətɪ/ n. entité f.

entrails /'entreɪlz/ n. pl. entrailles f. pl.

entrance [1] /'entrəns/ n. (*entering, way in*) entrée f. (**to**, de); (*right to enter*) admission f. ● a. (*charge, exam*) d'entrée.

entrance [2] /ɪn'trɑ:ns/ v.t. transporter.

entrant /'entrənt/ n. (*sport*) concurrent(e) m. (f.); (*in exam*) candidat(e) m. (f.).

entreat /ɪn'tri:t/ v.t. supplier.

entrenched /ɪn'trentʃt/ a. ancré.

entrepreneur /ɒntrəprə'nɜ:(r)/ n. entrepreneur m.

entrust /ɪn'trʌst/ v.t. confier.

entry /'entrɪ/ n. (*entrance*) entrée f.; (*word on list*) mot inscrit m. ~ **form**, feuille d'inscription f.

enumerate /ɪ'nju:məreɪt/ v.t. énumérer.

enunciate /ɪ'nʌnsɪeɪt/ v.t. (*word*) articuler; (*ideas*) énoncer.

envelop /ɪn'veləp/ v.t. (*p.t.* **enveloped**) envelopper.

envelope /'envələʊp/ n. enveloppe f.

enviable /'envɪəbl/ a. enviable.

envious /'envɪəs/ a. envieux (**of sth.**, de qch.). ~ **of s.o.**, jaloux de qn. ~**ly** adv. avec envie.

environment /ɪn'vaɪərənmənt/ n. milieu m.; (*ecological*) environnement m. ~**al** /-'mentl/ a. du milieu; de l'environnement. ~**alist** n. spécialiste de l'environnement m./f.

envisage /ɪn'vɪzɪdʒ/ v.t. envisager.

envoy /'envɔɪ/ n. envoyé(e) m. (f.).

envy /'envɪ/ n. envie f. ● v.t. envier.

enzyme /'enzaɪm/ n. enzyme m.

ephemeral /ɪ'femərəl/ a. éphémère.

epic /'epɪk/ n. épopée f. ● a. épique.

epidemic /epɪ'demɪk/ n. épidémie f.

epilep|sy /'epɪlepsɪ/ n. épilepsie f. ~**tic** /-'leptɪk/ a. & n. épileptique (m./f.).

episode /'epɪsəʊd/ n. épisode m.

epistle /ɪ'pɪsl/ n. épître f.

epitaph /'epɪtɑ:f/ n. épitaphe f.

epithet /'epɪθet/ n. épithète f.

epitom|e /ɪ'pɪtəmɪ/ n. (*embodiment*) modèle m.; (*summary*) résumé m. ~**ize** v.t. incarner.

epoch /'i:pɒk/ n. époque f. ~-**making** a. qui fait époque.

equal /'i:kwəl/ a. & n. égal(e) (m.f.). ● v.t. (*p.t.* **equalled**) égaler. ~ **opportunities/rights**, égalité des chances/droits f. ~ **to**, (*task*) à la hauteur de. ~**ity** /ɪ'kwɒlətɪ/ n. égalité f. ~**ly** adv. également; (*just as*) tout aussi.

equalize /ˈiːkwəlaɪz/ v.t./i. égaliser. ~r /-ə(r)/ n. (goal) but égalisateur m.

equanimity /ekwəˈnɪmətɪ/ n. égalité d'humeur f., calme m.

equate /ɪˈkweɪt/ v.t. assimiler, égaler (with, à).

equation /ɪˈkweɪʒn/ n. équation f.

equator /ɪˈkweɪtə(r)/ n. équateur m. ~ial /ekwəˈtɔːrɪəl/ a. équatorial.

equilibrium /iːkwɪˈlɪbrɪəm/ n. équilibre m.

equinox /ˈiːkwɪnɒks/ n. équinoxe m.

equip /ɪˈkwɪp/ v.t. (p.t. equipped) équiper (with, de). ~ment n. équipement m.

equitable /ˈekwɪtəbl/ a. équitable.

equity /ˈekwɪtɪ/ n. équité f.

equivalen|t /ɪˈkwɪvələnt/ a. & n. équivalent (m.). ~ce n. équivalence f.

equivocal /ɪˈkwɪvəkl/ a. équivoque.

era /ˈɪərə/ n. ère f., époque f.

eradicate /ɪˈrædɪkeɪt/ v.t. supprimer, éliminer.

erase /ɪˈreɪz/ v.t. effacer. ~r/-ə(r)/ n. (rubber) gomme f.

erect /ɪˈrekt/ a. droit. ● v.t. ériger. ~ion /-kʃn/ n. érection f.

ermine /ˈɜːmɪn/ n. hermine f.

ero|de /ɪˈrəʊd/ v.t. ronger. ~sion n. érosion f.

erotic /ɪˈrɒtɪk/ a. érotique. ~ism /-sɪzəm/ n. érotisme m.

err /ɜː(r)/ v.i. (be mistaken) se tromper; (sin) pécher.

errand /ˈerənd/ n. course f.

erratic /ɪˈrætɪk/ a. (uneven) irrégulier; (person) capricieux.

erroneous /ɪˈrəʊnɪəs/ a. erroné.

error /ˈerə(r)/ n. erreur f.

erudit|e /ˈeruːdaɪt, Amer. ˈerjʊdaɪt/ a. érudit. ~ion /-ˈdɪʃn/ n. érudition f.

erupt /ɪˈrʌpt/ v.i. (volcano) entrer en éruption; (fig.) éclater. ~ion /-pʃn/ n. éruption f.

escalat|e /ˈeskəleɪt/ v.t./i. (s')intensifier; (of prices) monter en flèche. ~ion /-ˈleɪʃn/ n. escalade f.

escalator /ˈeskəleɪtə(r)/ n. escalier mécanique m., escalator m.

escapade /eskəˈpeɪd/ n. fredaine f.

escape /ɪˈskeɪp/ v.i. s'échapper (from a place, d'un lieu); (prisoner) s'évader. ● v.t. échapper à. ● n. fuite f., évasion f.; (of gas etc.) fuite f. ~ from s.o., échapper à qn. ~ to, s'enfuir dans. **have a lucky** or **narrow** ~, l'échapper belle.

escapism /ɪˈskeɪpɪzəm/ n. évasion (de la réalité) f.

escort[1] /ˈeskɔːt/ n. (guard) escorte f.; (of lady) cavalier m.

escort[2] /ɪˈskɔːt/ v.t. escorter.

Eskimo /ˈeskɪməʊ/ n. (pl. -os) Esquimau(de) m. (f.).

especial /ɪˈspeʃl/ a. particulier. ~ly adv. particulièrement.

espionage /ˈespɪənɑːʒ/ n. espionnage m.

esplanade /espləˈneɪd/ n. esplanade f.

espresso /eˈspresəʊ/ n. (pl. -os) (café) express m.

essay /ˈeseɪ/ n. essai m.; (schol.) rédaction f.; (univ.) dissertation f.

essence /ˈesns/ n. essence f.; (main point) essentiel m.

essential /ɪˈsenʃl/ a. essentiel. ● n. pl. the ~s, l'essentiel m. ~ly adv. essentiellement.

establish /ɪˈstæblɪʃ/ v.t. établir; (business, state) fonder. ~ment n. établissement m.; fondation f. **the E~ment**, les pouvoirs établis m.pl.

estate /ɪˈsteɪt/ n. (land) propriété f.; (possessions) biens m. pl.; (inheritance) succession f.; (district) cité f., complexe m. ~ **agent**, agent immobilier m. ~ **car**, break m.

esteem /ɪˈstiːm/ v.t. estimer. ● n. estime f.

esthetic /esˈθetɪk/ a. (Amer.) = **aesthetic**.

estimate[1] /ˈestɪmət/ n. (calculation) estimation f.; (comm.) devis m.

estimat|e[2] /ˈestɪmeɪt/ v.t. estimer. ~ion /-ˈmeɪʃn/ n. jugement m.; (high regard) estime f.

estuary /ˈestʃʊərɪ/ n. estuaire m.

etc. /etˈsetərə/ adv. etc.

etching /ˈetʃɪŋ/ n. eau-forte f.

eternal /ɪˈtɜːnl/ a. éternel.

eternity /ɪˈtɜːnətɪ/ n. éternité f.

ether /ˈiːθə(r)/ n. éther m.

ethic /ˈeθɪk/ n. éthique f. ~s, moralité f. ~al a. éthique.

ethnic /ˈeθnɪk/ a. ethnique.

ethos /ˈiːθɒs/ n. génie m.

etiquette /ˈetɪket/ n. étiquette f.

etymology /etɪˈmɒlədʒɪ/ n. étymologie f.

eucalyptus /juːkəˈlɪptəs/ n. (pl. -tuses) eucalyptus m.

eulogy /ˈjuːlədʒɪ/ n. éloge m.

euphemism /ˈjuːfəmɪzəm/ n. euphémisme m.

euphoria /juːˈfɔːrɪə/ n. euphorie f.

eurocheque /'juərəutʃek/ *n.* euro-chèque *m.*

Europe /'juərəp/ *n.* Europe *f.* **~an** /-'prən/ *a. & n.* européen(ne) (*m.* (*f.*)). **E~an Community,** Communauté Européenne *f.*

euthanasia /juːθə'neızıə/ *n.* euthanasie *f.*

evacuat|e /ı'vækjʊeıt/ *v.t.* évacuer. **~ion** /-'eıʃn/ *n.* évacuation *f.*

evade /ı'veıd/ *v.t.* esquiver. **~ tax,** frauder le fisc.

evaluate /ı'væljʊeıt/ *v.t.* évaluer.

evangelical /iːvæn'dʒelıkl/ *a.* évangélique.

evangelist /ı'vændʒəlıst/ *n.* évangéliste *m.*

evaporat|e /ı'væpəreıt/ *v.i.* s'évaporer. **~ed milk,** lait concentré *m.* **~ion** /-'reıʃn/ *n.* évaporation *f.*

evasion /ı'veıʒn/ *n.* fuite *f.* (**of,** devant); (*excuse*) subterfuge *m.* **tax ~,** fraude fiscale.

evasive /ı'veısıv/ *a.* évasif.

eve /iːv/ *n.* veille *f.* (**of,** de).

even /'iːvn/ *a.* régulier; (*surface*) uni; (*equal, unvarying*) égal; (*number*) pair. ● *v.t./i.* **~ (out** *or* **up),** (s')égaliser. ● *adv.* même. **~ better/***etc.***,** (*still*) encore mieux/*etc.* **get ~ with,** se venger de. **~ly** *adv.* régulièrement; (*equally*) de manière égale.

evening /'iːvnıŋ/ *n.* soir *m.*; (*whole evening, event*) soirée *f.*

event /ı'vent/ *n.* événement *m.*; (*sport*) épreuve *f.* **in the ~ of,** en cas de. **~ful** *a.* mouvementé.

eventual /ı'ventʃʊəl/ *a.* final, définitif. **~ity** /-'ælətı/ *n.* éventualité *f.* **~ly** *adv.* en fin de compte; (*in future*) un jour ou l'autre.

ever /'evə(r)/ *adv.* jamais; (*at all times*) toujours. **~ since** *prep. & adv.* depuis (ce moment-là); *conj.* depuis que. **~ so,** (*fam.*) vraiment.

evergreen /'evəgriːn/ *n.* arbre à feuilles persistantes *m.*

everlasting /evə'lɑːstıŋ/ *a.* éternel.

every /'evrı/ *a.* chaque. **~ one,** chacun(e). **~ other day,** un jour sur deux, tous les deux jours.

everybody /'evrıbɒdı/ *pron.* tout le monde.

everyday /'evrıdeı/ *a.* quotidien.

everyone /'evrıwʌn/ *pron.* tout le monde.

everything /'evrıθıŋ/ *pron.* tout.

everywhere /'evrıweə(r)/ *adv.* partout. **~ he goes,** partout où il va.

evict /ı'vıkt/ *v.t.* expulser. **~ion** /-kʃn/ *n.* expulsion *f.*

evidence /'evıdəns/ *n.* (*proof*) preuve(s) *f.* (*pl.*); (*certainty*) évidence *f.*; (*signs*) signes *m. pl.*; (*testimony*) témoignage *m.* **give ~,** témoigner. **in ~,** en vue.

evident /'evıdənt/ *a.* évident. **~ly** *adv.* de toute évidence.

evil /'iːvl/ *a.* mauvais. ● *n.* mal *m.*

evo|ke /ı'vəuk/ *v.t.* évoquer. **~cative** /ı'vɒkətıv/ *a.* évocateur.

evolution /iːvə'luːʃn/ *n.* évolution *f.*

evolve /ı'vɒlv/ *v.i.* se développer, évoluer. ● *v.t.* développer.

ewe /juː/ *n.* brebis *f.*

ex- /eks/ *pref.* ex-, ancien.

exacerbate /ıg'zæsəbeıt/ *v.t.* exacerber.

exact[1] /ıg'zækt/ *a.* exact. **~ly** *adv.* exactement. **~ness** *n.* exactitude *f.*

exact[2] /ıg'zækt/ *v.t.* exiger (**from,** de). **~ing** *a.* exigeant.

exaggerat|e /ıg'zædʒəreıt/ *v.t./i.* exagérer. **~ion** /-'reıʃn/ *n.* exagération *f.*

exalted /ıg'zɔːltıd/ *a.* (*in rank*) de haut rang; (*ideal*) élevé.

exam /ıg'zæm/ *n.* (*fam.*) examen *m.*

examination /ıgzæmı'neıʃn/ *n.* examen *m.*

examine /ıg'zæmın/ *v.t.* examiner; (*witness etc.*) interroger. **~r** /-ə(r)/ *n.* examina|teur, -trice *m., f.*

example /ıg'zɑːmpl/ *n.* exemple *m.* **for ~,** par exemple. **make an ~ of,** punir pour l'exemple.

exasperat|e /ıg'zæspəreıt/ *v.t.* exaspérer. **~ion** /-'reıʃn/ *n.* exaspération *f.*

excavat|e /'ekskəveıt/ *v.t.* creuser; (*uncover*) déterrer. **~ions** /-'veıʃnz/ *n. pl.* (*archaeol.*) fouilles *f. pl.*

exceed /ık'siːd/ *v.t.* dépasser. **~ingly** *adv.* extrêmement.

excel /ık'sel/ *v.i.* (*p.t.* **excelled**) exceller. ● *v.t.* surpasser.

excellen|t /'eksələnt/ *a.* excellent. **~ce** *n.* excellence *f.* **~tly** *adv.* admirablement, parfaitement.

except /ık'sept/ *prep.* sauf, excepté. ● *v.t.* excepter. **~ for,** à part. **~ing** *prep.* sauf, excepté.

exception /ık'sepʃn/ *n.* exception *f.* **take ~ to,** s'offenser de.

exceptional /ɪk'sepʃənl/ *a.* exceptionnel. **~ly** *adv.* exceptionnellement.

excerpt /'eksɜ:pt/ *n.* extrait *m.*

excess [1] /ɪk'ses/ *n.* excès *m.*

excess [2] /'ekses/ *a.* excédentaire. **~ fare,** supplément *m.* **~ luggage,** excédent de bagages *m.*

excessive /ɪk'sesɪv/ *a.* excessif. **~ly** *adv.* excessivement.

exchange /ɪks'tʃeɪndʒ/ *v.t.* échanger. ● *n.* échange *m.*; (*between currencies*) change *m.* **~ rate,** taux d'échange *m.* **(telephone) ~,** central (téléphonique) *m.*

exchequer /ɪks'tʃekə(r)/ *n.* (*British pol.*) Échiquier *m.*

excise /'eksaɪz/ *n.* impôt (indirect) *m.*

excit|e /ɪk'saɪt/ *v.t.* exciter; (*enthuse*) enthousiasmer. **~able** *a.* excitable. **~ed** *a.* excité. **get ~ed,** s'exciter. **~ement** *n.* excitation *f.* **~ing** *a.* passionnant.

exclaim /ɪk'skleɪm/ *v.t./i.* exclamer, s'écrier.

exclamation /eksklə'meɪʃn/ *n.* exclamation *f.* **~ mark** *or* **point** (*Amer.*), point d'exclamation *m.*

exclu|de /ɪk'sklu:d/ *v.t.* exclure. **~sion** *n.* exclusion *f.*

exclusive /ɪk'sklu:sɪv/ *a.* (*rights etc.*) exclusif; (*club etc.*) sélect; (*news item*) en exclusivité. **~ of service/** *etc.,* service/*etc.* non compris. **~ly** *adv.* exclusivement.

excrement /'ekskrəmənt/ *n.* excrément(s) *m.* (*pl.*).

excruciating /ɪk'skru:ʃɪeɪtɪŋ/ *a.* atroce, insupportable.

excursion /ɪk'skɜ:ʃn/ *n.* excursion *f.*

excus|e [1] /ɪk'skju:z/ *v.t.* excuser. **~e from,** (*exempt*) dispenser de. **~e me!,** excusez-moi!, pardon! **~able** *a.* excusable.

excuse [2] /ɪk'skju:s/ *n.* excuse *f.*

ex-directory /eksdɪ'rektərɪ/ *a.* qui n'est pas dans l'annuaire.

execute /'eksɪkju:t/ *v.t.* exécuter.

execution /eksɪ'kju:ʃn/ *n.* exécution *f.* **~er** *n.* bourreau *m.*

executive /ɪg'zekjʊtɪv/ *n.* (pouvoir) exécutif *m.*; (*person*) cadre *m.* ● *a.* exécutif.

exemplary /ɪg'zemplərɪ/ *a.* exemplaire.

exemplify /ɪg'zemplɪfaɪ/ *v.t.* illustrer.

exempt /ɪg'zempt/ *a.* exempt (**from,** de). ● *v.t.* exempter. **~ion** /-pʃn/ *n.* exemption *f.*

exercise /'eksəsaɪz/ *n.* exercice *m.* ● *v.t.* exercer; (*restraint, patience*) faire preuve de. ● *v.i.* prendre de l'exercice. **~ book,** cahier *m.*

exert /ɪg'zɜ:t/ *v.t.* exercer. **~ o.s.,** se dépenser, faire des efforts. **~ion** /-ʃn/ *n.* effort *m.*

exhaust /ɪg'zɔ:st/ *v.t.* épuiser. ● *n.* (*auto.*) (pot d')échappement *m.* **~ed** *a.* épuisé. **~ion** /-stʃən/ *n.* épuisement *m.*

exhaustive /ɪg'zɔ:stɪv/ *a.* complet.

exhibit /ɪg'zɪbɪt/ *v.t.* exposer; (*fig.*) faire preuve de. ● *n.* objet exposé *m.* **~or** *n.* exposant(e) *m.* (*f.*).

exhibition /eksɪ'bɪʃn/ *n.* exposition *f.*; (*act of showing*) démonstration *f.* **~ist** *n.* exhibitionniste *m./f.*

exhilarat|e /ɪg'zɪləreɪt/ *v.t.* transporter de joie; (*invigorate*) stimuler. **~ing** *a.* euphorisant. **~ion** /-'reɪʃn/ *n.* joie *f.*

exhort /ɪg'zɔ:t/ *v.t.* exhorter (**to,** à).

exhume /eks'hju:m/ *v.t.* exhumer.

exile /'eksaɪl/ *n.* exil *m.*; (*person*) exilé(e) *m.* (*f.*). ● *v.t.* exiler.

exist /ɪg'zɪst/ *v.i.* exister. **~ence** *n.* existence *f.* **be in ~ence,** exister. **~ing** *a.* actuel.

exit /'eksɪt/ *n.* sortie *f.* ● *v.t./i.* (*comput.*) sortir (de).

exodus /'eksədəs/ *n.* exode *m.*

exonerate /ɪg'zɒnəreɪt/ *v.t.* disculper, innocenter.

exorbitant /ɪg'zɔ:bɪtənt/ *a.* exorbitant.

exorcize /'eksɔ:saɪz/ *v.t.* exorciser.

exotic /ɪg'zɒtɪk/ *a.* exotique.

expan|d /ɪk'spænd/ *v.t./i.* (*develop*) (se) développer; (*extend*) (s')étendre; (*metal, liquid*) (se) dilater. **~sion** *n.* développement *m.*; dilatation *f.*; (*pol., comm.*) expansion *f.*

expanse /ɪk'spæns/ *n.* étendue *f.*

expatriate /eks'pætrɪət, *Amer.* eks'peɪtrɪət/ *a. & n.* expatrié(e) (*m.* (*f.*)).

expect /ɪk'spekt/ *v.t.* attendre, s'attendre à; (*suppose*) supposer; (*demand*) exiger; (*baby*) attendre. **~ to do,** compter faire. **~ation** /ekspek'teɪʃn/ *n.* attente *f.*

expectan|t /ɪk'spektənt/ *a.* **~t look,** air d'attente *m.* **~t mother,** future maman *f.* **~cy** *n.* attente *f.*

expedient /ɪk'spi:dɪənt/ *a.* opportun. ● *n.* expédient *m.*

expedite /'ekspɪdaɪt/ *v.t.* hâter.

expedition /ekspɪˈdɪʃn/ n. expédition f.

expel /ɪkˈspel/ v.t. (p.t. **expelled**) expulser; (from school) renvoyer.

expend /ɪkˈspend/ v.t. dépenser. ~**able** a. remplaçable.

expenditure /ɪkˈspendɪtʃə(r)/ n. dépense(s) f. (pl.).

expense /ɪkˈspens/ n. dépense f.; frais m. pl. **at s.o.'s** ~, aux dépens de qn. ~ **account**, note de frais f.

expensive /ɪkˈspensɪv/ a. cher, coûteux; (tastes, habits) de luxe. ~**ly** adv. coûteusement.

experience /ɪkˈspɪərɪəns/ n. expérience f.; (adventure) aventure f. ● v.t. (undergo) connaître; (feel) éprouver. ~**d** a. expérimenté.

experiment /ɪkˈsperɪmənt/ n. expérience f. ● v.i. faire une expérience. ~**al** /-ˈmentl/ a. expérimental.

expert /ˈekspɜːt/ n. expert(e) m. (f.). ● a. expert. ~**ly** adv. habilement.

expertise /eksˈpɜːˈtiːz/ n. compétence f. (**in**, en).

expir|e /ɪkˈspaɪə(r)/ v.i. expirer. ~**ed** a. périmé. ~**y** n. expiration f.

expl|ain /ɪkˈsplein/ v.t. expliquer. ~**anation** /eksplaˈneɪʃn/ n. explication f. ~**anatory** /-ˈænətəri/ a. explicatif.

expletive /ɪkˈspliːtɪv, Amer. ˈeksplətɪv/ n. juron m.

explicit /ɪkˈsplɪsɪt/ a. explicite.

explo|de /ɪkˈspləʊd/ v.t./i. (faire) exploser. ~**sion** n. explosion f. ~**sive** a. & n. explosif (m.).

exploit[1] /ˈeksplɔɪt/ n. exploit m.

exploit[2] /ɪkˈsplɔɪt/ v.t. exploiter. ~**ation** /eksplɔɪˈteɪʃn/ n. exploitation f.

exploratory /ɪkˈsplɒrətri/ a. (talks: pol.) exploratoire.

explor|e /ɪkˈsplɔː(r)/ v.t. explorer; (fig.) examiner. ~**ation** /ekspləˈreɪʃn/ n. exploration f. ~**er** n. explorateur, -trice m., f.

exponent /ɪkˈspəʊnənt/ n. interprète m. (**of**, de).

export[1] /ɪkˈspɔːt/ v.t. exporter. ~**er** n. exportateur m.

export[2] /ˈekspɔːt/ n. exportation f.

expos|e /ɪkˈspəʊz/ v.t. exposer; (disclose) dévoiler. ~**ure** /-ʒə(r)/ n. exposition f.; (photo.) pose f. **die of** ~**ure**, mourir de froid.

expound /ɪkˈspaʊnd/ v.t. exposer.

express[1] /ɪkˈspres/ a. formel, exprès; (letter) exprès invar. ● adv. (by

express post) (par) exprès. ● n. (train) rapide m.; (less fast) express m. ~**ly** adv. expressément.

express[2] /ɪkˈspres/ v.t. exprimer. ~**ion** /-ʃn/ n. expression f. ~**ive** a. expressif.

expressway /ɪkˈspreswei/ n. voie express f.

expulsion /ɪkˈspʌlʃn/ n. expulsion f.; (from school) renvoi m.

expurgate /ˈekspəgeɪt/ v.t. expurger.

exquisite /ˈekskwɪzɪt/ a. exquis. ~**ly** adv. d'une façon exquise.

ex-serviceman /eksˈsɜːvɪsmən/ n. (pl. -**men**) ancien combattant m.

extant /ekˈstænt/ a. existant.

extempore /ekˈstempəri/ a. & adv. impromptu.

exten|d /ɪkˈstend/ v.t. (increase) étendre, agrandir; (arm, leg) étendre; (prolong) prolonger; (house) agrandir; (grant) offrir. ● v.i. (stretch) s'étendre; (in time) se prolonger. ~**sion** n. (of line, road) prolongement m.; (in time) prolongation f.; (building) annexe f.; (of phone) appareil supplémentaire m.; (phone number) poste m.; (cable, hose, etc.) rallonge f.

extensive /ɪkˈstensɪv/ a. vaste; (study) profond; (damage etc.) important. ~**ly** adv. (much) beaucoup; (very) très.

extent /ɪkˈstent/ n. (size, scope) étendue f.; (degree) mesure f. **to some** ~, dans une certaine mesure. **to such an** ~ **that**, à tel point que.

extenuating /ɪkˈstenjʊeɪtɪŋ/ a. ~ **circumstances,** circonstances atténuantes.

exterior /ɪkˈstɪərɪə(r)/ a. & n. extérieur (m.).

exterminat|e /ɪkˈstɜːmɪneɪt/ v.t. exterminer. ~**ion** /-ˈneɪʃn/ n. extermination f.

external /ɪkˈstɜːnl/ a. extérieur; (cause, medical use) externe. ~**ly** adv. extérieurement.

extinct /ɪkˈstɪŋkt/ a. (species) disparu; (volcano, passion) éteint. ~**ion** /-kʃn/ n. extinction f.

extinguish /ɪkˈstɪŋgwɪʃ/ v.t. éteindre. ~**er** n. extincteur m.

extol /ɪkˈstəʊl/ v.t. (p.t. **extolled**) exalter, chanter les louanges de.

extort /ɪkˈstɔːt/ v.t. extorquer (**from**, à). ~**ion** /-ʃn/ n. (jurid.) extorsion (de fonds) f.

extortionate /ɪk'stɔːʃənət/ a. exorbitant.

extra /'ekstrə/ a. de plus, supplémentaire. ● adv. plus (que d'habitude). **~ strong,** extra-fort. ● n. (additional thing) supplément m.; (cinema) figurant(e) m. (f.). **~ charge,** supplément m. **~ time,** (football) prolongation f.

extra- /'ekstrə/ pref. extra-.

extract [1] /ɪk'strækt/ v.t. extraire; (promise, tooth) arracher; (fig.) obtenir. **~ion** /-kʃn/ n. extraction f.

extract [2] /'ekstrækt/ n. extrait m.

extra-curricular /ekstrəkə'rɪkjʊlə(r)/ a. parascolaire.

extradit|e /'ekstrədaɪt/ v.t. extrader. **~ion** /-'dɪʃn/ n. extradition f.

extramarital /ekstrə'mærɪtl/ a. extra-conjugal.

extramural /ekstrə'mjʊərəl/ a. (univ.) hors faculté.

extraordinary /ɪk'strɔːdnrɪ/ a. extraordinaire.

extravagan|t /ɪk'strævəgənt/ a. extravagant; (wasteful) prodigue. **~ce** n. extravagance f.; prodigalité f.

extrem|e /ɪk'striːm/ a. & n. extrême (m.). **~ely** adv. extrêmement. **~ist** n. extrémiste m./f.

extremity /ɪk'stremətɪ/ n. extrémité f.

extricate /'ekstrɪkeɪt/ v.t. dégager.

extrovert /'ekstrəvɜːt/ n. extraverti(e) m. (f.).

exuberan|t /ɪg'zjuːbərənt/ a. exubérant. **~ce** n. exubérance f.

exude /ɪg'zjuːd/ v.t. (charm etc.) dégager.

exult /ɪg'zʌlt/ v.i. exulter.

eye /aɪ/ n. œil m. (pl. yeux). ● v.t. (p.t. eyed, pres. p. eyeing) regarder. **keep an ~ on,** surveiller. **~-catching** a. qui attire l'attention. **~-opener** n. révélation f. **~-shadow** n. ombre à paupières f.

eyeball /'aɪbɔːl/ n. globe oculaire m.

eyebrow /'aɪbraʊ/ n. sourcil m.

eyeful /'aɪfʊl/ n. **get an ~,** (fam.) se rincer l'œil.

eyelash /'aɪlæʃ/ n. cil m.

eyelet /'aɪlɪt/ n. œillet m.

eyelid /'aɪlɪd/ n. paupière f.

eyesight /'aɪsaɪt/ n. vue f.

eyesore /'aɪsɔː(r)/ n. horreur f.

eyewitness /'aɪwɪtnɪs/ n. témoin oculaire m.

F

fable /'feɪbl/ n. fable f.

fabric /'fæbrɪk/ n. (cloth) tissu m.

fabrication /fæbrɪ'keɪʃn/ n. (invention) invention f.

fabulous /'fæbjʊləs/ a. fabuleux; (marvellous: fam.) formidable.

façade /fə'sɑːd/ n. façade f.

face /feɪs/ n. visage m., figure f.; (aspect) face f.; (of clock) cadran m. ● v.t. être en face de; (risk) devoir affronter; (confront) faire face à, affronter. ● v.i. se tourner; (of house) être exposé. **~-flannel** n. gant de toilette m. **~-lift** n. lifting m. **give a ~-lift to,** donner un coup de neuf à. **~ value,** (comm.) valeur nominale. **take sth. at ~ value,** prendre qch. au premier degré. **~ to face,** face à face. **in the ~ of, ~d with,** face à. **make a (funny) ~,** faire une grimace.

faceless /'feɪslɪs/ a. anonyme.

facet /'fæsɪt/ n. facette f.

facetious /fə'siːʃəs/ a. facétieux.

facial /'feɪʃl/ a. de la face, facial. ● n. soin du visage m.

facile /'fæsaɪl, Amer. 'fæsl/ a. facile, superficiel.

facilitate /fə'sɪlɪteɪt/ v.t. faciliter.

facilit|y /fə'sɪlətɪ/ n. facilité f. **~ies,** (equipment) équipements m. pl.

facing /'feɪsɪŋ/ n. parement m. ● prep. en face de. ● a. en face.

facsimile /fæk'sɪmɪlɪ/ n. facsimilé m. **~ transmission,** télécopie f.

fact /fækt/ n. fait m. **as a matter of ~, in ~,** en fait.

faction /'fækʃn/ n. faction f.

factor /'fæktə(r)/ n. facteur m.

factory /'fæktərɪ/ n. usine f.

factual /'fæktʃʊəl/ a. basé sur les faits.

faculty /'fækltɪ/ n. faculté f.

fad /fæd/ n. manie f., folie f.

fade /feɪd/ v.i. (sound) s'affaiblir; (memory) s'évanouir; (flower) se faner; (material) déteindre; (colour) passer.

fag /fæg/ n. (chore: fam.) corvée f.; (cigarette: sl.) sèche f.; (homosexual: Amer., sl.) pédé m.

fagged /fægd/ a. (tired) éreinté.

fail /feɪl/ v.i. échouer; (grow weak)
(s'af)faiblir; (run short) manquer;
(engine etc.) tomber en panne.
● v.t. (exam) échouer à; (candidate)
refuser, recaler; (disappoint)
décevoir. ~ s.o., (of words etc.)
manquer à qn. ~ to do, (not do)
ne pas faire; (not be able) ne pas
réussir à faire. without ~, à coup
sûr.

failing /'feɪlɪŋ/ n. défaut m. ● prep. à
défaut de.

failure /'feɪljə(r)/ n. échec m.; (person) raté(e) m. (f.); (breakdown)
panne f. ~ to do, (inability) incapacité de faire f.

faint /feɪnt/ a. (-er, -est) léger, faible.
● v.i. s'évanouir. ● n. évanouissement m. feel ~, (ill) se trouver mal.
I haven't the ~est idea, je n'en ai
pas la moindre idée. ~-hearted a.
timide. ~ly adv. (weakly) faiblement; (slightly) légèrement. ~ness
n. faiblesse f.

fair ¹ /feə(r)/ n. foire f. ~-ground n.
champ de foire m.

fair ² /feə(r)/ a. (-er, -est) (hair, person) blond; (skin etc.) clair; (just)
juste, équitable; (weather) beau;
(amount, quality) raisonnable.
● adv. (play) loyalement. ~ play,
le fair-play. ~ly adv. (justly) équitablement; (rather) assez. ~ness n.
justice f.

fairy /'feərɪ/ n. fée f. ~ story, ~-tale
n. conte de fées m.

faith /feɪθ/ n. foi. f. ~-healer n.
guérisseu|r, -se m., f.

faithful /'feɪθfl/ a. fidèle. ~ly adv.
fidèlement. ~ness n. fidélité f.

fake /feɪk/ n. (forgery) faux m.; (person) imposteur m. it is a ~, c'est
faux. ● a. faux. ● v.t. (copy) faire
un faux de; (alter) falsifier, truquer;
(illness) simuler.

falcon /'fɔːlkən/ n. faucon m.

fall /fɔːl/ v.i. (p.t. fell, p.p. fallen)
tomber. ● n. chute f.; (autumn:
Amer.) automne m. Niagara F~s,
chutes de Niagara. ~ back on, se
rabattre sur. ~ behind, prendre du
retard. ~ down or off, tomber. ~
for, (person: fam.) tomber amoureux
de; (a trick: fam.) se laisser prendre
à. ~ in, (mil.) se mettre en rangs.
~ off, (decrease) diminuer. ~ out,
se brouiller (with, avec). ~-out
n. retombées f. pl. ~ over, tomber (par terre). ~ short, être

insuffisant. ~ through, (plans)
tomber à l'eau.

fallacy /'fæləsɪ/ n. erreur f.

fallible /'fæləbl/ a. faillible.

fallow /'fæləʊ/ a. en jachère.

false /fɔːls/ a. faux. ~hood n. mensonge m. ~ly adv. faussement.
~ness n. fausseté f.

falsetto /fɔːl'setəʊ/ n. (pl. -os) fausset
m.

falsify /'fɔːlsɪfaɪ/ v.t. falsifier.

falter /'fɔːltə(r)/ v.i. vaciller; (nerve)
faire défaut.

fame /feɪm/ n. renommée f.

famed /feɪmd/ a. renommé.

familiar /fə'mɪlɪə(r)/ a. familier. be
~ with, connaître. ~ity /-'ærətɪ/ n.
familiarité f. ~ize v.t. familiariser.

family /'fæməlɪ/ n. famille f. ● a. de
famille, familial.

famine /'fæmɪn/ n. famine f.

famished /'fæmɪʃt/ a. affamé.

famous /'feɪməs/ a. célèbre. ~ly adv.
(very well: fam.) à merveille.

fan ¹ /fæn/ n. ventilateur m.; (handheld) éventail m. ● v.t. (p.t.
fanned) éventer; (fig.) attiser.
● v.i. ~ out, se déployer en
éventail. ~ belt, courroie de ventilateur f.

fan ² /fæn/ n. (of person) fan m./f.,
admira|teur, -trice m., f.; (enthusiast)
fervent(e) m. (f.), passionné(e) m.
(f.).

fanatic /fə'nætɪk/ n. fanatique m./f.
~al a. fanatique. ~ism /-sɪzəm/ n.
fanatisme m.

fancier /'fænsɪə(r)/ n. (dog/etc.) ~,
amateur (de chiens/etc.) m.

fanciful /'fænsɪfl/ a. fantaisiste.

fancy /'fænsɪ/ n. (whim, fantasy)
fantaisie f.; (liking) goût m. ● a.
(buttons etc.) fantaisie invar.;
(prices) extravagant; (impressive)
impressionnant. ● v.t. s'imaginer;
(want: fam.) avoir envie de; (like:
fam.) aimer. take a ~ to s.o., se
prendre d'affection pour qn. it took
my ~, ça m'a plu. ~ dress, déguisement m.

fanfare /'fænfeə(r)/ n. fanfare f.

fang /fæŋ/ n. (of dog etc.) croc m.; (of
snake) crochet m.

fanlight /'fænlaɪt/ n. imposte f.

fantastic /fæn'tæstɪk/ a. fantastique.

fantas|y /'fæntəsɪ/ n. fantaisie f.;
(day-dream) fantasme m. ~ize v.i.
fantasmer.

far /fɑː(r)/ adv. loin; (much) beaucoup; (very) très. ● a. lointain; (end, side) autre. ~ **away**, ~ **off**, au loin. **as ~ as**, (up to) jusqu'à. **as ~ as I know**, autant que je sache. ~ **away** a. lointain. **by ~**, de loin. ~ **from**, loin de. **the Far East**, l'Extrême-Orient m. ~-**fetched** a. bizarre, exagéré. ~-**reaching** a. de grande portée.

farc|e /fɑːs/ n. farce f. ~**ical** a. ridicule, grotesque.

fare /feə(r)/ n. (prix du) billet m.; (food) nourriture f. ● v.i. (progress) aller; (manage) se débrouiller.

farewell /feə'wel/ int. & n. adieu (m.).

farm /fɑːm/ n. ferme f. ● v.t. cultiver. ● v.i. être fermier. ~ **out**, céder en sous-traitance. ~ **worker**, ouvrier, -ère agricole m., f. ~**er** n. fermier m. ~**ing** n. agriculture f.

farmhouse /'fɑːmhaʊs/ n. ferme f.

farmyard /'fɑːmjɑːd/ n. basse-cour f.

fart /fɑːt/ v.i. péter. ● n. pet m.

farth|er /'fɑːðə(r)/ adv. plus loin. ● a. plus éloigné. ~**est** adv. le plus loin; a. le plus éloigné.

fascinat|e /'fæsɪneɪt/ v.t. fasciner. ~**ion** /-'neɪʃn/ n. fascination f.

Fascis|t /'fæʃɪst/ n. fasciste m./f. ~**m** /-zəm/ n. fascisme m.

fashion /'fæʃn/ n. (current style) mode f.; (manner) façon f. ● v.t. façonner. ~ **designer**, styliste m./f. **in ~**, à la mode. **out of ~**, démodé. ~**able** a., ~**ably** adv. à la mode.

fast¹ /fɑːst/ a. (-er, -est) rapide; (colour) grand teint invar., fixe; (firm) fixe, solide. ● adv. vite; (firmly) ferme. **be ~**, (clock etc.) avancer. ~ **asleep**, profondément endormi. ~ **food**, fast food m. restauration rapide f.

fast² /fɑːst/ v.i. (go without food) jeûner. ● n. jeûne m.

fasten /'fɑːsn/ v.t./i. (s')attacher. ~**er**, ~**ing** ns. attache f., fermeture f.

fastidious /fə'stɪdɪəs/ a. difficile.

fat /fæt/ n. graisse f.; (on meat) gras m. ● a. (**fatter, fattest**) gros, gras; (meat) gras; (sum, volume: fig.) gros. **a ~ lot**, (sl.) bien peu (**of**, de). ~-**head** n. (fam.) imbécile m.,/f. ~**ness** n. corpulence f.

fatal /'feɪtl/ a. mortel; (fateful, disastrous) fatal. ~**ity** /fə'tælətɪ/ n. mort m. ~**ly** adv. mortellement.

fatalist /'feɪtəlɪst/ n. fataliste m./f.

fate /feɪt/ n. (controlling power) destin m., sort m.; (one's lot) sort m. ~**ful** a. fatidique.

fated /'feɪtɪd/ a. destiné (**to**, à).

father /'fɑːðə(r)/ n. père m. ~-**in-law** n. (pl. ~**s-in-law**) beau-père m. ~**hood** n. paternité f. ~**ly** a. paternel.

fathom /'fæðəm/ n. brasse f. (= 1.8 m.). ● v.t. ~ (**out**), comprendre.

fatigue /fə'tiːg/ n. fatigue f. ● v.t. fatiguer.

fatten /'fætn/ v.t./i. engraisser. ~**ing** a. qui fait grossir.

fatty /'fætɪ/ a. gras; (tissue) adipeux. ● n. (person: fam.) gros(se) m. (f.).

fatuous /'fætʃʊəs/ a. stupide.

faucet /'fɔːsɪt/ n. (Amer.) robinet m.

fault /fɔːlt/ n. (defect, failing) défaut m.; (blame) faute f.; (geol.) faille f. ● v.t. ~ **sth./s.o.**, trouver des défauts à qch./chez qn. **at ~**, fautif. **find ~ with**, critiquer. ~**less** a. irréprochable. ~**y** a. défectueux.

fauna /'fɔːnə/ n. faune f.

favour, (Amer.) **favor** /'feɪvə(r)/ n. faveur f. ● v.t. favoriser; (support) être en faveur de; (prefer) préférer. **do s.o. a ~**, rendre service à qn. **in ~ of**, pour. ~**able** a. favorable. ~**ably** adv. favorablement.

favourit|e /'feɪvərɪt/ a. & n. favori(te) (m. (f.)). ~**ism** n. favoritisme m.

fawn¹ /fɔːn/ n. faon m. ● a. fauve.

fawn² /fɔːn/ v.i. ~ **on**, flatter bassement, flagorner.

fax /fæks/ n. fax m., télécopie f. ● v.t. faxer, envoyer par télécopie. ~ **machine**, télécopieur m.

FBI abbr. (Federal Bureau of Investigation) (Amer.) service d'enquêtes du Ministère de la Justice m.

fear /fɪə(r)/ n. crainte f., peur f.; (fig.) risque m. ● v.t. craindre. **for ~ of/ that**, de peur de/que. ~**ful** a. (terrible) affreux; (timid) craintif. ~**less** a. intrépide. ~**lessness** n. intrépidité f.

fearsome /'fɪəsəm/ a. redoutable.

feasib|le /'fiːzəbl/ a. faisable; (likely) plausible. ~**ility** /-'bɪlətɪ/ n. possibilité f.; plausibilité f.

feast /fiːst/ n. festin m.; (relig.) fête f. ● v.i. festoyer. ● v.t. régaler. ~ **on**, se régaler de.

feat /fiːt/ n. exploit m.

feather /'feðə(r)/ n. plume f. ● v.t. ~ **one's nest**, s'enrichir. ~ **duster**, plumeau m.

featherweight /'feðəweɪt/ n. poids plume m. invar.

feature /'fi:tʃə(r)/ n. caractéristique f.; (of person, face) trait m.; (film) long métrage m.; (article) article vedette m. ● v.t. représenter; (give prominence to) mettre en vedette. ● v.i. figurer (in, dans).

February /'februərɪ/ n. février m.

feckless /'feklɪs/ a. inepte.

fed /fed/ see feed. ● a. be ~ up, (fam.) en avoir marre (with, de).

federa|l /'fedərəl/ a. fédéral. ~tion /-'reɪʃn/ n. fédération f.

fee /fi:/ n. (for entrance) prix m. ~(s), (of doctor etc.) honoraires m. pl.; (of actor, artist) cachet m.; (for tuition) frais m. pl.; (for enrolment) droits m. pl.

feeble /fi:bl/ a. (-er, -est) faible. ~-minded a. faible d'esprit.

feed /fi:d/ v.t. (p.t. fed) nourrir, donner à manger à; (suckle) allaiter; (supply) alimenter. ● v.i. se nourrir (on, de). ● n. nourriture f.; (of baby) tétée f. ~ in information, rentrer des données. ~er n. alimentation. f.

feedback /'fi:dbæk/ n. réaction(s) f. (pl.); (med., techn.) feed-back m.

feel /fi:l/ v.t. (p.t. felt) (touch) tâter; (be conscious of) sentir; (emotion) ressentir; (experience) éprouver; (think) estimer. ● v.i. (tired, lonely, etc.) se sentir. ~ hot/thirsty/etc., avoir chaud/soif/etc. ~ as if, avoir l'impression que. ~ awful, (ill) se sentir malade. ~ like, (want: fam.) avoir envie de.

feeler /'fi:lə(r)/ n. antenne f. put out a ~, lancer un ballon d'essai.

feeling /'fi:lɪŋ/ n. sentiment m.; (physical) sensation f.

feet /fi:t/ see foot.

feign /feɪn/ v.t. feindre.

feint /feɪnt/ n. feinte f.

felicitous /fə'lɪsɪtəs/ a. heureux.

feline /'fi:laɪn/ a. félin.

fell [1] /fel/ v.t. (cut down) abattre.

fell [2] /fel/ see fall.

fellow /'feləʊ/ n. compagnon m., camarade m.; (of society) membre m.; (man: fam.) type m. ~-countryman n. compatriote m. ~-passenger n. ~-traveller n. compagnon de voyage m. ~ship n. camaraderie f.; (group) association f.

felony /'felənɪ/ n. crime m.

felt [1] /felt/ n. feutre m. ~-tip n. feutre m.

felt [2] /felt/ see feel.

female /'fi:meɪl/ a. (animal etc.) femelle; (voice, sex, etc.) féminin. ● n. femme f.; (animal) femelle f.

feminin|e /'femənɪn/ a. & n. féminin (m.). ~ity /-'nɪnətɪ/ n. féminité f.

feminist /'femɪnɪst/ n. féministe m./f.

fenc|e /fens/ n. barrière f.; (person: jurid.) receleu|r, -se m., f. ● v.t. ~e (in), clôturer. ● v.i. (sport) faire de l'escrime. ~er n. escrimeu|r, -se m., f. ~ing n. escrime f.

fend /fend/ v.i. ~ for o.s., se débrouiller tout seul. ● v.t. ~ off, (blow, attack) parer.

fender /'fendə(r)/ n. (for fireplace) garde-feu m. invar.; (mudguard: Amer.) garde-boue m. invar.

fennel /'fenl/ n. (culin.) fenouil m.

ferment [1] /fə'ment/ v.t./i. (faire) fermenter. ~ation /fɜ:men'teɪʃn/ n. fermentation f.

ferment [2] /'fɜ:ment/ n. ferment m.; (excitement: fig.) agitation f.

fern /fɜ:n/ n. fougère f.

feroc|ious /fə'rəʊʃəs/ a. féroce. ~ity /-'rɒsətɪ/ n. férocité f.

ferret /'ferɪt/ n. (animal) furet m. ● v.i. (p.t. ferreted) fureter. ● v.t. ~ out, dénicher.

ferry /'ferɪ/ n. ferry m., bac m. ● v.t. transporter.

fertil|e /'fɜ:taɪl, Amer. 'fɜ:tl/ a. fertile; (person, animal) fécond. ~ity /fə'tɪlətɪ/ n. fertilité f.; fécondité f. ~ize /-əlaɪz/ v.t. fertiliser; féconder.

fertilizer /'fɜ:təlaɪzə(r)/ n. engrais m.

fervent /'fɜ:vənt/ a. fervent.

fervour /'fɜ:və(r)/ n. ferveur f.

fester /'festə(r)/ v.i. (wound) suppurer; (fig.) rester sur le cœur.

festival /'festɪvl/ n. festival m.; (relig.) fête f.

festiv|e /'festɪv/ a. de fête, gai. ~e season, période des fêtes f. ~ity /fe'stɪvətɪ/ n. réjouissance f. pl.

festoon /fe'stu:n/ v.i. ~ with, orner de.

fetch /fetʃ/ v.t. (go for) aller chercher; (bring person) amener; (bring thing) apporter; (be sold for) rapporter.

fête /feɪt/ n. fête f. ● v.t. fêter.

fetid /'fetɪd/ a. fétide.

fetish /'fetɪʃ/ n. (object) fétiche m.; (psych.) obsession f.

fetter /'fetə(r)/ *v.t.* enchaîner. **~s** *n. pl.* chaînes *f. pl.*

feud /fju:d/ *n.* querelle *f.*

feudal /'fju:dl/ *a.* féodal.

fever /'fi:və(r)/ *n.* fièvre *f.* **~ish** *a.* fiévreux.

few /fju:/ *a. & n.* peu (de). **~ books,** peu de livres. **they are ~,** ils sont peu nombreux. **a ~** *a.* quelques; *n.* quelques-un(e)s. **a good ~, quite a ~,** (*fam.*) bon nombre (de). **~er** *a. & n.* moins (de). **be ~er,** être moins nombreux (**than,** que). **~est** *a. & n.* le moins (de).

fiancé /fɪ'ɒnseɪ/ *n.* fiancé *m.*

fiancée /fɪ'ɒnseɪ/ *n.* fiancée *f.*

fiasco /fræskəʊ/ *n.* (*pl.* **-os**) fiasco *m.*

fib /fɪb/ *n.* mensonge *m.* **~ber** *n.* menteu|r, -se *m., f.*

fibre, *Amer.* **fiber** /'faɪbə(r)/ *n.* fibre *f.* **~ optics,** fibres optiques.

fibreglass, *Amer.* **fiberglass** /'faɪbəglɑ:s/ *n.* fibre de verre *f.*

fickle /'fɪkl/ *a.* inconstant.

fiction /'fɪkʃn/ *n.* fiction *f.* **(works of) ~,** romans *m. pl.* **~al** *a.* fictif.

fictitious /fɪk'tɪʃəs/ *a.* fictif.

fiddle /'fɪdl/ *n.* (*fam.*) violon *m.*; (*swindle*: *sl.*) combine *f.* ● *v.i.* (*sl.*) frauder. ● *v.t.* (*sl.*) falsifier. **~ with,** (*fam.*) tripoter. **~r** /-ə(r)/ *n.* (*fam.*) violoniste *m./f.*

fidelity /fɪ'delətɪ/ *n.* fidélité *f.*

fidget /'fɪdʒɪt/ *v.i.* (*p.t.* **fidgeted**) remuer sans cesse. ● *n.* **be a ~,** être remuant. **~ with,** tripoter. **~y** *a.* remuant.

field /fi:ld/ *n.* champ *m.*; (*sport*) terrain *m.*; (*fig.*) domaine *m.* ● *v.t* (*ball*: *cricket*) bloquer. **~-day** *n.* grande occasion *f.* **~-glasses** *n. pl.* jumelles *f. pl.* **F~ Marshal,** maréchal *m.*

fieldwork /'fi:ldwɜ:k/ *n.* travaux pratiques *m. pl.*

fiend /fi:nd/ *n.* démon *m.* **~ish** *a.* diabolique.

fierce /fɪəs/ *a.* (**-er, -est**) féroce; (*storm, attack*) violent. **~ness** *n.* férocité *f.*; violence *f.*

fiery /'faɪərɪ/ *a.* (**-ier, -iest**) (*hot*) ardent; (*spirited*) fougueux.

fiesta /frˈestə/ *n.* fiesta *f.*

fifteen /fɪfˈti:n/ *a. & n.* quinze (*m.*). **~th** *a. & n.* quinzième (*m./f.*).

fifth /fɪfθ/ *a. & n.* cinquième (*m./f.*). **~ column,** cinquième colonne *f.*

fift|y /'fɪftɪ/ *a. & n.* cinquante (*m.*). **~ieth** *a. & n.* cinquantième (*m./f.*).

a ~y-fifty chance, (*equal*) une chance sur deux.

fig /fɪg/ *n.* figue *f.*

fight /faɪt/ *v.i.* (*p.t.* **fought**) se battre; (*struggle*: *fig.*) lutter; (*quarrel*) se disputer. ● *v.t.* se battre avec; (*evil etc.*: *fig.*) lutter contre. ● *n.* (*struggle*) lutte *f.*; (*quarrel*) dispute *f.*; (*brawl*) bagarre *f.*; (*mil.*) combat *m.* **~ back,** se défendre. **~ off,** surmonter. **~ over sth.,** se disputer qch. **~ shy of,** fuir devant. **~er** *n.* (*brawler, soldier*) combattant *m.*; (*fig.*) battant *m.*; (*aircraft*) chasseur *m.* **~ing** *n.* combats *m. pl.*

figment /'fɪgmənt/ *n.* invention *f.*

figurative /'fɪgjərətɪv/ *a.* figuré.

figure /'fɪgə(r)/ *n.* (*number*) chiffre *m.*; (*diagram*) figure *f.*; (*shape*) forme *f.*; (*body*) ligne *f.* **~s,** arithmétique *f.* ● *v.t.* s'imaginer. ● *v.i.* (*appear*) figurer. **~ out,** comprendre. **~-head** *n.* (*person with no real power*) prête-nom *m.* **~ of speech,** façon de parler *f.* **that ~s,** (*Amer., fam.*) c'est logique.

filament /'fɪləmənt/ *n.* filament *m.*

filch /fɪltʃ/ *v.t.* voler, piquer.

file[1] /faɪl/ *n.* (*tool*) lime *f.* ● *v.t.* limer. **~ings** *n. pl.* limaille *f.*

file[2] /faɪl/ *n.* dossier *m.*, classeur *m.*; (*comput.*) fichier *m.*; (*row*) file *f.* ● *v.t.* (*papers*) classer; (*jurid.*) déposer. ● *v.i.* **~e in,** entrer en file. **~e past,** défiler devant. **~ing cabinet,** classeur *m.*

fill /fɪl/ *v.t./i.* (se) remplir. ● *n.* **eat one's ~,** manger à sa faim. **have had one's ~,** en avoir assez. **~ in** *or* **up,** (*form*) remplir. **~ out,** (*get fat*) grossir. **~ up,** (*auto.*) faire le plein (d'essence).

fillet /'fɪlɪt, *Amer.* frˈleɪ/ *n.* filet *m.* ● *v.t.* (*p.t.* **filleted**) découper en filets.

filling /'fɪlɪŋ/ *n.* (*of tooth*) plombage *m.*; (*of sandwich*) garniture *f.* **~ station,** station-service *f.*

filly /'fɪlɪ/ *n.* pouliche *f.*

film /fɪlm/ *n.* film *m.*; (*photo.*) pellicule *f.* ● *v.t.* filmer. **~-goer** *n.* cinéphile *m./f.* **~ star,** vedette de cinéma *f.*

filter /'fɪltə(r)/ *n.* filtre *m.*; (*traffic signal*) flèche *f.* ● *v.t./i.* filtrer; (*of traffic*) suivre la flèche. **~ coffee,** café-filtre *m.* **~-tip** *n.* bout filtre *m.*

filth /fɪlθ/ **,~iness** /fɪlθ, fɪlθməs/ *n.* saleté *f.* **~y** *a.* sale.

fin /fɪn/ *n*. (*of fish, seal*) nageoire *f*.; (*of shark*) aileron *m*.

final /'faɪml/ *a*. dernier; (*conclusive*) définitif. ● *n*. (*sport*) finale *f*. ~ist *n*. finaliste *m*./*f*. ~ly *adv*. (*lastly, at last*) enfin, finalement; (*once and for all*) définitivement.

finale /fɪ'nɑːlɪ/ *n*. (*mus*.) final(e) *m*.

finalize /'faɪməlaɪz/ *v.t*. mettre au point, fixer.

financ|e /'faɪmæns/ *n*. finance *f*. ● *a*. financier. ● *v.t*. financer. ~ier /-'nænsɪə(r)/ *n*. financier *m*.

financial /faɪ'nænʃl/ *a*. financier. ~ly *adv*. financièrement.

find /faɪnd/ *v.t*. (*p.t*. **found**) trouver; (*sth. lost*) retrouver. ● *n*. trouvaille *f*. ~ **out** *v.t*. découvrir; *v.i*. se renseigner (**about**, sur). ~ings *n. pl*. conclusions *f. pl*.

fine [1] /faɪn/ *n*. amende *f*. ● *v.t*. condamner à une amende.

fine [2] /faɪn/ *a*. (**-er, -est**) fin; (*excellent*) beau. ● *adv*. (très) bien; (*small*) fin. ~ **arts**, beaux-arts *m. pl*. ~ly *adv*. (*admirably*) magnifiquement; (*cut*) fin.

finery /'faɪnərɪ/ *n*. atours *m. pl*.

finesse /fɪ'nes/ *n*. finesse *f*.

finger /'fɪŋɡə(r)/ *n*. doigt *m*. ● *v.t*. palper. ~-nail *n*. ongle *m*. ~-stall *n*. doigtier *m*.

fingerprint /'fɪŋɡəprɪnt/ *n*. empreinte digitale *f*.

fingertip /'fɪŋɡətɪp/ *n*. bout du doigt *m*.

finicking, finicky /'fɪnɪkɪŋ, 'fɪnɪkɪ/ *adjs*. méticuleux.

finish /'fɪnɪʃ/ *v.t./i*. finir. ● *n*. fin *f*.; (*of race*) arrivée *f*.; (*appearance*) finition *f*. ~ **doing**, finir de faire. ~ **up doing**, finir par faire. ~ **up in**, (*land up in*) se retrouver à.

finite /'faɪnaɪt/ *a*. fini.

Fin|land /'fɪnlənd/ *n*. Finlande *f*. ~n *n*. Finlandais(e) *m*. (*f*.). ~nish *a*. finlandais; *n*. (*lang*.) finnois *m*.

fir /fɜː(r)/ *n*. sapin *m*.

fire /'faɪə(r)/ *n*. feu *m*.; (*conflagration*) incendie *m*.; (*heater*) radiateur *m*. ● *v.t*. (*bullet etc*.) tirer; (*dismiss*) renvoyer; (*fig*.) enflammer. ● *v.i*. tirer (**at**, sur). ~ **a gun**, tirer un coup de revolver *or* de fusil. **set** ~ **to**, mettre le feu à. ~ **alarm**, avertisseur d'incendie *m*. ~ **brigade**, pompiers *m. pl*. ~-engine *n*. voiture de pompiers *f*. ~-escape *n*. escalier de secours *m*. ~ **extinguisher**, ex-

tincteur d'incendie *m*. ~ **station**, caserne de pompiers *f*.

firearm /'faɪərɑːm/ *n*. arme à feu *f*.

firecracker /'faɪəkrækə(r)/ *n*. (*Amer*.) pétard *m*.

firelight /'faɪəlaɪt/ *n*. lueur du feu *f*.

fireman /'faɪəmən/ *n*. (*pl*. **-men**) pompier *m*.

fireplace /'faɪəpleɪs/ *n*. cheminée *f*.

fireside /'faɪəsaɪd/ *n*. coin du feu *m*.

firewood /'faɪəwʊd/ *n*. bois de chauffage *m*.

firework /'faɪəwɜːk/ *n*. feu d'artifice *m*.

firing-squad /'faɪərɪŋskwɒd/ *n*. peloton d'exécution *m*.

firm [1] /fɜːm/ *n*. firme *f*., société *f*.

firm [2] /fɜːm/ *a*. (**-er, -est**) ferme; (*belief*) solide. ~ly *adv*. fermement. ~ness *n*. fermeté *f*.

first /fɜːst/ *a*. premier. ● *n*. prem|ier, -ière *m*., *f*. ● *adv*. d'abord, premièrement; (*arrive etc*.) le premier, la première. **at** ~, d'abord. **at** ~ **hand**, de première main. **at** ~ **sight**, à première vue. ~ **aid**, premiers soins *m. pl*. ~-**class** *a*. de première classe. ~ **floor**, (*Amer*.) rez-de-chaussée *m. invar*. ~ **(gear)**, première (vitesse) *f*. **F~ Lady**, (*Amer*.) épouse du Président *f*. ~ **name**, prénom *m*. ~ **of all**, tout d'abord. ~-**rate** *a*. de premier ordre. ~ly *adv*. premièrement.

fiscal /'fɪskl/ *a*. fiscal.

fish /fɪʃ/ *n*. (*usually invar*.) poisson *m*. ● *v.i*. pêcher. ~ **for**, (*cod etc*.) pêcher; (*take out: fam*.) sortir. ~ **out**, (*from water*) repêcher; (*take out: fam*.) sortir. ~ **shop**, poissonnerie *f*. ~ing *n*. pêche *f*. **go** ~ing, aller à la pêche. ~ing **rod**, canne à pêche *f*. ~y *a*. de poisson; (*fig*.) louche.

fisherman /'fɪʃəmən/ *n*. (*pl*. **-men**) *n*. pêcheur *m*.

fishmonger /'fɪʃmʌŋɡə(r)/ *n*. poissonn|ier, -ière *m*., *f*.

fission /'fɪʃn/ *n*. fission *f*.

fist /fɪst/ *n*. poing *m*.

fit [1] /fɪt/ *n*. (*bout*) accès *m*., crise *f*.

fit [2] /fɪt/ *a*. (**fitter, fittest**) en bonne santé; (*proper*) convenable; (*good enough*) bon; (*able*) capable. ● *v.t./i*. (*p.t*. **fitted**) (*clothes*) aller (à); (*match*) s'accorder (avec); (*put or go in or on*) (s')adapter (**to**, à); (*into space*) aller; (*install*) poser. ● *n*. **be a good** ~, (*dress*) être à la bonne taille. **in no** ~ **state to do**, pas en état de faire. **~ in,** *v.t.* caser; *v.i.* (*newcomer*) s'intégrer. **~ out, ~ up,** équiper. **~ness** *n.* santé *f.*; (*of remark*) justesse *f.*

fitful /'fɪtfl/ *a.* irrégulier.

fitment /'fɪtmənt/ *n.* meuble fixe *m.*

fitted /'fɪtɪd/ *a.* (*wardrobe*) encastré. **~ carpet,** moquette *f.*

fitting /'fɪtɪŋ/ *a.* approprié. ● *n.* essayage *m.* **~ room,** cabine d'essayage *f.*

fittings /'fɪtɪŋz/ *n. pl.* (*in house*) installations *f. pl.*

five /faɪv/ *a. & n.* cinq (*m.*).

fiver /'faɪvə(r)/ *n.* (*fam.*) billet de cinq livres *m.*

fix /fɪks/ *v.t.* (*make firm, attach, decide*) fixer; (*mend*) réparer; (*deal with*) arranger. ● *n.* **in a ~,** dans le pétrin. **~ s.o. up with sth.,** trouver qch. à qn. **~ed** *a.* fixe.

fixation /fɪk'seɪʃn/ *n.* fixation *f.*

fixture /'fɪkstʃə(r)/ *n.* (*sport*) match *m.* **~s,** (*in house*) installations *f. pl.*

fizz /fɪz/ *v.i.* pétiller. ● *n.* pétillement *m.* **~y** *a.* gazeux.

fizzle /'fɪzl/ *v.i.* pétiller. **~ out,** (*plan etc.*) finir en queue de poisson.

flab /flæb/ *n.* (*fam.*) corpulence *f.* **~by** /'flæbɪ/ *a.* flasque.

flabbergast /'flæbəgɑːst/ *v.t.* sidérer, ahurir.

flag¹ /flæg/ *n.* drapeau *m.*; (*naut.*) pavillon *m.* ● *v.t.* (*p.t.* **flagged**). **~ (down),** faire signe de s'arrêter à. **~-pole** *n.* mât *m.*

flag² /flæg/ *v.i.* (*p.t.* **flagged**) (*weaken*) faiblir; (*sick person*) s'affaiblir; (*droop*) dépérir.

flagon /'flægən/ *n.* bouteille *f.*

flagrant /'fleɪgrənt/ *a.* flagrant.

flagstone /'flægstəʊn/ *n.* dalle *f.*

flair /fleə(r)/ *n.* flair *m.*

flak /flæk/ *n.* (*fam.*) critiques *f. pl.*

flak|e /fleɪk/ *n.* flocon *m.*; (*of paint, metal*) écaille *f.* ● *v.i.* s'écailler. **~y** *a.* (*paint*) écailleux.

flamboyant /flæm'bɔɪənt/ *a.* (*colour*) éclatant; (*manner*) extravagant.

flame /fleɪm/ *n.* flamme *f.* ● *v.i.* flamber. **burst into ~s,** exploser. **go up in ~s,** brûler.

flamingo /flə'mɪŋgəʊ/ *n.* (*pl.* **-os**) flamant (rose) *m.*

flammable /'flæməbl/ *a.* inflammable.

flan /flæn/ *n.* tarte *f.*; (*custard tart*) flan *m.*

flank /flæŋk/ *n.* flanc *m.* ● *v.t.* flanquer.

flannel /'flænl/ *n.* flannelle *f.*; (*for face*) gant de toilette *m.*

flannelette /flænə'let/ *n.* pilou *m.*

flap /flæp/ *v.i.* (*p.t.* **flapped**) battre. ● *v.t.* **~ its wings,** battre des ailes. ● *n.* (*of pocket*) rabat *m.*; (*of table*) abattant *m.* **get into a ~,** (*fam.*) s'affoler.

flare /fleə(r)/ *v.i.* **~ up,** s'enflammer, flamber; (*fighting*) éclater; (*person*) s'emporter. ● *n.* flamboiement *m.*; (*mil.*) fusée éclairante *f.*; (*in skirt*) évasement *m.* **~d** *a.* (*skirt*) évasé.

flash /flæʃ/ *v.i.* briller; (*on and off*) clignoter. ● *v.t.* faire briller; (*aim torch*) diriger (**at,** sur); (*flaunt*) étaler. ● *n.* éclair *m.*, éclat *m.*; (*of news, camera*) flash *m.* **in a ~,** en un éclair. **~ one's headlights,** faire un appel de phares. **~ past,** passer à toute vitesse.

flashback /'flæʃbæk/ *n.* retour en arrière *m.*

flashlight /'flæʃlaɪt/ *n.* (*torch*) lampe électrique *f.*

flashy /'flæʃɪ/ *a.* voyant.

flask /flɑːsk/ *n.* flacon *m.*; (*vacuum flask*) thermos *m./f. invar.* (P.).

flat /flæt/ *a.* (**flatter, flattest**) plat; (*tyre*) à plat; (*refusal*) catégorique; (*fare, rate*) fixe. ● *adv.* (*say*) carrément. ● *n.* (*rooms*) appartement *m.*; (*tyre: fam.*) crevaison *f.*; (*mus.*) bémol *m.* **~ out,** (*drive*) à toute vitesse; (*work*) d'arrache-pied. **~-pack** *a.* en kit. **~ly** *adv.* catégoriquement. **~ness** *n.* égalité *f.*

flatten /'flætn/ *v.t./i.* (s')aplatir.

flatter /'flætə(r)/ *v.t.* flatter. **~er** *n.* flatteu|r, -se *f.* **~ing** *a.* flatteur. **~y** *n.* flatterie *f.*

flatulence /'flætjʊləns/ *n.* flatulence *f.*

flaunt /flɔːnt/ *v.t.* étaler, afficher.

flautist /'flɔːtɪst/ *n.* flûtiste *m./f.*

flavour, (*Amer.*) **flavor** /'fleɪvə(r)/ *n.* goût *m.*; (*of ice-cream etc.*) parfum *m.* ● *v.t.* parfumer, assaisonner. **~ing** *n.* arôme artificiel *m.*

flaw /flɔː/ *n.* défaut *m.* **~ed** *a.* imparfait. **~less** *a.* parfait.

flax /flæks/ *n.* lin *m.* **~en** *a.* de lin.

flea /fliː/ *n.* puce *f.* **~ market,** marché aux puces *m.*

fleck /flek/ *n.* petite tache *f.*

fled /fled/ *see* flee.

fledged /fledʒd/ a. fully-~, (doctor etc.) diplômé; (member, citizen) à part entière.

flee /fliː/ v.i. (p.t. **fled**) s'enfuir. ● v.t. s'enfuir de; (danger) fuir.

fleece /fliːs/ n. toison f. ● v.t. voler.

fleet /fliːt/ n. (naut., aviat.) flotte f. a ~ of vehicles, un parc automobile.

fleeting /ˈfliːtɪŋ/ a. très bref.

Flemish /ˈflemɪʃ/ a. flamand. ● n. (lang.) flamand m.

flesh /fleʃ/ n. chair f. one's (own) ~ and blood, les siens m. pl. ~y a. charnu.

flew /fluː/ see fly[2].

flex[1] /fleks/ v.t. (knee etc.) fléchir; (muscle) faire jouer.

flex[2] /fleks/ n. (electr.) fil souple m.

flexib|le /ˈfleksəbl/ a. flexible. ~ility /-ˈbɪlɪti/ n. flexibilité f.

flexitime /ˈfleksɪtaɪm/ n. horaire variable m.

flick /flɪk/ n. petit coup m. ● v.t. donner un petit coup à. ~-knife n. couteau à cran d'arrêt m. ~ through, feuilleter.

flicker /ˈflɪkə(r)/ v.i. vaciller. ● n. vacillement m.; (light) lueur f.

flier /ˈflaɪə(r)/ n. = flyer.

flies /flaɪz/ n. pl. (on trousers: fam.) braguette f.

flight[1] /flaɪt/ n. (of bird, plane, etc.) vol m. ~-deck n. poste de pilotage m. ~ of stairs, escalier m.

flight[2] /flaɪt/ n. (fleeing) fuite f. put to ~, mettre en fuite. take ~, prendre la fuite.

flimsy /ˈflɪmzi/ a. (-ier, -iest) (pej.) mince, peu solide.

flinch /flɪntʃ/ v.i. (wince) broncher; (draw back) reculer.

fling /flɪŋ/ v.t. (p.t. **flung**) jeter. ● n. have a ~, faire la fête.

flint /flɪnt/ n. silex m.; (for lighter) pierre f.

flip /flɪp/ v.t. (p.t. **flipped**) donner un petit coup à. ● n. chiquenaude f. ~ through, feuilleter. ~-flops n. pl. tongs f. pl.

flippant /ˈflɪpənt/ a. désinvolte.

flipper /ˈflɪpə(r)/ n. (of seal etc.) nageoire f.; (of swimmer) palme f.

flirt /flɜːt/ v.i. flirter. ● n. flirteu|r, -se m., f. ~ation /-ˈteɪʃn/ n. flirt m.

flit /flɪt/ v.i. (p.t. **flitted**) voltiger.

float /fləʊt/ v.t./i. (faire) flotter. ● n. flotteur m.; (cart) char m.

flock /flɒk/ n. (of sheep etc.) troupeau m.; (of people) foule f. ● v.i. venir en foule.

flog /flɒɡ/ v.t. (p.t. **flogged**) (beat) fouetter; (sell: sl.) vendre.

flood /flʌd/ n. inondation f.; (fig.) flot m. ● v.t. inonder. ● v.i. (building etc.) être inondé; (river) déborder; (people: fig.) affluer.

floodlight /ˈflʌdlaɪt/ n. projecteur m. ● v.t. (p.t. **floodlit**) illuminer.

floor /flɔː(r)/ n. sol m., plancher m.; (for dancing) piste f.; (storey) étage m. ● v.t. (knock down) terrasser; (baffle) stupéfier. ~-board n. planche f.

flop /flɒp/ v.i. (p.t. **flopped**) s'agiter faiblement; (drop) s'affaler; (fail: sl.) échouer. ● n. (sl.) échec m., fiasco m. ~py a. lâche, flasque. ~py (disk), disquette f.

flora /ˈflɔːrə/ n. flore f.

floral /ˈflɔːrəl/ a. floral.

florid /ˈflɒrɪd/ a. fleuri.

florist /ˈflɒrɪst/ n. fleuriste m./f.

flounce /flaʊns/ n. volant m.

flounder[1] /ˈflaʊndə(r)/ v.i. patauger (avec difficulté).

flounder[2] /ˈflaʊndə(r)/ n. (fish: Amer.) flet m., plie f.

flour /ˈflaʊə(r)/ n. farine f. ~y a. farineux.

flourish /ˈflʌrɪʃ/ v.i. prospérer. ● v.t. brandir. ● n. geste élégant m.; (curve) fioriture f.

flout /flaʊt/ v.t. faire fi de.

flow /fləʊ/ v.i. couler; (circulate) circuler; (traffic) s'écouler; (hang loosely) flotter. ● n. (of liquid, traffic) écoulement m.; (of tide) flux m.; (of orders, words: fig.) flot m. ~ chart, organigramme m. ~ in, affluer. ~ into, (of river) se jeter dans.

flower /ˈflaʊə(r)/ n. fleur f. ● v.i. fleurir. ~-bed n. plate-bande f. ~ed a. à fleurs. ~y a. fleuri.

flown /fləʊn/ see fly[2].

flu /fluː/ n. (fam.) grippe f.

fluctuat|e /ˈflʌktʃʊeɪt/ v.i. varier. ~ion /-ˈeɪʃn/ n. variation f.

flue /fluː/ n. (duct) tuyau m.

fluen|t /ˈfluːənt/ a. (style) aisé. be ~t (in a language), parler (une langue) couramment. ~cy n. facilité f. ~tly adv. avec facilité; (lang.) couramment.

fluff /flʌf/ n. peluche(s) f. (pl.); (down) duvet m. ~y a. pelucheux.

fluid /ˈfluːɪd/ *a. & n.* fluide (*m.*).

fluke /fluːk/ *n.* coup de chance *m.*

flung /flʌŋ/ *see* fling.

flunk /flʌŋk/ *v.t./i.* (*Amer., fam.*) être collé (à).

fluorescent /fluəˈresnt/ *a.* fluorescent.

fluoride /ˈfluəraɪd/ *n.* (*in toothpaste, water*) fluor *m.*

flurry /ˈflʌrɪ/ *n.* (*squall*) rafale *f.*; (*fig.*) agitation *f.*

flush¹ /flʌʃ/ *v.i.* rougir. ● *v.t.* nettoyer à grande eau. ● *n.* (*blush*) rougeur *f.*; (*fig.*) excitation *f.* ● *a.* ~ **with**, (*level with*) au ras de. ~ **the toilet**, tirer la chasse d'eau.

flush² /flʌʃ/ *v.t.* ~ **out**, chasser.

fluster /ˈflʌstə(r)/ *v.t.* énerver.

flute /fluːt/ *n.* flûte *f.*

flutter /ˈflʌtə(r)/ *v.i.* voleter; (*of wings*) battre. ● *n.* (*of wings*) battement *m.*; (*fig.*) agitation *f.*; (*bet: fam.*) pari *m.*

flux /flʌks/ *n.* changement continuel *m.*

fly¹ /flaɪ/ *n.* mouche *f.*

fly² /flaɪ/ *v.i.* (*p.t.* **flew**, *p.p.* **flown**) voler; (*of passengers*) voyager en avion; (*of flag*) flotter; (*rush*) filer. ● *v.t.* (*aircraft*) piloter; (*passengers, goods*) transporter par avion; (*flag*) arborer. ● *n.* (*of trousers*) braguette *f.* ~ **off**, s'envoler.

flyer /ˈflaɪə(r)/ *n.* aviateur *m.*; (*circular: Amer.*) prospectus *m.*

flying /ˈflaɪɪŋ/ *a.* (*saucer etc.*) volant. ● *n.* (*activity*) aviation *f.* ~ **buttress**, arc-boutant *m.* **with ~ colours**, haut la main. ~ **start**, excellent départ *m.* ~ **visit**, visite éclair *f.* (*a. invar.*).

flyover /ˈflaɪəʊvə(r)/ *n.* (*road*) toboggan *m.*, saut-de-mouton *m.*

flyweight /ˈflaɪweɪt/ *n.* poids mouche *m.*

foal /fəʊl/ *n.* poulain *m.*

foam /fəʊm/ *n.* écume *f.*, mousse *f.* ● *v.i.* écumer, mousser. ~ **(rubber)** *n.* caoutchouc mousse *m.*

fob /fɒb/ *v.t.* (*p.t.* **fobbed**) ~ **off on (to) s.o.**, (*palm off*) refiler à qn. ~ **s.o. off with**, forcer qn. à se contenter de.

focal /ˈfəʊkl/ *a.* focal.

focus /ˈfəʊkəs/ *n.* (*pl.* **-cuses** *or* **-ci** /-saɪ/) foyer *m.*; (*fig.*) centre *m.* ● *v.t./i.* (*p.t.* **focused**) (faire) converger; (*instrument*) mettre au point; (*with camera*) faire la mise au point (**on**,

sur; (*fig.*) (se) concentrer. **be in/out of ~**, être/ne pas être au point.

fodder /ˈfɒdə(r)/ *n.* fourrage *m.*

foe /fəʊ/ *n.* ennemi(e) *m.(f.).*

foetus /ˈfiːtəs/ *n.* (*pl.* **-tuses**) fœtus *m.*

fog /fɒg/ *n.* brouillard *m.* ● *v.t./i.* (*p.t.* **fogged**) (*window etc.*) (s')embuer. ~**-horn** *n.* (*naut.*) corne de brume *f.* ~**gy** *a.* brumeux. **it is ~gy**, il fait du brouillard.

fog(e)y /ˈfəʊgɪ/ *n.* (**old**) ~, vieille baderne *f.*

foible /ˈfɔɪbl/ *n.* faiblesse *f.*

foil¹ /fɔɪl/ *n.* (*tin foil*) papier d'aluminium *m.*; (*fig.*) repoussoir *m.*

foil² /fɔɪl/ *v.t.* (*thwart*) déjouer.

foist /fɔɪst/ *v.t.* imposer (**on**, à).

fold¹ /fəʊld/ *v.t./i.* (se) plier; (*arms*) croiser; (*fail*) s'effondrer. ● *n.* pli *m.* ~**er** *n.* (*file*) chemise *f.*; (*leaflet*) dépliant *m.* ~**ing** *a.* pliant.

fold² /fəʊld/ *n.* (*for sheep*) parc à moutons *m.*; (*relig.*) bercail *m.*

foliage /ˈfəʊlɪɪdʒ/ *n.* feuillage *m.*

folk /fəʊk/ *n.* gens *m. pl.* ~**s**, parents *m. pl.* ● *a.* folklorique.

folklore /ˈfəʊklɔː(r)/ *n.* folklore *m.*

follow /ˈfɒləʊ/ *v.t./i.* suivre. **it ~s that**, il s'ensuit que. ~ **suit**, en faire autant. ~ **up**, (*letter etc.*) donner suite à. ~**er** *n.* partisan *m.* ~**ing** *n.* partisans *m. pl.*; *a.* suivant; *prep.* à la suite de.

folly /ˈfɒlɪ/ *n.* sottise *f.*

foment /fəʊˈment/ *v.t.* fomenter.

fond /fɒnd/ *a.* (**-er, -est**) (*loving*) affectueux; (*hope*) cher. **be ~ of**, aimer. ~**ness** *n.* affection *f.*; (*for things*) attachement *m.*

fondle /ˈfɒndl/ *v.t.* caresser.

food /fuːd/ *n.* nourriture *f.* ● *a.* alimentaire. **French ~**, la cuisine française. ~ **processor**, robot (ménager) *m.*

fool /fuːl/ *n.* idiot(e) *m.* (*f.*). ● *v.t.* duper. ● *v.i.* ~ **around**, faire l'idiot.

foolhardy /ˈfuːlhɑːdɪ/ *a.* téméraire.

foolish /ˈfuːlɪʃ/ *a.* idiot. ~**ly** *adv.* sottement. ~**ness** *n.* sottise *f.*

foolproof /ˈfuːlpruːf/ *a.* infaillible.

foot /fʊt/ *n.* (*pl.* **feet**) pied *m.*; (*measure*) pied *m.* (= 30.48 *cm.*); (*of stairs, page*) bas *m.* ● *v.t.* (*bill*) payer. ~**-bridge** *n.* passerelle *f.* **on ~**, à pied. **on** *or* **to one's feet**, debout. **under s.o.'s feet**, dans les jambes de qn.

footage /'fʊtɪdʒ/ n. (of film) métrage m.

football /'fʊtbɔːl/ n. (ball) ballon m.; (game) football m. **~ pools**, paris sur les matchs de football m. pl. **~er** n. footballeur m.

foothills /'fʊthɪlz/ n. pl. contreforts m. pl.

foothold /'fʊthəʊld/ n. prise f.

footing /'fʊtɪŋ/ n. prise (de pied) f., équilibre m.; (fig.) situation f. **on an equal ~**, sur un pied d'égalité.

footlights /'fʊtlaɪts/ n. pl. rampe f.

footman /'fʊtmən/ n. (pl. **-men**) valet de pied m.

footnote /'fʊtnəʊt/ n. note (en bas de la page) f.

footpath /'fʊtpɑːθ/ n. sentier m.; (at the side of the road) chemin m.

footprint /'fʊtprɪnt/ n. empreinte (de pied) f.

footsore /'fʊtsɔː(r)/ a. **be ~**, avoir les pieds douloureux.

footstep /'fʊtstep/ n. pas m.

footwear /'fʊtweə(r)/ n. chaussures f. pl.

for /fɔː(r), unstressed fə(r)/ prep. pour; (during) pendant; (before) avant. ● conj. car. **a liking ~**, le goût de. **look ~**, chercher. **pay ~**, payer. **he has been away ~**, il est absent depuis. **he stopped ~ ten minutes**, il s'est arrêté (pendant) dix minutes. **it continues ~ ten kilometres**, ça continue pendant dix kilomètres. **~ ever**, pour toujours. **~ good**, pour de bon. **~ all my work**, malgré mon travail.

forage /'fɒrɪdʒ/ v.i. fourrager. ● n. fourrage m.

foray /'fɒreɪ/ n. incursion f.

forbade /fə'bæd/ see forbid.

forbear /fɔː'beə(r)/ v.t./i. (p.t. **forbore**, p.p. **forborne**) s'abstenir. **~ance** n. patience f.

forbid /fə'bɪd/ v.t. (p.t. **forbade**, p.p. **forbidden**) interdire, défendre (**s.o. to do**, à qn. de faire). **~ s.o. sth.**, interdire or défendre qch. à qn. **you are ~den to leave**, il vous est interdit de partir.

forbidding /fə'bɪdɪŋ/ a. menaçant.

force /fɔːs/ n. force f. ● v.t. forcer. **~ into**, faire entrer de force. **~ on**, imposer à. **come Into ~**, entrer en vigueur. **the ~s**, les forces armées f. pl. **~d** a. forcé. **~ful** a. énergique.

force-feed /'fɔːsfiːd/ v.t. (p.t. **-fed**) nourrir de force.

forceps /'fɔːseps/ n. invar. forceps m.

forcibl|e /'fɔːsəbl/ a., **~y** adv. de force.

ford /fɔːd/ n. gué m. ● v.t. passer à gué.

fore /fɔː(r)/ a. antérieur. ● n. **to the ~**, en évidence.

forearm /'fɔːrɑːm/ n. avant-bras m. invar.

foreboding /fɔː'bəʊdɪŋ/ n. pressentiment m.

forecast /'fɔːkɑːst/ v.t. (p.t. **forecast**) prévoir. ● n. prévision f.

forecourt /'fɔːkɔːt/ n. (of garage) devant m.; (of station) cour f.

forefathers /'fɔːfɑːðəz/ n. pl. aïeux m. pl.

forefinger /'fɔːfɪŋgə(r)/ n. index m.

forefront /'fɔːfrʌnt/ n. premier rang m.

foregone /'fɔːgɒn/ a. **~ conclusion**, résultat à prévoir m.

foreground /'fɔːgraʊnd/ n. premier plan m.

forehead /'fɒrɪd/ n. front m.

foreign /'fɒrən/ a. étranger; (trade) extérieur; (travel) à l'étranger. **~er** n. étrang|er, -ère m., f.

foreman /'fɔːmən/ n. (pl. **-men**) contremaître m.

foremost /'fɔːməʊst/ a. le plus éminent. ● adv. **first and ~**, tout d'abord.

forename /'fɔːneɪm/ n. prénom m.

forensic /fə'rensɪk/ a. médico-légal. **~ medicine**, médecine légale f.

foreplay /'fɔːpleɪ/ n. préliminaires m. pl.

forerunner /'fɔːrʌnə(r)/ n. précurseur m.

foresee /fɔː'siː/ v.t. (p.t. **-saw**, p.p. **-seen**) prévoir. **~able** a. prévisible.

foreshadow /fɔː'ʃædəʊ/ v.t. présager, laisser prévoir.

foresight /'fɔːsaɪt/ n. prévoyance f.

forest /'fɒrɪst/ n. forêt f.

forestall /fɔː'stɔːl/ v.t. devancer.

forestry /'fɒrɪstrɪ/ n. sylviculture f.

foretaste /'fɔːteɪst/ n. avant-goût m.

foretell /fɔː'tel/ v.t. (p.t. **foretold**) prédire.

forever /fə'revə(r)/ adv. toujours.

forewarn /fɔː'wɔːn/ v.t. avertir.

foreword /'fɔːwɜːd/ n. avant-propos m. invar.

forfeit /'fɔːfɪt/ n. (penalty) peine f.; (in game) gage m. ● v.t. perdre.

forgave /fə'geɪv/ see forgive.

forge[1] /fɔːdʒ/ v.i. ~ **ahead,** aller de l'avant, avancer.

forge[2] /fɔːdʒ/ n. forge f. ● v.t. (metal, friendship) forger; (copy) contrefaire, falsifier. ~**r** /-ə(r)/ n. faussaire m. ~**ry** /-ərɪ/ n. faux m., contrefaçon f.

forget /fə'get/ v.t./i. (p.t. **forgot,** p.p. **forgotten**) oublier. ~**-me-not** n. myosotis m. ~ **o.s.,** s'oublier. ~**ful** a. distrait. ~**ful of,** oublieux de.

forgive /fə'gɪv/ v.t. (p.t. **forgave,** p.p. **forgiven**) pardonner (s.o. for sth., qch. à qn.). ~**ness** n. pardon m.

forgo /fɔː'gəʊ/ v.t. (p.t. **forwent,** p.p. **forgone**) renoncer à.

fork /fɔːk/ n. fourchette f.; (for digging etc.) fourche f.; (in road) bifurcation f. ● v.i. (road) bifurquer. ~**-lift truck,** chariot élévateur m. ~ **out,** (sl.) payer. ~**ed** a. fourchu.

forlorn /fə'lɔːn/ a. triste, abandonné. ~ **hope,** mince espoir m.

form /fɔːm/ n. forme f.; (document) formulaire m.; (schol.) classe f. ● v.t./i. (se) former. **on ~,** en forme.

formal /'fɔːml/ a. officiel, en bonne et due forme; (person) compassé, cérémonieux; (dress) de cérémonie; (denial, grammar) formel; (language) soutenu. ~**ity** /-'mælətɪ/ n. cérémonial m.; (requirement) formalité f. ~**ly** adv. officiellement.

format /'fɔːmæt/ n. format m. ● v.t. (p.t. **formatted**) (disk) initialiser, formater.

formation /fɔː'meɪʃn/ n. formation f.

formative /'fɔːmətɪv/ a. formateur.

former /'fɔːmə(r)/ a. ancien; (first of two) premier. ● n. **the ~,** celui-là, celle-là. ~**ly** adv. autrefois.

formidable /'fɔːmɪdəbl/ a. redoutable, terrible.

formula /'fɔːmjʊlə/ n. (pl. **-ae** /-iː/ or **-as**) formule f.

formulate /'fɔːmjʊleɪt/ v.t. formuler.

forsake /fə'seɪk/ v.t. (p.t. **forsook,** p.p. **forsaken**) abandonner.

fort /fɔːt/ n. (mil.) fort m.

forte /'fɔːteɪ/ n. (talent) fort m.

forth /fɔːθ/ adv. en avant. **and so ~,** et ainsi de suite. **go back and ~,** aller et venir.

forthcoming /fɔːθ'kʌmɪŋ/ a. à venir, prochain; (sociable: fam.) communicatif.

forthright /'fɔːθraɪt/ a. direct.

forthwith /fɔːθ'wɪθ/ adv. sur-le-champ.

fortif|y /'fɔːtɪfaɪ/ v.t. fortifier. ~**ication** /-ɪ'keɪʃn/ n. fortification f.

fortitude /'fɔːtɪtjuːd/ n. courage m.

fortnight /'fɔːtnaɪt/ n. quinze jours m. pl., quinzaine f. ~**ly** a. bimensuel; adv. tous les quinze jours.

fortress /'fɔːtrɪs/ n. forteresse f.

fortuitous /fɔː'tjuːɪtəs/ a. fortuit.

fortunate /'fɔːtʃənət/ a. heureux. **be ~,** avoir de la chance. ~**ly** adv. heureusement.

fortune /'fɔːtʃuːn/ n. fortune f. ~**-teller** n. diseuse de bonne aventure f. **have the good ~ to,** avoir la chance de.

fort|y /'fɔːtɪ/ a. & n. quarante (m.). ~**y winks,** un petit somme. ~**ieth** a. & n. quarantième (m./f.).

forum /'fɔːrəm/ n. forum m.

forward /'fɔːwəd/ a. en avant; (advanced) précoce; (pert) effronté. ● n. (sport) avant m. ● adv. en avant. ● v.t. (letter) faire suivre; (goods) expédier; (fig.) favoriser. **come ~,** se présenter. **go ~,** avancer. ~**ness** n. précocité f.

forwards /'fɔːwədz/ adv. en avant.

fossil /'fɒsl/ n. & a. fossile (m.).

foster /'fɒstə(r)/ v.t. (promote) encourager; (child) élever. ~**-child** n. enfant adoptif m. ~**-mother** n. mère adoptive f.

fought /fɔːt/ see fight.

foul /faʊl/ a. (**-er, -est**) (smell, weather, etc.) infect; (place, action) immonde; (language) ordurier. ● n. (football) faute f. ● v.t. souiller, encrasser. ~**-mouthed** a. au langage ordurier. ~ **play,** jeu irrégulier m.; (crime) acte criminel m. ~ **up,** (sl.) gâcher.

found[1] /faʊnd/ see find.

found[2] /faʊnd/ v.t. fonder. ~**ation** /-'deɪʃn/ n. fondation f.; (basis) fondement m.; (make-up) fond de teint m. ~**er**[1] n. fonda|teur, -trice m., f.

founder[2] /'faʊndə(r)/ v.i. sombrer.

foundry /'faʊndrɪ/ n. fonderie f.

fountain /'faʊntɪn/ n. fontaine f. ~**-pen** n. stylo à encre m.

four /fɔː(r)/ a. & n. quatre (m.). ~**fold** a. quadruple; adv. au quadruple. ~**th** a. & n. quatrième (m./f.). ~**-wheel drive,** quatre roues motrices; (car) quatre-quatre m.

foursome /'fɔːsəm/ n. partie à quatre f.

fourteen /fɔːˈtiːn/ *a. & n.* quatorze (*m.*). **~th** *a. & n.* quatorzième (*m./ f.*).

fowl /faʊl/ *n.* volaille *f.*

fox /fɒks/ *n.* renard *m.* ● *v.t.* (*baffle*) mystifier; (*deceive*) tromper.

foyer /ˈfɔɪeɪ/ *n.* (*hall*) foyer *m.*

fraction /ˈfrækʃn/ *n.* fraction *f.*

fracture /ˈfræktʃə(r)/ *n.* fracture *f.* ● *v.t./i.* (se) fracturer.

fragile /ˈfrædʒaɪl, Amer. ˈfrædʒəl/ *a.* fragile.

fragment /ˈfrægmənt/ *n.* fragment *m.* **~ary** *a.* fragmentaire.

fragran|t /ˈfreɪɡrənt/ *a.* parfumé. **~ce** *n.* parfum *m.*

frail /freɪl/ *a.* (**-er, -est**) frêle.

frame /freɪm/ *n.* charpente *f.*; (*of picture*) cadre *m.*; (*of window*) châssis *m.*; (*of spectacles*) monture *f.* ● *v.t.* encadrer; (*fig.*) formuler; (*jurid., sl.*) monter un coup contre. **~ of mind,** humeur *f.*

framework /ˈfreɪmwɜːk/ *n.* structure *f.*; (*context*) cadre *m.*

franc /fræŋk/ *n.* franc *m.*

France /frɑːns/ *n.* France *f.*

franchise /ˈfræntʃaɪz/ *n.* (*pol.*) droit de vote *m.*; (*comm.*) franchise *f.*

Franco- /ˈfræŋkəʊ/ *pref.* franco-.

frank[1] /fræŋk/ *a.* franc. **~ly** *adv.* franchement. **~ness** *n.* franchise *f.*

frank[2] /fræŋk/ *v.t.* affranchir.

frantic /ˈfræntɪk/ *a.* frénétique. **~ with,** fou de.

fratern|al /frəˈtɜːnl/ *a.* fraternel. **~ity** *n.* (*bond*) fraternité *f.*; (*group, club*) confrérie *f.*

fraternize /ˈfrætənaɪz/ *v.i.* fraterniser (**with,** avec).

fraud /frɔːd/ *n.* (*deception*) fraude *f.*; (*person*) imposteur *m.* **~ulent** *a.* frauduleux.

fraught /frɔːt/ *a.* (*tense*) tendu. **~ with,** chargé de.

fray[1] /freɪ/ *n.* rixe *f.*

fray[2] /freɪ/ *v.t./i.* (s')effilocher.

freak /friːk/ *n.* phénomène *m.* ● *a.* anormal. **~ish** *a.* anormal.

freckle /ˈfrekl/ *n.* tache de rousseur *f.* **~d** *a.* couvert de taches de rousseur.

free /friː/ *a.* (**freer** /ˈfriːə(r)/, **freest** /ˈfriːɪst/) libre; (*gratis*) gratuit; (*lavish*) généreux. ● *v.t.* (*p.t.* **freed**) libérer; (*clear*) dégager. **~ enterprise,** libre entreprise. **a ~ hand,** carte blanche *f.* **~ kick,** coup franc *m.* **~lance** *a. & n.* free-lance (*m./f.*), indépendant(e) *m., f.* **~ (of charge),**

gratuit(ement). **~-range** *a.* (*eggs*) de ferme. **~-wheel** *v.i.* descendre en roue libre. **~-wheeling** *a.* sans contraintes. **~ly** *adv.* librement.

freedom /ˈfriːdəm/ *n.* liberté *f.*

Freemason /ˈfriːmeɪsn/ *n.* franc-maçon *m.* **~ry** *n.* francmaçonnerie *f.*

freeway /ˈfriːweɪ/ *n.* (*Amer.*) autoroute *f.*

freez|e /friːz/ *v.t./i.* (*p.t.* **froze**, *p.p.* **frozen**) geler; (*culin.*) (se) congeler; (*wages etc.*) bloquer. ● *n.* gel *m.*; blocage *m.* **~e-dried** *a.* lyophilisé. **~er** *n.* congélateur *m.* **~ing** *a.* glacial. **below ~ing,** au-dessous de zéro.

freight /freɪt/ *n.* fret *m.* **~er** *n.* (*ship*) cargo *m.*

French /frentʃ/ *a.* français. ● *n.* (*lang.*) français *m.* **~ bean,** haricot vert *m.* **~ fries,** frites *f. pl.* **~-speaking** *a.* francophone. **~ window** *n.* porte-fenêtre *f.* **the ~,** les Français *m. pl.* **~man** *n.* Français *m.* **~woman** *n.* Française *f.*

frenz|y /ˈfrenzɪ/ *n.* frénésie *f.* **~ied** *a.* frénétique.

frequen|t[1] /ˈfriːkwənt/ *a.* fréquent. **~cy** *n.* fréquence *f.* **~tly** *adv.* fréquemment.

frequent[2] /frɪˈkwent/ *v.t.* fréquenter.

fresco /ˈfreskəʊ/ *n.* (*pl.* **-os**) fresque *f.*

fresh /freʃ/ *a.* (**-er, -est**) frais; (*different, additional*) nouveau; (*cheeky: fam.*) culotté. **~ly** *adv.* nouvellement. **~ness** *n.* fraîcheur *f.*

freshen /ˈfreʃn/ *v.i.* (*weather*) fraîchir. **~ up,** (*person*) se rafraîchir.

fresher /ˈfreʃə(r)/ *n.,* **freshman** /ˈfreʃmən/ *n.* (*pl.* **-men**) bizuth *m./f.*

freshwater /ˈfreʃwɔːtə(r)/ *a.* d'eau douce.

fret /fret/ *v.i.* (*p.t.* **fretted**) se tracasser. **~ful** *a.* ronchon, insatisfait.

friar /ˈfraɪə(r)/ *n.* moine *m.*, frère *m.*

friction /ˈfrɪkʃn/ *n.* friction *f.*

Friday /ˈfraɪdɪ/ *n.* vendredi *m.*

fridge /frɪdʒ/ *n.* frigo *m.*

fried /fraɪd/ *see* fry. ● *a.* frit. **~ eggs,** œufs sur le plat *m. pl.*

friend /frend/ *n.* ami(e) *m.* (*f.*). **~ship** *n.* amitié *f.*

friendl|y /ˈfrendlɪ/ *a.* (**-ier, -iest**) amical, gentil. **F~y Society,** mutuelle *f.*, société de prévoyance *f.* **~iness** *n.* gentillesse *f.*

frieze /friːz/ *n.* frise *f.*

frigate /ˈfrɪgət/ n. frégate f.

fright /fraɪt/ n. peur f.; (person, thing) horreur f. **~ful** a. affreux. **~fully** adv. affreusement.

frighten /ˈfraɪtn/ v.t. effrayer. **~ off,** faire fuir. **~ed** a. effrayé. **be ~ed,** avoir peur (**of,** de). **~ing** a. effrayant.

frigid /ˈfrɪdʒɪd/ a. froid, glacial; (psych.) frigide. **~ity** /-ˈdʒɪdətɪ/ n. frigidité f.

frill /frɪl/ n. (trimming) fanfreluche f. **with no ~s,** très simple.

fringe /frɪndʒ/ n. (edging, hair) frange f.; (of area) bordure f.; (of society) marge f. **~ benefits,** avantages sociaux m. pl.

frisk /frɪsk/ v.t. (search) fouiller.

frisky /ˈfrɪskɪ/ a. (-ier, -iest) fringant, frétillant.

fritter[1] /ˈfrɪtə(r)/ n. beignet m.

fritter[2] /ˈfrɪtə(r)/ v.t. **~ away,** gaspiller.

frivol|ous /ˈfrɪvələs/ a. frivole. **~ity** /-ˈvɒlətɪ/ n. frivolité f.

frizzy /ˈfrɪzɪ/ a. crépu, crêpelé.

fro /frəʊ/ see to and fro.

frock /frɒk/ n. robe f.

frog /frɒg/ n. grenouille f. **a ~ in one's throat,** un chat dans la gorge.

frogman /ˈfrɒgmən/ n. (pl. -men) homme-grenouille m.

frolic /ˈfrɒlɪk/ v.i. (p.t. **frolicked**) s'ébattre. ● n. ébats m. pl.

from /frɒm, unstressed frəm/ prep. de; (with time, prices, etc.) à partir de, de; (habit, conviction, etc.) par; (according to) d'après. **take ~ s.o.,** prendre à qn. **take ~ one's pocket,** prendre dans sa poche.

front /frʌnt/ n. (of car, train, etc.) avant m.; (of garment, building) devant m.; (mil., pol.) front m.; (of book, pamphlet, etc.) début m.; (appearance: fig.) façade f. ● a. de devant, avant invar.; (first) premier. **~ door,** porte d'entrée f. **~-wheel drive,** traction avant f. **in ~ (of),** devant. **~age** n. façade f. **~al** a. frontal; (attack) de front.

frontier /ˈfrʌntɪə(r)/ n. frontière f.

frost /frɒst/ n. gel m., gelée f.; (on glass etc.) givre m. ● v.t./i. (se) givrer. **~-bite** n. gelure f. **~-bitten** a. gelé. **~ed** a. (glass) dépoli. **~ing** n. (icing: Amer.) glace f. **~y** a. (weather, welcome) glacial; (window) givré.

froth /frɒθ/ n. mousse f., écume f. ● v.i. mousser, écumer. **~y** a. mousseux.

frown /fraʊn/ v.i. froncer les sourcils. ● n. froncement de sourcils m. **~ on,** désapprouver.

froze /frəʊz/ see freeze.

frozen /ˈfrəʊzn/ see freeze. ● a. congelé.

frugal /ˈfruːgl/ a. (person) économe; (meal, life) frugal. **~ly** adv. (live) simplement.

fruit /fruːt/ n. fruit m.; (collectively) fruits m. pl. **~ machine,** machine à sous f. **~ salad,** salade de fruits f. **~erer** n. fruit|ier, -ière m., f. **~y** a. (taste) fruité.

fruit|ful /ˈfruːtfl/ a. (discussions) fructueux. **~less** a. stérile.

fruition /fruːˈɪʃn/ n. **come to ~,** se réaliser.

frustrat|e /frʌˈstreɪt/ v.t. (plan) faire échouer; (person: psych.) frustrer; (upset: fam.) exaspérer. **~ion** /-ʃn/ n. (psych.) frustration f.; (disappointment) déception f.

fry[1] /fraɪ/ v.t./i. (p.t. **fried**) (faire) frire. **~ing-pan** n. poêle (à frire) f.

fry[2] /fraɪ/ n. **the small ~,** le menu fretin.

fuddy-duddy /ˈfʌdɪdʌdɪ/ n. **be a ~,** (sl.) être vieux jeu invar.

fudge /fʌdʒ/ n. (sorte de) caramel mou m. ● v.t. se dérober à.

fuel /ˈfjuːəl/ n. combustible m.; (for car engine) carburant m. ● v.t. (p.t. **fuelled**) alimenter en combustible.

fugitive /ˈfjuːdʒətɪv/ n. & a. fugiti|f, -ve (m., f.).

fugue /fjuːg/ n. (mus.) fugue f.

fulfil /fʊlˈfɪl/ v.t. (p.t. **fulfilled**) accomplir, réaliser; (condition) remplir. **~ o.s.,** s'épanouir. **~ling** a. satisfaisant. **~ment** n. réalisation f.; épanouissement m.

full /fʊl/ a. (-er, -est) plein (**of,** de); (bus, hotel) complet; (programme) chargé; (name) complet; (skirt) ample. ● n. **in ~,** intégral(ement). **to the ~,** complètement. **be ~ (up),** n'avoir plus faim. **~ back,** (sport) arrière m. **~ moon,** pleine lune f. **~-scale** a. (drawing etc.) grandeur nature invar.; (fig.) de grande envergure. **at ~ speed,** à toute vitesse. **~ stop,** point m. **~-time** a. & adv. à plein temps. **~y** adv. complètement.

fulsome /ˈfʊlsəm/ a. excessif.

fumble /'fʌmbl/ v.i. tâtonner, fouiller. ~ **with,** tripoter.

fume /fjuːm/ v.i. rager. ~**s** n. pl. exhalaisons f. pl., vapeurs f. pl.

fumigate /'fjuːmɪɡeɪt/ v.t. désinfecter.

fun /fʌn/ n. amusement m. **be ~,** être chouette. **for ~,** pour rire. ~-**fair** n. fête foraine f. **make ~ of,** se moquer de.

function /'fʌŋkʃn/ n. (purpose, duty) fonction f.; (event) réception f. ● v.i. fonctionner. ~**al** a. fonctionnel.

fund /fʌnd/ n. fonds m. ● v.t. fournir les fonds pour.

fundamental /fʌndə'mentl/ a. fondamental. ~**ist** n. intégriste m./ f. ~**ism** n. intégrisme m.

funeral /'fjuːnərəl/ n. enterrement m., funérailles f. pl. ● a. funèbre.

fungus /'fʌŋɡəs/ n. (pl. -**gi** /-ɡaɪ/) (plant) champignon m.; (mould) moisissure f.

funicular /fjuː'nɪkjʊlə(r)/ n. funiculaire m.

funk /fʌŋk/ m. **be in a ~,** (afraid: sl.) avoir la frousse; (depressed: Amer., sl.) être déprimé.

funnel /'fʌnl/ n. (for pouring) entonnoir m.; (of ship) cheminée f.

funn|y /'fʌnɪ/ a. (-**ier, -iest**) drôle; (odd) bizarre. ~**y business,** quelque chose de louche. ~**ily** adv. drôlement; bizarrement.

fur /fɜː(r)/ n. fourrure f.; (in kettle) tartre m.

furious /'fjʊərɪəs/ a. furieux. ~**ly** adv. furieusement.

furnace /'fɜːnɪs/ n. fourneau m.

furnish /'fɜːnɪʃ/ v.t. (with furniture) meubler; (supply) fournir. ~**ings** n. pl. ameublement m.

furniture /'fɜːnɪtʃə(r)/ n. meubles m. pl., mobilier m.

furrow /'fʌrəʊ/ n. sillon m.

furry /'fɜːrɪ/ a. (animal) à fourrure; (toy) en peluche.

furth|er /'fɜːðə(r)/ a. plus éloigné; (additional) supplémentaire. ● adv. plus loin; (more) davantage. ● v.t. avancer. ~**er education,** formation continue f. ~**est** a. le plus éloigné; adv. le plus loin.

furthermore /'fɜːðəmɔː(r)/ adv. en outre, de plus.

furtive /'fɜːtɪv/ a. furtif.

fury /'fjʊərɪ/ n. fureur f.

fuse[1] /fjuːz/ v.t./i. (melt) fondre; (unite: fig.) fusionner. ● n. fusible

m., plomb m. ~ **the lights** etc., faire sauter les plombs.

fuse[2] /fjuːz/ n. (of bomb) amorce f.

fuselage /'fjuːzəlɑːʒ/ n. fuselage m.

fusion /'fjuːʒn/ n. fusion f.

fuss /fʌs/ n. (when upset) histoire(s) f. (pl.); (when excited) agitation f. ● v.i. s'agiter. **make a ~,** faire des histoires; s'agiter; (about food) faire des chichis. **make a ~ of,** faire grand cas de. ~**y** a. (finicky) tatillon; (hard to please) difficile.

futile /'fjuːtaɪl/ a. futile, vain.

future /'fjuːtʃə(r)/ a. futur. ● n. avenir m.; (gram.) futur m. **in ~,** à l'avenir.

fuzz /fʌz/ n. (fluff, growth) duvet m.; (police: sl.) flics m. pl.

fuzzy /'fʌzɪ/ a. (hair) crépu; (photograph) flou; (person: fam.) à l'esprit confus.

G

gabardine /ɡæbə'diːn/ n. gabardine f.

gabble /'ɡæbl/ v.t./i. bredouiller. ● n. baragouin m.

gable /'ɡeɪbl/ n. pignon m.

gad /ɡæd/ v.i. (p.t. **gadded**). ~ **about,** se promener, aller çà et là.

gadget /'ɡædʒɪt/ n. gadget m.

Gaelic /'ɡeɪlɪk/ n. gaélique m.

gaffe /ɡæf/ n. (blunder) gaffe f.

gag /ɡæɡ/ n. bâillon m.; (joke) gag m. ● v.t. (p.t. **gagged**) bâillonner.

gaiety /'ɡeɪətɪ/ n. gaieté f.

gaily /'ɡeɪlɪ/ adv. gaiement.

gain /ɡeɪn/ v.t. gagner; (speed, weight) prendre. ● v.i. (of clock) avancer. ● n. acquisition f.; (profit) gain m. ~**ful** a. profitable.

gait /ɡeɪt/ n. démarche f.

gala /'ɡɑːlə/ n. (festive occasion) gala m.; (sport) concours m.

galaxy /'ɡæləksɪ/ n. galaxie f.

gale /ɡeɪl/ n. tempête f.

gall /ɡɔːl/ n. bile f.; (fig.) fiel m.; (impudence: sl.) culot m. ~-**bladder** n. vésicule biliaire f.

gallant /'ɡælənt/ a. (brave) courageux; (chivalrous) galant. ~**ry** n. courage m.

galleon /'ɡælɪən/ n. galion m.

gallery /'ɡælərɪ/ n. galerie f. (art) ~, (public) musée m.

galley /'gælɪ/ n. (*ship*) galère f.; (*kitchen*) cambuse f.

Gallic /'gælɪk/ a. français. **~ism** /-sɪzəm/ n. gallicisme m.

gallivant /gælɪ'vænt/ v.i. (*fam.*) se promener, aller çà et là.

gallon /'gælən/ n. gallon m. (*imperial = 4.546 litres; Amer. = 3.785 litres*).

gallop /'gæləp/ n. galop m. ● v.i. (*p.t.* **galloped**) galoper.

gallows /'gæləʊz/ n. potence f.

galore /gə'lɔː(r)/ adv. en abondance, à gogo.

galosh /gə'lɒʃ/ n. (*overshoe*) caoutchouc m.

galvanize /'gælvənaɪz/ v.t. galvaniser.

gambit /'gæmbɪt/ n. (**opening**) **~**, (*move*) première démarche f.; (*ploy*) stratagème m.

gambl|e /'gæmbl/ v.t./i. jouer. ● n. (*venture*) entreprise risquée f.; (*bet*) pari m.; (*risk*) risque m. **~e on,** miser sur. **~er** n. joueur|r, -se m., f. **~ing** n. le jeu.

game ¹ /geɪm/ n. jeu m.; (*football*) match m.; (*tennis*) partie f.; (*animals, birds*) gibier m. ● a. (*brave*) brave. **~ for,** prêt à.

game ² /geɪm/ a. (*lame*) estropié.

gamekeeper /'geɪmkiːpə(r)/ n. garde-chasse m.

gammon /'gæmən/ n. jambon fumé m.

gamut /'gæmət/ n. gamme f.

gamy /'geɪmɪ/ a. faisandé.

gang /gæŋ/ n. bande f.; (*of workmen*) équipe f. ● v.i. **~ up,** se liguer (**on, against,** contre).

gangling /'gæŋglɪŋ/ a. dégingandé, grand et maigre.

gangrene /'gæŋgriːn/ n. gangrène f.

gangster /'gæŋstə(r)/ n. gangster m.

gangway /'gæŋweɪ/ n. passage m.; (*aisle*) allée f.; (*of ship*) passerelle f.

gaol /dʒeɪl/ n. & v.t. = **jail.**

gap /gæp/ n. trou m., vide m.; (*in time*) intervalle m.; (*in education*) lacune f.; (*difference*) écart m.

gap|e /geɪp/ v.i. rester bouche bée. **~ing** a. béant.

garage /'gærɑːʒ, *Amer.* gə'rɑːʒ/ n. garage m. ● v.t. mettre au garage.

garb /gɑːb/ n. costume m.

garbage /'gɑːbɪdʒ/ n. ordures f. pl.

garble /'gɑːbl/ v.t. déformer.

garden /'gɑːdn/ n. jardin m. ● v.i. jardiner. **~er** n. jardin|ier, -ière m., f. **~ing** n. jardinage m.

gargle /'gɑːgl/ v.i. se gargariser. ● n. gargarisme m.

gargoyle /'gɑːgɔɪl/ n. gargouille f.

garish /'geərɪʃ/ a. voyant, criard.

garland /'gɑːlənd/ n. guirlande f.

garlic /'gɑːlɪk/ n. ail m.

garment /'gɑːmənt/ n. vêtement m.

garnish /'gɑːnɪʃ/ v.t. garnir (**with,** de). ● n. garniture f.

garret /'gærət/ n. mansarde f.

garrison /'gærɪsn/ n. garnison f.

garrulous /'gærələs/ a. loquace.

garter /'gɑːtə(r)/ n. jarretière f. **~-belt** n. porte-jarretelles n.m. invar.

gas /gæs/ n. (*pl.* **gases**) gaz m.; (*med.*) anesthésique m.; (*petrol: Amer., fam.*) essence f. ● a. (*mask, pipe*) à gaz. ● v.t. asphyxier; (*mil.*) gazer. ● v.i. (*fam.*) bavarder.

gash /gæʃ/ n. entaille f. ● v.t. entailler.

gasket /'gæskɪt/ n. (*auto.*) joint de culasse m.; (*for pressure cooker*) rondelle f.

gasoline /'gæsəliːn/ n. (*petrol: Amer.*) essence f.

gasp /gɑːsp/ v.i. haleter; (*in surprise: fig.*) avoir le souffle coupé. ● n. halètement m.

gassy /'gæsɪ/ a. gazeux.

gastric /'gæstrɪk/ a. gastrique.

gastronomy /gæ'strɒnəmɪ/ n. gastronomie f.

gate /geɪt/ n. porte f.; (*of metal*) grille f.; (*barrier*) barrière f.

gatecrash /'geɪtkræʃ/ v.t./i. venir sans invitation (à). **~er** n. intrus(e) m.(f).

gateway /'geɪtweɪ/ n. porte f.

gather /'gæðə(r)/ v.t. (*people, objects*) rassembler; (*pick up*) ramasser; (*flowers*) cueillir; (*fig.*) comprendre; (*sewing*) froncer. ● v.i. (*people*) se rassembler; (*crowd*) se former; (*pile up*) s'accumuler. **~ speed,** prendre de la vitesse. **~ing** n. rassemblement m.

gaudy /'gɔːdɪ/ a. (**-ier, -iest**) voyant, criard.

gauge /geɪdʒ/ n. jauge f., indicateur m. ● v.t. jauger, évaluer.

gaunt /gɔːnt/ a. (*lean*) émacié; (*grim*) lugubre.

gauntlet /'gɔːntlɪt/ n. **run the ~ of,** subir (l'assaut de).

gauze /gɔːz/ n. gaze f.

gave /geɪv/ *see* give.

gawky /'gɔːkɪ/ a. (**-ier, -iest**) gauche, maladroit.

gawp (*or* **gawk**) /gɔ:p, gɔ:k/ *v.i.* ~ **(at),** regarder bouche bée.

gay /geɪ/ *a.* (**-er, -est**) (*joyful*) gai; (*fam.*) gay *invar.* ● *n.* gay *m./f.*

gaze /geɪz/ *v.i.* ~ **(at),** regarder (fixement). ● *n.* regard (fixe) *m.*

gazelle /gə'zel/ *n.* gazelle *f.*

gazette /gə'zet/ *n.* journal (officiel) *m.*

GB *abbr. see* Great Britain.

gear /gɪə(r)/ *n.* équipement *m.*; (*techn.*) engrenage *m.*; (*auto.*) vitesse *f.* ● *v.t.* adapter. ~**-lever,** (*Amer.*) ~**-shift** *ns.* levier de vitesse *m.* **in** ~, en prise. **out of** ~, au point mort.

gearbox /'gɪəbɒks/ *n.* (*auto.*) boîte de vitesses *f.*

geese /gi:s/ *see* goose.

gel /dʒel/ *n.* gelée *f.*; (*for hair*) gel *m.*

gelatine /'dʒelətiːn/ *n.* gélatine *f.*

gelignite /'dʒelɪgnaɪt/ *n.* nitroglycérine *f.*

gem /dʒem/ *n.* pierre précieuse *f.*

Gemini /'dʒemɪnaɪ/ *n.* les Gémeaux *m. pl.*

gender /'dʒendə(r)/ *n.* genre *m.*

gene /dʒi:n/ *n.* gène *m.*

genealogy /dʒi:nɪ'ælədʒɪ/ *n.* généalogie *f.*

general /'dʒenrəl/ *a.* général. ● *n.* général *m.* ~ **election,** élections législatives *f. pl.* ~ **practitioner,** (*med.*) généraliste *m.* **in** ~, en général. ~**ly** *adv.* généralement.

generaliz|e /'dʒenrəlaɪz/ *v.t./i.* généraliser. ~**ation** /-'zeɪʃn/ *n.* généralisation *f.*

generate /'dʒenəreɪt/ *v.t.* produire.

generation /dʒenə'reɪʃn/ *n.* génération *f.*

generator /'dʒenəreɪtə(r)/ *n.* (*electr.*) groupe électrogène *m.*

gener|ous /'dʒenərəs/ *a.* généreux; (*plentiful*) copieux. ~**osity** /-'rɒsətɪ/ *n.* générosité *f.*

genetic /dʒɪ'netɪk/ *a.* génétique. ~**s** *n.* génétique *f.*

Geneva /dʒɪ'ni:və/ *n.* Genève *m./f.*

genial /'dʒi:nɪəl/ *a.* affable, sympathique; (*climate*) doux.

genital /'dʒenɪtl/ *a.* génital. ~**s** *n. pl.* organes génitaux *m. pl.*

genius /'dʒi:nɪəs/ *n.* (*pl.* -uses) génie *m.*

genocide /'dʒenəsaɪd/ *n.* génocide *m.*

gent /dʒent/ *n.* (*sl.*) monsieur *m.*

genteel /dʒen'ti:l/ *a.* distingué.

gentl|e /'dʒentl/ *a.* (**-er, -est**) (*mild, kind*) doux; (*slight*) léger; (*hint*) discret. ~**eness** *n.* douceur *f.* ~**y** *adv.* doucement.

gentleman /'dʒentlmən/ *n.* (*pl.* -men) (*man*) monsieur *m.*; (*wellbred*) gentleman *m.*

genuine /'dʒenjʊɪn/ *a.* (*true*) véritable; (*person, belief*) sincère.

geograph|y /dʒɪ'ɒgrəfɪ/ *n.* géographie *f.* ~**er** *n.* géographe *m./f.* ~**ical** /dʒɪə'græfɪkl/ *a.* géographique.

geolog|y /dʒɪ'ɒlədʒɪ/ *n.* géologie *f.* ~**ical** /dʒɪə'lɒdʒɪkl/ *a.* géologique. ~**ist** *n.* géologue *m./f.*

geometr|y /dʒɪ'ɒmɪtrɪ/ *n.* géométrie *f.* ~**ic(al)** /dʒɪə'metrɪk(l)/ *a.* géométrique.

geranium /dʒə'reɪnɪəm/ *n.* géranium *m.*

geriatric /dʒerɪ'ætrɪk/ *a.* gériatrique.

germ /dʒɜ:m/ *n.* (*rudiment, seed*) germe *m.*; (*med.*) microbe *m.*

German /'dʒɜ:mən/ *a.* & *n.* allemand(e) (*m.* (*f.*)); (*lang.*) allemand *m.* ~ **measles,** rubéole *f.* ~ **shepherd,** (*dog*: *Amer.*) berger allemand *m.* ~**ic** /dʒə'mænɪk/ *a.* germanique. ~**y** *n.* Allemagne *f.*

germinate /'dʒɜ:mɪneɪt/ *v.t./i.* (faire) germer.

gestation /dʒe'steɪʃn/ *n.* gestation *f.*

gesticulate /dʒe'stɪkjʊleɪt/ *v.i.* gesticuler.

gesture /'dʒestʃə(r)/ *n.* geste *m.*

get /get/ *v.t.* (*p.t.* & *p.p.* got, *p.p. Amer.* **gotten,** *pres. p.* **getting**) avoir, obtenir, recevoir; (*catch*) prendre; (*buy*) acheter, prendre; (*find*) trouver; (*fetch*) aller chercher; (*understand*: *sl.*) comprendre. ~ **s.o. to do sth.,** faire faire qch. à qn. ~ **sth. done,** faire faire qch. **did you** ~ **that number?,** tu as relevé le numéro? ● *v.i.* aller, arriver **(to,** à); (*become*) devenir; (*start*) se mettre **(to,** à); (*manage*) parvenir **(to,** à). ~ **married/ready/etc.,** se marier/se préparer/*etc.* ~ **promoted/hurt/etc.,** être promu/blessé/*etc.* ~ **arrested/robbed/etc.,** se faire arrêter/voler/*etc.* **you** ~ **to use the computer,** vous utilisez l'ordinateur. **it's** ~**ting to be annoying,** ça commence a être agaçant. ~ **about,** (*person*) se déplacer. ~ **across,** (*cross*) traverser. ~ **along** *or* **by,** (*manage*) se débrouiller. **~ along** or **on**, (*progress*) avancer. **~ along** or **on with**, s'entendre avec. **~ at**, (*reach*) parvenir à. **what are you ~ting at?**, où veux-tu en venir? **~ away**, partir; (*escape*) s'échapper. **~ back** *v.i.* revenir; *v.t.* (*recover*) récupérer. **~ by** or **through**, (*pass*) passer. **~ down** *v.t./i.* descendre; (*depress*) déprimer. **~ in**, entrer, arriver. **~ into**, (*car*) monter dans; (*dress*) mettre. **~ into trouble**, avoir des ennuis. **~ off** *v.i.* (*from bus etc.*) descendre; (*leave*) partir; (*jurid.*) être acquitté; *v.t.* (*remove*) enlever. **~ on**, (*on train etc.*) monter; (*succeed*) réussir. **~ on with**, (*job*) attaquer; (*person*) s'entendre de. **~ out**, sortir. **~ out of**, (*fig.*) se soustraire à. **~ over**, (*illness*) se remettre de. **~ round**, (*rule*) contourner; (*person*) entortiller. **~ through**, (*finish*) finir. **~ up** *v.i.* se lever; *v.t.* (*climb, bring*) monter. **~-up** *n.* (*clothes: fam.*) mise *f.*

getaway /'getəweɪ/ *n.* fuite *f.*

geyser /'giːzə(r)/ *n.* chauffe-eau *m. invar.*; (*geol.*) geyser *m.*

Ghana /'gɑːnə/ *n.* Ghana *m.*

ghastly /'gɑːstlɪ/ *a.* (**-ier, -iest**) affreux; (*pale*) blême.

gherkin /'gɜːkɪn/ *n.* cornichon *m.*

ghetto /'getəʊ/ *n.* (*pl.* **-os**) ghetto *m.*

ghost /gəʊst/ *n.* fantôme *m.* **~ly** *a.* spectral.

giant /'dʒaɪənt/ *n.* & *a.* géant (*m.*).

gibberish /'dʒɪbərɪʃ/ *n.* baragouin *m.*, charabia *m.*

gibe /dʒaɪb/ *n.* raillerie *f.* ● *v.i.* **(at)**, railler.

giblets /'dʒɪblɪts/ *n. pl.* abattis *m. pl.*, abats *m. pl.*

gidd|y /'gɪdɪ/ *a.* (**-ier, -iest**) vertigineux. **be** or **feel ~y**, avoir le vertige. **~iness** *n.* vertige *m.*

gift /gɪft/ *n.* cadeau *m.*; (*ability*) don *m.* **~-wrap** *v.t.* (*p.t.* **-wrapped**) faire un paquet-cadeau de.

gifted /'gɪftɪd/ *a.* doué.

gig /gɪg/ *n.* (*fam.*) concert *m.*

gigantic /dʒaɪˈgæntɪk/ *a.* gigantesque.

giggle /'gɪgl/ *v.i.* ricaner (sottement), glousser. ● *n.* ricanement *m.* **the ~s**, le fou rire.

gild /gɪld/ *v.t.* dorer.

gill /dʒɪl/ *n.* (*approx.*) décilitre (*imperial = 0.15 litre; Amer. = 0.12 litre*).

gills /gɪlz/ *n. pl.* ouïes *f. pl.*

gilt /gɪlt/ *a.* doré. ● *n.* dorure *f.* **~-edged** *a.* (*comm.*) de tout repos.

gimmick /'gɪmɪk/ *n.* truc *m.*

gin /dʒɪn/ *n.* gin *m.*

ginger /'dʒɪndʒə(r)/ *n.* gingembre *m.* ● *a.* roux. **~ ale**, **~ beer**, boisson gazeuse au gingembre *f.*

gingerbread /'dʒɪndʒəbred/ *n.* pain d'épice *m.*

gingerly /'dʒɪndʒəlɪ/ *adv.* avec précaution.

gipsy /'dʒɪpsɪ/ *n.* = **gypsy**.

giraffe /dʒɪˈrɑːf/ *n.* girafe *f.*

girder /'gɜːdə(r)/ *n.* poutre *f.*

girdle /'gɜːdl/ *n.* (*belt*) ceinture *f.*; (*corset*) gaine *f.*

girl /gɜːl/ *n.* (petite) fille *f.*; (*young woman*) (jeune) fille *f.* **~-friend** *n.* amie *f.*; (*of boy*) petite amie *f.* **~hood** *n.* enfance *f.*, jeunesse *f.* **~ish** *a.* de (jeune) fille.

giro /'dʒaɪərəʊ/ *n.* (*pl.* **-os**) virement bancaire *m.*; (*cheque: fam.*) mandat *m.*

girth /gɜːθ/ *n.* circonférence *f.*

gist /dʒɪst/ *n.* essentiel *m.*

give /gɪv/ *v.t.* (*p.t.* **gave**, *p.p.* **given**) donner; (*gesture*) faire; (*laugh, sigh, etc.*) pousser. **~ s.o. sth.**, donner qch. à qn. ● *v.i.* donner; (*yield*) céder; (*stretch*) se détendre. ● *n.* élasticité *f.* **~ away**, donner; (*secret*) trahir. **~ back**, rendre. **~ in**, (*yield*) se rendre. **~ off**, dégager. **~ out** *v.t.* distribuer; *v.i.* (*become used up*) s'épuiser. **~ over**, (*devote*) consacrer; (*stop: fam.*) cesser. **~ up** *v.t./i.* (*renounce*) renoncer (à); (*yield*) céder. **~ o.s. up**, se rendre. **~ way**, céder; (*collapse*) s'effondrer.

given /'gɪvn/ *see* give. ● *a.* donné. **~ name**, prénom *m.*

glacier /'glæsɪə(r), Amer. 'gleɪʃər/ *n.* glacier *m.*

glad /glæd/ *a.* content. **~ly** *adv.* avec plaisir.

gladden /'glædn/ *v.t.* réjouir.

gladiolus /glædrˈəʊləs/ *n.* (*pl.* **-li** /-laɪ/) glaïeul *m.*

glam|our /'glæmə(r)/ *n.* enchantement *m.*, séduction *f.* **~orize** *v.t.* rendre séduisant. **~orous** *a.* séduisant, ensorcelant.

glance /glɑːns/ *n.* coup d'œil *m.* ● *v.i.* **~ at**, jeter un coup d'œil à.

gland /glænd/ *n.* glande *f.*

glar|e /gleə(r)/ *v.i.* briller très fort. ● *n.* éclat (aveuglant) *m.*; (*stare: fig.*) regard furieux *m.* **~e at**, regarder d'un air furieux. **~ing** a. éblouissant; (*obvious*) flagrant.

glass /glɑːs/ n. verre m.; (*mirror*) miroir m. ; (*spectacles*) lunettes f. pl. **~y** a. vitreux.

glaze /gleɪz/ v.t. (*door etc.*) vitrer; (*pottery*) vernisser. ● n. vernis m.

gleam /gliːm/ n. lueur f. ● v.i. luire.

glean /gliːn/ v.t. glaner.

glee /gliː/ n. joie f. **~ club**, chorale f. **~ful** a. joyeux.

glen /glen/ n. vallon m.

glib /glɪb/ a. (*person: pej.*) qui a la parole facile or du bagou; (*reply, excuse*) désinvolte, spécieux. **~ly** adv. avec désinvolture.

glide /glaɪd/ v.i. glisser; (*of plane*) planer. **~r** /-ə(r)/ n. planeur m.

glimmer /'glɪmə(r)/ n. lueur f. ● v.i. luire.

glimpse /glɪmps/ n. aperçu m. **catch a ~ of**, entrevoir.

glint /glɪnt/ n. éclair m. ● v.i. étinceler.

glisten /'glɪsn/ v.i. briller, luire.

glitter /'glɪtə(r)/ v.i. scintiller. ● n. scintillement m.

gloat /gləʊt/ v.i. jubiler (**over**, à l'idée de).

global /'gləʊbl/ a. (*world-wide*) mondial; (*all-embracing*) global.

globe /gləʊb/ n. globe m.

gloom /gluːm/ n. obscurité f.; (*sadness: fig.*) tristesse f. **~y** a. triste; (*pessimistic*) pessimiste.

glorif|y /'glɔːrɪfaɪ/ v.t. glorifier. **a ~ied waitress/etc.**, à peine plus qu'une serveuse/etc.

glorious /'glɔːrɪəs/ a. splendide; (*deed, hero, etc.*) glorieux.

glory /'glɔːrɪ/ n. gloire f.; (*beauty*) splendeur f. ● v.i. **~ in**, s'enorgueillir de.

gloss /glɒs/ n. lustre m., brillant m. ● a. brillant. ● v.i. **~ over**, (*make light of*) glisser sur; (*cover up*) dissimuler. **~y** a. brillant.

glossary /'glɒsərɪ/ n. glossaire m.

glove /glʌv/ n. gant m. **~ compartment**, (*auto.*) vide-poches m. invar. **~d** a. ganté.

glow /gləʊ/ v.i. rougeoyer; (*person, eyes*) rayonner. ● n. rougeoiement m., éclat m. **~ing** a. (*account etc.*) enthousiaste.

glucose /'gluːkəʊs/ n. glucose m.

glue /gluː/ n. colle f. ● v.t. (*pres. p. gluing*) coller.

glum /glʌm/ a. (**glummer, glummest**) triste, morne.

glut /glʌt/ n. surabondance f.

glutton /'glʌtn/ n. glouton(ne) m. (f.). **~ous** a. glouton. **~y** n. gloutonnerie f.

glycerine /'glɪsəriːn/ n. glycérine f.

gnarled /nɑːld/ a. noueux.

gnash /næʃ/ v.t. **~ one's teeth**, grincer des dents.

gnat /næt/ n. (*fly*) cousin m.

gnaw /nɔː/ v.t./i. ronger.

gnome /nəʊm/ n. gnome m.

go /gəʊ/ v.i. (*p.t.* **went**, *p.p.* **gone**) aller; (*leave*) partir; (*work*) marcher; (*become*) devenir; (*be sold*) se vendre; (*vanish*) disparaître. **my coat's gone**, mon manteau n'est plus là. **~ via Paris**, passer par Paris. **~ by car/on foot**, aller en voiture/à pied. **~ for a walk/ride**, aller se promener/faire un tour en voiture. **go red/dry/etc.**, rougir/tarir/etc. **don't ~ telling him**, ne va pas lui dire. **~ riding/shopping/etc.**, faire du cheval/les courses/etc. ● n. (*pl.* **goes**) (*try*) coup m.; (*success*) réussite f.; (*turn*) tour m.; (*energy*) dynamisme m. **have a ~**, essayer. **be ~ing to do**, aller faire. **~ across**, traverser. **~ ahead!**, allez-y! **~-ahead** n. feu vert m.; a. dynamique. **~ away**, s'en aller. **~ back**, retourner; (*go home*) rentrer. **~ back on**, (*promise etc.*) revenir sur. **~ bad** *or* **off**, se gâter. **~-between** n. intermédiaire m./f. **~ by**, (*pass*) passer. **~ down**, descendre; (*sun*) se coucher. **~ for**, aller chercher; (*like*) aimer; (*attack: sl.*) attaquer. **~ in**, (r)entrer. **~ in for**, (*exam*) se présenter à. **~ into**, entrer dans; (*subject*) examiner. **~-kart** n. kart m. **~ off**, partir; (*explode*) sauter; (*ring*) sonner; (*take place*) se dérouler; (*dislike*) revenir de. **~ on**, continuer; (*happen*) se passer. **~ out**, sortir; (*light, fire*) s'éteindre. **~ over**, (*cross*) traverser; (*pass*) passer. **~ over** *or* **through**, (*check*) vérifier; (*search*) fouiller. **~ round**, (*be enough*) suffire. **~-slow** n. grève perlée f. **~ through**, (*suffer*) subir. **~ under**, (*sink*) couler; (*fail*) échouer. **~ up**, monter. **~ without**, se passer de. **on the ~**, actif.

goad /gəʊd/ v.t. aiguillonner.

goal /gəʊl/ n. but m. **~-post** n. poteau de but m.

goalkeeper /'gəʊlkiːpə(r)/ n. gardien de but m.

goat /gəʊt/ n. chèvre f.

goatee /gəʊ'tiː/ n. barbiche f.

gobble /'gɒbl/ v.t. engouffrer.

goblet /'gɒblɪt/ n. verre à pied m.

goblin /'gɒblɪn/ n. lutin m.

God /gɒd/ n. Dieu m. **~-forsaken** a. perdu.

god /gɒd/ n. dieu m. **~dess** n. déesse f. **~ly** a. dévot.

god|**child** /'gɒdtʃaɪld/ n. (pl. **-children**) filleul(e) m. (f.). **~daughter** n. filleule f. **~father** n. parrain m. **~mother** n. marraine f. **~son** n. filleul m.

godsend /'gɒdsend/ n. aubaine f.

goggle /'gɒgl/ v.i. **~ (at)**, regarder avec de gros yeux.

goggles /'gɒglz/ n. pl. lunettes (protectrices) f. pl.

going /'gəʊɪŋ/ n. **it is slow/hard ~**, c'est lent/difficile. ● a. (price, rate) actuel. **~s-on** n. pl. activités (bizarres) f. pl.

gold /gəʊld/ n. or m. ● a. en or, d'or. **~-mine** n. mine d'or f.

golden /'gəʊldən/ a. d'or; (in colour) doré; (opportunity) unique. **~ wedding**, noces d'or f. pl.

goldfish /'gəʊldfɪʃ/ n. invar. poisson rouge m.

gold-plated /gəʊld'pleɪtɪd/ a. plaqué or.

goldsmith /'gəʊldsmɪθ/ n. orfèvre m.

golf /gɒlf/ n. golf m. **~ ball**, balle de golf f.; (on typewriter) boule f. **~-course** n. terrain de golf m. **~er** n. joueu|r, -se de golf m., f.

gondol|**a** /'gɒndələ/ n. gondole f. **~ier** /-'lɪə(r)/ n. gondolier m.

gone /gɒn/ see go. ● a. parti. **~ six o'clock**, six heures passées. **the butter's all ~**, il n'y a plus de beurre.

gong /gɒŋ/ n. gong m.

good /gʊd/ a. (**better, best**) bon; (weather) beau; (well-behaved) sage. ● n. bien m. **as ~ as**, (almost) pratiquement. **that's ~ of you**, c'est gentil (de ta part). **be ~ with**, savoir s'y prendre avec. **do ~**, faire du bien. **feel ~**, se sentir bien. **~-for-nothing** a. & n. propre à rien (m./f.). **G~ Friday**, Vendredi saint m. **~-afternoon**, **~-morning** ints. bonjour. **~-evening** int. bonsoir.

~-looking a. beau. **~-natured** a. gentil. **~ name**, réputation f. **~-night** int. bonsoir, bonne nuit. **it is ~ for you**, ça vous fait du bien. **is it any ~?**, est-ce que c'est bien? **it's no ~**, ça ne vaut rien. **it is no ~ shouting**/etc., ça ne sert à rien de crier/etc. **for ~**, pour toujours. **~ness** n. bonté f. **my ~ness!**, mon Dieu!

goodbye /gʊd'baɪ/ int. & n. au revoir (m. invar.).

goods /gʊdz/ n. pl. marchandises f. pl.

goodwill /gʊd'wɪl/ n. bonne volonté f.

goody /'gʊdɪ/ n. (fam.) bonne chose f. **~-goody** n. petit(e) saint(e) m. (f.).

gooey /'guːɪ/ a. (sl.) poisseux.

goof /guːf/ v.i. (Amer.) gaffer.

goose /guːs/ n. (pl. **geese**) oie f. **~-flesh**, **~-pimples** ns. chair de poule f.

gooseberry /'gʊzbərɪ/ n. groseille f. maquereau f.

gore[1] /gɔː(r)/ n. (blood) sang m.

gore[2] /gɔː(r)/ v.t. encorner.

gorge /gɔːdʒ/ n. (geog.) gorge f. ● v.t. **~ o.s.**, se gorger.

gorgeous /'gɔːdʒəs/ a. magnifique, splendide, formidable.

gorilla /gə'rɪlə/ n. gorille m.

gormless /'gɔːmlɪs/ a. (sl.) stupide.

gorse /gɔːs/ n. invar. ajonc(s) m. (pl.).

gory /'gɔːrɪ/ a. (**-ier, -iest**) sanglant; (horrific: fig.) horrible.

gosh /gɒʃ/ int. mince (alors).

gospel /'gɒspl/ n. évangile m. **the G~**, l'Évangile m.

gossip /'gɒsɪp/ n. bavardage(s) m. (pl.), commérage(s) m. (pl.); (person) bavard(e) m. (f.). ● v.i. (p.t. **gossiped**) bavarder. **~y** a. bavard.

got /gɒt/ see get. ● **have ~**, avoir. **have ~ to do**, devoir faire.

Gothic /'gɒθɪk/ a. gothique.

gouge /gaʊdʒ/ v.t. **~ out**, arracher.

gourmet /'gʊəmeɪ/ n. gourmet m.

gout /gaʊt/ n. (med.) goutte f.

govern /'gʌvn/ v.t./i. gouverner. **~ess** /-ənɪs/ n. gouvernante f. **~or** /-ənə(r)/ n. gouverneur m.

government /'gʌvənmənt/ n. gouvernement m. **~al** /-'mentl/ a. gouvernemental.

gown /gaʊn/ n. robe f.; (of judge, teacher) toge f.

GP abbr. see general practitioner.

grab /græb/ v.t. (p.t. **grabbed**) saisir.

grace /greɪs/ n. grâce f. ● v.t. (*honour*) honorer; (*adorn*) orner. **~ful** a. gracieux.

gracious /'greɪʃəs/ a. (*kind*) bienveillant; (*elegant*) élégant.

gradation /grə'deɪʃn/ n. gradation f.

grade /greɪd/ n. catégorie f.; (*of goods*) qualité f.; (*on scale*) grade m.; (*school mark*) note f.; (*class: Amer.*) classe f. ● v.t. classer; (*school work*) noter. **~ crossing,** (*Amer.*) passage à niveau m. **~ school,** (*Amer.*) école primaire f.

gradient /'greɪdɪənt/ n. (*slope*) inclinaison f.

gradual /'grædʒʊəl/ a. progressif, graduel. **~ly** adv. progressivement, peu à peu.

graduate[1] /'grædʒʊət/ n. (*univ.*) diplômé(e) m. (f.).

graduat[e][2] /'grædʒʊeɪt/ v.i. obtenir son diplôme. ● v.t. graduer. **~ion** /-'eɪʃn/ n. remise de diplômes f.

graffiti /grə'fiːtiː/ n. pl. graffiti m. pl.

graft[1] /grɑːft/ n. (*med., bot.*) greffe f. (*work*) boulot m. ● v.t. greffer; (*work*) trimer.

graft[2] /grɑːft/ n. (*bribery: fam.*) corruption f.

grain /greɪn/ n. (*seed, quantity, texture*) grain m.; (*in wood*) fibre f.

gram /græm/ n. gramme m.

gramm[ar] /'græmə(r)/ n. grammaire f. **~atical** /grə'mætɪkl/ a. grammatical.

grand /grænd/ a. (-er, -est) magnifique; (*duke, chorus*) grand. **~ piano,** piano à queue m.

grandad /'grændæd/ n. (*fam.*) papy m.

grand[child] /'græn(d)tʃaɪld/ n. (*pl.* -children) petit(e)-enfant m. (f.). **~daughter** n. petite-fille f. **~father** n. grand-père m. **~mother** n. grand-mère f. **~parents** n. pl. grands-parents m. pl. **~son** n. petit-fils m.

grandeur /'grændʒə(r)/ n. grandeur f.

grandiose /'grændɪəʊs/ a. grandiose.

grandma /'grændmɑː/ n. = **granny.**

grandstand /'græn(d)stænd/ n. tribune f.

granite /'grænɪt/ n. granit m.

granny /'grænɪ/ n. (*fam.*) grandmaman f., mémé f., mamie f.

grant /grɑːnt/ v.t. (*give*) accorder; (*request*) accéder à; (*admit*) admettre (**that,** que). ● n. subvention f.; (*univ.*) bourse f. **take sth. for ~ed,**

considérer qch. comme une chose acquise.

granulated /'grænjʊleɪtɪd/ a. **~ sugar,** sucre semoule m.

granule /'grænjuːl/ n. granule m.

grape /greɪp/ n. grain de raisin m. **~s,** raisin(s) m. (pl.).

grapefruit /'greɪpfruːt/ n. invar. pamplemousse m.

graph /grɑːf/ n. graphique m.

graphic /'græfɪk/ a. (*arts etc.*) graphique; (*fig.*) vivant, explicite. **~s** n. pl. (*comput.*) graphiques m. pl.

grapple /græpl/ v.i. **~ with,** affronter, être aux prises avec.

grasp /grɑːsp/ v.t. saisir. ● n. (*hold*) prise f.; (*strength of hand*) poigne f.; (*reach*) portée f.; (*fig.*) compréhension f.

grasping /'grɑːspɪŋ/ a. rapace.

grass /grɑːs/ n. herbe f. **~ roots,** peuple m.; (*pol.*) base f. **~-roots** a. populaire. **~y** a. herbeux.

grasshopper /'grɑːshɒpə(r)/ n. sauterelle f.

grassland /'grɑːslænd/ n. prairie f.

grate[1] /greɪt/ n. (*fireplace*) foyer m.; (*frame*) grille f.

grate[2] /greɪt/ v.t. râper. ● v.i. grincer. **~r** /-ə(r)/ n. râpe f.

grateful /'greɪtfl/ a. reconnaissant. **~ly** adv. avec reconnaissance.

gratif[y] /'grætɪfaɪ/ v.t. satisfaire; (*please*) faire plaisir à **~ied** a. très heureux. **~ying** a. agréable.

grating /'greɪtɪŋ/ n. grille f.

gratis /'greɪtɪs, 'grætɪs/ a. & adv. gratis (a. invar.).

gratitude /'grætɪtjuːd/ n. gratitude f.

gratuitous /grə'tjuːɪtəs/ a. gratuit.

gratuity /grə'tjuːətɪ/ n. (*tip*) pourboire m.; (*bounty: mil.*) prime f.

grave[1] /greɪv/ n. tombe f. **~-digger** n. fossoyeur m.

grave[2] /greɪv/ a. (-er, -est) (*serious*) grave. **~ly** adv. gravement.

grave[3] /grɑːv/ a. **~ accent,** accent grave m.

gravel /'grævl/ n. gravier m.

gravestone /'greɪvstəʊn/ n. pierre tombale f.

graveyard /'greɪvjɑːd/ n. cimetière m.

gravitat[e] /'grævɪteɪt/ v.i. graviter. **~ion** /-'teɪʃn/ n. gravitation f.

gravity /'grævətɪ/ n. (*seriousness*) gravité f.; (*force*) pesanteur f.

gravy /'greɪvɪ/ n. jus (de viande) m.

gray /greɪ/ a. & n. = **grey.**

graze[1] /greɪz/ v.t./i. (eat) paître.

graze[2] /greɪz/ v.t. (touch) frôler; (scrape) écorcher. ● n. écorchure f.

greas|e /griːs/ n. graisse f. ● v.t. graisser. **~e-proof paper,** papier sulfurisé m. **~y** a. graisseux.

great /greɪt/ a. (-er, -est) grand; (very good: fam.) magnifique. **~ Britain,** Grande-Bretagne f. **~-grandfather** n. arrière-grand–père m. **~-grandmother** n. arrière-grand-mère f. **~ly** adv. (very) très; (much) beaucoup. **~ness** n. grandeur f.

Greece /griːs/ n. Grèce f.

greed /griːd/ n. avidité f.; (for food) gourmandise f. **~y** a. avide; gourmand.

Greek /griːk/ a. & n. grec(que) (m. (f.)); (lang.) grec m.

green /griːn/ a. (-er, -est) vert; (fig.) naïf. ● n. vert m.; (grass) pelouse f.; (golf) green m. **~s,** légumes verts m. pl. **~ belt,** ceinture verte f. **~ light,** feu vert m. **~ery** n. verdure f.

greengage /ˈgriːngeɪdʒ/ n. (plum) reine-claude f.

greengrocer /ˈgriːngrəʊsə(r)/ n. marchand(e) de fruits et légumes m. (f.).

greenhouse /ˈgriːnhaʊs/ n. serre f.

greet /griːt/ v.t. (receive) accueillir; (address politely) saluer. **~ing** n. accueil m. **~ings** n. pl. compliments m. pl.; (wishes) vœux m. pl. **~ings card,** carte de vœux f.

gregarious /grɪˈgeərɪəs/ a. (instinct) grégaire; (person) sociable.

grenade /grɪˈneɪd/ n. grenade f.

grew /gruː/ see grow.

grey /greɪ/ a. (-er, -est) gris; (fig.) triste. ● n. gris m. **go ~,** (hair, person) grisonner.

greyhound /ˈgreɪhaʊnd/ n. lévrier m.

grid /grɪd/ n. grille f.; (network: electr.) réseau m.; (culin.) gril m.

grief /griːf/ n. chagrin m. **come to ~,** (person) avoir un malheur; (fail) tourner mal.

grievance /ˈgriːvns/ n. grief m.

grieve /griːv/ v.t./i. (s')affliger. **~ for,** pleurer.

grill /grɪl/ n. (cooking device) gril m.; (food) grillade f.; (auto.) calandre f. ● v.t./i. griller; (interrogate) cuisiner.

grille /grɪl/ n. grille f.

grim /grɪm/ a. (**grimmer, grimmest**) sinistre.

grimace /grɪˈmeɪs/ n. grimace f. ● v.i. grimacer.

grim|e /graɪm/ n. crasse f. **~y** a. crasseux.

grin /grɪn/ v.i. (p.t. **grinned**) sourire. ● n. (large) sourire m.

grind /graɪnd/ v.t. (p.t. **ground**) écraser; (coffee) moudre; (sharpen) aiguiser. ● n. corvée f. **~ one's teeth,** grincer des dents. **~ to a halt,** devenir paralysé.

grip /grɪp/ v.t. (p.t. **gripped**) saisir; (interest) passionner. ● n. prise f.; (strength of hand) poigne f.; (bag) sac de voyage m. **come to ~s,** en venir aux prises.

gripe /graɪp/ n. **~s,** (med.) coliques f. pl. ● v.i. (grumble: sl.) râler.

grisly /ˈgrɪzlɪ/ a. (-ier, -iest) macabre, horrible.

gristle /ˈgrɪsl/ n. cartilage m.

grit /grɪt/ n. gravillon m., sable m.; (fig.) courage m. ● v.t. (p.t. **gritted**) (road) sabler; (teeth) serrer.

grizzle /ˈgrɪzl/ v.i. (cry) pleurnicher.

groan /grəʊn/ v.i. gémir. ● n. gémissement m.

grocer /ˈgrəʊsə(r)/ n. épic|ier, -ière m., f. **~ies** n. pl. (goods) épicerie f. **~y** n. (shop) épicerie f.

grog /grɒg/ n. grog m.

groggy /ˈgrɒgɪ/ a. (weak) faible; (unsteady) chancelant; (ill) mal fichu.

groin /grɔɪn/ n. aine f.

groom /gruːm/ n. marié m.; (for horses) valet d'écurie m. ● v.t. (horse) panser; (fig.) préparer.

groove /gruːv/ n. (for door etc.) rainure f.; (in record) sillon m.

grope /grəʊp/ v.i. tâtonner. **~ for,** chercher à tâtons.

gross /grəʊs/ a. (-er, -est) (coarse) grossier; (comm.) brut. ● n. invar. grosse f. **~ly** adv. grossièrement; (very) extrêmement.

grotesque /grəʊˈtesk/ a. grotesque, horrible.

grotto /ˈgrɒtəʊ/ n. (pl. **-oes**) grotte f.

grotty /ˈgrɒtɪ/ a. (sl.) moche.

grouch /graʊtʃ/ v.i. (grumble: fam.) rouspéter, râler.

ground[1] /graʊnd/ n. terre f., sol m.; (area) terrain m.; (reason) raison f.; (electr., Amer.) masse f. **~s,** terres f. pl., parc m.; (of coffee) marc m. ● v.t./i. (naut.) échouer; (aircraft) retenir au sol. **on the ~,** par terre. **lose ~,** perdre du terrain. **~ floor,**

rez-de-chaussée *m. invar.* ~ **rule,** règle de base *f.* ~**less** *a.* sans fondement. ~ **swell,** lame de fond *f.*

ground² /graʊnd/ *see* grind. ● *a.* ~ **beef,** (*Amer.*) bifteck haché *m.*

grounding /'graʊndɪŋ/ *n.* connaissances (de base) *f. pl.*

groundsheet /'graʊndʃiːt/ *n.* tapis de sol *m.*

groundwork /'graʊndwɜːk/ *n.* travail préparatoire *m.*

group /gruːp/ *n.* groupe *m.* ● *v.t./i.* (se) grouper.

grouse¹ /graʊs/ *n. invar.* (*bird*) coq de bruyère *m.*, grouse *f.*

grouse² /graʊs/ *v.i.* (*grumble: fam.*) rouspéter, râler.

grove /grəʊv/ *n.* bocage *m.*

grovel /'grɒvl/ *v.i.* (*p.t.* **grovelled**) ramper. ~**ling** *a.* rampant.

grow /grəʊ/ *v.i.* (*p.t.* **grew,** *p.p.* **grown**) grandir; (*of plant*) pousser; (*become*) devenir. ● *v.t.* cultiver. ~ **up,** devenir adulte, grandir. ~**er** *n.* cultiva|teur, -trice *m.*, *f.* ~**ing** *a.* grandissant.

growl /graʊl/ *v.i.* grogner. ● *n.* grognement *m.*

grown /grəʊn/ *see* grow. ● *a.* adulte. ~-**up** *a.* & *n.* adulte (*m./f.*).

growth /grəʊθ/ *n.* croissance *f.*; (*in numbers*) accroissement *m.*; (*of hair, tooth*) pousse *f.*; (*med.*) tumeur *f.*

grub /grʌb/ *n.* (*larva*) larve *f.*; (*food: sl.*) bouffe *f.*

grubby /'grʌbɪ/ *a.* (-**ier,** -**iest**) sale.

grudge /grʌdʒ/ *v.t.* ~ **doing,** faire à contrecœur. ~ **s.o. sth.,** (*success, wealth*) en vouloir à qn. de qch. ● *n.* rancune *f.* **have a** ~ **against,** en vouloir à. **grudgingly** *adv.* à contrecœur.

gruelling /'gruːəlɪŋ/ *a.* exténuant.

gruesome /'gruːsəm/ *a.* macabre.

gruff /grʌf/ *a.* (-**er,** -**est**) bourru.

grumble /'grʌmbl/ *v.i.* ronchonner, grogner (**at,** après).

grumpy /'grʌmpɪ/ *a.* (-**ier,** -**iest**) grincheux, grognon.

grunt /grʌnt/ *v.i.* grogner. ● *n.* grognement *m.*

guarant|ee /gærən'tiː/ *n.* garantie *f.* ● *v.t.* garantir. ~**or** *n.* garant(e) *m.* (*f.*).

guard /gɑːd/ *v.t.* protéger; (*watch*) surveiller. ● *v.i.* ~ **against,** se protéger contre. ● *n.* (*vigilance, mil., group*) garde *f.*; (*person*) garde *m.*; (*on train*) chef de train *m.* ~**ian** *n.* gardien(ne) *m.* (*f.*); (*of orphan*) tu|teur, -trice *m.*, *f.*

guarded /'gɑːdɪd/ *a.* prudent.

guerrilla /gə'rɪlə/ *n.* guérillero *m.* ~ **warfare,** guérilla *f.*

guess /ges/ *v.t./i.* deviner; (*suppose*) penser. ● *n.* conjecture *f.*

guesswork /'geswɜːk/ *n.* conjectures *f. pl.*

guest /gest/ *n.* invité(e) *m.* (*f.*); (*in hotel*) client(e) *m.* (*f.*). ~-**house** *n.* pension *f.* ~-**room** *n.* chambre d'ami *f.*

guffaw /gə'fɔː/ *n.* gros rire *m.* ● *v.i.* s'esclaffer, rire bruyamment.

guidance /'gaɪdns/ *n.* (*advice*) conseils *m. pl.*; (*information*) information *f.*

guide /gaɪd/ *n.* (*person, book*) guide *m.* ● *v.t.* guider. ~**d** /-ɪd/ *a.* ~**d missile,** missile téléguidé *m.* ~-**dog** *n.* chien d'aveugle *m.* ~-**lines** *n. pl.* grandes lignes *f. pl.*

Guide /gaɪd/ *n.* (*girl*) guide *f.*

guidebook /'gaɪdbʊk/ *n.* guide *m.*

guild /gɪld/ *n.* corporation *f.*

guile /gaɪl/ *n.* ruse *f.*

guillotine /'gɪlətiːn/ *n.* guillotine *f.*; (*for paper*) massicot *m.*

guilt /gɪlt/ *n.* culpabilité *f.* ~**y** *a.* coupable.

guinea-pig /'gɪnɪpɪg/ *n.* cobaye *m.*

guinea-fowl /'gɪnɪfaʊl/ *n.* pintade *f.*

guise /gaɪz/ *n.* apparence *f.*

guitar /gɪ'tɑː(r)/ *n.* guitare *f.* ~**ist** *n.* guitariste *m./f.*

gulf /gʌlf/ *n.* (*part of sea*) golfe *m.*; (*hollow*) gouffre *m.*

gull /gʌl/ *n.* mouette *f.*, goéland *m.*

gullet /'gʌlɪt/ *n.* gosier *m.*

gullible /'gʌləbl/ *a.* crédule.

gully /'gʌlɪ/ *n.* (*ravine*) ravine *f.*; (*drain*) rigole *f.*

gulp /gʌlp/ *v.t.* ~ (**down**), avaler en vitesse. ● *v.i.* (*from fear etc.*) avoir un serrement de gorge. ● *n.* gorgée *f.*

gum¹ /gʌm/ *n.* (*anat.*) gencive *f.*

gum² /gʌm/ *n.* (*from tree*) gomme *f.*; (*glue*) colle *f.*; (*for chewing*) chewing-gum *m.* ● *v.t.* (*p.t.* **gummed**) gommer.

gumboil /'gʌmbɔɪl/ *n.* abcès dentaire *m.*

gumboot /'gʌmbuːt/ *n.* botte de caoutchouc *f.*

gumption /'gʌmpʃn/ *n.* (*fam.*) initiative *f.*, courage *m.*, audace *f.*

gun /gʌn/ n. (*pistol*) revolver m.; (*rifle*) fusil m.; (*large*) canon m. ● v.t. (*p.t.* **gunned**). ~ **down**, abattre. ~**ner** n. artilleur m.

gunfire /'gʌnfaɪə(r)/ n. fusillade f.

gunge /gʌndʒ/ n. (*sl.*) crasse f.

gunman /'gʌnmən/ n. (*pl.* -**men**) bandit armé m.

gunpowder /'gʌnpaʊdə(r)/ n. poudre à canon f.

gunshot /'gʌnʃɒt/ n. coup de feu m.

gurgle /'gɜːgl/ n. glouglou m. ● v.i. glouglouter.

guru /'guːruː/ n. (*pl.* -**us**) gourou m.

gush /gʌʃ/ v.i. ~ (**out**), jaillir. ● n. jaillissement m.

gust /gʌst/ n. rafale f.; (*of smoke*) bouffée f. ~**y** a. venteux.

gusto /'gʌstəʊ/ n. enthousiasme m.

gut /gʌt/ n. boyau m. ~**s**, boyaux m. pl., ventre m.; (*courage: fam.*) cran m. ● v.t. (*p.t.* **gutted**) (*fish*) vider; (*of fire*) dévaster.

gutter /'gʌtə(r)/ n. (*on roof*) gouttière f.; (*in street*) caniveau m.

guttural /'gʌtərəl/ a. guttural.

guy /gaɪ/ n. (*man: fam.*) type m.

guzzle /'gʌzl/ v.t./i. (*eat*) bâfrer; (*drink: Amer.*) boire d'un trait.

gym /dʒɪm/ n. (*fam.*) gymnase m.; (*fam.*) gym(nastique) f. ~-**slip** n. tunique f. ~**nasium** n. gymnase m.

gymnast /'dʒɪmnæst/ n. gymnaste m./f. ~**ics** /-'næstɪks/ n. pl. gymnastique f.

gynaecolog|y /gaɪnɪ'kɒlədʒɪ/ n. gynécologie f. ~**ist** n. gynécologue m./f.

gypsy /'dʒɪpsɪ/ n. bohémien(ne) m. (f.).

gyrate /dʒaɪ'reɪt/ v.i. tournoyer.

H

haberdashery /hæbə'dæʃərɪ/ n. mercerie f.

habit /'hæbɪt/ n. habitude f.; (*costume: relig.*) habit m. **be in/get into the** ~ **of**, avoir/prendre l'habitude de.

habit|able /'hæbɪtəbl/ a. habitable. ~**ation** /-'teɪʃn/ n. habitation f.

habitat /'hæbɪtæt/ n. habitat m.

habitual /hə'bɪtʃʊəl/ a. (*usual*) habituel; (*smoker, liar*) invétéré. ~**ly** adv. habituellement.

hack [1] /hæk/ n. (*old horse*) haridelle f.; (*writer*) nègre m., écrivailleu|r, -se m., f.

hack [2] /hæk/ v.t. hacher, tailler.

hackneyed /'hæknɪd/ a. rebattu.

had /hæd/ *see* have.

haddock /'hædək/ n. *invar.* églefin m. **smoked** ~, haddock m.

haemorrhage /'hemərɪdʒ/ n. hémorragie f.

haemorrhoids /'hemərɔɪdz/ n. pl. hémorroïdes f. pl.

hag /hæg/ n. (vieille) sorcière f.

haggard /'hægəd/ a. (*person*) qui a le visage défait; (*face, look*) défait, hagard.

haggle /'hægl/ v.i. marchander. ~ **over**, (*object*) marchander; (*price*) discuter.

Hague (The) /(ðə)'heɪg/ n. La Haye.

hail [1] /heɪl/ v.t. (*greet*) saluer; (*taxi*) héler. ● v.i. ~ **from**, venir de.

hail [2] /heɪl/ n. grêle f. ● v.i. grêler.

hailstone /'heɪlstəʊn/ n. grêlon m.

hair /heə(r)/ n. (*on head*) cheveux m. pl.; (*on body, of animal*) poils m. pl.; (*single strand on head*) cheveu m.; (*on body*) poil m. ~-**do** n. (*fam.*) coiffure f. ~-**drier** n. séchoir (à cheveux) m. ~-**grip** n. pince à cheveux f. ~-**raising** a. horrifiant. ~ **remover**, dépilatoire m. ~-**style** n. coiffure f.

hairbrush /'heəbrʌʃ/ n. brosse à cheveux f.

haircut /'heəkʌt/ n. coupe de cheveux f. **have a** ~, se faire couper les cheveux.

hairdresser /'heədresə(r)/ n. coiffeu|r, -se m., f.

hairpin /'heəpɪn/ n. épingle à cheveux f.

hairy /'heərɪ/ a. (-**ier**, -**iest**) poilu; (*terrifying: sl.*) horrifiant.

hake /heɪk/ n. *invar.* colin m.

hale /heɪl/ a. vigoureux.

half /hɑːf/ n. (*pl.* **halves**) moitié f., demi(e) m. (f.). ● a. demi. ● adv. à moitié. ~ **a dozen**, une demi-douzaine. ~ **an hour**, une demi-heure. **four and a** ~, quatre et demi(e). ~ **and half**, moitié moitié. **in** ~, en deux. ~-**back** n. (*sport*) demi m. ~-**caste** n. métis(se) m. (f.). ~-**hearted** a. tiède. **at** ~-**mast** adv. en berne. ~ **measure**, demi-mesure f. ~ **price**, moitié prix. ~-**term** n. congé de (de)mi-trimestre m. ~-**time** n. mi-temps f. ~-**way** adv. à mi-chemin. ~-**wit** n. imbécile m./f.

halibut /'hælɪbət/ n. *invar.* (*fish*) flétan m.

hall 365 **happen**

hall /hɔːl/ *n.* (*room*) salle *f.*; (*entrance*) vestibule *m.*; (*mansion*) manoir *m.*; (*corridor*) couloir *m.* ~ **of residence,** foyer d'étudiants *m.*

hallelujah /hælɪˈluːjə/ *int. & n.* = **alleluia.**

hallmark /ˈhɔːlmɑːk/ *n.* (*on gold etc.*) poinçon *m.*; (*fig.*) sceau *m.*

hallo /həˈləʊ/ *int. & n.* bonjour (*m.*). ~!, (*on telephone*) allô!; (*in surprise*) tiens!

hallow /ˈhæləʊ/ *v.t.* sanctifier.

Hallowe'en /hæləʊˈiːn/ *n.* la veille de la Toussaint.

hallucination /həluːsɪˈneɪʃn/ *n.* hallucination *f.*

halo /ˈheɪləʊ/ *n.* (*pl.* **-oes**) auréole *f.*

halt /hɔːlt/ *n.* halte *f.* ● *v.t./i.* (s')arrêter.

halve /hɑːv/ *v.t.* diviser en deux; (*time etc.*) réduire de moitié.

ham /hæm/ *n.* jambon *m.*; (*theatre: sl.*) cabotin(e) *m.* (*f.*). ~**-fisted** *a.* maladroit.

hamburger /ˈhæmbɜːɡə(r)/ *n.* hamburger *m.*

hamlet /ˈhæmlɪt/ *n.* hameau *m.*

hammer /ˈhæmə(r)/ *n.* marteau *m.* ● *v.t./i.* marteler, frapper; (*defeat*) battre à plate couture. ~ **out,** (*differences*) arranger; (*agreement*) arriver à.

hammock /ˈhæmək/ *n.* hamac *m.*

hamper[1] /ˈhæmpə(r)/ *n.* panier *m.*

hamper[2] /ˈhæmpə(r)/ *v.t.* gêner.

hamster /ˈhæmstə(r)/ *n.* hamster *m.*

hand /hænd/ *n.* main *f.*; (*of clock*) aiguille *f.*; (*writing*) écriture *f.*; (*worker*) ouvr|ier, -ière *m., f.*; (*cards*) jeu *m.* ● *v.t.* donner. **at** ~, proche. ~**-baggage** *n.* bagages à main *m. pl.* **give s.o. a** ~, donner un coup de main à qn. ~ **in** *or* **over,** remettre. ~ **out,** distribuer. ~**-out** *n.* prospectus *m.*; (*money*) aumône *f.* **on** ~, disponible. **on one's** ~**s,** (*fig.*) sur les bras. **on the one** ~ . . . **on the other** ~, d'une part . . . d'autre part. **to** ~, à portée de la main.

handbag /ˈhændbæɡ/ *n.* sac à main *m.*

handbook /ˈhændbʊk/ *n.* manuel *m.*

handbrake /ˈhændbreɪk/ *n.* frein à main *m.*

handcuffs /ˈhændkʌfs/ *n. pl.* menottes *f. pl.*

handful /ˈhændfʊl/ *n.* poignée *f.*; **he's a** ~!, c'est du boulot!

handicap /ˈhændɪkæp/ *n.* handicap *m.* ● *v.t.* (*p.t.* **handicapped**) handicaper.

handicraft /ˈhændɪkrɑːft/ *n.* travaux manuels *m. pl.*, artisanat *m.*

handiwork /ˈhændɪwɜːk/ *n.* ouvrage *m.*

handkerchief /ˈhæŋkətʃɪf/ *n.* (*pl.* **-fs**) mouchoir *m.*

handle /ˈhændl/ *n.* (*of door etc.*) poignée *f.*; (*of implement*) manche *m.*; (*of cup etc.*) anse *f.*; (*of pan etc.*) queue *f.*; (*for turning*) manivelle *f.* ● *v.t.* manier; (*deal with*) s'occuper de; (*touch*) toucher à.

handlebar /ˈhændlbɑː(r)/ *n.* guidon *m.*

handshake /ˈhændʃeɪk/ *n.* poignée de main *f.*

handsome /ˈhænsəm/ *a.* (*goodlooking*) beau; (*generous*) généreux; (*large*) considérable.

handwriting /ˈhændraɪtɪŋ/ *n.* écriture *f.*

handy /ˈhændɪ/ *a.* (**-ier, -iest**) (*useful*) commode, utile; (*person*) adroit; (*near*) accessible.

handyman /ˈhændɪmæn/ *n.* (*pl.* **-men**) bricoleur *m.*; (*servant*) homme à tout faire *m.*

hang /hæŋ/ *v.t.* (*p.t.* **hung**) suspendre, accrocher; (*p.t.* **hanged**) (*criminal*) pendre. ● *v.i.* pendre. ● *n.* **get the** ~ **of doing,** trouver le truc pour faire. ~ **about,** traîner. ~**-gliding** *n.* vol libre *m.* ~ **on,** (*hold out*) tenir bon; (*wait: sl.*) attendre. ~ **out** *v.i.* pendre; (*live: sl.*) crécher; (*spend time: sl.*) passer son temps; *v.t.* (*washing*) étendre. ~ **up,** (*telephone*) raccrocher. ~**-up** *n.* (*sl.*) complexe *m.*

hangar /ˈhæŋə(r)/ *n.* hangar *m.*

hanger /ˈhæŋə(r)/ *n.* (*for clothes*) cintre *m.* ~**-on** *n.* parasite *m.*

hangover /ˈhæŋəʊvə(r)/ *n.* (*after drinking*) gueule de bois *f.*

hanker /ˈhæŋkə(r)/ *v.i.* ~ **after,** avoir envie de. ~**ing** *n.* envie *f.*

hanky-panky /ˈhæŋkɪpæŋkɪ/ *n.* (*trickery: sl.*) manigances *f. pl.*

haphazard /hæpˈhæzəd/ *a.*, ~**ly** *adv.* au petit bonheur, au hasard.

hapless /ˈhæplɪs/ *a.* infortuné.

happen /ˈhæpən/ *v.i.* arriver, se passer. **it so** ~**s that,** il se trouve que. **he** ~**s to know that,** il se trouve qu'il sait que. ~**ing** *n.* événement *m.*

happ|y /'hæpɪ/ a. (-ier, -iest) heureux. **I'm not ~y about the idea,** je n'aime pas trop l'idée. **~y with sth.,** satisfait de qch. **~y medium** or **mean,** juste milieu m. **~ily** adv. joyeusement; (fortunately) heureusement. **~iness** n. bonheur m. **~y-go-lucky** a. insouciant.

harass /'hærəs/ v.t. harceler. **~ment** n. harcèlement m.

harbour, (Amer.) **harbor** /'ha:bə(r)/ n. port m. ● v.t. (shelter) héberger.

hard /ha:d/ a. (-er, -est) dur; (difficult) difficile, dur. ● adv. dur; (think) sérieusement; (pull) fort. **~ and fast,** concret. **~-boiled egg,** œuf dur m. **~ by,** tout près. **~ disk,** disque dur m. **~ done by,** mal traité. **~-headed** a. réaliste. **~ of hearing,** dur d'oreille. **the ~ of hearing,** les malentendants m. pl. **~-line** a. pur et dur. **~ shoulder,** accotement stabilisé m. **~ up,** (fam.) fauché. **~-wearing** a. solide. **~-working** a. travailleur. **~ness** n. dureté f.

hardboard /'ha:dbɔ:d/ n. Isorel m. (P.).

harden /'ha:dn/ v.t./i. durcir.

hardly /'ha:dlɪ/ adv. à peine. **~ ever,** presque jamais.

hardship /'ha:dʃɪp/ n. **~(s),** épreuves f. pl., souffrance f.

hardware /'ha:dweə(r)/ n. (metal goods) quincaillerie f.; (machinery, of computer) matériel m.

hardy /'ha:dɪ/ a. (-ier, iest) résistant.

hare /heə(r)/ n. lièvre m. **~ around,** courir partout. **~-brained** a. écervelé.

hark /ha:k/ v.i. écouter. **~ back to,** revenir sur.

harm /ha:m/ n. (hurt) mal m.; (wrong) tort m. ● v.t. (hurt) faire du mal à; (wrong) faire du tort à; (object) endommager. **there is no harm in,** il n'y a pas de mal à. **~ful** a. nuisible. **~less** a. inoffensif.

harmonica /ha:'mɒnɪkə/ n. harmonica m.

harmon|y /'ha:mənɪ/ n. harmonie f. **~ious** /-'məʊnɪəs/ a. harmonieux. **~ize** v.t./i. (s')harmoniser.

harness /'ha:nɪs/ n. harnais m. ● v.t. (horse) harnacher; (control) maîtriser; (use) exploiter.

harp /ha:p/ n. harpe f. ● v.i. **~ on (about),** rabâcher. **~ist** n. harpiste m./f.

harpoon /ha:'pu:n/ n. harpon m.

harpsichord /'ha:psɪkɔ:d/ n. clavecin m.

harrowing /'hærəʊɪŋ/ a. déchirant, qui déchire le cœur.

harsh /ha:ʃ/ a. (-er, -est) dur, rude; (taste) âpre; (sound) rude, âpre. **~ly** adv. durement. **~ness** n. dureté f.

harvest /'ha:vɪst/ n. moisson f., récolte f. **the wine ~,** les vendanges f. pl. ● v.t. moissonner, récolter. **~er** n. moissonneuse f.

has /hæz/ see have.

hash /hæʃ/ n. (culin.) hachis m.; (fig.) gâchis m. **make a ~ of,** (bungle: sl.) saboter.

hashish /'hæʃɪʃ/ n. ha(s)chisch m.

hassle /'hæsl/ n. (fam.) difficulté(s) f. (pl.); (bother, effort: fam.) mal m., peine f.; (quarrel: fam.) chamaillerie f. ● v.t. (harass: fam.) harceler.

haste /heɪst/ n. hâte f. **in ~,** à la hâte. **make ~,** se hâter.

hasten /'heɪsn/ v.t./i. (se) hâter.

hast|y /'heɪstɪ/ a. (-ier, -iest) précipité. **~ily** adv. à la hâte.

hat /hæt/ n. chapeau m. **a ~ trick,** trois succès consécutifs.

hatch[1] /hætʃ/ n. (for food) passeplat m.; (naut.) écoutille f.

hatch[2] /hætʃ/ v.t./i. (faire) éclore.

hatchback /'hætʃbæk/ n. voiture avec hayon arrière f.

hatchet /'hætʃɪt/ n. hachette f.

hate /heɪt/ n. haine f. ● v.t. haïr. **~ful** a. haïssable.

hatred /'heɪtrɪd/ n. haine f.

haughty /'hɔ:tɪ/ a. (-ier, -iest) hautain.

haul /hɔ:l/ v.t. traîner, tirer. ● n. (of thieves) butin m.; (catch) prise f.; (journey) voyage m. **~age** n. camionnage m. **~ier** n. camionneur m.

haunch /hɔ:ntʃ/ n. **on one's ~es,** accroupi.

haunt /hɔ:nt/ v.t. hanter. ● n. endroit favori m.

have /hæv/ v.t. (3 sing. present tense **has;** p.t. **had**) avoir; (meal, bath, etc.) prendre; (walk, dream, etc.) faire. ● v. aux. avoir; (with aller, partir, etc. & pronominal verbs) être. **~ it out with,** s'expliquer avec. **~ just done,** venir de faire. **~ sth. done,** faire faire qch. **~ to do,** devoir faire. **the ~s and have-nots,** les riches et les pauvres m. pl.

haven /'heɪvn/ n. havre m., abri m.

haversack /'hævəsæk/ n. musette f.

havoc /'hævək/ n. ravages m. pl.

haw /hɔː/ see hum.

hawk[1] /hɔːk/ n. faucon m.

hawk[2] /hɔːk/ v.t. colporter. **~er** n. colporteu|r, -se m., f.

hawthorn /'hɔːθɔːn/ n. aubépine f.

hay /heɪ/ n. foin m. **~ fever,** rhume des foins m.

haystack /'heɪstæk/ n. meule de foin f.

haywire /'heɪwaɪə(r)/ a. **go ~,** (plans) se désorganiser; (machine) se détraquer.

hazard /'hæzəd/ n. risque m. ● v.t. risquer, hasarder. **~ warning lights,** feux de détresse m. pl. **~ous** a. hasardeux, risqué.

haze /heɪz/ n. brume f.

hazel /'heɪzl/ n. (bush) noisetier m. **~-nut** n. noisette f.

hazy /'heɪzɪ/ a. (-ier, -iest) (misty) brumeux; (fig.) flou, vague.

he /hiː/ pron. il; (emphatic) lui. ● n. mâle m.

head /hed/ n. tête f.; (leader) chef m.; (of beer) mousse f. ● a. principal. ● v.t. être à la tête de. ● v.i. **~ for,** se diriger vers. **~-dress** n. coiffure f.; (lady's) coiffe f. **~-on** a. & adv. de plein fouet. **~ first,** la tête la première. **~s or tails?,** pile ou face? **~ office,** siège m. **~ rest,** appui-tête m. **~ the ball,** faire une tête. **~ waiter,** maître d'hôtel m. **~er** n. (football) tête f.

headache /'hedeɪk/ n. mal de tête m.

heading /'hedɪŋ/ n. titre m.; (subject category) rubrique f.

headlamp /'hedlæmp/ n. phare m.

headland /'hedlənd/ n. cap m.

headlight /'hedlaɪt/ n. phare m.

headline /'hedlaɪn/ n. titre m.

headlong /'hedlɒŋ/ adv. (in a rush) à toute allure.

head|master /hed'mɑːstə(r)/ n. (of school) directeur m. **~mistress** n. directrice f.

headphone /'hedfəʊn/ n. écouteur m. **~s,** casque (à écouteurs) m.

headquarters /'hedkwɔːtəz/ n. pl. siège m., bureau central m.; (mil.) quartier général m.

headstrong /'hedstrɒŋ/ a. têtu.

headway /'hedweɪ/ n. progrès m. (pl.) **make ~,** faire des progrès.

heady /'hedɪ/ a. (-ier, -iest) (wine) capiteux; (exciting) grisant.

heal /hiːl/ v.t./i. guérir.

health /helθ/ n. santé f. **~ centre,** dispensaire m. **~ foods,** aliments diététiques m. pl. **~ insurance,** assurance médicale f. **~y** a. sain; (person) en bonne santé.

heap /hiːp/ n. tas m. ● v.t. entasser. **~s of,** (fam.) des tas de.

hear /hɪə(r)/ v.t./i. (p.t. **heard** /hɜːd/) entendre. **hear, hear!,** bravo! **~ from,** recevoir des nouvelles de. **~ of or about,** entendre parler de. **not ~ of,** (refuse to allow) ne pas entendre parler de. **~ing** n. ouïe f.; (of witness) audition f.; (of case) audience f. **~ing-aid** n. appareil acoustique m.

hearsay /'hɪəseɪ/ n. ouï-dire m. invar. **from ~,** par ouï-dire.

hearse /hɜːs/ n. corbillard m.

heart /hɑːt/ n. cœur m. **~s,** (cards) cœur m. **at ~,** au fond. **by ~,** par cœur. **~ attack,** crise cardiaque f. **~-break** n. chagrin m. **~-breaking** a. navrant. **be ~-broken,** avoir le cœur brisé. **~-to-heart** a. à cœur ouvert. **lose ~,** perdre courage.

heartache /'hɑːteɪk/ n. chagrin m.

heartburn /'hɑːtbɜːn/ n. brûlures d'estomac f. pl.

hearten /'hɑːtn/ v.t. encourager.

heartfelt /'hɑːtfelt/ a. sincère.

hearth /hɑːθ/ n. foyer m.

heartless /'hɑːtlɪs/ a. cruel.

heart|y /'hɑːtɪ/ a. (-ier, -iest) (sincere) chaleureux; (meal) gros. **~ily** adv. (eat) avec appétit.

heat /hiːt/ n. chaleur f.; (excitement: fig.) feu m.; (contest) éliminatoire f. ● v.t./i. chauffer. **~ stroke,** insolation f. **~ up,** (food) réchauffer. **~ wave,** vague de chaleur f. **~er** n. radiateur m. **~ing** n. chauffage m.

heated /'hiːtɪd/ a. (fig.) passionné.

heath /hiːθ/ n. (area) lande f.

heathen /'hiːðn/ n. païen(ne) m. (f.).

heather /'heðə(r)/ n. bruyère f.

heave /hiːv/ v.t./i. (lift) (se) soulever; (a sigh) pousser; (throw: fam.) lancer; (retch) avoir des nausées.

heaven /'hevn/ n. ciel m. **~ly** a. céleste; (pleasing: fam.) divin.

heav|y /'hevɪ/ a. (-ier, -iest) lourd; (cold, work, etc.) gros; (traffic) dense. **~y goods vehicle,** poids lourd m. **~y-handed** a. maladroit. **~ily** adv. lourdement; (smoke, drink) beaucoup.

heavyweight /'hevɪweɪt/ n. poids lourd m.

Hebrew /'hi:bru:/ *a.* hébreu (*m. only*), hébraïque. ● *n.* (*lang.*) hébreu *m.*

heckle /'hekl/ *v.t.* (*speaker*) interrompre, interpeller.

hectic /'hektɪk/ *a.* très bousculé, trépidant, agité.

hedge /hedʒ/ *n.* haie *f.* ● *v.t.* entourer. ● *v.i.* (*in answering*) répondre évasivement. ~ **one's bets,** protéger ses arrières.

hedgehog /'hedʒhɒg/ *n.* hérisson *m.*

heed /hi:d/ *v.t.* faire attention à. ● *n.* **pay ~ to,** faire attention à. **~less** *a.* **~less of,** inattentif à.

heel /hi:l/ *n.* talon *m.*; (*man: sl.*) salaud *m.* **down at ~,** (*Amer.*) **down at the ~s,** miteux.

hefty /'heftɪ/ *a.* (**-ier, -iest**) gros, lourd.

heifer /'hefə(r)/ *n.* génisse *f.*

height /haɪt/ *n.* hauteur *f.*; (*of person*) taille *f.*; (*of plane, mountain*) altitude *f.*; (*of fame, glory*) apogée *m.*; (*of joy, folly, pain*) comble *m.*

heighten /'haɪtn/ *v.t.* (*raise*) rehausser; (*fig.*) augmenter.

heinous /'heɪnəs/ *a.* atroce.

heir /eə(r)/ *n.* héritier *m.* **~ess** *n.* héritière *f.*

heirloom /'eəlu:m/ *n.* bijou (meuble, tableau, *etc.*) de famille *m.*

held /held/ *see* hold[1].

helicopter /'helɪkɒptə(r)/ *n.* hélicoptère *m.*

heliport /'helɪpɔ:t/ *n.* héliport *m.*

hell /hel/ *n.* enfer *m.* **~-bent** *a.* acharné (**on,** à). **~ish** *a.* infernal.

hello /hə'ləʊ/ *int. & n.* = **hallo.**

helm /helm/ *n.* (*of ship*) barre *f.*

helmet /'helmɪt/ *n.* casque *m.*

help /help/ *v.t./i.* aider. ● *n.* aide *f.*; (*employees*) personnel *m.*; (*charwoman*) femme de ménage *f.* **~ o.s. to,** se servir de. **he cannot ~ laughing,** il ne peut pas s'empêcher de rire. **~er** *n.* aide *m./f.* **~ful** *a.* utile; (*person*) serviable. **~less** *a.* impuissant.

helping /'helpɪŋ/ *n.* portion *f.*

helter-skelter /heltə'skeltə(r)/ *n.* toboggan *m.* ● *adv.* pêle-mêle.

hem /hem/ *n.* ourlet *m.* ● *v.t.* (*p.t.* **hemmed**) ourler. **~ in,** enfermer.

hemisphere /'hemɪsfɪə(r)/ *n.* hémisphère *m.*

hemorrhage /'hemərɪdʒ/ *n.* (*Amer.*) = **haemorrhage.**

hemorrhoids /'hemərɔɪdz/ *n. pl.* (*Amer.*) = **haemorrhoids.**

hen /hen/ *n.* poule *f.*

hence /hens/ *adv.* (*for this reason*) d'où; (*from now*) d'ici. **~forth** *adv.* désormais.

henchman /'hentʃmən/ *n.* (*pl.* **-men**) acolyte *m.*, homme de main *m.*

henpecked /'henpekt/ *a.* dominé *or* harcelé par sa femme.

hepatitis /hepə'taɪtɪs/ *n.* hépatite *f.*

her /hɜ:(r)/ *pron.* la, l'*; (*after prep.*) elle. **(to) ~,** lui. **I know ~,** je la connais. ● *a.* son, sa, *pl.* ses.

herald /'herəld/ *v.t.* annoncer.

herb /hɜ:b, *Amer.* ɜ:b/ *n.* herbe *f.* **~s,** (*culin.*) fines herbes *f. pl.*

herd /hɜ:d/ *n.* troupeau *m.* ● *v.t./i.* **~ together,** (s')entasser.

here /hɪə(r)/ *adv.* ici. **~!,** (*take this*) tenez! **~ is, ~ are,** voici. **I'm ~,** je suis là. **~abouts** *adv.* par ici.

hereafter /hɪər'ɑ:ftə(r)/ *adv.* après; (*in book*) ci-après.

hereby /hɪə'baɪ/ *adv.* par le présent acte; (*in letter*) par la présente.

hereditary /hə'redɪtərɪ/ *a.* héréditaire.

heredity /hə'redɪtɪ/ *n.* hérédité *f.*

here|sy /'herəsɪ/ *n.* hérésie *f.* **~tic** *n.* hérétique *m./f.*

herewith /hɪə'wɪð/ *adv.* (*comm.*) avec ceci, ci-joint.

heritage /'herɪtɪdʒ/ *n.* patrimoine *m.*, héritage *m.*

hermit /'hɜ:mɪt/ *n.* ermite *m.*

hernia /'hɜ:nɪə/ *n.* hernie *f.*

hero /'hɪərəʊ/ *n.* (*pl.* **-oes**) héros *m.* **~ine** /'herəʊɪn/ *n.* héroïne *f.* **~ism** /'herəʊɪzəm/ *n.* héroïsme *m.*

heroic /hɪ'rəʊɪk/ *a.* héroïque.

heroin /'herəʊɪn/ *n.* héroïne *f.*

heron /'herən/ *n.* héron *m.*

herpes /'hɜ:pi:z/ *n.* herpès *m.*

herring /'herɪŋ/ *n.* hareng *m.*

hers /hɜ:z/ *poss. pron.* le sien, la sienne, les sien(ne)s. **it is ~,** c'est à elle *or* le sien.

herself /hɜ:'self/ *pron.* elle-même; (*reflexive*) se; (*after prep.*) elle.

hesitant /'hezɪtənt/ *a.* hésitant.

hesitat|e /'hezɪteɪt/ *v.i.* hésiter. **~ion** /-'teɪʃn/ *n.* hésitation *f.*

het /het/ *a.* **~ up,** (*sl.*) énervé.

heterosexual /hetərəʊ'seksjʊəl/ *a. & n.* hétérosexuel(le) (*m.* (*f.*)).

hexagon /'heksəgən/ *n.* hexagone *m.* **~al** /-'ægənl/ *a.* hexagonal.

hey /heɪ/ *int.* dites donc.

heyday /'heɪdeɪ/ n. apogée m.

HGV abbr. see heavy goods vehicle.

hi /haɪ/ int. (greeting: Amer.) salut.

hibernat|e /'haɪbəneɪt/ v.i. hiberner. ~ion /-'neɪʃn/ n. hibernation f.

hiccup /'hɪkʌp/ n. hoquet m. ● v.i. hoqueter. **(the) ~s**, le hoquet.

hide[1] /haɪd/ v.t. (p.t. hid, p.p. hidden) cacher (from, à). ● v.i. se cacher (from, de). **go into hiding**, se cacher. ~-out n. (fam.) cachette f.

hide[2] /haɪd/ n. (skin) peau f.

hideous /'hɪdɪəs/ a. (dreadful) atroce; (ugly) hideux.

hiding /'haɪdɪŋ/ n. (thrashing: fam.) correction f.

hierarchy /'haɪərɑːkɪ/ n. hiérarchie f.

hi-† /haɪ'faɪ/ a. & n. hi-fi a. & f. invar.; (machine) chaîne hi-fi f.

high /haɪ/ a. (-er, -est) haut; (price, number) élevé; (priest, speed) grand; (voice) aigu. ● n. **a (new) ~**, (recorded level) un record. ● adv. haut. **~ chair**, chaise haute f. **~-handed** a. autoritaire. **~-jump**, saut en hauteur m. **~-level** a. de haut niveau. **~-rise building**, tour f. **~ road**, grand-route f. **~ school**, lycée m. **in the ~ season**, en pleine saison. **~- speed** a. ultra-rapide. **~ spot**, (fam.) point culminant m. **~ street**, grand-rue f. **~-strung** a. (Amer.) nerveux. **~ tea**, goûter-dîner m. **~er education**, enseignement supérieur m.

highbrow /'haɪbraʊ/ a. & n. intellectuel(le) (m. (f.)).

highlight /'haɪlaɪt/ n. (vivid moment) moment fort m. **~s**, (in hair) balayage m. **recorded ~s**, extraits enregistrés m. pl. ● v.t. (emphasize) souligner.

highly /'haɪlɪ/ adv. extrêmement; (paid) très bien. **~-strung** a. nerveux. **speak/think ~ of**, dire/penser du bien de.

Highness /'haɪnɪs/ n. Altesse f.

highway /'haɪweɪ/ n. route nationale f. **~ code**, code de la route m.

hijack /'haɪdʒæk/ v.t. détourner. ● n. détournement m. **~er** n. pirate (de l'air) m.

hike /haɪk/ n. randonnée f. ● v.i. faire de la randonnée. **price ~**, hausse de prix f. **~r** /-ə(r)/ n. randonneu|r, -se m., f.

hilarious /hɪ'leərɪəs/ a. (funny) désopilant.

hill /hɪl/ n. colline f.; (slope) côte f. **~y** a. accidenté.

hillside /'hɪlsaɪd/ n. coteau m.

hilt /hɪlt/ n. (of sword) garde f. **to the ~**, tout à fait, au maximum.

him /hɪm/ pron. le, l'*; (after prep.) lui. **(to) ~**, lui. **I know ~**, je le connais.

himself /hɪm'self/ pron. lui-même; (reflexive) se; (after prep.) lui.

hind /haɪnd/ a. de derrière.

hind|er /'hɪndə(r)/ v.t. (hamper) gêner; (prevent) empêcher. **~rance** n. obstacle m., gêne f.

hindsight /'haɪndsaɪt/ n. **with ~**, rétrospectivement.

Hindu /hɪn'duː/ a. & n. hindou(e) (m. (f.)). **~ism** /'hɪnduːɪzəm/ n. hindouisme m.

hinge /hɪndʒ/ n. charnière f. ● v.i. **~ on**, (depend on) dépendre de.

hint /hɪnt/ n. allusion f.; (advice) conseil m. ● v.t. laisser entendre. ● v.i. **~ at**, faire allusion à.

hip /hɪp/ n. hanche f.

hippie /'hɪpɪ/ n. hippie m./f.

hippopotamus /hɪpə'pɒtəməs/ n. (pl. -muses) hippopotame m.

hire /'haɪə(r)/ v.t. (thing) louer; (person) engager. ● n. location f. **~-car** n. voiture de location f. **~-purchase** n. achat à crédit m., vente à crédit f.

his /hɪz/ a. son, sa, pl. ses. ● poss. pron. le sien, la sienne, les sien(ne)s. **it is ~**, c'est à lui or le sien.

hiss /hɪs/ n. sifflement m. ● v.t./i. siffler.

historian /hɪ'stɔːrɪən/ n. historien(ne) m. (f.).

histor|y /'hɪstərɪ/ n. histoire f. **make ~y**, entrer dans l'histoire. **~ic(al)** /hɪ'stɒrɪk(l)/ a. historique.

hit /hɪt/ v.t. (p.t. hit, pres. p. hitting) frapper; (knock against, collide with) heurter; (find) trouver; (affect, reach) toucher. ● v.i. **~ on**, (find) tomber sur. ● n. (blow) coup m.; (fig.) succès m.; (song) tube m. **~ it off**, s'entendre bien (with, avec). **~-or-miss** a. fait au petit bonheur.

hitch /hɪtʃ/ v.t. (fasten) accrocher. ● n. (snag) anicroche f. **~ a lift**, **~-hike** v.i. faire de l'auto-stop. **~-hiker** n. auto-stoppeu|r, -se m., f. **~ up**, (pull up) remonter.

hi-tech /haɪ'tek/ a. & n. high-tech (m.) invar.

hitherto /hɪðə'tuː/ adv. jusqu'ici.

HIV *abbr.* HIV. **~-positive** *a.* séropositif.

hive /haɪv/ *n.* ruche *f.* ● *v.t.* **~ off,** séparer; (*industry*) vendre.

hoard /hɔːd/ *v.t.* amasser. ● *n.* réserve(s) *f.* (*pl.*); (*of money*) magot *m.*, trésor *m.*

hoarding /ˈhɔːdɪŋ/ *n.* panneau d'affichage *m.*

hoar-frost /ˈhɔːfrɒst/ *n.* givre *m.*

hoarse /hɔːs/ *a.* (**-er, -est**) enroué. **~ness** *n.* enrouement *m.*

hoax /həʊks/ *n.* canular *m.* ● *v.t.* faire un canular à.

hob /hɒb/ *n.* plaque chauffante *f.*

hobble /ˈhɒbl/ *v.i.* clopiner.

hobby /ˈhɒbɪ/ *n.* passe-temps *m. invar.* **~-horse** *n.* (*fig.*) dada *m.*

hob-nob /ˈhɒbnɒb/ *v.i.* (*p.t.* **hobnobbed**) **~ with,** frayer avec.

hock[1] /hɒk/ *n.* vin du Rhin *m.*

hock[2] /hɒk/ *v.t.* (*pawn: sl.*) mettre au clou.

hockey /ˈhɒkɪ/ *n.* hockey *m.*

hoe /həʊ/ *n.* binette *f.* ● *v.t.* (*pres. p.* **hoeing**) biner.

hog /hɒg/ *n.* cochon *m.* ● *v.t.* (*p.t.* **hogged**) (*fam.*) accaparer.

hoist /hɔɪst/ *v.t.* hisser. ● *n.* palan *m.*

hold[1] /həʊld/ *v.t.* (*p.t.* **held**) tenir; (*contain*) contenir; (*interest, breath, etc.*) retenir; (*possess*) avoir; (*believe*) maintenir. ● *v.i.* (*of rope, weather, etc.*) tenir. ● *n.* prise *f.* **get ~ of,** saisir; (*fig.*) trouver. **on ~,** en suspens. **~ back,** (*contain*) retenir; (*hide*) cacher. **~ down,** (*job*) garder; (*in struggle*) retenir. **~ on,** (*stand firm*) tenir bon; (*wait*) attendre. **~ on to,** (*keep*) garder; (*cling to*) se cramponner à. **~ one's tongue,** se taire. **~ out** *v.t.* (*offer*) offrir; *v.i.* (*resist*) tenir le coup. **~ (the line), please,** ne quittez pas. **~ up,** (*support*) soutenir; (*delay*) retarder; (*rob*) attaquer. **~-up** *n.* retard *m.*; (*of traffic*) bouchon *m.*; (*robbery*) hold-up *m. invar.* **not ~ with,** désapprouver. **~er** *n.* détenteur, -trice *m., f.*; (*of post*) titulaire *m./f.*; (*for object*) support *m.*

hold[2] /həʊld/ *n.* (*of ship*) cale *f.*

holdall /ˈhəʊldɔːl/ *n.* (*bag*) fourretout *m. invar.*

holding /ˈhəʊldɪŋ/ *n.* (*possession, land*) possession *f.* **~ company,** holding *m.*

hole /həʊl/ *n.* trou *m.* ● *v.t.* trouer.

holiday /ˈhɒlədeɪ/ *n.* vacances *f. pl.*; (*public*) jour férié *m.*; (*day off*) congé *m.* ● *v.i.* passer ses vacances. ● *a.* de vacances. **~-maker** *n.* vacancier, -ière *m., f.*

holiness /ˈhəʊlɪnɪs/ *n.* sainteté *f.*

holistic /həʊˈlɪstɪk/ *a.* holistique.

Holland /ˈhɒlənd/ *n.* Hollande *f.*

hollow /ˈhɒləʊ/ *a.* creux; (*fig.*) faux. ● *n.* creux *m.* ● *v.t.* creuser.

holly /ˈhɒlɪ/ *n.* houx *m.*

holster /ˈhəʊlstə(r)/ *n.* étui de revolver *m.*

holy /ˈhəʊlɪ/ *a.* (**-ier, -iest**) saint, sacré; (*water*) bénit. **H~ Ghost, H~ Spirit,** Saint-Esprit *m.*

homage /ˈhɒmɪdʒ/ *n.* hommage *m.*

home /həʊm/ *n.* maison *f.*, foyer *m.*; (*institution*) maison *f.*; (*for soldiers, workers*) foyer *m.*; (*country*) pays natal *m.* ● *a.* de la maison, du foyer; (*of family*) de famille; (*pol.*) national, intérieur; (*match, visit*) à domicile. ● *adv.* (**at**) **~,** à la maison, chez soi. **come** *or* **go ~,** rentrer; (*from abroad*) rentrer dans son pays. **feel at ~ with,** être à l'aise avec. **H~ Counties,** région autour de Londres *f.* **~-made** *a.* (*food*) fait maison; (*clothes*) fait à la maison. **H~ Office,** ministère de l'Intérieur *m.* **H~ Secretary,** ministre de l'Intérieur *m.* **~ town,** ville natale *f.* **~ truth,** vérité bien sentie *f.* **~less** *a.* sans abri.

homeland /ˈhəʊmlænd/ *n.* patrie *f.*

homely /ˈhəʊmlɪ/ *a.* (**-ier, -iest**) simple; (*person: Amer.*) assez laid.

homesick /ˈhəʊmsɪk/ *a.* **be ~,** avoir le mal du pays.

homeward /ˈhəʊmwəd/ *a.* (*journey*) de retour.

homework /ˈhəʊmwɜːk/ *n.* devoirs *m. pl.*

homicide /ˈhɒmɪsaɪd/ *n.* homicide *m.*

homœopath|y /ˈhəʊmɪˈɒpəθɪ/ *n.* homéopathie *f.* **~ic** *a.* homéopathique.

homogeneous /hɒməˈdʒiːnɪəs/ *a.* homogène.

homosexual /hɒməˈseksjʊəl/ *a. & n.* homosexuel(le) (*m.* (*f.*)).

honest /ˈɒnɪst/ *a.* honnête; (*frank*) franc. **~ly** *adv.* honnêtement; franchement. **~y** *n.* honnêteté *f.*

honey /ˈhʌnɪ/ *n.* miel *m.*; (*person: fam.*) chéri(e) *m.* (*f.*).

honeycomb /ˈhʌnɪkəʊm/ *n.* rayon de miel *m.*

honeymoon /'hʌnɪmuːn/ *n.* lune de miel *f.*

honk /hɒŋk/ *v.i.* klaxonner.

honorary /'ɒnərərɪ/ *a.* (*person*) honoraire; (*duties*) honorifique.

honour, (*Amer.*) **honor** /'ɒnə(r)/ *n.* honneur *m.* ● *v.t.* honorer. **~able** *a.* honorable.

hood /hʊd/ *n.* capuchon *m.*; (*car roof*) capote *f.*; (*car engine cover*: *Amer.*) capot *m.*

hoodlum /'huːdləm/ *n.* voyou *m.*

hoodwink /'hʊdwɪŋk/ *v.t.* tromper.

hoof /huːf/ *n.* (*pl.* **-fs**) sabot *m.*

hook /hʊk/ *n.* crochet *m.*; (*on garment*) agrafe *f.*; (*for fishing*) hameçon *m.* ● *v.t./i.* (s')accrocher; (*garment*) (s')agrafer. **off the ~,** tiré d'affaire; (*phone*) décroché.

hooked /hʊkt/ *a.* crochu. **~ on,** (*sl.*) adonné à.

hooker /'hʊkə(r)/ *n.* (*rugby*) talonneur *m.*; (*Amer., sl.*) prostituée *f.*

hookey /'hʊkɪ/ *n.* **play ~,** (*Amer., sl.*) faire l'école buissonnière.

hooligan /'huːlɪgən/ *n.* houligan *m.*

hoop /huːp/ *n.* (*toy etc.*) cerceau *m.*

hooray /hʊ'reɪ/ *int.* & *n.* = **hurrah.**

hoot /huːt/ *n.* (h)ululement *m.*; coup de klaxon *m.*; huée *f.* ● *v.i.* (*owl*) (h)ululer; (*of car*) klaxonner; (*jeer*) huer. **~er** *n.* klaxon *m.* (P.); (*of factory*) sirène *f.*

Hoover /'huːvə(r)/ *n.* (P.) aspirateur *m.* ● *v.t.* passer à l'aspirateur.

hop[1] /hɒp/ *v.i.* (*p.t.* **hopped**) sauter (à cloche-pied). ● *n.* saut *m.*; (*flight*) étape *f.* **~ in,** (*fam.*) monter. **~ it,** (*sl.*) décamper. **~ out,** (*fam.*) descendre.

hop[2] /hɒp/ *n.* **~(s),** houblon *m.*

hope /həʊp/ *n.* espoir *m.* ● *v.t./i.* espérer. **~ for,** espérer (avoir). **I ~ so,** je l'espère. **~ful** *a.* encourageant. **be ~ful (that),** avoir bon espoir (que). **~fully** *adv.* avec espoir; (*it is hoped*) on l'espère. **~less** *a.* sans espoir; (*useless*: *fig.*) nul. **~lessly** *adv.* sans espoir *m.*

hopscotch /'hɒpskɒtʃ/ *n.* marelle *f.*

horde /hɔːd/ *n.* horde *f.*, foule *f.*

horizon /hə'raɪzn/ *n.* horizon *m.*

horizontal /hɒrɪ'zɒntl/ *a.* horizontal.

hormone /'hɔːməʊn/ *n.* hormone *f.*

horn /hɔːn/ *n.* corne *f.*; (*of car*) klaxon *m.* (P.); (*mus.*) cor *m.* ● *v.i.* **~ in,** (*sl.*) interrompre. **~y** *a.* (*hands*) calleux.

hornet /'hɔːnɪt/ *n.* frelon *m.*

horoscope /'hɒrəskəʊp/ *n.* horoscope *m.*

horrible /'hɒrəbl/ *a.* horrible.

horrid /'hɒrɪd/ *a.* horrible.

horrific /hə'rɪfɪk/ *a.* horrifiant.

horr|or /'hɒrə(r)/ *n.* horreur *f.* ● *a.* (*film etc.*) d'épouvante. **~ify** *v.t.* horrifier.

hors-d'œuvre /ɔː'dɜːvrə/ *n.* hors-d'œuvre *m. invar.*

horse /hɔːs/ *n.* cheval *m.* **~-chestnut** *n.* marron (d'Inde) *m.* **~-race** *n.* course de chevaux *f.* **~-radish** *n.* raifort *m.* **~ sense,** (*fam.*) bon sens *m.*

horseback /'hɔːsbæk/ *n.* **on ~,** à cheval.

horseman /'hɔːsmən/ *n.* (*pl.* **-men**) cavalier *m.*

horsepower /'hɔːspaʊə(r)/ *n.* (*unit*) cheval (vapeur) *m.*

horseshoe /'hɔːsʃuː/ *n.* fer à cheval *m.*

horsy /'hɔːsɪ/ *a.* (*face etc.*) chevalin.

horticultur|e /'hɔːtɪkʌltʃə(r)/ *n.* horticulture *f.* **~al** /-'kʌltʃərəl/ *a.* horticole.

hose /həʊz/ *n.* (*tube*) tuyau *m.* ● *v.t.* arroser. **~-pipe** *n.* tuyau *m.*

hosiery /'həʊzɪərɪ/ *n.* bonneterie *f.*

hospice /'hɒspɪs/ *n.* hospice *m.*

hospit|able /hɒ'spɪtəbl/ *a.* hospitalier. **~ably** *adv.* avec hospitalité. **~ality** /-'tælətɪ/ *n.* hospitalité *f.*

hospital /'hɒspɪtl/ *n.* hôpital *m.*

host[1] /həʊst/ *n.* (*to guests*) hôte *m.*; (*on TV*) animateur *m.* **~ess** *n.* hôtesse *f.*

host[2] /həʊst/ *n.* **a ~ of,** une foule de.

host[3] /həʊst/ *n.* (*relig.*) hostie *f.*

hostage /'hɒstɪdʒ/ *n.* otage *m.*

hostel /'hɒstl/ *n.* foyer *m.* **(youth) ~,** auberge (de jeunesse) *f.*

hostil|e /'hɒstaɪl, *Amer.* 'hɒstl/ *a.* hostile. **~ity** /hɒ'stɪlətɪ/ *n.* hostilité *f.*

hot /hɒt/ *a.* (**hotter, hottest**) chaud; (*culin.*) épicé; (*news*) récent. **be or feel ~,** avoir chaud. **it is ~,** il fait chaud. ● *v.t./i.* (*p.t.* **hotted**) **~ up,** (*fam.*) chauffer. **~ dog,** hot-dog *m.* **~ line,** téléphone rouge *m.* **~ shot,** (*Amer., sl.*) crack *m.* **~-water bottle,** bouillotte *f* **in ~ water,** (*fam.*) dans le pétrin. **~ly** *adv.* vivement.

hotbed /'hɒtbed/ *n.* foyer *m.*

hotchpotch /'hɒtʃpɒtʃ/ *n.* fatras *m.*

hotel /həʊ'tel/ *n.* hôtel *m.* **~ier** /-ɪeɪ/ *n.* hôtel|ier, -ière *m., f.*

hothead /'hɒthed/ n. tête brûlée f. ~ed a. impétueux.

hotplate /'hɒtpleɪt/ n. plaque chauffante f.

hound /haʊnd/ n. chien courant m. ● v.t. poursuivre.

hour /'aʊə(r)/ n. heure f. ~ly a. & adv. toutes les heures. ~ly rate, tarif horaire m. **paid ~ly**, payé à l'heure.

house[1] /haʊs/ n. (pl. -s /'haʊzɪz/) n. maison f.; (theatre) salle f.; (pol.) chambre f. ~-proud a. méticuleux. ~-warming n. pendaison de la crémaillère f.

house[2] /haʊz/ v.t. loger; (of building) abriter; (keep) garder.

housebreaking /'haʊsbreɪkɪŋ/ n. cambriolage m.

housecoat /'haʊskəʊt/ n. blouse f., tablier m.

household /'haʊshəʊld/ n. (house, family) ménage m. ● a. ménager. ~er n. occupant(e) m. (f.); (owner) propriétaire m./f.

housekeep|er /'haʊskiːpə(r)/ n. gouvernante f. ~ing n. ménage m.

housewife /'haʊswaɪf/ n. (pl. -wives) ménagère f.

housework /'haʊswɜːk/ n. ménage m. travaux de ménage m. pl.

housing /'haʊzɪŋ/ n. logement m. ~ association, service de logement m. ~ development, cité f.

hovel /'hɒvl/ n. taudis m.

hover /'hɒvə(r)/ v.i. (bird, threat, etc.) planer; (loiter) rôder.

hovercraft /'hɒvəkrɑːft/ n. aéroglisseur m.

how /haʊ/ adv. comment. ~ long/tall is . . .?, quelle est la longueur/hauteur de . . .? ~ pretty!, comme or que c'est joli! ~ about a walk?, si on faisait une promenade? ~ are you?, comment allez-vous? ~ do you do?, (introduction) enchanté. ~ many?, ~ much?, combien?

however /haʊ'evə(r)/ adv. de quelque manière que; (nevertheless) cependant. ~ small/delicate/etc. it may be, quelque petit/délicat/etc. que ce soit.

howl /haʊl/ n. hurlement m. ● v.i. hurler.

howler /'haʊlə(r)/ n. (fam.) bévue f.

HP abbr. see hire-purchase.

hp abbr. see horsepower.

HQ abbr. see headquarters.

hub /hʌb/ n. moyeu m.; (fig.) centre m. ~-cap n. enjoliveur m.

hubbub /'hʌbʌb/ n. vacarme m.

huddle /'hʌdl/ v.i. se blottir.

hue[1] /hjuː/ n. (colour) teinte f.

hue[2] /hjuː/ n. ~ and cry, clameur f.

huff /hʌf/ n. in a ~, fâché, vexé.

hug /hʌɡ/ v.t. (p.t. hugged) serrer dans ses bras; (keep close to) serrer. ● n. étreinte f.

huge /hjuːdʒ/ a. énorme. ~ly adv. énormément.

hulk /hʌlk/ n. (of ship) épave f.; (person) mastodonte m.

hull /hʌl/ n. (of ship) coque f.

hullo /hə'ləʊ/ int. & n. = hallo.

hum /hʌm/ v.t./i. (p.t. hummed) (person) fredonner; (insect) bourdonner; (engine) vrombir. ● n. bourdonnement m.; vrombissement m. ~ and haw, hésiter.

human /'hjuːmən/ a. humain. ● n. être humain m. ~itarian /-mænɪ'teərɪən/ a. humanitaire.

humane /hjuː'meɪn/ a. humain, plein d'humanité.

humanity /hjuː'mænətɪ/ n. humanité f.

humbl|e /'hʌmbl/ a. (-er, -est) humble. ● v.t. humilier. ~y adv. humblement.

humbug /'hʌmbʌɡ/ n. (false talk) hypocrisie f.

humdrum /'hʌmdrʌm/ a. monotone.

humid /'hjuːmɪd/ a. humide. ~ity /-'mɪdətɪ/ n. humidité f.

humiliat|e /hjuː'mɪlɪeɪt/ v.t. humilier. ~ion /-'eɪʃn/ n. humiliation f.

humility /hjuː'mɪlətɪ/ n. humilité f.

humorist /'hjuːmərɪst/ n. humoriste m./f.

hum|our, (Amer.) **hum|or** /'hjuːmə(r)/ n. humour m.; (mood) humeur f. ● v.t. ménager. ~ous a. humoristique; (person) plein d'humour. ~orously adv. avec humour.

hump /hʌmp/ n. bosse f. ● v.t. voûter. **the ~**, (sl.) le cafard.

hunch[1] /hʌntʃ/ v.t. voûter.

hunch[2] /hʌntʃ/ n. petite idée f.

hunchback /'hʌntʃbæk/ n. bossu(e) m. (f.).

hundred /'hʌndrəd/ a. & n. cent (m.). ~s of, des centaines de. ~fold a. centuple; adv. au centuple. ~th a. & n. centième (m./f.).

hundredweight /'hʌndrədweɪt/ n. 50.8 kg.; (Amer.) 45.36 kg.

hung /hʌŋ/ *see* hang.
Hungar|y /'hʌŋgərɪ/ *n.* Hongrie *f.*
~**ian** /-'geərɪən/ *a. & n.* hongrois(e)
(*m. (f.)*).
hunger /'hʌŋgə(r)/ *n.* faim *f.* ● *v.i.* ~
for, avoir faim de. ~**-strike** *n.* grève
de la faim *f.*
hungr|y /'hʌŋgrɪ/ *a.* (-**ier**, -**iest**)
affamé. **be** ~**y**, avoir faim. ~**ily**
adv. avidement.
hunk /hʌŋk/ *n.* gros morceau *m.*
hunt /hʌnt/ *v.t./i.* chasser. ● *n.*
chasse *f.* ~ **for**, chercher. ~**er** *n.*
chasseur *m.* ~**ing** *n.* chasse *f.*
hurdle /'hɜːdl/ *n.* (*sport*) haie *f.*; (*fig.*)
obstacle *m.*
hurl /hɜːl/ *v.t.* lancer.
hurrah, hurray /hʊ'rɑː, hʊ'reɪ/ *int. &
n.* hourra (*m.*).
hurricane /'hʌrɪkən, *Amer.* 'hʌrɪ-
keɪn/ *n.* ouragan *m.*
hurried /'hʌrɪd/ *a.* précipité. ~**ly**
adv. précipitamment.
hurry /'hʌrɪ/ *v.i.* se dépêcher, se
presser. ● *v.t.* presser, activer.
● *n.* hâte *f.* **in a** ~, pressé.
hurt /hɜːt/ *v.t./i.* (*p.t.* **hurt**) faire mal
(à); (*injure, offend*) blesser. ● *a.*
blessé. ● *n.* mal *m.* ~**ful** *a.* blessant.
hurtle /'hɜːtl/ *v.t.* lancer. ● *v.i.* ~
along, avancer à toute vitesse.
husband /'hʌzbənd/ *n.* mari *m.*
hush /hʌʃ/ *v.t.* faire taire. ● *n.*
silence *m.* ~**-hush** *a.* (*fam.*) ultra-
secret. ~ **up**, (*news etc.*) étouffer.
husk /hʌsk/ *n.* (*of grain*) enveloppe *f.*
husky /'hʌskɪ/ *a.* (-**ier**, -**iest**) (*hoarse*)
rauque; (*burly*) costaud. ● *n.* chien
de traîneau *m.*
hustle /'hʌsl/ *v.t.* (*push, rush*)
bousculer. ● *v.i.* (*work busily*:
Amer.) se démener. ● *n.* bousculade
f. ~ **and bustle**, agitation *f.*
hut /hʌt/ *n.* cabane *f.*
hutch /hʌtʃ/ *n.* clapier *m.*
hyacinth /'haɪəsɪnθ/ *n.* jacinthe *f.*
hybrid /'haɪbrɪd/ *a. & n.* hybride
(*m.*).
hydrangea /haɪ'dreɪndʒə/ *n.* hortensia *m.*
hydrant /'haɪdrənt/ *n.* (**fire**) ~,
bouche d'incendie *f.*
hydraulic /haɪ'drɔːlɪk/ *a.* hydraulique.
hydroelectric /haɪdrəʊɪ'lektrɪk/ *a.*
hydro-électrique.
hydrofoil /'haɪdrəʊfɔɪl/ *n.* hydrop-
tère *m.*

hydrogen /'haɪdrədʒən/ *n.* hydrogène *m.* ~ **bomb**, bombe à hydrogène *f.*
hyena /haɪ'iːnə/ *n.* hyène *f.*
hygiene /'haɪdʒiːn/ *n.* hygiène *f.*
hygienic /haɪ'dʒiːnɪk/ *a.* hygiénique.
hymn /hɪm/ *n.* cantique *m.*, hymne *m.*
hype /haɪp/ *n.* tapage publicitaire *m.*
● *v.t.* faire du tapage autour de.
hyper- /'haɪpə(r)/ *pref.* hyper-.
hypermarket /'haɪpəmɑːkɪt/ *n.* hypermarché *m.*
hyphen /'haɪfn/ *n.* trait d'union *m.*
~**ate** *v.t.* mettre un trait d'union à.
hypno|sis /hɪp'nəʊsɪs/ *n.* hypnose *f.*
~**tic** /-'nɒtɪk/ *a.* hypnotique.
hypnot|ize /'hɪpnətaɪz/ *v.t.* hyp-
notiser. ~**ism** *n.* hypnotisme *m.*
hypochondriac /haɪpə'kɒndrɪæk/ *n.*
malade imaginaire *m./f.*
hypocrisy /hɪ'pɒkrəsɪ/ *n.* hypocrisie
f.
hypocrit|e /'hɪpəkrɪt/ *n.* hypocrite
m./f. ~**ical** /-'krɪtɪkl/ *a.* hypocrite.
hypodermic /haɪpə'dɜːmɪk/ *a.*
hypodermique. ● *n.* seringue hypodermique *f.*
hypothermia /haɪpə'θɜːmɪə/ *n.* hy-
pothermie *f.*
hypothe|sis /haɪ'pɒθəsɪs/ *n.* (*pl.*
-**theses** /-siːz/) hypothèse *f.* ~**tical**
/-ə'θetɪkl/ *a.* hypothétique.
hyster|ia /hɪ'stɪərɪə/ *n.* hystérie *f.*
~**ical** /-erɪkl/ *a.* hystérique; (*person*) surexcité.
hysterics /hɪ'sterɪks/ *n. pl.* crise de
nerfs *or* de rire *f.*

I

I /aɪ/ *pron.* je, j'*; (*stressed*) moi.
ice /aɪs/ *n.* glace *f.*; (*on road*) verglas
m. ● *v.t.* (*cake*) glacer. ● *v.i.* ~
(**up**), (*window*) se givrer; (*river*)
geler. ~**-cream** *n.* glace *f.* ~**-cube**
n. glaçon *m.* ~ **hockey**, hockey sur
glace *m.* ~ **lolly**, glace (*sur
bâtonnet*) *f.* ~ **rink**, patinoire *f.* ~
skate, patin à glace *m.*
iceberg /'aɪsbɜːg/ *n.* iceberg *m.*
icebox /'aɪsbɒks/ *n.* (*Amer.*) réfrigérateur *m.*
Iceland /'aɪslənd/ *n.* Islande *f.* ~**er** *n.*
Islandais(e) *m.* (*f.*). ~**ic** /-'lændɪk/ *a.*
islandais; *n.* (*lang.*) islandais *m.*
icicle /'aɪsɪkl/ *n.* glaçon *m.*

icing /ˈaɪsɪŋ/ n. (*sugar*) glace f.
icon /ˈaɪkɒn/ n. icône f.
icy /ˈaɪsɪ/ a. (**-ier, -iest**) (*hands, wind*) glacé; (*road*) verglacé; (*manner, welcome*) glacial.
idea /aɪˈdɪə/ n. idée f.
ideal /aɪˈdɪəl/ a. idéal. ● n. idéal m. **~ize** v.t. idéaliser. **~ly** adv. idéalement.
idealis|t /aɪˈdɪəlɪst/ n. idéaliste m./f. **~m** /-zəm/ n. idéalisme m. **~tic** /-ˈlɪstɪk/ a. idéaliste.
identical /aɪˈdentɪkl/ a. identique.
identif|y /aɪˈdentɪfaɪ/ v.t. identifier. ● v.i. **~y with,** s'identifier à. **~ication** /-ɪˈkeɪʃn/ n. identification f.; (*papers*) une pièce d'identité.
identikit /aɪˈdentɪkɪt/ n. **~ picture,** portrait-robot m.
identity /aɪˈdentətɪ/ n. identité f.
ideolog|y /aɪdrˈɒlədʒɪ/ n. idéologie f. **~ical** /-əˈlɒdʒɪkl/ a. idéologique.
idiocy /ˈɪdɪəsɪ/ n. idiotie f.
idiom /ˈɪdɪəm/ n. expression idiomatique f.; (*language*) idiome m. **~atic** /-ˈmætɪk/ a. idiomatique.
idiosyncrasy /ɪdɪəˈsɪŋkrəsɪ/ n. particularité f.
idiot /ˈɪdɪət/ n. idiot(e) m. (f.). **~ic** /-ˈɒtɪk/ a. idiot.
idle /ˈaɪdl/ a. (**-er, -est**) désœuvré, oisif; (*lazy*) paresseux; (*unemployed*) sans travail; (*machine*) au repos; (*fig.*) vain. ● v.i. (*engine*) tourner au ralenti. ● v.t. **~ away,** gaspiller. **~ness** n. oisiveté f. **~r** /-ə(r)/ n. oisi|f, -ve m., f.
idol /ˈaɪdl/ n. idole f. **~ize** v.t. idolâtrer.
idyllic /ˈɪdɪlɪk, Amer. aɪˈdɪlɪk/ a. idyllique.
i.e. abbr. c'est-à-dire.
if /ɪf/ conj. si.
igloo /ˈɪgluː/ n. igloo m.
ignite /ɪgˈnaɪt/ v.t./i. (s')enflammer.
ignition /ɪgˈnɪʃn/ n. (*auto.*) allumage m. **~ key,** clé de contact f. **~ (switch),** contact m.
ignoran|t /ˈɪgnərənt/ a. ignorant (**of,** de). **~ce** n. ignorance f. **~tly** adv. par ignorance.
ignore /ɪgˈnɔː(r)/ v.t. ne faire or prêter aucune attention à; (*person in street etc.*) faire semblant de ne pas voir; (*facts*) ne pas tenir compte de.
ilk /ɪlk/ n. (*kind: fam.*) acabit m.
ill /ɪl/ a. malade; (*bad*) mauvais. ● adv. mal. ● n. mal m. **~-advised** a. peu judicieux. **~ at**

ease, mal à l'aise. **~-bred** a. mal élevé. **~-fated** a. malheureux. **~-feeling,** ressentiment m. **~-gotten** a. mal acquis. **~-natured** a. désagréable. **~-treat** v.t. maltraiter. **~ will,** malveillance f.
illegal /ɪˈliːgl/ a. illégal.
illegible /ɪˈledʒəbl/ a. illisible.
illegitima|te /ɪlɪˈdʒɪtɪmət/ a. illégitime. **~cy** n. illégitimité f.
illitera|te /ɪˈlɪtərət/ a. & n. illettré(e) (m. (f.)), analphabète m./f. **~cy** n. analphabétisme m.
illness /ˈɪlnɪs/ n. maladie f.
illogical /ɪˈlɒdʒɪkl/ a. illogique.
illuminat|e /ɪˈluːmɪneɪt/ v.t. éclairer; (*decorate with lights*) illuminer. **~ion** /-ˈneɪʃn/ n. éclairage m.; illumination f.
illusion /ɪˈluːʒn/ n. illusion f.
illusory /ɪˈluːsərɪ/ a. illusoire.
illustrat|e /ˈɪləstreɪt/ v.t. illustrer. **~ion** /-ˈstreɪʃn/ n. illustration f. **~ive** /-ətɪv/ a. qui illustre.
illustrious /ɪˈlʌstrɪəs/ a. illustre.
image /ˈɪmɪdʒ/ n. image f. (*of firm, person*) image de marque f. **~ry** /-ərɪ/ n. images f. pl.
imaginary /ɪˈmædʒɪnərɪ/ a. imaginaire.
imaginat|ion /ɪmædʒɪˈneɪʃn/ n. imagination f. **~ive** /ɪˈmædʒɪnətɪv/ a. plein d'imagination.
imagin|e /ɪˈmædʒɪn/ v.t. (*picture to o.s.*) (s')imaginer; (*suppose*) imaginer. **~able** a. imaginable.
imbalance /ɪmˈbæləns/ n. déséquilibre m.
imbecile /ˈɪmbəsiːl/ n. & a. imbécile (m./f.).
imbue /ɪmˈbjuː/ v.t. imprégner.
imitat|e /ˈɪmɪteɪt/ v.t. imiter. **~ion** /-ˈteɪʃn/ n. imitation f. **~or** n. imita|teur, -trice m., f.
immaculate /ɪˈmækjʊlət/ a. (*room, dress, etc.*) impeccable.
immaterial /ɪməˈtɪərɪəl/ a. sans importance (**to,** pour; **that,** que).
immature /ɪməˈtjʊə(r)/ a. pas mûr; (*person*) immature.
immediate /ɪˈmiːdɪət/ a. immédiat. **~ly** adv. immédiatement; conj. dès que.
immens|e /ɪˈmens/ a. immense. **~ely** adv. extrêmement, immensément. **~ity** n. immensité f.
immers|e /ɪˈmɜːs/ v.t. plonger, immerger. **~ion** /-ɜːʃn/ n. immer-

sion *f.* **~ion heater,** chauffe-eau
(électrique) *m. invar.*

immigr|ate /'ɪmɪgreɪt/ *v.i.* immigrer.
~ant *n. & a.* immigré(e) (*m. (f.)*);
(*newly-arrived*) immigrant(e) (*m.
(f.)*). **~ation** /-'greɪʃn/ *n.* immigra-
tion *f.* **go through ~ation,** passer le
contrôle des passeports.

imminen|t /'ɪmɪnənt/ *a.* imminent.
~ce *n.* imminence *f.*

immobil|e /ɪ'məʊbaɪl, *Amer.* ɪ'məʊbl/
a. immobile. **~ize** /-əlaɪz/ *v.t.* immobiliser.

immoderate /ɪ'mɒdərət/ *a.* immodéré.

immoral /ɪ'mɒrəl/ *a.* immoral. **~ity**
/ɪmə'ræləti/ *n.* immoralité *f.*

immortal /ɪ'mɔːtl/ *a.* immortel. **~ity**
/-'tæləti/ *n.* immortalité *f.* **~ize** *v.t.*
immortaliser.

immun|e /ɪ'mjuːn/ *a.* immunisé
(**from, to,** contre). **~ity** *n.* immunité
f.

immuniz|e /'ɪmjʊnaɪz/ *v.t.* immu-
niser. **~ation** /-'zeɪʃn/ *n.* immuni-
sation *f.*

imp /ɪmp/ *n.* lutin *m.*

impact /'ɪmpækt/ *n.* impact *m.*

impair /ɪm'peə(r)/ *v.t.* détériorer.

impart /ɪm'pɑːt/ *v.t.* communiquer,
transmettre.

impartial /ɪm'pɑːʃl/ *a.* impartial.
~ity /-'ræləti/ *n.* impartialité *f.*

impassable /ɪm'pɑːsəbl/ *a.* (*barrier
etc.*) infranchissable; (*road*) impraticable.

impasse /'æmpɑːs, *Amer.* 'ɪmpæs/ *n.*
impasse *f.*

impassioned /ɪm'pæʃnd/ *n.* passionné.

impassive /ɪm'pæsɪv/ *a.* impassible.

impatien|t /ɪm'peɪʃnt/ *a.* impatient.
get ~t, s'impatienter. **~ce** *n.* impatience *f.* **~tly** *adv.* impatiemment.

impeccable /ɪm'pekəbl/ *a.* impeccable.

impede /ɪm'piːd/ *v.t.* gêner.

impediment /ɪm'pedɪmənt/ *n.* obstacle *m.* (**speech**) **~,** défaut d'élocution *m.*

impel /ɪm'pel/ *v.t.* (*p.t.* **impelled**)
pousser, forcer (**to do,** à faire).

impending /ɪm'pendɪŋ/ *a.* imminent.

impenetrable /ɪm'penɪtrəbl/ *a.* impénétrable.

imperative /ɪm'perətɪv/ *a.* nécessaire; (*need etc.*) impérieux. ● *n.*
(*gram.*) impératif *m.*

imperceptible /ɪmpə'septəbl/ *a.* imperceptible.

imperfect /ɪm'pɜːfɪkt/ *a.* imparfait;
(*faulty*) défectueux. **~ion** /-ə'fekʃn/
n. imperfection *f.*

imperial /ɪm'pɪərɪəl/ *a.* impérial;
(*measure*) légal (au Royaume-Uni).
~ism *n.* impérialisme *m.*

imperil /ɪm'perəl/ *v.t.* (*p.t.* **imper-
illed**) mettre en péril.

imperious /ɪm'pɪərɪəs/ *a.* impérieux.

impersonal /ɪm'pɜːsənl/ *a.* impersonnel.

impersonat|e /ɪm'pɜːsəneɪt/ *v.t.* se
faire passer pour; (*mimic*) imiter.
~ion /-'neɪʃn/ *n.* imitation *f.* **~or** *n.*
imita|teur, -trice *m., f.*

impertinen|t /ɪm'pɜːtɪnənt/ *a.* im-
pertinent. **~ce** *n.* impertinence *f.*
~tly *adv.* avec impertinence.

impervious /ɪm'pɜːvɪəs/ *a.* **~ to,**
imperméable à.

impetuous /ɪm'petʃʊəs/ *a.* impétueux.

impetus /'ɪmpɪtəs/ *n.* impulsion *f.*

impinge /ɪm'pɪndʒ/ *v.i.* **~ on,** affecter; (*encroach*) empiéter sur.

impish /'ɪmpɪʃ/ *a.* espiègle.

implacable /ɪm'plækəbl/ *a.* implacable.

implant /ɪm'plɑːnt/ *v.t.* implanter.
● *n.* implant *m.*

implement[1] /'ɪmplɪmənt/ *n.* (*tool*)
outil *m.*; (*utensil*) ustensile *m.*

implement[2] /'ɪmplɪment/ *v.t.* exécuter, mettre en pratique.

implicat|e /'ɪmplɪkeɪt/ *v.t.* impliquer.
~ion /-'keɪʃn/ *n.* implication *f.*

implicit /ɪm'plɪsɪt/ *a.* (*implied*) implicite; (*unquestioning*) absolu.

implore /ɪm'plɔː(r)/ *v.t.* implorer.

impl|y /ɪm'plaɪ/ *v.t.* (*assume, mean*)
impliquer; (*insinuate*) laisser
entendre. **~ied** *a.* implicite.

impolite /ɪmpə'laɪt/ *a.* impoli.

imponderable /ɪm'pɒndərəbl/ *a. &
n.* impondérable (*m.*).

import[1] /ɪm'pɔːt/ *v.t.* importer.
~ation /-'teɪʃn/ *n.* importation *f.*
~er *n.* importa|teur, -trice *m., f.*

import[2] /'ɪmpɔːt/ *n.* (*article*) importation *f.*; (*meaning*) sens *m.*

importan|t /ɪm'pɔːtnt/ *a.* important.
~ce *n.* importance *f.*

impos|e /ɪm'pəʊz/ *v.t.* imposer. ● *v.i.*
~e on, abuser de l'amabilité de.
~ition /-ə'zɪʃn/ *n.* imposition *f.*;
(*fig.*) dérangement *m.*

imposing /ɪm'pəʊzɪŋ/ *a.* imposant.

impossib|le /ɪm'pɒsəbl/ a. impossible. ~**ility** /-'bɪlətɪ/ n. impossibilité f.

impostor /ɪm'pɒstə(r)/ n. imposteur m.

impoten|t /'ɪmpətənt/ a. impuissant. ~**ce** n. impuissance f.

impound /ɪm'paʊnd/ v.t. confisquer, saisir.

impoverish /ɪm'pɒvərɪʃ/ v.t. appauvrir.

impracticable /ɪm'præktɪkəbl/ a. impraticable.

impractical /ɪm'præktɪkl/ a. peu pratique.

imprecise /ɪmprɪ'saɪs/ a. imprécis.

impregnable /ɪm'pregnəbl/ a. imprenable; (fig.) inattaquable.

impregnate /'ɪmpregneɪt/ v.t. imprégner (**with**, de).

impresario /ɪmprɪ'sɑːrɪəʊ/ n. (pl. -os) impresario m.

impress /ɪm'pres/ v.t. impressionner; (imprint) imprimer. ~ **on s.o.**, faire comprendre à qn.

impression /ɪm'preʃn/ n. impression f. ~**able** a. impressionnable.

impressive /ɪm'presɪv/ a. impressionnant.

imprint[1] /'ɪmprɪnt/ n. empreinte f.

imprint[2] /ɪm'prɪnt/ v.t. imprimer.

imprison /ɪm'prɪzn/ v.t. emprisonner. ~**ment** n. emprisonnement m., prison f.

improbab|le /ɪm'prɒbəbl/ a. (not likely) improbable; (incredible) invraisemblable. ~**ility** /-'bɪlətɪ/ n. improbabilité f.

impromptu /ɪm'prɒmptjuː/ a. & adv. impromptu.

improp|er /ɪm'prɒpə(r)/ a. inconvenant, indécent; (wrong) incorrect. ~**riety** /-ə'praɪətɪ/ n. inconvenance f.

improve /ɪm'pruːv/ v.t./i. (s')améliorer. ~**ment** n. amélioration f.

improvis|e /'ɪmprəvaɪz/ v.t./i. improviser. ~**ation** /-'zeɪʃn/ n. improvisation f.

imprudent /ɪm'pruːdnt/ a. imprudent.

impuden|t /'ɪmpjʊdənt/ a. impudent. ~**ce** n. impudence f.

impulse /'ɪmpʌls/ n. impulsion f. **on ~**, sur un coup de tête.

impulsive /ɪm'pʌlsɪv/ a. impulsif. ~**ly** adv. par impulsion.

impunity /ɪm'pjuːnətɪ/ n. impunité f. **with ~**, impunément.

impur|e /ɪm'pjʊə(r)/ a. impur. ~**ity** n. impureté f.

impute /ɪm'pjuːt/ v.t. imputer.

in /ɪn/ prep. dans, à, en. ● adv. (inside) dedans; (at home) là, à la maison; (in fashion) à la mode. **in the box/garden**, dans la boîte/le jardin. **in Paris/school**, à Paris/l'école. **in town**, en ville. **in the country**, à la campagne. **in English**, en anglais. **in India**, en Inde. **in Japan**, au Japon. **in a firm manner/voice**, d'une manière/voix ferme. **in blue**, en bleu. **in ink**, à l'encre. **in uniform**, en uniforme. **in a skirt**, en jupe. **in a whisper**, en chuchotant. **in a loud voice**, d'une voix forte. **in winter**, en hiver. **in spring**, au printemps. **in an hour**, (at end of) au bout d'une heure. **in an hour('s time)**, dans une heure. **in (the space of) an hour**, en une heure. **in doing**, en faisant. **in the evening**, le soir. **one in ten**, un sur dix. **in between**, entre les deux; (time) entretemps. **the best in**, le meilleur de. **we are in for**, on va avoir. **in-laws** n. pl. (fam.) beaux-parents m. pl. ~**-patient** n. malade hospitalisé(e) m.(f.). **the ins and outs of**, les tenants et aboutissants de. **in so far as**, dans la mesure où.

inability /ɪnə'bɪlətɪ/ n. incapacité f. (**to do**, de faire).

inaccessible /ɪnæk'sesəbl/ a. inaccessible.

inaccurate /ɪn'ækjərət/ a. inexact.

inaction /ɪn'ækʃn/ n. inaction f.

inactiv|e /ɪn'æktɪv/ a. inactif. ~**ity** /-'tɪvətɪ/ n. inaction f.

inadequa|te /ɪn'ædɪkwət/ a. insuffisant. ~**cy** n. insuffisance f.

inadmissible /ɪnəd'mɪsəbl/ a. inadmissible.

inadvertently /ɪnəd'vɜːtntlɪ/ adv. par mégarde.

inadvisable /ɪnəd'vaɪzəbl/ a. déconseillé, pas recommandé.

inane /ɪ'neɪm/ a. inepte.

inanimate /ɪn'ænɪmət/ a. inanimé.

inappropriate /ɪnə'prəʊprɪət/ a. inopportun; (term) inapproprié.

inarticulate /ɪnɑː'tɪkjʊlət/ a. qui a du mal à s'exprimer.

inasmuch as /ɪnəz'mʌtʃəz/ adv. en ce sens que; (because) vu que.

inattentive /ɪnə'tentɪv/ a. inattentif.

inaudible /ɪn'ɔːdɪbl/ *a.* inaudible.

inaugural /ɪ'nɔːgjʊrəl/ *a.* inaugural.

inaugurat|e /ɪ'nɔːgjʊreɪt/ *v.t.* (*open, begin*) inaugurer; (*person*) investir. ~**ion** /-'reɪʃn/ *n.* inauguration *f.*; investiture *f.*

inauspicious /mɔː'spɪʃəs/ *a.* peu propice.

inborn /ɪn'bɔːn/ *a.* inné.

inbred /ɪn'bred/ *a.* (*inborn*) inné.

inc. *abbr.* (*incorporated*) S.A.

incalculable /ɪn'kælkjʊləbl/ *a.* incalculable.

incapable /ɪn'keɪpəbl/ *a.* incapable.

incapacit|y /ɪnkə'pæsəti/ *n.* incapacité *f.* ~**ate** *v.t.* rendre incapable (*de travailler etc.*).

incarcerate /ɪn'kɑːsəreɪt/ *v.t.* incarcérer.

incarnat|e /ɪn'kɑːneɪt/ *a.* incarné. ~**ion** /-'neɪʃn/ *n.* incarnation *f.*

incendiary /ɪn'sendɪərɪ/ *a.* incendiaire. ● *n.* (*bomb*) bombe incendiaire *f.*

incense[1] /'ɪnsens/ *n.* encens *m.*

incense[2] /ɪn'sens/ *v.t.* mettre en fureur.

incentive /ɪn'sentɪv/ *n.* motivation *f.*; (*payment*) prime (d'encouragement) *f.*

inception /ɪn'sepʃn/ *n.* début *m.*

incessant /ɪn'sesnt/ *a.* incessant. ~**ly** *adv.* sans cesse.

incest /'ɪnsest/ *n.* inceste *m.* ~**uous** /ɪn'sestjʊəs/ *a.* incestueux.

inch /ɪntʃ/ *n.* pouce *m.* (=2.54 cm.). ● *v.i.* avancer doucement.

incidence /'ɪnsɪdəns/ *n.* fréquence *f.*

incident /'ɪnsɪdənt/ *n.* incident *m.*; (*in play, film, etc.*) épisode *m.*

incidental /ɪnsɪ'dentl/ *a.* accessoire. ~**ly** *adv.* accessoirement; (*by the way*) à propos.

incinerat|e /ɪn'sɪnəreɪt/ *v.t.* incinérer. ~**or** *n.* incinérateur *m.*

incipient /ɪn'sɪpɪənt/ *a.* naissant.

incision /ɪn'sɪʒn/ *n.* incision *f.*

incisive /ɪn'saɪsɪv/ *a.* incisif.

incite /ɪn'saɪt/ *v.t.* inciter, pousser. ~**ment** *n.* incitation *f.*

inclement /ɪn'klemənt/ *a.* inclément, rigoureux.

inclination /ɪnklɪ'neɪʃn/ *n.* (*propensity, bowing*) inclination *f.*

incline[1] /ɪn'klaɪn/ *v.t./i.* incliner. **be** ~**d to,** avoir tendance à.

incline[2] /'ɪnklaɪn/ *n.* pente *f.*

inclu|de /ɪn'kluːd/ *v.t.* comprendre, inclure. ~**ding** *prep.* (y) compris. ~**sion** *n.* inclusion *f.*

inclusive /ɪn'kluːsɪv/ *a. & adv.* inclus, compris. **be** ~ **of,** comprendre, inclure.

incognito /ɪnkɒg'niːtəʊ/ *adv.* incognito.

incoherent /ɪnkəʊ'hɪərənt/ *a.* incohérent.

income /'ɪnkʌm/ *n.* revenu *m.* ~ **tax,** impôt sur le revenu *m.*

incoming /'ɪnkʌmɪŋ/ *a.* (*tide*) montant; (*tenant etc.*) nouveau.

incomparable /ɪn'kɒmprəbl/ *a.* incomparable.

incompatible /ɪnkəm'pætəbl/ *a.* incompatible.

incompeten|t /ɪn'kɒmpɪtənt/ *a.* incompétent. ~**ce** *n.* incompétence *f.*

incomplete /ɪnkəm'pliːt/ *a.* incomplet.

incomprehensible /ɪnkɒmprɪ'hensəbl/ *a.* incompréhensible.

inconceivable /ɪnkən'siːvəbl/ *a.* inconcevable.

inconclusive /ɪnkən'kluːsɪv/ *a.* peu concluant.

incongruous /ɪn'kɒŋgrʊəs/ *a.* déplacé, incongru.

inconsequential /ɪnkɒnsɪ'kwenʃl/ *a.* sans importance.

inconsiderate /ɪnkən'sɪdərət/ *a.* (*person*) qui ne se soucie pas des autres; (*act*) irréfléchi.

inconsisten|t /ɪnkən'sɪstənt/ *a.* (*treatment*) sans cohérence, inconséquent; (*argument*) contradictoire; (*performance*) irrégulier. ~**t with,** incompatible avec. ~**cy** *n.* inconséquence *f.*, contradiction *f.*; irrégularité *f.*

inconspicuous /ɪnkən'spɪkjʊəs/ *a.* peu en évidence.

incontinen|t /ɪn'kɒntɪnənt/ *a.* incontinent. ~**ce** *n.* incontinence *f.*

inconvenien|t /ɪnkən'viːnɪənt/ *a.* incommode, peu pratique; (*time*) mal choisi. **be** ~**t for,** ne pas convenir à. ~**ce** *n.* dérangement *m.*; (*drawback*) inconvénient *m.*; *v.t.* déranger.

incorporate /ɪn'kɔːpəreɪt/ *v.t.* incorporer; (*include*) contenir.

incorrect /ɪnkə'rekt/ *a.* inexact.

incorrigible /ɪn'kɒrɪdʒəbl/ *a.* incorrigible.

incorruptible /ɪnkə'rʌptəbl/ *a.* incorruptible.

increas|e [1] /ɪn'kriːs/ *v.t./i.* augmenter. **~ing** *a.* croissant. **~ingly** *adv.* de plus en plus.

increase [2] /'ɪnkriːs/ *n.* augmentation *f.* (**in, of,** de). **be on the ~,** augmenter.

incredible /ɪn'kredəbl/ *a.* incroyable.

incredulous /ɪn'kredjʊləs/ *a.* incrédule.

increment /'ɪnkrəmənt/ *n.* augmentation *f.*

incriminat|e /ɪn'krɪmɪneɪt/ *v.t.* incriminer. **~ing** *a.* compromettant.

incubat|e /'ɪnkjʊbeɪt/ *v.t.* (*eggs*) couver. **~ion** /-'beɪʃn/ *n.* incubation *f.* **~or** *n.* couveuse *f.*

inculcate /'ɪnkʌlkeɪt/ *v.t.* inculquer.

incumbent /ɪn'kʌmbənt/ *n.* (*pol., relig.*) titulaire *m./f.*

incur /ɪn'kɜː(r)/ *v.t.* (*p.t.* **incurred**) encourir; (*debts*) contracter; (*anger*) s'exposer à.

incurable /ɪn'kjʊərəbl/ *a.* incurable.

incursion /ɪn'kɜːʃn/ *n.* incursion *f.*

indebted /ɪn'detɪd/ *a.* **~ to s.o.,** redevable à qn. (**for,** de).

indecen|t /ɪn'diːsnt/ *a.* indécent. **~cy** *n.* indécence *f.*

indecision /ɪndɪ'sɪʒn/ *n.* indécision *f.*

indecisive /ɪndɪ'saɪsɪv/ *a.* indécis; (*ending*) peu concluant.

indeed /ɪn'diːd/ *adv.* en effet, vraiment.

indefensible /ɪndɪ'fensɪbl/ *a.* indéfendable.

indefinable /ɪndɪ'faɪnəbl/ *a.* indéfinissable.

indefinite /ɪn'defɪnɪt/ *a.* indéfini; (*time*) indéterminé. **~ly** *adv.* indéfiniment.

indelible /ɪn'deləbl/ *a.* indélébile.

indemni|fy /ɪn'demnɪfaɪ/ *v.t.* (*compensate*) indemniser (**for,** de); (*safeguard*) garantir. **~ty** /-nətɪ/ *n.* indemnité *f.*; garantie *f.*

indent /ɪn'dent/ *v.t.* (*text*) renfoncer. **~ation** /-'teɪʃn/ *n.* (*outline*) découpure *f.*

independen|t /ɪndɪ'pendənt/ *a.* indépendant. **~ce** *n.* indépendance *f.* **~tly** *adv.* de façon indépendante. **~tly of,** indépendamment de.

indescribable /ɪndɪ'skraɪbəbl/ *a.* indescriptible.

indestructible /ɪndɪ'strʌktəbl/ *a.* indestructible.

indeterminate /ɪndɪ'tɜːmɪnət/ *a.* indéterminé.

index /'ɪndeks/ *n.* (*pl.* **indexes**) (*figure*) indice *m.*; (*in book*) index *m.*; (*in library*) catalogue *m.* ● *v.t.* classer. **~ card,** fiche *f.* **~ finger** index *m.* **~-linked** *a.* indexé.

India /'ɪndɪə/ *n.* Inde *f.* **~n** *a.* & *n.* indien(ne) (*m.* (*f.*)). **~n summer,** été de la Saint-Martin *m.*

indicat|e /'ɪndɪkeɪt/ *v.t.* indiquer. **~ion** /-'keɪʃn/ *n.* indication *f.* **~or** *n.* (*device*) indicateur *m.*; (*on vehicle*) clignotant *m.*; (*board*) tableau *m.*

indicative /ɪn'dɪkətɪv/ *a.* indicatif. ● *n.* (*gram.*) indicatif *m.*

indict /ɪn'daɪt/ *v.t.* accuser. **~ment** *n.* accusation *f.*

indifferen|t /ɪn'dɪfrənt/ *a.* indifférent; (*not good*) médiocre. **~ce** *n.* indifférence *f.*

indigenous /ɪn'dɪdʒɪnəs/ *a.* indigène.

indigest|ion /ɪndɪ'dʒestʃən/ *n.* indigestion *f.* **~ible** /-təbl/ *a.* indigeste.

indign|ant /ɪn'dɪgnənt/ *a.* indigné. **~ation** /-'neɪʃn/ *n.* indignation *f.*

indigo /'ɪndɪgəʊ/ *n.* indigo *m.*

indirect /ɪndɪ'rekt/ *a.* indirect. **~ly** *adv.* indirectement.

indiscr|eet /ɪndɪ'skriːt/ *a.* indiscret; (*not wary*) imprudent. **~etion** /-eʃn/ *n.* indiscrétion *f.*

indiscriminate /ɪndɪ'skrɪmɪnət/ *a.* qui manque de discernement; (*random*) fait au hasard. **~ly** *adv.* sans discernement; au hasard.

indispensable /ɪndɪ'spensəbl/ *a.* indispensable.

indispos|ed /ɪndɪ'spəʊzd/ *a.* indisposé, souffrant. **~ition** /-ə'zɪʃn/ *n.* indisposition *f.*

indisputable /ɪndɪ'spjuːtəbl/ *a.* incontestable.

indistinct /ɪndɪ'stɪŋkt/ *a.* indistinct.

indistinguishable /ɪndɪ'stɪŋgwɪʃəbl/ *a.* indifférenciable.

individual /ɪndɪ'vɪdʒʊəl/ *a.* individuel. ● *n.* individu *m.* **~ist** *n.* individualiste *m./f.* **~ity** /-'ælətɪ/ *n.* individualité *f.* **~ly** *adv.* individuellement.

indivisible /ɪndɪ'vɪzəbl/ *a.* indivisible.

indoctrinat|e /ɪn'dɒktrɪneɪt/ *v.t.* endoctriner. **~ion** /-'neɪʃn/ *n.* endoctrinement *m.*

indolen|t /'ɪndələnt/ *a.* indolent. **~ce** *n.* indolence *f.*

indomitable /ɪn'dɒmɪtəbl/ *a.* indomptable.

Indonesia /ɪndəʊ'niːzɪə/ n. Indonésie f. ~n a. & n. indonésien(ne) (m. (f.)).

indoor /'ɪndɔː(r)/ a. (clothes etc.) d'intérieur; (under cover) couvert. ~s /ɪn'dɔːz/ adv. à l'intérieur.

induce /ɪn'djuːs/ v.t. (influence) persuader; (cause) provoquer. ~ment n. encouragement m.

induct /ɪn'dʌkt/ v.t. investir, installer; (mil., Amer.) incorporer.

indulge /ɪn'dʌldʒ/ v.t. (desires) satisfaire; (person) se montrer indulgent pour, gâter. ● v.i. ~ in, se livrer à, s'offrir.

indulgen|t /ɪn'dʌldʒənt/ a. indulgent. ~ce n. indulgence f.; (treat) gâterie f.

industrial /ɪn'dʌstrɪəl/ a. industriel; (unrest etc.) ouvrier; (action) revendicatif; (accident) du travail. ~ist n. industriel(le) m.(f.). ~ized a. industrialisé.

industrious /ɪn'dʌstrɪəs/ a. travailleur, appliqué.

industry /'ɪndəstrɪ/ n. industrie f.; (zeal) application f.

inebriated /ɪ'niːbrɪeɪtɪd/ a. ivre.

inedible /ɪn'edɪbl/ a. (food) immangeable.

ineffective /ɪnɪ'fektɪv/ a. inefficace; (person) incapable.

ineffectual /ɪnɪ'fektʃʊəl/ a. inefficace; (person) incapable.

inefficien|t /ɪnɪ'fɪʃnt/ a. inefficace; (person) incompétent. ~cy n. inefficacité f.; incompétence f.

ineligible /ɪn'elɪdʒəbl/ a. inéligible. be ~ for, ne pas avoir droit à.

inept /ɪ'nept/ a. (absurd) inepte; (out of place) mal à propos.

inequality /ɪnɪ'kwɒlətɪ/ n. inégalité f.

inert /ɪ'nɜːt/ a. inerte.

inertia /ɪ'nɜːʃə/ n. inertie f.

inescapable /ɪnɪ'skeɪpəbl/ a. inéluctable.

inevitabl|e /ɪn'evɪtəbl/ a. inévitable. ~y adv. inévitablement.

inexact /ɪnɪg'zækt/ a. inexact.

inexcusable /ɪnɪk'skjuːzəbl/ a. inexcusable.

inexhaustible /ɪnɪg'zɔːstəbl/ a. inépuisable.

inexorable /ɪn'eksərəbl/ a. inexorable.

inexpensive /ɪnɪk'spensɪv/ a. bon marché invar., pas cher.

inexperience /ɪnɪk'spɪərɪəns/ n. inexpérience f. ~d a. inexpérimenté.

inexplicable /ɪnɪk'splɪkəbl/ a. inexplicable.

inextricable /ɪnɪk'strɪkəbl/ a. inextricable.

infallib|le /ɪn'fæləbl/ a. infaillible. ~ility /-'bɪlətɪ/ n. infaillibilité f.

infam|ous /'ɪnfəməs/ a. infâme. ~y n. infamie f.

infan|t /'ɪnfənt/ n. (baby) nourrisson m.; (at school) petit(e) enfant m.(f.). ~cy n. petite enfance f.; (fig.) enfance f.

infantile /'ɪnfəntaɪl/ a. infantile.

infantry /'ɪnfəntrɪ/ n. infanterie f.

infatuat|ed /ɪn'fætʃʊeɪtɪd/ a. ~ed with, engoué de. ~ion /-'eɪʃn/ n. engouement m., béguin m.

infect /ɪn'fekt/ v.t. infecter. ~ s.o. with, communiquer à qn. ~ion /-kʃn/ n. infection f.

infectious /ɪn'fekʃəs/ a. (med.) infectieux; (fig.) contagieux.

infer /ɪn'fɜː(r)/ v.t. (p.t. inferred) déduire. ~ence /'ɪnfərəns/ n. déduction f.

inferior /ɪn'fɪərɪə(r)/ a. inférieur (to, à); (work, product) de qualité inférieure. ● n. inférieur(e) m. (f.). ~ity /-'ɒrətɪ/ n. infériorité f.

infernal /ɪn'fɜːnl/ a. infernal. ~ly adv. (fam.) atrocement.

inferno /ɪn'fɜːnəʊ/ n. (pl. -os) (hell) enfer m.; (blaze) incendie m.

infertil|e /ɪn'fɜːtaɪl, Amer. ɪn'fɜːtl/ a. infertile. ~ity /-ə'tɪlətɪ/ n. infertilité f.

infest /ɪn'fest/ v.t. infester.

infidelity /ɪnfɪ'delətɪ/ n. infidélité f.

infighting /'ɪnfaɪtɪŋ/ n. querelles internes f. pl.

infiltrat|e /'ɪnfɪltreɪt/ v.t./i. s'infiltrer (dans). ~ion /-'treɪʃn/ n. infiltration f.

infinite /'ɪnfɪnɪt/ a. infini. ~ly adv. infiniment.

infinitesimal /ɪnfɪnɪ'tesɪml/ a. infinitésimal.

infinitive /ɪn'fɪnətɪv/ n. infinitif m.

infinity /ɪn'fɪnətɪ/ n. infinité f.

infirm /ɪn'fɜːm/ a. infirme. ~ity n. infirmité f.

infirmary /ɪn'fɜːmərɪ/ n. hôpital m.; (sick-bay) infirmerie f.

inflam|e /ɪn'fleɪm/ v.t. enflammer. ~mable /-æməbl/ a. inflammable. ~mation /-ə'meɪʃn/ n. inflammation f.

inflammatory /ɪn'flæmətrɪ/ a. incendiaire.

inflat|e /ɪnˈfleɪt/ v.t. (*balloon, prices, etc.*) gonfler. **~able** a. gonflable.

inflation /ɪnˈfleɪʃn/ n. inflation f. **~ary** a. inflationniste.

inflection /ɪnˈflekʃn/ n. inflexion f.; (*suffix*: *gram.*) désinence f.

inflexible /ɪnˈfleksəbl/ a. inflexible.

inflict /ɪnˈflɪkt/ v.t. infliger (**on**, à).

influence /ˈɪnfluəns/ n. influence f. ● v.t. influencer. **under the ~**, (*drunk*: *fam.*) en état d'ivresse.

influential /ɪnfluˈenʃl/ a. influent.

influenza /ɪnfluˈenzə/ n. grippe f.

influx /ˈɪnflʌks/ n. afflux m.

inform /ɪnˈfɔːm/ v.t. informer (**of**, de). **keep ~ed**, tenir au courant. **~ant** n. informa|teur, -trice m., f. **~er** n. indica|teur, -trice m., f.

informal /ɪnˈfɔːml/ a. (*simple*) simple, sans cérémonie; (*unofficial*) officieux; (*colloquial*) familier. **~ity** /-ˈmælətɪ/ n. simplicité f. **~ly** adv. sans cérémonie.

information /ɪnfəˈmeɪʃn/ n. renseignement(s) m. (*pl.*), information(s) f. (*pl.*). **some ~**, un renseignement. **~ technology**, informatique f.

informative /ɪnˈfɔːmətɪv/ a. instructif.

infra-red /ɪnfrəˈred/ a. infrarouge.

infrastructure /ˈɪnfrəstrʌktʃə(r)/ n. infrastructure f.

infrequent /ɪnˈfriːkwənt/ a. peu fréquent. **~ly** adv. rarement.

infringe /ɪnˈfrɪndʒ/ v.t. contrevenir à. **~ on**, empiéter sur. **~ment** n. infraction f.

infuriate /ɪnˈfjʊərɪeɪt/ v.t. exaspérer, rendre furieux.

infus|e /ɪnˈfjuːz/ v.t. infuser. **~ion** /-ʒn/ n. infusion f.

ingen|ious /ɪnˈdʒiːnɪəs/ a. ingénieux. **~uity** /-ɪˈnjuːətɪ/ n. ingéniosité f.

ingenuous /ɪnˈdʒenjʊəs/ a. ingénu.

ingot /ˈɪŋgət/ n. lingot m.

ingrained /ɪnˈgreɪnd/ a. enraciné.

ingratiate /ɪnˈgreɪʃɪeɪt/ v.t. **~ o.s. with**, gagner les bonnes grâces de.

ingratitude /ɪnˈgrætɪtjuːd/ n. ingratitude f.

ingredient /ɪnˈgriːdɪənt/ n. ingrédient m.

inhabit /ɪnˈhæbɪt/ v.t. habiter. **~able** a. habitable. **~ant** n. habitant(e) m. (f.).

inhale /ɪnˈheɪl/ v.t. inhaler; (*tobacco smoke*) avaler. **~r** n. spray m.

inherent /ɪnˈhɪərənt/ a. inhérent. **~ly** adv. en soi, intrinsèquement.

inherit /ɪnˈherɪt/ v.t. hériter (de). **~ance** n. héritage m.

inhibit /ɪnˈhɪbɪt/ v.t. (*hinder*) gêner; (*prevent*) empêcher. **be ~ed**, avoir des inhibitions. **~ion** /-ˈbɪʃn/ n. inhibition f.

inhospitable /ɪnhɒˈspɪtəbl/ a. inhospitalier.

inhuman /ɪnˈhjuːmən/ a. (*brutal, not human*) inhumain. **~ity** /-ˈmænətɪ/ n. inhumanité f.

inhumane /ɪnhjuːˈmeɪn/ a. (*unkind*) inhumain.

inimitable /ɪˈnɪmɪtəbl/ a. inimitable.

iniquit|ous /ɪˈnɪkwɪtəs/ a. inique. **~y** /-ətɪ/ n. iniquité f.

initial /ɪˈnɪʃl/ n. initiale f. ● v.t. (*p.t.* **initialled**) parapher. ● a. initial. **~ly** adv. initialement.

initiat|e /ɪˈnɪʃɪeɪt/ v.t. (*begin*) amorcer; (*scheme*) lancer; (*person*) initier (**into**, à). **~ion** /-ˈeɪʃn/ n. initiation f.; (*start*) amorce f.

initiative /ɪˈnɪʃətɪv/ n. initiative f.

inject /ɪnˈdʒekt/ v.t. injecter; (*new element*: *fig.*) insuffler. **~ion** /-kʃn/ n. injection f., piqûre f.

injunction /ɪnˈdʒʌŋkʃn/ n. (*court order*) ordonnance f.

injure /ˈɪndʒə(r)/ v.t. blesser; (*do wrong to*) nuire à.

injury /ˈɪndʒərɪ/ n. (*physical*) blessure f.; (*wrong*) préjudice m.

injustice /ɪnˈdʒʌstɪs/ n. injustice f.

ink /ɪŋk/ n. encre f. **~-well** n. encrier m. **~y** a. taché d'encre.

inkling /ˈɪŋklɪŋ/ n. petite idée f.

inland /ˈɪnlənd/ a. à l'intérieur. ● adv. /ɪnˈlænd/ à l'intérieur. **I~ Revenue**, fisc m.

in-laws /ˈɪnlɔːz/ n. pl. (*parents*) beaux-parents m. pl.; (*family*) belle-famille f.

inlay [1] /ɪnˈleɪ/ v.t. (*p.t.* **inlaid**) incruster.

inlay [2] /ˈɪnleɪ/ n. incrustation f.

inlet /ˈɪnlet/ n. bras de mer m.; (*techn.*) arrivée f.

inmate /ˈɪnmeɪt/ n. (*of asylum*) interné(e) m. (f.); (*of prison*) détenu(e) m. (f.).

inn /ɪn/ n. auberge f.

innards /ˈɪnədz/ n. pl. (*fam.*) entrailles f. pl.

innate /ɪˈneɪt/ a. inné.

inner /ˈɪnə(r)/ a. intérieur, interne; (*fig.*) profond, intime. **~ city**, quartiers défavorisés *m. pl.* ~most *a.* le plus profond. ~ **tube,** chambre à air *f.*

innings /'mɪŋz/ *n. invar.* tour de batte *m.*; (*fig.*) tour *m.*

innkeeper /'ɪnkiːpə(r)/ *n.* aubergiste *m./f.*

innocen|t /'ɪnəsnt/ *a. & n.* innocent(e) (*m. (f.)*). ~**ce** *n.* innocence *f.*

innocuous /ɪ'nɒkjʊəs/ *a.* inoffensif.

innovat|e /'ɪnəveɪt/ *v.i.* innover. ~**ion** /-'veɪʃn/ *n.* innovation *f.* ~**or** *n.* innova|teur, -trice *m., f.*

innuendo /mjuː'endəʊ/ *n.* (*pl.* -oes) insinuation *f.*

innumerable /ɪ'njuːmərəbl/ *a.* innombrable.

inoculat|e /ɪ'nɒkjʊleɪt/ *v.t.* inoculer. ~**ion** /-'leɪʃn/ *n.* inoculation *f.*

inoffensive /ɪnə'fensɪv/ *a.* inoffensif.

inoperative /m'ɒpərətɪv/ *a.* inopérant.

inopportune /m'ɒpətjuːn/ *a.* inopportun.

inordinate /ɪ'nɔːdmət/ *a.* excessif. ~**ly** *adv.* excessivement.

input /'ɪnpʊt/ *n.* (*data*) données *f. pl.*; (*computer process*) entrée *f.*; (*power*; *electr.*) énergie *f.*

inquest /'ɪnkwest/ *n.* enquête *f.*

inquire /m'kwaɪə(r)/ *v.t./i.* = **enquire.**

inquiry /m'kwaɪərɪ/ *n.* enquête *f.*

inquisition /ɪnkwɪ'zɪʃn/ *n.* inquisition *f.*

inquisitive /m'kwɪzətɪv/ *a.* curieux; (*prying*) indiscret.

inroad /'ɪnrəʊd/ *n.* incursion *f.*

insan|e /m'sem/ *a.* fou. ~**ity** /m-'sænətɪ/ *n.* folie *f.,* démence *f.*

insanitary /m'sænɪtrɪ/ *a.* insalubre, malsain.

insatiable /m'seɪʃəbl/ *a.* insatiable.

inscri|be /m'skraɪb/ *v.t.* inscrire; (*book*) dédicacer. ~**ption** /-ɪpʃn/ *n.* inscription *f.;* dédicace *f.*

inscrutable /m'skruːtəbl/ *a.* impénétrable.

insect /'ɪnsekt/ *n.* insecte *m.*

insecticide /m'sektɪsaɪd/ *n.* insecticide *m.*

insecur|e /msɪ'kjʊə(r)/ *a.* (*not firm*) peu solide; (*unsafe*) peu sûr; (*worried*) anxieux. ~**ity** *n* insécurité *f.*

insemination /msemɪ'neɪʃn/ *n.* insémination *f.*

insensible /m'sensəbl/ *a.* insensible; (*unconscious*) inconscient.

insensitive /m'sensətɪv/ *a.* insensible.

inseparable /m'seprəbl/ *a.* inséparable.

insert[1] /'mɜːt/ *v.t.* insérer. ~**ion** /-ʃn/ *n.* insertion *f.*

insert[2] /'mɜːt/ *n.* insertion *f.;* (*advertising*) encart *m.*

in-service /'mɜːvɪs/ *a.* (*training*) continu.

inshore /m'ʃɔː(r)/ *a.* côtier.

inside /m'saɪd/ *n.* intérieur *m.* ~**(s),** (*fam.*) entrailles *f. pl.* ● *a.* intérieur. ● *adv.* à l'intérieur, dedans. ● *prep.* à l'intérieur de; (*of time*) en moins de. ~ **out,** à l'envers; (*thoroughly*) à fond.

insidious /m'sɪdɪəs/ *a.* insidieux.

insight /'msaɪt/ *n.* (*perception*) perspicacité *f.;* (*idea*) aperçu *m.*

insignia /m'sɪgnɪə/ *n. pl.* insignes *m. pl.*

insignificant /msɪg'nɪfɪkənt/ *a.* insignifiant.

insincer|e /msm'sɪə(r)/ *a.* peu sincère. ~**ity** /-'serətɪ/ *n.* manque de sincérité *m.*

insinuat|e /m'sɪnjʊeɪt/ *v.t.* insinuer. ~**ion** /-'eɪʃn/ *n.* insinuation *f.*

insipid /m'sɪpɪd/ *a.* insipide.

insist /m'sɪst/ *v.t./i.* insister. ~ **on,** affirmer; (*demand*) exiger. ~ **on doing,** insister pour faire.

insisten|t /m'sɪstənt/ *a.* insistant. ~**ce** *n.* insistance *f.* ~**tly** *adv.* avec insistance.

insole /'msəʊl/ *n.* (*separate*) semelle *f.*

insolen|t /'msələnt/ *a.* insolent. ~**ce** *n.* insolence *f.*

insoluble /m'sɒljʊbl/ *a.* insoluble.

insolvent /m'sɒlvənt/ *a.* insolvable.

insomnia /m'sɒmnɪə/ *n.* insomnie *f.* ~**c** /-ræk/ *n.* insomniaque *m./f.*

inspect /m'spekt/ *v.t.* inspecter; (*tickets*) contrôler. ~**ion** /-kʃn/ *n.* inspection *f.;* contrôle *m.* ~**or** *n.* inspec|teur, -trice *m., f.;* (*on train, bus*) contrôleu|r, -se *m., f.*

inspir|e /m'spaɪə(r)/ *v.t.* inspirer. ~**ation** /-ə'reɪʃn/ *n.* inspiration *f.*

instability /mstə'bɪlətɪ/ *n.* instabilité *f.*

install /m'stɔːl/ *v.t.* installer. ~**ation** /-ə'leɪʃn/ *n.* installation *f.*

instalment /m'stɔːlmənt/ *n.* (*payment*) acompte *m.,* versement *m.;* (*of serial*) épisode *m.*

instance /'ɪnstəns/ n. exemple m.; (*case*) cas m. **for ~,** par exemple. **in the first ~,** en premier lieu.

instant /'ɪnstənt/ a. immédiat; (*food*) instantané. ● n. instant m. **~ly** adv. immédiatement.

instantaneous /ɪnstən'teɪnɪəs/ a. instantané.

instead /ɪn'sted/ adv. plutôt. **~ of doing,** au lieu de faire. **~ of s.o.,** à la place de qn.

instep /'ɪnstep/ n. cou-de-pied m.

instigat|e /'ɪnstɪɡeɪt/ v.t. provoquer. **~ion** /-'ɡeɪʃn/ n. instigation f. **~or** n. instiga|teur, -trice m., f.

instil /ɪn'stɪl/ v.t. (p.t. **instilled**) inculquer; (*inspire*) insuffler.

instinct /'ɪnstɪŋkt/ n. instinct m. **~ive** /ɪn'stɪŋktɪv/ a. instinctif.

institut|e /'ɪnstɪtjuːt/ n. institut m. ● v.t. instituer; (*inquiry etc.*) entamer. **~ion** /-'tjuːʃn/ n. institution f.; (*school, hospital*) établissement m.

instruct /ɪn'strʌkt/ v.t. instruire; (*order*) ordonner. **~ s.o. in sth.,** enseigner qch. à qn. **~ s.o. to do,** ordonner à qn. de faire. **~ion** /-kʃn/ n. instruction f. **~ions** /-kʃnz/ n. pl. (*for use*) mode d'emploi m. **~ive** a. instructif. **~or** n. professeur m.; (*skiing, driving*) moni|teur, -trice m., f.

instrument /'ɪnstrʊmənt/ n. instrument m. **~ panel,** tableau de bord m.

instrumental /ɪnstrʊ'mentl/ a. instrumental. **be ~ in,** contribuer à. **~ist** n. instrumentaliste m./f.

insubordinat|e /ɪnsə'bɔːdɪnət/ a. insubordonné. **~ion** /-'neɪʃn/ n. insubordination f.

insufferable /ɪn'sʌfrəbl/ a. intolérable, insupportable.

insufficient /ɪnsə'fɪʃnt/ a. insuffisant. **~ly** adv. insuffisamment.

insular /'ɪnsjʊlə(r)/ a. insulaire; (*mind, person: fig.*) borné.

insulat|e /'ɪnsjʊleɪt/ v.t. (*room, wire, etc.*) isoler. **~ing tape,** chatterton m. **~ion** /-'leɪʃn/ n. isolation f.

insulin /'ɪnsjʊlɪn/ n. insuline f.

insult[1] /ɪn'sʌlt/ v.t. insulter.

insult[2] /'ɪnsʌlt/ n. insulte f.

insuperable /ɪn'sjuːprəbl/ a. insurmontable.

insur|e /ɪn'ʃʊə(r)/ v.t. assurer. **~e that,** (*ensure: Amer.*) s'assurer que. **~ance** n. assurance f.

insurmountable /ɪnsə'maʊntəbl/ a. insurmontable.

insurrection /ɪnsə'rekʃn/ n. insurrection f.

intact /ɪn'tækt/ a. intact.

intake /'ɪnteɪk/ n. admission(s) f. (*pl.*); (*techn.*) prise f.

intangible /ɪn'tændʒəbl/ a. intangible.

integral /'ɪntɪɡrəl/ a. intégral. **be an ~ part of,** faire partie intégrante de.

integrat|e /'ɪntɪɡreɪt/ v.t./i. (s')intégrer. **~ion** /-'ɡreɪʃn/ n. intégration f.; (*racial*) déségrégation f.

integrity /ɪn'teɡrətɪ/ n. intégrité f.

intellect /'ɪntəlekt/ n. intelligence f. **~ual** /-'lektʃʊəl/ a. & n. intellectuel(le) (m. (f.)).

intelligen|t /ɪn'telɪdʒənt/ a. intelligent. **~ce** n. intelligence f.; (*mil.*) renseignements m. pl. **~tly** adv. intelligemment.

intelligentsia /ɪntelɪ'dʒentsɪə/ n. intelligentsia f.

intelligible /ɪn'telɪdʒəbl/ a. intelligible.

intemperance /ɪn'tempərəns/ n. (*drunkenness*) ivrognerie f.

intend /ɪn'tend/ v.t. destiner. **~ to do,** avoir l'intention de faire. **~ed** a. (*deliberate*) intentionnel; (*planned*) prévu; n. (*future spouse: fam.*) promis(e) m. (f.).

intens|e /ɪn'tens/ a. intense; (*person*) passionné. **~ely** adv. (*to live etc.*) intensément; (*very*) extrêmement. **~ity** n. intensité f.

intensif|y /ɪn'tensɪfaɪ/ v.t. intensifier. **~ication** /-ɪ'keɪʃn/ n. intensification f.

intensive /ɪn'tensɪv/ a. intensif. **in ~ care,** en réanimation.

intent /ɪn'tent/ n. intention f. ● a. attentif. **~ on,** absorbé par. **~ on doing,** résolu à faire. **~ly** adv. attentivement.

intention /ɪn'tenʃn/ n. intention f. **~al** a. intentionnel.

inter /ɪn'tɜː(r)/ v.t. (p.t. **interred**) enterrer.

inter- /ɪntə(r)/ pref. inter-.

interact /ɪntə'rækt/ v.i. avoir une action réciproque. **~ion** /-kʃn/ n. interaction f.

intercede /ɪntə'siːd/ v.i. intercéder.

intercept /mtə'sept/ *v.t.* intercepter. **~ion** /-pʃn/ *n.* interception *f.*

interchange /'mtətʃemdʒ/ *n.* (*road junction*) échangeur *m.*

interchangeable /mtə'tʃemdʒəbl/ *a.* interchangeable.

intercom /'mtəkɒm/ *n.* interphone *m.*

interconnected /mtəkə'nektɪd/ *a.* (*facts, events, etc.*) lié.

intercourse /'mtəkɔ:s/ *n.* (*sexual, social*) rapports *m. pl.*

interest /'mtrəst/ *n.* intérêt *m.*; (*stake*) intérêts *m. pl.* ● *v.t.* intéresser. **~ rates,** taux d'intérêt *m. pl.* **~ed** *a.* intéressé. **be ~ed in,** s'intéresser à. **~ing** *a.* intéressant.

interface /'mtəfeɪs/ *n.* (*comput.*) interface *f.*; (*fig.*) zone de rencontre *f.*

interfer|e /mtə'fɪə(r)/ *v.i.* se mêler des affaires des autres. **~e in,** s'ingérer dans. **~e with,** (*plans*) créer un contretemps avec; (*work*) s'immiscer dans; (*radio*) faire des interférences avec; (*lock*) toucher à. **~ence** *n.* ingérence *f.*; (*radio*) parasites *m. pl.*

interim /'mtərɪm/ *n.* intérim *m.* ● *a.* intérimaire.

interior /m'tɪərɪə(r)/ *n.* intérieur *m.* ● *a.* intérieur.

interjection /mtə'dʒekʃn/ *n.* interjection *f.*

interlinked /mtə'lɪŋkt/ *a.* lié.

interlock /mtə'lɒk/ *v.t./i.* (*techn.*) (s')emboîter, (s')enclencher.

interloper /'mtələʊpə(r)/ *n.* intrus(e) *m.* (*f.*).

interlude /'mtəlu:d/ *n.* intervalle *m.*; (*theatre, mus.*) intermède *m.*

intermarr|iage /mtə'mærɪdʒ/ *n.* mariage entre membres de races différentes *m.* **~y** *v.i.* se marier (entre eux).

intermediary /mtə'mi:dɪərɪ/ *a. & n.* intermédiaire (*m./f.*).

intermediate /mtə'mi:dɪət/ *a.* intermédiaire; (*exam etc.*) moyen.

interminable /m'tɜ:mɪnəbl/ *a.* interminable.

intermission /mtə'mɪʃn/ *n.* pause *f.*; (*theatre etc.*) entracte *m.*

intermittent /mtə'mɪtnt/ *a.* intermittent. **~ly** *adv.* par intermittence.

intern[1] /m'tɜ:n/ *v.t.* interner. **~ee** /-'ni:/ *n.* interné(e) *m.* (*f.*). **~ment** *n.* internement *m.*

intern[2] /'mtɜ:n/ *n.* (*doctor: Amer.*) interne *m./f.*

internal /m'tɜ:nl/ *a.* interne; (*domestic: pol.*) intérieur. **I~ Revenue,** (*Amer.*) fisc *m.* **~ly** *adv.* intérieurement.

international /mtə'næʃnəl/ *a. & n.* international (*m.*).

interplay /'mtəpleɪ/ *n.* jeu *m.*, interaction *f.*

interpolate /m'tɜ:pəleɪt/ *v.t.* interpoler.

interpret /m'tɜ:prɪt/ *v.t.* interpréter. ● *v.i.* faire l'interprète. **~ation** /-'teɪʃn/ *n.* interprétation *f.* **~er** *n.* interprète *m./f.*

interrelated /mtərɪ'leɪtɪd/ *a.* en corrélation, lié.

interrogat|e /m'terəgeɪt/ *v.t.* interroger. **~ion** /-'geɪʃn/ *n.* interrogation *f.* (**of,** de); (*session of questions*) interrogatoire *m.*

interrogative /mtə'rɒgətɪv/ *a. & n.* interrogatif (*m.*).

interrupt /mtə'rʌpt/ *v.t.* interrompre. **~ion** /-pʃn/ *n.* interruption *f.*

intersect /mtə'sekt/ *v.t./i.* (*lines, roads*) (se) couper. **~ion** /-kʃn/ *n.* intersection *f.*; (*crossroads*) croisement *m.*

interspersed /mtə'spɜ:st/ *a.* (*scattered*) dispersé. **~ with,** parsemé de.

intertwine /mtə'twaɪn/ *v.t./i.* (s')entrelacer.

interval /'mtəvl/ *n.* intervalle *m.*; (*theatre*) entracte *m.* **at ~s,** par intervalles.

interven|e /mtə'vi:n/ *v.i.* intervenir; (*of time*) s'écouler (**between,** entre); (*happen*) survenir. **~tion** /-'venʃn/ *n.* intervention *f.*

interview /'mtəvju:/ *n.* (*with reporter*) interview *f.*; (*for job etc.*) entrevue *f.* ● *v.t.* interviewer. **~er** *n.* interviewer *m.*

intestin|e /m'testɪn/ *n.* intestin *m.* **~al** *a.* intestinal.

intima|te[1] /'mtɪmət/ *a.* intime; (*detailed*) profond. **~cy** *n.* intimité *f.* **~tely** *adv.* intimement.

intimate[2] /'mtɪmeɪt/ *v.t.* (*state*) annoncer; (*imply*) suggérer.

intimidat|e /m'tɪmɪdeɪt/ *v.t.* intimider. **~ion** /-'deɪʃn/ *n.* intimidation *f.*

into /'mtu:, *unstressed* 'mtə/ *prep.* (*put, go, fall, etc.*) dans; (*divide, translate, etc.*) en.

intolerable /ɪnˈtɒlərəbl/ a. intolérable.

intoleran|t /ɪnˈtɒlərənt/ a. intolérant. **~ce** n. intolérance f.

intonation /ɪntəˈneɪʃn/ n. intonation f.

intoxicat|e /ɪnˈtɒksɪkeɪt/ v.t. enivrer. **~ed** a. ivre. **~ion** /-ˈkeɪʃn/ n. ivresse f.

intra- /ˈɪntrə/ pref. intra-.

intractable /ɪnˈtræktəbl/ a. très difficile.

intransigent /ɪnˈtrænsɪdʒənt/ a. intransigeant.

intransitive /ɪnˈtrænsətɪv/ a. (verb) intransitif.

intravenous /ɪntrəˈviːnəs/ a. (med.) intraveineux.

intrepid /ɪnˈtrepɪd/ a. intrépide.

intrica|te /ˈɪntrɪkət/ a. complexe. **~cy** n. complexité f.

intrigu|e /ɪnˈtriːg/ v.t./i. intriguer. ● n. intrigue f. **~ing** a. très intéressant; (curious) curieux.

intrinsic /ɪnˈtrɪnsɪk/ a. intrinsèque. **~ally** /-klɪ/ adv. intrinsèquement.

introduce /ɪntrəˈdjuːs/ v.t. (bring in, insert) introduire; (programme, question) présenter. **~ s.o. to,** (person) présenter qn. à; (subject) faire connaître à qn.

introduct|ion /ɪntrəˈdʌkʃn/ n. introduction f.; (to person) présentation f. **~ory** /-tərɪ/ a. (letter, words) d'introduction.

introspective /ɪntrəˈspektɪv/ a. introspectif.

introvert /ˈɪntrəvɜːt/ n. introverti(e) m. (f.).

intru|de /ɪnˈtruːd/ v.i. (person) s'imposer (on s.o., à qn.), déranger. **~der** n. intrus(e) m. (f.). **~sion** n. intrusion f.

intuit|ion /ɪntjuːˈɪʃn/ n. intuition f. **~ive** /ɪnˈtjuːɪtɪv/ a. intuitif.

inundat|e /ˈɪnʌndeɪt/ v.t. inonder (with, de). **~ion** /-ˈdeɪʃn/ n. inondation f.

invade /ɪnˈveɪd/ v.t. envahir. **~r** /-ə(r)/ n. envahisseu|r, -se m., f.

invalid[1] /ˈɪnvəlɪd/ n. malade m./f.; (disabled) infirme m./f.

invalid[2] /ɪnˈvælɪd/ a. non valable. **~ate** v.t. invalider.

invaluable /ɪnˈvæljʊəbl/ a. inestimable.

invariabl|e /ɪnˈveərɪəbl/ a. invariable. **~y** adv. invariablement.

invasion /ɪnˈveɪʒn/ n. invasion f.

invective /ɪnˈvektɪv/ n. invective f.

inveigh /ɪnˈveɪ/ v.i. invectiver.

inveigle /ɪnˈveɪgl/ v.t. persuader.

invent /ɪnˈvent/ v.t. inventer. **~ion** /-enʃn/ n. invention f. **~ive** a. inventif. **~or** n. inven|teur, -trice m., f.

inventory /ˈɪnvəntrɪ/ n. inventaire m.

inverse /ɪnˈvɜːs/ a. & n. inverse (m.). **~ly** adv. inversement.

inver|t /ɪnˈvɜːt/ v.t. intervertir. **~ted commas,** guillemets m. pl. **~sion** n. inversion f.

invest /ɪnˈvest/ v.t. investir; (time, effort: fig.) consacrer. ● v.i. faire un investissement. **~ in,** (buy: fam.) se payer. **~ment** n. investissement m. **~or** n. actionnaire m./f.; (saver) épargnant(e) m. (f.).

investigat|e /ɪnˈvestɪgeɪt/ v.t. étudier; (crime etc.) enquêter sur. **~ion** /-ˈgeɪʃn/ n. investigation f. **under ~ion,** à l'étude. **~or** n. (police) enquêteu|r, -se m., f.

inveterate /ɪnˈvetərət/ a. invétéré.

invidious /ɪnˈvɪdɪəs/ a. (hateful) odieux; (unfair) injuste.

invigilat|e /ɪnˈvɪdʒɪleɪt/ v.i. (schol.) être de surveillance. **~or** n. surveillant(e) m. (f.).

invigorate /ɪnˈvɪgəreɪt/ v.t. vivifier; (encourage) stimuler.

invincible /ɪnˈvɪnsəbl/ a. invincible.

invisible /ɪnˈvɪzəbl/ a. invisible.

invit|e /ɪnˈvaɪt/ v.t. inviter; (ask for) demander. **~ation** /ɪnvɪˈteɪʃn/ n. invitation f. **~ing** a. (meal, smile, etc.) engageant.

invoice /ˈɪnvɔɪs/ n. facture f. ● v.t. facturer.

invoke /ɪnˈvəʊk/ v.t. invoquer.

involuntary /ɪnˈvɒləntrɪ/ a. involontaire.

involve /ɪnˈvɒlv/ v.t. entraîner; (people) faire participer. **~d** a. (complex) compliqué; (at stake) en jeu. **be ~d in,** (work) participer à; (crime) être mêlé à. **~ment** n. participation f. (in, à).

invulnerable /ɪnˈvʌlnərəbl/ a. invulnérable.

inward /ˈɪnwəd/ a. & adv. vers l'intérieur; (feeling etc.) intérieur. **~ly** adv. intérieurement. **~s** adv. vers l'intérieur.

iodine /ˈaɪədiːn/ n. iode m.; (antiseptic) teinture d'iode f.

iota /aɪˈəʊtə/ n. (amount) brin m.

IOU /aɪəʊˈjuː/ *abbr.* (*I owe you*) reconnaissance de dette *f.*

IQ /aɪˈkjuː/ *abbr.* (*intelligence quotient*) QI *m.*

Iran /ɪˈrɑːn/ *n.* Iran *m.* **~ian** /ɪˈreɪnɪən/ *a. & n.* iranien(ne) (*m.* (*f.*)).

Iraq /ɪˈrɑːk/ *n.* Irak *m.* **~i** *a. & n.* irakien(ne) (*m.* (*f.*)).

irascible /ɪˈræsəbl/ *a.* irascible.

irate /aɪˈreɪt/ *a.* en colère, furieux.

ire /ˈaɪə(r)/ *n.* courroux *m.*

Ireland /ˈaɪələnd/ *n.* Irlande *f.*

iris /ˈaɪərɪs/ *n.* (*anat.*, *bot.*) iris *m.*

Irish /ˈaɪərɪʃ/ *a.* irlandais. ● *n.* (*lang.*) irlandais *m.* **~man** *n.* Irlandais *m.* **~woman** *n.* Irlandaise *f.*

irk /ɜːk/ *v.t.* ennuyer. **~some** *a.* ennuyeux.

iron /ˈaɪən/ *n.* fer *m.*; (*appliance*) fer (à repasser) *m.* ● *a.* de fer. ● *v.t.* repasser. **I~ Curtain,** rideau de fer *m.* **~ out,** faire disparaître. **~ingboard** *n.* planche à repasser *f.*

ironic(al) /aɪˈrɒnɪk(l)/ *a.* ironique.

ironmonger /ˈaɪənmʌŋgə(r)/ *n.* quincaillier *m.* **~y** *n.* quincaillerie *f.*

ironwork /ˈaɪənwɜːk/ *n.* ferronnerie *f.*

irony /ˈaɪərənɪ/ *n.* ironie *f.*

irrational /ɪˈræʃənl/ *a.* irrationnel; (*person*) pas rationnel.

irreconcilable /ɪrekənˈsaɪləbl/ *a.* irréconciliable; (*incompatible*) inconciliable.

irrefutable /ɪˈrefjʊtəbl/ *a.* irréfutable.

irregular /ɪˈregjʊlə(r)/ *a.* irrégulier. **~ity** /-ˈlærətɪ/ *n.* irrégularité *f.*

irrelevan|t /ɪˈreləvənt/ *a.* sans rapport (**to,** avec). **~ce** *n.* manque de rapport *m.*

irreparable /ɪˈrepərəbl/ *a.* irréparable, irrémédiable.

irreplaceable /ɪrɪˈpleɪsəbl/ *a.* irremplaçable.

irrepressible /ɪrɪˈpresəbl/ *a.* irrépressible.

irresistible /ɪrɪˈzɪstəbl/ *a.* irrésistible.

irresolute /ɪˈrezəluːt/ *a.* irrésolu.

irrespective /ɪrɪˈspektɪv/ *a.* **~ of,** sans tenir compte de.

irresponsible /ɪrɪˈspɒnsəbl/ *a.* irresponsable.

irretrievable /ɪrɪˈtriːvəbl/ *a.* irréparable.

irreverent /ɪˈrevərənt/ *a.* irrévérencieux.

irreversible /ɪrɪˈvɜːsəbl/ *a.* irréversible; (*decision*) irrévocable.

irrevocable /ɪˈrevəkəbl/ *a.* irrévocable.

irrigat|e /ˈɪrɪgeɪt/ *v.t.* irriguer. **~ion** /-ˈgeɪʃn/ *n.* irrigation *f.*

irritable /ˈɪrɪtəbl/ *a.* irritable.

irritat|e /ˈɪrɪteɪt/ *v.t.* irriter. **be ~ed by,** être énervé par. **~ing** *a.* énervant. **~ion** /-ˈteɪʃn/ *n.* irritation *f.*

is /ɪz/ *see* be.

Islam /ˈɪzlɑːm/ *n.* Islam *m.* **~ic** /ɪzˈlæmɪk/ *a.* islamique.

island /ˈaɪlənd/ *n.* île *f.* **traffic ~,** refuge *m.* **~er** *n.* insulaire *m./f.*

isle /aɪl/ *n.* île *f.*

isolat|e /ˈaɪsəleɪt/ *v.t.* isoler. **~ion** /-ˈleɪʃn/ *n.* isolement *m.*

isotope /ˈaɪsətəʊp/ *n.* isotope *m.*

Israel /ˈɪzreɪl/ *n.* Israël *m.* **~i** /ɪzˈreɪlɪ/ *a. & n.* israélien(ne) (*m.* (*f.*)).

issue /ˈɪʃuː/ *n.* question *f.*; (*outcome*) résultat *m.*; (*of magazine etc.*) numéro *m.*; (*of stamps etc.*) émission *f.*; (*offspring*) descendance *f.* ● *v.t.* distribuer, donner; (*stamps etc.*) émettre; (*book*) publier; (*order*) donner. ● *v.i.* **~ from,** sortir de. **at ~,** en cause. **take ~,** engager une controverse.

isthmus /ˈɪsməs/ *n.* isthme *m.*

it /ɪt/ *pron.* (*subject*) il, elle; (*object*) le, la, l'*; (*impersonal subject*) il; (*non-specific*) ce, c'*, cela, ça. **it is,** (*quiet, my book, etc.*) c'est. **it is/cold/warm/late/** *etc.*, il fait froid/chaud/tard/*etc.* **that's it,** c'est ça. **who is it?,** qui est-ce? **of it, from it,** en. **in it, at it, to it,** y.

IT *abbr. see* information technology.

italic /ɪˈtælɪk/ *a.* italique. **~s** *n. pl.* italique *m.*

Ital|y /ˈɪtəlɪ/ *n.* Italie *f.* **~ian** /ɪˈtælɪən/ *a. & n.* italien(ne) (*m.* (*f.*)); (*lang.*) italien *m.*

itch /ɪtʃ/ *n.* démangeaison *f.* ● *v.i.* démanger. **my arm ~es,** mon bras me démange. **I am ~ing to,** ça me démange de. **~y** *a.* qui démange.

item /ˈaɪtəm/ *n.* article *m.*, chose *f.*; (*on agenda*) question *f.* **news ~,** nouvelle *f.* **~ize** *v.t.* détailler.

itinerant /aɪˈtɪnərənt/ *a.* itinérant; (*musician, actor*) ambulant.

itinerary /aɪˈtɪnərərɪ/ *n.* itinéraire *m.*

its /ɪts/ *a.* son, sa, *pl.* ses.

it's /ɪts/ = **it is, it has.**

itself /ɪt'self/ *pron.* lui-même, elle-même; (*reflexive*) se.

IUD *abbr.* (*intrauterine device*) stérilet *m.*

ivory /'aɪvərɪ/ *n.* ivoire *m.* ~ **tower,** tour d'ivoire *f.*

ivy /'aɪvɪ/ *n.* lierre *m.*

J

jab /dʒæb/ *v.t.* (*p.t.* **jabbed**) (*thrust*) enfoncer; (*prick*) piquer. ● *n.* coup *m.*; (*injection*) piqûre *f.*

jabber /'dʒæbə(r)/ *v.i.* jacasser, bavarder; (*indistinctly*) bredouiller. ● *n.* bavardage *m.*

jack /dʒæk/ *n.* (*techn.*) cric *m.*; (*cards*) valet *m.*; (*plug*) fiche *f.* ● *v.t.* ~ **up,** soulever (avec un cric).

jackal /'dʒækɔːl/ *n.* chacal *m.*

jackass /'dʒækæs/ *n.* âne *m.*

jackdaw /'dʒækdɔː/ *n.* choucas *m.*

jacket /'dʒækɪt/ *n.* veste *f.*, veston *m.*; (*of book*) jaquette *f.*

jack-knife /'dʒæknaɪf/ *n.* couteau pliant *m.* ● *v.i.* (*lorry*) faire un tête-à-queue.

jackpot /'dʒækpɒt/ *n.* gros lot *m.* **hit the ~,** gagner le gros lot.

Jacuzzi /dʒə'kuːzɪ/ *n.* (P.) bain à remous *m.*

jade /dʒeɪd/ *n.* (*stone*) jade *m.*

jaded /'dʒeɪdɪd/ *a.* las; (*appetite*) blasé.

jagged /'dʒægɪd/ *a.* dentelé.

jail /dʒeɪl/ *n.* prison *f.* ● *v.t.* mettre en prison. ~**er** *n.* geôlier *m.*

jalopy /dʒə'lɒpɪ/ *n.* vieux tacot *m.*

jam¹ /dʒæm/ *n.* confiture *f.*

jam² /dʒæm/ *v.t./i.* (*p.t.* **jammed**) (*wedge, become wedged*) (se) coincer; (*cram*) (s')entasser; (*street etc.*) encombrer; (*thrust*) enfoncer; (*radio*) brouiller. ● *n.* foule *f.*; (*of traffic*) embouteillage *m.*; (*situation: fam.*) pétrin *m.* ~**-packed** *a.* (*fam.*) bourré.

Jamaica /dʒə'meɪkə/ *n.* Jamaïque *f.*

jangle /'dʒæŋgl/ *n.* cliquetis *m.* ● *v.t./i.* (faire) cliqueter.

janitor /'dʒænɪtə(r)/ *n.* concierge *m.*

January /'dʒænjʊərɪ/ *n.* janvier *m.*

Japan /dʒə'pæn/ *n.* Japon *m.* ~**ese** /dʒæpə'niːz/ *a.* & *n.* japonais(e) (*m.* (*f.*)); (*lang.*) japonais *m.*

jar¹ /dʒɑː(r)/ *n.* pot *m.*, bocal *m.*

jar² /dʒɑː(r)/ *v.i.* (*p.t.* **jarred**) grincer; (*of colours etc.*) détonner. ● *v.t.* ébranler. ● *n.* son discordant *m.* ~**ring** *a.* discordant.

jargon /'dʒɑːgən/ *n.* jargon *m.*

jasmine /'dʒæsmɪn/ *n.* jasmin *m.*

jaundice /'dʒɔːndɪs/ *n.* jaunisse *f.*

jaundiced /'dʒɔːndɪst/ *a.* (*envious*) envieux; (*bitter*) aigri.

jaunt /dʒɔːnt/ *n.* (*trip*) balade *f.*

jaunty /'dʒɔːntɪ/ *a.* (-ier, -iest) (*cheerful, sprightly*) allègre.

javelin /'dʒævlɪn/ *n.* javelot *m.*

jaw /dʒɔː/ *n.* mâchoire *f.* ● *v.i.* (*talk: sl.*) jacasser.

jay /dʒeɪ/ *n.* geai *m.* ~**-walk** *v.i.* traverser la chaussée imprudemment.

jazz /dʒæz/ *n.* jazz *m.* ● *v.t.* ~ **up,** animer. ~**y** *a.* tape-à-l'œil *invar.*

jealous /'dʒeləs/ *a.* jaloux. ~**y** *n.* jalousie *f.*

jeans /dʒiːnz/ *n. pl.* (blue-)jean *m.*

jeep /dʒiːp/ *n.* jeep *f.*

jeer /dʒɪə(r)/ *v.t./i.* ~ **(at),** railler; (*boo*) huer. ● *n.* raillerie *f.*; huée *f.*

jell /dʒel/ *v.i.* (*set: fam.*) prendre. ~**ied** *a.* en gelée.

jelly /'dʒelɪ/ *n.* gelée *f.*

jellyfish /'dʒelɪfɪʃ/ *n.* méduse *f.*

jeopard|y /'dʒepədɪ/ *n.* péril *m.* ~**ize** *v.t.* mettre en péril.

jerk /dʒɜːk/ *n.* secousse *f.*; (*fool: sl.*) idiot *m.*; (*creep: sl.*) salaud *m.* ● *v.t.* donner une secousse à. ~**ily** *adv.* par saccades. ~**y** *a.* saccadé.

jersey /'dʒɜːzɪ/ *n.* (*garment*) chandail *m.*, tricot *m.*; (*fabric*) jersey *m.*

jest /dʒest/ *n.* plaisanterie *f.* ● *v.i.* plaisanter. ~**er** *n.* bouffon *m.*

Jesus /'dʒiːzəs/ *n.* Jésus *m.*

jet¹ /dʒet/ *n.* (*mineral*) jais *m.* ~**-black** *a.* de jais.

jet² /dʒet/ *n.* (*stream*) jet *m.*; (*plane*) avion à réaction *m.*, jet *m.* ~ **lag,** fatigue due au décalage horaire *f.* ~**-propelled** *a.* à réaction.

jettison /'dʒetɪsn/ *v.t.* jeter à la mer; (*aviat.*) larguer; (*fig.*) abandonner.

jetty /'dʒetɪ/ *n.* (*breakwater*) jetée *f.*

Jew /dʒuː/ *n.* Juif *m.* ~**ess** *n.* Juive *f.*

jewel /'dʒuːəl/ *n.* bijou *m.* ~**led** *a.* orné de bijoux. ~**ler** *n.* bijout|ier, -ière *m.*, *f.* ~**lery** *n.* bijoux *m. pl.*

Jewish /'dʒuːɪʃ/ *a.* juif.

Jewry /'dʒʊərɪ/ *n.* les Juifs *m. pl.*

jib /dʒɪb/ *v.i.* (*p.t.* **jibbed**) regimber (**at,** devant). ● *n.* (*sail*) foc *m.*

jibe /dʒaɪb/ *n.* = **gibe.**

jiffy /'dʒɪfɪ/ n. (fam.) instant m.

jig /dʒɪg/ n. (dance) gigue f.

jiggle /'dʒɪgl/ v.t. secouer légèrement.

jigsaw /'dʒɪgsɔ:/ n. puzzle m.

jilt /dʒɪlt/ v.t. laisser tomber.

jingle /'dʒɪŋgl/ v.t./i. (faire) tinter. ● n. tintement m.; (advertising) jingle m., sonal m.

jinx /dʒɪŋks/ n. (person: fam.) portemalheur m. invar.; (spell: fig.) mauvais sort m.

jitter|s /'dʒɪtəz/ n. pl. the ~s, (fam.) la frousse f. ~y /-ərɪ/ a. be ~y, (fam.) avoir la frousse.

job /dʒɒb/ n. travail m.; (post) poste m. **have a ~ doing**, avoir du mal à faire. **it is a good ~ that**, heureusement que. ~less a. sans travail, au chômage.

jobcentre /'dʒɒbsentə(r)/ n. agence (nationale) pour l'emploi f.

jockey /'dʒɒkɪ/ n. jockey m. ● v.i. (manœuvre) manœuvrer.

jocular /'dʒɒkjʊlə(r)/ a. jovial.

jog /dʒɒg/ v.t. (p.t. **jogged**) pousser; (memory) rafraîchir. ● v.i. faire du jogging. ~**ging** n. jogging m.

join /dʒɔɪn/ v.t. joindre, unir; (club) devenir membre de; (political group) adhérer à; (army) s'engager dans. ~ **s.o.**, (in activity) se joindre à qn.; (meet) rejoindre qn. ● v.i. (roads etc.) se rejoindre. ● n. joint m. ~ **in**, participer (à). ~ **up**, (mil.) s'engager.

joiner /'dʒɔɪnə(r)/ n. menuisier m.

joint /dʒɔɪnt/ a. (account, venture) commun. ● n. (join) joint m.; (anat.) articulation f.; (culin.) rôti m.; (place: sl.) boîte f. ~ **author**, coauteur m. **out of ~**, déboîté. ~**ly** adv. conjointement.

joist /dʒɔɪst/ n. solive f.

jok|e /dʒəʊk/ n. plaisanterie f.; (trick) farce f. ● v.i. plaisanter. **it's no ~e**, ce n'est pas drôle. ~**er** n. blagueu|r, -se m., f.; (pej.) petit malin m.; (cards) joker m. ~**ingly** adv. pour rire.

joll|y /'dʒɒlɪ/ a. (-ier, -iest) gai. ● adv. (fam.) rudement. ~**ification** /-fɪ'keɪ-ʃn/, ~**ity** ns. réjouissances f. pl.

jolt /dʒəʊlt/ v.t./i. (vehicle, passenger) cahoter; (shake) secouer. ● n. cahot m.; secousse f.

Jordan /'dʒɔ:dn/ n. Jordanie f.

jostle /'dʒɒsl/ v.t./i. (push) bousculer; (push each other) se bousculer.

jot /dʒɒt/ n. brin m. ● v.t. (p.t. **jotted**) ~ **down**, noter. ~**ter** n. (pad) bloc-notes m.

journal /'dʒɜ:nl/ n. journal m. ~**ism** n. journalisme m. ~**ist** n. journaliste m./f. ~**ese** /-'li:z/ n. jargon des journalistes m.

journey /'dʒɜ:nɪ/ n. voyage m.; (distance) trajet m. ● v.i. voyager.

jovial /'dʒəʊvɪəl/ a. jovial.

joy /dʒɔɪ/ n. joie f. ~-**riding** n. courses en voitures volées f. pl. ~**ful**, ~**ous** adjs. joyeux.

joystick /'dʒɔɪstɪk/ n. (comput.) manette f.

jubil|ant /'dʒu:bɪlənt/ a. débordant de joie. **be ~ant**, jubiler. ~**ation** /-'leɪʃn/ n. jubilation f.

jubilee /'dʒu:bɪli:/ n. jubilé m.

Judaism /'dʒu:deɪɪzəm/ n. judaïsme m.

judder /'dʒʌdə(r)/ v.i. vibrer. ● n. vibration f.

judge /dʒʌdʒ/ n. juge m. ● v.t. juger. **judging by**, à juger de. ~**ment** n. jugement m.

judic|iary /dʒu:'dɪʃərɪ/ n. magistrature f. ~**ial** a. judiciaire.

judicious /dʒu:'dɪʃəs/ a. judicieux.

judo /'dʒu:dəʊ/ n. judo m.

jug /dʒʌg/ n. cruche f., pichet m.

juggernaut /'dʒʌgənɔ:t/ n. (lorry) poids lourd m., mastodonte m.

juggle /'dʒʌgl/ v.t./i. jongler (avec). ~**r** /-ə(r)/ n. jongleu|r, -se m., f.

juic|e /dʒu:s/ n. jus m. ~**y** a. juteux; (details etc.: fam.) croustillant.

juke-box /'dʒu:kbɒks/ n. juke-box m.

July /dʒu:'laɪ/ n. juillet m.

jumble /'dʒʌmbl/ v.t. mélanger. ● n. (muddle) fouillis m. ~ **sale**, vente (de charité) f.

jumbo /'dʒʌmbəʊ/ a. ~ **jet**, avion géant m., jumbo-jet m.

jump /dʒʌmp/ v.t./i. sauter; (start) sursauter; (of price etc.) faire un bond. ● n. saut m.; sursaut m.; (increase) hausse f. ~ **at**, sauter sur. ~-**leads** n. pl. câbles de démarrage m. pl. ~ **the gun**, agir prématurément. ~ **the queue**, resquiller.

jumper /'dʒʌmpə(r)/ n. pull(-over) m.; (dress: Amer.) robe chasuble f.

jumpy /'dʒʌmpɪ/ a. nerveux.

junction /'dʒʌŋkʃn/ n. jonction f.; (of roads etc.) embranchement m.

juncture /'dʒʌŋktʃə(r)/ n. moment m.; (state of affairs) conjoncture f.

June /dʒuːn/ *n.* juin *m.*

jungle /'dʒʌŋgl/ *n.* jungle *f.*

junior /'dʒuːnɪə(r)/ *a.* (*in age*) plus jeune (**to,** que); (*in rank*) subalterne; (*school*) élémentaire; (*executive, doctor*) jeune. ● *n.* cadet(te) *m.* (*f.*); (*schol.*) petit(e) élève *m.*(*f.*); (*sport*) junior *m./f.*

junk /dʒʌŋk/ *n.* bric-à-brac *m. invar.*; (*poor material*) camelote *f.* ● *v.t.* (*Amer., sl.*) balancer. **~ food,** saloperies *f. pl.* **~-shop** *n.* boutique de brocanteur *f.*

junkie /'dʒʌŋkɪ/ *n.* (*sl.*) drogué(e) *m.* (*f.*).

junta /'dʒʌntə/ *n.* junte *f.*

jurisdiction /dʒʊərɪs'dɪkʃn/ *n.* juridiction *f.*

jurisprudence /dʒʊərɪs'pruːdəns/ *n.* jurisprudence *f.*

juror /'dʒʊərə(r)/ *n.* juré *m.*

jury /'dʒʊərɪ/ *n.* jury *m.*

just /dʒʌst/ *a.* (*fair*) juste. ● *adv.* juste, exactement; (*only, slightly*) juste; (*simply*) tout simplement. **he has/had ~ left/etc.,** il vient/venait de partir/*etc.* **have ~ missed,** avoir manqué de peu. **it's ~ a cold,** ce n'est qu'un rhume. **~ as tall/etc.,** tout aussi grand/*etc.* (**as,** que). **~ as well,** heureusement (que). **~ listen!,** écoutez donc! **~ly** *adv.* avec justice.

justice /'dʒʌstɪs/ *n.* justice *f.* **J~ of the Peace,** juge de paix *m.*

justifiabl|e /dʒʌstɪ'faɪəbl/ *a.* justifiable. **~y** *adv.* avec raison.

justif|y /'dʒʌstɪfaɪ/ *v.t.* justifier. **~ication** /-ɪ'keɪʃn/ *n.* justification *f.*

jut /dʒʌt/ *v.i.* (*p.t.* **jutted**). **~ out,** faire saillie, dépasser.

juvenile /'dʒuːvənaɪl/ *a.* (*youthful*) juvénile; (*childish*) puéril; (*delinquent*) jeune; (*court*) pour enfants. ● *n.* jeune *m./f.*

juxtapose /dʒʌkstə'pəʊz/ *v.t.* juxtaposer.

K

kaleidoscope /kə'laɪdəskəʊp/ *n.* kaléidoscope.

kangaroo /kæŋgə'ruː/ *n.* kangourou *m.*

karate /kə'rɑːtɪ/ *n.* karaté *m.*

kebab /kə'bæb/ *n.* brochette *f.*

keel /kiːl/ *n.* (*of ship*) quille *f.* ● *v.i.* **~ over,** chavirer.

keen /kiːn/ *a.* (**-er, -est**) (*interest, wind, feeling, etc.*) vif; (*mind, analysis*) pénétrant; (*edge, appetite*) aiguisé; (*eager*) enthousiaste. **be ~ on,** (*person, thing: fam.*) aimer beaucoup. **be ~ to do** *or* **on doing,** tenir beaucoup à faire. **~ly** *adv.* vivement; avec enthousiasme. **~ness** *n.* vivacité *f.*; enthousiasme *m.*

keep /kiːp/ *v.t.* (*p.t.* **kept**) garder; (*promise, shop, diary, etc.*) tenir; (*family*) entretenir; (*animals*) élever; (*rule etc.*) respecter; (*celebrate*) célébrer; (*delay*) retenir; (*prevent*) empêcher; (*conceal*) cacher. ● *v.i.* (*food*) se garder; (*remain*) rester. **~ (on),** continuer (**doing,** à faire). ● *n.* subsistance *f.*; (*of castle*) donjon *m.* **for ~s,** (*fam.*) pour toujours. **~ back** *v.t.* retenir; *v.i.* ne pas s'approcher. **~ s.o. from doing,** empêcher qn. de faire. **~ in/out,** empêcher d'entrer/de sortir. **~ up,** (se) maintenir. **~ up (with),** suivre. **~er** *n.* gardien(ne) *m.* (*f.*). **~-fit** *n.* exercices physiques *m. pl.*

keeping /'kiːpɪŋ/ *n.* garde *f.* **in ~ with,** en accord avec.

keepsake /'kiːpseɪk/ *n.* (*thing*) souvenir *m.*

keg /keg/ *n.* tonnelet *m.*

kennel /'kenl/ *n.* niche *f.*

Kenya /'kenjə/ *n.* Kenya *m.*

kept /kept/ *see* keep.

kerb /kɜːb/ *n.* bord du trottoir *m.*

kerfuffle /kə'fʌfl/ *n.* (*fuss: fam.*) histoire(s) *f.* (*pl.*).

kernel /'kɜːnl/ *n.* amande *f.*

kerosene /'kerəsiːn/ *n.* (*aviation fuel*) kérosène *m.*; (*paraffin*) pétrole (lampant) *m.*

ketchup /'ketʃəp/ *n.* ketchup *m.*

kettle /'ketl/ *n.* bouilloire *f.*

key /kiː/ *n.* clef *f.*; (*of piano etc.*) touche *f.* ● *a.* clef (*f. invar.*). **~-ring** *n.* porte-clefs *m. invar.* ● *v.t.* **~ in,** (*comput.*) saisir. **~ up,** surexciter.

keyboard /'kiːbɔːd/ *n.* clavier *m.*

keyhole /'kiːhəʊl/ *n.* trou de la serrure *m.*

keynote /'kiːnəʊt/ *n.* (*of speech etc.*) note dominante *f.*

keystone /'kiːstəʊn/ *n.* (*archit., fig.*) clef de voûte *f.*

khaki /'kɑːkɪ/ *a.* kaki *invar.*

kibbutz /kɪˈbʊts/ n. (pl. **-im** /-iːm/) n. kibboutz m.

kick /kɪk/ v.t./i. donner un coup de pied (à); (of horse) ruer. ● n. coup de pied m.; ruade f.; (of gun) recul m.; (thrill: fam.) (malin) plaisir m. **~-off** n. coup d'envoi m. **~ out,** (fam.) flanquer dehors. **~ up,** (fuss, racket: fam.) faire.

kid /kɪd/ n. (goat, leather) chevreau m.; (child: sl.) gosse m./f. ● v.t./i. (p.t. **kidded**) blaguer.

kidnap /ˈkɪdnæp/ v.t. (p.t. **kidnapped**) enlever, kidnapper. **~ping** n. enlèvement m.

kidney /ˈkɪdnɪ/ n. rein m.; (culin.) rognon m.

kill /kɪl/ v.t. tuer; (fig.) mettre fin à. ● n. mise à mort f. **~er** n. tueu|r, -se m., f. **~ing** n. massacre m., meurtre m.; a. (funny: fam.) tordant; (tiring: fam.) tuant.

killjoy /ˈkɪldʒɔɪ/ n. rabat-joie m. invar., trouble-fête m./f. invar.

kiln /kɪln/ n. four m.

kilo /ˈkiːləʊ/ n. (pl. **-os**) kilo m.

kilobyte /ˈkɪləbaɪt/ n. kilo-octet m.

kilogram /ˈkɪləgræm/ n. kilogramme m.

kilohertz /ˈkɪləhɜːts/ n. kilohertz m.

kilometre /ˈkɪləmiːtə(r)/ n. kilomètre m.

kilowatt /ˈkɪləwɒt/ n. kilowatt m.

kilt /kɪlt/ n. kilt m.

kin /kɪn/ n. parents m. pl.

kind [1] /kaɪnd/ n. genre m., sorte f., espèce f. **in ~,** en nature f. **~ of,** (somewhat: fam.) un peu. **be two of a ~,** se rassembler.

kind [2] /kaɪnd/ a. (**-er, -est**) gentil, bon. **~-hearted** a. bon. **~ness** n. bonté f.

kindergarten /ˈkɪndəgɑːtn/ n. jardin d'enfants m.

kindle /ˈkɪndl/ v.t./i. (s')allumer.

kindly /ˈkaɪndlɪ/ a. (**-ier, -iest**) bienveillant. ● adv. avec bonté. **~ wait/etc.,** voulez-vous avoir la bonté d'attendre/etc.

kindred /ˈkɪndrɪd/ a. apparenté. **~ spirit,** personne qui a les mêmes goûts f., âme sœur f.

kinetic /kɪˈnetɪk/ a. cinétique.

king /kɪŋ/ n. roi m. **~-size(d)** a. géant.

kingdom /ˈkɪŋdəm/ n. royaume m.; (bot.) règne m.

kingfisher /ˈkɪŋfɪʃə(r)/ n. martin-pêcheur m.

kink /kɪŋk/ n. (in rope) entortillement m., déformation f.; (fig.) perversion f. **~y** a. (fam.) perverti.

kiosk /ˈkiːɒsk/ n. kiosque m. **telephone ~,** cabine téléphonique f.

kip /kɪp/ n. (sl.) roupillon m. ● v.i. (p.t. **kipped**) (sl.) roupiller.

kipper /ˈkɪpə(r)/ n. hareng fumé m.

kirby-grip /ˈkɜːbɪgrɪp/ n. pince à cheveux f.

kiss /kɪs/ n. baiser m. ● v.t./i. (s')embrasser.

kit /kɪt/ n. équipement m.; (clothing) affaires f. pl.; (set of tools etc.) trousse f.; (for assembly) kit m. ● v.t. (p.t. **kitted**). **~ out,** équiper.

kitbag /ˈkɪtbæg/ n. sac m. (de marin etc.).

kitchen /ˈkɪtʃɪn/ n. cuisine f. **~ garden,** jardin potager m.

kitchenette /kɪtʃɪˈnet/ n. kitchenette f.

kite /kaɪt/ n. (toy) cerf-volant m.

kith /kɪθ/ n. **~ and kin,** parents et amis m. pl.

kitten /ˈkɪtn/ n. chaton m.

kitty /ˈkɪtɪ/ n. (fund) cagnotte f.

knack /næk/ n. truc m., chic m.

knapsack /ˈnæpsæk/ n. sac à dos m.

knave /neɪv/ n. (cards) valet m.

knead /niːd/ v.t. pétrir.

knee /niː/ n. genou m.

kneecap /ˈniːkæp/ n. rotule f.

kneel /niːl/ v.i. (p.t. **knelt**). **~ (down),** s'agenouiller.

knell /nel/ n. glas m.

knew /njuː/ see **know**.

knickers /ˈnɪkəz/ n. pl. (woman's undergarment) culotte f., slip m.

knife /naɪf/ n. (pl. **knives**) couteau m. ● v.t. poignarder.

knight /naɪt/ n. chevalier m.; (chess) cavalier m. ● v.t. faire or armer chevalier. **~hood** n. titre de chevalier m.

knit /nɪt/ v.t./i. (p.t. **knitted** or **knit**) tricoter; (bones etc.) (se) souder. **~ one's brow,** froncer les sourcils. **~ting** n. tricot m.

knitwear /ˈnɪtweə(r)/ n. tricots m. pl.

knob /nɒb/ n. bouton m.

knock /nɒk/ v.t./i. frapper, cogner; (criticize: sl.) critiquer. ● n. coup m. **~ about** v.t. malmener; v.i. vadrouiller. **~ down,** (chair, pedestrian) renverser; (demolish) abattre; (reduce) baisser. **~-down** a. (price) très bas. **~-kneed** a. cagneux. **~ off** v.t. faire tomber; (fam.) expédier; v.i.

(*fam.*) s'arrêter de travailler. **~ out**, (*by blow*) assommer; (*tire*) épuiser. **~-out** *n.* (*boxing*) knock-out *m.* **~ over**, renverser. **~ up**, (*meal etc.*) préparer en vitesse. **~er** *n.* heurtoir *m.*

knot /nɒt/ *n.* nœud *m.* ● *v.t.* (*p.t.* **knotted**) nouer. **~ty** /ˈnɒtɪ/ *a.* noueux; (*problem*) épineux.

know /nəʊ/ *v.t./i.* (*p.t.* **knew**, *p.p.* **known**) savoir (**that**, que); (*person, place*) connaître. **~ how to do**, savoir comment faire. ● *n.* **in the ~**, (*fam.*) dans le secret, au courant. **~ about**, (*cars etc.*) s'y connaître en. **~-all**, (*Amer.*) **~-it-all** *n.* je-sais-tout *m./f.* **~-how** *n.* technique *f.* **~ of**, connaître, avoir entendu parler de. **~ingly** *adv.* (*consciously*) sciemment.

knowledge /ˈnɒlɪdʒ/ *n.* connaissance *f.*; (*learning*) connaissances *f. pl.* **~able** *a.* bien informé.

known /nəʊn/ *see* know. ● *a.* connu; (*recognized*) reconnu.

knuckle /ˈnʌkl/ *n.* articulation du doigt *f.* ● *v.i.* **~ under**, se soumettre.

Koran /kəˈrɑːn/ *n.* Coran *m.*

Korea /kəˈrɪə/ *n.* Corée *f.*

kosher /ˈkəʊʃə(r)/ *a.* kascher *invar.*

kowtow /kaʊˈtaʊ/ *v.i.* se prosterner (**to**, devant).

kudos /ˈkjuːdɒs/ *n.* (*fam.*) gloire *f.*

Kurd /kɜːd/ *a. & n.* kurde *m./f.*

L

lab /læb/ *n.* (*fam.*) labo *m.*

label /ˈleɪbl/ *n.* étiquette *f.* ● *v.t.* (*p.t.* **labelled**) étiqueter.

laboratory /ləˈbɒrətrɪ, *Amer.* ˈlæbrətɔːrɪ/ *n.* laboratoire *m.*

laborious /ləˈbɔːrɪəs/ *a.* laborieux.

labour /ˈleɪbə(r)/ *n.* travail *m.*; (*workers*) main-d'œuvre *f.* ● *v.i.* peiner. ● *v.t.* trop insister sur. **in ~**, en train d'accoucher, en couches. **~ed** *a.* laborieux.

Labour /ˈleɪbə(r)/ *n.* le parti travailliste *m.* ● *a.* travailliste.

labourer /ˈleɪbərə(r)/ *n.* manœuvre *m.*; (*on farm*) ouvrier agricole *m.*

labyrinth /ˈlæbərɪnθ/ *n.* labyrinthe *m.*

lace /leɪs/ *n.* dentelle *f.*; (*of shoe*) lacet *m.* ● *v.t.* (*fasten*) lacer; (*drink*) arroser. **~-ups** *n. pl.* chaussures à lacets *f. pl.*

lacerate /ˈlæsəreɪt/ *v.t.* lacérer.

lack /læk/ *n.* manque *m.* ● *v.t.* manquer de. **be ~ing**, manquer (**in**, de). **for ~ of**, faute de.

lackadaisical /lækəˈdeɪzɪkl/ *a.* indolent, apathique.

lackey /ˈlækɪ/ *n.* laquais *m.*

laconic /ləˈkɒnɪk/ *a.* laconique.

lacquer /ˈlækə(r)/ *n.* laque *f.*

lad /læd/ *n.* garçon *m.*, gars *m.*

ladder /ˈlædə(r)/ *n.* échelle *f.*; (*in stocking*) maille filée *f.* ● *v.t./i.* (*stocking*) filer.

laden /ˈleɪdn/ *a.* chargé (**with**, de).

ladle /ˈleɪdl/ *n.* louche *f.*

lady /ˈleɪdɪ/ *n.* dame *f.* **~ friend**, amie *f.* **~-in-waiting** *n.* dame d'honneur *f.* **young ~**, jeune femme *or* fille *f.* **~like** *a.* distingué.

lady|bird /ˈleɪdɪbɜːd/ *n.* coccinelle *f.* **~bug** *n.* (*Amer.*) coccinelle *f.*

lag[1] /læg/ *v.i.* (*p.t.* **lagged**) traîner. ● *n.* (*interval*) décalage *m.*

lag[2] /læg/ *v.t.* (*p.t.* **lagged**) (*pipes*) calorifuger.

lager /ˈlɑːgə(r)/ *n.* bière blonde *f.*

lagoon /ləˈguːn/ *n.* lagune *f.*

laid /leɪd/ *see* lay[2]. ● **~-back** *a.* (*fam.*) cool.

lain /leɪn/ *see* lie[2].

lair /leə(r)/ *n.* tanière *f.*

laity /ˈleɪətɪ/ *n.* laïques *m. pl.*

lake /leɪk/ *n.* lac *m.*

lamb /læm/ *n.* agneau *m.*

lambswool /ˈlæmzwʊl/ *n.* laine d'agneau *f.*

lame /leɪm/ *a.* (**-er**, **-est**) boiteux; (*excuse*) faible. **~ly** *adv.* (*argue*) sans conviction. **~ duck**, canard boiteux *m.*

lament /ləˈment/ *n.* lamentation *f.* ● *v.t./i.* se lamenter (sur). **~able** *a.* lamentable.

laminated /ˈlæmɪneɪtɪd/ *a.* laminé.

lamp /læmp/ *n.* lampe *f.*

lamppost /ˈlæmppəʊst/ *n.* réverbère *m.*

lampshade /ˈlæmpʃeɪd/ *n.* abat-jour *m. invar.*

lance /lɑːns/ *n.* lance *f.* ● *v.t.* (*med.*) inciser.

lancet /ˈlɑːnsɪt/ *n.* bistouri *m.*

land /lænd/ *n.* terre *f.*; (*plot*) terrain *m.*; (*country*) pays *m.* ● *a.* terrestre; (*policy, reform*) agraire. ● *v.t./i.*

débarquer; (*aircraft*) (se) poser, (faire) atterrir; (*fall*) tomber; (*obtain*) décrocher; (*put*) mettre; (*a blow*) porter. ~-**locked** *a.* sans accès à la mer. ~ **up,** se retrouver.

landed /'lændɪd/ *a.* foncier.

landing /'lændɪŋ/ *n.* débarquement *m.*; (*aviat.*) atterrissage *m.*; (*top of stairs*) palier *m.* ~-**stage** débarcadère *m.*

land|lady /'lændleɪdɪ/ *n.* propriétaire *f.*; (*of inn*) patronne *f.* ~**lord** *n.* propriétaire *m.*; patron *m.*

landmark /'lændmɑːk/ *n.* (point de) repère *m.*

landscape /'læn(d)skeɪp/ *n.* paysage *m.* ● *v.t.* aménager.

landslide /'lændslaɪd/ *n.* glissement de terrain *m.*; (*pol.*) raz-de-marée (électoral) *m. invar.*

lane /leɪn/ *n.* (*path, road*) chemin *m.*; (*strip of road*) voie *f.*; (*of traffic*) file *f.*; (*aviat.*) couloir *m.*

language /'læŋgwɪdʒ/ *n.* langue *f.*; (*speech, style*) langage *m.* ~ **laboratory,** laboratoire de langue *m.*

languid /'læŋgwɪd/ *a.* languissant.

languish /'læŋgwɪʃ/ *v.i.* languir.

lank /læŋk/ *a.* grand et maigre.

lanky /'læŋkɪ/ *a.* (-**ier, -iest**) dégingandé, grand et maigre.

lanolin /'lænəʊlɪn/ *n.* lanoline *f.*

lantern /'læntən/ *n. m. invar.*

lap[1] /læp/ *n.* genoux *m. pl.*; (*sport*) tour (de piste) *m.* ● *v.t./i.* (*p.t.* lapped) ~ **over,** (se) chevaucher.

lap[2] /læp/ *v.t.* (*p.t.* lapped). ~ **up,** laper. ● *v.i.* (*waves*) clapoter.

lapel /lə'pel/ *n.* revers *m.*

lapse /læps/ *v.i.* (*decline*) se dégrader; (*expire*) se périmer. ● *n.* défaillance *f.*, erreur *f.*; (*of time*) intervalle *m.* ~ **into,** retomber dans.

larceny /'lɑːsənɪ/ *n.* vol simple *m.*

lard /lɑːd/ *n.* saindoux *m.*

larder /'lɑːdə(r)/ *n.* garde-manger *m. invar.*

large /lɑːdʒ/ *a.* (-**er, -est**) grand, gros. **at** ~, en liberté. **by and** ~, en général. ~**ly** *adv.* en grande mesure. ~**ness** *n.* grandeur *f.*

lark[1] /lɑːk/ *n.* (*bird*) alouette *f.*

lark[2] /lɑːk/ *n.* (*bit of fun: fam.*) rigolade *f.* ● *v.i.* (*fam.*) rigoler.

larva /'lɑːvə/ *n.* (*pl.* -**vae** /-viː/) larve *f.*

laryngitis /lærɪn'dʒaɪtɪs/ *n.* laryngite *f.*

larynx /'lærɪŋks/ *n.* larynx *m.*

lasagne /lə'zænjə/ *n.* lasagne *f.*

lascivious /lə'sɪvɪəs/ *a.* lascif.

laser /'leɪzə(r)/ *n.* laser *m.* ~ **printer,** imprimante laser *f.*

lash /læʃ/ *v.t.* fouetter. ● *n.* coup de fouet *m.*; (*eyelash*) cil *m.* ~ **out,** (*spend*) dépenser follement. ~ **out against,** attaquer.

lashings /'læʃɪŋz/ *n. pl.* ~ **of,** (*cream etc.: sl.*) des masses de.

lass /læs/ *n.* jeune fille *f.*

lasso /læ'suː/ *n.* (*pl.* -**os**) lasso *m.*

last[1] /lɑːst/ *a.* dernier. ● *adv.* en dernier; (*most recently*) la dernière fois. ● *n.* dern|ier, -ière *m.*, *f.*; (*remainder*) reste *m.* **at (long)** ~, enfin. ~-**ditch** *a.* ultime. ~-**minute** *a.* de dernière minute. ~ **night,** hier soir. **the** ~ **straw,** le comble. **the** ~ **word,** le mot de la fin. **on its** ~ **legs,** sur le point de rendre l'âme. ~**ly** *adv.* en dernier lieu.

last[2] /lɑːst/ *v.i.* durer. ~**ing** *a.* durable.

latch /lætʃ/ *n.* loquet *m.*

late /leɪt/ *a.* (-**er, -est**) (*not on time*) en retard; (*recent*) récent; (*former*) ancien; (*hour, fruit, etc.*) tardif; (*deceased*) défunt. **the** ~ **Mrs X,** feu Mme X. ~**st** /-ɪst/ (*last*) dernier. ● *adv.* (*not early*) tard; (*not on time*) en retard. **in** ~ **July,** fin juillet. **of** ~, dernièrement. ~**ness** *n.* retard *m.*; (*of event*) heure tardive *f.*

latecomer /'leɪtkʌmə(r)/ *n.* retardataire *m./f.*

lately /'leɪtlɪ/ *adv.* dernièrement.

latent /'leɪtnt/ *a.* latent.

lateral /'lætərəl/ *a.* latéral.

lathe /leɪð/ *n.* tour *m.*

lather /'lɑːðə(r)/ *n.* mousse *f.* ● *v.t.* savonner. ● *v.i.* mousser.

Latin /'lætɪn/ *n.* (*lang.*) latin *m.* ● *a.* latin. ~ **America,** Amérique latine *f.*

latitude /'lætɪtjuːd/ *n.* latitude *f.*

latrine /lə'triːn/ *n.* latrines *f. pl.*

latter /'lætə(r)/ *a.* dernier. ● *n.* **the** ~, celui-ci, celle-ci. ~-**day** *a.* moderne. ~**ly** *adv.* dernièrement.

lattice /'lætɪs/ *n.* treillage *m.*

laudable /'lɔːdəbl/ *a.* louable.

laugh /lɑːf/ *v.i.* rire (**at,** de). ● *n.* rire *m.* ~**able** *a.* ridicule. ~**ing-stock** *n.* objet de risée *m.*

laughter /'lɑːftə(r)/ *n.* (*act*) rire *m.*; (*sound of laughs*) rires *m. pl.*

launch[1] /lɔːntʃ/ *v.t.* lancer. ● *n.* lancement *m.* ~ (**out**) **into,** se lancer dans. ~**ing pad,** aire de lancement *f.*

launch[2] /lɔːntʃ/ *n.* (*boat*) vedette *f.*

launder /'lɔːndə(r)/ *v.t.* blanchir.

launderette /lɔːnˈdret/ n. laverie automatique f.

laundry /ˈlɔːndrɪ/ n. (place) blanchisserie f.; (clothes) linge m.

laurel /ˈlɒrəl/ n. laurier m.

lava /ˈlɑːvə/ n. lave f.

lavatory /ˈlævətrɪ/ n. cabinets m. pl.

lavender /ˈlævəndə(r)/ n. lavande f.

lavish /ˈlævɪʃ/ a. (person) prodigue; (plentiful) copieux; (lush) somptueux. ● v.t. prodiguer (on, à). ~ly adv. copieusement.

law /lɔː/ n. loi f.; (profession, subject of study) droit m. ~-abiding a. respectueux des lois. ~ and order, l'ordre public. ~ful a. légal. ~fully adv. légalement. ~less a. sans loi.

lawcourt /ˈlɔːkɔːt/ n. tribunal m.

lawn /lɔːn/ n. pelouse f., gazon m. ~-mower n. tondeuse à gazon f. ~ tennis, tennis (sur gazon) m.

lawsuit /ˈlɔːsuːt/ n. procès m.

lawyer /ˈlɔːjə(r)/ n. avocat m.

lax /læks/ a. négligent; (morals etc.) relâché. ~ity n. négligence f.

laxative /ˈlæksətɪv/ n. laxatif m.

lay[1] /leɪ/ a. (non-clerical) laïque; (opinion etc.) d'un profane.

lay[2] /leɪ/ v.t. (p.t. laid) poser, mettre; (trap) tendre; (table) mettre; (plan) former; (eggs) pondre. ● v.i. pondre. ~ aside, mettre de côté. ~ down, (dé)poser; (condition) (im)poser. ~ hold of, saisir. ~ off v.t. (worker) licencier; v.i. (fam.) arrêter. ~-off n. licenciement m. ~ on, (provide) fournir. ~ out, (design) dessiner; (display) disposer; (money) dépenser. ~ up, (store) amasser. ~ waste, ravager.

lay[3] /leɪ/ see lie[2].

layabout /ˈleɪəbaʊt/ n. fainéant(e) m. (f.).

lay-by /ˈleɪbaɪ/ n. (pl. -bys) petite aire de stationnement f.

layer /ˈleɪə(r)/ n. couche f.

layman /ˈleɪmən/ n. (pl. -men) profane m.

layout /ˈleɪaʊt/ n. disposition f.

laze /leɪz/ v.i. paresser.

laz|y /ˈleɪzɪ/ a. (-ier, -iest) paresseux. ~iness n. paresse f. ~y-bones n. flemmard(e) m. (f.).

lead[1] /liːd/ v.t./i. (p.t. led) mener; (team etc.) diriger; (life) mener; (induce) amener. ~ to, conduire à, mener à. ● n. avance f.; (clue) indice m.; (leash) laisse f.; (theatre) premier rôle m.; (wire) fil m.; (ex-

ample) exemple m. in the ~, en tête. ~ away, emmener. ~ up to, (come to) en venir à; (precede) précéder.

lead[2] /led/ n. plomb m.; (of pencil) mine f. ~en a. (sky) de plomb; (humour) lourd.

leader /ˈliːdə(r)/ n. chef m.; (of country, club, etc.) dirigeant(e) m. (f.); (leading article) éditorial m. ~ship n. direction f.

leading /ˈliːdɪŋ/ a. principal. ~ article, éditorial m.

leaf /liːf/ n. (pl. leaves) feuille f.; (of table) rallonge f. ● v.i. ~ through, feuilleter. ~y a. feuillu.

leaflet /ˈliːflɪt/ n. prospectus m.

league /liːg/ n. ligue f.; (sport) championnat m. in ~ with, de mèche avec.

leak /liːk/ n. fuite f. ● v.i. fuir; (news: fig.) s'ébruiter. ● v.t. répandre; (fig.) divulguer. ~age n. fuite f. ~y a. qui a une fuite.

lean[1] /liːn/ a. (-er, -est) maigre. ● n. (of meat) maigre m. ~ness n. maigreur f.

lean[2] /liːn/ v.t./i. (p.t. leaned or leant /lent/) (rest) (s')appuyer; (slope) pencher. ~ out, se pencher à l'extérieur. ~ over, (of person) se pencher. ~-to n. appentis m.

leaning /ˈliːnɪŋ/ a. penché ● n. tendance f.

leap /liːp/ v.i. (p.t. leaped or leapt /lept/) bondir. ● n. bond m. ~-frog n. saute-mouton m. invar.; v.i. (p.t. -frogged) sauter (over, par-dessus). ~ year, année bissextile f.

learn /lɜːn/ v.t./i. (p.t. learned or learnt) apprendre (to do, à faire). ~er n. débutant(e) m. (f.).

learn|ed /ˈlɜːnɪd/ a. érudit. ~ing n. érudition f., connaissances f. pl.

lease /liːs/ n. bail m. ● v.t. louer à bail.

leaseback /ˈliːsbæk/ n. cession-bail f.

leash /liːʃ/ n. laisse f.

least /liːst/ a. the ~, (smallest amount of) le moins de; (slightest) le or la moindre. ● n. le moins. ● adv. le moins; (with adjective) le or la moins. at ~, au moins.

leather /ˈleðə(r)/ n. cuir m.

leave /liːv/ v.t. (p.t. left) laisser; (depart from) quitter. ● n. (holiday) congé m.; (consent) permission f. **be left (over)**, rester. ~ alone, (thing) ne pas toucher à; (person) laisser tranquille. ~ behind,

laisser. **~ out**, omettre. **on ~**, (*mil.*)
en permission. **take one's ~**, prendre congé (**of**, de).

leavings /'li:vɪŋz/ *n. pl.* restes *m. pl.*

Leban|on /'lebənən/ *n.* Liban *m.*
~ese /-'ni:z/ *a. & n.* libanais(e) (*m.*
(*f.*)).

lecher /'letʃə(r)/ *n.* débauché *m.*
~ous *a.* lubrique. **~y** *n.* lubricité *f.*

lectern /'lektən/ *n.* lutrin *m.*

lecture /'lektʃə(r)/ *n.* cours *m.*, conférence *f.*; (*rebuke*) réprimande *f.*
● *v.t./i.* faire un cours *or* une conférence (à); (*rebuke*) réprimander.
~r /-ə(r)/ *n.* conférenc|ier, -ière *m.*,
f., (*univ.*) enseignant(e) *m.* (*f.*).

led /led/ *see* lead¹.

ledge /ledʒ/ *n.* (*window*) rebord *m.*;
(*rock*) saillie *f.*

ledger /'ledʒə(r)/ *n.* grand livre *m.*

lee /li:/ *n.* côté sous le vent *m.*

leech /li:tʃ/ *n.* sangsue *f.*

leek /li:k/ *n.* poireau *m.*

leer /lɪə(r)/ *v.i.* **~ (at)**, lorgner. ● *n.*
regard sournois *m.*

leeway /'li:weɪ/ *n.* (*naut.*) dérive *f.*;
(*fig.*) liberté d'action *f.* **make up ~**,
rattraper le retard.

left¹ /left/ *see* leave. **~ luggage
(office)**, consigne *f.* **~-overs** *n. pl.*
restes *m. pl.*

left² /left/ *a.* gauche. ● *adv.* à
gauche. ● *n.* gauche *f.* **~-hand** *a.* à
or de gauche. **~-handed** *a.* gaucher.
~-wing *a.* (*pol.*) de gauche.

leftist /'leftɪst/ *n.* gauchiste *m./f.*

leg /leg/ *n.* jambe *f.*; (*of animal*) patte
f.; (*of table*) pied *m.*; (*of chicken*)
cuisse *f.*; (*of lamb*) gigot *m.*; (*of
journey*) étape *f.* **~-room** *n.* place
pour les jambes *f.* **~-warmers** *n. pl.*
jambières *f. pl.*

legacy /'legəsɪ/ *n.* legs *m.*

legal /'li:gl/ *a.* légal; (*affairs etc.*)
juridique. **~ity** /li:'gælətɪ/ *n.* légalité
f. **~ly** *adv.* légalement.

legalize /'li:gəlaɪz/ *v.t.* légaliser.

legend /'ledʒənd/ *n.* légende *f.* **~ary**
a. légendaire.

leggings /'legɪŋz/ *n. pl.* collant sans
pieds *m.*

legib|le /'ledʒəbl/ *a.* lisible. **~ility**
/-'bɪlətɪ/ *n.* lisibilité *f.* **~ly** *adv.* lisi-
blement.

legion /'li:dʒən/ *n.* légion *f.* **~naire** *n.*
légionnaire *m.* **~naire's disease**,
maladie du légionnaire *f.*

legislat|e /'ledʒɪsleɪt/ *v.i.* légiférer.
~ion /-'leɪʃn/ *n.* (*body of laws*)
législation *f.*; (*law*) loi *f.*

legislat|ive /'ledʒɪslətɪv/ *a.* législatif.
~ure /-eɪtʃə(r)/ *n.* corps législatif *m.*

legitima|te /lɪ'dʒɪtɪmət/ *a.* légitime.
~cy *n.* légitimité *f.*

leisure /'leʒə(r)/ *n.* loisir(s) *m.* (*pl.*).
at one's ~, à tête reposée. **~ centre**,
centre de loisirs *m.* **~ly** *a.* lent; *adv.*
sans se presser.

lemon /'lemən/ *n.* citron *m.*

lemonade /lemə'neɪd/ *n.* (*fizzy*) limonade *f.*; (*still*) citronnade *f.*

lend /lend/ *v.t.* (*p.t.* lent) prêter;
(*contribute*) donner. **~ itself to**, se
prêter à. **~er** *n.* prêteu|r, -se *m.*, *f.*
~ing *n.* prêt *m.*

length /leŋθ/ *n.* longueur *f.*; (*in time*)
durée *f.*; (*section*) morceau *m.* **at ~**,
(*at last*) enfin. **at (great) ~**,
longuement. **~y** *a.* long.

lengthen /'leŋθən/ *v.t./i.* (s')allonger.

lengthways /'leŋθweɪz/ *adv.* dans le
sens de la longueur.

lenien|t /'li:nɪənt/ *a.* indulgent. **~cy**
n. indulgence *f.* **~tly** *adv.* avec
indulgence.

lens /lenz/ *n.* lentille *f.*; (*of spectacles*)
verre *m.*; (*photo.*) objectif *m.*

lent /lent/ *see* lend.

Lent /lent/ *n.* Carême *m.*

lentil /'lentl/ *n.* (*bean*) lentille *f.*

Leo /'li:əʊ/ *n.* le Lion.

leopard /'lepəd/ *n.* léopard *m.*

leotard /'li:əta:d/ *n.* body *m.*

leper /'lepə(r)/ *n.* lépreu|x, -se *m.*, *f.*

leprosy /'leprəsɪ/ *n.* lèpre *f.*

lesbian /'lezbɪən/ *n.* lesbienne *f.* ● *a.*
lesbien.

lesion /'li:ʒn/ *n.* lésion *f.*

less /les/ *a.* (*in quantity etc.*) moins de
(**than**, que). ● *adv.*, *n.* & *prep.*
moins. **~ than**, (*with numbers*)
moins de. **work/etc. ~ than**, travail-
ler/*etc.* moins que. **ten pounds/etc.
~**, dix livres/*etc.* de moins. **~ and
less**, de moins en moins. **~er** *a.*
moindre.

lessen /'lesn/ *v.t./i.* diminuer.

lesson /'lesn/ *n.* leçon *f.*

lest /lest/ *conj.* de peur que *or* de.

let /let/ *v.t.* (*p.t.* let, *pres. p.* letting)
laisser; (*lease*) louer. ● *v. aux.* **~ us
do**, **~'s do**, faisons. **~ him do**, qu'il
fasse. **~ me know the results**,
informe-moi des résultats. ● *n.* location *f.* **~ alone**, (*thing*) ne pas
toucher à; (*person*) laisser tran-

quille; (*never mind*) encore moins.
~ down, baisser; (*deflate*) dégonfler; (*fig.*) décevoir. **~-down** *n.* déception *f.* **~ go** *v.t.* lâcher; *v.i.* lâcher
prise. **~ sb. in/out,** laisser *or* faire
entrer/sortir qn. **~ a dress out,**
élargir une robe. **~ o.s. in for,**
(*task*) s'engager à; (*trouble*)
s'attirer. **~ off,** (*explode, fire*) faire
éclater or partir; (*excuse*) dispenser;
(*not punish*) ne pas punir. **~ up,**
(*fam.*) s'arrêter. **~-up** *n.* répit *m.*

lethal /'li:θl/ *a.* mortel; (*weapon*)
meurtrier.

letharg|y /'leθədʒɪ/ *n.* léthargie *f.* **~ic**
/lɪ'θɑ:dʒɪk/ *a.* léthargique.

letter /'letə(r)/ *n.* lettre *f.* **~-bomb** *n.*
lettre piégée *f.* **~-box** *n.* boîte à *or*
aux lettres *f.* **~ing** *n.* (*letters*) caractères *m. pl.*

lettuce /'letɪs/ *n.* laitue *f.*, salade *f.*

leukaemia /lu:'ki:mɪə/ *n.* leucémie *f.*

level /'levl/ *a.* plat, uni; (*on surface*)
horizontal; (*in height*) au même
niveau (**with,** que); (*in score*) à
égalité. ● *n.* niveau *m.* (**spirit**) **~,**
niveau à bulle *m.* ● *v.t.* (*p.t.* **le-
velled**) niveler; (*aim*) diriger. **be on
the ~,** (*fam.*) être franc. **~ crossing,** passage à niveau *m.* **~-headed**
a. équilibré.

lever /'li:və(r)/ *n.* levier *m.* ● *v.t.*
soulever au moyen d'un levier.

leverage /'li:vərɪdʒ/ *n.* influence *f.*

levity /'levətɪ/ *n.* légèreté *f.*

levy /'levɪ/ *v.t.* (*tax*) (pré)lever. ● *n.*
impôt *m.*

lewd /lju:d/ *a.* (**-er, -est**) obscène.

liable /'laɪəbl/ *a.* **be ~ to do,** avoir
tendance à faire, pouvoir faire. **~
to,** (*illness etc.*) sujet à; (*fine*) passible de. **~ for,** responsable de.

liabilit|y /laɪə'bɪlətɪ/ *n.* responsabilité
f.; (*fam.*) handicap *m.* **~ies,** (*debts*)
dettes *f. pl.*

liais|e /lɪ'eɪz/ *v.i.* (*fam.*) faire la
liaison. **~on** /-ɒn/ *n.* liaison *f.*

liar /'laɪə(r)/ *n.* menteu|r, -se *m., f.*

libel /'laɪbl/ *n.* diffamation *f.* ● *v.t.*
(*p.t.* **libelled**) diffamer.

liberal /'lɪbərəl/ *a.* libéral; (*generous*)
généreux, libéral. **~ly** *adv.* libérale-
ment.

Liberal /'lɪbərəl/ *a. & n.* (*pol.*) libé-
ral(e) (*m. (f.)*).

liberat|e /'lɪbəreɪt/ *v.t.* libérer. **~ion**
/-'reɪʃn/ *n.* libération *f.*

libert|y /'lɪbətɪ/ *n.* liberté *f.* **at ~y to,**
libre de. **take ~ies,** prendre des
libertés.

libido /lɪ'bi:dəʊ/ *n.* libido *f.*

Libra /'li:brə/ *n.* la Balance.

librar|y /'laɪbrərɪ/ *n.* bibliothèque *f.*
~ian /-'breərɪən/ *n.* bibliothécaire
m./f.

libretto /lɪ'bretəʊ/ *n.* (*pl.* **-os**) (*mus.*)
livret *m.*

Libya /'lɪbɪə/ *n.* Libye *f.* **~n** *a. & n.*
libyen(ne) (*m. (f.)*).

lice /laɪs/ *see* louse.

licence, *Amer.* **license** [1] /'laɪsns/ *n.*
permis *m.*; (*for television*) redevance
f.; (*comm.*) licence *f.*; (*liberty: fig.*)
licence *f.* **~ plate,** plaque minéralogique *f.*

license [2] /'laɪsns/ *v.t.* accorder un
permis à, autoriser.

licentious /laɪ'senʃəs/ *a.* licencieux.

lichen /'laɪkən/ *n.* lichen *m.*

lick /lɪk/ *v.t.* lécher; (*defeat: sl.*)
rosser. ● *n.* coup de langue *m.* **~
one's chops,** se lécher les babines.

licorice /'lɪkərɪs/ *n.* (*Amer.*) réglisse
f.

lid /lɪd/ *n.* couvercle *m.*

lido /'laɪdəʊ/ *n.* (*pl.* **-os**) piscine en
plein air *f.*

lie [1] /laɪ/ *n.* mensonge *m.* ● *v.i.* (*p.t.*
lied, *pres. p.* lying) (*tell lies*) mentir.
give the ~ to, démentir.

lie [2] /laɪ/ *v.i.* (*p.t.* lay, *p.p.* lain, *pres. p.*
lying) s'allonger; (*remain*) rester;
(*be*) se trouver, être; (*in grave*)
reposer. **be lying,** être allongé. **~
down,** s'allonger. **~ in, have a ~-
in,** faire la grasse matinée. **~ low,** se
cacher.

lieu /lju:/ *n.* **in ~ of,** au lieu de.

lieutenant /lef'tenənt, *Amer.* lu:-
'tenənt/ *n.* lieutenant *m.*

life /laɪf/ *n.* (*pl.* lives) vie *f.* **~ cycle,**
cycle de vie *m.* **~-guard** *n.* sauve-
teur *m.* **~ insurance,** assurance-vie
f. **~-jacket,** **~ preserver,** *n.* gilet de
sauvetage *m.* **~- size(d)** *a.* grandeur
nature *invar.* **~-style** *n.* style de vie
m.

lifebelt /'laɪfbelt/ *n.* bouée de sauvetage *f.*

lifeboat /'laɪfbəʊt/ *n.* canot de sauvetage *m.*

lifebuoy /'laɪfbɔɪ/ *n.* bouée de sauvetage *f.*

lifeless /'laɪflɪs/ *a.* sans vie.

lifelike /'laɪflaɪk/ *a.* très ressemblant.

lifelong /'laɪflɒŋ/ *a.* de toute la vie.

lifetime /'laiftaim/ n. vie f. **in one's ~,** de son vivant.

lift /lift/ v.t. lever; (*steal: fam.*) voler. ● v.i. (*of fog*) se lever. ● n. (*in building*) ascenseur m. **give a ~ to,** emmener (en voiture). **~-off** n. (*aviat.*) décollage m.

ligament /'ligəmənt/ n. ligament m.

light¹ /lait/ n. lumière f.; (*lamp*) lampe f.; (*for fire, on vehicle, etc.*) feu m.; (*headlight*) phare m. ● a. (*not dark*) clair. ● v.t. (*p.t.* **lit** or **lighted**) allumer; (*room etc.*) éclairer; (*match*) frotter. **bring to ~,** révéler. **come to ~,** être révélé. **have you got a ~?,** vous avez du feu? **~ bulb,** ampoule f. **~ pen,** crayon optique m. **~ up** v.i. s'allumer; v.t. (*room*) éclairer. **~-year** n. année lumière f.

light² /lait/ a. (**-er, -est**) (*not heavy*) léger. **~-fingered** a. chapardeur. **~-headed** a. (*dizzy*) qui a un vertige; (*frivolous*) étourdi. **~-hearted** a. gai. **~ly** adv. légèrement. **~ness** n. légèreté f.

lighten¹ /'laitn/ v.t. (*give light to*) éclairer; (*make brighter*) éclaircir.

lighten² /'laitn/ v.t. (*make less heavy*) alléger.

lighter /'laitə(r)/ n. briquet m.; (*for stove*) allume-gaz m. invar.

lighthouse /'laithaus/ n. phare m.

lighting /'laitiŋ/ n. éclairage m. **~ technician,** éclairagiste m./f.

lightning /'laitniŋ/ n. éclair(s) m. (*pl.*), foudre f. ● a. éclair invar.

lightweight /'laitweit/ a. léger. ● n. (*boxing*) poids léger m.

like¹ /laik/ a. semblable, pareil. ● prep. comme. ● conj. (*fam.*) comme. ● n. pareil m. **be ~-minded,** avoir les mêmes sentiments. **the ~s of you,** des gens comme vous.

like² /laik/ v.t. aimer (bien). **~s** n. pl. goûts m. pl. **I should ~,** je voudrais, j'aimerais. **would you ~?,** voulez-vous? **~able** a. sympathique.

likel|y /'laikli/ a. (**-ier, -iest**) probable. ● adv. probablement. **he is ~y to do,** il fera probablement. **not ~y!,** (*fam.*) pas question! **~ihood** n. probabilité f.

liken /'laikən/ v.t. comparer.

likeness /'laiknis/ n. ressemblance f.

likewise /'laikwaiz/ adv. de même.

liking /'laikiŋ/ n. (*for thing*) penchant m.; (*for person*) affection f.

lilac /'lailək/ n. lilas m. ● a. lilas invar.

lily /'lili/ n. lis m., lys m. **~ of the valley,** muguet m.

limb /lim/ n. membre m. **out on a ~,** isolé (et vulnérable).

limber /'limbə(r)/ v.i. **~ up,** faire des exercices d'assouplissement.

limbo /'limbəu/ n. **be in ~,** (*forgotten*) être tombé dans l'oubli.

lime¹ /laim/ n. chaux f.

lime² /laim/ n. (*fruit*) citron vert m.

lime³ /laim/ n. **~(-tree),** tilleul m.

limelight /'laimlait/ n. **in the ~,** en vedette.

limerick /'limərik/ n. poème humoristique m. (*de cinq vers*).

limit /'limit/ n. limite f. ● v.t. limiter. **~ed company,** société anonyme f. **~ation** /-'teiʃn/ n. limitation f. **~less** a. sans limites.

limousine /'liməzi:n/ n. (*car*) limousine f.

limp¹ /limp/ v.i. boiter. ● n. **have a ~,** boiter.

limp² /limp/ a. (**-er, -est**) mou.

limpid /'limpid/ a. limpide.

linctus /'liŋktəs/ n. sirop m.

line¹ /lain/ n. ligne f.; (*track*) voie f.; (*wrinkle*) ride f.; (*row*) rangée f., file f.; (*of poem*) vers m.; (*rope*) corde f.; (*of goods*) gamme f.; (*queue: Amer.*) queue f. ● v.t. (*paper*) régler; (*streets etc.*) border. **be in ~ for,** avoir de bonnes chances d'avoir. **in ~ with,** en accord avec. **stand in ~,** faire la queue. **~ up,** (s')aligner; (*in queue*) faire la queue. **~ sth. up,** prévoir qch.

line² /lain/ v.t. (*garment*) doubler; (*fill*) remplir, garnir.

lineage /'liniidʒ/ n. lignée f.

linear /'liniə(r)/ a. linéaire.

linen /'linin/ n. (*sheets etc.*) linge m.; (*material*) lin m., toile de lin f.

liner /'lainə(r)/ n. paquebot m.

linesman /'lainzmən/ n. (*football*) juge de touche m.

linger /'liŋgə(r)/ v.i. s'attarder; (*smells etc.*) persister.

lingerie /'lænʒəri/ n. lingerie f.

lingo /'liŋgəu/ n. (*pl.* **-os**) (*hum., fam.*) jargon m.

linguist /'liŋgwist/ n. linguiste m./f.

linguistic /liŋ'gwistik/ a. linguistique. **~s** n. linguistique f.

lining /'lainiŋ/ n. doublure f.

link /liŋk/ n. lien m.; (*of chain*) maillon m. ● v.t. relier; (*relate*) (re)lier. **~ up,** (*of roads*) se rejoindre. **~age** *n*. lien *m*. **~-up** *n*. liaison *f*.

links /lɪŋks/ *n. invar.* terrain de golf *m*.

lino /'laɪnəʊ/ *n.* (*pl.* **-os**) lino *m*.

linoleum /lɪ'nəʊlɪəm/ *n.* linoléum *m*.

lint /lɪnt/ *n.* (*med.*) tissu ouaté *m.*; (*fluff*) peluche(s) *f.* (*pl.*).

lion /'laɪən/ *n.* lion *m*. **take the ~'s share,** se tailler la part du lion. **~ess** *n*. lionne *f*.

lip /lɪp/ *n.* lèvre *f.*; (*edge*) rebord *m*. **~-read** *v.t./i.* lire sur les lèvres. **pay ~-service to,** n'approuver que pour la forme.

lipsalve /'lɪpsælv/ *n.* baume pour les lèvres *m*.

lipstick /'lɪpstɪk/ *n.* rouge (à lèvres) *m*.

liquefy /'lɪkwɪfaɪ/ *v.t./i.* (se) liquéfier.

liqueur /lɪ'kjʊə(r)/ *n.* liqueur *f*.

liquid /'lɪkwɪd/ *n. & a.* liquide (*m.*). **~ize** *v.t.* passer au mixeur. **~izer** *n.* mixeur *m*.

liquidat|e /'lɪkwɪdeɪt/ *v.t.* liquider. **~ion** /-'deɪʃn/ *n.* liquidation *f*. **go into ~ion,** déposer son bilan.

liquor /'lɪkə(r)/ *n.* alcool *m*.

liquorice /'lɪkərɪs/ *n.* réglisse *f*.

lira /'lɪərə/ *n.* (*pl.* **lire** /'lɪəreɪ/ *or* **liras**) lire *f*.

lisp /lɪsp/ *n.* zézaiement *m*. ● *v.i.* zézayer. **with a ~,** en zézayant.

list [1] /lɪst/ *n.* liste *f*. ● *v.t.* dresser la liste de.

list [2] /lɪst/ *v.i.* (*ship*) gîter.

listen /'lɪsn/ *v.i.* écouter. **~ to, ~ in (to),** écouter. **~er** *n.* audi|teur, -trice *m./f.*

listless /'lɪstlɪs/ *a.* apathique.

lit /lɪt/ *see* **light** [1].

litany /'lɪtənɪ/ *n.* litanie *f*.

liter /'liːtə(r)/ *see* **litre**.

literal /'lɪtərəl/ *a.* littéral; (*person*) prosaïque. **~ly** *adv.* littéralement.

literary /'lɪtərərɪ/ *a.* littéraire.

litera|te /'lɪtərət/ *a.* qui sait lire et écrire. **~cy** *n.* capacité de lire et écrire *f*.

literature /'lɪtrətʃə(r)/ *n.* littérature *f.*; (*fig.*) documentation *f*.

lithe /laɪð/ *a.* souple, agile.

litigation /lɪtɪ'geɪʃn/ *n.* litige *m*.

litre, (*Amer.*) **liter** /'liːtə(r)/ *n.* litre *m*.

litter /'lɪtə(r)/ *n.* détritus *m. pl.*, papiers *m. pl.*; (*animals*) portée *f*. ● *v.t.* éparpiller; (*make untidy*) lais-

ser des détritus dans. **~bin** *n.* poubelle *f*. **~ed with,** jonché de.

little /'lɪtl/ *a.* petit; (*not much*) peu de. ● *n.* peu *m*. ● *adv.* peu. **a ~,** un peu (de).

liturgy /'lɪtədʒɪ/ *n.* liturgie *f*.

live [1] /laɪv/ *a.* vivant; (*wire*) sous tension; (*broadcast*) en direct. **be a ~ wire,** être très dynamique.

live [2] /lɪv/ *v.t./i.* vivre; (*reside*) habiter, vivre. **~ down,** faire oublier. **~ it up,** mener la belle vie. **~ on,** (*feed o.s. on*) vivre de; (*continue*) survivre. **~ up to,** se montrer à la hauteur de.

livelihood /'laɪvlɪhʊd/ *n.* moyens d'existence *m. pl.*

livel|y /'laɪvlɪ/ *a.* (**-ier, -iest**) vif, vivant. **~iness** *n.* vivacité *f*.

liven /'laɪvn/ *v.t./i.* **~ up,** (s')animer; (*cheer up*) (s')égayer.

liver /'lɪvə(r)/ *n.* foie *m*.

livery /'lɪvərɪ/ *n.* livrée *f*.

livestock /'laɪvstɒk/ *n.* bétail *m*.

livid /'lɪvɪd/ *a.* livide; (*angry: fam.*) furieux.

living /'lɪvɪŋ/ *a.* vivant. ● *n.* vie *f*. **make a ~,** gagner sa vie. **~ conditions,** conditions de vie *f. pl.* **~room** *n.* salle de séjour *f*.

lizard /'lɪzəd/ *n.* lézard *m*.

llama /'lɑːmə/ *n.* lama *m*.

load /ləʊd/ *n.* charge *f.*; (*loaded goods*) chargement *m.*, charge *f.*; (*weight, strain*) poids *m*. **~s of,** (*fam.*) des masses de. ● *v.t.* charger. **~ed** *a.* (*dice*) pipé; (*wealthy: sl.*) riche.

loaf [1] /ləʊf/ *n.* (*pl.* **loaves**) pain *m*.

loaf [2] /ləʊf/ *v.i.* **~ (about),** fainéanter. **~er** *n.* fainéant(e) *m. (f.*).

loam /ləʊm/ *n.* terreau *m*.

loan /ləʊn/ *n.* prêt *m.*; (*money borrowed*) emprunt *m*. ● *v.t.* (*lend: fam.*) prêter.

loath /ləʊθ/ *a.* peu disposé (**to,** à).

loath|e /ləʊð/ *v.t.* détester. **~ing** *n.* dégoût *m*. **~some** *a.* dégoûtant.

lobby /'lɒbɪ/ *n.* entrée *f.*, vestibule *m.*; (*pol.*) lobby *m.*, groupe de pression *m*. ● *v.t.* faire pression sur.

lobe /ləʊb/ *n.* lobe *m*.

lobster /'lɒbstə(r)/ *n.* homard *m*.

local /'ləʊkl/ *a.* local; (*shops etc.*) du quartier. ● *n.* personne du coin *f.*; (*pub: fam.*) pub du coin *m*. **~ government,** administration locale *f*. **~ly** *adv.* localement; (*nearby*) dans les environs.

locale /ləʊ'kɑːl/ *n.* lieu *m.*

locality /ləʊ'kælətɪ/ *n.* (*district*) région *f.*; (*position*) lieu *m.*

localized /'ləʊkəlaɪzd/ *a.* localisé.

locat|e /ləʊ'keɪt/ *v.t.* (*situate*) situer; (*find*) repérer. **~ion** /-ʃn/ *n.* emplacement *m.* **on ~ion,** (*cinema*) en extérieur.

lock¹ /lɒk/ *n.* mèche (de cheveux) *f.*

lock² /lɒk/ *n.* (*of door etc.*) serrure *f.*; (*on canal*) écluse *f.* ● *v.t./i.* fermer à clef; (*wheels: auto.*) (se) bloquer. **~ in** *or* **up,** (*person*) enfermer. **~ out,** (*by mistake*) enfermer dehors. **~-out** *n.* lockout *m. invar.* **~-up** *n.* (*shop*) boutique *f.*; (*garage*) box *m.*

locker /'lɒkə(r)/ *n.* casier *m.*

locket /'lɒkɪt/ *n.* médaillon *m.*

locksmith /'lɒksmɪθ/ *n.* serrurier *m.*

locomotion /ləʊkə'məʊʃn/ *n.* locomotion *f.*

locomotive /'ləʊkəməʊtɪv/ *n.* locomotive *f.*

locum /'ləʊkəm/ *n.* (*doctor etc.*) remplaçant(e) *m.* (*f.*).

locust /'ləʊkəst/ *n.* criquet *m.*, sauterelle *f.*

lodge /lɒdʒ/ *n.* (*house*) pavillon (de gardien *or* de chasse) *m.*; (*of porter*) loge *f.* ● *v.t.* loger; (*money, complaint*) déposer. ● *v.i.* être logé (**with,** chez); (*become fixed*) se loger. **~r** /-ə(r)/ *n.* locataire *m./f.*, pensionnaire *m./f.*

lodgings /'lɒdʒɪŋz/ *n.* chambre (meublée) *f.*; (*flat*) logement *m.*

loft /lɒft/ *n.* grenier *m.*

lofty /'lɒftɪ/ *a.* (**-ier, -iest**) (*tall, noble*) élevé; (*haughty*) hautain.

log /lɒg/ *n.* (*of wood*) bûche *f.* **~(-book),** (*naut.*) journal de bord *m.*; (*auto.*) (*équivalent de la*) carte grise *f.* ● *v.t.* (*p.t.* **logged**) noter; (*distance*) parcourir. **~ on,** entrer. **~ off,** sortir.

logarithm /'lɒgərɪðəm/ *n.* logarithme *m.*

loggerheads /'lɒgəhedz/ *n. pl.* **at ~,** en désaccord.

logic /'lɒdʒɪk/ *a.* logique. **~al** *a.* logique. **~ally** *adv.* logiquement.

logistics /lə'dʒɪstɪks/ *n.* logistique *f.*

logo /'ləʊgəʊ/ *n.* (*pl.* **-os**) (*fam.*) emblème *m.*

loin /lɔɪn/ *n.* (*culin.*) filet *m.* **~s,** reins *m. pl.*

loiter /'lɔɪtə(r)/ *v.i.* traîner.

loll /lɒl/ *v.i.* se prélasser.

loll|ipop /'lɒlɪpɒp/ *n.* sucette *f.* **~y** *n.* (*fam.*) sucette *f.*; (*sl.*) fric *m.*

London /'lʌndən/ *n.* Londres *m./f.* **~er** *n.* Londonien(ne) *m.* (*f.*).

lone /ləʊn/ *a.* solitaire. **~r** /-ə(r)/ *n.* solitaire *m./f.* **~some** *a.* solitaire.

lonely /'ləʊnlɪ/ *a.* (**-ier, -iest**) solitaire; (*person*) seul, solitaire.

long¹ /lɒŋ/ *a.* (**-er, -est**) long. ● *adv.* longtemps. **how ~ is?,** quelle est la longueur de?; (*in time*) quelle est la durée de? **how ~?,** combien de temps? **he will not be ~,** il n'en a pas pour longtemps. **a ~ time,** longtemps. **as** *or* **so ~ as,** pourvu que. **before ~,** avant peu. **I no ~er do,** je ne fais plus. **~-distance** *a.* (*flight*) sur long parcours; (*phone call*) interurbain. **~ face,** grimace *f.* **~ johns,** (*fam.*) caleçon long *m.* **~ jump,** saut en longueur *m.* **~-playing record,** microsillon *m.* **~-range** *a.* à longue portée; (*forecast*) à long terme. **~-sighted** *a.* presbyte. **~-standing** *a.* de longue date. **~-suffering** *a.* très patient. **~-term** *a.* à long terme. **~ wave,** grandes ondes *f. pl.* **~-winded** *a.* (*speaker etc.*) verbeux.

long² /lɒŋ/ *v.i.* avoir bien *or* très envie (**for, to,** de). **~ for s.o.,** (*pine for*) languir après qn. **~ing** *n.* envie *f.*; (*nostalgia*) nostalgie *f.*

longevity /lɒn'dʒevətɪ/ *n.* longévité *f.*

longhand /'lɒŋhænd/ *n.* écriture courante *f.*

longitude /'lɒndʒɪtjuːd/ *n.* longitude *f.*

loo /luː/ *n.* (*fam.*) toilettes *f. pl.*

look /lʊk/ *v.t./i.* regarder; (*seem*) avoir l'air. ● *n.* regard *m.*; (*appearance*) air *m.*, aspect *m.* (**good**) **~s,** beauté *f.* **~ after,** s'occuper de, soigner. **~ at,** regarder. **~ back on,** repenser à. **~ down on,** mépriser. **~ for,** chercher. **~ forward to,** attendre avec impatience. **~ in on,** passer voir. **~ into,** examiner. **~ like,** ressembler à, avoir l'air de. **~ out,** faire attention. **~ out for,** chercher; (*watch*) guetter. **~-out** *n.* (*mil.*) poste de guet *m.*; (*person*) guetteur *m.* **be on the ~-out for,** rechercher. **~ round,** se retourner. **~ up,** (*word*) chercher; (*visit*) passer voir. **~ up to,** respecter. **~-alike** *n.* sosie *m.* **~ing-glass** *n.* glace *f.*

loom¹ /luːm/ *n.* métier à tisser *m.*

loom[2] /luːm/ v.i. surgir; (event etc.: fig.) paraître imminent.

loony /ˈluːnɪ/ n. & a. (sl.) fou, folle (m., f.).

loop /luːp/ n. boucle f. ● v.t. boucler.

loophole /ˈluːphəʊl/ n. (in rule) échappatoire f.

loose /luːs/ a. (-er, -est) (knot etc.) desserré; (page etc.) détaché; (clothes) ample, lâche; (tooth) qui bouge; (lax) relâché; (not packed) en vrac; (inexact) vague; (pej.) immoral. **at a ~ end**, (Amer.) **~ ends**, désœuvré. **come ~**, bouger. **~ly** adv. sans serrer; (roughly) vaguement.

loosen /ˈluːsn/ v.t. (slacken) desserrer; (untie) défaire.

loot /luːt/ n. butin m. ● v.t. piller. **~er** n. pillard(e) m. (f.). **~ing** n. pillage m.

lop /lɒp/ v.t. (p.t. lopped). **~ off**, couper.

lop-sided /lɒpˈsaɪdɪd/ a. de travers.

lord /lɔːd/ n. seigneur m.; (British title) lord m. **the L~**, le Seigneur. **(good) L~!**, mon Dieu! **~ly** a. noble; (haughty) hautain.

lore /lɔː(r)/ n. traditions f. pl.

lorry /ˈlɒrɪ/ n. camion m.

lose /luːz/ v.t./i. (p.t. lost) perdre. **get lost**, se perdre. **~r** /-ə(r)/ n. perdant(e) m. (f.).

loss /lɒs/ n. perte f. **be at a ~**, être perplexe. **be at a ~ to**, être incapable de. **heat ~**, déperdition de chaleur f.

lost /lɒst/ see lose. ● a. perdu. **~ property**, (Amer.) **~ and found**, objets trouvés m. pl.

lot[1] /lɒt/ n. (fate) sort m.; (at auction) lot m.; (land) lotissement m.

lot[2] /lɒt/ n. **the ~**, (le) tout m.; (people) tous m. pl., toutes f. pl. **a ~ (of), ~s (of)**, (fam.) beaucoup (de). **quite a ~ (of)**, (fam.) pas mal (de).

lotion /ˈləʊʃn/ n. lotion f.

lottery /ˈlɒtərɪ/ n. loterie f.

loud /laʊd/ a. (-er, -est) bruyant, fort. ● adv. fort. **~ hailer**, portevoix m. invar. **out ~**, tout haut. **~ly** adv. fort.

loudspeaker /laʊdˈspiːkə(r)/ n. haut-parleur m.

lounge /laʊndʒ/ v.i. paresser. ● n. salon m. **~ suit**, costume m.

louse /laʊs/ n. (pl. lice) pou m.

lousy /ˈlaʊzɪ/ a. (-ier, -iest) pouilleux; (bad: sl.) infect.

lout /laʊt/ n. rustre m.

lovable /ˈlʌvəbl/ a. adorable.

love /lʌv/ n. amour m.; (tennis) zéro m. ● v.t. aimer; (like greatly) aimer (beaucoup) (**to do**, faire). **in ~**, amoureux (**with**, de). **~ affair**, liaison amoureuse f. **~ life**, vie amoureuse f. **make ~**, faire l'amour.

lovely /ˈlʌvlɪ/ a. (-ier, -iest) joli; (delightful: fam.) très agréable.

lover /ˈlʌvə(r)/ n. amant m.; (devotee) amateur m. (**of**, de).

lovesick /ˈlʌvsɪk/ a. amoureux.

loving /ˈlʌvɪŋ/ a. affectueux.

low[1] /ləʊ/ v.i. meugler.

low[2] /ləʊ/ a. & adv. (-er, -est) bas. ● n. (low pressure) dépression f. **reach a (new) ~**, atteindre son niveau le plus bas. **~ in sth.**, à faible teneur en qch. **~-calorie** a. basses-calories. **~-cut** a. décolleté. **~-down** a. méprisable; n. (fam.) renseignements m. pl. **~-fat** a. maigre. **~-key** a. modéré; (discreet) discret. **~-lying** a. à faible altitude.

lowbrow /ˈləʊbraʊ/ a. peu intellectuel.

lower /ˈləʊə(r)/ a. & adv. see low[2]. ● v.t. baisser. **~ o.s.**, s'abaisser.

lowlands /ˈləʊləndz/ n. pl. plaine(s) f. (pl.).

lowly /ˈləʊlɪ/ a. (-ier, -iest) humble.

loyal /ˈlɔɪəl/ a. loyal. **~ly** adv. loyalement. **~ty** n. loyauté f.

lozenge /ˈlɒzɪndʒ/ n. (shape) losange m.; (tablet) pastille f.

LP abbr. see long-playing record.

Ltd. abbr. (Limited) SA.

lubric|ate /ˈluːbrɪkeɪt/ v.t. graisser, lubrifier. **~ant** n. lubrifiant m. **~ation** /-ˈkeɪʃn/ n. graissage m.

lucid /ˈluːsɪd/ a. lucide. **~ity** /luːˈsɪdətɪ/ n. lucidité f.

luck /lʌk/ n. chance f. **bad ~**, malchance f. **good ~!**, bonne chance!

luck|y /ˈlʌkɪ/ a. (-ier, -iest) qui a de la chance, heureux; (event) heureux; (number) qui porte bonheur. **it's ~y that**, c'est une chance que. **~ily** adv. heureusement.

lucrative /ˈluːkrətɪv/ a. lucratif.

ludicrous /ˈluːdɪkrəs/ a. ridicule.

lug /lʌg/ v.t. (p.t. lugged) traîner.

luggage /ˈlʌgɪdʒ/ n. bagages m. pl. **~-rack** n. porte-bagages m. invar.

lukewarm /ˈluːkwɔːm/ a. tiède.

lull /lʌl/ v.t. (soothe, send to sleep) endormir. ● n. accalmie f.
lullaby /'lʌləbaɪ/ n. berceuse f.
lumbago /lʌm'beɪgəʊ/ n. lumbago m.
lumber /'lʌmbə(r)/ n. bric-à-brac m. invar.; (wood) bois de charpente m. ● v.t. ~ s.o. with, (chore etc.) coller à qn.
lumberjack /'lʌmbədʒæk/ n. (Amer.) bûcheron m.
luminous /'lu:mɪnəs/ a. lumineux.
lump /lʌmp/ n. morceau m.; (swelling on body) grosseur f.; (in liquid) grumeau m. ● v.t. ~ together, réunir. ~ sum, somme globale f. ~y a. (sauce) grumeleux; (bumpy) bosselé.
lunacy /'lu:nəsɪ/ n. folie f.
lunar /'lu:nə(r)/ a. lunaire.
lunatic /'lu:nətɪk/ n. fou, folle m., f.
lunch /lʌntʃ/ n. déjeuner m. ● v.i. déjeuner. ~ box, cantine f.
luncheon /'lʌntʃən/ n. déjeuner m. ~ meat, (approx.) saucisson m. ~ voucher, chèque-repas m.
lung /lʌŋ/ n. poumon m.
lunge /lʌndʒ/ n. mouvement brusque en avant m. ● v.i. s'élancer (at, sur).
lurch[1] /lɜ:tʃ/ n. leave in the ~, planter là, laisser en plan.
lurch[2] /lɜ:tʃ/ v.i. (person) tituber.
lure /lʊə(r)/ v.t. appâter, attirer. ● n. (attraction) attrait m., appât m.
lurid /'lʊərɪd/ a. choquant, affreux; (gaudy) voyant.
lurk /lɜ:k/ v.i. se cacher; (in ambush) s'embusquer; (prowl) rôder. a ~ing suspicion, un petit soupçon.
luscious /'lʌʃəs/ a. appétissant.
lush /lʌʃ/ a. luxuriant. ● n. (Amer., fam.) ivrogne(sse) m. (f.).
lust /lʌst/ n. luxure f.; (fig.) convoitise f. ● v.i. ~ after, convoiter.
lustre /'lʌstə(r)/ n. lustre m.
lusty /'lʌstɪ/ a. (-ier, -iest) robuste.
lute /lu:t/ n. (mus.) luth m.
Luxemburg /'lʌksəmbɜ:g/ n. Luxembourg m.
luxuriant /lʌg'ʒʊərɪənt/ a. luxuriant.
luxurious /lʌg'ʒʊərɪəs/ a. luxueux.
luxury /'lʌkʃərɪ/ n. luxe m. ● a. de luxe.
lying /'laɪŋ/ see lie[1], lie[2]. ● n. le mensonge.
lynch /lɪntʃ/ v.t. lyncher.
lynx /lɪŋks/ n. lynx m.
lyric /'lɪrɪk/ a. lyrique. ~s n. pl. paroles f. pl. ~al a. lyrique. ~ism /-sɪzəm/ n. lyrisme m.

M

MA abbr. see Master of Arts.
mac /mæk/ n. (fam.) imper m.
macaroni /mækə'rəʊnɪ/ n. macaronis m. pl.
macaroon /mækə'ru:n/ n. macaron m.
mace /meɪs/ n. (staff) masse f.
Mach /mɑ:k/ n. ~ (number), (nombre de) Mach m.
machiavellian /mækɪə'velɪən/ a. machiavélique.
machinations /mækɪ'neɪʃnz/ n. pl. machinations f. pl.
machine /mə'ʃi:n/ n. machine f. ● v.t. (sew) coudre à la machine; (techn.) usiner. ~ code, code machine m. ~-gun n. mitrailleuse f.; v.t. (p.t. -gunned) mitrailler. ~-readable a. en langage machine. ~-tool, machine-outil f.
machinery /mə'ʃi:nərɪ/ n. machinerie f.; (working parts & fig.) mécanisme(s) m. (pl.).
machinist /mə'ʃi:nɪst/ n. (operator) opéra|teur, -trice sur machine m., f.; (on sewing-machine) piqueu|r, -se m., f.
macho /'mætʃəʊ/ n. (pl. -os) macho m. ● a. macho invar.
mackerel /'mækrəl/ n. invar. (fish) maquereau m.
mackintosh /'mækɪntɒʃ/ n. imperméable m.
macrobiotic /mækrəʊbaɪ'ɒtɪk/ a. macrobiotique.
mad /mæd/ a. (madder, maddest) fou; (foolish) insensé; (dog etc.) enragé; (angry: fam.) furieux. be ~ about, se passionner pour; (person) être fou de. drive s.o. ~, exaspérer qn. like ~, comme un fou. ~ly adv. (interested, in love, etc.) follement; (frantically) comme un fou. ~ness n. folie f.
Madagascar /mædə'gæskə(r)/ n. Madagascar f.
madam /'mædəm/ n. madame f.; (unmarried) mademoiselle f.
madden /'mædn/ v.t. exaspérer.
made /meɪd/ see make. ~ to measure, fait sur mesure.
Madeira /mə'dɪərə/ n. (wine) madère m.
madhouse /'mædhaʊs/ n. (fam.) maison de fous f.

madman /'mædmən/ n. (pl. **-men**) fou m.

madrigal /'mædrɪgl/ n. madrigal m.

magazine /mægə'zi:n/ n. revue f., magazine m.; (of gun) magasin m.

magenta /mə'dʒentə/ a. magenta (invar.).

maggot /'mægət/ n. ver m., asticot m. **~y** a. véreux.

magic /'mædʒɪk/ n. magie f. ● a. magique. **~al** a. magique.

magician /mə'dʒɪʃn/ n. magicien(ne) m. (f.).

magistrate /'mædʒɪstreɪt/ n. magistrat m.

magnanim|ous /mæg'nænɪməs/ a. magnanime. **~ity** /-ə'nɪmətɪ/ n. magnanimité f.

magnate /'mægneɪt/ n. magnat m.

magnesia /mæg'ni:ʃə/ n. magnésie f.

magnet /'mægnɪt/ n. aimant m. **~ic** /-'netɪk/ a. magnétique. **~ism** n. magnétisme m. **~ize** v.t. magnétiser.

magneto /mæg'ni:təʊ/ n. (pl. **os**) magnéto f.

magnificen|t /mæg'nɪfɪsnt/ a. magnifique. **~ce** n. magnificence f.

magnif|y /'mægnɪfaɪ/ v.t. grossir; (sound) amplifier; (fig.) exagérer. **~ication** /-ɪ'keɪʃn/ n. grossissement m.; amplification f. **~ier** n., **~ying glass,** loupe f.

magnitude /'mægnɪtju:d/ n. (importance) ampleur f.; (size) grandeur f.

magnolia /mæg'nəʊlɪə/ n. magnolia m.

magnum /'mægnəm/ n. magnum m.

magpie /'mægpaɪ/ n. pie f.

mahogany /mə'hɒgənɪ/ n. acajou m.

maid /meɪd/ n. (servant) bonne f.; (girl: old use) jeune fille f.

maiden /'meɪdn/ n. (old use) jeune fille f. ● a. (aunt) célibataire; (voyage) premier. **~ name,** nom de jeune fille m. **~hood** n. virginité f. **~ly** a. virginal.

mail¹ /meɪl/ n. poste f.; (letters) courrier m. ● a. (bag, van) postal. ● v.t. envoyer par la poste. **mail box,** boîte à lettres f. **~ing list,** liste d'adresses f. **~ order,** vente par correspondance f. **~ shot,** publipostage m.

mail² /meɪl/ n. (armour) cotte de mailles f.

mailman /'meɪlmæn/ n. (pl. **-men**) (Amer.) facteur m.

maim /meɪm/ v.t. mutiler.

main¹ /meɪn/ a. principal. ● n. **in the ~,** en général. **~ line,** grande ligne f. **a ~ road,** une grande route. **~ly** adv. principalement, surtout.

main² /meɪn/ n. **(water/gas) ~,** conduite d'eau/de gaz f. **the ~s,** (electr.) le secteur.

mainframe n. unité centrale f.

mainland /'meɪnlənd/ n. continent m.

mainspring /'meɪnsprɪŋ/ n. ressort principal m.; (motive: fig.) mobile principal m.

mainstay /'meɪnsteɪ/ n. soutien m.

mainstream /'meɪnstri:m/ n. tendance principale f., ligne f.

maintain /meɪn'teɪn/ v.t. (continue, keep, assert) maintenir; (house, machine, family) entretenir; (rights) soutenir.

maintenance /'meɪntənəns/ n. (care) entretien m.; (continuation) maintien m.; (allowance) pension alimentaire f.

maisonette /meɪzə'net/ n. duplex m.

maize /meɪz/ n. maïs m.

majestic /mə'dʒestɪk/ a. majestueux.

majesty /'mædʒəstɪ/ n. majesté f.

major /'meɪdʒə(r)/ a. majeur. ● n. commandant m. ● v.i. **~ in,** (univ., Amer.) se spécialiser en. **~ road,** route à priorité f.

Majorca /mə'dʒɔ:kə/ n. Majorque f.

majority /mə'dʒɒrətɪ/ n. majorité f. ● a. majoritaire. **the ~ of people,** la plupart des gens.

make /meɪk/ v.t./i. (p.t. **made**) faire; (manufacture) fabriquer; (friends) se faire; (money) gagner, se faire; (decision) prendre; (destination) arriver à; (cause to be) rendre. **~ s.o. do sth.,** faire faire qch. à qn.; (force) obliger qn. à faire qch. ● n. fabrication f.; (brand) marque f. **be made of,** être fait de. **~ o.s. at home,** se mettre à l'aise. **~ s.o. happy,** rendre qn. heureux. **~ it,** arriver; (succeed) réussir. **I ~ it two o'clock,** j'ai deux heures. **I ~ it 150,** d'après moi, ça fait 150. **I cannot ~ anything of it,** je n'y comprends rien. **can you ~ Friday?,** vendredi, c'est possible? **~ as if to,** faire mine de. **~ believe,** faire semblant. **~-believe,** a. feint, illusoire; n. fantaisie f. **~ do,** (manage) se débrouiller (**with,** avec). **~ do with,** (content o.s.) se contenter de. **~ for,** se diriger vers; (cause) tendre à créer. **~ good** v.i. réussir;

v.t. compenser; (*repair*) réparer. **~ off,** filer (**with,** avec). **~ out** *v.t.* distinguer; (*understand*) comprendre; (*draw up*) faire; (*assert*) prétendre; *v.i.* (*fam.*) se débrouiller. **~ over,** céder (**to,** à); (*convert*) transformer. **~ up** *v.t.* faire, former; (*story*) inventer; (*deficit*) combler; *v.i.* se réconcilier. **~ up (one's face),** se maquiller. **~-up** *n.* maquillage *m.*; (*of object*) constitution *f.*; (*psych.*) caractère *m.* **~ up for,** compenser; (*time*) rattraper. **~ up one's mind,** se décider. **~ up to,** se concilier les bonnes grâces de.

maker /'meɪkə(r)/ *n.* fabricant *m.*

makeshift /'meɪkʃɪft/ *n.* expédient *m.* ● *a.* provisoire.

making /'meɪkɪŋ/ *n.* **be the ~ of,** faire le succès de. **he has the ~s of,** il a l'étoffe de.

maladjusted /mælə'dʒʌstɪd/ *a.* inadapté.

maladministration /mælədmɪnɪ'streɪʃn/ *n.* mauvaise gestion *f.*

malaise /mæ'leɪz/ *n.* malaise *m.*

malaria /mə'leərɪə/ *n.* malaria *f.*

Malay /mə'leɪ/ *a. & n.* malais(e) (*m.* (*f.*)). **~sia** *n.* Malaisie *f.*

Malaya /mə'leɪə/ *n.* Malaisie *f.*

male /meɪl/ *a.* (*voice, sex*) masculin; (*bot., techn.*) mâle. ● *n.* mâle *m.*

malevolen|t /mə'levələnt/ *a.* malveillant. **~ce** *n.* malveillance *f.*

malform|ation /mælfɔː'meɪʃn/ *n.* malformation *f.* **~ed** *a.* difforme.

malfunction /mæl'fʌŋkʃn/ *n.* mauvais fonctionnement *m.* ● *v.i.* mal fonctionner.

malice /'mælɪs/ *n.* méchanceté *f.*

malicious /mə'lɪʃəs/ *a.* méchant. **~ly** *adv.* méchamment.

malign /mə'laɪn/ *a.* pernicieux. ● *v.t.* calomnier.

malignan|t /mə'lɪgnənt/ *a.* malveillant; (*tumour*) malin. **~cy** *n.* malveillance *f.*; malignité *f.*

malinger /mə'lɪŋgə(r)/ *v.i.* feindre la maladie. **~er** *n.* simula|teur, -trice *m., f.*

mall /mɔːl/ *n.* (**shopping**) **~,** centre commercial *m.*

malleable /'mælɪəbl/ *a.* malléable.

mallet /'mælɪt/ *n.* maillet *m.*

malnutrition /mælnjuː'trɪʃn/ *n.* sous-alimentation *f.*

malpractice /mæl'præktɪs/ *n.* faute professionnelle *f.*

malt /mɔːlt/ *n.* malt *m.* **~ whisky,** whisky pur malt *m.*

Malt|a /'mɔːltə/ *n.* Malte *f.* **~ese** /-'tiːz/ *a. & n.* maltais(e) (*m.* (*f.*)).

maltreat /mæl'triːt/ *v.t.* maltraiter. **~ment** *n.* mauvais traitement *m.*

mammal /'mæml/ *n.* mammifère *m.*

mammoth /'mæməθ/ *n.* mammouth *m.* ● *a.* monstre.

man /mæn/ *n.* (*pl.* **men**) homme *m.*; (*in sports team*) joueur *m.*; (*chess*) pièce *f.* ● *v.t.* (*p.t.* **manned**) pourvoir en hommes; (*ship*) armer; (*guns*) servir; (*be on duty at*) être de service à. **~-hour** *n.* heure de main-d'œuvre *f.* **~ in the street,** homme de la rue *m.* **~-made** *a.* artificiel. **~-sized** *a.* grand. **~ to man,** d'homme à homme. **~ned space flight,** vol spatial habité *m.*

manage /'mænɪdʒ/ *v.t.* diriger; (*shop, affairs*) gérer; (*handle*) manier. **I could ~ another drink,** (*fam.*) je prendrais bien encore un verre. **can you ~ Friday?,** vendredi, c'est possible? ● *v.i.* se débrouiller. **~ to do,** réussir à faire. **~able** *a.* (*tool, size, person, etc.*) maniable; (*job*) faisable. **~ment** *n.* direction *f.*; (*of shop*) gestion *f.* **managing director,** directeur général *m.*

manager /'mænɪdʒə(r)/ *n.* direc|teur, -trice *m.,f.*; (*of shop*) gérant(e) *m.(f.)*; (*of actor*) impresario *m.* **~ess** /-'res/ *n.* directrice *f.*; gérante *f.* **~ial** /-'dʒɪərɪəl/ *a.* directorial. **~ial staff,** cadres *m. pl.*

mandarin /'mændərɪn/ *n.* mandarin *m.*; (*orange*) mandarine *f.*

mandate /'mændeɪt/ *n.* mandat *m.*

mandatory /'mændətrɪ/ *a.* obligatoire.

mane /meɪn/ *n.* crinière *f.*

manful /'mænfl/ *a.* courageux.

manganese /mæŋgə'niːz/ *n.* manganèse *m.*

mangetout /mɒnʒ'tuː/ *n.* mange-tout *m. invar.*

mangle[1] /'mæŋgl/ *n.* (*for wringing*) essoreuse *f.*; (*for smoothing*) calandre *f.*

mangle[2] /'mæŋgl/ *v.t.* mutiler.

mango /'mæŋgəʊ/ *n.* (*pl.* **-oes**) mangue *f.*

manhandle /'mænhændl/ *v.t.* maltraiter, malmener.

manhole /'mænhəʊl/ *n.* trou d'homme *m.*, regard *m.*

manhood /'mænhʊd/ n. âge d'homme m.; (*quality*) virilité f.

mania /'meɪnɪə/ n. manie f. **~c** /-ɪæk/ n. maniaque m./f., fou m., folle f.

manic-depressive /'mænɪk-dɪ'presɪv/ a & n. maniaco-dépressif(-ive) (m. (f.)).

manicur|e /'mænɪkjʊə(r)/ n. soin des mains m. ● v.t. soigner, manucurer. **~ist** n. manucure m./f.

manifest /'mænɪfest/ a. manifeste. ● v.t. manifester. **~ation** /-'steɪʃn/ n. manifestation f.

manifesto /mænɪ'festəʊ/ n. (pl. -os) manifeste m.

manifold /'mænɪfəʊld/ a. multiple. ● n. (*auto.*) collecteur m.

manipulat|e /mə'nɪpjʊleɪt/ v.t. (*tool, person*) manipuler. **~ion** /-'leɪʃn/ n. manipulation f.

mankind /mæn'kaɪnd/ n. genre humain m.

manly /'mænlɪ/ a. viril.

manner /'mænə(r)/ n. manière f.; (*attitude*) attitude f.; (*kind*) sorte f. **~s**, (*social behaviour*) manières f. pl. **~ed** a. maniéré.

mannerism /'mænərɪzəm/ n. trait particulier m.

manœuvre /mə'nu:və(r)/ n. manœuvre f. ● v.t./i. manœuvrer.

manor /'mænə(r)/ n. manoir m.

manpower /'mænpaʊə(r)/ n. main-d'œuvre f.

manservant /'mænsɜ:vənt/ n. (pl. **menservants**) domestique m.

mansion /'mænʃn/ n. château m.

manslaughter /'mænslɔ:tə(r)/ n. homicide involontaire m.

mantelpiece /'mæntlpi:s/ n. (*shelf*) cheminée f.

manual /'mænjʊəl/ a. manuel. ● n. (*handbook*) manuel m.

manufacture /mænjʊ'fæktʃə(r)/ v.t. fabriquer. ● n. fabrication f. **~r** /-ə(r)/ n. fabricant m.

manure /mə'njʊə(r)/ n. fumier m.; (*artificial*) engrais m.

manuscript /'mænjʊskrɪpt/ n. manuscrit m.

many /'menɪ/ a. & n. beaucoup (de). **a great** or **good ~**, un grand nombre (de). **~ a**, bien des.

Maori /'maʊrɪ/ a. maori. ● n. Maori(e) m. (f.).

map /mæp/ n. carte f.; (*of streets etc.*) plan m. ● v.t. (p.t. **mapped**) faire la carte de. **~ out**, (*route*) tracer; (*arrange*) organiser.

maple /'meɪpl/ n. érable m.

mar /mɑ:(r)/ v.t. (p.t. **marred**) gâter; (*spoil beauty of*) déparer.

marathon /'mærəθən/ n. marathon m.

marble /'mɑ:bl/ n. marbre m.; (*for game*) bille f.

March /mɑ:tʃ/ n. mars m.

march /mɑ:tʃ/ v.i. (*mil.*) marcher (au pas). **~ off/etc.**, partir/etc. allégrement. ● v.t. **~ off**, (*lead away*) emmener. ● n. marche f. **~-past** n. défilé m.

mare /meə(r)/ n. jument f.

margarine /mɑ:dʒə'ri:n/ n. margarine f.

margin /'mɑ:dʒɪn/ n. marge f. **~al** a. marginal; (*increase etc.*) léger, faible. **~al seat**, (*pol.*) siège chaudement disputé m. **~alize** v.t. marginaliser. **~ally** adv. très légèrement.

marigold /'mærɪɡəʊld/ n. souci m.

marijuana /mærɪ'wɑ:nə/ n. marijuana f.

marina /mə'ri:nə/ n. marina f.

marinate /'mærɪmeɪt/ v.t. mariner.

marine /mə'ri:n/ a. marin. ● n. (*shipping*) marine f.; (*sailor*) fusilier marin m.

marionette /mærɪə'net/ n. marionnette f.

marital /'mærɪtl/ a. conjugal. **~ status**, situation de famille f.

maritime /'mærɪtaɪm/ a. maritime.

marjoram /'mɑ:dʒərəm/ n. marjolaine f.

mark¹ /mɑ:k/ n. (*currency*) mark m.

mark² /mɑ:k/ n. marque f.; (*trace*) trace f., marque f.; (*schol.*) note f.; (*target*) but m. ● v.t. marquer; (*exam*) corriger. **~ out**, délimiter; (*person*) désigner. **~ time**, marquer le pas. **~er** n. marque f. **~ing** n. (*marks*) marques f.pl.

marked /mɑ:kt/ a. marqué. **~ly** /-ɪdlɪ/ adv. visiblement.

market /'mɑ:kɪt/ n. marché m. ● v.t. (*sell*) vendre; (*launch*) commercialiser. **~ garden**, jardin maraîcher m. **~ -place** n. marché m. **~ research**, étude de marché f. **~ value**, valeur marchande f. **on the ~**, en vente. **~ing** n. marketing m.

marksman /'mɑ:ksmən/ n. (pl. -men) tireur d'élite m.

marmalade /'mɑ:məleɪd/ n. confiture d'oranges f.

maroon /mə'ru:n/ *n*. bordeaux *m*. *invar*. ● *a*. bordeaux *invar*.

marooned /mə'ru:nd/ *a*. abandonné; (*snow-bound etc.*) bloqué.

marquee /mɑ:'ki:/ *n*. grande tente *f*.; (*awning*: *Amer.*) marquise *f*.

marquis /'mɑ:kwɪs/ *n*. marquis *m*.

marriage /'mærɪdʒ/ *n*. mariage *m*. **~able** *a*. nubile, mariable.

marrow /'mærəʊ/ *n*. (*of bone*) moelle *f*.; (*vegetable*) courge *f*.

marr|y /'mærɪ/ *v.t*. épouser; (*give or unite in marriage*) marier. ● *v.i*. se marier. **~ied** *a*. marié; (*life*) conjugal. **get ~ied**, se marier (**to,** avec).

Mars /mɑ:z/ *n*. (*planet*) Mars *f*.

marsh /mɑ:ʃ/ *n*. marais *m*. **~y** *a*. marécageux.

marshal /'mɑ:ʃl/ *n*. maréchal *m*.; (*at event*) membre du service d'ordre *m*. ● *v.t*. (*p.t.* **marshalled**) rassembler.

marshmallow /mɑ:ʃ'mæləʊ/ *n*. guimauve *f*.

martial /'mɑ:ʃl/ *a*. martial. **~ law,** loi martiale *f*.

martyr /'mɑ:tə(r)/ *n*. martyr(e) *m*. (*f*.). ● *v.t*. martyriser. **~dom** *n*. martyre *m*.

marvel /'mɑ:vl/ *n*. merveille *f*. ● *v.i*. (*p.t.* **marvelled**) s'émerveiller (**at,** de).

marvellous /'mɑ:vələs/ *a*. merveilleux.

Marxis|t /'mɑ:ksɪst/ *a*. & *n*. marxiste (*m./f.*). **~m** /-zəm/ *n*. marxisme *m*.

marzipan /'mɑ:zɪpæn/ *n*. pâte d'amandes *f*.

mascara /mæ'skɑ:rə/ *n*. mascara *m*.

mascot /'mæskət/ *n*. mascotte *f*.

masculin|e /'mæskjʊlɪn/ *a*. & *n*. masculin (*m*.). **~ity** /-'lɪnətɪ/ *n*. masculinité *f*.

mash /mæʃ/ *n*. pâtée *f*.; (*potatoes*: *fam.*) purée *f*. ● *v.t*. écraser. **~ed potatoes,** purée (de pommes de terre) *f*.

mask /mɑ:sk/ *n*. masque *m*. ● *v.t*. masquer.

masochis|t /'mæsəkɪst/ *n*. masochiste *m./f*. **~m** /-zəm/ *n*. masochisme *m*.

mason /'meɪsn/ *n*. (*builder*) maçon *m*. **~ry** *n*. maçonnerie *f*.

Mason /'meɪsn/ *n*. maçon *m*. **~ic** /mə'sɒnɪk/ *a*. maçonnique

masquerade /mɑ:skə'reɪd/ *n*. mascarade *f*. ● *v.i*. **~ as,** se faire passer pour.

mass [1] /mæs/ *n*. (*relig.*) messe *f*.

mass [2] /mæs/ *n*. masse *f*. ● *v.t./i*. (se) masser. **~-produce** *v.t*. fabriquer en série. **the ~es,** les masses *f.pl*. **the ~ media,** les média *m.pl*.

massacre /'mæsəkə(r)/ *n*. massacre *m*. ● *v.t*. massacrer.

massage /'mæsɑ:ʒ, *Amer*. mə'sɑ:ʒ/ *n*. massage *m*. ● *v.t*. masser.

masseu|r /mæ'sɜ:(r)/ *n*. masseur *m*. **~se** /-ɜ:z/ *n*. masseuse *f*.

massive /'mæsɪv/ *a*. (*large*) énorme; (*heavy*) massif.

mast /mɑ:st/ *n*. mât *m*.; (*for radio, TV*) pylône *m*.

master /'mɑ:stə(r)/ *n*. maître *m*.; (*in secondary school*) professeur *m*. ● *v.t*. maîtriser. **~-key** *n*. passepartout *m. invar*. **~-mind** *n*. (*of scheme etc.*) cerveau *m*.; *v.t*. diriger. **M~ of Arts**/*etc.*, titulaire d'une maîtrise ès lettres/*etc. m./f*. **~-stroke** *n*. coup de maître *m*. **~y** *n*. maîtrise *f*.

masterly /'mɑ:stəlɪ/ *a*. magistral.

masterpiece /'mɑ:stəpi:s/ *n*. chef-d'œuvre *m*.

mastiff /'mæstɪf/ *n*. dogue *m*.

masturbat|e /'mæstəbeɪt/ *v.i*. se masturber. **~ion** /-'beɪʃn/ *n*. masturbation *f*.

mat /mæt/ *n*. (petit) tapis *m*., natte *f*.; (*at door*) paillasson *m*.

match [1] /mætʃ/ *n*. allumette *f*.

match [2] /mætʃ/ *n*. (*sport*) match *m*.; (*equal*) égal(e) *m*. (*f.*); (*marriage*) mariage *m*.; (*s.o. to marry*) parti *m*. ● *v.t*. opposer; (*go with*) aller avec; (*cups etc.*) assortir; (*equal*) égaler. **be a ~ for,** pouvoir tenir tête à. ● *v.i*. (*be alike*) être assorti. **~ing** *a*. assorti.

matchbox /'mætʃbɒks/ *n*. boîte à allumettes *f*.

mate [1] /meɪt/ *n*. camarade *m./f.*; (*of animal*) compagnon *m*., compagne *f.*; (*assistant*) aide *m./f*. ● *v.t./i*. (s')accoupler (**with,** avec).

mate [2] /meɪt/ *n*. (*chess*) mat *m*.

material /mə'tɪərɪəl/ *n*. matière *f.*; (*fabric*) tissu *m*.; (*documents, for building*) matériau(x) *m*. (*pl.*). **~s,** (*equipment*) matériel *m*. ● *a*. matériel; (*fig.*) important. **~istic** /-'lɪstɪk/ *a*. matérialiste.

materialize /məˈtɪərɪəlaɪz/ *v.i.* se matérialiser, se réaliser.

maternal /məˈtɜ:nl/ *a.* maternel.

maternity /məˈtɜ:nətɪ/ *n.* maternité *f.* ● *a.* (*clothes*) de grossesse. **~ hospital,** maternité *f.* **~ leave,** congé maternité *m.*

mathematic|s /mæθəˈmætɪks/ *n.* & *n. pl.* mathématiques *f. pl.* **~ian** /-əˈtɪʃn/ *n.* mathématicien(ne) *m.* (*f.*). **~al** *a.* mathématique.

maths /mæθs/ (*Amer.* **math** /mæθ/) *n.* & *n. pl.* (*fam.*) maths *f. pl.*

matinée /ˈmætɪneɪ/ *n.* matinée *f.*

mating /ˈmeɪtɪŋ/ *n.* accouplement *m.* **~ season,** saison des amours *f.*

matriculat|e /məˈtrɪkjʊleɪt/ *v.t./i.* (s')inscrire. **~ion** /-ˈleɪʃn/ *n.* inscription *f.*

matrimon|y /ˈmætrɪmənɪ/ *n.* mariage *m.* **~ial** /-ˈməʊnɪəl/ *a.* matrimonial.

matrix /ˈmeɪtrɪks/ *n.* (*pl.* **matrices** /-ɪsi:z/) matrice *f.*

matron /ˈmeɪtrən/ *n.* (*married, elderly*) dame âgée *f.*; (*in hospital; former use*) infirmière-major *f.* **~ly** *a.* d'âge mûr; (*manner*) très digne.

matt /mæt/ *a.* mat.

matted /ˈmætɪd/ *a.* (*hair*) emmêlé.

matter /ˈmætə(r)/ *n.* (*substance*) matière *f.*; (*affair*) affaire *f.*; (*pus*) pus *m.* ● *v.i.* importer. **as a ~ of fact,** en fait. **it does not ~,** ça ne fait rien. **~-of-fact** *a.* terre à terre *invar.* **no ~ what happens,** quoi qu'il arrive. **what is the ~?,** qu'est-ce qu'il y a?

mattress /ˈmætrɪs/ *n.* matelas *m.*

matur|e /məˈtjʊə(r)/ *a.* mûr. ● *v.t./i.* (se) mûrir. **~ity** *n.* maturité *f.*

maul /mɔ:l/ *v.t.* déchiqueter.

Mauritius /məˈrɪʃəs/ *n.* île Maurice *f.*

mausoleum /mɔ:səˈlɪəm/ *n.* mausolée *m.*

mauve /məʊv/ *a.* & *n.* mauve (*m.*).

maverick /ˈmævərɪk/ *n.* non-conformiste.

maxim /ˈmæksɪm/ *n.* maxime *f.*

maxim|um /ˈmæksɪməm/ *a.* & *n.* (*pl.* **-ima**) maximum (*m.*). **~ize** *v.t.* porter au maximum.

may /meɪ/ *v. aux.* (*p.t.* **might**) pouvoir. **he ~/might come,** il peut/pourrait venir. **you might have,** vous auriez pu. **you ~ leave,** vous pouvez partir. **~ I smoke?,** puis-je fumer? **~ he be happy,** qu'il

soit heureux. **I ~ or might as well stay,** je ferais aussi bien de rester.

May /meɪ/ *n.* mai *m.* **~ Day,** le Premier Mai.

maybe /ˈmeɪbɪ/ *adv.* peut-être.

mayhem /ˈmeɪhem/ *n.* (*havoc*) ravages *m. pl.*

mayonnaise /meɪəˈneɪz/ *n.* mayonnaise *f.*

mayor /meə(r)/ *n.* maire *m.* **~ess** *n.* (*wife*) femme du maire *f.*

maze /meɪz/ *n.* labyrinthe *m.*

MBA (*abbr.*) (*Master of Business Administration*) magistère en gestion commerciale *m.*

me /mi:/ *pron.* me, m'*; (*after prep.*) moi. **(to) ~,** me, m'*. **he knows ~,** il me connaît.

meadow /ˈmedəʊ/ *n.* pré *m.*

meagre /ˈmi:gə(r)/ *a.* maigre.

meal[1] /mi:l/ *n.* repas *m.*

meal[2] /mi:l/ *n.* (*grain*) farine *f.*

mealy-mouthed /mi:lɪˈmaʊðd/ *a.* mielleux.

mean[1] /mi:n/ *a.* (**-er, -est**) (*poor*) misérable; (*miserly*) avare; (*unkind*) méchant. **~ness** *n.* avarice *f.*; méchanceté *f.*

mean[2] /mi:n/ *a.* moyen. ● *n.* milieu *m.*; (*average*) moyenne *f.* **in the ~ time,** en attendant.

mean[3] /mi:n/ *v.t.* (*p.t.* **meant**) vouloir dire, signifier; (*involve*) entraîner. **I ~ that!,** je suis sérieux. **be meant for,** être destiné à. **~ to do,** avoir l'intention de faire.

meander /mɪˈændə(r)/ *v.i.* faire des méandres.

meaning /ˈmi:nɪŋ/ *n.* sens *m.*, signification *f.* **~ful** *a.* significatif. **~less** *a.* denué de sens.

means /mi:nz/ *n.* moyen(s) *m.* (*pl.*). **by ~ of sth.,** au moyen de qch. ● *n. pl.* (*wealth*) moyens financiers *m. pl.* **by all ~,** certainement. **by no ~,** nullement.

meant /ment/ *see* mean[2].

mean|time /ˈmi:ntaɪm/, **~while** *advs.* en attendant.

measles /ˈmi:zlz/ *n.* rougeole *f.*

measly /ˈmi:zlɪ/ *a.* (*sl.*) minable.

measurable /ˈmeʒərəbl/ *a.* mesurable.

measure /ˈmeʒə(r)/ *n.* mesure *f.*; (*ruler*) règle *f.* ● *v.t./i.* mesurer. **~ up to,** être à la hauteur de. **~d** *a.* mesuré. **~ment** *n.* mesure *f.*

meat /mi:t/ *n.* viande *f.* **~y** *a.* de viande; (*fig.*) substantiel.

mechanic /mɪˈkænɪk/ a. mécanicien(ne) m. (f.).

mechanic|al /mɪˈkænɪkl/ d. mécanique. ~**s** n. (science) mécanique f.; n. pl. mécanisme m.

mechan|ism /ˈmekənɪzəm/ n. mécanisme m. ~**ize** v.t. mécaniser.

medal /ˈmedl/ n. médaille f. ~**list** n. médaillé(e) m. (f.). **be a gold ~list,** être médaille d'or.

medallion /mɪˈdælɪən/ n. (medal, portrait, etc.) médaillon m.

meddle /ˈmedl/ v.i. (interfere) se mêler (in, de); (tinker) toucher (with, à). ~**some** a. importun.

media /ˈmiːdɪə/ see **medium.** ● n. pl. **the ~,** les média m. pl. **talk to the ~,** parler à la presse.

median /ˈmiːdɪən/ a. médian. ● n. médiane f.

mediat|e /ˈmiːdɪeɪt/ v.i. servir d'intermédiaire. ~**ion** /-ˈeɪʃn/ n. médiation f. ~**or** n. média|teur, -trice m., f.

medical /ˈmedɪkl/ a. médical; (student) en médecine. ● n. (fam.) visite médicale f.

medicat|ed /ˈmedɪkeɪtɪd/ a. médical. ~**ion** /-ˈkeɪʃn/ n. médicaments m. pl.

medicin|e /ˈmedsn/ n. (science) médecine f.; (substance) médicament m. ~**al** /mɪˈdɪsɪnl/ a. médicinal.

medieval /medrˈiːvl/ a. médiéval.

mediocr|e /ˌmiːdɪˈəʊkə(r)/ a. médiocre. ~**ity** /-ˈɒkrətɪ/ n. médiocrité f.

meditat|e /ˈmedɪteɪt/ v.t./i. méditer. ~**ion** /-ˈteɪʃn/ n. méditation f.

Mediterranean /medɪtəˈreɪnɪən/ a. méditerranéen. ● n. **the ~,** la Méditerranée f.

medium /ˈmiːdɪəm/ n. (pl. **media**) milieu m.; (for transmitting data etc.) support m.; (pl. **mediums**) (person) médium m. ● a. moyen.

medley /ˈmedlɪ/ n. mélange m.; (mus.) pot-pourri m.

meek /miːk/ a. (-er, -est) doux.

meet /miːt/ v.t. (p.t. **met**) rencontrer; (see again) retrouver; (fetch) (aller) chercher; (be introduced to) faire la connaissance de; (face) faire face à; (requirement) satisfaire. ● v.i. se rencontrer; (see each other again) se retrouver; (in session) se réunir.

meeting /ˈmiːtɪŋ/ n. réunion f.; (between two people) rencontre f.

megalomania /megələʊˈmeɪnɪə/ n. mégalomanie f. ~**c** /-æk/ n. mégalomane m./f.

megaphone /ˈmegəfəʊn/ n. porte-voix m. invar.

melamine /ˈmeləmiːn/ n. mélamine f.

melanchol|y /ˈmelənkəlɪ/ n. mélancolie f. ● a. mélancolique. ~**ic** /-ˈkɒlɪk/ a. mélancolique.

mellow /ˈmeləʊ/ a. (-er, -est) (fruit) mûr; (sound, colour) moelleux, doux; (person) mûri. ● v.t./i. (mature) mûrir; (soften) (s')adoucir.

melodious /mɪˈləʊdɪəs/ a. mélodieux.

melodrama /ˈmelədrɑːmə/ n. mélodrame m. ~**tic** /-əˈmætɪk/ a. mélodramatique.

melod|y /ˈmelədɪ/ n. mélodie f. ~**ic** /mɪˈlɒdɪk/ a. mélodique.

melon /ˈmelən/ n. melon m.

melt /melt/ v.t./i. (faire) fondre. ~**ing-pot** n. creuset m.

member /ˈmembə(r)/ n. membre m. **M~ of Parliament,** député m. ~**ship** n. adhésion f.; (members) membres m. pl.; (fee) cotisation f.

membrane /ˈmembreɪn/ n. membrane f.

memento /mɪˈmentəʊ/ n. (pl. -**oes**) (object) souvenir m.

memo /ˈmeməʊ/ n. (pl. -**os**) (fam.) note f.

memoir /ˈmemwɑː(r)/ n. (record, essay) mémoire m.

memorable /ˈmemərəbl/ a. mémorable.

memorandum /meməˈrændəm/ n. (pl. -**ums**) note f.

memorial /mɪˈmɔːrɪəl/ n. monument m. ● a. commémoratif.

memorize /ˈmeməraɪz/ v.t. apprendre par cœur.

memory /ˈmemərɪ/ n. (mind, in computer) mémoire f.; (thing remembered) souvenir m. **from ~,** de mémoire. **in ~ of,** à la mémoire de.

men /men/ see **man.**

menac|e /ˈmenəs/ n. menace f.; (nuisance) peste f. ● v.t. menacer. ~**ing** a. menaçant.

menagerie /mɪˈnædʒərɪ/ n. ménagerie f.

mend /mend/ v.t. réparer; (darn) raccommoder. ● n. raccommodage m. ~ **one's ways,** s'amender. **on the ~,** en voie de guérison.

menial /ˈmiːnɪəl/ a. servile.

meningitis /menm'dʒaɪtɪs/ n. méningite f.

menopause /'menəpɔːz/ n. ménopause f.

menstruation /menstrʊ'eɪʃn/ n. menstruation f.

mental /'mentl/ a. mental; (hospital) psychiatrique. **~ block,** blocage m.

mentality /men'tælətɪ/ n. mentalité f.

menthol /'menθɒl/ n. menthol m. ● a. mentholé.

mention /'menʃn/ v.t. mentionner. ● n. mention f. **don't ~ it!,** il n'y a pas de quoi!, je vous en prie!

mentor /'mentɔː(r)/ n. mentor m.

menu /'menjuː/ n. (food, on computer) menu m.; (list) carte f.

MEP (abbr.) (member of the European Parliament) député européen m.

mercenary /'mɜːsɪnərɪ/ a. & n. mercenaire (m.).

merchandise /'mɜːtʃəndaɪz/ n. marchandise f. pl.

merchant /'mɜːtʃənt/ n. marchand m. ● a. (ship, navy) marchand. **~ bank,** banque de commerce f.

merciful /'mɜːsɪfl/ a. miséricordieux. **~ly** adv. (fortunately: fam.) Dieu merci.

merciless /'mɜːsɪlɪs/ a. impitoyable, implacable.

mercury /'mɜːkjʊrɪ/ n. mercure m.

mercy /'mɜːsɪ/ n. pitié f. **at the ~ of,** à la merci de.

mere /mɪə(r)/ a. simple. **~ly** adv. simplement.

merest /'mɪərɪst/ a. moindre.

merge /mɜːdʒ/ v.t./i. (se) mêler (**with,** à); (companies: comm.) fusionner. **~r** /-ə(r)/ n. fusion f.

meridian /mə'rɪdɪən/ n. méridien m.

meringue /mə'ræŋ/ n. meringue f.

merit /'merɪt/ n. mérite m. ● v.t. (p.t. **merited**) mériter.

mermaid /'mɜːmeɪd/ n. sirène f.

merriment /'merɪmənt/ n. gaieté f.

merry /'merɪ/ a. (-ier, -iest) gai. **make ~,** faire la fête. **~-go-round** n. manège m. **~-making** n. réjouissances f. pl. **merrily** adv. gaiement.

mesh /meʃ/ n. maille f.; (fabric) tissu à mailles m.; (network) réseau m.

mesmerize /'mezməraɪz/ v.t. hypnotiser.

mess /mes/ n. désordre m., gâchis m.; (dirt) saleté f.; (mil.) mess m. ● v.t. **~ up,** gâcher. ● v.i. **~ about,** s'amuser; (dawdle) traîner. **~**

with, (tinker with) tripoter. **make a ~ of,** gâcher.

message /'mesɪdʒ/ n. message m.

messenger /'mesɪndʒə(r)/ n. messager m.

Messrs /'mesəz/ n. pl. **~ Smith,** Messieurs or MM. Smith.

messy /'mesɪ/ a. (-ier, -iest) en désordre; (dirty) sale.

met /met/ see meet.

metabolic /metə'bɒlɪk/ adj. métabolique.

metabolism /mɪ'tæbəlɪzəm/ n. métabolisme m.

metal /'metl/ n. métal m. ● a. de métal. **~lic** /mɪ'tælɪk/ a. métallique; (paint, colour) métallisé.

metallurgy /mɪ'tælədʒɪ, Amer. 'metələːdʒɪ/ n. métallurgie f.

metamorphosis /metə'mɔːfəsɪs/ n. (pl. **-phoses** /-siːz/) métamorphose f.

metaphor /'metəfə(r)/ n. métaphore f. **~ical** /-'fɒrɪkl/ a. métaphorique.

mete /miːt/ v.t. **~ out,** donner, distribuer; (justice) rendre.

meteor /'miːtɪə(r)/ n. météore m.

meteorite /'miːtɪəraɪt/ n. météorite m.

meteorolog|y /miːtɪə'rɒlədʒɪ/ n. météorologie f. **~ical** /-ə'lɒdʒɪkl/ a. météorologique.

meter [1] /'miːtə(r)/ n. compteur m.

meter [2] /'miːtə(r)/ n. (Amer.) = **metre.**

method /'meθəd/ n. méthode f.

methodical /mɪ'θɒdɪkl/ a. méthodique.

Methodist /'meθədɪst/ n. & a. méthodiste (m./f.).

methodology /meθə'dɒlədʒɪ/ n. méthodologie f.

methylated /'meθɪleɪtɪd/ a. **~ spirit,** alcool à brûler m.

meticulous /mɪ'tɪkjʊləs/ a. méticuleux.

metre /'miːtə(r)/ n. mètre m.

metric /'metrɪk/ a. métrique. **~ation** /-'keɪʃn/ n. adoption du système métrique f.

metropol|is /mə'trɒpəlɪs/ n. (city) métropole f. **~itan** /metrə'pɒlɪtən/ a. métropolitain.

mettle /'metl/ n. courage m.

mew /mjuː/ n. miaulement m. ● v.i. miauler.

mews /mjuːz/ n. pl. (dwellings) appartements chic aménagés dans des anciennes écuries m. pl.

Mexic|o /'meksɪkəʊ/ *n.* Mexique *m.* **~an** *a.* & *n.* mexicain(e) (*m.* (*f.*)).
miaow /mi:'aʊ/ *n.* & *v.i.* = **mew**.
mice /maɪs/ *see* **mouse**.
mickey /'mɪkɪ/ *n.* **take the ~ out of,** (*sl.*) se moquer de.
micro- /'maɪkrəʊ/ *pref.* micro-.
microbe /'maɪkrəʊb/ *n.* microbe *m.*
microchip /'maɪkrəʊtʃɪp/ *n.* micro-plaquette *f.*, puce *f.*
microclimate /'maɪkrəʊklaɪmət/ *n.* microclimat *n.*
microcomputer /maɪkrəʊ-kəm'pju:tə(r)/ *n.* micro(-ordinateur) *m.*
microcosm /'maɪkrəʊkɒzm/ *n.* microcosme *m.*
microfilm /'maɪkrəʊfɪlm/ *n.* micro-film *m.*
microlight /'maɪkrəʊlaɪt/ *n.* U.L.M. *m.*
microphone /'maɪkrəfəʊn/ *n.* microphone *m.*
microprocessor /maɪkrəʊ-'prəʊsesə(r)/ *n.* microprocesseur *m.*
microscop|e /'maɪkrəskəʊp/ *n.* microscope *m.* **~ic** /-'skɒpɪk/ *a.* microscopique.
microwave /'maɪkrəʊweɪv/ *n.* micro-onde *f.* **~ oven,** four à micro-ondes *m.*
mid /mɪd/ *a.* **in ~ air**/*etc.*, en plein ciel/*etc.* **in ~ March**/*etc.*, à la mi-mars/*etc.* **in ~ ocean**/*etc.*, au milieu de l'océan/*etc.*
midday /mɪd'deɪ/ *n.* midi *m.*
middle /'mɪdl/ *a.* du milieu; (*quality*) moyen. ● *n.* milieu *m.* **in the ~ of,** au milieu de. **~-aged** *a.* d'un certain âge. **M~ Ages,** moyen âge *m.* **~ class,** classe moyenne *f.* **~-class** *a.* bourgeois. **M~ East,** Proche-Orient *m.*
middleman /'mɪdlmæn/ *n.* (*pl.* **-men**) intermédiaire *m.*
middling /'mɪdlɪŋ/ *a.* moyen.
midge /mɪdʒ/ *n.* moucheron *m.*
midget /'mɪdʒɪt/ *n.* nain(e) *m.* (*f.*). ● *a.* minuscule.
Midlands /'mɪdləndz/ *n. pl.* région du centre de l'Angleterre *f.*
midnight /'mɪdnaɪt/ *n.* minuit *f.*
midriff /'mɪdrɪf/ *n.* ventre *m.*
midst /mɪdst/ *n.* **in the ~ of,** au milieu de. **in our ~,** parmi nous.
midsummer /mɪd'sʌmə(r)/ *n.* milieu de l'été *m.*; (*solstice*) solstice d'été *m.*
midway /mɪdweɪ/ *adv.* à mi-chemin.

midwife /'mɪdwaɪf/ *n.* (*pl.* **-wives**) sage-femme *f.*
might [1] /maɪt/ *n.* puissance *f.* **~y** *a.* puissant; (*very great*: *fam.*) très grand; *adv.* (*fam.*) rudement.
might [2] /maɪt/ *see* **may**.
migraine /'mi:greɪn, *Amer.* 'maɪ-greɪn/ *n.* migraine *f.*
migrant /'maɪgrənt/ *a.* & *n.* (*bird*) migrateur (*m.*); (*worker*) migrant(e) (*m.* (*f.*)).
migrat|e /maɪ'greɪt/ *v.i.* émigrer. **~ion** /-ʃn/ *n.* migration *f.*
mike /maɪk/ *n.* (*fam.*) micro *m.*
mild /maɪld/ *a.* (**-er, -est**) doux; (*illness*) bénin. **~ly** *adv.* doucement. **to put it ~ly,** pour ne rien exagérer. **~ness** *n.* douceur *f.*
mildew /'mɪldju:/ *n.* moisissure *f.*
mile /maɪl/ *n.* mille *m.* (= 1.6 km.). **~s too big**/*etc.*, (*fam.*) beaucoup trop grand/*etc.* **~age** *n.* (*loosely*) kilo-métrage *m.*
milestone /'maɪlstəʊn/ *n.* borne *f.*; (*event, stage*: *fig.*) jalon *m.*
militant /'mɪlɪtənt/ *a.* & *n.* militant(e) (*m.* (*f.*)).
military /'mɪlɪtrɪ/ *a.* militaire.
militate /'mɪlɪteɪt/ *v.i.* militer.
militia /mɪ'lɪʃə/ *n.* milice *f.*
milk /mɪlk/ *n.* lait *m.* ● *a.* (*product*) laitier. ● *v.t.* (*cow etc.*) traire; (*fig.*) exploiter. **~ shake,** milk-shake *m.* **~y** *a.* (*diet*) lacté; (*colour*) laiteux; (*tea etc.*) au lait. **M~y Way,** Voie lactée *f.*
milkman /'mɪlkmən, *Amer.* 'mɪlk-mæn/ *n.* (*pl.* **-men**) laitier *m.*
mill /mɪl/ *n.* moulin *m.*; (*factory*) usine *f.* ● *v.t.* moudre. ● *v.i.* **~ around,** tourner en rond; (*crowd*) grouiller. **~er** *n.* meunier *m.*
millennium /mɪ'lenɪəm/ *n.* (*pl.* **-ums**) millénaire *m.*
millet /'mɪlɪt/ *n.* millet *m.*
milli- /'mɪlɪ/ *pref.* milli-.
millimetre /'mɪlɪmi:tə(r)/ *n.* milli-mètre *m.*
milliner /'mɪlɪnə(r)/ *n.* modiste *f.*
million /'mɪljən/ *n.* million *m.* **a ~ pounds,** un million de livres. **~aire** /-'neə(r)/ *n.* millionnaire *m.*
millstone /'mɪlstəʊn/ *n.* meule *f.*; (*burden*: *fig.*) boulet *m.*
milometer /maɪ'lɒmɪtə(r)/ *n.* comp-teur kilométrique *m.*
mime /maɪm/ *n.* (*actor*) mime *m.*/*f.*; (*art*) (art du) mime *m.* ● *v.t.*/*i.* mimer.

mimic /'mɪmɪk/ v.t. (p.t. **mimicked**) imiter. ● n. imita|teur, -trice m., f. ~**ry** n. imitation f.

mince /mɪns/ v.t. hacher. ● n. viande hachée f. ~ **pie**, tarte aux fruits confits f. **not to ~ matters**, ne pas mâcher ses mots. ~**r** /-ə(r)/ n. (machine) hachoir m.

mincemeat /'mɪnsmiːt/ n. hachis de fruits confits m. **make ~ of**, anéantir, pulvériser.

mind /maɪnd/ n. esprit m.; (sanity) raison f.; (opinion) avis m. ● v.t. (have charge of) s'occuper de; (heed) faire attention à. **be on s.o.'s ~**, préoccuper qn. **bear that in ~**, ne l'oubliez pas. **change one's ~**, changer d'avis. **make up one's ~**, se décider (**to**, à). **I do not ~ the noise**/etc., le bruit/etc. ne me dérange pas. **I do not ~**, ça m'est égal. **would you ~ checking?**, je peux vous demander de vérifier? ~**ful** a. attentif (**of**, à). ~**less** a. irréfléchi.

minder /'maɪndə(r)/ n. (for child) gardien(ne) m. (f.); (for protection) ange gardien m.

mine[1] /maɪn/ poss. pron. le mien, la mienne, les mien(ne)s. **it is ~**, c'est à moi or le mien.

mine[2] /maɪn/ n. mine f. ● v.t. extraire; (mil.) miner. ~**r** n. mineur m. ~**ing** n. exploitation minière f.; a. minier.

minefield /'maɪnfiːld/ n. champ de mines m.

mineral /'mɪnərəl/ n. & a. minéral (m.). ~ (**water**), (fizzy soft drink) boisson gazeuse f. ~ **water**, (natural) eau minérale f.

minesweeper /'maɪnswiːpə(r)/ n. (ship) dragueur de mines m.

mingle /'mɪŋgl/ v.t./i. (se) mêler (**with**, à).

mingy /'mɪndʒɪ/ a. (fam.) radin.

mini- /'mɪnɪ/ pref. mini-.

miniatur|e /'mɪnɪtʃə(r)/ a. & n. miniature (f.). ~**ize** v.t. miniaturiser.

minibus /'mɪnɪbʌs/ n. minibus m.

minicab /'mɪnɪkæb/ n. taxi m.

minim /'mɪnɪm/ n. blanche f.

minim|um /'mɪnɪməm/ a. & n. (pl. -**ima**) minimum (m.). ~**al** a. minimal. ~**ize** v.t. minimiser.

minist|er /'mɪnɪstə(r)/ n. ministre m. ~**erial** /-'stɪərɪəl/ a. ministériel. ~**ry** n. ministère m.

mink /mɪŋk/ n. vison m.

minor /'maɪnə(r)/ a. petit, mineur. ● n. (jurid.) mineur(e) m. (f.).

minority /maɪ'nɒrətɪ/ n. minorité f. ● a. minoritaire.

mint[1] /mɪnt/ n. **the M~**, l'Hôtel de la Monnaie m. **a ~**, une fortune. ● v.t. frapper. **in ~ condition**, à l'état neuf.

mint[2] /mɪnt/ n. (plant) menthe f.; (sweet) pastille de menthe f.

minus /'maɪnəs/ prep. moins; (without: fam.) sans. ● n. (sign) moins m. ~ **sign**, moins m.

minute[1] /'mɪnɪt/ n. minute f. ~**s**, (of meeting) procès-verbal m.

minute[2] /maɪ'njuːt/ a. (tiny) minuscule; (detailed) minutieux.

mirac|le /'mɪrəkl/ n. miracle m. ~**ulous** /mɪ'rækjʊləs/ a. miraculeux.

mirage /'mɪrɑːʒ/ n. mirage m.

mire /maɪə(r)/ n. fange f.

mirror /'mɪrə(r)/ n. miroir m., glace f. ● v.t. refléter.

mirth /mɜːθ/ n. gaieté f.

misadventure /mɪsəd'ventʃə(r)/ n. mésaventure f.

misanthropist /mɪs'ænθrəpɪst/ n. misanthrope m./f.

misapprehension /mɪsæprɪ'henʃn/ n. malentendu m.

misbehav|e /mɪsbɪ'heɪv/ v.i. se conduire mal. ~**iour** n. mauvaise conduite f.

miscalculat|e /mɪs'kælkjʊleɪt/ v.t. mal calculer. ● v.i. se tromper. ~**ion** /-'leɪʃn/ n. erreur de calcul f.

miscarr|y /mɪs'kærɪ/ v.i. faire une fausse couche. ~**iage** /-ɪdʒ/ n. fausse couche f. ~**iage of justice**, erreur judiciaire f.

miscellaneous /mɪsə'leɪnɪəs/ a. divers.

mischief /'mɪstʃɪf/ n. (foolish conduct) espièglerie f.; (harm) mal m. **get into ~**, faire des sottises.

mischievous /'mɪstʃɪvəs/ a. espiègle; (malicious) méchant.

misconception /mɪskən'sepʃn/ n. idée fausse f.

misconduct /mɪs'kɒndʌkt/ n. mauvaise conduite f.

misconstrue /mɪskən'struː/ v.t. mal interpréter.

misdeed /mɪs'diːd/ n. méfait m.

misdemeanour /mɪsdɪ'miːnə(r)/ n. (jurid.) délit m.

misdirect /mɪsdɪ'rekt/ v.t. (person) mal renseigner.

miser /'maɪzə(r)/ n. avare m./f. ~ly a. avare.

miserable /'mɪzrəbl/ a. (sad) malheureux; (wretched) misérable; (unpleasant) affreux.

misery /'mɪzərɪ/ n. (unhappiness) malheur m.; (pain) souffrances f. pl.; (poverty) misère f.; (person: fam.) grincheu|x, -se m., f.

misfire /mɪs'faɪə(r)/ v.i. (plan etc.) rater; (engine) avoir des ratés.

misfit /'mɪsfɪt/ n. inadapté(e) m. (f.).

misfortune /mɪs'fɔːtʃuːn/ n. malheur m.

misgiving /mɪs'gɪvɪŋ/ n. (doubt) doute m.; (apprehension) crainte f.

misguided /mɪs'gaɪdɪd/ a. (foolish) imprudent; (mistaken) erroné. **be ~,** (person) se tromper.

mishap /'mɪshæp/ n. mésaventure f., contretemps m.

misinform /mɪsɪn'fɔːm/ v.t. mal renseigner.

misinterpret /mɪsɪn'tɜːprɪt/ v.t. mal interpréter.

misjudge /mɪs'dʒʌdʒ/ v.t. mal juger.

mislay /mɪs'leɪ/ v.t. (p.t. **mislaid**) égarer.

mislead /mɪs'liːd/ v.t. (p.t. **misled**) tromper. ~ing a. trompeur.

mismanage /mɪs'mænɪdʒ/ v.t. mal gérer. ~ment n. mauvaise gestion f.

misnomer /mɪs'nəʊmə(r)/ n. terme impropre m.

misplace /mɪs'pleɪs/ v.t. mal placer; (lose) égarer.

misprint /'mɪsprɪnt/ n. faute d'impression f., coquille f.

misread /mɪs'riːd/ v.t. (p.t. **misread** /mɪs'red/) mal lire; (intentions) mal comprendre.

misrepresent /mɪsreprɪ'zent/ v.t. présenter sous un faux jour.

miss[1] /mɪs/ v.t./i. manquer; (deceased person etc.) regretter. **he ~es her/Paris/**etc., elle/Paris/etc. lui manque. **I ~ you,** tu me manques. **you're ~ing the point,** vous n'avez rien compris. ● n. coup manqué m. **it was a near ~,** on l'a échappé belle or de peu. ~ **out,** omettre. ~ **out on sth,** rater qch.

miss[2] /mɪs/ n. (pl. **misses**) mademoiselle f. (pl. **mesdemoiselles**). **M~ Smith,** Mademoiselle or Mlle Smith.

misshapen /mɪs'ʃeɪpən/ a. difforme.

missile /'mɪsaɪl/ n. (mil.) missile m.; (object thrown) projectile m.

missing /'mɪsɪŋ/ a. (person) disparu; (thing) qui manque. **something's ~,** il manque quelque chose.

mission /'mɪʃn/ n. mission f.

missionary /'mɪʃənrɪ/ n. missionnaire m./f.

missive /'mɪsɪv/ n. missive f.

misspell /mɪs'spel/ v.t. (p.t. **misspelt** or **misspelled**) mal écrire.

mist /mɪst/ n. brume f.; (on window) buée f. ● v.t./i. (s')embuer.

mistake /mɪ'steɪk/ n. erreur f. ● v.t. (p.t. **mistook,** p.p. **mistaken**) mal comprendre; (choose wrongly) se tromper de. **by ~,** par erreur. **make a ~,** faire une erreur. ~ **for,** prendre pour. ~n /-ən/ a. erroné. **be ~n,** se tromper. ~nly /-ənlɪ/ adv. par erreur.

mistletoe /'mɪsltəʊ/ n. gui m.

mistreat /mɪs'triːt/ v.t. maltraiter.

mistress /'mɪstrɪs/ n. maîtresse f.

mistrust /mɪs'trʌst/ v.t. se méfier de. ● n. méfiance f.

misty /'mɪstɪ/ a. (-ier, -iest) brumeux; (window) embué.

misunderstand /mɪsʌndə'stænd/ v.t. (p.t. **-stood**) mal comprendre. ~ing n. malentendu m.

misuse[1] /mɪs'juːz/ v.t. mal employer; (power etc.) abuser de.

misuse[2] /mɪs'juːs/ n. mauvais emploi m.; (unfair use) abus m.

mitigat|e /'mɪtɪgeɪt/ v.t. atténuer. ~ing circumstances, circonstances atténuantes f. pl.

mitten /'mɪtn/ n. moufle f.

mix /mɪks/ v.t./i. (se) mélanger. ● n. mélange m. ~ **up,** mélanger; (bewilder) embrouiller; (mistake, confuse) confondre (**with,** avec). ~-up n. confusion f. ~ **with,** (people) fréquenter. ~er n. (culin.) mélangeur m. **be a good ~er,** être sociable. ~er tap, mélangeur m.

mixed /mɪkst/ a. (school etc.) mixte; (assorted) assorti. **be ~-up,** (fam.) avoir des problèmes.

mixture /'mɪkstʃə(r)/ n. mélange m.; (for cough) sirop m.

moan /məʊn/ n. gémissement m. ● v.i. gémir; (complain) grogner. ~er n. (grumbler) grognon m.

moat /məʊt/ n. douve(s) f. (pl.).

mob /mɒb/ n. (crowd) cohue f.; (gang: sl.) bande f. ● v.t. (p.t. **mobbed**) assiéger.

mobil|e /'məʊbaɪl/ *a.* mobile. **~e home,** caravane *f.* ● *n.* mobile *m.* **~ity** /-'bɪlətɪ/ *n.* mobilité *f.*

mobiliz|e /'məʊbɪlaɪz/ *v.t./i.* mobiliser. **~ation** /-'zeɪʃn/ *n.* mobilisation *f.*

moccasin /'mɒkəsɪn/ *n.* mocassin *m.*

mock /mɒk/ *v.t./i.* se moquer (de). ● *a.* faux. **~-up** *n.* maquette *f.*

mockery /'mɒkərɪ/ *n.* moquerie *f.* **a ~ of,** une parodie de.

mode /məʊd/ *n.* (*way, method*) mode *m.*; (*fashion*) mode *f.*

model /'mɒdl/ *n.* modèle *m.*; (*of toy*) modèle réduit *m.*; (*artist's*) modèle *m.*; (*for fashion*) mannequin *m.* ● *a.* modèle; (*car etc.*) modèle réduit *invar.* ● *v.t.* (*p.t.* **modelled**) modeler; (*clothes*) présenter. ● *v.i.* être mannequin; (*pose*) poser. **~ling** *n.* métier de mannequin *m.*

modem /'məʊdem/ *n.* modem *m.*

moderate[1] /'mɒdərət/ *a. & n.* modéré(e) (*m.* (*f.*)). **~ly** *adv.* (*in moderation*) modérément; (*fairly*) moyennement.

moderat|e[2] /'mɒdəreɪt/ *v.t./i.* (se) modérer. **~ion** /-'reɪʃn/ *n.* modération *f.* **in ~ion,** avec modération.

modern /'mɒdn/ *a.* moderne. **~ languages,** langues vivantes *f. pl.* **~ize** *v.t.* moderniser.

modest /'mɒdɪst/ *a.* modeste. **~y** *n.* modestie *f.*

modicum /'mɒdɪkəm/ *n.* **a ~ of,** un peu de.

modif|y /'mɒdɪfaɪ/ *v.t.* modifier. **~ication** /-ɪ'keɪʃn/ *n.* modification *f.*

modular /'mɒdjʊlə(r)/ *a.* modulaire

modulat|e /'mɒdjʊleɪt/ *v.t./i.* moduler. **~ion** /-'leɪʃn/ *n.* modulation *f.*

module /'mɒdju:l/ *n.* module *m.*

mohair /'məʊheə(r)/ *n.* mohair *m.*

moist /mɔɪst/ *a.* (**-er, -est**) humide, moite. **~ure** /'mɔɪstʃə(r)/ *n.* humidité *f.* **~urizer** /'mɔɪstʃəraɪzə(r)/ *n.* produit hydratant *m.*

moisten /'mɔɪsn/ *v.t.* humecter.

molar /'məʊlə(r)/ *n.* molaire *f.*

molasses /mə'læsɪz/ *n.* mélasse *f.*

mold /məʊld/ (*Amer.*) = **mould.**

mole[1] /məʊl/ *n.* grain de beauté *m.*

mole[2] /məʊl/ *n.* (*animal*) taupe *f.*

molecule /'mɒlɪkju:l/ *n.* molécule *f.*

molest /mə'lest/ *v.t.* (*pester*) importuner; (*ill-treat*) molester.

mollusc /'mɒləsk/ *n.* mollusque *m.*

mollycoddle /'mɒlɪkɒdl/ *v.t.* dorloter, chouchouter.

molten /'məʊltən/ *a.* en fusion.

mom /mɒm/ *n.* (*Amer.*) maman *f.*

moment /'məʊmənt/ *n.* moment *m.*

momentar|y /'məʊməntrɪ, *Amer.* -terɪ/ *a.* momentané. **~ily** (*Amer.* /-'terəlɪ/) *adv.* momentanément; (*soon: Amer.*) très bientôt.

momentous /mə'mentəs/ *a.* important.

momentum /mə'mentəm/ *n.* élan *m.*

Monaco /'mɒnəkəʊ/ *n.* Monaco *f.*

monarch /'mɒnək/ *n.* monarque *m.* **~y** *n.* monarchie *f.*

monast|ery /'mɒnəstrɪ/ *n.* monastère *m.* **~ic** /mə'næstɪk/ *a.* monastique.

Monday /'mʌndɪ/ *n.* lundi *m.*

monetarist /'mʌnɪtərɪst/ *n.* monétariste *m./f.*

monetary /'mʌnɪtrɪ/ *a.* monétaire.

money /'mʌnɪ/ *n.* argent *m.* **~s,** sommes d'argent *f. pl.* **~-box** *n.* tirelire *f.* **~-lender** *n.* prêteu|r, -se *m., f.* **~ order,** mandat *m.* **~-spinner** *n.* mine d'or *f.*

mongrel /'mʌŋgrəl/ *n.* (chien) bâtard *m.*

monitor /'mɒnɪtə(r)/ *n.* (*pupil*) chef de classe *m.*; (*techn.*) moniteur *m.* ● *v.t.* contrôler; (*a broadcast*) écouter.

monk /mʌŋk/ *n.* moine *m.*

monkey /'mʌŋkɪ/ *n.* singe *m.* **~-nut** *n.* cacahuète *f.* **~-wrench** *n.* clef à molette *f.*

mono /'mɒnəʊ/ *n.* (*pl.* **-os**) mono *f.* ● *a.* mono *invar.*

monochrome /'mɒnəkrəʊm/ *a. & n.* (en) noir et blanc (*m.*).

monogram /'mɒnəgræm/ *n.* monogramme *m.*

monologue /'mɒnəlɒg/ *n.* monologue *m.*

monopol|y /mə'nɒpəlɪ/ *n.* monopole *m.* **~ize** *v.t.* monopoliser.

monotone /'mɒnətəʊn/ *n.* ton uniforme *m.*

monoton|ous /mə'nɒtənəs/ *a.* monotone. **~y** *n.* monotonie *f.*

monsoon /mɒn'su:n/ *n.* mousson *f.*

monst|er /'mɒnstə(r)/ *n.* monstre *m.* **~rous** *a.* monstrueux.

monstrosity /mɒn'strɒsətɪ/ *n.* monstruosité *f.*

month /mʌnθ/ *n.* mois *m.*

monthly /'mʌnθlɪ/ *a.* mensuel. ● *adv.* mensuellement. ● *n.* (*periodical*) mensuel *m.*

monument /'mɒnjʊmənt/ *n.* monument *m.* ~**al** /-'mentl/ *a.* monumental.

moo /mu:/ *n.* meuglement *m.* ● *v.i.* meugler.

mooch /mu:tʃ/ *v.i.* (*sl.*) flâner. ● *v.t.* (*Amer., sl.*) se procurer.

mood /mu:d/ *n.* humeur *f.* **in a good/bad ~,** de bonne/mauvaise humeur. ~**y** *a.* d'humeur changeante; (*sullen*) maussade.

moon /mu:n/ *n.* lune *f.*

moon|light /'mu:nlaɪt/ *n.* clair de lune *m.* ~**lit** *a.* éclairé par la lune.

moonlighting /'mu:nlaɪtɪŋ/ *n.* (*fam.*) travail au noir *m.*

moor [1] /mʊə(r)/ *n.* lande *f.*

moor [2] /mʊə(r)/ *v.t.* amarrer. ~**ings** *n. pl.* (*chains etc.*) amarres *f. pl.*; (*place*) mouillage *m.*

moose /mu:s/ *n. invar.* élan *m.*

moot /mu:t/ *a.* discutable. ● *v.t.* (*question*) soulever.

mop /mɒp/ *n.* balai à franges *m.* ● *v.t.* (*p.t.* **mopped**). ~ **(up),** éponger. ~ **of hair,** tignasse *f.*

mope /məʊp/ *v.i.* se morfondre.

moped /'məʊped/ *n.* cyclomoteur *m.*

moral /'mɒrəl/ *a.* moral. ● *n.* morale *f.* ~**s,** moralité *f.* ~**ize** *v.i.* moraliser. ~**ly** *adv.* moralement.

morale /mə'rɑ:l/ *n.* moral *m.*

morality /mə'rælətɪ/ *n.* moralité *f.*

morass /mə'ræs/ *n.* marais *m.*

morbid /'mɔ:bɪd/ *a.* morbide.

more /mɔ:(r)/ *a.* (*a greater amount of*) plus de (**than,** que). ● *n. & adv.* plus (**than,** que). **(some) ~ tea/pens/etc.,** (*additional*) encore du thé/des stylos/*etc.* **no ~ bread**/*etc.,* plus de pain/*etc.* **I want no ~, I do not want any ~,** je n'en veux plus. ~ **or less,** plus ou moins.

moreover /mɔ:'rəʊvə(r)/ *adv.* de plus, en outre.

morgue /mɔ:g/ *n.* morgue *f.*

moribund /'mɒrɪbʌnd/ *a.* moribond.

morning /'mɔ:nɪŋ/ *n.* matin *m.*; (*whole morning*) matinée *f.*

Morocc|o /mə'rɒkəʊ/ *n.* Maroc *m.* ~**an** *a. & n.* marocain(e) (*m.* (*f.*)).

moron /'mɔ:rɒn/ *n.* crétin(e) *m.* (*f.*).

morose /mə'rəʊs/ *a.* morose.

morphine /'mɔ:fi:n/ *n.* morphine *f.*

Morse /mɔ:s/ *n.* ~ **(code),** morse *m.*

morsel /'mɔ:sl/ *n.* petit morceau *m.*; (*of food*) bouchée *f.*

mortal /'mɔ:tl/ *a. & n.* mortel(le) (*m.*(*f.*)). ~**ity** /mɔ:'tælətɪ/ *n.* mortalité *f.*

mortar /'mɔ:tə(r)/ *n.* mortier *m.*

mortgage /'mɔ:gɪdʒ/ *n.* crédit immobilier *m.* ● *v.t.* hypothéquer.

mortify /'mɔ:tɪfaɪ/ *v.t.* mortifier.

mortise /'mɔ:tɪs/ *n.* ~ **lock** serrure encastrée *f.*

mortuary /'mɔ:tʃərɪ/ *n.* morgue *f.*

mosaic /məʊ'zeɪɪk/ *n.* mosaïque *f.*

Moscow /'mɒskəʊ/ *n.* Moscou *m.*/*f.*

Moses /'məʊzɪz/ *a.* ~ **basket,** moïse *m.*

mosque /mɒsk/ *n.* mosquée *f.*

mosquito /mə'ski:təʊ/ *n.* (*pl.* -oes) moustique *m.*

moss /mɒs/ *n.* mousse *f.* ~**y** *a.* moussu.

most /məʊst/ *a.* (*the greatest amount of*) le plus de; (*the majority of*) la plupart de. ● *n.* le plus. ● *adv.* (le) plus; (*very*) fort. ~ **of,** la plus grande partie de; (*majority*) la plupart de. **at ~,** tout au plus. **for the ~ part,** pour la plupart. **make the ~ of,** profiter de. ~**ly** *adv.* surtout.

motel /məʊ'tel/ *n.* motel *m.*

moth /mɒθ/ *n.* papillon de nuit *m.*; (*in cloth*) mite *f.* ~**-ball** *n.* boule de naphtaline *f.*; *v.t.* mettre en réserve. ~**-eaten** *a.* mité.

mother /'mʌðə(r)/ *n.* mère *f.* ● *v.t.* entourer de soins maternels, materner. ~**hood** *n.* maternité *f.* ~**-in-law** *n.* (*pl.* ~**s-in-law**) belle-mère *f.* ~**-of-pearl** *n.* nacre *f.* **M~'s Day,** la fête des mères. ~**-to-be** *n.* future maman *f.* ~ **tongue,** langue maternelle *f.*

motherly /'mʌðəlɪ/ *a.* maternel.

motif /məʊ'ti:f/ *n.* motif *m.*

motion /'məʊʃn/ *n.* mouvement *m.*; (*proposal*) motion *f.* ● *v.t./i.* ~ **(to)** **s.o. to,** faire signe à qn. de. ~**less** *a.* immobile. ~ **picture,** (*Amer.*) film *m.*

motivat|e /'məʊtɪveɪt/ *v.t.* motiver. ~**ion** /-'veɪʃn/ *n.* motivation *f.*

motive /'məʊtɪv/ *n.* motif *m.*

motley /'mɒtlɪ/ *a.* bigarré.

motor /'məʊtə(r)/ *n.* moteur *m.*; (*car*) auto *f.* ● *a.* (*anat.*) moteur; (*boat*) à moteur. ● *v.i.* aller en auto. ~ **car,** (*fam.*) moto *f.* ~ **car,** auto *f.* ~ **cycle,** motocyclette *f.* ~**-cyclist** *n.* motocycliste *m.*/*f.* ~ **home,** (*Amer.*) camping-car *m.* ~**ing** *n.* (*sport*) l'automobile *f.* ~**ized** *a.* motorisé ~ **vehicle,** véhicule automobile *m.*

motorist /'məʊtərɪst/ *n.* automobiliste *m./f.*

motorway /'məʊtəweɪ/ *n.* autoroute *f.*

mottled /'mɒtld/ *a.* tacheté.

motto /'mɒtəʊ/ *n.* (*pl.* **-oes**) devise *f.*

mould [1] /məʊld/ *n.* moule *m.* ● *v.t.* mouler; (*influence*) former. ~**ing** *n.* (*on wall etc.*) moulure *f.*

mould [2] /məʊld/ *n.* (*fungus, rot*) moisissure *f.* ~**y** *a.* moisi.

moult /məʊlt/ *v.i.* muer.

mound /maʊnd/ *n.* monticule *m.*, tertre *m.*; (*pile: fig.*) tas *m.*

mount [1] /maʊnt/ *n.* (*hill*) mont *m.*

mount [2] /maʊnt/ *v.t./i.* monter. ● *n.* monture *f.* ~ **up,** s'accumuler; (*add up*) chiffrer (**to,** à).

mountain /'maʊntɪn/ *n.* montagne *f.* ~ **bike,** (vélo) tout terrain *m.*, vtt *m.* ~**ous** *a.* montagneux.

mountaineer /maʊntɪ'nɪə(r)/ *n.* alpiniste *m./f.* ~**ing** *n.* alpinisme *m.*

mourn /mɔːn/ *v.t./i.* ~ (**for**), pleurer. ~**er** *n.* personne qui suit le cortège funèbre *f.* ~**ing** *n.* deuil *m.*

mournful /'mɔːnfl/ *a.* triste.

mouse /maʊs/ *n.* (*pl.* **mice**) souris *f.*

mousetrap /'maʊstræp/ *n.* souricière *f.*

mousse /muːs/ *n.* mousse *f.*

moustache /mə'stɑːʃ, *Amer.* 'mʌstæʃ/ *n.* moustache *f.*

mousy /'maʊsɪ/ *a.* (*hair*) d'un brun terne; (*fig.*) timide.

mouth /maʊθ/ *n.* bouche *f.*; (*of dog, cat, etc.*) gueule *f.* ~**-organ** *n.* harmonica *m.*

mouthful /'maʊθfʊl/ *n.* bouchée *f.*

mouthpiece /'maʊθpiːs/ *n.* (*mus.*) embouchure *f.*; (*person: fig.*) porte-parole *m. invar.*

mouthwash /'maʊθwɒʃ/ *n.* eau dentifrice *f.*

mouthwatering /'maʊθwɔːtrɪŋ/ *a.* qui fait venir l'eau à la bouche.

movable /'muːvəbl/ *a.* mobile.

move /muːv/ *v.t./i.* remuer, (se) déplacer, bouger; (*incite*) pousser; (*emotionally*) émouvoir; (*propose*) proposer; (*depart*) partir; (*act*) agir. ~ (**out**), déménager. ● *n.* mouvement *m.*; (*in game*) coup *m.*; (*player's turn*) tour *m.*; (*procedure: fig.*) démarche *f.*; (*house change*) déménagement *m.* ~ **back,** (faire) reculer. ~ **forward** *or* **on,** (faire)

avancer. ~ **in,** emménager. ~ **over,** se pousser. **on the** ~, en marche.

movement /'muːvmənt/ *n.* mouvement *m.*

movie /'muːvɪ/ *n.* (*Amer.*) film *m.* **the** ~**s,** le cinéma. ~ **camera,** (*Amer.*) caméra *f.*

moving /'muːvɪŋ/ *a.* en mouvement; (*touching*) émouvant.

mow /məʊ/ *v.t.* (*p.p.* **mowed** *or* **mown**) (*corn etc.*) faucher; (*lawn*) tondre. ~ **down,** faucher. ~**er** *n.* (*for lawn*) tondeuse *f.*

MP *abbr. see* Member of Parliament.

Mr /'mɪstə(r)/ *n.* (*pl.* **Messrs**). ~ **Smith,** Monsieur *or* M. Smith.

Mrs /'mɪsɪz/ *n.* (*pl.* **Mrs**). ~ **Smith,** Madame *or* Mme Smith. **the** ~ **Smith,** Mesdames *or* Mmes Smith.

Ms /mɪz/ *n.* (*title of married or unmarried woman*). ~ **Smith,** Madame *or* Mme Smith.

much /mʌtʃ/ *a.* beaucoup de. ● *adv.* & *n.* beaucoup.

muck /mʌk/ *n.* fumier *m.*; (*dirt: fam.*) saleté *f.* ● *v.i.* ~ **about,** (*sl.*) s'amuser. ~ **about with,** (*sl.*) tripoter. ~ **in,** (*sl.*) participer. ● *v.t.* ~ **up,** (*sl.*) gâcher. ~**y** *a.* sale.

mucus /'mjuːkəs/ *n.* mucus *m.*

mud /mʌd/ *n.* boue *f.* ~**dy** *a.* couvert de boue.

muddle /'mʌdl/ *v.t.* embrouiller. ● *v.i.* ~ **through,** se débrouiller. ● *n.* désordre *m.*, confusion *f.*; (*mix-up*) confusion *f.*

mudguard /'mʌdgɑːd/ *n.* garde-boue *m. invar.*

muff /mʌf/ *n.* manchon *m.*

muffin /'mʌfɪn/ *n.* muffin *m.* (*petit pain rond et plat*).

muffle /'mʌfl/ *v.t.* emmitoufler; (*sound*) assourdir. ~**r** /-ə(r)/ *n.* (*scarf*) cache-nez *m. invar.*; (*Amer.: auto.*) silencieux *m.*

mug /mʌg/ *n.* tasse *f.*; (*in plastic, metal*) gobelet *m.*; (*for beer*) chope *f.*; (*face: sl.*) gueule *f.*; (*fool: sl.*) idiot(e) *m.(f.)* ● *v.t.* (*p.t.* **mugged**) agresser. ~**ger** *n.* agresseur *m.* ~**ging** *n.* agression *f.*

muggy /'mʌgɪ/ *a.* lourd.

mule /mjuːl/ *n.* (*male*) mulet *m.*; (*female*) mule *f.*

mull [1] /mʌl/ *v.t.* (*wine*) chauffer.

mull [2] /mʌl/ *v.t.* ~ **over,** ruminer.

multi- /'mʌltɪ/ *pref.* multi-.

multicoloured /'mʌltɪkʌləd/ *a.* multicolore.

multifarious /mʌltɪˈfeərɪəs/ a. divers.

multinational /mʌltɪˈnæʃnəl/ a. & n. multinational(e) (f.).

multiple /ˈmʌltɪpl/ a. & n. multiple (m.). ~ **sclerosis**, sclérose en plaques f.

multipl|y /ˈmʌltɪplaɪ/ v.t./i. (se) multiplier. ~**ication** /-ɪˈkeɪʃn/ n. multiplication f.

multistorey /mʌltɪˈstɔːrɪ/ a. (car park) à étages.

multitude /ˈmʌltɪtjuːd/ n. multitude f.

mum [1] /mʌm/ a. **keep ~,** (fam.) garder le silence.

mum [2] /mʌm/ n. (fam.) maman f.

mumble /ˈmʌmbl/ v.t./i. marmotter, marmonner.

mummy [1] /ˈmʌmɪ/ n. (embalmed body) momie f.

mummy [2] /ˈmʌmɪ/ n. (mother: fam.) maman f.

mumps /mʌmps/ n. oreillons m. pl.

munch /mʌntʃ/ v.t./i. mastiquer.

mundane /mʌnˈdeɪn/ a. banal.

municipal /mjuːˈnɪsɪpl/ a. municipal. ~**ity** /-ˈpælətɪ/ n. municipalité f.

munitions /mjuːˈnɪʃnz/ n. pl. munitions f. pl.

mural /ˈmjʊərəl/ a. mural. ● n. peinture murale f.

murder /ˈmɜːdə(r)/ n. meurtre m. ● v.t. assassiner; (ruin: fam.) massacrer. ~**er** n. meurtrier m., assassin m. ~**ous** a. meurtrier.

murky /ˈmɜːkɪ/ a. (-ier, -iest) (night, plans, etc.) sombre, ténébreux; (liquid) épais, sale.

murmur /ˈmɜːmə(r)/ n. murmure m. ● v.t./i. murmurer.

muscle /ˈmʌsl/ n. muscle m. ● v.i. ~ **in,** (sl.) s'introduire de force (on, dans).

muscular /ˈmʌskjʊlə(r)/ a. musculaire; (brawny) musclé.

muse /mjuːz/ v.i. méditer.

museum /mjuːˈzɪəm/ n. musée m.

mush /mʌʃ/ n. (pulp, soft food) bouillie f. ~**y** a. mou.

mushroom /ˈmʌʃrʊm/ n. champignon m. ● v.i. pousser comme des champignons.

music /ˈmjuːzɪk/ n. musique f. ~**al** a. musical; (instrument) de musique; (talented) doué pour la musique; n. comédie musicale f.

musician /mjuːˈzɪʃn/ n. musicien(ne) m. (f.).

musk /mʌsk/ n. musc m.

Muslim /ˈmʊzlɪm/ a. & n. musulman(e) (m. (f.)).

muslin /ˈmʌzlɪn/ n. mousseline f.

mussel /ˈmʌsl/ n. moule f.

must /mʌst/ v. aux. devoir. **you ~ go,** vous devez partir, il faut que vous partiez. **he ~ be old,** il doit être vieux. **I ~ have done it,** j'ai dû le faire. ● n. **be a ~,** (fam.) être un must.

mustard /ˈmʌstəd/ n. moutarde f.

muster /ˈmʌstə(r)/ v.t./i. (se) rassembler.

musty /ˈmʌstɪ/ a. (-ier, -iest) (room, etc.) qui sent le moisi; (smell, taste) de moisi.

mutant /ˈmjuːtənt/ a. & n. mutant. (m.)

mutation /mjuːˈteɪʃn/ n. mutation f.

mute /mjuːt/ a. & n. muet(te) (m. (f.)). ~**d** /-ɪd/ a. (colour, sound) sourd, atténué; (criticism) voilé.

mutilat|e /ˈmjuːtɪleɪt/ v.t. mutiler. ~**ion** /-ˈleɪʃn/ n. mutilation f.

mutin|y /ˈmjuːtɪnɪ/ n. mutinerie f. ● v.i. se mutiner. ~**ous** a. (sailor etc.) mutiné; (fig.) rebelle.

mutter /ˈmʌtə(r)/ v.t./i. marmonner, murmurer.

mutton /ˈmʌtn/ n. mouton m.

mutual /ˈmjuːtʃʊəl/ a. mutuel; (common to two or more: fam.) commun. ~**ly** adv. mutuellement.

muzzle /ˈmʌzl/ n. (snout) museau m.; (device) muselière f.; (of gun) gueule f. ● v.t. museler.

my /maɪ/ a. mon, ma, pl. mes.

myopic /maɪˈɒpɪk/ a. myope.

myself /maɪˈself/ pron. moi-même; (reflexive) me, m'*; (after prep.) moi.

mysterious /mɪˈstɪərɪəs/ a. mystérieux.

mystery /ˈmɪstərɪ/ n. mystère m.

mystic /ˈmɪstɪk/ a. & n. mystique (m./f.) ~**al** a. mystique. ~**ism** /-sɪzəm/ n. mysticisme m.

mystify /ˈmɪstɪfaɪ/ v.t. laisser perplexe.

mystique /mɪˈstiːk/ n. mystique f.

myth /mɪθ/ n. mythe m. ~**ical** a. mythique.

mythology /mɪˈθɒlədʒɪ/ n. mythologie f.

N

nab /næb/ v.t. (p.t. **nabbed**) (arrest: sl.) épingler, attraper.

nag /næg/ v.t./i. (p.t. **nagged**) critiquer; (pester) harceler.

nagging /'nægɪŋ/ a. persistant.

nail /neɪl/ n. clou m.; (of finger, toe) ongle m. ● v.t. clouer. **~-brush** n. brosse à ongles f. **~-file** n. lime à ongles f. **~ polish**, vernis à ongles m. **on the ~,** (pay) sans tarder, tout de suite.

naïve /nar'i:v/ a. naïf.

naked /'neɪkɪd/ a. nu. **to the ~ eye,** à l'œil nu. **~ly** adv. à nu. **~ness** n. nudité f.

name /neɪm/ n. nom m.; (fig.) réputation f. ● v.t. nommer; (fix) fixer. **be ~d after,** porter le nom de. **~less** a. sans nom, anonyme.

namely /'neɪmlɪ/ adv. à savoir.

namesake /'neɪmseɪk/ n. (person) homonyme m.

nanny /'nænɪ/ n. nounou f. **~-goat** n. chèvre f.

nap /næp/ n. somme m. ● v.i. (p.t. **napped**) faire un somme. **catch ~ping,** prendre au dépourvu.

nape /neɪp/ n. nuque f.

napkin /'næpkɪn/ n. (at meals) serviette f.; (for baby) couche f.

nappy /'næpɪ/ n. couche f.

narcotic /nɑ:'kɒtɪk/ a. & n. narcotique (m.).

narrat|e /nə'reɪt/ v.t. raconter. **~ion** /-ʃn/ n. narration f. **~or** n. narrateur, -trice m., f.

narrative /'nærətɪv/ n. récit m.

narrow /'nærəʊ/ a. (-er, -est) étroit. ● v.t./i. (se) rétrécir; (limit) (se) limiter. **~ down the choices,** limiter les choix. **~ly** adv. étroitement; (just) de justesse. **~-minded** a. à l'esprit étroit; (ideas etc.) étroit. **~ness** n. étroitesse f.

nasal /'neɪzl/ a. nasal.

nast|y /'nɑ:stɪ/ a. (-ier, -iest) mauvais, désagréable; (malicious) méchant. **~ily** adv. désagréablement; méchamment; (malice) **~iness** n. (malice) méchanceté f.

nation /'neɪʃn/ n. nation f. **~-wide** a. dans l'ensemble du pays.

national /'næʃnəl/ a. national. ● n. ressortissant(e) m. (f.). **~ anthem,** hymne national m. **~ism** n. natio-

nalisme m. **~ize** v.t. nationaliser. **~ly** adv. à l'échelle nationale.

nationality /næʃə'nælətɪ/ n. nationalité f.

native /'neɪtɪv/ n. (local inhabitant) autochtone m./f.; (non-European) indigène m./f. ● a. indigène; (country) natal; (inborn) inné. **be a ~ of,** être originaire de. **~ language,** langue maternelle f. **~ speaker of French,** personne de langue maternelle française f.

Nativity /nə'tɪvətɪ/ n. **the ~,** la Nativité f.

natter /'nætə(r)/ v.i. bavarder.

natural /'nætʃrəl/ a. naturel. **~ history,** histoire naturelle f. **~ist** n. naturaliste m./f. **~ly** adv. (normally, of course) naturellement; (by nature) de nature.

naturaliz|e /'nætʃrəlaɪz/ v.t. naturaliser. **~ation** /-'zeɪʃn/ n. naturalisation f.

nature /'neɪtʃə(r)/ n. nature f.

naught /nɔ:t/ n. (old use) rien m.

naught|y /'nɔ:tɪ/ a. (-ier, -iest) vilain, méchant; (indecent) grivois. **~ily** adv. mal.

nause|a /'nɔ:sɪə/ n. nausée f. **~ous** a. nauséabond.

nauseate /'nɔ:sɪeɪt/ v.t. écœurer.

nautical /'nɔ:tɪkl/ a. nautique.

naval /'neɪvl/ a. (battle etc.) naval; (officer) de marine.

nave /neɪv/ n. (of church) nef f.

navel /'neɪvl/ n. nombril m.

navigable /'nævɪgəbl/ a. navigable.

navigat|e /'nævɪgeɪt/ v.t. (sea etc.) naviguer sur; (ship) piloter. ● v.i. naviguer. **~ion** /-'geɪʃn/ n. navigation f. **~or** n. navigateur m.

navvy /'nævɪ/ n. terrassier m.

navy /'neɪvɪ/ n. marine f. **~ (blue),** bleu marine invar.

near /nɪə(r)/ adv. près. ● prep. près de. ● a. proche. ● v.t. approcher de. **draw ~,** (s')approcher (**to,** de). **~ by** adv. tout près. **N~ East,** Proche-Orient m. **~ to,** près de. **~ness** n. proximité f. **~-sighted** a. myope.

nearby /nɪə'baɪ/ a. proche.

nearly /'nɪəlɪ/ adv. presque. **I ~ forgot,** j'ai failli oublier. **not ~ as pretty/etc. as,** loin d'être aussi joli/etc. que.

nearside /'nɪəsaɪd/ a. (auto.) du côté du passager.

neat /ni:t/ a. (-er, -est) soigné, net; (room etc.) bien rangé; (clever) ha-

bile; (*whisky, brandy, etc.*) sec. **~ly**
adv. avec soin; habilement. **~ness** *n.*
netteté *f.*
nebulous /'nebjʊləs/ *a.* nébuleux.
necessar|y /'nesəsərɪ/ *a.* nécessaire.
~ies *n. pl.* nécessaire *m.* **~ily** *adv.*
nécessairement.
necessitate /nɪ'sesɪteɪt/ *v.t.* nécessiter.
necessity /nɪ'sesɪtɪ/ *n.* nécessité *f.*;
(*thing*) chose indispensable *f.*
neck /nek/ *n.* cou *m.*; (*of dress*)
encolure *f.* **~ and neck**, à égalité.
necklace /'neklɪs/ *n.* collier *m.*
neckline /'neklaɪn/ *n.* encolure *f.*
necktie /'nektaɪ/ *n.* cravate *f.*
nectarine /'nektərɪn/ *n.* brugnon *m.*,
nectarine *f.*
need /niːd/ *n.* besoin *m.* ● *v.t.* avoir
besoin de; (*demand*) demander. **you
~ not come**, vous n'êtes pas obligé
de venir. **~less** *a.* inutile. **~lessly**
adv. inutilement.
needle /'niːdl/ *n.* aiguille *f.* ● *v.t.*
(*annoy: fam.*) asticoter, agacer.
needlework /'niːdlwɜːk/ *n.* couture
f.; (*object*) ouvrage (à l'aiguille) *m.*
needy /'niːdɪ/ *a.* (**-ier, -iest**) nécessi-
teux, indigent.
negation /nɪ'geɪʃn/ *n.* négation *f.*
negative /'negətɪv/ *a.* négatif. ● *n.*
(*of photograph*) négatif *m.*; (*word:
gram.*) négation *f.* **in the ~**, (*answer*) par la négative; (*gram.*) à la
forme négative. **~ly** *adv.* négative-
ment.
neglect /nɪ'glekt/ *v.t.* négliger, laisser
à l'abandon. ● *n.* manque de soins
m. (**state of**) **~**, abandon *m.* **~ to
do**, négliger de faire. **~ful** *a.* négligent.
négligé /'neglɪʒeɪ/ *n.* négligé *m.*
negligen|t /'neglɪdʒənt/ *a.* négligent.
~ce *a.* négligence *f.*
negligible /'neglɪdʒəbl/ *a.* négligeable.
negotiable /nɪ'gəʊʃəbl/ *a.* négocia-
ble.
negotiat|e /nɪ'gəʊʃɪeɪt/ *v.t./i.* négo-
cier. **~ion** /-'eɪʃn/ *n.* négociation
f. **~or** *n.* négocia|teur, -trice *m.*,
f.
Negr|o /'niːgrəʊ/ *n.* (*pl.* **-oes**) Noir *m.*
● *a.* noir; (*art, music*) nègre. **~ess**
n. Noire *f.*
neigh /neɪ/ *n.* hennissement *m.*
● *v.i.* hennir.
neighbour, *Amer.* **neighbor** /'neɪ-
bə(r)/ *n.* voisin(e) *m.* (*f.*). **~hood**

n. voisinage *m.*, quartier *m.* **in the
~hood of**, aux alentours de. **~ing**
a. voisin.
neighbourly /'neɪbəlɪ/ *a.* amical.
neither /'naɪðə(r)/ *a. & pron.* au-
cun(e) des deux, ni l'un(e) ni
l'autre. ● *adv.* ni. ● *conj.* non
plus. **~ big nor small**, ni grand ni
petit. **~ am I coming**, je ne viendrai
pas non plus.
neon /'niːɒn/ *n.* néon *m.* ● *a.* (*lamp
etc.*) au néon.
nephew /'nevjuː, *Amer.* 'nefjuː/ *n.*
neveu *m.*
nerve /nɜːv/ *n.* nerf *m.*; (*courage*)
courage *m.*; (*calm*) sang-froid *m.*;
(*impudence: fam.*) culot *m.* **~s**, (*before exams etc.*) le trac **~-racking**
a. éprouvant.
nervous /'nɜːvəs/ *a.* nerveux. **be or
feel ~**, (*afraid*) avoir peur. **~
breakdown**, dépression nerveuse *f.*
~ly *adv.* (*tensely*) nerveusement;
(*timidly*) craintivement. **~ness** *n.*
nervosité *f.*; (*fear*) crainte *f.*
nervy /'nɜːvɪ/ *a.* = **nervous**; (*Amer.,
fam.*) effronté.
nest /nest/ *n.* nid *m.* ● *v.i.* nicher. **~-
egg** *n.* pécule *m.*
nestle /'nesl/ *v.i.* se blottir.
net[1] /net/ *n.* filet *m.* ● *v.t.* (*p.t.*
netted) prendre au filet. **~ting** *n.*
(*nets*) filets *m. pl.*; (*wire*) treillis *m.*;
(*fabric*) voile *m.*
net[2] /net/ *a.* (*weight etc.*) net.
netball /'netbɔːl/ *n.* netball *m.*
Netherlands /'neðələndz/ *n. pl.* **the
~**, les Pays-Bas *m. pl.*
nettle /'netl/ *n.* ortie *f.*
network /'netwɜːk/ *n.* réseau *m.*
neuralgia /njʊə'rældʒə/ *n.* névralgie
f.
neuro|sis /njʊə'rəʊsɪs/ *n.* (*pl.*-oses
/-siːz/) névrose *f.* **~tic** /-'rɒtɪk/ *a. &
n.* névrosé(e) (*m.* (*f.*)).
neuter /'njuːtə(r)/ *a. & n.* neutre
(*m.*). ● *v.t.* (*castrate*) castrer.
neutral /'njuːtrəl/ *a.* neutre. **~
(gear)**, (*auto.*) point mort *m.* **~ity**
/-'trælətɪ/ *n.* neutralité *f.*
neutron /'njuːtrɒn/ *n.* neutron *m.* **~
bomb**, bombe à neutrons *f.*
never /'nevə(r)/ *adv.* (ne) jamais;
(*not: fam.*) (ne) pas. **he ~ refuses**,
il ne refuse jamais. **I ~ saw him**,
(*fam.*) je ne l'ai pas vu. **~ again**,
plus jamais. **~ mind**, (*don't worry*)
ne vous en faites pas; (*it doesn't*

matter) peu importe. **~-ending** *a.*
interminable.

nevertheless /nevəðə'les/ *adv.* néanmoins, toutefois.

new /nju:/ *a.* (**-er, -est**) nouveau;
(*brand-new*) neuf. **~-born** *a.* nou-
veau-né. **~-laid egg,** œuf frais *m.* **~
moon,** nouvelle lune *f.* **~ year,**
nouvel an *m.* **New Year's Day,** le
jour de l'an. **New Year's Eve,** la
Saint-Sylvestre. **New Zealand,** Nou-
velle-Zélande *f.* **New Zealander,**
Néo-Zélandais(e) *m.* (*f.*). **~ness** *n.*
nouveauté *f.*

newcomer /'nju:kʌmə(r)/ *n.* nouveau venu *m.*, nouvelle venue *f.*

newfangled /nju:'fæŋgld/ *a.* (*pej.*)
moderne, neuf.

newly /'nju:lɪ/ *adv.* nouvellement. **~-
weds** *n. pl.* nouveaux mariés *m. pl.*

news /nju:z/ *n.* nouvelle(s) *f.* (*pl.*);
(*radio, press*) informations *f. pl.*;
(*TV*) actualités *f. pl.*, informations
f. pl. **~ agency,** agence de presse *f.*
~caster, ~-reader *ns.* présenta|-
teur, trice *m.,f.*

newsagent /'nju:zeɪdʒənt/ *n.* mar-
chand(e) de journaux *m.*(*f.*).

newsletter /'nju:zletə(r)/ *n.* bulletin
m.

newspaper /'nju:speɪpə(r)/ *n.* journal *m.*

newsreel /'nju:zri:l/ *n.* actualités *f.
pl.*

newt /nju:t/ *n.* triton *m.*

next /nekst/ *a.* prochain; (*adjoining*)
voisin; (*following*) suivant. ● *adv.*
la prochaine fois; (*afterwards*)
ensuite. ● *n.* suivant(e) *m.*(*f.*). **~-
door,** à côté (**to,** de). **~-door** *a.* d'à
côté. **~ of kin,** parent le plus proche
m. **~ to,** à côté de.

nib /nɪb/ *n.* bec *m.*, plume *f.*

nibble /'nɪbl/ *v.t./i.* grignoter.

nice /naɪs/ *a.* (**-er, -est**) agréable, bon;
(*kind*) gentil; (*pretty*) joli; (*respectable*) bien *invar.*; (*subtle*) délicat.
~ly *adv.* agréablement; gentiment;
(*well*) bien.

nicety /'naɪsətɪ/ *n.* subtilité *f.*

niche /nɪtʃ, ni:ʃ/ *n.* (*recess*) niche *f.*;
(*fig.*) place *f.*, situation *f.*

nick /nɪk/ *n.* petite entaille *f.* ● *v.t.*
(*steal, arrest: sl.*) piquer. **in the ~ of
time,** juste à temps.

nickel /'nɪkl/ *n.* nickel *m.*; (*Amer.*)
pièce de cinq cents *f.*

nickname /'nɪkneɪm/ *n.* surnom *m.*;
(*short form*) diminutif *m.* ● *v.t.*
surnommer.

nicotine /'nɪkəti:n/ *n.* nicotine *f.*

niece /ni:s/ *n.* nièce *f.*

nifty /'nɪftɪ/ *a.* (*sl.*) chic *invar.*

Nigeria /naɪ'dʒɪərɪə/ *n.* Nigéria *m./f.*
~n *a. & n.* nigérian(e) (*m.* (*f.*)).

niggardly /'nɪgədlɪ/ *a.* chiche.

niggling /'nɪglɪŋ/ *a.* (*person*) tatillon;
(*detail*) insignifiant.

night /naɪt/ *n.* nuit *f.*; (*evening*) soir
m. ● *a.* de nuit. **~-cap** *n.* boisson *f.*
(*avant d'aller se coucher*). **~-club** *n.*
boîte de nuit *f.* **~-dress, ~-gown,
~ie** *ns.* chemise de nuit *f.* **~-life** *n.*
vie nocturne *f.* **~-school** *n.* cours du
soir *m. pl.* **~-time** *n.* nuit *f.* **~-
watchman** *n.* veilleur de nuit *m.*

nightfall /'naɪtfɔ:l/ *n.* tombée de la
nuit *f.*

nightingale /'naɪtɪŋgeɪl/ *n.* rossignol
m.

nightly /'naɪtlɪ/ *a. & adv.* (de) chaque
nuit *or* soir.

nightmare /'naɪtmeə(r)/ *n.* cauchemar *m.*

nil /nɪl/ *n.* rien *m.*; (*sport*) zéro *m.*
● *a.* (*chances, risk, etc.*) nul.

nimble /'nɪmbl/ *a.* (**-er, -est**) agile.

nin|e /naɪn/ *a. & n.* neuf (*m.*). **~th** *a.
& n.* neuvième (*m./f.*).

nineteen /naɪn'ti:n/ *a. & n.* dix-neuf
(*m.*). **~th** *a. & n.* dix-neuvième (*m./
f.*).

ninet|y /'naɪntɪ/ *a. & n.* quatre-vingt-
dix (*m.*). **~ieth** *a. & n.* quatre-
vingt-dixième (*m./f.*).

nip /nɪp/ *v.t./i.* (*p.t.* **nipped**) (*pinch*)
pincer; (*rush: sl.*) courir. **~ out/
back/etc.,** sortir/rentrer/*etc.* rapidement. ● *n.* pincement *m.*; (*cold*)
fraîcheur *f.*

nipper /'nɪpə(r)/ *n.* (*sl.*) gosse *m./f.*

nipple /'nɪpl/ *n.* bout de sein *m.*; (*of
baby's bottle*) tétine *f.*

nippy /'nɪpɪ/ *a.* (**-ier, -iest**) (*fam.*)
alerte; (*chilly: fam.*) frais.

nitrogen /'naɪtrədʒən/ *n.* azote *m.*

nitwit /'nɪtwɪt/ *n.* (*fam.*) imbécile *m./
f.*

no /nəʊ/ *a.* aucun(e); pas de. ● *adv.*
non. ● *n.* (*pl.* **noes**) non *m. invar.* **~
man/etc.,** aucun homme/*etc.* **~
money/time/etc.,** pas d'argent/de
temps/*etc.* **~ man's land,** no man's
land *m.* **~ one = nobody.** **~ smok-
ing/entry,** défense de fumer/

d'entrer. **~ way!**, (*fam.*) pas question!

nob|le /'nəʊbl/ *a.* (**-er, -est**) noble. **~ility** /-'bɪlətɪ/ *n.* noblesse *f.*

nobleman /'nəʊblmən/ *n.* (*pl.* **-men**) noble *m.*

nobody /'nəʊbədɪ/ *pron.* (ne) personne. ● *n.* nullité *f.* **he knows ~,** il ne connaît personne. **~ is there,** personne n'est là.

nocturnal /nɒk'tɜ:nl/ *a.* nocturne.

nod /nɒd/ *v.t./i.* (*p.t.* **nodded**). **~ (one's head),** faire un signe de tête. **~ off,** s'endormir. ● *n.* signe de tête *m.*

noise /nɔɪz/ *n.* bruit *m.* **~less** *a.* silencieux.

nois|y /'nɔɪzɪ/ *a.* (**-ier, -iest**) bruyant. **~ily** *adv.* bruyamment.

nomad /'nəʊmæd/ *n.* nomade *m./f.* **~ic** /-'mædɪk/ *a.* nomade.

nominal /'nɒmɪnl/ *a.* symbolique, nominal; (*value*) nominal. **~ly** *adv.* nominalement.

nominat|e /'nɒmɪneɪt/ *v.t.* nommer; (*put forward*) proposer. **~ion** /-'neɪʃn/ *n.* nomination *f.*

non- /nɒn/ *pref.* non-. **~-iron** *a.* qui ne se repasse pas. **~-skid** *a.* antidérapant. **~-stick** *a.* à revêtement antiadhésif.

non-commissioned /nɒnkə'mɪʃnd/ *a.* **~ officer,** sous-officier *m.*

non-committal /nɒnkə'mɪtl/ *a.* évasif.

nondescript /'nɒndɪskrɪpt/ *a.* indéfinissable.

none /nʌn/ *pron.* aucun(e). **~ of us,** aucun de nous. **I have ~,** je n'en ai pas. **~ of the money was used,** l'argent n'a pas du tout été utilisé. ● *adv.* **~ too,** (ne) pas tellement. **he is ~ the happier,** il n'en est pas plus heureux.

nonentity /nɒ'nentətɪ/ *n.* nullité *f.*

non-existent /nɒnɪg'zɪstənt/ *a.* inexistant.

nonplussed /nɒn'plʌst/ *a.* perplexe, déconcerté.

nonsens|e /'nɒnsəns/ *n.* absurdités *f. pl.* **~ical** /-'sensɪkl/ *a.* absurde.

non-smoker /nɒn'sməʊkə(r)/ *n.* non-fumeur *m.*

non-stop /nɒn'stɒp/ *a.* (*train, flight*) direct. ● *adv.* sans arrêt.

noodles /'nu:dlz/ *n. pl.* nouilles *f. pl.*

nook /nʊk/ *n.* (re)coin *m.*

noon /nu:n/ *n.* midi *m.*

noose /nu:s/ *n.* nœud coulant *m.*

nor /nɔ:(r)/ *adv.* ni. ● *conj.* (ne) non plus. **~ shall I come,** je ne viendrai pas non plus.

norm /nɔ:m/ *n.* norme *f.*

normal /'nɔ:ml/ *a.* normal. **~ity** /nɔ:'mælətɪ/ *n.* normalité *f.* **~ly** *adv.* normalement.

Norman /'nɔ:mən/ *a. & n.* normand(e) (*m.(f.*)). **~dy** *n.* Normandie *f.*

north /nɔ:θ/ *n.* nord *m.* ● *a.* nord *invar.*, du nord. ● *adv.* vers le nord. **N~ America,** Amérique du Nord *f.* **N~ American** *a. & n.* nord-américain(e) (*m. (f.*)). **~-east** *n.* nord-est *m.* **~erly** /'nɔ:ðəlɪ/ *a.* du nord. **~ward** *a.* au nord. **~wards** *adv.* vers le nord. **~-west** *n.* nord-ouest *m.*

northern /'nɔ:ðən/ *a.* du nord. **~er** *n.* habitant(e) du nord *m. (f.*).

Norw|ay /'nɔ:weɪ/ *n.* Norvège *f.* **~egian** /nɔ:'wi:dʒən/ *a. & n.* norvégien(ne) (*m. (f.*)).

nose /nəʊz/ *n.* nez *m.* ● *v.i.* **~ about,** fouiner.

nosebleed /'nəʊzbli:d/ *n.* saignement de nez *m.*

nosedive /'nəʊzdaɪv/ *n.* piqué *m.* ● *v.i.* descendre en piqué.

nostalg|ia /nɒ'stældʒə/ *n.* nostalgie *f.* **~ic** *a.* nostalgique.

nostril /'nɒstrəl/ *n.* narine *f.*; (*of horse*) naseau *m.*

nosy /'nəʊzɪ/ *a.* (**-ier, -iest**) (*fam.*) curieux, indiscret.

not /nɒt/ *adv.* (ne) pas. **I do ~ know,** je ne sais pas. **~ at all,** pas du tout. **~ yet,** pas encore. **I suppose ~,** je suppose que non.

notable /'nəʊtəbl/ *a.* notable. ● *n.* (*person*) notable *m.*

notably /'nəʊtəblɪ/ *adv.* notamment.

notary /'nəʊtərɪ/ *n.* notaire *m.*

notation /nəʊ'teɪʃn/ *n.* notation *f.*

notch /nɒtʃ/ *n.* entaille *f.* ● *v.t.* **~ up,** (*score etc.*) marquer.

note /nəʊt/ *n.* note *f.*; (*banknote*) billet *m.*; (*short letter*) mot *m.* ● *v.t.* noter; (*notice*) remarquer.

notebook /'nəʊtbʊk/ *n.* carnet *m.*

noted /'nəʊtɪd/ *a.* connu (**for,** pour).

notepaper /'nəʊtpeɪpə(r)/ *n.* papier à lettres *m.*

noteworthy /'nəʊtwɜ:ðɪ/ *a.* remarquable.

nothing /'nʌθɪŋ/ *pron.* (ne) rien. ● *n.* rien *m.*; (*person*) nullité *f.* ● *adv.* nullement. **he eats ~,** il ne mange rien. **~ big**/*etc.*, rien de grand/*etc.* **~ else,** rien d'autre. **~ much,** pas grand-chose. **for ~,** pour rien, gratis.

notice /'nəʊtɪs/ *n.* avis *m.*, annonce *f.*; (*poster*) affiche *f.* **(advance) ~,** préavis *m.* **at short ~,** dans des délais très brefs. **give in one's ~,** donner sa démission. ● *v.t.* remarquer, observer. **~-board** *n.* tableau d'affichage *m.* **take ~,** faire attention (**of,** à).

noticeabl|e /'nəʊtɪsəbl/ *a.* visible. **~y** *adv.* visiblement.

notif|y /'nəʊtɪfaɪ/ *v.t.* (*inform*) aviser; (*make known*) notifier. **~ication** /-ɪ'keɪʃn/ *n.* avis *m.*

notion /'nəʊʃn/ *n.* idée *f.*, notion *f.* **~s,** (*sewing goods etc.*: *Amer.*) mercerie *f.*

notor|ious /nəʊ'tɔːrɪəs/ *a.* (tristement) célèbre. **~iety** /-ə'raɪətɪ/ *n.* notoriété *f.* **~iously** *adv.* notoirement.

notwithstanding /nɒtwɪθ'stændɪŋ/ *prep.* malgré. ● *adv.* néanmoins.

nougat /'nuːgɑː/ *n.* nougat *m.*

nought /nɔːt/ *n.* zéro *m.*

noun /naʊn/ *n.* nom *m.*

nourish /'nʌrɪʃ/ *v.t.* nourrir. **~ing** *a.* nourrissant. **~ment** *n.* nourriture *f.*

novel /'nɒvl/ *n.* roman *m.* ● *a.* nouveau. **~ist** *n.* romanc|ier, -ière *m.*, *f.* **~ty** *n.* nouveauté *f.*

November /nəʊ'vembə(r)/ *n.* novembre *m.*

novice /'nɒvɪs/ *n.* novice *m.*/*f.*

now /naʊ/ *adv.* maintenant. ● *conj.* maintenant que. **just ~,** maintenant; (*a moment ago*) tout à l'heure. **~ and again, ~ and then,** de temps à autre.

nowadays /'naʊədeɪz/ *adv.* de nos jours.

nowhere /'nəʊweə(r)/ *adv.* nulle part.

nozzle /'nɒzl/ *n.* (*tip*) embout *m.*; (*of hose*) lance *f.*

nuance /'njuːɑːns/ *n.* nuance *f.*

nuclear /'njuːklɪə(r)/ *a.* nucléaire.

nucleus /'njuːklɪəs/ *n.* (*pl.* **-lei** /-lɪaɪ/) noyau *m.*

nud|e /njuːd/ *a.* nu. ● *n.* nu *m.* **in the ~e,** tout nu. **~ity** *n.* nudité *f.*

nudge /nʌdʒ/ *v.t.* pousser du coude. ● *n.* coup de coude *m.*

nudis|t /'njuːdɪst/ *n.* nudiste *m.*/*f.* **~m** /-zəm/ *n.* nudisme *m.*

nuisance /'njuːsns/ *n.* (*thing, event*) ennui *m.*; (*person*) peste *f.* **be a ~,** être embêtant.

null /nʌl/ *a.* nul. **~ify** *v.t.* infirmer.

numb /nʌm/ *a.* engourdi. ● *v.t.* engourdir.

number /'nʌmbə(r)/ *n.* nombre *m.*; (*of ticket, house, page, etc.*) numéro *m.* ● *v.t.* numéroter; (*count, include*) compter. **a ~ of people,** plusieurs personnes. **~-plate** *n.* plaque d'immatriculation *f.*

numeral /'njuːmərəl/ *n.* chiffre *m.*

numerate /'njuːmərət/ *a.* qui sait calculer.

numerical /njuː'merɪkl/ *a.* numérique.

numerous /'njuːmərəs/ *a.* nombreux.

nun /nʌn/ *n.* religieuse *f.*

nurs|e /nɜːs/ *n.* infirmière *f.*, infirmier *m.*; (*nanny*) nurse *f.* ● *v.t.* soigner; (*hope etc.*) nourrir. **~ing home,** clinique *f.*

nursemaid /'nɜːsmeɪd/ *n.* bonne d'enfants *f.*

nursery /'nɜːsərɪ/ *n.* chambre d'enfants *f.*; (*for plants*) pépinière *f.* **(day) ~,** crèche *f.* **~ rhyme,** chanson enfantine *f.*, comptine *f.* **~ school,** (école) maternelle *f.* **~ slope,** piste facile *f.*

nurture /'nɜːtʃə(r)/ *v.t.* élever.

nut /nʌt/ *n.* (*walnut, Brazil nut, etc.*) noix *f.*; (*hazelnut*) noisette *f.*; (*peanut*) cacahuète *f.*; (*techn.*) écrou *m.*; (*sl.*) idiot(e) *m.* (*f.*).

nutcrackers /'nʌtkrækəz/ *n. pl.* casse-noix *m. invar.*

nutmeg /'nʌtmeg/ *n.* muscade *f.*

nutrient /'njuːtrɪənt/ *n.* substance nutritive *f.*

nutrit|ion /njuː'trɪʃn/ *n.* nutrition *f.* **~ious** *a.* nutritif.

nuts /nʌts/ *a.* (*crazy: sl.*) cinglé.

nutshell /'nʌtʃel/ *n.* coquille de noix *f.* **in a ~,** en un mot.

nuzzle /'nʌzl/ *v.i.* **~ up to,** coller son museau à.

nylon /'naɪlɒn/ *n.* nylon *m.* **~s,** bas nylon *m. pl.*

O

oaf /əʊf/ *n.* (*pl.* **oafs**) lourdaud(e) *m.* (*f.*).

oak /əʊk/ *n.* chêne *m.*

OAP abbr. (old-age pensioner) retraité(e) m. (f.), personne âgée f.

oar /ɔː(r)/ n. aviron m., rame f.

oasis /əʊ'eɪsɪs/ n. (pl. **oases** /-siːz/) oasis f.

oath /əʊθ/ n. (promise) serment m.; (swear-word) juron m.

oatmeal /'əʊtmiːl/ n. farine d'avoine f., flocons d'avoine m. pl.

oats /əʊts/ n. pl. avoine f.

obedien|t /ə'biːdɪənt/ a. obéissant. **~ce** n. obéissance f. **~tly** adv. docilement, avec soumission.

obes|e /əʊ'biːs/ a. obèse. **~ity** n. obésité f.

obey /ə'beɪ/ v.t./i. obéir (à).

obituary /ə'bɪtʃʊərɪ/ n. nécrologie f.

object [1] /'ɒbdʒɪkt/ n. (thing) objet m.; (aim) but m., objet m.; (gram.) complément (d'objet) m. **money/etc. is no ~,** l'argent/etc. ne pose pas de problèmes.

object [2] /əb'dʒekt/ v.i. protester. ● v.t. **~ that,** objecter que. **~ to,** (behaviour) désapprouver; (plan) protester contre. **~ion** /-kʃn/ n. objection f.; (drawback) inconvénient m.

objectionable /əb'dʒekʃnəbl/ a. désagréable.

objectiv|e /əb'dʒektɪv/ a. objectif. ● n. objectif m. **~ity** /ɒbdʒek'tɪvətɪ/ n. objectivité f.

obligat|e /'ɒblɪɡeɪt/ v.t. obliger. **~ion** /-'ɡeɪʃn/ n. obligation f. **under an ~ion to s.o.,** redevable à qn. (**for,** de).

obligatory /ə'blɪɡətrɪ/ a. obligatoire.

oblig|e /ə'blaɪdʒ/ v.t. obliger. **~e to do,** obliger à faire. **~ed** a. obligé (**to,** de). **~ed to s.o.,** redevable à qn. **~ing** a. obligeant. **~ingly** adv. obligeamment.

oblique /ə'bliːk/ a. oblique; (reference etc.: fig.) indirect.

obliterat|e /ə'blɪtəreɪt/ v.t. effacer. **~ion** /-'reɪʃn/ n. effacement m.

oblivion /ə'blɪvɪən/ n. oubli m.

oblivious /ə'blɪvɪəs/ a. (unaware) inconscient (**to, of,** de).

oblong /'ɒblɒŋ/ a. oblong. ● n. rectangle m.

obnoxious /əb'nɒkʃəs/ a. odieux.

oboe /'əʊbəʊ/ n. hautbois m.

obscen|e /əb'siːn/ a. obscène. **~ity** /-enətɪ/ n. obscénité f.

obscur|e /əb'skjʊə(r)/ a. obscur. ● v.t. obscurcir; (conceal) cacher.

~ely adv. obscurément. **~ity** n. obscurité f.

obsequious /əb'siːkwɪəs/ a. obséquieux.

observan|t /əb'zɜːvənt/ a. observateur. **~ce** n. observance f.

observatory /əb'zɜːvətrɪ/ n. observatoire m.

observ|e /əb'zɜːv/ v.t. observer; (remark) remarquer. **~ation** /ɒbzə'veɪʃn/ n. observation f. **~er** n. observateur, -trice m., f.

obsess /əb'ses/ v.t. obséder. **~ion** /-ʃn/ n. obsession f. **~ive** a. obsédant; (psych.) obsessionnel.

obsolete /'ɒbsəliːt/ a. dépassé.

obstacle /'ɒbstəkl/ n. obstacle m.

obstetric|s /əb'stetrɪks/ n. obstétrique f. **~ian** /ɒbstɪ'trɪʃn/ n. médecin accoucheur m.

obstina|te /'ɒbstɪnət/ a. obstiné. **~cy** n. obstination f. **~tely** adv. obstinément.

obstruct /əb'strʌkt/ v.t. (block) boucher; (congest) encombrer; (hinder) entraver. **~ion** /-kʃn/ n. (act) obstruction f.; (thing) obstacle m.; (traffic jam) encombrement m.

obtain /əb'teɪn/ v.t. obtenir. ● v.i. avoir cours. **~able** a. disponible.

obtrusive /əb'truːsɪv/ a. importun; (thing) trop en évidence.

obtuse /əb'tjuːs/ a. obtus.

obviate /'ɒbvɪeɪt/ v.t. éviter.

obvious /'ɒbvɪəs/ a. évident, manifeste. **~ly** adv. manifestement.

occasion /ə'keɪʒn/ n. occasion f.; (big event) événement m. ● v.t. occasionner. **on ~,** à l'occasion.

occasional /ə'keɪʒənl/ a. fait, pris, etc. de temps en temps; (visitor etc.) qui vient de temps en temps. **~ly** adv. de temps en temps. **very ~ly,** rarement.

occult /ɒ'kʌlt/ a. occulte.

occupation /ɒkjʊ'peɪʃn/ n. (activity, occupying) occupation f.; (job) métier m., profession f. **~al** a. professionnel, du métier. **~al therapy** ergothérapie f.

occup|y /'ɒkjʊpaɪ/ v.i. occuper. **~ant, ~ier** ns. occupant(e) m. (f.).

occur /ə'kɜː(r)/ v.i. (p.t. **occurred**) se produire; (arise) se présenter. **~ to s.o.,** venir à l'esprit de qn.

occurrence /ə'kʌrəns/ n. événement m. **a frequent ~,** une chose qui arrive souvent.

ocean /'əʊʃn/ n. océan m.

o'clock /əˈklɒk/ adv. **it is six ~**/etc., il est six heures/etc.

octagon /ˈɒktəgən/ n. octogone m.

octane /ˈɒkteɪn/ n. octane m.

octave /ˈɒktɪv/ n. octave f.

October /ɒkˈtəʊbə(r)/ n. octobre m.

octopus /ˈɒktəpəs/ n. (pl. **-puses**) pieuvre f.

odd /ɒd/ a. (**-er, -est**) bizarre; (number) impair; (left over) qui reste; (not of set) dépareillé; (occasional) fait, pris, etc. de temps en temps. **~ jobs,** menus travaux m. pl. **twenty ~,** vingt et quelques. **~ity** n. bizarrerie f.; (thing) curiosité f. **~ly** adv. bizarrement.

oddment /ˈɒdmənt/ n. fin de série f.

odds /ɒdz/ n. pl. chances f. pl.; (in betting) cote f. (**on,** de). **at ~,** en désaccord. **it makes no ~,** ça ne fait rien. **~ and ends,** des petites choses.

ode /əʊd/ n. ode f.

odious /ˈəʊdɪəs/ a. odieux.

odour, Amer. **odor** /ˈəʊdə(r)/ n. odeur f. **~less** a. inodore.

of /ɒv, unstressed əv/ prep. de. **of the,** du, de la, pl. des. **of it,** en. **a friend of mine,** un de mes amis. **six of them,** six d'entre eux. **the fifth of June**/etc., le cinq juin/etc. **a litre of water,** un litre d'eau; **made of steel,** en acier.

off /ɒf/ adv. parti, absent; (switched off) éteint; (tap) fermé; (taken off) enlevé, détaché; (cancelled) annulé. ● prep. de; (distant from) éloigné de. **go ~,** (leave) partir; (milk) tourner; (food) s'abîmer. **be better ~,** (in a better position, richer) être mieux. **a day ~,** un jour de congé. **20% ~,** une réduction de 20%. **take sth. ~,** (a surface) prendre qch. sur. **~-beat** a. original. **on the ~ chance (that),** au cas où. **~ colour,** (ill) patraque. **~ color,** (improper: Amer.) scabreux. **~-licence** n. débit de vins m. **~-line** a. autonome; (switched off) déconnecté. **~-load** v.t. décharger. **~-peak** a. (hours) creux; (rate) des heures creuses. **~-putting** a. (fam.) rebutant. **~-stage** a. & adv. dans les coulisses. **~-white** a. blanc cassé invar.

offal /ˈɒfl/ n. abats m. pl.

offence /əˈfens/ n. délit m. **give ~ to,** offenser. **take ~,** s'offenser (**at,** de).

offend /əˈfend/ v.t. offenser; (fig.) choquer. **be ~ed,** s'offenser (**at,** de). **~er** n. délinquant(e) m. (f.).

offensive /əˈfensɪv/ a. offensant; (disgusting) dégoûtant; (weapon) offensif. ● n. offensive f.

offer /ˈɒfə(r)/ v.t. (p.t. **offered**) offrir. ● n. offre f. **on ~,** en promotion. **~ing** n. offrande f.

offhand /ɒfˈhænd/ a. désinvolte. ● adv. à l'improviste.

office /ˈɒfɪs/ n. bureau m.; (duty) fonction f.; (surgery: Amer.) cabinet m. ● a. de bureau. **good ~s,** bons offices m. pl. **in ~,** au pouvoir. **~ building,** immeuble de bureaux m.

officer /ˈɒfɪsə(r)/ n. (army etc.) officier m.; (policeman) agent m.

official /əˈfɪʃl/ a. officiel. ● n. officiel m.; (civil servant) fonctionnaire m./f. **~ly** adv. officiellement.

officiate /əˈfɪʃɪeɪt/ v.i. (priest) officier; (president) présider.

officious /əˈfɪʃəs/ a. trop zélé.

offing /ˈɒfɪŋ/ n. **in the ~,** en perspective.

offset /ˈɒfset/ v.t. (p.t. **-set,** pres. p. **-setting**) compenser.

offshoot /ˈɒfʃuːt/ n. (bot.) rejeton m.; (fig.) ramification f.

offshore /ɒfˈʃɔː(r)/ a. (waters) côtier; (exploration) en mer; (banking) dans les paladis fiscaux.

offside /ɒfˈsaɪd/ a. (sport) hors jeu invar.; (auto.) du côté du conducteur.

offspring /ˈɒfsprɪŋ/ n. invar. progéniture f.

often /ˈɒfn/ adv. souvent. **how ~?,** combien de fois? **every so ~,** de temps en temps.

ogle /ˈəʊgl/ v.t. lorgner.

ogre /ˈəʊgə(r)/ n. ogre m.

oh /əʊ/ int. oh, ah.

oil /ɔɪl/ n. huile f.; (petroleum) pétrole m.; (for heating) mazout m. ● v.t. graisser. **~-painting** n. peinture à l'huile f. **~-tanker** n. pétrolier m. **~y** a. graisseux.

oilfield /ˈɔɪlfiːld/ n. gisement pétrolifère m.

oilskins /ˈɔɪlskɪnz/ n. pl. ciré m.

ointment /ˈɔɪntmənt/ n. pommade f., onguent m.

OK /əʊˈkeɪ/ a. & adv. (fam.) bien.

old /əʊld/ a. (**-er, -est**) vieux; (person) vieux, âgé; (former) ancien. **how ~ is he?,** quel âge a-t-il? **he is eight years ~,** il a huit ans. **of ~,** jadis. **~ age,** vieillesse f. **~-age pensioner,** retraité(e) m. (f.). **~ boy,** ancien élève m.; (fellow: fam.) vieux m.

~er, ~est, (*son etc.*) aîné. ~-
fashioned *a.* démodé; (*person*)
vieux jeu *invar.* ~ **maid,** vieille fille
f. ~ **man,** vieillard *m.*, vieux *m.* ~-
time *a.* ancien. ~ **woman,** vieille *f.*
olive /'ɒlɪv/ *n.* olive *f.* ● *a.* olive
invar. ~ **oil,** huile d'olive *f.*
Olympic /ə'lɪmpɪk/ *a.* olympique. ~**s**
n. pl., ~ **Games,** Jeux olympiques
m. pl.
omelette /'ɒmlɪt/ *n.* omelette *f.*
omen /'əʊmen/ *n.* augure *m.*
ominous /'ɒmɪnəs/ *a.* de mauvais
augure; (*fig.*) menaçant.
omi|t /ə'mɪt/ *v.t.* (*p.t.* **omitted**)
omettre. ● ~**ssion** *n.* omission *f.*
on /ɒn/ *prep.* sur. ● *adv.* en avant;
(*switched on*) allumé; (*tap*) ouvert;
(*machine*) en marche; (*put on*) mis.
on foot/time/etc., à pied/l'heure/
etc. **on arriving,** en arrivant. **on
Tuesday,** mardi. **on Tuesdays,** le
mardi. **walk/etc. on,** continuer à
marcher/*etc.* **be on,** (*of film*)
passer. **the meeting/deal is still
on,** la réunion/le marché est
maintenu(e). **be on at,** (*fam.*) être
après. **on and off,** de temps en
temps.
once /wʌns/ *adv.* une fois; (*formerly*)
autrefois. ● *conj.* une fois que. **all at
~,** tout à coup. ~**-over** *n.* (*fam.*)
coup d'œil rapide *m.*
oncoming /'ɒnkʌmɪŋ/ *a.* (*vehicle
etc.*) qui approche.
one /wʌn/ *a. & n.* un(e) (*m.* (*f.*)).
● *pron.* un(e) *m.* (*f.*); (*impersonal*)
on. ~ **(and only),** seul (et unique). **a
big/red/etc.. ~,** un(e) grand(e)/
rouge/*etc.* **this/that ~,** celui-ci/-là,
celle-ci/-là. ~ **another,** l'un(e)
l'autre. ~**-eyed,** borgne. ~**-off** *a.*
(*fam.*), ~ **of a kind,** (*Amer.*) unique,
exceptionnel. ~**-sided** *a.* (*biased*)
partial; (*unequal*) inégal. ~**-way** *a.*
(*street*) à sens unique; (*ticket*) simple.
oneself /wʌn'self/ *pron.* soi-même;
(*reflexive*) se.
ongoing /'ɒngəʊɪŋ/ *a.* qui continue à
évoluer.
onion /'ʌnjən/ *n.* oignon *m.*
onlooker /'ɒnlʊkə(r)/ *n.* specta|teur, -
trice *m., f.*
only /'əʊnlɪ/ *a.* seul. **an ~ son/** *etc.*,
un fils/*etc.* unique. ● *adv. & conj.*
seulement. **he ~ has six,** il n'en a
que six, il en a six seulement. ~ **too,**
extrêmement.

onset /'ɒnset/ *n.* début *m.*
onslaught /'ɒnslɔːt/ *n.* attaque *f.*
onus /'əʊnəs/ *n.* **the ~ is on me/***etc.*,
c'est ma/*etc.* responsabilité (**to,** de).
onward(s) /'ɒnwəd(z)/ *adv.* en avant.
onyx /'ɒnɪks/ *n.* onyx *m.*
ooze /uːz/ *v.i.* suinter.
opal /'əʊpl/ *n.* opale *f.*
opaque /əʊ'peɪk/ *a.* opaque.
open /'əʊpən/ *a.* ouvert; (*view*) dégagé; (*free to all*) public; (*undis-
guised*) manifeste; (*question*) en
attente. ● *v.t./i.* (s')ouvrir; (*of
shop, play*) ouvrir. **in the ~ air,** en
plein air. ~**-ended** *a.* sans limite (*de
durée etc.*); (*system*) qui peut
évoluer. ~**-heart** *a.* (*surgery*) à
cœur ouvert. **keep ~ house,** tenir
table ouverte. ~ **out** *or* **up,**
(s')ouvrir. ~**-minded** *a.* à l'esprit
ouvert. ~**-plan** *a.* sans cloisons. ~
secret, secret de Polichinelle *m.*
opener /'əʊpənə(r)/ *n.* ouvre-boîte(s)
m., ouvre-bouteille(s) *m.*
opening /'əʊpənɪŋ/ *n.* ouverture *f.*;
(*job*) débouché *m.*, poste vacant *m.*
openly /'əʊpənlɪ/ *adv.* ouvertement.
opera /'ɒpərə/ *n.* opéra *m.* ~**-glasses**
n. pl. jumelles *f. pl.* ~**tic** /ɒpə'rætɪk/
a. d'opéra.
operat|e /'ɒpəreɪt/ *v.t./i.* opérer;
(*techn.*) (faire) fonctionner. ~**e on,**
(*med.*) opérer. ~**ing theatre,** salle
d'opération *f.* ~**ion** /-'reɪʃn/ *n.* opération *f.* **have an ~ion,** se faire
opérer. **in ~ion,** en vigueur; (*techn.*)
en service. ~**or** *n.* opéra|teur, -trice
m., f.; (*telephonist*) standardiste *m./
f.*
operational /ɒpə'reɪʃənl/ *a.* opérationnel.
operative /'ɒpərətɪv/ *a.* (*med.*) opératoire; (*law etc.*) en vigueur.
operetta /ɒpə'retə/ *n.* opérette *f.*
opinion /ə'pɪnjən/ *n.* opinion *f.*, avis
m. ~**ated** *a.* dogmatique.
opium /'əʊpɪəm/ *n.* opium *m.*
opponent /ə'pəʊnənt/ *n.* adversaire
m./f.
opportune /'ɒpətjuːn/ *a.* opportun.
opportunist /ɒpə'tjuːnɪst/ *n.* oppor-
tuniste *m./f.*
opportunity /ɒpə'tjuːnətɪ/ *n.* occasion *f.* (**to do,** de faire).
oppos|e /ə'pəʊz/ *v.t.* s'opposer à. ~**ed
to,** opposé à. ~**ing** *a.* opposé.
opposite /'ɒpəzɪt/ *a.* contraire. ● *n.*
contraire *m.*, opposé *m.* ● *adv.* en
face. ● *prep.* ~ **(to),** en face de.

one's ~ number, son homologue *m./f.*

opposition /ɒpə'zɪʃn/ *n.* opposition *f.*; (*mil.*) résistance *f.*

oppress /ə'pres/ *v.t.* opprimer. **~ion** /-ʃn/ *n.* oppression *f.* **~ive** *a.* (*cruel*) oppressif; (*heat*) oppressant. **~or** *n.* oppresseur *m.*

opt /ɒpt/ *v.i.* ~ **for,** opter pour. ~ **out,** refuser de participer (**of,** à). ~ **to do,** choisir de faire.

optical /'ɒptɪkl/ *a.* optique. ~ **illusion,** illusion d'optique *f.*

optician /ɒp'tɪʃn/ *n.* opticien(ne) *m.* (*f.*).

optimis|t /'ɒptɪmɪst/ *n.* optimiste *m./f.* **~m** /-zəm/ *n.* optimisme *m.* **~tic** /-'mɪstɪk/ *a.* optimiste. **~tically** /-'mɪstɪklɪ/ *adv.* avec optimisme.

optimum /'ɒptɪməm/ *a. & n.* (*pl.* **-ima**) optimum (*m.*).

option /'ɒpʃn/ *n.* choix *m.*, option *f.*

optional /'ɒpʃənl/ *a.* facultatif. ~ **extras,** accessoires en option *m. pl.*

opulen|t /'ɒpjʊlənt/ *a.* opulent. **~ce** *n.* opulence *f.*

or /ɔː(r)/ *conj.* ou; (*with negative*) ni.

oracle /'ɒrəkl/ *n.* oracle *m.*

oral /'ɔːrəl/ *a.* oral. ● *n.* (*examination: fam.*) oral *m.*

orange /'ɒrɪndʒ/ *n.* (*fruit*) orange *f.* ● *a.* (*colour*) orange *invar.*

orangeade /ɒrɪndʒ'eɪd/ *n.* orangeade *f.*

orator /'ɒrətə(r)/ *n.* ora|teur, -trice *m., f.* **~y** /-trɪ/ *n.* rhétorique *f.*

oratorio /ɒrə'tɔːrɪəʊ/ *n.* (*pl.* **-os**) oratorio *m.*

orbit /'ɔːbɪt/ *n.* orbite *f.* ● *v.t.* graviter autour de, orbiter.

orchard /'ɔːtʃəd/ *n.* verger *m.*

orchestra /'ɔːkɪstrə/ *n.* orchestre *m.* ~ **stalls** (*Amer.*), fauteuils d'orchestre *m. pl.* **~l** /-'kestrəl/ *a.* orchestral.

orchestrate /'ɔːkɪstreɪt/ *v.t.* orchestrer.

orchid /'ɔːkɪd/ *n.* orchidée *f.*

ordain /ɔː'deɪn/ *v.t.* décréter (**that,** que); (*relig.*) ordonner.

ordeal /ɔː'diːl/ *n.* épreuve *f.*

order /'ɔːdə(r)/ *n.* ordre *m.*; (*comm.*) commande *f.* ● *v.t.* ordonner; (*goods etc.*) commander. **in ~,** (*tidy*) en ordre; (*document*) en règle; (*fitting*) de règle. **in ~ that,** pour que. **in ~ to,** pour. ~ **s.o. to,** ordonner à qn. de.

orderly /'ɔːdəlɪ/ *a.* (*tidy*) ordonné; (*not unruly*) discipliné. ● *n.* (*mil.*) planton *m.*; (*med.*) garçon de salle *m.*

ordinary /'ɔːdɪnrɪ/ *a.* (*usual*) ordinaire; (*average*) moyen.

ordination /ɔːdɪ'neɪʃn/ *n.* (*relig.*) ordination *f.*

ore /ɔː(r)/ *n.* mineral *m.*

organ /'ɔːgən/ *n.* organe *m.*; (*mus.*) orgue *m.* **~ist** *n.* organiste *m./f.*

organic /ɔː'gænɪk/ *a.* organique.

organism /'ɔːgənɪzəm/ *n.* organisme *m.*

organiz|e /'ɔːgənaɪz/ *v.t.* organiser. **~ation** /-'zeɪʃn/ *n.* organisation *f.* **~er** *n.* organisa|teur, -trice *m., f.*

orgasm /'ɔːgæzəm/ *n.* orgasme *m.*

orgy /'ɔːdʒɪ/ *n.* orgie *f.*

Orient /'ɔːrɪənt/ *n.* **the ~,** l'Orient *m.* **~al** /-'entl/ *a.* Oriental(e) *m.* (*f.*).

oriental /ɔːrɪ'entl/ *a.* oriental.

orient(at|e /'ɔːrɪənt(eɪt)/ *v.t.* orienter. **~ion** /-'teɪʃn/ *n.* orientation *f.*

orifice /'ɒrɪfɪs/ *n.* orifice *m.*

origin /'ɒrɪdʒɪn/ *n.* origine *f.*

original /ə'rɪdʒənl/ *a.* (*first*) originel; (*not copied*) original. **~ity** /-'nælətɪ/ *n.* originalité *f.* **~ly** *adv.* (*at the outset*) à l'origine; (*write etc.*) originalement.

originat|e /ə'rɪdʒɪneɪt/ *v.i.* (*plan*) prendre naissance. ● *v.t.* être l'auteur de. **~e from,** provenir de; (*person*) venir de. **~or** *n.* auteur *m.*

ornament /'ɔːnəmənt/ *n.* (*decoration*) ornement *m.*; (*object*) objet décoratif *m.* **~al** /-'mentl/ *a.* ornemental. **~ation** /- en'teɪʃn/ *n.* ornementation *f.*

ornate /ɔː'neɪt/ *a.* richement orné.

ornithology /ɔːnɪ'θɒlədʒɪ/ *n.* ornithologie *f.*

orphan /'ɔːfn/ *n.* orphelin(e) *m.* (*f.*). ● *v.t.* rendre orphelin. **~age** *n.* orphelinat *m.*

orthodox /'ɔːθədɒks/ *a.* orthodoxe. **~y** *n.* orthodoxie *f.*

orthopaedic /ɔːθə'piːdɪk/ *a.* orthopédique.

oscillate /'ɒsɪleɪt/ *v.i.* osciller.

ostensibl|e /ɒs'tensəbl/ *a.* apparent, prétendu. **~y** *adv.* apparemment, prétendument.

ostentati|on /ɒsten'teɪʃn/ *n.* ostentation *f.* **~ous** *a.* prétentieux.

osteopath /'ɒstɪəpæθ/ *n.* ostéopathe *m./f.*

ostracize /'ɒstrəsaɪz/ v.t. frapper d'ostracisme.

ostrich /'ɒstrɪtʃ/ n. autruche f.

other /'ʌðə(r)/ a. autre. ● n. & pron. autre m./f. ● adv. ~ than, autrement que; (except) à part. (some) ~s, d'autres. the ~ one, l'autre m./f.

otherwise /'ʌðəwaɪz/ adv. autrement.

otter /'ɒtə(r)/ n. loutre f.

ouch /aʊtʃ/ int. aïe!

ought /ɔːt/ v. aux. devoir. you ~ to stay, vous devriez rester. he ~ to succeed, il devrait réussir. I ~ to have done it, j'aurais dû le faire.

ounce /aʊns/ n. once f. (= 28.35 g.).

our /aʊə(r)/ a. notre, pl. nos.

ours /'aʊəz/ poss. le or la nôtre, les nôtres.

ourselves /aʊə'selvz/ pron. nous-mêmes; (reflexive & after prep.) nous.

oust /aʊst/ v.t. évincer.

out /aʊt/ adv. dehors; (sun) levé. be ~, (person, book) être sorti; (light) être éteint; (flower) être épanoui; (tide) être bas; (secret) se savoir; (wrong) se tromper. be ~ to do, être résolu à faire. run/etc. ~, sortir en courant/etc. ~-and-out a. absolu. ~ of, hors de; (without) sans, à court de. ~ of pity/etc., par pitié/etc. made ~ or de. take ~ of, prendre dans. 5 ~ of 6, 5 sur 6. ~ of date, démodé; (not valid) périmé. ~ of doors, dehors. ~ of hand, (situation) dont on n'est plus maître. ~ of line, (impertinent: Amer.) incorrect. ~ of one's mind, fou. ~ of order, (broken) en panne. ~ of place, (object, remark) déplacé. ~ of the way, écarté. get ~ of the way! écarte-toi! ~ of work, sans travail. ~-patient n. malade en consultation externe m./f.

outbid /aʊt'bɪd/ v.t. (p.t. -bid, pres. p. -bidding) enchérir sur.

outboard /'aʊtbɔːd/ a. (motor) hors-bord invar.

outbreak /'aʊtbreɪk/ n. (of war etc.) début m.; (of violence, boils) éruption f.

outburst /'aʊtbɜːst/ n. explosion f.

outcast /'aʊtkɑːst/ n. paria m.

outclass /aʊt'klɑːs/ v.t. surclasser.

outcome /'aʊtkʌm/ n. résultat m.

outcrop /'aʊtkrɒp/ n. affleurement m.

outcry /'aʊtkraɪ/ n. tollé m.

outdated /aʊt'deɪtɪd/ a. démodé.

outdo /aʊt'duː/ v.t. (p.t. -did, p.p. -done) surpasser.

outdoor /'aʊtdɔː(r)/ a. de or en plein air. ~s /-'dɔːz/ adv. dehors.

outer /'aʊtə(r)/ a. extérieur. ~ space, espace (cosmique) m.

outfit /'aʊtfɪt/ n. (articles) équipement m.; (clothes) tenue f.; (group: fam.) équipe f. ~ter n. spécialiste de confection m./f.

outgoing /'aʊtgəʊɪŋ/ a. (minister, tenant) sortant; (sociable) ouvert. ~s n. pl. dépenses f. pl.

outgrow /aʊt'grəʊ/ v.t. (p.t. -grew, p.p. -grown) (clothes) devenir trop grand pour; (habit) dépasser.

outhouse /'aʊthaʊs/ n. appentis m.; (of mansion) dépendance f.; (Amer.) cabinets extérieurs m. pl.

outing /'aʊtɪŋ/ n. sortie f.

outlandish /aʊt'lændɪʃ/ a. bizarre, étrange.

outlaw /'aʊtlɔː/ n. hors-la-loi m. invar. ● v.t. proscrire.

outlay /'aʊtleɪ/ n. dépenses f. pl.

outlet /'aʊtlet/ n. (for water, gases) sortie f.; (for goods) débouché m.; (for feelings) exutoire m.

outline /'aʊtlaɪn/ n. contour m.; (summary) esquisse f. (main) ~s, grandes lignes f. pl. ● v.t. tracer le contour de; (summarize) exposer sommairement.

outlive /aʊt'lɪv/ v.t. survivre à.

outlook /'aʊtlʊk/ n. perspective f.

outlying /'aʊtlaɪɪŋ/ a. écarté.

outmoded /aʊt'məʊdɪd/ a. démodé.

outnumber /aʊt'nʌmbə(r)/ v.t. surpasser en nombre.

outpost /'aʊtpəʊst/ n. avant-poste m.

output /'aʊtpʊt/ n. rendement m.; (comput.) sortie f. ● v.t./i. (comput.) sortir.

outrage /'aʊtreɪdʒ/ n. atrocité f.; (scandal) scandale m. ● v.t. (morals) outrager; (person) scandaliser.

outrageous /aʊt'reɪdʒəs/ a. scandaleux, atroce.

outright /aʊt'raɪt/ adv. complètement; (at once) sur le coup; (frankly) carrément. ● a. /'aʊtraɪt/ complet; (refusal) net.

outset /'aʊtset/ n. début m.

outside [1] /aʊt'saɪd/ n. extérieur m. ● adv. (au) dehors. ● prep. en dehors de; (in front of) devant.

outside [2] /'aʊtsaɪd/ a. extérieur.

outsider /aʊt'saɪdə(r)/ n. étrang|er, -ère m., f.; (sport) outsider m.

outsize /'aʊtsaɪz/ a. grande taille invar.

outskirts /'aʊtskɜ:ts/ n. pl. banlieue f.

outspoken /aʊt'spəʊkən/ a. franc.

outstanding /aʊt'stændɪŋ/ a. exceptionnel; (not settled) en suspens.

outstretched /aʊt'stretʃt/ a. (arm) tendu.

outstrip /aʊt'strɪp/ v.t. (p.t. -stripped) devancer, surpasser.

outward /'aʊtwəd/ a. & adv. vers l'extérieur; (sign etc.) extérieur; (journey) d'aller. **~ly** adv. extérieurement. **~s** adv. vers l'extérieur.

outweigh /aʊt'weɪ/ v.t. (exceed in importance) l'emporter sur.

outwit /aʊt'wɪt/ v.t. (p.t. -witted) duper, être plus malin que.

oval /'əʊvl/ n. & a. ovale (m.).

ovary /'əʊvərɪ/ n. ovaire m.

ovation /ə'veɪʃn/ n. ovation f.

oven /'ʌvn/ n. four m.

over /'əʊvə(r)/ prep. sur, au-dessus de; (across) de l'autre côté de; (during) pendant; (more than) plus de. ● adv. (par-)dessus; (ended) fini; (past) passé; (too) trop; (more) plus. jump/etc. **~**, sauter/etc. par-dessus. **~ the radio**, à la radio. ask **~**, inviter chez soi. he has some **~**, il lui en reste. all **~ (the table)**, partout (sur la table). **~ and above**, en plus de. **~ and over**, à maintes reprises. **~ here**, par ici. **~ there**, là-bas.

over- /'əʊvə(r)/ pref. sur-, trop.

overall [1] /'əʊvərɔ:l/ n. blouse f. **~s**, bleu(s) de travail m. (pl.).

overall [2] /əʊvər'ɔ:l/ a. global, d'ensemble; (length, width) total. ● adv. globalement.

overawe /əʊvər'ɔ:/ v.t. intimider.

overbalance /əʊvə'bæləns/ v.t./i. (faire) basculer.

overbearing /əʊvə'beərɪŋ/ a. autoritaire.

overboard /'əʊvəbɔ:d/ adv. par-dessus bord.

overbook /əʊvə'bʊk/ v.t. accepter trop de réservations pour.

overcast /'əʊvəkɑ:st/ a. couvert.

overcharge /əʊvə'tʃɑ:dʒ/ v.t. **~ s.o. (for)**, faire payer trop cher à qn.

overcoat /'əʊvəkəʊt/ n. pardessus m.

overcome /əʊvə'kʌm/ v.t. (p.t. -came, p.p. -come) triompher de; (difficulty) surmonter, triompher de. **~ by**, accablé de.

overcrowded /əʊvə'kraʊdɪd/ a. bondé; (country) surpeuplé.

overdo /əʊvə'du:/ v.t. (p.t. -did, p.p. -done) exagérer; (culin.) trop cuire. **~ it**, (overwork) se surmener.

overdose /'əʊvədəʊs/ n. overdose f., surdose f.

overdraft /'əʊvədrɑ:ft/ n. découvert m.

overdraw /əʊvə'drɔ:/ v.t. (p.t. -drew, p.p. -drawn) (one's account) mettre à découvert.

overdrive /'əʊvədraɪv/ n. surmultipliée f.

overdue /əʊvə'dju:/ a. en retard; (belated) tardif; (bill) impayé.

overestimate /əʊvər'estɪmeɪt/ v.t. surestimer.

overexposed /əʊvərɪk'spəʊzd/ a. surexposé.

overflow [1] /əʊvə'fləʊ/ v.i. déborder.

overflow [2] /'əʊvəfləʊ/ n. (outlet) trop-plein m.

overgrown /əʊvə'grəʊn/ a. (garden etc.) envahi par la végétation.

overhang /əʊvə'hæŋ/ v.t. (p.t. -hung) surplomber. ● v.i. faire saillie.

overhaul [1] /əʊvə'hɔ:l/ v.t. réviser.

overhaul [2] /'əʊvəhɔ:l/ n. révision f.

overhead [1] /əʊvə'hed/ adv. au-dessus; (in sky) dans le ciel.

overhead [2] /'əʊvəhed/ a. aérien. **~s** n. pl. frais généraux m. pl. **~ projector**, rétroprojecteur m.

overhear /əʊvə'hɪə(r)/ v.t. (p.t. -heard) surprendre, entendre.

overjoyed /əʊvə'dʒɔɪd/ a. ravi.

overland a. /'əʊvəlænd/, adv. /əʊvə'lænd/ par voie de terre.

overlap /əʊvə'læp/ v.t./i. (p.t. -lapped) (se) chevaucher.

overleaf /əʊvə'li:f/ adv. au verso.

overload /əʊvə'ləʊd/ v.t. surcharger.

overlook /əʊvə'lʊk/ v.t. oublier, négliger; (of window, house) donner sur; (of tower) dominer.

overly /'əʊvəlɪ/ adv. excessivement.

overnight /əʊvə'naɪt/ adv. (pendant) la nuit; (instantly: fig.) du jour au lendemain. ● a. /'əʊvənaɪt/ (train etc.) de nuit; (stay etc.) d'une nuit; (fig.) soudain.

overpay /əʊvə'peɪ/ v.t. (p.t. -paid) (person) surpayer.

overpower /əʊvə'paʊə(r)/ v.t. subjuguer; (opponent) maîtriser; (fig.)

accabler. **~ing** *a.* irrésistible; (*heat, smell*) accablant.
overpriced /əʊvə'praɪst/ *a.* trop cher.
overrate /əʊvə'reɪt/ *v.t.* surestimer. **~d** /-ɪd/ *a.* surfait.
overreach /əʊvə'ri:tʃ/ *v. pr.* **~ o.s.**, trop entreprendre.
overreact /əʊvərɪ'ækt/ *v.i.* réagir excessivement.
overrid|e /əʊvə'raɪd/ *v.t.* (*p.t.* **-rode**, *p.p.* **-ridden**) passer outre à. **~ing** *a.* prépondérant; (*importance*) majeur.
overripe /'əʊvəraɪp/ *a.* trop mûr.
overrule /əʊvə'ru:l/ *v.t.* rejeter.
overrun /əʊvə'rʌn/ *v.t.* (*p.t.* **-ran**, *p.p.* **-run**, *pres. p.* **-running**) envahir; (*a limit*) aller au-delà de. ● *v.i.* (*meeting*) durer plus longtemps que prévu.
overseas /əʊvə'si:z/ *a.* d'outre-mer, étranger. ● *adv.* outre-mer, à l'étranger.
oversee /əʊvə'si:/ *v.t.* (*p.t.* **-saw**, *p.p.* **-seen**) surveiller. **~r** /'əʊvəsɪə(r)/ *n.* contremaître *m.*
overshadow /əʊvə'ʃædəʊ/ *v.t.* (*darken*) assombrir; (*fig.*) éclipser.
overshoot /əʊvə'ʃu:t/ *v.t.* (*p.t.* **-shot**) dépasser.
oversight /'əʊvəsaɪt/ *n.* omission *f.*
oversleep /əʊvə'sli:p/ *v.i.* (*p.t.* **-slept**) se réveiller trop tard.
overt /'əʊvɜ:t/ *a.* manifeste.
overtake /əʊvə'teɪk/ *v.t./i.* (*p.t.* **-took**, *p.p.* **-taken**) dépasser; (*vehicle*) doubler, dépasser; (*surprise*) surprendre.
overtax /əʊvə'tæks/ *v.t.* (*strain*) fatiguer; (*taxpayer*) surimposer.
overthrow /əʊvə'θrəʊ/ *v.t.* (*p.t.* **-threw**, *p.p.* **-thrown**) renverser.
overtime /'əʊvətaɪm/ *n.* heures supplémentaires *f. pl.*
overtone /'əʊvətəʊn/ *n.* nuance *f.*
overture /'əʊvətjʊə(r)/ *n.* ouverture *f.*
overturn /əʊvə'tɜ:n/ *v.t./i.* (se) renverser.
overweight /əʊvə'weɪt/ *a.* **be ~**, peser trop.
overwhelm /əʊvə'welm/ *v.t.* accabler; (*defeat*) écraser; (*amaze*) bouleverser. **~ing** *a.* accablant; (*victory*) écrasant; (*urge*) irrésistible.
overwork /əʊvə'wɜ:k/ *v.t./i.* (se) surmener. ● *n.* surmenage *m.*
overwrought /əʊvə'rɔ:t/ *a.* à bout.
ow|e /əʊ/ *v.t.* devoir. **~ing** *a.* dû. **~ing to**, à cause de.
owl /aʊl/ *n.* hibou *m.*

own¹ /əʊn/ *a.* propre. **a house**/*etc.* **of one's ~**, sa propre maison/*etc.*, une maison/*etc.* à soi. **get one's ~ back**, (*fam.*) prendre sa revanche. **hold one's ~**, bien se défendre. **on one's ~**, tout seul.
own² /əʊn/ *v.t.* posséder. **~ up (to)**, (*fam.*) avouer. **~er** *n.* propriétaire *m./f.* **~ership** *n.* possession *f.* (**of**, de); (*right*) propriété *f.*
ox /ɒks/ *n.* (*pl.* **oxen**) bœuf *m.*
oxygen /'ɒksɪdʒən/ *n.* oxygène *m.*
oyster /'ɔɪstə(r)/ *n.* huître *f.*
ozone /'əʊzəʊn/ *n.* ozone *m.* **~ layer**, couche d'ozone *f.*

P

pace /peɪs/ *n.* pas *m.*; (*speed*) allure *f.*; ● *v.t.* (*room etc.*) arpenter. ● *v.i.* **~ (up and down)**, faire les cent pas. **keep ~ with**, suivre.
pacemaker /'peɪsmeɪkə(r)/ *n.* (*med.*) stimulateur cardiaque *m.*
Pacific /pə'sɪfɪk/ *a.* pacifique. ● *n.* **~ (Ocean)**, Pacifique *m.*
pacifist /'pæsɪfɪst/ *n.* pacifiste *m./f.*
pacif|y /'pæsɪfaɪ/ *v.t.* (*country*) pacifier; (*person*) apaiser. **~ier** *n.* (*Amer.*) sucette *f.*
pack /pæk/ *n.* paquet *m.*; (*mil.*) sac *m.*; (*of hounds*) meute *f.*; (*of thieves*) bande *f.*; (*of lies*) tissu *m.* ● *v.t.* emballer; (*suitcase*) faire; (*box, room*) remplir; (*press down*) tasser. ● *v.i.* **~ (one's bags)**, faire ses valises. **~ into**, (*cram*) (s')entasser dans. **~ off**, expédier. **send ~ing**, envoyer promener. **~ed** *a.* (*crowded*) bondé. **~ed lunch**, repas froid *m.* **~ing** *n.* (*action, material*) emballage *m.* **~ing case**, caisse *f.*
package /'pækɪdʒ/ *n.* paquet *m.* ● *v.t.* empaqueter. **~ deal**, forfait *m.* **~ tour**, voyage organisé *m.*
packet /'pækɪt/ *n.* paquet *m.*
pact /pækt/ *n.* pacte *m.*
pad¹ /pæd/ *n.* bloc(-notes) *m.*; (*for ink*) tampon *m.* **(launching) ~**, rampe (de lancement) *f.* ● *v.t.* (*p.t.* **padded**) rembourrer; (*text: fig.*) délayer. **~ding** *n.* rembourrage *m.*; délayage *m.*
pad² /pæd/ *v.i.* (*p.t.* **padded**) (*walk*) marcher à pas feutrés.

paddle¹ /'pædl/ *n.* pagaie *f.* ● *v.t.* ~ a canoe, pagayer. ~-steamer *n.* bateau à roues *m.*

paddle² /'pædl/ *v.i.* barboter, se mouiller les pieds. ~ing pool, pataugeoire *f.*

paddock /'pædək/ *n.* paddock *m.*

paddy(-field) /'pædɪ(fiːld)/ *n.* rizière *f.*

padlock /'pædlɒk/ *n.* cadenas *m.* ● *v.t.* cadenasser.

paediatrician /piːdɪə'trɪʃn/ *n.* pédiatre *m./f.*

pagan /'peɪgən/ *a.* & *n.* païen(ne) (*m.* (*f.*)).

page¹ /peɪdʒ/ *n.* (*of book etc.*) page *f.*

page² /peɪdʒ/ *n.* (*in hotel*) chasseur *m.* (*at wedding*) page *m.* ● *v.t.* (faire) appeler.

pageant /'pædʒənt/ *n.* spectacle (historique) *m.* ~ry *n.* pompe *f.*

pagoda /pə'gəʊdə/ *n.* pagode *f.*

paid /peɪd/ *see* pay. ● *a.* put ~ to, (*fam.*) mettre fin à.

pail /peɪl/ *n.* seau *m.*

pain /peɪn/ *n.* douleur *f.* ~s, efforts *m. pl.* ● *v.t.* (*grieve*) peiner. be in ~, souffrir. take ~s to, se donner du mal pour. ~-killer *n.* analgésique *m.* ~less *a.* indolore.

painful /'peɪnfl/ *a.* douloureux; (*laborious*) pénible.

painstaking /'peɪnzteɪkɪŋ/ *a.* assidu, appliqué.

paint /peɪnt/ *n.* peinture *f.* ~s, (*in tube, box*) couleurs *f. pl.* ● *v.t./i.* peindre. ~er *n.* peintre *m.* ~ing *n.* peinture *f.*

paintbrush /'peɪntbrʌʃ/ *n.* pinceau *m.*

paintwork /'peɪntwɜːk/ *n.* peintures *f. pl.*

pair /peə(r)/ *n.* paire *f.*; (*of people*) couple *m.* a ~ of trousers, un pantalon. ● *v.i.* ~ off, (*at dance etc.*) former un couple.

pajamas /pə'dʒɑːməz/ *n.pl.* (*Amer.*) pyjama *m.*

Pakistan /pɑːkɪ'stɑːn/ *n.* Pakistan. *m.* ~i *a.* & *n.* pakistanais(e) (*m.* (*f.*)).

pal /pæl/ *n.* (*fam.*) cop|ain, -ine *m.*, *f.*

palace /'pælɪs/ *n.* palais *m.*

palat|e /'pælət/ *n.* (*of mouth*) palais *m.* ~able *a.* agréable au goût.

palatial /pə'leɪʃl/ *a.* somptueux.

palaver /pə'lɑːvə(r)/ *n.* (*fuss: fam.*) histoire *f.* (*pl.*).

pale /peɪl/ *a.* (-er, -est) pâle. ● *v.i.* pâlir. ~ness *n.* pâleur *f.*

Palestin|e /'pælɪstam/ *n.* Palestine *f.* ~ian /-'stɪnɪən/ *a.* & *n.* palestinien(ne) (*m.* (*f.*)).

palette /'pælɪt/ *n.* palette *f.*

pall /pɔːl/ *v.i.* devenir insipide.

pallet /'pælɪt/ *n.* palette *f.*

pallid /'pælɪd/ *a.* pâle.

palm /pɑːm/ *n.* (*of hand*) paume *f.*; (*tree*) palm|ier *m.*; (*symbol*) palme *f.* ● *v.t.* ~ off, (*thing*) refiler, coller (on, à); (*person*) coller. P~ Sunday, dimanche des Rameaux *m.*

palmist /'pɑːmɪst/ *n.* chiromancien(ne) *m.* (*f.*).

palpable /'pælpəbl/ *a.* manifeste.

palpitat|e /'pælpɪteɪt/ *v.i.* palpiter. ~ion /-'teɪʃn/ *n.* palpitation *f.*

paltry /'pɔːltrɪ/ *a.* (-ier, -iest) dérisoire, piètre.

pamper /'pæmpə(r)/ *v.t.* dorloter.

pamphlet /'pæmflɪt/ *n.* brochure *f.*

pan /pæn/ *n.* casserole *f.*; (*for frying*) poêle *f.*; (*of lavatory*) cuvette *f.* ● *v.t.* (*p.t.* panned) (*fam.*) critiquer.

panacea /pænə'sɪə/ *n.* panacée *f.*

panache /pə'næʃ/ *n.* panache *m.*

pancake /'pænkeɪk/ *n.* crêpe *f.*

pancreas /'pæŋkrɪəs/ *n.* pancréas *m.*

panda /'pændə/ *n.* panda *m.* ~ car, voiture pie (de la police) *f.*

pandemonium /pændɪ'məʊnɪəm/ *n.* tumulte *m.*, chaos *m.*

pander /'pændə(r)/ *v.i.* ~ to, (*person, taste*) flatter bassement.

pane /peɪn/ *n.* carreau *m.*, vitre *f.*

panel /'pænl/ *n.* (*of door etc.*) panneau *m.*; (*jury*) jury *m.*; (*speakers: TV*) invités *m. pl.* (**instrument**) ~, tableau de bord *m.* ~ of experts, groupe d'experts *m.* ~led *a.* lambrissé. ~ling *n.* lambrissage *m.* ~list *n.* (*TV*) invité(e) (de tribune) *m.* (*f.*).

pang /pæŋ/ *n.* pincement au cœur *m.* ~s, (*of hunger, death*) affres *f. pl.* ~s of conscience, remords *m. pl.*

panic /'pænɪk/ *n.* panique *f.* ● *v.t./i.* (*p.t.* panicked) (s')affoler, paniquer. ~-stricken *a.* pris de panique, affolé.

panorama /pænə'rɑːmə/ *n.* panorama *m.*

pansy /'pænzɪ/ *n.* (*bot.*) pensée *f.*

pant /pænt/ *v.i.* haleter.

panther /'pænθə(r)/ *n.* panthère *f.*

panties /'pæntɪz/ *n. pl.* (*fam.*) slip *m.*, culotte *f.* (*de femme*).

pantihose /'pæntɪhəʊz/ *n.* (*Amer.*) collant *m.*

pantomime /'pæntəmaɪm/ n. (*show*) spectacle de Noël m.; (*mime*) pantomime f.

pantry /'pæntrɪ/ n. office m.

pants /pænts/ n. pl. (*underwear: fam.*) slip m.; (*trousers: fam. & Amer.*) pantalon m.

papacy /'peɪpəsɪ/ n. papauté f.

papal /'peɪpl/ a. papal.

paper /'peɪpə(r)/ n. papier m.; (*newspaper*) journal m.; (*exam*) épreuve f.; (*essay*) exposé m.; (*wallpaper*) papier peint m. (*identity*) ~s papiers (d'identité) m. pl. ● v.t. (*room*) tapisser. **on** ~, par écrit. ~**-clip** n. trombone m.

paperback /'peɪpəbæk/ a. & n. ~ **(book)**, livre broché m.

paperweight /'peɪpəweɪt/ n. presse-papiers m. invar.

paperwork /'peɪpəwɜːk/ n. paperasserie f.

paprika /'pæprɪkə/ n. paprika m.

par /pɑː(r)/ n. **be below** ~, ne pas être en forme. **on a** ~ **with**, à égalité avec.

parable /'pærəbl/ n. parabole f.

parachut|e /'pærəʃuːt/ n. parachute m. ● v.i. descendre en parachute. ~**ist** n. parachutiste m./f.

parade /pə'reɪd/ n. (*procession*) défilé m.; (*ceremony, display*) parade f.; (*street*) avenue f. ● v.i. défiler. ● v.t. faire parade de.

paradise /'pærədaɪs/ n. paradis m.

paradox /'pærədɒks/ n. paradoxe m. ~**ical** /-'dɒksɪkl/ a. paradoxal.

paraffin /'pærəfɪn/ n. pétrole (lampant) m.; (*wax*) paraffine f.

paragon /'pærəgən/ n. modèle m.

paragraph /'pærəgrɑːf/ n. paragraphe m.

parallel /'pærəlel/ a. parallèle. ● n. (*line*) parallèle f.; (*comparison & geog.*) parallèle m. ● v.t. (*p.t.* **paralleled**) être semblable à; (*match*) égaler.

paralyse /'pærəlaɪz/ v.t. paralyser.

paraly|sis /pə'ræləsɪs/ n. paralysie f. ~**tic** /pærə'lɪtɪk/ a. & n. paralytique (m./f.).

paramedic /pærə'medɪk/ n. auxiliaire médical(e) m. (f.).

parameter /pə'ræmɪtə(r)/ n. paramètre m.

paramount /'pærəmaʊnt/ a. primordial, fondamental.

paranoi|a /pærə'nɔɪə/ n. paranoïa f. ~**d** a. paranoïaque; (*fam.*) parano invar.

parapet /'pærəpɪt/ n. parapet m.

paraphernalia /pærəfə'neɪlɪə/ n. attirail m., équipement m.

paraphrase /'pærəfreɪz/ n. paraphrase f. ● v.t. paraphraser.

parasite /'pærəsaɪt/ n. parasite m.

parasol /'pærəsɒl/ n. ombrelle f.; (*on table, at beach*) parasol m.

paratrooper /'pærətruːpə(r)/ n. (*mil.*) parachutiste m/f.

parcel /'pɑːsl/ n. colis m., paquet m. ● v.t. (*p.t.* **parcelled**). ~ **out**, diviser en parcelles.

parch /pɑːtʃ/ v.t. dessécher. **be** ~**ed**, (*person*) avoir très soif.

parchment /'pɑːtʃmənt/ n. parchemin m.

pardon /'pɑːdn/ n. pardon m.; (*jurid.*) grâce m. ● v.t. (*p.t.* **pardoned**) pardonner (**s.o. for sth.**, qch. à qn.); gracier. **I beg your** ~, pardon.

pare /peə(r)/ v.t. (*clip*) rogner; (*peel*) éplucher.

parent /'peərənt/ n. père m., mère f. ~**s**, parents m. pl. ~**al** /pə'rentl/ a. des parents. ~**hood** n. l'état de parent m.

parenthesis /pə'renθəsɪs/ n. (*pl.* -theses /-siːz/) parenthèse f.

Paris /'pærɪs/ n. Paris m./f. ~**ian** /pə'rɪzɪən, Amer. pə'riːʒn/ a. & n. parisien(ne) (m. (f.)).

parish /'pærɪʃ/ n. (*relig.*) paroisse f.; (*municipal*) commune f. ~**ioner** /pə'rɪʃənə(r)/ n. paroissien(ne) (m. (f.)).

parity /'pærətɪ/ n. parité f.

park /pɑːk/ n. parc m. ● v.t./i. (se) garer; (*remain parked*) stationner. ~**ing-lot** n. (*Amer.*) parking m. ~**ing-meter** n. parcmètre m. ~**ing ticket**, procès-verbal m.

parka /'pɑːkə/ n. parka m./f.

parlance /'pɑːləns/ n. langage m.

parliament /'pɑːləmənt/ n. parlement m. ~**ary** /-'mentrɪ/ a. parlementaire.

parlour, (*Amer.*) **parlor** /'pɑːlə(r)/ n. salon m.

parochial /pə'rəʊkɪəl/ a. (*relig.*) paroissial; (*fig.*) borné, provincial.

parody /'pærədɪ/ n. parodie f. ● v.t. parodier.

parole /pə'rəʊl/ n. **on** ~, en liberté conditionnelle.

parquet /'pɑːkeɪ/ n. parquet m.

parrot /'pærət/ n. perroquet m.

parry /'pærɪ/ v.t. (sport) parer; (question etc.) esquiver. ● n. parade f.

parsimonious /pɑ:sɪ'məʊnɪəs/ a. parcimonieux.

parsley /'pɑ:slɪ/ n. persil m.

parsnip /'pɑ:snɪp/ n. panais m.

parson /'pɑ:sn/ n. pasteur m.

part /pɑ:t/ n. partie f.; (of serial) épisode m.; (of machine) pièce f.; (theatre) rôle m.; (side in dispute) parti m. ● a. partiel. ● adv. en partie. ● v.t./i. (separate) (se) séparer. **in ~**, en partie. **on the ~ of**, de la part de. **~-exchange** n. reprise f. **~ of speech**, catégorie grammaticale f. **~-time** a. & adv. à temps partiel. **~ with**, se séparer de. **take ~ in**, participer à. **in these ~s**, dans la région, dans le coin.

partake /pɑ:'teɪk/ v.i. (p.t. **-took**, p.p. **-taken**) participer (**in**, à).

partial /'pɑ:ʃl/ a. partiel; (biased) partial. **be ~ to**, avoir une prédilection pour. **~ity** /-ɪ'ælətɪ/ n. (bias) partialité f.; (fondness) prédilection f. **~ly** adv. partiellement.

participate /pɑ:'tɪsɪpeɪt/ v.i. participer (**in**, à). **~ant** n. participant(e) m. (f.). **~ation** /-'peɪʃn/ n. participation f.

participle /'pɑ:tɪsɪpl/ n. participe m.

particle /'pɑ:tɪkl/ n. particule f.

particular /pə'tɪkjʊlə(r)/ a. particulier; (fussy) difficile; (careful) méticuleux. **that ~ man**, cet homme-là en particulier. **~s** n. pl. détails m. pl. **in ~**, en particulier. **~ly** adv. particulièrement.

parting /'pɑ:tɪŋ/ n. séparation f.; (in hair) raie f. ● a. d'adieu.

partisan /pɑ:tɪ'zæn, Amer. 'pɑ:tɪzn/ n. partisan(e) m. (f.).

partition /pɑ:'tɪʃn/ n. (of room) cloison f.; (pol.) partage m., partition f. ● v.t. (room) cloisonner; (country) partager.

partly /'pɑ:tlɪ/ adv. en partie.

partner /'pɑ:tnə(r)/ n. associé(e) m. (f.); (sport) partenaire m./f. **~ship** n. association f.

partridge /'pɑ:trɪdʒ/ n. perdrix f.

party /'pɑ:tɪ/ n. fête f.; (formal) réception f.; (for young people) boum f.; (group) groupe m., équipe f.; (pol.) parti m.; (jurid.) partie f. **~ line**, (telephone) ligne commune f.

pass /pɑ:s/ v.t./i. (p.t. **passed**) passer; (overtake) dépasser; (in exam) être reçu (à); (approve) accepter, autori-

ser; (remark) faire; (judgement) prononcer; (law, bill) voter. **~ (by)**, (building) passer devant; (person) croiser. ● n. (permit) laissez-passer m. invar.; (ticket) carte (d'abonnement) f.; (geog.) col m.; (sport) passe f. **~ (mark)**, (in exam) moyenne f. **make a ~ at**, (fam.) faire des avances à. **~ away**, mourir. **~ out or round**, distribuer. **~ out**, (faint: fam.) s'évanouir. **~ over**, (overlook) passer sur. **~ up**, (forego: fam.) laisser passer.

passable /'pɑ:səbl/ a. (adequate) passable; (road) praticable.

passage /'pæsɪdʒ/ n. (way through, text, etc.) passage m.; (voyage) traversée f.; (corridor) couloir m.

passenger /'pæsɪndʒə(r)/ n. passager, -ère m., f.; (in train) voyageu|r, -se m., f.

passer-by /pɑ:sə'baɪ/ n. (pl. **passers-by**) passant(e) m. (f.).

passing /'pɑ:sɪŋ/ a. (fleeting) fugitif, passager.

passion /'pæʃn/ n. passion f. **~ate** a. passionné. **~ately** adv. passionnément.

passive /'pæsɪv/ a. passif. **~ness** n. passivité f.

Passover /'pɑ:səʊvə(r)/ n. Pâque f.

passport /'pɑ:spɔ:t/ n. passeport m.

password /'pɑ:swɜ:d/ n. mot de passe m.

past /pɑ:st/ a. passé; (former) ancien. ● n. passé m. ● prep. au-delà de; (in front of) devant. ● adv. devant. **the ~ months**, ces derniers mois. **~ midnight**, minuit passé. **10 ~ 6**, six heures dix.

pasta /'pæstə/ n. pâtes f. pl.

paste /peɪst/ n. (glue) colle f.; (dough) pâte f.; (of fish, meat) pâté m.; (jewellery) strass m. ● v.t. coller.

pastel /'pæstl/ n. pastel m. ● a. pastel invar.

pasteurize /'pæstʃəraɪz/ v.t. pasteuriser.

pastiche /pæ'sti:ʃ/ n. pastiche m.

pastille /'pæstɪl/ n. pastille f.

pastime /'pɑ:staɪm/ n. passetemps m. invar.

pastoral /'pɑ:stərəl/ a. pastoral.

pastry /'peɪstrɪ/ n. (dough) pâte f.; (tart) pâtisserie f.

pasture /'pɑ:stʃə(r)/ n. pâturage m.

pasty[1] /'pæstɪ/ n. petit pâté m.

pasty[2] /'peɪstɪ/ a. pâteux.

pat /pæt/ v.t. (p.t. **patted**) tapoter. ● n. petite tape f. ● adv. & a. à propos; (ready) tout prêt.

patch /pætʃ/ n. pièce f.; (over eye) bandeau m.; (spot) tache f.; (of vegetables) carré m. ● v.t. ~ **up**, rapiécer; (fig.) régler. **bad ~**, période difficile f. **not be a ~ on**, ne pas arriver à la cheville de. **~y** a. inégal.

patchwork /'pætʃwɜːk/ n. patchwork m.

pâté /'pæteɪ/ n. pâté m.

patent /'peɪtnt/ a. patent. ● n. brevet (d'invention) m. ● v.t. breveter. **~ leather**, cuir verni m. **~ly** adv. manifestement.

paternal /pə'tɜːnl/ a. paternel.

paternity /pə'tɜːnəti/ n. paternité f.

path /pɑːθ/ n. (pl. **-s** /pɑːðz/) sentier m., chemin m.; (in park) allée f.; (of rocket) trajectoire f.

pathetic /pə'θetɪk/ a. pitoyable; (bad: fam.) minable.

pathology /pə'θɒlədʒɪ/ n. pathologie f.

pathos /'peɪθɒs/ n. pathétique m.

patience /'peɪʃns/ n. patience f.

patient /'peɪʃnt/ a. patient. ● n. malade m./f., patient(e) m. (f.). **~ly** adv. patiemment.

patio /'pætɪəʊ/ n. (pl. **-os**) patio m.

patriot /'pætrɪət, 'peɪtrɪət/ n. patriote m./f. **~ic** /-'ɒtɪk/ a. patriotique; (person) patriote. **~ism** n. patriotisme m.

patrol /pə'trəʊl/ n. patrouille f. ● v.t./i. patrouiller (dans). **~ car**, voiture de police f.

patrolman /pə'trəʊlmən/ n. (pl. **-men** /-men/) (Amer.) agent de police m.

patron /'peɪtrən/ n. (of the arts) mécène m. (customer) client(e) m. (f.). **~ saint**, saint(e) patron(ne) m. (f.).

patron|age /'pætrənɪdʒ/ n. clientèle f.; (support) patronage m. **~ize** v.t. être client de; (fig.) traiter avec condescendance.

patter[1] /'pætə(r)/ n. (of steps) bruit m.; (of rain) crépitement m.

patter[2] /'pætə(r)/ n. (speech) baratin m.

pattern /'pætn/ n. motif m., dessin m.; (for sewing) patron m.; (procedure, type) schéma m.; (example) exemple m.

paunch /pɔːntʃ/ n. panse f.

pauper /'pɔːpə(r)/ n. indigent(e) m. (f.), pauvre m., pauvresse f.

pause /pɔːz/ n. pause f. ● v.i. faire une pause; (hesitate) hésiter.

pav|e /peɪv/ v.t. paver. **~e the way**, ouvrir la voie (for, à). **~ing-stone** n. pavé m.

pavement /'peɪvmənt/ n. trottoir m.; (Amer.) chaussée f.

pavilion /pə'vɪljən/ n. pavillon m.

paw /pɔː/ n. patte f. ● v.t. (of animal) donner des coups de patte à; (touch: fam.) tripoter.

pawn[1] /pɔːn/ n. (chess & fig.) pion m.

pawn[2] /pɔːn/ v.t. mettre en gage. ● n. **in ~**, en gage. **~-shop** n. mont-de-piété m.

pawnbroker /'pɔːnbrəʊkə(r)/ n. prêteur sur gages m.

pay /peɪ/ v.t./i. (p.t. **paid**) payer; (yield: comm.) rapporter; (compliment, visit) faire. ● n. salaire m., paie f. **in the ~ of**, à la solde de. **~ attention**, faire attention (to, à). **~ back**, rembourser. **~ for**, payer. **~ homage**, rendre hommage (to, à). **~ in**, verser (to, à). **~ off**, (finir de) payer; (succeed: fam.) être payant. **~ out**, payer, verser.

payable /'peɪəbl/ a. payable.

payment /'peɪmənt/ n. paiement m.; (regular) versement m. (reward) récompense f.

payroll /'peɪrəʊl/ n. registre du personnel m. **be on the ~ of**, être membre du personnel de.

pea /piː/ n. (petit) pois m. **~-shooter** n. sarbacane f.

peace /piːs/ n. paix f. **~ of mind**, tranquillité d'esprit f. **~able** a. pacifique.

peaceful /'piːsfl/ a. paisible; (intention, measure) pacifique.

peacemaker /'piːsmeɪkə(r)/ n. concilia|teur, -trice m., f.

peach /piːtʃ/ n. pêche f.

peacock /'piːkɒk/ n. paon m.

peak /piːk/ n. sommet m.; (of mountain) pic m.; (maximum) maximum m. **~ hours**, heures de pointe f. pl. **~ed cap**, casquette f.

peaky /'piːkɪ/ a. (pale) pâlot; (puny) chétif; (ill) patraque.

peal /piːl/ n. (of bells) carillon m.; (of laughter) éclat m.

peanut /'piːnʌt/ n. cacahuète f. **~s**, (money: sl.) une bagatelle f.

pear /peə(r)/ n. poire f.

pearl /pɜːl/ n. perle f. **~y** a. nacré.

peasant /'peznt/ n. paysan(ne) m. (f.).

peat /pi:t/ n. tourbe f.

pebble /'pebl/ n. caillou m.; (on beach) galet m.

peck /pek/ v.t./i. (food etc.) picorer; (attack) donner des coups de bec (à). ● n. coup de bec m. **a ~ on the cheek,** une bise.

peckish /'pekɪʃ/ a. **be ~,** (fam.) avoir faim.

peculiar /pɪ'kju:lɪə(r)/ a. (odd) bizarre; (special) particulier (**to,** à). **~ity** /-'ærətɪ/ n. bizarrerie f.

pedal /'pedl/ n. pédale f. ● v.i. pédaler.

pedantic /pɪ'dæntɪk/ a. pédant.

peddle /'pedl/ v.t. colporter; (drugs) revendre.

pedestal /'pedɪstl/ n. piédestal m.

pedestrian /pɪ'destrɪən/ n. piéton m. ● a. (precinct, street) piétonnier; (fig.) prosaïque. **~ crossing,** passage piétons m.

pedigree /'pedɪgri:/ n. (of person) ascendance f.; (of animal) pedigree m. ● a. (cattle etc.) de race.

pedlar /'pedlə(r)/ n. camelot m.; (door-to-door) colporteu|r, -se m., f.

pee /pi:/ v.i. (fam.) faire pipi.

peek /pi:k/ v.i. & n. = peep[1].

peel /pi:l/ n. épluchure(s) f. (pl.); (of orange) écorce f. ● v.t. (fruit, vegetables) éplucher. ● v.i. (of skin) peler; (of paint) s'écailler. **~ings** n. pl. épluchures f. pl.

peep[1] /pi:p/ v.i. jeter un coup d'œil (furtif) (**at,** à). ● n. coup d'œil (furtif) m. **~-hole** n. judas m. **P~ing Tom,** voyeur m.

peep[2] /pi:p/ v.i. (chirp) pépier.

peer[1] /pɪə(r)/ v.i. **~ (at),** regarder attentivement, scruter.

peer[2] /pɪə(r)/ n. (equal, noble) pair m. **~age** n. pairie f.

peeved /pi:vd/ a. (sl.) irrité.

peevish /'pi:vɪʃ/ a. grincheux.

peg /peg/ n. cheville f.; (for clothes) pince à linge f.; (to hang coats etc.) patère f.; (for tent) piquet m. ● v.t. (p.t. **pegged**) (prices) stabiliser. **buy off the ~,** acheter en prêt-à-porter.

pejorative /pɪ'dʒɒrətɪv/ a. péjoratif.

pelican /'pelɪkən/ n. pélican m. **~ crossing,** passage clouté (avec feux de signalisation) m.

pellet /'pelɪt/ n. (round mass) boulette f.; (for gun) plomb m.

pelt[1] /pelt/ n. (skin) peau f.

pelt[2] /pelt/ v.t. bombarder (**with,** de). ● v.i. pleuvoir à torrents.

pelvis /'pelvɪs/ n. (anat.) bassin m.

pen[1] /pen/ n. (for sheep etc.) enclos m.; (for baby, cattle) parc m.

pen[2] /pen/ n. stylo m.; (to be dipped in ink) plume f. ● v.t. (p.t. **penned**) écrire. **~-friend** n. correspondant(e) m. (f.). **~-name** n. pseudonyme m.

penal /'pi:nl/ a. pénal. **~ize** v.t. pénaliser; (fig.) handicaper.

penalty /'penltɪ/ n. peine f.; (fine) amende f.; (sport) pénalité f.

penance /'penəns/ n. pénitence f.

pence /pens/ see penny.

pencil /'pensl/ n. crayon m. ● v.t. (p.t. **pencilled**) crayonner. **~ in,** noter provisoirement. **~-sharpener** n. taille-crayon(s) m.

pendant /'pendənt/ n. pendentif m.

pending /'pendɪŋ/ a. en suspens. ● prep. (until) en attendant.

pendulum /'pendjʊləm/ n. pendule m.; (of clock) balancier m.

penetrat|e /'penɪtreɪt/ v.t. (enter) pénétrer dans; (understand, permeate) pénétrer. ● v.i. pénétrer. **~ing** a. pénétrant. **~ion** /-'treɪʃn/ n. pénétration f.

penguin /'peŋgwɪn/ n. manchot m., pingouin m.

penicillin /penɪ'sɪlɪn/ n. pénicilline f.

peninsula /pə'nɪnsjʊlə/ n. péninsule f.

penis /'pi:nɪs/ n. pénis m.

peniten|t /'penɪtənt/ a. & n. pénitent(e) m. (f.)). **~ce** n. pénitence f.

penitentiary /penɪ'tenʃərɪ/ n. (Amer.) prison f., pénitencier m.

penknife /'pennaɪf/ n. (pl. **-knives**) canif m.

pennant /'penənt/ n. flamme f.

penniless /'penɪlɪs/ a. sans le sou.

penny /'penɪ/ n. (pl. **pennies** or **pence**) penny m.; (fig.) sou m.

pension /'penʃn/ n. pension f.; (for retirement) retraite f. ● v.t. **~ off,** mettre à la retraite. **~ scheme,** caisse de retraite f. **~able** a. qui a droit à une retraite. **~er** n. (old-age) **~er,** retraité(e) m. (f.), personne âgée f.

pensive /'pensɪv/ a. pensif.

Pentecost /'pentɪkɒst/ n. Pentecôte f. **~al** a. pentecôtiste.

penthouse /'penthaʊs/ n. appartement de luxe m. (sur le toit d'un immeuble).

pent-up /pent'ʌp/ a. refoulé.

penultimate /pen'ʌltɪmət/ a. avant-dernier.

people /'pi:pl/ n. pl. gens m. pl., personnes f. pl. ● n. peuple m. ● v.t. peupler. **English**/etc. ~, les Anglais/ etc. m. pl. ~ **say,** on dit.

pep /pep/ n. entrain m. ● v.t. ~ **up,** donner de l'entrain à. ~ **talk,** discours d'encouragement m.

pepper /'pepə(r)/ n. poivre m.; (vegetable) poivron m. ● v.t. (culin.) poivrer. ~**y** a. poivré.

peppermint /'pepəmɪnt/ n. (plant) menthe poivrée f.; (sweet) bonbon à la menthe m.

per /pɜ:(r)/ prep. par. ~ **annum,** par an. ~ **cent,** pour cent. ~ **kilo**/etc., le kilo/etc. **ten km.** ~ **hour,** dix km à l'heure.

perceive /pə'si:v/ v.t. percevoir; (notice) s'apercevoir de. ~ **that,** s'apercevoir que.

percentage /pə'sentɪdʒ/ n. pourcentage m.

perceptible /pə'septəbl/ a. perceptible.

percept|ion /pə'sepʃn/ n. perception f. ~**ive** /-tɪv/ a. pénétrant.

perch /pɜ:tʃ/ n. (of bird) perchoir m. ● v.i. (se) percher.

percolat|e /'pɜ:kəleɪt/ v.t. passer. ● v.i. filtrer. ~**or** n. cafetière f.

percussion /pə'kʌʃn/ n. percussion f.

peremptory /pə'remptərɪ/ a. péremptoire.

perennial /pə'renɪəl/ a. perpétuel; (plant) vivace.

perfect[1] /'pɜ:fɪkt/ a. parfait. ~**ly** adv. parfaitement.

perfect[2] /pə'fekt/ v.t. parfaire, mettre au point. ~**ion** /-kʃn/ n. perfection f. **to** ~**ion,** à la perfection. ~**ionist** /-kʃənɪst/ n. perfectionniste m./f.

perforat|e /'pɜ:fəreɪt/ v.t. perforer. ~**ion** /-'reɪʃn/ n. perforation f.; (line of holes) pointillé m.

perform /pə'fɔ:m/ v.t. exécuter, faire; (a function) remplir; (mus., theatre) interpréter, jouer. ● v.i. jouer; (behave, function) se comporter. ~**ance** n. exécution f.; interprétation f.; (of car, team) performance f.; (show) représentation f.; séance f.; (fuss) histoire f. ~**er** n. artiste m./f.

perfume /'pɜ:fju:m/ n. parfum m.

perfunctory /pə'fʌŋktərɪ/ a. négligent, superficiel.

perhaps /pə'hæps/ adv. peut-être.

peril /'perəl/ n. péril m. ~**ous** a. périlleux.

perimeter /pə'rɪmɪtə(r)/ n. périmètre m.

period /'pɪərɪəd/ n. période f., époque f.; (era) époque f.; (lesson) cours m.; (gram.) point m.; (med.) règles f. pl. ● a. d'époque. ~**ic** /-'ɒdɪk/ a. périodique. ~**ically** /-'ɒdɪklɪ/ adv. périodiquement.

periodical /pɪərɪ'ɒdɪkl/ n. périodique m.

peripher|y /pə'rɪfərɪ/ n. périphérie f. ~**al** a. périphérique; (of lesser importance: fig.) accessoire; n. (comput.) périphérique m.

periscope /'perɪskəʊp/ n. périscope m.

perish /'perɪʃ/ v.i. périr; (rot) se détériorer. ~**able** a. périssable.

perjur|e /'pɜ:dʒə(r)/ v. pr. ~**e o.s.,** se parjurer. ~**y** n. parjure m.

perk[1] /pɜ:k/ v.t./i. ~ **up,** (fam.) (se) remonter. ~**y** a. (fam.) gai.

perk[2] /pɜ:k/ n. (fam.) avantage m.

perm /pɜ:m/ n. permanente f. ● v.t. **have one's hair** ~**ed,** se faire faire une permanente.

permanen|t /'pɜ:mənənt/ a. permanent. ~**ce** n. permanence f. ~**tly** adv. à titre permanent.

permeable /'pɜ:mɪəbl/ a. perméable.

permeate /'pɜ:mɪeɪt/ v.t. imprégner, se répandre dans.

permissible /pə'mɪsəbl/ a. permis.

permission /pə'mɪʃn/ n. permission f.

permissive /pə'mɪsɪv/ a. tolérant, laxiste. ~**ness** n. laxisme m.

permit[1] /pə'mɪt/ v.t. (p.t. **permitted**) permettre (**s.o. to,** à qn. de), autoriser (**s.o. to,** qn. à).

permit[2] /'pɜ:mɪt/ n. permis m.; (pass) laissez-passer m. invar.

permutation /pɜ:mjʊ'teɪʃn/ n. permutation f.

pernicious /pə'nɪʃəs/ a. nocif, pernicieux; (med.) pernicieux.

peroxide /pə'rɒksaɪd/ n. eau oxygénée f.

perpendicular /pɜ:pən'dɪkjʊlə(r)/ a. & n. perpendiculaire (f.).

perpetrat|e /'pɜ:pɪtreɪt/ v.t. perpétrer. ~**or** n. auteur m.

perpetual /pə'petʃʊəl/ a. perpétuel.

perpetuate /pə'petʃʊeɪt/ v.t. perpétuer.

perplex /pə'pleks/ v.t. rendre perplexe. ~ed a. perplexe. ~ing a. déroutant. ~ity n. perplexité f.

persecut|e /'pɜːsɪkjuːt/ v.t. persécuter. ~ion /-'kjuːʃn/ n. persécution f.

persever|e /pɜːsɪ'vɪə(r)/ v.i. persévérer. ~ance n. persévérance f.

Persian /'pɜːʃn/ a. & n. (lang.) persan (m.). ~ Gulf, golfe persique m.

persist /pə'sɪst/ v.i. persister (in doing, à faire). ~ence n. persistance f. ~ent a. (cough, snow, etc.) persistant; (obstinate) obstiné; (continual) continuel. ~ently adv. avec persistance.

person /'pɜːsn/ n. personne f. in ~, en personne. ~able a. beau.

personal /'pɜːsənl/ a. personnel; (hygiene, habits) intime; (secretary) particulier. ~ly adv. personnellement. ~ stereo, baladeur m.

personality /pɜːsə'nælətɪ/ n. personnalité f.; (on TV) vedette f.

personify /pə'sɒnɪfaɪ/ v.t. personnifier.

personnel /pɜːsə'nel/ n. personnel m.

perspective /pə'spektɪv/ n. perspective f.

Perspex /'pɜːspeks/ n. (P.) plexiglas m. (f.).

perspir|e /pə'spaɪə(r)/ v.i. transpirer. ~ation /-ə'reɪʃn/ n. transpiration f.

persua|de /pə'sweɪd/ v.t. persuader (to, de). ~sion /-eɪʒn/ n. persuasion f.

persuasive /pə'sweɪsɪv/ a. (person, speech, etc.) persuasif. ~ly adv. d'une manière persuasive.

pert /pɜːt/ a. (saucy) impertinent; (lively) plein d'entrain. ~ly adv. avec impertinence.

pertain /pə'teɪn/ v.i. ~ to, se rapporter à.

pertinent /'pɜːtɪnənt/ a. pertinent. ~ly adv. pertinemment.

perturb /pə'tɜːb/ v.t. troubler.

Peru /pə'ruː/ n. Pérou m. ~vian a. & n. péruvien(ne) (m. (f.)).

perus|e /pə'ruːz/ v.t. lire (attentivement). ~al n. lecture f.

perva|de /pə'veɪd/ v.t. imprégner, envahir. ~sive a. (mood, dust) envahissant.

pervers|e /pə'vɜːs/ a. (stubborn) entêté; (wicked) pervers. ~ity n. perversité f.

pervert|t[1] /pə'vɜːt/ v.t. pervertir.

~sion n. perversion f.

pervert|t[2] /'pɜːvɜːt/ n. perverti(e) m. (f.), dépravé(e) m. (f.).

peseta /pə'seɪtə/ n. peseta f.

pessimis|t /'pesɪmɪst/ n. pessimiste m./f. ~m /-zəm/ n. pessimisme m. ~tic /-'mɪstɪk/ a. pessimiste. ~tically /-'mɪstɪklɪ/ adv. avec pessimisme.

pest /pest/ n. insecte or animal nuisible m.; (person: fam.) enquiquineu|r, -se m., f.

pester /'pestə(r)/ v.t. harceler.

pesticide /'pestɪsaɪd/ n. pesticide m., insecticide m.

pet /pet/ n. animal (domestique) m.; (favourite) chouchou(te) m. (f.). ● a. (tame) apprivoisé. ● v.t. (p.t. petted) caresser; (sexually) peloter. ~ hate, bête noire f. ~ name, diminutif m.

petal /'petl/ n. pétale m.

peter /'piːtə(r)/ v.i. ~ out, (supplies) s'épuiser; (road) finir.

petite /pə'tiːt/ a. (woman) menue.

petition /pɪ'tɪʃn/ n. pétition f. ● v.t. adresser une pétition à.

petrify /'petrɪfaɪ/ v.t. pétrifier; (scare: fig.) pétrifier de peur.

petrol /'petrəl/ n. essence f. ~ bomb, cocktail molotov m. ~ station, station-service f. ~ tank, réservoir d'essence m.

petroleum /pɪ'trəʊlɪəm/ n. pétrole m.

petticoat /'petɪkəʊt/ n. jupon m.

petty /'petɪ/ a. (-ier, -iest) (minor) petit; (mean) mesquin. ~ cash, petite caisse f.

petulan|t /'petjʊlənt/ a. irritable. ~ce n. irritabilité f.

pew /pjuː/ n. banc d'église m.

pewter /'pjuːtə(r)/ n. étain m.

phallic /'fælɪk/ a. phallique.

phantom /'fæntəm/ n. fantôme m.

pharmaceutical /fɑːmə'sjuːtɪkl/ a. pharmaceutique.

pharmac|y /'fɑːməsɪ/ n. pharmacie f. ~ist n. pharmacien(ne) m. (f.).

pharyngitis /færɪn'dʒaɪtɪs/ n. pharyngite f.

phase /feɪz/ n. phase f. ● v.t. ~ in/out, introduire/retirer progressivement.

pheasant /'feznt/ n. faisan m.

phenomen|on /fɪ'nɒmɪnən/ n. (pl. -ena) phénomène m. ~al a. phénoménal.

phew /fjuː/ int. ouf.

phial /'faɪəl/ n. fiole f.

philanderer /fɪ'lændərə(r)/ n. coureur (de femmes) m.

philanthrop|ist /fɪ'lænθrəpɪst/ n. philanthrope m./f. **~ic** /-ən'θrɒpɪk/ a. philanthropique.

philatel|y /fɪ'lætəlɪ/ n. philatélie f. **~ist** n. philatéliste m./f.

philharmonic /fɪlɑː'mɒnɪk/ a. philharmonique.

Philippines /'fɪlɪpiːnz/ n. pl. the ~, les Philippines f. pl.

philistine /'fɪlɪstam, Amer. 'fɪlɪstiːn/ n. philistin m.

philosoph|y /fɪ'lɒsəfɪ/ n. philosophie f. **~er** n. philosophe m./f. **~ical** /-ə'sɒfɪkl/ a. philosophique; (resigned) philosophe.

phlegm /flem/ n. (med.) mucosité f.

phlegmatic /fleg'mætɪk/ a. flegmatique.

phobia /'fəʊbɪə/ n. phobie f.

phone /fəʊn/ n. téléphone m. ● v.t. (person) téléphoner à; (message) téléphoner. ● v.i. téléphoner. ~ back, rappeler. on the ~, au téléphone. ~ book, annuaire m. ~ box, ~ booth, cabine téléphonique f. ~ call, coup de fil m. ~-in n. émission à ligne ouverte f.

phonecard /'fəʊnkɑːd/ n. télécarte f.

phonetic /fə'netɪk/ a. phonétique.

phoney /'fəʊnɪ/ a. (-ier, -iest) (sl.) faux. ● n. (person: sl.) charlatan m. it's a ~, (sl.) c'est faux.

phosphate /'fɒsfeɪt/ n. phosphate m.

phosphorus /'fɒsfərəs/ n. phosphore m.

photo /'fəʊtəʊ/ n. (pl. -os) (fam.) photo f.

photocop|y /'fəʊtəʊkɒpɪ/ n. photocopie f. ● v.t. photocopier. **~ier** n. photocopieuse f.

photogenic /fəʊtəʊ'dʒenɪk/ a. photogénique.

photograph /'fəʊtəɡrɑːf/ n. photographie f. ● v.t. photographier. **~er** /fə'tɒɡrəfə(r)/ n. photographe m./f. **~ic** /-'ɡræfɪk/ a. photographique. **~y** /fə'tɒɡrəfɪ/ n. (activity) photographie f.

phrase /freɪz/ n. expression f.; (idiom & gram.) locution f. ● v.t. exprimer, formuler. **~-book** n. guide de conversation m.

physical /'fɪzɪkl/ a. physique. **~ly** adv. physiquement.

physician /fɪ'zɪʃn/ n. médecin m.

physicist /'fɪzɪsɪst/ n. physicien(ne) m. (f.).

physics /'fɪzɪks/ n. physique f.

physiology /fɪzɪ'ɒlədʒɪ/ n. physiologie f.

physiotherap|y /fɪzɪəʊ'θerəpɪ/ n. kinésithérapie f. **~ist** n. kinésithérapeute m./f.

physique /fɪ'ziːk/ n. constitution f.; (appearance) physique m.

pian|o /pɪ'ænəʊ/ n. (pl. -os) piano m. **~ist** /'pɪənɪst/ n. pianiste m./f.

piazza /pɪ'ætsə/ n. (square) place f.

pick[1] /pɪk/ (tool) n. pioche f.

pick[2] /pɪk/ v.t. choisir; (flower etc.) cueillir; (lock) crocheter; (nose) se curer; (pockets) faire. ~ (off), enlever. ● n. choix m.; (best) meilleur(e) m. (f.). ~ a quarrel with, chercher querelle à. ~ holes in, relever les défauts de. the ~ of, ce qu'il y a de mieux dans. ~ off, (mil.) abattre un à un. ~ on, harceler. ~ out, choisir; (identify) distinguer. ~ up v.t. ramasser; (sth. fallen) relever; (weight) soulever; (habit, passenger, speed, etc.) prendre; (learn) apprendre; v.i. s'améliorer. **~-me-up** n. remontant m. **~-up** n. partenaire de rencontre m./ f.; (truck, stylus-holder) pick-up m.

pickaxe /'pɪkæks/ n. pioche f.

picket /'pɪkɪt/ n. (single striker) gréviste m./f.; (stake) piquet m. ~ (line), piquet de grève m. ● v.t. (p.t. picketed) mettre un piquet de grève devant.

pickings /'pɪkɪŋz/ n. pl. restes m. pl.

pickle /'pɪkl/ n. vinaigre m.; (brine) saumure f. ~s, pickles m. pl.; (Amer.) concombres m.pl. ● v.t. conserver dans du vinaigre or de la saumure. in a ~, (fam.) dans le pétrin.

pickpocket /'pɪkpɒkɪt/ n. (thief) pickpocket m.

picnic /'pɪknɪk/ n. pique-nique m. ● v.i. (p.t. picnicked) piqueniquer.

pictorial /pɪk'tɔːrɪəl/ a. illustré.

picture /'pɪktʃə(r)/ n. image f.; (painting) tableau m.; (photograph) photo f.; (drawing) dessin m.; (film) film m.; (fig.) description f., tableau m. ● v.t. s'imaginer; (describe) dépeindre. the ~s, (cinema) le cinéma. ~ book, livre d'images m.

picturesque /pɪktʃə'resk/ a. pittoresque.

piddling /'pɪdlɪŋ/ *a.* (*fam.*) dérisoire.

pidgin /'pɪdʒɪn/ *a.* ~ **English,** pidgin *m.*

pie /paɪ/ *n.* tarte *f.*; (*of meat*) pâté en croûte *m.* ~ **chart,** camembert *m.*

piebald /'paɪbɔːld/ *a.* pie *invar.*

piece /piːs/ *n.* morceau *m.*; (*of currency, machine, etc.*) pièce *f.* ● *v.t.* ~ (**together**), (r)assembler. a ~ **of advice/furniture/etc.**, un conseil/meuble/*etc.* ~-**work** *n.* travail à la pièce *m.* **go to** ~**s**, (*fam.*) s'effondrer. **take to** ~**s**, démonter.

piecemeal /'piːsmiːl/ *a.* par bribes.

pier /pɪə(r)/ *n.* (*promenade*) jetée *f.*

pierce /pɪəs/ *v.t.* percer. ~**ing** *a.* perçant; (*cold*) glacial.

piety /'paɪətɪ/ *n.* piété *f.*

piffle /'pɪfl/ *n.* (*sl.*) fadaises *f. pl.* ~**ing** *a.* (*sl.*) insignifiant.

pig /pɪg/ *n.* cochon *m.* ~-**headed** *a.* entêté.

pigeon /'pɪdʒɪn/ *n.* pigeon *m.* ~-**hole** *n.* casier *m.*; *v.t.* classer.

piggy /'pɪgɪ/ *a.* porcin; (*greedy. fam.*) goinfre. ~-**back** *adv.* sur le dos. ~ **bank,** tirelire *f.*

pigment /'pɪgmənt/ *n.* pigment *m.* ~**ation** /-en'teɪʃn/ *n.* pigmentation *f.*

pigsty /'pɪgstaɪ/ *n.* porcherie *f.*

pigtail /'pɪgteɪl/ *n.* natte *f.*

pike /paɪk/ *n. invar.* (*fish*) brochet *m.*

pilchard /'pɪltʃəd/ *n.* pilchard *m.*

pile /paɪl/ *n.* pile *f.*, tas *m.*; (*of carpet*) poils *m.pl.* ● *v.t.* ~ (**up**), (*stack*) empiler. ● *v.i.* ~ **into,** s'empiler dans. ~ **up,** (*accumulate*) (s')accumuler. **a** ~ **of,** (*fam.*) un tas de. ~-**up** *n.* (*auto.*) carambolage *m.*

piles /paɪlz/ *n. pl.* (*fam.*) hémorroïdes *f. pl.*

pilfer /'pɪlfə(r)/ *v.t.* chaparder. ~**age** *n.* chapardage *m.*

pilgrim /'pɪlgrɪm/ *n.* pèlerin *m.* ~**age** *n.* pèlerinage *m.*

pill /pɪl/ *n.* pilule *f.*

pillage /'pɪlɪdʒ/ *n.* pillage *m.* ● *v.t.* piller. ● *v.i.* se livrer au pillage.

pillar /'pɪlə(r)/ *n.* pilier *m.* ~-**box** *n.* boîte à *or* aux lettres *f.*

pillion /'pɪljən/ *n.* siège arrière *m.* **ride** ~, monter derrière.

pillory /'pɪlərɪ/ *n.* pilori *m.*

pillow /'pɪləʊ/ *n.* oreiller *m.*

pillowcase /'pɪləʊkeɪs/ *n.* taie d'oreiller *f.*

pilot /'paɪlət/ *n.* pilote *m.* ● *a.* pilote. ● *v.t.* (*p.t.* **piloted**) piloter. ~-**light** *n.* veilleuse *f.*

pimento /pɪ'mentəʊ/ *n.* (*pl.* -**os**) piment *m.*

pimp /pɪmp/ *n.* souteneur *m.*

pimple /'pɪmpl/ *n.* bouton *m.* ~**y** *a.* boutonneux.

pin /pɪn/ *n.* épingle *f.*; (*techn.*) goupille *f.* ● *v.t.* (*p.t.* **pinned**) épingler, attacher; (*hold down*) clouer. **have** ~**s and needles,** avoir des fourmis. ~ **s.o. down,** (*fig.*) forcer qn. à se décider. ~-**point** *v.t.* repérer, définir. ~ **up,** afficher. ~-**up** *n.* (*fam.*) pin-up *f. invar.*

pinafore /'pɪnəfɔː(r)/ *n.* tablier *m.*

pincers /'pɪnsəz/ *n. pl.* tenailles *f. pl.*

pinch /pɪntʃ/ *v.t.* pincer; (*steal: sl.*) piquer. ● *v.i.* (*be too tight*) serrer. ● *n.* (*mark*) pinçon *m.*; (*of salt*) pincée *f.* **at a** ~, au besoin.

pincushion /'pɪnkʊʃn/ *n.* pelote à épingles *f.*

pine [1] /paɪn/ *n.* (*tree*) pin *m.* ~-**cone** *n.* pomme de pin *f.*

pine [2] /paɪn/ *v.i.* ~ **away,** dépérir. ~ **for,** languir après.

pineapple /'paɪnæpl/ *n.* ananas *m.*

ping /pɪŋ/ *n.* bruit métallique *m.*

ping-pong /'pɪŋpɒŋ/ *n.* ping-pong *m.*

pink /pɪŋk/ *a. & n.* rose (*m.*).

pinnacle /'pɪnəkl/ *n.* pinacle *m.*

pint /paɪnt/ *n.* pinte *f.* (*imperial = 0.57 litre*; *Amer. = 0.47 litre*).

pioneer /paɪə'nɪə(r)/ *n.* pionnier *m.* ● *v.t.* être le premier à faire, utiliser, étudier, *etc.*

pious /'paɪəs/ *a.* pieux.

pip [1] /pɪp/ *n.* (*seed*) pépin *m.*

pip [2] /pɪp/ *n.* (*sound*) top *m.*

pipe /paɪp/ *n.* tuyau *m.*; (*of smoker*) pipe *f.*; (*mus.*) pipeau *m.* ● *v.t.* transporter par tuyau. ~-**cleaner** *n.* cure-pipe *m.* ~ **down,** se taire. ~-**dream** *n.* chimère *f.*

pipeline /'paɪplaɪn/ *n.* pipeline *m.* **in the** ~, en route.

piping /'paɪpɪŋ/ *n.* tuyau(x) *m.* (*pl.*). ~ **hot,** très chaud.

piquant /'piːkənt/ *a.* piquant.

pique /piːk/ *n.* dépit *m.*

pirate /'paɪərət/ *n.* pirate *m.* ● *v.t.* pirater. ~**cy** *n.* piraterie *f.*

Pisces /'paɪsiːz/ *n.* les Poissons *m. pl.*

pistachio /pɪ'stæʃɪəʊ/ *n.* (*pl.* -**os**) pistache *f.*

pistol /'pɪstl/ *n.* pistolet *m.*

piston /'pɪstən/ *n.* piston *m.*

pit /pɪt/ *n.* fosse *f.*, trou *m.*; (*mine*) puits *m.*; (*quarry*) carrière *f.*; (*for orchestra*) fosse *f.*; (*of stomach*)

creux *m.*; (*of cherry etc.*: *Amer.*)
noyau *m.* ● *v.t.* (*p.t.* pitted) trouer;
(*fig.*) opposer. ~ o.s. against, se
mesurer à.

pitch¹ /pɪtʃ/ *n.* (*tar*) poix *f.* ~-black
a. d'un noir d'ébène.

pitch² /pɪtʃ/ *v.t.* lancer; (*tent*)
dresser. ● *v.i.* (*of ship*) tanguer.
● *n.* degré *m.*; (*of voice*) hauteur *f.*;
(*mus.*) ton *m.*; (*sport*) terrain *m.*
~ed battle, bataille rangée *f.* a
high-~ed voice, une voix aiguë. ~
in, (*fam.*) contribuer. ~ into, (*fam.*)
s'attaquer à.

pitcher /ˈpɪtʃə(r)/ *n.* cruche *f.*

pitchfork /ˈpɪtʃfɔːk/ *n.* fourche à foin
f.

pitfall /ˈpɪtfɔːl/ *n.* piège *m.*

pith /pɪθ/ *n.* (*of orange*) peau blanche
f.; (*essence: fig.*) moelle *f.*

pithy /ˈpɪθɪ/ *a.* (-ier, -iest) (*terse*)
concis; (*forceful*) vigoureux.

piti|ful /ˈpɪtɪfl/ *a.* pitoyable. ~less *a.*
impitoyable.

pittance /ˈpɪtns/ *n.* revenu *or* salaire
dérisoire *m.*

pity /ˈpɪtɪ/ *n.* pitié *f.*; (*regrettable fact*)
dommage *m.* ● *v.t.* plaindre. take ~
on, avoir pitié de. what a ~, quel
dommage. it's a ~, c'est dommage.

pivot /ˈpɪvət/ *n.* pivot *m.* ● *v.i.* (*p.t.*
pivoted) pivoter.

pixie /ˈpɪksɪ/ *n.* lutin *m.*

pizza /ˈpiːtsə/ *n.* pizza *f.*

placard /ˈplækɑːd/ *n.* affiche *f.*

placate /pləˈkeɪt, *Amer.* ˈpleɪkeɪt/ *v.t.*
calmer.

place /pleɪs/ *n.* endroit *m.*, lieu *m.*;
(*house*) maison *f.*; (*seat, rank, etc.*)
place *f.* ● *v.t.* placer; (*an order*)
passer; (*remember*) situer. at *or* to
my ~, chez moi. be ~d, (*in race*) se
placer. change ~s, changer de
place. in the first ~, d'abord. out
of ~, déplacé. take ~, avoir lieu. ~-
mat *n.* set *m.*

placenta /pləˈsentə/ *n.* placenta *m.*

placid /ˈplæsɪd/ *a.* placide.

plagiar|ize /ˈpleɪdʒəraɪz/ *v.t.* plagier.
~ism *n.* plagiat *m.*

plague /pleɪg/ *n.* peste *f.*; (*nuisance*:
fam.) fléau *m.* ● *v.t.* harceler.

plaice /pleɪs/ *n. invar.* carrelet *m.*

plaid /plæd/ *n.* tissu écossais *m.*

plain /pleɪn/ *a.* (-er, -est) clair; (*candid*) franc; (*simple*) simple; (*not
pretty*) sans beauté; (*not patterned*)
uni. ● *adv.* franchement. ● *n.*
plaine *f.* ~ chocolate, chocolat

noir *m.* in ~ clothes, en civil.
~ly *adv.* clairement; franchement;
simplement. ~ness *n.* simplicité *f.*

plaintiff /ˈpleɪntɪf/ *n.* plaignant(e) *m.*
(*f.*).

plaintive /ˈpleɪntɪv/ *a.* plaintif.

plait /plæt/ *v.t.* tresser, natter. ● *n.*
tresse *f.*, natte *f.*

plan /plæn/ *n.* projet *m.*, plan *m.*;
(*diagram*) plan *m.* ● *v.t.* (*p.t.*
planned) prévoir, projeter; (*arrange*) organiser; (*design*) concevoir; (*economy, work*) planifier.
● *v.i.* faire des projets. ~ to do,
avoir l'intention de faire.

plane¹ /pleɪn/ *n.* (*tree*) platane *m.*

plane² /pleɪn/ *n.* (*level*) plan *m.*;
(*aeroplane*) avion *m.* ● *a.* plan.

plane³ /pleɪn/ *n.* (*tool*) rabot *m.*
● *v.t.* raboter.

planet /ˈplænɪt/ *n.* planète *f.* ~ary *a.*
planétaire.

plank /plæŋk/ *n.* planche *f.*

plankton /ˈplæŋktn/ *n.* plancton *m.*

planning /ˈplænɪŋ/ *n.* (*pol., comm.*)
planification *f.* family ~, planning
familial *m.* ~ permission, permis
de construire *m.*

plant /plɑːnt/ *n.* plante *f.*; (*techn.*)
matériel *m.*; (*factory*) usine *f.* ● *v.t.*
planter; (*bomb*) (dé)poser. ~ation
/-ˈteɪʃn/ *n.* plantation *f.*

plaque /plɑːk/ *n.* plaque *f.*

plasma /ˈplæzmə/ *n.* plasma *m.*

plaster /ˈplɑːstə(r)/ *n.* plâtre *m.*; (*adhesive*) sparadrap *m.* ● *v.t.* plâtrer;
(*cover*) tapisser (with, de). in ~,
dans le plâtre. ~ of Paris, plâtre à
mouler *m.* ~er *n.* plâtrier *m.*

plastic /ˈplæstɪk/ *a.* en plastique; (*art,
substance*) plastique. ● *n.* plastique
m. ~ surgery, chirurgie esthétique
f.

Plasticine /ˈplæstɪsiːn/ *n.* (P.) pâte à
modeler *f.*

plate /pleɪt/ *n.* assiette *f.*; (*of metal*)
plaque *f.*; (*gold or silver dishes*)
vaisselle plate *f.*; (*in book*) gravure
f. ● *v.t.* (*metal*) plaquer. ~ful *n.*
(*pl.* -fuls) assiettée *f.*

plateau /ˈplætəʊ/ *n.* (*pl.* -eaux /-əʊz/)
plateau *m.*

platform /ˈplætfɔːm/ *n.* (*in
classroom, hall, etc.*) estrade *f.*; (*for
speaking*) tribune *f.*; (*rail.*) quai *m.*;
(*of bus & pol.*) plate-forme *f.*

platinum /ˈplætɪnəm/ *n.* platine *m.*

platitude /ˈplætɪtjuːd/ *n.* platitude *f.*

platonic /pləˈtɒnɪk/ *a.* platonique.

platoon /plə'tu:n/ n. (mil.) section f.

platter /'plætə(r)/ n. plat m.

plausible /'plɔ:zəbl/ a. plausible.

play /pleɪ/ v.t./i. jouer; (instrument) jouer de; (record) passer; (game) jouer à; (opponent) jouer contre; (match) disputer. ● n. jeu m.; (theatre) pièce f. ~-act v.i. jouer la comédie. ~ down, minimiser. ~-group, ~-school ns. garderie f. ~-off n. (sport) belle f. ~ on, (take advantage of) jouer sur. ~ on words, jeu de mots m. ~ed out, épuisé. ~-pen n. parc m. ~ safe, ne pas prendre de risques (à). ~ up, (fam.) créer des problèmes (à). ~ up to, flatter. ~er n. joueu|r, -se m., f.

playboy /'pleɪbɔɪ/ n. play-boy m.

playful /'pleɪfl/ a. enjoué; (child) joueur. ~ly adv. avec espièglerie.

playground /'pleɪgraʊnd/ n. cour de récréation f.

playing /'pleɪɪŋ/ n. jeu m. ~-card n. carte à jouer f. ~-field n. terrain de sport m.

playmate /'pleɪmeɪt/ n. camarade m./f., cop|ain, -ine m., f.

plaything /'pleɪθɪŋ/ n. jouet m.

playwright /'pleɪraɪt/ n. dramaturge m./f.

plc abbr. (public limited company) SA.

plea /pli:/ n. (entreaty) supplication f.; (reason) excuse f.; (jurid.) défense f.

plead /pli:d/ v.t./i. (jurid.) plaider; (as excuse) alléguer. ~ for, (beg for) implorer. ~ with, (beg) implorer.

pleasant /'pleznt/ a. agréable. ~ly adv. agréablement.

please /pli:z/ v.t./i. plaire (à), faire plaisir (à). ● adv. s'il vous or te plaît. ~ o.s., do as one ~s, faire ce qu'on veut. ~d a. content (with, de). **pleasing** a. agréable.

pleasur|e /'pleʒə(r)/ n. plaisir m. ~able a. très agréable.

pleat /pli:t/ n. pli m. ● v.t. plisser.

plebiscite /'plebɪsɪt/ n. plébiscite m.

pledge /pledʒ/ n. (token) gage m.; (fig.) promesse f. ● v.t. promettre; (pawn) engager.

plentiful /'plentɪfl/ a. abondant.

plenty /'plentɪ/ n. abondance f. ~ (of), (a great deal) beaucoup (de); (enough) assez (de).

pleurisy /'plʊərəsɪ/ n. pleurésie f.

pliable /'plaɪəbl/ a. souple.

pliers /'plaɪəz/ n. pl. pince(s) f. (pl.).

plight /plaɪt/ n. triste situation f.

plimsoll /'plɪms(ə)l/ n. chaussure de gym f.

plinth /plɪnθ/ n. socle m.

plod /plɒd/ v.i. (p.t. plodded) avancer péniblement or d'un pas lent; (work) bûcher. ~der n. bûcheu|r, -se m., f. ~ding a. lent.

plonk /plɒŋk/ n. (sl.) pinard m. ● v.t. ~ down, poser lourdement.

plot /plɒt/ n. complot m.; (of novel etc.) intrigue f. ~ (of land), terrain m. ● v.t./i. (p.t. plotted) comploter; (mark out) tracer.

plough /plaʊ/ n. charrue f. ● v.t./i. labourer. ~ back, réinvestir. ~ into, rentrer dans. ~ through, avancer péniblement dans.

plow /plaʊ/ n. & v.t./i. (Amer.) = **plough**.

ploy /plɔɪ/ n. (fam.) stratagème m.

pluck /plʌk/ v.t. cueillir; (bird) plumer; (eyebrows) épiler; (strings: mus.) pincer. ● n. courage m. ~ up courage, prendre son courage à deux mains. ~y a. courageux.

plug /plʌg/ n. (of cloth, paper, etc.) tampon m.; (for sink etc.) bonde f.; (electr.) fiche f., prise f. ● v.t. (p.t. plugged) (hole) boucher; (publicize: fam.) faire du battage autour de. ● v.i. ~ away, (work: fam.) bosser. ~ in, brancher. ~-hole n. vidange f.

plum /plʌm/ n. prune f. ~ job, travail en or m. ~ pudding, (plum-) pudding m.

plumb /plʌm/ adv. tout à fait. ● v.t. (probe) sonder. ~-line n. fil à plomb m.

plumb|er /'plʌmə(r)/ n. plombier m. ~ing n. plomberie f.

plum|e /plu:m/ n. plume(s) f. (pl.). ~age n. plumage m.

plummet /'plʌmɪt/ v.i. (p.t. plummeted) tomber, plonger.

plump /plʌmp/ a. (-er, -est) potelé, dodu. ● v.i. ~ for, choisir. ~ness n. rondeur f.

plunder /'plʌndə(r)/ v.t. piller. ● n. (act) pillage m.; (goods) butin m.

plunge /plʌndʒ/ v.t./i. (dive, thrust) plonger; (fall) tomber. ● n. plongeon m.; (fall) chute f. take the ~, se jeter à l'eau.

plunger /'plʌndʒə(r)/ n. (for sink etc.) ventouse f., débouchoir m.

plural /'plʊərəl/ a. pluriel; (noun) au pluriel. ● n. pluriel m.

plus /plʌs/ *prep.* plus. ● *a.* (*electr. & fig.*) positif. ● *n.* signe plus *m.*; (*fig.*) atout *m.* **ten ~,** plus de dix.

plush(y) /'plʌʃ(ɪ)/ *a.* somptueux.

ply /plaɪ/ *v.t.* (*tool*) manier; (*trade*) exercer. ● *v.i.* faire la navette. **~ s.o. with drink,** offrir continuellement à boire à qn.

plywood /'plaɪwʊd/ *n.* contreplaqué *m.*

p.m. /piː'em/ *adv.* de l'après-midi *or* du soir.

pneumatic /njuː'mætɪk/ *a.* pneumatique. **~ drill,** marteau-piqueur *m.*

pneumonia /njuː'məʊnɪə/ *n.* pneumonie *f.*

PO *abbr. see* Post Office.

poach /pəʊtʃ/ *v.t./i.* (*game*) braconner; (*staff*) débaucher; (*culin.*) pocher. **~er** *n.* braconnier *m.*

pocket /'pɒkɪt/ *n.* poche *f.* ● *a.* de poche. ● *v.t.* empocher. **be out of ~,** avoir perdu de l'argent. **~-book** *n.* (*notebook*) carnet *m.*; (*wallet: Amer.*) portefeuille *m.*; (*handbag: Amer.*) sac à main *m.* **~-money** *n.* argent de poche *m.*

pock-marked /'pɒkmɑːkt/ *a.* (*face etc.*) grêlé.

pod /pɒd/ *n.* (*peas etc.*) cosse *f.*; (*vanilla*) gousse *f.*

podgy /'pɒdʒɪ/ *a.* (**-ier, -iest**) dodu.

poem /'pəʊɪm/ *n.* poème *m.*

poet /'pəʊɪt/ *n.* poète *m.* **~ic** /-'etɪk/ *a.* poétique.

poetry /'pəʊɪtrɪ/ *n.* poésie *f.*

poignant /'pɔɪnjənt/ *a.* poignant.

point /pɔɪnt/ *n.* point *m.*; (*tip*) pointe *f.*; (*decimal point*) virgule *f.*; (*meaning*) sens *m.*, intérêt *m.*; (*remark*) remarque *f.* **~s,** (*rail.*) aiguillage *m.* ● *v.t.* (*aim*) braquer; (*show*) indiquer. ● *v.i.* indiquer du doigt (**at** *or* **to s.o.,** qn.). **~ out that, make the ~ that,** faire remarquer que. **good ~s,** qualités *f. pl.* **make a ~ of doing,** ne pas manquer de faire. **on the ~ of,** sur le point de. **~-blank** *a. & adv.* à bout portant. **~ in time,** moment *m.* **~ of view,** point de vue *m.* **~ out,** signaler. **to the ~,** pertinent. **what is the ~?,** à quoi bon?

pointed /'pɔɪntɪd/ *a.* pointu; (*remark*) lourd de sens.

pointer /'pɔɪntə(r)/ *n.* (*indicator*) index *m.*; (*dog*) chien d'arrêt *m.*; (*advice: fam.*) tuyau *m.*

pointless /'pɔɪntlɪs/ *a.* inutile.

poise /pɔɪz/ *n.* équilibre *m.*; (*carriage*) maintien *m.*; (*fig.*) assurance *f.* **~d** *a.* en équilibre; (*confident*) assuré. **~d for,** prêt à.

poison /'pɔɪzn/ *n.* poison *m.* ● *v.t.* empoisonner. **~ous** *a.* (*substance etc.*) toxique; (*plant*) vénéneux; (*snake*) venimeux.

poke /pəʊk/ *v.t./i.* (*push*) pousser; (*fire*) tisonner; (*thrust*) fourrer. ● *n.* (petit) coup *m.* **~ about,** fureter. **~ fun at,** se moquer de. **~ out,** (*head*) sortir.

poker[1] /'pəʊkə(r)/ *n.* tisonnier *m.*

poker[2] /'pəʊkə(r)/ *n.* (*cards*) poker *m.*

poky /'pəʊkɪ/ *a.* (**-ier, -iest**) (*small*) exigu; (*slow: Amer.*) lent.

Poland /'pəʊlənd/ *n.* Pologne *f.*

polar /'pəʊlə(r)/ *a.* polaire. **~ bear,** ours blanc *m.*

polarize /'pəʊləraɪz/ *v.t.* polariser.

Polaroid /'pəʊlərɔɪd/ *n.* (P.) polaroïd (P.) *m.*

pole[1] /pəʊl/ *n.* (*fixed*) poteau *m.*; (*rod*) perche *f.*; (*for flag*) mât *m.* **~-vault** *n.* saut à la perche *m.*

pole[2] /pəʊl/ *n.* (*geog.*) pôle *m.*

Pole /pəʊl/ *n.* Polonais(e) *m.* (*f.*).

polemic /pə'lemɪk/ *n.* polémique *f.*

police /pə'liːs/ *n.* police *f.* ● *v.t.* faire la police dans. **~ state,** état policier *m.* **~ station,** commissariat de police *m.*

police|man /pə'liːsmən/ *n.* (*pl.* **-men**) agent de police *m.* **~woman** (*pl.* **-women**) femme-agent *f.*

policy[1] /'pɒlɪsɪ/ *n.* politique *f.*

policy[2] /'pɒlɪsɪ/ *n.* (*insurance*) police (d'assurance) *f.*

polio(myelitis) /'pəʊlɪəʊ(maɪə-'laɪtɪs)/ *n.* polio(myélite) *f.*

polish /'pɒlɪʃ/ *v.t.* polir; (*shoes, floor*) cirer. ● *n.* (*for shoes*) cirage *m.*; (*for floor*) encaustique *f.*; (*for nails*) vernis *m.*; (*shine*) poli *m.*; (*fig.*) raffinement *m.* **~ off,** finir en vitesse. **~ up,** (*language*) perfectionner. **~ed** *a.* raffiné.

Polish /'pəʊlɪʃ/ *a.* polonais. ● *n.* (*lang.*) polonais *m.*

polite /pə'laɪt/ *a.* poli. **~ly** *adv.* poliment. **~ness** *n.* politesse *f.*

political /pə'lɪtɪkl/ *a.* politique.

politician /pɒlɪ'tɪʃn/ *n.* homme politique *m.*, femme politique *f.*

politics /'pɒlətɪks/ *n.* politique *f.*

polka /'pɒlkə, *Amer.* 'pəʊlkə/ *n.* polka *f.* ~ **dots,** pois *m. pl.*

poll /pəʊl/ *n.* scrutin *m.*; (*survey*) sondage *m.* ● *v.t.* (*votes*) obtenir. **go to the ~s,** aller aux urnes. **~ing-booth** *n.* isoloir *m.* **~ing station,** bureau de vote *m.*

pollen /'pɒlən/ *n.* pollen *m.*

pollut|e /pə'luːt/ *v.t.* polluer. **~ion** /-ʃn/ *n.* pollution *f.*

polo /'pəʊləʊ/ *n.* polo *m.* ~ **neck,** col roulé *m.* ~ **shirt,** polo *m.*

polyester /pɒlɪ'estə(r)/ *n.* polyester *m.*

polygamy /pə'lɪgəmɪ/ *n.* polygamie *f.*

polytechnic /pɒlɪ'teknɪk/ *n.* institut universitaire de technologie *m.*

polythene /'pɒlɪθiːn/ *n.* polythène *m.*, polyéthylène *m.*

pomegranate /'pɒmɪgrænɪt/ *n.* (*fruit*) grenade *f.*

pomp /pɒmp/ *n.* pompe *f.*

pompon /'pɒmpɒn/ *n.* pompon *m.*

pomp|ous /'pɒmpəs/ *a.* pompeux. **~osity** /-'pɒsɪtɪ/ *n.* solennité *f.*

pond /pɒnd/ *n.* étang *m.*; (*artificial*) bassin *m.*; (*stagnant*) mare *f.*

ponder /'pɒndə(r)/ *v.t./i.* réfléchir (à), méditer (sur).

ponderous /'pɒndərəs/ *a.* pesant.

pong /pɒŋ/ *n.* (*stink: sl.*) puanteur *f.* ● *v.i.* (*sl.*) puer.

pony /'pəʊnɪ/ *n.* poney *m.* **~-tail** *n.* queue de cheval *f.*

poodle /'puːdl/ *n.* caniche *m.*

pool¹ /puːl/ *n.* (*puddle*) flaque *f.*; (*pond*) étang *m.*; (*of blood*) mare *f.*; (*for swimming*) piscine *f.*

pool² /puːl/ *n.* (*fund*) fonds commun *m.*, (*of ideas*) réservoir *m.*; (*of typists*) pool *m.*; (*snooker*) billard américain *m.* **~s,** pari mutuel sur le football *m.* ● *v.t.* mettre en commun.

poor /pɔː(r)/ *a.* (**-er, -est**) pauvre; (*not good*) médiocre, mauvais. **~ly** *adv.* mal; *a.* malade.

pop¹ /pɒp/ *n.* (*noise*) bruit sec *m.* ● *v.t./i.* (*p.t.* **popped**) (*burst*) crever; (*put*) mettre. ~ **in/out/off,** entrer/sortir/partir. ~ **over,** faire un saut (**to see s.o.,** chez qn.). ~ **up,** surgir.

pop² /pɒp/ *n.* (*mus.*) musique pop *f.* ● *a.* pop *invar.*

popcorn /'pɒpkɔːn/ *n.* pop-corn *m.*

pope /pəʊp/ *n.* pape *m.*

poplar /'pɒplə(r)/ *n.* peuplier *m.*

poppy /'pɒpɪ/ *n.* pavot *m.*; (*wild*) coquelicot *m.*

popsicle /'pɒpsɪkl/ *n.* (P.) (*Amer.*) glace à l'eau *f.*

popular /'pɒpjʊlə(r)/ *a.* populaire; (*in fashion*) en vogue. **be ~ with,** plaire à. **~ity** /-'lærətɪ/ *n.* popularité *f.* **~ize** *v.t.* populariser. **~ly** *adv.* communément.

populat|e /'pɒpjʊleɪt/ *v.t.* peupler. **~ion** /-'leɪʃn/ *n.* population *f.*

populous /'pɒpjʊləs/ *a.* populeux.

porcelain /'pɔːsəlɪn/ *n.* porcelaine *f.*

porch /pɔːtʃ/ *n.* porche *m.*

porcupine /'pɔːkjʊpaɪn/ *n.* (*rodent*) porc-épic *m.*

pore¹ /pɔː(r)/ *n.* pore *m.*

pore² /pɔː(r)/ *v.i.* ~ **over,** étudier minutieusement.

pork /pɔːk/ *n.* (*food*) porc *m.*

pornograph|y /pɔː'nɒgrəfɪ/ *n.* pornographie *f.* **~ic** /-ə'græfɪk/ *a.* pornographique.

porous /'pɔːrəs/ *a.* poreux.

porpoise /'pɔːpəs/ *n.* marsouin *m.*

porridge /'pɒrɪdʒ/ *n.* porridge *m.*

port¹ /pɔːt/ *n.* (*harbour*) port *m.* ~ **of call,** escale *f.*

port² /pɔːt/ *n.* (*left: naut.*) bâbord *m.*

port³ /pɔːt/ *n.* (*wine*) porto *m.*

portable /'pɔːtəbl/ *a.* portatif.

portal /'pɔːtl/ *n.* portail *m.*

porter¹ /'pɔːtə(r)/ *n.* (*carrier*) porteur *m.*

porter² /'pɔːtə(r)/ *n.* (*door-keeper*) portier *m.*

portfolio /pɔːt'fəʊlɪəʊ/ *n.* (*pl.* **-os**) (*pol., comm.*) portefeuille *m.*

porthole /'pɔːthəʊl/ *n.* hublot *m.*

portico /'pɔːtɪkəʊ/ *n.* (*pl.* **-oes**) portique *m.*

portion /'pɔːʃn/ *n.* (*share, helping*) portion *f.*; (*part*) partie *f.*

portly /'pɔːtlɪ/ *a.* (**-ier, -iest**) corpulent (et digne).

portrait /'pɔːtrɪt/ *n.* portrait *m.*

portray /pɔː'treɪ/ *v.t.* représenter. **~al** *n.* portrait *m.*, peinture *f.*

Portug|al /'pɔːtjʊgl/ *n.* Portugal *m.* **~uese** /-'giːz/ *a. & n. invar.* portugais(e) (*m.* (*f.*)).

pose /pəʊz/ *v.t./i.* poser. ● *n.* pose *f.* ~ **as,** (*expert etc.*) se poser en.

poser /'pəʊzə(r)/ *n.* colle *f.*

posh /pɒʃ/ *a.* (*sl.*) chic *invar.*

position /pə'zɪʃn/ *n.* position *f.*; (*job, state*) situation *f.* ● *v.t.* placer.

positive /'pɒzətɪv/ *a.* (*test, help, etc.*) positif; (*sure*) sûr, certain; (*real*)

réel, vrai. **~ly** adv. positivement;
(*absolutely*) complètement.
possess /pəˈzes/ v.t. posséder. **~ion**
/-ʃn/ n. possession f. **take ~ion
of,** prendre possession de. **~or** n.
possesseur m.
possessive /pəˈzesɪv/ a. possessif.
possib∣le /ˈpɒsəbl/ a. possible. **~ility**
/-ˈbɪlətɪ/ n. possibilité f.
possibly /ˈpɒsəblɪ/ adv. peut-être. **if I
~ can,** si cela m'est possible. **I
cannot ~ leave,** il m'est impossible
de partir.
post¹ /pəʊst/ n. (*pole*) poteau m.
● v.t. **~ (up),** (*a notice*) afficher.
post² /pəʊst/ n. (*station, job*) poste
m. ● v.t. poster; (*appoint*) affecter.
post³ /pəʊst/ n. (*mail service*) poste
f.; (*letters*) courrier m. ● a. postal.
● v.t. (*put in box*) poster; (*send*)
envoyer (par la poste). **catch the
last ~,** attraper la dernière levée.
keep ~ed, tenir au courant. **~box**
n. boîte à or aux lettres f. **~ code** n.
code postal m. **P~ Office,** postes f.
pl.; (*in France*) Postes et Télécommunications f. pl. **~ office,** bureau
de poste m., poste f.
post- /pəʊst/ pref. post-.
postage /ˈpəʊstɪdʒ/ n. tarif postal m.,
frais de port m.pl.
postal /ˈpəʊstl/ a. postal. **~ order,**
mandat m. **~ worker,** employé(e)
des postes m. (f.).
postcard /ˈpəʊstkɑːd/ n. carte postale
f.
poster /ˈpəʊstə(r)/ n. affiche f.; (*for
decoration*) poster m.
posterior /pɒˈstɪərɪə(r)/ n. postérieur
m.
posterity /pɒˈsterətɪ/ n. postérité f.
postgraduate /pəʊstˈgrædʒʊət/ n.
étudiant(e) de troisième cycle m. (f.).
posthumous /ˈpɒstjʊməs/ a. posthume. **~ly** adv. à titre posthume.
postman /ˈpəʊstmən/ n. (pl. **-men**)
facteur m.
postmark /ˈpəʊstmɑːk/ n. cachet de
la poste m.
postmaster /ˈpəʊstmɑːstə(r)/ n. rece-
veur des postes m.
post-mortem /pəʊstˈmɔːtəm/ n. autopsie f.
postpone /pəˈspəʊn/ v.t. remettre.
~ment n. ajournement m.
postscript /ˈpəʊskrɪpt/ n. (*to letter*)
post-scriptum m. invar.
postulate /ˈpɒstjʊleɪt/ v.t. postuler.

posture /ˈpɒstʃə(r)/ n. posture f.
● v.i. (*affectedly*) prendre des poses.
post-war /ˈpəʊstwɔː(r)/ a. d'après-
guerre.
pot /pɒt/ n. pot m.; (*for cooking*)
marmite f.; (*drug: sl.*) marie-jeanne
f. ● v.t. (*plants*) mettre en pot. **go
to ~,** (*sl.*) aller à la ruine. **~-belly**
n. gros ventre m. **take ~ luck,** tenter
sa chance. **take a ~-shot at,** faire
un carton sur.
potato /pəˈteɪtəʊ/ n. (pl. **-oes**)
pomme de terre f.
poten∣t /ˈpəʊtnt/ a. puissant; (*drink*)
fort. **~cy** n. puissance f.
potential /pəˈtenʃl/ a. & n. potentiel
(m.). **~ly** adv. potentiellement.
pot-hol∣e /ˈpɒthəʊl/ n. (*in rock*) caverne f.; (*in road*) nid de poule m.
~ing n. spéléologie f.
potion /ˈpəʊʃn/ n. potion f.
potted /ˈpɒtɪd/ a. (*plant etc.*) en pot;
(*preserved*) en conserve; (*abridged*)
condensé.
potter¹ /ˈpɒtə(r)/ n. potier m. **~y** n.
(*art*) poterie f.; (*objects*) poteries
f.pl.
potter² /ˈpɒtə(r)/ v.i. bricoler.
potty /ˈpɒtɪ/ a. (**-ier, -iest**) (*crazy: sl.*)
toqué. ● n. pot m.
pouch /paʊtʃ/ n. poche f.; (*for tobacco*) blague f.
pouffe /puːf/ n. pouf m.
poultice /ˈpəʊltɪs/ n. cataplasme m.
poult∣ry /ˈpəʊltrɪ/ n. volaille f. **~erer**
n. marchand de volailles m.
pounce /paʊns/ v.i. bondir (**on,** sur).
● n. bond m.
pound¹ /paʊnd/ n. (*weight*) livre f.
(= 454 g.); (*money*) livre f.
pound² /paʊnd/ n. (*for dogs, cars*)
fourrière f.
pound³ /paʊnd/ v.t. (*crush*) piler;
(*bombard*) pilonner. ● v.i. frapper
fort; (*of heart*) battre fort; (*walk*)
marcher à pas lourds.
pour /pɔː(r)/ v.t. verser. ● v.i. couler,
ruisseler (**from,** de); (*rain*) pleuvoir
à torrents. **~ in/out,** (*people*) arri-
ver/sortir en masse. **~ off** or **out,**
vider. **~ing rain,** pluie torrentielle f.
pout /paʊt/ v.t./i. **~ (one's lips),**
faire la moue. ● n. moue f.
poverty /ˈpɒvətɪ/ n. misère f., pau-
vreté f.
powder /ˈpaʊdə(r)/ n. poudre f.
● v.t. poudrer. **~ed** a. en poudre.
~y a. poudreux. **~-room** n. toilettes
pour dames f. pl.

power /'pauə(r)/ *n.* puissance *f.*; (*ability, authority*) pouvoir *m.*; (*energy*) énergie *f.*; (*electr.*) courant *m.* **~ cut,** coupure de courant *f.* **~ed by,** fonctionnant à; (*jet etc.*) propulsé par. **~less** *a.* impuissant. **~ point,** prise de courant *f.* **~-station** *n.* centrale électrique *f.*

powerful /'pauəfl/ *a.* puissant. **~ly** *adv.* puissamment.

practicable /'præktɪkəbl/ *a.* praticable.

practical /'præktɪkl/ *a.* pratique. **~ity** /-'kælətɪ/ *n.* sens *or* aspect pratique *m.* **~ joke,** farce *f.*

practically /'præktɪklɪ/ *adv.* pratiquement.

practice /'præktɪs/ *n.* pratique *f.*; (*of profession*) exercice *m.*; (*sport*) entraînement *m.*; (*clients*) clientèle *f.* **be in ~,** (*doctor, lawyer*) exercer. **in ~,** (*in fact*) en pratique; (*well-trained*) en forme. **out of ~,** rouillé. **put into ~,** mettre en pratique.

practis|e /'præktɪs/ *v.t./i.* (*musician, typist, etc.*) s'exercer (à); (*sport*) s'entraîner (à); (*put into practice*) pratiquer; (*profession*) exercer. **~ed** *a.* expérimenté. **~ing** *a.* (*Catholic etc.*) pratiquant.

practitioner /præk'tɪʃənə(r)/ *n.* praticien(ne) *m.* (*f.*).

pragmatic /præg'mætɪk/ *a.* pragmatique.

prairie /'preərɪ/ *n.* (*in North America*) prairie *f.*

praise /preɪz/ *v.t.* louer. ● *n.* éloge(s) *m.* (*pl.*), louange(s) *f.* (*pl.*).

praiseworthy /'preɪzwɜːðɪ/ *a.* digne d'éloges.

pram /præm/ *n.* voiture d'enfant *f.*, landau *m.*

prance /prɑːns/ *v.i.* caracoler.

prank /præŋk/ *n.* farce *f.*

prattle /'prætl/ *v.i.* jaser.

prawn /prɔːn/ *n.* crevette rose *f.*

pray /preɪ/ *v.i.* prier.

prayer /preə(r)/ *n.* prière *f.*

pre- /priː/ *pref.* pré-.

preach /priːtʃ/ *v.t./i.* prêcher. **~ at** *or* **to,** prêcher. **~er** *n.* prédicateur *m.*

preamble /priː'æmbl/ *n.* préambule *m.*

pre-arrange /priːə'reɪndʒ/ *v.t.* fixer à l'avance.

precarious /prɪ'keərɪəs/ *a.* précaire.

precaution /prɪ'kɔːʃn/ *n.* précaution *f.* **~ary** *a.* de précaution.

preced|e /prɪ'siːd/ *v.t.* précéder. **~ing** *a.* précédent.

precedence /'presɪdəns/ *n.* priorité *f.*; (*in rank*) préséance *f.*

precedent /'presɪdənt/ *n.* précédent *m.*

precept /'priːsept/ *n.* précepte *m.*

precinct /'priːsɪŋkt/ *n.* enceinte *f.*; (*pedestrian area*) zone *f.*; (*district: Amer.*) circonscription *f.*

precious /'preʃəs/ *a.* précieux. ● *adv.* (*very: fam.*) très.

precipice /'presɪpɪs/ *n.* (*geog.*) à-pic *m. invar.*; (*fig.*) précipice *m.*

precipitat|e /prɪ'sɪpɪteɪt/ *v.t.* (*person, event, chemical*) précipiter. ● *a.* /-ɪtət/ précipité. **~ion** /-'teɪʃn/ *n.* précipitation *f.*

précis /'preɪsiː/ *n. invar.* précis *m.*

precis|e /prɪ'saɪs/ *a.* précis; (*careful*) méticuleux. **~ely** *adv.* précisément. **~ion** /-'sɪʒn/ *n.* précision *f.*

preclude /prɪ'kluːd/ *v.t.* (*prevent*) empêcher; (*rule out*) exclure.

precocious /prɪ'kəuʃəs/ *a.* précoce.

preconc|eived /priːkən'siːvd/ *a.* préconçu. **~eption** *n.* préconception *f.*

pre-condition /priːkən'dɪʃn/ *n.* condition requise *f.*

predator /'predətə(r)/ *n.* prédateur *m.* **~y** *a.* rapace.

predecessor /'priːdɪsesə(r)/ *n.* prédécesseur *m.*

predicament /prɪ'dɪkəmənt/ *n.* mauvaise situation *or* passe *f.*

predict /prɪ'dɪkt/ *v.t.* prédire. **~able** *a.* prévisible. **~ion** /-kʃn/ *n.* prédiction *f.*

predispose /priːdɪ'spəuz/ *v.t.* prédisposer (**to do,** à faire).

predominant /prɪ'dɒmɪnənt/ *a.* prédominant. **~ly** *adv.* pour la plupart.

predominate /prɪ'dɒmɪneɪt/ *v.i.* prédominer.

pre-eminent /priː'emɪnənt/ *a.* prééminent.

pre-empt /priː'empt/ *v.t.* (*buy*) acquérir d'avance; (*stop*) prévenir. **~ive** *a.* preventief.

preen /priːn/ *v.t.* (*bird*) lisser. **~ o.s.,** (*person*) se bichonner.

prefab /'priːfæb/ *n.* (*fam.*) bâtiment préfabriqué *m.* **~ricated** /-'fæbrɪkeɪtɪd/ *a.* préfabriqué.

preface /'prefɪs/ *n.* préface *f.*

prefect /'pri:fekt/ n. (*pupil*) élève chargé(e) de la discipline m.(f.); (*official*) préfet m.

prefer /prɪ'fɜ:(r)/ v.t. (*p.t.* **preferred**) préférer (**to do**, faire). **~able** /'prefrəbl/ a. préférable. **~ably** adv. de préférence.

preferen|ce /'prefrəns/ n. préférence f. **~tial** /-ə'renʃl/ a. préférentiel.

prefix /'pri:fɪks/ n. préfixe m.

pregnan|t /'pregnənt/ a. (*woman*) enceinte; (*animal*) pleine. **~cy** n. (*of woman*) grossesse f.

prehistoric /pri:hɪ'stɒrɪk/ a. préhistorique.

prejudge /pri:'dʒʌdʒ/ v.t. préjuger de; (*person*) juger d'avance.

prejudice /'predʒudɪs/ n. préjugé(s) m. (*pl.*); (*harm*) préjudice m. ● v.t. (*claim*) porter préjudice à; (*person*) prévenir. **~d** a. partial; (*person*) qui a des préjugés.

preliminar|y /prɪ'lɪmɪnərɪ/ a. préliminaire. **~ies** n. pl. préliminaires m. pl.

prelude /'prelju:d/ n. prélude m.

pre-marital /pri:'mærɪtl/ a. avant le mariage.

premature /'premətjʊə(r)/ a. prématuré.

premeditated /pri:'medɪteɪtɪd/ a. prémédité.

premier /'premɪə(r)/ a. premier. ● n. premier ministre m.

première /'premɪeə(r)/ n. première f.

premises /'premɪsɪz/ n. pl. locaux m. pl. **on the ~**, sur les lieux.

premiss /'premɪs/ n. prémisse f.

premium /'pri:mɪəm/ n. prime f. **be at a ~**, faire prime.

premonition /pri:mə'nɪʃn/ n. prémonition f., pressentiment m.

preoccup|ation /pri:ɒkjʊ'peɪʃn/ n. préoccupation f. **~ied** /-'ɒkjʊpaɪd/ a. préoccupé.

prep /prep/ n. (*work*) devoirs m.pl. **~ school** = **preparatory school**.

preparation /prepə'reɪʃn/ n. préparation f. **~s**, préparatifs m. pl.

preparatory /prɪ'pærətrɪ/ a. préparatoire. **~ school**, école primaire privée f.; (*Amer.*) école secondaire privée f.

prepare /prɪ'peə(r)/ v.t./i. (se) préparer (**for**, à). **be ~d for**, (*expect*) s'attendre à **~d to**, prêt à.

prepay /pri:'peɪ/ v.t. (*p.t.* **-paid**) payer d'avance.

preponderance /prɪ'pɒndərəns/ n. prédominance f.

preposition /prepə'zɪʃn/ n. préposition f.

preposterous /prɪ'pɒstərəs/ a. absurde, ridicule.

prerequisite /pri:'rekwɪzɪt/ n. condition préalable f.

prerogative /prɪ'rɒgətɪv/ n. prérogative f.

Presbyterian /prezbɪ'tɪərɪən/ a. & n. presbytérien(ne) (m. (f.)).

prescri|be /prɪ'skraɪb/ v.t. prescrire. **~ption** /-ɪpʃn/ n. prescription f.; (*med.*) ordonnance f.

presence /'prezns/ n. présence f. **~ of mind**, présence d'esprit f.

present[1] /'preznt/ a. présent. ● n. présent m. **at ~**, à présent. **for the ~**, pour le moment. **~-day** a. actuel.

present[2] /'preznt/ n. (*gift*) cadeau m.

present[3] /prɪ'zent/ v.t. présenter; (*film, concert, etc.*) donner. **~ s.o. with**, offrir à qn. **~able** a. présentable. **~ation** /prezn'teɪʃn/ n. présentation f. **~er** n. présentateur, -trice m., f.

presently /'prezntlɪ/ adv. bientôt; (*now*: *Amer.*) en ce moment.

preservative /prɪ'zɜ:vətɪv/ n. (*culin.*) agent de conservation m.

preserv|e /prɪ'zɜ:v/ v.t. préserver; (*maintain & culin.*) conserver. ● n. réserve f.; (*fig.*) domaine m.; (*jam*) confiture f. **~ation** /prezə'veɪʃn/ n. conservation f.

preside /prɪ'zaɪd/ v.i. présider. **~ over**, présider.

presiden|t /'prezɪdənt/ n. président(e) m. (f.). **~cy** n. présidence f. **~tial** /-'denʃl/ a. présidentiel.

press /pres/ v.t./i. (*button etc.*) appuyer (sur); (*squeeze*) presser; (*iron*) repasser; (*pursue*) poursuivre. ● n. (*newspapers, machine*) presse f.; (*for wine*) pressoir m. **be ~ed for**, (*time etc.*) manquer de. **~ for sth.**, faire pression pour avoir qch. **~ s.o. to do sth.**, pousser qn. à faire qch. **~ conference/cutting**, conférence/coupure de presse f. **~ on**, continuer (**with sth.**, qch.). **~ release**, communiqué de presse m. **~-stud** n. bouton-pression m. **~-up** n. traction f.

pressing /'presɪŋ/ a. pressant.

pressure /'preʃə(r)/ n. pression f. ● v.t. faire pression sur. **~-cooker**

n. cocotte-minute *f.* **~ group,** groupe de pression *m.*

pressurize /'preʃəraɪz/ *v.t.* (*cabin etc.*) pressuriser; (*person*) faire pression sur.

prestige /pre'sti:ʒ/ *n.* prestige *m.*

prestigious /pre'stɪdʒəs/ *a.* prestigieux.

presumably /prɪ'zju:məblɪ/ *adv.* vraisemblablement.

presum|e /prɪ'zju:m/ *v.t.* (*suppose*) présumer. **~e to,** (*venture*) se permettre de. **~ption** /-'zʌmpʃn/ *n.* présomption *f.*

presumptuous /prɪ'zʌmptʃʊəs/ *a.* présomptueux.

pretence, (*Amer.*) **pretense** /prɪ'tens/ *n.* feinte *f.*, simulation *f.*; (*claim*) prétention *f.*; (*pretext*) prétexte *m.*

pretend /prɪ'tend/ *v.t./i.* faire semblant (**to do,** de faire). **~ to,** (*lay claim to*) prétendre à.

pretentious /prɪ'tenʃəs/ *a.* prétentieux.

pretext /'pri:tekst/ *n.* prétexte *m.*

pretty /'prɪtɪ/ *a.* (**-ier, -iest**) joli. ● *adv.* assez. **~ much,** presque.

prevail /prɪ'veɪl/ *v.i.* prédominer; (*win*) prévaloir. **~ on,** persuader (**to do,** de faire). **~ing** *a.* actuel; (*wind*) dominant.

prevalen|t /'prevələnt/ *a.* répandu. **~ce** *n.* fréquence *f.*

prevent /prɪ'vent/ *v.t.* empêcher (**from doing,** de faire). **~able** *a.* évitable. **~ion** /-enʃn/ *n.* prévention *f.* **~ive** *a.* préventif.

preview /'pri:vju:/ *n.* avant-première *f.*; (*fig.*) aperçu *m.*

previous /'pri:vɪəs/ *a.* précédent, antérieur. **~ to,** avant. **~ly** *adv.* précédemment, auparavant.

pre-war /'pri:wɔ:(r)/ *a.* d'avant-guerre.

prey /preɪ/ *n.* proie *f.* ● *v.i.* **~ on,** faire sa proie de; (*worry*) préoccuper. **bird of ~,** rapace *m.*

price /praɪs/ *n.* prix *m.* ● *v.t.* fixer le prix de. **~less** *a.* inestimable; (*amusing*: *sl.*) impayable.

pricey /'praɪsɪ/ *a.* (*fam.*) coûteux.

prick /prɪk/ *v.t.* (*with pin etc.*) piquer. ● *n.* piqûre *f.* **~ up one's ears,** dresser l'oreille.

prickl|e /'prɪkl/ *n.* piquant *m.*; (*sensation*) picotement *m.* **~y** *a.* piquant; (*person*) irritable.

pride /praɪd/ *n.* orgueil *m.*; (*satisfaction*) fierté *f.* ● *v. pr.* **~ o.s. on,** s'enorgueillir de. **~ of place,** place d'honneur *f.*

priest /pri:st/ *n.* prêtre *m.* **~hood** *n.* sacerdoce *m.* **~ly** *a.* sacerdotal.

prig /prɪg/ *n.* petit saint *m.*, pharisien(ne) *m.* (*f.*). **~gish** *a.* hypocrite.

prim /prɪm/ *a.* (**primmer, primmest**) guindé, méticuleux.

primar|y /'praɪmərɪ/ *a.* (*school, elections, etc.*) primaire; (*chief, basic*) premier, fondamental. ● *n.* (*pol.*: *Amer.*) primaire *m.* **~ily** *Amer.* /-'merɪlɪ/ *adv.* essentiellement.

prime[1] /praɪm/ *a.* principal, premier; (*first-rate*) excellent. **P~ Minister,** Premier Ministre *m.* **the ~ of life,** la force de l'âge.

prime[2] /praɪm/ *v.t.* (*pump, gun*) amorcer; (*surface*) apprêter. **~r**[1] /-ə(r)/ *n.* (*paint etc.*) apprêt *m.*

primer[2] /'praɪmə(r)/ *n.* (*school-book*) premier livre *m.*

primeval /praɪ'mi:vl/ *a.* primitif.

primitive /'prɪmɪtɪv/ *a.* primitif.

primrose /'prɪmrəʊz/ *n.* primevère (jaune) *f.*

prince /prɪns/ *n.* prince *m.* **~ly** *a.* princier.

princess /prɪn'ses/ *n.* princesse *f.*

principal /'prɪnsəpl/ *a.* principal. ● *n.* (*of school etc.*) direc|teur, -trice *m., f.* **~ly** *adv.* principalement.

principle /'prɪnsəpl/ *n.* principe *m.* **in/on ~,** en/par principe.

print /prɪnt/ *v.t.* imprimer; (*write in capitals*) écrire en majuscules. ● *n.* (*of foot etc.*) empreinte *f.*; (*letters*) caractères *m. pl.*; (*photograph*) épreuve *f.*; (*engraving*) gravure *f.* **in ~,** disponible. **out of ~,** épuisé. **~-out** *n.* listage *m.* **~ed matter,** imprimés *m. pl.*

print|er /'prɪntə(r)/ *n.* (*person*) imprimeur *m.*; (*comput.*) imprimante *f.* **~ing** *n.* impression *f.*

prior[1] /'praɪə(r)/ *a.* précédent. **~ to,** *prep.* avant (de).

prior[2] /'praɪə(r)/ *n.* (*relig.*) prieur *m.* **~y** *n.* prieuré *m.*

priority /praɪ'ɒrətɪ/ *n.* priorité *f.* **take ~,** avoir la priorité (**over,** sur).

prise /praɪz/ *v.t.* forcer. **~ open,** ouvrir en forçant.

prism /'prɪzəm/ *n.* prisme *m.*

prison /'prɪzn/ *n.* prison *f.* **~er** *n.* prisonn|ier, -ière *m., f.* **~ officer,** gardien(ne) de prison *m.* (*f.*).

pristine /'prɪstiːn/ *a.* primitif; (*condition*) parfait.

privacy /'prɪvəsɪ/ *n.* intimité *f.*, solitude *f.*

private /'praɪvɪt/ *a.* privé; (*confidential*) personnel; (*lessons, house, etc.*) particulier; (*ceremony*) intime. ● *n.* (*soldier*) simple soldat *m.* **in ~,** en privé; (*of ceremony*) dans l'intimité. **~ly** *adv.* en privé; dans l'intimité; (*inwardly*) intérieurement.

privation /praɪ'veɪʃn/ *n.* privation *f.*

privet /'prɪvɪt/ *n.* (*bot.*) troène *m.*

privilege /'prɪvɪlɪdʒ/ *n.* privilège *m.* **~d** *a.* privilégié. **be ~d to,** avoir le privilège de.

privy /'prɪvɪ/ *a.* **~ to,** au fait de.

prize /praɪz/ *n.* prix *m.* ● *a.* (*entry etc.*) primé; (*fool etc.*) parfait. ● *v.t.* (*value*) priser. **~-fighter** *n.* boxeur professionnel *m.* **~-winner** *n.* lauréat(e) *m.* (*f.*); (*in lottery etc.*) gagnant(e) *m.* (*f.*).

pro /prəʊ/ *n.* **the ~s and cons,** le pour et le contre.

pro- /prəʊ/ *pref.* pro-.

probab|le /'prɒbəbl/ *a.* probable. **~ility** /-'bɪlətɪ/ *n.* probabilité *f.* **~ly** *adv.* probablement.

probation /prə'beɪʃn/ *n.* (*testing*) essai *m.*; (*jurid.*) liberté surveillée *f.* **~ary** *a.* d'essai.

probe /prəʊb/ *n.* (*device*) sonde *f.*; (*fig.*) enquête *f.* ● *v.t.* sonder. ● *v.i.* **~ into,** sonder.

problem /'prɒbləm/ *n.* problème *m.* ● *a.* difficile. **~atic** /-'mætɪk/ *a.* problématique.

procedure /prə'siːdʒə(r)/ *n.* procédure *f.*; (*way of doing sth.*) démarche à suivre *f.*

proceed /prə'siːd/ *v.i.* (*go*) aller, avancer; (*pass*) passer (**to,** à); (*act*) procéder. **~ (with),** (*continue*) continuer. **~ to do,** se mettre à faire. **~ing** *n.* procédé *m.*

proceedings /prə'siːdɪŋz/ *n. pl.* (*discussions*) débats *m. pl.*; (*meeting*) réunion *f.*; (*report*) actes *m. pl.*; (*jurid.*) poursuites *f. pl.*

proceeds /'prəʊsiːdz/ *n. pl.* (*profits*) produit *m.*, bénéfices *m. pl.*

process /'prəʊses/ *n.* processus *m.*; (*method*) procédé *m.* ● *v.t.* (*material, data*) traiter. **in ~,** en cours. **in the ~ of doing,** en train de faire.

procession /prə'seʃn/ *n.* défilé *m.*

procl|aim /prə'kleɪm/ *v.t.* proclamer. **~amation** /prɒklə'meɪʃn/ *n.* proclamation *f.*

procrastinate /prə'kræstɪneɪt/ *v.i.* différer, tergiverser.

procreation /prəʊkrɪ'eɪʃn/ *n.* procréation *f.*

procure /prə'kjʊə(r)/ *v.t.* obtenir.

prod /prɒd/ *v.t./i.* (*p.t.* **prodded**) pousser. ● *n.* poussée *f.*, coup *m.*

prodigal /'prɒdɪgl/ *a.* prodigue.

prodigious /prə'dɪdʒəs/ *a.* prodigieux.

prodigy /'prɒdɪdʒɪ/ *n.* prodige *m.*

produc|e[1] /prə'djuːs/ *v.t./i.* produire; (*bring out*) sortir; (*show*) présenter; (*cause*) provoquer; (*theatre, TV*) mettre en scène; (*radio*) réaliser; (*cinema*) produire. **~er** *n.* metteur en scène *m.*; réalisateur *m.*; producteur *m.* /-'dʌkʃn/. **~tion** /-'dʌkʃn/ *n.* production *f.*; mise en scène *f.*; réalisation *f.*

produce[2] /'prɒdjuːs/ *n.* (*food etc.*) produits *m. pl.*

product /'prɒdʌkt/ *n.* produit *m.*

productiv|e /prə'dʌktɪv/ *a.* productif. **~ity** /prɒdʌk'tɪvətɪ/ *n.* productivité *f.*

profan|e /prə'feɪn/ *a.* sacrilège; (*secular*) profane. **~ity** /-'fænətɪ/ *n.* (*oath*) juron *m.*

profess /prə'fes/ *v.t.* professer. **~ to do,** prétendre faire.

profession /prə'feʃn/ *n.* profession *f.* **~al** *a.* professionnel; (*of high quality*) de professionnel; (*person*) qui exerce une profession libérale; *n.* professionnel(le) *m.* (*f.*).

professor /prə'fesə(r)/ *n.* professeur (titulaire d'une chaire) *m.*

proficien|t /prə'fɪʃnt/ *a.* compétent. **~cy** *n.* compétence *f.*

profile /'prəʊfaɪl/ *n.* profil *m.*

profit /'prɒfɪt/ *n.* profit *m.*, bénéfice *m.* ● *v.i.* (*p.t.* **profited**). **~ by,** tirer profit de. **~able** *a.* rentable.

profound /prə'faʊnd/ *a.* profond. **~ly** *adv.* profondément.

profus|e /prə'fjuːs/ *a.* abondant. **~e in,** (*lavish in*) prodigue de. **~ely** *adv.* en abondance; (*apologize*) avec effusion. **~ion** /-ʒn/ *n.* profusion *f.*

progeny /'prɒdʒənɪ/ *n.* progéniture *f.*

program /'prəʊgræm/ *n.* (*Amer.*) = **programme. (computer) ~,** programme *m.* ● *v.t.* (*p.t.* **programmed**) programmer. **~mer** *n.* programmeu|r, -se *m.*, *f.* **~ming** *n.* (*on computer*) programmation *f.*

programme /'prəʊgræm/ *n.* programme *m.*; (*broadcast*) émission *f.*

progress[1] /'prəʊgres/ *n.* progrès *m.* (*pl.*). **in ~**, en cours. **make ~**, faire des progrès. **~ report**, compterendu *m.*

progress[2] /prə'gres/ *v.i.* (*advance, improve*) progresser. **~ion** /-ʃn/ *n.* progression *f.*

progressive /prə'gresɪv/ *a.* progressif; (*reforming*) progressiste. **~ly** *adv.* progressivement.

prohibit /prə'hɪbɪt/ *v.t.* interdire (**s.o. from doing**, à qn. de faire).

prohibitive /prə'hɪbətɪv/ *a.* (*price etc.*) prohibitif.

project[1] /prə'dʒekt/ *v.t.* projeter. ● *v.i.* (*jut out*) être en saillie. **~ion** /-kʃn/ *n.* projection *f.*; saillie *f.*

project[2] /'prɒdʒekt/ *n.* (*plan*) projet *m.*; (*undertaking*) entreprise *f.*; (*schol.*) dossier *m.*

projectile /prə'dʒektaɪl/ *n.* projectile *m.*

projector /prə'dʒektə(r)/ *n.* (*cinema etc.*) projecteur *m.*

proletari|at /prəʊlɪ'teərɪət/ *n.* prolétariat *m.* **~an** *a.* prolétarien; *n.* prolétaire *m./f.*

proliferat|e /prə'lɪfəreɪt/ *v.i.* proliférer. **~ion** /-'reɪʃn/ *n.* prolifération *f.*

prolific /prə'lɪfɪk/ *a.* prolifique.

prologue /'prəʊlɒg/ *n.* prologue *m.*

prolong /prə'lɒŋ/ *v.t.* prolonger.

promenade /prɒmə'nɑːd/ *n.* promenade *f.* ● *v.t./i.* (se) promener.

prominen|t /'prɒmɪnənt/ *a.* (*projecting*) proéminent; (*conspicuous*) bien en vue; (*fig.*) important. **~ce** *n.* proéminence *f.*; importance *f.* **~tly** *adv.* bien en vue.

promiscu|ous /prə'mɪskjʊəs/ *a.* qui a plusieurs partenaires; (*pej.*) de mœurs faciles. **~ity** /prɒmɪ-'skjuːətɪ/ *n.* les partenaires multiples; (*pej.*) liberté de mœurs *f.*

promis|e /'prɒmɪs/ *n.* promesse *f.* ● *v.t./i.* promettre. **~ing** *a.* prometteur; (*person*) qui promet.

promot|e /prə'məʊt/ *v.t.* promouvoir; (*advertise*) faire la promotion de. **~ion** /-'məʊʃn/ *n.* (*of person, sales, etc.*) promotion *f.*

prompt /prɒmpt/ *a.* rapide; (*punctual*) à l'heure, ponctuel. ● *adv.* (*on the dot*) pile. ● *v.t.* inciter; (*cause*) provoquer; (*theatre*) souffler (son rôle) à. **~er** *n.* souffleu|r, -se *m.*, *f.*

~ly *adv.* rapidement; ponctuellement. **~ness** *n.* rapidité *f.*

prone /prəʊn/ *a.* couché sur le ventre. **~ to**, prédisposé à.

prong /prɒŋ/ *n.* (*of fork*) dent *f.*

pronoun /'prəʊnaʊn/ *n.* pronom *m.*

pron|ounce /prə'naʊns/ *v.t.* prononcer. **~ouncement** *n.* déclaration *f.* **~unciation** /-ʌnsɪ'eɪʃn/ *n.* prononciation *f.*

pronounced /prə'naʊnst/ *a.* (*noticeable*) prononcé.

proof /pruːf/ *n.* (*evidence*) preuve *f.*; (*test, trial copy*) épreuve *f.*; (*of liquor*) teneur en alcool *f.* ● *a.* **~ against**, à l'épreuve de.

prop[1] /prɒp/ *n.* support *m.* ● *v.t.* (*p.t.* **propped**). **~ (up)**, (*support*) étayer; (*lean*) appuyer.

prop[2] /prɒp/ *n.* (*theatre, fam.*) accessoire *m.*

propaganda /prɒpə'gændə/ *n.* propagande *f.*

propagat|e /'prɒpəgeɪt/ *v.t./i.* (se) propager. **~ion** /-'geɪʃn/ *n.* propagation *f.*

propane /'prəʊpeɪn/ *n.* propane *m.*

propel /prə'pel/ *v.t.* (*p.t.* **propelled**) propulser. **~ling pencil**, porte-mine *m. invar.*

propeller /prə'pelə(r)/ *n.* hélice *f.*

proper /'prɒpə(r)/ *a.* correct, bon; (*seemly*) convenable; (*real*) vrai; (*thorough: fam.*) parfait. **~ noun**, nom propre *m.* **~ly** *adv.* correctement, comme il faut; (*rightly*) avec raison.

property /'prɒpətɪ/ *n.* propriété *f.*; (*things owned*) biens *m. pl.*, propriété *f.* ● *a.* immobilier, foncier.

prophecy /'prɒfəsɪ/ *n.* prophétie *f.*

prophesy /'prɒfɪsaɪ/ *v.t./i.* prophétiser. **~ that**, prédire que.

prophet /'prɒfɪt/ *n.* prophète *m.* **~ic** /prə'fetɪk/ *a.* prophétique.

proportion /prə'pɔːʃn/ *n.* (*ratio, dimension*) proportion *f.*; (*amount*) partie *f.* **~al**, **~ate** *adjs.* proportionnel.

proposal /prə'pəʊzl/ *n.* proposition *f.*; (*of marriage*) demande en mariage *f.*

propos|e /prə'pəʊz/ *v.t.* proposer. ● *v.i.* **~e to**, faire une demande en mariage à. **~e to do**, se proposer de faire. **~ition** /prɒpə'zɪʃn/ *n.* proposition *f.*; (*matter: fam.*) affaire *f.*; *v.t.* (*fam.*) faire des propositions malhonnêtes à.

propound /prə'paʊnd/ v.t. (theory etc.) proposer.

proprietor /prə'praɪətə(r)/ n. propriétaire m./f.

propriety /prə'praɪətɪ/ n. (correct behaviour) bienséance f.

propulsion /prə'pʌlʃn/ n. propulsion f.

prosaic /prə'zeɪk/ a. prosaïque.

proscribe /prə'skraɪb/ v.t. proscrire.

prose /prəʊz/ n. prose f.; (translation) thème m.

prosecut|e /'prɒsɪkjuːt/ v.t. poursuivre. ~ion /-'kjuːʃn/ n. poursuites f. pl. ~or n. procureur m.

prospect[1] /'prɒspekt/ n. perspective f.; (chance) espoir m. **a job with ~s,** un travail avec des perspectives d'avenir.

prospect[2] /prə'spekt/ v.t./i. prospecter. ~or n. prospecteur m.

prospective /prə'spektɪv/ a. (future) futur; (possible) éventuel.

prospectus /prə'spektəs/ n. prospectus m.; (univ.) guide m.

prosper /'prɒspə(r)/ v.i. prospérer.

prosper|ous /'prɒspərəs/ a. prospère. ~ity /-'sperətɪ/ n. prospérité f.

prostate /'prɒsteɪt/ n. prostate f.

prostitut|e /'prɒstɪtjuːt/ n. prostituée f. ~ion /-'tjuːʃn/ n. prostitution f.

prostrate /'prɒstreɪt/ a. (prone) à plat ventre; (submissive) prosterné; (exhausted) prostré.

protagonist /prə'tægənɪst/ n. protagoniste m.

protect /prə'tekt/ v.t. protéger. ~ion /-kʃn/ n. protection f. ~or n. protec|teur, -trice m., f.

protective /prə'tektɪv/ a. protecteur; (clothes) de protection.

protégé /'prɒtɪʒeɪ/ n. protégé m. ~e n. protégée f.

protein /'prəʊtiːn/ n. protéine f.

protest[1] /'prəʊtest/ n. protestation f. **under ~,** en protestant.

protest[2] /prə'test/ v.t./i. protester. ~er n. (pol.) manifestant(e) m. (f.).

Protestant /'prɒtɪstənt/ a. & n. protestant(e) (m. (f.)).

protocol /'prəʊtəkɒl/ n. protocole m.

prototype /'prəʊtətaɪp/ n. prototype m.

protract /prə'trækt/ v.t. prolonger, faire traîner. ~ed a. prolongé.

protractor /prə'træktə(r)/ n. (for measuring) rapporteur m.

protrude /prə'truːd/ v.i. dépasser.

proud /praʊd/ a. (-er, -est) fier, orgueilleux. ~ly adv. fièrement.

prove /pruːv/ v.t. prouver. ● v.i. ~ (to be) easy/etc., se révéler facile/ etc. ~ o.s., faire ses preuves. ~n a. prouvé.

proverb /'prɒvɜːb/ n. proverbe m. ~ial /prə'vɜːbɪəl/ a. proverbial.

provide /prə'vaɪd/ v.t. fournir (s.o. with sth., qch. à qn.). ● v.i. ~ for, (allow for) prévoir; (guard against) parer à; (person) pourvoir aux besoins de.

provided /prə'vaɪdɪd/ conj. ~ that, à condition que.

providence /'prɒvɪdəns/ n. providence f.

providing /prə'vaɪdɪŋ/ conj. = provided.

provinc|e /'prɒvɪns/ n. province f.; (fig.) compétence f. ~ial /prə'vɪnʃl/ a. & n. provincial(e) (m. (f.)).

provision /prə'vɪʒn/ n. (stock) provision f.; (supplying) fourniture f.; (stipulation) disposition f. ~s, (food) provisions f. pl.

provisional /prə'vɪʒənl/ a. provisoire. ~ly adv. provisoirement.

proviso /prə'vaɪzəʊ/ n. (pl. -os) condition f., stipulation f.

provo|ke /prə'vəʊk/ v.t. provoquer. ~cation /prɒvə'keɪʃn/ n. provocation f. ~cative /-'vɒkətɪv/ a. provocant.

prow /praʊ/ n. proue f.

prowess /'praʊɪs/ n. prouesse f.

prowl /praʊl/ v.i. rôder. ● n. **be on the ~,** rôder. ~er n. rôdeu|r, -se m., f.

proximity /prɒk'sɪmətɪ/ n. proximité f.

proxy /'prɒksɪ/ n. **by ~,** par procuration.

prud|e /pruːd/ n. prude f. ~ish a. prude.

pruden|t /'pruːdnt/ a. prudent. ~ce n. prudence f. ~tly adv. prudemment.

prune[1] /pruːn/ n. pruneau m.

prune[2] /pruːn/ v.t. (cut) tailler.

pry[1] /praɪ/ v.i. être indiscret. ~ into, fourrer son nez dans.

pry[2] /praɪ/ v.t. (Amer.) = prise.

psalm /sɑːm/ n. psaume m.

pseudo- /'sjuːdəʊ/ pref. pseudo-.

pseudonym /'sjuːdənɪm/ n. pseudonyme m.

psoriasis /sə'raɪəsɪs/ n. psoriasis m.

psyche /ˈsaɪkɪ/ *n.* psyché *f.*

psychiatr|y /saɪˈkaɪətrɪ/ *n.* psychiatrie *f.* ~**ic** /-ɪˈætrɪk/ *a.* psychiatrique. ~**ist** *n.* psychiatre *m./f.*

psychic /ˈsaɪkɪk/ *a.* (*phenomenon etc.*) métapsychique; (*person*) doué de télépathie.

psychoanalys|e /saɪkəʊˈænəlaɪz/ *v.t.* psychanalyser. ~**t** /-ɪst/ *n.* psychanalyste *m./f.*

psychoanalysis /saɪkəʊəˈnælɪsɪs/ *n.* psychanalyse *f.*

psycholog|y /saɪˈkɒlədʒɪ/ *n.* psychologie *f.* ~**ical** /-əˈlɒdʒɪkl/ *a.* psychologique. ~**ist** *n.* psychologue *m./f.*

psychopath /ˈsaɪkəʊpæθ/ *n.* psychopathe *m./f.*

psychosomatic /saɪkəʊsəˈmætɪk/ *a.* psychosomatique.

psychotherap|y /saɪkəʊˈθerəpɪ/ *n.* psychothérapie *f.* ~**ist** *n.* psychothérapeute *m./f.*

pub /pʌb/ *n.* pub *m.*

puberty /ˈpjuːbətɪ/ *n.* puberté *f.*

public /ˈpʌblɪk/ *a.* public; (*library etc.*) municipal. **in** ~, en public. ~ **address system,** sonorisation *f.* (*dans un lieu public*). ~ **house,** pub *m.* ~ **relations,** relations publiques *f. pl.* ~ **school,** école privée *f.*; (*Amer.*) école publique *f.* ~ **servant,** fonctionnaire *m./f.* ~**-spirited** *a.* dévoué au bien public. ~ **transport,** transports en commun *m. pl.* ~**ly** *adv.* publiquement.

publican /ˈpʌblɪkən/ *n.* patron(ne) de pub *m.* (*f.*).

publication /pʌblɪˈkeɪʃn/ *n.* publication *f.*

publicity /pʌbˈlɪsətɪ/ *n.* publicité *f.*

publicize /ˈpʌblɪsaɪz/ *v.t.* faire connaître au public.

publish /ˈpʌblɪʃ/ *v.t.* publier. ~**er** *n.* éditeur *m.* ~**ing** *n.* édition *f.*

puck /pʌk/ *n.* (*ice hockey*) palet *m.*

pucker /ˈpʌkə(r)/ *v.t./i.* (se) plisser.

pudding /ˈpʊdɪŋ/ *n.* dessert *m.*; (*steamed*) pudding *m.* **black** ~, boudin *m.* **rice** ~, riz au lait *m.*

puddle /ˈpʌdl/ *n.* flaque d'eau *f.*

pudgy /ˈpʌdʒɪ/ *a.* (**-ier, -iest**) dodu.

puerile /ˈpjʊəraɪl/ *a.* puéril.

puff /pʌf/ *n.* bouffée *f.* ● *v.t./i.* souffler. ~ **at,** (*cigar*) tirer sur. ~ **out,** (*swell*) (se) gonfler.

puffy /ˈpʌfɪ/ *a.* gonflé.

pugnacious /pʌgˈneɪʃəs/ *a.* batailleur, combatif.

pug-nosed /ˈpʌgnəʊzd/ *a.* camus.

pull /pʊl/ *v.t./i.* tirer; (*muscle*) se froisser. ● *n.* traction *f.*; (*fig.*) attraction *f.*; (*influence*) influence *f.* **give a** ~, tirer. ~ **a face,** faire une grimace. ~ **one's weight,** faire sa part du travail. ~ **s.o.'s leg,** faire marcher qn. ~ **apart,** mettre en morceaux. ~ **away,** (*auto.*) démarrer. ~ **back** *or* **out,** (*withdraw*) (se) retirer. ~ **down,** baisser; (*building*) démolir. ~ **in,** (*enter*) entrer; (*stop*) s'arrêter. ~ **off,** enlever; (*fig.*) réussir. ~ **out,** (*from bag etc.*) sortir; (*extract*) arracher; (*auto.*) déboîter. ~ **over,** (*auto.*) se ranger. ~ **round** *or* **through,** s'en tirer. ~ **o.s. together,** se ressaisir. ~ **up,** remonter; (*uproot*) déraciner; (*auto.*) (s')arrêter.

pulley /ˈpʊlɪ/ *n.* poulie *f.*

pullover /ˈpʊləʊvə(r)/ *n.* pull(-over) *m.*

pulp /pʌlp/ *n.* (*of fruit*) pulpe *f.*; (*for paper*) pâte à papier *f.*

pulpit /ˈpʊlpɪt/ *n.* chaire *f.*

pulsate /pʌlˈseɪt/ *v.i.* battre.

pulse /pʌls/ *n.* (*med.*) pouls *m.*

pulverize /ˈpʌlvəraɪz/ *v.t.* (*grind, defeat*) pulvériser.

pummel /ˈpʌml/ *v.t.* (*p.t.* **pummelled**) bourrer de coups.

pump[1] /pʌmp/ *n.* pompe *f.* ● *v.t./i.* pomper; (*person*) soutirer des renseignements à. ~ **up,** gonfler.

pump[2] /pʌmp/ *n.* (*plimsoll*) tennis *m.*; (*for dancing*) escarpin *m.*

pumpkin /ˈpʌmpkɪn/ *n.* potiron *m.*

pun /pʌn/ *n.* jeu de mots *m.*

punch[1] /pʌntʃ/ *v.t.* donner un coup de poing à; (*perforate*) poinçonner; (*a hole*) faire. ● *n.* coup de poing *m.*; (*vigour: sl.*) punch *m.*; (*device*) poinçonneuse *f.* ~**-drunk** *a.* sonné. ~**-line,** chute *f.* ~**-up** *n.* (*fam.*) bagarre *f.*

punch[2] /pʌntʃ/ *n.* (*drink*) punch *m.*

punctual /ˈpʌŋktʃʊəl/ *a.* à l'heure; (*habitually*) ponctuel. ~**ity** /-ˈælətɪ/ *n.* ponctualité *f.* ~**ly** *adv.* à l'heure; ponctuellement.

punctuat|e /ˈpʌŋktʃʊeɪt/ *v.t.* ponctuer. ~**ion** /-ˈeɪʃn/ *n.* ponctuation *f.*

puncture /ˈpʌŋktʃə(r)/ *n.* (*in tyre*) crevaison *f.* ● *v.t./i.* crever.

pundit /ˈpʌndɪt/ *n.* expert *m.*

pungent /ˈpʌndʒənt/ *a.* âcre.

punish /'pʌnɪʃ/ v.t. punir (**for sth.**, de qch.). **~able** a. punissable (**by**, de). **~ment** n. punition f.

punitive /'pju:nɪtɪv/ a. punitif.

punk /pʌŋk/ n. (*music, fan*) punk m.; (*person: Amer., fam.*) salaud m.

punt¹ /pʌnt/ n. (*boat*) bachot m.

punt² /pʌnt/ v.i. (*bet*) parier.

puny /'pju:nɪ/ a. (-ier, -iest) chétif.

pup(py) /'pʌp(ɪ)/ n. chiot m.

pupil /'pju:pl/ n. (*person*) élève m./f.; (*of eye*) pupille f.

puppet /'pʌpɪt/ n. marionnette f.

purchase /'pɜ:tʃəs/ v.t. acheter (**from s.o.**, à qn.). ● n. achat m. **~r** /-ə(r)/ n. acheteu|r, -se m., f.

pur|e /pjʊə(r)/ a. (-er, -est) pur. **~ely** adv. purement. **~ity** n. pureté f.

purgatory /'pɜ:gətrɪ/ n. purgatoire m.

purge /pɜ:dʒ/ v.t. purger (**of**, de). ● n. purge f.

purif|y /'pjʊərɪfaɪ/ v.t. purifier. **~ication** /-ɪ'keɪʃn/ n. purification f.

purist /'pjʊərɪst/ n. puriste m./f.

puritan /'pjʊərɪtən/ n. puritain(e) m. (f.). **~ical** /-'tænɪkl/ a. puritain.

purple /'pɜ:pl/ a. & n. violet (m.).

purport /pə'pɔ:t/ v.t. **~ to be**, (*claim*) prétendre être.

purpose /'pɜ:pəs/ n. but m.; (*fig.*) résolution f. **on ~**, exprès. **~-built** a. construit spécialement. **to no ~**, sans résultat.

purr /pɜ:(r)/ n. ronronnement m. ● v.i. ronronner.

purse /pɜ:s/ n. porte-monnaie m. invar.; (*handbag: Amer.*) sac à main m. ● v.t. (*lips*) pincer.

pursue /pə'sju:/ v.t. poursuivre. **~r** /-ə(r)/ n. poursuivant(e) m. (f.).

pursuit /pə'sju:t/ n. poursuite f.; (*fig.*) activité f., occupation f.

purveyor /pə'veɪə(r)/ n. fournisseur m.

pus /pʌs/ n. pus m.

push /pʊʃ/ v.t./i. pousser; (*button*) appuyer sur; (*thrust*) enfoncer; (*recommend: fam.*) proposer avec insistance. ● n. poussée f.; (*effort*) gros effort m.; (*drive*) dynamisme m. **be ~ed for,** (*time etc.*) manquer de. **be ~ing thirty/** etc., (*fam.*) friser la trentaine/etc. **give the ~ to,** (*sl.*) flanquer à la porte. **~ s.o. around,** bousculer qn. **~ back,** repousser. **~-chair** n. poussette f. **~er** n. revendeu|r, -se (de drogue) m., f. **~ off,** (*sl.*) filer. **~ on,** continuer. **~-over**

n. jeu d'enfant m. **~ up,** (*lift*) relever; (*prices*) faire monter. **~-up** n. (*Amer.*) traction f. **~y** a. (*fam.*) autoritaire.

pushing /'pʊʃɪŋ/ a. arriviste.

puss /pʊs/ n. (*cat*) minet(te) m. (f.).

put /pʊt/ v.t./i. (*p.t.* put, *pres. p.* putting) mettre, placer, poser; (*question*) poser. **~ the damage at a million,** estimer les dégâts à un million; **I'd ~ it at a thousand,** je dirais un millier. **~ sth. tactfully,** dire qch. avec tact. **~ across,** communiquer. **~ away,** ranger; (*fig.*) enfermer. **~ back,** remettre; (*delay*) retarder. **~ by,** mettre de côté. **~ down,** (dé)poser; (*write*) inscrire; (*pay*) verser; (*suppress*) réprimer. **~ forward,** (*plan*) soumettre. **~ in,** (*insert*) introduire; (*fix*) installer; (*submit*) soumettre. **~ in for,** faire une demande de. **~ off,** (*postpone*) renvoyer à plus tard; (*disconcert*) déconcerter; (*displease*) rebuter. **~ s.o. off sth.,** dégoûter qn. de qch. **~ on,** (*clothes, radio*) mettre; (*light*) allumer; (*speed, accent, weight*) prendre. **~ out,** sortir; (*stretch*) (é)tendre; (*extinguish*) éteindre; (*disconcert*) déconcerter; (*inconvenience*) déranger. **~ up,** lever, remonter; (*building*) construire; (*notice*) mettre; (*price*) augmenter; (*guest*) héberger; (*offer*) offrir. **~-up job,** coup monté m. **~ up with,** supporter.

putt /pʌt/ n. (*golf*) putt m.

putter /'pʌtə(r)/ v.i. (*Amer.*) bricoler.

putty /'pʌtɪ/ n. mastic m.

puzzle /'pʌzl/ n. énigme f.; (*game*) casse-tête m. invar.; (*jigsaw*) puzzle m. ● v.t. rendre perplexe. ● v.i. se creuser la tête.

pygmy /'pɪgmɪ/ n. pygmée m.

pyjamas /pə'dʒɑ:məz/ n. pl. pyjama m.

pylon /'paɪlɒn/ n. pylône m.

pyramid /'pɪrəmɪd/ n. pyramide f.

Pyrenees /pɪrə'ni:z/ n. pl. **the ~**, les Pyrénées f. pl.

python /'paɪθn/ n. python m.

Q

quack¹ /kwæk/ n. (*of duck*) coin-coin m. invar.

quack [2] /kwæk/ *n.* charlatan *m.*

quad /kwɒd/ (*fam.*) = **quadrangle**, **quadruplet**.

quadrangle /'kwɒdræŋgl/ (*of college*) *n.* cour *f.*

quadruped /'kwɒdrʊped/ *n.* quadrupède *m.*

quadruple /kwɒ'dru:pl/ *a. & n.* quadruple (*m.*). ● *v.t./i.* quadrupler. **∼ts** /-plɪts/ *n. pl.* quadruplé(e)s *m.* (*f.*) *pl.*

quagmire /'kwægmaɪə(r)/ *n.* (*bog*) bourbier *m.*

quail /kweɪl/ *n.* (*bird*) caille *f.*

quaint /kweɪnt/ *a.* (**-er, -est**) pittoresque; (*old*) vieillot; (*odd*) bizarre. **∼ness** *n.* pittoresque *m.*

quake /kweɪk/ *v.i.* trembler. ● *n.* (*fam.*) tremblement de terre *m.*

Quaker /'kweɪkə(r)/ *n.* quaker(esse) *m.* (*f.*).

qualification /kwɒlɪfɪ'keɪʃn/ *n.* diplôme *m.*; (*ability*) compétence *f.*; (*fig.*) réserve *f.*, restriction *f.*

qualif|y /'kwɒlɪfaɪ/ *v.t.* qualifier; (*modify: fig.*) mettre des réserves à; (*statement*) nuancer. ● *v.i.* obtenir son diplôme (**as,** de); (*sport*) se qualifier; (*fig.*) remplir les conditions requises. **∼ied** *a.* diplômé; (*able*) qualifié (**to do,** pour faire); (*fig.*) conditionnel; (*success*) modéré. **∼ying** *a.* (*round*) éliminatoire; (*candidates*) qualifiés.

qualit|y /'kwɒlətɪ/ *n.* qualité *f.* **∼ative** /-ɪtətɪv/ *a.* qualitatif.

qualm /kwɑ:m/ *n.* scrupule *m.*

quandary /'kwɒndərɪ/ *n.* embarras *m.*, dilemme *m.*

quantit|y /'kwɒntətɪ/ *n.* quantité *f.* **∼ative** /-ɪtətɪv/ *a.* quantitatif.

quarantine /'kwɒrənti:n/ *n.* (*isolation*) quarantaine *f.*

quarrel /'kwɒrəl/ *n.* dispute *f.*, querelle *f.* ● *v.i.* (*p.t.* **quarrelled**) se disputer. **∼some** *a.* querelleur.

quarry [1] /'kwɒrɪ/ *n.* (*prey*) proie *f.*

quarry [2] /'kwɒrɪ/ *n.* (*excavation*) carrière *f.* ● *v.t.* extraire.

quart /kwɔ:t/ *n.* (*approx.*) litre *m.*

quarter /'kwɔ:tə(r)/ *n.* quart *m.*; (*of year*) trimestre *m.*; (*25 cents: Amer.*) quart de dollar *m.*; (*district*) quartier *m.* **∼s,** logement(s) *m.* (*pl.*) ● *v.t.* diviser en quatre; (*mil.*) cantonner. **from all ∼s,** de toutes parts. **∼-final** *n.* quart de finale *m.* **∼ly** *a.* trimestriel; *adv.* trimestriellement.

quartermaster /'kwɔ:təmɑ:stə(r)/ *n.* (*mil.*) intendant *m.*

quartet /kwɔ:'tet/ *n.* quatuor *m.*

quartz /kwɔ:ts/ *n.* quartz *m.* ● *a.* (*watch etc.*) à quartz.

quash /kwɒʃ/ *v.t.* (*suppress*) étouffer; (*jurid.*) annuler.

quasi- /'kweɪsaɪ/ *pref.* quasi-.

quaver /'kweɪvə(r)/ *v.i.* trembler, chevroter. ● *n.* (*mus.*) croche *f.*

quay /ki:/ *n.* (*naut.*) quai *m.* **∼side** *n.* (*edge of quay*) quai *m.*

queasy /'kwi:zɪ/ *a.* (*stomach*) délicat. **feel ∼,** avoir mal au cœur.

queen /kwi:n/ *n.* reine *f.*; (*cards*) dame *f.* **∼ mother,** reine mère *f.*

queer /kwɪə(r)/ *a.* (**-er, -est**) étrange; (*dubious*) louche; (*ill*) patraque. ● *n.* (*sl.*) homosexuel *m.*

quell /kwel/ *v.t.* réprimer.

quench /kwentʃ/ *v.t.* éteindre; (*thirst*) étancher; (*desire*) étouffer.

query /'kwɪərɪ/ *n.* question *f.* ● *v.t.* mettre en question.

quest /kwest/ *n.* recherche *f.*

question /'kwestʃən/ *n.* question *f.* ● *v.t.* interroger; (*doubt*) mettre en question, douter de. **a ∼ of money,** une question d'argent. **in ∼,** en question. **no ∼ of,** pas question de. **out of the ∼,** hors de question. **∼ mark,** point d'interrogation *m.*

questionable /'kwestʃənəbl/ *a.* discutable.

questionnaire /kwestʃə'neə(r)/ *n.* questionnaire *m.*

queue /kju:/ *n.* queue *f.* ● *v.i.* (*pres. p.* **queuing**) faire la queue.

quibble /'kwɪbl/ *v.i.* ergoter.

quick /kwɪk/ *a.* (**-er, -est**) rapide. ● *adv.* vite. ● *n.* **a ∼ one,** (*fam.*) un petit verre. **cut to the ∼,** piquer au vif. **be ∼,** (*hurry*) se dépêcher. **have a ∼ temper,** s'emporter facilement. **∼ly** *adv.* rapidement, vite. **∼-witted** *a.* vif.

quicken /'kwɪkən/ *v.t./i.* (s')accélérer.

quicksand /'kwɪksænd/ *n.* **∼(s),** sables mouvants *m. pl.*

quid /kwɪd/ *n. invar.* (*sl.*) livre *f.*

quiet /'kwaɪət/ *a.* (**-er, -est**) (*calm, still*) tranquille; (*silent*) silencieux; (*gentle*) doux; (*discreet*) discret. ● *n.* tranquillité *f.* **keep ∼,** se taire. **on the ∼,** en cachette. **∼ly** *adv.* tranquillement; silencieusement; doucement; discrètement. **∼ness** *n.* tranquillité *f.*

quieten /'kwaɪətn/ *v.t./i.* (se) calmer.

quill /kwɪl/ n. plume (d'oie) f.

quilt /kwɪlt/ n. édredon m. (**continental**) ~, couette f. ● v.t. matelasser.

quinine /'kwɪniːn, Amer. 'kwamaɪn/ n. quinine f.

quintet /kwɪn'tet/ n. quintette m.

quintuplets /kwɪn'tjuːplɪts/ n. pl. quintuplé(e)s m. (f.) pl.

quip /kwɪp/ n. mot piquant m.

quirk /kwɜːk/ n. bizarrerie f.

quit /kwɪt/ v.t. (p.t. **quitted**) quitter. ● v.i. abandonner; (resign) démissionner. ~ **doing**, (cease: Amer.) cesser de faire.

quite /kwaɪt/ adv. tout à fait, vraiment; (rather) assez. ~ (**so**)!, parfaitement! ~ **a few**, un assez grand nombre (de).

quits /kwɪts/ a. quitte (**with**, envers). **call it** ~, en rester là.

quiver /'kwɪvə(r)/ v.i. trembler.

quiz /kwɪz/ n. (pl. **quizzes**) test m.; (game) jeu-concours m. ● v.t. (p.t. **quizzed**) questionner.

quizzical /'kwɪzɪkl/ a. moqueur.

quorum /'kwɔːrəm/ n. quorum m.

quota /'kwəʊtə/ n. quota m.

quotation /kwəʊ'teɪʃn/ n. citation f.; (price) devis m.; (stock exchange) cotation f. ~ **marks**, guillemets m. pl.

quote /kwəʊt/ v.t. citer; (reference: comm.) rappeler; (price) indiquer; (share price) coter. ● v.i. ~ **for**, faire un devis pour. ~ **from**, citer. ● n. (estimate) devis m. (fam.) = **quotation**. **in** ~**s**, (fam.) entre guillemets.

quotient /'kwəʊʃnt/ n. quotient m.

R

rabbi /'ræbaɪ/ n. rabbin m.

rabbit /'ræbɪt/ n. lapin m.

rabble /'ræbl/ n. (crowd) cohue f. **the** ~, (pej.) la populace.

rabid /'ræbɪd/ a. enragé.

rabies /'reɪbiːz/ n. (disease) rage f.

race[1] /reɪs/ n. course f. ● v.t. (horse) faire courir; (engine) emballer. ~ (**against**), faire la course à. ● v.i. courir; (rush) foncer. ~**-track** n. piste f.; (for horses) champ de courses m.

race[2] /reɪs/ n. (group) race f. ● a. racial; (relations) entre les races.

racecourse /'reɪskɔːs/ n. champ de courses m.

racehorse /'reɪshɔːs/ n. cheval de course m.

racial /'reɪʃl/ a. racial.

racing /'reɪsɪŋ/ n. courses f. pl. ~ **car**, voiture de course f.

racis|t /'reɪsɪst/ a. & n. raciste (m./f.). ~**m** /-zəm/ n. racisme m.

rack[1] /ræk/ n. (shelf) étagère f.; (pigeon-holes) casier m.; (for luggage) porte-bagages m. invar.; (for dishes) égouttoir m.; (on car roof) galerie f. ● v.t. ~ **one's brains**, se creuser la cervelle.

rack[2] /ræk/ n. **go to** ~ **and ruin**, aller à la ruine; (building) tomber en ruine.

racket[1] /'rækɪt/ n. raquette f.

racket[2] /'rækɪt/ n. (din) tapage m.; (dealings) combine f.; (crime) racket m. ~**eer** /-ə'tɪə(r)/ n. racketteur m.

racy /'reɪsɪ/ a. (-**ier**, -**iest**) fougueux, piquant; (Amer.) risqué.

radar /'reɪdɑː(r)/ n. radar m. ● a. (system etc.) radar invar.

radial /'reɪdɪəl/ a. (tyre) à carcasse radiale.

radian|t /'reɪdɪənt/ a. rayonnant. ~**ce** n. éclat m. ~**tly** adv. avec éclat.

radiat|e /'reɪdɪeɪt/ v.t. dégager. ● v.i. rayonner (**from**, de). ~**ion** /-'eɪʃn/ n. rayonnement m.; (radioactivity) radiation f.

radiator /'reɪdɪeɪtə(r)/ n. radiateur m.

radical /'rædɪkl/ a. radical. ● n. (person: pol.) radical(e) m. (f.).

radio /'reɪdɪəʊ/ n. (pl. -**os**) radio f. ● v.t. (message) envoyer par radio; (person) appeler par radio.

radioactiv|e /reɪdɪəʊ'æktɪv/ a. radioactif. ~**ity** /-'tɪvətɪ/ n. radioactivité f.

radiographer /reɪdɪ'ɒgrəfə(r)/ n. radiologue m./f.

radish /'rædɪʃ/ n. radis m.

radius /'reɪdɪəs/ n. (pl. -**dii** /-dɪaɪ/) rayon m.

raffle /'ræfl/ n. tombola f.

raft /rɑːft/ n. radeau m.

rafter /'rɑːftə(r)/ n. chevron m.

rag[1] /ræg/ n. lambeau m., loque f.; (for wiping) chiffon m.; (newspaper) torchon m. **in** ~**s**, (person) en haillons; (clothes) en lambeaux. ~ **doll**, poupée de chiffon f.

rag² /ræg/ v.t. (p.t. **ragged**) (tease: sl.) taquiner. ● n. (univ., sl.) carnaval m. (pour une œuvre de charité).

ragamuffin /'rægəmʌfɪn/ n. va-nupieds m. invar.

rage /reɪdʒ/ n. rage f., fureur f. ● v.i. rager; (storm, battle) faire rage. **be all the ~,** faire fureur.

ragged /'rægɪd/ a. (clothes, person) loqueteux; (edge) déchiqueté.

raging /'reɪdʒɪŋ/ a. (storm, fever, etc.) violent.

raid /reɪd/ n. (mil.) raid m.; (by police) rafle f.; (by criminals) hold-up m. invar. ● v.t. faire un raid or une rafle or un hold-up dans. **~er** n. (person) bandit m., pillard m. **~ers** n. pl. (mil.) commando m.

rail /reɪl/ n. (on balcony) balustrade f.; (stairs) main courante f., rampe f.; (for train) rail m.; (for curtain) tringle f. **by ~,** par chemin de fer.

railing /'reɪlɪŋ/ n. ~s, grille f.

railroad /'reɪlrəʊd/ n. (Amer.) = **railway.**

railway /'reɪlweɪ/ n. chemin de fer m. **~ line,** voie ferrée f. **~man** n. (pl. -men) cheminot m. **~ station,** gare f.

rain /reɪn/ n. pluie f. ● v.i. pleuvoir. **~ forest,** forêt (humide) tropicale f. **~-storm** n. trombe d'eau f. **~-water** n. eau de pluie f.

rainbow /'reɪnbəʊ/ n. arc-en-ciel m.

raincoat /'reɪnkəʊt/ n. imperméable m.

rainfall /'reɪnfɔːl/ n. précipitation f.

rainy /'reɪnɪ/ a. (-ier, -iest) pluvieux; (season) des pluies.

raise /reɪz/ v.t. lever; (breed, build) élever; (question etc.) soulever; (price etc.) relever; (money etc.) obtenir; (voice) élever. ● n. (Amer.) augmentation f.

raisin /'reɪzn/ n. raisin sec m.

rake¹ /reɪk/ n. râteau m. ● v.t. (garden) ratisser; (search) fouiller dans. **~ in,** (money) amasser. **~-off** n. (fam.) profit m. **~ up,** (memories, past) remuer.

rake² /reɪk/ n. (man) débauché m.

rally /'rælɪ/ v.t./i. (se) rallier; (strength) reprendre; (after illness) aller mieux. ● n. rassemblement m.; (auto.) rallye m.; (tennis) échange m. **~ round,** venir en aide.

ram /ræm/ n. bélier m. ● v.t. (p.t. **rammed**) (thrust) enfoncer; (crash into) emboutir, percuter.

RAM /ræm/ abbr. (random access memory) mémoire vive f.

ramble /'ræmbl/ n. randonnée f. ● v.i. faire une randonnée. **~e on,** parler (sans cesse), divaguer. **~er** n. randonneu|r, -se, m., f. **~ing** a. (speech) décousu.

ramification /ræmɪfɪ'keɪʃn/ n. ramification f.

ramp /ræmp/ n. (slope) rampe f.; (in garage) pont de graissage m.

rampage¹ /ræm'peɪdʒ/ v.i. se livrer à des actes de violence, se déchaîner.

rampage² /'ræmpeɪdʒ/ n. **go on the ~** = **rampage**¹.

rampant /'ræmpənt/ a. **be ~,** (disease etc.) sévir, être répandu.

rampart /'ræmpɑːt/ n. rempart m.

ramshackle /'ræmʃækl/ a. délabré.

ran /ræn/ see **run.**

ranch /rɑːntʃ/ n. ranch m.

rancid /'rænsɪd/ a. rance.

rancour /'ræŋkə(r)/ n. rancœur f.

random /'rændəm/ a. fait, pris, etc. au hasard, aléatoire (techn.). ● n. **at ~,** au hasard.

randy /'rændɪ/ a. (-ier, -iest) (fam.) excité, en chaleur.

rang /ræŋ/ see **ring**².

range /reɪndʒ/ n. (distance) portée f.; (of aircraft etc.) rayon d'action m.; (series) gamme f.; (scale) échelle f.; (choice) choix m.; (domain) champ m.; (of mountains) chaîne f.; (stove) cuisinière f. ● v.i. s'étendre; (vary) varier.

ranger /'reɪndʒə(r)/ n. garde forestier m.

rank¹ /ræŋk/ n. rang m.; (grade: mil.) grade m., rang m. ● v.t./i. **~ among,** compter parmi. **the ~ and file,** les gens ordinaires.

rank² /ræŋk/ a. (-er, -est) (plants: pej.) luxuriant; (smell) fétide; (complete) absolu.

rankle /'ræŋkl/ v.i. **~ with s.o.,** rester sur le cœur à qn.

ransack /'rænsæk/ v.t. (search) fouiller; (pillage) saccager.

ransom /'rænsəm/ n. rançon f. ● v.t. rançonner; (redeem) racheter. **hold to ~,** rançonner.

rant /rænt/ v.i. tempêter.

rap /ræp/ n. petit coup sec m. ● v.t./i. (p.t. **rapped**) frapper.

rape /reɪp/ v.t. violer. ● n. viol m.

rapid /'ræpɪd/ a. rapide. **~ity** /rə'pɪdətɪ/ n. rapidité f. **~s** n. pl. (of river) rapides m. pl.

rapist /'reɪpɪst/ n. violeur m.

rapport /ræ'pɔ:(r)/ n. rapport m.

rapt /ræpt/ a. (attention) profond. ~ **in**, plongé dans.

rapture /'ræptʃə(r)/ n. extase f. ~**ous** a. (person) en extase; (welcome etc.) frénétique.

rare[1] /reə(r)/ a. (-er, -est) rare. ~**ely** adv. rarement. ~**ity** n. rareté f.

rare[2] /reə(r)/ a. (-er, -est) (culin.) saignant.

rarefied /'reərɪfaɪd/ a. raréfié.

raring /'reərɪŋ/ a. ~ **to**, (fam.) impatient de.

rascal /'rɑ:skl/ n. coquin(e) m. (f.).

rash[1] /ræʃ/ n. (med.) éruption f., rougeurs f. pl.

rash[2] /ræʃ/ a. (-er, -est) imprudent. ~**ly** adv. imprudemment. ~**ness** n. imprudence f.

rasher /'ræʃə(r)/ n. tranche (de lard) f.

raspberry /'rɑ:zbrɪ/ n. framboise f.

rasping /'rɑ:spɪŋ/ a. grinçant.

rat /ræt/ n. rat m. ● v.i. (p.t. ratted). ~ **on**, (desert) lâcher; (inform on) dénoncer. ~ **race**, foire d'empoigne f.

rate /reɪt/ n. (ratio, level) taux m.; (speed) allure f.; (price) tarif m. ~**s**, (taxes) impôts locaux m. pl. ● v.t. évaluer; (consider) considérer; (deserve: Amer.) mériter. ● v.i. ~ **as**, être considéré comme. **at any** ~, en tout cas. **at the** ~ **of**, (on the basis of) à raison de.

ratepayer /'reɪtpeɪə(r)/ n. contribuable m./f.

rather /'rɑ:ðə(r)/ adv. (by preference) plutôt; (fairly) assez, plutôt; (a little) un peu. **I would** ~ **go**, j'aimerais mieux partir. ~ **than go**, plutôt que de partir.

ratif|**y** /'rætɪfaɪ/ v.t. ratifier. ~**ication** /-ɪ'keɪʃn/ n. ratification f.

rating /'reɪtɪŋ/ n. classement m.; (sailor) matelot m.; (number) indice m. **the** ~**s**, (TV) l'audimat (P.).

ratio /'reɪʃɪəʊ/ n. (pl. -os) proportion f.

ration /'ræʃn/ n. ration f. ● v.t. rationner.

rational /'ræʃnl/ a. rationnel; (person) raisonnable.

rationalize /'ræʃnəlaɪz/ v.t. tenter de justifier; (organize) rationaliser.

rattle /'rætl/ v.i. faire du bruit; (of bottles) cliqueter. ● v.t. secouer; (sl.) agacer. ● n. bruit (de ferraille) m.; cliquetis m.; (toy) hochet m. ~ **off**, débiter en vitesse.

rattlesnake /'rætlsneɪk/ n. serpent à sonnette m., crotale m.

raucous /'rɔ:kəs/ a. rauque.

raunchy /'rɔ:ntʃɪ/ a. (-ier, -iest) (Amer., sl.) cochon.

ravage /'rævɪdʒ/ v.t. ravager. ~**s** /-ɪz/ n. pl. ravages m. pl.

rav|**e** /reɪv/ v.i. divaguer; (in anger) tempêter. ~**e about**, s'extasier sur. ~**ings** n. pl. divagations f. pl.

raven /'reɪvn/ n. corbeau m.

ravenous /'rævənəs/ a. vorace. **I am** ~, je meurs de faim.

ravine /rə'vi:n/ n. ravin m.

raving /'reɪvɪŋ/ a. ~ **lunatic**, fou furieux m., folle furieuse f.

ravioli /rævɪ'əʊlɪ/ n. ravioli m. pl.

ravish /'rævɪʃ/ v.t. (rape) ravir. ~**ing** a. (enchanting) ravissant.

raw /rɔ:/ a. (-er, -est) cru; (not processed) brut; (wound) à vif; (immature) inexpérimenté. **get a** ~ **deal**, être mal traité. ~ **materials**, matières premières f. pl.

ray /reɪ/ n. (of light etc.) rayon m. ~ **of hope**, lueur d'espoir f.

raze /reɪz/ v.t. (destroy) raser.

razor /'reɪzə(r)/ n. rasoir m. ~**-blade** n. lame de rasoir f.

re /ri:/ prep. concernant.

re- /ri:/ pref. re-, ré-, r-.

reach /ri:tʃ/ v.t. atteindre, arriver à; (contact) joindre; (hand over) passer. ● v.i. s'étendre. ● n. portée f. ~ **for**, tendre la main pour prendre. **within** ~ **of**, à portée de; (close to) à proximité de.

react /rɪ'ækt/ v.i. réagir.

reaction /rɪ'ækʃn/ n. réaction f. ~**ary** a. & n. réactionnaire (m./f.).

reactor /rɪ'æktə(r)/ n. réacteur m.

read /ri:d/ v.t./i. (p.t. read /red/) lire; (fig.) comprendre; (study) étudier; (of instrument) indiquer. ● n. (fam.) lecture f. ~ **about s.o.**, lire un article sur qn. ~ **out**, lire à haute voix. ~**able** a. agréable or facile à lire. ~**ing** n. lecture f.; indication f. ~**ing-glasses** pl. n. lunettes pour lire f. pl. ~**ing-lamp** n. lampe de bureau f. ~**-out** n. affichage m.

reader /'ri:də(r)/ n. lec|teur, -trice m., f. ~**ship** n. lecteurs m. pl.

readily /'redɪlɪ/ adv. (willingly) volontiers; (easily) facilement.

readiness /'redmɪs/ n. empressement m. **in** ~, prêt (**for**, à).

readjust /riːˈdʒʌst/ v.t. rajuster. ● v.i. se réadapter (**to,** à).

ready /ˈredɪ/ a. (-ier, -iest) prêt; (*quick*) prompt. ● n. **at the ~,** tout prêt. **~-made** a. tout fait. **~ money,** (argent) liquide m. **~ reckoner,** barème m. **~-to-wear** a. prêt-à-porter.

real /rɪəl/ a. vrai, véritable, réel. ● adv. (*Amer., fam.*) vraiment. **~ estate,** biens fonciers m. pl.

realis|t /ˈrɪəlɪst/ n. réaliste m./f. **~m** /-zəm/ n. réalisme m. **~tic** /-ˈlɪstɪk/ a. réaliste. **~tically** /-ˈlɪstɪklɪ/ adv. avec réalisme.

reality /rɪˈælətɪ/ n. réalité f.

realiz|e /ˈrɪəlaɪz/ v.t. se rendre compte de, comprendre; (*fulfil, turn into cash*) réaliser; (*price*) atteindre. **~ation** /-ˈzeɪʃn/ n. prise de conscience f.; réalisation f.

really /ˈrɪəlɪ/ adv. vraiment.

realtor /ˈrɪəltə(r)/ n. (*Amer.*) agent immobilier m.

realm /relm/ n. royaume m.

reap /riːp/ v.t. (*crop, field*) moissonner; (*fig.*) récolter.

reappear /riːəˈpɪə(r)/ v.i. réapparaître, reparaître.

reappraisal /riːəˈpreɪzl/ n. réévaluation f.

rear [1] /rɪə(r)/ n. arrière m., derrière m. ● a. arrière *invar.*, de derrière. **~-view mirror,** rétroviseur m.

rear [2] /rɪə(r)/ v.t. (*bring up, breed*) élever. ● v.i. (*horse*) se cabrer. **~ one's head,** dresser la tête.

rearguard /ˈrɪəɡɑːd/ n. (*mil.*) arrière-garde f.

rearm /riːˈɑːm/ v.t./i. réarmer.

rearrange /riːəˈreɪndʒ/ v.t. réarranger.

reason /ˈriːzn/ n. raison f. ● v.i. raisonner. **it stands to ~ that,** de toute évidence. **we have ~ to believe that,** on a tout lieu de croire que. **there is no ~ to panic,** il n'y a pas de raison de paniquer. **~ with,** raisonner. **everything within ~,** tout dans les limites normales. **~ing** n. raisonnement m.

reasonable /ˈriːznəbl/ a. raisonnable.

reassur|e /riːəˈʃʊə(r)/ v.t. rassurer. **~ance** n. réconfort m.

rebate /ˈriːbeɪt/ n. remboursement (partiel) m.; (*discount*) rabais m.

rebel [1] /ˈrebl/ n. & a. rebelle (m./f.).

rebel [2] /rɪˈbel/ v.i. (*p.t.* **rebelled**) se rebeller. **~lion** n. rébellion f. **~lious** a. rebelle.

rebound /rɪˈbaʊnd/ v.i. rebondir. **~ on,** (*backfire*) se retourner contre. ● n. /ˈriːbaʊnd/ n. rebond m.

rebuff /rɪˈbʌf/ v.t. repousser. ● n. rebuffade f.

rebuild /riːˈbɪld/ v.t. reconstruire.

rebuke /rɪˈbjuːk/ v.t. réprimander. ● n. réprimande f., reproche m.

rebuttal /rɪˈbʌtl/ n. réfutation f.

recall /rɪˈkɔːl/ v.t. (*to s.o., call back*) rappeler; (*remember*) se rappeler. ● n. rappel m.

recant /rɪˈkænt/ v.i. se rétracter.

recap /ˈriːkæp/ v.t./i. (*p.t.* **recapped**) (*fam.*) récapituler. ● n. (*fam.*) récapitulation f.

recapitulat|e /riːkəˈpɪtʃʊleɪt/ v.t./i. récapituler. **~ion** /-ˈleɪʃn/ n. récapitulation f.

recapture /riːˈkæptʃə(r)/ v.t. reprendre; (*recall*) recréer.

reced|e /rɪˈsiːd/ v.i. s'éloigner. **his hair is ~ing,** son front se dégarnit. **~ing** a. (*forehead*) fuyant.

receipt /rɪˈsiːt/ n. (*written*) reçu m.; (*of letter*) réception f. **~s,** (*money: comm.*) recettes f. pl.

receive /rɪˈsiːv/ v.t. recevoir. **~r** /-ə(r)/ n. (*of stolen goods*) receleu|r, -se m., f.; (*telephone*) combiné m.

recent /ˈriːsnt/ a. récent. **~ly** adv. récemment.

receptacle /rɪˈseptəkl/ n. récipient m.

reception /rɪˈsepʃn/ n. réception f. **give s.o. a warm ~,** donner un accueil chaleureux à qn. **~ist** n. réceptionniste m./f.

receptive /rɪˈseptɪv/ a. réceptif.

recess /rɪˈses/ n. (*alcove*) renfoncement m.; (*nook*) recoin m.; (*holiday*) vacances f. pl.; (*schol., Amer.*) récréation f.

recession /rɪˈseʃn/ n. récession f.

recharge /riːˈtʃɑːdʒ/ v.t. recharger.

recipe /ˈresəpɪ/ n. recette f.

recipient /rɪˈsɪpɪənt/ n. (*of honour*) récipiendaire m.; (*of letter*) destinataire m./f.

reciprocal /rɪˈsɪprəkl/ a. réciproque.

reciprocate /rɪˈsɪprəkeɪt/ v.t. offrir en retour. ● v.i. en faire autant.

recital /rɪˈsaɪtl/ n. récital m.

recite /rɪˈsaɪt/ v.t. (*poem, lesson, etc.*) réciter; (*list*) énumérer.

reckless /ˈreklɪs/ a. imprudent. **~ly** adv. imprudemment.

reckon /'rekən/ *v.t./i.* calculer; (*judge*) considérer; (*think*) penser. **~ on/with,** compter sur/avec. **~ing** *n.* calcul(s) *m.* (*pl.*).

reclaim /rɪ'kleɪm/ *v.t.* (*seek return of*) réclamer; (*land*) défricher; (*flooded land*) assécher.

reclin|e /rɪ'klaɪn/ *v.i.* être étendu. **~ing** *a.* (*person*) étendu; (*seat*) à dossier réglable.

recluse /rɪ'kluːs/ *n.* reclus(e) *m.* (*f.*), ermite *m.*

recognition /rekəg'nɪʃn/ *n.* reconnaissance *f.* **beyond ~,** méconnaissable. **gain ~,** être reconnu.

recognize /'rekəgnaɪz/ *v.t.* reconnaître.

recoil /rɪ'kɔɪl/ *v.i.* reculer (**from,** devant).

recollect /rekə'lekt/ *v.t.* se souvenir de, se rappeler. **~ion** /-kʃn/ *n.* souvenir *m.*

recommend /rekə'mend/ *v.t.* recommander. **~ation** /-'deɪʃn/ *n.* recommandation *f.*

recompense /'rekəmpens/ *v.t.* (ré)compenser. ● *n.* récompense *f.*

reconcil|e /'rekənsaɪl/ *v.t.* (*people*) réconcilier; (*facts*) concilier. **~e o.s. to,** se résigner à. **~iation** /-sɪlɪ'eɪʃn/ *n.* réconciliation *f.*

recondition /riːkən'dɪʃn/ *v.t.* remettre à neuf, réviser.

reconn|oitre /rekə'nɔɪtə(r)/ *v.t.* (*pres. p.* **-tring**) (*mil.*) reconnaître. **~aissance** /rɪ'kɒnɪsns/ *n.* reconnaissance *f.*

reconsider /riːkən'sɪdə(r)/ *v.t.* reconsidérer. ● *v.i.* se déjuger.

reconstruct /riːkən'strʌkt/ *v.t.* reconstruire; (*crime*) reconstituer.

record [1] /rɪ'kɔːd/ *v.t./i.* (*in register, on tape, etc.*) enregistrer; (*in diary*) noter. **~ that,** rapporter que. **~ing** *n.* enregistrement *m.*

record [2] /'rekɔːd/ *n.* (*report*) rapport *m.*; (*register*) registre *m.*; (*mention*) mention *f.*; (*file*) dossier *m.*; (*fig.*) résultats *m. pl.*; (*mus.*) disque *m.*; (*sport*) record *m.* **(criminal) ~,** casier judiciaire *m.* ● *a.* record *invar.* **off the ~,** officieusement. **~-holder** *n.* déten|teur, -trice du record *m.*, *f.* **~-player** *n.* électrophone *m.*

recorder /rɪ'kɔːdə(r)/ *n.* (*mus.*) flûte à bec *f.*

recount /rɪ'kaʊnt/ *v.t.* raconter.

re-count /riː'kaʊnt/ *v.t.* recompter.

recoup /rɪ'kuːp/ *v.t.* récupérer.

recourse /rɪ'kɔːs/ *n.* recours *m.* **have ~ to,** avoir recours à.

recover /rɪ'kʌvə(r)/ *v.t.* récupérer. ● *v.i.* se remettre; (*med.*) se rétablir; (*economy*) se redresser. **~y** *n.* récupération *f.*; (*med.*) rétablissement *m.*

recreation /rekrɪ'eɪʃn/ *n.* récréation *f.* **~al** *a.* de récréation.

recrimination /rɪkrɪmɪ'neɪʃn/ *n.* contre-accusation *f.*

recruit /rɪ'kruːt/ *n.* recrue *f.* ● *v.t.* recruter. **~ment** *n.* recrutement *m.*

rectang|le /'rektæŋgl/ *n.* rectangle *m.* **~ular** /-'tæŋgjʊlə(r)/ *a.* rectangulaire.

rectif|y /'rektɪfaɪ/ *v.t.* rectifier. **~ication** /-ɪ'keɪʃn/ *n.* rectification *f.*

recuperate /rɪ'kjuːpəreɪt/ *v.t.* récupérer. ● *v.i.* (*med.*) se rétablir.

recur /rɪ'kɜː(r)/ *v.i.* (*p.t.* **recurred**) revenir, se répéter.

recurren|t /rɪ'kʌrənt/ *a.* fréquent. **~ce** *n.* répétition *f.*, retour *m.*

recycle /riː'saɪkl/ *v.t.* recycler.

red /red/ *a.* (**redder, reddest**) rouge; (*hair*) roux. ● *n.* rouge *m.* **in the ~,** en déficit. **roll out the ~ carpet for,** recevoir en grande pompe. **Red Cross,** Croix-Rouge *f.* **~-handed** *a.* en flagrant délit. **~ herring,** fausse piste *f.* **~-hot** *a.* brûlant. **the ~ light,** le feu rouge *m.* **~ tape,** paperasserie *f.*, bureaucratie *f.*

redcurrant /red'kʌrənt/ *n.* groseille *f.*

redden /'redn/ *v.t./i.* rougir.

reddish /'redɪʃ/ *a.* rougeâtre.

redecorate /riː'dekəreɪt/ *v.t.* (*repaint etc.*) repeindre, refaire.

redeem /rɪ'diːm/ *v.t.* racheter. **~ing quality,** qualité qui rachète les défauts *f.*

redemption *n.* /rɪ'dempʃn/ rachat *m.*

redeploy /riːdɪ'plɔɪ/ *v.t.* réorganiser; (*troops*) répartir.

redirect /riːdaɪə'rekt/ *v.t.* (*letter*) faire suivre.

redness /'rednɪs/ *n.* rougeur *f.*

redo /riː'duː/ *v.t.* (*p.t.* **-did,** *p.p.* **-done**) refaire.

redolent /'redələnt/ *a.* **~ of,** qui évoque.

redouble /rɪ'dʌbl/ *v.t.* redoubler.

redress /rɪ'dres/ *v.t.* (*wrong etc.*) redresser. ● *n.* réparation *f.*

reduc|e /rɪ'dju:s/ v.t. réduire; (temperature etc.) faire baisser. **~tion** /rɪ'dʌkʃn/ n. réduction f.

redundan|t /rɪ'dʌndənt/ a. superflu; (worker) licencié. **make ~,** licencier. **~cy** n. licenciement m.; (word, phrase) pléonasme m.

reed /ri:d/ n. (plant) roseau m.; (mus.) anche f.

reef /ri:f/ n. récif m., écueil m.

reek /ri:k/ n. puanteur f. ● v.i. ~ (of), puer.

reel /ri:l/ n. (of thread) bobine f.; (of film) bande f.; (winding device) dévidoir m. ● v.i. chanceler. ● v.t. ~ **off,** réciter.

refectory /rɪ'fektərɪ/ n. réfectoire m.

refer /rɪ'fɜ:(r)/ v.t./i. (p.t. referred). ~ **to,** (allude to) faire allusion à; (concern) s'appliquer à; (consult) consulter; (submit) soumettre à; (direct) renvoyer à.

referee /refə'ri:/ n. arbitre m.; (for job) répondant(e) m. (f.). ● v.t. (p.t. refereed) arbitrer.

reference /'refrəns/ n. référence f.; (mention) allusion f.; (person) répondant(e) m. (f.). **in** or **with ~ to,** en ce qui concerne; (comm.) suite à. ~ **book,** ouvrage de référence m.

referendum /refə'rendəm/ n. (pl. -ums) référendum m.

refill[1] /ri:fɪl/ v.t. remplir (à nouveau); (pen etc.) recharger.

refill[2] /'ri:fɪl/ n. (of pen, lighter, lipstick) recharge f.

refine /rɪ'faɪn/ v.t. raffiner. **~d** a. raffiné. **~ment** n. raffinement m.; (techn.) raffinage m. **~ry** /-ərɪ/ n. raffinerie f.

reflate /ri:'fleɪt/ v.t. relancer.

reflect /rɪ'flekt/ v.t. refléter; (of mirror) réfléchir, refléter. ● v.i. réfléchir (**on,** à). ~ **on s.o.,** (glory etc.) (faire) rejaillir sur qn.; (pej.) donner une mauvaise impression de qn. **~ion** /-kʃn/ n. réflexion f.; (image) reflet m. **on ~ion,** réflexion faite. **~or** n. réflecteur m.

reflective /rɪ'flektɪv/ a. réfléchissant.

reflex /'ri:fleks/ a. & n. réflexe (m.).

reflexive /rɪ'fleksɪv/ a. (gram.) réfléchi.

reform /rɪ'fɔ:m/ v.t. réformer. ● v.i. (person) s'amender. ● n. réforme f. **~er** n. réforma|teur, -trice m., f.

refract /rɪ'frækt/ v.t. réfracter.

refrain[1] /rɪ'freɪn/ n. refrain m.

refrain[2] /rɪ'freɪn/ v.i. s'abstenir (**from,** de).

refresh /rɪ'freʃ/ v.t. rafraîchir; (of rest etc.) ragaillardir, délasser. **~ing** a. (drink) rafraîchissant; (sleep) réparateur. **~ments** n. pl. rafraîchissements m. pl.

refresher /rɪ'freʃə(r)/ a. (course) de perfectionnement.

refrigerat|e /rɪ'frɪdʒəreɪt/ v.t. réfrigérer. **~or** n. réfrigérateur m.

refuel /ri:'fju:əl/ v.t./i. (p.t. re-fuelled) (se) ravitailler.

refuge /'refju:dʒ/ n. refuge m. **take ~,** se réfugier.

refugee /refjʊ'dʒi:/ n. réfugié(e) m. (f.).

refund /rɪ'fʌnd/ v.t. rembourser. ● n. /'ri:fʌnd/ remboursement m.

refurbish /ri:'fɜ:bɪʃ/ v.t. remettre à neuf.

refus|e[1] /rɪ'fju:z/ v.t./i. refuser. **~al** n. refus m.

refuse[2] /'refju:s/ n. ordures f. pl.

refute /rɪ'fju:t/ v.t. réfuter.

regain /rɪ'geɪn/ v.t. retrouver; (lost ground) regagner.

regal /'ri:gl/ a. royal, majestueux.

regalia /rɪ'geɪlɪə/ n. pl. (insignia) insignes (royaux) m. pl.

regard /rɪ'ga:d/ v.t. considérer. ● n. considération f., estime f. **~s,** amitiés f. pl. **in this ~,** à cet égard. **as ~s, ~ing** prep. en ce qui concerne.

regardless /rɪ'ga:dlɪs/ adv. quand même. ~ **of,** sans tenir compte de.

regatta /rɪ'gætə/ n. régates f. pl.

regenerat|e /rɪ'dʒenəreɪt/ v.t. régénérer. **~ion** /-'reɪʃn/ n. régénération f.

regen|t /'ri:dʒənt/ n. régent(e) m. (f.). **~cy** n. régence f.

regime /reɪ'ʒi:m/ n. régime m.

regiment /'redʒmənt/ n. régiment m. **~al** /-'mentl/ a. d'un régiment. **~ation** /-en'teɪʃn/ n. discipline excessive f.

region /'ri:dʒən/ n. région f. **in the ~ of,** environ. **~al** a. régional.

regist|er /'redʒɪstə(r)/ n. registre m. ● v.t. enregistrer; (vehicle) immatriculer; (birth) déclarer; (letter) recommander; (indicate) indiquer; (express) exprimer. ● v.i. (enrol) s'inscrire; (fig.) être compris. **~er office,** bureau d'état civil m. **~ration** /-'streɪʃn/ n. enregistrement m.; inscription f.; (vehicle document) carte grise f. **~ration**

(number), (*auto.*) numéro d'immatriculation *m.*

registrar /redʒɪ'strɑ:(r)/ *n.* officier de
l'état civil *m.*; (*univ.*) secrétaire
général *m.*

regret /rɪ'gret/ *n.* regret *m.* ● *v.t.*
(*p.t.* **regretted**) regretter (**to do,** de
faire). **~fully** *adv.* à regret. **~table**
a. regrettable, fâcheux. **~tably** *adv.*
malheureusement; (*small, poor, etc.*)
fâcheusement.

regroup /riː'gruːp/ *v.t./i.* (se) regrouper.

regular /'regjʊlə(r)/ *a.* régulier;
(*usual*) habituel; (*thorough.* *fam.*)
vrai. ● *n.* (*fam.*) habitué(e) *m.* (*f.*).
~ity /-'lærətɪ/ *n.* régularité *f.* **~ly**
adv. régulièrement.

regulat|e /'regjʊleɪt/ *v.t.* régler. **~ion**
/-'leɪʃn/ *n.* réglage *m.*; (*rule*) règlement *m.*

rehabilitat|e /riːə'bɪlɪteɪt/ *v.t.* réa-
dapter; (*in public esteem*) réhabili-
ter. **~ion** /-'teɪʃn/ *n.* réadaptation
f.; réhabilitation *f.*

rehash [1] /riː'hæʃ/ *v.t.* remanier.

rehash [2] /'riː'hæʃ/ *n.* réchauffé *m.*

rehears|e /rɪ'hɜːs/ *v.t./i.* (*theatre*)
répéter. **~al** *n.* répétition *f.*

re-heat /riː'hiːt/ *v.t.* réchauffer.

reign /reɪn/ *n.* règne *m.* ● *v.i.* régner
(**over,** sur).

reimburse /riːɪm'bɜːs/ *v.t.* rembourser.

rein /reɪn/ *n.* rêne *f.*

reindeer /'reɪndɪə(r)/ *n. invar.* renne
m.

reinforce /riːɪn'fɔːs/ *v.t.* renforcer.
~ment *n.* renforcement *m.*
~ments *n. pl.* renforts *m. pl.* **~d
concrete,** béton armé *m.*

reinstate /riːɪn'steɪt/ *v.t.* réintégrer,
rétablir.

reiterate /riː'ɪtəreɪt/ *v.t.* réitérer.

reject [1] /rɪ'dʒekt/ *v.t.* (*offer, plea, etc.*)
rejeter; (*book, goods, etc.*) refuser.
~ion /-kʃn/ *n.* rejet *m.*; refus *m.*

reject [2] /'riːdʒekt/ *n.* (article de) rebut
m.

rejoic|e /rɪ'dʒɔɪs/ *v.i.* se réjouir. **~ing**
n. réjouissance *f.*

rejuvenate /rɪ'dʒuːvəneɪt/ *v.t.* rajeunir.

relapse /rɪ'læps/ *n.* rechute *f.* ● *v.i.*
rechuter. **~ into,** retomber dans.

relate /rɪ'leɪt/ *v.t.* raconter; (*associate*) rapprocher. ● *v.i.* **~ to,** se
rapporter à; (*get on with*) s'entendre

avec. **~d** /-ɪd/ *a.* (*ideas etc.*) lié. **~d
to s.o.,** parent(e) de qn.

relation /rɪ'leɪʃn/ *n.* rapport *m.*; (*person*) parent(e) *m.* (*f.*). **~ship** *n.* lien
de parenté *m.*; (*link*) rapport *m.*;
(*affair*) liaison *f.*

relative /'relətɪv/ *n.* parent(e) *m.* (*f.*).
● *a.* relatif; (*respective*) respectif.
~ly *adv.* relativement.

relax /rɪ'læks/ *v.t./i.* (*less tense*) (se)
relâcher; (*for pleasure*) (se)
détendre. **~ation** /riːlæk'seɪʃn/ *n.*
relâchement *m.*; détente *f.* **~ing** *a.*
délassant.

relay [1] /'riːleɪ/ *n.* relais *m.* **~ race,**
course de relais *f.*

relay [2] /rɪ'leɪ/ *v.t.* relayer.

release /rɪ'liːs/ *v.t.* libérer; (*bomb*)
lâcher; (*film*) sortir; (*news*) publier;
(*smoke*) dégager; (*spring*) déclencher. ● *n.* libération *f.*; sortie *f.*;
(*record*) nouveau disque *m.* (*of pol-
lution*) émission *f.*

relegate /'relɪgeɪt/ *v.t.* reléguer.

relent /rɪ'lent/ *v.i.* se laisser fléchir.
~less *a.* impitoyable.

relevan|t /'reləvənt/ *a.* pertinent. **be
~t to,** avoir rapport à. **~ce** *n.*
pertinence *f.*, rapport *m.*

reliab|le /rɪ'laɪəbl/ *a.* sérieux, sûr;
(*machine*) fiable. **~ility** /-'bɪlətɪ/ *n.*
sérieux *m.*; fiabilité *f.*

reliance /rɪ'laɪəns/ *n.* dépendance *f.*;
(*trust*) confiance *f.*

relic /'relɪk/ *n.* relique *f.* **~s,** (*of past*)
vestiges *m. pl.*

relief /rɪ'liːf/ *n.* soulagement *m.*
(**from,** à); (*assistance*) secours *m.*;
(*outline, design*) relief *m.* **~ road,**
route de délestage *f.*

relieve /rɪ'liːv/ *v.t.* soulager; (*help*)
secourir; (*take over from*) relayer.

religion /rɪ'lɪdʒən/ *n.* religion *f.*

religious /rɪ'lɪdʒəs/ *a.* religieux.

relinquish /rɪ'lɪŋkwɪʃ/ *v.t.* abandonner; (*relax hold of*) lâcher.

relish /'relɪʃ/ *n.* plaisir *m.*, goût *m.*;
(*culin.*) assaisonnement *m.* ● *v.t.*
savourer; (*idea etc.*) aimer.

relocate /riːləʊ'keɪt/ *v.t.* (*company*)
déplacer; (*employee*) muter. ● *v.i.*
se déplacer, déménager.

reluctan|t /rɪ'lʌktənt/ *a.* fait, donné,
etc. à contrecœur. **~t to,** peu disposé
à. **~ce** *n.* répugnance *f.* **~tly** *adv.* à
contrecœur.

rely /rɪ'laɪ/ *v.i.* **~ on,** compter sur;
(*financially*) dépendre de.

remain /rɪ'mem/ v.i. rester. **~s** n. pl. restes m. pl.

remainder /rɪ'memdə(r)/ n. reste m.; (book) invendu soldé m.

remand /rɪ'mɑːnd/ v.t. mettre en détention préventive. ● n. **on ~,** en détention préventive.

remark /rɪ'mɑːk/ n. remarque f. ● v.t. remarquer. ● v.i. **~ on,** faire des commentaires sur. **~able** a. remarquable.

remarry /riː'mærɪ/ v.i. se remarier.

remed|y /'remədɪ/ n. remède m. ● v.t. remédier à. **~ial** /rɪ'miːdɪəl/ a. (class etc.) de rattrapage; (treatment: med.) curatif.

rememb|er /rɪ'membə(r)/ v.t. se souvenir de, se rappeler. **~er to do,** ne pas oublier de faire. **~rance** n. souvenir m.

remind /rɪ'mamd/ v.t. rappeler (s.o. of sth., qch. à qn.). **~ s.o. to do,** rappeler à qn. qu'il doit faire. **~er** n. (letter, signal) rappel m.

reminisce /remɪ'nɪs/ v.i. évoquer ses souvenirs. **~nces** n. pl. réminiscences f. pl.

reminiscent /remɪ'nɪsnt/ a. **~ of,** qui rappelle, qui évoque.

remiss /rɪ'mɪs/ a. négligent.

remission /rɪ'mɪʃn/ n. rémission f.; (jurid.) remise (de peine) f.

remit /rɪ'mɪt/ v.t. (p.t. **remitted**) (money) envoyer; (debt) remettre. **~tance** n. paiement m.

remnant /'remnənt/ n. reste m., débris m.; (trace) vestige m.; (of cloth) coupon m.

remodel /riː'mɒdl/ v.t. (p.t. **remodelled**) remodeler.

remorse /rɪ'mɔːs/ n. remords m. (pl.). **~ful** a. plein de remords. **~less** a. implacable.

remote /rɪ'məʊt/ a. (place, time) lointain; (person) distant; (slight) vague. **~ control,** télécommande f. **~ly** adv. au loin; vaguement. **~ness** n. éloignement m.

removable /rɪ'muːvəbl/ a. (detachable) amovible.

remov|e /rɪ'muːv/ v.t. enlever; (lead away) emmener; (dismiss) renvoyer; (do away with) supprimer. **~al** n. enlèvement m.; renvoi m.; suppression f.; (from house) déménagement m. **~al men,** déménageurs m. pl. **~er** n. (for paint) décapant m.

remunerat|e /rɪ'mjuːnəreɪt/ v.t. rémunérer. **~ion** /-'reɪʃn/ n. rémunération f.

rename /riː'neɪm/ v.t. rebaptiser.

render /'rendə(r)/ v.t. (give, make) rendre; (mus.) interpréter. **~ing** n. interprétation f.

rendezvous /'rɒndeɪvuː/ n. (pl. **-vous** /-vuːz/) rendez-vous m. invar.

renegade /'renɪgeɪd/ n. renégat(e) m. (f.).

renew /rɪ'njuː/ v.t. renouveler; (resume) reprendre. **~able** a. renouvelable. **~al** n. renouvellement m.; reprise f.

renounce /rɪ'naʊns/ v.t. renoncer à; (disown) renier.

renovat|e /'renəveɪt/ v.t. rénover. **~ion** /-'veɪʃn/ n. rénovation f.

renown /rɪ'naʊn/ n. renommée f. **~ed** a. renommé.

rent /rent/ n. loyer m. ● v.t. louer. **for ~,** à louer. **~al** n. prix de location m.

renunciation /rɪnʌnsɪ'eɪʃn/ n. renonciation f.

reopen /riː'əʊpən/ v.t./i. rouvrir. **~ing** n. réouverture f.

reorganize /riː'ɔːɡənaɪz/ v.t. réorganiser.

rep /rep/ n. (comm., fam.) représentant(e) m. (f.).

repair /rɪ'peə(r)/ v.t. réparer. ● n. réparation f. **in good/bad ~,** en bon/mauvais état. **~er** n. réparateur m.

repartee /repɑː'tiː/ n. repartie f.

repatriat|e /riː'pætrɪeɪt/ v.t. rapatrier. **~ion** /-'eɪʃn/ n. rapatriement m.

repay /riː'peɪ/ v.t. (p.t. **repaid**) rembourser; (reward) récompenser. **~ment** n. remboursement m.; récompense f. **monthly ~ments,** mensualités f. pl.

repeal /rɪ'piːl/ v.t. abroger, annuler. ● n. abrogation f.

repeat /rɪ'piːt/ v.t./i. répéter; (renew) renouveler. ● n. répétition f.; (broadcast) reprise f. **~ itself, ~ o.s.,** se répéter.

repeatedly /rɪ'piːtɪdlɪ/ adv. à maintes reprises.

repel /rɪ'pel/ v.t. (p.t. **repelled**) repousser. **~lent** a. repoussant.

repent /rɪ'pent/ v.i. se repentir (of, de). **~ance** n. repentir m. **~ant** a. repentant.

repercussion /ri:pə'kʌʃn/ n. réper-cussion f.

repertoire /'repətwɑː(r)/ n. réper-toire m.

repertory /'repətrɪ/ n. répertoire m. ~ **(theatre)**, théâtre de répertoire m.

repetit|ion /repɪ'tɪʃn/ n. répétition f. ~**ious** /-'tɪʃəs/, ~**ive** /rɪ'petətɪv/ adjs. plein de répétitions.

replace /rɪ'pleɪs/ v.t. remettre; (take the place of) remplacer. ~**ment** n. remplacement m. (**of,** de); (person) remplaçant(e) m. (f.); (new part) pièce de rechange f.

replay /'ri:pleɪ/ n. (sport) match rejoué m.; (recording) répétition im-médiate f.

replenish /rɪ'plenɪʃ/ v.t. (refill) remplir; (renew) renouveler.

replica /'replɪkə/ n. copie exacte f.

reply /rɪ'plaɪ/ v.t./i. répondre. ● n. réponse f.

report /rɪ'pɔːt/ v.t. rapporter, annon-cer (**that,** que); (notify) signaler; (denounce) dénoncer. ● v.i. faire un rapport. ~ **(on),** (news item) faire un reportage sur. ~ **to,** (go) se présenter chez. ● n. rapport m.; (in press) reportage m.; (schol.) bulletin m.; (sound) détonation f. ~**edly** adv. selon ce qu'on dit.

reporter /rɪ'pɔːtə(r)/ n. reporter m.

repose /rɪ'pəʊz/ n. repos m.

repossess /ri:pə'zes/ v.t. reprendre.

represent /reprɪ'zent/ v.t. représenter. ~**ation** /-'teɪʃn/ n. re-présentation f. **make** ~**ations to,** protester auprès de.

representative /reprɪ'zentətɪv/ a. re-présentatif, typique (**of,** de). ● n. représentant(e) m. (f.).

repress /rɪ'pres/ v.t. réprimer. ~**ion** /-ʃn/ n. répression f. ~**ive** a. répres-sif.

reprieve /rɪ'priːv/ n. (delay) sursis m.; (pardon) grâce f. ● v.t. accorder un sursis à; gracier.

reprimand /'reprɪmɑːnd/ v.t. ré-primander. ● n. réprimande f.

reprint /'riːprɪnt/ n. réimpression f.; (offprint) tiré à part m.

reprisals /rɪ'praɪzlz/ n. pl. repré-sailles f. pl.

reproach /rɪ'prəʊtʃ/ v.t. reprocher (s.o. for sth., qch. à qn.). ● n. reproche m. ~**ful** a. de reproche, réprobateur. ~**fully** adv. avec re-proche.

reproduc|e /riːprə'djuːs/ v.t./i. (se) reproduire. ~**tion** /-'dʌkʃn/ n. re-production f. ~**tive** /-'dʌktɪv/ a. reproducteur.

reptile /'reptaɪl/ n. reptile m.

republic /rɪ'pʌblɪk/ n. république f. ~**an** a. & n. républicain(e) (m. (f.)).

repudiate /rɪ'pjuːdɪeɪt/ v.t. répudier; (treaty) refuser d'honorer.

repugnan|t /rɪ'pʌgnənt/ a. ré-pugnant. ~**ce** n. répugnance f.

repuls|e /rɪ'pʌls/ v.t. repousser. ~**ion** /-ʃn/ n. répulsion f. ~**ive** a. repous-sant.

reputable /'repjʊtəbl/ a. honorable, de bonne réputation.

reputation /repjʊ'teɪʃn/ n. réputa-tion f.

repute /rɪ'pjuːt/ n. réputation f. ~**d** /-ɪd/ a. réputé. ~**dly** /-ɪdlɪ/ adv. d'après ce qu'on dit.

request /rɪ'kwest/ n. demande f. ● v.t. demander (**of, from,** à). ~ **stop,** arrêt facultatif m.

requiem /'rekwɪem/ n. requiem m.

require rɪ'kwaɪə(r) v.t. (of thing) demander; (of person) avoir besoin de; (demand, order) exiger. ~**d** a. requis. ~**ment** n. exigence f.; (con-dition) condition (requise) f.

requisite /'rekwɪzɪt/ a. nécessaire. ● n. chose nécessaire f. ~**s,** (for travel etc.) articles m. pl.

requisition /rekwɪ'zɪʃn/ n. réquisi-tion f. ● v.t. réquisitionner.

re-route /riː'ruːt/ v.t. dérouter.

resale /'riːseɪl/ n. revente f.

rescind /rɪ'sɪnd/ v.t. annuler.

rescue /'reskjuː/ v.t. sauver. ● n. sauvetage m. (**of,** de); (help) secours m. ~**r** /-ə(r)/ n. sauveteur m.

research /rɪ'sɜːtʃ/ n. recherche(s) f.(pl.). ● v.t./i. faire des recherches (sur). ~**er** n. chercheu|r, -se m., f.

resembl|e /rɪ'zembl/ v.t. ressembler à ~**ance** n. ressemblance f.

resent /rɪ'zent/ v.t. être indigné de, s'offenser de. ~**ful** a. plein de ressentiment, indigné. ~**ment** n. ressentiment m.

reservation /rezə'veɪʃn/ n. réserve f.; (booking) réservation f.; (Amer.) réserve (indienne) f. **make a** ~, réserver.

reserve /rɪ'zɜːv/ v.t. réserver. ● n. (reticence, stock, land) réserve f.; (sport) remplaçant(e) m. (f.). **in** ~, en réserve. **the** ~**s,** (mil.) les réserves *f. pl.* **~d** *a.* (*person, room*) réservé.

reservist /rɪˈzɜːvɪst/ *n.* (*mil.*) réserviste *m.*

reservoir /ˈrezəvwɑː(r)/ *n.* (*lake, supply, etc.*) réservoir *m.*

reshape /riːˈʃeɪp/ *v.t.* remodeler.

reshuffle /riːˈʃʌfl/ *v.t.* (*pol.*) remanier. ● *n.* (*pol.*) remaniement (ministériel) *m.*

reside /rɪˈzaɪd/ *v.i.* résider.

residen|t /ˈrezɪdənt/ *a.* résidant. be ~t, résider. ● *n.* habitant(e) *m.* (*f.*); (*foreigner*) résident(e) *m.* (*f.*); (*in hotel*) pensionnaire *m./f.* **~ce** *n.* résidence *f.*; (*of students*) foyer *m.* in ~ce, (*doctor*) résidant; (*students*) au foyer.

residential /rezɪˈdenʃl/ *a.* résidentiel.

residue /ˈrezɪdjuː/ *n.* résidu *m.*

resign /rɪˈzaɪn/ *v.t.* abandonner; (*job*) démissionner de. ● *v.i.* démissionner. ~ o.s. to, se résigner à. **~ation** /rezɪgˈneɪʃn/ *n.* résignation *f.*; (*from job*) démission *f.* **~ed** *a.* résigné.

resilien|t /rɪˈzɪlɪənt/ *a.* élastique; (*person*) qui a du ressort. **~ce** *n.* élasticité *f.*; ressort *m.*

resin /ˈrezɪn/ *n.* résine *f.*

resist /rɪˈzɪst/ *v.t./i.* résister (à). **~ance** *n.* résistance *f.* **~ant** *a.* (*med.*) rebelle; (*metal*) résistant.

resolut|e /ˈrezəluːt/ *a.* résolu. **~ion** /-ˈluːʃn/ *n.* résolution *f.*

resolve /rɪˈzɒlv/ *v.t.* résoudre (to do, de faire). ● *n.* résolution *f.* **~d** *a.* résolu (to do, à faire).

resonan|t /ˈrezənənt/ *a.* résonnant. **~ce** *n.* résonance *f.*

resort /rɪˈzɔːt/ *v.i.* ~ to, avoir recours à. ● *n.* (*recourse*) recours *m.*; (*place*) station *f.* in the last ~, en dernier ressort.

resound /rɪˈzaʊnd/ *v.i.* retentir (with, de). **~ing** *a.* retentissant.

resource /rɪˈsɔːs/ *n.* (*expedient*) ressource *f.* **~s**, (*wealth etc.*) ressources *f. pl.* **~ful** *a.* ingénieux. **~fulness** *n.* ingéniosité *f.*

respect /rɪˈspekt/ *n.* respect *m.*; (*aspect*) égard *m.* ● *v.t.* respecter. with ~ to, à l'égard de, relativement à. **~ful** *a.* respectueux.

respectab|le /rɪˈspektəbl/ *a.* respectable. **~ility** /-ˈbɪlətɪ/ *n.* respectabilité *f.* **~ly** *adv.* convenablement.

respective /rɪˈspektɪv/ *a.* respectif. **~ly** *adv.* respectivement.

respiration /respəˈreɪʃn/ *n.* respiration *f.*

respite /ˈresp(a)ɪt/ *n.* répit *m.*

resplendent /rɪˈsplendənt/ *a.* resplendissant.

respond /rɪˈspɒnd/ *v.i.* répondre (to, à) ~ to, (*react to*) réagir à.

response /rɪˈspɒns/ *n.* réponse *f.*

responsib|le /rɪˈspɒnsəbl/ *a.* responsable: (*job*) qui comporte des responsabilités. **~ility** /-ˈbɪlətɪ/ *n.* responsabilité *f.* **~ly** *adv.* de façon responsable.

responsive /rɪˈspɒnsɪv/ *a.* qui réagit bien. ~ to, sensible à.

rest[1] /rest/ *v.t./i.* (se) reposer; (*lean*) (s')appuyer (on, sur); (*be buried, lie*) reposer. ● *n.* (*repose*) repos *m.*; (*support*) support *m.* have a ~, se reposer; (*at work*) prendre une pause. **~-room** *n.* (*Amer.*) toilettes *f. pl.*

rest[2] /rest/ *v.i.* (*remain*) demeurer. ● *n.* (*remainder*) reste *m.* (of, de). the ~ (of the), (*others, other*) les autres. it ~s with him to, il lui appartient de.

restaurant /ˈrestərɒnt/ *n.* restaurant *m.*

restful /ˈrestfl/ *a.* reposant.

restitution /restɪˈtjuːʃn/ *n.* (*for injury*) compensation *f.*

restive /ˈrestɪv/ *a.* rétif.

restless /ˈrestlɪs/ *a.* agité. **~ly** *adv.* avec agitation, fébrilement.

restor|e /rɪˈstɔː(r)/ *v.t.* rétablir; (*building*) restaurer. ~e sth. to s.o., restituer qch. à qn. **~ation** /restəˈreɪʃn/ *n.* rétablissement *m.*; restauration *f.* **~er** *n.* (*art*) restaura|teur, -trice *m.*, *f.*

restrain /rɪˈstreɪn/ *v.t.* contenir. ~ s.o. from, retenir qn. de. **~ed** *a.* (*moderate*) mesuré; (*in control of self*) maître de soi. **~t** *n.* contrainte *f.*; (*moderation*) retenue *f.*

restrict /rɪˈstrɪkt/ *v.t.* restreindre. **~ion** /-kʃn/ *n.* restriction *f.* **~ive** *a.* restrictif.

restructure /riːˈstrʌktʃə(r)/ *v.t.* restructurer.

result /rɪˈzʌlt/ *n.* résultat *m.* ● *v.i.* résulter. ~ in, aboutir à.

resum|e /rɪˈzjuːm/ *v.t./i.* reprendre. **~ption** /rɪˈzʌmpʃn/ *n.* reprise *f.*

résumé /'rezju:meɪ/ n. résumé m.; (of career: Amer.) CV m., curriculum vitae m.

resurgence /rɪ'sɜːdʒəns/ n. réapparition f.

resurrect /rezə'rekt/ v.t. ressusciter. **~ion** -kʃn/ n. résurrection f.

resuscitate /rɪ'sʌsɪteɪt/ v.t. réanimer.

retail /'riːteɪl/ n. détail m. ● a. & adv. au détail. ● v.t./i. (se) vendre (au détail). **~er** n. détaillant(e) m. (f.).

retain /rɪ'teɪn/ v.t. (hold back, remember) retenir; (keep) conserver.

retaliat|e /rɪ'tælɪeɪt/ v.i. riposter. **~ion** -'eɪʃn/ n. représailles f. pl.

retarded /rɪ'tɑːdɪd/ a. arriéré.

retch /retʃ/ v.i. avoir un haut-le-cœur.

retentive /rɪ'tentɪv/ a. (memory) fidèle. **~ of**, qui retient.

rethink /riː'θɪŋk/ v.t. (p.t. **rethought**) repenser.

reticen|t /'retɪsnt/ a. réticent. **~ce** n. réticence f.

retina /'retɪnə/ n. rétine f.

retinue /'retɪnjuː/ n. suite f.

retire /rɪ'taɪə(r)/ v.i. (from work) prendre sa retraite; (withdraw) se retirer; (go to bed) se coucher. ● v.t. mettre à la retraite. **~d** a. retraité. **~ment** n. retraite f.

retiring /rɪ'taɪərɪŋ/ a. réservé.

retort /rɪ'tɔːt/ v.t./i. répliquer. ● n. réplique f.

retrace /riː'treɪs/ v.t. **~ one's steps**, revenir sur ses pas.

retract /rɪ'trækt/ v.t./i. (se) rétracter.

retrain /riː'treɪn/ v.t./i. (se) recycler.

retread /riː'tred/ n. pneu rechapé m.

retreat /rɪ'triːt/ v.i. (mil.) battre en retraite. ● n. retraite f.

retrial /riː'traɪəl/ n. nouveau procès m.

retribution /retrɪ'bjuːʃn/ n. châtiment m.; (vengeance) vengeance f.

retriev|e /rɪ'triːv/ v.t. (recover) récupérer; (restore) rétablir; (put right) réparer. **~al** n. récupération f.; (of information) recherche documentaire f. **~er** n. (dog) chien d'arrêt m.

retrograde /'retrəgreɪd/ a. rétrograde ● v.i. rétrograder.

retrospect /'retrəspekt/ n. **in ~**, rétrospectivement.

return /rɪ'tɜːn/ v.i. (come back) revenir; (go back) retourner; (go home) rentrer. ● v.t. (give back) rendre; (bring back) rapporter; (send back) renvoyer; (put back) remettre. ● n.

retour m.; (yield) rapport m. **~s**, (comm.) bénéfices m. pl. **in ~ for**, en échange de. **~ journey**, voyage de retour m. **~ match**, match retour m. **~ ticket**, aller-retour m.

reunion /riː'juːnɪən/ n. réunion f.

reunite /riːjuː'naɪt/ v.t. réunir.

rev /rev/ n. (auto., fam.) tour m. ● v.t./i. (p.t. **revved**). **~ (up)**, (engine: fam.) (s')emballer.

revamp /riː'væmp/ v.t. rénover.

reveal /rɪ'viːl/ v.t. révéler; (allow to appear) laisser voir. **~ing** a. révélateur.

revel /'revl/ v.i. (p.t. **revelled**) faire bombance. **~ in**, se délecter de. **~ry** n. festivités f. pl.

revelation /revə'leɪʃn/ n. révélation f.

revenge /rɪ'vendʒ/ n. vengeance f.; (sport) revanche f. ● v.t. venger.

revenue /'revənjuː/ n. revenu m.

reverberate /rɪ'vɜːbəreɪt/ v.i. (sound, light) se répercuter.

revere /rɪ'vɪə(r)/ v.t. révérer. **~nce** /'revərəns/ n. vénération f.

reverend /'revərənd/ a. révérend.

reverent /'revərənt/ a. respectueux.

reverie /'revərɪ/ n. rêverie f.

revers|e /rɪ'vɜːs/ a. contraire, inverse. ● n. contraire m.; (back) revers m., envers m.; (gear) marche arrière f. ● v.t. (situation, bracket, etc.) renverser; (order) inverser; (decision) annuler. ● v.i. (auto.) faire marche arrière. **~al** n. renversement m.; (of view) revirement m.

revert /rɪ'vɜːt/ v.i. **~ to**, revenir à.

review /rɪ'vjuː/ n. (inspection, magazine) revue f.; (of book etc.) critique f. ● v.t. passer en revue; (situation) réexaminer; faire la critique de. **~er** n. critique m.

revis|e /rɪ'vaɪz/ v.t. réviser; (text) revoir. **~ion** -ɪʒn/ n. révision f.

revitalize /riː'vaɪtəlaɪz/ v.t. revitaliser, revivifier.

reviv|e /rɪ'vaɪv/ v.t. (person, hopes) ranimer; (play) reprendre; (custom) rétablir. ● v.i. se ranimer. **~al** n. (resumption) reprise f.; (of faith) renouveau m.

revoke /rɪ'vəʊk/ v.t. révoquer.

revolt /rɪ'vəʊlt/ v.t./i. (se) révolter. ● n. révolte f.

revolting /rɪ'vəʊltɪŋ/ a. dégoûtant.

revolution /revə'luːʃn/ n. révolution f. **~ary** a. & n. révolutionnaire (m./f.). **~ize** v.t. révolutionner.

revolve /rɪ'vɒlv/ v.i. tourner. ~ing door, tambour m.

revolver /rɪ'vɒlvə(r)/ n. revolver m.

revulsion /rɪ'vʌlʃn/ n. dégoût m.

reward /rɪ'wɔːd/ n. récompense f. ● v.t. récompenser (for, de). ~ing a. rémunérateur; (worthwhile) qui (en) vaut la peine.

rewind /riː'waɪnd/ v.t. (p.t. rewound) (tape, film) rembobiner.

rewire /riː'waɪə(r)/ v.t. refaire l'installation électrique de.

reword /riː'wɜːd/ v.t. reformuler.

rewrite /riː'raɪt/ v.t. récrire.

rhapsody /'ræpsədɪ/ n. rhapsodie f.

rhetoric /'retərɪk/ n. rhétorique f. ~al /rɪ'tɒrɪkl/ a. (de) rhétorique; (question) de pure forme.

rheumatic /ruː'mætɪk/ a. (pain) rhumatismal; (person) rhumatisant. ~sm /'ruːmətɪzəm/ n. rhumatisme m.

rhinoceros /raɪ'nɒsərəs/ n. (pl. -oses) rhinocéros m.

rhubarb /'ruːbɑːb/ n. rhubarbe f.

rhyme /raɪm/ n. rime f.; (poem) vers m. pl. ● v.t./i. (faire) rimer.

rhythm /'rɪðəm/ n. rythme m. ~ic(al) /'rɪðmɪk(l)/ a. rythmique.

rib /rɪb/ n. côte f.

ribald /'rɪbld/ a. grivois.

ribbon /'rɪbən/ n. ruban m. in ~s, (torn pieces) en lambeaux.

rice /raɪs/ n. riz m.

rich /rɪtʃ/ a. (-er, -est) riche. ~es n. pl. richesses f. pl. ~ly adv. richement. ~ness n. richesse f.

rickety /'rɪkətɪ/ a. branlant.

ricochet /'rɪkəʃeɪ/ n. ricochet m. ● v.i. (p.t. ricocheted /-ʃeɪd/) ricocher.

rid /rɪd/ v.t. (p.t. rid, pres. p. ridding) débarrasser (of, de). get ~ of, se débarrasser de.

riddance /'rɪdns/ n. good ~!, bon débarras!

ridden /'rɪdn/ see ride.

riddle[1] /'rɪdl/ n. énigme f.

riddle[2] /'rɪdl/ v.t. ~ with, (bullets) cribler de; (mistakes) bourrer de.

ride /raɪd/ v.i. (p.t. rode, p.p. ridden) aller (à bicyclette, à cheval, etc.); (in car) rouler. ~ (a horse), (go riding as sport) monter (à cheval). ● v.t. (a particular horse) monter; (distance) parcourir. ● n. promenade f., tour m.; (distance) trajet m. give s.o. a ~, (Amer.) prendre qn. en voiture. go for a ~, aller faire un tour (à

bicyclette, à cheval, etc.). ~r /-ə(r)/ n. cavalier, -ière m., f.; (in horse race) jockey m.; (cyclist) cycliste m./ f.; (motorcyclist) motocycliste m./f.; (in document) annexe f.

ridge /rɪdʒ/ n. arête f., crête f.

ridicule /'rɪdɪkjuːl/ n. ridicule m. ● v.t. ridiculiser.

ridiculous /rɪ'dɪkjʊləs/ a. ridicule.

riding /'raɪdɪŋ/ n. équitation f.

rife /raɪf/ a. be ~, être répandu, sévir. ~ with, abondant en.

riff-raff /'rɪfræf/ n. canaille f.

rifle /'raɪfl/ n. fusil m. ● v.t. (rob) dévaliser.

rift /rɪft/ n. (crack) fissure f.; (between people) désaccord m.

rig[1] /rɪg/ v.t. (p.t. rigged) (equip) équiper. ● n. (for oil) derrick m. ~ out, habiller. ~-out n. (fam.) tenue f. ~ up, (arrange) arranger.

rig[2] /rɪg/ v.t. (p.t. rigged) (election, match, etc.) truquer.

right /raɪt/ a. (morally) bon; (fair) juste; (best) bon, qu'il faut; (not left) droit. be ~, (person) avoir raison (to, de); (calculation, watch) être exact. ● n. (entitlement) droit m.; (not left) droite f.; (not evil) le bien. ● v.t. (a wrong, sth. fallen, etc.) redresser. ● adv. (not left) à droite; (directly) tout droit; (exactly) bien, juste; (completely) tout (à fait). be in the ~, avoir raison. by ~s, normalement. on the ~, à droite. put ~, arranger, rectifier. ~ angle, angle droit m. ~ away, tout de suite. ~-hand a. à or de droite. ~-hand man, bras droit m. ~-handed a. droitier. ~ now, (at once) tout de suite; (at present) en ce moment. ~ of way, (auto.) priorité f. ~-wing a. (pol.) de droite.

righteous /'raɪtʃəs/ a. (person) vertueux; (cause, anger) juste.

rightful /'raɪtfl/ a. légitime. ~ly adv. à juste titre.

rightly /'raɪtlɪ/ adv. correctement; (with reason) à juste titre.

rigid /'rɪdʒɪd/ a. rigide. ~ity /rɪ-'dʒɪdətɪ/ n. rigidité f.

rigmarole /'rɪgmərəʊl/ n. charabia m.; (procedure) comédie f.

rig|our /'rɪgə(r)/ n. rigueur f. ~orous a. rigoureux.

rile /raɪl/ v.t. (fam.) agacer.

rim /rɪm/ n. bord m.; (of wheel) jante f. ~med a. bordé.

rind /raɪnd/ n. (*on cheese*) croûte f.; (*on bacon*) couenne f.; (*on fruit*) écorce f.

ring [1] /rɪŋ/ n. anneau m.; (*with stone*) bague f.; (*circle*) cercle m.; (*boxing*) ring m.; (*arena*) piste f. ● v.t. entourer; (*word in text etc.*) entourer d'un cercle. (**wedding**) ~, alliance f. ~ **road**, périphérique m.

ring [2] /rɪŋ/ v.t./i. (*p.t.* **rang**, *p.p.* **rung**) sonner; (*of words etc.*) retentir. ● n. sonnerie f. **give s.o. a** ~, donner un coup de fil à qn. ~ **the bell**, sonner. ~ **back**, rappeler. ~ **off**, raccrocher. ~ **up**, téléphoner (à). ~**ing** n. (*of bell*) sonnerie f. ~**ing tone**, tonalité f.

ringleader /ˈrɪŋliːdə(r)/ n. chef m.

rink /rɪŋk/ n. patinoire f.

rinse /rɪns/ v.t. rincer. ~ **out**, rincer. ● n. rinçage n.

riot /ˈraɪət/ n. émeute f.; (*of colours*) orgie f. ● v.i. faire une émeute. **run** ~, se déchaîner. ~**er** n. émeut|ier, -ière m., f.

riotous /ˈraɪətəs/ a. turbulent.

rip /rɪp/ v.t./i. (*p.t.* **ripped**) (se) déchirer. ● n. déchirure f. **let** ~, (*not check*) laisser courir. ~ **off**, (*sl.*) rouler. ~**-off** n. (*sl.*) vol m.

ripe /raɪp/ a. (**-er, -est**) mûr. ~**ness** n. maturité f.

ripen /ˈraɪpən/ v.t./i. mûrir.

ripple /ˈrɪpl/ n. ride f., ondulation f.; (*sound*) murmure m. ● v.t./i. (*water*) (se) rider.

rise /raɪz/ v.i. (*p.t.* **rose**, *p.p.* **risen**) (*go upwards, increase*) monter, s'élever; (*stand up, get up from bed*) se lever; (*rebel*) se soulever; (*sun, curtain*) se lever; (*water*) monter. ● n. (*slope*) pente f.; (*of curtain*) lever m.; (*increase*) hausse f.; (*in pay*) augmentation f.; (*progress, boom*) essor m. **give** ~ **to**, donner lieu à. ~ **up**, se soulever. ~**r** /-ə(r)/ n. **be an early** ~**r**, se lever tôt.

rising /ˈraɪzɪŋ/ n. (*revolt*) soulèvement m. ● a. (*increasing*) croissant; (*price*) qui monte; (*tide*) montant; (*sun*) levant. ~ **generation**, nouvelle génération f.

risk /rɪsk/ n. risque m. ● v.t. risquer. **at** ~, menacé. ~ **doing**, (*venture*) se risquer à faire. ~**y** a. risqué.

rissole /ˈrɪsəʊl/ n. croquette f.

rite /raɪt/ n. rite m. **last** ~**s**, derniers sacrements m. pl.

ritual /ˈrɪtʃʊəl/ a. & n. rituel (m.).

rival /ˈraɪvl/ n. rival(e) m. (f.). ● a. rival; (*claim*) opposé. ● v.t. (*p.t.* **rivalled**) rivaliser avec. ~**ry** n. rivalité f.

river /ˈrɪvə(r)/ n. rivière f.; (*flowing into sea & fig.*) fleuve m. ● a. (*fishing, traffic, etc.*) fluvial.

rivet /ˈrɪvɪt/ n. (*bolt*) rivet m. ● v.t. (*p.t.* **riveted**) river, riveter. ~**ing** a. fascinant.

Riviera /rɪvɪˈeərə/ n. **the (French)** ~, la Côte d'Azur.

road /rəʊd/ n. route f.; (*in town*) rue f.; (*small*) chemin m. ● a. (*sign, safety*) routier. **the** ~ **to**, (*glory etc.*: *fig.*) le chemin de. ~**-block** n. barrage routier m. ~**-hog** n. chauffard m. ~**-map** n. carte routière f. ~**works** n. pl. travaux m. pl.

roadside /ˈrəʊdsaɪd/ n. bord de la route m.

roadway /ˈrəʊdweɪ/ n. chaussée f.

roadworthy /ˈrəʊdwɜːðɪ/ a. en état de marche.

roam /rəʊm/ v.i. errer. ● v.t. (*streets, seas, etc.*) parcourir.

roar /rɔː(r)/ n. hurlement m.; rugissement m.; grondement m. ● v.t./i. hurler; (*of lion, wind*) rugir; (*of lorry, thunder*) gronder. ~ **with laughter**, rire aux éclats.

roaring /ˈrɔːrɪŋ/ a. (*trade, success*) très gros. ~ **fire**, belle flambée f.

roast /rəʊst/ v.t./i. rôtir. ● n. (*roast or roasting meat*) rôti m. ● a. rôti. ~ **beef**, rôti de bœuf m.

rob /rɒb/ v.t. (*p.t.* **robbed**) voler (**s.o. of sth.**, qch. à qn.); (*bank, house*) dévaliser; (*deprive*) priver (**of**, de). ~**ber** n. voleu|r, -se m., f. ~**bery** n. vol m.

robe /rəʊb/ n. (*of judge etc.*) robe f.; (*dressing-gown*) peignoir m.

robin /ˈrɒbɪn/ n. rouge-gorge m.

robot /ˈrəʊbɒt/ n. robot m.

robust /rəʊˈbʌst/ a. robuste.

rock [1] /rɒk/ n. roche f.; (*rock face, boulder*) rocher m.; (*hurled stone*) pierre f.; (*sweet*) sucre d'orge m. **on the** ~**s**, (*drink*) avec des glaçons; (*marriage*) en crise. ~**-bottom** a. (*fam.*) très bas. ~**-climbing** n. varappe f.

rock [2] /rɒk/ v.t./i. (se) balancer; (*shake*) (faire) trembler; (*child*) bercer. ● n. (*mus.*) rock m. ~**ing-chair** n. fauteuil à bascule m.

rockery /ˈrɒkərɪ/ n. rocaille f.

rocket /ˈrɒkɪt/ n. fusée f.

rocky /'rɒkɪ/ a. (-ier, -iest) (ground) rocailleux; (hill) rocheux; (shaky: fig.) branlant.

rod /rɒd/ n. (metal) tige f.; (for curtain) tringle f.; (wooden) baguette f.; (for fishing) canne à pêche f.

rode /rəʊd/ see ride.

rodent /'rəʊdnt/ n. rongeur m.

rodeo /rəʊ'deɪəʊ, Amer. 'rəʊdɪəʊ/ n. (pl. -os) rodéo m.

roe[1] /rəʊ/ n. œufs de poisson m. pl.

roe[2] /rəʊ/ n. (pl. roe or roes) (deer) chevreuil m.

rogue /rəʊg/ n. (dishonest) bandit m., voleur, -se m., f.; (mischievous) coquin(e) m. (f.). **~ish** a. coquin.

role /rəʊl/ n. rôle m. **~-playing** n. jeu de rôle m.

roll /rəʊl/ v.t./i. rouler. **~ (about)**, (child, dog) se rouler. ● n. rouleau m.; (list) liste f.; (bread) petit pain m.; (of drum, thunder) roulement m.; (of ship) roulis m. **be ~ing (in money)**, (fam.) rouler sur l'or. **~-bar** n. arceau de sécurité m. **~-call** n. appel m. **~ing-pin** n. rouleau à pâtisserie m. **~ out**, étendre. **~ over**, (turn over) se retourner. **~ up** v.t. (sleeves) retrousser; v.i. (fam.) s'amener.

roller /'rəʊlə(r)/ n. rouleau m. **~-blind** n. store m. **~-coaster** n. montagnes russes f. pl. **~-skate** n. patin à roulettes m.

rollicking /'rɒlɪkɪŋ/ a. exubérant.

rolling /'rəʊlɪŋ/ a. onduleux.

ROM (abbr.) (read-only memory) mémoire morte f.

Roman /'rəʊmən/ a. & n. romain(e) (m. (f.)). **~ Catholic** a. & n. catholique (m./f.). **~ numerals**, chiffres romains m. pl.

romance /rə'mæns/ n. roman d'amour m.; (love) amour m.; (affair) idylle f.; (fig.) poésie f.

Romania /rəʊ'meɪnɪə/ n. Roumanie f. **~n** a. & n. roumain(e) (m. (f.)).

romantic /rə'mæntɪk/ a. (of love etc.) romantique; (of the imagination) romanesque. **~ally** adv. (behave) en romantique.

romp /rɒmp/ v.i. s'ébattre; (fig.) réussir. ● n. have a ~, s'ébattre.

roof /ruːf/ n. (pl. roofs) toit m.; (of tunnel) plafond m.; (of mouth) palais m. ● v.t. recouvrir. **~ing** n. toiture f. **~-rack** n. galerie f. **~-top** n. toit m.

rook[1] /rʊk/ n. (bird) corneille f.

rook[2] /rʊk/ n. (chess) tour f.

room /ruːm/ n. pièce f.; (bedroom) chambre f.; (large hall) salle f.; (space) place f. **~mate** n. camarade de chambre m./f. **~y** a. spacieux; (clothes) ample.

roost /ruːst/ n. perchoir m. ● v.i. percher. **~er** /'ruːstə(r)/ n. coq m.

root[1] /ruːt/ n. racine f.; (source) origine f. ● v.t./i. (s')enraciner. **~out**, extirper. **take ~**, prendre racine. **~less** a. sans racines.

root[2] /ruːt/ v.i. **~ about**, fouiller. **~ for**, (Amer., fam.) encourager.

rope /rəʊp/ n. corde f. ● v.t. attacher. **know the ~s**, être au courant. **~ in**, (person) enrôler.

rosary /'rəʊzərɪ/ n. chapelet m.

rose[1] /rəʊz/ n. (flower) rose f.; (colour) rose m.; (nozzle) pomme f.

rose[2] /rəʊz/ see rise.

rosé /'rəʊzeɪ/ n. rosé m.

rosette /rəʊ'zet/ n. (sport) cocarde f.; (officer's) rosette f.

roster /'rɒstə(r)/ n. liste (de service) f., tableau (de service) m.

rostrum /'rɒstrəm/ n. (pl. -tra) tribune f.; (sport) podium m.

rosy /'rəʊzɪ/ a. (-ier, -iest) rose; (hopeful) plein d'espoir.

rot /rɒt/ v.t./i. (p.t. rotted) pourrir. ● n. pourriture f.; (nonsense: sl.) bêtises f. pl., âneries f. pl.

rota /'rəʊtə/ n. liste (de service) f.

rotary /'rəʊtərɪ/ a. rotatif.

rotate /rəʊ'teɪt/ v.t./i. (faire) tourner; (change round) alterner. **~ing** a. tournant. **~ion** /-ʃn/ n. rotation f.

rote /rəʊt/ n. by ~, machinalement.

rotten /'rɒtn/ a. pourri; (tooth) gâté; (bad: fam.) mauvais, sale.

rotund /rəʊ'tʌnd/ a. rond.

rouge /ruːʒ/ n. rouge (à joues) m.

rough /rʌf/ a. (-er, -est) (manners) rude; (to touch) rugueux; (ground) accidenté; (violent) brutal; (bad) mauvais; (estimate etc.) approximatif; (diamond) brut. ● adv. (live) à la dure; (play) brutalement. ● n. (ruffian) voyou m. ● v.t. **it**, vivre à la dure. **~-and-ready** a. (solution etc.) grossier (mais efficace). **~-and-tumble** n. mêlée f. **~ out**, ébaucher. **~ paper**, papier brouillon m. **~ly** adv. rudement; (approximately) à peu près. **~ness** n. rudesse f.; brutalité f.

roughage /'rʌfɪdʒ/ n. fibres (alimentaires) f. pl.

roulette /ruːˈlet/ n. roulette f.
round /raʊnd/ a. (**-er, -est**) rond. ● n. (*circle*) rond m.; (*slice*) tranche f.; (*of visits, drinks*) tournée f.; (*mil.*) ronde f.; (*competition*) partie f., manche f.; (*boxing*) round m.; (*of talks*) série f. ● prep. autour de. ● adv. autour. ● v.t. (*object*) arrondir; (*corner*) tourner. **go** *or* **come ~ to,** (*a friend etc.*) passer chez. **I'm going ~ the corner,** je vais juste à côté. **enough to go ~,** assez pour tout le monde. **go the ~ s,** circuler. **she lives ~ here** elle habite par ici. **~ about,** (*near by*) par ici; (*fig.*) à peu près. **~ of applause,** applaudissements m. pl. **~ off,** terminer. **~ the clock,** vingt-quatre heures sur vingt-quatre. **~ trip,** voyage allerretour m. **~ up,** rassembler. **~-up** n. rassemblement m.; (*of suspects*) rafle f.
roundabout /ˈraʊndəbaʊt/ n. manège m.; (*for traffic*) rond-point (à sens giratoire) m. ● a. indirect.
rounders /ˈraʊndəz/ n. sorte de baseball f.
roundly /ˈraʊndlɪ/ adv. (*bluntly*) franchement.
rous|e /raʊz/ v.t. éveiller; (*wake up*) réveiller. **be ~ed,** (*angry*) être en colère. **~ing** a. (*speech, music*) excitant; (*cheers*) frénétique.
rout /raʊt/ n. (*defeat*) déroute f. ● v.t. mettre en déroute.
route /ruːt/ n. itinéraire m., parcours m.; (*naut., aviat.*) route f.
routine /ruːˈtiːn/ n. routine f. ● a. de routine. **daily ~,** travail quotidien m.
rov|e /rəʊv/ v.t./i. errer (dans). **~ing** a. (*life*) vagabond.
row[1] /rəʊ/ n. rangée f., rang m. **in a ~,** (*consecutive*) consécutif.
row[2] /rəʊ/ v.i. ramer; (*sport*) faire de l'aviron. ● v.t. faire aller à la rame. **~ing** n. aviron m. **~(ing)-boat** n. bateau à rames m.
row[3] /raʊ/ n. (*noise: fam.*) tapage m.; (*quarrel: fam.*) engueulade f. ● v.i. (*fam.*) s'engueuler.
rowdy /ˈraʊdɪ/ a. (**-ier, -iest**) tapageur. ● n. voyou m. fr.
royal /ˈrɔɪəl/ a. royal. **~ly** adv. (*treat, live, etc.*) royalement.
royal|ty /ˈrɔɪəltɪ/ n. famille royale f. **~ies,** droits d'auteur m. pl.
rub /rʌb/ v.t./i. (*p.t.* **rubbed**) frotter. ● n. friction f. **~ it in,** insister là-

dessus. **~ off on,** déteindre sur. **~ out,** (s')effacer.
rubber /ˈrʌbə(r)/ n. caoutchouc m.; (*eraser*) gomme f. **~ band,** élastique m. **~ stamp,** tampon m. **~-stamp** v.t. approuver. **~y** a. caoutchouteux.
rubbish /ˈrʌbɪʃ/ n. (*refuse*) ordures f. pl.; (*junk*) saletés f. pl.; (*fig.*) bêtises f. pl. **~y** a. sans valeur.
rubble /ˈrʌbl/ n. décombres m. pl.
ruby /ˈruːbɪ/ n. rubis m.
rucksack /ˈrʌksæk/ n. sac à dos m.
rudder /ˈrʌdə(r)/ n. gouvernail m.
ruddy /ˈrʌdɪ/ a. (**-ier, -iest**) coloré, rougeâtre; (*damned: sl.*) fichu.
rude /ruːd/ a. (**-er, -est**) impoli, grossier; (*improper*) indécent; (*shock, blow*) brutal. **~ly** adv. impoliment. **~ness** n. impolitesse f.; indécence f.; brutalité f.
rudiment /ˈruːdɪmənt/ n. rudiment m. **~ary** /-ˈmentrɪ/ a. rudimentaire.
rueful /ˈruːfl/ a. triste.
ruffian /ˈrʌfɪən/ n. voyou m.
ruffle /ˈrʌfl/ v.t. (*hair*) ébouriffer; (*clothes*) froisser; (*person*) contrarier. ● n. (*frill*) ruche f.
rug /rʌg/ n. petit tapis m.
Rugby /ˈrʌgbɪ/ n. ● **(football),** rugby m.
rugged /ˈrʌgɪd/ a. (*surface*) rude, rugueux; (*ground*) accidenté; (*character, features*) rude.
ruin /ˈruːɪn/ n. ruine f. ● v.t. (*destroy*) ruiner; (*damage*) abîmer; (*spoil*) gâter. **~ous** a. ruineux.
rule /ruːl/ n. règle f.; (*regulation*) règlement m.; (*pol.*) gouvernement m. ● v.t. gouverner; (*master*) dominer; (*decide*) décider. ● v.i. régner. **as a ~,** en règle générale. **~ out,** exclure. **~d paper,** papier réglé m. **~r** /-ə(r)/ n. dirigeant(e) m. (f.), gouvernant m.; (*measure*) règle f.
ruling /ˈruːlɪŋ/ a. (*class*) dirigeant; (*party*) au pouvoir. ● n. décision f.
rum /rʌm/ n. rhum m.
rumble /ˈrʌmbl/ v.i. gronder; (*stomach*) gargouiller. ● n. grondement m.; gargouillement m.
rummage /ˈrʌmɪdʒ/ v.i. fouiller.
rumour, (*Amer.*) **rumor** /ˈruːmə(r)/ n. bruit m., rumeur f. **there's a ~ that,** le bruit court que.
rump /rʌmp/ n. (*of horse etc.*) croupe f.; (*of fowl*) croupion m.; (*steak*) romsteck m.
rumpus /ˈrʌmpəs/ n. (*uproar: fam.*) chahut m.

run /rʌn/ *v.i.* (*p.t.* **ran**, *p.p.* **run**, *pres. p.* **running**) courir; (*flow*) couler; (*pass*) passer; (*function*) marcher; (*melt*) fondre; (*extend*) s'étendre; (*of bus etc.*) circuler; (*of play*) se jouer; (*last*) durer; (*of colour in washing*) déteindre; (*in election*) être candidat. ● *v.t.* (*manage*) diriger; (*event*) organiser; (*risk, race*) courir; (*house*) tenir; (*blockade*) forcer; (*temperature, errand*) faire; (*comput.*) exécuter. ● *n.* course *f.*; (*journey*) parcours *m.*; (*outing*) promenade *f.*; (*rush*) ruée *f.*; (*series*) série *f.*; (*in cricket*) point *m.* **have the ~ of**, avoir à sa disposition. **in the long ~**, avec le temps. **on the ~**, en fuite. **~ across**, rencontrer par hasard. **~ away**, s'enfuir. **~ down**, descendre en courant; (*of vehicle*) renverser; (*production*) réduire progressivement; (*belittle*) dénigrer. **be ~ down**, (*weak etc.*) être sans forces *or* mal fichu. **~ in**, (*vehicle*) roder. **~ into**, (*hit*) heurter. **~ off**, (*copies*) tirer. **~-of-the-mill** *a.* ordinaire. **~ out**, (*be used up*) s'épuiser; (*of lease*) expirer. **~ out of**, manquer de. **~ over**, (*of vehicle*) écraser; (*details*) revoir. **~ through sth.**, regarder qch. rapidement. **~ sth. through sth.**, passer qch. à travers qch. **~ up**, (*bill*) accumuler. **the ~-up to**, la période qui précède.

runaway /'rʌnəweɪ/ *n.* fugiti|f, -ve *m., f.* ● *a.* fugitif; (*horse, vehicle*) fou; (*inflation*) galopant.

rung[1] /rʌŋ/ *n.* (*of ladder*) barreau *m.*

rung[2] /rʌŋ/ *see* ring[2].

runner /'rʌnə(r)/ *n.* coureu|r, -se *m., f.* **~ bean**, haricot (grimpant) *m.* **~-up** *n.* second(e) *m.* (*f.*).

running /'rʌnɪŋ/ *n.* course *f.*; (*of business*) gestion *f.*; (*of machine*) marche *f.* ● *a.* (*commentary*) suivi; (*water*) courant. **be in the ~ for**, être sur les rangs pour. **four days/ etc. ~**, quatre jours/*etc.* de suite.

runny /'rʌnɪ/ *a.* (*nose*) qui coule.

runt /rʌnt/ *n.* avorton *m.*

runway /'rʌnweɪ/ *n.* piste *f.*

rupture /'rʌptʃə(r)/ *n.* (*breaking, breach*) rupture *f.*; (*med.*) hernie *f.* ● *v.t./i.* (se) rompre. **~ o.s.**, se donner une hernie.

rural /'rʊərəl/ *a.* rural.

ruse /ruːz/ *n.* (*trick*) ruse *f.*

rush[1] /rʌʃ/ *n.* (*plant*) jonc *m.*

rush[2] /rʌʃ/ *v.i.* (*move*) se précipiter; (*be in a hurry*) se dépêcher. ● *v.t.* faire, envoyer, *etc.* en vitesse; (*person*) bousculer; (*mil.*) prendre d'assaut. ● *n.* ruée *f.*; (*haste*) bousculade *f.* **in a ~**, pressé. **~-hour** *n.* heure de pointe *f.*

rusk /rʌsk/ *n.* biscotte *f.*

russet /'rʌsɪt/ *a.* roussâtre, roux.

Russia /'rʌʃə/ *n.* Russie *f.* **~n** *a. & n.* russe (*m./f.*); (*lang.*) russe *m.*

rust /rʌst/ *n.* rouille *f.* ● *v.t./i.* rouiller. **~-proof** *a.* inoxydable. **~y** *a.* (*tool, person, etc.*) rouillé.

rustic /'rʌstɪk/ *a.* rustique.

rustle /'rʌsl/ *v.t./i.* (*leaves*) (faire) bruire; (*steal: Amer.*) voler. **~ up**, (*food etc.: fam.*) préparer.

rut /rʌt/ *n.* ornière *f.* **be in a ~**, rester dans l'ornière.

ruthless /'ruːθlɪs/ *a.* impitoyable. **~ness** *n.* cruauté *f.*

rye /raɪ/ *n.* seigle *m.*; (*whisky*) whisky *m.* (*à base de seigle*).

S

sabbath /'sæbəθ/ *n.* (*Jewish*) sabbat *m.*; (*Christian*) dimanche *m.*

sabbatical /sə'bætɪkl/ *a.* (*univ.*) sabbatique.

sabot|age /'sæbətɑːʒ/ *n.* sabotage *m.* ● *v.t.* saboter. **~eur** /-'tɜː(r)/ *n.* saboteu|r, -se *m., f.*

saccharin /'sækərɪn/ *n.* saccharine *f.*

sachet /'sæʃeɪ/ *n.* sachet *m.*

sack[1] /sæk/ *n.* (*bag*) sac *m.* ● *v.t.* (*fam.*) renvoyer. **get the ~**, (*fam.*) être renvoyé. **~ing** *n.* toile à sac *f.*; (*dismissal: fam.*) renvoi *m.*

sack[2] /sæk/ *v.t.* (*plunder*) saccager.

sacrament /'sækrəmənt/ *n.* sacrement *m.*

sacred /'seɪkrɪd/ *a.* sacré.

sacrifice /'sækrɪfaɪs/ *n.* sacrifice *m.* ● *v.t.* sacrifier.

sacrileg|e /'sækrɪlɪdʒ/ *n.* sacrilège *m.* **~ious** /-'lɪdʒəs/ *a.* sacrilège.

sad /sæd/ *a.* (**sadder, saddest**) triste. **~ly** *adv.* tristement; (*unfortunately*) malheureusement. **~ness** *n.* tristesse *f.*

sadden /'sædn/ *v.t.* attrister.

saddle /'sædl/ *n.* selle *f.* ● *v.t.* (*horse*) seller. **~ s.o. with**, (*task,* *person*) coller à qn. **in the ~,** bien en selle. **~-bag** *n.* sacoche *f.*

sadis|t /'seɪdɪst/ *n.* sadique *m./f.* **~m** /-zəm/ *n.* sadisme *m.* **~tic** /sə'dɪstɪk/ *a.* sadique.

safari /sə'fɑːrɪ/ *n.* safari *m.*

safe /seɪf/ *a.* (**-er, -est**) (*not dangerous*) sans danger; (*reliable*) sûr; (*out of danger*) en sécurité; (*after accident*) sain et sauf; (*wise: fig.*) prudent. ● *n.* coffre-fort *m.* **to be on the ~ side,** pour être sûr. **in ~ keeping,** en sécurité. **~ conduct,** sauf-conduit *m.* **~ from,** à l'abri de. **~ly** *adv.* sans danger; (*in safe place*) en sûreté.

safeguard /'seɪfgɑːd/ *n.* sauvegarde *f.* ● *v.t.* sauvegarder.

safety /'seɪftɪ/ *n.* sécurité *f.* **~-belt** *n.* ceinture de sécurité *f.* **~-pin** *n.* épingle de sûreté *f.* **~-valve** *n.* soupape de sûreté *f.*

saffron /'sæfrən/ *n.* safran *m.*

sag /sæg/ *v.i.* (*p.t.* **sagged**) s'affaisser, fléchir. **~ging** *a.* affaissé.

saga /'sɑːgə/ *n.* saga *f.*

sage [1] /seɪdʒ/ *n.* (*herb*) sauge *f.*

sage [2] /seɪdʒ/ *a.* & *n.* sage (*m.*).

Sagittarius /sædʒɪ'teərɪəs/ *n.* le Sagittaire.

said /sed/ *see* say.

sail /seɪl/ *n.* voile *f.*; (*journey*) tour en bateau *m.* ● *v.i.* naviguer; (*leave*) partir; (*sport*) faire de la voile; (*glide*) glisser. ● *v.t.* (*boat*) piloter. **~ing-boat, ~ing-ship** *ns.* bateau à voiles *m.*

sailor /'seɪlə(r)/ *n.* marin *m.*

saint /seɪnt/ *n.* saint(e) *m.* (*f.*). **~ly** *a.* (*person, act, etc.*) saint.

sake /seɪk/ *n.* **for the ~ of,** pour, pour l'amour de.

salad /'sæləd/ *n.* salade *f.* **~-dressing** *n.* vinaigrette *f.*

salami /sə'lɑːmɪ/ *n.* salami *m.*

salar|y /'sælərɪ/ *n.* traitement *m.*, salaire *m.* **~ied** *a.* salarié.

sale /seɪl/ *n.* vente *f.* **~s,** (*at reduced prices*) soldes *m. pl.* **~s assistant,** (*Amer.*) **~s clerk,** vendeu|r, -se *m.,f.* **for ~,** à vendre. **on ~,** en vente; (*at a reduced price: Amer.*) en solde. **~-room** *n.* salle des ventes *f.*

saleable /'seɪləbl/ *a.* vendable.

sales|man /'seɪlzmən/ *n.* (*pl.* **-men**) (*in shop*) vendeur *m.*; (*traveller*) représentant *m.* **~woman** *n.* (*pl.* **-women**) vendeuse *f.*; représentante *f.*

salient /'seɪlɪənt/ *a.* saillant.

saline /'seɪlaɪn/ *a.* salin. ● *n.* sérum physiologique *m.*

saliva /sə'laɪvə/ *n.* salive *f.*

sallow /'sæləʊ/ *a.* (**-er, -est**) (*complexion*) jaunâtre.

salmon /'sæmən/ *n. invar.* saumon *m.*

salon /'sælɒn/ *n.* salon *m.*

saloon /sə'luːn/ *n.* (*on ship*) salon *m.*; (*bar: Amer.*) bar *m.,* saloon *m.* **~ (car),** berline *f.*

salt /sɔːlt/ *n.* sel *m.* ● *a.* (*culin.*) salé; (*water*) de mer. ● *v.t.* saler. **~-cellar** *n.* salière *f.* **~y** *a.* salé.

salutary /'sæljʊtrɪ/ *a.* salutaire.

salute /sə'luːt/ *n.* (*mil.*) salut *m.* ● *v.t.* saluer. ● *v.i.* faire un salut.

salvage /'sælvɪdʒ/ *n.* sauvetage *m.*; (*of waste*) récupération *f.*; (*goods*) objets sauvés *m. pl.* ● *v.t.* sauver; (*for re-use*) récupérer.

salvation /sæl'veɪʃn/ *n.* salut *m.*

salvo /'sælvəʊ/ *n.* (*pl.* **-oes**) salve *f.*

same /seɪm/ *a.* même (**as,** que). ● *pron.* **the ~,** le *or* la même, les mêmes. **at the ~ time,** en même temps. **the ~ (thing),** la même chose.

sample /'sɑːmpl/ *n.* échantillon *m.*; (*of blood*) prélèvement *m.* ● *v.t.* essayer; (*food*) goûter.

sanatorium /sænə'tɔːrɪəm/ *n.* (*pl.* **-iums**) sanatorium *m.*

sanctify /'sæŋktɪfaɪ/ *v.t.* sanctifier.

sanctimonious /sæŋktɪ'məʊnɪəs/ *a.* (*person*) bigot; (*air, tone*) de petit saint.

sanction /'sæŋkʃn/ *n.* sanction *f.* ● *v.t.* sanctionner.

sanctity /'sæŋktətɪ/ *n.* sainteté *f.*

sanctuary /'sæŋktʃʊərɪ/ *n.* (*relig.*) sanctuaire *m.*; (*for animals*) réserve *f.*; (*refuge*) asile *m.*

sand /sænd/ *n.* sable *m.* **~s,** (*beach*) plage *f.* ● *v.t.* sabler. **~-castle** *n.* château de sable *m.* **~-pit,** (*Amer.*) **~-box** *n.* bac à sable *m.*

sandal /'sændl/ *n.* sandale *f.*

sandpaper /'sændpeɪpə(r)/ *n.* papier de verre *m.* ● *v.t.* poncer.

sandstone /'sændstəʊn/ *n.* grès *m.*

sandwich /'sænwɪdʒ/ *n.* sandwich *m.* ● *v.t.* **~ed between,** pris en sandwich entre. **~ course,** stage de formation continue à mi-temps *m.*

sandy /'sændɪ/ *a.* sablonneux, de sable; (*hair*) blond roux *invar.*

sane /seɪn/ a. (**-er, -est**) (view etc.) sain; (person) sain d'esprit. **~ly** adv. sainement.

sang /sæŋ/ see sing.

sanitary /'sænɪtrɪ/ a. (clean) hygiénique; (system etc.) sanitaire. **~ towel**, (Amer.) **~ napkin**, serviette hygiénique f.

sanitation /sænɪ'teɪʃn/ n. hygiène (publique) f.; (drainage etc.) système sanitaire m.

sanity /'sænətɪ/ n. santé mentale f.; (good sense: fig.) bon sens m.

sank /sæŋk/ see sink.

Santa Claus /'sæntəklɔːz/ n. le père Noël.

sap /sæp/ n. (of plants) sève f. ● v.t. (p.t. **sapped**) (undermine) saper.

sapphire /'sæfaɪə(r)/ n. saphir m.

sarcasm /'sɑːkæzəm/ n. sarcasme m. **~tic** /sɑː'kæstɪk/ a. sarcastique.

sardine /sɑː'diːn/ n. sardine f.

Sardinia /sɑː'dɪnɪə/ n. Sardaigne f.

sardonic /sɑː'dɒnɪk/ a. sardonique.

sash /sæʃ/ n. (on uniform) écharpe f.; (on dress) ceinture f. **~-window** n. fenêtre à guillotine f.

sat /sæt/ see sit.

satanic /sə'tænɪk/ a. satanique.

satchel /'sætʃl/ n. cartable m.

satellite /'sætəlaɪt/ n. & a. satellite (m.). **~ dish**, antenne parabolique f.

satin /'sætɪn/ n. satin m.

satir|e /'sætaɪə(r)/ n. satire f. **~ical** /sə'tɪrɪkl/ a. satirique.

satisfactor|y /sætɪs'fæktərɪ/ a. satisfaisant. **~ily** adv. d'une manière satisfaisante.

satisf|y /'sætɪsfaɪ/ v.t. satisfaire; (convince) convaincre. **~action** /-'fæk-ʃn/ n. satisfaction f. **~ying** a. satisfaisant.

satsuma /sæt'suːmə/ n. mandarine f.

saturat|e /'sætʃəreɪt/ v.t. saturer. **~ed** a. (wet) trempé. **~ion** /-'reɪ-ʃn/ n. saturation f.

Saturday /'sætədɪ/ n. samedi m.

sauce /sɔːs/ n. sauce f.; (impudence: sl.) toupet m.

saucepan /'sɔːspən/ n. casserole f.

saucer /'sɔːsə(r)/ n. soucoupe f.

saucy /'sɔːsɪ/ a. (**-ier, -iest**) impertinent; (boldly smart) coquin.

Saudi Arabia /saʊdɪə'reɪbɪə/ n. Arabie Séoudite f.

sauna /'sɔːnə/ n. sauna m.

saunter /'sɔːntə(r)/ v.i. flâner.

sausage /'sɒsɪdʒ/ n. saucisse f.; (precooked) saucisson m.

savage /'sævɪdʒ/ a. (fierce) féroce; (wild) sauvage. ● n. sauvage m./f. ● v.t. attaquer férocement. **~ry** n. sauvagerie f.

sav|e /seɪv/ v.t. sauver; (money) économiser; (time) (faire) gagner; (keep) garder; (prevent) éviter (from, de). ● n. (football) arrêt m. ● prep. sauf. **~er** n. épargnant(e) m. (f.). **~ing** n. (of time, money) économie f. **~ings** n. pl. économies f. pl.

saviour, (Amer.) **savior** /'seɪvɪə(r)/ n. sauveur m.

savour, (Amer.) **savor** /'seɪvə(r)/ n. saveur f. ● v.t. savourer. **~y** a. (tasty) savoureux; (culin.) salé.

saw[1] /sɔː/ see see[1].

saw[2] /sɔː/ n. scie f. ● v.t. (p.t. **sawed**, p.p. **sawn** /sɔːn/ or **sawed**) scier.

sawdust /'sɔːdʌst/ n. sciure f.

saxophone /'sæksəfəʊn/ n. saxophone m.

say /seɪ/ v.t./i. (p.t. **said** /sed/) dire; (prayer) faire. ● n. **have a ~**, dire son mot; (in decision) avoir voix au chapitre. **I ~!**, dites donc!

saying /'seɪɪŋ/ n. proverbe m.

scab /skæb/ n. (on sore) croûte f.; (blackleg: fam.) jaune m.

scaffold /'skæfəʊld/ n. (gallows) échafaud m. **~ing** /-əldɪŋ/ n. (for workmen) échafaudage m.

scald /skɔːld/ v.t. (injure, cleanse) ébouillanter. ● n. brûlure f.

scale[1] /skeɪl/ n. (of fish) écaille f.

scale[2] /skeɪl/ n. (for measuring, size, etc.) échelle f.; (mus.) gamme f.; (of salaries, charges) barème m. **on a small/**etc. **~**, sur une petite etc. échelle. **~ model**, maquette f. ● v.t. (climb) escalader. **~ down**, réduire (proportionnellement).

scales /skeɪlz/ n. pl. (for weighing) balance f.

scallop /'skɒləp/ n. coquille Saint-Jacques f.

scalp /skælp/ n. cuir chevelu m. ● v.t. (mutilate) scalper.

scalpel /'skælp(ə)l/ n. scalpel m.

scamper /'skæmpə(r)/ v.i. courir, trotter. **~ away**, détaler.

scampi /'skæmpɪ/ n. pl. grosses crevettes f. pl., gambas f. pl.

scan /skæn/ v.t. (p.t. **scanned**) scruter; (quickly) parcourir; (poetry) scander; (of radar) balayer. ● n. (ultrasound) échographie f.

scandal /'skændl/ *n.* (*disgrace, outrage*) scandale *m.*; (*gossip*) cancans *m. pl.* **~ous** *a.* scandaleux.

scandalize /'skændəlaız/ *v.t.* scandaliser.

Scandinavia /skændɪ'neɪvɪə/ *n.* Scandinavie *f.* **~n** *a.* & *n.* scandinave (*m./f.*).

scant /skænt/ *a.* insuffisant.

scant|y /'skæntɪ/ *a.* (**-ier, -iest**) insuffisant; (*clothing*) sommaire. **~ily** *adv.* insuffisamment. **~ily dressed**, à peine vêtu.

scapegoat /'skeɪpgəʊt/ *n.* bouc émissaire *m.*

scar /skɑː(r)/ *n.* cicatrice *f.* ● *v.t.* (*p.t.* **scarred**) marquer d'une cicatrice; (*fig.*) marquer.

scarc|e /skeəs/ *a.* (**-er, -est**) rare. **make o.s. ~e**, (*fam.*) se sauver. **~ity** *n.* rareté *f.*, pénurie *f.*

scarcely /'skeəslɪ/ *adv.* à peine.

scare /'skeə(r)/ *v.t.* faire peur à. ● *n.* peur *f.* **be ~d**, avoir peur. **bomb ~**, alerte à la bombe *f.*

scarecrow /'skeəkrəʊ/ *n.* épouvantail *m.*

scarf /skɑːf/ *n.* (*pl.* **scarves**) écharpe *f.*; (*over head*) foulard *m.*

scarlet /'skɑːlət/ *a.* écarlate. **~ fever**, scarlatine *f.*

scary /'skeərɪ/ *a.* (**-ier, -iest**) (*fam.*) qui fait peur, effrayant.

scathing /'skeɪðɪŋ/ *a.* cinglant.

scatter /'skætə(r)/ *v.t.* (*throw*) éparpiller, répandre; (*disperse*) disperser. ● *v.i.* se disperser. **~brain** *n.* écervelé(e) *m.* (*f.*).

scavenge /'skævɪndʒ/ *v.i.* fouiller (dans les ordures). **~r** /-ə(r)/ *n.* (*vagrant*) personne qui fouille dans les ordures *f.*

scenario /sɪ'nɑːrɪəʊ/ *n.* (*pl.* **-os**) scénario *m.*

scene /siːn/ *n.* scène *f.*; (*of accident, crime*) lieu(x) *m.* (*pl.*); (*sight*) spectacle *m.*; (*incident*) incident *m.* **behind the ~s**, en coulisse. **to make a ~**, faire un esclandre.

scenery /'siːnərɪ/ *n.* paysage *m.*; (*theatre*) décor(s) *m.* (*pl.*).

scenic /'siːnɪk/ *a.* pittoresque.

scent /sent/ *n.* (*perfume*) parfum *m.*; (*trail*) piste *f.* ● *v.t.* flairer; (*make fragrant*) parfumer.

sceptic /'skeptɪk/ *n.* sceptique *m./f.* **~al** *a.* sceptique. **~ism** /-sɪzəm/ *n.* scepticisme *m.*

schedule /'ʃedjuːl, *Amer.* 'skedʒʊl/ *n.* horaire *m.*; (*for job*) planning *m.* ● *v.t.* prévoir. **behind ~**, en retard. **on ~**, (*train*) à l'heure; (*work*) dans les temps. **~d flight**, vol régulier *m.*

scheme /skiːm/ *n.* plan *m.*; (*dishonest*) combine *f.*; (*fig.*) arrangement *m.* ● *v.i.* intriguer. **pension ~**, caisse de retraite *f.* **~r** /-ə(r)/ *n.* intrigant(e) *m.* (*f.*).

schism /'sɪzəm/ *n.* schisme *m.*

schizophrenic /skɪtsəʊ'frenɪk/ *a.* & *n.* schizophrène (*m./f.*).

scholar /'skɒlə(r)/ *n.* érudit(e) *m.* (*f.*) **~ly** *a.* érudit. **~ship** *n.* érudition *f.*; (*grant*) bourse *f.*

school /skuːl/ *n.* école *f.*; (*secondary*) lycée *m.*; (*of university*) faculté *f.* ● *a.* (*age, year, holidays*) scolaire. ● *v.t.* (*person*) éduquer; (*animal*) dresser. **~ing** *n.* (*education*) instruction *f.*; (*attendance*) scolarité *f.*

school|boy /'skuːlbɔɪ/ *n.* écolier *m.* **~girl** *n.* écolière *f.*

school|master /'skuːlmɑːstə(r)/, **~mistress, ~teacher** *ns.* (*primary*) institu|teur, -trice *m.*, *f.*; (*secondary*) professeur *m.*

schooner /'skuːnə(r)/ *n.* goélette *f.*

sciatica /saɪ'ætɪkə/ *n.* sciatique *f.*

scien|ce /'saɪəns/ *n.* science *f.* **~ce fiction**, science-fiction *f.* **~tific** /-'tɪfɪk/ *a.* scientifique.

scientist /'saɪəntɪst/ *n.* scientifique *m./f.*

scintillate /'sɪntɪleɪt/ *v.i.* scintiller; (*person: fig.*) briller.

scissors /'sɪzəz/ *n. pl.* ciseaux *m. pl.*

scoff[1] /skɒf/ *v.i.* **~ at**, se moquer de.

scoff[2] /skɒf/ *v.t.* (*eat: sl.*) bouffer.

scold /skəʊld/ *v.t.* réprimander. **~ing** *n.* réprimande *f.*

scone /skɒn/ *n.* petit pain au lait *m.*, galette *f.*

scoop /skuːp/ *n.* (*for grain, sugar*) pelle (à main) *f.*; (*for food*) cuiller *f.*; (*ice cream*) boule *f.*; (*news*) exclusivité *f.* ● *v.t.* (*pick up*) ramasser. **~ out**, creuser. **~ up**, ramasser.

scoot /skuːt/ *v.i.* (*fam.*) filer.

scooter /'skuːtə(r)/ *n.* (*child's*) trottinette *f.*; (*motor cycle*) scooter *m.*

scope /skəʊp/ *n.* étendue *f.*; (*competence*) compétence *f.*; (*opportunity*) possibilité(s) *f.* (*pl.*).

scorch /skɔːtʃ/ *v.t.* brûler, roussir. **~ing** *a.* brûlant, très chaud.

score /skɔː(r)/ *n.* score *m.*; (*mus.*) partition *f.* ● *v.t.* marquer; (*suc-*

cess) remporter. ● *v.i.* marquer un point; (*football*) marquer un but; (*keep score*) compter les points. **a ~ (of)**, (*twenty*) vingt. **on that ~**, à cet égard. **~ out**, rayer. **~-board** *n.* tableau *m.* **~r** /-ə(r)/ *n.* (*sport*) marqueur *m.*

scorn /skɔːn/ *n.* mépris *m.* ● *v.t.* mépriser. **~ful** *a.* méprisant. **~fully** *adv.* avec mépris.

Scorpio /'skɔːpɪəʊ/ *n.* le Scorpion.

scorpion /'skɔːpɪən/ *n.* scorpion *m.*

Scot /skɒt/ *n.* Écossais(e) *m.* (*f.*). **~tish** *a.* écossais.

Scotch /skɒtʃ/ *a.* écossais. ● *n.* whisky *m.*, scotch *m.*

scotch /skɒtʃ/ *v.t.* mettre fin à.

scot-free /skɒt'friː/ *a. & adv.* sans être puni; (*gratis*) sans payer.

Scotland /'skɒtlənd/ *n.* Écosse *f.*

Scots /skɒts/ *a.* écossais. **~man** *n.* Écossais *m.* **~woman** *n.* Écossaise *f.*

scoundrel /'skaʊndrəl/ *n.* vaurien *m.*, bandit *m.*, gredin(e) *m.* (*f.*).

scour[1] /'skaʊə(r)/ *v.t.* (*pan*) récurer. **~er** *n.* tampon à récurer *m.*

scour[2] /'skaʊə(r)/ *v.t.* (*search*) parcourir.

scourge /skɜːdʒ/ *n.* fléau *m.*

scout /skaʊt/ *n.* (*mil.*) éclaireur *m.* ● *v.i.* **~ around (for)**, chercher.

Scout /skaʊt/ *n.* (*boy*) scout *m.*, éclaireur *m.* **~ing** *n.* scoutisme *m.*

scowl /skaʊl/ *n.* air renfrogné *m.* ● *v.i.* faire la tête (**at**, à).

scraggy /'skrægɪ/ *a.* (**-ier, -iest**) décharné, efflanqué.

scram /skræm/ *v.i.* (*sl.*) se tirer.

scramble /'skræmbl/ *v.i.* (*clamber*) grimper. ● *v.t.* (*eggs*) brouiller. ● *n.* bousculade *f.*, ruée *f.* **~ for**, se bousculer pour avoir.

scrap[1] /skræp/ *n.* petit morceau *m.*, **~s**, (*of metal, fabric, etc.*) déchets *m. pl.*; (*of food*) restes *m. pl.* ● *v.t.* (*p.t.* **scrapped**) mettre au rebut; (*plan etc.*) abandonner. **~-book** *n.* album *m.* **on the ~-heap**, mis au rebut. **~-iron** *n.* ferraille *f.* **~-paper** *n.* brouillon *m.* **~py** *a.* fragmentaire.

scrap[2] /skræp/ *n.* (*fight: fam.*) bagarre *f.*, dispute *f.*

scrape /skreɪp/ *v.t.* racler, gratter; (*graze*) érafler. ● *v.i.* (*rub*) frotter. ● *n.* raclement *m.*; éraflure *f.* **in a ~**, dans une mauvaise passe. **~ through**, réussir de justesse. **~ together**, réunir. **~r** /-ə(r)/ *n.* racloir *m.*

scratch /skrætʃ/ *v.t./i.* (se) gratter; (*with claw, nail*) griffer; (*graze*) érafler; (*mark*) rayer. ● *n.* éraflure *f.* **start from ~**, partir de zéro. **up to ~**, au niveau voulu.

scrawl /skrɔːl/ *n.* gribouillage *m.* ● *v.t./i.* gribouiller.

scrawny /'skrɔːnɪ/ *a.* (**-ier, -iest**) décharné, émacié.

scream /skriːm/ *v.t./i.* crier, hurler. ● *n.* cri (perçant) *m.*

scree /skriː/ *n.* éboulis *m.*

screech /skriːtʃ/ *v.i.* (*scream*) hurler; (*of brakes*) grincer. ● *n.* hurlement *m.*; grincement *m.*

screen /skriːn/ *n.* écran *m.*; (*folding*) paravent *m.* ● *v.t.* masquer; (*protect*) protéger; (*film*) projeter; (*candidates*) filtrer; (*med.*) faire subir un test de dépistage. **~ing** *n.* projection *f.*

screenplay /'skriːnpleɪ/ *n.* scénario *m.*

screw /skruː/ *n.* vis *f.* ● *v.t.* visser. **~ up**, (*eyes*) plisser; (*ruin: sl.*) bousiller.

screwdriver /'skruːdraɪvə(r)/ *n.* tournevis *m.*

screwy /'skruːɪ/ *a.* (**-ier, -iest**) (*crazy: sl.*) cinglé.

scribble /'skrɪbl/ *v.t./i.* griffonner. ● *n.* griffonnage *m.*

scribe /skraɪb/ *n.* scribe *m.*

script /skrɪpt/ *n.* écriture *f.*; (*of film*) scénario *m.*; (*of play*) texte *m.* **~writer** *n.* scénariste *m./f.*

Scriptures /'skrɪptʃəz/ *n. pl.* **the ~**, l'Écriture (sainte) *f.*

scroll /skrəʊl/ *n.* rouleau *m.* ● *v.t./i.* (*comput.*) (faire) défiler.

scrounge /skraʊndʒ/ *v.t.* (*meal*) se faire payer; (*steal*) chiper. ● *v.i.* (*beg*) quémander. **~ money from**, taper. **~r** /-ə(r)/ *n.* parasite *m.*; (*of money*) tapeu|r, -se *m., f.*

scrub[1] /skrʌb/ *n.* (*land*) broussailles *f. pl.*

scrub[2] /skrʌb/ *v.t./i.* (*p.t.* **scrubbed**) nettoyer (à la brosse), frotter. ● *n.* nettoyage *m.*

scruff /skrʌf/ *n.* **by the ~ of the neck**, par la peau du cou.

scruffy /'skrʌfɪ/ *a.* (**-ier, -iest**) (*fam.*) miteux, sale.

scrum /skrʌm/ *n.* (*Rugby*) mêlée *f.*

scruple /'skruːpl/ *n.* scrupule *m.*

scrupulous /'skruːpjʊləs/ *a.* scrupuleux. **~ly** *adv.* scrupuleusement. **~ly clean,** impeccable.

scrutin|y /'skru:tɪnɪ/ n. examen minutieux m. **~ize** v.t. scruter.

scuba-diving /'sku:bədaɪvɪŋ/ n. plongée sous-marine f.

scuff /skʌf/ v.t. (scratch) érafler.

scuffle /'skʌfl/ n. bagarre f.

sculpt /skʌlpt/ v.t./i. sculpter. **~or** n. sculpteur m. **~ure** /-tʃə(r)/ n. sculpture f.; v.t./i. sculpter.

scum /skʌm/ n. (on liquid) écume f.; (people: pej.) racaille f.

scurf /skɜ:f/ n. pellicules f. pl.

scurrilous /'skʌrɪləs/ a. grossier, injurieux, venimeux.

scurry /'skʌrɪ/ v.i. courir (**for,** pour chercher). **~ off,** filer.

scuttle[1] /'skʌtl/ v.t. (ship) saborder.

scuttle[2] /'skʌtl/ v.i. **~ away,** se sauver, filer.

scythe /saɪð/ n. faux f.

sea /si:/ n. mer f. ● a. de (la) mer, marin. **at ~,** en mer. **by ~,** par mer. **~-green** a. vert glauque invar. **~-level** n. niveau de la mer m. **~ shell,** coquillage m. **~shore** n. rivage m.

seaboard /'si:bɔ:d/ n. littoral m.

seafarer /'si:feərə(r)/ n. marin m.

seafood /'si:fu:d/ n. fruits de mer m. pl.

seagull /'si:gʌl/ n. mouette f.

seal[1] /si:l/ n. (animal) phoque m.

seal[2] /si:l/ n. sceau m.; (with wax) cachet m. ● v.t. sceller; cacheter; (stick down) coller. **~ing-wax** n. cire à cacheter f. **~ off,** (area) boucler.

seam /si:m/ n. (in cloth etc.) couture f.; (of coal) veine f.

seaman /'si:mən/ n. (pl. -men) marin m.

seamy /'si:mɪ/ a. **~ side,** côté sordide m.

seance /'seɪɑ:ns/ n. séance de spiritisme f.

seaplane /'si:pleɪn/ n. hydravion m.

seaport /'si:pɔ:t/ n. port de mer m.

search /sɜ:tʃ/ v.t./i. fouiller; (study) examiner. ● n. fouille f.; (quest) recherche(s) f. (pl.). **in ~ of,** à la recherche de. **~ for,** chercher. **~-party** n. équipe de secours f. **~-warrant** n. mandat de perquisition m. **~ing** a. (piercing) pénétrant.

searchlight /'sɜ:tʃlaɪt/ n. projecteur m.

seasick /'si:sɪk/ a. **be ~,** avoir le mal de mer.

seaside /'si:saɪd/ n. bord de la mer m.

season /'si:zn/ n. saison f. ● v.t. assaisonner. **in ~,** de saison. **~able** a. qui convient à la saison. **~al** a. saisonnier. **~ing** n. assaisonnement m. **~-ticket** n. carte d'abonnement f.

seasoned /'si:znd/ a. expérimenté.

seat /si:t/ n. siège m.; (place) place f.; (of trousers) fond m. ● v.t. (put) placer; (have seats for) avoir des places assises pour. **be ~ed, take a ~,** s'asseoir. **~-belt** n. ceinture de sécurité f.

seaweed /'si:wi:d/ n. algues f. pl.

seaworthy /'si:wɜ:ðɪ/ a. en état de naviguer.

secateurs /sekə'tɜ:z/ n. pl. sécateur m.

sece|de /sɪ'si:d/ v.i. faire sécession. **~ssion** /-eʃn/ n. sécession f.

seclu|de /sɪ'klu:d/ v.t. isoler. **~ded** a. isolé. **~sion** /-ʒn/ n. solitude f.

second[1] /'sekənd/ a. deuxième, second. ● n. deuxième m./f., second(e) m. (f.); (unit of time) seconde f. **~s,** (goods) articles de second choix m. pl. ● adv. (in race etc.) en seconde place. ● v.t. (proposal) appuyer. **~-best** a. de second choix, numéro deux invar. **~-class** a. de deuxième classe. **at ~ hand,** de seconde main. **~-hand** a. & adv. d'occasion; n. (on clock) trotteuse f. **~-rate** a. médiocre. **have ~ thoughts,** avoir des doutes, changer d'avis. **on ~ thoughts,** (Amer.) **on ~ thought,** à la réflexion. **~ly** adv. deuxièmement.

second[2] /sɪ'kɒnd/ v.t. (transfer) détacher (**to,** à). **~ment** n. détachement m.

secondary /'sekəndrɪ/ a. secondaire. **~ school,** lycée m., collège m.

secrecy /'si:krəsɪ/ n. secret m.

secret /'si:krɪt/ a. secret. ● n. secret m. **in ~,** en secret. **~ly** adv. en secret, secrètement.

secretariat /sekrə'teərɪət/ n. secrétariat m.

secretar|y /'sekrətrɪ/ n. secrétaire m./f. **S~y of State,** ministre m.; (Amer.) ministre des Affaires étrangères m. **~ial** /-'teərɪəl/ a. (work etc.) de secrétaire.

secret|e /sɪ'kri:t/ v.t. (med.) sécréter. **~ion** /-ʃn/ n. sécrétion f.

secretive /'si:krətɪv/ a. cachottier.

sect /sekt/ *n.* secte *f.* **~arian**
/-'teərɪən/ *a.* sectaire.

section /'sekʃn/ *n.* section *f.*; (*of
country, town*) partie *f.*; (*in store*)
rayon *m.*; (*newspaper column*) rubrique *f.*

sector /'sektə(r)/ *n.* secteur *m.*

secular /'sekjʊlə(r)/ *a.* (*school etc.*)
laïque; (*art, music, etc.*) profane.

secure /sɪ'kjʊə(r)/ *a.* (*safe*) en sûreté;
(*in mind*) tranquille; (*psychologically*) sécurisé; (*firm*) solide;
(*against attack*) sûr; (*window etc.*)
bien fermé. ● *v.t.* attacher; (*obtain*)
s'assurer; (*ensure*) assurer. **~ly** *adv.*
solidement; (*safely*) en sûreté.

security /sɪ'kjʊərətɪ/ *n.* (*safety*) sécurité *f.*; (*for loan*) caution *f.* **~
guard,** vigile *m.*

sedan /sɪ'dæn/ *n.* (*Amer.*) berline *f.*

sedate [1] /sɪ'deɪt/ *a.* calme.

sedat|e [2] /sɪ'deɪt/ *v.t.* donner un séda-
tif à. **~ion** /-ʃn/ *n.* sédation *f.*

sedative /'sedətɪv/ *n.* sédatif *m.*

sedentary /'sedntrɪ/ *a.* sédentaire.

sediment /'sedɪmənt/ *n.* sédiment *m.*

sedition /sɪ'dɪʃn/ *n.* sédition *f.*

seduce /sɪ'dju:s/ *v.t.* séduire. **~r**
/-ə(r)/ *n.* séduc|teur, -trice *m., f.*

seduct|ion /sɪ'dʌkʃn/ *n.* séduction *f.*
~ive /-tɪv/ *a.* séduisant.

see [1] /si:/ *v.t./i.* (*p.t.* **saw,** *p.p.* **seen**)
voir; (*escort*) (r)accompagner. **~
about** *or* **to,** s'occuper de. **~
through,** (*task*) mener à bonne fin;
(*person*) deviner (le jeu de). **~ (to it)
that,** veiller à ce que. **see you
(soon)!,** à bientôt! **~ing that,** vu
que.

see [2] /si:/ *n.* (*of bishop*) évêché *m.*

seed /si:d/ *n.* graine *f.*; (*collectively*)
graines *f. pl.*; (*origin: fig.*) germe *m.*;
(*tennis*) tête de série *f.* **go to ~,**
(*plant*) monter en graine; (*person*)
se laisser aller. **~ling** *n.* plant *m.*

seedy /'si:dɪ/ *a.* (**-ier, -iest**) miteux.

seek /si:k/ *v.t.* (*p.t.* **sought**) chercher.
~ out, aller chercher.

seem /si:m/ *v.i.* sembler. **~ingly** *adv.*
apparemment.

seemly /'si:mlɪ/ *adv.* convenable.

seen /si:n/ *see* see [1].

seep /si:p/ *v.i.* (*ooze*) suinter. **~ into,**
s'infiltrer dans. **~age** *n.* suintement
m.; infiltration *f.*

see-saw /'si:sɔ:/ *n.* balançoire *f.*, tape-
cul *m.* ● *v.t.* osciller.

seethe /si:ð/ *v.i.* **~ with,** (*anger*)
bouillir de; (*people*) grouiller de.

segment /'segmənt/ *n.* segment *m.*;
(*of orange*) quartier *m.*

segregat|e /'segrɪgeɪt/ *v.t.* séparer.
~ion /-'geɪʃn/ *n.* ségrégation *f.*

seize /si:z/ *v.t.* saisir; (*take possession
of*) s'emparer de. ● *v.i.* **~ on,**
(*chance etc.*) saisir. **~ up,** (*engine
etc.*) se gripper.

seizure /'si:ʒə(r)/ *n.* (*med.*) crise *f.*

seldom /'seldəm/ *adv.* rarement.

select /sɪ'lekt/ *v.t.* choisir, sélec-
tionner. ● *a.* choisi; (*exclusive*)
sélect. **~ion** /-kʃn/ *n.* sélection *f.*

selective /sɪ'lektɪv/ *a.* sélectif.

self /self/ *n.* (*pl.* **selves**) (*on cheque*)
moi-même. **the ~,** le moi *m. invar.*
your good ~, vous-même.

self- /self/ *pref.* **~-assurance** *n.* assurance *f.* **~-assured** *a.* sûr de soi.
~-catering *a.* où l'on fait la cuisine
soi-même. **~-centred,** (*Amer.*) **~-
entered** *a.* égocentrique. **~-co-
loured,** (*Amer.*) **~-colored** *a.* uni.
~-confidence *n.* confiance en soi *f.*
~-confident *a.* sûr de soi. **~-
conscious** *a.* gêné, timide. **~-
contained** *a.* (*flat*) indépendant. **~-
control** *n.* maîtrise de soi *f.* **~-
defence** *n.* autodéfense *f.*; (*jurid.*)
légitime défense *f.* **~-denial** *n.* abné-
gation *f.* **~-employed** *a.* qui travaille à son compte. **~-esteem** *n.*
amour-propre *m.* **~-evident** *a.*
évident. **~-government** *n.* autono-
mie *f.* **~-indulgent** *a.* qui se permet
tout. **~-interest** *n.* intérêt personnel
m. **~-portrait** *n.* autoportrait *m.*
~-possessed *a.* assuré. **~-reliant** *a.*
indépendant. **~-respect** *n.* respect
de soi *m.*, dignité *f.* **~-righteous** *a.*
satisfait de soi. **~-sacrifice** *n.* abné-
gation *f.* **~-satisfied** *a.* content de
soi. **~-seeking** *a.* égoïste. **~-service**
n. & *a.* libre-service (*m.*). **~-styled**
a. soi-disant. **~-sufficient** *a.*
indépendant. **~-willed** *a.* entêté.

selfish /'selfɪʃ/ *a.* égoïste; (*motive*)
intéressé. **~ness** *n.* égoïsme *m.*

selfless /'selflɪs/ *a.* désintéressé.

sell /sel/ *v.t./i.* (*p.t.* **sold**) (se) vendre.
~-by date, date limite de vente *f.* **be
sold out of,** n'avoir plus de. **~ off,**
liquider. **~-out,** *n.* trahison *f.* **it was
a ~-out,** on a vendu tous les billets.
~ up, vendre son fonds, sa maison,
etc. **~er** *n.* vendeu|r, -se *m., f.*

Sellotape /'seləʊteɪp/ *n.* (P.) scotch
m. (P.).

semantic /sɪ'mæntɪk/ a. sémantique.
~s n. sémantique f.

semaphore /'seməfɔ:(r)/ n. signaux à
bras m. pl.; (device: rail.) sémaphore
m.

semblance /'sembləns/ n. semblant
m.

semen /'si:mən/ n. sperme m.

semester /sɪ'mestə(r)/ n. (univ.,
Amer.) seméstre m.

semi- /'semɪ/ pref. semi-, demi-.

semibreve /'semɪbri:v/ n. (mus.)
ronde f.

semicirc|le /'semɪsɜ:kl/ n. demi-cer-
cle m. **~ular** /-'sɜ:kjʊlə(r)/ a. en
demi-cercle.

semicolon /semɪ'kəʊlən/ n. point-
virgule m.

semiconductor /semɪkən'dʌktə(r)/
n. semi-conducteur n.

semi-detached /semɪ'dɪtætʃt/ a. **~
house,** maison jumelée f.

semifinal /semɪ'faɪnl/ n. demi-finale
f.

seminar /'semɪnɑ:(r)/ n. séminaire m.

seminary /'semɪnərɪ/ n. séminaire m.

semiquaver /'semɪkweɪvə(r)/ n.
(mus.) double croche f.

Semit|e /'si:maɪt, Amer. 'semaɪt/ n.
Sémite m./f. **~ic** /sɪ'mɪtɪk/ a. sémite;
(lang.) sémitique.

semolina /semə'li:nə/ n. semoule f.

senat|e /'senɪt/ n. sénat m. **~or**
/-ətə(r)/ n. sénateur m.

send /send/ v.t./i. (p.t. **sent**) envoyer.
~ away, (dismiss) renvoyer. **~
(away or off) for,** commander (par
la poste). **~ back,** renvoyer. **~ for,**
(person, help) envoyer chercher. **~
a player off,** renvoyer un joueur. **~
off,** adieux chaleureux m. pl. **~
up,** (fam.) parodier. **~er** n. expédi|-
teur, -trice m., f.

senil|e /'si:naɪl/ a. sénile. **~ity**
/sɪ'nɪlətɪ/ n. sénilité f.

senior /'si:nɪə(r)/ a. plus âgé (**to,** que);
(in rank) supérieur; (teacher, part-
ner) principal. ● n. aîné(e) m. (f.);
(schol.) grand(e) m. (f.). **~ citizen,**
personne âgée f. **~ity** /-'ɒrətɪ/ n.
priorité d'âge f.; supériorité f.; (in
service) ancienneté f.

sensation /sen'seɪʃn/ n. sensation f.
~al a. (event) qui fait sensation;
(wonderful) sensationnel.

sense /sens/ n. sens m.; (sensation)
sensation f.; (mental impression)
sentiment m.; (common sense) bon
sens m. **~s,** (mind) raison f. ● v.t.

(pres)sentir. **make ~,** avoir du sens.
make ~ of, comprendre. **~less** a.
stupide; (med.) sans connaissance.

sensibilit|y /sensə'bɪlətɪ/ n. sensibi-
lité f. **~ies,** susceptibilité f.

sensible /'sensəbl/ a. raisonnable,
sensé; (clothing) fonctionnel.

sensitiv|e /'sensətɪv/ a. sensible
(**to,** à); (touchy) susceptible. **~ity**
/-'tɪvətɪ/ n. sensibilité f.

sensory /'sensərɪ/ a. sensoriel.

sensual /'senʃʊəl/ a. sensuel. **~ity**
/-'ælətɪ/ n. sensualité f.

sensuous /'senʃʊəs/ a. sensuel.

sent /sent/ see send.

sentence /'sentəns/ n. phrase f.;
(decision: jurid.) jugement m., condamnation f.; (punishment) peine f.
● v.t. **~ to,** condamner à.

sentiment /'sentɪmənt/ n. sentiment
m.

sentimental /sentɪ'mentl/ a. sentimental. **~ity** /-'tælətɪ/ n. sentimen-
talité f.

sentry /'sentrɪ/ n. sentinelle f.

separable /'sepərəbl/ a. séparable.

separate¹ /'seprət/ a. séparé, différent; (independent) indépendant. **~s**
n. pl. coordonnés m. pl. **~ly** adv.
séparément.

separat|e² /'sepəreɪt/ v.t./i. (se)
séparer. **~ion** /-'reɪʃn/ n. séparation
f.

September /sep'tembə(r)/ n. septembre m.

septic /'septɪk/ a. (wound) infecté. **~
tank,** fosse septique f.

sequel /'si:kwəl/ n. suite f.

sequence /'si:kwəns/ n. (order)
ordre m.; (series) suite f.; (of film)
séquence f.

sequin /'si:kwɪn/ n. paillette f.

serenade /serə'neɪd/ n. sérénade f.
● v.t. donner une sérénade à.

seren|e /sɪ'ri:n/ a. serein. **~ity**
/-enətɪ/ n. sérénité f.

sergeant /'sɑ:dʒənt/ n. (mil.) sergent
m.; (policeman) brigadier m.

serial /'sɪərɪəl/ n. (story) feuilleton
m. ● a. (number) de série.

series /'sɪərɪz/ n. invar. série f.

serious /'sɪərɪəs/ a. sérieux; (very
bad, critical) grave, sérieux. **~ly**
adv. sérieusement, gravement. **take
~ly,** prendre au sérieux. **~ness** n.
sérieux m.

sermon /'sɜ:mən/ n. sermon m.

serpent /'sɜ:pənt/ n. serpent m.

serrated /sɪˈreɪtɪd/ a. (edge) en dents de scie.

serum /ˈsɪərəm/ n. (pl. -a) sérum m.

servant /ˈsɜːvənt/ n. domestique m./f.; (of God etc.) serviteur m.

serve /sɜːv/ v.t./i. servir; (undergo, carry out) faire; (of transport) desservir. ● n. (tennis) service m. ~ as/to, servir de/à. ~ its purpose, remplir sa fonction.

service /ˈsɜːvɪs/ n. service m.; (maintenance) révision f.; (relig.) office m. ~s, (mil.) forces armées f. pl. ● v.t. (car etc.) réviser. of ~ to, utile à. ~ area, (auto.) aire de services f. ~ charge, service m. ~ station, station-service f.

serviceable /ˈsɜːvɪsəbl/ a. (usable) utilisable; (useful) commode; (durable) solide.

serviceman /ˈsɜːvɪsmən/ n. (pl. -men) militaire m.

serviette /sɜːvɪˈet/ n. serviette f.

servile /ˈsɜːvaɪl/ a. servile.

session /ˈseʃn/ n. séance f.; (univ.) année (universitaire) f.; (univ., Amer.) semestre m.

set /set/ v.t. (p.t. set, pres. p. setting) mettre; (put down) poser, mettre; (limit etc.) fixer; (watch, clock) régler; (example, task) donner; (for printing) composer; (in plaster) plâtrer. ● v.i. (of sun) se coucher; (of jelly) prendre. ● n. (of chairs, stamps, etc.) série f.; (of knives, keys, etc.) jeu m.; (of people) groupe m.; (TV, radio) poste m.; (style of hair) mise en plis f.; (theatre) décor m.; (tennis) set m.; (mathematics) ensemble m. ● a. fixe; (in habits) régulier; (meal) à prix fixe; (book) au programme. ~ against sth., opposé à. be ~ on doing, être résolu à faire. ~ about or to, se mettre à. ~ back, (delay) retarder; (cost: sl.) coûter. ~-back n. revers m. ~ fire to, mettre le feu à. ~ free, libérer. ~ in, (take hold) s'installer, commencer. ~ off or out, partir. ~ off, (mechanism, activity) déclencher; (bomb) faire éclater. ~ out, (state) exposer; (arrange) disposer. ~ out to do sth., entreprendre de faire qch. ~ sail, partir. ~ square, équerre f. ~ to, (about to) sur le point de. ~-to n. querelle f. ~ to music, mettre en musique. ~ up, (establish) fonder, établir;

(launch) lancer. ~-up n. (fam.) affaire f.

settee /seˈtiː/ n. canapé m.

setting /ˈsetɪŋ/ n. cadre m.

settle /ˈsetl/ v.t. (arrange, pay) régler; (date) fixer; (nerves) calmer. ● v.i. (come to rest) se poser; (live) s'installer. ~ down, se calmer; (become orderly) se ranger. ~ for, accepter. ~ in, s'installer. ~ up (with), régler. ~r /-ə(r)/ n. colon m.

settlement /ˈsetlmənt/ n. règlement m. (of, de); (agreement) accord m.; (place) colonie f.

seven /ˈsevn/ a. & n. sept (m.). ~th a. & n. septième (m./f.).

seventeen /sevnˈtiːn/ a. & n. dix-sept (m.). ~th a. & n. dix-septième (m./f.).

sevent|y /ˈsevntɪ/ a. & n. soixante-dix (m.). ~ieth a. & n. soixante-dixième (m./f.).

sever /ˈsevə(r)/ v.t. (cut) couper; (relations) rompre. ~ance n. (breaking off) rupture f. ~ance pay, indemnité de licenciement f.

several /ˈsevrəl/ a. & pron. plusieurs.

sever|e /sɪˈvɪə(r)/ a. (-er, -est) sévère; (violent) violent; (serious) grave. ~ely adv. sévèrement; gravement. ~ity /sɪˈverətɪ/ n. sévérité f.; violence f.; gravité f.

sew /səʊ/ v.t./i. (p.t. sewed, p.p. sewn or sewed) coudre. ~ing n. couture f. ~ing-machine n. machine à coudre f.

sewage /ˈsjuːɪdʒ/ n. eaux d'égout f. pl., vidanges f. pl.

sewer /ˈsuːə(r)/ n. égout m.

sewn /səʊn/ see sew.

sex /seks/ n. sexe m. ● a. sexuel. have ~, avoir des rapports (sexuels). ~ maniac, obsédé(e) sexuel(le) m. (f.). ~y a. sexy invar.

sexist /ˈseksɪst/ a. & n. sexiste (m./f.).

sextet /seksˈtet/ n. sextuor m.

sexual /ˈsekʃʊəl/ a. sexuel. ~ intercourse, rapports sexuels m. pl. ~ity /-ˈælətɪ/ n. sexualité f.

shabb|y /ˈʃæbɪ/ a. (-ier, -iest) (place, object) minable, miteux; (person) pauvrement vêtu; (mean) mesquin. ~ily adv. (dress) pauvrement; (act) mesquinement.

shack /ʃæk/ n. cabane f.

shackles /ˈʃæklz/ n. pl. chaînes f. pl.

shade /ʃeɪd/ n. ombre f.; (of colour, opinion) nuance f.; (for lamp) abat-jour m.; (blind: Amer.) store m. a ~

bigger/*etc.*, légèrement plus grand/ *etc.* ● *v.t.* (*of person etc.*) abriter; (*of tree*) ombrager.

shadow /ˈʃædəʊ/ *n.* ombre *f.* ● *v.t.* (*follow*) filer. **S~ Cabinet,** cabinet fantôme *m.* **~y** *a.* ombragé; (*fig.*) vague.

shady /ˈʃeɪdɪ/ *a.* (**-ier, -iest**) ombragé; (*dubious: fig.*) louche.

shaft /ʃɑːft/ *n.* (*of arrow*) hampe *f.*; (*axle*) arbre *m.*; (*of mine*) puits *m.*; (*of light*) rayon *m.*

shaggy /ˈʃægɪ/ *a.* (**-ier, -iest**) (*beard*) hirsute; (*hair*) broussailleux; (*animal*) à longs poils.

shake /ʃeɪk/ *v.t.* (*p.t.* **shook,** *p.p.* **shaken**) secouer; (*bottle*) agiter; (*house, belief, etc.*) ébranler. ● *v.i.* trembler. ● *n.* secousse *f.* **~ hands with,** serrer la main à. **~ off,** (*get rid of*) se débarrasser de. **~ one's head,** (*in refusal*) dire non de la tête. **~ up,** (*disturb, rouse, mix contents of*) secouer. **~-up** *n.* (*upheaval*) remaniement *m.*

shaky /ˈʃeɪkɪ/ *a.* (**-ier, -iest**) (*hand, voice*) tremblant; (*table etc.*) branlant; (*weak: fig.*) faible.

shall /ʃæl, *unstressed* ʃ(ə)l/ *v. aux.* **I ~ do,** je ferai. **we ~ do,** nous ferons.

shallot /ʃəˈlɒt/ *n.* échalote *f.*

shallow /ˈʃæləʊ/ *a.* (**-er, -est**) peu profond; (*fig.*) superficiel.

sham /ʃæm/ *n.* comédie *f.*; (*person*) imposteur *m.*; (*jewel*) imitation *f.* ● *a.* faux; (*affected*) feint. ● *v.t.* (*p.t.* **shammed**) feindre.

shambles /ˈʃæmblz/ *n. pl.* (*mess: fam.*) désordre *m.*, pagaille *f.*

shame /ʃeɪm/ *n.* honte *f.* ● *v.t.* faire honte à. **it's a ~,** c'est dommage. **~ful** *a.* honteux. **~fully** *adv.* honteusement. **~less** *a.* éhonté.

shamefaced /ˈʃeɪmfeɪst/ *a.* honteux.

shampoo /ʃæmˈpuː/ *n.* shampooing *m.* ● *v.t.* faire un shampooing à, shampooiner.

shandy /ˈʃændɪ/ *n.* panaché *m.*

shan't /ʃɑːnt/ = **shall not.**

shanty /ˈʃæntɪ/ *n.* (*shack*) baraque *f.* **~ town,** bidonville *m.*

shape /ʃeɪp/ *n.* forme *f.* ● *v.t.* (*fashion, mould*) façonner; (*future etc.: fig.*) déterminer. ● *v.i.* **~ up,** (*plan etc.*) prendre tournure *or* forme; (*person etc.*) faire des progrès. **~less** *a.* informe.

shapely /ˈʃeɪplɪ/ *a.* (**-ier, -iest**) (*leg, person*) bien tourné.

share /ʃeə(r)/ *n.* part *f.*; (*comm.*) action *f.* ● *v.t./i.* partager; (*feature*) avoir en commun. **~-out** *n.* partage *m.*

shareholder /ˈʃeəhəʊldə(r)/ *n.* actionnaire *m./f.*

shark /ʃɑːk/ *n.* requin *m.*

sharp /ʃɑːp/ *a.* (**-er, -est**) (*knife etc.*) tranchant; (*pin etc.*) pointu; (*point*) aigu; (*acute*) vif; (*sudden*) brusque; (*dishonest*) peu scrupuleux. ● *adv.* (*stop*) net. **six o'clock**/*etc.* **~,** six heures/*etc.* pile. ● *n.* (*mus.*) dièse *m.* **~ly** *adv.* (*harshly*) vivement; (*suddenly*) brusquement.

sharpen /ˈʃɑːpən/ *v.t.* aiguiser; (*pencil*) tailler. **~er** *n.* (*for pencil*) taille-crayon(s) *m.*

shatter /ˈʃætə(r)/ *v.t./i.* (*glass etc.*) (faire) voler en éclats, (se) briser; (*upset, ruin*) anéantir.

shav|e /ʃeɪv/ *v.t./i.* (sc) raser. ● *n.* **have a ~e,** se raser. **~en** *a.* rasé. **~er** *n.* rasoir électrique *m.* **~ing-brush** *n.* blaireau *m.* **~ing-cream** *n.* crème à raser *f.*

shaving /ˈʃeɪvɪŋ/ *n.* copeau *m.*

shawl /ʃɔːl/ *n.* châle *m.*

she /ʃiː/ *pron.* elle. ● *n.* femelle *f.*

sheaf /ʃiːf/ *n.* (*pl.* **sheaves**) gerbe *f.*

shear /ʃɪə(r)/ *v.t.* (*p.p.* **shorn** *or* **sheared**) (*sheep etc.*) tondre. **~ off,** se détacher.

shears /ʃɪəz/ *n. pl.* cisaille(s) *f.* (*pl.*).

sheath /ʃiːθ/ *n.* (*pl.* **-s** /ʃiːðz/) gaine *f.*, fourreau *m.*; (*contraceptive*) préservatif *m.*

sheathe /ʃiːð/ *v.t.* rengainer.

shed[1] /ʃed/ *n.* remise *f.*

shed[2] /ʃed/ *v.t.* (*p.t.* **shed,** *pres. p.* **shedding**) perdre; (*light, tears*) répandre.

sheen /ʃiːn/ *n.* lustre *m.*

sheep /ʃiːp/ *n. invar.* mouton *m.* **~-dog** *n.* chien de berger *m.*

sheepish /ˈʃiːpɪʃ/ *a.* penaud. **~ly** *adv.* d'un air penaud.

sheepskin /ˈʃiːpskɪn/ *n.* peau de mouton *f.*

sheer /ʃɪə(r)/ *a.* pur (et simple); (*steep*) à pic; (*fabric*) très fin. ● *adv.* à pic, verticalement.

sheet /ʃiːt/ *n.* drap *m.*; (*of paper*) feuille *f.*; (*of glass, ice*) plaque *f.*

sheikh /ʃeɪk/ *n.* cheik *m.*

shelf /ʃelf/ *n.* (*pl.* **shelves**) rayon *m.* étagère *f.* **on the ~,** (*person*) laissé pour compte.

shell /ʃel/ n. coquille f.; (on beach) coquillage m.; (of building) carcasse f.; (explosive) obus m. ● v.t. (nut etc.) décortiquer; (peas) écosser; (mil.) bombarder.

shellfish /ʃelfɪʃ/ n. invar. (lobster etc.) crustacé(s) m. (pl.); (mollusc) coquillage(s) m. (pl.).

shelter /ʃeltə(r)/ n. abri m. ● v.t./i. (s')abriter; (give lodging to) donner asile à. ~ed a. (life etc.) protégé.

shelve /ʃelv/ v.t. (plan etc.) laisser en suspens, remettre à plus tard.

shelving /ʃelvɪŋ/ n. (shelves) rayonnage(s) m. (pl.).

shepherd /ʃepəd/ n. berger m. ● v.t. (people) guider. ~'s pie, hachis Parmentier m.

sherbet /ʃɜːbət/ n. jus de fruits m.; (powder) poudre acidulée f.; (water-ice: Amer.) sorbet m.

sheriff /ʃerɪf/ n. shérif m.

sherry /ʃerɪ/ n. xérès m.

shield /ʃiːld/ n. bouclier m.; (screen) écran m. ● v.t. protéger.

shift /ʃɪft/ v.t./i. (se) déplacer, bouger; (exchange, alter) changer de. ● n. changement m.; (workers) équipe f.; (work) poste m.; (auto.: Amer.) levier de vitesse m. **make ~,** se débrouiller. **~ work,** travail par roulement m.

shiftless /ʃɪftlɪs/ a. paresseux.

shifty /ʃɪftɪ/ a. (-ier, -iest) louche.

shilling /ʃɪlɪŋ/ n. shilling m.

shilly-shally /ʃɪlɪʃælɪ/ v.i. hésiter, balancer.

shimmer /ʃɪmə(r)/ v.i. chatoyer. ● n. chatoiement m.

shin /ʃɪn/ n. tibia m.

shine /ʃaɪn/ v.t./i. (p.t. **shone** /ʃɒn/) (faire) briller. ● n. éclat m., brillant m. **~ one's torch or the light (on),** éclairer.

shingle /ʃɪŋgl/ n. (pebbles) galets m. pl.; (on roof) bardeau m.

shingles /ʃɪŋglz/ n. pl. (med.) zona m.

shiny /ʃaɪnɪ/ a. (-ier, -iest) brillant.

ship /ʃɪp/ n. bateau m., navire m. ● v.t. (p.t. **shipped**) transporter; (send) expédier; (load) embarquer. **~ment** n. cargaison f., envoi m. **~per** n. expéditeur m. **~ping** n. (ships) navigation f., navires m. pl.

shipbuilding /ʃɪpbɪldɪŋ/ n. construction navale f.

shipshape /ʃɪpʃeɪp/ adv. & a. parfaitement en ordre.

shipwreck /ʃɪprek/ n. naufrage m. **~ed** a. naufragé. **be ~ed,** faire naufrage.

shipyard /ʃɪpjɑːd/ n. chantier naval m.

shirk /ʃɜːk/ v.t. esquiver. **~er** n. tire-au-flanc m. invar.

shirt /ʃɜːt/ n. chemise f.; (of woman) chemisier m. **in ~-sleeves,** en bras de chemise.

shiver /ʃɪvə(r)/ v.i. frissonner. ● n. frisson m.

shoal /ʃəʊl/ n. (of fish) banc m.

shock /ʃɒk/ n. choc m., secousse f.; (electr.) décharge f.; (med.) choc m. ● a. (result) choc invar.; (tactics) de choc. ● v.t. choquer. **~ absorber,** amortisseur m. **be a ~er,** (fam.) être affreux. **~ing** a. choquant; (bad: fam.) affreux. **~ingly** adv. (fam.) affreusement.

shoddy /ʃɒdɪ/ a. (-ier, -iest) mal fait, mauvais. **~ily** adv. mal.

shoe /ʃuː/ n. chaussure f., soulier m.; (of horse) fer (à cheval) m.; (in vehicle) sabot (de frein) m. ● v.t. (p.t. **shod** /ʃɒd/, pres. p. **shoeing**) (horse) ferrer. **~ repairer,** cordonnier m. **on a ~string,** avec très peu d'argent.

shoehorn /ʃuːhɔːn/ n. chausse-pied m.

shoelace /ʃuːleɪs/ n. lacet m.

shoemaker /ʃuːmeɪkə(r)/ n. cordonnier m.

shone /ʃɒn/ see shine.

shoo /ʃuː/ v.t. chasser.

shook /ʃʊk/ see shake.

shoot /ʃuːt/ v.t. (p.t. **shot**) (gun) tirer un coup de; (missile, glance) lancer; (kill, wound) tuer, blesser (d'un coup de fusil, de pistolet, etc.); (execute) fusiller; (hunt) chasser; (film) tourner. ● v.i. tirer (at, sur). ● n. (bot.) pousse f. **~ down,** abattre. **~ out,** (rush) sortir en vitesse. **~ up,** (spurt) jaillir; (grow) pousser vite. **hear ~ing,** entendre des coups de feu. **~ing-range** n. stand de tir m. **~ing star,** étoile filante f.

shop /ʃɒp/ n. magasin m., boutique f.; (workshop) atelier m. ● v.i. (p.t. **shopped**) faire ses courses. **~ around,** comparer les prix. **~ assistant,** vendeu|r, -se m., f. **~- floor** n. (workers) ouvriers m. pl. **~-per** n. acheteu|r, -se m., f. **~-soiled,** (Amer.) **~-worn** adjs. abîmé. **~**

steward, délégué(e) syndical(e) *m.* (*f.*). **~ window,** vitrine *f.*

shopkeeper /'ʃɒpkiːpə(r)/ *n.* commerçant(e) *m.* (*f.*).

shoplift|er /'ʃɒplɪftə(r)/ *n.* voleu|r, -se à l'étalage *m.*, *f.* **~ing** *n.* vol à l'étalage *m.*

shopping /'ʃɒpɪŋ/ *n.* (*goods*) achats *m. pl.* **go ~,** faire ses courses. **~ bag,** sac à provisions *m.* **~ centre,** centre commercial *m.*

shore /ʃɔː(r)/ *n.* rivage *m.*

shorn /ʃɔːn/ *see* shear. ● *a.* **~ of,** dépouillé de.

short /ʃɔːt/ *a.* **(-er, -est)** court; (*person*) petit; (*brief*) court, bref; (*curt*) brusque. **be ~ (of),** (*lack*) manquer (de). ● *adv.* (*stop*) net. ● *n.* (*electr.*) court-circuit *m.*; (*film*) court-métrage *m.* **~s,** (*trousers*) short *m.* **~ of money,** à court d'argent. **I'm two ~,** il m'en manque deux. **~ of doing sth,** à moins de faire qch. **everything ~ of,** tout sauf. **nothing ~ of,** rien de moins que. **cut ~,** écourter. **cut s.o. ~,** couper court à qn. **fall ~ of,** ne pas arriver à. **he is called Tom for ~,** son diminutif est Tom. **in ~,** en bref. **~-change** *v.t.* (*cheat*) rouler. **~ circuit,** court-circuit *m.* **~-circuit** *v.t.* court-circuiter. **~ cut,** raccourci *m.* **~-handed** *a.* à court de personnel. **~ list,** liste des candidats choisis *f.* **~-lived** *a.* éphémère. **~-sighted** *a.* myope. **~-staffed** *a.* à court de personnel. **~ story,** nouvelle *f.* **~-term** *a.* à court terme. **~ wave,** ondes courtes *f. pl.*

shortage /'ʃɔːtɪdʒ/ *n.* manque *m.*

shortbread /'ʃɔːtbred/ *n.* sablé *m.*

shortcoming /'ʃɔːtkʌmɪŋ/ *n.* défaut *m.*

shorten /'ʃɔːtn/ *v.t.* raccourcir.

shortfall /'ʃɔːtfɔːl/ *n.* déficit *m.*

shorthand /'ʃɔːthænd/ *n.* sténo(-graphie) *f.* **~ typist,** sténodactylo *f.*

shortly /'ʃɔːtlɪ/ *adv.* bientôt.

shot /ʃɒt/ *see* shoot. ● *n.* (*firing, attempt, etc.*) coup de feu *m.*; (*person*) tireur *m.*; (*bullet*) balle *f.*; (*photograph*) photo *f.*; (*injection*) piqûre *f.* **like a ~,** comme une flèche. **~-gun** *n.* fusil de chasse *m.*

should /ʃʊd, unstressed ʃəd/ *v.aux.* devoir. **you ~ help me,** vous devriez m'aider. **I ~ have stayed,** j'aurais dû rester. **I ~ like to,**

j'aimerais bien. **if he ~ come,** s'il vient.

shoulder /'ʃəʊldə(r)/ *n.* épaule *f.* ● *v.t.* (*responsibility*) endosser; (*burden*) se charger de. **~-bag** *n.* sac à bandoulière *m.* **~-blade** *n.* omoplate *f.* **~-pad** *n.* épaulette *f.*

shout /ʃaʊt/ *n.* cri *m.* ● *v.t./i.* crier. **~ at,** engueuler. **~ down,** huer.

shove /ʃʌv/ *n.* poussée *f.* ● *v.t./i.* pousser; (*put: fam.*) ficher. **~ off,** (*depart: fam.*) se tirer.

shovel /'ʃʌvl/ *n.* pelle *f.* ● *v.t.* (*p.t.* **shovelled**) pelleter.

show /ʃəʊ/ *v.t.* (*p.t.* **showed**, *p.p.* **shown**) montrer; (*of dial, needle*) indiquer; (*put on display*) exposer; (*film*) donner; (*conduct*) conduire. ● *v.i.* (*be visible*) se voir. ● *n.* démonstration *f.*; (*ostentation*) parade *f.*; (*exhibition*) exposition *f.*, salon *m.*; (*theatre*) spectacle *m.*; (*cinema*) séance *f.* **for ~,** pour l'effet. **on ~,** exposé. **~-down** *n.* épreuve de force *f.* **~-jumping** *n.* concours hippique *m.* **~ off** *v.t.* étaler; *v.i.* poser, crâner. **~-off** *n.* poseu|r, -se *m.*, *f.* **~-piece** *n.* modèle du genre *m.* **~ s.o. in/out,** faire entrer/sortir qn. **~ up,** (faire) ressortir; (*appear: fam.*) se montrer. **~ing** *n.* performance *f.*; (*cinema*) séance *f.*

shower /'ʃaʊə(r)/ *n.* (*of rain*) averse *f.*; (*of blows etc.*) grêle *f.*; (*for washing*) douche *f.* ● *v.t.* **~ with,** couvrir de. ● *v.i.* se doucher. **~y** *a.* pluvieux.

showerproof /'ʃaʊəpruːf/ *a.* imperméable.

showmanship /'ʃəʊmənʃɪp/ *n.* art de la mise en scène *m.*

shown /ʃəʊn/ *see* show.

showroom /'ʃəʊrʊm/ *n.* salle d'exposition *f.*

showy /'ʃəʊɪ/ *a.* **(-ier, -iest)** voyant; (*manner*) prétentieux.

shrank /ʃræŋk/ *see* shrink.

shrapnel /'ʃræpn(ə)l/ *n.* éclats d'obus *m. pl.*

shred /ʃred/ *n.* lambeau *m.*; (*least amount: fig.*) parcelle *f.* ● *v.t.* (*p.t.* **shredded**) déchiqueter; (*culin.*) râper. **~der** *n.* destructeur de documents *m.*

shrew /ʃruː/ *n.* (*woman*) mégère *f.*

shrewd /ʃruːd/ *a.* **(-er, -est)** astucieux. **~ness** *n.* astuce *f.*

shriek /ʃriːk/ n. hurlement m. ● v.t./i. hurler.

shrift /ʃrɪft/ n. **give s.o. short ~,** traiter qn. sans ménagement.

shrill /ʃrɪl/ a. strident, aigu.

shrimp /ʃrɪmp/ n. crevette f.

shrine /ʃraɪn/ n. (place) lieu saint m.; (tomb) châsse f.

shrink /ʃrɪŋk/ v.t./i. (p.t. **shrank**, p.p. **shrunk**) rétrécir; (lessen) diminuer. **~ from,** reculer devant. **~age** n. rétrécissement m.

shrivel /ˈʃrɪvl/ v.t./i. (p.t. **shrivelled**) (se) ratatiner.

shroud /ʃraʊd/ n. linceul m. ● v.t. (veil) envelopper.

Shrove /ʃrəʊv/ n. **~ Tuesday,** Mardi gras m.

shrub /ʃrʌb/ n. arbuste m. **~bery** n. arbustes m. pl.

shrug /ʃrʌg/ v.t. (p.t. **shrugged**). **~ one's shoulders,** hausser les épaules. ● n. haussement d'épaules m. **~ sth. off,** réagir avec indifférence à qch.

shrunk /ʃrʌŋk/ see shrink. **~en** a. rétréci; (person) ratatiné.

shudder /ˈʃʌdə(r)/ v.i. frémir. ● n. frémissement m.

shuffle /ˈʃʌfl/ v.t. (feet) traîner; (cards) battre. ● v.i. traîner les pieds. ● n. démarche traînante f.

shun /ʃʌn/ v.t. (p.t. **shunned**) éviter, fuir.

shunt /ʃʌnt/ v.t. (train) aiguiller.

shush /ʃʊʃ/ int. (fam.) chut.

shut /ʃʌt/ v.t. (p.t. **shut**, pres. p. **shutting**) fermer. ● v.i. se fermer; (of shop, bank, etc.) fermer. **~ down** or **up,** fermer. **~-down** n. fermeture f. **~ in** or **up,** enfermer. **~ up** v.i. (fam.) se taire; v.t. (fam.) faire taire.

shutter /ˈʃʌtə(r)/ n. volet m.; (photo.) obturateur m.

shuttle /ˈʃʌtl/ n. (bus etc.) navette f. ● v.i. faire la navette. ● v.t. transporter. **~ service,** navette f.

shuttlecock /ˈʃʌtlkɒk/ n. (badminton) volant m.

shy /ʃaɪ/ a. (-er, -est) timide. ● v.i. reculer. **~ness** n. timidité f.

Siamese /saɪəˈmiːz/ a. siamois.

sibling /ˈsɪblɪŋ/ n. frère m., sœur f.

Sicily /ˈsɪsɪlɪ/ n. Sicile f.

sick /sɪk/ a. malade; (humour) macabre. **be ~,** (vomit) vomir. **be ~ of,** en avoir assez or marre de. **feel ~,** avoir mal au cœur. **~-bay** n. infirmerie f. **~-leave** n. congé maladie m. **~-pay** n. assurance-maladie f. **~room** n. chambre de malade f.

sicken /ˈsɪkən/ v.t. écœurer. ● v.i. **be ~ing for,** (illness) couver.

sickle /ˈsɪkl/ n. faucille f.

sickly /ˈsɪklɪ/ a. (-ier, -iest) (person) maladif; (taste, smell, etc.) écœurant.

sickness /ˈsɪknɪs/ n. maladie f.

side /saɪd/ n. côté m.; (of road, river) bord m.; (of hill) flanc m.; (sport) équipe f. ● v.i. **~ with,** se ranger du côté de. **on the ~,** (extra) en plus; (secretly) en catimini. **~ by side,** côte à côte. **~-car** n. side-car m. **~-effect** n. effet secondaire m. **~-saddle** adv. en amazone. **~-show** n. petite attraction f. **~-step** v.t. (p.t. **-stepped**) éviter. **~-street** n. rue latérale f. **~-track** v.t. faire dévier de son sujet.

sideboard /ˈsaɪdbɔːd/ n. buffet m. **~s,** (whiskers: sl.) pattes f. pl.

sideburns /ˈsaɪdbɜːnz/ n. pl. pattes f. pl., rouflaquettes f. pl.

sidelight /ˈsaɪdlaɪt/ n. (auto.) veilleuse f., lanterne f.

sideline /ˈsaɪdlaɪn/ n. activité secondaire f.

sidewalk /ˈsaɪdwɔːk/ n. (Amer.) trottoir m.

side|ways /ˈsaɪdweɪz/, **~long** adv. & a. de côté.

siding /ˈsaɪdɪŋ/ n. voie de garage f.

sidle /ˈsaɪdl/ v.i. avancer furtivement (up to, vers).

siege /siːdʒ/ n. siège m.

siesta /sɪˈestə/ n. sieste f.

sieve /sɪv/ n. tamis m.; (for liquids) passoire f. ● v.t. tamiser.

sift /sɪft/ v.t. tamiser. ● v.i. **~ through,** examiner.

sigh /saɪ/ n. soupir m. ● v.t./i. soupirer.

sight /saɪt/ n. vue f.; (scene) spectacle m.; (on gun) mire f. ● v.t. apercevoir. **at** or **on ~,** à vue. **catch ~ of,** apercevoir. **in ~,** visible. **lose ~ of,** perdre de vue.

sightsee|ing /ˈsaɪtsiːɪŋ/ n. tourisme m. **~r** /-ə(r)/ n. touriste m./f.

sign /saɪn/ n. signe m.; (notice) panneau m. ● v.t./i. signer. **~ language,** (for deaf) langage des sourds-muets m. **~ on,** (when unemployed) s'inscrire au chômage. **~ up,** (s')enrôler.

signal /ˈsɪgnəl/ n. signal m. ● v.t. (p.t. **signalled**) communiquer (par signaux); (*person*) faire signe à. **~-box** *n.* poste d'aiguillage *m.*

signalman /'sɪgnəlmən/ *n.* (*pl.* **-men**) (*rail.*) aiguilleur *m.*

signatory /'sɪgnətrɪ/ *n.* signataire *m./f.*

signature /'sɪgnətʃə(r)/ *n.* signature *f.* **~ tune,** indicatif musical *m.*

signet-ring /'sɪgnɪtrɪŋ/ *n.* chevalière *f.*

significan|t /sɪg'nɪfɪkənt/ *a.* important; (*meaningful*) significatif. **~ce** *n.* importance *f.*; (*meaning*) signification *f.* **~tly** *adv.* (*much*) sensiblement.

signify /'sɪgnɪfaɪ/ *v.t.* signifier.

signpost /'saɪnpəʊst/ *n.* poteau indicateur *m.*

silence /'saɪləns/ *n.* silence *m.* ● *v.t.* faire taire. **~r** /-ə(r)/ *n.* (*on gun, car*) silencieux *m.*

silent /'saɪlənt/ *a.* silencieux; (*film*) muet. **~ly** *adv.* silencieusement.

silhouette /sɪlu:'et/ *n.* silhouette *f.* ● *v.t.* be **~d against,** se profiler contre.

silicon /'sɪlɪkən/ *n.* silicium *m.* **~ chip,** microplaquette *f.*

silk /sɪlk/ *n.* soie *f.* **~en, ~y** *adjs.* soyeux.

sill /sɪl/ *n.* rebord *m.*

silly /'sɪlɪ/ *a.* (**-ier, -iest**) bête, idiot.

silo /'saɪləʊ/ *n.* (*pl.* **-os**) silo *m.*

silt /sɪlt/ *n.* vase *f.*

silver /'sɪlvə(r)/ *n.* argent *m.*; (*silverware*) argenterie *f.* ● *a.* en argent, d'argent. **~ wedding,** noces d'argent *f. pl.* **~y** *a.* argenté; (*sound*) argentin.

silversmith /'sɪlvəsmɪθ/ *n.* orfèvre *m.*

silverware /'sɪlvəweə(r)/ *n.* argenterie *f.*

similar /'sɪmɪlə(r)/ *a.* semblable (**to,** à). **~ity** /-ə'lærətɪ/ *n.* ressemblance *f.* **~ly** *adv.* de même.

simile /'sɪmɪlɪ/ *n.* comparaison *f.*

simmer /'sɪmə(r)/ *v.t./i.* (*soup etc.*) mijoter; (*water*) (laisser) frémir; (*smoulder: fig.*) couver. **~ down,** se calmer.

simper /'sɪmpə(r)/ *v.i.* minauder. **~ing** *a.* minaudier.

simpl|e /'sɪmpl/ *a.* (**-er, -est**) simple. **~e-minded** *a.* simple d'esprit. **~icity** /-'plɪsətɪ/ *n.* simplicité *f.* **~y** *adv.* simplement; (*absolutely*) absolument.

simplif|y /'sɪmplɪfaɪ/ *v.t.* simplifier. **~ication** /-ɪ'keɪʃn/ *n.* simplification *f.*

simplistic /sɪm'plɪstɪk/ *a.* simpliste.

simulat|e /'sɪmjʊleɪt/ *v.t.* simuler. **~ion** /-'leɪʃn/ *n.* simulation *f.*

simultaneous /sɪml'teɪnɪəs, *Amer.* saɪml'teɪnɪəs/ *a.* simultané. **~ly** *adv.* simultanément.

sin /sɪn/ *n.* péché *m.* ● *v.i.* (*p.t.* **sinned**) pécher.

since /sɪns/ *prep. & adv.* depuis. ● *conj.* depuis que; (*because*) puisque. **~ then,** depuis.

sincere /sɪn'sɪə(r)/ *a.* sincère. **~ely** *adv.* sincèrement. **~ity** /-'serətɪ/ *n.* sincérité *f.*

sinew /'sɪnju:/ *n.* tendon *m.* **~s,** muscles *m. pl.*

sinful /'sɪnfl/ *a.* (*act*) coupable, qui constitue un péché; (*shocking*) scandaleux.

sing /sɪŋ/ *v.t./i.* (*p.t.* **sang,** *p.p.* **sung**) chanter. **~er** *n.* chanteu|r, -se *m., f.*

singe /sɪndʒ/ *v.t.* (*pres. p.* **singeing**) brûler légèrement, roussir.

single /'sɪŋgl/ *a.* seul; (*not double*) simple; (*unmarried*) célibataire; (*room, bed*) pour une personne; (*ticket*) simple. ● *n.* (*ticket*) aller simple *m.*; (*record*) 45 tours *m. invar.* **~s,** (*tennis*) simple *m.* **~s bar,** bar pour les célibataires *m.* ● *v.t.* **~ out,** choisir. **in ~ file,** en file indienne. **~-handed** *a.* sans aide. **~-minded** *a.* tenace. **~ parent,** parent seul *m.* **singly** *adv.* un à un.

singlet /'sɪŋglɪt/ *n.* maillot de corps *m.*

singsong /'sɪŋsɒŋ/ *n.* **have a ~,** chanter en chœur. ● *a.* (*voice*) monotone.

singular /'sɪŋgjʊlə(r)/ *n.* singulier *m.* ● *a.* (*uncommon & gram.*) singulier; (*noun*) au singulier. **~ly** *adv.* singulièrement.

sinister /'sɪnɪstə(r)/ *a.* sinistre.

sink /sɪŋk/ *v.t./i.* (*p.t.* **sank,** *p.p.* **sunk**) (faire) couler; (*of ground, person*) s'affaisser; (*well*) creuser; (*money*) investir. ● *n.* (*in kitchen*) évier *m.*; (*wash-basin*) lavabo *m.* **~ in,** (*fig.*) être compris. **~ into,** (*thrust*) enfoncer dans; *v.i.* (*go deep*) s'enfoncer dans. **~ unit,** bloc-évier *m.*

sinner /'sɪnə(r)/ *n.* péch|eur, -eresse *m., f.*

sinuous /'sɪnjʊəs/ *a.* sinueux.

sinus /'samǝs/ n. (pl. **-uses**) (anat.) sinus m.

sip /sɪp/ n. petite gorgée f. ● v.t. (p.t. **sipped**) boire à petites gorgées.

siphon /'saɪfn/ n. siphon m. ● v.t. ~ **off**, siphonner.

sir /sɜ:(r)/ n. monsieur m. **Sir,** (title) Sir m.

siren /'saɪǝrǝn/ n. sirène f.

sirloin /'sɜ:lɔɪn/ n. faux-filet m., aloyau m.; (Amer.) romsteck m.

sissy /'sɪsɪ/ n. personne efféminée f.; (coward) dégonflé(e) m. (f.).

sister /'sɪstǝ(r)/ n. sœur f.; (nurse) infirmière en chef f. **~-in-law** (pl. **~s-in-law**) belle-sœur f. **~ly** a. fraternel.

sit /sɪt/ v.t./i. (p.t. **sat,** pres. p. **sitting**) (s')asseoir; (of committee etc.) siéger. ~ **(for),** (exam) se présenter à. be **~ting,** être assis. ~ **around,** ne rien faire. ~ **down,** s'asseoir. ~ **in on a meeting,** assister à une réunion pour écouter. **~-in** n. sit-in m. invar. **~ting** n. séance f.; (in restaurant) service m. **~ting-room** n. salon m.

site /saɪt/ n. emplacement m. **(building)** ~, chantier m. ● v.t. placer, construire, situer.

situat|e /'sɪtʃʊeɪt/ v.t. situer. **be ~ed,** être situé. **~ion** /-'eɪʃn/ n. situation f.

six /sɪks/ a. & n. six (m.). **~th** a. & n. sixième (m./f.).

sixteen /sɪk'sti:n/ a. & n. seize (m.). **~th** a. & n. seizième (m./f.).

sixt|y /'sɪkstɪ/ a. & n. soixante (m.). **~ieth** a. & n. soixantième (m./f.).

size /saɪz/ n. dimension f.; (of person, garment, etc.) taille f.; (of shoes) pointure f.; (of sum, salary) montant m.; (extent) ampleur f. ● v.t. ~ **up,** (fam.) jauger, juger. **~able** a. assez grand.

sizzle /'sɪzl/ v.i. grésiller.

skate[1] /skeɪt/ n. invar. (fish) raie f.

skat|e[2] /skeɪt/ n. patin m. ● v.i. patiner. **~er** n. patineu|r, -se m., f. **~ing** n. patinage m. **~ing-rink** n. patinoire f.

skateboard /'skeɪtbɔ:d/ n. skateboard m., planche à roulettes f.

skelet|on /'skelɪtǝn/ n. squelette m. **~on crew** or **staff,** effectifs minimums m. pl. **~al** a. squelettique.

sketch /sketʃ/ n. esquisse f., croquis m.; (theatre) sketch m. ● v.t. faire un croquis de, esquisser. ● v.i. faire

des esquisses. ~ **out,** esquisser. **~ pad,** bloc à dessins m.

sketchy /'sketʃɪ/ a. (**-ier, -iest**) sommaire, incomplet.

skew /skju:/ n. **on the ~,** de travers. **~-whiff** a. (fam.) de travers.

skewer /'skjʊǝ(r)/ n. brochette f.

ski /ski:/ n. (pl. **-is**) ski m. ● a. de ski. ● v.i. (p.t. **ski'd** or **skied,** pres. p. **skiing**) skier; (go skiing) faire du ski. ~ **jump,** saut à skis m. ~ **lift,** remonte-pente m. **~er** n. skieu|r, -se m., f. **~ing** n. ski m.

skid /skɪd/ v.i. (p.t. **skidded**) déraper. ● n. dérapage m.

skilful /'skɪlfl/ a. habile.

skill /skɪl/ n. habileté f.; (craft) métier m. **~s,** aptitudes f. pl. **~ed** a. habile; (worker) qualifié.

skim /skɪm/ v.t. (p.t. **skimmed**) écumer; (milk) écrémer; (pass or glide over) effleurer. ● v.i. ~ **through,** parcourir.

skimp /skɪmp/ v.t./i. ~ **(on),** lésiner (sur).

skimpy /'skɪmpɪ/ a. (**-ier, -iest**) (clothes) étriqué; (meal) chiche.

skin /skɪn/ n. peau f. ● v.t. (p.t. **skinned**) (animal) écorcher; (fruit) éplucher. **~-diving** n. plongée sous-marine f. **~-tight** a. collant.

skinflint /'skɪnflɪnt/ n. avare m./f.

skinny /'skɪnɪ/ a. (**-ier, -iest**) maigre, maigrichon.

skint /skɪnt/ a. (sl.) fauché.

skip[1] /skɪp/ v.i. (p.t. **skipped**) sautiller; (with rope) sauter à la corde. ● v.t. (page, class, etc.) sauter. ● n. petit saut m. **~ping-rope** n. corde à sauter f.

skip[2] /skɪp/ n. (container) benne f.

skipper /'skɪpǝ(r)/ n. capitaine m.

skirmish /'skɜ:mɪʃ/ n. escarmouche f., accrochage m.

skirt /skɜ:t/ n. jupe f. ● v.t. contourner. **~ing-board** n. plinthe f.

skit /skɪt/ n. sketch satirique m.

skittle /'skɪtl/ n. quille f.

skive /skaɪv/ v.i. (sl.) tirer au flanc.

skivvy /'skɪvɪ/ n. (fam.) boniche f.

skulk /skʌlk/ v.i. (move) rôder furtivement; (hide) se cacher.

skull /skʌl/ n. crâne m. **~-cap** n. calotte f.

skunk /skʌŋk/ n. (animal) mouffette f.; (person: sl.) salaud m.

sky /skaɪ/ n. ciel m. **~-blue** a. & n. bleu ciel m. invar.

skylight /'skaɪlaɪt/ n. lucarne f.

skyscraper /'skaɪskreɪpə(r)/ n. gratte-ciel m. invar.

slab /slæb/ n. plaque f., bloc m.; (of paving-stone) dalle f.

slack /slæk/ a. (-er, -est) (rope) lâche; (person) négligent; (business) stagnant; (period) creux. ● n. the ~, (in rope) du mou ● v.t./i. (se) relâcher.

slacken /'slækən/ v.t./i. (se) relâcher; (slow) (se) ralentir.

slacks /slæks/ n. pl. pantalon m.

slag /slæg/ n. scories f. pl. ~-heap n. crassier m.

slain /sleɪn/ see slay.

slake /sleɪk/ v.t. étancher.

slalom /'slɑːləm/ n. slalom m.

slam /slæm/ v.t./i. (p.t. slammed) (door etc.) claquer; (throw) flanquer; (criticize: sl.) critiquer. ● n. (noise) claquement m.

slander /'slɑːndə(r)/ n. diffamation f., calomnie f. ● v.t. diffamer, calomnier. ~ous a. diffamatoire.

slang /slæŋ/ n. argot m. ~y a. argotique.

slant /slɑːnt/ v.t./i. (faire) pencher; (news) présenter sous un certain jour. ● n. inclinaison f.; (bias) angle m. ~ed a. partial. be ~ing, être penché.

slap /slæp/ v.t. (p.t. slapped) (strike) donner une claque à; (face) gifler; (put) flanquer. ● n. claque f.; gifle f. ● adv. tout droit. ~-happy a. (carefree: fam.) insouciant; (dazed: fam.) abruti. ~-up meal, (sl.) gueuleton m.

slapdash /'slæpdæʃ/ a. fait, qui travaille etc. n'importe comment.

slapstick /'slæpstɪk/ n. grosse farce f.

slash /slæʃ/ v.t. (cut) taillader; (sever) trancher; (fig.) réduire (radicalement). ● n. taillade f.

slat /slæt/ n. (in blind) lamelle f.; (on bed) latte f.

slate /sleɪt/ n. ardoise f. ● v.t. (fam.) critiquer, éreinter.

slaughter /'slɔːtə(r)/ v.t. massacrer; (animals) abattre. ● n. massacre m.; abattage m.

slaughterhouse /'slɔːtəhaʊs/ n. abattoir m.

Slav /slɑːv/ a. & n. slave (m./f.). ~onic /slə'vɒnɪk/ a. (lang.) slave.

slave /sleɪv/ n. esclave m./f. ● v.i. trimer. ~-driver n. négr|ier, -ière m., f. ~ry /-ərɪ/ n. esclavage m.

slavish /'sleɪvɪʃ/ a. servile.

slay /sleɪ/ v.t. (p.t. slew, p.p. slain) tuer.

sleazy /'sliːzɪ/ a. (-ier, -iest) (fam.) sordide, miteux.

sledge /sledʒ/ n. luge f.; (horse-drawn) traîneau m. ~-hammer n. marteau de forgeron m.

sleek /sliːk/ a. (-er, -est) lisse, brillant; (manner) onctueux.

sleep /sliːp/ n. sommeil m. ● v.i. (p.t. slept) dormir; (spend the night) coucher. ● v.t. loger. go to ~, s'endormir. ~ in, faire la grasse matinée. ~er n. dormeu|r, -se m., f.; (beam: rail) traverse f.; (berth) couchette f. ~ing-bag n. sac de couchage m. ~ing pill, somnifère m. ~less a. sans sommeil. ~-walker n. somnambule m./f.

sleep|y /'sliːpɪ/ a. (-ier, -iest) somnolent. be ~y, avoir sommeil. ~ily adv. à moitié endormi.

sleet /sliːt/ n. neige fondue f.; (coat of ice: Amer.) verglas m. ● v.i. tomber de la neige fondue.

sleeve /sliːv/ n. manche f.; (of record) pochette f. up one's ~, en réserve. ~less a. sans manches.

sleigh /sleɪ/ n. traîneau m.

sleight /slaɪt/ n. ~ of hand, prestidigitation f.

slender /'slendə(r)/ a. mince, svelte; (scanty: fig.) faible.

slept /slept/ see sleep.

sleuth /sluːθ/ n. limier m.

slew[1] /sluː/ v.i. (turn) virer.

slew[2] /sluː/ see slay.

slice /slaɪs/ n. tranche f. ● v.t. couper (en tranches).

slick /slɪk/ a. (unctuous) mielleux; (cunning) astucieux. ● n. (oil) ~, nappe de pétrole f., marée noire f.

slide /slaɪd/ v.t./i. (p.t. slid) glisser. ● n. glissade f.; (fall: fig.) baisse f.; (in playground) toboggan m.; (for hair) barrette f.; (photo.) diapositive f. ~ into, (go silently) se glisser dans. ~-rule n. règle à calcul f. **sliding** a. (door, panel) à glissière, à coulisse. **sliding scale**, échelle mobile f.

slight /slaɪt/ a. (-er, -est) petit, léger; (slender) mince; (frail) frêle. ● v.t. (insult) offenser. ● n. affront m. ~est a. moindre. ~ly adv. légèrement, un peu.

slim /slɪm/ a. (**slimmer, slimmest**) mince. ● v.i. (p.t. **slimmed**) maigrir. ~**ness** n. minceur f.

slim|e /slaɪm/ n. (weapon, toy) boue (visqueuse) f.; (on river-bed) vase f. ~**y** a. boueux; vaseux; (sticky, servile) visqueux.

sling /slɪŋ/ n. (weapon, toy) fronde f.; (bandage) écharpe f. ● v.t. (p.t. **slung**) jeter, lancer.

slip /slɪp/ v.t./i. (p.t. **slipped**) glisser. ● n. faux pas m.; (mistake) erreur f.; (petticoat) combinaison f.; (paper) fiche f. **give the ~ to,** fausser compagnie à. ~ **away,** s'esquiver. ~**-cover** n. (Amer.) housse f. ~ **into,** (go) se glisser dans; (clothes) mettre. ~ **of the tongue,** lapsus m. ~**ped disc,** hernie discale f. ~**-road** n. bretelle f. ~ **s.o.'s mind,** échapper à qn. ~**-stream** n. sillage m. ~ **up,** (fam.) gaffer. ~**-up** n. (fam.) gaffe f.

slipper /'slɪpə(r)/ n. pantoufle f.

slippery /'slɪpərɪ/ a. glissant.

slipshod /'slɪpʃɒd/ a. (person) négligent; (work) négligé.

slit /slɪt/ n. fente f. ● v.t. (p.t. **slit,** pres. p. **slitting**) couper, fendre.

slither /'slɪðə(r)/ v.i. glisser.

sliver /'slɪvə(r)/ n. (of cheese etc.) lamelle f.; (splinter) éclat m.

slob /slɒb/ n. (fam.) rustre m.

slobber /'slɒbə(r)/ v.i. baver.

slog /slɒg/ v.t. (p.t. **slogged**) (hit) frapper dur. ● v.i. (work) trimer. ● n. (work) travail dur m.; (effort) gros effort m.

slogan /'sləʊgən/ n. slogan m.

slop /slɒp/ v.t./i. (p.t. **slopped**) (se) répandre. ~**s** n. pl. eaux sales f. pl.

slop|e /sləʊp/ v.i. être en pente; (of handwriting) pencher. ● n. pente f.; (of mountain) flanc m. ~**ing** a. en pente.

sloppy /'slɒpɪ/ a. (-ier, -iest) (ground) détrempé; (food) liquide; (work) négligé; (person) négligent; (fig.) sentimental.

slosh /slɒʃ/ v.t. (fam.) répandre; (hit: sl.) frapper. ● v.i. patauger.

slot /slɒt/ n. fente f. ● v.t./i. (p.t. **slotted**) (s')insérer. ~**-machine** n. distributeur automatique m.; (for gambling) machine à sous f.

sloth /sləʊθ/ n. paresse f.

slouch /slaʊtʃ/ v.i. avoir le dos voûté; (move) marcher le dos voûté.

slovenl|y /'slʌvnlɪ/ a. débraillé. ~**iness** n. débraillé m.

slow /sləʊ/ a. (-er, -est) lent. ● adv. lentement. ● v.t./i. ralentir. **be ~,** (clock etc.) retarder. **in ~ motion,** au ralenti. ~**ly** adv. lentement. ~**ness** n. lenteur f.

slow|coach /'sləʊkəʊtʃ/, (Amer.) ~**poke** ns. lambin(e) m. (f.).

sludge /slʌdʒ/ n. gadoue f., boue f.

slug /slʌg/ n. (mollusc) limace f.; (bullet) balle f.; (blow) coup m.

sluggish /'slʌgɪʃ/ a. lent, mou.

sluice /sluːs/ n. (gate) vanne f.

slum /slʌm/ n. taudis m.

slumber /'slʌmbə(r)/ n. sommeil. m. ● v.i. dormir.

slump /slʌmp/ n. effondrement m.; baisse f.; (in business) marasme m. ● v.i. (collapse, fall limply) s'effondrer; (decrease) baisser.

slung /slʌŋ/ see sling.

slur /slɜː(r)/ v.t./i. (p.t. **slurred**) (spoken words) mal articuler. ● n. bredouillement m.; (discredit) atteinte f. (**on,** à).

slush /slʌʃ/ n. (snow) neige fondue f. ~ **fund,** fonds servant à des pots-de-vin m. ~**y** a. (road) couvert de neige fondue.

slut /slʌt/ n. (dirty) souillon f.; (immoral) dévergondée f.

sly /slaɪ/ a. (slyer, slyest) (crafty) rusé; (secretive) sournois. ● n. **on the ~,** en cachette. ~**ly** adv. sournoisement.

smack[1] /smæk/ n. tape f.; (on face) gifle f. ● v.t. donner une tape à; gifler. ● adv. (fam.) tout droit.

smack[2] /smæk/ v.i. ~ **of sth.,** (have flavour) sentir qch.

small /smɔːl/ a. (-er, -est) petit. ● n. ~ **of the back,** creux des reins m. ● adv. (cut etc.) menu. ~**ness** n. petitesse f. ~ **ads,** petites annonces f. pl. ~ **businesses,** les petites entreprises. ~ **change,** petite monnaie f. ~ **talk,** menus propos m. pl. ~**-time** a. petit, peu important.

smallholding /'smɔːlhəʊldɪŋ/ n. petite ferme f.

smallpox /'smɔːlpɒks/ n. variole f.

smarmy /'smɑːmɪ/ a. (-ier, -iest) (fam.) obséquieux, patelin.

smart /smɑːt/ a. (-er, -est) élégant; (clever) astucieux, intelligent; (brisk) rapide. ● v.i. (of wound etc.) brûler. ~**ly** adv. élégamment. ~**ness** n. élégance f.

smarten /'smɑːtn/ v.t./i. ~ (up), embellir. ~ (o.s.) up, se faire beau; (tidy) s'arranger.

smash /smæʃ/ v.t./i. (se) briser, (se) fracasser; (opponent, record) pulvériser. ● n. (noise) fracas m.; (blow) coup m.; (fig.) collision f.

smashing /'smæʃɪŋ/ a. (fam.) formidable, épatant.

smattering /'smætərɪŋ/ n. a ~ of, des notions de.

smear /smɪə(r)/ v.t. (stain) tacher; (coat) enduire; (discredit: fig.) entacher. ● n. tache f. ~ test, frottis m.

smell /smel/ n. odeur f.; (sense) odorat m. ● v.t./i. (p.t. smelt or smelled) sentir. ~ of, sentir. ~y a. malodorant, qui pue.

smelt [1] /smelt/ see smell.

smelt [2] /smelt/ v.t. (ore) fondre.

smil|e /smaɪl/ n. sourire. ● v.i. sourire. ~ing a. souriant.

smirk /smɜːk/ n. sourire affecté m.

smith /smɪθ/ n. forgeron m.

smithereens /smɪðə'riːnz/ n. pl. to or in ~, en mille morceaux.

smitten /'smɪtn/ a. (in love) épris (with, de).

smock /smɒk/ n. blouse f.

smog /smɒg/ n. brouillard mélangé de fumée m., smog m.

smoke /sməʊk/ n. fumée f. ● v.t./i. fumer. have a ~, fumer. ~d a. fumé. ~less a. (fuel) non polluant. ~r /-ə(r)/ n. fumeu|r, -se m., f. ~screen n. écran de fumée m.; (fig.) manœuvre de diversion f. smoky a. (air) enfumé.

smooth /smuːð/ a. (-er, -est) lisse; (movement) régulier; (manners, cream) onctueux; (flight) sans turbulence; (changes) sans heurt. ● v.t. lisser. ~ out, (fig.) faire disparaître. ~ly adv. facilement, doucement.

smother /'smʌðə(r)/ v.t. (stifle) étouffer; (cover) couvrir.

smoulder /'sməʊldə(r)/ v.i. (fire, discontent, etc.) couver.

smudge /smʌdʒ/ n. tache f. ● v.t./i. (se) salir, (se) tacher.

smug /smʌg/ a. (smugger, smuggest) suffisant. ~ly adv. avec suffisance. ~ness n. suffisance f.

smuggl|e /'smʌgl/ v.t. passer (en contrebande). ~er n. contreband|ier, -ière m., f. ~ing n. contrebande f.

smut /smʌt/ n. saleté f. ~ty a. indécent.

snack /snæk/ n. casse-croûte m. invar. ~-bar n. snack(-bar) m.

snag /snæg/ n. difficulté f., inconvénient m.; (in cloth) accroc m.

snail /sneɪl/ n. escargot m. at a ~'s pace, à un pas de tortue.

snake /sneɪk/ n. serpent m.

snap /snæp/ v.t./i. (p.t. snapped) (whip, fingers, etc.) (faire) claquer; (break) (se) casser net; (say) dire sèchement. ● n. claquement m.; (photograph) instantané m.; (press-stud: Amer.) bouton-pression m. ● a. soudain. ~ at, (bite) happer; (angrily) être cassant avec. ~ up, (buy) sauter sur.

snappy /'snæpɪ/ a. (-ier, -iest) (brisk: fam.) prompt, rapide. make it ~, (fam.) se dépêcher.

snapshot /'snæpʃɒt/ n. instantané m., photo f.

snare /sneə(r)/ n. piège m.

snarl /snɑːl/ v.i. gronder (en montrant les dents). ● n. grondement m. ~-up, n. embouteillage m.

snarl /snɑːl/ v.i. gronder (en montrant les dents). ● n. grondement m. ~-up n. embouteillage m.

snatch /snætʃ/ v.t. (grab) saisir; (steal) voler. ~ from s.o., arracher à qn. ● n. (theft) vol m.; (short part) fragment m.

sneak /sniːk/ v.i. aller furtivement. ● n. (schol., sl.) rapporteu|r, -se m., f. ~y a. sournois.

sneakers /'sniːkəz/ n. pl. (shoes) tennis m. pl.

sneaking /'sniːkɪŋ/ a. caché.

sneer /snɪə(r)/ n. ricanement m. ● v.i. ricaner.

sneeze /sniːz/ n. éternuement m. ● v.i. éternuer.

snide /snaɪd/ a. (fam.) narquois.

sniff /snɪf/ v.t./i. renifler. ● n. reniflement m.

snigger /'snɪgə(r)/ n. ricanement m. ● v.i. ricaner.

snip /snɪp/ v.t. (p.t. snipped) couper. ● n. morceau coupé m.; (bargain: sl.) bonne affaire f.

snipe /snaɪp/ v.i. canarder. ~r /-ə(r)/ n. tireur embusqué m.

snippet /'snɪpɪt/ n. bribe f.

snivel /'snɪvl/ v.i. (p.t. snivelled) pleurnicher.

snob /snɒb/ n. snob m./f. ~bery n. snobisme m. ~bish a. snob invar.

snooker /'snuːkə(r)/ n. (*sorte de*) jeu de billard m.

snoop /snuːp/ v.i. (*fam.*) fourrer son nez partout. **~ on,** espionner.

snooty /'snuːtɪ/ a. (**-ier, -iest**) (*fam.*) snob *invar.*, hautain.

snooze /snuːz/ n. petit somme m. ● v.i. faire un petit somme.

snore /snɔː(r)/ n. ronflement m. ● v.i. ronfler.

snorkel /'snɔːkl/ n. tuba m.

snort /snɔːt/ n. grognement m. ● v.i. (*person*) grogner; (*horse*) s'ébrouer.

snotty /'snɒtɪ/ a. morveux.

snout /snaʊt/ n. museau m.

snow /snəʊ/ n. neige f. ● v.i. neiger. **be ~ed under with,** être submergé de. **~-bound** a. bloqué par la neige. **~-drift** n. congère f. **~-plough** n. chasse-neige m. *invar.* **~-shoe** n. raquette f. **~y** a. neigeux.

snowball /'snəʊbɔːl/ n. boule de neige f. ● v.i. faire boule de neige.

snowdrop /'snəʊdrɒp/ n. perce-neige m./f. *invar.*

snowfall /'snəʊfɔːl/ n. chute de neige f.

snowflake /'snəʊfleɪk/ n. flocon de neige m.

snowman /'snəʊmæn/ n. (*pl.* **-men**) bonhomme de neige m.

snowstorm /'snəʊstɔːm/ n. tempête de neige f.

snub /snʌb/ v.t. (*p.t.* **snubbed**) (*person*) snober; (*offer*) repousser. ● n. rebuffade f.

snub-nosed /'snʌbnəʊzd/ a. au nez retroussé.

snuff[1] /snʌf/ n. tabac à priser m.

snuff[2] /snʌf/ v.t. (*candle*) moucher.

snuffle /'snʌfl/ v.i. renifler.

snug /snʌg/ a. (**snugger, snuggest**) (*cosy*) confortable; (*tight*) bien ajusté; (*safe*) sûr.

snuggle /'snʌgl/ v.i. se pelotonner.

so /səʊ/ adv. si, tellement; (*thus*) ainsi. ● conj. donc, alors. **so am I,** moi aussi. **so good/***etc.* **as,** aussi bon/*etc.* que. **so does he,** lui aussi. **that is so,** c'est ça. **I think so,** je pense que oui. **five or so,** environ cinq. **so-and-so** n. un(e) tel(le) m. (f.). **so as to,** de manière à. **so-called** a. soi-disant *invar.* **~ far,** jusqu'ici. **so long!,** (*fam.*) à bientôt! **so many, so much,** tant (de). **so-so** a. & adv. comme ci comme ça. **so that,** pour que.

soak /səʊk/ v.t./i. (faire) tremper (**in, dans**). **~ in** or **up,** absorber. **~ing** a. trempé.

soap /səʊp/ n. savon m. ● v.t. savonner. **~ opera,** feuilleton m. **~ powder,** lessive f. **~y** a. savonneux.

soar /sɔː(r)/ v.i. monter (en flèche).

sob /sɒb/ n. sanglot m. ● v.i. (*p.t.* **sobbed**) sangloter.

sober /'səʊbə(r)/ a. qui n'est pas ivre; (*serious*) sérieux; (*colour*) sobre. ● v.t./i. **~ up,** dessoûler.

soccer /'sɒkə(r)/ n. (*fam.*) football m.

sociable /'səʊʃəbl/ a. sociable.

social /'səʊʃl/ a. social; (*gathering, life*) mondain. ● n. réunion (amicale) f., fête f. **~ly** adv. socialement; (*meet*) en société. **~ security,** aide sociale f.; (*for old age: Amer.*) pension (de retraite) f. **~ worker,** assistant(e) social(e) m. (f.).

socialis|t /'səʊʃəlɪst/ n. socialiste m./f. **~m** /-zəm/ n. socialisme m.

socialize /'səʊʃəlaɪz/ v.i. se mêler aux autres. **~ with,** fréquenter.

society /sə'saɪətɪ/ n. société f.

sociolog|y /səʊsɪ'ɒlədʒɪ/ n. sociologie f. **~ical** /-ə'lɒdʒɪkl/ a. sociologique. **~ist** n. sociologue m./f.

sock[1] /sɒk/ n. chaussette f.

sock[2] /sɒk/ v.t. (*hit: sl.*) flanquer un coup (de poing) à.

socket /'sɒkɪt/ n. cavité f.; (*for lamp*) douille f.; (*electr.*) prise (de courant) f.; (*of tooth*) alvéole f.

soda /'səʊdə/ n. soude f. **~(-pop),** (*Amer.*) soda m. **~(-water),** soda m., eau de Seltz f.

sodden /'sɒdn/ a. détrempé.

sodium /'səʊdɪəm/ n. sodium m.

sofa /'səʊfə/ n. canapé m., sofa m.

soft /sɒft/ a. (**-er, -est**) (*gentle, lenient*) doux; (*not hard*) doux, mou; (*heart, wood*) tendre; (*silly*) ramolli; (*easy: sl.*) facile. **~ drink,** boisson non alcoolisée f. **~ly** adv. doucement. **~ness** n. douceur f. **~ spot,** faible m.

soften /'sɒfn/ v.t./i. (se) ramollir; (*tone down, sound*) (s')adoucir.

software /'sɒftweə(r)/ n. (*for computer*) logiciel m.

softwood /'sɒftwʊd/ n. bois tendre m.

soggy /'sɒgɪ/ a. (**-ier, -iest**) détrempé; (*bread etc.*) ramolli.

soil[1] /sɔɪl/ n. sol m., terre f.

soil[2] /sɔɪl/ v.t./i. (se) salir.

solar /'səʊlə(r)/ a. solaire.

sold /səʊld/ *see* sell. ● *a.* ~ **out,** épuisé.

solder /'sɒldə(r), *Amer.* 'sɒdər/ *n.* soudure *f.* ● *v.t.* souder. ~**ing iron,** fer à souder *m.*

soldier /'səʊldʒə(r)/ *n.* soldat *m.* ● *v.i.* ~ **on,** (*fam.*) persévérer.

sole [1] /səʊl/ *n.* (*of foot*) plante *f.*; (*of shoe*) semelle *f.*

sole [2] /səʊl/ *n.* (*fish*) sole *f.*

sole [3] /səʊl/ *a.* unique, seul. ~**ly** *adv.* uniquement.

solemn /'sɒləm/ *a.* (*formal*) solennel; (*not cheerful*) grave. ~**ity** /sə-'lemnəti/ *n.* solennité *f.* ~**ly** *adv.* solennellement; gravement.

solicit /sə'lɪsɪt/ *v.t.* (*seek*) solliciter. ● *v.i.* (*of prostitute*) racoler.

solicitor /sə'lɪsɪtə(r)/ *n.* avoué *m.*

solid /'sɒlɪd/ *a.* solide; (*not hollow*) plein; (*gold*) massif; (*mass*) compact; (*meal*) substantiel. ● *n.* solide *m.* ~**s,** (*food*) aliments solides *m. pl.* ~-**state** *a.* à circuits intégrés. ~**ity** /sə'lɪdəti/ *n.* solidité *f.* ~**ly** *adv.* solidement.

solidarity /sɒlɪ'dærəti/ *n.* solidarité *f.*

solidify /sə'lɪdɪfaɪ/ *v.t./i.* (se) solidifier.

soliloquy /sə'lɪləkwi/ *n.* monologue *m.*, soliloque *m.*

solitary /'sɒlɪtri/ *a.* (*alone, lonely*) solitaire; (*only, single*) seul.

solitude /'sɒlɪtjuːd/ *n.* solitude *f.*

solo /'səʊləʊ/ *n.* (*pl.* -os) solo *m.* ● *a.* (*mus.*) solo *invar.*; (*flight*) en solitaire. ~**ist** *n.* soliste *m./f.*

solstice /'sɒlstɪs/ *n.* solstice *m.*

soluble /'sɒljʊbl/ *a.* soluble.

solution /sə'luːʃn/ *n.* solution *f.*

solv|e /sɒlv/ *v.t.* résoudre. ~**able** *a.* soluble.

solvent /'sɒlvənt/ *a.* (*comm.*) solvable. ● *n.* (dis)solvant *m.*

sombre /'sɒmbə(r)/ *a.* sombre.

some /sʌm/ *a.* (*quantity, number*) du, de l'*, de la, des; (*unspecified, some or other*) un(e), quelque; (*a little*) un peu de; (*a certain*) un(e) certain(e), quelque; (*contrasted with others*) quelques, certain(e)s. ● *pron.* quelques-un(e)s; (*certain quantity of it or them*) en; (*a little*) un peu. ● *adv.* (*approximately*) quelque. **pour ~ milk,** versez du lait. **buy ~ flowers,** achetez des fleurs. **~ people like them,** il y a des gens qui les aiment. **~ of my friends,** quelques amis à moi. **he wants ~,** il en veut. **~**

book (or other), un livre (quelconque), quelque livre. **~ time ago,** il y a un certain temps.

somebody /'sʌmbədi/ *pron.* quelqu'un. ● *n.* **be a ~,** être quelqu'un.

somehow /'sʌmhaʊ/ *adv.* d'une manière ou d'une autre; (*for some reason*) je ne sais pas pourquoi.

someone /'sʌmwʌn/ *pron. & n.* = somebody.

someplace /'sʌmpleɪs/ *adv.* (*Amer.*) = somewhere.

somersault /'sʌməsɔːlt/ *n.* culbute *f.* ● *v.i.* faire la culbute.

something /'sʌmθɪŋ/ *pron. & n.* quelque chose (*m.*). ~ **good/***etc.* quelque chose de bon/*etc.* ~ **like,** un peu comme.

sometime /'sʌmtaɪm/ *adv.* un jour. ● *a.* (*former*) ancien. ~ **in June,** en juin.

sometimes /'sʌmtaɪmz/ *adv.* quelquefois, parfois.

somewhat /'sʌmwɒt/ *adv.* quelque peu, un peu.

somewhere /'sʌmweə(r)/ *adv.* quelque part.

son /sʌn/ *n.* fils *m.* ~-**in-law** *n.* (*pl.* ~**s-in-law**) beau-fils *m.*, gendre *m.*

sonar /'səʊnɑː(r)/ *n.* sonar *m.*

sonata /sə'nɑːtə/ *n.* sonate *f.*

song /sɒŋ/ *n.* chanson *f.* **going for a ~,** à vendre pour une bouchée de pain.

sonic /'sɒnɪk/ *a.* ~ **boom,** bang supersonique *m.*

sonnet /'sɒnɪt/ *n.* sonnet *m.*

sonny /'sʌni/ *n.* (*fam.*) fiston *m.*

soon /suːn/ *adv.* (-er, -est) bientôt; (*early*) tôt. **I would ~er stay,** j'aimerais mieux rester. **~ after,** peu après. **~er or later,** tôt ou tard.

soot /sʊt/ *n.* suie *f.* ~**y** *a.* couvert de suie.

sooth|e /suːð/ *v.t.* calmer. ~**ing** *a.* (*remedy, words, etc.*) calmant.

sophisticated /sə'fɪstɪkeɪtɪd/ *a.* raffiné; (*machine etc.*) sophistiqué.

sophomore /'sɒfəmɔː(r)/ *n.* (*Amer.*) étudiant(e) de seconde année *m.* (*f.*).

soporific /sɒpə'rɪfɪk/ *a.* soporifique.

sopping /'sɒpɪŋ/ *a.* trempé.

soppy /'sɒpi/ *a.* (-ier, -iest) (*fam.*) sentimental; (*silly: fam.*) bête.

soprano /sə'prɑːnəʊ/ *n.* (*pl.* -os) (*voice*) soprano *m.*; (*singer*) soprano *m./f.*

sorcerer /'sɔːsərə(r)/ *n.* sorcier *m.*

sordid /'sɔ:dɪd/ a. sordide.

sore /'sɔ:(r)/ a. (**-er, -est**) douloureux; (*vexed*) en rogne (**at, with,** contre). ● n. plaie f.

sorely /'sɔ:lɪ/ adv. fortement.

sorrow /'sɒrəʊ/ n. chagrin m. **~ful** a. triste.

sorry /'sɒrɪ/ a. (**-ier, -iest**) (*regretful*) désolé (**to,** de; **that,** que); (*wretched*) triste. **feel ~ for,** plaindre. **~!,** pardon!

sort /sɔ:t/ n. genre m., sorte f., espèce f.; (*person: fam.*) type m. ● v.t. **~ (out),** (*classify*) trier. **what ~ of?,** quel genre de? **be out of ~s,** ne pas être dans son assiette. **~ out,** (*tidy*) ranger; (*arrange*) arranger; (*problem*) régler.

SOS /esəʊˈes/ n. SOS m.

soufflé /'su:fleɪ/ n. soufflé m.

sought /sɔ:t/ *see* seek.

soul /səʊl/ n. âme f. **~-destroying** a. démoralisant.

soulful /'səʊlfl/ a. plein de sentiment, très expressif.

sound[1] /saʊnd/ n. son m., bruit m. ● v.t./i. sonner; (*seem*) sembler (**as if,** que). **~ a horn,** klaxonner. **~ barrier,** mur du son m. **~ like,** sembler être. **~-proof** a. insonorisé; v.t. insonoriser. **~-track** n. bande sonore f.

sound[2] /saʊnd/ a. (**-er, -est**) solide; (*healthy*) sain; (*sensible*) sensé. **~ asleep,** profondément endormi. **~ly** adv. solidement; (*sleep*) profondément.

sound[3] /saʊnd/ v.t. (*test*) sonder. **~ out,** sonder.

soup /su:p/ n. soupe f., potage m. **in the ~,** (*sl.*) dans le pétrin.

sour /'saʊə(r)/ a. (**-er, -est**) aigre. ● v.t./i. (s')aigrir.

source /sɔ:s/ n. source f.

south /saʊθ/ n. sud m. ● a. sud invar., du sud. ● adv. vers le sud. **S~ Africa/America,** Afrique/Amérique du Sud f. **S~ African** a. & n. sud-africain(e) (m. (f.)). **S~ American** a. & n. sud-américain(e) (m. (f.)). **~-east** n. sud-est m. **~erly** /'saʊðəlɪ/ a. du sud. **~-ward** a. au sud. **~wards** adv. vers le sud. **~-west** n. sud-ouest m.

southern /'sʌðən/ a. du sud. **~er** n. habitant(e) du sud m. (f.).

souvenir /su:vəˈnɪə(r)/ n. (*thing*) souvenir m.

sovereign /'sɒvrɪn/ n. & a. souverain(e) (m. (f.)). **~ty** n. souveraineté f.

Soviet /'səʊvɪət/ a. soviétique. **the ~ Union,** l'Union soviétique f.

sow[1] /səʊ/ v.t. (p.t. **sowed,** p.p. **sowed** or **sown**) (*seed etc.*) semer; (*land*) ensemencer.

sow[2] /saʊ/ n. (*pig*) truie f.

soya, soy /'sɔɪə, sɔɪ/ n. **~ bean,** graine de soja f. **~ sauce,** sauce soja f.

spa /spɑ:/ n. station thermale f.

space /speɪs/ n. espace m.; (*room*) place f.; (*period*) période f. ● a. (*research etc.*) spatial. ● v.t. **~ (out),** espacer.

space|craft /'speɪskrɑ:ft/ n. invar., **~ship** n. engin spatial m.

spacesuit /'speɪssu:t/ n. scaphandre m.

spacious /'speɪʃəs/ a. spacieux.

spade[1] /speɪd/ n. (*large, for garden*) bêche f.; (*child's*) pelle f.

spade[2] /speɪd/ n. (*cards*) pique m.

spadework /'speɪdwɜ:k/ n. (*fig.*) travail préparatoire m.

spaghetti /spəˈgetɪ/ n. spaghetti m. pl.

Spa|in /speɪn/ n. Espagne f. **~niard** /'spænɪəd/ n. Espagnol(e) m. (f.). **~nish** /'spænɪʃ/ a. espagnol; n. (*lang.*) espagnol m.

span[1] /spæn/ n. (*of arch*) portée f.; (*of wings*) envergure f.; (*of time*) durée f. ● v.t. (p.t. **spanned**) enjamber; (*in time*) embrasser.

span[2] /spæn/ *see* spick.

spaniel /'spænɪəl/ n. épagneul m.

spank /spæŋk/ v.t. donner une fessée à. **~ing** n. fessée f.

spanner /'spænə(r)/ n. (*tool*) clé (plate) f.; (*adjustable*) clé à molette f.

spar /spɑ:(r)/ v.i. (p.t. **sparred**) s'entraîner (à la boxe).

spare /speə(r)/ v.t. épargner; (*do without*) se passer de; (*afford to give*) donner, accorder; (*use with restraint*) ménager. ● a. en réserve; (*surplus*) de trop; (*tyre, shoes, etc.*) de rechange; (*room, bed*) d'ami. ● n. **~ (part),** pièce de rechange f. **~ time,** loisirs m. pl. **are there any ~ tickets?** y a-t-il encore des places?

sparing /'speərɪŋ/ a. frugal. **~ of,** avare de. **~ly** adv. en petite quantité.

spark /spɑːk/ n. étincelle f. ● v.t. ~ **off**, (*initiate*) provoquer. ~(**ing**)-**plug** n. bougie f.

sparkle /'spɑːkl/ v.i. étinceler. ● n. étincellement m.

sparkling /'spɑːklɪŋ/ a. (*wine*) mousseux, pétillant; (*eyes*) pétillant.

sparrow /'spærəʊ/ n. moineau m.

sparse /spɑːs/ a. clairsemé. ~**ly** adv. (*furnished etc.*) peu.

spartan /'spɑːtn/ a. spartiate.

spasm /'spæzəm/ n. (*of muscle*) spasme m.; (*of coughing, anger, etc.*) accès m.

spasmodic /spæz'mɒdɪk/ a. intermittent.

spastic /'spæstɪk/ n. handicapé(e) moteur m. (f.).

spat /spæt/ *see* spit[1].

spate /speɪt/ n. **a ~ of**, (*letters etc.*) une avalanche de.

spatter /'spætə(r)/ v.t. éclabousser (**with**, de).

spatula /'spætjʊlə/ n. spatule f.

spawn /spɔːn/ n. frai m., œufs m. pl. ● v.t. pondre. ● v.i. frayer.

speak /spiːk/ v.i. (*p.t.* **spoke**, *p.p.* **spoken**) parler. ● v.t. (*say*) dire; (*language*) parler. ~ **up**, parler plus fort.

speaker /'spiːkə(r)/ n. (*in public*) orateur m.; (*pol.*) président m.; (*loudspeaker*) baffle m. **be a French/a good**/*etc.* ~, parler français/bien/ *etc.*

spear /spɪə(r)/ n. lance f.

spearhead /'spɪəhed/ n. fer de lance m. ● v.t. (*lead*) mener.

spearmint /'spɪəmɪnt/ n. menthe verte f. ● a. à la menthe.

spec /spek/ n. **on ~**, (*as speculation: fam.*) à tout hasard.

special /'speʃl/ a. spécial; (*exceptional*) exceptionnel. ~**ity** /-ɪ'ælətɪ/, (*Amer.*) ~**ty** n. spécialité f. ~**ly** adv. spécialement.

specialist /'speʃəlɪst/ n. spécialiste m./f.

specialize /'speʃəlaɪz/ v.i. se spécialiser (**in**, en). ~**d** a. spécialisé.

species /'spiːʃiːz/ n. invar. espèce f.

specific /spə'sɪfɪk/ a. précis, explicite. ~**ally** adv. explicitement; (*exactly*) précisément.

specif|y /'spesɪfaɪ/ v.t. spécifier. ~**ication** /-ɪ'keɪʃn/ n. spécification f.; (*details*) prescriptions f. pl.

specimen /'spesɪmɪn/ n. spécimen m., échantillon m.

speck /spek/ n. (*stain*) (petite) tache f.; (*particle*) grain m.

speckled /'spekld/ a. tacheté.

specs /speks/ n. pl. (*fam.*) lunettes f. pl.

spectacle /'spektəkl/ n. spectacle m. ~**s**, lunettes f. pl.

spectacular /spek'tækjʊlə(r)/ a. spectaculaire.

spectator /spek'teɪtə(r)/ n. spectateur, -trice m., f.

spectre /'spektə(r)/ n. spectre m.

spectrum /'spektrəm/ n. (*pl.* **-tra**) spectre m.; (*of ideas etc.*) gamme f.

speculat|e /'spekjʊleɪt/ v.i. s'interroger (**about**, sur); (*comm.*) spéculer. ~**ion** /-'leɪʃn/ n. conjectures f. pl.; (*comm.*) spéculation f. ~**or** n. spécula|teur, -trice m., f.

speech /spiːtʃ/ n. (*faculty*) parole f.; (*diction*) élocution f.; (*dialect*) langage m.; (*address*) discours m. ~**less** a. muet (**with**, de).

speed /spiːd/ n. (*of movement*) vitesse f.; (*swiftness*) rapidité f. ● v.i. (*p.t.* **sped** /sped/) aller vite; (*p.t.* **speeded**) (*drive too fast*) aller trop vite. ~ **limit**, limitation de vitesse f. ~ **up**, accélérer; (*of pace*) s'accélérer. ~**ing** n. excès de vitesse m.

speedboat /'spiːdbəʊt/ n. vedette f.

speedometer /spiː'dɒmɪtə(r)/ n. compteur (de vitesse) m.

speedway /'spiːdweɪ/ n. piste pour motos f.; (*Amer.*) autodrome m.

speed|y /'spiːdɪ/ a. (**-ier**, **-iest**) rapide. ~**ily** adv. rapidement.

spell[1] /spel/ n. (*magic*) charme m., sortilège m.; (*curse*) sort m.

spell[2] /spel/ v.t./i. (*p.t.* **spelled** or **spelt**) écrire; (*mean*) signifier. ~ **out**, épeler; (*explain*) expliquer. ~**ing** n. orthographe f. ~**ing mistake**, faute d'orthographe f.

spell[3] /spel/ n. (courte) période f.

spend /spend/ v.t. (*p.t.* **spent**) (*money*) dépenser (**on**, pour); (*time, holiday*) passer; (*energy*) consacrer (**on**, à). ● v.i. dépenser.

spendthrift /'spendθrɪft/ n. dépens|ier, -ière m., f.

spent /spent/ *see* spend. ● a. (*used*) utilisé; (*person*) épuisé.

sperm /spɜːm/ n. (*pl.* **sperms** or **sperm**) (*semen*) sperme m.; (*cell*) spermatozoïde m. ~**icide** n. spermicide m.

spew /spjuː/ v.t./i. vomir.

sphere /sfɪə(r)/ *n.* sphère *f.*

spherical /'sferɪkl/ *a.* sphérique.

spic|e /spaɪs/ *n.* épice *f.*; (*fig.*) piquant *m.* **~y** *a.* épicé; piquant.

spick /spɪk/ *a.* **~ and span,** impeccable, d'une propreté parfaite.

spider /'spaɪdə(r)/ *n.* araignée *f.*

spiel /ʃpiːl, (*Amer.*) spiːl/ *n.* baratin *m.*

spik|e /spaɪk/ *n.* (*of metal etc.*) pointe *f.* **~y** *a.* garni de pointes.

spill /spɪl/ *v.t.* (*p.t.* **spilled** *or* **spilt**) renverser, répandre. ● *v.i.* se répandre. **~ over,** déborder.

spin /spɪn/ *v.t./i.* (*p.t.* **spun,** *pres. p.* **spinning**) (*wool, web, of spinner*) filer; (*turn*) (faire) tourner; (*story*) débiter. ● *n.* (*movement, excursion*) tour *m.* **~ out,** faire durer. **~-drier** *n.* essoreuse *f.* **~ning-wheel** *n.* rouet *m.* **~-off** *n.* avantage accessoire *m.*; (*by-product*) dérivé *m.*

spinach /'spɪnɪdʒ/ *n.* (*plant*) épinard *m.*; (*as food*) épinards *m. pl.*

spinal /'spaɪnl/ *a.* vertébral. **~ cord,** moelle épinière *f.*

spindl|e /'spɪndl/ *n.* fuseau *m.* **~y** *a.* filiforme, grêle.

spine /spaɪn/ *n.* colonne vertébrale *f.*; (*prickle*) piquant *m.*

spineless /'spaɪnlɪs/ *a.* (*fig.*) sans caractère, mou, lâche.

spinster /'spɪnstə(r)/ *n.* célibataire *f.*; (*pej.*) vieille fille *f.*

spiral /'spaɪərəl/ *a.* en spirale; (*staircase*) en colimaçon. ● *n.* spirale *f.* ● *v.i.* (*p.t.* **spiralled**) (*prices*) monter (en flèche).

spire /'spaɪə(r)/ *n.* flèche *f.*

spirit /'spɪrɪt/ *n.* esprit *m.*; (*boldness*) courage *m.* **~s,** (*morale*) moral *m.*; (*drink*) spiritueux *m. pl.* ● *v.t.* **~ away,** faire disparaître. **~-level** *n.* niveau à bulle *m.*

spirited /'spɪrɪtɪd/ *a.* fougueux.

spiritual /'spɪrɪtʃʊəl/ *a.* spirituel. ● *n.* (*song*) (negro-)spiritual *m.*

spit¹ /spɪt/ *v.t./i.* (*p.t.* **spat** *or* **spit,** *pres. p.* **spitting**) cracher; (*of rain*) crachiner. ● *n.* crachat(s) *m.* (*pl.*) **~ out,** cracher. **the ~ting image of,** le portrait craché *or* vivant de.

spit² /spɪt/ *n.* (*for meat*) broche *f.*

spite /spaɪt/ *n.* rancune *f.* ● *v.t.* contrarier. **in ~ of,** malgré. **~ful** *a.* méchant, rancunier. **~fully** *adv.* méchamment.

spittle /'spɪtl/ *n.* crachat(s) *m.* (*pl.*).

splash /splæʃ/ *v.t.* éclabousser. ● *v.i.* faire des éclaboussures. **~ (about),** patauger. ● *n.* (*act, mark*) éclaboussure *f.*; (*sound*) plouf *m.*; (*of colour*) tache *f.*

spleen /spliːn/ *n.* (*anat.*) rate *f.*

splendid /'splendɪd/ *a.* magnifique, splendide.

splendour /'splendə(r)/ *n.* splendeur *f.*, éclat *m.*

splint /splɪnt/ *n.* (*med.*) attelle *f.*

splinter /'splɪntə(r)/ *n.* éclat *m.*; (*in finger*) écharde *f.* **~ group,** groupe dissident *m.*

split /splɪt/ *v.t./i.* (*p.t.* **split,** *pres. p.* **splitting**) (se) fendre; (*tear*) (se) déchirer; (*divide*) (se) diviser; (*share*) partager. ● *n.* fente *f.*; déchirure *f.*; (*share: fam.*) part *f.*, partage *m.*; (*quarrel*) rupture *f.*; (*pol.*) scission *f.* **~ up,** (*couple*) rompre. **a ~ second,** un rien de temps. **~ one's sides,** se tordre (de rire).

splurge /splɜːdʒ/ *v.i.* (*fam.*) faire de folles dépenses.

splutter /'splʌtə(r)/ *v.i.* crachoter; (*stammer*) bafouiller; (*engine*) tousser; (*fat*) crépiter.

spoil /spɔɪl/ *v.t.* (*p.t.* **spoilt** *or* **spoiled**) (*pamper*) gâter; (*ruin*) abîmer; (*mar*) gâcher, gâter. ● *n.* **~(s),** (*plunder*) butin *m.* **~-sport** *n.* trouble-fête *m./f. invar.*

spoke¹ /spəʊk/ *n.* rayon *m.*

spoke², spoken /spəʊk, 'spəʊkən/ *see* speak.

spokesman /'spəʊksmən/ *n.* (*pl.* **-men**) porte-parole *m. invar.*

sponge /spʌndʒ/ *n.* éponge *f.* ● *v.t.* éponger. ● *v.i.* **~ on,** vivre aux crochets de. **~-bag** *n.* trousse de toilette *f.* **~-cake** *n.* génoise *f.* **~r** /-ə(r)/ *n.* parasite *m.* **spongy** *a.* spongieux.

sponsor /'spɒnsə(r)/ *n.* (*of concert*) parrain *m.*, sponsor *m.*; (*surety*) garant *m.*; (*for membership*) parrain *m.*, marraine *f.* ● *v.t.* parrainer, sponsoriser; (*member*) parrainer. **~ship** *n.* patronage *m.*; parrainage *m.*

spontane|ous /spɒn'teɪnɪəs/ *a.* spontané. **~ity** /-tə'niːətɪ/ *n.* spontanéité *f.* **~ously** *adv.* spontanément.

spoof /spuːf/ *n.* (*fam.*) parodie *f.*

spool /spuːl/ *n.* bobine *f.*

spoon /spuːn/ *n.* cuiller *f.* **~-feed** *v.t.* (*p.t.* **-fed**) nourrir à la cuiller; (*help*:

fig.) mâcher la besogne à. **~ful** *n.* (*pl.* **-fuls**) cuillerée *f.*

sporadic /spə'rædɪk/ *a.* sporadique.

sport /spɔːt/ *n.* sport *m.* **(good) ~,** (*person: sl.*) chic type *m.* ● *v.t.* (*display*) exhiber, arborer. **~s car/coat,** voiture/veste de sport *f.* **~y** *a.* (*fam.*) sportif.

sporting /'spɔːtɪŋ/ *a.* sportif. **a ~ chance,** une assez bonne chance.

sports|man /'spɔːtsmən/ *n.* (*pl.* **-men**) sportif *m.* **~manship** *n.* sportivité *f.* **~woman** *n.* (*pl.* **-women**) sportive *f.*

spot /spɒt/ *n.* (*mark, stain*) tache *f.*; (*dot*) point *m.*; (*in pattern*) pois *m.*; (*drop*) goutte *f.*; (*place*) endroit *m.*; (*pimple*) bouton *m.* ● *v.t.* (*p.t.* **spotted**) (*fam.*) apercevoir. **a ~ of,** (*fam.*) un peu de. **be in a ~,** (*fam.*) avoir un problème. **on the ~,** sur place; (*without delay*) sur le coup. **~ check,** contrôle à l'improviste *m.* **~ted** *a.* tacheté; (*fabric*) à pois. **~ty** *a.* (*skin*) boutonneux.

spotless /'spɒtlɪs/ *a.* impeccable.

spotlight /'spɒtlaɪt/ *n.* (*lamp*) projecteur *m.*, spot *m.*

spouse /spaʊs/ *n.* époux *m.*, épouse *f.*

spout /spaʊt/ *n.* (*of vessel*) bec *m.*; (*of liquid*) jet *m.* ● *v.i.* jaillir. **up the ~,** (*ruined: sl.*) fichu.

sprain /spreɪn/ *n.* entorse *f.*, foulure *f.* ● *v.t.* **~ one's wrist/etc.,** se fouler le poignet/etc.

sprang /spræŋ/ *see* spring.

sprawl /sprɔːl/ *v.i.* (*town, person, etc.*) s'étaler. ● *n.* étalement *m.*

spray [1] /spreɪ/ *n.* (*of flowers*) gerbe *f.*

spray [2] /spreɪ/ *n.* (*water*) gerbe d'eau *f.*; (*from sea*) embruns *m. pl.*; (*device*) bombe *f.*, atomiseur *m.* ● *v.t.* (*surface, insecticide*) vaporiser; (*plant etc.*) arroser; (*crops*) traiter.

spread /spred/ *v.t./i.* (*p.t.* **spread**) (*stretch, extend*) (s')étendre; (*news, fear, etc.*) (se) répandre; (*illness*) (se) propager; (*butter etc.*) (s')étaler. ● *n.* propagation *f.*; (*of population*) distribution *f.*; (*paste*) pâte à tartiner *f.*; (*food*) belle table *f.* **~-eagled** *a.* bras et jambes écartés.

spreadsheet /'spredʃiːt/ *n.* tableur *m.*

spree /spriː/ *n.* **go on a ~,** (*have fun: fam.*) faire la noce.

sprig /sprɪg/ *n.* (*shoot*) brin *m.*; (*twig*) brindille *f.*

sprightly /'spraɪtlɪ/ *a.* (**-ier, -iest**) alerte, vif.

spring /sprɪŋ/ *v.i.* (*p.t.* **sprang,** *p.p.* **sprung**) bondir. ● *v.t.* faire, annoncer, *etc.* à l'improviste (**on,** à). ● *n.* bond *m.*; (*device*) ressort *m.*; (*season*) printemps *m.*; (*of water*) source *f.* **~-clean** *v.t.* nettoyer de fond en comble. **~ from,** provenir de. **~ onion,** oignon blanc *m.* **~ up,** surgir.

springboard /'sprɪŋbɔːd/ *n.* tremplin *m.*

springtime /'sprɪŋtaɪm/ *n.* printemps *m.*

springy /'sprɪŋɪ/ *a.* (**-ier, -iest**) élastique.

sprinkle /'sprɪŋkl/ *v.t.* (*with liquid*) arroser (**with,** de); (*with salt, flour*) saupoudrer (**with,** de). **~ sand/etc.,** répandre du sable/etc. **~r** /-ə(r)/ *n.* (*in garden*) arroseur *m.*; (*for fires*) extincteur (à déclenchement) automatique *m.*

sprinkling /'sprɪŋklɪŋ/ *n.* (*amount*) petite quantité *f.*

sprint /sprɪnt/ *v.i.* (*sport*) sprinter. ● *n.* sprint *m.* **~er** *n.* sprinteu|r, -se *m.*, *f.*

sprout /spraʊt/ *v.t./i.* pousser. ● *n.* (*on plant etc.*) pousse *f.* **(Brussels) ~s,** choux de Bruxelles *m. pl.*

spruce [1] /spruːs/ *a.* pimpant. ● *v.t.* **~ o.s. up,** se faire beau.

spruce [2] /spruːs/ *n.* (*tree*) épicéa *m.*

sprung /sprʌŋ/ *see* spring. ● *a.* (*mattress etc.*) à ressorts.

spry /spraɪ/ *a.* (**spryer, spryest**) alerte, vif.

spud /spʌd/ *n.* (*sl.*) patate *f.*

spun /spʌn/ *see* spin.

spur /spɜː(r)/ *n.* (*of rider, cock, etc.*) éperon *m.*; (*stimulus*) aiguillon *m.* ● *v.t.* (*p.t.* **spurred**) éperonner. **on the ~ of the moment,** sous l'impulsion du moment.

spurious /'spjʊərɪəs/ *a.* faux.

spurn /spɜːn/ *v.t.* repousser.

spurt /spɜːt/ *v.i.* jaillir; (*fig.*) accélérer. ● *n.* jet *m.*; (*at work*) coup de collier *m.*

spy /spaɪ/ *n.* espion(ne) *m.* (*f.*). ● *v.i.* espionner. ● *v.t.* apercevoir. **~ on,** espionner. **~ out,** reconnaître.

squabble /'skwɒbl/ *v.i.* se chamailler. ● *n.* chamaillerie *f.*

squad /skwɒd/ *n.* (*of soldiers etc.*) escouade *f.*; (*sport*) équipe *f.*

squadron /'skwɒdrən/ n. (*mil.*) escadron m.; (*aviat.*) escadrille f.; (*naut.*) escadre f.

squal|id /'skwɒlɪd/ a. sordide. **~or** n. conditions sordides f. pl.

squall /skwɔːl/ n. rafale f.

squander /'skwɒndə(r)/ v.t. (*money, time, etc.*) gaspiller.

square /skweə(r)/ n. carré m.; (*open space in town*) place f.; (*instrument*) équerre f. ● a. carré; (*honest*) honnête; (*meal*) solide; (*fam.*) ringard. **(all) ~,** (*quits*) quitte. ● v.t. (*settle*) régler. ● v.i. (*agree*) cadrer (**with,** avec). **~ up to,** faire face à. **~ metre,** mètre carré m. **~ly** adv. carrément.

squash /skwɒʃ/ v.t. écraser; (*crowd*) serrer. ● n. (*game*) squash m.; (*marrow: Amer.*) courge f. **lemon ~,** citronnade f. **orange ~,** orangeade f. **~y** a. mou.

squat /skwɒt/ v.i. (*p.t.* **squatted**) s'accroupir. ● a. (*dumpy*) trapu. **~ in a house,** squatteriser une maison. **~ter** n. squatter m.

squawk /skwɔːk/ n. cri rauque m. ● v.i. pousser un cri rauque.

squeak /skwiːk/ n. petit cri m.; (*of door etc.*) grincement m. ● v.i. crier; grincer. **~y** a. grinçant.

squeal /skwiːl/ n. cri aigu m. ● v.i. pousser un cri aigu. **~ on,** (*inform on: sl.*) dénoncer.

squeamish /'skwiːmɪʃ/ a. (trop) délicat, facilement dégoûté.

squeeze /skwiːz/ v.t. presser; (*hand, arm*) serrer; (*extract*) exprimer (**from,** de); (*extort*) soutirer (**from,** à). ● v.i. (*force one's way*) se glisser. ● n. pression f.; (*comm.*) restrictions de crédit f. pl.

squelch /skweltʃ/ v.i. faire flic flac. ● v.t. (*suppress*) supprimer.

squid /skwɪd/ n. calmar m.

squiggle /'skwɪɡl/ n. ligne onduleuse f.

squint /skwɪnt/ v.i. loucher; (*with half-shut eyes*) plisser les yeux. ● n. (*med.*) strabisme m.

squire /'skwaɪə(r)/ n. propriétaire terrien m.

squirm /skwɜːm/ v.i. se tortiller.

squirrel /'skwɪrəl, *Amer.* 'skwɜːrəl/ n. écureuil m.

squirt /skwɜːt/ v.t./i. (faire) jaillir. ● n. jet m.

stab /stæb/ v.t. (*p.t.* **stabbed**) (*with knife etc.*) poignarder. ● n. coup (de couteau) m. **have a ~ at sth.,** essayer de faire qch.

stabilize /'steɪbəlaɪz/ v.t. stabiliser.

stab|le ¹ /'steɪbl/ a. (**-er, -est**) stable. **~ility** /stə'bɪlətɪ/ n. stabilité f.

stable ² /'steɪbl/ n. écurie f. **~-boy** n. lad m.

stack /stæk/ n. tas m. ● v.t. **~ (up),** entasser, empiler.

stadium /'steɪdɪəm/ n. stade m.

staff /stɑːf/ n. personnel m.; (*in school*) professeurs m. pl.; (*mil.*) état-major m.; (*stick*) bâton m. ● v.t. pourvoir en personnel.

stag /stæɡ/ n. cerf m. **have a ~-party,** enterrer sa vie de garçon.

stage /steɪdʒ/ n. (*theatre*) scène f.; (*phase*) stade m., étape f.; (*platform in hall*) estrade f. ● v.t. mettre en scène; (*fig.*) organiser. **go on the ~,** faire du théâtre. **~-coach** n. (*old use*) diligence f. **~ door,** entrée des artistes f. **~ fright,** trac m. **~-manage** v.t. monter, organiser. **~-manager** n. régisseur m.

stagger /'stæɡə(r)/ v.i. chanceler. ● v.t. (*shock*) stupéfier; (*holidays etc.*) étaler. **~ing** a. stupéfiant.

stagnant /'stæɡnənt/ a. stagnant.

stagnat|e /stæɡ'neɪt/ v.i. stagner. **~ion** /-ʃn/ n. stagnation f.

staid /steɪd/ a. sérieux.

stain /steɪn/ v.t. tacher; (*wood etc.*) colorer. ● n. tache f.; (*colouring*) colorant m. **~ed glass window,** vitrail m. **~less steel,** acier inoxydable m. **~ remover,** détachant m.

stair /steə(r)/ n. marche f. **the ~s,** l'escalier m.

stair|case /'steəkeɪs/, **~way** ns. escalier m.

stake /steɪk/ n. (*post*) pieu m.; (*wager*) enjeu m. ● v.t. (*area*) jalonner; (*wager*) jouer. **at ~,** en jeu. **~ a claim to,** revendiquer.

stale /steɪl/ a. (**-er, -est**) pas frais; (*bread*) rassis; (*smell*) de renfermé; (*news*) vieux. **~ness** n. manque de fraîcheur m.

stalemate /'steɪlmeɪt/ n. (*chess*) pat m.; (*fig.*) impasse f.

stalk ¹ /stɔːk/ n. (*of plant*) tige f.

stalk ² /stɔːk/ v.i. marcher de façon guindée. ● v.t./i. (*prey*) traquer.

stall /stɔːl/ n. (*in stable*) stalle f.; (*in market*) éventaire m. **~s,** (*theatre*) orchestre m. ● v.t./i. (*auto.*) caler. **~ (for time),** temporiser.

stallion /'stæljən/ n. étalon m.

stalwart /'stɔːlwət/ n. (*supporter*) partisan(e) fidèle m. (f.).

stamina /'stæmɪnə/ n. résistance f.

stammer /'stæmə(r)/ v.t./i. bégayer. ● n. bégaiement m.

stamp /stæmp/ v.t./i. ~ (**one's foot**), taper du pied. ● v.t. (*letter etc.*) timbrer. ● n. (*for postage, marking*) timbre m.; (*mark: fig.*) sceau m. ~**collecting** n. philatélie f. ~ **out,** supprimer.

stampede /stæm'piːd/ n. fuite désordonnée f.; (*rush: fig.*) ruée f. ● v.i. s'enfuir en désordre; se ruer.

stance /stæns/ n. position f.

stand /stænd/ v.i. (*p.t.* **stood**) être *or* se tenir (debout); (*rise*) se lever; (*be situated*) se trouver; (*rest*) reposer; (*pol.*) être candidat (**for,** à). ● v.t. mettre (debout); (*tolerate*) supporter. ● n. position f.; (*mil.*) résistance f.; (*for lamp etc.*) support m.; (*at fair*) stand m.; (*in street*) kiosque m.; (*for spectators*) tribune f.; (*jurid., Amer.*) barre f. **make a ~,** prendre position. ~ **a chance,** avoir une chance. ~ **back,** reculer. ~ **by** *or* **around,** ne rien faire. ~ **by,** (*be ready*) se tenir prêt; (*promise, person*) rester fidèle à. ~**-by** a. de réserve; n. **be a ~-by,** être de réserve. ~ **down,** se désister. ~ **for,** représenter; (*fam.*) supporter. ~ **in for,** remplacer. ~**-in** n. remplaçant(e) m. (f.). ~ **in line,** (*Amer.*) faire la queue. ~**-offish** a. (*fam.*) distant. ~ **out,** (*be conspicuous*) ressortir. ~ **to reason,** être logique. ~ **up,** se lever. ~ **up for,** défendre. ~ **up to,** résister à.

standard /'stændəd/ n. norme f.; (*level*) niveau (voulu) m.; (*flag*) étendard m. ~**s,** (*morals*) principes m. pl. ● a. ordinaire. ~ **lamp,** lampadaire m. ~ **of living,** niveau de vie m.

standardize /'stændədaɪz/ v.t. standardiser.

standing /'stændɪŋ/ a. debout *invar.*; (*army, offer*) permanent. ● n. position f., réputation f.; (*duration*) durée f. ~ **order,** prélèvement bancaire m. ~ **room,** places debout f. pl.

standpoint /'stændpɔɪnt/ n. point de vue m.

standstill /'stændstɪl/ n. **at a ~,** immobile. **bring/come to a ~,** (s')immobiliser.

stank /stæŋk/ *see* stink.

stanza /'stænzə/ n. strophe f.

staple[1] /'steɪpl/ n. agrafe f. ● v.t. agrafer. ~**r** /-ə(r)/ n. agrafeuse f.

staple[2] /'steɪpl/ a. principal, de base.

star /stɑː(r)/ n. étoile f.; (*famous person*) vedette f. ● v.t. (*p.t.* **starred**) (*of film*) avoir pour vedette. ● v.i. ~ **in,** être la vedette de. ~**dom** n. célébrité f.

starboard /'stɑːbəd/ n. tribord m.

starch /stɑːtʃ/ n. amidon m.; (*in food*) fécule f. ● v.t. amidonner. ~**y** a. féculent; (*stiff*) guindé.

stare /steə(r)/ v.i. ~ **at,** regarder fixement. ● n. regard fixe m.

starfish /'stɑːfɪʃ/ n. étoile de mer f.

stark /stɑːk/ a. (**-er, -est**) (*desolate*) désolé; (*severe*) austère; (*utter*) complet; (*fact etc.*) brutal. ● adv. complètement.

starling /'stɑːlɪŋ/ n. étourneau m.

starlit /'stɑːlɪt/ a. étoilé.

starry /'stɑːrɪ/ a. étoilé. ~**-eyed** a. naïf, (trop) optimiste.

start /stɑːt/ v.t./i. commencer; (*machine*) (se) mettre en marche; (*fashion etc.*) lancer; (*cause*) provoquer; (*jump*) sursauter; (*of vehicle*) démarrer. ● n. commencement m., début m.; (*of race*) départ m.; (*lead*) avance f.; (*jump*) sursaut m. ~ **to do,** commencer *or* se mettre à faire. ~ **off doing,** commencer par faire. ~ **out,** partir. ~ **up a business,** lancer une affaire. ~**er** n. (*auto.*) démarreur m.; (*runner*) partant m.; (*culin.*) entrée f. ~**ing point,** point de départ m. ~**ing tomorrow,** à partir de demain.

startle /'stɑːtl/ v.t. (*make jump*) faire tressaillir; (*shock*) alarmer.

starv|e /stɑːv/ v.i. mourir de faim. ● v.t. affamer; (*deprive*) priver. ~**ation** /-'veɪʃn/ n. faim f.

stash /stæʃ/ v.t. (*hide: sl.*) cacher.

state /steɪt/ n. état m.; (*pomp*) apparat m. **S~,** (*pol.*) État m. ● a. d'État, de l'État; (*school*) public. ● v.t. affirmer (**that,** que); (*views*) exprimer; (*fix*) fixer. **the S~s,** les États-Unis. **get into a ~,** s'affoler.

stateless /'steɪtlɪs/ a. apatride.

stately /'steɪtlɪ/ a. (**-ler, -lest**) majestueux. ~ **home,** château m.

statement /'steɪtmənt/ n. déclaration f.; (*of account*) relevé m.

statesman /'steɪtsmən/ n. (*pl.* **-men**) homme d'État m.

static /'stætɪk/ a. statique. ● n. (radio, TV) parasites m. pl.

station /'steɪʃn/ n. station f.; (rail.) gare f.; (mil.) poste m.; (rank) condition f. ● v.t. poster, placer. **~ed at** or **in**, (mil.) en garnison à. **~ wagon**, (Amer.) break m.

stationary /'steɪʃənrɪ/ a. immobile, stationnaire; (vehicle) à l'arrêt.

stationer /'steɪʃnə(r)/ n. papet|ier, -ière m., f. **~'s shop**, papeterie f. **~y** n. papeterie f.

statistic /stə'tɪstɪk/ n. statistique f. **~s**, statistique f. **~al** a. statistique.

statue /'stætʃuː/ n. statue f.

stature /'stætʃə(r)/ n. stature f.

status /'steɪtəs/ n. (pl. -uses) situation f., statut m.; (prestige) standing m. **~ quo**, statu quo m.

statut|e /'stætʃuːt/ n. loi f. **~es**, (rules) statuts m. pl. **~ory** /-ʊtrɪ/ a. statutaire; (holiday) légal.

staunch /stɔːntʃ/ a. (-er, -est) (friend etc.) loyal, fidèle.

stave /steɪv/ n. (mus.) portée f. ● v.t. **~ off**, éviter, conjurer.

stay /steɪ/ v.i. rester; (spend time) séjourner; (reside) loger. ● v.t. (hunger) tromper. ● n. séjour m. **~ away from**, (school etc.) ne pas aller à. **~ behind/on/late/**etc., rester. **~ in/out**, rester à la maison/dehors. **~ up (late)**, veiller, se coucher tard.

stead /sted/ n. **stand s.o. in good ~**, être bien utile à qn.

steadfast /'stedfɑːst/ a. ferme.

stead|y /'stedɪ/ a. (-ier, -iest) stable; (hand, voice) ferme; (regular) régulier; (staid) sérieux. ● v.t. maintenir, assurer; (calm) calmer. **~ily** adv. fermement; régulièrement.

steak /steɪk/ n. steak m., bifteck m.; (of fish) darne f.

steal /stiːl/ v.t./i. (p.t. **stole**, p.p. **stolen**) voler (**from s.o.**, à qn.).

stealth /stelθ/ n. **by ~**, furtivement. **~y** a. furtif.

steam /stiːm/ n. vapeur f.; (on glass) buée f. ● v.t. (cook) cuire à la vapeur; (window) embuer. ● v.i. fumer. **~-engine** n. locomotive à vapeur f. **~ iron**, fer à vapeur m. **~y** a. humide.

steam|er /'stiːmə(r)/ n. (culin.) cuit-vapeur m.; (also **~ship**) (bateau à) vapeur m.

steamroller /'stiːmrəʊlə(r)/ n. rouleau compresseur m.

steel /stiːl/ n. acier m. ● v. pr. **~ o.s.**, s'endurcir, se cuirasser. **~ industry**, sidérurgie f.

steep[1] /stiːp/ v.t. (soak) tremper. **~ed in**, (fig.) imprégné de.

steep[2] /stiːp/ a. (-er, -est) raide, rapide; (price: fam.) excessif. **~ly** adv. **rise ~ly**, (slope, price) monter rapidement.

steeple /'stiːpl/ n. clocher m.

steeplechase /'stiːpltʃeɪs/ n. (race) steeple(-chase) m.

steer[1] /stɪə(r)/ n. (ox) bouvillon m.

steer[2] /stɪə(r)/ v.t. diriger; (ship) gouverner; (fig.) guider. ● v.i. (in ship) gouverner. **~ clear of**, éviter. **~ing** n. (auto.) direction f. **~ing-wheel** n. volant m.

stem[1] /stem/ n. tige f.; (of glass) pied m. ● v.i. (p.t. **stemmed**). **~ from**, provenir de.

stem[2] /stem/ v.t. (p.t. **stemmed**) (check, stop) endiguer, contenir.

stench /stentʃ/ n. puanteur f.

stencil /'stensl/ n. pochoir m.; (for typing) stencil m. ● v.t. (p.t. **stencilled**) (document) polycopier.

stenographer /ste'nɒɡrəfə(r)/ n. (Amer.) sténodactylo f.

step /step/ v.i. (p.t. **stepped**) marcher, aller. ● v.t. **~ up**, augmenter. ● n. pas m.; (stair) marche f.; (of train) marchepied m.; (action) mesure f. **~s**, (ladder) escabeau m. **in ~**, au pas; (fig.) conforme (**with**, à). **~ down**, (resign) démissionner; (from ladder) descendre. **~ forward**, (faire un) pas en avant. **~ up**, (pressure) augmenter. **~ in**, (intervene) intervenir. **~-ladder** n. escabeau m. **~ping-stone** n. (fig.) tremplin m.

step|brother /'stepbrʌðə(r)/ n. demi-frère m. **~daughter** n. belle-fille f. **~father** n. beau-père m. **~mother** n. belle-mère f. **~sister** n. demi-sœur f. **~son** n. beau-fils m.

stereo /'sterɪəʊ/ n. (pl. -os) stéréo f.; (record-player) chaîne stéréo f. ● a. stéréo invar. **~phonic** /-ə'fɒnɪk/ a. stéréophonique.

stereotype /'sterɪətaɪp/ n. stéréotype m. **~d** a. stéréotypé.

steril|e /'steraɪl, Amer. 'sterəl/ a. stérile. **~ity** /stə'rɪlətɪ/ n. stérilité f.

steriliz|e /'sterəlaɪz/ v.t. stériliser. **~ation** /-'zeɪʃn/ n. stérilisation f.

sterling /'stɜːlɪŋ/ n. livre(s) sterling f. (pl.). ● a. sterling invar.; (silver) fin; (fig.) excellent.

stern¹ /stɜːn/ a. (-er, -est) sévère.

stern² /stɜːn/ n. (of ship) arrière m.

steroid /'steroɪd/ n. stéroïde m.

stethoscope /'steθəskəʊp/ n. stéthoscope m.

stew /stjuː/ v.t./i. cuire à la casserole. ● n. ragoût m. ~ed fruit, compote f. ~ed tea, thé trop infusé m. ~pan n. cocotte f.

steward /stjʊəd/ n. (of club etc.) intendant m.; (on ship etc.) steward m. ~ess /-'des/ n. hôtesse f.

stick¹ /stɪk/ n. bâton m.; (for walking) canne f.

stick² /stɪk/ v.t. (p.t. stuck) (glue) coller; (thrust) enfoncer; (put: fam.) mettre; (endure: sl.) supporter. ● v.i. (adhere) coller, adhérer; (to pan) attacher; (remain: fam.) rester; (be jammed) être coincé. be stuck with s.o., (fam.) se farcir qn. ~-in-the-mud n. encroûté(e) m. (f.). ~ at, persévérer dans. ~ out v.t. (head etc.) sortir; (tongue) tirer; v.i. (protrude) dépasser. ~ to, (promise etc.) rester fidèle à. ~ up for, (fam.) défendre. ~ing-plaster n. sparadrap m.

sticker /'stɪkə(r)/ n. autocollant m.

stickler /'stɪklə(r)/ n. be a ~ for, insister sur.

sticky /'stɪkɪ/ a. (-ier, -iest) poisseux; (label, tape) adhésif.

stiff /stɪf/ a. (-er, -est) raide; (limb, joint) ankylosé; (tough) dur; (drink) fort; (price) élevé; (manner) guindé. ~ neck, torticolis m. ~ness n. raideur f.

stiffen /'stɪfn/ v.t./i. (se) raidir.

stifle /'staɪfl/ v.t./i. étouffer.

stigma /'stɪɡmə/ n. (pl. -as) stigmate m. ~tize v.t. stigmatiser.

stile /staɪl/ n. échalier m.

stiletto /stɪ'letəʊ/ a. & n. (pl. -os) ~s, ~ heels talons aiguille m. pl.

still¹ /stɪl/ a. immobile; (quiet) calme, tranquille. ● n. silence m. ● adv. encore, toujours; (even) encore; (nevertheless) tout de même. keep ~!, arrête de bouger! ~ life, nature morte f.

still² /stɪl/ n. (apparatus) alambic m.

stillborn /'stɪlbɔːn/ a. mort-né.

stilted /'stɪltɪd/ a. guindé.

stilts /stɪlts/ n. pl. échasses f. pl.

stimulate /'stɪmjʊleɪt/ v.t. stimuler. ~ant n. stimulant m. ~ation /-'leɪʃn/ n. stimulation f.

stimulus /'stɪmjʊləs/ n. (pl. -li /-laɪ/) (spur) stimulant m.

sting /stɪŋ/ n. piqûre f.; (organ) dard m. ● v.t./i. (p.t. stung) piquer. ~ing a. (fig.) cinglant.

stingy /'stɪndʒɪ/ a. (-ier, -iest) avare (with, de).

stink /stɪŋk/ n. puanteur f. ● v.i. (p.t. stank or stunk, p.p. stunk). ~ (of), puer. ● v.t. ~ out, (room etc.) empester.

stinker /'stɪŋkə(r)/ n. (thing: sl.) vacherie f.; (person: sl.) vache f.

stint /stɪnt/ v.i. ~ on, lésiner sur. ● n. (work) tour m.

stipulate /'stɪpjʊleɪt/ v.t. stipuler. ~ion /-'leɪʃn/ n. stipulation f.

stir /stɜː(r)/ v.t./i. (p.t. stirred) (move) remuer; (excite) exciter. ● n. agitation f. ~ up, (trouble etc.) provoquer.

stirrup /'stɪrəp/ n. étrier m.

stitch /stɪtʃ/ n. point m.; (in knitting) maille f.; (med.) point de suture m.; (muscle pain) point de côté m. ● v.t. coudre. be in ~es, (fam.) avoir le fou rire.

stoat /stəʊt/ n. hermine f.

stock /stɒk/ n. réserve f.; (comm.) stock m.; (financial) valeurs f. pl.; (family) souche f.; (soup) bouillon m. ● a. (goods) courant. ● v.t. (shop etc.) approvisionner; (sell) vendre. ● v.i. ~ up, s'approvisionner (with, de). ~-car n. stock-car m. ~ cube, bouillon-cube m. S~ Exchange, ~ market, Bourse f. ~ phrase, cliché m. ~-taking n. (comm.) inventaire m. in ~, en stock. we're out of ~, il n'y en a plus. take ~, (fig.) faire le point.

stockbroker /'stɒkbrəʊkə(r)/ n. agent de change m.

stocking /'stɒkɪŋ/ n. bas m.

stockist /'stɒkɪst/ n. stockiste m.

stockpile /'stɒkpaɪl/ n. stock m. ● v.t. stocker; (arms) amasser.

stocky /'stɒkɪ/ a. (-ier, -iest) trapu.

stodge /stɒdʒ/ n. (fam.) aliment(s) lourd(s) m. (pl.). ~y a. lourd.

stoic /'stəʊɪk/ n. stoïque m./f. ~al a. stoïque. ~ism /-sɪzəm/ n. stoïcisme m.

stoke /stəʊk/ v.t. (boiler, fire) garnir, alimenter.

stole¹ /stəʊl/ n. (garment) étole f.

stole[2], **stolen** /stəʊl, 'stəʊlən/ *see* steal.

stolid /'stɒlɪd/ *a.* flegmatique.

stomach /'stʌmək/ *n.* estomac *m.*; (*abdomen*) ventre *m.* ● *v.t.* (*put up with*) supporter. **~-ache** *n.* mal à l'estomac *or* au ventre *m.*

ston|e /stəʊn/ *n.* pierre *f.*; (*pebble*) caillou *m.*; (*in fruit*) noyau *m.*; (*weight*) 6.350 kg. ● *a.* de pierre. ● *v.t.* lapider; (*fruit*) dénoyauter. **~e-cold/-deaf**, complètement froid/sourd. **~y** *a.* pierreux. **~y-broke** *a.* (*sl.*) fauché.

stonemason /'stəʊnmeɪsn/ *n.* maçon *m.*, tailleur de pierre *m.*

stood /stʊd/ *see* stand.

stooge /stuːdʒ/ *n.* (*actor*) comparse *m.*/*f.*; (*fig.*) fantoche *m.*, laquais *m.*

stool /stuːl/ *n.* tabouret *m.*

stoop /stuːp/ *v.i.* (*bend*) se baisser; (*condescend*) s'abaisser. ● *n.* have a **~**, être voûté.

stop /stɒp/ *v.t./i.* (*p.t.* **stopped**) arrêter; (*doing*, de faire); (*moving*, *talking*) s'arrêter; (*prevent*) empêcher (*from*, de); (*hole*, *leak*, *etc.*) boucher; (*of pain*, *noise*, *etc.*) cesser; (*stay: fam.*) rester. ● *n.* arrêt *m.*; (*full stop*) point *m.* **~ off**, s'arrêter. **~ up**, boucher. **~(-over)**, halte *f.*; (*port of call*) escale *f.* **~-light** *n.* (*on vehicle*) stop *m.* **~-watch** *n.* chronomètre *m.*

stopgap /'stɒpgæp/ *n.* bouche-trou *m.* ● *a.* intérimaire.

stoppage /'stɒpɪdʒ/ *n.* arrêt *m.*; (*of work*) arrêt de travail *m.*; (*of pay*) retenue *f.*

stopper /'stɒpə(r)/ *n.* bouchon *m.*

storage /'stɔːrɪdʒ/ *n.* (*of goods*, *food*, *etc.*) emmagasinage *m.* **~ heater**, radiateur électrique à accumulation *m.* **~ space**, espace de rangement *m.*

store /stɔː(r)/ *n.* réserve *f.*; (*warehouse*) entrepôt *m.*; (*shop*) grand magasin *m.*; (*Amer.*) magasin *m.* ● *v.t.* (*for future*) mettre en réserve; (*in warehouse*, *mind*) emmagasiner. have in **~ for**, réserver à. set **~ by**, attacher du prix à. **~-room** *n.* réserve *f.*

storey /'stɔːrɪ/ *n.* étage *m.*

stork /stɔːk/ *n.* cigogne *f.*

storm /stɔːm/ *n.* tempête *f.*, orage *m.* ● *v.t.* prendre d'assaut. ● *v.i.* (*rage*) tempêter. **~y** *a.* orageux.

story /'stɔːrɪ/ *n.* histoire *f.*; (*in press*) article *m.*; (*storey*: *Amer.*) étage *m.* **~**

book, livre d'histoires *m.* **~-teller** *n.* conteu|r, -se *m.*, *f.*; (*liar*: *fam.*) menteu|r, -se *m.*, *f.*

stout /staʊt/ *a.* (**-er**, **-est**) corpulent; (*strong*) solide. ● *n.* bière brune *f.* **~ness** *n.* corpulence *f.*

stove /stəʊv/ *n.* (*for cooking*) cuisinière *f.*; (*heater*) poêle *m.*

stow /stəʊ/ *v.t.* **~ away**, (*put away*) ranger; (*hide*) cacher. ● *v.i.* voyager clandestinement.

stowaway /'stəʊəweɪ/ *n.* passag|er, -ère clandestin(e) *m.*, *f.*

straddle /'strædl/ *v.t.* être à cheval sur, enjamber.

straggle /'strægl/ *v.i.* (*lag behind*) traîner en désordre. **~r** /-ə(r)/ *n.* traînard(e) *m.* (*f.*).

straight /streɪt/ *a.* (**-er**, **-est**) droit; (*tidy*) en ordre; (*frank*) franc. ● *adv.* (*in straight line*) droit; (*direct*) tout droit. ● *n.* ligne droite *f.* **~ ahead** *or* **on,** tout droit. **~ away,** tout de suite. **~ face,** visage sérieux *m.* get sth. **~,** mettre qch. au clair. **~ off,** (*fam.*) sans hésiter.

straighten /'streɪtn/ *v.t.* (*nail*, *situation*, *etc.*) redresser; (*tidy*) arranger.

straightforward /streɪt'fɔːwəd/ *a.* honnête; (*easy*) simple.

strain[1] /streɪn/ *n.* (*breed*) race *f.*; (*streak*) tendance *f.*

strain[2] /streɪn/ *v.t.* (*rope*, *ears*) tendre; (*limb*) fouler; (*eyes*) fatiguer; (*muscle*) froisser; (*filter*) passer; (*vegetables*) égoutter; (*fig.*) mettre à l'épreuve. ● *v.i.* fournir des efforts. ● *n.* tension *f.*; (*fig.*) effort *m.* **~s,** (*tune*: *mus.*) accents *m.* *pl.* **~ed** *a.* forcé; (*relations*) tendu. **~er** *n.* passoire *f.*

strait /streɪt/ *n.* détroit *m.* **~s,** détroit *m.*; (*fig.*) embarras *m.* **~-jacket** *n.* camisole de force *f.* **~-laced** *a.* collet monté *invar.*

strand /strænd/ *n.* (*thread*) fil *m.*, brin *m.*; (*lock of hair*) mèche *f.*

stranded /'strændɪd/ *a.* (*person*) en rade; (*ship*) échoué.

strange /streɪndʒ/ *a.* (**-er**, **-est**) étrange; (*unknown*) inconnu. **~ly** *adv.* étrangement. **~ness** *n.* étrangeté *f.*

stranger /'streɪndʒə(r)/ *n.* inconnu(e) *m.* (*f.*).

strangle /'stræŋgl/ *v.t.* étrangler.

stranglehold /'stræŋglhəʊld/ *n.* have a **~ on,** tenir à la gorge.

strap /stræp/ *n.* (*of leather etc.*) courroie *f.*; (*of dress*) bretelle *f.*; (*of watch*) bracelet *m.* ● *v.t.* (*p.t.* **strapped**) attacher.

strapping /'stræpɪŋ/ *a.* costaud.

stratagem /'strætədʒəm/ *n.* stratagème *m.*

strategic /strə'tiːdʒɪk/ *a.* stratégique.

strategy /'strætədʒɪ/ *n.* stratégie *f.*

stratum /'strɑːtəm/ *n.* (*pl.* **strata**) couche *f.*

straw /strɔː/ *n.* paille *f.* **the last ~,** le comble.

strawberry /'strɔːbrɪ/ *n.* fraise *f.*

stray /streɪ/ *v.i.* s'égarer; (*deviate*) s'écarter. ● *a.* perdu; (*isolated*) isolé. ● *n.* animal perdu *m.*

streak /striːk/ *n.* raie *f.*, bande *f.*; (*trace*) trace *f.*; (*period*) période *f.*; (*tendency*) tendance *f.* ● *v.t.* (*mark*) strier. ● *v.i.* filer à toute allure. **~y** *a.* strié.

stream /striːm/ *n.* ruisseau *m.*; (*current*) courant *m.*; (*flow*) flot *m.*; (*in schools*) classe (de niveau) *f.* ● *v.i.* ruisseler (**with,** de); (*eyes, nose*) couler.

streamer /'striːmə(r)/ *n.* (*of paper*) serpentin *m.*; (*flag*) banderole *f.*

streamline /'striːmlaɪn/ *v.t.* rationaliser. **~d** *a.* (*shape*) aérodynamique.

street /striːt/ *n.* rue *f.* **~ lamp,** réverbère *m.* **~ map,** plan des rues *m.*

streetcar /'striːtkɑː(r)/ *n.* (*Amer.*) tramway *m.*

strength /streŋθ/ *n.* force *f.*; (*of wall, fabric, etc.*) solidité *f.* **on the ~ of,** en vertu de.

strengthen /'streŋθn/ *v.t.* renforcer, fortifier.

strenuous /'strenjʊəs/ *a.* énergique; (*arduous*) ardu; (*tiring*) fatigant. **~ly** *adv.* énergiquement.

stress /stres/ *n.* accent *m.*; (*pressure*) pression *f.*; (*med.*) stress *m.* ● *v.t.* souligner, insister sur.

stretch /stretʃ/ *v.t.* (*pull taut*) tendre; (*arm, leg*) étendre; (*neck*) tendre; (*clothes*) étirer; (*truth etc.*) forcer. ● *v.i.* s'étendre; (*of person, clothes*) s'étirer. ● *n.* etendue *f.*; (*period*) période *f.*; (*of road*) tronçon *m.* ● *a.* (*fabric*) extensible. **~ one's legs,** se dégourdir les jambes. **at a ~,** d'affilée.

stretcher /'stretʃə(r)/ *n.* brancard *m.*

strew /struː/ *v.t.* (*p.t.* **strewed,** *p.p.* **strewed** *or* **strewn**) (*scatter*) répandre; (*cover*) joncher.

stricken /'strɪkən/ *a.* **~ with,** frappé *or* atteint de.

strict /strɪkt/ *a.* (-er, -est) strict. **~ly** *adv.* strictement. **~ness** *n.* sévérité *f.*

stride /straɪd/ *v.i.* (*p.t.* **strode,** *p.p.* **stridden**) faire de grands pas. ● *n.* grand pas *m.*

strident /'straɪdnt/ *a.* strident.

strife /straɪf/ *n.* conflit(s) *m.* (*pl.*).

strike /straɪk/ *v.t.* (*p.t.* **struck**) frapper; (*blow*) donner; (*match*) frotter; (*gold etc.*) trouver. ● *v.i.* faire grève; (*attack*) attaquer; (*clock*) sonner. ● *n.* (*of workers*) grève *f.*; (*mil.*) attaque *f.*; (*find*) découverte *f.* **on ~,** en grève. **~ off** *or* **out,** rayer. **~ up a friendship,** lier amitié (**with,** avec).

striker /'straɪkə(r)/ *n.* gréviste *m./f.*; (*football*) buteur *m.*

striking /'straɪkɪŋ/ *a.* frappant.

string /strɪŋ/ *n.* ficelle *f.*; (*of violin, racket, etc.*) corde *f.*; (*of pearls*) collier *m.*; (*of lies etc.*) chapelet *m.* ● *v.t.* (*p.t.* **strung**) (*thread*) enfiler. **the ~s,** (*mus.*) les cordes. **~ bean,** haricot vert *m.* **pull ~s,** faire jouer ses relations, faire marcher le piston. **~ out,** (s')échelonner. **~ed** *a.* (*instrument*) à cordes. **~y** *a.* filandreux.

stringent /'strɪndʒənt/ *a.* rigoureux, strict.

strip¹ /strɪp/ *v.t./i.* (*p.t.* **stripped**) (*undress*) (se) déshabiller; (*machine*) démonter; (*deprive*) dépouiller. **~per** *n.* strip-teaseuse *f.*; (*solvent*) décapant *m.* **~-tease** *n.* strip-tease *m.*

strip² /strɪp/ *n.* bande *f.* **comic ~,** bande dessinée *f.* **~ light,** néon *m.*

stripe /straɪp/ *n.* rayure *f.*, raie *f.* **~d** *a.* rayé.

strive /straɪv/ *v.i.* (*p.t.* **strove,** *p.p.* **striven**) s'efforcer (**to,** de).

strode /strəʊd/ *see* stride.

stroke¹ /strəʊk/ *n.* coup *m.*; (*of pen*) trait *m.*; (*swimming*) nage *f.*; (*med.*) attaque *f.*, congestion *f.* **at a ~,** d'un seul coup.

stroke² /strəʊk/ *v.t.* (*with hand*) caresser. ● *n.* caresse *f.*

stroll /strəʊl/ *v.i.* flâner. ● *n.* petit tour *m.* **~ in**/*etc.,* entrer/*etc.*

tranquillement. **~er** n. (*Amer.*) poussette f.

strong /strɒŋ/ a. (**-er, -est**) fort; (*shoes, fabric, etc.*) solide. **be fifty/ etc. ~,** être au nombre de cinquante/ etc. **~-box** n. coffre-fort m. **~- minded** a. résolu. **~- room** n. chambre forte f. **~ly** adv. (*greatly*) fortement; (*with energy*) avec force; (*deeply*) profondément.

stronghold /ˈstrɒŋhəʊld/ n. bastion m.

strove /strəʊv/ see strive.

struck /strʌk/ see strike. ● a. **~ on**, (*sl.*) impressionné par.

structur|e /ˈstrʌktʃə(r)/ n. (*of cell, poem, etc.*) structure f.; (*building*) construction f. **~al** a. structural; de (la) construction.

struggle /ˈstrʌgl/ v.i. lutter, se battre. ● n. lutte f.; (*effort*) effort m. **have a ~ to,** avoir du mal à.

strum /strʌm/ v.t. (p.t. **strummed**) (*banjo etc.*) gratter de.

strung /strʌŋ/ see string. ● a. **~ up**, (*tense*) nerveux.

strut /strʌt/ n. (*support*) étai m. ● v.i. (p.t. **strutted**) se pavaner.

stub /stʌb/ n. bout m.; (*of tree*) souche f.; (*counterfoil*) talon m. ● v.t. (p.t. **stubbed**) **~ one's toe,** se cogner le doigt de pied. **~ out,** écraser.

stubble /ˈstʌbl/ n. (*on chin*) barbe de plusieurs jours f.; (*remains of wheat*) chaume m.

stubborn /ˈstʌbən/ a. opiniâtre, obstiné. **~ly** adv. obstinément. **~ness** n. opiniâtreté f.

stubby /ˈstʌbɪ/ a. (**-ier, -iest**) (*finger*) épais; (*person*) trapu.

stuck /stʌk/ see stick². ● a. (*jammed*) coincé. **I'm ~,** (*for answer*) je sèche. **~-up** a. (*sl.*) prétentieux.

stud¹ /stʌd/ n. clou m.; (*for collar*) bouton m. ● v.t. (p.t. **studded**) clouter. **~ded with,** parsemé de.

stud² /stʌd/ n. (*horses*) écurie f. **~ (-farm)** n. haras m.

student /ˈstjuːdnt/ n. (*univ.*) étudiant(e) m. (f.); (*schol.*) élève m./f. ● a. (*restaurant, life, residence*) universitaire.

studied /ˈstʌdɪd/ a. étudié.

studio /ˈstjuːdɪəʊ/ n. (pl. **-os**) studio m. **~ flat,** studio m.

studious /ˈstjuːdɪəs/ a. (*person*) studieux; (*deliberate*) étudié. **~ly** adv. (*carefully*) avec soin.

study /ˈstʌdɪ/ n. étude f.; (*office*) bureau m. ● v.t./i. étudier.

stuff /stʌf/ n. substance f.; (*sl.*) chose(s) f. (*pl.*). ● v.t. rembourrer; (*animal*) empailler; (*cram*) bourrer; (*culin.*) farcir; (*block up*) boucher; (*put*) fourrer. **~ing** n. bourre f.; (*culin.*) farce f.

stuffy /ˈstʌfɪ/ a. (**-ier, -iest**) mal aéré; (*dull: fam.*) vieux jeu *invar*.

stumbl|e /ˈstʌmbl/ v.i. trébucher. **~e across** or **on,** tomber sur. **~ing- block** n. pierre d'achoppement f.

stump /stʌmp/ n. (*of tree*) souche f.; (*of limb*) moignon m.; (*of pencil*) bout m.

stumped /stʌmpt/ a. (*baffled: fam.*) embarrassé.

stun /stʌn/ v.t. (p.t. **stunned**) étourdir; (*bewilder*) stupéfier.

stung /stʌŋ/ see sting.

stunk /stʌŋk/ see stink.

stunning /ˈstʌnɪŋ/ a. (*delightful: fam.*) sensationnel.

stunt¹ /stʌnt/ v.t. (*growth*) retarder. **~ed** a. (*person*) rabougri.

stunt² /stʌnt/ n. (*feat: fam.*) tour de force m.; (*trick: fam.*) truc m.; (*dangerous*) cascade f. **~man** n. cascadeur m.

stupefy /ˈstjuːpɪfaɪ/ v.t. abrutir; (*amaze*) stupéfier.

stupendous /stjuːˈpendəs/ a. prodigieux, formidable.

stupid /ˈstjuːpɪd/ a. stupide, bête. **~ity** /-ˈpɪdətɪ/ n. stupidité f. **~ly** adv. stupidement, bêtement.

stupor /ˈstjuːpə(r)/ n. stupeur f.

sturd|y /ˈstɜːdɪ/ a. (**-ier, -iest**) robuste. **~iness** n. robustesse f.

stutter /ˈstʌtə(r)/ v.i. bégayer. ● n. bégaiement m.

sty¹ /staɪ/ n. (*pigsty*) porcherie f.

sty² /staɪ/ n. (*on eye*) orgelet m.

styl|e /staɪl/ n. style m.; (*fashion*) mode f.; (*sort*) genre m.; (*pattern*) modèle m. ● v.t. (*design*) créer. **do sth. in ~e,** faire qch. avec classe. **~e s.o.'s hair,** coiffer qn. **~ist** n. (*of hair*) coiffeu|r, -se m., f.

stylish /ˈstaɪlɪʃ/ a. élégant.

stylized /ˈstaɪlaɪzd/ a. stylisé.

stylus /ˈstaɪləs/ n. (pl. **-uses**) (*of record-player*) saphir m.

suave /swɑːv/ a. (*urbane*) courtois; (*smooth: pej.*) doucereux.

sub- /sʌb/ *pref.* sous-, sub-.

subconscious /sʌb'kɒnʃəs/ *a. & n.* inconscient (*m.*), subconscient (*m.*). **~ly** *adv.* inconsciemment.

subcontract /sʌbkən'trækt/ *v.t.* sous-traiter.

subdivide /sʌbdɪ'vaɪd/ *v.t.* subdiviser.

subdue /səb'dju:/ *v.t.* (*feeling*) maîtriser; (*country*) subjuguer. **~d** *a.* (*weak*) faible; (*light*) tamisé; (*person, criticism*) retenu.

subject[1] /'sʌbdʒɪkt/ *a.* (*state etc.*) soumis. ● *n.* sujet *m.*; (*schol., univ.*) matière *f.*; (*citizen*) ressortissant(e) *m.* (*f.*), sujet(te) *m.* (*f.*). **~matter** *n.* contenu *m.* **~ to,** soumis à; (*liable to, dependent on*) sujet à.

subject[2] /səb'dʒekt/ *v.t.* soumettre. **~ion** /-kʃn/ *n.* soumission *f.*

subjective /səb'dʒektɪv/ *a.* subjectif.

subjunctive /səb'dʒʌŋktɪv/ *a. & n.* subjonctif (*m.*).

sublet /sʌb'let/ *v.t.* sous-louer.

sublime /sə'blaɪm/ *a.* sublime.

submarine /sʌbmə'ri:n/ *n.* sous-marin *m.*

submerge /səb'mɜ:dʒ/ *v.t.* submerger. ● *v.i.* plonger.

submissive /səb'mɪsɪv/ *a.* soumis.

submit /səb'mɪt/ *v.t./i.* (*p.t.* **submitted**) (se) soumettre (**to,** à). **~ssion** *n.* soumission *f.*

subordinate[1] /sə'bɔ:dɪnət/ *a.* subalterne; (*gram.*) subordonné. ● *n.* subordonné(e) *m.* (*f.*).

subordinate[2] /sə'bɔ:dɪneɪt/ *v.t.* subordonner (**to,** à).

subpoena /səb'pi:nə/ *n.* (*pl.* **-as**) (*jurid.*) citation *f.*, assignation *f.*

subroutine /'sʌbru:ti:n/ *n.* sous-programme *m.*

subscribe /səb'skraɪb/ *v.t./i.* verser (de l'argent) (**to,** à). **~ to,** (*loan, theory*) souscrire à; (*newspaper*) s'abonner à, être abonné à. **~r** /-ə(r)/ *n.* abonné(e) *m.* (*f.*).

subscription /səb'skrɪpʃn/ *n.* souscription *f.*; abonnement *m.*; (*membership dues*) cotisation *f.*

subsequent /'sʌbsɪkwənt/ *a.* (*later*) ultérieur; (*next*) suivant. **~ly** *adv.* par la suite.

subside /səb'saɪd/ *v.i.* (*land etc.*) s'affaisser; (*flood, wind*) baisser. **~nce** /-əns/ *n.* affaissement *m.*

subsidiary /səb'sɪdɪərɪ/ *a.* accessoire. ● *n.* (*comm.*) filiale *f.*

subsid|y /'sʌbsədɪ/ *n.* subvention *f.* **~ize** /-ɪdaɪz/ *v.t.* subventionner.

subsist /səb'sɪst/ *v.i.* subsister. **~ence** *n.* subsistance *f.*

substance /'sʌbstəns/ *n.* substance *f.*

substandard /sʌb'stændəd/ *a.* de qualité inférieure.

substantial /səb'stænʃl/ *a.* considérable; (*meal*) substantiel. **~ly** *adv.* considérablement.

substantiate /səb'stænʃɪeɪt/ *v.t.* justifier, prouver.

substitut|e /'sʌbstɪtju:t/ *n.* succédané *m.*; (*person*) remplaçant(e) *m.* (*f.*). ● *v.t.* substituer (**for,** à). **~ion** /-'tju:ʃn/ *n.* substitution *f.*

subterfuge /'sʌbtəfju:dʒ/ *n.* subterfuge *m.*

subterranean /sʌbtə'reɪnɪən/ *a.* souterrain.

subtitle /'sʌbtaɪtl/ *n.* sous-titre *m.*

subtle /'sʌtl/ *a.* (**-er, -est**) subtil. **~ty** *n.* subtilité *f.*

subtotal /sʌb'təʊtl/ *n.* total partiel *m.*

subtract /səb'trækt/ *v.t.* soustraire. **~ion** /-kʃn/ *n.* soustraction *f.*

suburb /'sʌbɜ:b/ *n.* faubourg *m.*, banlieue *f.* **~s,** banlieue *f.* **~an** /sə-'bɜ:bən/ *a.* de banlieue.

suburbia /sə'bɜ:bɪə/ *n.* la banlieue.

subversive /səb'vɜ:sɪv/ *a.* subversif.

subver|t /səb'vɜ:t/ *v.t.* renverser. **~sion** /-ʃn/ *n.* subversion *f.*

subway /'sʌbweɪ/ *n.* passage souterrain *m.*; (*Amer.*) métro *m.*

succeed /sək'si:d/ *v.i.* réussir (**in doing,** à faire). ● *v.t.* (*follow*) succéder à. **~ing** *a.* suivant.

success /sək'ses/ *n.* succès *m.*, réussite *f.*

successful /sək'sesfl/ *a.* réussi, couronné de succès; (*favourable*) heureux; (*in exam*) reçu. **be ~ in doing,** réussir à faire. **~ly** *adv.* avec succès.

succession /sək'seʃn/ *n.* succession *f.* **in ~,** de suite.

successive /sək'sesɪv/ *a.* successif. **six ~ days,** six jours consécutifs.

successor /sək'sesə(r)/ *n.* successeur *m.*

succinct /sək'sɪŋkt/ *a.* succinct.

succulent /'sʌkjʊlənt/ *a.* succulent.

succumb /sə'kʌm/ *v.i.* succomber.

such /sʌtʃ/ *a. & pron.* tel(le), tel(le)s; (*so much*) tant (de). ● *adv.* si. **~ a book**/*etc.*, un tel livre/*etc.* **~ books**/*etc.*, de tels livres/*etc.* **~ courage**/*etc.*, tant de courage/ *etc.* **~ a big house,** une si grande maison. **~ as,**

comme, tel que. **as ~,** en tant que tel. **there's no ~ thing,** ça n'existe pas. **~-and-such** a. tel ou tel.

suck /sʌk/ v.t. sucer. **~ in** or **up,** aspirer. **~er** n. (*rubber pad*) ventouse f.; (*person: sl.*) dupe f.

suction /'sʌkʃn/ n. succion f.

sudden /'sʌdn/ a. soudain, subit. **all of a ~,** tout à coup. **~ly** adv. subitement, brusquement. **~ness** n. soudaineté f.

suds /sʌdz/ n. pl. (*froth*) mousse de savon f.

sue /su:/ v.t. (*pres. p.* **suing**) poursuivre (en justice).

suede /sweid/ n. daim m.

suet /'su:it/ n. graisse de rognon f.

suffer /'sʌfə(r)/ v.t./i. souffrir; (*loss, attack, etc.*) subir. **~er** n. victime f., malade m./f. **~ing** n. souffrance(s) f. (*pl.*).

suffice /sə'fais/ v.i. suffire.

sufficient /sə'fiʃnt/ a. (*enough*) suffisamment de; (*big enough*) suffisant. **~ly** adv. suffisamment.

suffix /'sʌfiks/ n. suffixe m.

suffocat|e /'sʌfəkeit/ v.t./i. suffoquer. **~ion** /-'keiʃn/ n. suffocation f.; (*med.*) asphyxie f.

suffused /sə'fju:zd/ a. **~ with,** (*light, tears*) baigné de.

sugar /'ʃʊgə(r)/ n. sucre m. ● v.t. sucrer. **~y** a. sucré.

suggest /sə'dʒest/ v.t. suggérer. **~ion** /-tʃn/ n. suggestion f.

suggestive /sə'dʒestiv/ a. suggestif. **be ~ of,** suggérer.

suicid|e /'su:isaid/ n. suicide m. **commit ~e,** se suicider. **~al** /-'saidl/ a. suicidaire.

suit /su:t/ n. costume m.; (*woman's*) tailleur m.; (*cards*) couleur f. ● v.t. convenir à; (*of garment, style, etc.*) aller à; (*adapt*) adapter. **~ability** n. (*of action etc.*) à-propos m.; (*of candidate*) aptitude(s) f. (*pl.*). **~able** a. qui convient (**for,** à), convenable. **~ably** adv. convenablement. **~ed** a. (**well**) **~ed,** (*matched*) bien assorti. **~ed to,** fait pour, apte à.

suitcase /'su:tkeis/ n. valise f.

suite /swi:t/ n. (*rooms, retinue*) suite f.; (*furniture*) mobilier m.

suitor /'su:tə(r)/ n. soupirant m.

sulfur /'sʌlfər/ n. (*Amer.*) = **sulphur.**

sulk /sʌlk/ v.i. bouder. **~y** a. boudeur, maussade.

sullen /'sʌlən/ a. maussade. **~ly** adv. d'un air maussade.

sulphur /'sʌlfə(r)/ n. soufre m. **~ic** /-'fjʊərik/ a. **~ic acid,** acide sulfurique m.

sultan /'sʌltən/ n. sultan m.

sultana /sʌl'tɑ:nə/ n. raisin de Smyrne m., raisin sec m.

sultry /'sʌltri/ a. (**-ier, -iest**) étouffant, lourd; (*fig.*) sensuel.

sum /sʌm/ n. somme f.; (*in arithmetic*) calcul m. ● v.t./i. (*p.t.* **summed**). **~ up,** résumer, récapituler; (*assess*) évaluer.

summar|y /'sʌməri/ n. résumé m. ● a. sommaire. **~ize** v.t. résumer.

summer /'sʌmə(r)/ n. été m. ● a. d'été. **~-time** n. (*season*) été m. **~y** a. estival.

summit /'sʌmit/ n. sommet m. **~ (conference),** (*pol.*) (conférence f. au) sommet m.

summon /'sʌmən/ v.t. appeler; (*meeting, s.o. to meeting*) convoquer. **~ up,** (*strength, courage, etc.*) rassembler.

summons /'sʌmənz/ n. (*jurid.*) assignation f. ● v.t. assigner.

sump /sʌmp/ n. (*auto.*) carter m.

sumptuous /'sʌmptʃʊəs/ a. somptueux, luxueux.

sun /sʌn/ n. soleil m. ● v.t. (*p.t.* **sunned**). **~ o.s.,** se chauffer au soleil. **~-glasses** n. pl. lunettes de soleil f. pl. **~-roof** n. toit ouvrant m. **~-tan** n. bronzage m. **~-tanned** a. bronzé.

sunbathe /'sʌnbeið/ v.i. prendre un bain de soleil.

sunburn /'sʌnbɜ:n/ n. coup de soleil m. **~t** a. brûlé par le soleil.

Sunday /'sʌndi/ n. dimanche m. **~ school,** catéchisme m.

sundial /'sʌndaiəl/ n. cadran solaire m.

sundown /'sʌndaʊn/ n. = sunset.

sundr|y /'sʌndri/ a. divers. **~ies** n. pl. articles divers m. pl. **all and ~y,** tout le monde.

sunflower /'sʌnflaʊə(r)/ n. tournesol m.

sung /sʌŋ/ see sing.

sunk /sʌŋk/ see sink.

sunken /'sʌŋkən/ a. (*ship etc.*) submergé; (*eyes*) creux.

sunlight /'sʌnlait/ n. soleil m.

sunny /'sʌni/ a. (**-ier, -iest**) (*room, day, etc.*) ensoleillé.

sunrise /'sʌnraiz/ n. lever du soleil m.

sunset /'sʌnset/ n. coucher du soleil m.

sunshade /'sʌnʃeɪd/ n. (lady's) ombrelle f.; (awning) parasol m.

sunshine /'sʌnʃaɪn/ n. soleil m.

sunstroke /'sʌnstrəʊk/ n. insolation f.

super /'su:pə(r)/ a. (sl.) formidable.

superb /su:'pɜ:b/ a. superbe.

supercilious /su:pə'sɪlɪəs/ a. hautain, dédaigneux.

superficial /su:pə'fɪʃl/ a. superficiel. **~ity** /-ɪ'rælətɪ/ n. caractère superficiel m. **~ly** adv. superficiellement.

superfluous /su:'pɜ:flʊəs/ a. superflu.

superhuman /su:pə'hju:mən/ a. surhumain.

superimpose /su:pərɪm'pəʊz/ v.t. superposer (on, à).

superintendent /su:pərɪn'tendənt/ n. direc|teur, -trice m., f.; (of police) commissaire m.

superior /su:'pɪərɪə(r)/ a. & n. supérieur(e) (m. (f.)). **~ity** /-'ɒrətɪ/ n. supériorité f.

superlative /su:'pɜ:lətɪv/ a. suprême. ● n. (gram.) superlatif m.

superman /'su:pəmæn/ n. (pl. -men) surhomme m.

supermarket /'su:pəmɑ:kɪt/ n. supermarché m.

supernatural /su:pə'nætʃrəl/ a. surnaturel.

superpower /'su:pəpaʊə(r)/ n. superpuissance f.

supersede /su:pə'si:d/ v.t. remplacer, supplanter.

supersonic /su:pə'sɒnɪk/ a. supersonique.

superstiti|on /su:pə'stɪʃn/ n. superstition f. **~ous** a. superstitieux.

superstore /'su:pəstɔ:(r)/ n. hypermarché m.

supertanker /'su:pətæŋkə(r)/ n. pétrolier géant m.

supervis|e /'su:pəvaɪz/ v.t. surveiller, diriger. **~ion** /-'vɪʒn/ n. surveillance f. **~or** n. surveillant(e) m. (f.); (shop) chef de rayon m.; (firm) chef de service m. **~ory** /-'vaɪzərɪ/ a. de surveillance.

supper /'sʌpə(r)/ n. dîner m.; (late at night) souper m.

supple /'sʌpl/ a. souple.

supplement[1] /'sʌplɪmənt/ n. supplément m. **~ary** /-'mentrɪ/ a. supplémentaire.

supplement[2] /'sʌplɪment/ v.t. compléter.

supplier /sə'plaɪə(r)/ n. fournisseur m.

suppl|y /sə'plaɪ/ v.t. fournir; (equip) pourvoir; (feed) alimenter (with, en). ● n. provision f.; (of gas etc.) alimentation f. **~ies**, (food) vivres m. pl.; (material) fournitures f. pl. **~y teacher**, (professeur) suppléant(e) m. (f.).

support /sə'pɔ:t/ v.t. soutenir; (family) assurer la subsistance de; (endure) supporter. ● n. soutien m., appui m.; (techn.) support m. **~er** n. partisan(e) m. (f.); (sport) supporter m. **~ive** a. qui soutient et encourage.

suppos|e /sə'pəʊz/ v.t./i. supposer. **be ~ed to do**, être censé faire, devoir faire. **~ing he comes**, supposons qu'il vienne. **~ition** /sʌpə'zɪʃn/ n. supposition f.

supposedly /sə'pəʊzɪdlɪ/ adv. soi-disant, prétendument.

suppress /sə'pres/ v.t. (put an end to) supprimer; (restrain) réprimer; (stifle) étouffer. **~ion** /-ʃn/ n. suppression f.; répression f.

suprem|e /su:'pri:m/ a. suprême. **~acy** /-əməsɪ/ n. suprématie f.

surcharge /'sɜ:tʃɑ:dʒ/ n. prix supplémentaire m.; (tax) surtaxe f.; (on stamp) surcharge f.

sure /ʃɔ:(r)/ a. (-er, -est) sûr. ● adv. (Amer., fam.) pour sûr. **make ~ of**, s'assurer de. **make ~ that**, vérifier que. **~ly** adv. sûrement.

surety /'ʃɔ:rətɪ/ n. caution f.

surf /sɜ:f/ n. (waves) ressac m. **~ing** n. surf m.

surface /'sɜ:fɪs/ n. surface f. ● a. superficiel. ● v.t. revêtir. ● v.i. faire surface; (fig.) réapparaître. **~ mail**, courrier maritime m.

surfboard /'sɜ:fbɔ:d/ n. planche de surf f.

surfeit /'sɜ:fɪt/ n. excès m. (of, de).

surge /sɜ:dʒ/ v.i. (of crowd) déferler; (of waves) s'enfler; (increase) monter. ● n. (wave) vague f.; (rise) montée f.

surgeon /'sɜ:dʒən/ n. chirurgien m.

surg|ery /'sɜ:dʒərɪ/ n. chirurgie f.; (office) cabinet m.; (session) consultation f. **need ~ery**, devoir être opéré. **~ical** a. chirurgical. **~ical spirit**, alcool à 90 degrés m.

surly /'sɜ:lɪ/ a. (-ier, -iest) bourru.

surmise /sə'maɪz/ v.t. conjecturer. ● n. conjecture f.

surmount /sə'maʊnt/ v.t. (overcome, cap) surmonter.

surname /'sɜːneɪm/ n. nom de famille m.

surpass /sə'pɑːs/ v.t. surpasser.

surplus /'sɜːpləs/ n. surplus m. ● a. en surplus.

surpris|e /sə'praɪz/ n. surprise f. ● v.t. surprendre. ~ed a. surpris (at, de). ~ing a. surprenant. ~ingly adv. étonnamment.

surrender /sə'rendə(r)/ v.i. se rendre. ● v.t. (hand over) remettre; (mil.) rendre. ● n. (mil.) reddition f.; (of passport etc.) remise f.

surreptitious /sʌrəp'tɪʃəs/ a. subreptice, furtif.

surround /sə'raʊnd/ v.t. entourer; (mil.) encercler. ~ing a. environnant. ~ings n. pl. environs m. pl.; (setting) cadre m.

surveillance /sɜː'veɪləns/ n. surveillance f.

survey¹ /sə'veɪ/ v.t. (review) passer en revue; (inquire into) enquêter sur; (building) inspecter. ~or n. expert (géomètre) m.

survey² /'sɜːveɪ/ n. (inquiry) enquête f.; inspection f.; (general view) vue d'ensemble f.

survival /sə'vaɪvl/ n. survie f.; (relic) vestige m.

surviv|e /sə'vaɪv/ v.t./i. survivre (à). ~or n. survivant(e) m. (f.).

susceptib|le /sə'septəbl/ a. sensible (to, à). ~le to, (prone to) prédisposé à. ~ility /-'bɪlətɪ/ n. sensibilité f.; prédisposition f.

suspect¹ /sə'spekt/ v.t. soupçonner; (doubt) douter de.

suspect² /'sʌspekt/ n. & a. suspect(e) (m. (f.)).

suspen|d /sə'spend/ v.t. (hang, stop) suspendre; (licence) retirer provisoirement. ~ded sentence, condamnation avec sursis f. ~sion n. suspension f.; retrait provisoire m. ~sion bridge, pont suspendu m.

suspender /sə'spendə(r)/ n. jarretelle f. ~s, (braces: Amer.) bretelles f. pl. ~ belt, porte-jarretelles m.

suspense /sə'spens/ n. attente f.; (in book etc.) suspense m.

suspicion /sə'spɪʃn/ n. soupçon m.; (distrust) méfiance f.

suspicious /səs'pɪʃəs/ a. soupçonneux; (causing suspicion) suspect. be ~ of, (distrust) se méfier de. ~ly adv. de façon suspecte.

sustain /səs'teɪn/ v.t. supporter; (effort etc.) soutenir; (suffer) subir.

sustenance /'sʌstɪnəns/ n. (food) nourriture f.; (quality) valeur nutritive f.

swab /swɒb/ n. (pad) tampon m.

swagger /'swægə(r)/ v.i. (walk) se pavaner, parader.

swallow¹ /'swɒləʊ/ v.t./i. avaler. ~ up, (absorb, engulf) engloutir.

swallow² /'swɒləʊ/ n. hirondelle f.

swam /swæm/ see swim.

swamp /swɒmp/ n. marais m. ● v.t. (flood, overwhelm) submerger. ~y a. marécageux.

swan /swɒn/ n. cygne m. ~-song n. (fig.) chant du cygne m.

swank /swæŋk/ n. (behaviour: fam.) épate f., esbroufe f.; (person: fam.) crâneu|r, -se m., f. ● v.i. (show off: fam.) crâner.

swap /swɒp/ v.t./i. (p.t. swapped) (fam.) échanger. ● n. (fam.) échange m.

swarm /swɔːm/ n. (of insects, people) essaim m. ● v.i. fourmiller. ~ into or round, (crowd) envahir.

swarthy /'swɔːðɪ/ a. (-ier, -iest) noiraud; (complexion) basané.

swastika /'swɒstɪkə/ n. (Nazi) croix gammée f.

swat /swɒt/ v.t. (p.t. swatted) (fly etc.) écraser.

sway /sweɪ/ v.t./i. (se) balancer; (influence) influencer. ● n. balancement m.; (rule) empire m.

swear /sweə(r)/ v.t./i. (p.t. swore, p.p. sworn) jurer (to sth., de qch.). ~ at, injurier. ~ by sth., (fam.) ne jurer que par qch. ~-word n. juron m.

sweat /swet/ n. sueur f. ● v.i. suer. ~-shirt n. sweat-shirt m. ~y a. en sueur.

sweater /'swetə(r)/ n. pull-over m.

swede /swiːd/ n. rutabaga m.

Swed|e /swiːd/ n. Suédois(e) m. (f.). ~en n. Suède f. ~ish a. suédois; n. (lang.) suédois m.

sweep /swiːp/ v.t./i. (p.t. swept) balayer; (carry away) emporter, entraîner; (chimney) ramonner. ● n. coup de balai m.; (curve) courbe f.; (mouvement) geste m., mouvement m.; (for chimneys) ramoneur m. ~ by, passer rapidement or majestueusement. ~ out, balayer.

~er n. (for carpet) balai mécanique m.; (football) arrière volant m. **~ing** a. (gesture) large; (action) qui va loin; (statement) trop général.

sweet /swiːt/ a. (-er, -est) (not sour, pleasant) doux; (not savoury) sucré; (charming: fam.) gentil. ● n. bonbon m.; (dish) dessert m.; (person) chéri(e) m. (f.). **have a ~ tooth,** aimer les sucreries. **~ corn,** maïs m. **~ pea,** pois de senteur m. **~ shop,** confiserie f. **~ly** adv. gentiment. **~ness** n. douceur f.; goût sucré m.

sweeten /ˈswiːtn/ v.t. sucrer; (fig.) adoucir. **~er** n. édulcorant m.

sweetheart /ˈswiːthɑːt/ n. petit(e) ami(e) m. (f.); (term of endearment) chéri(e) m. (f.).

swell /swel/ v.t./i. (p.t. swelled, p.p. swollen or swelled) (increase) grossir; (expand) (se) gonfler; (of hand, face) enfler. ● n. (of sea) houle f. ● a. (fam.) formidable. **~ing** n. (med.) enflure f.

swelter /ˈsweltə(r)/ v.i. étouffer. **~ing** a. étouffant.

swept /swept/ see sweep.

swerve /swɜːv/ v.i. faire un écart.

swift /swɪft/ a. (-er, -est) rapide. ● n. (bird) martinet m. **~ly** adv. rapidement. **~ness** n. rapidité f.

swig /swɪɡ/ v.t. (p.t. swigged) (drink: fam.) lamper. ● n. (fam.) lampée f., coup m.

swill /swɪl/ v.t. rincer; (drink) lamper. ● n. (pig-food) pâtée f.

swim /swɪm/ v.i. (p.t. swam, p.p. swum, pres. p. swimming) nager; (be dizzy) tourner. ● v.t. traverser à la nage; (distance) nager. ● n. baignade f. **go for a ~,** aller se baigner. **~mer** n. nageu|r, -se m., f. **~ming** n. natation f. **~ming-bath, ~ming-pool** ns. piscine f. **~-suit** n. maillot (de bain) m.

swindle /ˈswɪndl/ v.t. escroquer. ● n. escroquerie f. **~r** /-ə(r)/ n. escroc m.

swine /swaɪn/ n. pl. (pigs) pourceaux m. pl. ● n. invar. (person: fam.) salaud m.

swing /swɪŋ/ v.t./i. (p.t. swung) (se) balancer, (turn round) tourner; (of pendulum) osciller. ● n. balancement m.; (seat) balançoire f.; (of opinion) revirement m. **(towards,** en faveur de); (mus.) rythme m. **be in full ~,** battre son plein. **~ round,** (of person) se retourner.

swingeing /ˈswɪndʒɪŋ/ a. écrasant.

swipe /swaɪp/ v.t. (hit: fam.) frapper; (steal: fam.) piquer. ● n. (hit: fam.) grand coup m.

swirl /swɜːl/ v.i. tourbillonner. ● n. tourbillon m.

swish /swɪʃ/ v.i. (hiss) siffler, cingler l'air. ● a. (fam.) chic invar.

Swiss /swɪs/ a. suisse. ● n. invar. Suisse(sse) m. (f.).

switch /swɪtʃ/ n. bouton (électrique) m., interrupteur m.; (shift) changement m., revirement m. ● v.t. (transfer) transférer; (exchange) échanger (for, contre); (reverse positions of) changer de place. **~ trains/** etc., (change) changer de train/etc. ● v.i. (go over) passer. **~ off,** éteindre. **~ on,** mettre, allumer.

switchback /ˈswɪtʃbæk/ n. montagnes russes f. pl.

switchboard /ˈswɪtʃbɔːd/ n. (telephone) standard m.

Switzerland /ˈswɪtsələnd/ n. Suisse f.

swivel /ˈswɪvl/ v.t./i. (p.t. swivelled) (faire) pivoter.

swollen /ˈswəʊlən/ see swell.

swoon /swuːn/ v.i. se pâmer.

swoop /swuːp/ v.i. (bird) fondre; (police) faire une descente, foncer. ● n. (police raid) descente f.

sword /sɔːd/ n. épée f.

swore /swɔː(r)/ see swear.

sworn /swɔːn/ see swear. ● a. (enemy) juré; (ally) dévoué.

swot /swɒt/ v.t./i. (p.t. swotted) (study: sl.) bûcher. ● n. (sl.) bûcheu|r, -se m., f.

swum /swʌm/ see swim.

swung /swʌŋ/ see swing.

sycamore /ˈsɪkəmɔː(r)/ n. (maple) sycomore m.; (Amer.) platane m.

syllable /ˈsɪləbl/ n. syllabe f.

syllabus /ˈsɪləbəs/ n. (pl. -uses) (schol., univ.) programme m.

symbol /ˈsɪmbl/ n. symbole m. **~ic(al)** /-ˈbɒlɪk(l)/ a. symbolique. **~ism** n. symbolisme m.

symbolize /ˈsɪmbəlaɪz/ v.t. symboliser.

symmetr|y /ˈsɪmətrɪ/ n. symétrie f. **~ical** /sɪˈmetrɪkl/ a. symétrique.

sympathize /ˈsɪmpəθaɪz/ v.i. **~ with,** (pity) plaindre; (fig.) comprendre les sentiments de. **~r** /-ə(r)/ n. sympathisant(e) m. (f.).

sympath|y /ˈsɪmpəθɪ/ n. (pity) compassion f.; (fig.) compréhension f.; (solidarity) solidarité f.; (condo-

lences) condoléances _f. pl._ **be in ~y with,** comprendre, être en accord avec. **~etic** /-'θetɪk/ _a._ compatissant; (_fig._) compréhensif. **~etically** /-'θetɪklɪ/ _adv._ avec compassion; (_fig._) avec compréhension.

symphon|y /'sɪmfənɪ/ _n._ symphonie _f._ ● _a._ symphonique. **~ic** /-'fɒnɪk/ _a._ symphonique.

symposium /sɪm'pəʊzɪəm/ _n._ (_pl._ **-ia**) symposium _m._

symptom /'sɪmptəm/ _n._ symptôme _m._ **~atic** /-'mætɪk/ _a._ symptomatique (**of,** de).

synagogue /'sɪnəgɒg/ _n._ synagogue _f._

synchronize /'sɪŋkrənaɪz/ _v.t._ synchroniser.

syndicate /'sɪndɪkət/ _n._ syndicat _m._

syndrome /'sɪndrəʊm/ _n._ syndrome _m._

synonym /'sɪnənɪm/ _n._ synonyme _m._ **~ous** /sɪ'nɒnɪməs/ _a._ synonyme.

synopsis /sɪ'nɒpsɪs/ _n._ (_pl._ **-opses** /-siːz/) résumé _m._

syntax /'sɪntæks/ _n._ syntaxe _f._

synthesis /'sɪnθəsɪs/ _n._ (_pl._ **-theses** /-siːz/) synthèse _f._

synthetic /sɪn'θetɪk/ _a._ synthétique.

syphilis /'sɪfɪlɪs/ _n._ syphilis _f._

Syria /'sɪrɪə/ _n._ Syrie _f._ **~n** _a._ & _n._ syrien(ne) (_m._ (_f._)).

syringe /sɪ'rɪndʒ/ _n._ seringue _f._

syrup /'sɪrəp/ _n._ (_liquid_) sirop _m._; (_treacle_) mélasse raffinée _f._ **~y** _a._ sirupeux.

system /'sɪstəm/ _n._ système _m._; (_body_) organisme _m._; (_order_) méthode _f._ **~s analyst,** analyste-programmeu|r, -se _m., f._ **~s disk,** disque système _m._

systematic /sɪstə'mætɪk/ _a._ systématique.

T

tab /tæb/ _n._ (_flap_) languette _f._, patte _f._; (_loop_) attache _f._; (_label_) étiquette _f._; (_Amer., fam._) addition _f._ **keep ~s on,** (_fam._) surveiller.

table /'teɪbl/ _n._ table _f._ ● _v.t._ présenter; (_postpone_) ajourner. ● _a._ (_lamp, wine_) de table. **at ~,** à table. **lay** or **set the ~,** mettre la table. **~-cloth** _n._ nappe _f._ **~-mat** _n._ dessous-de-plat _m. invar._; (_cloth_) set _m._ **~ of**

contents, table des matières _f._ **~ tennis,** ping-pong _m._

tablespoon /'teɪblspuːn/ _n._ cuiller à soupe _f._ **~ful** _n._ (_pl._ **~fuls**) cuillerée à soupe _f._

tablet /'tæblɪt/ _n._ (_of stone_) plaque _f._; (_drug_) comprimé _m._

tabloid /'tæblɔɪd/ _n._ tabloïd _m._ **the ~ press,** la presse populaire.

taboo /tə'buː/ _n._ & _a._ tabou (_m._).

tabulator /'tæbjʊleɪtə(r)/ _n._ (_on typewriter_) tabulateur _m._

tacit /'tæsɪt/ _a._ tacite.

taciturn /'tæsɪtɜːn/ _a._ taciturne.

tack /tæk/ _n._ (_nail_) broquette _f._; (_stitch_) point de bâti _m._; (_course of action_) voie _f._ ● _v.t._ (_nail_) clouer; (_stitch_) bâtir; (_add_) ajouter. ● _v.i._ (_naut._) louvoyer.

tackle /'tækl/ _n._ équipement _m._, matériel _m._; (_football_) plaquage _m._ ● _v.t._ (_problem etc._) s'attaquer à; (_football player_) plaquer.

tacky /'tækɪ/ _a._ (**-ier, -iest**) poisseux, pas sec; (_shabby, mean: Amer._) moche.

tact /tækt/ _n._ tact _m._ **~ful** _a._ plein de tact. **~fully** _adv._ avec tact. **~less** _a._ qui manque de tact. **~lessly** _adv._ sans tact.

tactic /'tæktɪk/ _n._ tactique _f._ **~s** _n._ & _n. pl._ tactique _f._ **~al** _a._ tactique.

tactile /'tæktaɪl/ _a._ tactile.

tadpole /'tædpəʊl/ _n._ têtard _m._

tag /tæg/ _n._ (_label_) étiquette _f._; (_end piece_) bout _m._; (_phrase_) cliché _m._ ● _v.t._ (_p.t._ **tagged**) étiqueter; (_join_) ajouter. ● _v.i._ **~ along,** (_fam._) suivre.

tail /teɪl/ _n._ queue _f._; (_of shirt_) pan _m._ **~s,** (_coat_) habit _m._ **~s!,** (_tossing coin_) pile! ● _v.t._ (_follow_) filer. ● _v.i._ **~ away** or **off,** diminuer. **~-back** _n._ (_traffic_) bouchon _m._ **~-end** _n._ fin _f._, bout _m._ **~-gate** _n._ hayon arrière _m._

tailcoat /'teɪlkəʊt/ _n._ habit _m._

tailor /'teɪlə(r)/ _n._ tailleur _m._ ● _v.t._ (_garment_) façonner; (_fig._) adapter. **~-made** _a._ fait sur mesure. **~-made for,** (_fig._) fait pour.

tainted /'teɪntɪd/ _a._ (_infected_) infecté; (_decayed_) gâté; (_fig._) souillé.

take /teɪk/ _v.t./i._ (_p.t._ **took,** _p.p._ **taken**) prendre; (_carry_) (ap)porter (**to,** à); (_escort_) accompagner, amener; (_contain_) contenir; (_tolerate_) supporter; (_prize_) remporter; (_exam_) passer; (_choice_) faire; (_precedence_) avoir. **~ sth. from s.o.,** prendre

qch. à qn. **~ sth. from a place,**
prendre qch. d'un endroit. **~ s.o.
home,** ramener qn. chez lui. **be ~n
by** or **with,** être impressionné par.
be ~n ill, tomber malade. **it ~s
time/courage/etc. to,** il faut du
temps/du courage/etc. pour. **~
after,** ressembler à. **~ apart,**
démonter. **~ away,** (object) emporter; (person) emmener; (remove)
enlever (**from,** à). **~-away** n.
(meal) plat à emporter m.; (shop)
restaurant qui fait des plats à emporter m. **~ back,** reprendre; (return) rendre; (accompany) raccompagner; (statement) retirer. **~
down,** (object) descendre; (notes)
prendre. **~ in,** (object) rentrer; (include) inclure; (cheat) tromper;
(grasp) saisir. **~ it that,** supposer
que. **~ off** v.t. enlever; (mimic)
imiter; v.i. (aviat.) décoller. **~-off**
n. imitation f.; (aviat.) décollage m.
~ on, (task, staff, passenger, etc.)
prendre; (challenger) relever le défi
de. **~ out,** sortir; (stain etc.)
enlever. **~ over** v.t. (factory,
country, etc.) prendre la direction
de; (firm: comm.) racheter; v.i. (of
dictator) prendre le pouvoir. **~ over
from,** (relieve) prendre la relève de;
(succeed) prendre la succession de.
~-over n. (pol.) prise de pouvoir f.;
(comm.) rachat m. **~ part,** participer (**in,** à). **~ place,** avoir lieu. **~
sides,** prendre parti (**with,** pour). **~
to,** se prendre d'amitié pour; (activity) prendre goût à. **~ to doing,** se
mettre à faire. **~ up,** (object) monter; (hobby) se mettre à; (occupy)
prendre; (resume) reprendre. **~ up
with,** se lier avec.

takings /'teɪkɪŋz/ n. pl. recette f.

talcum /'tælkəm/ n. talc m. **~ powder,** talc m.

tale /teɪl/ n. conte m.; (report) récit
m.; (lie) histoire f.

talent /'tælənt/ n. talent m. **~ed** a.
doué, qui a du talent.

talk /tɔːk/ v.t./i. parler; (say) dire;
(chat) bavarder. ● n. conversation
f., entretien m.; (words) propos m.
pl.; (lecture) exposé m. **~ into
doing,** persuader de faire. **~ over,**
discuter (de). **~-show** n. talk-show
m. **~er** n. causeu|r, -se m., f. **~ing-to**
n. (fam.) réprimande f.

talkative /'tɔːkətɪv/ a. bavard.

tall /tɔːl/ a. (-er, -est) (high) haut;
(person) grand. **~ story,** (fam.)
histoire invraisemblable f.

tallboy /'tɔːlbɔɪ/ n. commode f.

tally /'tælɪ/ v.i. correspondre (**with,**
à), s'accorder (**with,** avec).

tambourine /tæmbə'riːn/ n. tambourin m.

tame /teɪm/ a. (-er, -est) apprivoisé;
(dull) insipide. ● v.t. apprivoiser;
(lion) dompter. **~r** /-ə(r)/ n. domp-
teu|r, -se m., f.

tamper /'tæmpə(r)/ v.i. **~ with,** toucher à, tripoter; (text) altérer.

tampon /'tæmpɒn/ n. (med.) tampon
hygiénique m.

tan /tæn/ v.t./i. (p.t. **tanned**) bronzer;
(hide) tanner. ● n. bronzage m.
● a. marron clair invar.

tandem /'tændəm/ n. (bicycle) tandem m. **in ~,** en tandem.

tang /tæŋ/ n. (taste) saveur forte f.;
(smell) odeur forte f.

tangent /'tændʒənt/ n. tangente f.

tangerine /tændʒə'riːn/ n. mandarine f.

tangible /'tændʒəbl/ a. tangible.

tangle /'tæŋgl/ v.t. enchevêtrer. ● n.
enchevêtrement m. **become ~d,**
s'enchevêtrer.

tango /'tæŋgəʊ/ n. (pl. **-os**) tango m.

tank /tæŋk/ n. réservoir m.; (vat)
cuve f.; (for fish) aquarium m.; (mil.)
char m., tank m.

tankard /'tæŋkəd/ n. chope f.

tanker /'tæŋkə(r)/ n. camion-citerne
m.; (ship) pétrolier m.

tantaliz|e /'tæntəlaɪz/ v.t. tour-
menter. **~ing** a. tentant.

tantamount /'tæntəmaʊnt/ a. **be ~
to,** équivaloir à.

tantrum /'tæntrəm/ n. crise de colère
or de rage f.

tap¹ /tæp/ n. (for water etc.) robinet
m. ● v.t. (p.t. **tapped**) (resources)
exploiter; (telephone) mettre sur
table d'écoute. **on ~,** (fam.) disponible.

tap² /tæp/ v.t./i. (p.t. **tapped**) frapper (doucement). ● n. petit coup m.
~-dance n. claquettes f. pl.

tape /teɪp/ n. ruban m.; (sticky)
ruban adhésif m. **(magnetic) ~,**
bande (magnétique) f. ● v.t. (tie)
attacher; (stick) coller; (record)
enregistrer. **~-measure** n. mètre
(à) ruban m. **~ recorder,** magnétophone m.

taper /'teɪpə(r)/ n. (for lighting) bougie f. ● v.t./i. (s')effiler. ~ **off,** (diminish) diminuer. ~**ed,** ~**ing** adjs. (fingers etc.) effilé, fuselé; (trousers) étroit du bas.

tapestry /'tæpɪstrɪ/ n. tapisserie f.

tapioca /tæpɪ'əʊkə/ n. tapioca m.

tar /tɑ:(r)/ n. goudron m. ● v.t. (p.t. **tarred**) goudronner.

tardy /'tɑ:dɪ/ a. (-ier, -iest) (slow) lent; (belated) tardif.

target /'tɑ:gɪt/ n. cible f.; (objective) objectif m. ● v.t. prendre pour cible.

tariff /'tærɪf/ n. (charges) tarif m.; (on imports) tarif douanier m.

Tarmac /'tɑ:mæk/ n. (P.) macadam (goudronné) m.; (runway) piste f.

tarnish /'tɑ:nɪʃ/ v.t./i. (se) ternir.

tarpaulin /tɑ:'pɔ:lɪn/ n. bâche goudronnée f.

tarragon /'tærəgən/ n. estragon m.

tart¹ /tɑ:t/ a. (-er, -est) acide.

tart² /tɑ:t/ n. tarte f.; (prostitute; sl.) poule f. ● v.t. ~ **up,** (pej.; sl.) embellir (sans le moindre goût).

tartan /'tɑ:tn/ n. tartan m. ● a. écossais.

tartar /'tɑ:tə(r)/ n. tartre m. ~ **sauce,** sauce tartare f.

task /tɑ:sk/ n. tâche f., travail m. **take to ~,** réprimander. ~ **force,** détachement spécial m.

tassel /'tæsl/ n. gland m., pompon m.

taste /teɪst/ n. goût m. ● v.t. (eat, enjoy) goûter; (try) goûter à; (perceive taste of) sentir le goût de. ● v.i. ~ **of** or **like,** avoir un goût de. **have a ~ of,** (experience) goûter de. ~**less** a. sans goût; (fig.) de mauvais goût.

tasteful /'teɪstfl/ a. de bon goût. ~**ly** adv. avec goût.

tasty /'teɪstɪ/ a. (-ier, -iest) délicieux, savoureux.

tat /tæt/ see tit².

tatter|s /'tætəz/ n. pl. lambeaux m. pl. ~**ed** /'tætəd/ a. en lambeaux.

tattoo¹ /tə'tu:/ n. (mil.) spectacle militaire m.

tattoo² /tə'tu:/ v.t. tatouer. ● n. tatouage m.

tatty /'tætɪ/ a. (-ier, -iest) (shabby: fam.) miteux, minable.

taught /tɔ:t/ see teach.

taunt /tɔ:nt/ v.t. railler. ● n. raillerie f. ~**ing** a. railleur.

Taurus /'tɔ:rəs/ n. le Taureau.

taut /tɔ:t/ a. tendu.

tavern /'tævn/ n. taverne f.

tawdry /'tɔ:drɪ/ a. (-ier, -iest) (showy) tape-à-l'œil invar.

tax /tæks/ n. taxe f., impôt m.; (on income) impôts m. pl. ● v.t. imposer; (put to test: fig.) mettre à l'épreuve. ~**able** a. imposable. ~**ation** /-'seɪʃn/ n. imposition f.; (taxes) impôts m. pl. ~**collector** n. percepteur m. ~**deductible** a. déductible d'impôts. ~ **disc,** vignette f. ~**free** a. exempt d'impôts. ~**ing** a. (fig.) éprouvant. ~ **haven** paradis fiscal m. ~ **inspector,** inspecteur des impôts m. ~ **relief,** dégrèvement fiscal m. ~ **return,** déclaration d'impôts f.

taxi /'tæksɪ/ n. (pl. -is) taxi m. ● v.i. (p.t. **taxied,** pres. p. **taxiing**) (aviat.) rouler au sol. ~-**cab** n. taxi m. ~-**rank,** (Amer.) ~ **stand,** station de taxi f.

taxpayer /'tækspeɪə(r)/ n. contribuable m./f.

tea /ti:/ n. thé m.; (snack) goûter m. ~-**bag** n. sachet de thé m. ~-**break** n. pause-thé f. ~-**leaf** n. feuille de thé f. ~-**set** n. service à thé m. ~-**shop** n. salon de thé m. ~-**towel** n. torchon m.

teach /ti:tʃ/ v.t. (p.t. **taught**) apprendre (s.o. sth., qch. à qn.); (in school) enseigner (s.o. sth., qch. à qn.). ● v.i. enseigner. ~**er** n. professeur m.; (primary) institu|teur, -trice m., f.; (member of teaching profession) enseignant(e) m. (f.). ~**ing** n. enseignement m.; a. pédagogique; (staff) enseignant.

teacup /'ti:kʌp/ n. tasse à thé f.

teak /ti:k/ n. (wood) teck m.

team /ti:m/ n. équipe f.; (of animals) attelage m. ● v.i. ~ **up,** faire équipe (with, avec). ~-**work** n. travail d'équipe m.

teapot /'ti:pɒt/ n. théière f.

tear¹ /teə(r)/ v.t./i. (p.t. **tore,** p.p. **torn**) (se) déchirer; (snatch) arracher (from, à); (rush) aller à toute vitesse. ● n. déchirure f.

tear² /tɪə(r)/ n. larme f. **in ~s,** en larmes. ~-**gas** n. gaz lacrymogène m.

tearful /'tɪəfl/ a. (voice) larmoyant; (person) en larmes. ~**ly** adv. en pleurant, les larmes aux yeux.

tease /ti:z/ v.t. taquiner. ● n. (person: fam.) taquin(e) m. (f.).

teaspoon /'ti:spu:n/ n. petite cuiller f. ~**ful** n. (pl. -**fuls**) cuillerée à café f.

teat /tiːt/ n. (of bottle, animal) tétine f.

technical /'teknɪkl/ a. technique. **~ity** /-'kælətɪ/ n. détail technique m. **~ly** adv. techniquement.

technician /tek'nɪʃn/ n. technicien(ne) m. (f.).

technique /tek'niːk/ n. technique f.

technolog|y /tek'nɒlədʒɪ/ n. technologie f. **~ical** /-ə'lɒdʒɪkl/ a. technologique.

teddy /'tedɪ/ a. **~ bear,** ours en peluche m.

tedious /'tiːdɪəs/ a. fastidieux.

tedium /'tiːdɪəm/ n. ennui m.

tee /tiː/ n. (golf) tee m.

teem[1] /tiːm/ v.i. (swarm) grouiller (with, de).

teem[2] /tiːm/ v.i. **~ (with rain),** pleuvoir à torrents.

teenage /'tiːneɪdʒ/ a. (d')adolescent. **~d** a. adolescent. **~r** /-ə(r)/ n. adolescent(e) m. (f.).

teens /tiːnz/ n. pl. **in one's ~,** adolescent.

teeny /'tiːnɪ/ a. (-ier, -iest) (tiny: fam.) minuscule.

teeter /'tiːtə(r)/ v.i. chanceler.

teeth /tiːθ/ see tooth.

teeth|e /tiːð/ v.i. faire ses dents. **~ing troubles,** (fig.) difficultés initiales f. pl.

teetotaller /tiː'təʊtlə(r)/ n. personne qui ne boit pas d'alcool f.

telecommunications /telɪkəmjuː-nɪ'keɪʃnz/ n. pl. télécommunications f. pl.

telegram /'telɪɡræm/ n. télégramme m.

telegraph /'telɪɡrɑːf/ n. télégraphe m. ● a. télégraphique. **~ic** /-'ɡræfɪk/ a. télégraphique.

telepath|y /tɪ'lepəθɪ/ n. télépathie f. **~ic** /telɪ'pæθɪk/ a. télépathique.

telephone /'telɪfəʊn/ n. téléphone m. ● v.t. (person) téléphoner à; (message) téléphoner. ● v.i. téléphoner. **~ book,** annuaire m. **~-box** n., **~ booth,** cabine téléphonique f. **~ call,** coup de téléphone m. **~ number,** numéro de téléphone m.

telephonist /tɪ'lefənɪst/ n. (in exchange) téléphoniste m./f.

telephoto /telɪ'fəʊtəʊ/ a. **~ lens,** téléobjectif m.

telescop|e /'telɪskəʊp/ n. télescope m. ● v.t./i. (se) télescoper. **~ic** /-'skɒpɪk/ a. télescopique.

teletext /'telɪtekst/ n. télétexte m.

televise /'telɪvaɪz/ v.t. téléviser.

television /'telɪvɪʒn/ n. télévision f. **~ set,** poste de télévision m.

telex /'teleks/ n. télex m. ● v.t. envoyer par télex.

tell /tel/ v.t. (p.t. **told**) dire (s.o. sth., qch. à qn.); (story) raconter; (distinguish) distinguer. ● v.i. avoir un effet; (know) savoir. **~ of,** parler de. **~ off,** (fam.) gronder. **~-tale** n. rapporteu|r, -se m., f.; a. révélateur. **~ tales,** rapporter.

teller /'telə(r)/ n. (in bank) caiss|ier, -ière m., f.

telling /'telɪŋ/ a. révélateur.

telly /'telɪ/ n. (fam.) télé f.

temerity /tɪ'merətɪ/ n. témérité f.

temp /temp/ n. (temporary employee: fam.) intérimaire m./f. ● v.i. faire de l'intérim.

temper /'tempə(r)/ n. humeur f.; (anger) colère f. ● v.t. (metal) tremper; (fig.) tempérer. **lose one's ~,** se mettre en colère.

temperament /'temprəmənt/ n. tempérament m. **~al** /-'mentl/ a. capricieux; (innate) inné.

temperance /'tempərəns/ n. (in drinking) tempérance f.

temperate /'tempərət/ a. tempéré.

temperature /'temprətʃə(r)/ n. température f. **have a ~,** avoir (de) la fièvre or de la température.

tempest /'tempɪst/ n. tempête f.

tempestuous /tem'pestʃʊəs/ a. (meeting etc.) orageux.

template /'templ(e)ɪt/ n. patron m.

temple[1] /'templ/ n. temple m.

temple[2] /'templ/ n. (of head) tempe f.

tempo /'tempəʊ/ n. (pl. -os) tempo m.

temporal /'tempərəl/ a. temporel.

temporar|y /'temprərɪ/ a. temporaire, provisoire. **~ily** adv. temporairement, provisoirement.

tempt /tempt/ v.t. tenter. **~ s.o. to do,** donner envie à qn. de faire. **~ation** /-'teɪʃn/ n. tentation f. **~ing** a. tentant.

ten /ten/ a. & n. dix (m.).

tenable /'tenəbl/ a. défendable.

tenac|ious /tɪ'neɪʃəs/ a. tenace. **~ity** /-'æsɪtɪ/ n. ténacité f.

tenancy /'tenənsɪ/ n. location f.

tenant /'tenənt/ n. locataire m./f.

tend[1] /tend/ v.t. s'occuper de.

tend[2] /tend/ v.i. **~ to,** (be apt to) avoir tendance à.

tendency /'tendənsɪ/ n. tendance f.

tender [1] /'tendə(r)/ a. tendre; (*sore, painful*) sensible. **~ly** adv. tendrement. **~ness** n. tendresse f.

tender [2] /'tendə(r)/ v.t. offrir, donner. ● v.i. faire une soumission. ● n. (*comm.*) soumission f. **be legal ~**, (*money*) avoir cours. **put sth. out to ~**, faire un appel d'offres pour qch.

tendon /'tendən/ n. tendon m.

tenement /'tenəmənt/ n. maison de rapport f., H.L.M. m./f.; (*slum: Amer.*) taudis m.

tenet /'tenɪt/ n. principe m.

tenner /'tenə(r)/ n. (*fam.*) billet de dix livres m.

tennis /'tenɪs/ n. tennis m. ● a. de tennis **~ shoes**, tennis m. pl.

tenor /'tenə(r)/ n. (*meaning*) sens général m.; (*mus.*) ténor m.

tense [1] /tens/ n. (*gram.*) temps m.

tense [2] /tens/ a. (**-er, -est**) tendu. ● v.t. (*muscles*) tendre, raidir. ● v.i. (*of face*) se crisper. **~ness** n. tension f.

tension /'tenʃn/ n. tension f.

tent /tent/ n. tente f.

tentacle /'tentəkl/ n. tentacule m.

tentative /'tentətɪv/ a. provisoire; (*hesitant*) timide. **~ly** adv. provisoirement; timidement.

tenterhooks /'tentəhʊks/ n. pl. **on ~**, sur des charbons ardents.

tenth /tenθ/ a. & n. dixième (m./f.).

tenuous /'tenjʊəs/ a. ténu.

tenure /'tenjʊə(r)/ n. (*in job, office*) (période de) jouissance f. **have ~**, être titulaire.

tepid /'tepɪd/ a. tiède.

term /tɜːm/ n. (*word, limit*) terme m.; (*of imprisonment*) temps m.; (*in school etc.*) trimestre m.; (*Amer.*) semestre m. **~s**, conditions f. pl. ● v.t. appeler, **on good/bad ~s**, en bons/mauvais termes. **in the short/long ~**, à court/long terme **come to ~s**, arriver à un accord. **come to ~s with sth.**, accepter qch. **~ of office**, (*pol.*) mandat m.

terminal /'tɜːmɪnl/ a. terminal, final; (*med.*) en phase terminale. ● n. (*oil, computer*) terminal m.; (*rail.*) terminus m.; (*electr.*) borne f. **(air) ~**, aérogare f.

terminat|e /'tɜːmɪneɪt/ v.t. mettre fin à. ● v.i. prendre fin. **~ion** /-'neɪʃn/ n. fin f.

terminology /tɜːmɪ'nɒlədʒɪ/ n. terminologie f.

terminus /'tɜːmɪnəs/ n. (*pl.* **-ni** /-naɪ/) (*station*) terminus m.

terrace /'terəs/ n. terrasse f.; (*houses*) rangée de maisons contiguës f. **the ~s**, (*sport*) les gradins m. pl.

terracotta /terə'kɒtə/ n. terre cuite f.

terrain /te'reɪn/ n. terrain m.

terribl|e /'terəbl/ a. affreux, atroce. **~y** adv. affreusement; (*very*) terriblement.

terrier /'terɪə(r)/ n. (*dog*) terrier m.

terrific /tə'rɪfɪk/ a. (*fam.*) terrible. **~ally** /-klɪ/ adv. (*very: fam.*) terriblement; (*very well: fam.*) terriblement bien.

terrif|y /'terɪfaɪ/ v.t. terrifier. **be ~ied of**, avoir très peur de.

territorial /terɪ'tɔːrɪəl/ a. territorial.

territory /'terɪtərɪ/ n. territoire m.

terror /'terə(r)/ n. terreur f.

terroris|t /'terərɪst/ n. terroriste m./f. **~m** /-zəm/ n. terrorisme m.

terrorize /'terəraɪz/ v.t. terroriser.

terse /tɜːs/ a. concis, laconique.

test /test/ n. examen m., analyse f.; (*of goods*) contrôle m.; (*of machine etc.*) essai m.; (*in school*) interrogation f.; (*of strength etc.: fig.*) épreuve f. ● v.t. examiner, analyser; (*check*) contrôler; (*try*) essayer; (*pupil*) donner une interrogation à; (*fig.*) éprouver. **driving ~**, (épreuve f. du) permis de conduire m. **~ match**, match international m. **~ pilot** pilote d'essai m. **~-tube** n. éprouvette f.

testament /'testəmənt/ n. testament m. **Old/New T~**, Ancien/Nouveau Testament m.

testicle /'testɪkl/ n. testicule m.

testify /'testɪfaɪ/ v.t./i. témoigner (**to**, de). **~ that**, témoigner que.

testimony /'testɪmənɪ/ n. témoignage m.

testy /'testɪ/ a. grincheux.

tetanus /'tetənəs/ n. tétanos m.

tetchy /'tetʃɪ/ a. grincheux.

tether /'teðə(r)/ v.t. attacher. ● n. **at the end of one's ~**, à bout.

text /tekst/ n. texte m.

textbook /'tekstbʊk/ n. manuel m.

textile /'tekstaɪl/ n. & a. textile (m.).

texture /'tekstʃə(r)/ n. (*of paper etc.*) grain m.; (*of fabric*) texture f.

Thai /taɪ/ a. & n. thaïlandais(e) (m. (f.)). **~land** n. Thaïlande f.

Thames /temz/ n. Tamise f.

than /ðæn, *unstressed* ðən/ *conj.* que, qu'*; (*with numbers*) de. **more/less ~ ten**, plus/moins de dix.

thank /θæŋk/ *v.t.* remercier. **~s** *n. pl.* remerciements *m. pl.* **~ you!**, merci! **~s!**, (*fam.*) merci! **~s to**, grâce à. **T~sgiving (Day)**, (*Amer.*) jour d'action de grâces *m.* (*fête nationale*).

thankful /'θæŋkfl/ *a.* reconnaissant (**for**, de). **~ly** *adv.* (*happily*) heureusement.

thankless /'θæŋklɪs/ *a.* ingrat.

that /ðæt, *unstressed* ðet/ *a. pl.* **those**) ce *or* cet*, cette. **those**, ces. ● *pron.* ce *or* c'*, cela, ça. **~ (one)**, celui-là, celle-là. **those (ones)**, ceux-là, celles-là. ● *adv.* si, aussi. ● *rel. pron.* (*subject*) qui; (*object*) que, qu'*. ● *conj.* que, qu'*. **~ boy**, ce garçon (*with emphasis*) ce garçon-là. **~ is**, c'est. **~ is (to say)**, c'est-à-dire. **after ~**, après ça *or* cela. **the day ~**, le jour où. **the man ~ married her**, l'homme qui l'a épousée. **the man ~ she married**, l'homme qu'elle a épousé. **the car ~ I came in**, la voiture dans laquelle je suis venu. **~ big**, grand comme ça. **~ many**, **~ much**, tant que ça.

thatch /θætʃ/ *n.* chaume *m.* **~ed** *a.* en chaume. **~ed cottage**, chaumière *f.*

thaw /θɔː/ *v.t./i.* (faire) dégeler; (*snow*) (faire) fondre. ● *n.* dégel *m.*

the /*before vowel* ði, *before consonant* ðə, *stressed* ðiː/ *a.* le *or* l'*, la *or* l'*, *pl.* les. **of ~**, **from ~**, du, de l'*, de la, *pl.* des. **to ~**, **at ~**, au, à l'*, à la, *pl.* aux. **~ third of June**, le trois juin.

theatre /'θɪətə(r)/ *n.* théâtre *m.*

theatrical /θɪ'ætrɪkl/ *a.* théâtral.

theft /θeft/ *n.* vol *m.*

their /ðeə(r)/ *a.* leur, *pl.* leurs.

theirs /ðeəz/ *poss. pron.* le *or* la leur, les leurs.

them /ðem, *unstressed* ðəm/ *pron.* les; (*after prep.*) eux, elles. (**to**) **~**, leur. **I know ~**, je les connais.

theme /θiːm/ *n.* thème *m.* **~ song**, (*in film etc.*) chanson principale *f.*

themselves /ðəm'selvz/ *pron.* euxmêmes, elles-mêmes; (*reflexive*) se; (*after prep.*) eux, elles.

then /ðen/ *adv.* alors; (*next*) ensuite, puis; (*therefore*) alors, donc. ● *a.* d'alors. **from ~ on**, dès lors.

theolog|y /θɪ'ɒlədʒɪ/ *n.* théologie *f.* **~ian** /θɪə'ləʊdʒən/ *n.* théologien(ne) *m.* (*f.*).

theorem /'θɪərəm/ *n.* théorème *m.*

theor|y /'θɪərɪ/ *n.* théorie *f.* **~etical** /-'retɪkl/ *a.* théorique.

therapeutic /θerə'pjuːtɪk/ *a.* thérapeutique.

therapy /'θerəpɪ/ *n.* thérapie *f.*

there /ðeə(r)/ *adv.* là; (*with verb*) y; (*over there*) là-bas. ● *int.* allez. **he goes ~**, il y va. **on ~**, là-dessus. **~ is**, **~ are**, il y a; (*pointing*) voilà. **~**, **~!**, allons, allons! **~abouts** *adv.* par là. **~after** *adv.* par la suite. **~by** *adv.* de cette manière.

therefore /'ðeəfɔː(r)/ *adv.* donc.

thermal /'θɜːml/ *a.* thermique.

thermometer /θə'mɒmɪtə(r)/ *n.* thermomètre *m.*

thermonuclear /θɜːməʊ'njuːklɪə(r)/ *a.* thermonucléaire.

Thermos /'θɜːməs/ *n.* (P.) thermos *m./f. invar.* (P.).

thermostat /'θɜːməstæt/ *n.* thermostat *m.*

thesaurus /θɪ'sɔːrəs/ *n.* (*pl.* **-ri** /-raɪ/) dictionnaire de synonymes *m.*

these /ðiːz/ *see* this.

thesis /'θiːsɪs/ *n.* (*pl.* **theses** /-siːz/) thèse *f.*

they /ðeɪ/ *pron.* ils, elles; (*emphatic*) eux, elles; (*people in general*) on.

thick /θɪk/ *a.* (**-er**, **-est**) épais; (*stupid*) bête; (*friends: fam.*) très lié. ● *adv.* = **thickly**. ● *n.* **in the ~ of**, au plus gros de. **~ly** *adv.* (*grow*) dru; (*spread*) en couche épaisse. **~ness** *n.* épaisseur *f.* **~-skinned** *a.* peu sensible.

thicken /'θɪkən/ *v.t./i.* (s')épaissir.

thickset /θɪk'set/ *a.* trapu.

thief /θiːf/ *n.* (*pl.* **thieves**) voleu|r, -se *m.*, *f.*

thigh /θaɪ/ *n.* cuisse *f.*

thimble /'θɪmbl/ *n.* dé (à coudre) *m.*

thin /θɪn/ *a.* (**thinner**, **thinnest**) mince; (*person*) maigre, mince; (*sparse*) clairsemé; (*fine*) fin. ● *adv.* = **thinly**. ● *v.t./i.* (*p.t.* **thinned**) (*liquid*) (s')éclaircir. **~ out**, (*in quantity*) (s')éclaircir. **~ly** *adv.* (*slightly*) légèrement. **~ner** *n.* diluant *m.* **~ness** *n.* minceur *f.*; maigreur *f.*

thing /θɪŋ/ *n.* chose *f.* **~s**, (*belongings*) affaires *f. pl.* **the best ~ is to**, le mieux est de. **the (right) ~**, ce qu'il faut (**for s.o.**, à qn.).

think /θɪŋk/ *v.t./i.* (*p.t.* **thought**) penser (**about, of**, à); (*carefully*) réfléchir (**about, of**, à); (*believe*) croire. **I ~ so,** je crois que oui. **~ better of it,** se raviser. **~ nothing of,** trouver naturel de. **~ of,** (*hold opinion of*) penser de. **I'm ~ing of going,** je pense que j'irai peut-être. **~ over,** bien réfléchir à. **~-tank** *n.* comité d'experts *m.* **~ up,** inventer. **~er** *n.* penseu|r, -se *m., f.*

third /θɜːd/ *a.* troisième. ● *n.* troisième *m./f.*; (*fraction*) tiers *m.* **~ly** *adv.* troisièmement. **~-rate** *a.* très inférieur. **T~ World,** Tiers-Monde *m.*

thirst /θɜːst/ *n.* soif *f.* **~y** *a.* **be ~y,** avoir soif. **make ~y,** donner soif à.

thirteen /θɜːˈtiːn/ *a. & n.* treize (*m.*). **~th** *a. & n.* treizième (*m./f.*).

thirt|y /ˈθɜːtɪ/ *a. & n.* trente (*m.*). **~ieth** *a. & n.* trentième (*m./f.*).

this /ðɪs/ *a.* (*pl.* **these**) ce *or* cet*, cette. **these,** ces. ● *pron.* ce *or* c'*, ceci. **~ (one),** celui-ci, celle-ci. **these (ones),** ceux-ci, celles-ci. **~ boy,** ce garçon; (*with emphasis*) ce garçon-ci. **~ is a mistake,** c'est une erreur. **~ is the book,** voici le livre. **~ is my son,** je vous présente mon fils. **~ is Anne speaking,** c'est Anne à l'appareil. **after ~,** après ceci.

thistle /ˈθɪsl/ *n.* chardon *m.*

thorn /θɔːn/ *n.* épine *f.* **~y** *a.* épineux.

thorough /ˈθʌrə/ *a.* consciencieux; (*deep*) profond; (*cleaning, washing*) à fond. **~ly** *adv.* (*clean, study, etc.*) à fond; (*very*) tout à fait.

thoroughbred /ˈθʌrəbred/ *n.* (*horse etc.*) pur-sang *m.* invar.

thoroughfare /ˈθʌrəfeə(r)/ *n.* grande artère *f.*

those /ðəʊz/ *see* that.

though /ðəʊ/ *conj.* bien que. ● *adv.* (*fam.*) cependant.

thought /θɔːt/ *see* think. ● *n.* pensée *f.*; (*idea*) idée *f.*

thoughtful /ˈθɔːtfl/ *a.* pensif; (*considerate*) attentionné. **~ly** *adv.* pensivement; avec considération.

thoughtless /ˈθɔːtlɪs/ *a.* étourdi. **~ly** *adv.* étourdiment.

thousand /ˈθaʊznd/ *a. & n.* mille (*m. invar.*). **~s of,** des milliers de.

thrash /θræʃ/ *v.t.* rosser; (*defeat*) écraser. **~ about,** se débattre. **~ out,** discuter à fond.

thread /θred/ *n.* (*yarn & fig.*) fil *m.*; (*of screw*) pas *m.* ● *v.t.* enfiler. **~ one's way,** se faufiler.

threadbare /ˈθredbeə(r)/ *a.* râpé.

threat /θret/ *n.* menace *f.*

threaten /ˈθretn/ *v.t./i.* menacer (**with,** de). **~ingly** *adv.* d'un air menaçant.

three /θriː/ *a. & n.* trois (*m.*). **~-dimensional** *a.* en trois dimensions.

thresh /θreʃ/ *v.t.* (*corn etc.*) battre.

threshold /ˈθreʃəʊld/ *n.* seuil *m.*

threw /θruː/ *see* throw.

thrift /θrɪft/ *n.* économie *f.* **~y** *a.* économe.

thrill /θrɪl/ *n.* émotion *f.*, frisson *m.* ● *v.t.* transporter (de joie). ● *v.i.* frissonner (de joie). **be ~ed,** être ravi. **~ing** *a.* excitant.

thriller /ˈθrɪlə(r)/ *n.* livre *or* film à suspense *m.*

thriv|e /θraɪv/ *v.i.* (*p.t.* **thrived** *or* **throve,** *p.p.* **thrived** *or* **thriven**) prospérer. **he ~es on it,** cela lui réussit. **~ing** *a.* prospère.

throat /θrəʊt/ *n.* gorge *f.* **have a sore ~,** avoir mal à la gorge.

throb /θrɒb/ *v.i.* (*p.t.* **throbbed**) (*wound*) causer des élancements; (*heart*) palpiter; (*fig.*) vibrer. ● *n.* (*pain*) élancement *m.*; palpitation *f.* **~bing** *a.* (*pain*) lancinant.

throes /θrəʊz/ *n. pl.* **in the ~ of,** au milieu de, aux prises avec.

thrombosis /θrɒmˈbəʊsɪs/ *n.* thrombose *f.*

throne /θrəʊn/ *n.* trône *m.*

throng /θrɒŋ/ *n.* foule *f.* ● *v.t.* (*streets etc.*) se presser dans. ● *v.i.* (*arrive*) affluer.

throttle /ˈθrɒtl/ *n.* (*auto.*) accélérateur *m.* ● *v.t.* étrangler.

through /θruː/ *prep.* à travers; (*during*) pendant; (*by means or way of, out of*) par; (*by reason of*) grâce à, à cause de. ● *adv.* à travers; (*entirely*) jusqu'au bout. ● *a.* (*train etc.*) direct. **be ~,** (*finished*) avoir fini. **come** *or* **go ~,** (*cross, pierce*) traverser. **I'm putting you ~,** je vous passe votre correspondant.

throughout /θruːˈaʊt/ *prep.* **~ the country**/*etc.,* dans tout le pays/*etc.* **~ the day**/*etc.,* pendant toute la journée/*etc.* ● *adv.* (*place*) partout; (*time*) tout le temps.

throw /θrəʊ/ *v.t.* (*p.t.* **threw,** *p.p.* **thrown**) jeter, lancer; (*baffle: fam.*) déconcerter. ● *n.* jet *m.*; (*of dice*) coup *m.* **~ a party,** (*fam.*) faire une fête. **~ away,** jeter. **~-away** *a.* à jeter. **~ off,** (*get rid of*) se débarrasser de. **~ out,** jeter; (*person*) expulser; (*reject*) rejeter. **~ over,** (*desert*) plaquer. **~ up,** (*one's arms*) lever; (*resign from*) abandonner; (*vomit: fam.*) vomir.

thru /θru:/ *prep., adv. & a.* (*Amer.*) = **through.**

thrush /θrʌʃ/ *n.* (*bird*) grive *f.*

thrust /θrʌst/ *v.t.* (*p.t.* **thrust**) pousser. ● *n.* poussée *f.* **~ into,** (*put*) enforcer dans, mettre dans. **~ upon,** (*force on*) imposer à.

thud /θʌd/ *n.* bruit sourd *m.*

thug /θʌg/ *n.* voyou *m.*, bandit *m.*

thumb /θʌm/ *n.* pouce *m.* ● *v.t.* (*book*) feuilleter. **~ a lift,** faire de l'auto-stop. **~-index,** répertoire à onglets *m.*

thumbtack /'θʌmtæk/ *n.* (*Amer.*) punaise *f.*

thump /θʌmp/ *v.t./i.* cogner (sur); (*of heart*) battre fort. ● *n.* grand coup *m.* **~ing** *a.* (*fam.*) énorme.

thunder /'θʌndə(r)/ *n.* tonnerre *m.* ● *v.i.* (*weather, person, etc.*) tonner. **~ past,** passer dans un bruit de tonnerre. **~y** *a.* orageux.

thunderbolt /'θʌndəbəʊlt/ *n.* coup de foudre *m.*; (*event: fig.*) coup de tonnerre *m.*

thunderstorm /'θʌndəstɔːm/ *n.* orage *m.*

Thursday /'θɜːzdɪ/ *n.* jeudi *m.*

thus /ðʌs/ *adv.* ainsi.

thwart /θwɔːt/ *v.t.* contrecarrer.

thyme /taɪm/ *n.* thym *m.*

thyroid /'θaɪrɔɪd/ *n.* thyroïde *f.*

tiara /tɪ'ɑːrə/ *n.* diadème *m.*

tic /tɪk/ *n.* tic (nerveux) *m.*

tick¹ /tɪk/ *n.* (*sound*) tic-tac *m.*; (*mark*) coche *f.*; (*moment: fam.*) instant *m.* ● *v.i.* faire tic-tac. **~ (off),** cocher. **~ off,** (*fam.*) réprimander. **~ over,** (*engine, factory*) tourner au ralenti.

tick² /tɪk/ *n.* (*insect*) tique *f.*

ticket /'tɪkɪt/ *n.* billet *m.*; (*for bus, cloakroom, etc.*) ticket *m.*; (*label*) étiquette *f.* **~-collector** *n.* contrôleu|r, -se *m., f.* **~-office** *n.* guichet *m.*

tickle /'tɪkl/ *v.t.* chatouiller; (*amuse: fig.*) amuser. ● *n.* chatouillement *m.*

ticklish /'tɪklɪʃ/ *a.* chatouilleux.

tidal /'taɪdl/ *a.* qui a des marées. **~ wave,** raz-de-marée *m. invar.*

tiddly-winks /'tɪdlɪwɪŋks/ *n.* (*game*) jeu de puce *m.*

tide /taɪd/ *n.* marée *f.*; (*of events*) cours *m.* ● *v.t.* **~ over,** dépanner.

tidings /'taɪdɪŋz/ *n. pl.* nouvelles *f. pl.*

tid|y /'taɪdɪ/ *a.* (**-ier, -iest**) (*room*) bien rangé; (*appearance, work*) soigné; (*methodical*) ordonné; (*amount: fam.*) joli. ● *v.t./i.* ranger. **~ily** *adv.* avec soin. **~iness** *n.* ordre *m.*

tie /taɪ/ *v.t.* (*pres. p.* **tying**) attacher, nouer; (*a knot*) faire; (*link*) lier. ● *v.i.* (*darts etc.*) finir à égalité de points; (*football*) faire match nul; (*in race*) être ex aequo. ● *n.* attache *f.*; (*necktie*) cravate *f.*; (*link*) lien *m.*; égalité (de points) *f.*; match nul *m.* **~ down,** attacher; (*job*) bloquer. **~ s.o. down to,** (*date*) forcer qn. à respecter. **~ in with,** être lié à. **~ up,** attacher; (*money*) immobiliser; (*occupy*) occuper. **~-up** *n.* (*link*) lien *m.*; (*auto., Amer.*) bouchon *m.*

tier /tɪə(r)/ *n.* étage *m.*, niveau *m.*; (*in stadium etc.*) gradin *m.*

tiff /tɪf/ *n.* petite querelle *f.*

tiger /'taɪgə(r)/ *n.* tigre *m.*

tight /taɪt/ *a.* (**-er, -est**) (*clothes*) étroit, juste; (*rope*) tendu; (*lid*) solidement fixé; (*control*) strict; (*knot, collar, schedule*) serré; (*drunk: fam.*) ivre. ● *adv.* (*hold, sleep, etc.*) bien; (*squeeze*) fort. **~ corner,** situation difficile *f.* **~-fisted** *a.* avare. **~ly** *adv.* bien; (*squeeze*) fort.

tighten /'taɪtn/ *v.t./i.* (se) tendre; (*bolt etc.*) (se) resserrer; (*control etc.*) renforcer. **~ up on,** se montrer plus strict à l'égard de.

tightrope /'taɪtrəʊp/ *n.* corde raide *f.* **~ walker,** funambule *m./f.*

tights /taɪts/ *n. pl.* collant *m.*

tile /taɪl/ *n.* (*on wall, floor*) carreau *m.*; (*on roof*) tuile *f.* ● *v.t.* carreler; couvrir de tuiles.

till¹ /tɪl/ *v.t.* (*land*) cultiver.

till² /tɪl/ *prep. & conj.* = **until.**

till³ /tɪl/ *n.* caisse (enregistreuse) *f.*

tilt /tɪlt/ *v.i./i.* pencher. ● *n.* (*slope*) inclinaison *f.* **(at) full ~,** à toute vitesse.

timber /'tɪmbə(r)/ *n.* bois (de construction) *m.*; (*trees*) arbres *m. pl.*

time /taɪm/ *n.* temps *m.*; (*moment*) moment *m.*; (*epoch*) époque *f.*; (*by clock*) heure *f.*; (*occasion*) fois *f.*; (*rhythm*) mesure *f.* **~s,** (*multiplying*) fois *f. pl.* ● *v.t.* choisir le moment de; (*measure*) minuter; (*sport*) chronométrer. **any ~,** n'importe quand. **behind the ~s,** en retard sur son temps. **for the ~ being,** pour le moment. **from ~ to time,** de temps en temps. **have a good ~,** s'amuser. **in no ~,** en un rien de temps. **in ~,** à temps; (*eventually*) avec le temps. **a long ~,** longtemps. **on ~,** à l'heure. **what's the ~?,** quelle heure est-il? **~ bomb,** bombe à retardement *f.* **~- honoured** *a.* consacré (par l'usage). **~-lag** *n.* décalage *m.* **~-limit** *n.* délai *m.* **~-scale** *n.* délais fixés *m. pl.* **~ off,** du temps libre. **~ zone,** fuseau horaire *m.*

timeless /'taɪmlɪs/ *a.* éternel.

timely /'taɪmlɪ/ *a.* à propos.

timer /'taɪmə(r)/ *n.* (*for cooker etc.*) minuteur *m.*; (*on video*) programmateur; (*culin.*) compte-minutes *m. invar.*; (*with sand*) sablier *m.*

timetable /'taɪmteɪbl/ *n.* horaire *m.*

timid /'tɪmɪd/ *a.* timide; (*fearful*) peureux. **~ly** *adv.* timidement.

timing /'taɪmɪŋ/ *n.* (*measuring*) minutage *m.*; (*moment*) moment *m.*; (*of artist*) rythme *m.*

tin /tɪn/ *n.* étain *m.*; (*container*) boîte *f.* **~(plate),** fer-blanc *m.* ● *v.t.* (*p.t.* **tinned**) mettre en boîte. **~ foil,** papier d'aluminium *m.* **~ny** *a.* métallique. **~-opener** *n.* ouvre-boîte(s) *m.*

tinge /tɪndʒ/ *v.t.* teinter (**with,** de). ● *n.* teinte *f.*

tingle /'tɪŋɡl/ *v.i.* (*prickle*) picoter. ● *n.* picotement *m.*

tinker /'tɪŋkə(r)/ *n.* rétameur *m.* ● *v.i.* **~ (with),** bricoler.

tinkle /'tɪŋkl/ *n.* tintement *m.*; (*fam.*) coup de téléphone *m.*

tinsel /'tɪnsl/ *n.* cheveux d'ange *m. pl.*, guirlandes de Noël *f. pl.*

tint /tɪnt/ *n.* teinte *f.*; (*for hair*) shampooing colorant *m.* ● *v.t.* (*glass, paper*) teinter.

tiny /'taɪnɪ/ *a.* (**-ier, -iest**) minuscule, tout petit.

tip[1] /tɪp/ *n.* bout *m.*; (*cover*) embout *m.* **~ped cigarette,** cigarette (à bout) filtre *f.*

tip[2] /tɪp/ *v.t./i.* (*p.t.* **tipped**) (*tilt*) pencher; (*overturn*) (faire) basculer; (*pour*) verser; (*empty*) déverser; (*give money*) donner un pourboire à. ● *n.* (*money*) pourboire *m.*; (*advice*) tuyau *m.*; (*for rubbish*) décharge *f.* **~ off,** prévenir. **~-off** *n.* tuyau *m.* (*pour prévenir*).

tipsy /'tɪpsɪ/ *a.* un peu ivre, gris.

tiptoe /'tɪptəʊ/ *n.* **on ~,** sur la pointe des pieds.

tiptop /'tɪptɒp/ *a.* (*fam.*) excellent.

tir|e[1] /'taɪə(r)/ *v.t./i.* (se) fatiguer. **~e of,** se lasser de. **~eless** *a.* infatigable. **~ing** *a.* fatigant.

tire[2] /'taɪə(r)/ *n.* (*Amer.*) pneu *m.*

tired /'taɪəd/ *a.* fatigué. **be ~ of,** en avoir assez de.

tiresome /'taɪəsəm/ *a.* ennuyeux.

tissue /'tɪʃuː/ *n.* tissu *m.*; (*handkerchief*) mouchoir en papier *m.* **~-paper** *n.* papier de soie *m.*

tit[1] /tɪt/ *n.* (*bird*) mésange *f.*

tit[2] /tɪt/ *n.* **give ~ for tat,** rendre coup pour coup.

titbit /'tɪtbɪt/ *n.* friandise *f.*

titillate /'tɪtɪleɪt/ *v.t.* exciter.

title /'taɪtl/ *n.* titre *m.* **~-deed** *n.* titre de propriété *m.* **~-role** *n.* rôle principal *m.*

titter /'tɪtə(r)/ *v.i.* rigoler.

titular /'tɪtjʊlə(r)/ *a.* (*ruler etc.*) nominal.

to /tuː, *unstressed* tə/ *prep.* à; (*towards*) vers; (*of attitude*) envers. ● *adv.* **push** *or* **pull to,** (*close*) fermer. **to France**/*etc.*, en France/*etc.* **to town,** en ville. **to Canada**/*etc.*, au Canada/*etc.* **to the baker's**/*etc.*, chez le boulanger/*etc.* **the road/door**/*etc.* **to,** la route/porte/*etc.* de. **to me/her**/*etc.*, me/lui/*etc.* **to do/sit**/*etc.*, faire/s'asseoir/*etc.* **I wrote to tell her,** j'ai écrit pour lui dire. **I tried to help you,** j'ai essayé de t'aider. **ten to six,** (*by clock*) six heures moins dix. **go to and fro,** aller et venir. **husband**/*etc.***-to-be** *n.* futur mari/ *etc. m.*

toad /təʊd/ *n.* crapaud *m.*

toadstool /'təʊdstuːl/ *n.* champignon (vénéneux) *m.*

toast /təʊst/ *n.* pain grillé *m.*, toast *m.*; (*drink*) toast *m.* ● *v.t.* (*bread*) faire griller; (*drink to*) porter un toast à; (*event*) arroser. **~er** *n.* grille-pain *m. invar.*

tobacco /tə'bækəʊ/ *n.* tabac *m.*

tobacconist /tə'bækənɪst/ *n.* marchand(e) de tabac *m.* (*f.*). **~'s shop,** tabac *m.*

toboggan /tə'bɒɡən/ *n.* toboggan *m.*, luge *f.*

today /tə'deɪ/ *n. & adv.* aujourd'hui (*m.*).

toddler /'tɒdlə(r)/ *n.* tout(e) petit(e) enfant *m.(f.)*

toddy /'tɒdɪ/ *n.* (*drink*) grog *m.*

toe /təʊ/ n. orteil m.; (of shoe) bout m. ● v.t. ~ **the line,** se conformer. **on one's ~s,** vigilant. **~-hold** n. prise (précaire) f.

toffee /'tɒfɪ/ n. caramel m. **~-apple** n. pomme caramélisée f.

together /tə'geðə(r)/ adv. ensemble; (at same time) en même temps. **~ with,** avec. **~ness** n. camaraderie f.

toil /tɔɪl/ v.i. peiner. ● n. labeur m.

toilet /'tɔɪlɪt/ n. toilettes f. pl.; (grooming) toilette f. **~-paper** n. papier hygiénique m. **~-roll** n. rouleau de papier hygiénique m. **~ water,** eau de toilette f.

toiletries /'tɔɪlɪtrɪz/ n. pl. articles de toilette m. pl.

token /'təʊkən/ n. témoignage m., marque f.; (voucher) bon m.; (coin) jeton m. ● a. symbolique.

told /təʊld/ see tell. ● a. **all ~,** (all in all) en tout.

tolerabl|e /'tɒlərəbl/ a. tolérable; (not bad) passable. **~y** adv. (work, play, etc.) passablement.

toleran|t /'tɒlərənt/ a. tolérant (of, à l'égard de). **~ce** n. tolérance f. **~tly** adv. avec tolérance.

tolerate /'tɒlərett/ v.t. tolérer.

toll [1] /təʊl/ n. péage m. **death ~,** nombre de morts m. **take its ~,** (of age) faire sentir son poids.

toll [2] /təʊl/ v.i. (of bell) sonner.

tom /tɒm/, **~-cat** ns. matou m.

tomato /tə'mɑːtəʊ, Amer. tə'meɪtəʊ/ n. (pl. -oes) tomate f.

tomb /tuːm/ n. tombeau m.

tombola /tɒm'bəʊlə/ n. tombola f.

tomboy /'tɒmbɔɪ/ n. garçon manqué m.

tombstone /'tuːmstəʊn/ n. pierre tombale f.

tomfoolery /tɒm'fuːlərɪ/ n. âneries f. pl., bêtises f. pl.

tomorrow /tə'mɒrəʊ/ n. & adv. demain (m.). **~ morning/night,** demain matin/soir. **the day after ~,** après-demain.

ton /tʌn/ n. tonne f. (= 1016 kg.). **(metric) ~,** tonne f. (= 1000 kg.). **~s of,** (fam.) des masses de.

tone /təʊn/ n. ton m.; (of radio, telephone, etc.) tonalité f. ● v.t. ~ **down,** atténuer. ● v.i. ~ **in,** s'harmoniser (**with,** avec). **~-deaf** a. qui n'a pas d'oreille. **~ up,** (muscles) tonifier.

tongs /tɒŋz/ n. pl. pinces f. pl.; (for sugar) pince f.; (for hair) fer m.

tongue /tʌŋ/ n. langue f. **~-tied** a. muet. **~-twister** n. phrase difficile à prononcer f. **with one's ~ in one's cheek,** ironiquement.

tonic /'tɒnɪk/ n. (med.) tonique m. ● a. (effect, accent) tonique. ~ **(water),** tonic m.

tonight /tə'naɪt/ n. & adv. cette nuit (f.); (evening) ce soir (m.).

tonne /tʌn/ n. (metric) tonne f.

tonsil /'tɒnsl/ n. amygdale f.

tonsillitis /tɒnsɪ'laɪtɪs/ n. amygdalite f.

too /tuː/ adv. trop; (also) aussi. ~ **many** a. trop de; n. trop. ~ **much** a. trop de; adv. & n. trop.

took /tʊk/ see take.

tool /tuːl/ n. outil m. **~-bag** n. trousse à outils f.

toot /tuːt/ n. coup de klaxon m. ● v.t./i. ~ **(the horn),** klaxonner.

tooth /tuːθ/ n. (pl. **teeth**) dent f. **~less** a. édenté.

toothache /'tuːθeɪk/ n. mal de dents m.

toothbrush /'tuːθbrʌʃ/ n. brosse à dents f.

toothcomb /'tuːθkəʊm/ n. peigne fin m.

toothpaste /'tuːθpeɪst/ n. dentifrice m., pâte dentifrice f.

toothpick /'tuːθpɪk/ n. cure-dent m.

top [1] /tɒp/ n. (highest point) sommet m.; (upper part) haut m.; (upper surface) dessus m.; (lid) couvercle m.; (of bottle, tube) bouchon m.; (of beer bottle) capsule f.; (of list) tête f. ● a. (shelf etc.) du haut; (floor) dernier; (in rank) premier; (best) meilleur; (distinguished) éminent; (maximum) maximum. ● v.t. (p.t. topped) (exceed) dépasser; (list) venir en tête de. **from ~ to bottom,** de fond en comble. **on ~ of,** sur; (fig.) en plus de. ~ **hat,** haut-de-forme m. **~-heavy** a. trop lourd du haut. **~-level** a. du plus haut niveau. **~-notch** a. excellent. **~-quality** a. de la plus haute qualité. ~ **secret,** ultra-secret. ~ **up,** remplir. **~ped with,** surmonté de; (cream etc.: culin.) nappé de.

top [2] /tɒp/ n. (toy) toupie f.

topic /'tɒpɪk/ n. sujet m.

topical /'tɒpɪkl/ a. d'actualité.

topless /'tɒplɪs/ a. aux seins nus.

topple /'tɒpl/ v.t./i. (faire) tomber, (faire) basculer.

topsy-turvy /ˈtɒpsɪˈtɜːvɪ/ *adv. & a.* sens dessus dessous.

torch /tɔːtʃ/ *n.* (*electric*) lampe de poche *f.*; (*flaming*) torche *f.*

tore /tɔː(r)/ *see* tear[1].

torment[1] /ˈtɔːment/ *n.* tourment *m.*

torment[2] /tɔːˈment/ *v.t.* tourmenter; (*annoy*) agacer.

torn /tɔːn/ *see* tear[1].

tornado /tɔːˈneɪdəʊ/ *n.* (*pl.* **-oes**) tornade *f.*

torpedo /tɔːˈpiːdəʊ/ *n.* (*pl.* **-oes**) torpille *f.* ● *v.t.* torpiller.

torrent /ˈtɒrənt/ *n.* torrent *m.* ~**ial** /təˈrenʃl/ *a.* torrentiel.

torrid /ˈtɒrɪd/ *a.* (*climate etc.*) torride; (*fig.*) passionné.

torso /ˈtɔːsəʊ/ *n.* (*pl.* **-os**) torse *m.*

tortoise /ˈtɔːtəs/ *n.* tortue *f.*

tortoiseshell /ˈtɔːtəsʃel/ *n.* (*for ornaments etc.*) écaille *f.*

tortuous /ˈtɔːtʃʊəs/ *a.* tortueux.

torture /ˈtɔːtʃə(r)/ *n.* torture *f.*, supplice *m.* ● *v.t.* torturer. ~**r** /-ə(r)/ *n.* tortionnaire *m.*

Tory /ˈtɔːrɪ/ *n.* tory *m.* ● *a.* tory (*f. invar.*).

toss /tɒs/ *v.t.* jeter, lancer; (*shake*) agiter. ● *v.i.* s'agiter. ~ **a coin,** ~ **up,** tirer à pile ou face (**for,** pour).

tot[1] /tɒt/ *n.* petit(e) enfant *m.(f.*; (*glass: fam.*) petit verre *m.*

tot[2] /tɒt/ *v.t.* (*p.t.* **totted**). ~ **up,** (*fam.*) additionner.

total /ˈtəʊtl/ *a.* total. ● *n.* total *m.* ● *v.t.* (*p.t.* **totalled**) (*find total of*) totaliser; (*amount to*) s'élever à. ~**ity** /-ˈtælətɪ/ *n.* totalité *f.* ~**ly** *adv.* totalement.

totalitarian /təʊtælɪˈteərɪən/ *a.* totalitaire.

totter /ˈtɒtə(r)/ *v.i.* chanceler.

touch /tʌtʃ/ *v.t./i.* toucher; (*of ends, gardens, etc.*) se toucher; (*tamper with*) toucher à. ● *n.* (*sense*) toucher *m.*; (*contact*) contact *m.*; (*of colour*) touche *f.*; (*football*) touche *f.* **a ~ of,** (*small amount*) un peu de. **get in ~ with,** contacter. **lose ~,** perdre contact. **be out of ~,** n'être plus dans le coup. ~**-and-go** *a.* douteux. ~ **down,** (*aviat.*) atterrir. ~**-line** *n.* (ligne de) touche *f.* ~ **off,** (*explode*) faire partir; (*cause*) déclencher. ~ **on,** (*mention*) aborder. ~ **up,** retoucher.

touchdown /ˈtʌtʃdaʊn/ *n.* atterrissage *m.*; (*sport, Amer.*) but *m.*

touching /ˈtʌtʃɪŋ/ *a.* touchant.

touchstone /ˈtʌtʃstəʊn/ *n.* pierre de touche *f.*

touchy /ˈtʌtʃɪ/ *a.* susceptible.

tough /tʌf/ *a.* (**-er, -est**) (*hard, difficult*) dur; (*strong*) solide; (*relentless*) acharné. ● *n.* ~ (**guy**), dur *m.* ~ **luck!,** (*fam.*) tant pis! ~**ness** *n.* dureté *f.*; solidité *f.*

toughen /ˈtʌfn/ *v.t.* (*strengthen*) renforcer; (*person*) endurcir.

toupee /ˈtuːpeɪ/ *n.* postiche *m.*

tour /tʊə(r)/ *n.* voyage *m.*; (*visit*) visite *f.*; (*by team etc.*) tournée *f.* ● *v.t.* visiter. **on ~,** en tournée. ~ **operator,** voyagiste *m.*

tourism /ˈtʊərɪzəm/ *n.* tourisme *m.*

tourist /ˈtʊərɪst/ *n.* touriste *m./f.* ● *a.* touristique. ~ **office,** syndicat d'initiative *m.*

tournament /ˈtɔːnəmənt/ *n.* (*sport & medieval*) tournoi *m.*

tousle /ˈtaʊzl/ *v.t.* ébouriffer.

tout /taʊt/ *v.i.* ~ (**for**), racoler. ● *v.t.* (*sell*) revendre. ● *n.* racoleu|r, -se *m., f.*; revendeu|r, -se *m., f.*

tow /təʊ/ *v.t.* remorquer. ● *n.* remorque *f.* **on ~,** en remorque. ~ **away,** (*vehicle*) (faire) enlever. ~**path** *n.* chemin de halage *m.* ~ **truck,** dépanneuse *f.*

toward(s) /təˈwɔːd(z), *Amer.* tɔːd(z)/ *prep.* vers; (*of attitude*) envers.

towel /ˈtaʊəl/ *n.* serviette *f.*; (*teatowel*) torchon *m.* ~**ling** *n.* tissuéponge *m.*

tower /ˈtaʊə(r)/ *n.* tour *f.* ● *v.i.* ~ **above,** dominer. ~ **block,** tour *f.*, immeuble *m.* ~**ing** *a.* très haut.

town /taʊn/ *n.* ville *f.* **go to ~,** (*fam.*) mettre le paquet. ~ **council,** conseil municipal *m.* ~ **hall,** hôtel de ville *m.*

toxic /ˈtɒksɪk/ *a.* toxique.

toxin /ˈtɒksɪn/ *n.* toxine *f.*

toy /tɔɪ/ *n.* jouet *m.* ● *v.i.* ~ **with,** (*object*) jouer avec; (*idea*) caresser.

toyshop /ˈtɔɪʃɒp/ *n.* magasin de jouets *m.*

trace /treɪs/ *n.* trace *f.* ● *v.t.* suivre *or* retrouver la trace de; (*draw*) tracer; (*with tracing-paper*) décalquer; (*relate*) retracer.

tracing /ˈtreɪsɪŋ/ *n.* calque *m.* ~**paper** *n.* papier-calque *m. invar.*

track /træk/ *n.* (*of person etc.*) trace *f.*, piste *f.*; (*path, race-track & of tape*) piste *f.*; (*on disc*) plage *f.*; (*of rocket etc.*) trajectoire *f.*; (*rail.*) voie *f.* ● *v.t.* suivre la trace *or* la trajectoire

de. **keep ~ of,** suivre. **~ down,**
(find) retrouver; (hunt) traquer. **~
suit,** survêtement m.; (with sweat-
shirt) jogging m.

tract [1] /trækt/ n. (land) étendue f.;
(anat.) appareil m.

tract [2] /trækt/ n. (pamphlet) tract m.

tractor /'træktə(r)/ n. tracteur m.

trade /treɪd/ n. commerce m.; (job)
métier m.; (swap) échange m. ● v.i.
faire du commerce. ● v.t. échanger.
~ deficit, déficit commercial m. **~
in,** (used article) faire reprendre. **~-
in** n. reprise f. **~ mark,** marque de
fabrique f.; (name) marque déposée
f. **~-off** n. (fam.) compromis m. **~
on,** (exploit) abuser de. **~ union,**
syndicat m. **~-unionist** n. syndica-
liste m./f. **~r** /-ə(r)/ n. négociant(e)
m. (f.), commerçant(e) m. (f.).

tradesman /'treɪdzmən/ n. (pl. -men)
commerçant m.

trading /'treɪdɪŋ/ n. commerce m. **~
estate,** zone industrielle f.

tradition /trə'dɪʃn/ n. tradition f.
~al a. traditionnel.

traffic /'træfɪk/ n. trafic m.; (on road)
circulation f. ● v.i. (p.t. **trafficked**)
trafiquer (**in,** de). **~ circle,** (Amer.)
rond-point m. **~ cone,** cône de
délimitation de voie m. **~ jam,**
embouteillage m. **~-lights** n. pl.
feux (de circulation) m. pl. **~ warden,** contractuel(le) m. (f.).

tragedy /'trædʒədɪ/ n. tragédie f.

tragic /'trædʒɪk/ a. tragique.

trail /treɪl/ v.t./i. traîner; (of plant)
ramper; (track) suivre. ● n. (of
powder etc.) traînée f.; (track) piste
f.; (beaten path) sentier m. **~ behind,** traîner.

trailer /'treɪlə(r)/ n. remorque f.;
(caravan: Amer.) caravane f.; (film)
bande-annonce f.

train /treɪn/ n. (rail.) train m.; (underground) rame f.; (procession) file
f.; (of dress) traîne f. ● v.t. (instruct,
develop) former; (sportsman) entraîner; (animal) dresser; (ear) exercer;
(aim) braquer. ● v.i. recevoir une
formation; s'entraîner. **~ed** a.
(skilled) qualifié; (doctor etc.)
diplômé. **~er** n. (sport) entraîneu|r,
-se m., f. **~ers,** (shoes) chaussures de
sport f. pl. **~ing** n. formation f.;
entraînement m.; dressage m.

trainee /treɪ'niː/ n. stagiaire m./f.

traipse /treɪps/ v.i. (fam.) traîner.

trait /treɪ(t)/ n. trait m.

traitor /'treɪtə(r)/ n. traître m.

tram /træm/ n. tram(way) m.

tramp /træmp/ v.i. marcher (d'un pas
lourd). ● v.t. parcourir. ● n. pas
lourds m. pl.; (vagrant) clochard(e)
m. (f.); (Amer., sl.) dévergondée f.;
(hike) randonnée f.

trample /'træmpl/ v.t./i. **~ (on),**
piétiner; (fig.) fouler aux pieds.

trampoline /'træmpəliːn/ n. (canvas
sheet) trampoline m.

trance /trɑːns/ n. transe f.

tranquil /'træŋkwɪl/ a. tranquille.
~lity /-'kwɪlətɪ/ n. tranquillité f.

tranquillizer /'træŋkwɪlaɪzə(r)/ n.
(drug) tranquillisant m.

transact /træn'zækt/ v.t. traiter.
~ion /-kʃn/ n. transaction f.

transatlantic /trænzət'læntɪk/ a.
transatlantique.

transcend /træn'send/ v.t.
transcender. **~ent** a. transcendant.

transcript /'trænskrɪpt/ n. (written
copy) transcription f.

transfer [1] /træns'fɜː(r)/ v.t. (p.t.
transferred) transférer; (power)
faire passer. ● v.i. être transféré.
~ the charges, (telephone) téléphoner en PCV.

transfer [2] /'trænsfɜː(r)/ n. transfert
m.; (of power) passation f.; (image)
décalcomanie f.; (sticker) autocollant m.

transform /træns'fɔːm/ v.t.
transformer. **~ation** /-ə'meɪʃn/ n.
transformation f. **~er** n. (electr.)
transformateur m.

transfusion /træns'fjuːʒn/ n. (of
blood) transfusion f.

transient /'trænzɪənt/ a. transitoire,
éphémère.

transistor /træn'zɪstə(r)/ n. (device,
radio set) transistor m.

transit /'trænsɪt/ n. transit m.

transition /træn'zɪʃn/ n. transition f.
~al a. transitoire.

transitive /'trænsətɪv/ a. transitif.

transitory /'trænsɪtərɪ/ a. transitoire.

translat|e /trænz'leɪt/ v.t. traduire.
~ion /-ʃn/ n. traduction f. **~or** n.
traduc|teur, -trice m., f.

translucent /trænz'luːsnt/ a. translucide.

transmi|t /trænz'mɪt/ v.t. (p.t. **trans-
mitted**) (pass on etc.) transmettre;
(broadcast) émettre. **~ssion** n.
transmission f.; émission f. **~tter**
n. émetteur m.

transparen|t /træns'pærənt/ *a.* transparent. **~cy** *n.* transparence *f.*; (*photo.*) diapositive *f.*

transpire /træn'spaɪə(r)/ *v.i.* s'avérer; (*happen: fam.*) arriver.

transplant¹ /træns'plɑːnt/ *v.t.* transplanter; (*med.*) greffer.

transplant² /'trænsplɑːnt/ *n.* transplantation *f.*; greffe *f.*

transport¹ /træn'spɔːt/ *v.t.* (*carry, delight*) transporter. **~ation** /-'teɪʃn/ *n.* transport *m.*

transport² /'trænspɔːt/ *n.* (*of goods, delight, etc.*) transport *m.*

transpose /træn'spəʊz/ *v.t.* transposer.

transverse /'trænzvɜːs/ *a.* transversal.

transvestite /trænz'vestaɪt/ *n.* travesti(e) *m.* (*f.*).

trap /træp/ *n.* piège *m.* ● *v.t.* (*p.t.* **trapped**) (*jam, pin down*) coincer; (*cut off*) bloquer; (*snare*) prendre au piège. **~per** *n.* trappeur *m.*

trapdoor /træp'dɔː(r)/ *n.* trappe *f.*

trapeze /trə'piːz/ *n.* trapèze *m.*

trappings /'træpɪŋz/ *n. pl.* (*fig.*) signes extérieurs *m. pl.*, apparat *m.*

trash /træʃ/ *n.* (*junk*) saleté(s) *f.* (*pl.*); (*refuse*) ordures *f. pl.*; (*nonsense*) idioties *f. pl.* **~can** *n.* (*Amer.*) poubelle *f.* **~y** *a.* qui ne vaut rien, de mauvaise qualité.

trauma /'trɔːmə/ *n.* traumatisme *m.* **~tic** /-'mætɪk/ *a.* traumatisant.

travel /'trævl/ *v.i.* (*p.t.* **travelled,** *Amer.* **traveled**) voyager; (*of vehicle, bullet, etc.*) aller. ● *v.t.* parcourir. ● *n.* voyage(s) *m.* (*pl.*). **~ agent,** agent de voyage *m.* **~ler** *n.* voyageu|r, -se *m., f.* **~ler's cheque,** chèque de voyage *m.* **~ling** *n.* voyage(s) *m.* (*pl.*). **~ sickness,** mal des transports *m.*

travesty /'trævəstɪ/ *n.* parodie *f.*, simulacre *m.* ● *v.t.* travestir.

trawler /'trɔːlə(r)/ *n.* chalutier *m.*

tray /treɪ/ *n.* plateau *m.*; (*on office desk*) corbeille *f.*

treacherous /'tretʃərəs/ *a.* traître. **~ly** *adv.* traîtreusement.

treachery /'tretʃərɪ/ *n.* traîtrise *f.*

treacle /'triːkl/ *n.* mélasse *f.*

tread /tred/ *v.i.* (*p.t.* **trod,** *p.p.* **trodden**) marcher (**on,** sur). ● *v.t.* parcourir (à pied); (*soil: fig.*) fouler. ● *n.* démarche *f.*; (*sound*) (bruit *m.* de) pas *m. pl.*; (*of tyre*) chape *f.* **~**

sth. **into,** (*carpet*) étaler qch. sur (avec les pieds).

treason /'triːzn/ *n.* trahison *f.*

treasure /'treʒə(r)/ *n.* trésor *m.* ● *v.t.* attacher une grande valeur à; (*store*) conserver. **~r** /-ə(r)/ *n.* trésor|ier, -ière *m., f.*

treasury /'treʒərɪ/ *n.* trésorerie *f.* **the T~,** le ministère des Finances.

treat /triːt/ *v.t.* traiter; (*consider*) considérer. ● *n.* (*pleasure*) plaisir *m.*, régal *m.*; (*present*) gâterie *f.*; (*food*) régal *m.* **~ s.o. to sth.,** offrir qch. à qn.

treatise /'triːtɪz/ *n.* traité *m.*

treatment /'triːtmənt/ *n.* traitement *m.*

treaty /'triːtɪ/ *n.* (*pact*) traité *m.*

treble /'trebl/ *a.* triple. ● *v.t./i.* tripler. ● *n.* (*voice: mus.*) soprano *m.* **~e clef,** clé de sol *f.* **~y** *adv.* triplement.

tree /triː/ *n.* arbre *m.* **~-top** *n.* cime (d'un arbre) *f.*

trek /trek/ *n.* voyage pénible *m.*; (*sport*) randonnée *f.* ● *v.i.* (*p.t.* **trekked**) voyager (péniblement); (*sport*) faire de la randonnée.

trellis /'trelɪs/ *n.* treillage *m.*

tremble /'trembl/ *v.i.* trembler.

tremendous /trɪ'mendəs/ *a.* énorme; (*excellent: fam.*) fantastique. **~ly** *adv.* fantastiquement.

tremor /'tremə(r)/ *n.* tremblement *m.* (**earth**) **~,** secousse (sismique) *f.*

trench /trentʃ/ *n.* tranchée *f.*

trend /trend/ *n.* tendance *f.*; (*fashion*) mode *f.* **~-setter** *n.* lanceu|r, -se de mode *m., f.* **~y** *a.* (*fam.*) dans le vent.

trepidation /trepɪ'deɪʃn/ *n.* (*fear*) inquiétude *f.*

trespass /'trespəs/ *v.i.* s'introduire sans autorisation (**on,** dans). **~er** *n.* intrus(e) *m.* (*f.*).

tresses /'tresɪz/ *n. pl.* chevelure *f.*

trestle /'tresl/ *n.* tréteau *m.* **~-table** *n.* table à tréteaux *f.*

tri- /traɪ/ *pref.* tri-.

trial /'traɪəl/ *n.* (*jurid.*) procès *m.*; (*test*) essai *m.*; (*ordeal*) épreuve *f.* **go on ~,** passer en jugement. **~ and error,** tâtonnements *m. pl.* **~ run,** galop d'essai *m.*

triang|le /'traɪæŋgl/ *n.* triangle *m.* **~ular** /-'æŋgjʊlə(r)/ *a.* triangulaire.

trib|e /traɪb/ *n.* tribu *f.* **~al** *a.* tribal.

tribulation /trɪbjʊ'leɪʃn/ *n.* tribulation *f.*

tribunal /traɪˈbjuːnl/ n. tribunal m.; (mil.) commission f.

tributary /ˈtrɪbjʊtəri/ n. affluent m.

tribute /ˈtrɪbjuːt/ n. tribut m. **pay ~ to,** rendre hommage à.

trick /trɪk/ n. astuce f., ruse f.; (joke, feat of skill) tour m.; (habit) manie f. ● v.t. tromper. **do the ~,** (fam.) faire l'affaire.

trickery /ˈtrɪkəri/ n. ruse f.

trickle /ˈtrɪkl/ v.i. dégouliner. **~ in/ out,** arriver or partir en petit nombre. ● n. filet m.; (fig.) petit nombre m.

tricky /ˈtrɪkɪ/ a. (crafty) rusé; (problem) délicat, difficile.

tricycle /ˈtraɪsɪkl/ n. tricycle m.

trifle /ˈtraɪfl/ n. bagatelle f.; (cake) diplomate m. ● v.i. **~ with,** jouer avec. **a ~,** (small amount) un peu.

trifling /ˈtraɪflɪŋ/ a. insignifiant.

trigger /ˈtrɪgə(r)/ n. (of gun) gâchette f., détente f. ● v.t. **~ (off),** (initiate) déclencher.

trilby /ˈtrɪlbɪ/ n. (hat) feutre m.

trim /trɪm/ a. (**trimmer, trimmest**) net, soigné; (figure) svelte. ● v.t. (p.t. **trimmed**) (cut) couper légèrement; (hair) rafraîchir; (budget) réduire. ● n. (cut) coupe légère f.; (decoration) garniture f. **in ~,** en bon ordre; (fit) en forme. **~ with,** (decorate) orner de. **~ming(s)** n. (pl.) garniture(s) f. (pl.).

Trinity /ˈtrɪnətɪ/ n. Trinité f.

trinket /ˈtrɪŋkɪt/ n. colifichet m.

trio /ˈtriːəʊ/ n. (pl. -os) trio m.

trip /trɪp/ v.t./i. (p.t. **tripped**) (faire) trébucher; (go lightly) marcher d'un pas léger. ● n. (journey) voyage m.; (outing) excursion f.; (stumble) faux pas m.

tripe /traɪp/ n. (food) tripes f. pl.; (nonsense: sl.) bêtises f. pl.

triple /ˈtrɪpl/ a. triple. ● v.t./i. tripler. **~ts** /-plɪts/ n. pl. triplé(e)s m. (f.) pl.

tripod /ˈtraɪpɒd/ n. trépied m.

trite /traɪt/ a. banal.

triumph /ˈtraɪəmf/ n. triomphe m. ● v.i. triompher (**over,** de). **~al** /-ˈʌmfl/ a. triomphal. **~ant** /-ˈʌmfənt/ a. triomphant, triomphal. **~antly** /-ˈʌmfəntlɪ/ adv. en triomphe.

trivial /ˈtrɪvɪəl/ a. insignifiant. **~ize** v.t. considérer comme insignifiant.

trod, trodden /trɒd, ˈtrɒdn/ see tread.

trolley /ˈtrɒlɪ/ n. chariot m. (**tea-)~,** table roulante f. **~-bus** n. trolleybus m.

trombone /trɒmˈbəʊn/ n. (mus.) trombone m.

troop /truːp/ n. bande f. **~s,** (mil.) troupes f. pl. ● v.i. **~ in/out,** entrer/sortir en bande. **~er** n. soldat de cavalerie m. **~ing the colour,** le salut au drapeau.

trophy /ˈtrəʊfɪ/ n. trophée m.

tropic /ˈtrɒpɪk/ n. tropique m. **~s,** tropiques m. pl. **~al** a. tropical.

trot /trɒt/ n. trot m. ● v.i. (p.t. **trotted**) trotter. **on the ~,** (fam.) de suite. **~ out,** (produce: fam.) sortir; (state: fam.) formuler.

trouble /ˈtrʌbl/ n. ennui(s) m. (pl.), difficulté(s) f. (pl.); (pains, effort) mal m., peine f. **~(s),** ennuis m. pl.; (unrest) conflits m. pl. ● v.t./i. (bother) (se) déranger; (worry) ennuyer. **be in ~,** avoir des ennuis. **go to a lot of ~,** se donner du mal. **what's the ~?,** quel est le problème? **~d** a. inquiet; (period) agité. **~-maker** n. provoca|teur, -trice m., f. **~-shooter** n. personne appelée pour désamorcer une crise.

troublesome /ˈtrʌblsəm/ a. ennuyeux, pénible.

trough /trɒf/ n. (drinking) abreuvoir m.; (feeding) auge f. **~ (of low pressure),** dépression f.

trounce /traʊns/ v.t. (defeat) écraser; (thrash) rosser.

troupe /truːp/ n. (theatre) troupe f.

trousers /ˈtraʊzəz/ n. pl. pantalon m. **short ~,** culotte courte f.

trousseau /ˈtruːsəʊ/ n. (pl. -s /-əʊz/) (of bride) trousseau m.

trout /traʊt/ n. invar. truite f.

trowel /ˈtraʊəl/ n. (garden) déplantoir m.; (for mortar) truelle f.

truan|t /ˈtruːənt/ n. absentéiste m./f.; (schol.) élève absent(e) sans permission m.(f.). **play ~t,** sécher les cours. **~cy** n. absentéisme m.

truce /truːs/ n. trêve f.

truck /trʌk/ n. (lorry) camion m.; (cart) chariot m.; (rail.) wagon m., plateforme f. **~-driver** n. camionneur m.

truculent /ˈtrʌkjʊlənt/ a. agressif.

trudge /trʌdʒ/ v.i. marcher péniblement, se traîner.

true /truː/ a. (-er, -est) vrai; (accurate) exact; (faithful) fidèle.

truffle /ˈtrʌfl/ n. truffe f.

truly /'tru:lɪ/ adv. vraiment; (faith-fully) fidèlement; (truthfully) sin-cèrement.

trump /trʌmp/ n. atout m. ● v.t. ~ up, inventer. ~ card, atout m.

trumpet /'trʌmpɪt/ n. trompette f.

truncate /trʌŋ'keɪt/ v.t. tronquer.

trundle /'trʌndl/ v.t./i. rouler bruyamment.

trunk /trʌŋk/ n. (of tree, body) tronc m.; (of elephant) trompe f.; (box) malle f.; (auto., Amer.) coffre m. ~s, (for swimming) slip de bain m. ~-call n. communication interurbaine f. ~-road n. route nationale f.

truss /trʌs/ n. (med.) bandage her-niaire m. ● v.t. (fowl) trousser.

trust /trʌst/ n. confiance f.; (associa-tion) trust m. ● v.t. avoir confiance en. ● v.i. ~ in or to, s'en remettre à. in ~, en dépôt. ~ s.o. with, confier à qn. ~ed a. (friend etc.) éprouvé, sûr. ~ful, ~ing adjs. confiant. ~y a. fidèle.

trustee /trʌs'ti:/ n. administra|teur, -trice m., f.

trustworthy /'trʌstwɜ:ðɪ/ a. digne de confiance.

truth /tru:θ/ n. (pl. -s /tru:ðz/) vérité f. ~ful a. (account etc.) véridique; (person) qui dit la vérité. ~fully adv. sincèrement.

try /traɪ/ v.t./i. (p.t. tried) essayer; (be a strain on) éprouver; (jurid.) juger. ● n. (attempt) essai m.; (Rugby) essai m. ~ on or out, essayer. ~ to do, essayer de faire. ~ing a. éprouvant.

tsar /zɑ:(r)/ n. tsar m.

T-shirt /'ti:ʃɜ:t/ n. tee-shirt m.

tub /tʌb/ n. baquet m., cuve f.; (bath: fam.) baignoire f.

tuba /'tju:bə/ n. tuba m.

tubby /'tʌbɪ/ a. (-ier, -iest) dodu.

tub|e /tju:b/ n. tube m.; (railway: fam.) métro m.; (in tyre) chambre à air f. ~ing n. tubes m. pl.

tuberculosis /tju:bɜ:kjʊ'ləʊsɪs/ n. tu-berculose f.

tubular /'tju:bjʊlə(r)/ a. tubulaire.

tuck /tʌk/ n. (fold) rempli m., (re)pli m. ● v.t. (put away, place) ranger; (hide) cacher. ● v.i. ~ in or into, (eat: sl.) attaquer. ~ in, (shirt) rentrer; (blanket, person) border. ~-shop n. (schol.) boutique à provi-sions f.

Tuesday /'tju:zdɪ/ n. mardi m.

tuft /tʌft/ n. (of hair etc.) touffe f.

tug /tʌg/ v.t. (p.t. tugged) tirer fort (sur). ● v.i. tirer fort. ● n. (boat) remorqueur m. ~ of war, jeu de la corde tirée m.

tuition /tju:'ɪʃn/ n. cours m. pl.; (fee) frais de scolarité m. pl.

tulip /'tju:lɪp/ n. tulipe f.

tumble /'tʌmbl/ v.i. (fall) dé-gringoler. ● n. chute f. ~-drier n. séchoir à linge (à air chaud) m. ~ to, (realize: fam.) piger.

tumbledown /'tʌmbldaʊn/ a. déla-bré, en ruine.

tumbler /'tʌmblə(r)/ n. gobelet m.

tummy /'tʌmɪ/ n. (fam.) ventre m.

tumour /'tju:mə(r)/ n. tumeur f.

tumult /'tju:mʌlt/ n. tumulte m. ~uous /-'mʌltʃʊəs/ a. tumultueux.

tuna /'tju:nə/ n. invar. thon m.

tune /tju:n/ n. air m. ● v.t. (engine) régler; (mus.) accorder. ● v.i. ~ in (to), (radio, TV) écouter. be in ~/out of ~, (instrument) être ac-cordé/désaccordé; (singer) chanter juste/faux. ~ful a. mélodieux. tun-ing-fork n. diapason m. ~ up, (orchestra) accorder leurs instru-ments.

tunic /'tju:nɪk/ n. tunique f.

Tunisia /tju:'nɪzɪə/ n. Tunisie f. ~n a. & n. tunisien(ne) (m. (f.)).

tunnel /'tʌnl/ n. tunnel m.; (in mine) galerie f. ● v.i. (p.t. tunnelled) creuser un tunnel (into, dans).

turban /'tɜ:bən/ n. turban m.

turbine /'tɜ:baɪn/ n. turbine f.

turbo /'tɜ:bəʊ/ n. turbo m.

turbulen|t /'tɜ:bjʊlənt/ a. turbulent. ~ce n. turbulence f.

tureen /tjʊ'ri:n/ n. soupière f.

turf /tɜ:f/ n. (pl. turf or turves) gazon m. ● v.t. ~ out, (sl.) jeter dehors. the ~, (racing) le turf.

turgid /'tɜ:dʒɪd/ a. (speech, style) boursouflé, ampoulé.

Turk /tɜ:k/ n. Turc m., Turque f. ~ey n. Turquie f. ~ish a. turc; n. (lang.) turc m.

turkey /'tɜ:kɪ/ n. dindon m., dinde f.; (as food) dinde f.

turmoil /'tɜ:mɔɪl/ n. trouble m., chaos m. in ~, en ébullition.

turn /tɜ:n/ v.t./i. tourner; (of person) se tourner; (to other side) retourner; (change) (se) transformer (into, en); (become) devenir; (deflect) détour-ner; (milk) tourner. ● n. tour m.; (in road) tournant m.; (of mind, *events*) tournure *f.*; (*illness: fam.*) crise *f.* **do a good ~**, rendre service. **in ~**, à tour de rôle. **speak out of ~**, commettre une indiscrétion. **take ~s**, se relayer. **~ against**, se retourner contre. **~ away** *v.i.* se détourner; *v.t.* (*avert*) détourner; (*refuse*) refuser; (*send back*) renvoyer. **~ back** *v.i.* (*return*) retourner; (*vehicle*) faire demi-tour; *v.t.* (*fold*) rabattre. **~ down**, refuser; (*fold*) rabattre; (*reduce*) baisser. **~ in**, (*go to bed: fam.*) se coucher. **~ off**, (*light etc.*) éteindre; (*engine*) arrêter; (*tap*) fermer; (*of driver*) tourner. **~-off** *n.* (*auto.*) embranchement *m.* **~ on**, (*light etc.*) allumer; (*engine*) allumer; (*tap*) ouvrir. **~ out** *v.t.* (*light*) éteindre; (*empty*) vider; (*produce*) produire; *v.i.* (*transpire*) s'avérer; (*come: fam.*) venir. **~-out** *n.* assistance *f.* **~ over**, (se) retourner. **~ round** *n.* revirement *m.* **~ up** *v.i.* arriver; (*be found*) se retrouver; *v.t.* (*find*) déterrer; (*collar*) remonter. **~-up** *n.* (*of trousers*) revers *m.*

turning /'tɜːnɪŋ/ *n.* rue (latérale) *f.*; (*bend*) tournant *m.* **~-point** *n.* tournant *m.*

turnip /'tɜːnɪp/ *n.* navet *m.*

turnover /'tɜːnəʊvə(r)/ *n.* (*pie, tart*) chausson *m.*; (*money*) chiffre d'affaires *m.*

turnpike /'tɜːnpaɪk/ *n.* (*Amer.*) autoroute à péage *f.*

turnstile /'tɜːnstaɪl/ *n.* (*gate*) tourniquet *m.*

turntable /'tɜːnteɪbl/ *n.* (*for record*) platine *f.*, plateau *m.*

turpentine /'tɜːpəntaɪn/ *n.* térébenthine *f.*

turquoise /'tɜːkwɔɪz/ *a.* turquoise *invar.*

turret /'tʌrɪt/ *n.* tourelle *f.*

turtle /'tɜːtl/ *n.* tortue (de mer) *f.* **~-neck** *a.* à col montant, roulé.

tusk /tʌsk/ *n.* (*tooth*) défense *f.*

tussle /'tʌsl/ *n.* bagarre *f.*, lutte *f.*

tutor /'tjuːtə(r)/ *n.* précep|teur, -trice *m.*, *f.*; (*univ.*) direc|teur, -trice d'études *m.*, *f.*

tutorial /tjuː'tɔːrɪəl/ *n.* (*univ.*) séance d'études *or* de travaux pratiques *f.*

tuxedo /tak'siːdəʊ/ *n.* (*pl.* -os) (*Amer.*) smoking *m.*

TV /tiː'viː/ *n.* télé *f.*

twaddle /'twɒdl/ *n.* fadaises *f. pl.*

twang /twæŋ/ *n.* (*son: mus.*) pincement *m.*; (*in voice*) nasillement *m.* ● *v.t./i.* (faire) vibrer.

tweed /twiːd/ *n.* tweed *m.*

tweezers /'twiːzəz/ *n. pl.* pince (à épiler) *f.*

twel|ve /twelv/ *a. & n.* douze (*m.*). **~fth** *a. & n.* douzième (*m./f.*). **~ve (o'clock)**, midi *m. or* minuit *m.*

twent|y /'twentɪ/ *a. & n.* vingt (*m.*). **~ieth** *a. & n.* vingtième (*m./f.*).

twice /twaɪs/ *adv.* deux fois.

twiddle /'twɪdl/ *v.t./i.* **~ (with)**, (*fiddle with*) tripoter. **~ one's thumbs**, se tourner les pouces.

twig[1] /twɪg/ *n.* brindille *f.*

twig[2] /twɪg/ *v.t./i.* (*p.t.* **twigged**) (*understand: fam.*) piger.

twilight /'twaɪlaɪt/ *n.* crépuscule *m.* ● *a.* crépusculaire.

twin /twɪn/ *n. & a.* jum|eau, -elle (*m.*, *f.*). ● *v.t.* (*p.t.* **twinned**) jumeler. **~ning** *n.* jumelage *m.*

twine /twaɪn/ *n.* ficelle *f.* ● *v.t./i.* (*wind*) (s')enlacer.

twinge /twɪndʒ/ *n.* élancement *m.*; (*remorse*) remords *m.*

twinkle /'twɪŋkl/ *v.i.* (*star etc.*) scintiller; (*eye*) pétiller. ● *n.* scintillement *m.*; pétillement *m.*

twirl /twɜːl/ *v.t./i.* (faire) tournoyer.

twist /twɪst/ *v.t.* tordre; (*weave together*) entortiller; (*roll*) enrouler; (*distort*) déformer. ● *v.i.* (*rope etc.*) s'entortiller; (*road*) zigzaguer. ● *n.* torsion *f.*; (*in rope*) tortillon *m.*; (*in road*) tournant *m.*; (*of events*) tournure *f.*, tour *m.*

twit /twɪt/ *n.* (*fam.*) idiot(e) *m.* (*f.*).

twitch /twɪtʃ/ *v.t./i.* (se) contracter nerveusement. ● *n.* (*tic*) tic *m.*; (*jerk*) secousse *f.*

two /tuː/ *a. & n.* deux (*m.*). **in *or* of ~ minds**, indécis. **put ~ and two together**, faire le rapport. **~-faced** *a.* hypocrite. **~fold** *a.* double; *adv.* au double. **~-piece** *n.* (*garment*) deux-pièces *m. invar.*

twosome /'tuːsəm/ *n.* couple *m.*

tycoon /taɪ'kuːn/ *n.* magnat *m.*

tying /'taɪɪŋ/ *see* tie.

type /taɪp/ *n.* (*example*) type *m.*; (*kind*) genre *m.*, sorte *f.*; (*person: fam.*) type *m.*; (*print*) caractères *m. pl.* ● *v.t./i.* (*write*) taper (à la machine). **~-cast** *a.* catégorisé (**as**, comme).

typescript /'taɪpskrɪpt/ *n.* manuscrit dactylographié *m.*

typewrit|er /'taɪpraɪtə(r)/ *n.* machine à écrire *f.* **~ten** /-rtn/ *a.* dactylographié.

typhoid /'taɪfɔɪd/ *n.* ~ **(fever),** typhoïde *f.*

typhoon /taɪ'fuːn/ *n.* typhon *m.*

typical /'tɪpɪkl/ *a.* typique. **~ly** *adv.* typiquement.

typify /'tɪpɪfaɪ/ *v.t.* être typique de.

typing /'taɪpɪŋ/ *n.* dactylo(graphie) *f.*

typist /'taɪpɪst/ *n.* dactylo *f.*

tyrann|y /'tɪrənɪ/ *n.* tyrannie *f.* **~ical** /tɪ'rænɪkl/ *a.* tyrannique.

tyrant /'taɪərənt/ *n.* tyran *m.*

tyre /'taɪə(r)/ *n.* pneu *m.*

U

ubiquitous /juː'bɪkwɪtəs/ *a.* omniprésent, qu'on trouve partout.

udder /'ʌdə(r)/ *n.* pis *m.*, mamelle *f.*

UFO /'juːfəʊ/ *n.* (*pl.* **-Os**) OVNI *m.*

Uganda /juː'gændə/ *n.* Ouganda *m.*

ugl|y /'ʌglɪ/ *a.* (**-ier, -iest**) laid. **~iness** *n.* laideur *f.*

UK *abbr.* *see* United Kingdom.

ulcer /'ʌlsə(r)/ *n.* ulcère *m.*

ulterior /ʌl'tɪərɪə(r)/ *a.* ultérieur. ~ **motive,** arrière-pensée *f.*

ultimate /'ʌltɪmət/ *a.* dernier, ultime; (*definitive*) définitif; (*basic*) fondamental. **~ly** *adv.* à la fin; (*in the last analysis*) en fin de compte.

ultimatum /ʌltɪ'meɪtəm/ *n.* (*pl.* **-ums**) ultimatum *m.*

ultra- /'ʌltrə/ *pref.* ultra-.

ultrasound /'ʌltrəsaʊnd/ *n.* ultrason *m.*

ultraviolet /ʌltrə'vaɪələt/ *a.* ultraviolet.

umbilical /ʌm'bɪlɪkl/ *a.* ~ **cord,** cordon ombilical *m.*

umbrella /ʌm'brelə/ *n.* parapluie *m.*

umpire /'ʌmpaɪə(r)/ *n.* (*sport*) arbitre *m.* ● *v.t.* arbitrer.

umpteen /'ʌmptiːn/ *a.* (*many: sl.*) un tas de. **~th** *a.* (*fam.*) énième.

UN *abbr.* (*United Nations*) ONU *f.*

un- /ʌn/ *pref.* in-, dé(s)-, non, peu, mal, sans.

unabated /ʌnə'beɪtɪd/ *a.* non diminué, aussi fort qu'avant.

unable /ʌn'eɪbl/ *a.* incapable; (*through circumstances*) dans l'impossibilité (**to do,** de faire).

unacceptable /ʌnək'septəbl/ *a.* inacceptable, inadmissible.

unaccountabl|e /ʌnə'kaʊntəbl/ *a.* (*strange*) inexplicable. **~y** *adv.* inexplicablement.

unaccustomed /ʌnə'kʌstəmd/ *a.* inaccoutumé. ~ **to,** peu habitué à.

unadulterated /ʌnə'dʌltəreɪtɪd/ *a.* (*pure, sheer*) pur.

unaided /ʌn'eɪdɪd/ *a.* sans aide.

unanim|ous /juː'nænɪməs/ *a.* unanime. **~ity** /-ə'nɪmətɪ/ *n.* unanimité *f.* **~ously** *adv.* à l'unanimité.

unarmed /ʌn'ɑːmd/ *a.* non armé.

unashamed /ʌnə'ʃeɪmd/ *a.* éhonté. **~ly** /-ɪdlɪ/ *adv.* sans vergogne.

unassuming /ʌnə'sjuːmɪŋ/ *a.* modeste, sans prétention.

unattached /ʌnə'tætʃt/ *a.* libre.

unattainable /ʌnə'teɪnəbl/ *a.* inaccessible.

unattended /ʌnə'tendɪd/ *a.* (laissé) sans surveillance.

unattractive /ʌnə'træktɪv/ *a.* peu séduisant, laid; (*offer*) peu intéressant.

unauthorized /ʌn'ɔːθəraɪzd/ *a.* non autorisé.

unavailable /ʌnə'veɪləbl/ *a.* pas disponible.

unavoidabl|e /ʌnə'vɔɪdəbl/ *a.* inévitable. **~y** *adv.* inévitablement.

unaware /ʌnə'weə(r)/ *a.* be ~ **of,** ignorer. **~s** /-eəz/ *adv.* au dépourvu.

unbalanced /ʌn'bælənst/ *a.* (*mind, person*) déséquilibré.

unbearable /ʌn'beərəbl/ *a.* insupportable.

unbeat|able /ʌn'biːtəbl/ *a.* imbattable. **~en** *a.* non battu.

unbeknown(st) /ʌnbɪ'nəʊn(st)/ *a.* **~(st) to,** (*fam.*) à l'insu de.

unbelievable /ʌnbɪ'liːvəbl/ *a.* incroyable.

unbend /ʌn'bend/ *v.i.* (*p.t.* **unbent**) (*relax*) se détendre.

unbiased /ʌn'baɪəst/ *a.* impartial.

unblock /ʌn'blɒk/ *v.t.* déboucher.

unborn /ʌn'bɔːn/ *a.* futur, à venir.

unbounded /ʌn'baʊndɪd/ *a.* illimité.

unbreakable /ʌn'breɪkəbl/ *a.* incassable.

unbridled /ʌn'braɪdld/ *a.* débridé.

unbroken /ʌn'brəʊkən/ *a.* (*intact*) intact; (*continuous*) continu.

unburden /ʌn'bɜːdn/ *v. pr.* ~ **o.s.,** (*open one's heart*) s'épancher.

unbutton /ʌn'bʌtn/ *v.t.* déboutonner.

uncalled-for /ʌnˈkɔːldfɔː(r)/ a. injustifié, superflu.

uncanny /ʌnˈkænɪ/ a. (**-ier, -iest**) étrange, mystérieux.

unceasing /ʌnˈsiːsɪŋ/ a. incessant.

unceremonious /ʌnserɪˈməʊnɪəs/ a. sans façon, brusque.

uncertain /ʌnˈsɜːtn/ a. incertain. **be ~ whether**, ne pas savoir exactement si (**to do**, on doit faire). **~ty** n. incertitude f.

unchang|ed /ʌnˈtʃeɪndʒd/ a. inchangé. **~ing** a. immuable.

uncivilized /ʌnˈsɪvɪlaɪzd/ a. barbare.

uncle /ˈʌŋkl/ n. oncle m.

uncomfortable /ʌnˈkʌmftəbl/ a. (*thing*) peu confortable; (*unpleasant*) désagréable. **feel** *or* **be ~**, (*person*) être mal à l'aise.

uncommon /ʌnˈkɒmən/ a. rare. **~ly** adv. remarquablement.

uncompromising /ʌnˈkɒmprəmaɪzɪŋ/ a. intransigeant.

unconcerned /ʌnkənˈsɜːnd/ a. (*indifferent*) indifférent (**by**, à).

unconditional /ʌnkənˈdɪʃənl/ a. inconditionnel.

unconscious /ʌnˈkɒnʃəs/ a. sans connaissance, inanimé; (*not aware*) inconscient (**of**, de) ● n. inconscient m. **~ly** adv. inconsciemment.

unconventional /ʌnkənˈvenʃənl/ a. peu conventionnel.

uncooperative /ʌnkəʊˈɒpərətɪv/ a. peu coopératif.

uncork /ʌnˈkɔːk/ v.t. déboucher.

uncouth /ʌnˈkuːθ/ a. grossier.

uncover /ʌnˈkʌvə(r)/ v.t. découvrir.

undecided /ʌndɪˈsaɪdɪd/ a. indécis.

undefinable /ʌndɪˈfaɪnəbl/ a. indéfinissable.

undeniable /ʌndɪˈnaɪəbl/ a. indéniable, incontestable.

under /ˈʌndə(r)/ prep. sous; (*less than*) moins de; (*according to*) selon. ● adv. au-dessous. **~ age**, mineur. **~ it/there**, là-dessous. **~side** n. dessous m. **~ way**, (*in progress*) en cours; (*on the way*) en route.

under- /ˈʌndə(r)/ pref. sous-.

undercarriage /ˈʌndəkærɪdʒ/ n. (*aviat.*) train d'atterrissage m.

underclothes /ˈʌndəkləʊðz/ n. pl. sous-vêtements m. pl.

undercoat /ˈʌndəkəʊt/ n. (*of paint*) couche de fond f.

undercover /ʌndəˈkʌvə(r)/ (*agent, operation*) a. secret.

undercurrent /ˈʌndəkʌrənt/ n. courant (profond) m.

undercut /ʌndəˈkʌt/ v.t. (p.t. **undercut**, pres. p. **undercutting**) (*comm.*) vendre moins cher que.

underdeveloped /ʌndədɪˈveləpt/ a. sous-développé.

underdog /ˈʌndədɒg/ n. (*pol.*) opprimé(e) m. (f.); (*socially*) déshérité(e) m. (f.).

underdone /ʌndədʌn/ a. pas assez cuit; (*steak*) saignant.

underestimate /ʌndərˈestɪmeɪt/ v.t. sous-estimer.

underfed /ʌndəˈfed/ a. sous-alimenté.

underfoot /ʌndəˈfʊt/ adv. sous les pieds.

undergo /ʌndəˈgəʊ/ v.t. (p.t. **-went**, pp. **-gone**) subir.

undergraduate /ʌndəˈgrædʒʊət/ n. étudiant(e) (qui prépare la licence) m. (f.).

underground¹ /ʌndəˈgraʊnd/ adv. sous terre.

underground² /ˈʌndəgraʊnd/ a. souterrain; (*secret*) clandestin. ● n. (*rail.*) métro m.

undergrowth /ˈʌndəgrəʊθ/ n. sous-bois m. invar.

underhand /ˈʌndəhænd/ a. (*deceitful*) sournois.

under|lie /ʌndəˈlaɪ/ v.t. (p.t. **-lay**, p.p. **-lain**, pres. p. **-lying**) sous-tendre. **~lying** a. fondamental.

underline /ʌndəˈlaɪn/ v.t. souligner.

undermine /ʌndəˈmaɪn/ v.t. (*cliff, society, etc.*) miner, saper.

underneath /ʌndəˈniːθ/ prep. sous. ● adv. (en) dessous.

underpaid /ʌndəˈpeɪd/ a. sous-payé.

underpants /ˈʌndəpænts/ n. pl. (*man's*) slip m.

underpass /ˈʌndəpɑːs/ n. (*for cars, people*) passage souterrain m.

underprivileged /ʌndəˈprɪvəlɪdʒd/ a. défavorisé.

underrate /ʌndəˈreɪt/ v.t. sous-estimer.

undershirt /ˈʌndəʃɜːt/ n. (*Amer.*) maillot (de corps) m.

undershorts /ˈʌndəʃɔːts/ n. pl. (*Amer.*) caleçon m.

underskirt /ˈʌndəskɜːt/ n. jupon m.

understand /ʌndəˈstænd/ v.t./i. (p.t. **-stood**) comprendre. **~able** a. compréhensible. **~ing** a. compréhensif; n. compréhension f.; (*agreement*) entente f.

understatement /'ʌndəsteɪtmənt/ *n.*
litote *f.* **that's an ~,** c'est en deçà de
la vérité.

understudy /'ʌndəstʌdɪ/ *n.* (*theatre*)
doublure *f.*

undertak|e /ʌndə'teɪk/ *v.t.* (*p.t.*
-took, *p.p.* **-taken**) entreprendre;
(*responsibility*) assumer. **~e to,**
s'engager à. **~ing** *n.* (*task*) entreprise *f.;* (*promise*) promesse *f.*

undertaker /'ʌndəteɪkə(r)/ *n.* entrepreneur de pompes funèbres *m.*

undertone /'ʌndətəʊn/ *n.* **in an ~,** à
mi-voix.

undervalue /ʌndə'vælju:/ *v.t.* sous-
évaluer.

underwater /ʌndə'wɔ:tə(r)/ *a.* sous-
marin. ● *adv.* sous l'eau.

underwear /'ʌndəweə(r)/ *n.* sous-
vêtements *m. pl.*

underwent /ʌndə'went/ *see* undergo.

underworld /'ʌndəwɜ:ld/ *n.* (*of
crime*) milieu *m.,* pègre *f.*

undeserved /ʌndɪ'zɜ:vd/ *a.* immé-
rité.

undesirable /ʌndɪ'zaɪərəbl/ *a.* peu
souhaitable; (*person*) indésirable.

undies /'ʌndɪz/ *n. pl.* (*female
underwear*: *fam.*) dessous *m. pl.*

undignified /ʌn'dɪgnɪfaɪd/ *a.* qui
manque de dignité, sans dignité.

undisputed /ʌndɪ'spju:tɪd/ *a.* incon-
testé.

undistinguished /ʌndɪ'stɪŋgwɪʃt/ *a.*
médiocre.

undo /ʌn'du:/ *v.t.* (*p.t.* **-did,** *p.p.* -
done /-dʌn/) défaire, détacher; (*a
wrong*) réparer. **leave ~ne,** ne pas
faire.

undoubted /ʌn'daʊtɪd/ *a.* indu-
bitable. **~ly** *adv.* indubitablement.

undreamt /ʌn'dremt/ *a.* **~ of,** in-
soupçonné, inimaginable.

undress /ʌn'dres/ *v.t./i.* (se) déshabiller. **get ~ed,** se déshabiller.

undu|e /ʌn'dju:/ *a.* excessif. **~ly** *adv.*
excessivement.

undulate /'ʌndjʊleɪt/ *v.i.* onduler.

undying /ʌn'daɪɪŋ/ *a.* éternel.

unearth /ʌn'ɜ:θ/ *v.t.* déterrer.

unearthly /ʌn'ɜ:θlɪ/ *a.* mystérieux. **~
hour,** (*fam.*) heure indue *f.*

uneasy /ʌn'i:zɪ/ *a.* (*ill at ease*) mal à
l'aise; (*worried*) inquiet; (*situation*)
difficile.

uneducated /ʌn'edʒʊkeɪtɪd/ *a.* (*person*) inculte; (*speech*) populaire.

unemploy|ed /ʌnɪm'plɔɪd/ *a.* en
chômage. **~ment** *n.* chômage *m.*
~ment benefit, allocations de
chômage *f. pl.*

unending /ʌn'endɪŋ/ *a.* interminable, sans fin.

unequal /ʌn'i:kwəl/ *a.* inégal. **~led**
a. inégalé.

unerring /ʌn'ɜ:rɪŋ/ *a.* infaillible.

uneven /ʌn'i:vn/ *a.* inégal.

uneventful /ʌnɪ'ventfl/ *a.* sans incident.

unexpected /ʌnɪk'spektɪd/ *a.* inattendu, imprévu. **~ly** *adv.* subitement; (*arrive*) à l'improviste.

unfailing /ʌn'feɪlɪŋ/ *a.* constant, continuel; (*loyal*) fidèle.

unfair /ʌn'feə(r)/ *a.* injuste. **~ness** *n.*
injustice *f.*

unfaithful /ʌn'feɪθfl/ *a.* infidèle.

unfamiliar /ʌnfə'mɪlɪə(r)/ *a.* inconnu, peu familier. **be ~ with,** ne
pas connaître.

unfashionable /ʌn'fæʃənəbl/ *a.*
(*clothes*) démodé. **it's ~ to,** ce n'est
pas à la mode de.

unfasten /ʌn'fɑ:sn/ *v.t.* défaire.

unfavourable /ʌn'feɪvərəbl/ *a.* défa-
vorable.

unfeeling /ʌn'fi:lɪŋ/ *a.* insensible.

unfinished /ʌn'fɪnɪʃt/ *a.* inachevé.

unfit /ʌn'fɪt/ *a.* (*med.*) peu en forme;
(*unsuitable*) impropre (**for,** à). **~ to,**
(*unable*) pas en état de.

unflinching /ʌn'flɪntʃɪŋ/ *a.* (*fearless*)
intrépide.

unfold /ʌn'fəʊld/ *v.t.* déplier; (*ex-
pose*) exposer. ● *v.i.* se dérouler.

unforeseen /ʌnfɔ:'si:n/ *a.* imprévu.

unforgettable /ʌnfə'getəbl/ *a.* inoubliable.

unforgivable /ʌnfə'gɪvəbl/ *a.* impardonnable, inexcusable.

unfortunate /ʌn'fɔ:tʃʊnət/ *a.* malheureux; (*event*) fâcheux. **~ly** *adv.*
malheureusement.

unfounded /ʌn'faʊndɪd/ *a.* (*rumour
etc.*) sans fondement.

unfriendly /ʌn'frendlɪ/ *a.* peu amical, froid.

ungainly /ʌn'geɪnlɪ/ *a.* gauche.

ungodly /ʌn'gɒdlɪ/ *a.* impie. **~ hour,**
(*fam.*) heure indue *f.*

ungrateful /ʌn'greɪtfl/ *a.* ingrat.

unhapp|y /ʌn'hæpɪ/ *a.* (**-ier, -iest**)
malheureux, triste; (*not pleased*)
mécontent (**with,** de). **~ily** *adv.*
malheureusement. **~iness** *n.* tristesse *f.*

unharmed /ʌnˈhɑːmd/ a. indemne, sain et sauf.

unhealthy /ʌnˈhelθɪ/ a. (-ier, -iest) (*climate etc.*) malsain; (*person*) en mauvaise santé.

unheard-of /ʌnˈhɜːdɒv/ a. inouï.

unhinge /ʌnˈhɪndʒ/ v.t. (*person, mind*) déséquilibrer.

unholy /ʌnˈhəʊlɪ/ a. (-ier, -iest) (*person, act, etc.*) impie; (*great: fam.*) invraisemblable.

unhook /ʌnˈhʊk/ v.t. décrocher; (*dress*) dégrafer.

unhoped /ʌnˈhəʊpt/ a. ~ for, inespéré.

unhurt /ʌnˈhɜːt/ a. indemne.

unicorn /ˈjuːnɪkɔːn/ n. licorne f.

uniform /ˈjuːnɪfɔːm/ n. uniforme m. ● a. uniforme. ~ity /-ˈfɔːmɪtɪ/ n. uniformité f. ~ly adv. uniformément.

unif|y /ˈjuːnɪfaɪ/ v.t. unifier. ~ication /-ɪˈkeɪʃn/ n. unification f.

unilateral /juːnɪˈlætrəl/ a. unilatéral.

unimaginable /ʌnɪˈmædʒɪnəbl/ a. inimaginable.

unimportant /ʌnɪmˈpɔːtnt/ a. peu important.

uninhabited /ʌnɪnˈhæbɪtɪd/ a. inhabité.

unintentional /ʌnɪnˈtenʃənl/ a. involontaire.

uninterest|ed /ʌnˈɪntrəstɪd/ a. indifférent (**in**, à). ~ing a. peu intéressant.

union /ˈjuːnɪən/ n. union f.; (*trade union*) syndicat m. ~ist n. syndiqué(e) m. (f.). U~ Jack, drapeau britannique m.

unique /juːˈniːk/ a. unique. ~ly adv. exceptionnellement.

unisex /ˈjuːnɪseks/ a. unisexe.

unison /ˈjuːnɪsn/ n. in ~, à l'unisson.

unit /ˈjuːnɪt/ n. unité f.; (*of furniture etc.*) élément m., bloc m. ~ trust, (*équivalent d'une*) SICAV f.

unite /juːˈnaɪt/ v.t./i. (s')unir. U~d Kingdom, Royaume-Uni m. U~d Nations, Nations Unies f. pl. U~d States (of America), États-Unis (d'Amérique) m. pl.

unity /ˈjuːnɪtɪ/ n. unité f.; (*harmony: fig.*) harmonie f.

universal /juːnɪˈvɜːsl/ a. universel.

universe /ˈjuːnɪvɜːs/ n. univers m.

university /juːnɪˈvɜːsətɪ/ n. université f. ● a. universitaire; (*student, teacher*) d'université.

unjust /ʌnˈdʒʌst/ a. injuste.

unkempt /ʌnˈkempt/ a. négligé.

unkind /ʌnˈkaɪnd/ a. pas gentil, méchant. ~ly adv. méchamment.

unknowingly /ʌnˈnəʊɪŋlɪ/ adv. sans le savoir, inconsciemment.

unknown /ʌnˈnəʊn/ a. inconnu. ● n. the ~, l'inconnu m.

unleash /ʌnˈliːʃ/ v.t. déchaîner.

unless /ənˈles/ conj. à moins que.

unlike /ʌnˈlaɪk/ a. (*brothers etc.*) différents. ● prep. à la différence de; (*different from*) très différent de.

unlik|ely /ʌnˈlaɪklɪ/ a. improbable. ~ihood n. improbabilité f.

unlimited /ʌnˈlɪmɪtɪd/ a. illimité.

unlisted /ʌnˈlɪstɪd/ a. (*comm.*) non inscrit à la cote; (*Amer.*) qui n'est pas dans l'annuaire.

unload /ʌnˈləʊd/ v.t. décharger.

unlock /ʌnˈlɒk/ v.t. ouvrir.

unluck|y /ʌnˈlʌkɪ/ a. (-ier, -iest) malheureux; (*number*) qui porte malheur. ~ily adv. malheureusement.

unmarried /ʌnˈmærɪd/ a. célibataire, qui n'est pas marié.

unmask /ʌnˈmɑːsk/ v.t. démasquer.

unmistakable /ʌnmɪˈsteɪkəbl/ a. (*voice etc.*) facilement reconnaissable; (*clear*) très net.

unmitigated /ʌnˈmɪtɪgeɪtɪd/ a. (*absolute*) absolu.

unmoved /ʌnˈmuːvd/ a. indifférent (**by**, à), insensible (**by**, à).

unnatural /ʌnˈnætʃrəl/ a. pas naturel, anormal.

unnecessary /ʌnˈnesəsərɪ/ a. inutile; (*superfluous*) superflu.

unnerve /ʌnˈnɜːv/ v.t. troubler.

unnoticed /ʌnˈnəʊtɪst/ a. inaperçu.

unobtainable /ʌnəbˈteɪnəbl/ n. impossible à obtenir.

unobtrusive /ʌnəbˈtruːsɪv/ a. (*person, object*) discret.

unofficial /ʌnəˈfɪʃl/ a. officieux.

unorthodox /ʌnˈɔːθədɒks/ a. peu orthodoxe.

unpack /ʌnˈpæk/ v.t. (*suitcase etc.*) défaire; (*contents*) déballer. ● v.i. défaire sa valise.

unpalatable /ʌnˈpælətəbl/ a. (*food, fact, etc.*) désagréable.

unparalleled /ʌnˈpærəleld/ a. incomparable.

unpleasant /ʌnˈpleznt/ a. désagréable (**to**, avec).

unplug /ʌnˈplʌg/ v.t. (*electr.*) débrancher; (*unblock*) déboucher.

unpopular /ʌn'pɒpjʊlə(r)/ *a.* impopulaire. **~ with,** mal vu de.

unprecedented /ʌn'presɪdentɪd/ *a.* sans précédent.

unpredictable /ʌnprɪ'dɪktəbl/ *a.* imprévisible.

unprepared /ʌnprɪ'peəd/ *a.* non préparé; (*person*) qui n'a rien préparé. **be ~ for,** (*not expect*) ne pas s'attendre à.

unpretentious /ʌnprɪ'tenʃəs/ *a.* sans prétention(s).

unprincipled /ʌn'prɪnsəpld/ *a.* sans scrupules.

unprofessional /ʌnprə'feʃənl/ *a.* (*work*) d'amateur; (*conduct*) contraire au code professionel.

unpublished /ʌn'pʌblɪʃt/ *a.* inédit.

unqualified /ʌn'kwɒlɪfaɪd/ *a.* non diplômé; (*success etc.*) total. **be ~ to,** ne pas être qualifié pour.

unquestionable /ʌn'kwestʃənəbl/ *a.* incontestable. **~y** *adv.* incontestablement.

unravel /ʌn'rævl/ *v.t.* (*p.t.* **unravelled**) démêler, débrouiller.

unreal /ʌn'rɪəl/ *a.* irréel.

unreasonable /ʌn'ri:znəbl/ *a.* déraisonnable, peu raisonnable.

unrecognizable /ʌnrekəg'naɪzəbl/ *a.* méconnaissable.

unrelated /ʌnrɪ'leɪtɪd/ *a.* (*facts*) sans rapport (**to,** avec).

unreliable /ʌnrɪ'laɪəbl/ *a.* peu sérieux; (*machine*) peu fiable.

unremitting /ʌnrɪ'mɪtɪŋ/ *a.* (*effort*) acharné; (*emotion*) inaltérable.

unreservedly /ʌnrɪ'zɜ:vɪdlɪ/ *adv.* sans réserve.

unrest /ʌn'rest/ *n.* troubles *m. pl.*

unrivalled /ʌn'raɪvld/ *a.* sans égal, incomparable.

unroll /ʌn'rəʊl/ *v.t.* dérouler.

unruffled /ʌn'rʌfld/ *a.* (*person*) qui n'a pas perdu son calme.

unruly /ʌn'ru:lɪ/ *a.* indiscipliné.

unsafe /ʌn'seɪf/ *a.* (*dangerous*) dangereux; (*person*) en danger.

unsaid /ʌn'sed/ *a.* **leave ~,** passer sous silence.

unsatisfactory /ʌnsætɪs'fæktərɪ/ *a.* peu satisfaisant.

unsavoury /ʌn'seɪvərɪ/ *a.* désagréable, répugnant.

unscathed /ʌn'skeɪðd/ *a.* indemne.

unscheduled /ʌn'ʃedju:ld, *Amer.* ʌn'skedju:ld/ *a.* pas prévu.

unscrew /ʌn'skru:/ *v.t.* dévisser.

unscrupulous /ʌn'skru:pjʊləs/ *a.* sans scrupules, malhonnête.

unseemly /ʌn'si:mlɪ/ *a.* inconvenant, incorrect, incongru.

unseen /ʌn'si:n/ *a.* inaperçu. ● *n.* (*translation*) version *f.*

unsettle /ʌn'setl/ *v.t.* troubler. **~d** *a.* (*weather*) instable.

unshakeable /ʌn'ʃeɪkəbl/ *a.* (*person, belief, etc.*) inébranlable.

unshaven /ʌn'ʃeɪvn/ *a.* pas rasé.

unsightly /ʌn'saɪtlɪ/ *a.* laid.

unskilled /ʌn'skɪld/ *a.* inexpert; (*worker*) non qualifié.

unsociable /ʌn'səʊʃəbl/ *a.* insociable, farouche.

unsophisticated /ʌnsə'fɪstɪkeɪtɪd/ *a.* peu sophistiqué, simple.

unsound /ʌn'saʊnd/ *a.* peu solide. **of ~ mind,** fou.

unspeakable /ʌn'spi:kəbl/ *a.* indescriptible; (*bad*) innommable.

unspecified /ʌn'spesɪfaɪd/ *a.* indéterminé.

unstable /ʌn'steɪbl/ *a.* instable.

unsteady /ʌn'stedɪ/ *a.* (*step*) chancelant; (*ladder*) instable; (*hand*) mal assuré.

unstuck /ʌn'stʌk/ *a.* décollé. **come ~,** (*fail: fam.*) échouer.

unsuccessful /ʌnsək'sesfl/ *a.* (*result, candidate*) malheureux; (*attempt*) infructueux. **be ~,** ne pas réussir (**in doing,** à faire).

unsuitable /ʌn'su:təbl/ *a.* qui ne convient pas (**for,** à), peu approprié. **~ed** *a.* inapte (**to,** à).

unsure /ʌn'ʃɔ:(r)/ *a.* incertain.

unsuspecting /ʌnsə'spektɪŋ/ *a.* qui ne se doute de rien.

unsympathetic /ʌnsɪmpə'θetɪk/ *a.* (*unhelpful*) peu compréhensif; (*unpleasant*) antipathique.

untangle /ʌn'tæŋgl/ *v.t.* démêler.

untenable /ʌn'tenəbl/ *a.* intenable.

unthinkable /ʌn'θɪŋkəbl/ *a.* impensable, inconcevable.

untidy /ʌn'taɪdɪ/ *a.* (**-ier, -iest**) (*person*) désordonné; (*clothes, hair, room*) en désordre; (*work*) mal soigné. **~ily** *adv.* sans soin.

untie /ʌn'taɪ/ *v.t.* (*knot, parcel*) défaire; (*person*) détacher.

until /ən'tɪl/ *prep.* jusqu'à. **not ~,** pas avant. ● *conj.* jusqu'à ce que; (*before*) avant que.

untimely /ʌn'taɪmlɪ/ *a.* inopportun; (*death*) prématuré.

untold /ʌn'təʊld/ *a.* incalculable.

untoward /ʌntə'wɔːd/ a. fâcheux.

untrue /ʌn'truː/ a. faux.

unused¹ /ʌn'juːzd/ a. (*new*) neuf; (*not in use*) inutilisé.

unused² /ʌn'juːst/ a. ~ **to**, peu habitué à.

unusual /ʌn'juːʒʊəl/ a. exceptionnel; (*strange*) insolite, étrange. ~**ly** adv. exceptionnellement.

unveil /ʌn'veɪl/ v.t. dévoiler.

unwanted /ʌn'wɒntɪd/ a. (*useless*) superflu; (*child*) non désiré.

unwelcome /ʌn'welkəm/ a. fâcheux; (*guest*) importun.

unwell /ʌn'wel/ a. indisposé.

unwieldy /ʌn'wiːldɪ/ a. difficile à manier.

unwilling /ʌn'wɪlɪŋ/ a. peu disposé (**to**, à); (*victim*) récalcitrant. ~**ly** adv. à contrecœur.

unwind /ʌn'waɪnd/ v.t./i. (*p.t.* **unwound** /ʌn'waʊnd/) (se) dérouler; (*relax: fam.*) se détendre.

unwise /ʌn'waɪz/ a. imprudent.

unwittingly /ʌn'wɪtɪŋlɪ/ adv. involontairement.

unworkable /ʌn'wɜːkəbl/ a. (*plan etc.*) irréalisable.

unworthy /ʌn'wɜːðɪ/ a. indigne.

unwrap /ʌn'ræp/ v.t. (*p.t.* **unwrapped**) ouvrir, défaire.

unwritten /ʌn'rɪtn/ a. (*agreement*) verbal, tacite.

up /ʌp/ adv. en haut, en l'air; (*sun, curtain*) levé; (*out of bed*) levé, debout; (*finished*) fini. **be up**, (*level, price*) avoir monté. ● prep. (*a hill*) en haut de; (*a tree*) dans; (*a ladder*) sur. ● v.t. (*p.t.* **upped**) augmenter. **come** *or* **go up**, monter. **up in the bedroom**, là-haut dans la chambre. **up there**, là-haut. **up to**, jusqu'à; (*task*) à la hauteur de. **it is up to you**, ça dépend de vous (**to**, de). **be up to sth.**, (*able*) être capable de qch.; (*do*) faire qch.; (*plot*) préparer qch. **be up to**, (*in book*) en être à. **be up against**, faire face à. **be up in**, (*fam.*) s'y connaître en. **feel up to doing**, (*able*) être de taille à faire. **have ups and downs**, connaître des hauts et des bas. **up-and-coming** a. prometteur. **up-market** a. haut-de-gamme. **up to date**, moderne; (*news*) récent.

upbringing /'ʌpbrɪŋɪŋ/ n. éducation f.

update /ʌp'deɪt/ v.t. mettre à jour.

upgrade /ʌp'greɪd/ v.t. (*person*) promouvoir; (*job*) revaloriser.

upheaval /ʌp'hiːvl/ n. bouleversement m.

uphill /ʌp'hɪl/ a. qui monte; (*fig.*) difficile. ● adv. **go** ~, monter.

uphold /ʌp'həʊld/ v.t. (*p.t.* **upheld**) maintenir.

upholster /ʌp'həʊlstə(r)/ v.t. (*pad*) rembourrer; (*cover*) recouvrir. ~**y** n. (*in vehicle*) garniture f.

upkeep /'ʌpkiːp/ n. entretien m.

upon /ə'pɒn/ prep. sur.

upper /'ʌpə(r)/ a. supérieur. ● n. (*of shoe*) empeigne f. **have the** ~ **hand**, avoir le dessus. ~ **class**, aristocratie f. ~**most** a. (*highest*) le plus haut.

upright /'ʌpraɪt/ a. droit. ● n. (*post*) montant m.

uprising /'ʌpraɪzɪŋ/ n. soulèvement m., insurrection f.

uproar /'ʌprɔː(r)/ n. tumulte m.

uproot /ʌp'ruːt/ v.t. déraciner.

upset¹ /ʌp'set/ v.t. (*p.t.* **upset**, *pres. p.* **upsetting**) (*overturn*) renverser; (*plan, stomach*) déranger; (*person*) contrarier, affliger. ● a. peiné.

upset² /'ʌpset/ n. dérangement m.; (*distress*) chagrin m.

upshot /'ʌpʃɒt/ n. résultat m.

upside-down /ʌpsaɪd'daʊn/ adv. (*in position, in disorder*) à l'envers, sens dessus dessous.

upstairs /ʌp'steəz/ adv. en haut. ● a. (*flat etc.*) d'en haut.

upstart /'ʌpstɑːt/ n. (*pej.*) parvenu(e) m. (f.).

upstream /ʌp'striːm/ adv. en amont.

upsurge /'ʌpsɜːdʒ/ n. recrudescence f.; (*of anger*) accès m.

uptake /'ʌpteɪk/ n. **be quick on the** ~, comprendre vite.

uptight /ʌp'taɪt/ a. (*tense: fam.*) crispé; (*angry: fam.*) en colère.

upturn /'ʌptɜːn/ n. amélioration f.

upward /'ʌpwəd/ a. & adv., ~**s** adv. vers le haut.

uranium /jʊ'reɪnɪəm/ n. uranium m.

urban /'ɜːbən/ a. urbain.

urbane /ɜː'beɪn/ a. courtois.

urchin /'ɜːtʃɪn/ n. garnement m.

urge /ɜːdʒ/ v.t. conseiller vivement (**to do**, de faire). ● n. forte envie f. ~ **on**, (*impel*) encourager.

urgen|t /'ɜːdʒənt/ a. urgent; (*request*) pressant. ~**cy** n. urgence f.; (*of request, tone*) insistance f. ~**tly** adv. d'urgence.

urinal /jʊə'raɪnl/ n. urinoir m.

V

urin|e /'jʊərɪn/ n. urine f. **~ate** v.i. uriner.

urn /ɜ:n/ n. urne f.; (for tea, coffee) fontaine f.

us /ʌs, unstressed əs/ pron. nous. **(to) us,** nous.

US abbr. see United States.

USA abbr. see United States of America.

usable /'ju:zəbl/ a. utilisable.

usage /'ju:sɪdʒ/ n. usage m.

use [1] /ju:z/ v.t. se servir de, utiliser; (consume) consommer. **~ up,** épuiser. **~r** /-ə(r)/ n. usager m. **~r-friendly** a. facile d'emploi.

use [2] /ju:s/ n. usage m., emploi m. **in ~,** en usage. **it is no ~ shouting/** etc., ça ne sert à rien de crier/etc. **make ~ of,** se servir de. **of ~,** utile.

used [1] /ju:zd/ a. (second-hand) d'occasion.

used [2] /ju:st/ p.t. **he ~ to do,** il faisait (autrefois), il avait l'habitude de faire. ● a. (accustomed) habitué à.

use|ful /'ju:sfl/ a. utile. **~fully** adv. utilement. **~less** a. inutile; (person) incompétent.

usher /'ʌʃə(r)/ n. (in theatre, hall) placeur m. ● v.t. **~ in,** faire entrer. **~ette** n. ouvreuse f.

USSR abbr. (Union of Soviet Socialist Republics) URSS f.

usual /'ju:ʒʊəl/ a. habituel, normal. **as ~,** comme d'habitude. **~ly** adv. d'habitude.

usurp /ju:'zɜ:p/ v.t. usurper.

utensil /ju:'tensl/ n. ustensile m.

uterus /'ju:tərəs/ n. utérus m.

utilitarian /ju:tɪlɪ'teərɪən/ a. utilitaire.

utility /ju:'tɪlətɪ/ n. utilité f. **(public) ~,** service public m.

utilize /'ju:tɪlaɪz/ v.t. utiliser.

utmost /'ʌtməʊst/ a. (furthest, most intense) extrême. **the ~ care/**etc., (greatest) le plus grand soin/etc. ● n. **do one's ~,** faire tout son possible.

Utopia /ju:'təʊpɪə/ n. utopie f. **~n** a. utopique.

utter [1] /'ʌtə(r)/ a. complet, absolu. **~ly** adv. complètement.

utter [2] /'ʌtə(r)/ v.t. proférer; (sigh, shout) pousser. **~ance** n. déclaration f. **give ~ance to,** exprimer.

U-turn /'ju:tɜ:n/ n. demi-tour m.

vacan|t /'veɪkənt/ a. (post) vacant; (seat etc.) libre; (look) vague. **~cy** n. (post) poste vacant m.; (room) chambre disponible f.

vacate /və'keɪt, Amer. 'veɪkeɪt/ v.t. quitter.

vacation /veɪ'keɪʃn/ n. (Amer.) vacances f. pl.

vaccinat|e /'væksɪneɪt/ v.t. vacciner. **~ion** /-'neɪʃn/ n. vaccination f.

vaccine /'væksi:n/ n. vaccin m.

vacuum /'vækjʊəm/ n. (pl. -cuums or -cua) vide m. **~ cleaner,** aspirateur m. **~ flask,** bouteille thermos f. (P.). **~-packed** a. emballé sous vide.

vagabond /'vægəbɒnd/ n. vagabond(e) m. (f.).

vagina /və'dʒaɪnə/ n. vagin m.

vagrant /'veɪɡrənt/ n. vagabond(e) m. (f.), clochard(e) m. (f.).

vague /veɪɡ/ a. (-er, -est) vague; (outline) flou. **be ~ about,** ne pas préciser. **~ly** adv. vaguement.

vain /veɪn/ a. (-er, -est) (conceited) vaniteux; (useless) vain. **in ~,** en vain. **~ly** adv. en vain.

valentine /'væləntaɪn/ n. (card) carte de la Saint-Valentin f.

valet /'vælɪt, 'væleɪ/ n. (manservant) valet de chambre m.

valiant /'vælɪənt/ a. courageux.

valid /'vælɪd/ a. valable. **~ity** /və'lɪdətɪ/ n. validité f.

validate /'vælɪdeɪt/ v.t. valider.

valley /'vælɪ/ n. vallée f.

valour, (Amer.) **valor** /'vælə(r)/ n. courage m.

valuable /'væljʊəbl/ a. (object) de valeur; (help etc.) précieux. **~s** n. pl. objets de valeur m. pl.

valuation /væljʊ'eɪʃn/ n. expertise f.; (of house) évaluation f.

value /'vælju:/ n. valeur f. ● v.t. (appraise) évaluer; (cherish) attacher de la valeur à. **~ added tax,** taxe à la valeur ajoutée f., TVA f. **~d** a. estimé. **~r** /-ə(r)/ n. expert m.

valve /vælv/ n. (techn.) soupape f.; (of tyre) valve f.; (radio) lampe f.

vampire /'væmpaɪə(r)/ n. vampire m.

van /væn/ n. (vehicle) camionnette f.; (rail.) fourgon m.

vandal /'vændl/ n. vandale m./f. **~ism** /-əlɪzəm/ n. vandalisme m.

vandalize /'vændəlaɪz/ v.t. abîmer, détruire, saccager.

vanguard /'vænɡɑːd/ n. (of army, progress, etc.) avant-garde f.

vanilla /və'nɪlə/ n. vanille f.

vanish /'vænɪʃ/ v.i. disparaître.

vanity /'vænətɪ/ n. vanité f. ~ **case**, mallette de toilette f.

vantage-point /'vɑːtɪdʒpɔɪnt/ n. (place) excellent point de vue m.

vapour /'veɪpə(r)/ n. vapeur f.

vari|able /'veərɪəbl/ a. variable. ~**ation** /-'eɪʃn/ n. variation f. ~**ed** /-ɪd/ a. varié.

variance /'veərɪəns/ n. at ~, en désaccord (with, avec).

variant /'veərɪənt/ a. différent. ● n. variante f.

varicose /'værɪkəʊs/ a. ~ **veins**, varices f. pl.

variety /və'raɪətɪ/ n. variété f.; (entertainment) variétés f. pl.

various /'veərɪəs/ a. divers. ~**ly** adv. diversement.

varnish /'vɑːnɪʃ/ n. vernis m. ● v.t. vernir.

vary /'veərɪ/ v.t./i. varier.

vase /vɑːz, Amer. veɪs/ n. vase m.

vast /vɑːst/ a. vaste, immense. ~**ly** adv. infiniment, extrêmement. ~**ness** n. immensité f.

vat /væt/ n. cuve f.

VAT /viːeɪ'tiː, væt/ abbr. (value added tax) TVA f.

vault¹ /vɔːlt/ n. (roof) voûte f.; (in bank) chambre forte f.; (tomb) caveau m.; (cellar) cave f.

vault² /vɔːlt/ v.t./i. sauter. ● n. saut m.

vaunt /vɔːnt/ v.t. vanter.

VCR abbr. see video cassette recorder.

VDU abbr. see visual display unit.

veal /viːl/ n. (meat) veau m.

veer /vɪə(r)/ v.i. tourner, virer.

vegan /'viːɡən/ a. & n. végétalien(-ne) (m. (f.)).

vegetable /'vedʒtəbl/ n. légume m. ● a. végétal. ~ **garden**, (jardin) potager m.

vegetarian /vedʒɪ'teərɪən/ a. & n. végétarien(ne) (m. (f.)).

vegetate /'vedʒɪteɪt/ v.i. végéter.

vegetation /vedʒɪ'teɪʃn/ n. végétation f.

vehement /'viːəmənt/ a. véhément. ~**ly** adv. avec véhémence.

vehicle /'viːɪkl/ n. véhicule m.

veil /veɪl/ n. voile m. ● v.t. voiler.

vein /veɪn/ n. (in body, rock) veine f.; (on leaf) nervure f. (mood) esprit m.

velocity /vɪ'lɒsətɪ/ n. vélocité f.

velvet /'velvɪt/ n. velours m.

vending-machine /'vendɪnməʃiːn/ n. distributeur automatique m.

vendor /'vendə(r)/ n. vendeu|r, -se m., f.

veneer /və'nɪə(r)/ n. placage m.; (appearance: fig.) vernis m.

venerable /'venərəbl/ a. vénérable.

venereal /və'nɪərɪəl/ a. vénérien.

venetian /və'niːʃn/ a. ~ **blind**, jalousie f.

vengeance /'vendʒəns/ n. vengeance f. with a ~, furieusement.

venison /'venɪzn/ n. venaison f.

venom /'venəm/ n. venin m. ~**ous** /'venəməs/ a. venimeux.

vent¹ /vent/ n. (in coat) fente f.

vent² /vent/ n. (hole) orifice m.; (for air) bouche d'aération f. ● v.t. (anger) décharger (on, sur). give ~ to, donner libre cours à.

ventilat|e /'ventɪleɪt/ v.t. ventiler. ~**ion** /-'leɪʃn/ n. ventilation f. ~**or** n. ventilateur m.

ventriloquist /ven'trɪləkwɪst/ n. ventriloque m./f.

venture /'ventʃə(r)/ n. entreprise f. ● v.t./i. (se) risquer.

venue /'venjuː/ n. lieu de rencontre or de rendez-vous m.

veranda /və'rændə/ n. véranda f.

verb /vɜːb/ n. verbe m.

verbal /'vɜːbl/ a. verbal.

verbatim /vɜː'beɪtɪm/ adv. textuellement, mot pour mot.

verdict /'vɜːdɪkt/ n. verdict m.

verge /vɜːdʒ/ n. bord m. ● v.i. ~ on, friser, frôler. on the ~ of doing, sur le point de faire.

verif|y /'verɪfaɪ/ v.t. vérifier. ~**ication** /-ɪ'keɪʃn/ n. vérification f.

vermicelli /vɜːmɪ'selɪ/ n. vermicelle(s) m. (pl.).

vermin /'vɜːmɪn/ n. vermine f.

vermouth /'vɜːməθ/ n. vermouth m.

vernacular /və'nækjʊlə(r)/ n. langue f.; (regional) dialecte m.

versatil|e /'vɜːsətaɪl, Amer. 'vɜːsətl/ a. (person) aux talents variés; (mind) souple. ~**ity** /-'tɪlətɪ/ n. souplesse f. her ~**ity**, la variété de ses talents.

verse /vɜːs/ n. strophe f.; (of Bible) verset m.; (poetry) vers m. pl.

versed /vɜːst/ a. ~ **in**, versé dans.

version /'vɜːʃn/ n. version f.

versus /'vɜːsəs/ prep. contre.

vertebra /'vɜːtɪbrə/ *n.* (*pl.* **-brae** /-briː/) vertèbre *f.*

vertical /'vɜːtɪkl/ *a.* vertical. **~ly** *adv.* verticalement.

vertigo /'vɜːtɪgəʊ/ *n.* vertige *m.*

verve /vɜːv/ *n.* fougue *f.*

very /'verɪ/ *adv.* très. ● *a.* (*actual*) même. **the ~ day**/*etc.*, le jour/*etc.* même. **at the ~ end**, tout à la fin. **the ~ first**, le tout premier. **~ much**, beaucoup.

vessel /'vesl/ *n.* (*duct, ship*) vaisseau *m.*

vest /vest/ *n.* maillot de corps *m.*; (*waistcoat*: *Amer.*) gilet *m.*

vested /'vestɪd/ *a.* **~ interests**, droits acquis *m. pl.*, intérêts *m. pl.*

vestige /'vestɪdʒ/ *n.* vestige *m.*

vestry /'vestrɪ/ *n.* sacristie *f.*

vet /vet/ *n.* (*fam.*) vétérinaire *m.*/*f.* ● *v.t.* (*p.t.* **vetted**) (*candidate etc.*) examiner (de près).

veteran /'vetərən/ *n.* vétéran *m.* (**war**) **~**, ancien combattant *m.*

veterinary /'vetərɪnərɪ/ *a.* vétérinaire. **~ surgeon**, vétérinaire *m.* /*f.*

veto /'viːtəʊ/ *n.* (*pl.* **-oes**) veto *m.*; (*right*) droit de veto *m.* ● *v.t.* mettre son veto à.

vex /veks/ *v.t.* contrarier, irriter; **~ed question**, question controversée *f.*

via /'vaɪə/ *prep.* via, par.

viable /'vaɪəbl/ *a.* (*baby, plan, firm*) viable.

viaduct /'vaɪədʌkt/ *n.* viaduc *m.*

vibrant /'vaɪbrənt/ *a.* vibrant.

vibrat|e /vaɪ'breɪt/ *v.t./i.* (faire) vibrer. **~ion** /-ʃn/ *n.* vibration *f.*

vicar /'vɪkə(r)/ *n.* pasteur *m.* **~age** /-ɪdʒ/ *n.* presbytère *m.*

vicarious /vɪ'keərɪəs/ *a.* (*emotion*) ressenti indirectement.

vice¹ /vaɪs/ *n.* (*depravity*) vice *m.*

vice² /vaɪs/ *n.* (*techn.*) étau *m.*

vice- /vaɪs/ *pref.* vice-.

vice versa /'vaɪsɪ'vɜːsə/ *adv.* vice versa.

vicinity /vɪ'sɪnətɪ/ *n.* environs *m. pl.* **in the ~ of**, aux environs de.

vicious /'vɪʃəs/ *a.* (*spiteful*) méchant; (*violent*) brutal. **~ circle**, cercle vicieux *m.* **~ly** *adv.* méchamment; brutalement.

victim /'vɪktɪm/ *n.* victime *f.*

victimiz|e /'vɪktɪmaɪz/ *v.t.* persécuter, martyriser. **~ation** /-'zeɪʃn/ *n.* persécution *f.*

victor /'vɪktə(r)/ *n.* vainqueur *m.*

Victorian /vɪk'tɔːrɪən/ *a.* & *n.* victorien(ne) (*m.* (*f.*)).

victor|y /'vɪktərɪ/ *n.* victoire *f.* **~ious** /-'tɔːrɪəs/ *a.* victorieux.

video /'vɪdɪəʊ/ *a.* (*game, camera*) vidéo *invar.* ● *n.* (*recorder*) magnétoscope *m.*; (*film*) vidéo *f.* **~ cassette**, vidéocassette *f.* **~ (cassette) recorder**, magnétoscope *m.* ● *v.t.* (*programme*) enregistrer.

videotape /'vɪdɪəʊteɪp/ *n.* bande vidéo *f.* ● *v.t.* (*programme*) enregistrer; (*wedding*) filmer avec une caméra vidéo.

vie /vaɪ/ *v.i.* (*pres. p.* **vying**) rivaliser (**with**, avec).

view /vjuː/ *n.* vue *f.* ● *v.t.* (*watch*) regarder; (*consider*) considérer (**as**, comme); (*house*) visiter. **in my ~**, à mon avis. **in ~ of**, compte tenu de. **on ~**, exposé. **with a ~ to**, dans le but de. **~er** *n.* (*TV*) téléspecta|teur, -trice *m.*, *f.*; (*for slides*) visionneuse *f.*

viewfinder /'vjuːfaɪndə(r)/ *n.* viseur *m.*

viewpoint /'vjuːpɔɪnt/ *n.* point de vue *m.*

vigil /'vɪdʒɪl/ *n.* veille *f.*; (*over sick person, corpse*) veillée *f.*

vigilan|t /'vɪdʒɪlənt/ *a.* vigilant. **~ce** *n.* vigilance *f.*

vig|our, (*Amer.*) **vigor** /'vɪgə(r)/ *n.* vigueur *f.* **~orous** *a.* vigoureux.

vile /vaɪl/ *a.* (*base*) infâme, vil; (*bad*) abominable, exécrable.

vilify /'vɪlɪfaɪ/ *v.t.* diffamer.

villa /'vɪlə/ *n.* villa *f.*, pavillon *m.*

village /'vɪlɪdʒ/ *n.* village *m.* **~r** /-ə(r)/ *n.* villageois(e) *m.* (*f.*).

villain /'vɪlən/ *n.* scélérat *m.*, bandit *m.*; (*in story etc.*) méchant *m.* **~y** *n.* infamie *f.*

vindicat|e /'vɪndɪkeɪt/ *v.t.* justifier. **~ion** /-'keɪʃn/ *n.* justification *f.*

vindictive /vɪn'dɪktɪv/ *a.* vindicatif.

vine /vaɪn/ *n.* vigne *f.*

vinegar /'vɪnɪgə(r)/ *n.* vinaigre *m.*

vineyard /'vɪnjəd/ *n.* vignoble *m.*

vintage /'vɪntɪdʒ/ *n.* (*year*) année *f.*, millésime *m.* ● *a.* (*wine*) de grand cru; (*car*) d'époque.

vinyl /'vaɪnɪl/ *n.* vinyle *m.*

viola /vɪ'əʊlə/ *n.* (*mus.*) alto *m.*

violat|e /'vaɪəleɪt/ *v.t.* violer. **~ion** /-'leɪʃn/ *n.* violation *f.*

violen|t /'vaɪələnt/ *a.* violent. **~ce** *n.* violence *f.* **~tly** *adv.* violemment, avec violence.

violet /'vaɪələt/ *n.* (*bot.*) violette *f.*; (*colour*) violet *m.* ● *a.* violet.

violin /vaɪə'lɪn/ *n.* violon *m.* **~ist** *n.* violoniste *m./f.*

VIP /viːaɪ'piː/ *abbr.* (*very important person*) personnage de marque *m.*

viper /'vaɪpə(r)/ *n.* vipère *f.*

virgin /'vɜːdʒɪn/ *n.* (*woman*) vierge *f.* ● *a.* vierge. **be a ~,** (*woman, man*) être vierge. **~ity** /və'dʒɪnətɪ/ *n.* virginité *f.*

Virgo /'vɜːgəʊ/ *n.* la Vierge.

viril|e /'vɪraɪl, *Amer.* 'vɪrəl/ *a.* viril. **~ity** /vɪ'rɪlətɪ/ *n.* virilité *f.*

virtual /'vɜːtʃʊəl/ *a.* vrai. **a ~ failure**/*etc.*, pratiquement un échec/*etc.* **~ly** *adv.* pratiquement.

virtue /'vɜːtʃuː/ *n.* (*goodness, chastity*) vertu *f.*; (*merit*) mérite *m.* **by or in ~ of,** en raison de.

virtuos|o /vɜːtʃʊ'əʊsəʊ/ *n.* (*pl.* **-si** /-siː/) virtuose *m./f.* **~ity** /-'ɒsətɪ/ *n.* virtuosité *f.*

virtuous /'vɜːtʃʊəs/ *a.* vertueux.

virulent /'vɪrʊlənt/ *a.* virulent.

virus /'vaɪərəs/ *n.* (*pl.* **-uses**) virus *m.*

visa /'viːzə/ *n.* visa *m.*

viscount /'vaɪkaʊnt/ *n.* vicomte *m.*

viscous /'vɪskəs/ *a.* visqueux.

vise /vaɪs/ *n.* (*Amer.*) étau *m.*

visib|le /'vɪzəbl/ *a.* (*discernible, obvious*) visible. **~ility** /-'bɪlətɪ/ *n.* visibilité *f.* **~ly** *adv.* visiblement.

vision /'vɪʒn/ *n.* vision *f.*

visionary /'vɪʒənərɪ/ *a. & n.* visionnaire (*m./f.*).

visit /'vɪzɪt/ *v.t.* (*p.t.* **visited**) (*person*) rendre visite à; (*place*) visiter. ● *v.i.* être en visite. ● *n.* (*tour, call*) visite *f.*; (*stay*) séjour *m.* **~or** *n.* visiteu|r, -se *m., f.*; (*guest*) invité(e) *m.* (*f.*); (*in hotel*) client(e) *m.* (*f.*).

visor /'vaɪzə(r)/ *n.* visière *f.*

vista /'vɪstə/ *n.* perspective *f.*

visual /'vɪʒʊəl/ *a.* visuel. **~ display unit,** visuel *m.*, console de visualisation *f.* **~ly** *adv.* visuellement.

visualize /'vɪʒʊəlaɪz/ *v.t.* se représenter; (*foresee*) envisager.

vital /'vaɪtl/ *a.* vital. **~ statistics,** (*fam.*) mensurations *f. pl.*

vitality /vaɪ'tælətɪ/ *n.* vitalité *f.*

vitally /'vaɪtəlɪ/ *adv.* extrêmement.

vitamin /'vɪtəmɪn/ *n.* vitamine *f.*

vivac|ious /vɪ'veɪʃəs/ *a.* plein d'entrain, animé. **~ity** /-æsətɪ/ *n.* vivacité *f.*, entrain *m.*

vivid /'vɪvɪd/ *a.* vif; (*graphic*) vivant. **~ly** *adv.* vivement; (*describe*) de façon vivante.

vivisection /vɪvɪ'sekʃn/ *n.* vivisection *f.*

vocabulary /və'kæbjʊlərɪ/ *n.* vocabulaire *m.*

vocal /'vəʊkl/ *a.* vocal; (*person: fig.*) qui s'exprime franchement. **~ cords,** cordes vocales *f. pl.* **~ist** *n.* chanteu|r, -se *m., f.*

vocation /və'keɪʃn/ *n.* vocation *f.* **~al** *a.* professionnel.

vociferous /və'sɪfərəs/ *a.* bruyant.

vodka /'vɒdkə/ *n.* vodka *f.*

vogue /vəʊg/ *n.* (*fashion, popularity*) vogue *f.* **in ~,** en vogue.

voice /vɔɪs/ *n.* voix *f.* ● *v.t.* (*express*) formuler.

void /vɔɪd/ *a.* vide (**of,** de); (*not valid*) nul. ● *n.* vide *m.*

volatile /'vɒlətaɪl, *Amer.* 'vɒlətl/ *a.* (*person*) versatile; (*situation*) variable.

volcan|o /vɒl'keɪnəʊ/ *n.* (*pl.* **-oes**) volcan *m.* **~ic** /-ænɪk/ *a.* volcanique.

volition /və'lɪʃn/ *n.* **of one's own ~,** de son propre gré.

volley /'vɒlɪ/ *n.* (*of blows etc., in tennis*) volée *f.*; (*of gunfire*) salve *f.* **~-ball** *n.* volley(-ball) *m.*

volt /vəʊlt/ *n.* (*electr.*) volt *m.* **~age** *n.* voltage *m.*

voluble /'vɒljʊbl/ *a.* volubile.

volume /'vɒljuːm/ *n.* volume *m.*

voluntar|y /'vɒləntərɪ/ *a.* volontaire; (*unpaid*) bénévole. **~ily** /-trəlɪ, *Amer.* -'terəlɪ/ *adv.* volontairement.

volunteer /vɒlən'tɪə(r)/ *n.* volontaire *m./f.* ● *v.i.* s'offrir (**to do,** pour faire); (*mil.*) s'engager comme volontaire. ● *v.t.* offrir.

voluptuous /və'lʌptʃʊəs/ *a.* voluptueux.

vomit /'vɒmɪt/ *v.t./i.* (*p.t.* **vomited**) vomir. ● *n.* vomi(ssement) *m.*

voracious /və'reɪʃəs/ *a.* vorace.

vot|e /vəʊt/ *n.* vote *m.*; (*right*) droit de vote *m.* ● *v.t./i.* voter. **~ (in),** (*person*) élire. **~er** *n.* élec|teur, -trice *m., f.* **~ing** *n.* vote *m.* (**of,** de); (*poll*) scrutin *m.*

vouch /vaʊtʃ/ *v.i.* **~ for,** se porter garant de, répondre de.

voucher /'vaʊtʃə(r)/ *n.* bon *m.*

vow /vaʊ/ *n.* vœu *m.* ● *v.t.* (*loyalty etc.*) jurer (**to**, à). ~ **to do,** jurer de faire.

vowel /'vaʊəl/ *n.* voyelle *f.*

voyage /'vɔɪɪdʒ/ *n.* voyage (par mer) *m.*

vulgar /'vʌlɡə(r)/ *a.* vulgaire. ~**ity** /-'ɡærətɪ/ *n.* vulgarité *f.*

vulnerab|le /'vʌlnərəbl/ *a.* vulnérable. ~**ility** /-'bɪlətɪ/ *n.* vulnérabilité *f.*

vulture /'vʌltʃə(r)/ *n.* vautour *m.*

W

wad /wɒd/ *n.* (*pad*) tampon *m.*; (*bundle*) liasse *f.*

wadding /'wɒdɪŋ/ *n.* rembourrage *m.*, ouate *f.*

waddle /'wɒdl/ *v.i.* se dandiner.

wade /weɪd/ *v.i.* ~ **through,** (*mud etc.*) patauger dans; (*book: fig.*) avancer péniblement dans.

wafer /'weɪfə(r)/ *n.* (*biscuit*) gaufrette *f.*; (*relig.*) hostie *f.*

waffle[1] /'wɒfl/ *n.* (*talk: fam.*) verbiage *m.* ● *v.i.* (*fam.*) divaguer.

waffle[2] /'wɒfl/ *n.* (*cake*) gaufre *f.*

waft /wɒft/ *v.i.* flotter. ● *v.t.* porter.

wag /wæɡ/ *v.t./i.* (*p.t.* **wagged**) (*tail*) remuer.

wage[1] /weɪdʒ/ *v.t.* (*campaign*) mener. ~ **war,** faire la guerre.

wage[2] /weɪdʒ/ *n.* (*weekly, daily*) salaire *m.* ~**s,** salaire *m.* ~**-earner** *n.* salarié(e) *m.* (*f.*).

wager /'weɪdʒə(r)/ *n.* (*bet*) pari *f.* ● *v.t.* parier (**that,** que).

waggle /'wæɡl/ *v.t./i.* remuer.

wagon /'wæɡən/ *n.* (*horse-drawn*) chariot *m.*; (*rail.*) wagon (de marchandises) *m.*

waif /weɪf/ *n.* enfant abandonné(e) *m.*(*f.*).

wail /weɪl/ *v.i.* (*utter cry or complaint*) gémir. ● *n.* gémissement *m.*

waist /weɪst/ *n.* taille *f.*

waistcoat /'weɪskəʊt/ *n.* gilet *m.*

wait /weɪt/ *v.t./i.* attendre. ● *n.* attente *f.* **I can't** ~, je n'en peux plus d'impatience. **let's** ~ **and see,** attendons voir. **while you** ~, sur place. ~ **for,** attendre. ~ **on,** servir. ~**ing-list** *n.* liste d'attente *f.* ~**ing-room** *n.* salle d'attente *f.*

wait|er /'weɪtə(r)/ *n.* garçon *m.*, serveur *m.* ~**ress** *n.* serveuse *f.*

waive /weɪv/ *v.t.* renoncer à

wake[1] /weɪk/ *v.t./i.* (*p.t.* **woke**, *p.p.* **woken**). ~ (**up**), (se) réveiller.

wake[2] /weɪk/ *n.* (*track*) sillage *m.* **in the** ~ **of,** (*after*) à la suite de.

waken /'weɪkən/ *v.t./i.* (se) réveiller, (s')éveiller.

Wales /weɪlz/ *n.* pays de Galles *m.*

walk /wɔːk/ *v.i.* marcher; (*not ride*) aller à pied; (*stroll*) se promener. ● *v.t.* (*streets*) parcourir; (*distance*) faire à pied; (*dog*) promener. ● *n.* promenade *f.*, tour *m.*; (*gait*) démarche *f.*; (*pace*) marche *f.*, pas *m.*; (*path*) allée *f.* ~ **of life,** condition sociale *f.* ~ **out,** (*go away*) partir; (*worker*) faire grève. ~**-out** *n.* grève surprise *f.* ~ **out on,** abandonner. ~**-over** *n.* victoire facile *f.*

walker /'wɔːkə(r)/ *n.* (*person*) marcheu|r, -se *m.*, *f.*

walkie-talkie /wɔːkɪ'tɔːkɪ/ *n.* talkie-walkie *m.*

walking /'wɔːkɪŋ/ *n.* marche (à pied) *f.* ● *a.* (*corpse, dictionary: fig.*) vivant. ~**-stick** *n.* canne *f.*

Walkman /'wɔːkmən/ *n.* (P.) Walkman (P.) *m.*, baladeur *m.*

wall /wɔːl/ *n.* mur *m.*; (*of tunnel, stomach, etc.*) paroi *f.* ● *a.* mural. ● *v.t.* (*city*) fortifier. **go to the** ~, (*firm*) faire faillite.

wallet /'wɒlɪt/ *n.* portefeuille *m.*

wallflower /'wɔːlflaʊə(r)/ *n.* (*bot.*) giroflée *f.*

wallop /'wɒləp/ *v.t.* (*p.t.* **walloped**) (*hit: sl.*) taper sur. ● *n.* (*blow: sl.*) grand coup *m.*

wallow /'wɒləʊ/ *v.i.* se vautrer.

wallpaper /'wɔːlpeɪpə(r)/ *n.* papier peint *m.* ● *v.t.* tapisser.

walnut /'wɔːlnʌt/ *n.* (*nut*) noix *f.*; (*tree*) noyer *m.*

walrus /'wɔːlrəs/ *n.* morse *m.*

waltz /wɔːls/ *n.* valse *f.* ● *v.i.* valser.

wan /wɒn/ *a.* pâle, blême.

wand /wɒnd/ *n.* baguette (magique) *f.*

wander /'wɒndə(r)/ *v.i.* errer; (*stroll*) flâner; (*digress*) s'écarter du sujet; (*in mind*) divaguer. ~**er** *n.* vagabond(e) *m.* (*f.*).

wane /weɪn/ *v.i.* décroître. ● *n.* **on the** ~, (*strength, fame, etc.*) en déclin; (*person*) sur son déclin.

wangle /'wæŋɡl/ *v.t.* (*obtain: sl.*) se débrouiller pour avoir.

want /wɒnt/ *v.t.* vouloir (**to do,** faire); (*need*) avoir besoin de (**doing,** d'être fait); (*ask for*) demander. ● *v.i.* ~ **for,** manquer de. ● *n.* (*need, poverty*) besoin *m.*; (*desire*) désir *m.*; (*lack*) manque *m.* **I** ~ **you to do it,** je veux que vous le fassiez. **for** ~ **of,** faute de. **~ed** *a.* (*criminal*) recherché par la police.

wanting /'wɒntɪŋ/ *a.* **be** ~, manquer (**in,** de).

wanton /'wɒntən/ *a.* (*cruelty*) gratuit; (*woman*) impudique.

war /wɔ:(r)/ *n.* guerre *f.* **at** ~, en guerre. **on the ~-path,** sur le sentier de la guerre.

ward /wɔ:d/ *n.* (*in hospital*) salle *f.*; (*minor: jurid.*) pupille *m./f.*; (*pol.*) division électorale *f.* ● *v.t.* ~ **off,** (*danger*) prévenir; (*blow, anger*) détourner.

warden /'wɔ:dn/ *n.* direc|teur, -trice *m., f.*; (*of park*) gardien(ne) *m.* (*f.*). (**traffic**) ~, contractuel(le) *m.* (*f.*).

warder /'wɔ:də(r)/ *n.* gardien (de prison) *m.*

wardrobe /'wɔ:drəʊb/ *n.* (*place*) armoire *f.*; (*clothes*) garde-robe *f.*

warehouse /'weəhaʊs/ *n.* (*pl.* **-s** /-haʊzɪz/) entrepôt *m.*

wares /weəz/ *n. pl.* (*goods*) marchandises *f. pl.*

warfare /'wɔ:feə(r)/ *n.* guerre *f.*

warhead /'wɔ:hed/ *n.* ogive *f.*

warily /'weərɪlɪ/ *adv.* avec prudence.

warm /wɔ:m/ *a.* (**-er, -est**) chaud; (*hearty*) chaleureux. **be** *or* **feel** ~, avoir chaud. **it is** ~, il fait chaud. ● *v.t./i.* ~ (**up**), (se) réchauffer; (*food*) chauffer; (*liven up*) (s')animer; (*exercise*) s'échauffer. **~-hearted** *a.* chaleureux. **~ly** *adv.* (*wrap up etc.*) chaudement; (*heartily*) chaleureusement. **~th** *n.* chaleur *f.*

warn /wɔ:n/ *v.t.* avertir, prévenir. ~ **s.o. off sth.,** (*advise against*) mettre qn. en garde contre qch.; (*forbid*) interdire qch. à qn. **~ing** *n.* avertissement *m.*; (*notice*) avis *m.* **without ~ing,** sans prévenir. **~ing light,** voyant *m.* **~ing triangle,** triangle de sécurité *m.*

warp /wɔ:p/ *v.t./i.* (*wood etc.*) (se) voiler; (*pervert*) pervertir.

warrant /'wɒrənt/ *n.* (*for arrest*) mandat (d'arrêt) *m.*; (*comm.*) autorisation *f.* ● *v.t.* justifier.

warranty /'wɒrəntɪ/ *n.* garantie *f.*

warring /'wɔ:rɪŋ/ *a.* en guerre.

warrior /'wɒrɪə(r)/ *n.* guerr|ier, -ière *m., f.*

warship /'wɔ:ʃɪp/ *n.* navire de guerre *m.*

wart /wɔ:t/ *n.* verrue *f.*

wartime /'wɔ:taɪm/ *n.* **in** ~, en temps de guerre.

wary /'weərɪ/ *a.* (**-ier, -iest**) prudent.

was /wɒz, *unstressed* wəz/ *see* be.

wash /wɒʃ/ *v.t./i.* (se) laver; (*flow over*) baigner. ● *n.* lavage *m.*; (*clothes*) lessive *f.*; (*of ship*) sillage *m.* **have a** ~, se laver. **~-basin** *n.* lavabo *m.* **~-cloth** *n.* (*Amer.*) gant de toilette *m.* ~ **down,** (*meal*) arroser. ~ **one's hands of,** se laver les mains de. ~ **out,** (*cup etc.*) laver; (*stain*) (faire) partir. **~-out** *n.* (*sl.*) fiasco *m.* **~-room** *n.* (*Amer.*) toilettes *f. pl.* ~ **up,** faire la vaisselle; (*Amer.*) se laver. **~able** *a.* lavable. **~ing** *n.* lessive *f.* **~ing-machine** *n.* machine à laver *f.* **~ing-powder** *n.* lessive *f.* **~ing-up** *n.* vaisselle *f.*; **~ing-up liquid,** produit pour la vaisselle *m.*

washed-out /wɒʃt'aʊt/ *a.* (*faded*) délavé; (*tired*) lessivé; (*ruined*) anéanti.

washer /'wɒʃə(r)/ *n.* rondelle *f.*

wasp /wɒsp/ *n.* guêpe *f.*

wastage /'weɪstɪdʒ/ *n.* gaspillage *m.* **some** ~, (*in goods, among candidates, etc.*) du déchet.

waste /weɪst/ *v.t.* gaspiller; (*time*) perdre. ● *v.i.* ~ **away,** dépérir. ● *a.* superflu; (*product*) de rebut. ● *n.* gaspillage *m.*; (*of time*) perte *f.*; (*rubbish*) déchets *m. pl.* **lay** ~, dévaster. ~ **disposal unit,** broyeur d'ordures *m.* ~ (**land**), (*desolate*) terre désolée *f.*; (*unused*) terre inculte *f.*; (*in town*) terrain vague *m.* ~ **paper,** vieux papiers *m. pl.* **~-paper basket,** corbeille (à papier) *f.* **~-pipe** *n.* vidange *f.*

wasteful /'weɪstfl/ *a.* peu économique; (*person*) gaspilleur.

watch /wɒtʃ/ *v.t./i.* (*television*) regarder; (*observe*) observer; (*guard, spy on*) surveiller; (*be careful about*) faire attention à. ● *n.* (*for telling time*) montre *f.*; (*naut.*) quart. **be on the** ~, guetter. **keep** ~ **on,** surveiller. **~-dog** *n.* chien de garde *m.* ~ **out,** (*take care*) faire attention (**for,** à). ~ **out for,** guetter. **~-tower** *n.* tour de guet *f.* **~ful** *a.* vigilant.

watchmaker /ˈwɒtʃmeɪkə(r)/ n. horlog|er, -ère m., f.

watchman /ˈwɒtʃmən/ n. (pl. -men) (of building) gardien m.

water /ˈwɔːtə(r)/ n. eau f. ● v.t. arroser. ● v.i. (of eyes) larmoyer. **my/his/**etc. **mouth** ~s, l'eau me/ lui/etc. vient à la bouche. **by** ~, en bateau. ~-**bottle** n. bouillotte f. ~-**closet** n. waters m. pl. ~-**colour** n. couleur pour aquarelle f.; (painting) aquarelle f. ~ **down**, couper (d'eau); (tone down) édulcorer. ~ **heater**, chauffe-eau m. ~-**ice** n. sorbet m. ~-**lily** n. nénuphar m. ~-**main** n. canalisation d'eau f. ~-**melon** n. pastèque f. ~-**pistol** n. pistolet à eau m. ~ **polo**, water-polo m. ~ **power**, énergie hydraulique f. ~-**skiing** n. ski nautique m.

watercress /ˈwɔːtəkres/ n. cresson (de fontaine) m.

waterfall /ˈwɔːtəfɔːl/ n. chute d'eau f., cascade f.

watering-can /ˈwɔːtərɪŋkæn/ n. arrosoir m.

waterlogged /ˈwɔːtəlɒɡd/ a. imprégné d'eau; (land) détrempé.

watermark /ˈwɔːtəmaːk/ n. (in paper) filigrane m.

waterproof /ˈwɔːtəpruːf/ a. (material) imperméable.

watershed /ˈwɔːtəʃed/ n. (in affairs) tournant décisif m.

watertight /ˈwɔːtətaɪt/ a. étanche.

waterway /ˈwɔːtəweɪ/ n. voie navigable f.

waterworks /ˈwɔːtəwɜːks/ n. (place) station hydraulique f.

watery /ˈwɔːtərɪ/ a. (colour) délavé; (eyes) humide; (soup) trop liquide; (tea) faible.

watt /wɒt/ n. watt m.

wav|e /weɪv/ n. vague f.; (in hair) ondulation f.; (radio) onde f.; (sign) signe m. ● v.t. agiter. ● v.i. faire signe (de la main); (move in wind) flotter. ~**y** a. (line) onduleux; (hair) ondulé.

wavelength /ˈweɪvleŋθ/ n. (radio & fig.) longueur d'ondes f.

waver /ˈweɪvə(r)/ v.i. vaciller.

wax[1] /wæks/ n. cire f.; (for skis) fart m. ● v.t. cirer; farter; (car) astiquer. ~**en**, ~**y** adjs. cireux.

wax[2] /wæks/ v.i. (of moon) croître.

waxwork /ˈwækswɜːk/ n. (dummy) figure de cire f.

way /weɪ/ n. (road, path) chemin m. (**to**, de); (distance) distance f.; (direction) direction f.; (manner) façon f.; (means) moyen m.; (particular) égard m. ~**s**, (habits) habitudes f. pl. ● adv. (fam.) loin. **be in the** ~, bloquer le passage; (hindrance: fig.) gêner (qn.). **be on one's** or **the** ~, être sur son or le chemin. **by the** ~, à propos. **by the** ~**side**, au bord de la route. **by** ~ **of**, comme; (via) par. **go out of one's** ~, se donner du mal pour. **in a** ~, dans un sens. **make one's** ~ **somewhere**, se rendre quelque part. **push one's** ~ **through**, se frayer un passage. **that** ~, par là. **this** ~, par ici. ~ **in**, entrée f. ~ **out**, sortie f. ~-**out** a. (strange: fam.) original.

waylay /ˈweɪleɪ/ v.t. (p.t. -**laid**) (assail) assaillir; (stop) accrocher.

wayward /ˈweɪwəd/ a. capricieux.

WC /dʌb(ə)ljuːˈsiː/ n. w.-c. m. pl.

we /wiː/ pron. nous.

weak /wiːk/ a. (-**er**, -**est**) faible; (delicate) fragile. ~**ly** adv. faiblement; a. faible. ~**ness** n. faiblesse f.; (fault) point faible m. **a** ~**ness for**, (liking) un faible pour.

weaken /ˈwiːkən/ v.t. affaiblir ● v.i. s'affaiblir, faiblir.

weakling /ˈwiːklɪŋ/ n. gringalet m.

wealth /welθ/ n. richesse f.; (riches, resources) richesses f. pl.; (quantity) profusion f.

wealthy /ˈwelθɪ/ a. (-**ier**, -**iest**) riche. ● n. **the** ~, les riches m. pl.

wean /wiːn/ v.t. (baby) sevrer.

weapon /ˈwepən/ n. arme f.

wear /weə(r)/ v.t. (p.t. **wore**, p.p. **worn**) porter; (put on) mettre; (expression etc.) avoir. ● v.i. (last) durer. ~ (**out**), (s')user. ● n. usage m.; (damage) usure f.; (clothing) vêtements m. pl. ~ **down**, user. ~ **off**, (colour, pain) passer. ~ **on**, (time) passer. ~ **out**, (exhaust) épuiser.

wear|y /ˈwɪərɪ/ a. (-**ier**, -**iest**) fatigué, las; (tiring) fatigant. ● v.i. ~**y of**, se lasser de. ~**ily** adv. avec lassitude. ~**iness** n. lassitude f., fatigue f.

weasel /ˈwiːzl/ n. belette f.

weather /ˈweðə(r)/ n. temps m. ● a. météorologique. ● v.t. (survive) réchapper de or à. **under the** ~, patraque. ~-**beaten** a. tanné. ~

forecast, météo *f.* **~-vane** *n.* girouette *f.*

weathercock /'weðəkɒk/ *n.* girouette *f.*

weave /wiːv/ *v.t./i.* (*p.t.* **wove,** *p.p.* **woven**) tisser; (*basket etc.*) tresser; (*move*) se faufiler. ● *n.* (*style*) tissage *m.* **~r** /-ə(r)/ *n.* tisserand(e) *m.* (*f.*).

web /web/ *n.* (*of spider*) toile *f.*; (*fabric*) tissu *m.*; (*on foot*) palmure *f.* **~bed** *a.* (*foot*) palmé. **~bing** *n.* (*in chair*) sangles *f. pl.*

wed /wed/ *v.t.* (*p.t.* **wedded**) épouser. ● *v.i.* se marier. **~ded to,** (*devoted to: fig.*) attaché à.

wedding /'wedɪŋ/ *n.* mariage *m.* **~-ring** *n.* alliance *f.*

wedge /wedʒ/ *n.* coin *m.*; (*under wheel etc.*) cale *f.* ● *v.t.* caler; (*push*) enfoncer; (*crowd*) coincer.

Wednesday /'wenzdɪ/ *n.* mercredi *m.*

wee /wiː/ *a.* (*fam.*) tout petit.

weed /wiːd/ *n.* mauvaise herbe *f.* ● *v.t./i.* désherber. **~-killer** *n.* désherbant *m.* ● **out,** extirper. **~y** *a.* (*person: fig.*) faible, maigre.

week /wiːk/ *n.* semaine *f.* **a ~ today/ tomorrow,** aujourd'hui/demain en huit. **~ly** *adv.* toutes les semaines; *a. & n.* (*periodical*) hebdomadaire (*m.*).

weekday /'wiːkdeɪ/ *n.* jour de semaine *m.*

weekend /wiːk'end/ *n.* week-end *m.*, fin de semaine *f.*

weep /wiːp/ *v.t./i.* (*p.t.* **wept**) pleurer (**for** s.o., qn.). **~ing willow,** saule pleureur *m.*

weigh /weɪ/ *v.t./i.* peser. **~ anchor,** lever l'ancre. **~ down,** faire plier; (*fig.*) accabler. **~ up,** (*examine*: *fam.*) calculer.

weight /weɪt/ *n.* poids *m.* **lose/put on ~,** perdre/prendre du poids. **~lessness** *n.* apesanteur *f.* **~-lifting** *n.* haltérophilie *f.* **~y** *a.* lourd; (*subject etc.*) de poids.

weighting /'weɪtɪŋ/ *n.* indemnité *f.*

weir /wɪə(r)/ *n.* barrage *m.*

weird /wɪəd/ *a.* (**-er, -est**) mystérieux; (*strange*) bizarre.

welcome /'welkəm/ *a.* agréable; (*timely*) opportun. **be ~,** être le *or* la bienvenu(e), être les bienvenu(e)s. **you're ~!,** (*after thank you*) il n'y a pas de quoi! **~ to do,** libre de faire. ● *int.* soyez le *or* la bienvenu(e),

soyez les bienvenu(e)s. ● *n.* accueil *m.* ● *v.t.* accueillir; (*as greeting*) souhaiter la bienvenue à; (*fig.*) se réjouir de.

weld /weld/ *v.t.* souder. ● *n.* soudure *f.* **~er** *n.* soudeur *m.* **~ing** *n.* soudure *f.*

welfare /'welfeə(r)/ *n.* bien-être *m.*; (*aid*) aide sociale *f.* **W~ State,** État-providence *m.*

well[1] /wel/ *n.* (*for water, oil*) puits *m.*; (*of stairs*) cage *f.*

well[2] /wel/ *adv.* (**better, best**) bien. ● *a.* bien *invar.* **as ~,** aussi. **be ~,** (*healthy*) aller bien. ● *int.* eh bien; (*surprise*) tiens. **do ~,** (*succeed*) réussir. **~-behaved** *a.* sage. **~-being** *n.* bien-être *m.* **~-built** *a.* bien bâti. **~-disposed** *a.* bien disposé. **~ done!,** bravo! **~-dressed** *a.* bien habillé. **~-heeled** *a.* (*fam.*) nanti. **~-informed** *a.* bien informé. **~-known** *a.* (bien) connu. **~-meaning** *a.* bien intentionné. **~ off,** aisé, riche. **~-read** *a.* instruit. **~-spoken** *a.* qui parle bien. **~-to-do** *a.* riche. **~-wisher** *n.* admirateur, -trice *m., f.*

wellington /'welɪŋtən/ *n.* (*boot*) botte de caoutchouc *f.*

Welsh /welʃ/ *a.* gallois. ● *n.* (*lang.*) gallois *m.* **~man** *n.* Gallois *m.* **~ rabbit,** croûte au fromage *f.* **~woman** *n.* Galloise *f.*

welsh /welʃ/ *v.i.* **~ on,** (*debt, promise*) ne pas honorer.

welterweight /'weltəweɪt/ *n.* poids mi-moyen *m.*

wench /wentʃ/ *n.* (*old use*) jeune fille *f.*

wend /wend/ *v.t.* **~ one's way,** se diriger, aller son chemin.

went /went/ *see* go.

wept /wept/ *see* weep.

were /wɜː(r)/, *unstressed* wə(r)/ *see* be.

west /west/ *n.* ouest *m.* **the W~,** (*pol.*) l'Occident *m.* ● *a.* d'ouest. ● *adv.* vers l'ouest. **the W~ Country,** le sud-ouest (de l'Angleterre). **W~ Germany,** Allemagne de l'Ouest *f.* **W~ Indian** *a. & n.* antillais(e) (*m.* (*f.*)). **the W~ Indies,** les Antilles *f. pl.* **~erly** *a.* d'ouest. **~ern** *a.* de l'ouest; (*pol.*) occidental; (*film*) western *m.* **~erner** *n.* occidental(e) *m.* (*f.*). **~ward** *a.* à l'ouest. **~wards** *adv.* vers l'ouest.

westernize /'westənaɪz/ *v.t.* occidentaliser.

wet /wet/ a. (**wetter, wettest**) mouillé; (*damp, rainy*) humide; (*paint*) frais. ● v.t. (*p.t.* **wetted**) mouiller. ● n. the ~, l'humidité f.; (*rain*) la pluie f. **get** ~, se mouiller. ~ **blanket**, rabat-joie m. invar. ~**ness** n. humidité f. ~ **suit**, combinaison de plongée f.

whack /wæk/ n. (*fam.*) grand coup m. ● v.t. (*fam.*) taper sur.

whacked /wækt/ a. (*fam.*) claqué.

whacking /ˈwækɪŋ/ a. énorme.

whale /weɪl/ n. baleine f.

wham /wæm/ int. vlan.

wharf /wɔːf/ n. (pl. **wharfs**) (*for ships*) quai m.

what /wɒt/ a. (*in questions*) quel(le), quel(le)s. ● pron. (*in questions*) qu'est-ce qui; (*object*) (qu'est-ce) que or qu'*; (*after prep.*) quoi; (*that which*) ce qui; (*object*) ce que, ce qu'*. ● int. quoi, comment. ~ **date?**, quelle date? ~ **time?**, à quelle heure? ~ **happened?**, qu'est-ce qui s'est passé? ~ **did he say?**, qu'est-ce qu'il a dit? ~ **he said,** ce qu'il a dit. ~ **is important,** ce qui est important. ~ **is it?**, qu'est-ce que c'est? ~ **you need,** ce dont vous avez besoin. ~ **a fool**/*etc.*, quel idiot/*etc.* ~ **about me/him**/*etc.*?, et moi/lui/*etc.*? ~ **about doing?**, si on faisait? ~ **for?**, pourquoi?

whatever /wɒtˈevə(r)/ a. ~ **book**/*etc.*, quel que soit le livre/*etc.* ● pron. (*no matter what*) quoi que, quoi qu'*; (*anything that*) tout ce qui; (*object*) tout ce que or qu'*. ~ **happens,** quoi qu'il arrive. ~ **happened?**, qu'est-ce qui est arrivé? ~ **the problems,** quels que soient les problèmes. ~ **you want,** tout ce que vous voulez. **nothing** ~, rien du tout.

whatsoever /wɒtsəʊˈevər/ a. & pron. = **whatever**.

wheat /wiːt/ n. blé m., froment m.

wheedle /ˈwiːdl/ v.t. cajoler.

wheel /wiːl/ n. roue f. ● v.t. pousser. ● v.i. tourner. **at the ~,** (*of vehicle*) au volant; (*helm*) au gouvernail. ~ **and deal,** faire des combines.

wheelbarrow /ˈwiːlbærəʊ/ n. brouette f.

wheelchair /ˈwiːltʃeə(r)/ n. fauteuil roulant m.

wheeze /wiːz/ v.i. siffler (en respirant). ● n. sifflement m.

when /wen/ adv. & pron. quand. ● conj. quand, lorsque. **the day/ moment ~,** le jour/moment où.

whenever /wenˈevə(r)/ conj. & adv. (*at whatever time*) quand; (*every time that*) chaque fois que.

where /weə(r)/ adv., conj., & pron. où; (*whereas*) alors que; (*the place that*) là où. ~**abouts** adv. (à peu près) où; n. s.o.'s ~**abouts,** l'endroit où se trouve qn. ~**by** adv. par quoi. ~**upon** adv. sur quoi.

whereas /weərˈæz/ conj. alors que.

wherever /weərˈevə(r)/ conj. & adv. où que; (*everywhere*) partout où; (*anywhere*) (là) où; (*emphatic where*) où donc.

whet /wet/ v.t. (*p.t.* **whetted**) (*appetite, desire*) aiguiser.

whether /ˈweðə(r)/ conj. si. **not know ~,** ne pas savoir si. ~ **I go or not,** que j'aille ou non.

which /wɪtʃ/ a. (*in questions*) quel(le), quel(le)s. ● pron. (*in questions*) lequel, laquelle, lesquel(le)s; (*the one or ones that*) celui (celle, ceux, celles) qui; (*object*) celui (celle, ceux, celles) que or qu'*; (*referring to whole sentence,* = *and that*) ce qui; (*object*) ce que, ce qu'*; (*after prep.*) lequel/*etc.* ● rel. pron. qui; (*object*) que, qu'*. ~ **house?,** quelle maison? ~ **(one) do you want?,** lequel voulez-vous? ~ **are ready?,** lesquels sont prêts? **the bird ~ flies,** l'oiseau qui vole. **the hat ~ he wears,** le chapeau qu'il porte. **of ~, from ~,** duquel/*etc.* **to ~, at ~,** auquel/*etc.* **the book of ~,** le livre dont or duquel. **after ~,** après quoi. **she was there, ~ surprised me,** elle était là, ce qui m'a surpris.

whichever /wɪtʃˈevə(r)/ a. ~ **book**/*etc.*, quel que soit le livre/*etc.* que or qui. **take ~ book you wish,** prenez le livre que vous voulez. ● pron. celui (celle, ceux, celles) qui or que.

whiff /wɪf/ n. (*puff*) bouffée f.

while /waɪl/ n. moment m. ● conj. (*when*) pendant que; (*although*) bien que; (*as long as*) tant que. ● v.t. ~ **away,** (*time*) passer.

whilst /waɪlst/ conj. = **while**.

whim /wɪm/ n. caprice m.

whimper /ˈwɪmpə(r)/ v.i. geindre, pleurnicher. ● n. pleurnichement m.

whimsical /ˈwɪmzɪkl/ a. (*person*) capricieux; (*odd*) bizarre.

whine /waɪn/ v.i. gémir, se plaindre.
● n. gémissement m.

whip /wɪp/ n. fouet m. ● v.t. (p.t.
whipped) fouetter; (culin.) fouetter,
battre; (seize) enlever brusquement. ● v.i. (move) aller en vitesse. **~-round** n. (fam.) collecte
f. **~ out**, (gun etc.) sortir. **~ up**,
exciter; (cause) provoquer; (meal:
fam.) préparer.

whirl /wɜːl/ v.t./i. (faire) tourbillonner. ● n. tourbillon m.

whirlpool /ˈwɜːlpuːl/ n. (in sea etc.)
tourbillon m.

whirlwind /ˈwɜːlwɪnd/ n. tourbillon
(de vent) m.

whirr /wɜː(r)/ v.i. vrombir.

whisk /wɪsk/ v.t. (snatch) enlever or
emmener brusquement; (culin.)
fouetter. ● n. (culin.) fouet m.;
(broom, brush) petit balai m. **~
away**, (brush away) chasser.

whisker /ˈwɪskə(r)/ n. poil m. **~s**,
(man's) barbe f., moustache f.; (side-
boards) favoris m. pl.

whisky /ˈwɪskɪ/ n. whisky m.

whisper /ˈwɪspə(r)/ v.t./i. chuchoter.
● n. chuchotement m.; (rumour:
fig.) rumeur f., bruit m.

whistle /ˈwɪsl/ n. sifflement m.; (instrument) sifflet m. ● v.t./i. siffler.
~ at or **for**, siffler.

Whit /wɪt/ a. **~ Sunday**, dimanche de
Pentecôte m.

white /waɪt/ a. (-er, -est) blanc. ● n.
blanc m.; (person) blanc(he) m. (f.).
~ coffee, café au lait m. **~-collar
worker**, employé(e) de bureau m.
(f.). **~ elephant**, objet, projet, etc.
inutile m. **~ lie**, pieux mensonge m.
W~ Paper, livre blanc m. **~ness** n.
blancheur f.

whiten /ˈwaɪtn/ v.t./i. blanchir.

whitewash /ˈwaɪtwɒʃ/ n. blanc de
chaux m. ● v.t. blanchir à la chaux;
(person: fig.) blanchir.

whiting /ˈwaɪtɪŋ/ n. invar. (fish)
merlan m.

Whitsun /ˈwɪtsn/ n. la Pentecôte.

whittle /ˈwɪtl/ v.t. **~ down**, tailler (au
couteau); (fig.) réduire.

whiz /wɪz/ v.i. (p.t. **whizzed**)
(through air) fendre l'air; (hiss)
siffler; (rush) aller à toute vitesse.
~-kid n. jeune prodige m.

who /huː/ pron. qui.

whodunit /huːˈdʌnɪt/ n. (story: fam.)
roman policier m.

whoever /huːˈevə(r)/ pron. (no matter who) qui que ce soit qui or que;
(the one who) quiconque. **tell ~ you
want**, dites-le à qui vous voulez.

whole /həʊl/ a. entier; (intact)
intact. **the ~ house/etc.**, toute la
maison/etc. ● n. totalité f.; (unit)
tout m. **on the ~**, dans l'ensemble.
~-hearted a., **~-heartedly** adv.
sans réserve.

wholefoods /ˈhəʊlfuːdz/ n. pl. aliments naturels et diététiques m. pl.

wholemeal /ˈhəʊlmiːl/ a. **~ bread**,
pain complet m.

wholesale /ˈhəʊlseɪl/ n. gros m. ● a.
(firm) de gros; (fig.) systématique.
● adv. (in large quantities) en gros;
(buy or sell one item) au prix de gros;
(fig.) en masse. **~r** /-ə(r)/ n. grossiste
m./f.

wholesome /ˈhəʊlsəm/ a. sain.

wholewheat /ˈhəʊlwiːt/ a. =
wholemeal.

wholly /ˈhəʊlɪ/ adv. entièrement.

whom /huːm/ pron. (that) que, qu'*;
(after prep. & in questions) qui. **of
~**, dont. **with ~**, avec qui.

whooping cough /ˈhuːpɪŋkɒf/ n.
coqueluche f.

whopping /ˈwɒpɪŋ/ a. (sl.) énorme.

whore /hɔː(r)/ n. putain f.

whose /huːz/ pron. & a. à qui, de qui.
~ hat is this?, ~ is this hat?, à qui
est ce chapeau? **~ son are you?**,
de qui êtes-vous le fils? **the man ~
hat I see**, l'homme dont je vois le
chapeau.

why /waɪ/ adv. pourquoi. ● int. eh
bien, ma parole, tiens. **the reason
~**, la raison pour laquelle.

wick /wɪk/ n. (of lamp etc.) mèche f.

wicked /ˈwɪkɪd/ a. méchant, mauvais,
vilain. **~ly** adv. méchamment.
~ness n. méchanceté f.

wicker /ˈwɪkə(r)/ n. osier m. **~work**
n. vannerie f.

wicket /ˈwɪkɪt/ n. guichet m.

wide /waɪd/ a. (-er, -est) large; (ocean
etc.) vaste. ● adv. (fall etc.) loin du
but. **open ~**, ouvrir tout grand. **~
open**, grand ouvert. **~-angle lens**
grand-angle m. **~ awake**, éveillé.
~ly adv. (spread, space) largement;
(travel) beaucoup; (generally) généralement; (extremely) extrêmement.

widen /ˈwaɪdn/ v.t./i. (s')élargir.

widespread /ˈwaɪdspred/ a. très répandu.

widow /'wɪdəʊ/ n. veuve. f. ~ed a.
(man) veuf; (woman) veuve. be
~ed, (become widower or widow)
devenir veuf or veuve. ~er n. veuf
m.

width /wɪdθ/ n. largeur f.

wield /wiːld/ v.t. (axe etc.) manier;
(power: fig.) exercer.

wife /waɪf/ n. (pl. wives) femme f.,
épouse f. ~ly a. d'épouse.

wig /wɪg/ n. perruque f.

wiggle /'wɪgl/ v.t./i. remuer; (hips)
tortiller; (of worm) se tortiller.

wild /waɪld/ a. (-er, -est) sauvage;
(sea, enthusiasm) déchaîné; (mad)
fou; (angry) furieux. ● adv. (grow)
à l'état sauvage. ~s n. pl. régions
sauvages f. pl. run ~, (free) courir
en liberté. ~-goose chase, fausse
piste f. ~ly adv. violemment;
(madly) follement.

wildcat /'waɪldkæt/ a. ~ strike,
grève sauvage f.

wilderness /'wɪldənɪs/ n. désert m.

wildlife /'waɪldlaɪf/ n. faune f.

wile /waɪl/ n. ruse f., artifice m.

wilful /'wɪlfl/ a. (intentional, obstinate) volontaire.

will [1] /wɪl/ v. aux. he ~ do/you ~
sing/etc., (future tense) il fera/tu
chanteras/etc. ~ you have a coffee?, voulez-vous prendre un café?

will [2] /wɪl/ n. volonté f.; (document)
testament m. ● v.t. (wish) vouloir.
at ~, quand or comme on veut. ~-
power n. volonté f. ~ o.s. to do,
faire un effort de volonté pour faire.

willing /'wɪlɪŋ/ a. (help, offer) spontané; (helper) bien disposé. ~ to,
disposé à. ~ly adv. (with pleasure)
volontiers; (not forced) volon-
tairement. ~ness n. empressement
m. (to do, à faire); (goodwill) bonne
volonté f.

willow /'wɪləʊ/ n. saule m.

willy-nilly /'wɪlɪ'nɪlɪ/ adv. bon gré mal
gré.

wilt /wɪlt/ v.i. (plant etc.) dépérir.

wily /'waɪlɪ/ a. (-ier, -iest) rusé.

win /wɪn/ v.t./i. (p.t. won, pres. p.
winning) gagner; (victory, prize)
remporter; (fame, fortune) acquérir,
trouver. ● n. victoire f. ~ round,
convaincre.

wince /wɪns/ v.i. se crisper,
tressaillir. without ~ing, sans
broncher.

winch /wɪntʃ/ n. treuil m. ● v.t.
hisser au treuil.

wind [1] /wɪnd/ n. vent m.; (breath)
souffle m. ● v.t. essouffler. get ~
of, avoir vent de. in the ~, dans
l'air. ~cheater, (Amer.) ~breaker
ns. blouson m. ~ instrument, instrument à vent m. ~-swept a.
balayé par les vents.

wind [2] /waɪnd/ v.t./i. (p.t. wound)
(s')enrouler; (of path, river)
serpenter. ~ (up), (clock etc.)
remonter. ~ up, (end) (se)
terminer. ~ up in hospital, finir à
l'hôpital. ~ing a. (path) sinueux.

windfall /'wɪndfɔːl/ n. fruit tombé m.;
(money: fig.) aubaine f.

windmill /'wɪndmɪl/ n. moulin à vent
m.

window /'wɪndəʊ/ n. fenêtre f.; (glass
pane) vitre f.; (in vehicle, train) vitre
f.; (in shop) vitrine f.; (counter)
guichet m. ~-box n. jardinière f.
~-cleaner n. laveur de carreaux m.
~-dresser n. étalagiste m./f.
~ledge n. rebord de (la) fenêtre m.;
~-shopping n. lèche-vitrines m. ~-
sill n. (inside) appui de (la) fenêtre
m.; (outside) rebord de (la) fenêtre
m.

windpipe /'wɪndpaɪp/ n. trachée f.

windscreen /'wɪndskriːn/, (Amer.)
windshield /'wɪndʃiːld/ n. pare-
brise m. invar. ~ washer, lave-glace
m. ~ wiper, essuie-glace m.

windsurf|ing /'wɪndsɜːfɪŋ/ n.
planche à voile f. ~er n. véliplanchiste m./f.

windy /'wɪndɪ/ a. (-ier, -iest) venteux.
it is ~, il y a du vent.

wine /waɪn/ n. vin m. ~-cellar n.
cave (à vin) f. ~-grower n. viticul-
teur m. ~-growing n. viticulture f.;
a. viticole. ~ list, carte des vins f. ~-
tasting n. dégustation de vins f. ~-
waiter, sommelier m.

wineglass /'waɪnglɑːs/ n. verre à vin
m.

wing /wɪŋ/ n. aile f. ~s, (theatre)
coulisses f. pl. under one's ~, sous
son aile. ~ mirror, rétroviseur extérieur m. ~ed a. ailé. ~er n.
(sport) ailier m.

wink /wɪŋk/ v.i. faire un clin d'œil;
(light, star) clignoter. ● n. clin
d'œil m.; clignotement m.

winner /'wɪnə(r)/ n. (of game) ga-
gnant(e) m. (f.); (of fight) vainqueur
m.

winning /'wɪnɪŋ/ see win. ● a.
(number, horse) gagnant; (team)

victorieux; (*smile*) engageant. ~s *n. pl.* gains *m. pl.*

wint|er /'wɪntə(r)/ *n.* hiver *m.* ● *v.i.* hiverner. ~ry *a.* hivernal.

wipe /waɪp/ *v.t.* essuyer. ● *v.i.* ~ up, essuyer la vaisselle. ● *n.* coup de torchon *or* d'éponge *m.* ~ off *or* out, essuyer. ~ out, (*destroy*) anéantir; (*remove*) effacer.

wir|e /'waɪə(r)/ *n.* fil *m.*; (*Amer.*) télégramme *m.* ~e netting, grillage *m.* ~ing *n.* (*electr.*) installation électrique *f.*

wireless /'waɪəlɪs/ *n.* radio *f.*

wiry /'waɪərɪ/ *a.* (-ier, -iest) (*person*) nerveux et maigre.

wisdom /'wɪzdəm/ *n.* sagesse *f.*

wise /waɪz/ *a.* (-er, -est) prudent, sage; (*look*) averti. ~ guy, (*fam.*) petit malin *m.* ~ man, sage *m.* ~ly *adv.* prudemment.

wisecrack /'waɪzkræk/ *n.* (*fam.*) mot d'esprit *m.*, astuce *f.*

wish /wɪʃ/ *n.* (*specific*) souhait *m.*, vœu *m.*; (*general*) désir *m.* ● *v.t.* souhaiter, vouloir, désirer (to do, faire); (*bid*) souhaiter. ● *v.i.* ~ for, souhaiter. I ~ he'd leave, je voudrais bien qu'il parte. best ~es, (*in letter*) amitiés *f. pl.*; (*on greeting card*) meilleurs vœux *m. pl.*

wishful /'wɪʃfl/ *a.* it's ~ thinking, on se fait des illusions.

wishy-washy /'wɪʃɪwɒʃɪ/ *a.* fade.

wisp /wɪsp/ *n.* (*of smoke*) volute *f.*

wistful /'wɪstfl/ *a.* mélancolique.

wit /wɪt/ *n.* intelligence *f.*; (*humour*) esprit *m.*; (*person*) homme d'esprit *m.*, femme d'esprit *f.* be at one's ~'s or ~s' end, ne plus savoir que faire.

witch /wɪtʃ/ *n.* sorcière *f.* ~craft *n.* sorcellerie *f.*

with /wɪð/ *prep.* avec; (*having*) à; (*because of*) de; (*at house of*) chez. the man ~ the beard, l'homme à la barbe. fill/*etc.* ~, remplir/*etc.* de. pleased/shaking/*etc.* ~, content/ frémissant/ *etc.* de. ~ it, (*fam.*) dans le vent.

withdraw /wɪð'drɔː/ *v.t./i.* (*p.t.* **withdrew**, *p.p.* **withdrawn**) (se) retirer. ~al *n.* retrait *m.* ~n *a.* (*person*) renfermé.

wither /'wɪðə(r)/ *v.t./i.* (se) flétrir. ~ed *a.* (*person*) desséché.

withhold /wɪð'həʊld/ *v.t.* (*p.t.* **withheld**) refuser (de donner); (*retain*) retenir; (*conceal, not tell*) cacher (from, à).

within /wɪ'ðɪn/ *prep. & adv.* à l'intérieur (de); (*in distances*) à moins de. ~ a month, (*before*) avant un mois. ~ sight, en vue.

without /wɪ'ðaʊt/ *prep.* sans. ~ my knowing, sans que je sache.

withstand /wɪð'stænd/ *v.t.* (*p.t.* **withstood**) résister à.

witness /'wɪtnɪs/ *n.* témoin *m.*; (*evidence*) témoignage *m.* ● *v.t.* être le témoin de, voir; (*document*) signer. bear ~ to, témoigner de. ~ box or stand, barre des témoins *f.*

witticism /'wɪtɪsɪzəm/ *n.* bon mot *m.*

witt|y /'wɪtɪ/ *a.* (-ier, -iest) spirituel. ~iness *n.* esprit *m.*

wives /waɪvz/ *see* wife.

wizard /'wɪzəd/ *n.* magicien *m.*; (*genius*: fig.) génie *m.*

wobbl|e /'wɒbl/ *v.i.* (*of jelly, voice, hand*) trembler; (*stagger*) chanceler; (*of table, chair*) branler. ~y *a.* tremblant; branlant.

woe /wəʊ/ *n.* malheur *m.*

woke, woken /wəʊk, 'wəʊkən/ *see* wake[1].

wolf /wʊlf/ *n.* (*pl.* wolves) loup *m.* ● *v.t.* (*food*) engloutir. cry ~, crier au loup. ~-whistle *n.* sifflement admiratif *m.*

woman /'wʊmən/ *n.* (*pl.* women) femme *f.* ~ doctor, femme médecin *f.* ~ driver, femme au volant *f.* ~ friend, amie *f.* ~hood *n.* féminité *f.* ~ly *a.* féminin.

womb /wuːm/ *n.* utérus *m.*

women /'wɪmɪn/ *see* woman.

won /wʌn/ *see* win.

wonder /'wʌndə(r)/ *n.* émerveillement *m.*; (*thing*) merveille *f.* ● *v.t.* se demander (if, si). ● *v.i.* s'étonner (at, de); (*reflect*) songer (about, à). it is no ~, ce *or* il n'est pas étonnant (that, que).

wonderful /'wʌndəfl/ *a.* merveilleux. ~ly *adv.* merveilleusement; (*work, do, etc.*) à merveille.

won't /wəʊnt/ = will not.

woo /wuː/ *v.t.* (*woman*) faire la cour à; (*please*) chercher à plaire à.

wood /wʊd/ *n.* bois *m.* ~ed *a.* boisé. ~en *a.* en or de bois; (*stiff*: fig.) raide, comme du bois.

woodcut /'wʊdkʌt/ *n.* gravure sur bois *f.*

woodland /'wʊdlənd/ *n.* région boisée *f.*, bois *m. pl.*

woodpecker /'wʊdpekə(r)/ *n.* (*bird*) pic *m.*, pivert *m.*

woodwind /'wʊdwɪnd/ n. (mus.) bois m. pl.

woodwork /'wʊdwɜːk/ n. (craft, objects) menuiserie f.

woodworm /'wʊdwɜːm/ n. (larvae) vers (de bois) m. pl.

woody /'wʊdɪ/ a. (wooded) boisé; (like wood) ligneux.

wool /wʊl/ n. laine f. **~len** a. de laine. **~lens** n. pl. lainages m. pl. **~ly** a. laineux; (vague) nébuleux; n. (garment: fam.) lainage m.

word /wɜːd/ n. mot m.; (spoken) parole f., mot m.; (promise) parole f.; (news) nouvelles f. pl. ● v.t. rédiger. **by ~ of mouth**, de vive voix. **give/keep one's ~**, donner/tenir sa parole. **have a ~ with**, parler à. **in other ~s**, autrement dit. **~ processor**, machine de traitement de texte f. **~ing** n. termes m. pl.

wordy /'wɜːdɪ/ a. verbeux.

wore /wɔː(r)/ see wear.

work /wɜːk/ n. travail m.; (product, book, etc.) œuvre f., ouvrage m.; (building etc. work) travaux m. pl. **~s**, (techn.) mécanisme m.; (factory) usine f. ● v.t./i. (of person) travailler; (shape, hammer, etc.) travailler; (techn.) (faire) fonctionner, (faire) marcher; (land, mine) exploiter; (of drug etc.) agir. **~ s.o.**, (make work) faire travailler qn. **~-force** n. main-d'œuvre f. **~ in**, (s')introduire. **~-load** n. travail (à faire) m. **~ off**, (get rid of) se débarrasser de. **~ out** v.t. (solve) résoudre; (calculate) calculer; (elaborate) élaborer; v.i. (succeed) marcher; (sport) s'entraîner. **~-station** n. poste de travail m. **~-to-rule** n. grève du zèle f. **~ up** v.t. développer; v.i. (to climax) monter vers. **~ed up**, (person) énervé.

workable /'wɜːkəbl/ a. réalisable.

workaholic /wɜːkə'hɒlɪk/ n. (fam.) bourreau de travail m.

worker /'wɜːkə(r)/ n. travailleu|r, -se m., f.; (manual) ouvr|ier, -ière m., f.

working /'wɜːkɪŋ/ a. (day, lunch, etc.) de travail. **~s** n. pl. mécanisme m. **~ class**, classe ouvrière f. **~-class** a. ouvrier. **in ~ order**, en état de marche.

workman /'wɜːkmən/ n. (pl. -men) ouvrier m. **~ship** n. maîtrise f.

workshop /'wɜːkʃɒp/ n. atelier m.

world /wɜːld/ n. monde m. ● a. (power etc.) mondial; (record etc.)

du monde. **best in the ~**, meilleur au monde. **~-wide** a. universel.

worldly /'wɜːldlɪ/ a. de ce monde, terrestre. **~-wise** a. qui a l'expérience du monde.

worm /wɜːm/ n. ver m. ● v.t. **~ one's way into**, s'insinuer dans. **~-eaten** a. (wood) vermoulu; (fruit) véreux.

worn /wɔːn/ see wear. ● a. usé. **~-out** a. (thing) complètement usé; (person) épuisé.

worr|y /'wʌrɪ/ v.t./i. (s')inquiéter. ● n. souci m. **~ied** a. inquiet. **~ier** n. inqu|et, -iète m., f.

worse /wɜːs/ a. pire, plus mauvais. ● adv. plus mal. ● n. pire m. **be ~ off**, perdre.

worsen /'wɜːsn/ v.t./i. empirer.

worship /'wɜːʃɪp/ n. (adoration) culte m. ● v.t. (p.t. **worshipped**) adorer. ● v.i. faire ses dévotions. **~per** n. (in church) fidèle m./f.

worst /wɜːst/ a. pire, plus mauvais. ● adv. (the) ~, (sing etc.) le plus mal. ● n. **the ~ (one)**, (person, object) le or la pire. **the ~ (thing)**, le pire (that, que). **get the ~ of it**, (be defeated) avoir le dessous.

worsted /'wʊstɪd/ n. worsted m.

worth /wɜːθ/ a. **be ~**, valoir. **it is ~ waiting**/etc., ça vaut la peine d'attendre/etc. ● n. valeur f. **ten pence ~ of**, (pour) dix pence de. **it is ~ (one's) while**, ça (en) vaut la peine. **~less** a. qui ne vaut rien.

worthwhile /wɜːθ'waɪl/ a. qui (en) vaut la peine.

worthy /'wɜːðɪ/ a. (-ier, -iest) digne (of, de); (laudable) louable. ● n. (person) notable m.

would /wʊd, unstressed wəd/ v. aux. **he ~ do/you ~ sing**/etc., (conditional tense) il ferait/tu chanterais/etc. **he ~ have done**, il aurait fait. **I ~ come every day**, (used to) je venais chaque jour. **I ~ like some tea**, je voudrais du thé. **~ you come here?**, voulez-vous venir ici? **he ~n't come**, il a refusé de venir. **~-be** a. soi-disant.

wound¹ /wuːnd/ n. blessure f. ● v.t. blesser. **the ~ed**, les blessés m. pl.

wound² /waʊnd/ see wind².

wove, woven /wəʊv, 'wəʊvn/ see weave.

wow /waʊ/ int. mince (alors).

wrangle /'ræŋgl/ v.i. se disputer. ● n. dispute f.

wrap /ræp/ *v.t.* (*p.t.* **wrapped**). ~ **(up)**, envelopper. ● *v.i.* ~ **up**, (*dress warmly*) se couvrir. ● *n.* châle *m.* ~**ped up in**, (*engrossed*) absorbé dans. ~**per** *n.* (*of book*) jaquette *f.*; (*of sweet*) papier *m.* ~**ping** *n.* emballage *m.*; ~**ping paper**, papier d'emballage *m.*

wrath /rɒθ/ *n.* courroux *m.*

wreak /riːk/ *v.t.* ~ **havoc,** (*of storm etc.*) faire des ravages.

wreath /riːθ/ *n.* (*pl.* **-s** /-ðz/) (*of flowers, leaves*) couronne *f.*

wreck /rek/ *n.* (*sinking*) naufrage *m.*; (*ship, remains, person*) épave *f.*; (*vehicle*) voiture accidentée *or* délabrée *f.* ● *v.t.* détruire; (*ship*) provoquer le naufrage de. ~**age** *n.* (*pieces*) débris *m. pl.*; (*wrecked building*) décombres *m. pl.*

wren /ren/ *n.* roitelet *m.*

wrench /rentʃ/ *v.t.* (*pull*) tirer sur; (*twist*) tordre; (*snatch*) arracher (**from**, à). ● *n.* (*tool*) clé *f.*

wrest /rest/ *v.t.* arracher (**from**, à).

wrestl|e /'resl/ *v.i.* lutter, se débattre (**with**, contre). ~**er** *n.* lutteu|r, -se *m.*, *f.*; catcheu|r, -se *m.*, *f.* ~**ing** *n.* lutte *f.* (**all-in**) ~**ing**, catch *m.*

wretch /retʃ/ *n.* malheureu|x, -se *m.*, *f.*; (*rascal*) misérable *m./f.*

wretched /'retʃɪd/ *a.* (*pitiful, poor*) misérable; (*bad*) affreux.

wriggle /'rɪgl/ *v.t./i.* (se) tortiller.

wring /rɪŋ/ *v.t.* (*p.t.* **wrung**) tordre; (*clothes*) essorer. ~ **out of,** (*obtain from*) arracher à. ~**ing wet**, trempé (jusqu'aux os).

wrinkle /'rɪŋkl/ *n.* (*crease*) pli *m.*; (*on skin*) ride *f.* ● *v.t./i.* (se) rider.

wrist /rɪst/ *n.* poignet *m.* ~**-watch** *n.* montre-bracelet *f.*

writ /rɪt/ *n.* acte judiciaire *m.*

write /raɪt/ *v.t./i.* (*p.t.* **wrote**, *p.p.* **written**) écrire. ~ **back**, répondre. ~ **down**, noter. ~ **off**, (*debt*) passer aux profits et pertes; (*vehicle*) considérer bon pour la casse. ~**-off** *n.* perte totale *f.* ~ **up**, (*from notes*) rédiger. ~**-up** *n.* compte rendu *m.*

writer /'raɪtə(r)/ *n.* auteur *m.*, écrivain *m.* ~ **of,** auteur de.

writhe /raɪð/ *v.i.* se tordre.

writing /'raɪtɪŋ/ *n.* écriture *f.* ~**(s),** (*works*) écrits *m. pl.* **in ~,** par écrit. ~**-paper** *n.* papier à lettres *m.*

written /'rɪtn/ *see* write.

wrong /rɒŋ/ *a.* (*incorrect, mistaken*) faux, mauvais; (*unfair*) injuste; (*amiss*) qui ne va pas; (*clock*) pas à l'heure. **be ~,** (*person*) avoir tort (**to**, de); (*be mistaken*) se tromper. ● *adv.* mal. ● *n.* injustice *f.*; (*evil*) mal *m.* ● *v.t.* faire (du) tort à. **be in the ~,** avoir tort. **go ~,** (*err*) se tromper; (*turn out badly*) mal tourner; (*vehicle*) tomber en panne. **it is ~ to,** (*morally*) c'est mal de. **what's ~?,** qu'est-ce qui ne va pas? **what is ~ with you?,** qu'est-ce que vous avez? ~**ly** *adv.* mal; (*blame etc.*) à tort.

wrongful /'rɒŋfl/ *a.* injustifié, injuste. ~**ly** *adv.* à tort.

wrote /rəʊt/ *see* write.

wrought /rɔːt/ *a.* ~ **iron,** fer forgé *m.*

wrung /rʌŋ/ *see* wring.

wry /raɪ/ *a.* (**wryer, wryest**) (*smile*) désabusé, forcé. ~ **face,** grimace *f.*

X

xerox /'zɪərɒks/ *v.t.* photocopier.

Xmas /'krɪsməs/ *n.* Noël *m.*

X-ray /'eksreɪ/ *n.* rayon X *m.*; (*photograph*) radio(graphie) *f.* ● *v.t.* radiographier.

xylophone /'zaɪləfəʊn/ *n.* xylophone *m.*

Y

yacht /jɒt/ *n.* yacht *m.* ~**ing** *n.* yachting *m.*

yank /jæŋk/ *v.t.* tirer brusquement. ● *n.* coup brusque *m.*

Yank /jæŋk/ *n.* (*fam.*) Américain(e) *m.* (*f.*), Amerloque *m./f.*

yap /jæp/ *v.i.* (*p.t.* **yapped**) japper.

yard[1] /jɑːd/ *n.* (*measure*) yard *m.* (= 0.9144 *metre*).

yard[2] /jɑːd/ *n.* (*of house etc.*) cour *f.*; (*garden: Amer.*) jardin *m.*; (*for storage*) chantier *m.*, dépôt *m.*

yardstick /'jɑːdstɪk/ *n.* mesure *f.*

yarn /jɑːn/ *n.* (*thread*) fil *m.*; (*tale: fam.*) (longue) histoire *f.*

yawn /jɔːn/ *v.i.* bâiller. ● *n.* bâillement *m.* ~**ing** *a.* (*gaping*) béant.

year /jɪə(r)/ *n.* an *m.*, année *f.*; **school/ tax/**etc. ~, année scolaire/fiscale/ etc. **be ten/**etc. ~**s old,** avoir dix/etc.

ans. **~-book** *n.* annuaire *m.* **~ly** *a.* annuel; *adv.* annuellement.

yearn /jɜːn/ *v.i.* avoir bien *or* très envie (**for, to,** de). **~ing** *n.* envie *f.*

yeast /jiːst/ *n.* levure *f.*

yell /jel/ *v.t./i.* hurler. ● *n.* hurlement *m.*

yellow /'jeləʊ/ *a.* jaune; (*cowardly: fam.*) froussard. ● *n.* jaune *m.*

yelp /jelp/ *n.* (*of dog etc.*) jappement *m.* ● *v.i.* japper.

yen /jen/ *n.* (*desire*) grande envie *f.*

yes /jes/ *adv.* oui; (*as answer to negative question*) si. ● *n.* oui *m. invar.*

yesterday /'jestədɪ/ *n. & adv.* hier (*m.*).

yet /jet/ *adv.* encore; (*already*) déjà. ● *conj.* pourtant, néanmoins.

yew /juː/ *n.* (*tree, wood*) if *m.*

Yiddish /'jɪdɪʃ/ *n.* yiddish *m.*

yield /jiːld/ *v.t.* (*produce*) produire, rendre; (*profit*) rapporter; (*surrender*) céder. ● *v.i.* (*give way*) céder. ● *n.* rendement *m.*

yoga /'jəʊgə/ *n.* yoga *m.*

yoghurt /'jɒgət, Amer. 'jəʊgərt/ *n.* yaourt *m.*

yoke /jəʊk/ *n.* joug *m.*

yokel /'jəʊkl/ *n.* rustre *m.*

yolk /jəʊk/ *n.* jaune (d'œuf) *m.*

yonder /'jɒndə(r)/ *adv.* là-bas.

you /juː/ *pron.* (*familiar form*) tu, *pl.* vous; (*polite form*) vous; (*object*) te, t'*, *pl.* vous; (*polite*) vous; (*after prep.*) toi, *pl.* vous; (*polite*) vous; (*indefinite*) on; (*object*) vous. (**to**) **~,** te, t'*, *pl.* vous; (*polite*) vous. **I gave ~ a pen,** je vous ai donné un stylo. **I know ~,** je te connais; je vous connais.

young /jʌŋ/ *a.* (**-er, -est**) jeune. ● *n.* (*people*) jeunes *m. pl.*; (*of animals*) petits *m. pl.* **~er** *a.* (*brother etc.*) cadet. **~est** *a.* **my ~est brother,** le cadet de mes frères.

youngster /'jʌŋstə(r)/ *n.* jeune *m./f.*

your /jɔː(r)/ *a.* (*familiar form*) ton, ta, *pl.* tes; (*polite form, & familiar form pl.*) votre, *pl.* vos.

yours /jɔːz/ *poss. pron.* (*familiar form*) le tien, la tienne, les tien(ne)s; (*polite form, & familiar form pl.*) le *or* la vôtre, les vôtres. **~ faithfully/ sincerely,** je vous prie d'agréer/de croire en l'expression de mes sentiments les meilleurs.

yoursel|f /jɔːˈself/ *pron.* (*familiar form*) toi-même; (*polite form*) vous-même; (*reflexive & after prep.*) te, t'*;

vous. **~ves** *pron. pl.* vous-mêmes; (*reflexive*) vous.

youth /juːθ/ *n.* (*pl.* **-s** /-ðz/) jeunesse *f.*; (*young man*) jeune *m.* **~ club,** centre de jeunes *m.* **~hostel,** auberge de jeunesse *f.* **~ful** *a.* juvénile, jeune.

yo-yo /'jəʊjəʊ/ *n.* (*pl.* **-os**) (P.) yo-yo *m. invar.* (P.).

Yugoslav /'juːgəslɑːv/ *a. & n.* Yougoslave (*m./f.*) **~ia** /-'slɑːvɪə/ *n.* Yougoslavie *f.*

yuppie /'jʌpɪ/ *n.* yuppie *m.*

Z

zany /'zeɪnɪ/ *a.* (**-ier, -iest**) farfelu.

zap /zæp/ *v.t.* (*fam.*) (*kill*) descendre; (*comput.*) enlever; (*TV*) zapper.

zeal /ziːl/ *n.* zèle *m.*

zealous /'zeləs/ *a.* zélé. **~ly** *a.* zèle.

zebra /'zebrə, 'ziːbrə/ *n.* zèbre *m.* **~ crossing,** passage pour piétons *m.*

zenith /'zenɪθ/ *n.* zénith *m.*

zero /'zɪərəʊ/ *n.* (*pl.* **-os**) zéro *m.* **~ hour,** l'heure H *f.*

zest /zest/ *n.* (*gusto*) entrain *m.*; (*spice: fig.*) piment *m.*; (*of orange or lemon peel*) zeste *m.*

zigzag /'zɪgzæg/ *n.* zigzag *m.* ● *a. & adv.* en zigzag. ● *v.i.* (*p.t.* **zig-zagged**) zigzaguer.

zinc /zɪŋk/ *n.* zinc *m.*

Zionism /'zaɪənɪzəm/ *n.* sionisme *m.*

zip /zɪp/ *n.* (*vigour*) allant *m.* **~(-fastener),** fermeture éclair *f.* (P.). ● *v.t.* (*p.t.* **zipped**) fermer avec une fermeture éclair (P.). ● *v.i.* aller à toute vitesse. **Zip code,** (*Amer.*) code postal *m.*

zipper /'zɪpə(r)/ *n.* (*Amer.*) = **zip (-fastener).**

zither /'zɪðə(r)/ *n.* cithare *f.*

zodiac /'zəʊdɪæk/ *n.* zodiaque *m.*

zombie /'zɒmbɪ/ *n.* mort(e) vivant(e) *m.* (*f.*); (*fam.*) automate *m.*

zone /zəʊn/ *n.* zone *f.*

zoo /zuː/ *n.* zoo *m.*

zoolog|y /zəʊˈɒlədʒɪ/ *n.* zoologie *f.* **~ical** /-əˈlɒdʒɪkl/ *a.* zoologique. **~ist** *n.* zoologiste *m./f.*

zoom /zuːm/ *v.i.* (*rush*) se précipiter. **~ lens,** zoom *m.* **~ off** *or* **past,** filer (comme une flèche).

zucchini /zuːˈkiːnɪ/ *n. invar.* (*Amer.*) courgette *f.*

French Verb Tables

Notes: The conditional may be formed by substituting the following endings for those of the future: *ais* for *ai* and *as*, *ait* for *a*, *ions* for *ons*, *iez* for *ez*, *aient* for *ont*. The present participle is formed (unless otherwise indicated) by substituting *ant* for *ons* in the first person plural of the present tense (e.g. *finissant* and *donnant* may be derived from *finissons* and *donnons*). The imperative forms are (unless otherwise indicated) the same as the second persons singular and plural and the first person plural of the present tense. The second person singular does not take *s* after *e* or *a* (e.g. *donne*, *va*), except when followed by *y* or *en* (e.g. *vas-y*).

Regular verbs:

1. in -*er* (e.g. **donn|er**)
   Present. ~e, ~es, ~e, ~ons, ~ez, ~ent.
   Imperfect. ~ais, ~ais, ~ait, ~ions, ~iez, ~aient.
   Past historic. ~ai, ~as, ~a, ~âmes, ~âtes, ~èrent.
   Future. ~erai, ~eras, ~era, ~erons, ~erez, ~eront.
   Present subjunctive. ~e, ~es, ~e, ~ions, ~iez, ~ent.
   Past participle. ~é.

2. in -*ir* (e.g. **fin|ir**)
   Pres. ~is, ~is, ~it, ~issons, ~issez, ~issent.
   Impf. ~issais, ~issais, ~issait, ~issions, ~issiez, ~issaient.
   Past hist. ~is, ~is, ~it, ~îmes, ~îtes, ~irent.
   Fut. ~irai, ~iras, ~ira, ~irons, ~irez, ~iront.
   Pres. sub. ~isse, ~isses, ~isse, ~issions, ~issiez, ~issent.
   Past part. ~i.

3. in -*re* (e.g. **vend|re**)
   Pres. ~s, ~s, ~, ~ons, ~ez, ~ent.
   Impf. ~ais, ~ais, ~ait, ~ions, ~iez, ~aient.
   Past hist. ~is, ~is, ~it, ~îmes, ~îtes, ~irent.
   Fut. ~rai, ~ras, ~ra, ~rons, ~rez, ~ront.
   Pres. sub. ~e, ~es, ~e, ~ions, ~iez, ~ent.
   Past part. ~u.

Peculiarities of -*er* verbs:

In verbs in -*cer* (e.g. **commencer**) and -*ger* (e.g. **manger**), *c* becomes *ç* and *g* becomes *ge* before *a* and *o* (e.g. commença, commençons; mangea, mangeons).

In verbs in -*yer* (e.g. **nettoyer**), *y* becomes *i* before mute *e* (e.g. nettoie, nettoierai). Verbs in -*ayer* (e.g. **payer**) may retain *y* before mute *e* (e.g. paye or paie, payerai or paierai).

In verbs in -*eler* (e.g. **appeler**) and in -*eter* (e.g. **jeter**), *l* becomes *ll* and *t* becomes *tt* before a syllable containing mute *e* (c.g. appelle, appellerai; jette, jetterai). In the verbs **celer, ciseler, congeler, déceler, démanteler, écarteler, geler, marteler, modeler** and **peler**, and in the verbs **acheter, crocheter, fureter, haleter** and **racheter**, *e* becomes *è* before a syllable containing mute *e* (e.g. cèle, cèlerai; achète, achèterai).

In verbs in which the penultimate syllable contains mute *e* (e.g. **semer**) or *é* (e.g. **révéler**), both *e* and *é* become *è* before a syllable containing mute *e* (e.g. sème, sèmerai; révèle). However, in the verbs in which the penultimate syllable containx *é*, *é* remains unchanged in the future and conditional (e.g. révéleral).

Irregular verbs

At least the first persons singular and plural of the present tense are shown. Forms not listed may be derived from these. Thought the base form of the imperfect, future, and present subjunctive may be irregular, the endings of these tenses are as shown in the regular verb section. Only the first person singular of these tenses is given in most cases. The base form of the past historic may also be irregular but the endings of this tense shown in the verbs below fall (with few exceptions) into the 'u' category, listed under **être** and **avoir**, and the 'i' category shown under **finir** and **vendre** in the regular verb section.

Only the first person singular of the past historic is listed in most cases. Additional forms appear throughout when these cannot be derived from the forms given or when it is considered helpful to list them. Only those irregular verbs judged to be the most useful are shown in the tables.

abbattre *as* BATTRE.
accueillir *as* CUEILLIR.
acquérir ● *Pres.* acquiers, acquérons, acquièrent. ● *Impf.* acquérais. ● *Past hist.* acquis. ● *Fut.* acquerrai. ● *Pres. sub.* acquière. ● *Past part.* acquis.
admettre *as* METTRE.
aller ● *Pres.* vais, vas, va, allons, allez, vont. ● *Fut.* irai. ● *Pres. sub.* aille, allions.
apercevoir *as* RECEVOIR.
apparaître *as* CONNAÎTRE.
appartenir *as* TENIR.
apprendre *as* PRENDRE.
asseoir ● *Pres.* assieds, asseyons, asseyent. ● *Impf.* asseyais. ● *Past hist.* assis. ● *Fut.* assiérai. ● *Pres. sub.* asseye. ● *Past part.* assis.
atteindre ● *Pres.* atteins, atteignons, atteignent. ● *Impf.* atteignais. ● *Past hist.* atteignis. ● *Fut.* atteindrai. ● *Pres. sub.* atteigne. ● *Past part.* atteint.
avoir ● *Pres.* ai, as, a, avons, avez, ont. ● *Impf.* avais. ● *Past hist.* eus, eut, eûmes, eûtes, eurent. ● *Fut.* aurai. ● *Pres. sub.* aie, aies, ait, ayons, ayez, aient. ● *Pres. part.* ayant. ● *Past part.* eu. ● *Imp.* aie, ayons, ayez.
battre ● *Pres.* bats, bat, battons, battez, battent.
boire ● *Pres.* bois, buvons, boivent. ● *Impf.* buvais. ● *Past hist.* bus. ● *Pres. sub.* boive, buvions. ● *Past part.* bu.
bouillir ● *Pres.* bous, bouillons, bouillent. ● *Impf.* bouillais. ● *Pres. sub.*

bouille.
combattre *as* BATTRE.
commettre *as* METTRE.
comprendre *as* PRENDRE.
concevoir *as* RECEVOIR.
conclure ● *Pres.* conclus, concluons, concluent. ● *Past hist.* conclus. ● *Past part.* conclu.
conduire ● *Pres.* conduis, conduisons, conduisent. ● *Impf.* conduisais. ● *Past hist.* conduisis. ● *Pres. sub.* conduise. ● *Past part.* conduit.
connaître ● *Pres.* connais, connaît, connaissons. ● *Impf.* connaissais. ● *Past hist.* connus. ● *Pres. sub.* connaisse. ● *Past part.* connu.
construire *as* CONDUIRE.
contenir *as* TENIR.
contraindre *as* ATTEINDRE (except *ai* replaces *ei*).
contredire *as* DIRE, except ● *Pres.* vous contredisez.
convaincre *as* VAINCRE.
convenir *as* TENIR.
corrompre *as* ROMPRE.
coudre ● *Pres.* couds, cousons, cousent. ● *Impf.* cousais. ● *Past hist.* cousis. ● *Pres. sub.* couse. ● *Past part.* cousu.
courir ● *Pres.* cours, courons, courent. ● *Impf.* courais. ● *Past hist.* courus. ● *Fut.* courrai. ● *Pres. sub.* coure. ● *Past part.* couru.
couvrir ● *Pres.* couvre, couvrons. ● *Impf.* couvrais. ● *Pres. sub.* couvre. ● *Past part.* couvert.
craindre *as* ATTEINDRE (except *ai* replaces *ei*).
croire ● *Pres.* crois, croit, croyons, croyez, croient. ● *Impf.* croyais. ● *Past hist.* crus. ● *Pres. sub.* croie, croyions. ● *Past part.* cru.
croître ● *Pres.* crois, croît, croissons. ● *Impf.* croissais. ● *Past hist.* crûs. ● *Pres. sub.* croisse. ● *Past part.* crû, crue.

cueillir
- *Pres.* cueille, cueillons.
- *Impf.* cueillais.
- *Fut.* cueillerai.
- *Pres. sub.* cueille.

débattre *as* BATTRE.

décevoir *as* RECEVOIR.

découvrir *as* COUVRIR.

décrire *as* éCRIRE.

déduire *as* CONDUIRE.

défaire *as* FAIRE.

détenir *as* TENIR.

détruire *as* CONDUIRE.

devenir *as* TENIR.

devoir
- *Pres.* dois, devons, doivent. ● *Impf.* devais.
- *Past hist.* dus. ● *Fut.* devrai. ● *Pres. sub.* doive.
- *Past part.* dû, due.

dire
- *Pres.* dis, dit, disons, dites, disent. ● *Impf.* disais. ● *Past hist.* dis.
- *Past part.* dit.

disparaître *as* CONNAîTRE.

dissoudre
- *Pres.* dissous. dissolvons. ● *Impf.* dissolvais. ● *Pres. sub.* dissolve. ● *Past part.* dissous, dissoute.

distraire *as* EXTRAIRE.

dormir
- *Pres.* dors, dormons.
- *Impf.* dormais.
- *Pres. sub* dorme.

écrire
- *Pres.* écris, écrivons.
- *Impf.* écrivais. ● *Past hist.* écrivis. ● *Pres. sub.* écrive. ● *Past part.* écrit.

élire *as* LIRE.

émettre *as* METTRE.

s'enfuir *as* FUIR.

entreprendre *as* PRENDRE.

entretenir *as* TENIR.

envoyer ● *Fut.* enverrai.

éteindre *as* ATTEINDRE.

être
- *Pres.* suis, es, est, sommes, êtes, sont.
- *Impf.* étais. ● *Past hist.* fus, futm fûmes, fûtes, furent. ● *Fut.* serai. ● *Pres. sub.* sois, soit, soyons, soyez, soient.
- *Pres. part.* étant. ● *Past part.* été. ● *Imp.* sois, soyons, soyez.

exclure *as* CONCLURE.

extraire
- *Pres.* extrais, extrayons. ● *Impf.* extrayais. ● *Pres. sub.* extraie. ● *Past part.* extrait.

faire
- *Pres.* fais, fait, faisons, faites, font. ● *Impf.* faisais. ● *Past hist.* fis.
- *Fut.* ferai. ● *Pres. sub.* fasse. ● *Past part.* fait.

falloir
(Impersonal) ● *Pres.* faut. ● *Impf.* fallait. ● *Past hist.* fallut. ● *Fut.* faudra. ● *Pres. sub.* faille. ● *Past part.* fallu.

feindre *as* ATTEINDRE.

fuir
- *Pres.* fuis, fuyons, fuient. ● *Impf.* fuyais. ● *Past hist.* fuis. ● *Pres sub.* fuie. ● *Past part.* fui.

inscrire *as* éCRIRE.

instruire *as* CONDUIRE.

interdire *as* DIRE, except ● *Pres.* vous interdisez.

interrompre *as* ROMPRE.

intervenir *as* TENIR.

introduire *as* CONDUIRE.

joindre *as* ATTEINDRE (except *oi* replaces *ei*).

lire
- *Pres.* lis, lit, lisons, lisez, lisent. ● *Impf.* lisais. ● *Past hist.* lus. ● *Pres. sub.* lise. ● *Past part.* lu.

luire
- *Pres.* luis, luisons. ● *Impf.* luisais. ● *Past hist.* luisis. ● *Pres. sub.* luise. ● *Past part.* lui.

maintenir *as* TENIR.

maudire
- *Pres.* maudis, maudissons.
- *Impf.* maudissais.
- *Past hist.* maudis.
- *Pres. sub.* maudisse.
- *Past part.* maudit.

mentir *as* SORTIR (except *en* replaces *or*).

mettre
- *Pres.* mets, met. mettons, mettez. mettent.
- *Past hist.* mis. ● *Past part.* mis.

mourir
- *Pres.* meurs, mourons, meurent. ● *Impf.* mourais. ● *Past hist.* mourus. ● *Fut.* mourrai.
- *Pres sub.* meure, mourions. ● *Past part.* mort.

mouvoir
- *Pres.* meus, mouvons, meuvent. ● *Impf.* mouvais. ● *Fut.* mouvrai. ● *Pres. sub.* meuve, mouvions. ●

Past part. mû, mue.

naître ● Pres. nais, nait, naissons. ● Impf. naissais. ● Past hist. naquis. ● Pres. sub. naisse. ● Past part. né.

nuire as LUIRE.
obtenir as TENIR.
offrir, ouvrir as COUVRIR.
omettre as METTRE.
paraître as CONNAîTRE.
parcourir as COURIR.
partir as SORTIR (except ar replaces or).
parvenir as TENIR.
peindre as ATTEINDRE.
percevoir as RECEVOIR.
permettre as METTRE.
plaindre as ATTEINDRE (except ai replaces ei).
plaire ● Pres. plais, plait, plaisons. ● Impf. plaisais. ● Past hist. plus. ● Pres. sub. plaise. ● Past part. plu.
pleuvoir (impersonal) ● Pres. pleut. ● Impf. pleuvait. ● Past hist. plut. ● Fut. pleuvra. ● Pres. sub. pleuve. ● Past part. plu.
poursuivre as SUIVRE.
pourvoir as VOIR, except ● Fut. pourvoirai.
pouvoir ● Pres. peux. peut, pouvons, pouvez, peuvent. ● Impf. pouvais. ● Past hist. pus. ● Fut. pourrai. ● Pres. sub. puisse. ● Past part. pu.
prédire as DIRE, except ● Pres. vous prédisez.
prendre ● Pres. prends, prenons, prennent. ● Impf. prenais. ● Past hist. pris. ● Pres. sub. prenne, prenions. ● Past part. pris.
prescrire as ÉCRIRE.
prévenir as TENIR.
prévoir as VOIR, except ● Fut. prévoirai.
produire as CONDUIRE.
prommettre as METTRE.
provenir as TENIR.
recevoir ● Pres. reçois, recevons, reçoivent. ● Impf. recevais. ● Past hist. reçus. ● Fut. recevrai.

● Pres. sub. reçoive, recevions. ● Past part. reçu.

reconduire as CONDUIRE.
reconnaître as CONNAîTRE.
reconstruire as CONDUIRE.
recouvrir as COUVRIR.
recueillir as CUEILLIR..
redire as DIRE.
réduire as CONDUIRE.
refaire as FAIRE.
rejoindre as ATTEINDRE (except oi replaces ei).
remettre as METTRE.
renvoyer as ENVOYER.
repartir as SORTIR (except ar replaces or.
reprendre as PRENDRE.
reproduire as vconduire.
résoudre ● Pres. résous, résolvons. ● Impf. résolvais. ● Past hist. résolus. ● Pres. sub. résolve. ● Past part. résolu.
ressortir as SORTIR.
restreindre as ATTEINDRE.
retenir, revenir as TENIR.
revivre as vvivre.
revoir as VOIR.
rire ● Pres. ris, rit, rions, riez, rient. ● Impf. riais. ● Past hist. ris. ● Pres. sub. rie, riions. ● Past part. ri.
rompre as VENDRE (regular), except ● Pres. il rompt.
satisfaire as FAIRE.
savoir ● Pres. sais, sait, savons, savez, savent. ● Impf. savais. ● Past hist. sus. ● Fut. saurai. ● Pres. sub. sache, sachions. ● Pres. part. sachant. ● Past part. su. ● Impt. sache, sachons, sachez.
séduire as CONDUIRE.
sentir as SORTIR (except en replaces or).
servir ● Pres. sers, servons. ● Impf. servais. ● Pres. sub. serve.
sortir ● Pres. sors, sortons. ● Impf. sortais. ● Pres. sub. sorte.
souffrir as COUVRIR.
soumettre as METTRE.
soustraire as VEXTRAIRE.
soutenir as TENIR.

suffire
- *Pres.* suffis, suffisons.
- *Impf.* suffisais.
- *Past hist.* suffis.
- *Pres. sub.* suffise.
- *Past part.* suffi.

suivre
- *Pres.* suis, suivons.
- *Impf.* suivais. ● *Past hist.* suivis. ● *Pres. sub.* suive. ● *Past part.* suivi.

surprendre *as* PRENDRE.

survivre *as* VIVRE.

taire
- *Pres.* tais, taisond. ● *Impf.* taisais. ● *Past hist.* tus. ● *Pres. sub.* taise. ● *Past part.* tu.

teindre *as* ATTEINDRE.

tenir
- *Pres.* tiens, tenons, tiennent. ● *Impf.* tenais. ● *Past hist.* tins, tint, tinmes, tintes, tinrent. ● *Fut.* tiendrai. ● *Pres. sub.* tienne. ● *Past part.* tenu.

traduire *as* CONDUIRE.

traire *as* EXTRAIRE.

transmettre *as* METTRE.

vaincre
- *Pres.* vaincs, vaine, vainquons.
- *Impf.* vain-quais.
- *Past hist.* vainquis.
- *Pres. sub.* vainque.
- *Past part.* vaincu.

valoir
- *Pres.* vaux, vaut, valons, valez, valent. ● *Impf.* valais. ● *Past hist.* valus. ● *Fut.* vaudrai. ● *Pres. sub.* vaille. ● *Past part.* valu. *as* TENIR. ● *Pres.* vis, vit, vivons, vivez, vivent. ● *Impf.* vivais. ● *Past hist.* vécus. ● *Pres. sub* vive. ● *Past part.* vécu. ● *Pres.* vois, voyons, voient. ● *Impf.* voyais. ● *Past hist.* vis. ● *Fut.* verrai. ● *Pres. sub.* voie, voyions. ● *Past part.* vu. ● *Pres.* veux, veut, voulons, voulez, veulent. ● *Impf.* voulais. ● *Past hist.* voulus. ● *Fut.* voudrai. ● *Pres. sub.* veuille, voulions. ● *Past part.* voulu. ● *Imp.* veuille, veuillons, veuillez.

PENGUIN PUTNAM INC.
Online

Your Internet gateway to a virtual environment with
hundreds of entertaining and enlightening books
from Penguin Putnam Inc.

*While you're there, get the latest buzz on
the best authors and books around—*

Tom Clancy, Patricia Cornwell, W.E.B. Griffin,
Nora Roberts, William Gibson, Robin Cook,
Brian Jacques, Catherine Coulter, Stephen King,
Jacquelyn Mitchard, and many more!

**Penguin Putnam Online is located at
http://www.penguinputnam.com**

PENGUIN PUTNAM NEWS

Every month you'll get an inside look at our upcoming books and new features on our site. This is an
ongoing effort to provide you with the most
up-to-date information about
our books and authors.

**Subscribe to Penguin Putnam News at
http://www.penguinputnam.com/ClubPPI**